For Reference

Not to be taken from this room

ROCK&ROLL

Reference Series
Tom Schultheiss, Series Editor

**Available only through Popular Culture, Ink., P.O. Box 1839, Ann Arbor, Michigan 48106
Phone 1(800) 678-8828 or (313) 973-1460.**

Remembrances Series
Tom Schultheiss, Series Editor

Trivia Series
Tom Schultheiss, Series Editor

**Available only through Popular Culture, Ink., P.O. Box 1839, Ann Arbor, Michigan 48106
Phone 1(800) 678-8828 or (313) 973-1460.**

Heat WAVE

THE MOTOWN FACT BOOK

BY

DAVID BIANCO

POPULAR CULTURE, INK.
1988

TO THE SPIRIT OF MOTOWN

CONTENTS

PART II: MOTOWN CHRONOLOGY

PART III: MOTOWN & RELATED LABELS

PART V: MOTOWN DISCOGRAPHY (UNITED KINGDOM)

ILLUSTRATIONS

FOREWORD

Many reviewers and filmgoers found 1983's "The Big Chill" to be a well-acted if rather shallow portrait of a group of aging sixties hippies caught up in the throes of their various mid-life crises. They also found that half the soundtrack music used to define the sixties and to evoke in the audience nostalgic memories of a bygone era were songs by The Temptations, Marvin Gaye, and Smokey Robinson. The apparent contradiction of an all white cast of players grooving to the strains of tunes sung by some of Motown's major black artists is at once true to history, for the sixties was a watershed period for the black performer previously co-opted by whites who covered the "Negro" music of the fifties to their own advantage. But it is also - probably unintentionally - the quintessence of what Motown was, what it was intended to be, what it has persisted in becoming: a wellspring of "America's music," music without color.

Motown destroyed, albeit not single-handedly, the line drawn between white music and black music; the appeal and legitimization that a white Elvis Presley gave to black music blossomed into the appeal and legitimization of the black performer largely because of Motown. In that sense, Motown can't be viewed simply as a record company; it assumes the role of catalyst for social change by default, by virtue of its existence; it becomes a shaper of race relations, of human relationships, as much as it is a business, a money-maker, a hit factory, "Hitsville U.S.A." The simple fact is, you can't preserve your prejudices for very long when you're laughing *with* someone of another skin color, any more than you can hate and sing along with Smokey at the same time. It just isn't possible. And the *best* rendition of the "Star-Spangled Banner" ever recorded isn't by the Marine Corps Band - it's by Marvin Gaye (no matter a Marvin Gaye freshly uprooted from Motown, recording for Columbia).

With that as background, it is time to turn to the absolutely staggering reference work David Bianco has produced in *Heat Wave*. As one who has been editing and publishing rock-and-roll music books for more than twelve years, virtually all of them concerned with the oeuvre of a single artist or group, the dedication and effort involved in undertaking the codification of the recording history of *an entire record company* for a period exceeding a quarter-century simply blows my mind. Yet, sixties clichés aside, here it is. And what better company to begin with - if you are bent on such a rash and foolhardy course! - than Berry Gordy, Jr.'s Motown Record Corporation. The stars, the hits, the story of Motown is like no other.

Many years have been required to gather, edit, and keyboard the information contained in this book, to proofread it, correct it, index it, write the computer programs used to format it, and finally to assemble the hundreds of pages, the scores of photographs and other illustrations, into a whole which unarguably represents the most fact-filled and exhaustive look at Motown's recording history published to date. An incredible recording history has here been favored with an equally monumental body of scholarly documentation.

"Heat Wave," apart from having earned for Martha & The Vandellas and for Motown the much deserved recognition (and dollars) that it has, apart from being the song title selected (from among many outstanding possibilities) to serve as the title of this work - one that says, as succinctly as possible, "this is about Motown" - "Heat Wave," in two short words, bespeaks the spirit of Motown's music, music filled with the energy of life, music to raise the spirit, the temperature, to excite the imagination, music to set fingers popping, feet moving, and pulses jumping. America's music.

Tom Schultheiss

INTRODUCTION

During the more than twenty-five years covered by this reference book, Motown has consistently exerted a strong influence on American popular music. As this volume goes to press, Motown continues to maintain its presence on both the popular and the black-oriented music charts through the strength of its new artists, as well as the continued popularity of such mainstays as Smokey Robinson, Stevie Wonder, and Lionel Richie. Throughout its history, Motown has diversified, venturing into country and western, gospel, spoken word, and jazz recordings, all without losing its basic popular music focus or its ability to produce great stars and great hit songs. All of these songs, styles, and artists are covered in this work, which contains over 5,500 discographical entries for recordings released on more than thirty different labels in the U.S. and England. Almost 6,700 references to the names of Motown artists, as well as over 8,500 references to Motown-produced songs and record titles, fill several of the indexes included herein, weighty testimony to power and potency of the Motown catalog. As Motown looks ahead to its thirtieth anniversary, there is every reason to believe it will continue to be a strong and vital force in contemporary music.

SCOPE & INCLUSIVENESS

Heat Wave was designed as a basic reference source on Motown's recording history, and to that end contains the most extensive and detailed discographies of the company's first issues ever published. These sections are supported by eight indexes, and are supplemented by concise biographical, chronological, and other features added with a view to rounding out the book as a single-source introduction to and handbook of Motown facts, dates, and personalities. It is hoped that this combination of detail on one hand and brevity on the other will satisfy the needs of both the most casual Motown enthusiast, as well as those of the most dedicated record collector and recording history

researcher.

Ease of use, accessibility, and quick reference were the decisive factors in the selection, arrangement, and presentation of the various sections in this work. Alphabetical approaches allow the location of information about a particular recording artist, song, or record; chronologically arranged sections provide an approach to a particular time period in Motown history; numerical formats and indexes allow matching of a record number with an artist or recording. The following paragraphs describe the book in greater detail, providing additional notes concerning the scope and content of each section.

ARRANGEMENT

Heat Wave is divided into eight distinct sections, some of which include photographs and reproductions of record labels and other materials important in Motown history.

Part I: BIOGRAPHY

Over twenty-five years of recording activity has provided Motown with an unparalleled list of hits and "names" important in popular music history; hundreds upon hundreds of artists from a variety of musical genres have recorded for Motown on its many labels. Included in the biographical section are the major Motown artists and groups, as well as some of the more obscure and lesser-known acts. In addition to recording artists, some producers and songwriters are included in the alphabetical sequence, the whole preceded by a capsule biography of Berry Gordy, Jr., founder of the Motown Record Corporation.

This section is admittedly incomplete in its coverage of Motown artists (for a complete list of all the individuals and groups to receive recording credits, see the personal and group name indexes included in this work). For example, the biographical section does not include any information about the country and western singers that recorded on Motown's c&w subsidiaries, nor does it list any jazz groups. As a general rule, artists who made their reputations at other labels, either before or after joining Motown, are not given extensive coverage in this section, although some exceptions have been made for performers who may have begun their careers with Motown but achieved greater fame recording for another label or labels at a later time.

For recording artists and groups covered in this section, an individual discography of their Motown singles and albums has been included to compensate for the order of the main discography, which is arranged by label and record number. In many cases, a "non-Motown" discography has also been provided for recordings issued while at other labels, although these should be considered selective rather than comprehensive lists (every effort has been made to make them as complete as possible, however). Non-Motown recordings by artists who had very substantial recording careers before or after joining Motown are generally not given, although some exceptions have been made. The absence of a "non-Motown" discography in a performer's entry should not be taken as an indication that they had no career outside of the time they spent at Motown.

Also included in the biographical entries in this section are personnel information and career highlights. These career summaries indicate the role each group or artist played in the history of Motown, but generally do not go into too much detail concerning events following departure from Motown.

Part II: CHRONOLOGY

Starting with the birthdate of Motown founder Berry Gordy, Jr., the Motown chronology goes on to provide an historical perspective on the development of Motown up through the end of 1987. A wide range of significant events are listed, including the major hits of each year, notable tours, artistic debuts, new labels, and other landmarks concerning Motown and its stable of recording stars.

Part III: LABELS

Each of Motown's labels, as well as some of the early Detroit-based labels associated with Motown in some way, are briefly profiled in this alphabetically arranged section. Illustrations of many of the original label designs are included.

Parts IV & V: DISCOGRAPHIES

Motown has enjoyed immense popularity throughout the world, and has probably issued recordings in nearly every country on earth, either directly or through licensing agreements. Indeed, many Motown stars have recorded some of their hits in languages other than English as a consequence of this international appeal. Inasmuch as Motown established its own British-based label as early as 1965, and has been every bit as popular in the United Kingdom as it has in the United States, a British discography has been included in this work to augment the U.S. listing. The American and British discographies are presented in different sections and are indexed separately.

The U.S. discography provides a complete listing of commercially released first issues from 1959 to nearly the end of 1986. It covers 7-inch (45 rpm) singles, EPs (extended play 7-inch recordings), 12-inch singles, albums, compact discs (CDs), cardboard records, color vinyl singles, and a few of the Motown special issue singles which have become notable Motown rarities. Inasmuch as many of Motown's U.S. labels developed simultaneously, label discographies in this section are listed alphabetically by the label-based entry number prefix assigned (for indexing purposes) to each label. This approach does place the U.S. discographies in rough alphabetical sequence by label name; the order is not perfectly alphabetical as a result of some of the prefixes selected to distinguish the labels, however. Within each distinct grouping, records are ordered sequentially by record number.

A key to the label prefixes used for each country appears at the beginning of each national discography, together with an indication of the meaning of the prefix (more on this in the discussion of indexes below), and the page number marking the beginning of each label listing. Additionally, the complete entry numbers for the first and last entry on each page within the discography appear as headings at the top of every page.

Throughout its history, Motown has entered into numerous distribution agreements with various other labels. Some, but not all, of the labels affiliated with Motown through such distribution arrangements are listed in the discography sections.

It should be stressed that *Heat Wave* discographies are concerned primarily with Motown first commercial issues; as massive as these record listings and their attendant indexes are, they do not pretend to deal comprehensively with promotional only or with reissued recordings, excepting that the former may have been noted incidentally in the main discographies, and the latter not mentioned at all except if released within the numerical sequences assigned to original issues.

The U.K. discography includes singles, EPs and albums from the pre-Tamla Motown period through the middle of 1986. In contrast to the U.S. discography, the British list has been arranged chronologically as it pertains to what eventually became the Motown label in England (London America, Fontana, Oriole, Stateside, Tamla Motown, Motown), followed by related labels (beginning with Gaiee), and then by special Motown album series exclusive to the U.K.

Parts VI & VII: INDEXES

Each national discography is supported by four different indexes: personal and group names; song and record titles; release dates; record numbers. At the top of every index page are headings which indicate the first and last name, title, date or number mentioned on that page.

It was felt that a dimension could and should be added to the indexes in this book which would serve to delineate more clearly the index references, to give them a "meaning" which would clarify the citation in such a way as to make the various discographies even more accessible, improve the prospects for speedily finding specific recordings with ease, and reduce the number of wasted minutes often spent locating what ultimately proves to be undesired information. Sequentially numbering each recording mentioned in well-defined lists of recordings is itself a vast improvement over merely citing the page number on which a record is listed; assigning each numbered recording a "letter prefix" which identifies both the label on which the recording was issued and the type of recording in question was felt to be the ideal way of enhancing the utility of the indexes still further. A system of four- and five-letter prefixes (actually, the word "character" could be substituted for "letter," as

many prefixes include numbers) was therefore developed to this end.

A key to entry number letter prefixes appears at the beginning of each of the separate sections of indexes devoted to the U.S. and British discographies, and is repeated at the beginning of each national discography itself. Prefixes usually consist of two letters which identify the record label (MO for the Motown label, TA for Tamla, GO for Gordy, etc.), followed by two or three letters or numbers which indicate the recording format (45 for 7-inch singles, 12 for 12-inch singles, EP for extended play 7-inch singles, LP for albums, CA for cardboard records, CO for color vinyl singles, and so on). See the appropriate national prefix key for a full delineation of the meaning of each combination of letters and numbers.

The benefits of this numbering system become immediately apparent when answers to the following types of questions are desired (assuming you have developed a familiarity with the entry number prefixes): On which Motown label did Shorty Long record, and how many albums by him were issued? Apart from the Tamla-label singles on which The Supremes sang before their move to the Motown label, were any Tamla albums by them released? How many Motown labels did Pat Boone record on, and which ones were they? How many Tamla singles feature Marvin Gaye duets with Tammi Terrell? Was Stevie Wonder's album, MY CHERIE AMOUR, issued as a CD? Was the Divinity label active before May 1963? How many first issue recordings did Motown release in the U.S. in September 1970, on what labels, and in what formats? Virtually all of these questions can be answered *without ever leaving the index section.*

There are four parallel indexes provided for each national discography:

Personal & Group Name Indexes

The names of individual performers and groups are listed alphabetically, each followed by a list of discography entries which mention their names (incidental appearances as backing vocalists are also indexed). Solo appearances are listed in advance of duets or other combinations of artists, although the solo list usually also includes references to the latter as well (for duets only, consult only the duet references). There are over

4,000 references to performer names in the American discography, and close to 2,600 references to those names in the British discography.

Song & Record Title Indexes

Alphabetically lists over 5,300 references to song titles, EP and album titles, etc., found in the U.S. discography, and over 3,200 such titles in the British record list. When different record formats have the same title, smaller formats are listed first - songs on singles - followed by CDs, EPs, LPs, and so forth. Formats are identified by these same parenthetical qualifiers in all cases: (song), (EP), (LP), etc.

Date Indexes

Year or month and year of release have been determined for fully 99.9% of the recordings listed in each national discography. This has allowed the creation of indexes ordered by date of release which provide profiles of Motown's record release activity over more than a quarter of a century, virtually month by month. Entry number prefixes help identify which labels were most active during a certain month or other time frame, which formats were emphasized, how any given month compared with any other month in the same or different years, which songs and artists were being promoted in the U.S. as opposed to England (after referring to the discography sections), and so forth. Such first issue profiles help present an unparalleled panorama of Motown's record release activity for record historians; care should be taken to compensate for factors like: the number of recordings listed by year alone with no month designated; the admittedly incomplete nature of the discographies for the year 1986.

Record Number Indexes

Over 9,000 permutations of the record numbers listed in this volume comprise the record number indexes. Beginning with numbers which have letter prefixes, and moving on to sequences of record numbers consisting solely of numerals or of numerals with prefixed letters removed, these indexes are of matchless utility in finding recordings about which little is known except the record number. It should be noted that, because these indexes were ordered by computer, record numbers are not listed in strict numerical ascendancy (1, 2, 3, 10, 20, 100, etc.) but are instead grouped in a digit-by-digit progression. All numbers without letter prefixes are grouped together by the first digit, but they are then further grouped by the second numeral, the third numeral, and so forth. The progression may therefore appear as follows: 0001, 001, 002, 01, 1, 10, 1000, 102, 1168, 117, 2. In short, each numerical increase in successive digits dictates a record number's position relative to other record numbers, rather than quantitative value. For example, 001 follows 0001 because the third digit has increased from 0 to 1, and 2 follows 117 because the first digit has increased from 1 to 2.

Part VIII: MOTOWN-RELATED LABELS

For added reference, label discographies for five contemporaneous Detroit-based labels that were either purchased by Motown or dissolved as a result of having key personnel join the Motown organization have been included as an appendix to the national discographies. These labels - Anna, Golden World, Harvey, Ric-Tic, and Tri-Phi - are not covered in the U.S. index section. They are included merely to provide a contextual setting within which to gauge the initial releases of the Motown Record Corporation. Many of the artists who went on to achieve great fame and popularity recording for Motown labels got their start with these lesser known entities.

ACKNOWLEDGEMENTS

This volume would not have been possible without the contributions of the several individuals and institutions identified below. The author would like to give recognition and special thanks to:

REGINALD BARTLETTE, who was the primary source of the discographical information for U.S. Motown labels, and who is working on a more specialized Motown reference book for Pierian Press. Reggie provides mail-order discographies to Motown record collectors; his work is extremely accurate and reliable. Write to him at: Motown Magic, 40 Harwood Crescent,

Winnipeg, Manitoba R3R 1W5, Canada.

MARTIN KOPPEL, for his personal encouragement in this project, and for helping to clear up a lot of difficult questions. Martin owns Kops Kollectibles, a Toronto-based record store, and publishes "Soul Survivor," an r&b fanzine. He is an excellent source of information for Motown and other soul record collectors. Write to him at his store: 436 Queen Street West, Toronto, Ontario M5V 2A8, Canada.

WALLY PODRAZIK, world-renowned Beatles discographer, for furnishing supplemental discographical information and researching non-Motown labels.

PETER DOGGETT, ace U.K. discographer, for supplying information on Motown's British releases.

PETER BENJAMINSON, for his encouragement, and for graciously allowing use of photographs from his personal collection. Thanks for writing the pioneer study of Motown, too!

Very special thanks to **MRS. ESTHER GORDY EDWARDS** for establishing the Motown Archives at Eastern Michigan University, thereby allowing a rare glimpse into the history of Motown Records.

Special thanks to the staff of **EASTERN MICHIGAN UNIVERSITY's** Center of Educational Resources, administrators of Esther Gordy's bequest, the Motown Archives: Library Director, Morell Boone; Marge Eidy, Mary Lou Webster, and Jack Etsweiler; Sandy Yee, Patricia Ramsey, Jean Rauch, and Alex Sanford. Your patience and professionalism were outstanding!

Special thanks also to the librarians in the Performing Arts Department of the **DETROIT PUBLIC LIBRARY** for their gracious assistance in using the Azalia Hackley Collection.

Thanks to **ALEX PRZEBIENDA** at Pierian Press for coming through with outstanding computer programs.

Thanks to **ED WALL** at Pierian Press for his interest in this project and in popular culture in general.

And finally, special recognition for **TOM SCHULTHEISS**, managing editor of the "Rock & Roll Reference Series," for putting it all together.

xxiii

PART I

MOTOWN BIOGRAPHY

BERRY GORDY, JR.
Founder of the Motown Record Corp.

BERRY GORDY, JR., THE GORDY FAMILY & THE MOTOWN RECORD CORP.

"Mr. Speaker, ten years ago a Detroit assembly line worker, who had formerly been a prizefighter, saved $700 and started his own business. Like so many before him, he had ideas of what he could do and wanted to try them in a business of his own. His name was Berry Gordy, Jr., and the company he created was the Motown Record Corp.

"Starting from their own home, the Gordy family has built Motown into the largest independent record firm in the world, and the only major black company in the entertainment business.

"Berry Gordy realizes that even in America factory workers cannot all become successful businessmen. Therefore, he believes that it is essential that each and every young person receive the maximum education possible. He knows that education is the passport to the future and that tomorrow belongs to the people who prepare for it today.

"One of the many ways Gordy puts his belief to work is through the Sterling Ball, a benefit which directly provides assistance in the form of scholarships to inner city high school graduates who wish to continue their education but are financially unable to do so. This annual charitable event has, to date, helped scores of young men and women, black and white, reach an otherwise impossible goal--a college education.

"The benefit was originally conceived by Mr. Gordy and his sister, Mrs. Esther Edwards, vice president in the corporation, as a continuing and meaningful memorial to their late sister, Mrs. Loucye Gordy Wakefield, who had been the first vice president of Motown and a personal inspiration to all who knew her."

These excerpts from a speech by the Hon. John Conyers, Jr., of Michigan, in the House of Representatives on April 19, 1971, reflect the familial nature of the Motown enterprise. Even though none of the family members of Berry Gordy's generation made their names as entertainers or performers, the Gordy family is very much a musical family, in much the same way the Jacksons or the DeBarges are. Their musicality made itself known, not in performance, but in a continuing enterprise that has provided us with numerous performers and countless popular songs.

It was Berry Gordy, Jr., the seventh of eight children of Berry, Sr., (known affectionately as "Pops") and Bertha Gordy, who began the Motown Record Corporation in 1959, but all of the family members were called on to make their own special contributions. (References to Berry Gordy, Jr., often do not include the "Jr." and, after his father's death in 1978, he stopped using it as well. To avoid confusion, his father is usually referred to as Berry Gordy, Sr., or by his nickname, "Pops.") As new performers were signed to the company, they became new members of the "Motown family" as well. And like all families, there have been instances of dissension along the way. But the whole enterprise has been kept on course by Berry Gordy, and new performers have been discovered to replace those who have left.

In January 1988, Berry Gordy was inducted into the Rock and Roll Hall of Fame for his role as leader and founder of the Motown Record Corporation.

Before Motown: The 1950's

Born November 28, 1929, Berry Gordy, Jr., was just twenty years old when the 1950's began. In 1951, Berry was drafted into the army, where he would receive his high school equivalency diploma. In 1953, now out of the service, he married Thelma Coleman, and in 1954 their daughter, Hazel Joy, was born. They would have two more children, Berry IV and Terry, before being divorced in 1959.

Berry worked on the assembly line in Detroit and started a jazz-oriented record store, the 3-D Record Mart, around 1955, but it soon folded. Like Motown, it was financed largely by Berry's family.

Berry was writing songs constantly, and he always submitted songs to magazines and contests. His big break came in 1957, when Jackie Wilson recorded "Reet Petite," a song written by Berry, his sister Gwen, and Tyran Carlo (pseudonym for Billy Davis). Jackie Wilson had just signed with Brunswick in 1956, and "Reet Petite" turned out to be

"That's Why (I Love You So)" was one of five Brunswick-label songs that Berry Gordy co-wrote for Jackie Wilson.

The first Jobete song, released in 1958, was "I Need You," written and produced by Berry Gordy.

This 1959 release by The Miracles was produced by Berry Gordy and leased to Chess Records.

One of Motown's short-lived subsidiaries, Berry Gordy established the Miracle label in 1961.

his first hit. Gordy et al. wrote four more hits for Jackie over the next two years: "To Be Loved" and "Lonely Teardrops" in 1958, and "That's Why" and "I'll Be Satisfied" in 1959.

In 1957, Berry also "discovered" Smokey Robinson and the Miracles when they auditioned for Jackie Wilson's manager, Nat Tarnapol, who also owned Brunswick. Berry was the more impressed with Smokey and his group and began recording them. By 1958, Berry was acting as an independent producer and leasing recordings of the Miracles, Marv Johnson, and Eddie Holland to nationally distributed labels.

Perhaps on the strength of Jackie Wilson's hits, Gwen Gordy, Anna Gordy, and Billy Davis established the Anna label in Detroit. Billy Davis had close ties to Leonard Chess of Chess Records in Chicago, and Anna enjoyed wider distribution with the help of the Chicago label. When Barrett Strong's Tamla recording of "Money (That's What I Want)" started to take off in 1960, Berry leased it to Anna Records for wider distribution. Berry would produce a number of the Anna releases from 1958 to 1961, at which point Anna was absorbed into Berry's growing Motown Record Corporation.

Berry established Jobete in 1958 to publish his songs. The first Jobete song was Herman Griffin's "I Need You," released on the HOB label. HOB stands for House of Beauty, the name of a beauty parlor in Detroit whose owner established the label based on profits from the business.

Now that Berry had some experience as a songwriter, producer, and publisher, he was motivated to become a full-fledged entrepreneur by a number of factors. His family background certainly contributed to and supported this ambition. Smokey urged him to take full control of his operations. As a songwriter, Berry was forced to split his royalties with the publisher. And he didn't like the way his songs were being produced at Brunswick.

So it was that in January 1959, Berry borrowed $800 from the family loan fund, known as the Ber-Berry Coop, in order to found Motown Records.

The Gordy Family

Nearly all of Berry Gordy's brothers and sisters were involved with Motown and/or popular music, as are many of the next generation of Gordys. Listed below are family members of Berry Gordy's generation and their relation to Motown's founder.

ESTHER GORDY EDWARDS. Berry's oldest sister. Senior Vice President of Motown Records. Acted as chaperone for many of the girl groups and singers. Known also as the company historian. Remained in Detroit when the company relocated to Los Angeles.

ANNA GORDY GAYE. Sister. Co-owner of Anna Records. Married to Marvin Gaye (his first wife) from 1963 to 1977. Songwriter.

GWENDOLYN GORDY FUQUA. Sister. Married Harvey Fuqua, leader of the Moonglows and later producer at Motown. As a songwriter, she shared credit with Berry on a number of Jackie Wilson's songs, including "Reet Petite," "Lonely Teardrops," "To Be Loved," "I'll Be Satisfied," and "That's Why (I Love You So)." Co-founded Tri-Phi Records with her husband in 1961.

LOUCYE GORDY WAKEFIELD. Sister. At the time of her death in 1965, she was Vice-President of Motown and a director of Jobete. In 1964, she developed a system for collecting money from the distributors that contributed enormously to Motown's financial well-being. In 1968, a fund was established in her name to award $500 scholarships to "educationally disadvantaged students who are victims of society's misdirected priorities," but who have exhibited a potential for achievement.

ROBERT GORDY. Brother. Motown executive and director of Jobete. Also recorded under the pseudonym Robert Kayli for Anna Records and on Tamla.

FULLER GORDY. Brother. More involved with bowling, and noted for his achievements in that sport, but a Motown executive nonetheless.

GEORGE GORDY. Brother. Shared song credits on "Beechwood 4- 5789" and "Stubborn Kind of Fellow." Involved with Motown.

Songwriting and Producing at Motown

When the Motown Record Corporation began in 1959, Berry Gordy was the company's

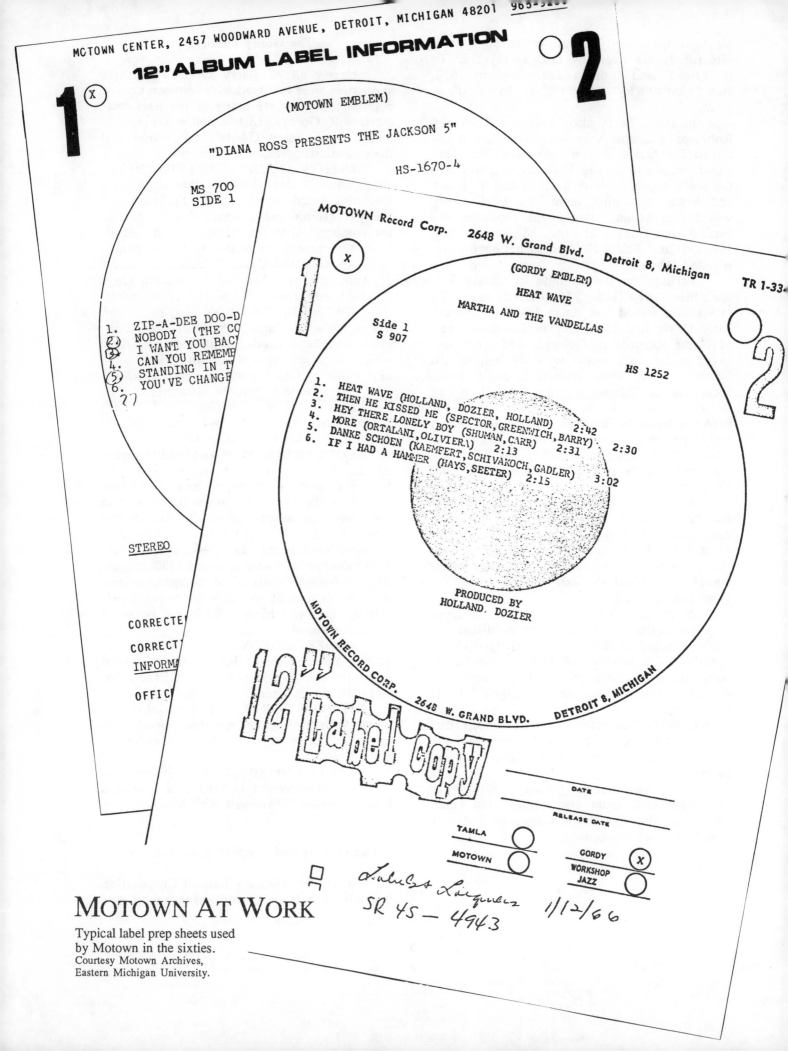

MOTOWN CENTER, 2457 WOODWARD AVENUE, DETROIT, MICHIGAN 48201 965-5151

12" ALBUM LABEL INFORMATION

1 (x)   ○ **2**

(MOTOWN EMBLEM)

"DIANA ROSS PRESENTS THE JACKSON 5"

HS-1670-4

MS 700
SIDE 1

1. ZIP-A-DEE DOO-D
2. NOBODY (THE CO
3. I WANT YOU BAC
4. CAN YOU REMEMF
5. STANDING IN T
6. YOU'VE CHANGE

?7

STEREO

CORRECTEI

CORRECTI

INFORM

OFFICI

MOTOWN Record Corp.   2648 W. Grand Blvd.   Detroit 8, Michigan   TR 1-33

1 (x)   ○ ○ **2**

(GORDY EMBLEM)

HEAT WAVE

MARTHA AND THE VANDELLAS

Side 1
S 907

HS 1252

1. HEAT WAVE (HOLLAND, DOZIER, HOLLAND)   2:42
2. THEN HE KISSED ME (SPECTOR, GREENWICH, BARRY)   2:30
3. HEY THERE LONELY BOY (SHUMAN, CARR)   2:31
4. MORE (ORTALANI, OLIVIERA)   2:13
5. DANKE SCHOEN (KAEMFERT, SCHIVAKOCH, GADLER)   3:02
6. IF I HAD A HAMMER (HAYS, SEETER)   2:15

PRODUCED BY
HOLLAND, DOZIER

MOTOWN RECORD CORP.   2648 W. GRAND BLVD.   DETROIT 8, MICHIGAN

12" Label Copy

DATE _____

RELEASE DATE _____

TAMLA ○

MOTOWN ○   GORDY (x)

     WORKSHOP JAZZ ○

□   _Lukas Loquez_

SR 45 — 4943   1/12/66

MOTOWN AT WORK

Typical label prep sheets used
by Motown in the sixties.
Courtesy Motown Archives,
Eastern Michigan University.

#1 songwriter and producer. A primary component of the company's success was Berry's ability to bring other talented individuals on board. Perhaps the most talented of these individuals was Smokey Robinson. During the 1960's, Smokey was the only Motown performer who was allowed to produce his own records. Smokey made his debut as a producer in 1962. Mary Wells, the Temptations, and the Miracles are three acts that initially were produced by Berry Gordy, but were later produced more successfully by Smokey.

Other producers who joined Motown in the early sixties included William "Mickey" Stevenson, Clarence Paul, Harvey Fuqua, the Holland-Dozier-Holland combination, Robert Bateman, Freddie Gorman, Johnny Bristol, Ivy Jo Hunter, and Norman Whitfield, to name a few of the most notable. Under Berry Gordy's direction, these talented producers and songwriters would be forced to compete fiercely to produce hits. It was a system that worked well and reflected the Gordy family's belief in the work ethic.

Stevenson and Paul were the initial components of Motown's A&R department. Another department was set up in the early sixties to groom and polish the Motown performers. It was headed by Maurice King, former bandleader at Detroit's Flame Show Bar, who provided musical instruction. Cholly Atkins was in charge of choreography, and Maxine Powell gave the performers instructions in manners and deportment. The need for an Artist Development Department became painfully apparent after a few embarrassingly unpolished performances of the Motown Revue on the road and at the Apollo Theater in New York. The results were well worth the effort, although some artists, notably Marvin Gaye and, later, Edwin Starr, rebelled against having to take such lessons.

Berry Gordy's Vision

Motown's musical roots were firmly planted in the soil of rhythm & blues and its predecessor, doo-wop. The company's earliest releases, like Mary Wells's "Bye Bye Baby," Barrett Strong's "Money (That's What I Want)," and the Contours' "Do You Love Me?" are all good examples of the earthy sound typical of r&b in the late fifties carried into the sixties. It was Berry Gordy's vision, though, that would take Motown far beyond the confining limitations of a black-oriented rhythm & blues sound to the broad-based, mass appeal of pop music.

The "Motown Sound," as it came to be known, was soon billed as "The Sound of Young America," a slogan that appears on the company's record jackets and sleeves. It was no secret that Motown wanted hits, right from the start, and that meant appealing to all teen-agers and young adults, not just a certain segment. Motown accomplished this goal with a vengeance in 1964, a banner year dominated by the Supremes and the songs of Holland-Dozier-Holland that began with Mary Wells's "My Guy" (written and produced by Smokey Robinson) reaching #1 on the pop charts.

As Motown became a successful record company, Berry Gordy's vision expanded to include other entertainment outlets. It was the company's intention to pursue opportunities in film, television, and the theatre. West Coast offices were established as early as 1966, and in 1972 the company fully relocated to Los Angeles from Detroit. The film, "Lady Sings The Blues," starring Diana Ross, opened in October 1972, and at the beginning of 1973, a corporate reorganization was announced. Motown Industries, an entertainment conglomerate, was established, with Berry Gordy as Chairman. At that time, Ewart Abner II was promoted from a Motown vice president to president of Motown Records. In 1973, the magazine *Black Enterprise* recognized Motown as the #1 black-owned or managed business. In less than fifteen years, Motown had grown from a Detroit-based record company specializing in r&b hits to a full-fledged entertainment corporation.

Produced by
BERRY GORDY, Jr.

MLP-600

An early Motown logo, reproduced from the back of the first Motown album jacket.

ASHFORD & SIMPSON

ANDANTES

Jackie Hicks
Marlene Barrow
Louvain Demps

Background vocalists for Motown artists during the early 1960s; also released records under their own name.

MOTOWN DISCOGRAPHY

1964: (Like A) Nightmare/If You Were Mine (V.I.P. 25006)

LAMONT ANTHONY
Pseudonym for Lamont Dozier.

(See LAMONT DOZIER; HOLLAND-DOZIER-HOLLAND.)

ASHFORD & SIMPSON

Nicholas "Nick" Ashford (born May 4, 1943, in Fairfield, South Carolina and grew up in Willow Run, Michigan), and Valerie Simpson (born August 26, 1948, Bronx, New York). Employed at Motown starting around 1967 as a songwriting and production team. Their songs were recorded at Motown primarily by the Marvin Gaye/Tammi Terrell duo, then later by Diana Ross. Ashford & Simpson acted as producers on the Diana Ross version of "Ain't No Mountain High Enough," while the Marvin Gaye/Tammi Terrell version was produced by Johnny Bristol and Harvey Fuqua. Song credits while at Motown include "Ain't No Mountain High Enough," "You're All I Need To Get By," "Ain't Nothing Like the Real Thing," "Reach Out and Touch Somebody's Hand," "If I Could Build My Whole World Around You," and "Remember Me." In 1975, they helped launch The Dynamic Superiors for Motown, producing their album PURE PLEASURE (M6-841S1). They also wrote and produced Diana Ross's 1979 album, *THE BOSS (Motown 923), and for Columbia Records, Gladys Knight and the Pips' THE TOUCH, released in 1981.

Ashford and Simpson met in New York, where they were members of a gospel group at the White Rock Baptist Church in Harlem. They began songwriting together and joined the staff of Scepter/Wand Records, writing rhythm & blues hits for Chuck Jackson and Maxine Brown. In 1964, as Valerie and Nick, they recorded "I'll Find You" on Glover Records. Success came when they wrote a song called "Let's Go Get Stoned," recorded by Ray Charles in 1966. Immediately afterward, they were signed by Motown as a staff songwriting and production team. In 1973, they began recording together for Warner Brothers while continuing as songwriters for Motown. Nick and Valerie got married in 1974 after working together for ten years.

NON-MOTOWN DISCOGRAPHY

1973: GIMME SOMETHING REAL (Warner Brothers BS 2739)

1973: Anywhere/I'm Determined (Warner Brothers 7745)

1974: I WANNA BE SELFISH (Warner Brothers WBS 2789)

1974: Time/Have You Ever Tried It (Warner Brothers 7781)

1974: Main Line/Don't Fight It (Warner Brothers 7811)

1975: Ain't Nothin' But A Maybe/Bend Me (Warner Brothers 8070)

1976: COME AS YOU ARE (Warner Brothers 2858)

1976: Caretaker/It'll Come, It'll Come, It'll Come (Warner Brothers 8179)

1976: It Came To Me/Somebody Told A Lie (Warner Brothers 8216)

1976: Believe In Me/Tried, Tested, and Found True (Warner Brothers 8286)

1977: SO, SO SATISFIED (Warner Brothers BS 2992)

1977: So, So Satisfied/Maybe I Can Find It (Warner Brothers 8337)

1977: It's You/Over and Over (Warner Brothers 8391)

1977: SEND IT (Warner Brothers BS 3088)

1977: Send It/Couldn't Get Enough (Warner Brothers 8453)

1977: Don't Cost You Nothing/Let Love Use Me (Warner Brothers 8514)

1978: IS IT STILL GOOD TO YA? (Warner Brothers 3219)

1978: By Way Of Love's Express/Too Bad (Warner Brothers 8571)

1978: It Seems To Hang On/Too Bad (Warner Brothers 8651)

1978: Is It Still Good To Ya?/As Long As It Holds You (Warner Brothers 8710)

1979: STAY FREE (Warner Brothers HS

Four Marvin Gaye-Tammi Terrell duets penned
by Ashford & Simpson, who acted as songwriters
and producers during their years at Motown. Later,
they achieved fame as performers in their own right,
recording for Capitol and Warner Bros.

3357)

1979: Flashback/Ain't It A Shame (Warner Brothers 8775)

1979: Found A Cure/You Always Could (Warner Brothers 8870)

1979: Crazy/Nobody Knows (Warner Brothers 49099)

1980: A MUSICAL AFFAIR (Warner Brothers HS 3458)

1980: Happy Endings/Make It To The Sky (Warner Brothers 49594)

1980: You Never Left Me Alone/Get Out Your Handkerchief (Warner Brothers 49646)

1981: PERFORMANCE (Warner Brothers 2WB 3524) two-album set, recorded live

1981: It Shows In The Eyes/Enough (Warner Brothers 49805)

1981: I Need Your Light/It's The Long Run (Warner Brothers 49867)

1982: STREET OPERA (Capitol ST-12207)

1982: Street Corner/Make It Work Again (Capitol 5109)

1982: Love It Away/Street Opera (Part 2) (Capitol 5146)

1982: I'll Take The Whole World On/ Mighty Mighty Love (Capitol 5190)

1983: HIGH-RISE (Capitol ST-12282)

1983: I'm Not That Tough/ (Capitol 5310)

1984: SOLID (Capitol ST-12366)

1984: Solid (part 1)/Solid (part 2) (Capitol 5397)

1984: Outta The World/ (Capitol 5434)

1986: REAL LOVE (Capitol ST-12469)

1986: Count Your Blessings/Side Effect (Capitol 5598)

FOR MORE INFORMATION
Ebony, February 1979.

(See also VALERIE SIMPSON.)

FLORENCE BALLARD

Born June 30, 1943, in Detroit; died February 22, 1976. Starting 1959-1960, Florence was an original member of the Primettes while attending Detroit's Northwestern High School (Diana Ross attended Cass Technical High School and Mary Wilson, Northeastern High School). She auditioned with the Primettes for Berry Gordy, who initially rejected them. Then the group recorded "Tears of Sorrow" and "Pretty Baby" for the Detroit label, Lupine (Lupine 120). They also sang backing vocals for other singers on that label. In 1961, the Primettes signed with Motown, and their name was changed to the Supremes. Flo sang lead on the group's second release, "Buttered Popcorn" (Tamla 54045). All subsequent Supremes releases were on the Motown label.

Called "the quiet one" by Diana Ross and Mary Wilson, Florence Ballard was a member of the Supremes until mid-1967, when she was asked to leave the group. Motown's official reason for her departure was that the strain of touring had become too great for her. She was replaced by Cindy Birdsong, a member of Patti LaBelle's backing group, The Blue Belles. Florence would later name Cindy Birdsong, Jean Terrell, Diana Ross, and Mary Wilson, along with Motown Records and International Management Corp., in a suit charging conspiracy to oust her from the Supremes.

Florence married Tom Chapman, a Motown staffer who was also Berry Gordy's chauffeur, on February 29, 1968. He became her manager, and in July 1968 she signed with ABC Records as a solo artist. Although her singles were released in the United States and England, none of them did well. She died tragically in 1976 of a cardiac arrest.

NON-MOTOWN DISCOGRAPHY

1968: It Doesn't Matter How I Say It/Goin' Out of My Head (ABC 11074)*

1968: Love Ain't Love/Forever Faithful (ABC 11144)*

*Also released in Great Britain on Stateside.

(See also PRIMETTES; SUPREMES.)

J. J. BARNES

J. J. is a sweet-soul singer. He recorded for several Detroit labels, including Kable, Ric-Tic, Groovesville, and Revilot. Ric-Tic's parent company, Golden World, was purchased by Motown in October, 1966. Although he is occasionally linked to Motown through his association with Ric-Tic and Edwin Starr, J. J. Barnes' recordings for Motown were never released. He performed with the Motown Revue, and appeared with them at Detroit's Fox Theater in December, 1966.

He began his recording career at age sixteen with his first release, "Won't You Let Me Know," on Detroit's Kable label. He recorded for Eddie Wingate's Ric-Tic label from 1965 to 1966. His most popular song for Ric-Tic was "Real Humdinger" (Ric-Tic 110). After he failed to get a follow-up hit, he signed with Solid Hitbound Productions in 1967 and began recording for their Groovesville label. Solid Hitbound also issued his records on their Revilot label, which recorded George Clinton's original Parliaments ["(I Wanna) Testify"] and Darrel Banks ["Open The Door To Your Heart"], among others.

NON-MOTOWN DISCOGRAPHY

1959: Won't You Let Me Know/ (Kable)
1965: I Think I Found A Love/Please Let Me In (Ric-Tic 106)
1966: Real Humdinger/ I Ain't Gonna Do It (Ric-Tic 110)
1966: Day Tripper/Don't Bring Me Bad News (Ric-Tic 115)
1967: Say It/Deeper In Love (Ric-Tic 117)
1967: Baby Please Come Back Home/ Chains Of Love (Groovesville 1006)
1967: Now That I Got You Back/Forgive Me (Groovesville 1008)
1967: Easy Living/ (Groovesville 1009)
1968: Hold On To It/Now She's Gone (Revilot 216)
1968: Sad Day A Coming/I'll Keep Coming Back (Revilot 218)
1968: Our Love (Is In The Pocket)/All Your Goodies Are Gone (Revilot 222)
1969: So Called Friends/Now She's Gone (Revilot 225)
1969: Snowflakes/Got To Get Rid Of You (Volt 4027)
----: Cloudy Days/. . . (Magic Touch 1001)
----: Touching You/Living Doll (Perception 546)
----: Won't You Let Me Know/. . . (Rich 1005 & 1737dj)

JOHNNY BRISTOL

Motown producer. Teamed with Harvey Fuqua to produce "Aint' No Mountain Enough," recorded by Marvin Gaye and Tammi Terrell. Other co-productions with Harvey Fuqua include "Your Precious Love" and "If I Could Build My Whole World Around You," both recorded by Marvin Gaye and Tammi Terrell, Tammi Terrell's "I Can't Believe You Love Me," and "Just Walk in My Shoes," recorded by Gladys Knight and the Pips.

G. C. CAMERON

Joined the Spinners in 1967 after serving in Vietnam as a marine. Noted for his lead vocals on such songs as "It's a Shame" and "We'll Have It Made." He stayed with Motown in 1971 as a solo artist when the Spinners left for Atlantic Records. His replacement in the Spinners was Phillipe Wynne.

MOTOWN DISCOGRAPHY

8/71: Act Like A Shotgun/Girl, I Really Love You (Mowest MW 55F)
3/72: What It Is, What It Is/You Are That Special One (Mowest MW 5015F)
1/73: Don't Wanna Play Pajama Games/ Jesus Help Me Find Another Way (Mowest MW 5036F)
4/73: No Matter Where/Have I Lost You (Motown 1234)
7/73: Time/Let Me Down Easy (Motown 1261)
8/74: If You Don't Love Me/Topics (Motown 1311)
11/74: LOVE SONGS & OTHER TRAGEDIES (Motown M6-819S1)
4/75: Tippin'/If You're Ever Gonna Love Me (Motown 1347)
9/75: It's So Hard To Say Goodbye To Yesterday/Haulin'+ Cold Blooded (Instrumental) (Motown 1364)
5/76: G. C. CAMERON (Motown M6-855S1)
7/76: Dream Lady/Tippin (Motown 1397)
1/77: YOU'RE WHAT'S MISSING IN MY LIFE (Motown M6-880S1)
3/77: You're What's Missing In My Life/ Kiss Me When You Want To (Motown 1412)
9/77: Let's Make A Deal/Love To The Rescue (Motown 1426) As by Syreeta and G.C. Cameron
9/77: RICH LOVE, POOR LOVE (Motown M6-891S1) As by Syreeta and G.C. Cameron

Come Get This Thang/My Woman
(Mowest MW 5035F) As by G. C.
Cameron and Willie Hutch
7TH SON (Mowest MW 107)
[ALBUM TITLE UNKNOWN] (Mowest
MW 124)
I'm Gonna Get You Pt. 1/I'm Gonna
Get You Pt. 2 (Mowest MW 5012F)

(See also SPINNERS)

CHOKER CAMPBELL

Played tenor sax and was the leader of
the road band used in the Motown Revue.
Also led big bands in recording sessions at
the Greystone Ballroom in Detroit. In 1969,
he established the Tri-City Recording Co.
in Saginaw, Michigan; labels included Tri-City,
Moonville USA, Ultra-City, and Gospel Train.

MOTOWN DISCOGRAPHY

12/64: Come See About Me/Pride And Joy
(Motown 1072)
3/65: HITS OF THE SIXTIES (Motown
MT-620)

CHARLENE

Born Charlene D'Angelo in Hollywood,
California, on June 1, 1950. She joined
Motown as a solo vocalist in 1974. She was
teamed with Ron Miller, songwriter-producer,
who rewrote "I've Never Been to Me" for
her. When it was released in 1977 on Motown
subsidiary Prodigal 636, it went unnoticed;
but it was revived in 1982 through the efforts
of deejay Scott Shannon in Tampa, Florida.
Motown then reissued the song on Motown
1611M, and it went to #3 on the pop charts.
Charlene had quit the music business in 1980,
but was signed again to Motown by President
Jay Lasker in 1982. Later that year, Charlene
recorded a duet with Stevie Wonder, "Used
To Be" (Motown 1650M).

MOTOWN DISCOGRAPHY

11/76: It Ain't Easy Comin' Down/On My
Way To You (Prodigal 632)

11/76: CHARLENE (Prodigal P6-115)
3/77: Freddie/Freddie (Instrumental)
(Prodigal 633)
5/77: SONGS OF LOVE (Prodigal 118)
7/77: I've Never Been To Me/It's Really
Nice To Be In Love Again (Prodigal
636)
7/80: Hungry/I Won't Remember Ever
Loving You (Motown 1492)
3/82: I've Never Been To Me/Somewhere
In My Life (Motown 1611MF)
3/82: I'VE NEVER BEEN TO ME
(Motown 69ML)
6/82: It Ain't Easy Comin' Down/If I
Could See Myself (Motown 1621MF)
6/82: Nunca He Ido A Mi/If I Could See
Myself (Latino 1624LF)
10/82: Used To Be/I Want To Come Back
As A Song (Motown 1650MF) 'A'
side by Charlene and Stevie Wonder
10/82: USED TO BE (Motown 6027ML)
1/83: THE SKY'S THE LIMIT (Motown
6024ML)
2/83: I Want To Go Back There Again/
Richie's Song (For Richard Oliver)
(Motown 1663MF)
7/84: We're Both In Love With You/I Want
The World To Know He's Mine
(Motown 1734MF)
7/84: HIT & RUN LOVER (Motown
6090ML)
9/84: Hit And Run Lover/The Last Song
(Motown 1761MF)

CHRIS CLARK

Signed with Motown in 1963 as a solo
recording artist. After her singing career,
she became an executive with Motown. She
collaborated on the script for the film, "Lady
Sings the Blues."

MOTOWN DISCOGRAPHY

12/65: Don't Be Too Long/Do Right Baby
Do Right (V.I.P. 25031)
8/66: Love's Gone Bad/Put Yourself In
My Place (V.I.P. 25038)
2/67: I Want To Go Back There Again/
I Love You (V.I.P. 25041)
8/67: SOUL SOUNDS (Motown MS-664)
9/67: From Head To Toe/The Beginning
Of The End (Motown 1114)
2/68: Whisper You Love Me Boy/The Begin-

Photo courtesy Peter Benjaminson.

CHOKER CAMPBELL

CHRIS CLARK

Recording artist Chris Clark became a Motown executive, and contributed to the film "Lady Sings The Blues."

ning Of The End (Motown 1121)
11/69: CC RIDES AGAIN (Weed 801)

THE COMMODORES

Lionel Richie - vocals, sax, piano (left in 1982 to pursue solo career)

Thomas McClary - guitar, vocals (left 1984 for solo career)

Ronald LaPread - bass, vocals

William King - trumpet, vocals

Walter Orange - drums

Milan Williams - keyboards, vocals

J.D. Nicholas - vocals (from England, joined late 1984)

The band formed in 1967 at Tuskegee Institute in Alabama, where all of the members were students. The group was originally known as The Mystics when they won a talent contest at Tuskegee, and before that as The Jays. They became The Commodores in 1969. From 1968-1972, they played the New York funk circuit, breaking in at Small's Paradise in Harlem after graduation. There is one pre-Motown album on Atlantic, the result of a one-off deal.

Original personnel had been maintained throughout their career until (a) Lionel Richie left in 1982 to become a solo artist; (b) Thomas McClary left in 1984; and (c) J. D. Nicholas was added. An important part of the Commodores was their manager, Bennie Ashburn (died 1982), who introduced them to Motown executive Suzanne De Passe in 1972. She let them audition as an opening act for the Jackson 5's European tour, and they subsequently went on the tour. The Commodores were Motown's best-selling act of the 1970s, and their success was not limited to American audiences. For the period 1974-1980, they averaged sales of two million albums per year in addition to their singles. Their first four albums went gold (500,000 units), then two platinum albums (1 million units), then a double-platinum album (two million units), and two triple-platinum albums (over three million units). Their first album, MACHINE GUN, went gold in five countries, while their single, "Three Times a Lady," reached the top five in twenty-five countries. During this period, their main competition was Earth, Wind, and Fire. In 1977, they played themselves in the movie, "Thank God It's Friday," which was released by Columbia in 1978; Motown co-produced the film with Casablanca Records. In 1978, The Commodores were named the #1 r&b group by *Rolling Stone* magazine.

The Commodores toured extensively with the Jackson 5 during the period 1972-1975. In 1976, they played a forty-two city tour with the O'Jays. In early 1977, they had a very successful Australian tour. 1977-78 saw a fifty-date world tour. In 1978, they also toured ninety U.S. cities, grossing over $9 million at small and medium-sized arenas. Their 1980 tour of larger arenas used a futuristic set, including a lucite piano. They have also toured with the Rolling Stones and Earth, Wind, and Fire. Their first album without Lionel Richie was COMMODORES 13 (Motown 6054ML), released in 1983. Their next album, NIGHTSHIFT (Motown 6124ML), came out in 1985 and produced the hit single of the same name. The lineup featured J. D. Nicholas, who replaced Thomas McClary. In 1986, they left Motown and released an album on Polydor, UNITED (Polydor 831-194-1-Y1).

MOTOWN DISCOGRAPHY

3/72: The Zoo (The Human Zoo)/I'm Looking For Love (Mowest MW 59F)

1/73: Don't You Be Worried/Determination (Mowest MW 5038F)

4/73: Are You Happy/There's A Song In My Heart (Motown 1268)

5/74: Machine Gun/There's A Song In My Heart (Motown 1307)

7/74: MACHINE GUN (Motown M6-798S1)

10/74: I Feel Sanctified/It Is As Good As You Make It (Motown 1319)

3/75: CAUGHT IN THE ACT (Motown M6-820S1)

4/75: Slippery When Wet/The Bump (Motown 1338)

9/75: This Is Your Life/Look What You've Done To Me (Motown 1361)

10/75: MOVIN' ON (Motown M6-848S1)

12/75: Sweet Love/Better Never Than Forever (Motown 1381)

6/76: HOT ON THE TRACKS (Motown M6-867S1)

8/76: Just To Be Close To You/Thumpin' Music (Motown 1402)

12/76: Fancy Dancer/Cebu (Motown 1408)

4/77: COMMODORES (Motown M7-884R1)

5/77: Easy/Can't Let You Tease Me (Motown 1418)

THE COMMODORES

THE CONTOURS

8/77: Brick House/Captain Quick Draw (Motown 1425)

11/77: COMMODORES LIVE! (Motown M9-894A2)

12/77: Too Hot Ta Trot/Funky Situation (Motown 1432)

5/78: Three Times A Lady/Look What You've Done To Me (Motown 1443)

5/78: NATURAL HIGH (Motown M7-902R1)

10/78: COMMODORES GREATEST HITS (Motown M7-912R1)

12/78: Flying High/X-Rated Movie (Motown 1452)

7/79: MIDNIGHT MAGIC (Motown M8-926M1)

8/79: Sail On/Thumpin' Music (Motown 1466)

9/79: Still/Such A Woman (Motown 1474)

12/79: Wonderland/Lovin' You (Motown 1479)

5/80: HEROES (Motown M8-939M1)

6/80: Old-Fashioned Love/Sexy Lady (Motown 1489)

9/80: Heroes/Funky Situation (Motown 1495)

11/80: Jesus Is Love/Mighty Spirit (Motown 1502)

5/81: IN THE POCKET (Motown M8-955M1)

6/81: Lady (You Bring Me Up)/Gettin' It (Motown 1514)

9/81: Oh No/Lovin' You (Motown 1527)

1/82: Why You Wanna Try Me/X-Rated Movie (Motown 1604MF)

11/82: Painted Picture/Reach High (Instrumental) (Motown 1651MF)

11/82: ALL THE GREAT HITS (Motown 6028ML)

2/83: Reach High/Sexy Lady (Motown 1661MF)

4/83: ANTHOLOGY (Motown 6044ML2)

8/83: Only You/Cebu (Motown 1694MF)

9/83: 13 (Motown 6054ML)

10/83: MACHINE GUN / MOVIN' ON (Motown 6074MC)

1/84: Turn Off The Lights/Been Lovin' You (Motown 1719MF)

2/84: COMPACT COMMAND PER-FORMANCES: 14 GREATEST HITS (Motown MCD06068MD)

9/84: ALL THE GREAT LOVE SONGS (Motown MCD06107MD)

12/84: Nightshift/I Keep Running (Motown 1773MF)

12/84: NIGHTSHIFT (Motown 6124ML)

4/85: Animal Instinct/Lightin' Up The Night (Motown 1788MF)

7/85: Janet/I'm In Love (Motown 1802MF)

7/85: LIONEL RICHIE THE COMPOSER: GREAT LOVE SONGS WITH THE COMMODORES AND DIANA ROSS (Motown MCD06143MD)

Unissued Motown Recordings

[ALBUM TITLE UNKNOWN] (Mowest MW 110)

Wide Open/ (Motown 1366)

Some Inside/Time (Motown 1394)

High On Sunshine/Thumpin' Music (Motown 1399)

Say Yeah/Thumpin' Music (Motown 1457)

ANTHOLOGY (Motown M8-954M1) Title later used with different number

NON-MOTOWN DISCOGRAPHY

1986: UNITED (Polydor 831-194-1-Y1)

1986: Goin' To The Bank/Serious Love (Polydor 885-358-7)

(See also LIONEL RICHIE.)

THE CONTOURS

The original Contours, formed in 1959, included Billy Gordon as lead vocalist, Billy Hoggs, Joe Billingslea, and Sylvester Potts. Hubert Johnson soon joined the group, and his distant cousin, singer Jackie Wilson, helped the group land a seven-year contract with Motown in 1961. Guitarist Hughey Davis joined the group in 1962 in time for their biggest hit, "Do You Love Me" (Gordy 7005). The group declined in popularity during the mid-1960s and underwent numerous personnel changes. Over the years, the group has included Gerald (Jerry) Green, Council Gay, Dennis Edwards (also Temptations), and Joe Stubbs (brother of the Four Tops' Levi Stubbs). They have performed at revival shows since 1972, and a 1984 line-up consisted of Joe Billingslea, Sylvester Potts, and Jerry Green. Hubert Johnson committed suicide in 1981.

2/61: Whole Lotta Woman/Come On And Be Mine (Motown 1008)

7/61: Funny/The Stretch (Motown 1012)

7/62: Do You Love Me/Move, Mr. Man (Gordy 7005)

10/62: DO YOU LOVE ME (NOW THAT I CAN DANCE) (Gordy G-901)

12/62: Shake Sherry/You Better Get In Line (Gordy 7012)

3/63: Don't Let Her Be Your Baby/It Must Be Love (Gordy 7016)

6/63: Pa I Need A Car/You Get Ugly (Gordy 7019)

3/64: Can You Do It/I'll Stand By You (Gordy 7029)

12/64: Can You Jerk Like Me/That Day When She Needed Me (Gordy 7037)

8/65: First I Look At The Purse/Searching For A Girl (Gordy 7044)

3/66: Just A Little Misunderstanding/ Determination (Gordy 7052)

3/67: It's So Hard Being A Loser/Your Love Grows More Precious Everyday (Gordy 7059)

THE CORPORATION

The Corporation was a songwriting production team at Motown that consisted of Freddie Perren, Deke Richards, Fonzie Mizell, and Berry Gordy, Jr. Their credits include the Jackson 5's "I Want You Back," "ABC," and "The Love You Save."

DARNELLS

This name was used for one 1963 single, "Too Hurt To Cry/Come On Home" (Gordy 7024). Appearing on "Come On Home" were Lamont Dozier, Eddie Kendricks, Brian Holland, and some of the Marvelettes. "Too Hurt To Cry" featured the renamed Marvelettes going for the Phil Spector-influenced "wall of sound."

MOTOWN DISCOGRAPHY

10/63: Too Hurt To Cry, Too Much In Love To Say Goodbye/Come On Home (Gordy 7024)

HAL DAVIS

Songwriter-producer. Joined Motown in the 1960s, but achieved his greatest successes in the 1970s with the Jackson 5's "I'll Be There" and "Slow Cruisin'," Diana Ross' "Love Hangover," and Thelma Houston's "Don't Leave Me T' Way."

DAZZ BAND

The group is divided into two units, the Dazz Horn Section and the Dazz Rhythm Section.

Dazz Horn Section:
Bobby Harris (leader) - tenor and alto sax, lead and background vocals
Pierre De Mudd - trumpet, lead and background vocals
Sennie "Skip" Martin - trumpet, lead and background vocals
Dazz Rhythm Section:
Steve Cox or Kevin Kendrick - keyboards
Keith Harrison (joined 1982) - keyboards, lead and background vocals
Eric Fearman or Marlon McClain - guitar
Kenny Pettus - percussion, lead and background vocals
Isaac Wiley, Jr. - drums, background vocals
Michael Wiley - bass

The group was formed in the early 1970s in Cleveland as a jazz-fusion band calling themselves Bell Telephunk. On the strength of their demos, they were signed by 20th-Century Fox Records, where they changed their name to Kinsman Dazz. Their two most popular singles from this period were "Might As Well Forget About Lovin' You" and "Catchin' Up On Love." In 1980, they signed with Motown and became known as the Dazz Band. In 1982, their single, "Let It Whip" (Motown 1609M), reached #5 on the pop charts. It was taken from their album, KEEP IT LIVE (Motown 6004M). Bobby Harris, the group's leader, has shared production credits with Reggie Andrews since 1983. The group left Motown in mid-1986 and signed with Geffen Records.

MOTOWN DISCOGRAPHY

10/80: INVITATION TO LOVE (Motown M8-946M1)

11/80: Shake It Up/Only Love (Motown 1500)

2/81: Invitation To Love/Magnetized (Motown 1507)

3/81: LET THE MUSIC PLAY (Motown M8-957M1)

8/81: Knock! Knock/Sooner Or Later (Motown 1515)

10/81: Let The Music Play/Hello Girl (Motown 1528)

2/82: KEEP IT LIVE (Motown 6004ML)

3/82: Let It Whip/Everyday Love (Motown 1609MF)

6/82: Keep It Live (On The K.I.L.)/This Time It's Forever (Motown 1622MF)

1/83: One The One For Fun/Just Believe In Love (Motown 1659MF)

1/83: ON THE ONE (Motown 6031ML)

4/83: Cheek To Cheek/Can We Dance (Motown 1676MF)

6/83: Party Right Here/Gamble With My Love (Motown 1680MF)

10/83: Joystick/Don't Get Caught Up In The Middle (Motown 1701MF)

11/83: JOYSTICK (Motown 6084ML)

4/84: Sweep/Bad Girl (Motown 1725MF)

9/84: Let It All Blow/Now That I Have You (Motown 1760MF)

9/84: JUKEBOX (Motown 6117ML)

1/85: Heartbeat/Rock With Me (Motown 1775MF)

6/85: Hot Spot/I've Been Waiting (Motown 1800MF)

6/85: HOT SPOT (Motown 6149ML)

Unissued Motown Recordings

When You Needed Roses/ (Motown 1820MF)

NON-MOTOWN DISCOGRAPHY

As by Kinsman Dazz:

1978: Might As Well Forget About Loving You/Dazzberry Jam (20th-Century Fox 2390)

1978: Get Down With The Feelin'/Makin' Music (20th-Century Fox 2401)

1979: I Searched Around/Keep On Rockin' (20th-Century Fox 2417)

1979: Catchin' Up On Love/I Searched Around (20th-Century Fox 2435)

1980: Dancin' Free/I Searched Around (20th-Century Fox 2453)

DeBARGE

Eldra DeBarge (born 1961) - guitar (left for solo career in 1986)
Mark DeBarge - percussion
Randy DeBarge - bass
Bunny DeBarge - vocals
Bobby DeBarge - keyboards (also a member of Switch)

Recording on the Gordy label, this musical family's first album was released under the name The DeBarges. The group consisted of four members, featuring the vocals of sister Bunny DeBarge, with Bobby receiving credit as one of the additional musicians. Bobby is the oldest brother; he produced DeBarge's first album and is also a member of Switch, for whom he produces on occasion. Eldra and Bunny received co-producer credits on the first album, too. The dedications on the family's first album note sisters Dedra, Alice, and Peaches, and brothers James (also in Switch), Chico, and Daryl - quite a talent pool. The group received its first national exposure in 1984 as the opening act on Luther Vandross' tour. Subsequent albums were released under the name DeBarge. In 1986, El DeBarge left the group and released a solo album, EL DeBARGE (Gordy 6181GL), containing "Who's Johnny?" (Gordy 1842GF), theme song of the movie "Short Circuit" and a #1 rhythm & blues hit. Younger brother Chico (born 1966) also records as a solo artist. His first album, CHICO DeBARGE (Motown 6214ML), ap-peared in the fall of 1986 and contained the Top 40 hit, "Talk To Me" (Motown 1858MF).

As of early 1987, the remaining members of the band were negotiating with other labels.

MOTOWN DISCOGRAPHY

3/81: THE DeBARGES (Gordy G8-1003M1)

6/81: What's Your Name/You're So Gentle, So Kind (Gordy 7203)

7/82: ALL THIS LOVE (Gordy 6012GL)

8/82: Stop! Don't Tease Me/Hesitated (Gordy 1635GF)

11/82: I Like It/Hesitated (Gordy 1645GF)

4/83: All This Love/I'm In Love With You (Gordy 1660GF)

10/83: Time Will Reveal/I'll Never Fall In Love Again (Gordy 1705GF)

10/83: IN A SPECIAL WAY (Gordy 6061GL)

2/84: Love Me In A Special Way/Dance The Night Away (Gordy 1723GF)

1/85: Rhythm Of The Night/Queen Of My Heart (Gordy 1770GF)

1/85: RHYTHM OF THE NIGHT (Gordy 6123GL)

5/85: Who's Holding Donna Now/Be My Lady (Gordy 1793GF)

8/85: You Wear It Well/Baby, Won't Cha Come Quick (Gordy 1804GF) El DeBarge with DeBarge

11/85: The Heart Is Not So Smart/Share My World (Gordy 1822GF) El DeBarge with DeBarge

3/86: GREATEST HITS (Gordy GCD06173GD)

4/86: Who's Johnny/Love Me In A Special Way (Gordy 1842GF) 'A' side as by El DeBarge; 'B' side as by El Debarge with DeBarge

4/86: EL DEBARGE (Gordy 6181GL) El DeBarge

7/86: Love Always/The Walls (Came Tumbling Down) (Gordy 1857GF) El DeBarge

8/86: Talk To Me/If It Takes All Night (Motown 1858MF) Chico DeBarge

10/86: Someone/Stop Don't Tease Me (Gordy 1867GF) El DeBarge

10/86: CHICO DE BARGE (Motown 6214ML) Chico DeBarge

11/86: Save The Best For Me (Best Of Your Lovin')/Life Begins With You (Gordy 1869GF) Bunny DeBarge, 'B' side as by Bunny Debarge with DeBarge

Unissued Motown Recordings

Dance The Night Away (Gordy 7198)

(See also SWITCH.)

BUNNY DeBARGE (See DeBARGE)

CHICO DeBARGE (See DeBARGE)

EL DeBARGE (See DeBARGE)

THE DeBARGES (See DeBARGE)

DEL-PHIS

An early version of Martha and the Vandellas that featured Gloria Williams on lead vocals. Released one single in 1961 on Check-Mate, a Detroit-based subsidiary of Chess Records: "It Takes Two/I'll Let You Know" (Check-Mate 1005). Can also be heard doing backup vocals for such Detroit artists as J.J. Barnes, Mike Hanks, and Leon Peterson.

(See also MARTHA & THE VANDELLAS.)

THE DISTANTS
Otis Williams
Elbridge (Al) Bryant
Melvin Franklin
Richard Street
James Crawford

In 1960, Berry Gordy heard the group playing at a Detroit location and asked them to come over to the Hitsville U.S.A. recording studio. Paul Williams and Eddie Kendricks had just replaced Richard Street and James Crawford, and the group was calling itself the Elgins. Their first record for Berry Gordy was released on the Miracle label in 1961 as the Temptations: "Oh, Mother O Mine/Romance Without Finance" (Miracle 5). Prior to becoming the Temptations, the Distants recorded for the Detroit label, Northern, and in 1959 released two singles on Warwick: "Always/Come On" (Warwick 546) "Open Up Your Heart/Always" (Warwick 577).

(See also THE TEMPTATIONS.)

THE DOWNBEATS
Cleo "Duke" Miller
Johnny Dawson
Robert Fleming

With the addition of Sandra Edwards in 1966, the group became the Elgins and had two Top 10 r&b hits, "Darling Baby" (V.I.P. 25029) and "Heaven Must Have Sent You" (V.I.P. 25037). First pressings of "Darling Baby" listed the group as the Downbeats.

MOTOWN DISCOGRAPHY

10/59: Your Baby's Back/Request Of A Fool

(Tamla 54026)
2/62: Your Baby's Back/Request Of A Fool
(Tamla 54056)

Unissued Motown Recordings

INTRODUCING THE DOWNBEATS
(Tamla TM-225)

(See also ELGINS.)

LAMONT DOZIER

Born June 16, 1941, in Detroit. He achieved greatest recognition as part of the songwriting-production team of Holland-Dozier-Holland. He was passed up as a songwriter by many New York record companies before coming to Motown. He also recorded as a vocalist with the Romeos, the Voice Masters, and as Lamont Anthony.

In 1962, he recorded an early Holland-Dozier-Holland collaboration, "Dearest One," for the Motown subsidiary, Mel-O-Dy. He then joined Brian Holland and Freddie Gorman to form a songwriting team at Motown; Eddie Holland soon replaced Freddie Gorman.

After H-D-H left Motown in 1968-69, they formed their own labels, Invictus and Hot Wax. Dozier left Invictus in 1972 to pursue a solo career. He recorded for ABC Records (1973-75) and then for Warner Brothers.

MOTOWN DISCOGRAPHY

6/62: Dearest One/Fortune Teller Tell Me
(Melody 102)
8/63: What Goes Up-Must Come Down/
Come On Home (Motown 1045) With
Eddie Holland

NON-MOTOWN DISCOGRAPHY

Records as by Lamont Anthony:

1960: Let's Talk It Over/Benny the Skinny
Man (Anna 1125)

First release of this single had "Popeye the Sailor Man" instead of "Benny the Skinny Man." It was withdrawn at the request of King Features, which owned the copyright to Popeye.

1961: Just To Be Loved/I Didn't Know
(Check-Mate 1001)

Records as by Lamont Dozier:

1973: Trying To Hold On To My Woman/
We Don't Want Nobody To Come
Between Us (ABC 11407)
1974: Fish Ain't Bitin'/Breaking Out All
Over (ABC 11438 and 12012; also
released on Dunhill 15012)
1974: Let Me Start Tonite/I Wanna Be With
You (ABC 12044)
1975: All Cried Out/Rose (ABC 12076)
1976: Out Here On My Own/Take Off
Your Makeup (ABC 12234)
1976: Can't Get Off Until The Feeling
Stops/Jump Right On In (Warner
Brothers 8240)
1977: Going Back To My Roots (Part 1)/
Going Back To My Roots (Part 2)
(Warner Brothers 8363)
1977: Sight For Sore Eyes/Tear Down The
Walls (Warner Brothers 8432)
1979: Boogie Business/True Love Is
Bittersweet (Warner Brothers 8792
and 8802)

Albums:

1974: BLACK BACH (ABC ABCD-839)
1976: RIGHT THERE (Warner Brothers BS
2929)
1977: PEDDLIN' MUSIC ON THE SIDE
(Warner Brothers BS 3039)
1979: BITTERSWEET (Warner Brothers
BSK 3282)

FOR MORE INFORMATION
Propes, Steve. "Lamont Dozier: An Insider's Inside Look At Motown," in *Goldmine*, June 20, 1986.

(See also HOLLAND-DOZIER-HOLLAND.)

DYNAMIC SUPERIORS
George Wesley Peterback, Jr.
Michael McCalpin
Tony Washington
George Spann
Maurice Washington

This vocal group started as teenagers in Washington, DC. They were discovered at an Atlanta, Georgia, talent show by Motown president, Ewart Abner, who was attending a disc jockey convention there. They signed with Motown in 1974, leaving the label in 1978. Their most popular song came from their first album (Motown 822) and was called "Shoe Shoe Shine" (Motown 1324). Their second album, PURE PLEASURE (Motown 841), was produced by Nick Ashford and Valerie Simpson.

MOTOWN DISCOGRAPHY

9/74: Shoe Shoe Shine/Release Me (Motown 1324)
JA75: THE DYNAMIC SUPERIORS (Motown M6-822S1)
3/75: Leave It Alone/One-Nighter (Motown 1342)
7/75: PURE PLEASURE (Motown M6-841S1)
8/75: Nobody's Gonna Change Me/I Got Away (Motown 1359)
10/75: Deception/One-Nighter (Motown 1365)
10/76: YOU NAME IT (Motown M6-875S1)
1/77: I Can't Stay Away (From Someone I Love)/Supersensousensation (Try Some Love) (Motown 1413)
6/77: Nowhere To Run Pt. 1/Nowhere To Run Pt. 2 (Motown 1419)
6/77: GIVE & TAKE (Motown M6-879S1)
10/77: You're What I Need/Here Comes That Feeling Again (Motown 1428)

Unissued Motown Recordings

Romeo/I Got Away (Motown 1357)
SKY'S THE LIMIT (Motown 862)

EIVETS REDNOW (See STEVIE WONDER)

ELGINS
Saundra Edwards (also Saundra Mallett) - lead vocals
Cleo "Duke" Miller
Johnny Dawson
Robert Fleming

In 1962, Saundra Mallett recorded "It's Gonna Be Hard Times" (Tamla 54067), with the Vandellas as backing group. That same year, Dawson, Miller, and Fleming recorded "Your Baby's Back" (Tamla 54056) as the Downbeats. The Elgins appeared on V.I.P. in 1965-66 with an album and two Top 10 r&b hits, "Darling Baby" and "Heaven Must Have Sent You." First pressings of "Darling Baby" list the group as the Downbeats rather than as the Elgins. (NOTE: The name, Elgins, was used briefly by the Temptations circa 1960, before their first release on the Miracle label.)

MOTOWN DISCOGRAPHY

12/65: Darling Baby/Put Yourself In My Place (V.I.P. 25029)
7/66: Heaven Must Have Sent You/Stay In My Lonely Arms (V.I.P. 25037)
10/66: DARLING BABY (V.I.P. VIPS-400)
6/67: I Understand My Man/It's Been A Long Long Time (V.I.P. 25043)
9/71: Heaven Must Have Sent You/Stay In My Lonely Arms (V.I.P. 25065)

(See also DOWNBEATS.)

FANTASTIC FOUR
James Epps
Joe Pruitt
Ralph Pruitt
William Hunter
Wallace Childs (replaced William Hunter)

Recording artists for the Detroit label, Ric-Tic, from 1966 to 1968, they were acquired by Motown when the company purchased Ric-Tic in 1968. After a few releases on Motown's V.I.P. label, the group was not re-signed by Motown and later recorded for Detroit's Solid Hitbound Productions on their labels, Eastbound and Westbound.

MOTOWN DISCOGRAPHY

9/68: I Love You Madly/I Love You Madly (Instrumental) (Soul 35052)
3/69: I Feel Like I'm Falling In Love Again/Pin Point It Down (Soul 35058)
3/69: BEST OF THE FANTASTIC FOUR (Soul SS-717)
9/69: Just Another Lonely Night/Don't Care Why You Want Me (Long As You Want Me) (Soul 35065)
3/70: On The Brighter Side Of A Blue World/I'm Gonna Carry On (Soul 35072)

HOW SWEET HE IS (Soul SS-722)

NON-MOTOWN DISCOGRAPHY

1966: Girl Have Pity/(I'm Gonna) Live Up To What She Thinks (Ric-Tic 119)

1967: Can't Stop Looking For My Baby/Just The Lonely (Ric-Tic 121)

1967: The Whole World Is A Stage/Ain't Love Wonderful (Ric-Tic 122)

1967: You Gave Me Something (And Everything's Alright)/I Don't Wanna Live Without You (Ric-Tic 128)

1967: As Long As I Live (I Live For You)/ To Share Your Love (Ric-Tic 130)

1968: Goddess Of Love/As Long As The Feeling Is There (Ric-Tic 134)

1968: Goddess Of Love/Love Is A Many Splendoured Thing (Ric-Tic 136)

1968: Man In Love/No Love Like Your Love (Ric-Tic 137)

1968: I've Got To Have You/Win Or Lose (Ric-Tic 139)

1968: I Love You Madly/I Love You Madly (Instrumental) (Ric-Tic 144)

1974: I Had This Whole World To Choose From/If You Need Me (Eastbound 620)

1974: I'm Falling In Love/I Believe In Miracles (Eastbound 620)

1975: Alvin Stone (The Birth & Death of a Gangster)/I Believe In Miracles (Westbound 5009)

1975: Have A Little Mercy/ (Westbound 5017)

1976: Hideaway/They Took The Show On The Road (Westbound 5032)

1977: Got To Have Your Love/Ain't I Been Good To You (Westbound 55403)

1977: Mixed Up Moods And Attitudes/ Disco Pool Blues (Westbound 55408)

1977: Sexy Lady/ (Westbound 55417)

1977: B.Y.O.F./If This Is Love (Westbound 55419)

FOUR TOPS

Levi Stubbs
Lawrence Payton
Abdul "Duke" Fakir
Renaldo "Obie" Benson

The line-up of this very successful quartet has remained stable since they released their first single in 1954 as The Four Aims. In 1956, they changed their name to The Four Tops for their single, "Kiss Me Baby" (Chess 1623). During the period 1956-1962, they played the national club circuit (e.g., Las Vegas, Miami, etc.) and put out records for three different labels that just didn't go anywhere. In 1962, they signed with Red Top records and recorded several tracks, none of which Red Top felt were good enough to be released. The turning point in their career came in 1963 when they met with Berry Gordy, who signed them for Motown. Initially, they were to record on Gordy's Workshop Jazz label, and one album in a jazz-pop style was recorded. They were then switched to the Motown label and, in an attempt to find suitable material for the group, were assigned to the Holland-Dozier-Holland team. Starting with "Baby I Need Your Loving" (Motown 1062), the group went on to record thirteen Top 10 hits for the period 1964-1971. Most of these hits were written and produced by Holland-Dozier-Hol-land.

"Baby I Need Your Loving" charted in August 1964, and the group made their first tour of Great Britain in 1965.

Indicative of their popularity in England, they sold out two complete houses at the Royal Albert Hall two years later. While "Baby I Need Your Loving" only reached #11 on the pop charts, the group scored two #1 pop hits with "I Can't Help Myself" (Motown 1076) in 1965, and "Reach Out I'll Be There" (Motown 1098) in 1966. In 1971 and 1972, the group joined with the Supremes for several recordings as a septet.

In late 1972, Four Tops' releases began appearing in the United States on Dunhill (and in England on Probe). They scored a "comeback" hit in 1973 with "Ain't No Woman (Like The One I've Got)" (Dunhill 4339), but were unable to match their earlier popularity. In 1975, they signed with ABC Records and began recording with Casablanca in 1981.

The Four Tops rejoined Motown in 1983 after they appeared on Motown's 25th anniversary show.

MOTOWN DISCOGRAPHY

7/64: Baby I Need Your Loving/Call On Me (Motown 1062)

11/64: Without The One You Love (Life's Not Worthwhile)/Love Has Gone

THE FOUR TOPS

The Four Tops' line-up has been stable throughout their long career.

Photo courtesy Motown Archives, Eastern Michigan University.

(Motown 1069)

1/65: Ask The Lonely/Where Did You Go (Motown 1073)

1/65: FOUR TOPS (Motown MS-622)

4/65: I Can't Help Myself/Sad Souvenirs (Motown 1076)

7/65: It's The Same Old Song/Your Love Is Amazing (Motown 1081)

10/65: Something About You/Darling I Hum Our Song (Motown 1084)

11/65: FOUR TOPS SECOND ALBUM (Motown MS-634)

2/66: Shake Me Wake Me (When It's Over)/ Just As Long As You Need Me (Motown 1090)

5/66: Loving You Is Sweeter Than Ever/I Like Everything About You (Motown 1096)

8/66: Reach Out I'll Be There/Until You Love Someone (Motown 1098)

8/66: FOUR TOPS ON TOP (Motown MS-647)

11/66: Standing In The Shadows Of Love/ Since You've Been Gone (Motown 1102)

11/66: FOUR TOPS LIVE! (Motown MS-654)

1/67: FOUR TOPS ON BROADWAY (Motown MS-657)

2/67: Bernadette/I Got A Feeling (Motown 1104)

5/67: 7 Rooms Of Gloom/I'll Turn To Stone (Motown 1110)

7/67: FOUR TOPS REACH OUT (Motown MS-660)

8/67: You Keep Running Away/If You Don't Want My Love (Motown 1113)

9/67: FOUR TOPS GREATEST HITS (Motown MS-662)

1/68: Walk Away Renee/Your Love Is Wonderful (Motown 1119)

4/68: If I Were A Carpenter/Wonderful Baby (Motown 1124)

6/68: For Once In My Life/Yesterday's Dreams (Motown 1127)

9/68: I'm In A Different World/Remember When (Motown 1132)

9/68: YESTERDAY'S DREAMS (Motown MS-669)

4/69: What Is A Man/Don't Bring Back Memories (Motown 1147)

6/69: NOW (Motown MS-675)

11/69: Don't Let Him Take Your Love From Me/The Key (Motown 1159)

11/69: SOUL SPIN (Motown MS-695)

3/70: It's All In The Game/Love (Motown 1164)

3/70: STILL WATERS RUN DEEP (Motown MS-704)

8/70: Still Water (Love)/Still Water (Peace) (Motown 1170)

9/70: CHANGING TIMES (Motown MS-721)

9/70: THE MAGNIFICENT 7 (Motown MS-717) Supremes and Four Tops

11/70: River Deep, Mountain High/Together We Can Make Such Sweet Music (Motown 1173) Supremes and Four Tops

12/70: Just Seven Numbers (Can Straighten Out My Life)/I Wish I Were Your Mirror (Motown 1175)

5/71: You Gotta Have Love In Your Heart/I'm Glad About It (Motown 1181) Supremes and Four Tops

5/71: In These Changing Times/Right Before My Eyes (Motown 1185)

6/71: THE RETURN OF THE MAGNIFICENT SEVEN (Motown MS-736) Supremes and Four Tops

8/71: MacArthur Park (Part 1)/MacArthur Park (Part 2) (Motown 1189)

9/71: GREATEST HITS VOL. 2 (Motown M-740L)

12/71: DYNAMITE (Motown M-745L) Supremes and Four Tops

1/72: A Simple Game/L.A. (My Town) (Motown 1196)

4/72: I Can't Quit Your Love/Happy (Is A Bumpy Road) (Motown 1198)

4/72: NATURE PLANNED IT (Motown M-748L)

8/72: (It's The Way) Nature Planned It/I'll Never Change (Motown 1210)

4/73: THE BEST OF THE FOUR TOPS (Motown M-764-D)

4/73: THE BEST OF THE FOUR TOPS (Motown 765)

7/74: ANTHOLOGY (Motown M9-809A3)

10/83: I Just Can't Walk Away/Hang (Motown 1706MF)

10/83: FOUR TOPS/REACH OUT (Motown 6075MC)

10/83: BACK WHERE I BELONG (Motown 6066ML)

3/84: Make Yourself At Home/Sing A Song Of Yesterday (Motown 1718MF)

9/84: COMPACT COMMAND PERFORMANCE: 19 GREATEST HITS (Motown MCD06106MD)

5/85: Sexy Ways/Body And Soul (Motown

1790MF)
5/85: MAGIC (Gordy 6130GL)
9/85: Don't Tell Me That It's Over/I'm Ready For Love (Motown 1811MF)
6/86: Hot Nights/Again (Motown 1854MF)
8/86: ANTHOLOGY (Motown MCD06188MD2)
8/86: HOT NIGHTS (Motown 6211ML)

Unissued Motown Recordings

BREAKING THROUGH (Workshop Jazz WSJ 217)
Hey Man - We Got To Get You A Woman/How Can I Forget You (Motown 1254)

NON-MOTOWN DISCOGRAPHY

1956: Kiss Me Baby/Could It Be You (Chess 1623)
1961: Ain't That Love/Lonely Summer (Columbia 41755)
1963: Pennies From Heaven/Where Are You (Riverside 4534)
1965: Ain't That Love/Lonely Summer (Columbia 43356; reissue of Columbia 41755)
1972: Keeper of the Castle/Jubilee With Soul (Dunhill 4330)
1972: Keeper of the Castle (Probe PRO 575) Great Britain
1972: KEEPER OF THE CASTLE (Dunhill DSX 50129)
1973: Ain't No Woman (Like The One I've Got)/The Good Lord Knows (Dunhill 4339)
1973: Are You Man Enough/Peace Of Mind (Dunhill 4354) From the film, "Shaft in Africa"
1973: Sweet Understanding Love/Main Street People (Dunhill 4366)
1973: Sweet Understanding Love/Main Street People (Probe PRO 604) Great Britain
1973: MAIN STREET PEOPLE (Dunhill DSX 50144)
1974: I Just Can't Get You Out of My Mind/Am I My Brother's Keeper (Dunhill 4377)
1974: MEETING OF THE MINDS (Dunhill DSD 50166)
1974: One Chain Don't Make No Prison/ Light of Your Love (Dunhill 4386)
1974: Midnight Flower/All My Love (Dunhill 15005)
1974: LIVE AND IN CONCERT (Dunhill DSD 50188)
1975: Seven Lonely Nights/I Can't Hold Out Much Longer (ABC 12096)
1975: We All Gotta Stick Together/(It Would Almost) Drive Me Out Of My Mind (ABC 12123)
1975: Mama You're All Right With Me/I'm So Glad You Walked Into My Life (ABC 12155)
1975: NIGHT LIGHTS HARMONY (ABC 862)
1976: Catfish/Look At My Baby (ABC 12214 and 12223)
1976: Feel Free/I Know You Like It (ABC 12236)
1976: CATFISH (ABC 968)
1977: Strung Out For Your Love/You Can't Hold Back On Love (ABC 12267)
1977: THE SHOW MUST GO ON (ABC 1014)
1977: Runnin' From Your Love/The Show Must Go On (ABC 12315)
1978: H.E.L.P./Inside A Brokenhearted Man (ABC 12427)
1978: AT THE TOP (ABC/MCA AA 1092)
1979: Just In Time/This House (ABC 12457)
1981: When She Was My Girl/Something To Remember (Casablanca 2338)
1981: Let Me Set You Free/From A Distance (Casablanca 2344)
1981: TONIGHT (Casablanca 7258) Also released as compact disc (Casablanca 800049-2)
1982: Tonight I'm Gonna Love You All Over/I'll Never Leave Again (Casablanca 2345)
1982: Back To School Again/Rock-A-Hula-Luau (RSO 1069) From the film "Grease 2"
1982: Sad Hearts/I Believe In You And Me (Casablanca 2353)

FOR MORE INFORMATION
Hirshey, Gerri. *Nowhere To Run*, pp. 193-200.
Langley, Brian. "Four Tops," in *Record Collector*, June 1980 (Issue No. 10).

HARVEY FUQUA

Producer and songwriter. Born in Louisville, Kentucky. Known as lead singer for the

Moonglows, who recorded for Chess Records in Chicago in the 1950s. Harvey came to Motown toward the end of 1962 when his own labels, Tri-Phi and Harvey, which he co-owned with his wife, Gwendolyn (Gordy) Fuqua, discon-tinued and merged with Berry Gordy's Motown family. He brought with him such artists as Shorty Long, Jr. Walker & the All Stars, and the Spinners. Harvey was also instrumental in bringing Marvin Gaye to Motown, for it was Harvey who discovered Marvin and re-cruited him for the Moonglows in the late 1950s. While Marvin recorded some sessions for Harvey at Anna Records, none were ever released. Both Harvey and Berry worked as producers for Anna in 1960, although Berry was already starting his own label and also worked as an independent producer. Harvey Fuqua's work at Motown as a songwriter and producer reflected his roots in the doo-wop or streetcorner sound of the early 1950s. The Moonglows were a highly polished doo-wop group at home with intricate harmonies and a cappella melodies. He co-wrote and produced with Johnny Bristol some of the Marvin Gaye-Tammi Terrell duets of the late 1960s, including "Ain't No Mountain High Enough" (Tamla 54149) and "If I Could Build My Whole World Around You" (Tamla 54161). Bristol and Fuqua also did Tammi's solo effort, "I Can't Believe You Love Me" (Motown 1086), and "Just Walk In My Shoes" (Soul 35023) for Gladys Knight & the Pips.

For Jr. Walker & the All Stars, Fuqua and Bristol co-wrote and produced "Pucker Up, Buttercup" (Soul 35030) and the Top 10 pop hit "What Does It Take (To Win Your Love)" (Soul 35062). Harvey left Motown in 1969 and has worked with a variety of r&b acts during the 1970s and 1980s. He participated in putting together some of Marvin Gaye's posthumous albums.

MARVIN GAYE

Born April 2, 1939, in Washington, D.C.; died April 1, 1984, of a gunshot wound inflicted by his father, in Los Angeles.

Marvin Gaye's singing career spanned three decades, starting in the mid-1950s as a member of the Washington, D.C.-based groups The Rainbows and The Marquees. In 1958, Harvey Fuqua arrived in D.C. looking for a new line-up for his group, The Moonglows. Choosing Marvin and his group, The Marquees, he recorded two singles with them for Chess in 1959. Through his association with Harvey Fuqua, Marvin recorded many unreleased songs for Chess and Anna. Both Berry Gordy and Harvey Fuqua were producing records for Anna, which was owned by Berry's sister, Anna Gordy (later to marry Marvin Gaye) and Billy Davis. Another sister, Gwen Gordy (later to marry Harvey Fuqua), worked at Anna and was also a songwriter. Berry wanted very much to sign Marvin to his own label, just starting in 1959, so the songs recorded for Anna were never released.

In 1959, Berry Gordy signed Marvin to the Tamla label, and Harvey Fuqua later became a songwriter-producer for Motown. Marvin's first solo record, "Let Your Conscience Be Your Guide" (Tamla 54041) was released in 1961. His first hit came the next year with "Stubborn Kind of Fellow" (Tamla 54068), on which the Vandellas sang backing vocals. He later co-wrote "Dancing in the Streets" for them. His biggest hit of the 1960s was "I Heard It Through The Grapevine" (Tamla 54176), which stayed at #1 in America for seven weeks starting November 23, 1968. It also reached #1 in England.

In addition to being a vocalist, Marvin could play drums and piano. He served as Motown's session drummer early in his career, and had played drums on some of Harvey Fuqua's productions for Anna Records. He was the drummer on Little Stevie Wonder's first single, "I Call It Pretty Music (But The Old People Call It The Blues)" (Tamla 54061), released in 1963.

Complementing Marvin's outstanding solo career at Motown are his numerous duets with some of Motown's best female vocalists. During the period 1964-1967, he recorded duets with Mary Wells, Kim Weston, and Tammi Terrell. In 1967, Tammi Terrell collapsed in his arms while performing onstage; she subsequently died in 1970 after numerous operations to remove a brain tumor. Her death had a profound effect on Marvin, who refrained from live performances and went into a period of reclusive exile. Other notable duets were recorded with Diana Ross in 1973 and 1974. In 1971, Marvin developed a new sound as writer, producer, singer, and instrumentalist on the album, WHAT'S GOING ON (Tamla 310). Based on this and subsequent albums,

MARVIN GAYE

Marvin has been credited with introducing a new vein of creativity into soul music. The latter half of the 1970s was a difficult period, too, that saw the breakup of two marriages and the release of the double-album dedicated to his first wife, Anna Gordy, titled HERE MY DEAR (Tamla 364), in 1978. In 1981, Motown released the album, IN OUR LIFETIME (Tamla 374), infuriating Marvin, who felt the album was incomplete and shouldn't have been released. He refused to record again, and in 1982 Motown released him from his contract. He signed with Columbia and released the very successful "Sexual Healing" (Columbia 03302) in the Fall of 1982. Since his death in 1984, Columbia has released material that was originally recorded both for Motown and for Columbia.

MOTOWN DISCOGRAPHY

1961: Masquerade (Is Over)/Witchcraft (Tamla promo) As by Marvin Gay

5/61: Let Your Conscience Be Your Guide/Never Let You Go (Tamla 54041)

6/61: THE SOULFUL MOODS OF MARVIN GAYE (Tamla TM-221)

1/62: Sandman/I'm Yours, You're Mine (Tamla 54055)

5/62: Soldier's Plea/Taking My Time (Tamla 54063)

7/62: Stubborn Kind Of Fellow/It Hurt Me Too (Tamla 54068)

12/62: Hitch Hike/Hello There Angel (Tamla 54075)

1/63: THAT STUBBORN KINDA' FELLOW (Tamla TM-239)

4/63: Pride And Joy/One Of These Days (Tamla 54079)

8/63: RECORDED LIVE: ON STAGE (Tamla TM-242)

9/63: Can I Get A Witness/I'm Crazy 'Bout My Baby (Tamla 54087)

2/64: You're A Wonderful One/When I'm Alone I Cry (Tamla 54093)

4/64: Try It Baby/If My Heart Could Sing (Tamla 54095)

4/64: WHEN I'M ALONE I CRY (Tamla TM-251)

4/64: MARVIN GAYE'S GREATEST HITS (Tamla TS-252)

4/64: Once Upon A Time/What's The Matter With You Baby (Motown 1057) Marvin Gaye and Mary Wells

4/64: TOGETHER (Motown MLP-613) Marvin Gaye and Mary Wells

8/64: Baby Don't You Do It/Walk On The Wild Side (Tamla 54101)

9/64: What Good Am I Without You/I Want You 'Round (Tamla 54104) Marvin Gaye and Kim Weston

11/64: How Sweet It Is (To Be Loved By You)/Forever (Tamla 54107)

11/64: HELLO BROADWAY (Tamla TS-259)

1/65: HOW SWEET IT IS TO BE LOVED BY YOU (Tamla TM-258)

2/65: I'll Be Doggone/You've Been A Long Time Coming (Tamla 54112)

6/65: Pretty Little Baby/Now That You've Won Me (Tamla 54117)

9/65: Ain't That Peculiar/She's Got To Be Real (Tamla 54122)

11/65: A TRIBUTE TO THE GREAT NAT KING COLE (Tamla TS-261)

1966: The Teen Beat Song/Loraine Alterman Interviews Marvin Gaye For Teen Beat Readers (Tamla promo)

1/66: One More Heartache/When I Had Your Love (Tamla 54129)

4/66: Take This Heart Of Mine/Need Your Lovin' (Want You Back) (Tamla 54132)

5/66: MOODS OF MARVIN GAYE (Tamla TS-266)

7/66: Little Darling, I Need You/Hey Diddle Diddle (Tamla 54138)

8/66: TAKE TWO (Tamla TS-270) Marvin Gaye and Kim Weston

12/66: It Takes Two/It's Got To Be A Miracle (This Thing Called Love) (Tamla 54141) Marvin Gaye and Kim Weston

4/67: Ain't No Mountain High Enough/ Give A Little Love (Tamla 54149) Marvin Gaye and Tammi Terrell

6/67: Your Unchanging Love/I'll Take Care Of You (Tamla 54153)

8/67: Your Precious Love/Hold Me Oh My Darling (Tamla 54156) Marvin Gaye and Tammi Terrell

8/67: UNITED (Tamla TS-277) Marvin Gaye and Tammi Terrell

8/67: MARVIN GAYE'S GREATEST HITS VOL. 2 (Tamla TS-278)

11/67: If I Could Build My Whole World Around You/If This World Were Mine (Tamla 54161) Marvin Gaye and Tammi Terrell

12/67: You/Change What You Can (Tamla

54160)

3/68: Ain't Nothing Like The Real Thing/Little Ole Boy, Little Ole Girl (Tamla 54163) Marvin Gaye and Tammi Terrell

6/68: His Eye Is On The Sparrow/Just A Closer Walk With Thee (Motown 1128) 'B' side by Gladys Knight and The Pips

7/68: You're All I Need To Get By/Two Can Have A Party (Tamla 54169) Marvin Gaye and Tammi Terrell

8/68: Chained/At Last (I Found A Love) (Tamla 54170)

8/68: IN THE GROOVE (Tamla TS-285)

8/68: YOU'RE ALL I NEED (Tamla TS-284) Marvin Gaye and Tammi Terrell

9/68: Keep On Lovin' Me Honey/You Ain't Livin' Till You're Lovin' (Tamla 54173) Marvin Gaye and Tammi Terrell

11/68: I Heard It Through The Grapevine/You're What's Happening (In The World Today) (Tamla 54176)

1/69: Good Lovin' Ain't Easy To Come By/Satisfied Feelin' (Tamla 54179) Marvin Gaye and Tammi Terrell

4/69: Too Busy Thinking About My Baby/Wherever I Lay My Hat (That's My Home) (Tamla 54181)

4/69: M.P.G. (Tamla TS-292)

5/69: MARVIN GAYE AND HIS GIRLS (Tamla TS-293) Duets

8/69: That's The Way Love Is/Gonna Keep On Tryin' Till I Win Your Love (Tamla 54185)

9/69: EASY (Tamla TS-294) Marvin Gaye and Tammi Terrell

11/69: What You Gave Me/How You Gonna Keep It (After You Get It) (Tamla 54187) Marvin Gaye and Tammi Terrell

12/69: Gonna Give Her All The Love I've Got/How Can I Forget (Tamla 54190)

1/70: THAT'S THE WAY LOVE IS (Tamla TS-299)

3/70: The Onion Song/California Soul (Tamla 54192) Marvin Gaye and Tammi Terrell

5/70: The End Of Our Road/Me And My Lonely Room (Tamla 54195)

5/70: GREATEST HITS (Tamla TS-302) Marvin Gaye and Tammi Terrell

9/70: SUPER HITS (Tamla TS-300)

1/71: What's Going On/God Is Love (Tamla 54201)

5/71: WHAT'S GOING ON (Tamla TS-310)

6/71: Mercy Mercy Me (The Ecology)/Sad Tomorrows (Tamla 54207)

9/71: Inner City Blues (Make Me Wanna Holler)/Wholy Holy (Tamla 54209)

4/72: You're The Man (Part 1)/You're The Man (Part 2) (Tamla 54221)

11/72: Trouble Man/Don't Mess With Mr. "T" (Tamla 54228)

12/72: TROUBLE MAN (SOUNDTRACK) (Tamla T-322L)

6/73: Let's Get It On/I Wish It Would Rain (Tamla 54234)

8/73: LET'S GET IT ON (Tamla T-329V1)

9/73: You're A Special Part Of Me/I'm Falling In Love With You (Motown 1280) Diana Ross and Marvin Gaye

10/73: Come Get To This/Distant Lovers (Tamla 54241)

10/73: DIANA & MARVIN (Motown M 803V1) Diana Ross and Marvin Gaye

1/74: You Sure Love To Ball/Just To Keep You Satisfied (Tamla 54244)

1/74: My Mistake (Was To Love You)/Include Me In Your Life (Motown 1269) Diana Ross and Marvin Gaye

4/74: ANTHOLOGY (Motown M9-791A3)

6/74: Don't Knock My Love/Just Say, Just Say (Motown 1296) Diana Ross and Marvin Gaye

6/74: LIVE (Tamla T6-333S1)

9/74: Distant Lover (Edited version)/Trouble Man (Tamla 54253)

9/74: Distant Lover (Live version)/Distant Lover (Live Version) (Tamla 54253)

9/74: Distant Lover (Edited Version)/Distant Lover (Edited Version) (Tamla 54253)

3/76: I WANT YOU (Tamla T6-342S1)

4/76: I Want You (Long version)/I Want You (Instrumental) (Tamla 54264)

4/76: I Want You (Short Version) (Mono)/I Want You (Short Version) (Stereo) (Tamla 54264)

7/76: After The Dance/Feel All My Love Inside (Tamla 54273)

9/76: GREATEST HITS (Tamla T6-348S1)

3/77: Got To Give It Up (Pt. I)/Got To Give It Up (Pt. II) (Tamla 54280)

3/77: LIVE AT THE LONDON PALLADIUM (Tamla T7-352R2)

11/78: Pops, We Love You (Vocal)/Pops, We

Love You (Instrumental) (Motown 1455) As by Marvin Gaye, Smokey Robinson, Diana Ross, and Stevie Wonder

12/78: A Funky Space Reincarnation (Part I)/A Funky Space Reincarnation (Part II) (Tamla 54298)

12/78: HERE, MY DEAR (Tamla T-364LP2)

6/79: Anger/Time To Get It Together (Tamla 54300)

9/79: Ego Tripping Out/Ego Tripping Out (Instrumental) (Tamla 54305)

1/81: IN OUR LIFETIME (Tamla T8-374M1)

2/81: Praise/Funk Me (Tamla 54322)

4/81: Heavy Love Affair/Far Cry (Tamla 54326)

9/83: EVERY GREAT MOTOWN HIT OF MARVIN GAYE (Motown 6058ML)

10/83: LIVE / LET'S GET IT ON (Motown 6076MC)

10/83: YOU'RE ALL I NEED / UNITED (Motown 6083MC) Marvin Gaye and Tammi Terrell

2/84: COMPACT COMMAND PERFOR-MANCES: 15 GREATEST HITS (Tamla TCD06069TD)

10/85: MARVIN GAYE & HIS WOMEN: 21 CLASSIC DUETS (Tamla TCD06153TD) Duets

3/86: The World Is Rated X/The World Is Rated X (Instrumental) (Tamla 1836TF)

3/86: MOTOWN REMEMBERS MARVIN GAYE (Tamla 6172TL)

4/86: The World Is Rated X/No Greater Love (Tamla 1836TF-RE1)

8/86: LIVE AT THE LONDON PAL-LADIUM (Tamla TCD06191TD)

8/86: ANTHOLOGY (Motown MCD06199MD2)

8/86: COMPACT COMMAND PERFORM-ANCES VOLUME II: 20 GREATEST HITS (Tamla TCD06201TD)

Unissued Motown Recordings

I Want To Come Home For Christmas/ Christmas In The City (Tamla 54229)

MARVIN GAYE & KIM WESTON SIDE BY SIDE (Tamla 260)

YOU'RE THE MAN (Tamla 316)

[ALBUM TITLE UNKNOWN] (Tamla T-323)

HERE, MY DEAR (Tamla T6-354S1)

LOVE MAN (Tamla T8-369M1)

NON-MOTOWN DISCOGRAPHY

As member of the Rainbows (included Marvin Gaye, Don Covay, John Berry, Sonny Spencer, Chester Simmons, Billy Stewart):

1955: Mary Lee/Evening (Red Robin 134)

1956: Mary Lee/Evening (Pilgrim 703)

1956: Shirley/Stay (Pilgrim 711)

As member of the Marquees (included Marvin Gaye, Chester Simmons, Reese Palmer, James Nolan aka James Knowland):

1957: Baby You're My Only Love/Billy's Heartache (Okeh 7095) As by Billy Stewart

1957: Wyatt Earp/Little School Girl (Okeh 7096)

As member of Harvey and the Moonglows:

1958: Twelve Months Of The Year/Don't Be Afraid Of Love (Chess 1725) As by Harvey (Fuqua)

1958: Unemployment/Mama Loochie (Chess 1739) As by Harvey and the Moonglows

1959: Blue Skies/Ooh Ouch Stop (Chess 1749) As by Harvey (Fuqua)

1959: Beatnik/Junior (Chess 1770) As by the Moonglows

Post-Motown solo records for Columbia:

Albums:

1982: MIDNIGHT LOVE (Columbia 38197)

1985: DREAM OF A LIFETIME (Columbia 39916)

1985: ROMANTICALLY YOURS (Columbia 40208)

Singles:

1982: Sexual Healing (Vocal)/Sexual Heal-ing (Instrumental) (Columbia 03302)

1982: Sexual Healing (Columbia 03344) One-sided budget release

198?: Turn On Some Music/Star Spangled Banner (Columbia)

1983: 'Til Tommorrow/ (Columbia 03589)

1985: Sanctified Lady (Columbia)

HIGH INERGY

At one point, Motown billed High Inergy as
"The New Supremes."

198?: Ain't It Funny (How Things Turn Around)/It's Madness (Columbia 05442)
198?: Just Like/More (Columbia 05791)

FOR MORE INFORMATION

Contemporary Literary Criticism, Vol. 26. (Detroit: Gale Research Co., 1983).

Davis, Sharon. *Marvin Gaye*. New York: Proteus, 1985. A paperback picture biography with brief text.

Doggett, Peter. "Marvin Gaye," in *Record Collector*, April 1981 (Issue No. 20) and updated in *Record Collector*, February 1986 (Issue No. 78). Includes discography of British singles and albums.

Ritz, David. *Divided Soul: The Life of Marvin Gaye*. New York: McGraw-Hill, 1985. The definitive biography. Includes discography of albums. Also available in paperback edition.

"Sex and Soul: The Consuming Passions of Marvin Gaye," interview in *Face*, April 1983, pp. 49-53.

HERMAN GRIFFIN

A Detroit-based singer associated with Berry Gordy while Gordy was an independent producer and working at Anna. Griffin recorded for various Detroit labels, including the HOB label, Anna, and Motown. He has the distinction of recording the first song published by Berry Gordy's publishing arm, Jobete, "I Need You" (HOB 112), written by Berry and released in 1958.

MOTOWN DISCOGRAPHY

11/60: True Love (That's Love)/It's You (Tamla 54032)
6/62: Uptight/Sleep (Little One) (Motown 1028)

HEARTS OF STONE

Rare Earth recording group from Boston.

MOTOWN DISCOGRAPHY

9/70: It's A Lonesome Road/Yesterday's Love Is Over (V.I.P. 25058)
10/70: STOP THE WORLD....WE WANNA GET ON (V.I.P. VIPS-402)

6/71: If I Could Give You The World/You Gotta Sacrifice (We Gotta Sacrifice) (V.I.P. 25064)

HIGH INERGY

Vernessa Mitchell (left June 1979, not replaced)
Barbara Mitchell
Linda Howard
Michelle Martin

High Inergy is a vocal group that was formed in 1976 when the Mitchell sisters joined forces with Linda Howard and Michelle Martin as part of Pasadena's Bicentennial Performing Arts Program. At Motown's request, they auditioned for Gwen Gordy, who signed the group and became their mentor. They had recently graduated from Pasadena's Blair High School, when their first album, TURNIN' ON (Gordy 978), went gold on the strength of the popular "You Can't Turn Me Off (In The Middle Of Turning Me On)" (Gordy 7155). At that time, they were billed as Motown's "Teen Queens." Two years later, they had become a trio and were managed by Gwen Gordy and Gwendolyn Joyce Fuller. The group disbanded shortly after appearing on Motown's 25th anniversary special in 1983. Barbara Mitchell later signed with Capitol as a solo artist.

MOTOWN DISCOGRAPHY

9/77: You Can't Turn Me Off (In The Middle Of Turning Me On)/Save It For A Rainy Day (Gordy 7155)
9/77: You Can't Turn Me Off (In The Middle Of Turning Me On)/Let Me Get Close To You (Gordy 7155)
10/77: TURNIN' ON (Gordy G6-978R1)
2/78: Love Is All You Need/Some Kinda Magic (Gordy 7157)
6/78: We Are The Future/High School (Gordy 7160)
6/78: STEPPIN' OUT (Gordy G7-982R1)
8/78: Lovin' Fever/Beware (Gordy 7161)
3/79: Shoulda Gone Dancin'/Peaceland (Gordy 7166)
4/79: SHOULDA GONE DANCIN' (Gordy G7-987R1)
9/79: Skate To The Rhythm/Midnight Music Man (Gordy 7174)
10/79: Come And Get It/Midnight Music

Man (Gordy 7172)
10/79: FRENZY (Gordy G7-989R1)
 1/80: I Love Makin' Love (To The
Music)/Somebody, Somewhere
(Gordy 7178)
 8/80: Make Me Yours/I Love Makin' Love
(To The Music) (Gordy 7187)
 8/80: HOLD ON (Gordy G8-996M1)
10/80: Hold On To My Love/If I Love You
Tonight (Gordy 7192)
 4/81: I Just Wanna Dance With You/Take
My Life (Gordy 7201)
 5/81: HIGH INERGY (Gordy G8-1005M1)
 8/81: Goin' Through The Motions/I Just
Can't Help Myself (Gordy 7207)
 9/81: Don't Park Your Loving/Now That
There's You (Gordy 7211)
 4/82: First Impressions/Could This Be
Love (Gordy 1613GF)
 4/82: SO RIGHT (Gordy 6006GL)
 7/82: Wrong Man, Right Touch/Beware
(Gordy 1632GF)
 9/82: Journey To Love/Could This Be
Love (Gordy 1641GF)
 1/83: So Right/Don't Let Up On The
Groove (Gordy 1656GF)
 1/83: He's A Pretender/Don't Let Up On
The Groove (Gordy 1662GF)
 4/83: GROOVE PATROL (Gordy 6041GL)
 6/83: Blame It Onn Love/Even Tho'
(Tamla 1684TF) 'A' side with Smokey
Robinson; 'B' side by Smokey
Robinson
 7/83: Back In My Arms Again/So Right
(Gordy 1688GF)

FOR MORE INFORMATION
McLane, Daisann. "Sweethearts of Soul,"
in *Circus*, October 3, 1978, p.21.

BRIAN HOLLAND

Born February 15, 1941, in Detroit. Like the other members of Motown's famed songwriting/production team, Holland-Dozier-Holland, Brian had a singing background. He sang lead with the Satintones for Motown, and then joined Barrett Strong on the road as his pianist. In 1958, the Detroit-based Kudo Records released "Shock," a Berry Gordy production with the vocals credited to Brian Holland, but it may have actually been Eddie Holland singing. Brian has a reputation for being the most enigmatic of the three

songwriters; he has been characterized as a backroom creative force in pop music. His contributions appear to have been more on the production and engineering side, although he shares songwriting credit on all H-D-H compositions. In 1961, before H-D-H had formed as a team, he co-produced the Marvelettes' "Please Mr. Postman" (Tamla 54046) with Robert Bateman, under the alias Brianbert. Brian, Lamont Dozier, and Freddie Gorman formed a songwriting team in 1962 at Motown. When Gorman left Motown, Eddie Holland took his place and the legendary Holland-Dozier-Holland team was formed.

NON-MOTOWN DISCOGRAPHY

1958: Shock/ (Kudo)
1972: Don't Leave Me Starvin' For Your
Love (Part 1)/Don't Leave Me
Starvin' For Your Love (Part 2)
(Invictus 9133)
1974: I'm So Glad (Part 1)/I'm So Glad
(Part 2) (Invictus 1265)
1974: Super Woman/Let's Get Together
(Invictus 1272)

(See also HOLLAND-DOZIER-HOLLAND.)

EDDIE HOLLAND

Born October 30, 1939, in Detroit. Probably the most successful solo vocalist of the Holland-Dozier-Holland songwriting and production team, Eddie's relationship with Berry Gordy goes back to Berry's days as an independent producer in the late 1950s. In 1958, Berry Gordy produced Eddie's "You/Little Miss Ruby," which was released on Mercury. Then, in 1959-1960, Berry Gordy placed four singles he had produced with United Artists, including "Merry Go Round," which was first released as Tamla 102 and then on United Artists. At that point, UA signed Eddie to an exclusive recording contract. Eddie returned to Motown in 1961 and soon joined his brother Brian and Lamont Dozier to form Holland-Dozier-Holland. Eddie continued to record for Motown as a solo artist, and his talent for writing lyrics led to his co-writing with Norman Whitfield several songs for the Temptations, as well as for other artists and with other collaborators. Some of his songwriting credits, in addition to those with H-D-H, include:

Function At The Junction (with Shorty Long)

He Was Really Saying Something (with Norman Whitfield)

(I Know) I'm Losing You (with Norman Whitfield)

Ain't Too Proud To Beg (with Norman Whitfield)

Beauty Is Only Skin Deep (with Norman Whitfield)

The Girl's Alright With Me (with Norman Whitfield)

Girl (Why You Wanna Make Me Blue) (with Norman Whitfield)

Too Many Fish In The Sea (with Norman Whitfield)

MOTOWN DISCOGRAPHY

1/59: Merry-Go-Round/It Moves Me (Tamla 102)

10/61: Jamie/Take A Chance On Me (Motown 1021)

4/62: You Deserve What You Get/Last Night I Had A Vision (Motown 1026)

5/62: If Cleopatra Took A Chance/What About Me (Motown 1030)

5/62: EDDIE HOLLAND (Motown MT-604)

8/62: If It's Love (It's Alright)/It's Not Too Late (Motown 1031)

12/62: Darling I Hum Our Song/Just A Few More Days (Motown 1036)

6/63: Baby Shake/Brenda (Motown 1043)

8/63: What Goes Up - Must Come Down/Come On Home (Motown 1045) With Lamont Dozier

10/63: I Couldn't Cry If I Wanted To/I'm On The Outside Looking In (Motown 1049)

12/63: Leaving Here/Brenda (Motown 1052)

5/64: Just Ain't Enough Love/Last Night I Had A Vision (Motown 1058)

8/64: Candy To Me/If You Don't Want My Love (Motown 1063)

NON-MOTOWN DISCOGRAPHY

1958: You/Little Miss Ruby (Mercury)

1959: Merry Go Round/It Moves Me (United Artists 172) Also on Tamla 102

1960: Because I Love Her/Everybody's Going (United Artists 191)

1960: Magic Mirror/Will You Love Me (United Artists 207)

1960: The Last Laugh/Why Do You Want To Let Me Go (United Artists 280)

(See also HOLLAND-DOZIER-HOLLAND.)

HOLLAND-DOZIER-HOLLAND

Motown's ace songwriting/production team consisted of Eddie Holland (born Detroit, October 30, 1939), Lamont Dozier (born Detroit, June 16, 1941), and Brian Holland (born Detroit, February 15, 1941). Brian and Eddie are brothers. While all three are talented composers, Eddie Holland was noted for his lyrics, Lamont Dozier for his melodies, and Brian Holland for production and engineering. Of course, other writers and producers contributed to the Motown sound, but H-D-H songs are synonymous with "The Motown Sound" because of their hits of the 1963-1967 period. In those five years, they wrote twenty-five Top 10 pop records, of which twelve reached the #1 spot, plus twelve others that made Top 10 on the rhythm and blues chart, for a total of thirty-seven Top 10 hits in twelve years. H-D-H are considered pioneers in changing the sound of rhythm and blues to "crossover music" or pop/r&b. They combined many influences in their music, including soul, pop, country, and r&b. Their music appealed to both black and white audiences, thus "crossing over" from one market to the other. Hence, "The Motown Sound" was also billed as "The Sound of Young America" because of its wide appeal. The very first H-D-H collaboration is alternately given as "Dearest One" (Melody 102), recorded by Lamont Dozier in 1962, or "Locking Up My Heart" (Tamla 54077), recorded by the Marvelettes.

While many Motown artists recorded songs written and/or produced by H-D-H, they were most notably associated with Martha and the Vandellas, the Supremes, and the Four Tops. The Four Tops were virtually unknown after performing for nearly ten years, until they were teamed up with H-D-H and recorded such hits as "Baby, I Need Your Loving" (- Motown 1062), "Bernadette" (Motown 1104), "I Can't Help Myself (Sugar Pie, Honey Bunch)" (Motown 1076), "It's The Same Old Song" (Motown 1081), "Reach Out I'll Be There" (Motown 1098), "7 Rooms Of Gloom" (Motown 1110), and "Standing In The Shadows of Love" (Motown 1102). The Supremes similarly were

BRENDA HOLLOWAY

Berry Gordy discovered Brenda Holloway while
attending a disc jockey convention in Los Angeles.

hitless; then H-D-H wrote five consecutive #1 hits for them in 1964 and 1965: "Where Did Our Love Go" (Motown 1060), "Baby Love" (Motown 1066), "Come See About Me" (Motown 1072), "Stop! In The Name of Love" (Motown 1074), and "Back In My Arms Again" (Motown 1075). In 1966 and 1967, the Supremes scored four more consecutive #1 hits, all by H-D-H: "You Can't Hurry Love" (Motown 1097), "You Keep Me Hangin' On" (Motown 1101), "Love Is Here And Now You're Gone" (Motown 1103), and "The Happening" (Motown 1107). Martha and the Vandellas also found H-D-H a boost to their popularity, as they recorded five Top 10 pop hits from 1963 through 1967 by H-D-H: "Heatwave" (Gordy 7022), "Quicksand" (Gordy 7025), "Nowhere To Run" (Gordy 7039), "I'm Ready For Love" (Gordy 7056), and "Jimmy Mack" (Gordy 7058). In addition, H-D-H compositions were recorded by such artists as Marvin Gaye: "Can I Get A Witness" (Tamla 54087), "Little Darling (I Need You)" (Tamla 54138), "How Sweet It Is (To Be Loved By You)" (Tamla 54107), "You're A Wonderful One" (Tamla 54093); the Marvelettes: "Please Mr. Postman" (Tamla 54046), "Playboy" (Tamla 54060), "Locking Up My Heart" (Tamla 54077); the Miracles: "Mickey's Monkey" (Tamla 54083), "(Come 'Round Here) I'm The One You Need" (Tamla 54140); Kim Weston: "Take Me In Your Arms (Rock Me A Little While)" (Gordy 7046); the Isley Brothers "This Ole Heart Of Mine (Is Weak For You)" (Tamla 54128); and countless others.

H-D-H left Motown in 1968 and were inactive for two years due to lawsuits concerning their departure. In 1970, they established two labels, Invictus (distributed by Capitol) and Hot Wax (distributed by Buddah). Lamont Dozier left to pursue a solo career as a vocalist, and by 1974 these labels were defunct, but not before producing some r&b hits for groups like Chairmen of the Board, Honey Cone, and Freda Payne. During the 1970s, they worked separately and as a team for various labels, in some cases producing ex-Motown artists like the Temptations, Edwin Starr, and the Originals. In the early 1980s, a reunited H-D-H was writing and producing songs for such artists as Herb Alpert, Musical Youth, and the Four Tops.

NON-MOTOWN DISCOGRAPHY

1971: Don't Leave Me (Part 1)/Don't Leave Me (Part 2) (Invictus 9110)
1972: Why Can't We Be Lovers/Don't Leave Me (Invictus 9125)
1973: Can't Get Enough/Slipping Away (Invictus 1253)
1973: If You Don't Want To Be In My Life/New Breed Kinda Woman (Invictus 1254)
1973: I'm Gonna Hijack Ya, Kidnap Ya, Take What I Want/You Took Me From A World Outside (Invictus 1258)

(See also LAMONT DOZIER; BRIAN HOLLAND; EDDIE HOLLAND.)

BRENDA HOLLOWAY

Born Atascadero, California, June 21, 1946. Brenda was discovered at the age of seventeen in 1964 by Berry Gordy, who was attending a disc jockey convention in Los Angeles. She had grown up in the Watts section of Los Angeles and had recorded for some local L.A. labels. A now-forgotten high point of her career occurred in 1965, when she was the only female vocalist to accompany the Beatles on their North American tour. The story goes that Brian Epstein, the Beatles' manager, heard her British single, "Every Little Bit Hurts," and invited her on the tour. Other groups accompanying the Beatles on that tour were the King Curtis band, Cannibal & the Headhunters, and a British instrumental group called Sounds, Inc. Brenda performed with the Beatles that summer at such locations as Shea Stadium (August 14, 1965), Toronto, Atlanta, Houston, Chicago, Minneapolis, Portland, San Diego, Los Angeles, and San Francisco. Following the Beatles tour, she was in great demand for television and nightclub appearances. Her 1967 version of "You've Made Me So Very Happy" (Tamla 54155), for which she received songwriting credit, was described as "soft and smooth." It became a very big hit when recorded in a "psychedelic" style by Blood, Sweat, and Tears in 1969.

Brenda married Alfred Davis, a minister, and she became a reborn Christian. Her religion led to her leave the pop music business.

Photo courtesy Peter Benjaminson.

THE ISLEY BROTHERS

The original Isley Brothers trio, and the later "3+3" expanded line-up.

MOTOWN DISCOGRAPHY

3/64: Every Little Bit Hurts/Land Of A Thousand Boys (Tamla 54094)

7/64: I'll Always Love You/Sad Song (Tamla 54099)

7/64: EVERY LITTLE BIT HURTS (Tamla TM-257)

2/65: When I'm Gone/I've Been Good To You (Tamla 54111)

5/65: Operator/I'll Be Available (Tamla 54115)

8/65: You Can Cry On My Shoulder/How Many Times Did You Mean It (Tamla 54121)

11/65: Together 'Til The End Of Time/Sad Song (Tamla 54125)

7/66: Hurt A Little Everyday/Where Were You (Tamla 54137)

4/67: Just Look What You've Done/Starting The Hurt All Over Again (Tamla 54148)

8/67: You've Made Me So Very Happy/I've Got To Find It (Tamla 54155)

Unissued Motown Recordings

'Til Johnny Comes/Where Were You (Tamla 54144)
BRENDA HOLLOWAY (Tamla 273)

NON-MOTOWN DISCOGRAPHY

1963: I Ain't Gonna Take You Back/ You're My Only Love (Catch 109)

1963: It's You/Unless I Have You (Minasa 6714) As by Hal (Davis) and Brenda (Holloway)

ISLEY BROTHERS

The original line-up in the 1950s consisted of Ronald Isley (born May 21, 1941), Rudolph Isley (born April 1, 1939), O'Kelly Isley (born December 25, 1937; died March 1986), and Vernon Isley, who was killed in an auto crash. The trio added three members in 1969 for their "3+3" lineup. The new members were two more brothers, Ernest Isley and Marvin Isley, and brother-in-law Chris Jasper. In 1984, Chris, Ernie, and Marvin split from the original trio and began performing as Isley/Jasper/Isley. The group's biggest hits happened before and after their Tamla years (1966-1969). They first achieved national recognition with "Shout, Part 1" (RCA 7588) in 1959 (reissued in 1962 on RCA 0589). They also recorded "Twist and Shout" (Wand 124) in 1962, a song that became a big hit for the Beatles. The group recorded for several labels from 1957 to 1964 before signing with Motown's Tamla label in 1966. Their first release on Tamla, "This Old Heart of Mine (Is Weak for You)" (Tamla 54128), was their biggest hit while on that label. That song was written by Holland-Dozier-Holland. In 1968, they toured England and have been fairly popular in that country. In 1969, they left Motown and recorded on their own label, T-Neck, which they had established in 1964 for one release, "Testify, Parts 1 and 2" (T-Neck 501), notable in that Jimi Hendrix played guitar on it. Their first 1969 release on T-Neck featured their new "3+3" line-up. "It's Your Thing" (T-Neck 901) reached the #2 spot on the pop charts and was the biggest hit of their career. They also scored well in 1973 with "That Lady (Part 1)" (T-Neck 2251) and again in 1975 with "Fight the Power-Part 1" (T-Neck 2256).

MOTOWN DISCOGRAPHY

1965: I Hear A Symphony/Who Could Ever Doubt My Love (V.I.P. 25020)

1/66: This Old Heart Of Mine (Is Weak For You)/There's No Love Left (Tamla 54128)

5/66: Take Some Time Out For Love/Who Could Ever Doubt My Love (Tamla 54133)

6/66: I Guess I'll Always Love You/I Hear A Symphony (Tamla 54135)

6/66: THIS OLD HEART OF MINE (IS WEAK FOR YOU) (Tamla TS-269)

4/67: Just Ain't Enough Love/Got To Have You Back (Tamla 54146)

7/67: That's The Way Love Is/One Too Many Heartaches (Tamla 54154)

9/67: SOUL ON THE ROCKS (Tamla TS-275)

3/68: Take Me In Your Arms (Rock Me A Little While)/Why When Love Is Gone (Tamla 54164)

10/68: All Because I Love You/Behind A Painted Smile (Tamla 54175)

4/69: Just Ain't Enough Love/Take Some Time Out For Love (Tamla 54182)

4/69: DOIN' THEIR THING (Tamla TS-287)

THE JACKSON 5

FOR MORE INFORMATION
Doggett, Peter. "The Isley Brothers," in *Record Collector*, March 1982.

JACKSON 5

From Gary, Indiana, a family group that started performing at an early age in the mid-1960s, consisting of Jackie Jackson (born Sigmund Esco Jackson, May 4, 1951), Tito Jackson (born Toriano Adaryll Jackson, October 15, 1953), Jermaine Jackson (born Jermaine Lajuane Jackson, December 11, 1954), Marlon Jackson (born Marlon David Jackson, March 12, 1957), and Michael Jackson (born Michael Joseph Jackson, August 29, 1958).

According to Motown press releases, the Jackson 5 were discovered and brought to Berry Gordy's attention by Diana Ross, who was invited to see the group by Gary's mayor, Richard Hatcher. That this may have been a publicity hype is supported by the fact that the group's first album, DIANA ROSS PRESENTS THE JACKSON 5 (Motown 700) was originally to have been called simply INTRODUCING THE JACKSON 5 as late as June 1969. Michael Jackson has since revealed that Diana Ross had nothing to do with their discovery, but he couldn't say so while still under contract to Motown. Others taking credit for the discovery of the group are Bobby Taylor of Bobby Taylor & the Vancouvers, and Gladys Knight, who first saw the group perform at a concert in Gary in September, 1968.

If nothing else, the Jackson 5 were an incredibly popular group. Four of their first six singles for Motown, released between late 1969 and mid-1971, went to #1 on the pop charts, and the other two reached the #2 spot. The four number one songs were "I Want You Back" (Motown 1157), "ABC" (Motown 1163), "The Love You Save" (Motown 1166), and "I'll Be There" (Motown 1171). "Mama's Pearl" (Motown 1177) and "Never Can Say Goodbye" (Motown 1179) were the #2 hits. "I Want You Back," "ABC," and "The Love You Save" were all written and produced by The Corporation, a team consisting of Berry Gordy, Freddie Perren, Deke Richards, and Fonzie Mizell. The group's next five singles (1971-72) only reached the top twenty on the charts, but Michael picked up the slack with his solo releases. His first on Motown, "Got to Be There" (Motown 1191) reached #4, followed by "Rockin' Robin" (Motown 1197) to #2. In August 1972, "Ben" (Motown 1207) was #1 and charted for sixteen weeks. In 1971, the television cartoon series, "The Jackson 5," appeared. In 1974, the Jackson 5 appeared in the concert film, "Save the Children."

Jermaine began his solo career in 1972, and his second release, "Daddy's Home" (Motown 1216) reached #9. He had his second Top 10 hit for Motown in 1980 with "Let's Get Serious" (Motown 1469), after he had separated from the group. The Jackson 5's contract was up in 1975, and they decided to switch labels and signed with Epic. Jermaine, who had married Berry Gordy's daughter, Hazel Joy, in 1973, chose to remain with Motown as a solo artist. He was replaced by Randy (born Steven Randall Jackson, October 29, 1962), and the group was renamed The Jacksons. Motown was serious about Jermaine's solo career and engaged CBS/Epic in lawsuits to prevent Jermaine's name and photo appearing in connection with the Jacksons. The Jacksons' subsequent career at Epic has been extremely successful, as has Michael's solo career. When the group began recording for Epic, they performed songs they had written themselves, leading many to speculate that artistic freedom was a major issue in their leaving Motown.

MOTOWN DISCOGRAPHY

10/69: I Want You Back/Who's Lovin' You (Motown 1157)

12/69: DIANA ROSS PRESENTS THE JACKSON 5 (Motown MS-700)

2/70: ABC/The Young Folks (Motown 1163)

5/70: The Love You Save/I Found That Girl (Motown 1166)

5/70: ABC (Motown MS-709)

8/70: I'll Be There/One More Chance (Motown 1171)

9/70: THIRD ALBUM (Motown MS-718)

10/70: CHRISTMAS ALBUM (Motown MS-713)

11/70: Santa Claus Is Coming To Town/ Christmas Won't Be The Same This Year (Motown 1174)

1/71: Mama's Pearl/Darling Dear (Motown 1177)

3/71: Never Can Say Goodbye/She's Good (Motown 1179)

4/71: MAYBE TOMORROW (Motown MS-735)

6/71: Maybe Tomorrow/I Will Find A Way (Motown 1186)

9/71: GOIN' BACK TO INDIANA (Motown M-742L)

11/71: Sugar Daddy/I'm So Happy (Motown 1194)

12/71: GREATEST HITS (Motown M-741L)

4/72: Little Bitty Pretty One/If I Have To Move A Mountain (Motown 1199)

5/72: LOOKIN' THROUGH THE WINDOWS (Motown M-750L)

6/72: Lookin' Through The Windows/Love Song (Motown 1205)

10/72: The Corner Of The Sky/To Know (Motown 1214)

2/73: You Made Me What I Am/Hallelujah Day (Motown 1224)

3/73: SKYWRITER (Motown M-761L)

8/73: Get It Together/Touch (Motown 1277)

9/73: GET IT TOGETHER (Motown M-783V1)

2/74: Dancing Machine/It's Too Late To Change The Time (Motown 1286)

9/74: DANCING MACHINE (Motown M6-780S1)

10/74: Whatever You Got, I Want/I Can't Quit Your Love (Motown 1308)

12/74: I Am Love/I Am Love Pt. II (Motown 1310)

5/75: MOVING VIOLATION (Motown M6-829S1)

6/75: Forever Came Today/All I Do Is Think of You (Motown 1356)

6/76: ANTHOLOGY (Motown M7-868R3)

10/76: JOYFUL JUKEBOX MUSIC (Motown M6-865S1)

2/84: COMPACT COMMAND PER-FORMANCES: 18 GREATEST HITS (Motown MCD06070MD)

5/84: 14 GREATEST HITS (Motown 6099ML)

5/84: 16 GREATEST HITS (Motown 6100MC)

8/86: ANTHOLOGY (Motown MCD06194MD2)

Unissued Motown Recordings

Boogie Man/Don't Let Your Baby Catch You (Motown 1230)

Body Language (Do The Love Dance)/ Call Of The Wild (Motown 1375)

NON-MOTOWN DISCOGRAPHY

The Jackson 5's first records were issued on Steeltown, a Gary-based label.

1968: Big Boy/You've Changed (Steeltown 681)

1971: We Don't Have to Be Over 21 (To Fall In Love)/Jam Session (Steeltown 682) Recorded 1968

1971?: You Don't Have To Be Over 21 (To Fall In Love)/Some Girls Want Me For Their Lover (Dynamo 146) Re-issue of Steeltown 682A with slight title change

1971: Let Me Carry Your School Books/I Never Had a Girl (Steeltown 688) Probably issued while the J5 were under contract to Motown; group is identified as "The Ripples & Waves, plus Michael." Songs were copyrighted in 1971.

As by the Jacksons:

1976: Enjoy Yourself/Style of Life (Epic 50289)

1976: THE JACKSONS (Epic PE-34229)

1977: Show You The Way To Go/Blues Away (Epic 50350)

1977: Goin' Places/Do What You Wanna (Epic 50454)

1977: GOIN' PLACES (Epic PE-34835)

1978: Different Kind of Lady/Find Me A Girl (Epic 50496)

1978: Blame It On The Boogie/Do What You Wanna (Epic 50595)

1978: DESTINY (Epic JE-35552)

1979: Shake Your Body (Down To The Ground)/That's What You Get (For Being Polite) (Epic 50656) Reissued on Epic 50721

1980: Lovely One/Bless His Soul (Epic 50938)

1980: TRIUMPH (Epic FE-36424)

1980: Heartbreak Hotel/Things I Do For You (Epic 50959)

1981: Can You Feel It/Wondering Who (Epic 01032)

1981: Walk Right Now/Your Ways (Epic 02132)

1981: JACKSONS LIVE (Epic KE2-37545) Two-LP set

1984: State of Shock/Your Ways (Epic 34-04503) A-side features Michael

CHUCK JACKSON

Jackson-Mick Jagger duet
1984: VICTORY (Epic QE-38946)
1984: Torture/Torture (Instrumental) (Epic 34-04575)
1984: Body/Body (Instrumental) (Epic 34-04673)

FOR MORE INFORMATION

Brown, Dave. "The Jacksons," in *Record Collector*, May 1982. Includes discography of British releases.

Terry, Carol D. *Sequins & Shades: The Michael Jackson Reference Guide*. Ann Arbor, MI: Pierian Press, 1987. Extensive treatment of J5 and Jacksons material.

(See also JERMAINE JACKSON; MICHAEL JACKSON.)

CHUCK JACKSON

Born July 22, 1937, in Winston-Salem, North Carolina. Although known as a polished performer in r&b circles, Chuck Jackson never had a major pop hit. His two best-known records, "I Don't Want To Cry" (Wand 106) and "Any Day Now" (Wand 122), only reached #36 and #23 on the pop charts. These were recorded in the early 1960s for Scepter/Wand and appeared on the Wand label.

In September 1967, he bought his contract from Scepter and signed with Motown. His move to Motown probably reflected his desire for a chart hit and his confidence in Motown as a hit-making record company.

He stayed with Motown for four years, recording on the V.I.P. and Motown labels, without achieving that chart success.

MOTOWN DISCOGRAPHY

1/68: (You Can't Let The Boy Overpower) The Man In You/Girls, Girls, Girls (Motown 1118)
2/68: CHUCK JACKSON ARRIVES! (Motown MS-667)
4/69: Are You Lonely For Me Baby/Your Wonderful Love (Motown 1144)
6/69: GOIN' BACK TO CHUCK JACKSON (Motown MS-687)
9/69: Honey Come Back/What Am I Gonna Do Without You (Motown 1152)
11/69: The Day The World Stood Still/Baby,

I'll Get It (V.I.P. 25052)
5/70: Two Feet From Happiness/Let Somebody Love Me (V.I.P. 25056)
9/70: TEARDROPS KEEP FALLING ON MY HEART (V.I.P. VIPS-403)
1/71: Pet Names/Is There Anything Love Can't Do (V.I.P. 25059)

Unissued Motown Recordings

Who You Gonna Run To/Forgive My Jealousy (V.I.P. 25067)
Baby, I'll Get It/The Day The World Stood Still (Motown 1160)

JERMAINE JACKSON

Born Jermaine Lajuane Jackson, December 11, 1954, in Gary, Indiana.

1973 was a big year for Jermaine Jackson. He married the boss's daughter and added a second gold single as a solo artist, in addition to his duties as a member of the Jackson 5. Jermaine's first solo releases came while he was still a member of the Jackson 5. "That's How Love Goes" (Motown 1201) and "Daddy's Home" (Motown 1216) were both released in 1972. Both went gold.

When his brothers left Motown in 1975 and signed with Epic, he stayed with Motown as a solo artist. He was replaced by Randy in the group, which was renamed The Jacksons. Motown supported Jermaine's solo career in part by engaging CBS/Epic in lawsuits to prevent his name and photo from appearing in connection with The Jacksons. He rejoined his brothers temporarily in 1983 for Motown's 25th anniversary show and again for their 1984 "Victory" tour.

On December 15, 1973, Jermaine married Berry Gordy's only daughter, Hazel Joy. They were both nineteen at the time; the reception was held at the Beverly Hills Hotel. By all accounts, it was a very opulent occasion.

In mid-1983, Jermaine was released from his Motown contract to pursue his solo career. He signed with Arista Records.

MOTOWN DISCOGRAPHY

7/72: JERMAINE (Motown M-752L)
8/72: That's How Love Goes/I Lost My Love In The Big City (Motown 1201)
11/72: Daddy's Home/Take Me In Your

Arms (Rock Me A Little While)
(Motown 1216)

5/73: COME INTO MY LIFE (Motown
M-775L)

9/73: You're In Good Hands/Does Your
Mama Know About Me (Motown 1244)

8/76: Let's Be Young Tonight/Bass Odyssey
(Motown 1401)

8/76: MY NAME IS JERMAINE (Motown
M6-842S1)

10/76: My Touch Of Madness/You Need To
Be Loved (Motown 1409)

8/77: FEEL THE FIRE (Motown M-888S1)

2/78: FRONTIERS (Motown M7-898R1)

4/78: Castles Of Sand/I Love Every Little
Thing About You (Motown 1441)

10/79: LET'S GET SERIOUS (Motown
M7-928R1)

3/80: Let's Get Serious/Je Vous Aime
Beaucoup (I Love You) (Motown 1469)

8/80: You're Supposed To Keep Your
Love For Me/Let It Ride (Motown
1490)

11/80: Little Girl Don't You Worry/We Can
Put It Back Together (Motown 1499)

12/80: JERMAINE (Motown M8-948M1)

2/81: You Like Me Don't You/You Like
Me Don't You (Instrumental)
(Motown 1503)

9/81: I LIKE YOUR STYLE (Motown
M8-952M1)

10/81: I'm Just Too Shy/All Because Of
You (Motown 1525)

1/82: Paradise In Your Eyes/I'm My
Brother's Keeper (Motown 1600MF)

7/82: Let Me Tickle Your Fancy/Maybe
Next Time (Motown 1628MF)

7/82: LET ME TICKLE YOUR FANCY
(Motown 6017ML)

10/82: Very Special Part/You're Givin' Me
The Runaround (Motown 1649MF)

Unissued Motown Recordings

She's The Ideal Girl/I Am So Glad You
Chose Me (Motown 1386)
DO UNTO OTHERS (Motown 830)
LIVING (Motown M7-913R1)

NON-MOTOWN DISCOGRAPHY

1984: Dynamite/Tell Me I'm Not Dreaming
(Arista 9190 and 9346)

1984: Dynamite/Dynamite (Instrumental)/

Tell Me I'm Not Dreaming (Arista
9222) 12"

1984: Take Good Care Of My Heart/Tell
Me I'm Not Dreaming (Arista 9275)

1984: Do What You Do/Tell Me I'm Not
Dreaming (Arista 9279)

1984: JERMAINE JACKSON (Arista AL8-
8203)

1985: When The Rain Begins To Fall/Come
To Me (Arista 9317 and 9340)

1985: (Closest Thing To) Perfect/ (Arista
9356)

1986: I Think It's Love/ (Arista 9444)

1986: Words Into Action/Our Love Story
(Arista 9494)

1986: Do You Remember Me?/ (Arista 9502)

(See also JACKSON FIVE.)

MICHAEL JACKSON

Born Michael Joseph Jackson, August 29, 1958, in Gary, Indiana.

Lead singer with the Jackson 5, Michael's first solo record appeared in 1971. "Got To Be There" (Motown 1191) reached #4 on the pop charts, to be followed in 1972 with "Rockin' Robin" (Motown 1197), a song that went to #2. Michael continued to record solo discs while performing with the Jackson 5.

Michael and his brothers left Motown in 1975 to sign with Epic (Jermaine remained at Motown). Since the group left Motown, Michael has appeared in the movie, "The Wiz" (1978), as the scarecrow, produced Diana Ross's 1982 hit, "Muscles," and co-produced with Quincy Jones his extremely popular Epic album, THRILLER. Michael and his brothers (and sisters) continue to be very popular with audiences around the world.

MOTOWN DISCOGRAPHY

10/71: Got To Be There/Maria (You Were
The Only One) (Motown 1191)

1/72: GOT TO BE THERE (Motown M-
747L)

2/72: Rockin' Robin/Love Is Here And
Now You're Gone (Motown 1197)

5/72: I Wanna Be Where You Are/We've
Got A Good Thing Going (Motown
1202)

7/72: Ben/You Can Cry On My Shoulder
(Motown 1207)

8/72: BEN (Motown M-755L)

4/73: With A Child's Heart/Morning Glow (Motown 1218)

4/73: MUSIC AND ME (Motown M-767L)

1/75: FOREVER MICHAEL (Motown M6-825S1)

2/75: We're Almost There/Take Me Back (Motown 1341)

4/75: Just A Little Bit Of You/Dear Michael (Motown 1349)

8/75: THE BEST OF MICHAEL JACKSON (Motown M6-851S1)

10/76: JOYFUL JUKEBOX MUSIC (Motown M6-865S1)

3/81: One Day In Your Life/Take Me Back (Motown 1512)

3/81: ONE DAY IN YOUR LIFE (Motown M8-956M1)

10/83: GOT TO BE THERE/BEN (Motown 6077MC)

2/84: COMPACT COMMAND PERFORM- ANCES: 18 GREATEST HITS (Motown MCD06070MD)

5/84: Farewell My Summer Love/Call On Me (Motown 1739MF)

5/84: FAREWELL MY SUMMER LOVE (Motown 6101ML)

5/84: 14 GREATEST HITS (Motown 6099ML)

5/84: 16 GREATEST HITS (Motown 6100MC)

8/84: Girl You're So Together/Touch The One You Love (Motown 1757MF)

8/86: ANTHOLOGY (Motown MCD06195MD2)

Unissued Motown Recordings

Doggin' Around/Up Again (Motown 1270)

NON-MOTOWN DISCOGRAPHY

1979: You Can't Win (Part 1)/You Can't Win (Part 2) (Epic 50654)

1979: Don't Stop 'Til You Get Enough/I Can't Help It (Epic 50742)

1979: Rock With You/Working Day And Night (Epic 50797)

1980: Off The Wall/Get On The Floor (Epic 50838)

1980: She's Out Of My Life/Get On The Floor (Epic 50871)

1982: The Girl Is Mine/Can't Get Outta The Rain (Epic 34-03288) A-side is duet with Paul McCartney

1982: THRILLER (Epic QE 38112)

1983: Billie Jean/Can't Get Outta The Rain (Epic 34-03509)

1983: Beat It/Get On The Floor (Epic 34-03759)

1983: Wanna Be Startin' Somethin'/Wanna Be Startin' Somethin' (Part 2) (Epic 34-03914)

1983: Say Say Say (part 1)/Say Say Say (part 2) (Columbia 04168) Duet with Paul McCartney

1983: Human Nature/Baby Be Mine (Epic 34-04026)

1983: P.Y.T. (Pretty Young Thing)/Working Day And Night (Epic 34-04165) With the Jacksons

1984: Thriller/Can't Get Outta The Rain (Epic 34-04364)

FOR MORE INFORMATION

Jackson, Richard. "Michael Jackson," in *Record Collector*, October 1984. Includes discography of British releases.

Terry, Carol D. *Sequins & Shades: The Michael Jackson Reference Guide*. Ann Arbor, MI: Pierian Press, 1987. Bibliography, chronology, U.S. and U.K. discographies, etc.

(See also JACKSON 5.)

RICK JAMES

Born James Johnson, Jr., in Buffalo, N.Y., on February 1, 1948. Rick James is credited with establishing the "punk-funk" style. He has a rebellious, outspoken, tough, streetwise image, and his musical talents include writing, producing, singing and playing a variety of instruments.

Rick joined the navy at age fifteen, but soon went AWOL to Canada, where he formed the Mynah Birds in Toronto. This group in- cluded Neil Young, who later achieved fame with Buffalo Springfield and as a solo artist, Bill Palmer, and Goldie McJohn, who later joined Steppenwolf. The Mynah Birds apparent- ly combined folk rock with rhythm & blues in their playing. Motown offered the Mynah Birds a contract, but the group broke up when most of the members went to Los Angeles. The Mynah Birds are said to have recorded for Motown, but nothing was released.

In the late 1960s, Rick got a job at Motown as a staff songwriter, but his break as an artist came in 1978 when he went to Motown's Los Angeles office with a finished album. He signed with Motown's Gordy label and the album was released as COME GET IT (Gordy 981), which eventually sold over two million copies. Two singles from the album both charted, "You and I" (Gordy 7156) and "Mary Jane" (Gordy 7162). His commercial break-through came in 1981, when the album STREET SONGS (Gordy 1002) sold over three million copies.

In 1979, Rick took a singer named Prince with him on his "Fire It Up" tour. This was a big break for Prince, and the two artists are frequently compared. Also in 1979, Rick came down with a severe case of hepatitis, and his general health has since forced a number of tour cancellations. In August 1982, he was hospitalized in Dallas after collapsing onstage at the Reunion Arena. He had to cancel the remaining twenty dates of his concert tour that year, and his summer 1983 tour was to have been his last. He was again reported hospitalized in 1984 in Buffalo. Rick is a nephew of the Temptations' Melvin Franklin, and he assisted the Temptations' 1982 comeback with "Standing On The Top" (Gordy 1616G), taken from their REUNION album (Gordy 6008G).

Rick presented the Mary Jane Girls in 1983, and the comparison was quickly drawn with Prince's similar group, Vanity 6. By this time, Rick was outspoken in his dislike of being compared to Prince. He continues to write, produce, and record for Motown. In addition to the Mary Jane Girls, he writes and produces material for Teena Marie.

MOTOWN DISCOGRAPHY

4/78: COME GET IT (Gordy G7-981R1)
5/78: You And I/Hollywood (Gordy 7156)
9/78: Mary Jane/Dream Maker (Gordy 7162)
1/79: High On Your Love Suite/Stone City Band, Hi! (Gordy 7164)
1/79: BUSTIN' OUT OF L SEVEN (Gordy G7-984R1)
4/79: Bustin' Out/Sexy Lady (Gordy 7167)
7/79: Fool On The Street/Jefferson Ball (Gordy 7171)
10/79: Love Gun/Stormy Love (Gordy 7176)
10/79: FIRE IT UP (Gordy G8-990M1)
12/79: Come Into My Life (Part 1)/Come Into My Life (Part 2) (Gordy 7177)
6/80: Big Time/Island Lady (Gordy 7185)
7/80: GARDEN OF LOVE (Gordy G8-995M1)
9/80: Summer Love/Gettin' It On (In The Sunshine) (Gordy 7191)
3/81: Give It To Me Baby/Don't Give Up On Love Gordy 7197)
3/81: STREET SONGS (Gordy G8-1002M1)
8/81: Super Freak (Part I)/Super Freak (Part II) (Gordy 7205)
11/81: Ghetto Life/Below The Funk (Pass The J) (Gordy 7215)
4/82: Standing On The Top (Part 1)/ Standing On The Top (Part 2) (Gordy 1616GF) The Temptations featuring Rick James
5/82: Dance Wit' Me (Part 1)/Dance Wit' Me (Part 2) (Gordy 1619GF)
5/82: THROWIN' DOWN (Gordy 6005GL)
7/82: Hard To Get/My Love (Gordy 1634GF)
10/82: She Blew My Mind (69 Times)/She Blew My Mind (69 Times) (Gordy 1646GF)
1/83: Teardrops/Throwdown (Gordy 1658GF)
7/83: Cold Blooded/Cold Blooded (Instrumental) (Gordy 1687GF)
8/83: COLD BLOODED (Gordy 6043GL)
10/83: U Bring The Freak Out/Money Talks (Gordy 1703GF)
10/83: COME GET IT/FIRE UP (Motown 6078MC)
11/83: Ebony Eyes/1, 2, 3, (You, Her And Me) (Gordy 1714GF) 'A' side with Smokey Robinson
5/84: REFLECTIONS: ALL THE GREATEST HITS (Gordy 6095GL)
6/84: 17/17 (Instrumental) (Gordy 1730GF)
9/84: You Turn Me On/Fire & Desire (Gordy 1763GF)
3/85: Can't Stop/Oh What A Night (4 Luv) (Gordy 1776GF)
4/85: THE GLOW (Gordy 6135GL)
5/85: Glow/Glow (Instrumental) (Gordy 1796GF)
8/85: Spend The Night With Me/Spend The Night With Me (Instrumental) (Gordy 1806GF)
4/86: THE FLAG (Gordy 6185GL
6/86: Sweet And Sexy Thing/Sweet And Sexy Thing (Instrumental) (Gordy 1844GF)
9/86: Forever And A Day/Forever And A Day (Instrumental) (Gordy 1862GF)

MARV JOHNSON

In the early 1960s, Berry Gordy wrote and produced
several songs for Marv Johnson that were leased to
United Artists Records.

Born Detroit, Michigan, October 15, 1938. Marv Johnson met Berry Gordy in 1958 while working in a record store in Detroit. Berry was at that time an independent record producer. Marv's first record, "Once Upon A Time/My Baby-O," was a Berry Gordy production (Sonny Woods co-produced) that was released on the Detroit-based gospel label, Kudo Records, run by Robert West, who also operated Lupine Records.

Marv had graduated from Detroit's Cass Technical High School in 1957 and was a member of a group called the Serenaders that toured with carnival shows in Florida and the South, playing rhythm & blues in the summers between school. In the summer of 1957, Marv was involved in a serious car accident that left him laid up for about a year.

Marv has the distinction of having the first record released on Berry Gordy's Tamla label, "Come To Me/Whisper" (Tamla 101). It was quickly licensed to United Artists and was released on UA 160. As a result of UA's national distribution, the record charted for fifteen weeks in 1959, reaching a peak position of #30 on the pop charts. His subsequent records were released on United Artists until 1965, when he began recording for the Gordy label. While Marv was with UA, Berry Gordy wrote and produced his material, usually making the master recordings in Detroit.

Marv's third release on United Artists was also a hit. "You Got What It Takes" (UA 185) was his third 1959 release; the song was written by Berry Gordy, Gwen Gordy, and Tyran Carlo (pseudonym for Billy Davis), and published by Jobete. It reached #10, making it the first Berry Gordy production to reach pop's Top 10, and charted for twenty-two weeks. The follow-up, "I Love The Way You Love" (UA 208), reached #9 and stayed on the charts for thirteen weeks.

Marv released three singles on the Gordy label in 1965, 1966, and 1968. The last, "I'll Pick A Rose For My Rose" (Gordy 7077) enjoyed some chart success in England, and Marv spent March and April of 1969 on a three-week tour there. Marv did not accompany Motown Records to Los Angeles from Detroit, and he was sadly not included in the company's 25th anniversary show in

MOTOWN DISCOGRAPHY

1/59: Come To Me/Whisper (Tamla 101)
6/65: Why Do You Want To Let Me Go/ I'm Not A Plaything (Gordy 7042)
3/66: I Miss You Baby (How I Miss You)/ Just The Way You Are (Gordy 7051)
9/68: I'll Pick A Rose For My Rose/You Got The Love I Love (Gordy 7077)

Unissued Motown Recordings

MARV (Gordy GS-937)

NON-MOTOWN DISCOGRAPHY

1958: Once Upon A Time/My Baby-O (Kudo 663)
1959: Come To Me/Whisper (United Artists 160) Also Tamla 101
1959: I'm Coming Home/River of Tears (United Artists 175)
1959: You Got What It Takes/Don't Leave Me (United Artists 185)
1960: I Love The Way You Love/Let Me Love You (United Artists 208)
1960: Ain't Gonna Be That Way/All The Love I've Got (United Artists 226)
1960: (You've Got To) Move Two Mountains/I Need You (United Artists 241)
1960: Happy Days/Baby Baby (United Artists 273)
1961: Merry-Go-Round/Tell Me That You Love Me (United Artists 294)
1961: I've Got A Notion/How Can We Tell Him (United Artists 322)
1961: Oh Mary/Show Me (United Artists 359)
1961: Easier Said Than Done/Johnny One Stop (United Artists 386)
1961: Magic Mirror/With All That's In Me (United Artists 423)
1962: That's How Bad/He Gave Me You (United Artists 454)
1962: Let Yourself Go/That's Where I Lost My Baby (United Artists 483)
1962: Keep Tellin' Yourself/Everyone Who's Been In Love With You (United Artists 556)
1963: Another Tear Falls/He's Got The Whole World In His Hands (United Artists 590)

EDDIE KENDRICKS

Eddie Kendricks after he left The Temptations.

1963: Come On And Stop/Not Available
(United Artists 617)
1963: Unbreakable Love/Man Who Don't
Believe In Love (United Artists 691)

FOR MORE INFORMATION
Keegan, Kevin. "Marv Johnson," in *RPM: Record Profile Magazine*, No. 6, July 1984.

EDDIE KENDRICKS

Born December 17, 1939, in Birmingham, Alabama.

One of the original members of the Temptations, Eddie sang or shared lead vocals for the group until he left May 1971 to pursue a solo career. In 1960, Eddie's group, the Primes, had just broken up; he and Paul Williams joined the Distants, who were then calling themselves the Elgins, when Berry Gordy heard the group in Detroit and signed them. Eddie sang lead on the Temptations' first national chart hit, "The Way You Do The Things You Do" (Gordy 7028); his final song with the Temptations, "Just My Imagination (Running Away With Me)" (Gordy 7105), reached the #1 spot on the pop charts early in 1971.

The most popular of his solo releases on Tamla (1971-1976) was the #1 hit, "Keep On Truckin' (Part 1)" (Tamla 54238) in 1973.

The follow-up, "Boogie Down" (Tamla 54243), reached #2 in 1974. Throughout his career, Eddie seems to have enjoyed live performances. He launched his first major tour after leaving the Temptations in May 1973 from Detroit's Phelps Lounge. The tour continued on to Chicago, Boston, Philadelphia, and New York.

By 1976, Eddie's career stalled. He had no bookings during the latter half of 1976, so he changed management. 1977 began with a few club dates, then came the cross-country "Tour '77" that saw a sellout performance at Madison Square Garden. In 1978, he signed with Arista. In 1981, he again switched labels, this time to Atlantic. Eddie temporarily rejoined the Temptations in 1982 for their reunion tour and album, coordinated by Rick James.

Subsequent to the reunion, Eddie and David Ruffin (another former lead singer with the Temptations) began performing together. In 1985, they appeared on the Live Aid broadcast and released an album and single that was recorded live at New York's Apollo Theatre with Daryl Hall and John Oates.

MOTOWN DISCOGRAPHY

4/71: It's So Hard For Me To Say Good-Bye/This Use To Be The Home Of Johnnie Mae (Tamla 54203)

4/71: It's So Hard For Me To Say Good-bye (Short Version 3:40)/It's So Hard For Me To Say Good-bye (Long Version 5:04) (Tamla 54203)

4/71: This Use To Be The Home Of Johnnie Mae (Short Version 3:40)/ This Use To Be The Home Of Johnnie Mae (Long Version 5:40) (Tamla 54203)

4/71: ALL BY MYSELF (Tamla TS-309)

11/71: Can I/I Did It All For You (Tamla 54210)

11/71: Can I (Short Version 3:40)/Can I (Long Version 6:05) (Tamla 54210)

5/72: Eddie's Love/Let Me Run Into Your Lonely Heart (Tamla 54218)

5/72: PEOPLE...HOLD ON (Tamla T-315L)

8/72: If You Let Me/Just Memories (Tamla 54222)

1/73: Girl You Need A Change Of Mind (Part 1)/Girl You Need A Change Of Mind (Part 2) (Tamla 54230)

5/73: EDDIE KENDRICKS (Tamla T-327L)

6/73: Darling Come Back Home/Loving You The Second Time Around (Tamla 54236)

8/73: Keep On Truckin' (Part 1)/Keep On Truckin' (Part 2) (Tamla 54238)

12/73: Boogie Down/Can't Help What I Am (Tamla 54243)

2/74: BOOGIE DOWN! (Tamla T-330V1)

4/74: Son Of Sagittarius/Trust Your Heart (Tamla 54247)

7/74: Tell Her Love Has Felt The Need/ Loving You The Second Time Around (Tamla 54249)

11/74: One Tear/The Thin Man (Tamla 54255)

12/74: FOR YOU (Tamla T6-335S1)

1/75: Shoeshine Boy/Hooked On Your Love (Tamla 54257)

6/75: Get The Cream Off The Top/Honey Brown (Tamla 54260)

6/75: THE HIT MAN (Tamla T6-338S1)

9/75: Happy/Deep And Quiet Love (Tamla 54263)

GLADYS KNIGHT & THE PIPS

A very early photo.

1/76: He's A Friend/All Of My Love
(Tamla 54266)
2/76: HE'S A FRIEND (Tamla T6-343S1)
6/76: Get It While It's Hot/Never Gonna
Leave You (Tamla 54270)
9/76: GOIN' UP IN SMOKE (Tamla
T6-346S1)
11/76: Goin' Up In Smoke/Thanks For The
Memories (Tamla 54277)
7/77: Born Again/Date With The Rain
(Tamla 54285)
8/77: SLICK (Tamla T6-356S1)
12/77: Baby/Intimate Friends (Tamla 54290)
1/78: AT HIS BEST (Tamla T7-354R1)

NON-MOTOWN DISCOGRAPHY

1978: VINTAGE '78 (Arista 4170)
1978: Ain't No Smoke Without Fire/Love,
Love, Love (Arista 0325)
1978: The Best Of Strangers Now/Don't
Underestimate The Power Of Love
(Arista 0346)
1979: SOMETHING MORE (Arista 4250)
1980: Your Love Has Been So Good/I
Never Used To Dance (Arista 0500)
1981: LOVE KEYS (Atlantic SD 19294)
1981: (Oh I) Need Your Lovin'/Looking
For Love (Atlantic 3796)
1981: I Don't Need Nobody Else/(Atlantic
3874)
1982: Surprise Attack/ (Cornerstone)
1985: LIVE AT THE APOLLO WITH
DAVID RUFFIN AND EDDIE
KENDRICK [sic] (RCA AFL1-7035)
As by Daryl Hall and John Oates
1985: A Nite At The Apollo Live! The Way
You Do The Things You Do/My Girl
(RCA PB-14178) As by Daryl Hall
and John Oates Featuring David
Ruffin and Eddie Kendrick [sic]

MAURICE KING

Went from being the house bandleader at the Flame Show Bar in Detroit to the head of Motown's Artist Development Department, where Motown's singers and performers learned the art of performance and developed stage presence.

GLADYS KNIGHT AND THE PIPS

This family group has been together since the mid-1950s without a personnel change. From Atlanta, Georgia, the group consists of Gladys Knight (born May 28, 1944), Merald "Bubba" Knight (Gladys' brother, born September 4, 1942), Edward Patten (a cousin, born August 2, 1939), and William Guest (a cousin, born June 2, 1941). The name Pips was originally taken from a cousin's nickname; later it was used to stand for Perfection In Performance. In 1952, Gladys won first prize of $2,000 on the "Ted Mack Amateur Hour," the same year the Pips were formed to sing in church. She sang a version of Nat King Cole's "Too Young."

The group recorded for several labels from 1958 to 1965 before signing with Motown in 1966. Their first hit, "Every Beat Of My Heart," was released on three labels (Huntom 2510, Vee Jay 386, and Fury 1050) in 1961, and they never received any royalties for it. While they had some hits during their seven-year stay at Motown (1966-1973), they were more successful after leaving Motown. Gladys has stated that her choice of material while at Motown was too narrow, that she wanted to also sing gospel, country, and blues. While at Motown, the group's songs were issued primarily on the Soul label, where they were assigned to producer Norman Whitfield. Whitfield produced their biggest hit while they were at Motown, "I Heard It Through The Grapevine" (Soul 35039), which reached #2 in the pop charts in 1967. This Norman Whitfield-Barrett Strong composition was an even bigger hit for Marvin Gaye a year later.

It was three years before the group had another Top 10 hit, "If I Were Your Woman" (Soul 35078), and then another three years before "Neither One Of Us (Wants To Be The First To Say Goodbye)" (Soul 35098) reached #2. While 1973 began with that hit, the year ended with the group leaving Motown and signing with Buddah Records.

They began their post-Motown career in 1973 with a #1 hit for Buddah, "Midnight Train To Georgia" (Buddah 383), and their next three records all reached the top five on the pop charts: "I've Got To Use My Imagination" (Buddah 393), "Best Thing That Ever Happened To Me" (Buddah 403), and "On And On" (Buddah 423).

Motown issued a few singles on Soul after

the group had already signed with Buddah. In 1986, the group signed a long-term, worldwide, exclusive contract with MCA Records.

MOTOWN DISCOGRAPHY

7/66: Just Walk In My Shoes/Stepping Closer To Your Heart (Soul 35023)

3/67: Take Me In Your Arms And Love Me/Do You Love Me Just A Little, Honey (Soul 35033)

6/67: Everybody Needs Love/Stepping Closer To Your Heart (Soul 35034)

9/67: I Heard It Through The Grapevine/It's Time To Go Now (Soul 35039)

9/67: EVERYBODY NEEDS LOVE (Soul SS-706)

1/68: The End Of Our Road/Don't Let Her Take Your Love From Me (Soul 35042)

5/68: It Should Have Been Me/You Don't Love Me No More (Soul 35045)

5/68: FEELIN' BLUESY (Soul S-707)

8/68: I Wish It Would Rain/It's Summer (Soul 35047)

12/68: SILK N' SOUL (Soul SS-711)

2/69: Didn't You Know (You'd Have To Cry Sometime)/Keep An Eye (Soul 35057)

5/69: The Nitty Gritty/Got Myself A Good Man (Soul 35063)

9/69: NITTY GRITTY (Soul S-713)

10/69: Friendship Train/Cloud Nine (Soul 35068)

2/70: You Need Love Like I Do (Don't You)/You're My Everything (Soul 35071)

3/70: GREATEST HITS (Soul SS-723)

10/70: If I Were Your Woman/The Tracks Of My Tears (Soul 35078)

10/70: ALL IN A KNIGHT'S WORK (LIVE) (Soul SS-730)

4/71: IF I WERE YOUR WOMAN (Soul SS-731)

5/71: I Don't Want To Do Wrong/Is There A Place (In His Heart For Me) (Soul 35083)

11/71: Make Me The Woman That You Go Home To/It's All Over But The Shoutin' (Soul 35091)

12/71: STANDING OVATION (Soul S-736L)

3/72: Help Me Make It Through The Night /If You're Gonna Leave (Just Leave) (Soul 35094)

12/72: Neither One Of Us (Wants To Be The First To Say Goodbye)/Can't Give It Up No More (Soul 35098)

2/73: NEITHER ONE OF US (Soul S-737L)

4/73: Daddy Could Swear (I Declare)/For Once In My Life (Soul 35105)

6/33: ALL I NEED IS TIME (Soul S-739L)

7/73: All I Need Is Time/The Only Time You Love Me Is When You're Losing Me (Soul 35107)

1/74: ANTHOLOGY (Motown M-792S2)

2/74: KNIGHT TIME (Soul S-741V1)

6/74: Between Her Goodbye And My Hello/This Child Needs Its Father (Soul 35111)

3/75: A LITTLE KNIGHT MUSIC (Soul S-744V1)

11/84: COMPACT COMMAND PERFOR-MANCES: 17 GREATEST HITS (Motown 6109MD)

8/86: ANTHOLOGY (Motown MCD06200MDZ)

PRE-MOTOWN DISCOGRAPHY

1958: Ching Chong/Whistle My Love (Brunswick 55048) As by The Pips

1961: Every Beat Of My Heart/Room In Your Heart (Huntom 2510) Atlanta-based label; as by The Pips

1961: Every Beat Of My Heart/Room In Your Heart (Vee Jay 386) National release, same as Huntom 2510; as by The Pips

Subsequent releases as by Gladys Knight & the Pips:

1961: Love Call/What Shall I Do (Enjoy)

1961: I Had A Dream Last Night/Happiness (Everlast)

1961: Every Beat Of My Heart/Room In Your Heart (Fury 1050) Re-recorded version

1961: Guess Who/Stop Running Around (Fury 1052)

1961: Letter Full Of Tears/You Broke Your Promise (Fury 1054)

1961: LETTERS FULL OF TEARS (Fury F-1003)

1962: Operator/I'll Trust In You (Fury 1064)

1962: Darling/Linda (Fury 1067)

1962: Come See About Me/I Want That Kind Of Love (Fury 1073)

1963: Queen Of Tears/A Love Like Mine

SHORTY LONG

(Vee Jay 545)

1964: Giving Up/Maybe Maybe Baby (Maxx 326)

1964: Lovers Always Forgive/Another Love (Maxx 329)

1965: Either Way I Lose/Go Away Stay Away (Maxx 331)

1965: Who Knows/Stop And Think It Over (Maxx 334)

SHORTY LONG

Born Frederick Earl Long, May 20, 1940, in Birmingham, Alabama; died June 29, 1969, at the age of twenty-nine in a boating accident on the Detroit River.

Frederick "Shorty" Long came to Motown when Harvey and Gwen Fuqua's Tri-Phi/Harvey labels were consolidated with Berry Gordy's Motown empire in 1962-63. Although Long was first announced as a new signing to Tri-Phi's subsidiary, Harvey, in 1961, all of his records were released on Tri-Phi and, with Motown, on the Soul label.

Shorty Long sang and played many instruments, including piano, organ, drums, trumpet, and harmonica. He had traveled with the Ink Spots, and received his musical training from W.C. Handy and Alvin Robinson before signing with Harvey Fuqua. While at Motown, he acted as the master of ceremonies at many Motown Revue performances and on tours. His 1964 record, "Devil With A Blue Dress" (Soul 35001), was the first release for Motown's Soul label.

Shorty Long's songwriting credits include "Devil With A Blue Dress," "Here Comes The Judge," and "Function At The Junction."

MOTOWN DISCOGRAPHY

3/64: Devil With The Blue Dress/Wind It Up (Soul 35001)

8/64: It's A Crying Shame (The Way You Treat A Good Man Like Me)/Out To Get You (Soul 35005)

9/66: Function At The Junction/Call On Me (Soul 35021)

2/67: Chantilly Lace/Your Love Is Amazing (Soul 35031)

1/68: Night Fo' Last [Vocal]/Night Fo' Last (featuring Shorty Long on the organ) (Soul 35040)

5/68: Here Comes The Judge/Sing What You Wanna (Soul 35044)

1/69: I Had A Dream/Ain't No Justice (Soul 35054)

6/69: A Whiter Shade Of Pale/When You Are Available (Soul 35064)

9/68: HERE COMES THE JUDGE (Soul SS-709)

11/69: THE PRIME OF SHORTY LONG (Soul SS-719)

NON-MOTOWN DISCOGRAPHY

1962: Bad Willie/I'll Be There (Tri-Phi 1006)

1962: Too Smart/I'll Be There (Tri-Phi 1015)

1963: Going Away/What's The Matter (Tri-Phi 1021)

FOR MORE INFORMATION

Huston, Bruce. "Shorty Long Remembered," in *Soul Survivor*, Vol. 1, No. 2 (Spring 1985).

MARTHA & THE VANDELLAS

Martha Reeves was born in Alabama on July 18, 1941, but raised in Detroit. After high school graduation, she sang locally in Detroit as an amateur and in talent contests. In 1959, singing as blues singer Martha Lavaille, she met William "Mickey" Stevenson, head of Motown's A & R department. He got her a job as secretary there.

Martha & the Vandellas began in the early 1960s as the Del-Phis, consisting of Gloria Williams (lead), Martha Reeves, Rosalind (or Rosalyn) Ashford, and Annette Sterling (later Annette Sterling Beard). They sang backup for such Detroit r&b artists as J.J. Barnes and Mike Hanks. In 1961, they released "It Takes Two/I'll Let You Know" (Check-Mate 1005).

Their breaks started to happen at Motown while Martha was working for Mickey Stevenson. Mary Wells missed a recording session for "There He Is (At My Door)," and since one of Martha's duties was booking studio time, she called in her group. The record was released as by The Vels, with Gloria Williams singing lead, on Motown's subsidiary, Melody. When the record flopped, Gloria Williams left the group and the music business altogether, leaving Martha to sing lead.

The group's first release on the Gordy label featured Martha on lead, with backing by Rosalind Ashford and Annette Sterling,

MARTHA & THE VANDELLAS

MARTHA & THE VANDELLAS

The Gordy album G-915, the announced title of which was "Wild One" (as reflected on this 45 rpm label), was actually released as "Dance Party." It turned out that the song, "Dancing In The Street," also on the album, was a much bigger hit than "Wild One."

AUDITION COPY   **NOT FOR SALE**

G-7036
© 1964
Jobete BMI
DMAY-XL-106105
RK5M-6508
© 1964
Motown Record
Corporation

Produced by
STEVENSON
& HUNTER
Time 2:39
45 RPM

WILD ONE
(Stevenson, Hunter)
**MARTHA &
THE VANDELLAS**
Taken From Album
"Wild One" G 915

doing "I'll Have To Let Him Go" (Gordy 7011). Again, this session was originally scheduled for Mary Wells and the Andantes. The group's second release on Gordy, "Come And Get These Memories/Jealous Lover" (Gordy 7014) began their work with Motown's songwriting/production team, Holland-Dozier-Holland. Released early in 1963, this song is often cited as the beginning of "The Motown Sound."

During the period of 1963 to 1967, H-D-H wrote five Top 10 hits for the group: "Heatwave" (Gordy 7022), "Quicksand" (Gordy 7025), "Nowhere To Run" (Gordy 7039), "I'm Ready For Love" (Gordy 7056), and "Jimmy Mack" (Gordy 7058). The group's best chart performance, however, came in 1964 with "Dancing In The Street" (Gordy 7033), a song written by Mickey Stevenson and Marvin Gaye. It was produced by Mickey Stevenson and featured Marvin Gaye on piano.

The Vandellas have undergone some personnel changes through their career. Originally a quartet, they became a trio when Gloria Williams left in 1962. Annette Sterling left in 1963 after "Heatwave" to become Annette Sterling Beard. She was replaced by ex-Velvelette Betty Kelley, who stayed with the group until 1968, when she was replaced by Martha's younger sister, Lois Reeves. Lois first recorded with the group on "I Promise To Wait My Love/Forget Me Not" (Gordy 7070). Martha took ill in 1968, and the group disbanded temporarily, reforming with Martha, Lois, and Sandra Tilley, formerly with the Orlons and the Velvelettes. This line-up recorded the albums, SUGAR 'N' SPICE (Gordy 944) and NATURAL RESOURCES (Gordy 952). Martha Reeves was one artist who did not wish to relocate with Motown to Los Angeles. She was let out of her contract in 1971, in exchange for giving up future royalties. During the 1970s and 1980s, she has pursued a solo career and often performs at Motown revival shows with various backing singers.

MOTOWN DISCOGRAPHY

9/62: I'll Have To Let Him Go/My Baby Won't Come Back (Gordy 7011)

2/63: Come And Get These Memories/ Jealous Lover (Gordy 7014)

7/63: Heat Wave/A Love Like Yours (Don't Come Knocking Everyday) (Gordy 7022)

8/63: COME AND GET THESE MEMORIES (Gordy G-902)

9/63: HEAT WAVE (Gordy G-907)

11/63: Quicksand/Darling, I Hum Our Song (Gordy 7025)

1/64: Live Wire/Old Love (Let's Try It Again) (Gordy 7027)

3/64: In My Lonely Room/A Tear For The Girl (Gordy 7031)

7/64: Dancing In The Street/There He Is (At My Door) (Gordy 7033)

11/64: Wild One/Dancing Slow (Gordy 7036)

2/65: Nowhere To Run/Motoring (Gordy 7039)

5/65: DANCE PARTY (Gordy G-915)

7/65: Love (Makes Me Do Foolish Things)/You've Been In Love Too Long (Gordy 7045)

1/66: My Baby Loves Me/Never Leave Your Baby's Side (Gordy 7048)

4/66: What Am I Going To Do Without Your Love/Go Ahead And Laugh (Gordy 7053)

5/66: VANDELLAS GREATEST HITS (Gordy GS-917)

10/66: I'm Ready For Love/He Doesn't Love Her Anymore (Gordy 7056)

11/66: WATCHOUT! (Gordy GS-920)

2/67: Jimmy Mack/Third Finger, Left Hand (Gordy 7058)

8/67: Love Bug Leave My Heart Alone/ One Way Out (Gordy 7062)

9/67: MARTHA AND THE VANDELLAS LIVE! (Gordy GS-925)

Subsequent releases as by Martha Reeves and the Vandellas:

11/67: Honey Chile/Show Me The Way (Gordy 7067) First release as by Martha Reeves and the Vandellas

4/68: I Promise To Wait My Love/Forget Me Not (Gordy 7070)

5/68: RIDIN' HIGH (Gordy GS-926)

8/68: I Can't Dance To That Music You're Playing/I Tried (Gordy 7075)

10/68: Sweet Darlin'/Without You (Gordy 7080)

3/69: (We've Got) Honey Love/I'm In Love (And I Know It) (Gordy 7085)

8/69: Taking My Love (And Leaving Me)/Heartless (Gordy 7094)

10/69: SUGAR N' SPICE (Gordy GS-944)

3/70: I Should Be Proud/Love, Guess Who

MARTHA REEVES

(Gordy 7098)

9/70: NATURAL RESOURCES (Gordy GS-952)

11/70: I Gotta Let You Go/You're The Loser Now (Gordy 7103)

9/71: Bless You/Hope I Don't Get My Heart Broke (Gordy 7110)

12/71: In And Out Of My Life/Your Love Makes It All Worthwhile (Gordy 7113)

2/72: BLACK MAGIC (Gordy G-958L)

5/72: Tear It On Down/I Want You Back (Gordy 7118)

9/74: ANTHOLOGY (Motown M7-778R2)

2/86: COMPACT COMMAND PERFORMANCES: 26 GREATEST HITS (Gordy GCD06170GD)

NON-MOTOWN DISCOGRAPHY

1961: It Takes Two/I'll Let You Know (Check-Mate 1005) As by the Del-Phis

1962: There He Is (At My Door)/You'll Never Cherish A Love So True ('Till You Lose It) (Melody 103) As by The Vels

1984?: Spellbound/ (Tamtown) Striped label, British bootleg 45; as by The Vandellas

FOR MORE INFORMATION
Betrock, Alan. *Girl Groups*. pp. 156-162.
Hirshey, Gerri. *Nowhere To Run*, pp. 145-55.
O'Grady, Maureen. "Martha & the Vandellas," in *Record Collector*, June 1982. Includes discography of British releases.

(See also DEL-PHIS; VELS.)

MARVELETTES

The Marvelettes were discovered by Robert Bateman in 1960 at an Inkster High School talent show (Inkster is a Detroit suburb). The group was formed by Gladys Horton while in high school, originally as the Marvels. When they auditioned and signed with Tamla, Berry Gordy changed their name to the Marvelettes. Preceding the Supremes and Martha & the Vandellas, the Marvelettes were a quintessential "girl group," projecting an innocent teenage quality. The group auditioned as a quintet consisting of Gladys Horton, Wanda Young (later to marry Bobby Rogers of the Miracles), Katherine Anderson, Juanita Cowart, and Georgeanna Dobbins (also Georgeanna Tillman). This line-up sang on their first release, "Please Mr. Postman" (Tamla 54046), which shot to #1 on the pop charts and became their biggest hit. It was Motown's best chart performance to date, surpassing The Miracles' "Shop Around." They went on to release "Twistin' Postman" (Tamla 54054) and another Top 10 hit, "Playboy" (Tamla 54060,) before graduating from high school in 1962.

Following "Please Mr. Postman," Juanita Cowart left the group, and they recorded as a quartet until mid-1962, when Georgeanna Dobbins left to stay on at Motown as a secretary. Gladys Horton, Wanda Young, and Katherine Anderson carried on as a trio. The group's popularity declined after their 1962 hit, "Beechwood 4-5789" (Tamla 54065), a song co-written by William "Mickey" Stevenson, Marvin Gaye, and George Gordy. They bounced back somewhat with Norman Whitfield's production of "Too Many Fish In The Sea" (Tamla 54105) in 1964. Gladys sang lead on most of their hits, while Wanda sang lead on the ballads and some A-sides, such as their 1966 hit, "Don't Mess With Bill" (Tamla 54126).

Smokey Robinson wrote two Top 10 hits for the group in 1967, "The Hunter Gets Captured By The Game" (Tamla 54143) and "My Baby Must Be A Magician" (Tamla 54158). In 1969, their career virtually ended when Gladys Horton left to get married. She was replaced by Ann Bogan, but Wanda Young became the new leader. She appears as lead singer on their last album, THE RETURN OF THE MARVELETTES (Tamla 305).

The Marvelettes were another Motown group that did not relocate with the company to Los Angeles in 1971. Gladys Horton has revived the group's name for 1980s revival shows, utilizing various backing singers. Georgeanna Tillman died of sickle cell anemia on January 6, 1980.

MOTOWN DISCOGRAPHY

8/61: Please Mr. Postman/So Long Baby (Tamla 54046)

11/61: PLEASE MR. POSTMAN (Tamla TM-228)

1/62: Twistin' Postman/I Want A Guy

THE MARVELETTES

The original Marvelettes quintet that recorded
"Please Mr. Postman."

(Tamla 54054)

4/62: Playboy/All The Love I've Got
(Tamla 54060)

4/62: THE MARVELETTES SING (Tamla
TM-229)

7/62: Beechwood 4-5789/Someday,
Someway (Tamla 54065)

9/62: PLAYBOY (Tamla TM-231)

11/62: Strange I Know/Too Strong To Be
Strung Along (Tamla 54072)

3/63: Forever/Locking Up My Heart
(Tamla 54077)

5/63: MARVELOUS MARVELETTES
(Tamla TM-237)

7/63: My Daddy Knows Best/Tie A String
Around Your Finger) (Tamla 54082)

7/63: RECORDED LIVE: ON STAGE
(Tamla TM-243)

10/63: As Long As I Know He's Mine/
Little Girl Blue (Tamla 54088)

1/64: He's A Good Guy (Yes He Is)/
Goddess Of Love (Tamla 54091)

6/64: You're My Remedy/A Little Bit Of
Sympathy, A Little Bit Of Love
(Tamla 54097)

10/64: Too Many Fish In The Sea/A Need
For Love (Tamla 54105)

5/65: I'll Keep Holding On/No Time For
Tears (Tamla 54116)

7/65: Danger Heartbreak Dead Ahead/Your
Cheating Ways (Tamla 54120)

12/65: Don't Mess With Bill/Anything You
Wanna Do (Tamla 54126)

2/66: MARVELETTES GREATEST HITS
(Tamla TS-253)

4/66: You're The One/Paper Boy (Tamla
54131)

12/66: The Hunter Gets Captured By The
Game/I Think I Can Change You
(Tamla 54143)

3/67: THE MARVELETTES (Tamla TS-274)

4/67: When You're Young And In Love/
The Day You Take One, You Have
To Take The Other (Tamla 54150)

11/67: My Baby Must Be A Magician/I
Need Someone (Tamla 54158

5/68: Here I Am Baby/Keep Off, No
Trespassing (Tamla 54166)

8/68: SOPHISTICATED SOUL (Tamla TS-
286)

9/68: Destination: Anywhere/What's Easy
For Two Is So Hard For One (Tamla
54171)

12/68: I'm Gonna Hold On As Long As I
Can/Don't Make Hurting Me A Habit

(Tamla 54177)

10/69: That's How Heartaches Are Made/
Rainy Mourning (Tamla 54186)

10/69: IN FULL BLOOM (Tamla TS-288)

8/70: Marionette/After All (Tamla 54198)

10/70: THE RETURN OF THE
MARVELETTES (Tamla TS-305)

11/71: A Breath Taking Guy/You're The
One For Me Baby (Tamla 54213)

6/75: ANTHOLOGY (Motown M7-827R2)

2/86: COMPACT COMMAND PER-
FORMANCES: 23 GREATEST HITS
(Tamla TCD 06169TD)

FOR MORE INFORMATION
Betrock, Alan. *Girl Groups*, pp. 64-69.

MARY JANE GIRLS

Recording on the Gordy label, this all-girl group was introduced in 1983 by Rick James, who has continued to write, produce, and arrange their songs and albums. Their initial lineup consisted of Maxi, JoJo, Cheri, and Candi. Corvette Brooks replaced Cheri in 1985 and appears on their ONLY FOUR YOU (Gordy 6092GL) album.

MOTOWN DISCOGRAPHY

3/83: Candy Man (Vocal)/Candy Man
(Instrumental) (Gordy 1670GF)

3/83: MARY JANE GIRLS (Gordy 6040GL)

7/83: All Night Long/Musical Love (Gordy
1690GF)

10/83: Boys/Boys (Instrumental) (Gordy
1704GF)

1/84: Jealousy/You Are My Heaven (Gordy
1721GF)

5/84: In My House/In My House
(Instrumental) (Gordy 1741GF)

2/85: ONLY FOUR YOU (Gordy 6092GL)

6/85: Wild & Crazy Love/Wild & Crazy
Love (Instrumental) (Gordy 1798GF)

9/85: Break It Up/Break It Up
(Instrumental) (Gordy 1816GF)

6/86: Walk Like A Man/Shadow Lover
(Motown 1851MF)

MESSENGERS

Rare Earth recording artists from Milwaukee.

THE MIRACLES

7/67: Window Shopping/California Soul (Soul 35037)
8/69: MESSENGERS (Rare Earth RS 509)
7/71: That's The Way A Woman Is/In The Jungle (Rare Earth 5032)

RON MILLER

Songwriter-Producer. Song credits include "Let's All Save The Children," "For Once In My Life" (recorded by Stevie Wonder), "Touch Me In The Morning" (recorded by Diana Ross), "A Place In The Sun" (recorded by Stevie Wonder), "Heaven Help Us All" (recorded by Stevie Wonder), "Yester-Me, Yester-You, Yesterday" (recorded by Stevie Wonder), "I've Never Been To Me" (recorded by Charlene), "Green Grow The Lilacs" (recorded by The Originals).

THE MIRACLES

William "Smokey" Robinson (lead) (born February 19, 1940)
Robert "Bobby" Rogers (born February 19, 1940)
Claudette Rogers (later Claudette Robinson)
Warren "Pete" Moore (born November 19, 1939)
Ronnie White (born April 5, 1939)

The Miracles were formed in 1957 by Smokey after he graduated from high school in Detroit. Claudette Rogers and Bobby Rogers are cousins, and Bobby's brother, Sonny, was also an original member; Claudette replaced him when he joined the army. Claudette married Smokey in 1959. For a while, she appeared on record with the group but did not tour; by 1965 she stopped performing with the group entirely. The Miracles stayed together with essentially the same personnel until 1972, when Smokey left to spend more time with his family. After a three-year sabbatical, he began his solo career in earnest. The Miracles played a farewell concert tour in 1972, at which time Smokey introduced his replacement, William Griffin. The "new" Miracles continued to record on Tamla for another five years, then on Columbia. They disbanded in 1978 but were temporarily re-united for Motown's 25th anniversary show in 1983.

The Miracles have had a long and distinguished career that included having Motown's first million-unit seller, "Shop Around" (Tamla 54034), in 1960. Berry Gordy discovered them in 1957 when they auditioned for Jackie Wilson's manager. Acting as an independent producer, Berry began recording the Miracles and marketed the recordings to other labels, such as the Chicago-based Chess label and the New York-based label, End. Their first release, "Got A Job" (End 1016), was co-written by Smokey Robinson, Berry Gordy, and Tyran Carlo (pseudonym for Billy Davis). It was an "answer song" to the then-popular, "Get A Job." The Miracles were the first group Berry Gordy signed when he began to form his own Motown family of labels.

Two of the Miracles' early recordings are now among the rarest of any issued by Motown and related labels. "Bad Girl" (Chess 1734) was the first of two releases that Berry Gordy leased to Chicago's Chess label, but copies were also pressed on the Motown label (with two different numbers, G1/G2 and 2207). Most likely, these were not made available commercially, but were used as demos in marketing the song to other labels. (All subsequent Miracles' releases were on the Tamla label.) Of the two, #2207 is considered the rarest. The second Miracles' rarity concerns their very first release on Tamla. "Way Over There/Depend On Me" (Tamla 54028) is generally considered the label's first national release, all previous releases being limited to the Detroit area. However, this was preceded by "The Feeling Is So Fine/You Can Depend On Me," also on Tamla 54028. For some reason, it was quickly withdrawn and replaced by "Way Over There," making "The Feeling Is So Fine" an extremely rare record and one of the Miracles' "lost" recordings, as it has not appeared on any of their albums or on later compilation albums. "Way Over There" also exists in two versions, one with strings and one without. It seems that the use of strings in r&b and soul music was starting to take hold, and the first, local release of "Way Over There" did not have any string accompaniment. It was redone with strings for the national release.

While Tamla 54028, released in mid-1960, was the group's first release on Tamla, Ronnie White and Smokey Robinson had a mid-1959

SMOKEY ROBINSON
& THE MIRACLES

I'LL TRY SOMETHING NEW

SIDE 1   H 1199
TM 230   XCTV 83642

THE MIRACLES

I'LL TRY SOMETHING NEW (Wm. Robinson) - Jobete BMI
WHAT'S SO GOOD ABOUT GOOD-BYE (Wm. Robinson)
- Jobete BMI
HE DON'T CARE ABOUT ME (Wm. Robinson) - Jobete
BMI
A LOVE THAT CAN NEVER BE (Wylie, Bradford,
Bateman) - Jobete BMI
I'VE BEEN GOOD TO YOU (Wm. Robinson)
- Jobete BMI

The Miracles' third album.

release, "It/Don't Say Bye-Bye" (Tamla 54025), that was credited to "Ron & Bill." It was leased to Chicago's Argo label and appeared on Argo 5350 that same year. Both singers were, of course, members of the Miracles at the time. The Miracles had a broad enough appeal to have had seven Top 10 pop hits, including one after Smokey left the group. These included "Shop Around" (Tamla 54034) in 1961, "You've Really Got A Hold On Me" (Tamla 54073) in 1963, "Mickey's Monkey" (Tamla 54083), "I Second That Emotion" (Tamla 54159) in 1967, "Baby, Baby Don't Cry" (Tamla 54178) in 1969, "The Tears Of A Clown" (Tamla 54199) in 1970, and, with William Griffin on lead, "Love Machine (Part 1)" (Tamla 54262) in 1975-76.

Smokey Robinson and Berry Gordy have apparently been very close friends right from the start. Smokey was made a vice-president at Motown in 1963, and he has been a prolific songwriter and producer not only for the Miracles, but for other groups as well. More information about Smokey Robinson may be found in his separate entry.

MOTOWN DISCOGRAPHY

9/59: Bad Girl/I Love You Baby (Motown G1/G2)

9/59: Bad Girl/I Love You Baby (Motown TLX2207)

7/60: The Feeling Is So Fine/You Can Depend On Me (Tamla 54028)

7/60: Way Over There/Depend On Me (Tamla 54028)

10/60: Shop Around/Who's Lovin' You (Tamla 54034)

3/61: Ain't It Baby/The Only One I Love (Tamla 54036)

6/61: HI, WE'RE THE MIRACLES (Tamla TM-220)

7/61: Broken Hearted/Mighty Good Lovin' (Tamla 54044)

10/61: I Can't Believe/Everybody's Gotta Pay Some Dues (Tamla 54048)

12/61: What's So Good About Good-By/I've Been Good To You (Tamla 54053)

2/62: COOKIN' WITH THE MIRACLES (Tamla TM-223)

4/62: I'll Try Something New/You Never Miss A Good Thing (Tamla 54059)

8/62: Way Over There/If Your Mother Only Knew (Tamla 54069)

9/62: I'LL TRY SOMETHING NEW (Tamla TM-230)

11/62: You've Really Got A Hold On Me/ Happy Landing (Tamla 54073)

3/63: A Love She Can Count On/I Can Take A Hint (Tamla 54078)

5/63: THE FABULOUS MIRACLES (Tamla TM-238)

5/63: RECORDED LIVE: ON STAGE (Tamla TM-241)

7/63: Mickey's Monkey/Whatever Makes You Happy (Tamla 54083)

11/63: I Gotta Dance To Keep From Crying/Such Is Love, Such Is Life (Tamla 54089)

11/63: The Christmas Song/Christmas Everyday (Tamla EX-009)

11/63: CHRISTMAS WITH THE MIRACLES (Tamla TM-236)

11/63: THE MIRACLES DOIN' MICKEY'S MONKEY (Tamla TM-245)

2/64: (You Can't Let The Boy Overpower) The Man In You/Heartbreak Road (Tamla 54092)

6/64: I Like It Like That/You're So Fine And Sweet (Tamla 54098)

9/64: That's What Love Is Made Of/Would I Love You (Tamla 54102)

11/64: Come On Do The Jerk/Baby Don't You Go (Tamla 54109)

3/65: Ooo Baby Baby/All That's Good (Tamla 54113)

3/65: GREATEST HITS FROM THE BEGINNING (Tamla TS2-254)

6/65: The Tracks Of My Tears/A Fork In The Road (Tamla 54118)

9/65: My Girl Has Gone/Since You Won My Heart (Tamla 54123)

11/65: GOING TO A GO-GO (Tamla TS-267)

12/65: Going To A Go-Go/Choosey Beggar (Tamla 54127)

5/66: Whole Lot Of Shakin' In My Heart (Since I Met You)/Oh Be My Love (Tamla 54134)

10/66: (Come 'Round Here) I'm The One You Need/Save Me (Tamla 54140)

11/66: AWAY WE A GO-GO (Tamla TS-271)

Subsequent releases as by Smokey Robinson and the Miracles

1967: I Care About Detroit (Tamla 13090)

1/67: The Love I Saw In You Was Just A Mirage/Come Spy With Me (Tamla 54145) First release as by Smokey Robinson and The Miracles

5/67: More Love/Swept For You Baby (Tamla 54152)

9/67: SMOKEY ROBINSON AND THE MIRACLES MAKE IT HAPPEN (Tamla TS-276)

10/67: I Second That Emotion/You Must Be Love (Tamla 54159)

2/68: If You Can Want/When The Words From Your Heart Get Caught Up In Your Throat (Tamla 54162)

2/68: SMOKEY ROBINSON AND THE MIRACLES GREATEST HITS VOL. 2 (Tamla TS-280)

5/68: Yester Love/Much Better Off (Tamla 54167)

8/68: Special Occasion/Give Her Up (Tamla 54172)

9/68: SPECIAL OCCASION (Tamla TS-290)

12/68: Baby, Baby Don't Cry/Your Mother's Only Daughter (Tamla 54178)

1/69: LIVE (Tamla TS-289)

5/69: Here I Go Again/Doggone Right (Tamla 54183)

6/69: Abraham, Martin And John/Much Better Off (Tamla 54184)

7/69: TIME OUT FOR SMOKEY ROBINSON AND THE MIRACLES (Tamla TS-295)

11/69: Point It Out/Darling Dear (Tamla 54189)

11/69: FOUR IN BLUE (Tamla TS-297)

4/70: WHAT LOVE HAS JOINED TOGETHER (Tamla TS-301)

5/70: Who's Gonna Take The Blame/I Gotta Thing For You (Tamla 54194)

9/70: The Tears Of A Clown/Promise Me (Tamla 54199)

9/70: The Tears Of A Clown/The Love I Saw In You Was Just A Mirage (Tamla 54199)

9/70: A POCKET FULL OF MIRACLES (Tamla TS-306)

11/70: THE SEASON FOR MIRACLES (Tamla TS-307)

3/71: I Don't Blame You At All/That Girl (Tamla 54205)

6/71: Crazy About The La La La/Oh Baby Baby I Love You (Tamla 54206)

8/71: ONE DOZEN ROSES (Tamla T-312L)

11/71: Satisfaction/Flower Girl (Tamla 54211)

5/72: We've Come Too Far To End It Now/When Sundown Comes (Tamla 54220)

7/72: FLYING HIGH TOGETHER (Tamla T-318L)

11/72: I Can't Stand To See You Cry/With Your Love Came (Tamla 54225)

12/72: 1957-1972 (Tamla T-320D)

Subsequent releases as by The Miracles:

4/73: RENAISSANCE (Tamla T-325L)

7/73: Don't Let It End ('Til You Let It Begin)/Wigs And Lashes (Tamla 54237) As by The Miracles. William Griffin replaces Smokey Robinson as lead singer

11/73: Give Me Just Another Day/I Wanna Be With You (Tamla 54240)

1/74: ANTHOLOGY (Motown M793R3)

6/74: Do It Baby/I Wanna Be With You (Tamla 54248)

4/74: DO IT BABY (Tamla T6-334S1)

11/74: Don't Cha Love It/Up Again (Tamla 54256)

1/75: DON'TCHA LOVE IT (Tamla T6-336S1)

4/75: Gemini/You Are Love (Tamla 54259)

10/75: Love Machine (Pt. 1)/Love Machine (Pt. 2) (Tamla 54262)

10/75: CITY OF ANGELS (Tamla T6-339S1)

5/76: Night Life/Smog (Tamla 54268)

9/76: THE POWER OF MUSIC (Tamla T6-344S1)

8/77: GREATEST HITS (Tamla T6-357S1)

2/84: COMPACT COMMAND PER-FORMANCES: 18 GREATEST HITS (Tamla TCD 06071TD)

8/86: ANTHOLOGY (Tamla TCD 06196TD2)

8/86: COMPACT COMMAND PER-FORMANCES VOLUME II: 22 GREAT-EST HITS (Tamla TCD 06202TD)

Unissued Motown Recordings

Take It All (Tamla 54272)
THE MIRACLES SING MODERN (Tamla TM-234)

NON-MOTOWN DISCOGRAPHY

1958: Got A Job/My Mama Done Told Me (End 1016)

1958: I Cry/Money (End 1029) Also End 1084

1959: It/Don't Say Bye-Bye (Argo 5350) As by Ron & Bill; also Tamla 54025

1959: Bad Girl/I Love You Baby (Chess 1734)

1959: All I Want/I Need A Change (Chess

1768)

1977: LOVE CRAZY (Columbia PC-34460)

1977: Women (Make The World Go 'Round) /Spy For Brotherhood (Columbia 10515)

1977: Women (Make The World Go 'Round) /I Can Touch The Sky (Columbia 10517)

1978: THE MIRACLES (Columbia JC-34910)

1978: Mean Machine/The Magic Of Your Eyes (Laura's Eyes) (Columbia 10706)

----: After All/Embraceable You (Tamla 54022) bootleg

MONITORS
Sandra Fagin
John "Maurice" Fagin
Warren Harris
Richard Street (formerly with the Distants from 1956-1960, joined the Temptations in 1971).

Their only song to reach the pop charts is the 1966 release, "Greetings (This Is Uncle Sam)" (V.I.P. 25032), which reached #100 for one week. The song was originally recorded by Motown's Valadiers (Miracle 6) in 1961.

MOTOWN DISCOGRAPHY

12/65: Say You/All For Someone (V.I.P. 25028)

3/66: Greetings (This Is Uncle Sam)/Say You (V.I.P. 25032)

12/66: Since I Lost You Girl/Don't Put Off 'Til Tomorrow What You Can Do Today (V.I.P. 25039)

4/68: Bring Back The Love/The Further You Look, The Less You See (V.I.P. 25046)

7/68: Step By Step (Hand In Hand)/Time Is Passin' By (Soul 35049)

12/68: GREETINGS! . . . WE'RE THE MONITORS (Soul SS-714)

1969: Step By Step (Hand In Hand)/Time Is Passin' By (V.I.P. 25049)

SYLVIA MOY

Sylvia Moy achieved her greatest success at Motown as a songwriter. She worked for Motown from 1964 to 1970, writing some 150-200 songs. Many of her songs were recorded by Stevie Wonder. She shares songwriting credit on such hits as "Up Tight," "My Cherie Amour," "My Baby Loves Me," "I Was Made To Love Her," and "Nothing's Too Good For My Baby," all recorded by Stevie Wonder. Other credits include "Honey Chile" (recorded by Martha & the Vandellas) and "It Takes Two" (recorded by Marvin Gaye and Kim Weston). Raised in Detroit in a family of nine, she graduated from Detroit's Pershing High School and attended Highland Park Community College after not being accepted into Wayne State University's music school. She was discovered by Motown in 1964 while singing in supper clubs in the Detroit-Windsor area. Her songs have won many awards, and she has seventeen gold records for songs she wrote at Motown. In 1972, she built her own studio and became an independent producer. She uses her studio to help young people develop their own talent. Another of her distinctions is being the first woman producer at Motown. Even though her royalties provide her with a comfortable income, she maintains a rigorous work schedule.

FOR MORE INFORMATION
Pack, Richard. "Sylvia Moy: From Motown to MSR." in *Soul Survivor*, Number 6 (Winter 1986-87).

THE ORIGINALS
Freddie Gorman
Walter Gaines (ex-Five Stars, ex-Voice Masters)
C. P. Spencer (aka Crathman Spencer, aka Spencher Craftman) (ex-Five Stars, ex-Voice Masters)
Henry "Hank" Dixon
Joe Stubbs (left in 1966 to join 100 Proof Aged in Soul)
Ty Hunter (ex-Voice Masters; replaced C. P. Spencer in 1975)

Although the group didn't record on their own until 1966, their sound is rooted in the "doo-wop" sound of the 1950s. As members of Anna recording group, the Voice Masters, Spencer and Gaines had experience making records with Berry Gordy and Harvey Fuqua. Freddie Gorman's first solo release was in 1961 on the Motown subsidiary label, Miracle, "The Day Will Come/Just For You" (Miracle

11). He also recorded for Ric-Tic before it was purchased by Motown, and he was a writer-producer for Motown.

From 1965 to 1969, the Originals were the primary male vocal backing group for Motown artists like Marvin Gaye, Stevie Wonder, and Jimmy Ruffin. In 1966, Motown released their "Goodnight Irene/Need Your Loving (Want You Back)" (Soul 35029), with vocalist Joe Stubbs singing lead on "Need Your Loving (Want You Back)." He left the group after this record and joined 100 Proof Aged in Soul, a group that would later record for Holland-Dozier-Holland's label, Invictus. In 1969, Marvin Gaye co-wrote and produced "Baby, I'm For Real" for the group, bringing them some recognition. The next year, he co-wrote and produced "The Bells" (Soul 35069), which reached #12 on the pop charts.

The group's first album was originally issued under the title, GREEN GROW THE LILACS (Soul SS716), but was reissued as BABY, I'M FOR REAL when that song became the most popular on the album. The Originals disbanded in the early 1970s but re-formed in 1975 with Ty Hunter replacing C.P. Spencer. They recorded an album of Lamont Dozier songs, CALIFORNIA SUNSET (Motown M6- 826S1), in 1975, while Lamont was affiliated with ABC Records.

In 1978, they left Motown and released an album on Fantasy, ANOTHER TIME, ANOTHER PLACE (Fantasy F-9546). Their second album on Fantasy, COME AWAY WITH ME (Fantasy F-9577), came out in 1979 and featured the reunited Originals as a quintet, with Freddie Gorman, Hank Dixon, Walter Gaines, Ty Hunter, and C.P. Spencer. Ty Hunter has since died.

MOTOWN DISCOGRAPHY

1/67: Good Night Irene/Need Your Lovin' (Want You Back) (Soul 35029

1/69: We've Got A Way Out Love/You're The One (Soul 35056)

4/69: Green Grow The Lilacs/You're The One (Soul 35061)

7/69: GREEN GROW THE LILACS (Soul SS-716)

9/69: Baby, I'm For Real/Moment Of Truth (Soul 35066)

1/70: The Bells/I'll Wait For You (Soul 35069)

6/70: PORTRAIT OF THE ORIGINALS (Soul SS-724)

7/70: We Can Make It Baby/I Like Your Style (Soul 35074)

10/70: NATURALLY TOGETHER (Soul SS-729)

11/70: God Bless Whoever Sent You/ Desperate Young Man (Soul 35079)

7/71: Keep Me/A Man Without Love (Soul 35085)

1/72: I'm Someone Who Cares/Once I Have You (I Will Never Let You Go) (Soul 35093)

2/72: DEF.I.NI.TIONS (Soul S-734L)

4/73: Be My Love/Endlessly Love (Soul 35102)

9/73: There's A Chance When You Love You'll Lose/1st Lady (Sweet Mother's Love) (Soul 35109)

1/74: Supernatural Voodoo Woman (Pt. I)/Supernatural Voodoo Woman (Pt. II) (Soul 35112)

7/74: Game Called Love/Ooh You (Put A Crush On Me) (Soul 35113)

8/74: GAME CALLED LOVE (Soul S6-740S1)

12/74: You're My Only World/So Near (And Yet So Far) (Soul 35115)

3/75: CALIFORNIA SUNSET (Motown (M6-826S1)

6/75: Good Lovin' Is Just A Dime Away/Nothing Can Take The Place (Of Your Love) (Motown 1355)

10/75: 50 Years/Financial Affair (Motown 1370)

12/75: Everybody's Got To Do Something (Vocal)/Everybody's Got To Do Something (Instrumental) (Motown 1379)

5/76: Touch/Ooh You (Put A Crush On Me) (Soul 35117)

5/76: COMMUNIQUE (Soul S-746P1)

9/76: Down To Love Town/Just To Be Closer To You (Soul 35119)

1/77: DOWN TO LOVE TOWN (Soul S6-749S1)

Unissued Motown Recordings

CALIFORNIA SUNSET (Soul 743)
Supernatural Voodoo Woman/ Supernatural Voodoo Woman (Part 2) (Motown 1285)
(Call On Your) Six-Million Dollar Man/Mother Nature's Best (Soul 35121)

NON-MOTOWN DISCOGRAPHY

1978: ANOTHER TIME, ANOTHER PLACE (Fantasy F-9546)

1978: Take This Love/Ladies (We Need You) (Fantasy 820)

1979: COME AWAY WITH ME (Fantasy F-9577)

1979: Blue Moon/Ladies (We Need You) (Fantasy 847)

1979: J-E-A-L-O-U-S (Means I Love You)/Jezebel (You've Got Me Under Your Spell) (Fantasy 856)

THE PIRATES

Alias used in 1962 by the Temptations for "Mind Over Matter/I'll Love You 'Til I Die" (Melody 105) released on the Motown subsidiary.

MOTOWN DISCOGRAPHY

9/62: Mind Over Matter/I'll Love You 'Till I Die (Melody 105)

POOR BOYS

Rare Earth recording artists from New York.

NON-MOTOWN DISCOGRAPHY

5/70: AIN'T NOTHIN' IN OUR POCKET BUT LOVE (Rare Earth RS519)

POWER OF ZEUS

A Rare Earth recording group consisting of Joe Periano (guitar), Bill Jones (bass), Dennis Weber (organ, harpsichord, and piano), and Bob Michalski (drums).

MOTOWN DISCOGRAPHY

9/70: THE GOSPEL ACCORDING TO ZEUS (Rare Earth RS 516)

THE PRIMES

An unrecorded Detroit vocal group of the 1950s, with roots in Birmingham, Alabama, that contributed Eddie Kendricks and Paul Williams to the Temptations. The third member of this trio was Kel Osborn.

(See also THE TEMPTATIONS.)

THE PRIMETTES

Diana Ross
Mary Wilson
Florence Ballard
Betty Travis (also Betty Hutton, Betty Anderson)
Barbara Martin (replaced Betty Travis)

The Primettes were a "sister group" to the Primes, featuring Eddie Kendricks and Paul Williams, both founding members of the Temptations. While still attending various Detroit schools, the Primettes released one record in 1960 on the Detroit label, Lupine, "Tears Of Sorrow/Pretty Baby" (LR120). By that time, Barbara Martin had replaced original member Betty Travis. That same year, they auditioned for Berry Gordy, who felt they were too young. In 1961, they signed with Motown while still in high school, becoming the Supremes.

With increased interest in the Supremes, some of the Primettes' material is now available on compilation albums.

(See also THE SUPREMES.)

NON-MOTOWN DISCOGRAPHY

1960: Tears of Sorrow/Pretty Baby (Lupine LR120)

1968: LOOKING BACK WITH THE PRIMETTES (Ember EMB-3398)

1973: THE ROOTS OF DIANA ROSS (Windmill WMB 192)

19??: THE DETROIT GIRL GROUPS (Relic 8004) Includes the two songs by the Primettes released on Lupine LR120

1985: THE SOUL OF DETROIT (Relic/Lupine 8009) Includes two songs with the Primettes backing Gene Martin ("Lonely Nights") and Don Revel ("Return of Stagger Lee")

RARE EARTH

One of the many Rare Earth line-ups, this one
from a record on the Prodigal label.

RARE EARTH

Originally formed in 1961 as The Sunliners by Gil Bridges and Pete Rivera, this Detroit group represented Motown's entry into the "psychedelic" craze of the late 1960s. The group's debut album, GET READY (Rare Earth RS 507), was one of the first on the new Motown subsidiary of the same name that would present a number of white psychedelic rockers and other alternatives to r&b until 1976. The album itself features a twenty-minute version of the Temptations' hit, "Get Ready," that was produced by Norman Whitfield. Whitfield continued to produce several of the group's albums in the 1970s.

When the Rare Earth label folded in 1976, the group continued to release albums on the Motown subsidiary, Prodigal. Rare Earth underwent several personnel changes, with only co-founder Gil Bridges remaining with the group from their first album in 1969 until their last Prodigal album in 1978. The original personnel on GET READY were:

Gil Bridges - sax, tambourine, vocals
Pete Rivera - drums, vocals
Rod Richards - guitar, vocals (joined 1966)
John Parrish - bass, tambourine, vocals (joined 1962)
Kenny James - organ, electric piano (joined 1966)

A new lineup featuring Peter Hoorelbeke as lead vocalist and drummer (replacing co-founder Pete Rivera) recorded albums in 1973 (MA, Rare Earth R546L) and in 1978 (BAND TOGETHER, Prodigal P7-10025R1), and (GRAND SLAM, Prodigal P7-10027R1):

Peter Hoorelbeke - lead vocals, drums
Gil Bridges - background vocals, flute, sax
Michael Urso - background vocals, bass
Eddie Guzman - percussion
Mark Olson - keyboards and vocals
Ray Monette - lead guitar

The 1977 album, RAREARTH (Prodigal P6-10019S1), features a similar lineup, with Ron Fransen for Mark Olson on keyboards, and Daniel Ferguson for Ray Monette on lead guitar. Still another grouping recorded the 1975 album, BACK TO EARTH (Rare Earth R6-548S1):

Jerry La Croix - lead vocals, tenor sax, flute
Gil Bridges - tenor sax, flute, vocals
Ray Monette - guitar
Eddie Guzman - congas, percussion
Paul Warren - guitar, vocals
Reggie McBride - bass, vocals
Barry Eugene Frost - traps, percussion
Gabriel Katora - keyboards, vocals

Former Rare Earth members Peter Hoorelbeke, Gil Bridges, and Michael Urso subsequently recorded for Capitol Records as H.U.B., a name taken from their initials.

MOTOWN DISCOGRAPHY

8/69:	GET READY (Rare Earth RS 507)
11/69:	Generation (Light Up The Sky)/ Magic Key (Rare Earth 5010)
2/70:	Get Ready/Magic Key (Rare Earth 5012)
6/70:	ECOLOGY (Rare Earth RS 514)
7/70:	(I Know) I'm Losing You/When Joanie Smiles (Rare Earth 5017)
11/70:	Born To Wander/Here Comes The Night (Rare Earth 5021)
6/71:	I Just Want To Celebrate/The Seed (Rare Earth 5031)
6/71:	ONE WORLD (Rare Earth RS 520)
11/71:	He Big Brother/Under God's Light (Rare Earth 5038)
12/71:	IN CONCERT (Rare Earth R 534L)
3/72:	What'd I Say/Nice To Be With You (Rare Earth 5043)
10/72:	Good Time Sally/Love Shines Down (Rare Earth 5048)
10/72:	WILLIE REMEMBERS (Rare Earth R 543L)
12/72:	We're Gonna Have A Good Time/ Would You Like To Come Along (Rare Earth 5052)
3/73:	Ma (Vocal)/Ma (Instrumental) (Rare Earth 5053)
5/73:	MA (Rare Earth R 546L)
8/73:	Hum Along And Dance/Come With Me (Rare Earth 5054)
10/73:	Big John Is My Name/Ma (vocal) (Rare Earth 5056)
5/74:	Chained/Fresh From The Can (Rare Earth 5057)
6/75:	BACK TO EARTH (Rare Earth R6-548S1)
8/75:	Keepin' Me Out Of The Storm/Let Me Be Your Sunshine (Rare Earth

5059)

10/75:	It Makes You Happy (But It Ain't Gonna Last Too Long)/Boogie With Me Children (Rare Earth 5058)
3/76:	MIDNIGHT LADY (Rare Earth R6-550S1)
5/76:	Midnight Lady/Walking Schtick (Rare Earth 5060)
7/77:	RAREARTH (Prodigal P6-10019S1)
9/77:	Is Your Teacher Cool/Crazy Love (Prodigal 637)
3/78:	Warm Ride/Would You Like To Come Along (Prodigal 640)
4/78:	BAND TOGETHER (Prodigal P7-10025R1)
6/78:	I Can Feel My Love Risin'/S.O.S. (Stop Her On Sight) (Prodigal 643)
9/78:	GRAND SLAM (Prodigal P7-10027R 1)

Unissued Motown Recordings

GENERATION (Film Soundtrack) (Rare Earth RS 510)

RAYBER VOICES

Used as a backing vocal group on early Motown records as well on other local Detroit labels. Their first record credit was in 1958 backing Herman Griffin on Berry Gordy's production of "I Need You" (HOB 112). Their shifting personnel included Robert Bateman, Gwendolyn Murry, Brian Holland, and Raynoma Gordy. Raynoma was Berry Gordy's second wife, and the group's name, Rayber, was a combination of Raynoma and Berry.

MARTHA REEVES

(See MARTHA & THE VANDELLAS.)

LIONEL RICHIE

Born in Tuskegee, Alabama, where he went to college at Tuskegee Institute. The Commodores were formed at Tuskegee in 1967 when all six members were students. Lionel was the composer, pianist, and singer for the Commodores from 1967 to 1982, when he left the group to pursue his own solo career. During that period, he sang lead on and wrote such songs as "Easy" (Motown 1418) in 1977, "Three Times A Lady" (Motown 1443) in 1978, and in 1979, "Sail On" (Motown 1466) and "Still" (Motown 1474). "Three Times A Lady" and "Still" both reached #1 on the pop charts, and the other two songs were in the top five.

Lionel started having his own personal success outside the Commodores in 1980, when he wrote the #1 hit song, "Lady," for Kenny Rogers (released on Liberty 1380). In 1981, his duet with Diana Ross, "Endless Love" (Motown 1519) stayed at the #1 spot on the pop charts for nine weeks and was certified platinum (over two million units sold).

In 1982, amidst rumors pro and con, Lionel officially left the Commodores to pursue his own solo career. His first solo album, LIONEL RICHIE (Motown 6007M), yielded three hits: "Truly" (Motown 1644MF), "You Are" (Motown 1657MF), and "My Love" (Motown 1677MF). For "Truly," Lionel Richie received his first Grammy. In 1983, he made his first major solo tours, first in Japan in the spring, and then a three-month, forty-city concert tour of the United States in the fall. In 1984, he released his second solo album, CAN'T SLOW DOWN (Motown 6059). Accord-ing to *Ebony* magazine, it was the biggest selling album in Motown's history. It won Lionel two Grammys for Album of the Year and Producer of the Year (with co-producer James Anthony Carmichael). In 1985, he was the host for the 11th annual American Music Awards, where he won six awards himself. That same year he co-wrote with Michael Jackson "We Are The World," which won two Grammy awards (Lionel's fourth), and participated in the Live Aid concerts. "Say You, Say Me" (Motown 1819MF) was another #1 pop hit and appears on his 1986 album, DANCING ON THE CEILING (Motown 6158ML). "Say You, Say Me" won the 1985 Oscar for Song of the Year; it was the title song from the film, "White Nights."

Lionel continues to be very popular and quite visible as a solo artist and as a composer. His immense popularity is due largely to the ballads he writes and sings.

MOTOWN DISCOGRAPHY

8/81: Endless Love (Vocal)/Endless Love (Instrumental) (Motown 1519) Diana Ross and Lionel Richie

9/82: Truly/Just Put Some Love In Your Heart (Motown 1644MF)

9/82: LIONEL RICHIE (Motown 6007ML)

1/83: You Are/You Mean More To Me (Motown 1657MF)

4/83: My Love/Round And Round (Motown 1677MF)

9/83: All Night Long (All Night)/Wandering Stranger (Motown 1698MF)

10/83: CAN'T SLOW DOWN (Motown 6059ML)

11/83: Running With The Night/Serves You Right (Motown 1710MF)

2/84: Hello/You Mean More To Me (Motown 1722MF)

6/84: Stuck on You/Round And Round (Motown 1746MF)

9/84: Penny Lover/Tell Me (Motown 1762MF)

7/85: LIONEL RICHIE THE COMPOSER: GREAT LOVE SONGS WITH THE COMMODORES AND DIANA ROSS (Motown MCD06143MD)

11/85: Say You, Say Me/Can't Slow Down (Motown 1819MF)

6/86: Dancing On The Ceiling/Love Will Find A Way (Motown 1843MF)

8/86: DANCING ON THE CEILING (Motown 6158ML)

10/86: Love Will Conquer All/The Only One (Motown 1866MF)

12/86: Ballerina Girl/Deep River Woman (Motown 1873MF)

WILLIAM "SMOKEY" ROBINSON

Born Feb. 19, 1940, in Detroit as William Robinson, Jr. Graduate of Detroit's Northern High School, where he formed the Miracles, then known as the Matadors. He met Berry Gordy, then an independent producer and working for Anna Records; in 1958, Smokey Robinson & the Miracles were featured on several masters that Berry Gordy produced and leased to such record companies as End in New York and Chess in Chicago. Smokey was the lead singer in the group until 1972, when he left to spend more time with his family. He began his solo career in earnest afterwards. (For more information about the Miracles, see their entry.)

Smokey married Claudette Rogers, the female member of the Miracles, on November 7, 1959. Their son is named Berry, after Berry Gordy, and their daughter, Tamla, after the label on which all of Smokey Robinson's records appear.

In addition to being an outstanding male vocalist, Smokey is also well known for his songwriting, and he has produced many Motown artists. He was also named a Vice President of Motown in 1963, and has remained an executive of the company. He has appeared on several Motown-related television specials and in the fall of 1985 hosted a weekly series of Motown Revue shows for NBC.

He began producing for Motown in the early 1960s, starting with Mary Wells' hit, "The One Who Really Loves You" (Motown 1024) in 1962. He has also written and produced hits for the Temptations, the Miracles, the Marvelettes, and Marvin Gaye, among others.

Smokey is a prolific songwriter and has written at least a thousand songs in his career. Equally adept at soft ballads or uptempo songs, he is a master at rhyming couplets. His songs have contributed to the success of a number of Motown artists. Here is a selective list of some of the songs he has written for various Motown groups and artists:

Songs recorded by Mary Wells:
Laughing Boy, My Guy, The One Who Really Loves You, What's Easy For Two Is So Hard For One, You Beat Me To The Punch (with Ronnie White), Two Lovers, Your Old Standby (with Janie Bradford).

Songs recorded by the Temptations:
Slow Down Heart, I Want A Love I Can See, The Further You Look, The Less You See (with Norman Whitfield), The Way You Do The Things You Do, My Girl (with Ronnie White), It's Growing (with Warren "Pete" Moore), Since I Lost My Baby (with Warren Moore), Get Ready.

Songs recorded by Marvin Gaye:
Ain't That Peculiar (with Warren Moore, Marv Tarplin, and Bobbie Rogers), Take This Heart of Mine (with Warren Moore and Marv Tarplin), I'll Be Doggone (with Warren Moore and Marv Tarplin).

Songs recorded by the Marvelettes:
Don't Mess With Bill, The Hunter Gets Captured By The Game, My Baby Must Be A Magician, You're The One, Here

SMOKEY ROBINSON

Smokey Robinson left The Miracles in 1972 to
spend more time with his family, later pursuing
a solo career.

I Am Baby.

Songs recorded by the Miracles:
Going To A Go-Go (with Warren Moore, Bobbie Rogers, and Marv Tarplin), I Second That Emotion (with Alfred Cleveland), More Love, The Tracks Of My Tears (with Warren Moore and Marv Tarplin), You've Really Got A Hold On Me, If You Can Want, Ooo Baby Baby (with Warren Moore), Special Occasion (with Alfred Cleveland), The Tears of A Clown (with Henry "Hank" Cosby and Stevie Wonder), and many more.

MOTOWN DISCOGRAPHY

6/73: Sweet Harmony/Want To Know My Mind (Tamla 54233)

6/73: SMOKEY (Tamla T-328L)

10/73: Baby Come Close/A Silent Partner In A Three-Way Love Affair (Tamla 54239)

3/74: PURE SMOKEY (Tamla T6-331S1)

5/74: It's Her Turn To Live/Just My Soul Responding (Tamla 54246)

7/74: Virgin Man/Fulfill Your Need (Tamla 54250)

11/74: I Am I Am/The Family Song (Tamla 54251)

2/75: Baby That's Backatcha/Just Passing Through (Tamla 54258)

3/75: A QUIET STORM (Tamla T6-337S1)

8/75: The Agony And The Ecstasy/ Wedding Song (Tamla 54261)

12/75: Quiet Storm/Asleep On My Love (Tamla 54265)

2/76: SMOKEY'S FAMILY ROBINSON (Tamla T6-341S1)

4/76: Open/Coincidentally (Tamla 54267)

5/76: When You Came/Coincidentally (Tamla 54269)

10/76: An Old-Fashioned Man/Just Passing Through (Tamla 54276)

1/77: There Will Come A Day (I'm Gonna Happen To You)/The Humming Song (Lost For Words) (Tamla 54279)

1/77: DEEP IN MY SOUL (Tamla T6-350S1)

6/77: Vitamin U/Holly (Tamla 54284)

7/77: ORIGINAL MUSIC SCORE FROM THE MOTION PICTURE, "BIG TIME" (Tamla T6-355S1)

9/77: Theme From Big Time Pt. 1/Theme From Big Time Pt. 2 (Tamla 54288)

2/78: LOVE BREEZE (Tamla T7-359R1)

3/78: Why You Wanna See My Bad Side/ Daylight & Darkness (Tamla 54293)

10/78: Shoe Soul/I'm Loving You Softly (Tamla 54296)

11/78: SMOKIN' (Tamla T9-363A2)

11/78: Pops, We Love You (Vocal)/Pops, We Love You (Instrumental) Motown 1455) As by Marvin Gaye, Smokey Robinson, Diana Ross, and Stevie Wonder

5/79: WHERE THERE'S SMOKE . . . (Tamla T7-366R1)

6/79: Get Ready/Ever Had A Dream (Tamla 54301)

8/79: Cruisin'/Ever Had A Dream (Tamla 54306)

1/80: WARM THOUGHTS (Tamla T8-367M1)

3/80: Let Me Be The Clock/Travelin' Through (Tamla 54311)

6/80: Heavy On Pride (Light On Love)/I Love The Nearness Of You (Tamla 54313)

9/80: Wine, Women And Song/I Want To Be Your Love (Tamla 54318)

1/81: Being With You/What's In Your Life For Me (Tamla 54321)

2/81: BEING WITH YOU (Tamla T8-375M1)

5/81: Aqui Con Tigo/Being With You + Aqui Con Tigo (Tamla 54325)

5/81: You Are Forever/I Hear The Children Singing (Tamla 54327)

8/81: Who's Sad/Food For Thought (Tamla 54332)

1/82: Tell Me Tomorrow (Part 1)/Tell Me Tomorrow (Part 2) (Tamla 1601TF)

1/82: YES IT'S YOU LADY (Tamla 6001TL)

4/82: Old Fashioned Love/Destiny (Tamla 1615TF)

7/82: Yes It's You Lady/Are You Still Here (Tamla 1630TF)

12/82: TOUCH THE SKY (Tamla 6030TL)

1/83: I've Made Love To You A Thousand Times/Into Each Rain Some Life Must Fall (Tamla 1655TF)

4/83: Touch the Sky/All My Life's A Lie (Tamla 1678TF)

6/83: Blame It On Love/Even Tho' (Tamla 1684TF) 'A' side with High Inergy

8/83: BLAME IT ON LOVE AND ALL THE GREAT HITS (Tamla 6064TL)

10/83: Don't Play Another Love Song/ Wouldn't You Like To Know (Tamla 1700TF)

11/83: Ebony Eyes/1, 2, 3, (You, Her And

Me) (Gordy 1714GF) 'A' side with
Rick James. 'B' side by Rick James
5/84: And I Don't Love You/Dynamite
(Tamla 1735TF)
5/84: ESSAR (Tamla 6098TL)
8/84: I Can't Find/Gimme What You Want
(Tamla 1756TF)
3/85: First Time On A Ferris Wheel/Train
Of Thought (Tamla 1786TF) 'A' side
by Smokey Robinson and Syreeta
10/85: SMOKE SIGNALS (Tamla 6156TL)
1/86: Hold On To Your Love/Train Of
Thought (Tamla 1828TF)
3/86: A Fine Mess/Wishful Thinking
(Motown 1837MF) 'A' side by The
Temptations
3/86: Sleepless Nights/Close Encounters
Of The First Kind (Tamla 1839TF)
7/86: Because Of You (It's The Best It's
Ever Been)/Girl I'm Standing There
(Tamla 1855TF)

Unissued Motown Recordings

If You Wanna Make Love (Come
'Round Here)/I Hear The Children
Singing (Tamla 54327)

FOR MORE INFORMATION
Contemporary Literary Criticism, Vol. 21.
(Detroit: Gale Research Co., 1982).

(See also THE MIRACLES; RON AND BILL.)

ROCKWELL
(Performing name for Kennedy Gordy, Berry
Gordy's fourth son.) Born March 15, 1964.

Rockwell came to national attention with
his 1984 smash hit, "Somebody's Watching
Me" (Motown 1702MF), a record on which
Jermaine and Michael Jackson helped out.

MOTOWN DISCOGRAPHY

1/84: Somebody's Watching Me/Somebody's
Watching Me (Instrumental) (Motown
1702MF)
1/84: SOMEBODY'S WATCHING ME
(Motown 6052ML)
4/84: Obscene Phone Caller/Obscene Phone
Caller (Instrumental) (Motown
1731MF)
12/84: He's A Cobra/Change Your Ways

(Motown 1772MF)
1/85: CAPTURED (Motown 6122ML)
2/85: Keeping Tom/Tokyo (Instrumental)
(Motown 1782MF)
6/86: Carme (Part I)/Carme (Part II)
(Motown 1845MF)
6/86: GENIE (Motown 6178ML)
8/86: Grow Up/Grow Up (Instrumental)
(Motown 1863MF)

RON AND BILL

Ronnie White and William "Smokey"
Robinson of the Miracles. In August, Tamla
releases "It/Don't Say Bye Bye" (Tamla 54025)
as by Ron and Bill. Berry Gordy leased it
to Argo, a Chess subsidiary. This is Smokey's
only non-Miracles release prior to his leaving
the group in 1972.

MOTOWN DISCOGRAPHY

8/59: It/Don't Say Bye-Bye (Tamla 54025)
also released on Argo 5350

DIANA ROSS

Born March 26, 1944, in Detroit, Michigan.
Diana's career in pop music began in high
school as a member of the Primettes, an all-girl
group consisting of Diana, Mary Wilson, Florence
Ballard, and Barbara Martin. They auditioned
for Berry Gordy in 1960, who signed them
the next year and changed their name to the
Supremes. Diana was lead singer with the
Supremes until she left to pursue a solo career
in music and the cinema in January 1970.

Diana's solo releases for Motown spanned
the 1970s; in 1981 she left Motown to sign
with RCA. During that decade, she had five
number one pop hits: in 1971, "Ain't No
Mountain High Enough" (Motown 1169); 1973,
"Touch Me In The Morning" (Motown 1239);
1975, "Theme From Mahogany (Do You Know
Where You're Going To)" (Motown 1377); 1976,
"Love Hangover" (Motown 1392); and 1980,
"Upside Down" (Motown 1494). Four additional
releases reached the top ten. In addition,
she recorded duets with Marvin Gaye and,
in 1981, her duet with Lionel Richie, "Endless
Love" (Motown 1519), was a #1 hit.

Diana's film career began in 1972 with
her portrayal of Billie Holiday in the movie,

DIANA ROSS

"Lady Sings the Blues." She was nominated for an Academy Award as Best Actress, but lost out to Liza Minelli (for "Cabaret"). In 1975, she appeared in the film, "Mahogany," and in 1978, "The Wiz."

Diana was married from 1971 to 1977 to Robert Ellis Silberstein, a public relations executive, with whom she had three daughters. In 1986, she married Norwegian shipping tycoon Arne Naess.

MOTOWN DISCOGRAPHY

4/70: Reach Out And Touch (Somebody's Hand)/Dark Side Of The World (Motown 1165)

6/70: REACH OUT (Motown MS-711)

7/70: Ain't No Mountain High Enough/Can't It Wait Until Tomorrow (Motown 1169)

9/70: EVERYTHING IS EVERYTHING (Motown MS-724)

12/70: Remember Me/How About You (Motown 1176)

3/71: DIANA (Motown MS-719) Original T.V. Soundtrack

4/71: Reach Out I'll Be There/(They Long To Be) Close To You (Motown 1184)

7/71: Surrender/I'm A Winner (Motown 1188)

7/71: SURRENDER (Motown MS-723)

10/71: I'm Still Waiting/A Simple Thing Like Cry (Motown 1192)

10/72: LADY SINGS THE BLUES (SOUNDTRACK) (Motown M-758-D)

12/72: Good Morning Heartache/God Bless The Child (Motown 1211)

5/73: Touch Me In The Morning/I Won't Last A Day Without You (Motown 1211)

5/73: TOUCH ME IN THE MORNING (Motown 1239)

9/73: You're A Special Part Of Me/I'm Falling In Love With You (Motown 1280) Diana Ross and Marvin Gaye

10/73: DIANA & MARVIN (Motown M 803V1) Diana Ross and Marvin Gaye

12/73: Last Time I Saw Him/Save The Children (Motown 1278)

12/73: LAST TIME I SAW HIM (Motown M 812V1)

1/74: My Mistake (Was To Love You)/Include Me In Your Life (Motown 1269) Diana Ross and Marvin Gaye

4/74: Sleepin'/You (Motown 1295)

5/74: DIANA ROSS LIVE AT CAESARS PALACE (Motown M6-801S1)

6/74: Don't Knock My Love/Just Say, Just Say (Motown 1296) Diana Ross and Marvin Gaye

2/75: Sorry Doesn't Always Make It Right/Together (Motown 1335)

10/75: Theme From Mahogany (Do You Know Where You're Going To)/No One's Gonna Be A Fool Forever (Motown 1377)

10/75: MAHOGANY (ORIGINAL SOUND-TRACK) (Motown M6-858S1)

3/76: I Thought It Took A Little Time (But Today I Fell In Love)/ After You (Motown 1387)

3/76: Love Hangover/Kiss Me Now (Motown 1392)

3/76: DIANA ROSS (Motown M6-861S1)

7/76: One Love In My Lifetime/Smile (Motown 1398)

8/76: DIANA ROSS' GREATEST HITS (Motown M6-869S1)

1/77: AN EVENING WITH DIANA ROSS (Motown M7-877R2

9/77: BABY IT'S ME (Motown M7-890R1)

10/77: Gettin' Ready For Love/Confide In Me (Motown 1427)

2/78: Your Love Is So Good For Me/Baby It's Me (Motown 1436)

4/78: You Got It/Too Shy To Say (Motown 1442)

9/78: ROSS (Motown M7-907R1)

11/78: Pops, We Love You (Vocal)/Pops, We Love You (Instrumental) (Motown 1455) Marvin Gaye, Smokey Robinson, Diana Ross, and Stevie Wonder

1/79: What You Gave Me/Together (Motown 1456)

5/79: The Boss/I'm In The World (Motown 1462)

5/79: THE BOSS (Motown M7-923R1)

10/79: It's My House/Sparkle (Motown 1471)

3/80: DIANA (Motown M8-936)

6/80: Medley of Hits/Where Do We Go From Here (Motown 1488) 'A' side by Diana Ross and The Supremes; 'B' side by Diana Ross

6/80: Upside Down/Friend To Friend (Motown 1494)

8/80: I'm Coming Out/Give Up (Motown 1491)

8/80: I'm Coming Out/Friend To Friend (Motown 1491)

10/80: It's My Turn/Together (Motown 1496)
2/81: One More Chance/After You (Motown 1508)
2/81: TO LOVE AGAIN (Motown M8-951M1)
5/81: Cryin' My Heart Out For You/To Love Again (Motown 1513)
8/81: Endless Love (Vocal)/Endless Love (Instrumental) (Motown 1519) Diana Ross and Lionel Richie
8/81: Medley of Hits/Where Did We Go Wrong (Motown 1523) 'A' side by Diana Ross and The Supremes (same as 1488); 'B' side by Diana Ross
10/81: ALL THE GREAT HITS (Motown M13-960C2)
1/82: My Old Piano/Now That You're Gone (Motown 1531)
7/82: We Can Never Light That Old Flame Again/Old Funky Rolls (Motown 1626MF)
5/83: ANTHOLOGY (Motown 6049ML2)
1683: TOUCH ME IN THE MORNING / LIVE AT CAESAR'S PALACE (Motown 6082MC)
2/84: COMPACT COMMAND PER- FORMANCES: 14 GREATEST HITS (Motown MCD06072MD)
9/84: ALL THE GREAT LOVE SONGS (Motown MCD06105MD)
4/85: ORIGINAL SOUNDTRACK FROM THE MOTION PICTURE "LADY SINGS THE BLUES" (Motown MCD06133MD)
7/85: LIONEL RICHIE THE COMPOSER: GREAT LOVE SONGS WITH THE COMMODORES AND DIANA ROSS (Motown MCD06143MD) Includes duets by Lionel Richie and Diana Ross
8/86: ANTHOLOGY (Motown MCD06197M D2)

Unissued Motown Recordings

Top Of The World/ (Motown 1449)
Lovin', Livin' And Givin'/Baby Its Me (Motown 1450)
TIME AND LOVE (Motown MS-706)
THE BEST OF DIANA ROSS (Motown 817)
DIANA ROSS SINGS SONGS FROM THE "WIZ" (Motown M7-915R1)

NON-MOTOWN DISCOGRAPHY

1981: WHY DO FOOLS FALL IN LOVE (RCA AFL1-4153)
1981: Why Do Fools Fall In Love/Think I'm In Love (RCA 12349)
1981: Mirror, Mirror/Sweet Nothings (RCA 13021)
1982: Work That Body/Two Can Make It (RCA 13201)
1982: Muscles/I Am Me (RCA 13348)
1982: SILK ELECTRIC (RCA AFL1-4384)
1983: ROSS (RCA AFL1-4677)
1983: So Close/ (RCA 13424)
1983: Why Do Fools Fall In Love/Mirror, Mirror (RCA 13479)
1983: Pieces of Ice/ (RCA 13549)
1983: Let's Go Up/ (RCA 13671)
1984: All Of You/ (Columbia 04507) Duet with Julio Iglesias
1984: SWEPT AWAY (RCA AFL1-5009)
1984: Muscles/Pieces Of Ice (RCA 13798)
1984: Swept Away/ (RCA 13864)
1984: Missing You/We Are The Children Of The World (RCA 13966)
1985: EATEN ALIVE (RCA AFL1-5422)
1985: Telephone/ (RCA 14032)
1985: Eaten Alive/ (RCA 14181)
1985: Chain Reaction/ (RCA 14244) Remix reissued 1986

(See also THE PRIMETTES; THE SU-PREMES.)

DAVID RUFFIN

Born January 18, 1941, in Meridian, Mississippi. Moved to Detroit at a very early age. Younger brother of Jimmy Ruffin. Lead singer for the Temptations from late 1963 to 1968. His first record with the Temptations was their first national hit, "The Way You Do The Things You Do" (Gordy 7028). While with the Temptations, David shared lead duties with Eddie Kendricks.

Prior to joining the Temptations, David was known around the Detroit scene both as a solo act and as a member of various singing groups recording for Anna Records. In 1958, he joined the Voice Masters just after they recorded "Hope and Pray" (Anna 101). His first solo releases were in 1961, the first being "I'm In Love/One of These

DAVID RUFFIN

In 1968, David Ruffin left The Temptations (inset is a group period picture) to pursue a solo career at Motown.

Days" (Anna 1127), which was the next to last release for the label. David's second solo release was on the Detroit-based Chess subsidiary, Check-Mate, run by Billy Davis with financial help from Leonard Chess. Davis had also worked at Anna Record as a songwriter and is well known in blues circles for his compositions recorded by Chess blues artists. Davis and Chess were partners in Chevis Music, the blues publishing firm, and Davis wrote "Action Speaks Louder Than Words" and "Mr. Bus Driver - Hurry" for David Ruffin. As a further aside on Billy Davis, he also used the pseudonym Tyran Carlo and co-wrote with Berry Gordy the Jackie Wilson hits, "Lonely Teardrops" (Brunswick 55105) and "That's Why (I Love You So)" (Brunswick 55121), among others.

In 1968, David left the Temptations to pursue a solo career, a step taken by many of the Temptations' lead singers. He recorded for Motown for about ten more years, leaving in 1979 for Warner Brothers. In 1982, he rejoined the Temptations for their Reunion tour and album. Following that, he and Eddie Kendricks performed together. In 1985, they released material with Hall and Oates on RCA and appeared on the Live Aid television special.

MOTOWN DISCOGRAPHY

2/69: My Whole World Ended (The Moment You Left Me)/I've Got To Find Myself A Brand New Baby (Motown 1140)

5/69: MY WHOLE WORLD ENDED (Motown MS-685)

7/69: I've Lost Everything I've Ever Loved/We'll Have A Good Thing Going On (Motown 1149)

11/69: FEELIN' GOOD (Motown MS-696)

12/69: I'm So Glad I Fell For You/I Pray Everyday You Won't Regret Loving Me (Motown 1158)

10/70: Stand By Me/Your Love Was Worth Waiting For (Soul 35076) David and Jimmy Ruffin

10/70: I AM MY BROTHER'S KEEPER (Soul SS-0728) The Ruffin Brothers

2/71: Don't Stop Loving Me/Each Day Is A Lifetime (Motown 1178)

3/71: When My Love Hand Comes Down/Steppin' On A Dream (Soul 35082) David and Jimmy Ruffin

7/71: You Can Come Right Back To Me/Dinah (Motown 1187)

6/72: A Little More Trust/A Day In The Life Of A Working Man (Motown 1204)

2/73: DAVID RUFFIN (Motown M-762L)

4/73: Blood Donors Needed (Give All You Can)/Go On With Your Bad Self (Motown 1223)

7/73: Common Man/Just A Mortal Man (Motown 1259)

11/74: Me And Rock & Roll (Are Here To Stay)/Smiling Faces Sometimes (Motown 1327)

12/74: ME 'N ROCK 'N ROLL ARE HERE TO STAY (Motown M6-818S1)

3/75: Superstar (Remember How You Got Where You Are)/No Matter Where (Motown 1336)

10/75: Walk Away From Love/Love Can Be Hazardous To Your Health (Motown 1376)

10/75: WHO I AM (Motown M6-849S1)

2/76: Heavy Love/Love Can Be Hazardous To Your Health (Motown 1388)

5/76: Everything's Coming Up Love/No Matter Where (Motown 1393)

5/76: EVERYTHING'S COMING UP LOVE (Motown M6-866S1)

10/76: On And Off/Statue Of A Fool (Motown 1405)

6/77: IN MY STRIDE (Motown M-885P1)

7/77: Just Let Me Hold You For A Night/Just Rode By The Place (Where We Used To Stay) (Motown 1420)

1/78: You're My Peace Of Mind/Rode By The Place (Where We Used To Stay) (Motown 1435)

1/78: AT HIS BEST (Motown M7-895R1)

Unissued Motown Recordings

Take Me Clear From Here/I Just Want To Celebrate (Motown 1332)
DAVID (Motown MS-733)
Lo And Behold/The Things We Have To Do (Soul 35086) David and Jimmy Ruffin

NON-MOTOWN DISCOGRAPHY

1961: I'm In Love/One Of These Days (Anna 1127)

1961: Action Speaks Louder Than Words/You Can Get (Check-Mate 1003)

1962: Knock You Out/Mr. Bus Driver-

JIMMY RUFFIN

Photo courtesy Motown Archives,
Eastern Michigan University.

Hurry (Check-Mate 1010)

1979: SO SOON WE CHANGE (Warner Brothers BSK 3306)

1979: Break My Heart/Sexy Dancer (Warner Brothers 49030)

1979: I Get Excited/Chain On The Brain (Warner Brothers 49123)

1980: GENTLEMAN RUFFIN (Warner Brothers 3416)

1980: Slow Dance/ (Warner Brothers 49277)

1980: Still In Love With You/I Wanna Be With You (Warner Brothers 49577)

1985: LIVE AT THE APOLLO WITH DAVID RUFFIN AND EDDIE KENDRICK [sic] (RCA AFL1-7035) As by Daryl Hall and John Oates

1985: A Nite At The Apollo Live! The Way You Do The Things You Do/My Girl (RCA PB-14178) As by Daryl Hall and John Oates featuring David Ruffin and Eddie Kendrick [sic]

(See also THE TEMPTATIONS.)

JIMMY RUFFIN

Born May 7, 1939, in Mississippi, the older brother of David Ruffin. Jimmy was singing in Detroit clubs when he signed with Berry Gordy. His first record appeared on the Motown subsidiary, Miracle, in 1961, the same label as the first Temptations' records. Soon thereafter, Jimmy was drafted and served in the armed forces. Upon his return in 1964, he began recording for Motown's Soul label. His biggest popular hit in the U.S. was "What Becomes Of The Brokenhearted" (Soul 35022) in 1966.

He achieved greater popularity in England, though, where he had a three-week tour in 1969 to promote the British release of the follow-up, "I've Passed This Way Before." In 1970 and 1971, he spent much time in England and Europe, touring and performing, and "It's Wonderful (To Be Loved By You)" was his third British chart hit that year. In 1971, a musical poll in England named him the #2 vocalist behind Elvis Presley. Jimmy left Motown in 1974 and, in 1980, "Hold On To My Love" (RSO 1021) reached the #10 spot on the pop charts in America.

MOTOWN DISCOGRAPHY

1/61: Don't Feel Sorry For Me/Heart (Miracle M 1)

7/64: Since I've Lost You/I Want Her Love (Soul 35002)

10/65: As Long As There Is L-O-V-E Love/ How Can I Say I'm Sorry (Soul 35016)

7/66: What Becomes Of The Broken Hearted/Baby I've Got It (Soul 35022)

11/66: I've Passed This Way Before/ Tomorrow's Tears (Soul 35027)

1/67: TOP TEN (Soul S-704)

3/67: Gonna Give Her All The Love I've Got/World So Wide, Nowhere To Hide (From Your Heart) (Soul 35032)

7/67: Don't You Miss Me A Little Bit Baby/I Want Her Love (Soul 35035)

2/68: I'll Say Forever My Love/Everybody Needs Love (Soul 35043)

6/68: Don't Let Him Take Your Love From Me/Lonely Lonely Man Am I (Soul 35046)

10/68: Gonna Keep On Trying' Till I Win Your Love/Sad And Lonesome Feeling (Soul 35053)

1/69: Farewell Is A Lonely Sound/If You Will Let Me, I Know I Can (Soul 35060)

3/69: RUFF' N READY (Soul SS-708)

9/70: THE GROOVE GOVERNOR (Soul SS-727)

10/70: Stand By Me/Your Love Was Worth Waiting For (Soul 35076) David and Jimmy Ruffin

10/70: I AM MY BROTHER'S KEEPER (Soul SS-0728) The Ruffin Brothers

12/70: Maria (You Were The Only One)/ Living In A World I Created For Myself (Soul 35077)

3/71: When My Love Hand Comes Down/Steppin' On A Dream (Soul 35082) David and Jimmy Ruffin

12/71: Our Favorite Melody/You Gave Me Love (Soul 35092)

12/74: What Becomes Of The Brokenhearted/Baby I've Got It (Motown 1329)

Unissued Motown Recordings

Lo And Behold/The Things We Have To Do (Soul 35086) David and Jimmy Ruffin

G.C. Cameron remained with Motown, while the line-up pictured here went on to achieve supergroup status at Atlantic Records.

Photo courtesy Peter Benjaminson.

THE SPINNERS

The Spinners during their years at Motown.
Photo courtesy Motown Archives,
Eastern Michigan University.

In 1961, The Spinners first record launched Harvey Fuqua's Tri-Phi label. They subsequently joined Motown in 1963.

NON-MOTOWN DISCOGRAPHY

1974: Tell Me What You Want/Do You Know Me (Chess 2160)
1975: What You See (Ain't Always What You Get)/Boy From Mississippi (Chess 2168)
1980: Hold On To My Love (Vocal)/Hold On To My Love (Instrumental) (RSO 1021)
1980: SUNRISE (RSO RS-1-3078)
1980: Night Of Love/Searchin' (RSO 1042)

RUSTIX

Rare Earth recording artists from Rochester, New York, consisting of Chuck Brucate, Ron Collins, Dave Colen, Jr., Bob D'Andrea, Albin Galich, and Vince Strenk. They were produced by R. Dean Taylor.

MOTOWN DISCOGRAPHY

8/69: BEDLAM (Rare Earth RS 508)
11/69: Can't You Hear The Music Play/I Guess This Is Goodbye (Rare Earth 5011)
4/70: Come On People/Free Again (Non . . . C'est Rien) (Rare Earth 5014)
7/70: COME ON PEOPLE (Rare Earth RS 513)
7/71: My Peace Of Heaven/Down Down (Rare Earth 5034)
11/71: We All End Up In Boxes/Down Down (Rare Earth 5037)

VALERIE SIMPSON

Born August 26, 1948, in Bronx, New York. She recorded two solo albums for Motown that were produced by her singing partner, Nick Ashford. She married Ashford in 1974 after they had worked together for ten years.

MOTOWN DISCOGRAPHY

5/71: EXPOSED (Tamla TS-311)
7/71: Back To Nowhere/Can't It Wait Until Tomorrow (Tamla 54204)
7/72: VALERIE SIMPSON (Tamla T-317L)
11/72: Silly Wasn't I/I Believe I'm Gonna Take This Ride (Tamla 54224)
1/77: KEEP IT COMIN' (Tamla T6-351S1)

Unissued Motown Recordings

Genius II/One More Baby Child Born (Tamla 54231)

(See also ASHFORD & SIMPSON.)

THE SPINNERS

The original 1961 lineup of this Detroit-based quintet:
Henry Fambrough
Robert "Bobbie" Smith
Billy Henderson
Pervis Jackson
George W. Dixon

Additional members:
Edgar "Chico" Edwards (replaced George Dixon in 1962)
G.C. Cameron (replaced Chico Edwards, 1967-1971)
Phillipe Wynne (1971-1977, deceased July 13, 1984)
John Edwards (replaced Phillipe Wynne)

The Spinners have gone from a "doo-wop" 1950s style vocal group recording on Tri-Phi, to a polished soul group recording for Motown and V.I.P., to supergroup status on Atlantic Records. Their line-up has remained fairly stable, with core members Henry Fambrough, Bobbie Smith, Billy Henderson, and Pervis Jackson remaining with the group throughout their careers. Chico Edwards replaced George Dixon in 1962, and was later replaced by G. C. Cameron.

Most of the original Spinners were born in the south, but grew up in Detroit. They were a well-rehearsed nightclub act by the time they released their first record, "That's What Girls Are Made For" (Tri-Phi 1001) in June 1961. This record also marked the debut of Tri-Phi Records, a Detroit label established by Harvey Fuqua and Gwen Gordy, both of whom had been working at Anna Records, run by Gwen's sister, Anna Gordy. Harvey Fuqua worked closely with the Spinners and may have sung lead on their first record. By this time, Harvey's backing group, the Moonglows, had disbanded. In 1969, the Spinners recorded "In My Diary" (V.I.P. 25050), a song originally recorded by the Moonglows on Chess 1589. The Spinners' first song was also their most popular until their 1970 hit, "It's A Shame" (V.I.P. 25057), a Stevie Wonder production that featured G. C. Cameron on lead vocals.

Tri-Phi operations were discontinued by the end of 1963, and around this time Harvey Fuqua came to Motown. As part of this merger of Tri-Phi and its subsidiary label, Harvey, Motown acquired such artists as the Spinners, Shorty Long, and Junior Walker & the All Stars. Since many of Motown's top artists and groups were now enjoying great popularity and demand, it was difficult for the Spinners to find a place at Motown. It has been reported that they were often given demeaning jobs to do around Motown offices, and they left Motown in 1971 after their seven-year contract was up. They did not achieve great success while at Motown, with "It's A Shame" being their only release to reach the top twenty on the pop charts.

When the Spinners left Motown and signed with Atlantic (at the suggestion of Aretha Franklin), their lead singer, G.C. Cameron, decided to stay with Motown as a solo artist. He was replaced by Phillipe Wynne, and it was with Phillipe Wynne as lead vocalist that the group achieved its supergroup status. Wynne (born April 3, 1941) died tragically of a heart attack after collapsing on-stage during a live performance in Oakland, California, at the age of forty-three on July 13, 1984. John Edwards replaced Wynne in 1977, and appears on the album YESTERDAY, TODAY & TOMORROW (Atlantic SD 19100).

MOTOWN DISCOGRAPHY

10/64: Sweet Thing/How Can I (Motown 1067)

6/65: I'll Always Love You/Tomorrow May Never Come (Motown 1078)

4/66: Truly Yours/Where Is That Girl (Motown 1093)

4/67: For All We Know/I Cross My Heart (Motown 1109)

8/67: THE ORIGINAL SPINNERS (Motown MS-639)

11/68: I Just Can't Help But Feel The Pain/ Bad, Bad Weather (Till You Come Home) (Motown 1136)

10/69: In My Diary/(She's Gonna Love Me)

At Sundown (V.I.P. 25050)

2/70: Message From A Black Man/(She's Gonna Love Me) At Sundown (V.I.P. 25054)

7/70: It's A Shame/Together We Can Make Such Sweet Music (V.I.P. 25057)

10/70: 2ND TIME AROUND (V.I.P. VIPS-405)

12/70: We'll Have It Made/My Whole World Ended (The Moment You Left Me) (V.I.P. 25060)

3/73: Together We Can Make Such Sweet Music/Bad, Bad Weather (Till You Come Home) (Motown 1235)

4/73: THE BEST OF THE SPINNERS (Motown M-769L)

Unissued Motown Recordings

In My Diary/(She's Gonna Love Me) At Sundown (Motown 1155)

NON-MOTOWN DISCOGRAPHY

1961: That's What Girls Are Made For/ Heebie Jeebies (Tri-Phi 1001)

1961: Love (I Am So Glad I Found You)/Sudbuster (Tri-Phi 004)

1961: What Did She Use/Itching For My Baby But I Don't Know Where To Scratch (Tri-Phi 1007)

1962: She Loves Me So/Whistling About You (Tri-Phi 1010)

1962: I've Been Hurt/I Got Your Water Boiling Baby (Now I'm Gonna Cook Your Goose) (Tri-Phi 1013)

1962: She Don't Love Me/Too Young, Too Much, Too Soon (Tri-Phi 1018)

1972: How Could I Let You Get Away/I'll Be Around (Atlantic 2904)

1972: Could It Be I'm Falling In Love/Just You And Me Baby (Atlantic 2927)

1973: THE SPINNERS (Atlantic SD 7256)

1973: One Of A Kind/Don't Let The Grass Fool You (Atlantic 2962)

1973: Ghetto Child/We Belong Together (Atlantic 2973)

1973: Mighty Love (Part 1)/Mighty Love (Part 2) (Atlantic 3006)

1974: MIGHTY LOVE (Atlantic SD 7296)

1974: I'm Coming Home/He'll Never Love You Like I Do (Atlantic 3027)

1974: Then Came You/ (Atlantic 3202) With Dionne Warwick

1974: Love Don't Love Nobody (Part 1)/

Love Don't Love Nobody (Part 2) (Atlantic 3206)

1974: NEW AND IMPROVED (Atlantic SD 18118

1975: Living A Little, Laughing A Little/ Smile, We Have Each Other (Atlantic 3252)

1975: Sadie/Lazy Susan (Atlantic 3268)

1975: PICK OF THE LITTER (Atlantic SD 18141)

1975: They Just Can't Stop It (The Games People Play)/I Don't Want To Lose You (Atlantic 3284)

1975: Love Or Leave/You Made A Promise To Me (Atlantic 3309)

1975: SPINNERS LIVE (Atlantic SD2-910) Two-album set

1976: Wake Up Susan/If You Can't Be In Love (Atlantic 3341)

1976: Rubber Band Man/Now That We're Together (Atlantic 3355)

1976: HAPPINESS IS BEING WITH THE SPINNERS (Atlantic SD 18181)

1977: You're Throwing A Good Love Away/You're All I Need In Life (Atlantic 3382)

1977: Me And My Music/I'm Riding Your Shadow (Atlantic 3400)

1977: Heaven On Earth/I'm Tired Of Giving (Atlantic 3425)

1977?: MIGHTY LOVE (Atlantic SD 7296) Budget album

1977: YESTERDAY, TODAY, AND TOMORROW (Atlantic SD 19100)

1977: 8 (Atlantic SD 19146)

1978: Easy Come, Easy Go/Love Is One Step Away (Atlantic 3462)

1978: If You Wanna Do A Dance/Once In A Life Proposal (Atlantic 3493)

1978: THE BEST OF THE SPINNERS (Atlantic SD 19179)

1979: Are You Ready For Love/Once You Fall In Love (Atlantic 3546)

1979: I Love The Music/Don't Let The Man Get You (Atlantic 3590)

1979: Body Language/With My Eyes (Atlantic 3619)

1979: Working My Way Back To You + Forgive Me Girl/Disco Ride (Atlantic 3637)

1979: FROM HERE TO ETERNALLY (Atlantic SD 19219)

1979: DANCIN' AND LOVIN' (Atlantic SD 19256)

1980: LOVE TRIPPIN' (Atlantic SD 19270)

1980: Cupid, I've Loved You For A Long Time/Pipe Dreams (Atlantic 3664)

1980: Now That You're Mine Again/Love Trippin' (Atlantic 3757)

1980: I Just Want To Fall In Love/Heavy On The Sunshine (Atlantic 3765)

1981: LABOR OF LOVE (Atlantic SD 16032)

1981: Yesterday Once More + Nothing Remains The Same/Be My Love (Atlantic 3798)

1981: Long Live Soul Music/Give Your Lady What She Wants (Atlantic 3814)

1981: Winter Of Our Love/The Deacon (Atlantic 3827)

1981: Street Talk/What You Feel Is Real (Atlantic 3848) with Gino Soccio

1981: You Go Your Way (I'll Go Mine)/ Got To Be Love (Atlantic 3865)

1981: Love Connection/ (Atlantic 3882)

1981: CAN'T SHAKE THIS FEELIN' (Atlantic 19318)

1982: Never Thought I'd Fall In Love/Send A Little Love (Atlantic 4007)

1982: Magic In The Moonlight/So Far Away (Atlantic 89962)

1982: Funny How Time Slips Away/I'm Calling You Now (Atlantic 89922)

1982: GRAND SLAM (Atlantic 80020-1)

1983: City Full Of Memories/No Other Love (Atlantic 89862)

1984: CROSS FIRE (Atlantic 80150-1)

1984: Right Or Wrong/ Love Is In Season (Atlantic 89689)

1984: (We Have Come Into) Our Time For Love/All Your Love (Atlantic 89648)

198?: LOVIN FEELINGS (Mirage 90456-1) Distributed by ATCO

FOR MORE INFORMATION
Keegan, Kevin. "Pervis Jackson Remembers Philippe Wynne," in *RPM: Record Profile Magazine*, Number 7 (September–October 1984).

(See also G. C. CAMERON.)

EDWIN STARR

Born January 21, 1942, as Charles Hatcher in Nashville, Tennessee, and raised in Cleveland, Ohio. He began singing in Cleveland in 1956 with a group called the Future Tunes. In 1960, he joined the army and performed with a group of servicemen. After the army, he turned

EDWIN STARR

professional and toured for two years as featured vocalist with organist "Wild" Bill Doggett. He was spotted in Detroit by Eddie Wingate while playing with Bill Doggett at the 20 Grand, and signed with Eddie's Golden World label. His first recordings appeared on Wingate's Ric-Tic label, until both Golden World and Ric-Tic were acquired by Motown (Golden World in 1966, Ric-Tic in 1968).

Edwin Starr's first record, "Agent Double-O Soul" (Ric-Tic 103), hit the pop charts in August 1965 and was fairly popular with both white and black audiences. After "Back Street" (Ric-Tic 107) didn't fare as well, he had another Top 10 rhythm & blues hit with "Stop Her On Sight (S.O.S.)" (Ric-Tic 109) in early 1966. During this period, he appeared on many television shows, including "Shindig," "Where The Action Is," and "Hollywood A Go Go."

Edwin was in England when he discovered his contract had been sold to Motown and that he was now a Motown artist. By 1967, he was recording for the Gordy label. After signing with Motown, Edwin toured the U.S. and Europe. In February 1969, he had a major tour of the U.S. to promote his newly-released song, "Twenty-Five Miles" (Gordy 7083), which climbed to #6 on the pop charts. The song was produced by Johnny Bristol and Harvey Fuqua. That same year he performed on his ninth tour of England.

The biggest hit of his career would come the next year. In 1970, "War" (Gordy 7101) reached the #1 position on the pop charts. Produced by Norman Whitfield and written by Whitfield and Barrett Strong, the song was deemed too controversial for Motown's top male group of the time, the Temptations.

Edwin stayed with Motown until 1975, playing nightclubs and touring, but never matching his earlier successes. He also toured with r&b shows featuring Jackie Wilson, Otis Redding, and Sam & Dave. After leaving Motown, he recorded for Granite Records and 20th-Century Fox.

Edwin is also a noted songwriter. Among his songwriting credits are "Oh How Happy" (recorded by the Shades of Blue), "Agent Double-O Soul," "Stop Her On Sight (S.O.S.)," and "Twenty-Five Miles," as well as numerous other songs he recorded himself.

MOTOWN DISCOGRAPHY

11/67: I Want My Baby Back/Gonna Keep On Tryin' Till I Win Your Love (Gordy 7066)

4/68: I Am The Man For You Baby/My Weakness Is You (Gordy 7071)

9/68: SOUL MASTER (Gordy GS-931)

10/68: Way Over There/If My Heart Could Tell The Story (Gordy 7078)

1/69: Twenty-Five Miles/Love Is My Destination (Gordy 7083)

4/69: 25 MILES (Gordy GS-940)

6/69: I'm Still A Struggling Man/Pretty Little Angel (Gordy 7087)

7/69: Oh How Happy/Ooo Baby Baby (Gordy 7090)

10/69: JUST WE TWO (Gordy GS-945)

2/70: Time/Running Back and Forth (Gordy 7097)

6/70: War/He Who Picks A Rose (Gordy 7101)

8/70: WAR & PEACE (Gordy GS-948)

12/70: Stop The War Now/Gonna Keep On Tryin' Till I Win Your Love (Gordy 7104)

4/71: Funky Music Sho Nuff Turns Me On/Cloud Nine (Gordy 7107)

7/71: INVOLVED (Gordy G-956L)

3/72: Take Me Clear From Here/Ball Of Confusion (That's What The World Is Today) (Soul 35096)

8/72: Who Is The Leader Of The People/Don't Tell Me I'm Crazy (Soul 35100)

5/73: There You Go (Vocal)/There You Go (Instrumental) (Soul 35103)

9/73: You've Got My (Soul On Fire/Love (The Lonely People's Prayer) (Motown 1276)

1/74: HELL UP IN HARLEM (ORIGINAL SOUNDTRACK) (Motown M 802V1)

2/74: Ain't It Hell Up In Harlem/Don't It Feel Good To Be Free (Motown 1284)

6/74: Big Papa/Like We Used To Do (Motown 1300)

11/74: Who's Right Or Wrong/Lonely Rainy Days In San Diego (Motown 1326)

Unissued Motown Recordings

Ain't It Hell Up In Harlem/Don't It Feel Good To Be Free (Soul 35112)

NON-MOTOWN DISCOGRAPHY

1965: Agent Double-O Soul/Agent Double-O Soul (Instrumental) (Ric-Tic 103)

1965: Back Street/Back Street
(Instrumental) (Ric-Tic 107)

1966: Stop Her On Sight (S.O.S.)/I Have
Faith In You (Ric-Tic 109)

1966: Scott's On Swingers (S.O.S)/ (Ric-Tic
109X) Promotional release for
Detroit-area disc jockey, Scott
Regan, of WKNR-AM.

1966: Headline News/Harlem (Ric-Tic 114)

1966: Girls Are Getting Prettier/It's My
Turn Now (Ric-Tic 118)

1966: You're My Mellow/My Kind of
Woman (Ric-Tic 120)

1975: FREE TO BE MYSELF (Granite GS
-1005)

1975: Pain/I'll Never Forget You (Granite
522)

1975: Stay With Me/Party (Granite 528)

1975: Abyssinia Jones/Beginning (Granite
532)

1977: EDWIN STARR (20th-Century Fox
T-538)

1977: I Just Wanna Do My Thing/Mr.
Davenport & Mr. Jones (20th-
Century Fox 2338)

1978: CLEAN (20th-Century Fox T-559)

1978: I'm So Into You/Don't Waste Your
Time (20th-Century Fox 2389)

1978: Contact/Don't Waste Your Time
(20th-Century Fox 2396)

1979: HAPPY RADIO (20th-Century Fox)

1979: H.A.P.P.Y. Radio/My Friend
(20th-Century Fox 2408)

1979: It's Called The Rock/Patiently
(20th-Century Fox 2420)

1979: It's Called The Rock/H.A.P.P.Y.
Radio (20th-Century Fox 2423 and
2441)

1980: STRONGER THAN YOU THINK I
AM (20th-Century Fox T-615)

1980: Stronger Than You Think I Am
(Vocal)/Stronger Than You Think
I Am (Instrumental) (20th-Century
Fox 2445)

1980: Boop Boop Song/Tell-A-Star
(20th-Century Fox 2450)

1980: Get Up + Whirlpool/Bigger and
Better (20th-Century Fox 2455 and
2462)

1980: Twenty-Five Miles/Never Turn My
Back On You (20th-Century Fox 2477)

1981: Sweet/Real Live #10 (20th-Century
Fox 2496)

1981: THE BEST OF EDWIN STARR
(20th-Century Fox T-634)

WILLIAM "MICKEY" STEVENSON

Songwriter-producer. Mickey Stevenson was the head of Motown's A&R department from the beginning, in 1959, until he left Motown in January 1967. He was responsible for bringing Martha Reeves to Motown, where she began working as his secretary. In 1964, he and Ivy Jo Hunter would co-produce Martha & the Vandellas' most popular album, DANCE PARTY (Gordy 915). He shared writing credits for their hits from that album, "Wild One" (Gordy 7036), with Hunter, and "Dancing In The Streets" (Gordy 7033), with Marvin Gaye. That year, Mickey and Norman Whitfield co-wrote and produced "Needle In A Haystack" for the Velvelettes.

Stevenson also co-wrote and produced several hits for Marvin Gaye, including "Stubborn Kind Of Fellow" (Tamla 54068) and "Pride And Joy" (Tamla 54079). Along with Marvin Gaye and Gwen Gordy, he co-wrote "Beechwood 4-5789" (Tamla 54065) for the Marvelettes, as well as their 1962 hit, "Playboy" (Tamla 54060), with Brian Holland and Robert Bateman. Married to Motown singer Kim Weston, Stevenson produced and co-wrote her duet with Marvin Gaye, "It Takes Two" (Tamla 54141), just before leaving the label. Both Stevenson and Kim Weston left Motown in January 1967. He left to establish his own label, People. In April, Kim signed with MGM Records, and Mickey was offered a reported million-dollar contract to improve MGM's subsidiary, Venture Records.

BARRETT STRONG

Born February 5, 1941, in Mississippi. Moved to Detroit with his family at an early age. His cousin is Nolan Strong, lead singer for the Diablos ("Mind Over Matter"). Barrett Strong is perhaps best known for his hit, "Money," first released in 1959 on Tamla and then leased to Anna Records, which enjoyed national distribution with the help of Chess Records. The song charted in 1960 and reached the #23 position. It was covered in the 1960s by both the Beatles and the Rolling Stones. He met Berry Gordy while singing in Detroit clubs, and joined Motown as a vocalist and staff songwriter. He stayed with Motown until 1973, when he left for a solo career with

Capitol Records.

In 1961, Eddie Holland recorded "Jamie" (Motown 1021), a song written by Barrett Strong and William "Mickey" Stevenson. As a songwriter, Barrett Strong would achieve his greatest successes teamed with Norman Whitfield. Together, they co-wrote songs for Gladys Knight and the Pips, including "The End Of Our Road" (with Roger Penzabene), "Friendship Train," and "I Heard It Through The Grapevine." Starting in 1968, the Whitfield-Strong team would lead the Temptations into "psychedelic soul" with such Top 10 hits as "Cloud Nine" (Gordy 7081), "Run Away Child, Running Wild" (Gordy 7084), the #1 hit "I Can't Get Next To You" (Gordy 7093), "Psychedelic Shack" (Gordy 7096), and "Ball Of Confusion (That's What the World Is Today)" (Gordy 7099). They also wrote the #1 hit that was Eddie Kendricks' last single with the Temptations, "Just My Imagination (Running Away With Me)" (Gordy 7105). Another Whitfield-Strong composition, "War" (Gordy 7101), was probably written for the Temptations, but it became a #1 hit for Edwin Starr in 1970. In 1971, the Undisputed Truth scored their only Top 10 hit with the Whitfield-Strong song, "Smiling Faces Sometimes" (Gordy 7108).

MOTOWN DISCOGRAPHY

11/59: Money (That's What I Want)/Oh I Apologize (Tamla 54027)
 7/60: Yes, No, Maybe So/You Knows What To Do (Tamla 54029)
10/60: Whirlwind/I'm Gonna Cry (If You Quit Me) (Tamla 54033)
12/60: Money And Me/You Got What It Takes (Tamla 54035)
 6/61: Misery/Two Wrongs Don't Make A Right (Tamla 54043)

Unissued Motown Recordings

MONEY AND OTHER BIG HITS
(Tamla TM-226)

NON-MOTOWN DISCOGRAPHY

1960: Money/Oh I Apologize (Anna 1111)
1960: Yes, No, Maybe So/You Know What To Do (Anna 1116)
1975: STRONGHOLD (Capitol ST-11376)
1975: Is It True/Anywhere (Capitol 4052)

1975: Surrender/There's Something About You (Capitol 4120)
1976: Gonna Make It Right/Man Up In The Sky (Capitol 4223)
1976: LIVE AND LOVE (Capitol ST-11490)
19??: LOVE IS YOU (Coup CR-LP-2007)

THE SUPREMES

Diana Ross (born March 26, 1944; left Motown January 1970)

Florence Ballard (born June 30, 1943; left Motown July 1967; died February 22, 1976)

Mary Wilson (born March 4, 1944)

Betty Hutton (aka Betty Travis, Betty Anderson, Betty McGlown) (1958-1960) Does not appear on any records

Barbara Martin (1960-1962) Fourth member on early records

Cindy Birdsong (born December 15, 1939) (replaced Florence Ballard in July 1967; left May 1972; returned January 1974; left 1976)

Jean Terrell (replaced Diana Ross in January 1970; left January 1974)

Lynda Laurence (also Lawrence) (replaced Cindy Birdsong in May 1972; left January 1974)

Scherrie Payne (born November 14, 1944) (replaced Jean Terrell in January 1974)

Susaye Greene (replaced Cindy Birdsong in 1976)

Based on record sales, the Supremes currently rank third behind the Beatles and Elvis Presley as the most popular recording artists of all time. More than any other Motown group or artist, the Supremes achieved Motown's goal of appealing equally to white as well as black audiences. Although there have been several line-ups, the Supremes achieved their greatest popularity with Diana Ross as lead singer and Mary Wilson and Florence Ballard as backing vocalists. Their most popular songs have been written by the team of Holland-Dozier-Holland.

The Supremes began in Detroit in the late 1950s as a quartet known as the Primettes. They were either in late junior high school or just starting high school at the time. By the time they had graduated from high school, they had become a trio, signed a contract with Motown, and released several singles. Their first album commemorates their high

TAMLA

2648 W. Grand
Boulevard

Jobete B.M.I.

Detroit 8, Mich.
TR 1-3340

Time 2:49
H-620

I WANT A GUY
(B. Gordy Jr. - B. Holland - F. Gorman)
THE SUPREMES
Produced By
Berry Gordy, Jr.
T-54038

TAMLA

TAMLA RECORDS, DETROIT, MICHIGAN

Jobete
B.M.I.

Time 2:44
H-772

WHO'S LOVING YOU
(William Robinson)
SUPREMES
Produced By
BERRY GORDY, JR.
T-54045

THE SUPREMES

The group's line-up, 1962-1967: Diana Ross flanked
by Mary Wilson (left) and Florence Ballard (right).
The Supremes' first two releases for Motown appeared
on the Tamla label. All their subsequent records were
on the Motown label.

school graduation, according to the liner notes. Diana Ross graduated from Detroit's Cass Technical H.S., Mary Wilson from Northeastern H.S., and Florence Ballard from Northwestern H.S.

Their first six singles, including two on the Tamla label, were produced by Berry Gordy or Smokey Robinson, who had been generating hits for Mary Wells. The group didn't click until their seventh, released late in 1963. "When The Lovelight Starts Shining Through His Eyes" (Motown 1051) was their first recording of a Holland-Dozier-Holland song, and reached a respectable #23 on the pop charts. The follow-up song, "Run Run Run" (Motown 1054), flopped. Then began the string of #1 pop hits in July 1964.

The Supremes' string of five consecutive #1 pop hits, all written by Holland-Dozier-Holland, began with "Where Did Our Love Go" (Motown 1060), and was followed by "Baby Love" (Motown 1066), "Come See About Me" (Motown 1068), "Stop! In The Name Of Love" (Motown 1074), and "Back In My Arms Again" (Motown 1075). By the fall of 1965, they were in great demand for television appearances, which included several "Hullabaloo" shows, the "Red Skelton Show," Ed Sullivan, and Dean Martin. That year they appeared onstage at the Michigan State Fair, and added "I Hear A Symphony" (Motown 1083) to their list of #1 hits.

In 1966, Michigan's Schafer Bakeries, Inc., introduced a line of Supremes bread. The plastic wrappers featured likenesses of the Supremes, and are now in demand by collectors. That year, Holland-Dozier-Holland began another string of #1 pop hits for the Supremes that took them into 1967: "You Can't Hurry Love" (Motown 1097), "You Keep Me Hangin' On" (Motown 1101), "Love Is Here and Now You're Gone" (Motown 1103), and "The Happening" (Motown 1107). July 1967 marked a turning point for the Supremes. In live performances, the group was now billed as "Diana Ross and the Supremes," and Florence Ballard was replaced by Cindy Birdsong, who had been part of Patti LaBelle's backing group, the Blue Belles. Motown would explain Flo's withdrawal from the group by saying she was "exhausted from the girls' demanding schedule." In a lawsuit, Florence would later charge Motown as well as present and future Supremes with conspiracy to oust her from the group. (For more information about Flo Ballard, see her separate entry.)

In the years between Florence and Diana's departure, the Supremes only achieved two #1 pop singles, "Love Child" (Motown 1135), in 1968, and "Someday We'll Be Together" (Motown 1156), in 1969. "Reflections" (Motown 1111), the first song released by the Ross-Wilson-Birdsong lineup, reached #2, and their next song, "In And Out Of Love" (Motown 1116) went to #9. (Mary Wilson has stated that "Reflections" was recorded while Florence Ballard was still a member of the group.) In 1968, Diana, Mary, and Cindy appeared as three nuns on the television show, "Tarzan."

Motown had always groomed the Supremes for the nightclub circuit as well as for the charts. They usually performed their hits as well as other popular songs that would appeal to the typical nightclub crowds. It was appropriate, then, that the Supremes' farewell shows would be held at the Frontier Hotel in Las Vegas in January 1970. The Ross decade was over, and she would go on to even greater heights as a popular solo artist and film actress. (For more information about Diana Ross, see her separate entry.)

Diana Ross's replacement in the Supremes was Jean Terrell. Jean had been discovered in 1968 by Berry Gordy, who heard her singing at Miami's Fountainbleau Hotel with her brother's group, Ernie Terrell & The Heavyweights. She signed a contract as a solo artist with Motown in May 1969. In January 1970, she became lead vocalist with the Supremes. The Terrell-Wilson-Birdsong edition of the Supremes was the most popular post-Ross combination. They recorded such hits as "Stoned Love" (Motown 1172), which reached #7 on the charts in 1970; "Nathan Jones (Motown 1182) in 1971 reached #16; and "Floy Joy" (Motown 1195) in 1972. The latter two songs were Top 10 r&b hits.

Jean Terrell got married in 1973, and the Supremes didn't release any albums until she had been replaced by Scherrie Payne (Freda Payne's sister) in 1975. The Supremes as a group disbanded in 1977, although there was a 1978 tour of the United Kingdom with Mary Wilson, Karen Ragland, and Karen Jackson performing as the Supremes. Mary Wilson made her solo debut at the New York-New York disco in August 1979. A complete key to the various Supremes' lineups is given below.

THE SUPREMES

Another shot from later in the 1962-1967 period:
(from left) Diana Ross, Mary Wilson, Florence
Ballard.

KEY TO SUPREMES' LINE-UPS AND RECORDINGS

1960: Primettes (Diana Ross, Mary Wilson, Florence Ballard, Betty Hutton (aka Betty Travis, aka Betty Anderson)) No records

1960: Primettes (Diana Ross, Mary Wilson, Florence Ballard, Barbara Martin) Lupine LR 120

1962: Supremes (Diana Ross, Mary Wilson, Florence Ballard, Barbara Martin) Tamla 54038, Tamla 54045, Motown 1008 (promo only), Motown 1027. Barbara Martin left the group to get married in October 1962. She was not replaced.

1962-July 1967: Supremes (Diana Ross, Mary Wilson, Florence Ballard) Motown 1034, 1040, 1044, 1051, 1054, 1060, 1066, 1068, 1074, 1075, 1080, 1083, 1085, 1089, 1094, 1097, 1101, 1103, 1107. Also 1079 (promo on George Alexander label), 1125 (unissued)

> Albums: M606-MEET THE SUPREMES (12-63) through MS-2-663-DIANA ROSS & THE SUPREMES GREATEST HITS (9-67)

Feb. 1966: Issue a radio-only single, "Things Are Changing," a public-service message that is part of the Equal Employment Opportunity (EEO) campaign. July 1967 live performances when first billed as Diana Ross & the Supremes

1967-1969: Diana Ross & the Supremes (Diana Ross, Mary Wilson, Cindy Birdsong) Motown 1111 (may have been recorded while Ballard was still in the group), 1116, 1122, 1126, 1135, 1139, 1146, 1148, 1156. Also M1137, 1142, 1150, 1153 all with the Temptations.

> Albums: MS665-REFLECTIONS (4-68) through MS-2-708-FAREWELL (5-70).

Jean Terrell replaces Diana Ross in January 1970 after their farewell performances at the Frontier Hotel in Las Vegas. The new Supremes begin making live club appearances in February. Cindy Birdsong marries George Hewlett in May 1970.

1970-1972: Supremes (Jean Terrell, Mary Wilson, Cindy Birdsong) Motown 1162, 1172, 1182, 1190, 1195, 1200, 1206. Also M1173, 1181, both with the Four Tops.

> Albums: MS705-RIGHT ON (4-70) through M751-FLOY JOY (5-72).

In May 1972, Lynda Laurence, "a former gospel singer from Philadelphia," replaces Cindy Birdsong, who goes into temporary retirement.

1972-1973: Supremes (Jean Terrell, Mary Wilson, Lynda Laurence) Motown 1213, 1225.

> Album: M756-THE SUPREMES (11-72)

NOTE: No albums from 11-72 (THE SUPREMES, M756) until 5-75 (THE SUPREMES, M6-828S1)

1973: Both Jean Terrell and Lynda Laurence get married.

1974-1976: Supremes (Mary Wilson, Scherrie Payne (replaces Jean, who leaves to devote more time to her family), Cindy Birdsong (replaces Lynda, who is pregnant)) Motown 1350 (unissued), 1358, 1374, 1391

> Albums: M6-828S1-THE SUPREMES (5-75)

1976-77: Supremes (Mary Wilson, Scherrie Payne, Susaye Greene (formerly a member of Stevie Wonder's backing group, Wonderlove, replaces Cindy Birdsong)) Motown 1407, 1415

> Albums: M6-863S1-HIGH ENERGY (4-76); M6-873S1-MARY, SCHERRIE & SUSAYE (10-76)

1978: Supremes (Mary Wilson, Karen Ragland, Karen Jackson) (UK tour)

MOTOWN DISCOGRAPHY

4/61: I Want A Guy/Never Again (Tamla 54038)

7/61: Buttered Popcorn/Who's Loving You (Tamla 54045)

5/62: Your Heart Belongs To Me/(He's) Seventeen (Motown 1027)

11/62: Let Me Go The Right Way/Time Changes Things (Motown 1034)

3/63: My Heart Can't Take It No More/You Bring Back Memories (Motown 1040)

6/63: A Breath Taking, First Sight Soul Shaking, One Night Love Making, Next Day Heart Breaking Guy/(The Man With The) Rock and Roll Banjo Band (Motown 1044)

6/63: A Breath Taking Guy/(The Man With The) Rock And Roll Banjo Band (Motown 1044)

11/63: When The Lovelight Starts Shining Through His Eyes/Standing At The Crossroads Of Love (Motown 1051)

12/63: MEET THE SUPREMES (Motown MT-606)

2/64: Run, Run, Run/I'm Giving You Your Freedom (Motown 1054)

6/64: Where Did Our Love Go/He Means The World To Me (Motown 1060)

8/64: WHERE DID OUR LOVE GO (Motown MT-621)

9/64: Baby Love/Ask Any Girl (Motown 1066)

10/64: Come See About Me/Always In My Heart (Motown 1068)

10/64: A BIT OF LIVERPOOL (Motown MS-623)

2/65: Stop! In The Name Of Love/I'm In Love Again (Motown 1074)

2/65: SUPREMES SING COUNTRY, WESTERN AND POP (Motown MS-625)

4/65: Back In My Arms Again/Whisper You Love Me Baby (Motown 1075)

4/65: WE REMEMBER SAM COOKE (Motown MS-629)

7/65: Nothing But Heartaches/He Holds His Own (Motown 1080)

8/65: MORE HITS BY THE SUPREMES (Motown MS-627)

10/65: I Hear A Symphony/Who Could Ever Doubt My Love (Motown 1083)

11/65: MERRY CHRISTMAS (Motown MS-638)

11/65: SUPREMES AT THE COPA (Motown MS-636)

12/65: Children's Christmas Song/Twinkle Twinkle Little Me (Motown 1085)

12/65: My World Is Empty Without You/Everything Is Good About You (Motown 1089)

1966: Mother You, Smother You/Mother You, Smother You (Motown DM-L-294MO5) As by Christine Schumacher Sings With The Supremes. Promo only, contest record

2/66: I HEAR A SYMPHONY (Motown MS-643)

2/66: Things Are Changing (Tamla SL4M-3114) Radio-only single for Equal Employment Opportunity campaign

4/66: Love Is Like An Itching In My Heart/He's All I Got (Motown 1094)

7/66: You Can't Hurry Love/Put Yourself In My Place (Motown 1097)

8/66: SUPREMES A GO GO (Motown MS-649)

10/66: You Keep Me Hangin' On/Remove This Doubt (Motown 1101)

1/67: Love Is Here And Now You're Gone/There's No Stopping Us Now (Motown 1103)

1/67: SUPREMES SING HOLLAND, DOZIER, HOLLAND (Motown MS-650)

3/67: The Happening/All I Know About You (Motown 1107)

Subsequent releases as by Diana Ross and the Supremes:

6/67: SUPREMES SING RODGERS AND HART (Motown MS-659) Group name changed to Diana Ross and The Supremes

7/67: Reflections/Going Down For The Third Time (Motown 1111)

9/67: DIANA ROSS AND THE SUPREMES GREATEST HITS (Motown MS-2-663)

10/67: In And Out Of Love/I Guess I'll Always Love You (Motown 1116)

3/68: Forever Came Today/Time Changes Things (Motown 1122)

4/68: REFLECTIONS (Motown MS-665)

5/68: Some Things You Never Get Used To/You've Been So Wonderful To Me (Motown 1126)

9/68: Love Child/Will This Be The Day (Motown 1135)

9/68: DIANA ROSS AND THE SUPREMES SING AND PERFORM "FUNNY GIRL" (Motown MS-672)

9/68: DIANA ROSS AND THE SUPREMES 'LIVE' AT LONDON'S TALK OF THE TOWN (Motown MS-676)

11/68: I'm Gonna Make You Love Me/A Place In The Sun (Motown 1137) With the Temptations

11/68: DIANA ROSS & THE SUPREMES JOIN THE TEMPTATIONS (Motown

MS-679) With the Temptations

11/68: LOVE CHILD (Motown MS-670)

12/68: TCB (Motown MS-682) With the Temptations

1/69: I'm Livin' In Shame/I'm So Glad I Got Somebody (Like You Around) (Motown 1139)

2/69: I'll Try Something New/The Way You Do The Things You Do (Motown 1142) With the Temptations

3/69: The Composer/The Beginning Of The End (Motown 1146)

5/69: No Matter What Sign You Are/The Young Folks (Motown 1148)

5/69: LET THE SUNSHINE IN (Motown MS-689)

8/69: Stubborn Kind Of Fellow/Try It Baby (Motown 1150) With the Temptations

9/69: The Weight/For Better Or Worse (Motown 1153) With the Temptations

9/69: TOGETHER (Motown MS-692) With the Temptations

10/69: Someday We'll Be Together/He's My Sunny Boy (Motown 1156)

11/69: CREAM OF THE CROP (Motown MS-694)

11/69: ON BROADWAY (Motown MS-699) With the Temptations

1/70: DIANA ROSS AND THE SUPREMES GREATEST HITS VOLUME 3 (Motown MS-702)

Subsequent releases as by The Supremes:

2/70: Up The Ladder To The Roof/Bill, When Are You Coming Back (Motown 1162) As by The Supremes

4/70: RIGHT ON (Motown MS-705) As by The Supremes

5/70: FAREWELL (Motown MS2-7088) As by Diana Ross and The Supremes

7/70: Everybody's Got The Right To Love/ But I Love You More (Motown 1167)

9/70: THE MAGNIFICENT 7 (Motown MS-717) With the Four Tops

10/70: Stoned Love/Shine On Me (Motown 1172)

10/70: NEW WAYS BUT LOVE STAYS (Motown MS-720)

11/70: River Deep, Mountain High/Together We Can Make Such Sweet Music (Motown 1173) With the Four Tops

4/71: Nathan Jones/Happy (Is A Bumpy Road) (Motown 1182)

5/71: You Gotta Have Love In Your Heart/ I'm Glad About It (Motown 1181) With the Four Tops

6/71: THE RETURN OF THE MAGNIFI-CENT SEVEN (Motown MS-736) With the Four Tops

6/71: TOUCH (Motown MS-737)

9/71: Touch/It's So Hard For Me To Say Good-By (Motown 1190)

12/71: Floy Joy/This Is The Story (Motown 1195)

12/71: DYNAMITE (Motown M-745L) With the Four Tops

4/72: Automatically Sunshine/Precious Little Things (Motown 1200)

5/72: FLOY JOY (Motown M-751L)

7/72: Your Wonderful, Sweet Sweet Love/ The Wisdom Of Time (Motown 1206)

10/72: I Guess I'll Miss The Man/Over And Over (Motown 1213)

11/72: THE SUPREMES (Motown M-756L)

5/73: Bad Weather/Oh Be My Love (Motown 1225)

6/74: ANTHOLOGY (Motown M9-794A3)

6/75: THE SUPREMES (Motown M6-828S1)

7/75: He's My Man/Give Out, But Don't Give Up (Motown 1358)

10/75: Where Do I Go From Here/Give Out, But Don't Give Up (Motown 1374)

4/76: HIGH ENERGY (Motown M6-863S1)

5/76: I'm Gonna Let My Heart Do The Walking/Early Morning Love (Motown 1391)

10/76: You're My Driving Wheel/You're What's Missing In My Life (Motown 1407)

10/76: MARY, SCHERRIE & SUSAYE (Motown M6-873S1)

2/77: Let Yourself Go/You Are The Heart Of Me (Motown 1415)

7/78: AT THEIR BEST (Motown M7-904R1)

6/80: Medley of Hits/Where Do We Go From Here (Motown 1488) 'B'side by Diana Ross

8/81: Medley of Hits/Where Did We Go Wrong (Motown 1523) 'B' side by Diana Ross

2/84: COMPACT COMMAND PER-FORMANCES: 20 GREATEST HITS (Motown CD06073MD)

8/86: ANTHOLOGY (Motown MCD06198MD2)

8/86: THE SUPREMES 25TH ANNI-VERSARY (Motown MCD06193MD)

SYREETA

Unissued Motown Recordings

I Want A Guy/Never Again (Motown 1008)
The Only Time I'm Happy/Supreme's Interview (Motown 1079)
What The World Needs Now Is Love/ Your Kiss Of Fire (Motown 1125)
It's All Been Said Before/Give Out, But Don't Give Up (Motown 1350
THE SUPREMES SING BALLADS AND BLUES (Motown MLP-610
LIVE, LIVE, LIVE! (Motown MS-626)
THERE'S A PLACE FOR US (Motown MS-628)
A TRIBUTE TO THE GIRLS (Motown MS-635)
PURE GOLD (Motown MS-648)
THE SUPREMES AND THE MOTOWN SOUND (Motown MS-656)
PROMISES KEPT (Motown M-746L)
THE BEST OF THE SUPREMES (Motown 816)

FOR MORE INFORMATION

Betrock, Alan. *Girl Groups*. pp. 163-170.
About the Supremes after Diana Ross: *Ebony* (February 1970), *Life* (February 13, 1970), and *Time* (August 17, 1970).
Hirshey, Gerri. *Nowhere To Run*, pp. 156-83.
Wilson, Mary. *Dreamgirl, My Life As A Supreme* (NY: St. Martin's, 1986). Also available in paperback.

(See also THE PRIMETTES; DIANA ROSS; FLORENCE BALLARD.)

SWITCH

Bobby DeBarge - keyboards, background vocals
Eddie Fluellen - piano, guitar, trombone
Gregory Williams - synthesizer, organ, guitar, fluegelhorn, background vocals
Thomas DeBarge - bass, background vocals
Jody Sims - drums
Phillip Ingram - percussion, background vocals

Gordy recording artists from 1978 to 1981, Switch may be described as a funky dance band with close ties to DeBarge and Jermaine Jackson. Jermaine wrote two songs for their second album, SWITCH II (Gordy G7-988R1), and appears as a background

vocalist on those two songs. Bobby DeBarge joined his brothers and sister in the group, DeBarge, in 1982, although he appeared as an additional musician on their debut album in 1981, THE DeBARGES (Gordy G8-1003M1). He also produced songs for Switch on occasion, a role he has also assumed for DeBarge.

MOTOWN DISCOGRAPHY

7/78: There'll Never Be/You Pulled A Switch (Gordy 7159)
7/78: SWITCH (Gordy G7-980R1)
12/78: I Wanna Be Closer/Somebody's Watchin' You (Gordy 7163)
4/79: SWITCH II (Gordy G7-988R1)
5/79: Best Beat In Town/It's So Real (Gordy 7168)
9/79: I Call Your Name/Next To You (Gordy 7175)
9/79: I Call Your Name/Best Beat In Town (Gordy 7175)
3/80: REACHING FOR TOMORROW (Gordy G8-993M1)
5/80: Don't Take My Love Away/Don't Take My Love Away (Instrumental) (Gordy 7181)
9/80: My Friend In The Sky/Next To You (Gordy 7190)
10/80: Love Over And Over Again/Keep Movin' On (Gordy 7193)
11/80: THIS IS MY DREAM (Gordy G8-999M1)
4/81: You And I/Get Back With You (Gordy 7199)
10/81: I Do Love You/Without You In My Life (Gordy 7214)
11/81: SWITCH V (Gordy G8-1007M1)
1/82: Call On Me/Fallin' (Gordy 1603GF)

(See also DeBARGE.)

SYREETA

She first recorded for Motown in 1968 as Rita Wright, singing "I Can't Give Back The Love I Feel For You" (Gordy 7064). In 1970, she married Stevie Wonder, but they divorced after eighteen months. Solo releases as by Syreeta began appearing in 1972 on Mowest. In the latter part of the 1970s, she recorded duets with G. C. Cameron and Billy Preston. Her most popular recording was her duet with Billy Preston, "With You I'm Born Again" (Motown 1477), which reached the

#4 position early in 1980. The song was part of the film, "Fastbreak."

MOTOWN DISCOGRAPHY

6/67: I Can't Give Back The Love I Feel For You/Something On My Mind (Gordy 7064) As by Rita Wright

6/72: SYREETA (Mowest MW 113)

7/72: To Know You Is To Love You/ Happiness (Mowest MW 5021F)

9/72: I Love Every Little Thing About You/Black Magic (Mowest MW 5016F)

6/74: STEVIE WONDER PRESENTS SYREETA (Motown M-808V1)

7/74: Come And Get This Stuff/Black Magic (Motown 1297)

11/74: Heavy Day/I'm Goin' Left (Motown 1317)

12/74: Your Kiss Is Sweet/Spinnin' And Spinnin' (Motown 1328)

6/75: Harmour Love/Cause We've Ended As Lovers (Motown 1353)

1/77: ONE TO ONE (Tamla T6-349S1)

9/77: Let's Make A Deal/Love To The Rescue (Motown 1426) G. C Cameron and Syreeta

9/77: RICH LOVE, POOR LOVE (Motown M6-891S1) Syreeta and G. C. Cameron

3/79: MUSIC FROM THE MOTION PICTURE "FAST BREAK" (Motown M7-915R1) Billy Preston and Syreeta

4/79: Go For It/With You I'm Born Again (Instrumental) (Motown 1460) Billy Preston and Syreeta

11/79: With You I'm Born Again/All I Wanted Was You (Motown 1477) Billy Preston and Syreeta

4/80: SYREETA (Tamla T-372)

6/80: One More Time For Love/Dance For Me Children (Tamla 54312) 'A' side by Billy Preston and Syreeta

9/80: Please Stay/Signed, Sealed, Delivered (I'm Yours) (Tamla 54319) Billy Preston and Syreeta

8/81: Searchin'/Hey You (Motown 1520) Billy Preston and Syreeta

8/81: Just For You (Put the Boogie In Your Body)/Hey You (Motown 1522) Billy Preston and Syreeta

8/81: BILLY PRESTON & SYREETA (Motown M8-958M1) Billy Preston and Syreeta

11/81: SET MY LOVE IN MOTION (Tamla T8-376M1)

12/81: Quick Slick/I Don't Know (Tamla 54333)

3/82: I Must Be In Love/Wish Upon A Star (Tamla 1610TF)

4/83: Forever Is Not Enough/She's Leaving Home (Tamla 1675TF)

5/83: THE SPELL (Tamla 6039TL)

3/85: First Time On A Ferris Wheel/Train Of Thought (Tamla 1786TF) 'A' side by Smokey Robinson and Syreeta. 'B' side by Smokey Robinson

Unissued Motown Recordings

RITA WRIGHT (Gordy GS-941)
Please Stay/Signed, Sealed, Delivered (I'm Yours) (Motown 1497) Billy Preston and Syreeta
ONE TO ONE (Motown 844)
Forever Is Not Enough/Wish Upon A Star (Tamla 1675TF)

BOBBY TAYLOR AND THE VANCOUVERS

Bobby Taylor - lead vocals
Wes Henderson - guitar
Tommy Chong - guitar (later with Cheech and Chong)
Eddie Patterson - bass
Robbie King - organ
Ted Lewis - drums

Discovered while playing clubs in Vancouver, British Columbia, this group's first release for Motown, "Does Your Mama Know About Me?" (Gordy 7069), reached #29 on the pop charts in 1968. It was their most popular song, and by 1970 they had disbanded. Guitarist Thomas Chong achieved fame as a member of the comedy team, Cheech and Chong. Bobby Taylor went on to record as a solo artist.

MOTOWN DISCOGRAPHY

3/68: Does Your Mama Know About Me/ Fading Away (Gordy 7069) Bobby Taylor and the Vancouvers

6/68: I Am Your Man/If You Love Her (Gordy 7073) Bobby Taylor and the Vancouvers

9/68: BOBBY TAYLOR AND THE VANCOUVERS (Gordy GS-930) Bobby Taylor and the Vancouvers

11/68: Malinda/It's Growing (Gordy 7079)

Photo courtesy Peter Benjaminson.

R. Dean Taylor

Bobby Taylor and the Vancouvers

7/69: TAYLOR MADE SOUL (Gordy GS-942) Bobby Taylor

8/69: My Girl Has Gone/It Should Have Been Me Loving Her (Gordy 7092) Bobby Taylor

1/70: Oh, I've Been Bless'd/Blackmail (V.I.P. 25053) Bobby Taylor

11/71: Hey Lordy/Just A Little Bit Closer (Mowest MW 5006F) Bobby Taylor

Unissued Motown Recordings

Oh, I've Been Bless'd/It Should Have Been Me Loving Her (Gordy 7088) Bobby Taylor

R. DEAN TAYLOR

He came to Motown from Toronto in the mid-1960s as a staff songwriter and producer. He co-wrote "Love Child" for the Supremes, a song that became a #1 hit for them in 1968. As a vocalist, he recorded primarily for Motown's Rare Earth label and, in 1970, had a hit with "Indiana Wants Me" (Rare Earth 5013). He recorded for the Rare Earth label until 1973, when he left to form his own record company, Jane Records. By 1974, he had joined Polydor Records.

MOTOWN DISCOGRAPHY

11/65: Let's Go Somewhere/Poor Girl (V.I.P. 25027)

4/67: There's A Ghost In My House/Don't Fool Around (V.I.P. 25042)

4/68: Gotta See Jane/Don't Fool Around (V.I.P. 25045)

4/70: Indiana Wants Me/Love's Your Name (Rare Earth 5013)

12/70: I THINK THEREFORE I AM (Rare Earth RS 522)

1/71: Ain't It A Sad Thing/Back Street (Rare Earth 5023)

3/71: Gotta See Jane/Back Street (Rare Earth 5026)

6/71: Candy Apple Red/Woman Alive (Rare Earth 5030)

3/72: Taos New Mexico/Shadow (Rare Earth 5041)

THE TEMPTATIONS

The Temptations were formed in 1961 by former members of the Distants and the Primes. The Primes were a Birmingham, Alabama-based group that included Eddie Kendricks, Paul Williams, and Kel Osborn. The Distants were based in Detroit and, also known as Otis Williams and the Distants, consisted of Otis Williams, Melvin Franklin, Elbridge "Al" Bryant, Richard Street, and James Crawford (also Albert Harold for James Crawford). The Distants were active as a group from 1956 until 1960, releasing two singles on Warwick in 1959, "Always/Come On" (Warwick 546) and "Open Up Your Heart/ Always" (Warwick 577). Richard Street, who would rejoin the Temptations in 1971, and James Crawford left the Distants in 1960, paving the way for the formation of the Temptations in 1961. At first, the new group (Eddie Kendricks, Paul Williams, Otis Williams, Melvin Franklin, and Al Bryant) was known as the Elgins, but by the time of their first release on Berry Gordy's Miracle label in 1961, the group had been renamed the Temptations.

Berry produced two singles by the Temptations on the Miracle label in 1961. He launched his Gordy label in 1962, and its first release was by the Temptations, "Dream Come True/Isn't She Pretty" (Gordy 7001). Their second release on Gordy, "Paradise/Slow Down Heart" (Gordy 7010), offered one song written and produced by Berry Gordy ("Paradise"), and the other written and produced by Smokey Robinson ("Slow Down Heart"). This foreshadows the group's work with Smokey.

It would be another year and a few releases later (including the Robinson-penned "I Want A Love I Can See" b/w the Robinson-Whitfield collaboration "The Further You Look, The Less You See" on Gordy 7015) before the Temptations broke nationally with Smokey's composition, "The Way You Do the Things You Do" (Gordy 7028). Featuring Eddie Kendricks on lead, the record is the group's first with David Ruffin replacing Al Bryant (now deceased). David and Eddie would continue to share lead vocals until 1968, when David left for a solo career.

Smokey continued to pen the hits for the Temptations through 1966. "My Girl" (co-written with the Miracles' Ronnie White), "It's Growing" (co-written with the Miracles'

Warren "Pete" Moore), "Since I Lost My Baby" (also with Warren Moore), and "Get Ready" all reached the Top 30 on the pop charts. "My Girl" went all the way to #1 at the beginning of 1965, staying on the charts for some thirteen weeks.

"Ain't To Proud To Beg" (Gordy 7054), released in February 1966, marks another change in the behind-the-scenes team writing and producing the Temptations' material. Featuring the lead vocals of David Ruffin, the song was written by Eddie Holland and Norman Whitfield. From 1966 to 1968, these two would go on to write several hits for the Temptations, including "Beauty Is Only Skin Deep" (Gordy 7055), "(I Know) I'm Losing You" (Gordy 7057), "(Loneliness Made Me Realize) It's You That I Need" (Gordy 7065), and "I Wish It Would Rain" (Gordy 7068), the latter with Roger Penzabene. During this period, Eddie Holland, Frank Wilson, and R. Dean Taylor contributed the 1967 hit, "All I Need" (Gordy 7061), and Whitfield, Penzabene, and Cornelius Grant wrote the 1967 follow-up, "You're My Everything" (Gordy 7063).

Eddie Holland's talents as a lyricist led him to co-write songs with others outside of the Holland-Dozier-Holland team on an occasional basis, but Norman Whitfield would remain with the Temptations into the 1970s and bring them to the forefront of "psychedelic soul." His writing partner was none other than the multi-talented Barrett Strong, a vocalist, pianist, and songwriter at Motown. To most, Barrett Strong is inevitably linked to his 1959 hit, "Money," a song that was covered by the Beatles and the Rolling Stones.

Leading the Temptations into the chartbreaking territory of "psychedelic soul" was Dennis Edwards, a former Contour, who replaced David Ruffin as lead vocalist in mid-1968. Dennis Edwards would remain lead vocalist with the Temptations until 1977, when the group left Motown and recorded two albums for Atlantic. He rejoined the group when they returned to Motown in late 1979.

"Cloud Nine" (Gordy 7081) was the first of several Whitfield-Strong compositions to penetrate the Top 10. It was followed by "Run Away Child, Running Wild" (Gordy 7084), the #1 hit "I Can't Get Next To You" (Gordy 7093), "Psychedelic Shack" (Gordy 7096), and

"Ball Of Confusion (That's What The World Is Today)" (Gordy 7099). Eddie Kendricks and Dennis Edwards can be heard sharing lead vocals on these songs.

The group's next hit would be their last with Eddie Kendricks. Featuring Eddie on lead, it was a beautiful swan song, and "Just My Imagination (Running Away With Me)" (Gordy 7105) reached the #1 spot on the pop charts in early 1971. The song was another composition from Barrett Strong and Norman Whitfield. It would also be the last release with Paul Williams, who had to leave the group on doctor's orders. Paul would die tragically two years later, an apparent suicide in a car parked not more than a few blocks from Motown's old Detroit offices.

This same line-up (Dennis Edwards, Eddie Kendricks, Paul Williams, Otis Williams, Melvin Franklin) can be heard on the four albums the Temptations recorded with the Supremes in 1968-69.

Richard Street, an original Distant and sometime member of the Monitors, rejoined the Temptations in 1971 to replace Paul Williams, and Damon Harris was recruited to fill in for Eddie Kendricks. Having lost Eddie Kendricks and Paul Williams, the group released the fairly popular "Superstar (Remember How You Got Where You Are)" (Gordy 7111) late in 1971. They rebounded with a bang in 1972 with another #1 hit, "Papa Was a Rollin' Stone" (Gordy 7121). Written by Norman Whitfield and Barrett Strong, it was Motown's first Grammy winning record ("Rhythm & Blues Song of the Year"). It was followed by the Top 10 hit, "Masterpiece" (Gordy 7126), in early 1973.

With Barrett Strong leaving Motown in 1973 and Norman Whitfield leaving in 1975, the Temptations were unable to match their former success. In 1977, they left Motown and signed with Atlantic. They released two albums, HEAR TO TEMPT YOU (Atlantic SD 19143) in 1977 and BARE BACK (Atlantic SD 19188) in 1978. BARE BACK was produced by Brian and Eddie Holland, and most of the songs on that album were co-written by the Holland brothers and others. Louis Price replaced Dennis Edwards as lead vocalist for these records. The Temptations returned to Motown and Dennis Edwards at the beginning of the decade. Their releases in 1980 and 1981 failed to make any great impact, and the group was probably languishing in the shadow of Motown's

THE TEMPTATIONS

Line-up for the group, 1963-1968: (back row from left)
Paul Williams, Eddie Kendricks, Otis Williams; (front
from left) Melvin Franklin, David Ruffin.

THE TEMPTATIONS

An unusual photo of The Temptations which pictures
original lead singer Elbridge "Al" Bryant (top) together
with his replacement, David Ruffin (second from left).
Also shown (from left): Eddie Kendricks, Melvin
Franklin, and Paul Williams.

best-selling group, the Commodores. In 1982, Rick James, a nephew of Melvin Franklin, helped to organize the Temptations "Reunion" tour and album. Always an outstanding "live" act, the Temptations made the reunion tour a success. Eddie Kendricks and David Ruffin rejoined the group for this tour; performances included a tribute to Paul Williams. A single featuring Rick James, "Standing On The Top" (Gordy 1616), was released from the album.

Dennis Edwards left the group in 1984 to pursue his own solo career, a step taken by many of the Temptations' lead singers. The current lineup (Ollie Woodson, Ron Tyson, Richard Street, Otis Williams, Melvin Franklin) continues to record and tour; they often appear sharing the bill with the Four Tops, a group whose personnel has remained constant for some thirty years.

Co-written by Ollie Woodson and Otis Williams, the 1984 release "Treat Her Like A Lady" (Gordy 1765) did well, and the group recently appeared on the soundtrack to the motion picture, "A Fine Mess." They were co-featured with the Four Tops on the summer 1986 Showtime (a cable network) special on Motown.

Temptations line-ups since 1961:

1961-1963: Otis Williams, Melvin Franklin, Elbridge "Al" Bryant (now deceased), Eddie Kendricks, Paul Williams (now deceased). NOTE: Many accounts refer to Melvin Franklin by his given name, David Melvin English, and to Otis Williams as Otis Miles. Miracle 5, 12. Gordy 7001. Melody 105 (as by The Pirates). Gordy 7010, 7015, 7020.

1963-1968: David Ruffin (lead), Eddie Kendricks (alternate lead), Paul Williams, Otis Williams, Melvin Franklin. Gordy 7028, 7032, 7035, 7038, 7040, 7043, 7047, 7049, 7054, 7055, 7057, 7061, 7063, 7065, 7068, 7072, 7074.

1968-1971: Dennis Williams (lead), Eddie Kendricks (alternate lead), Paul Williams, Otis Williams, Melvin Franklin. Gordy 7081, 7082, 7084, 7086, 7093, 7096, 7099, 7102, 7105, 7109. Motown 1137, 1142, 1150, 1153 (with Diana Ross & the Supremes).

1971-1975: Dennis Edwards, Richard Street,

Damon Harris, Otis Williams, Melvin Franklin. Gordy 7111, 7115, 7119, 7121, 7126, 7129, 7131, 7133, 7135, 7136, 7138, 7142, 7144.

1975-1977: Dennis Edwards, Richard Street, Glenn Leonard, Otis Williams, Melvin Franklin. Gordy 7146, 7150, 7151, 7152.

1977-1979: Louis Price, Richard Street, Glenn Leonard, Otis Williams, Melvin Franklin.

Group records on Atlantic during this period:

HEAR TO TEMPT YOU (Atlantic SD 19143) (1977)
In A Lifetime/I Could Never Stop Loving You (Atlantic 3436) (1977)
Let's Live In Peace/Think For Yourself (Altantic 3461) (1978) With others
BARE BACK (Atlantic SD 19188) (1978)
Bare Back/I See My Child (Atlantic 3517) (1978)
Ever Ready Love/Touch Me Again (Atlantic 3538) (1978)
I Just Don't Know How To Let You Go/Mystic Woman (Atlantic 3567) (1979)

1979-1983: Dennis Edwards, Richard Street, Glenn Leonard, Otis Williams, Melvin Franklin. Gordy 7183, 7188. Motown 1501. Gordy 7208, 7213.

NOTE: Motown begins a new numbering system starting January 1982 at 1600; Motown, Tamla, and Gordy singles retain their label designs but share the same number sequence.

1982: Eddie Kendricks, David Ruffin, Dennis Edwards, Richard Street, Glenn Leonard, Otis Williams, Melvin Franklin ("Reunion" tour and album). Gordy 1616GF (as by The Temptations Featuring Rick James).

1982-1983: Same line-up minus Eddie Kendricks and David Ruffin. Gordy 1631GF, 1654GF, 1666GF, 1683GF.

1983-1984: Dennis Edwards, Richard Street, Ron Tyson, Otis Williams, Melvin Franklin. Gordy 1707GF, 1713GF, 1720GF.

1984-1986: Ollie Woodson, Ron Tyson, Richard Street, Otis Williams, Melvin Franklin. Gordy 1765GF, 1781GF, 1789GF, 1818GF, 1834GF. Motown

1836MF (B-side by Smokey
Robinson) Gordy 1856GF.

MOTOWN DISCOGRAPHY

7/61: Oh, Mother O Mine/Romance
Without Finance (Miracle M 5)

11/61: Check Yourself/Your Wonderful
Love (Miracle M 12)

4/62: Dream Come True/Isn't She Pretty
(Gordy 7001)

1/63: Paradise/Slow Down Heart (Gordy
7010)

3/63: I Want A Love I Can See/The
Further You Look The Less You See
(Gordy 7015)

7/63: May I Have This Dance/Farewell My
Love (Gordy 7020)

1/64: The Way You Do The Things You
Do/Just Let Me Know (Gordy 7028)

3/64: MEET THE TEMPTATIONS (Gordy
G-911)

4/64: The Girl's Alright With Me/I'll Be
In Trouble (Gordy 7032)

8/64: Girl (Why You Wanna Make Me
Blue)/Baby, Baby I Need You (Gordy
7035)

12/64: My Girl/(Talking 'Bout) Nobody But
My Baby (Gordy 7038

2/65: TEMPTATIONS SING SMOKEY
(Gordy G-912)

3/65: It's Growing/What Love Has Joined
Together (Gordy 7040

6/65: Since I Lost My Baby/You've Got
to Earn It (Gordy 7043

10/65: My Baby/Don't Look Back (Gordy
7047)

11/65: THE TEMPTIN' TEMPTATIONS
(Gordy G-914)

2/66: Get Ready/Fading Away (Gordy 7049)

5/66: Ain't Too Proud To Beg/You'll Lose
A Precious Love (Gordy 7054)

6/66: GETTIN' READY (Gordy GS-918)

8/66: Beauty Is Only Skin Deep/You're Not
An Ordinary Girl) (Gordy 7055)

11/66: (I Know) I'm Losing You/I Couldn't
Cry If I Wanted To (Gordy 7057)

11/66: TEMPTATIONS GREATEST HITS
(Gordy GS-919)

3/67: TEMPTATIONS LIVE! (Gordy
GS-921)

4/67: All I Need/Sorry Is A Sorry Word
(Gordy 7061)

6/67: You're My Everything/I've Been
Good To You (Gordy 7063

7/67: THE TEMPTATIONS WITH A LOT
O' SOUL (Gordy GS-922)

9/67: (Loneliness Made Me Realize) It's
You That I Need/Don't Send Me Away
(Gordy 7065)

11/67: THE TEMPTATIONS IN A
MELLOW MOOD (Gordy GS-924)

12/67: I Wish It Would Rain/I Truly, Truly
Believe (Gordy 7068)

4/68: I Could Never Love Another (After
Loving You)/Gonna Give Her All
The Love I've Got (Gordy 7072)

4/68: THE TEMPTATIONS WISH IT
WOULD RAIN (Gordy GS-927)

7/68: Please Return Your Love To Me/
How Can I Forget (Gordy 7074)

10/68: Cloud Nine/Why Did She Have To
Leave Me (Why Did She Have To
Go) (Gordy 7081)

11/68: I'm Gonna Make You Love Me/A
Place In The Sun (Motown 1137)
With Diana Ross and The Supremes

11/68: DIANA ROSS & THE SUPREMES
JOIN THE TEMPTATIONS (Motown
MS-679) With Diana Ross and The
Supremes

12/68: TCB (Motown MS-682) With Diana
Ross and The Supremes

12/68: Rudolph, The Red Nosed Reindeer/
Silent Night (Gordy 7082)

12/68: LIVE AT THE COPA (Gordy GS-938)

1/69: Run Away Child, Running Wild/I
Need Your Lovin' (Gordy 7084)

2/69: I'll Try Something New/The Way
You Do The Things You Do (Motown
1142) With Diana Ross and The
Supremes

2/69: CLOUD NINE (Gordy GS-939)

5/69: Don't Let The Joneses Get You
Down/Since I've Lost You (Gordy
7086)

7/69: I Can't Get Next To You/Running
Away (Ain't Gonna Help You)
(Gordy 7093)

7/69: THE TEMPTATIONS SHOW (Gordy
GS-933)

8/69: Stubborn Kind Of Fellow/Try It
Baby (Motown 1150) With Diana
Ross and The Supremes

9/69: The Weight/For Better Or Worse
(Motown 1153) With Diana Ross and
The Supremes

9/69: TOGETHER (Motown MS-692) With
Diana Ross and The Supremes

9/69: PUZZLE PEOPLE (Gordy GS-949)

11/69: ON BROADWAY (Motown MS-699) With Diana Ross and The Supremes

12/69: Psychedelic Shack/That's The Way Love Is (Gordy 7096)

3/70: PSYCHEDELIC SHACK (Gordy GS-947)

5/70: Ball of Confusion (That's What The World Is Today)/It's Summer (Gordy 7099)

8/70: LIVE AT LONDON'S TALK OF THE TOWN (Gordy GS-953)

9/70: Ungena Za Ulimwengu (Unite The World)/Hum Along And Dance (Gordy 7102)

9/70: GREATEST HITS VOLUME 2 (Gordy GS-954)

11/70: CHRISTMAS CARD (Gordy GS-951)

1/71: Just My Imagination (Running Away With Me)/You Make Your Own Heaven And Hell Right Here On Earth (Gordy 7105)

4/71: SKY'S THE LIMIT (Gordy GS-957)

7/71: It's Summer/I'm The Exception To The Rule (Gordy 7109

10/71: Superstar (Remember How You Got Where You Are)/Gonna Keep On Tryin' Till I Win Your Love (Gordy 7111)

1/72: SOLID ROCK (Gordy G-961L)

2/72: Take A Look Around/Smooth Sailing (From Now On) (Gordy 7115)

6/72: Mother Nature/Funky Music Sho Nuff Turns Me On (Gordy 7119)

8/72: ALL DIRECTIONS (Gordy G-962L)

9/72: Papa Was A Rollin' Stone/Papa Was A Rollin' Stone (Instrumental) (Gordy 7121)

2/73: Masterpiece (Vocal)/Masterpiece (Instrumental) (Gordy 7126)

2/73: MASTERPIECE (Gordy G-965L

6/73: Plastic Man/Hurry Tommorrow (Gordy 7129)

8/73: ANTHOLOGY (Motown M-782A3)

8/73: Hey Girl (I Like Your Style)/Ma (Gordy 7131)

12/73: Let Your Hair Down/Ain't No Justice (Gordy 7133)

12/73: 1990 (Gordy G-966V1)

2/74: Heavenly/Zoom (Gordy 7135)

5/74: You've Got My Soul On Fire/I Need You (Gordy 7136)

12/74: Happy People/Happy People (Instrumental) (Gordy 7138)

1/75: A SONG FOR YOU (Gordy G6-969S1)

2/75: Shakey Ground/I'm A Bachelor

(Gordy 7142)

7/75: Glasshouse/The Prophet (Gordy 7144)

11/75: HOUSE PARTY (Gordy G-973V1)

1/76: Keep Holding On/What You Need Most (I Do Best Of All) (Gordy 7146)

3/76: WINGS OF LOVE (Gordy G6-971S1)

5/76: Up The Creek (Without A Paddle)/Darling, Stand By Me (Song For My Woman) (Gordy 7150)

8/76: THE TEMPTATIONS DO THE TEMPTATIONS (Gordy G6-975S1)

10/76: Who Are You/Let Me Count The Ways (I Love You) (Gordy 7152)

4/80: Power (Vocal)/Power (Instrumental) (Gordy 7183)

4/80: POWER (Gordy G8-994M1)

7/80: Struck By Lightning Twice/I'm Coming Home (Gordy 7188)

10/80: GIVE LOVE AT CHRISTMAS (Gordy G8-998M1)

11/80: Take Me Away/There's More Where That Came From (Motown 1501)

8/81: Aiming At Your Heart/The Life Of A Cowboy (Gordy 7208)

8/81: THE TEMPTATIONS (Gordy G8-1006M1)

10/81: Oh, What A Night/Isn't The Night Fantastic (Gordy 7213   0482)

4/82: Standing On The Top (Part 1)/ Standing On The Top (Part 2) (Gordy 1616GF) As by The Temptations featuring Rick James

4/82: REUNION (Gordy 6008GL)

7/82: More On The Inside/Money's Hard To Get (Gordy 1631GF)

12/82: Silent Night/Everything For Christmas (Gordy 1654GF)

2/83: SURFACE THRILLS (Gordy 6032GL)

3/83: Love On My Mind Tonight/Bring Your Body (Exercise Chant) (Gordy 1666GF)

5/83: Surface Thrills/Made In America (Gordy 1683GF)

10/83: Miss Busy Body (Get Your Body Busy)/Miss Busy Body (Get Your Body Busy) (Part 2) (Instrumental) (Gordy 1707GF)

10/83: MEET THE TEMPTATIONS/ MASTERPIECE (Motown 6079MC)

10/83: BACK TO BASICS (Gordy 6085GL)

12/83: Silent Night (6:03)/Everything For Christmas (Gordy 1713GF)

2/84: Sail Away/Isn't the Night Fantastic (Gordy 1720GF)

10/84: Treat Her Like A Lady/Isn't The

Night Fantastic (Gordy 1765GF)

10/84: TRULY FOR YOU (Gordy 6119GL

2/85: My Love Is True (Truly For You)/Set Your Love Right (Gordy 1781GF)

3/85: COMPACT COMMAND PER- FORMANCES: 17 GREATEST HITS (Gordy GCD06125GD)

5/85: How Can You Say That It's Over/I'll Keep My Light In My Window (Gordy 1789GF)

10/85: Do You Really Love Your Baby/I'll Keep My Light In My Window (Gordy 1818GF)

11/85: TOUCH ME (Gordy 6164GL)

2/86: Touch/Set You Right (Gordy 1834GF)

3/86: A Fine Mess/Wishful Thinking (Motown 1837MF) 'B' side by Smokey Robinson

6/86: Lady Soul/Put Us Together Again (Gordy 1856GF)

8/86: ANTHOLOGY (Motown MCD06189MD2)

8/86: THE TEMPTATIONS 25TH ANNIVERSARY (Motown MCD06204MD2)

8/86: TO BE CONTINUED . . . (Gordy 6207GL)

11/86: To Be Continued . . . /You're The One (Gordy 1871GF)

Unissued Motown Recordings

Who Are You/Darling, Stand By Me (Song For My Woman) (Gordy 7151)

FOR MORE INFORMATION

Bianco, David. "The Temptations," in *Soul Survivor*, No. 6 (Winter 1986-87).

Hirshey, Gerri. *Nowhere To Run*, pp. 200- 209.

Williams, Otis, with Chet Flippo. *Temptations*. (NY: Putnam, 1987).

JEAN TERRELL

Born November 26, 194?. Jean Terrell replaced Diana Ross as lead singer of the Supremes in January 1970. Jean had been discovered by Berry Gordy in 1968 while singing at Miami's Fountainbleu Hotel with her brother, the famous boxer Ernie Terrell. She signed with Motown in May 1969 as a solo artist. Jean stayed with the Supremes until she got married in 1973, and in January 1974 she was officially replaced by Scherrie Payne.

NON-MOTOWN DISCOGRAPHY

1978: I HAD TO FALL IN LOVE (A&M SP 4676)

1978: Don't Stop Reaching For The Top/ No Limit (A&M 2039)

1978: I Had To Fall In Love/Rising Cost Of Love (A&M 2064)

(See also: THE SUPREMES.)

TAMMI TERRELL

Born April 29, 1945, in Philadelphia as Thomasina Montgomery. Died March 16, 1970, of a brain tumor. Known as a solo artist and for her duets with Marvin Gaye, Tammi Terrell died tragically at the age of twenty-four. An estimated crowd of over 3,000 people attended her funeral.

In the eighteen months prior to her death, she underwent six brain operations. Her career nearly came to an end three years earlier, in 1967, when she collapsed on-stage in Virginia while singing "Your Precious Love" with Marvin Gaye. Marvin went into a period of inactivity following this incident, so great was the shock.

Tammi Terrell broke into show business at the age of eleven, appearing in talent shows at the old Earle Theater in Philadelphia. She had her first recording contract when she was fifteen with Scepter/Wand. They kept her for two years and two releases. In 1963, she joined the James Brown revue and toured with them. She also released a single on James Brown's Try Me label, "I Cried/If You Don't Think" (Try Me 28001).

She enrolled in the University of Pennsylvania and spent two years there. At this time, she married the famous boxer, Ernie Terrell, whose sister Jean would later become lead singer of the Supremes, but the marriage was a brief one. From this time forward, however, she would be known as Tammi Terrell rather than Tammi Montgomery.

In 1965, while touring with Jerry Butler, she was heard by Berry Gordy at Detroit's Twenty Grand nightclub. Gordy immediately signed her to a contract, and her first Motown single appeared later that year. After two solo singles, she was teamed with Marvin Gaye,

TAMMI TERRELL

and together they recorded several Top 10 hits. "Ain't No Mountain High Enough" (Tamla 54149), their first of eleven duets recorded on the Tamla label, reached the Top 20; it was written and produced by Ashford & Simpson. Their next four releases rose to the Top 10: "Your Precious Love" (Tamla 54156), "If I Could Build My Whole World Around You" (Tamla 54161), "Ain't Nothing Like The Real Thing" (Tamla 54163), and "You're All I Need To Get By" (Tamla 54169).

After this string, Marvin released the massive solo hit "I Heard It Through The Grapevine" (Tamla 54176) in the fall of 1968. The duet's remaining four releases were not as successful.

Tammi's headaches began in 1967 and, following her on-stage collapse, she was diagnosed as having a brain tumor. Many rumors have circulated concerning her death, largely stemming from remarks by Smokey Robinson and Marvin Gaye, but none have been confirmed. It has also been revealed that Valerie Simpson had to sing Tammi's part on nine of the eleven songs appearing on the album, EASY (Tamla 294), including the singles "Good Lovin' Ain't Easy To Come By" (Tamla 54187), "What You Gave Me" (Tamla 54187), and the posthumously released "Onion Song" (Tamla 54192).

MOTOWN DISCOGRAPHY

12/65: I Can't Believe You Love Me/Hold Me Oh My Darling (Motown 1086)

5/66: Come On And See Me/Baby Dont'cha Worry (Motown 1095)

4/67: Ain't No Mountain High Enough/ Give A Little Love (Tamla 54149) As by Marvin Gaye and Tammi Terrell

8/67: Your Precious Love/Hold Me Oh My Darling (Tamla 54156) As by Marvin Gaye and Tammi Terrell

8/67: UNITED (Tamla TS-277) As by Marvin Gaye and Tammi Terrell

10/67: What A Good Man He Is/There Are Things (Motown 1115)

11/67: If I Could Build My Whole World Around You/If This World Were Mine (Tamla 54161) As by Marvin Gaye and Tammi Terrell

3/68: Ain't Nothing Like The Real Thing/ Little Ole Boy, Little Ole Girl (Tamla 54163) As by Marvin Gaye and Tammi Terrell

7/68: You're All I Need To Get By/Two Can Have A Party (Tamla 54169) As by Marvin Gaye and Tammi Terrell

8/68: YOU'RE ALL I NEED (Tamla TS-284) As by Marvin Gaye and Tammi Terrell

9/68: Keep On Lovin' Me Honey/You Ain't Livin' Till You're Lovin' (Tamla 54173) As by Marvin Gaye and Tammi Terrell

12/68: This Old Heart Of Mine (Is Weak For You)/Just Too Much To Hope For (Motown 1138)

1/69: Good Lovin' Ain't Easy To Come By/Satisfied Feelin' (Tamla 54179) As by Marvin Gaye and Tammi Terrell

1/69: IRRESISTIBLE TAMMI TERRELL (Motown MS-652)

9/69: EASY (Tamla TS-294) As by Marvin Gaye and Tammi Terrell

11/69: What You Gave Me/How You Gonna Keep It (After You Get It) (Tamla 54187) As by Marvin Gaye and Tammi Terrell

3/70: The Onion Song/California Soul (Tamla 54192) As by Marvin Gaye and Tammi Terrell

5/70: GREATEST HITS (Tamla TS-302) As by Marvin Gaye and Tammi Terrell

10/83: You're All I Need/United (Motown 6083MC) As by Marvin Gaye and Tammi Terrell

NON-MOTOWN DISCOGRAPHY

As by Tammi Montgomery

1961: If You See Bill/It's Mine (Scepter 1224)

1962: Voice Of Experience/I Wancha To Be Sure (Wand 123)

1963: I Cried/If You Don't Think (Try Me 28001)

1964: If I Would Marry You/This Time Tomorrow (Checker 1072)

FOR MORE INFORMATION
Huston, Bruce. "Tammi Terrell Remembered," in *Soul Survivor*, Volume 1, Number 4 (Winter 1985-86).

THE UNDERDOGS

A white garage band from Grosse Pointe,

Michigan, who recorded Holland-Dozier-Holland's "Love's Gone Bad," an underground classic that didn't achieve much in the way of popularity or sales.

MOTOWN DISCOGRAPHY

1/67: Love's Gone Bad/Mo Jo Hanna (V.I.P. 25040)

THE UNDISPUTED TRUTH
Joe Haris - lead vocals
Billie Calvin
Brenda Evans

Post-Motown line-up
Taka Boom
Joe Harris
Tyrone Barkley
Calvin Stephenson

Brought into the Motown fold in 1971 by producer/songwriter Norman Whitfield, who was working on the "psychedelic soul" sound of the Temptations at the time. That year the Undisputed Truth had their most popular release, "Smiling Faces Sometimes" (Gordy 7108), a Norman Whitfield-Barrett Strong composition that went to #3 on the pop charts.

In 1972, they released "Papa Was A Rolling Stone" (Gordy 7117) a few months before the Temptations' version. This and subsequent releases didn't do very well on the charts, and the group went on to record in the late 1970s on Norman Whitfield's own label, Whitfield, distributed by Warner Brothers. Throughout their career, they have had a shifting line-up of different singers.

MOTOWN DISCOGRAPHY

3/71: Save My Love For A Rainy Day/ Since I've Lost You (Gordy 7106)
6/71: Smiling Faces Sometimes/You Got The Love I Need (Gordy 7108)
7/71: THE UNDISPUTED TRUTH (Gordy G-955L)
12/71: You Make Your Own Heaven And Hell Right Here On Earth/Ball Of Confusion (That's What The World Is Today) (Gordy 7112)
1/72: FACE TO FACE WITH THE TRUTH (Gordy G-959L)

2/72: What It Is/California Soul (Gordy 7114)
6/72: Papa Was A Rollin' Stone/Friendship Train (Gordy 7117)
11/72: Girl You're Alright/With A Little Help From My Friends (Gordy 7122)
3/73: Mama I Gotta Brand New Thing (Don't Say No)/Gotta Keep On Tryin' Till I Win Your Love (Gordy 7124)
6/73: Law Of The Land/Just My Imagination (Running Away With Me) (Gordy 7130)
6/73: LAW OF THE LAND (Gordy G-963L)
4/74: Help Yourself/What's Going On (Gordy 7134)
7/74: I'm A Fool For You/The Girl's Alright With Me (Gordy 7139)
8/74: DOWN TO EARTH (Gordy G6-968S1)
10/74: Lil' Red Ridin' Hood/Big John Is My Name (Gordy 7140)
3/75: COSMIC TRUTH (Gordy G6-970S1)
4/75: UFO's/Got To Get My Hands On Some Lovin' (Gordy 7143)
9/75: Higher Than High/Spaced Out (Gordy 7145)
10/75: HIGHER THAN HIGH (Gordy G6-972S1)
3/76: Boogie Bump Boogie/I Saw You When You Met Her (Gordy 7147)

Unissued Motown Recordings

Earthquake Shake/Spaced Out (Gordy 7141)

THE VALADIERS

Motown's first all-white recording group was recommended to Berry Gordy by his pal, Jackie Wilson. Their 1961 release, "Greetings (This Is Uncle Sam)" (Miracle 6) became a minor hit for the Monitors in 1966 during the Vietnam War.

MOTOWN DISCOGRAPHY

10/61: Greetings (This Is Uncle Sam)/Take A Chance (Miracle M 6)
5/62: While I'm Away/Because I Love Her (Gordy 7003)
1/63: I Found A Girl/You'll Be Sorry Someday (Gordy 7013)

THE VELVELETTES

EARL VAN DYKE

EARL VAN DYKE

From 1962-1974 he was a keyboardist, prominent studio musician, and leader of Motown's house band for revues and various tours. He also released singles and albums for Motown under his own name.

MOTOWN DISCOGRAPHY

9/64: (Soul Stomp/Hot 'N' Tot (Soul 35006)
1965: I Can't Help Myself (Sugar Pie, Honey Bunch)/How Sweet It Is (To Be Loved By You) (Soul 35014) As by Earl Van Dyke and the Soul Brothers
11/65: The Flick (Part I)/The Flick (Part II) (Soul 35018) As by Earl Van Dyke and the Soul Brothers
12/66: 6 By 6/There Is No Greater Love (Soul 35028) As by Earl Van Dyke and the Motown Brass
3/69: Runaway Child, Running Wild/ Gonna Give Her All The Love I've Got (Soul 35059)
9/70: THE EARL OF FUNK (Soul SS-715)

Unissued Motown Recordings

All For You/Too Many Fish In The Sea (Soul 35009) As by Earl Van Dyke and the Soul Brothers

THE VELS
Gloria Williams - lead vocals
Rosalyn Ashford
Annette Sterling (later Annette Sterling Beard)
Martha Reeves

The Vels were an early version of Martha & The Vandellas, releasing one single in 1962 on Berry Gordy's Melody label, "There He Is (At My Door)/You'll Never Cherish A Love So True" (Melody 103). Gloria Williams sang lead at this point, but left the group after this particular record flopped. Their next release would be on the Gordy label as by Martha & The Vandellas.

MOTOWN DISCOGRAPHY

10/62: You'll Never Cherish A Love So True ('Till You Lose It)/There He Is (At My Door) (Melody 103)

(See also DEL-PHIS; MARTHA & THE VANDELLAS.)

THE VELVELETTES
Caldin ("Carolyn" or "Cal") Gill
Mildred Gill
Bertha Barbee
Norma Barbee
Betty Kelley (left 1963 to join Martha & the Vandellas)
Sandra Tilley (joined 1965)
Annette McMillan (joined 1965)

The Velvelettes were formed around 1962 in Kalamazoo, Michigan, where the Gill sisters and the Barbee cousins met at Western Michigan University. The Barbees had some previous experience in a family group that recorded a one-off 1957 single on the Detroit-based Stepp label, "Que Pasa?/The Wind" (Stepp 236), that was produced by William "Mickey" Stevenson, who would later be in charge of Motown's A&R department.

Robert Bullock, a nephew of Berry Gordy, brought the Velvelettes to Detroit to audition for Motown in 1963. While they didn't pass Motown's audition at this time, they did meet Mickey Stevenson at the audition and ended up releasing a single on the I.P.G. (Independent Producers Group) label that was produced by Stevenson.

After singing background at Motown recording sessions, the Velvelettes released their first single for Motown on the V.I.P. label in 1964. Written by Norman Whitfield and Mickey Stevenson, "Needle In A Haystack" (V.I.P. 25007) was recorded as a trio (Cal Gill, Bertha Barbee, Norma Barbee), and reached #45 on the pop charts. It would be their most popular song. The same line-up can be heard on the follow-up, "He Was Really Saying Somethin'" (V.I.P. 25013), which only reached #64 on the pop charts in 1965 but fared better with black audiences, as reflected on the soul and r&b charts.

Following these moderate successes, the group's line-up changed to Cal Gill, Sandra Tilley, and Annette McMillan, who recorded "Lonely Lonely Girl Am I/I'm The Exception To The Rule" (V.I.P. 25017). This same line-up recorded the group's next release, "A Bird In The Hand (Is Worth Two In The Bush)/Since

You've Been Loving Me" (V.I.P. 25030). Both records were released in 1965.

In 1966, "These Things Will Keep Me Loving You" (Soul 35025) was a moderate success on the r&b charts. It was a recording that dated back to the group's days as a quartet, but Motown also added the voices of Sandra Tilley and Annette McMillan. The group carried on with Cal Gill as leader and various backing vocalists until 1969, when she married Motown artist Richard Street, who would replace Paul Williams in the Temptations in 1971. The group disbanded at this point.

In 1984, the Gills and Barbees reunited to form the Velvelettes for Motown revival shows and various live performances.

MOTOWN DISCOGRAPHY

9/64: Needle In A Haystack/Should I Tell Them (V.I.P. 25007)

12/64: He Was Really Sayin' Somethin'/Throw A Farewell Kiss) (V.I.P. 25013)

5/65: Lonely Lonely Girl Am I/I'm The Exception To The Rule) (V.I.P. 25017)

11/65: A Bird In The Hand (Is Worth Two In The Bush)/Since You've Been Loving Me (V.I.P. 25030)

4/66: These Things Will Keep Me Loving You/Since You've Been Loving Me (V.I.P. 25034)

8/66: These Things Will Keep Me Loving You/Since You've Been Loving Me (Soul 35025)

Unissued Motown Recordings

A Bird In The Hand (Is Worth Two In The Bush)/Since You've Been Loving Me (V.I.P. 25021)
THE VELVELETTES (V.I.P. VIPS-401)

NON-MOTOWN DISCOGRAPHY

1963: There He Goes/That's The Reason Why (I.P.G. 1002)

FOR MORE INFORMATION
Towne, Steve and Max Oates. "The Velvelettes: Motown's Earthy Soulful Girl Group Sound," in *Goldmine*, September 12, 1986.

"The Velvelettes," in *Soul Survivor*, No. 6 (Winter 1986-87).

JR. WALKER & THE ALL STARS
Jr. Walker (born Autrey DeWalt, Jr., in 1942, in Blythesville, Arkansas) - tenor sax, piano, vocals
Willie Woods - guitar
Vic Thomas - organ
James Graves - drums

From the time of their first Top 10 pop hit, "Shotgun" (Soul 35008), in 1965, this was Motown's top instrumental group, noted for Jr. Walker's distinctive tenor sax sound. They began in the early 1960s with Harvey Fuqua's label, Harvey, and came to Motown with Harvey Fuqua in 1963 (along with such other groups as the Spinners). Their second Top 10 pop hit came in 1969 with "What Does It Take (To Win Your Love)" (Soul 35062), a song that marked a radical departure in style for the group.

Jr. Walker left Motown in mid-1978 to sign with ex-Motown producer Norman Whitfield's label, Whitfield (distributed by Warner Brothers). He returned to Motown in 1983. In 1981, he played sax on Foreigner's "Urgent."

MOTOWN DISCOGRAPHY

8/64: Satan's Blues/Monkey Jump (Soul 35003)

1/65: Shotgun/Hot Cha (Soul 35008) Some early copies give title as "Shot Gun" and group as Jr. Walker and All The Stars

5/65: Do The Boomerang/Tune Up (Soul 35012)

5/65: SHOTGUN (Soul SS-701)

7/65: Shake And Finger Pop/Cleo's Back (Soul 35013) Later copies give title as "Shake And Fingerpop"

12/65: Cleo's Mood/Baby You Know You Ain't Right) (Soul 35017)

3/66: (I'm A) Road Runner/Shoot Your Shot (Soul 35015)

3/66: SOUL SESSION (Soul S-702)

7/66: How Sweet It Is (To Be Loved By You)/Nothing But Soul (Soul 35024)

8/66: Money (That's What I Want) Part 1/Money (That's What I Want) Part 2 (Soul 35026)

JR. WALKER

Photo courtesy Peter Benjaminson.

8/66: ROAD RUNNER (Soul SS-703)
1/67: Pucker Up Buttercup/Anyway You Wanna (Soul 35030)
6/67: Shoot Your Shot/Ain't That The Truth (Soul 35036)
9/67: JR. WALKER & THE ALL STARS LIVE! (Soul S-705)
11/67: Come See About Me/Sweet Soul (Soul 35041)
7/68: Hip City (Pt. 1)/Hip City (Pt. 2) (Soul 35048)
12/68: Home Cookin/Mutiny (Soul 35055)
1/69: HOME COOKIN' (Soul SS-710)
4/69: What Does It Take (To Win You Love)/Brainwasher (Part 1) (Soul 35062)
8/69: JR. WALKER & THE ALL STARS GREATEST HITS (Soul SS-718)
10/69: These Eyes/I've Got To Find A Way To Win Maria Back (Soul 35067)
11/69: GOTTA HOLD ON TO THIS FEELING (Soul SS-721)
1/70: Gotta Hold On To This Feeling/Clinging To The Thought That She's Coming Back (Soul 35070)
5/70: JR. WALKER & THE ALL STARS LIVE (Soul SS-725)
6/70: Do You See My Love (For You Growing)/Groove And Move) (Soul 35073)
9/70: A GASSSSSSSSSS (Soul SS-726)
11/70: Holly Holy/Carry Your Own Load (Soul 35081)
7/71: Take Me Girl, I'm Ready/Right On Brothers And Sisters (Soul 35084)
7/71: RAINBOW FUNK (Soul S-732L)
11/71: Way Back Home (Vocal)/Way Back Home (Instrumental) (Soul 35090)
12/71: MOODY JR. (Soul S-733L)
2/72: Walk In The Night/I Don't Want To Do Wrong) (Soul 35095)
6/72: Groove Thang/Me And My Family (Soul 35097)
1/73: Gimme That Beat (Part 1)/Gimme That Beat (Part 2) (Soul 35104)
4/73: PEACE & UNDERSTANDING IS HARD TO FIND (Soul S-738L)
5/73: I Don't Need No Reason/Country Boy (Soul 35106)
7/73: Peace And Understanding (Is Hard To Find)/Soul Clappin' (Soul 35108)
5/74: Dancin' Like They Do On (Soul Train)/I Ain't That Easy To Lose (Soul 35110)
7/74: ANTHOLOGY (Motown M7-786R2)

5/75: What Does It Take (To Win Your Love)/Country Boy (Motown 1352)
12/75: I'm So Glad/Soul Clappin (Soul 35116) As by Jr. Walker
1/76: HOT SHOT (Soul S6-745S1)
6/76: Hot Shot/You Ain't No Ordinary Woman (Soul 35118) As by Jr. Walker
6/76: SAX APPEAL (Soul S747S1) As by Jr. Walker
10/76: WHOPPER BOPPER SHOW STOPPER (Soul S6-748S1) As by Jr. Walker
8/77: Hard Love/Whopper Bopper Show Stopper (Soul 35122) As by Jr. Walker
5/78: . . . SMOOTH (Soul S7-750R1) As by Jr. Walker
7/83: BLOW THE HOUSE DOWN (Motown 6053ML) As by Jr. Walker
8/83: Blow The House Down/Ball Baby (Instrumental) (Motown 1689MF) As by Jr. Walker
8/86: COMPACT COMMAND PER- FORMANCES: 19 GREATEST HITS) (Motown MCD6203MD)

Unissued Motown Recordings

JR. WALKER & THE ALL STARS (Soul S6-742S1)
Rise And Shine/Closer Than Close (Motown 1708MF)
You Are The Sunshine Of My Life/ Until You Come Back To Me (That's What I'm Gonna Do) (Soul 35114) As by Jr. Walker

NON-MOTOWN DISCOGRAPHY

19??: 2-2-5 Special/ (Von 704) As by The All Stars
1962: Twist Lackawanna/Willie's Blues (Harvey 113)
1962: Cleo's Mood/Brain Washer (Harvey 117)
1963: Brainwasher/Good Rockin' (Harvey 119)
1979: Back Street Boogie/Don't Let Me Go Astray (Whitfield 8861 or 8862)
1979: Hole In The Wall/Wishing On A Star (Whitfield 49052)
1979: BACK STREET BOOGIE (Whitfield WHK 3331)

FOR MORE INFORMATION
Hirshey, Gerri. *Nowhere To Run*, pp. 210-

MARY WELLS

MARY WELLS

Born May 13, 1943, in Detroit. She graduated from Detroit's Northwestern High School, where she was a featured soloist in the choir. In 1960, she obtained an audition with Berry Gordy through her friendship with Robert Bateman, a member of the Satintones who would later become Motown's chief engineer. She sang "Bye Bye Baby," a song she had written when she was fifteen, and was immediately signed to a contract. This song became her first release (Motown 1003); background vocals were by the Andantes.

From 1962 to 1964, she had four Top 10 hits, all written and produced by Smokey Robinson. The first three came out in 1962: "The One Who Really Loves You" (Motown 1024), "You Beat Me To The Punch" (Motown 1032), and "Two Lovers" (Motown 1035). "The One Who Really Loves You" marked Smokey's debut as a producer. He also wrote and produced her 1963 release, "What's Easy For Two Is So Hard For One" (Motown 1048), which reached #29 on the pop charts. The flip side of this two-sided hit was "You Lost The Sweetest Boy," a Holland-Dozier-Holland song that foreshadowed the material they would write for the Supremes in 1964.

Her biggest hit, "My Guy" (Motown 1056), charted in the spring of 1964. It would be the last song produced for her by Smokey. Largely on the strength of this #1 hit, she was named the top rhythm and blues songstress in *Billboard's* 1965 poll of disc jockeys. Later that year, she would accompany the Beatles on a tour of Great Britain after recording some duets with Marvin Gaye. During her tour with the Beatles, it was reported that she was afflicted with spinal meningitis, a condition she'd had since the age of twelve. In September 1964, when Mary Wells was just twenty-one, she left Motown and signed a four-year, $500,000 contract with Twentieth-Century Fox Records. At the time, she was married to Herman Griffin, a singer that had been associated with Berry Gordy since his days as an independent producer. Her stay at Fox was a short one, and in October 1965 there was an amicable parting. By that time, it was reported that she had contracted tuberculosis.

Fox would later release an album of Lennon-McCartney songs titled MARY WELLS SINGS LOVE SONGS TO THE BEATLES.

In August 1966, she married Cecil Womack, brother of vocalist Bobby Womack. After leaving Fox, she had signed with ATCO. She took some time off in 1967 for the birth of her first son, Cecil (December 29, 1967), and in 1968 was recording for Jubilee. In 1969, while expecting her second child, she returned to Great Britain for a tour.

Mary Wells has recorded for other labels since 1970, including Epic and Warner Brothers. She appeared on Motown's 25th Anniversary Special in 1983, and currently resides in Los Angeles with her husband and family of seven children. She has been performing before live audiences in the mid-1980s, often as part of a Motown revival show.

MOTOWN DISCOGRAPHY

12/60: Bye Bye Baby/Please Forgive Me (Motown 1003)

7/61: I Don't Want To Take A Chance/I'm So Sorry (Motown 1011)

9/61: Strange Love/Come To Me (Motown 1016)

11/61: BYE, BYE BABY, I DON'T WANT TO TAKE A CHANCE (Motown MLP-600)

2/62: The One Who Really Loves You/I'm Gonna Stay (Motown 1024)

8/62: You Beat Me To The Punch/Old Love (Let's Try It Again) (Motown 1032)

9/62: THE ONE WHO REALLY LOVES YOU (Motown MT-605)

10/62: Two Lovers/Operator (Motown 1035)

2/63: Laughing Boy/Two Wrongs Don't Make A Right (Motown 1039)

2/63: TWO LOVERS AND OTHER GREAT HITS (Motown MT-607)

5/63: What Love Has Joined Together/Your Old Standby (Motown 1042)

8/63: What's Easy For Two Is So Hard For One/You Lost The Sweetest Boy (Motown 1048)

9/63: RECORDED LIVE ON STAGE (Motown MT-611)

3/64: My Guy/Oh Little Boy (What Did You Do To Me) (Motown 1056)

4/64: Once Upon A Time/What's The Matter With You Baby (Motown 1057)
As by Marvin Gaye and Mary Wells

KIM WESTON

4/64: TOGETHER (Motown MLP-613) As by Marvin Gaye and Mary Wells

4/64: MARY WELLS' GREATEST HITS (Motown MS-616)

5/64: MY GUY (Motown MLP-617)

11/66: VINTAGE STOCK (Motown MS-653)

2/86: COMPACT COMMAND PER-FORMANCES: 22 GREATEST HITS (Motown MCD06171MD)

Unissued Motown Recordings

When I'm Gone/Guarantee (For A Lifetime) (Motown 1061)

Whisper You Love Me/I'll Be Available (Motown 1065)

NON-MOTOWN DISCOGRAPHY

1964: Ain't It The Truth/Stop Takin' Me For Granted (20th-Century Fox 544)

1964: Use Your Head/Everlovin' Boy (20th-Century Fox 555)

1965: Never, Never Leave Me/Why Don't You Let Yourself Go (20th-Century Fox 570)

1965: He's A Lover/I'm Learning (20th-Century Fox 590)

1965: Me Without You/I'm Sorry (20th-Century Fox 606)

1965: MARY WELLS SINGS LOVE SONGS TO THE BEATLES (20th-Century Fox)

1965: I Should Have Known Better/Please Please Me (20th-Century Fox 6619)

1966: Dear Lover/Can't You See (You're Losing Me) (ATCO 6392)

1966: Such A Sweet Thing/Keep Me In Suspense (ATCO 6423)

1966: THE TWO SIDES OF MARY WELLS (ATCO 33-199)

1966: Fancy Free/Me and My Baby (ATCO 6436)

1967: Coming Home/Hey You Set My Soul On Fire (ATCO 6469)

1968: The Doctor/Two Lovers History (Jubilee 5621)

1968: Woman In Love/Can't Get Away From Your Love (Jubilee 5629)

1968: Don't Look Back/500 Miles (Jubilee 5639)

1969: Can You Dig The Way I Feel/Love Shooting Bandit (Jubilee 5684)

1970: Sweet Love/It Must Be (Jubilee 5695)

19??: SERVIN' UP SOME SOUL (Jubilee JGS 8018)

1971: Mr. Tough/Never Give A Man The World (Jubilee 5718)

1981: Gigolo/Let's Mix It Up (Epic 02663) 12"

1981: Gigolo/I'm Changing My Ways (Epic 02664)

1981: IN AND OUT OF LOVE (Epic ARE 37540)

1982: These Arms/Spend The Night With Me (Epic 02855)

FOR MORE INFORMATION

Betrock, Alan. *Girl Groups*, pp. 58-64.

Hirshey, Gerri. *Nowhere To Run*, pp. 140-5.

KIM WESTON

Born December 20, 1939, in Detroit. Graduated from Detroit's Miller High School. Kim Weston was discovered by Johnny Thornton, a cousin of the Holland brothers, who got her first job at Detroit's Veteran's Memorial Building in 1962. He was instrumental in getting her a contract with Motown, and her first Motown record came out in 1963, "Love Me All The Way" (Tamla 54076). In 1964, she subbed for the Supremes at Detroit's 20 Grand nightclub, where she made a great impression. In 1965, she recorded the Holland-Dozier-Holland composition, "Take Me In Your Arms (Rock Me A Little While)" (Gordy 7046). While she recorded as a solo artist with Motown until the end of 1966, she is perhaps better known for her duets with Marvin Gaye, notably "It Takes Two" (Tamla 54141), released just before she left the company.

While she was with Motown, Kim toured Las Vegas, Reno, and Lake Tahoe with Billy Eckstine in 1965. Around this time, she also toured England with Gerry & the Pacemakers, the Kinks, and Gene Pitney. In 1966, she appeared on the television show, "Hullabaloo." Married to Motown producer William "Mickey" Stevenson, Kim Weston and her husband both left Motown in January 1967. Stevenson at that time was the head of Motown's A&R department, and left to establish his own label, People. In April, Kim signed with MGM Records, and Mickey Stevenson was offered a reported million-dollar contract to improve MGM's subsidiary, Venture Records. Kim's departure from Motown also marked a change in her singing style to one that included show tunes and the standards as well as her Motown-era songs.

A versatile performer who has also been involved in the theater, Kim introduced a new album, THIS IS AMERICA (MGM SE4561), while headlining at the Coconut Grove in Los Angeles in March 1968. This album contains the song, "Lift Every Voice and Sing," with words written by the poet James Weldon Johnson, later set to music by J. Rosamond Johnson. Almost immediately, this song became the un-official "Black National Anthem."

Other live performances following her departure from Motown included dates with the Count Basie Orchestra in New York (April 1967), Las Vegas in August 1968 with Harry Belafonte, and a summer of 1972 performance at the Watts-Stax Festival in the Los Angeles Coliseum that was included in the 1973 film, "Wattstax" (Columbia Pictures). In 1968, she starred in the road company version of "Hallelujah Baby" with Adam Wade and Julius LaRosa, but had to drop out after a few performances because of illness. She would later become involved in community theater and have her own plays produced.

Throughout her career, Kim has been involved in public service, fund-raisers, and youth training. In the summer of 1970, she gave concerts with the Reverend Jesse Jackson in connection with SCLC's Operation Breadbasket. In 1976, she founded the Festival of the Performing Arts, a summer program for young people in Detroit. In 1984, she led the eighth annual Festival for Performing Arts group at Detroit's Afro-American Festival. Her versatility is also exemplified by the 1976 album she recorded with a group known as the Hastings Street Jazz Experience, re-creating the Detroit jazz sound of the 1930's and 1940's.

MOTOWN DISCOGRAPHY

6/63: Love Me All The Way/It Should Have Been Me (Tamla 54076)

8/63: Just Loving You/Another Train Coming (Tamla 54085)

7/64: Looking For The Right Guy/Feel Alright Tonight (Tamla 54100)

9/64: What Good Am I Without You/I Want You 'Round (Tamla 54104) As

by Marvin Gaye and Kim Weston

10/64: A Little More Love/Go Ahead And Laugh (Tamla 54106)

1/65: I'm Still Loving You/Go Ahead And Laugh (Tamla 54110)

5/65: A Thrill A Moment/I'll Never See My Love Again (Gordy 7041)

9/65: Take Me In Your Arms (Rock Me A Little While)/Don't Compare Me With Her (Gordy 7046)

3/66: Helpless/A Love Like Yours (Don't Come Knocking Every Day) (Gordy 7050)

8/66: TAKE TWO (Tamla TS-270) As by Marvin Gaye and Kim Weston

12/66: It Takes Two/It's Got To Be A Miracle (This Thing Called Love) (Tamla 54141) As by Marvin Gaye and Kim Weston

Unissued Motown Recordings

MARVIN GAYE & KIM WESTON
SIDE BY SIDE (Tamla 260) As by Marvin Gaye and Kim Weston
TAKE ME IN YOUR ARMS (Gordy GS-934)

NON-MOTOWN DISCOGRAPHY

1967: I Got What You Need/Someone Like You (MGM K-13720)

1967: That's Groovy/Land of Tomorrow (MGM K-13804)

1967: FOR THE FIRST TIME (MGM E/SE-4477)

1967: Nobody/You're Just The Kind Of Guy (MGM 13881)

1968: THIS IS AMERICA (MGM SE 4561)

1968: Lift Every Voice And Sing/This Is America (MGM 13927)

1968: The Impossible Dream/When Johnny Comes Marching Home (MGM 13928)

1968: I Will Understand/Thankful (MGM 13992)

1970: Danger, Heartbreak Ahead/I'll Be Thinkin' (People 1001)

1972: Little By Little And Bit By Bit/

19??: KIM KIM KIM (Volt VOS-6014)

NORMAN WHITFIELD

Songwriter-producer. Soul-funk producer Norman Whitfield is perhaps best known for creating the "psychedelic soul" sound for the

Temptations. His association with Motown began in the early 1960s as a songwriter. Written in collaboration with Smokey Robinson, "The Further You Look, The Less You See" (Gordy 7015) was recorded by the Temptations and released in 1963.

From 1964 to 1966, the Temptations recorded several smash hits written and produced by Smokey Robinson. Whitfield took over the Temptations' production in 1966 with "Ain't Too Proud To Beg" (Gordy 7054). Beginning with that song, Norman Whitfield and Eddie Holland would co-write a string of hits for the Temptations, including "Beauty Is Only Skin Deep" (Gordy 7055), "(I Know) I'm Losing You" (Gordy 7057), "(Loneliness Made Me Realize) It's You That I Need" (Gordy 7065), and "I Wish It Would Rain" (Gordy 7068), the latter with Roger Penzabene.

In mid-1968, Dennis Edwards replaced David Ruffin as lead vocalist with the Temptations and Norman Whitfield teamed with Barrett Strong to write songs for the Temptations and lead them to the forefront of "psychedelic soul." "Cloud Nine" (Gordy 7081) was the first of several Whitfield-Strong compositions to penetrate the Top 10. It was followed by "Run Away Child, Running Wild" (Gordy 7084), the #1 hit "I Can't Get Next To You" (Gordy 7093), "Psychedelic Shack" (Gordy 7096), and "Ball of Confusion (That's What The World Is Today)" (Gordy 7099).

During the 1965-70 period, Whitfield also produced and wrote songs for Gladys Knight & the Pips, including "I Heard It Through The Grapevine" (Soul 35039) and "Friendship Train" (Soul 35068), both co-written with Barrett Strong. Whitfield also produced Marvin Gaye's popular version of "I Heard It Through The Grapevine" (Tamla 54176). He produced psychedelic versions for Rare Earth of songs he and Smokey had written for the Temptations, including "Get Ready" (Rare Earth 5012) and "(I Know) I'm Losing You" (Rare Earth 5017).

Continuing with the Temptations into the 1970s, Whitfield and Strong wrote Eddie Kendricks' last song with the Temptations, the #1 hit "Just My Imagination (Running Away With Me)" (Gordy 7105). This was followed by the fairly popular "Superstar (Remember How You Got Where You Are)" (Gordy 7111) late in 1971. In 1972, they wrote the #1 hit, "Papa Was A Rollin' Stone" (Gordy 7121), Motown's first Grammy winning record ("Rhythm & Blues Song of the Year"). It was followed by the Top 10 hit "Masterpiece" (Gordy 7126) in early 1973.

In 1973, Barrett Strong left Motown, and Whitfield was unable to match his earlier successes with the Temptations. In 1975, Whitfield also left Motown, and by 1977 had established his own label, Whitfield Records, with distribution by Warner Brothers. Former Motown group, The Undisputed Truth, was one group that recorded for his label.

STEVIE WONDER

Born May 13, 1950, in Saginaw, Michigan. Christened Stevland (or Steveland) Judkins (after father's surname); also uses Hardaway (mother's maiden name) and Morris (on birth certificate) as last name. Stevie's family moved to Detroit at an early age. His connection to Motown was through Ronnie White of the Miracles, a cousin of one of Stevie's friends. Ronnie White arranged a meeting with Berry Gordy, and Stevie entered the studio at age eleven. His first six singles were released as by "Little Stevie Wonder." With the seventh, "Hey Harmonica Man" (Tamla 54096), the "Little" was dropped.

His first hit, "Fingertips, Pt. 2" (Tamla 54080), was one of his biggest, reaching the #1 spot on the pop charts in 1963. It was recorded live at the Regal Theater in Chicago. In 1963, his album 12 YEAR OLD GENIUS (Tamla 240), was Motown's first #1 pop album, foreshadowing Stevie's immense popularity, not to mention critical acclaim.

In 1964, Stevie appeared in two movies, "Muscle Beach Party" and "Bikini Beach," both starring Frankie Avalon and Annette Funicello. That same year, the Rolling Stones opened for Stevie on his tour. In 1965, he toured as part of the first British Motortown revue to herald the debut of the Tamla Motown label in England.

Throughout his spectacular career with Motown, Stevie has had several #1 pop hits, including "Superstition" (Tamla 54226), "You Are The Sunshine Of My Life" (Tamla 54232), "You Haven't Done Nothin'" (Tamla 54252), "I Wish" (Tamla 54274), "Sir Duke" (Tamla 54281), the duet with Paul McCartney, "Ebony and Ivory" (Columbia 02860), and "I Just Called

STEVIE WONDER

Released in the U.S. only as a 12-inch record, this
single from Stevie Wonder's Wondirection label
(shown here in its Canadian 7-inch release) was
originally assigned a number in the Tamla label
sequence.

To Say I Love You" (Motown 1745MF). "Part Time Lover" (Tamla 1808TF), the first single from the Grammy-winning album IN SQUARE CIRCLE (Tamla 6134TF), became his twenty-sixth Top 10 hit. Only two artists have had more, Elvis Presley (thirty-eight) and the Beatles (thirty-three).

Stevie has been awarded more Grammys than any other Motown artist (sixteen through the 1987 award ceremonies) for his songs, albums, and vocals, starting with 1973 Album of the Year for INNERVISIONS (Tamla 326) through 1985 Rhythm & Blues Vocal-Male for IN SQUARE CIRCLE. In March 1985, he won an Oscar for Best Original Song for "I Just Called To Say I Love You," theme song from the film "Woman In Red."

Stevie is one of the few Motown artists to have been granted complete artistic freedom. In 1970 he began producing his own albums, and the next year he renegotiated his contract to get complete artistic control over his own recordings. His 1972 album, TALKING BOOK (Tamla 319) was the first album by an American artist to enter the *Billboard* charts at #1. Songs from the album were introduced during the 1972 tour, when he opened for the Rolling Stones, thus reaching a wider audience. The album resulted in two #1 hits, "Superstition" (Tamla 54226) and "You Are The Sunshine Of My Life" (Tamla 54232).

Stevie married Syreeta Wright in 1970, but they divorced after eighteen months. Syreeta is also a Motown recording artist. In 1971, he recorded material in New York for his next four albums: MUSIC OF MY MIND (Tamla 314), TALKING BOOK (Tamla 332), INNERVISIONS (Tamla 326), and FULFILLINGNESS' FIRST FINALE (Tamla 332). The latter two albums, released in 1973 and 1974 respectively, each won five Grammys; and FULFILLINGNESS' FIRST FINALE became the #1 album within three weeks of its release.

In 1973, Stevie was involved in a serious car accident that left him without a sense of smell. He was in a coma for three days. Following the accident and his recovery, his songs began to reflect deeper concerns.

Stevie signed a new contract with Motown in 1976 worth a reported $13 million. His next album was the successful and influential double-album, SONGS IN THE KEY OF LIFE. This was followed by the experimental but commercially disastrous JOURNEY THROUGH THE SECRET LIFE OF PLANTS (Tamla 371). It would not be until 1984 that he would have another #1 single, although "Send One Your Love" (Tamla 54303), "Master Blaster (Jammin')" (Tamla 54317), and "That Girl" (Tamla 1602TF) would all reach the Top Ten in the interim.

Blind since birth, Stevie has long been involved in the social issues of his time. Most recently, he was active in the U.S.A. for Africa's "We Are The World" fund-raising for hunger in Africa; the drive to get Rev. Martin Luther King, Jr.'s birthday recognized as a national holiday in the U.S.; several anti-drunk driving campaigns; the anti-apartheid movement in the U.S., and similar causes.

MOTOWN DISCOGRAPHY

5/62: I Call It Pretty Music, But The Old People Call It The Blues, Part 1/I Call It Pretty Music, But The Old People Call It The Blues, Part 2 (Tamla 54061) As by Little Stevie Wonder

10/62: La La La La La/Little Water Boy (Tamla 54070) As by Little Stevie Wonder

12/62: Contract Of Love/Sunset (Tamla 54074) As by Little Stevie Wonder

5/63: Fingertips - Part 1/Fingertips - Part 2 (Tamla 54080) As by Little Stevie Wonder

5/63: 12 YEAR OLD GENIUS (RECORDED LIVE) (Tamla TM-240) As by Little Stevie Wonder

7/63: TRIBUTE TO UNCLE RAY (Tamla TM-232) As by Little Stevie Wonder

7/63: THE JAZZ SOUL OF LITTLE STEVIE (Tamla TM-233) As by Little Stevie Wonder

9/63: Workout Stevie, Workout/Money Talk (Tamla 54086) As by Little Stevie Wonder

12/63: Castles In The Sand/Thank You (For Loving Me All The Way) (Tamla 54090) As by Little Stevie Wonder

12/63: WITH A SONG IN MY HEART (Tamla TM-250)

5/64: Hey Harmonica Man/This Little Girl (Tamla 54096)

7/64: STEVIE AT THE BEACH (Tamla TM-255)

9/64: Sad Boy/Happy Street (Tamla 54103)

STEVIE WONDER

3/65: Kiss Me Baby/Tears In Vain (Tamla 54114)

8/65: High Heel Sneakers/Music Talk (Tamla 54119)

8/65: High Heel Sneakers/Funny How Time Slips Away (Tamla 54119)

11/65: Uptight (Everything's Alright)/Purple Rain Drops (Tamla 54124)

3/66: Nothing's Too Good For My Baby/With A Child's Heart (Tamla 54130)

5/66: UP TIGHT (Tamla TS-268)

6/66: Blowin' In The Wind/Ain't That Asking For Trouble (Tamla 54136)

10/66: A Place In The Sun/Sylvia (Tamla 54139)

11/66: Some Day At Christmas/The Miracles Of Christmas (Tamla 54142)

11/66: DOWN TO EARTH (Tamla TS-272)

2/67: Travelin' Man/Hey Love (Tamla 54147)

5/67: I Was Made To Love Her/Hold Me (Tamla 54151)

9/67: I'm Wondering/Everytime I See You I Go Wild (Tamla 54157)

9/67: I WAS MADE TO LOVE HER (Tamla TS-279)

12/67: SOMEDAY AT CHRISTMAS (Tamla TS-281)

3/68: Shoo-Be-Doo-Be-Doo-Da-Day/Why Don't You Lead Me To Love (Tamla 54165)

3/68: STEVIE WONDER'S GREATEST HITS (Tamla TS-282)

6/68: You Met Your Match/My Girl (Tamla 54168)

8/68: Alfie/More Than A Dream (Gordy 7076) As by Eivets Rednow

10/68: For Once In My Life/Angie Girl (Tamla 54174)

12/68: ALFIE (Gordy GS-932) As by Evits Rednow

12/68: FOR ONCE IN MY LIFE (Tamla TS-291)

1/69: My Cherie Amour/Don't Know Why I Love You (Tamla 54180)

9/69: Yester-Me, Yester-You, Yesterday/I'd Be A Fool Right Now (Tamla 54188)

9/69: MY CHERIE AMOUR (Tamla TS-296)

1/70: Never Had A Dream Come True/Somebody Knows, Somebody Cares (Tamla 54191)

3/70: LIVE (Tamla TS-298)

6/70: Signed, Sealed, Delivered I'm Yours/I'm More Than Happy (I'm Satisfied) (Tamla 54196)

8/70: SIGNED, SEALED & DELIVERED (Tamla TS-304)

9/70: Heaven Help Us All/I Gotta Have A Song (Tamla 54200)

2/71: We Can Work It Out/Never Dreamed You'd Leave In Summer (Tamla 54202)

4/71: WHERE I'M COMING FROM (Tamla TS-308)

7/71: If You Really Love Me/Think Of Me As Your Soldier (Tamla 54208)

11/71: What Christmas Means To Me/Bedtime For Toys (Tamla 54214)

11/71: GREATEST HITS VOL. 2 (Tamla T-313L)

2/72: MUSIC OF MY MIND (Tamla T-314L)

4/72: Superwoman (Where Were You When I Needed You)/I Love Every Little Thing About You (Tamla 54216)

8/72: Keep On Running/Evil (Tamla 54223)

10/72: Superstition/You've Got It Bad Girl (Tamla 54226)

11/72: TALKING BOOK (Tamla T-319L)

2/73: You Are The Sunshine Of My Life/Tuesday Heartbreak (Tamla 54232)

7/73: Higher Ground/Too High (Tamla 54235)

7/73: INNERVISIONS (Tamla T-326L)

10/73: Living For The City/Visions (Tamla 54242)

3/74: Don't You Worry 'Bout A Thing/Blame It On The Sun (Tamla 54245)

7/74: You Haven't Done Nothin'/Big Brother (Tamla 54252)

7/74: FULFILLINGNESS' FIRST FINALE (Tamla T6-332S1)

10/74: Boogie On Reggae Woman/Seems So Long (Tamla 54254)

9/76: SONGS IN THE KEY OF LIFE (Tamla T13-340C2)

11/76: I Wish/You And I (Tamla 54274)

3/77: Sir Duke/He's Misstra Know-It-All (Tamla 54281)

8/77: Another Star/Creepin' (Tamla 54286)

10/77: As/Contusion (Tamla 54291)

12/77: LOOKING BACK (Motown M9-804A3)

10/78: SOMEDAY AT CHRISTMAS (Tamla T7-362R1)

11/78: Pops, We Love You (Vocal)/Pops, We Love You (Instrumental) (Motown 1455) As by Marvin Gaye, Smokey Robinson, Diana Ross, and Stevie Wonder

1/79: STEVIE WONDER'S JOURNEY

THROUGH THE SECRET LIFE OF PLANTS (Tamla T13-371N2)

10/79: Send One Your Love/Send One Your Love (Instrumental) (Tamla 54303)

2/80: Outside My Window/Same Old Story (Tamla 54308)

9/80: Master Blaster (Jammin')/Master Blaster (Dub) (Tamla 54317)

10/80: HOTTER THAN JULY (Tamla T8-373M1)

12/80: I Ain't Gonna Stand For It/Knocks Me Off My Feet (Tamla 54320)

3/81: Lately/If It's Magic (Tamla 54323)

7/81: Did I Hear You Say You Love Me/As If You Read My Mind (Tamla 54328)

1/82: That Girl/All I Do (Tamla 1602TF)

5/82: Do I Do/Rocket Love (Tamla 1612TF)

5/82: ORIGINAL MUSIQUARIUM VOLUMES I AND II (Tamla 6002TL2)

8/82: Ribbon In The Sky/Black Orchid (Tamla 1639TF)

10/82: Used To Be/I Want To Come Back As A Song (Motown 1650MF) 'A' side by Charlene and Stevie Wonder. 'B' side by Charlene

10/83: SIGNED, SEALED DELIVERED/MY CHERIE AMOUR (Motown 6081MC)

7/84: SELECTIONS FROM THE ORIGINAL MOTION PICTURE SOUNDTRACK FROM "THE WOMAN IN RED" (Motown 6108ML)

8/84: I Just Called To Say I Love You/I Just Called To Say I Love You (Instrumental) (Motown 1745MF)

11/84: Love Light In Flight/It's More Than You (Instrumental) (Motown 1769MF)

1/85: Don't Drive Drunk/Don't Drive Drunk (Instrumental) (Motown 1774MF)

1/85: ORIGINAL MUSIQUARIUM VOLS. I AND II (Tamla TCD06113TD2)

1/85: SONGS IN THE KEY OF LIFE VOLS. I AND II (Tamla TCD06115TD2)

3/85: JOURNEY THROUGH THE SECRET LIFE OF PLANTS (Tamla TCD06127TD2)

7/85: LOVE SONGS: 20 CLASSIC HITS (Tamla TCD06144TD)

7/85: TALKING BOOK (Tamla TCD06151TD)

7/85: INNERVISIONS (Tamla TCD06152TD)

8/85: Part-Time Lover/Part-Time Lover (Instrumental) (Tamla 1808TF)

10/85: IN SQUARE CIRCLE (Tamla 6134TL)

11/85: Go Home/Go Home (Instrumental) (Tamla 1817TF)

2/86: Overjoyed/Overjoyed (Instrumental) (Tamla 1832TF)

8/86: HOTTER THAN JULY (Tamla TCD06205TD)

Unissued Motown Recordings

Happy Birthday (Vocal)/Happy Birthday (Instrumental) (Tamla 54331)
WORKOUT STEVIE WORKOUT (Tamla TM-248)
PEOPLE MOVE, HUMAN PLAYS (Tamla 6047TL)
Pretty Little Angel/Tears In Vain (Tamla 54108) Promo

FOR MORE INFORMATION
(NOTE: For many, Stevie Wonder symbolizes the difficult struggle to overcome an individual handicap and lead a productive life. He is an inspiration to everyone faced with a physical handicap, and his musical legacy will live forever. As a result, he has been the subject of countless books and articles, a few of which are given below.)

Contemporary Literary Criticism, Vol. 12. (Detroit: Gale Research Co., 1980).

Dragonwagon, C. *Stevie Wonder*. (NY & London: Flash Books,1977.) Text, photographs, discography.

Edwards, Audrey and Gary Wohl. *The Picture Life of Stevie Wonder*. (NY & London: Franklin Watts, 1977.) For children.

Haskins, James. *The Story of Stevie Wonder*. (NY: Lothrop, Lee & Shepard Co., 1976.) Includes photographs. For adults and young adults.

Haskins, James with Kathleen Benson. *The Stevie Wonder Scrapbook*. (NY: Grosset & Dunlap, 1978.) Over 100 photographs, plus text. Includes bibliography.

Hill, George H. "Stevie Wonder," in *Bulletin of Bibliography*, Vol. 42, No. 3 (September 1985), pp. 163-168. Extensive bibliography.

Peisch, Jeffrey. *Stevie Wonder*. NY: Ballantine, 1985. Paperback.

Swenson, John. *Stevie Wonder*. NY: Harper & Row, 1986. An excellent work; includes discography.

Torgoff, Martin. "Stevie Wonder," cover story in *Interview*, Vol. XVI, No. 6 (June 1986).

Wilson, Beth P. *Stevie Wonder*. (NY: G.P. Putnam's Sons, 1979.) A large print "See and Read Biography" for children. Illustrated.

RITA WRIGHT

(See SYREETA.)

XIT
Obie Sullivan
Leeja Herrera
Jomac Suazo
R. C. Garris, Jr.
Chili Yazzie
Tom Bee
Tyrone King

This Rare Earth recording group is a group of American Indians whose name means "Crossing of Indian Tribes."

MOTOWN DISCOGRAPHY
2/72: PLIGHT OF THE REDMAN (Rare Earth R 536L)
4/72: Nihaa Shil Hozho (I Am Happy About You)/End (Rare Earth 5044)
4/73: SILENT WARRIOR (Rare Earth R 545L)
9/73: Reservation of Education/Color Nature Gone (Rare Earth 5055)
6/74: I Need Your Love (Give It To Me)/Movin' From The City (Motown 1304)
10/74: Renegade/Cement Prairie (Motown 1320)

Unissued Motown Recordings

RELOCATION (Motown 787)

GENERAL BIBLIOGRAPHY

The following books deal with the overall story of Motown Records. Works on specific artists and groups are listed in separate entries contained in the biographical section.

Benjaminson, Peter. *The Story of Motown.* New York: Grove Press, 1979.

The pioneering study of Motown. Includes a good selection of photographs not often seen elsewhere.

Brown, Ashley, and Michael Heatley. *The Motown Story.* London: Orbis, 1985.

George, Nelson. *Where Did Our Love Go? The Rise and Fall of the Motown Sound.* New York: St. Martin's Press, 1986.

A history of Motown by a long-time writer for Billboard and noted scholar of soul music.

The Motown Era: 112 Songs Arranged for Voice, Piano, Guitar. (Jobete/Grosset & Dunlap, 1971.) 319 pages. Sheet music and photos.

All songs included made the Top Ten in *Billboard* and *Cash Box*.

Ryan, Jack. *Recollections: The Detroit Years.* np: Whitlaker Marketing, 1982.

Written by a Detroit-area journalist, this work covers Motown artists in A-to-Z fashion. Many unusual photographs.

Taraborrelli, J. Randy. *Motown: Hot Wax, City Cool & Solid Gold.* Garden City, NY: Doubleday, 1986.

Numerous photographs, with chapters on the major performers and notes on the minor artists interwoven with a chronology of events.

Waller, Don. *The Motown Story.* New York: Charles Scribner's Sons, 1985.

An engagingly readable story covering many facets of Motown. Includes extensive discography of American singles and albums. Numerous photographs.

Books With Information On Motown Artists

Betrock, Alan. *Girl Groups: The Story of a Sound.* New York: Delilah Books, 1982.

Includes chapters on Martha & the Vandellas, the Supremes, the Marvelettes, Mary Wells, and others.

Hirshey, Gerri. *Nowhere to Run.* New York: Times Books, 1984.

An oral history of soul music and rhythm and blues, with quotes and conversations from many Motown artists, including Berry Gordy himself.

PART II

MOTOWN
CHRONOLOGY

BER-BERRY CO-OP
5139 St. Antoine
Detroit, Michigan

•SAVINGS SHARE LOAN NOTE

$800.⁼   SHARE LOAN NUMBER _____

FOR VALUE RECEIVED ON OR BEFORE ___Jan. 12, 1959___   DETROIT 2, MICHIGAN
BER-BERRY Co-op
HOME FEDERAL SAVINGS AND LOAN ASSOCIATION OF DETROIT, at its office in   I promise to pay
the City of Detroit at 9100 Woodward Avenue; the sum of
___Eight Hundred • ⁰⁰/₁₀₀___
with interest at the rate of _____   ($800.⁼)
per annum, payable _____Six_____   per cent (__)
_____ Monthly, Yearly, _____.

I hereby transfer, assign and pledge my share account # 113
of said Association owned by me and the Certificate evidencing the
same as security for the payment of said amount when due, and upon the
failure of full payment thereof when due, do authorise said Association to repurchase, in accordance with its charter and by-laws, sufficient of said share account and to apply so much of the purchase price
therefor as may be necessary to pay and discharge the amount then due
including interest and I hereby appoint the Treasurer of said Association or in his absence the President, my Attorney-in-fact to execute
for me any papers and to take any other action necessary to carry out
this agreement.

AMOUNT OF NOTE _____800.—_____
AMOUNT OF INTEREST ____48.—____   DATE OF NOTE ___Jan. 12, 1959___
TOTAL _____   DUE DATE OF NOTE ___Jan. 12, 1960___

SIGNATURE OF BORROWER

SIGNATURE OF BORROWER
1719 Gladstone
ADDRESS
TR 1-3340

In addition—
I also hereby assign from
my future earnings, the
amount necessary, at any
given date, to repay any
unpaid balance due at
this note
Berry Gordy 3

$800.⁼   ___January 12___ 1959   __promise to pay to___   __Dollars__
One year __after date__
the order of Ber-Berry Co-op
Eight Hundred • ⁰⁰/₁₀₀
file at Detroit, Michigan
with interest at 6 per cent per annum   Siy Jordy ?
No. _____

FROM LITTLE ACORNS
The Ber-Berry Co-op promissory note
and $800 loan agreement which helped
launch Berry Gordy, Jr.'s enterprise,
the Motown Record Corp., in 1959.

1929

November 28
  Berry Gordy, Jr., is born in Detroit.

1953

Berry Gordy marries Thelma Coleman.

1957

Berry Gordy first hears the Miracles when they audition for Jackie Wilson's manager, Nat Tarnapol, owner of Brunswick Records. Berry begins recording them as an independent producer and will begin leasing their records to other labels in 1958.

1958

Acting as an independent producer, Gordy leases the first Miracles record, "Got A Job/ My Mama Done Told Me" (End 1016), to the New York-based End label, operated by George Goldner. This year he will also place his productions of Eddie Holland with Mercury Records, and recordings of several other artists, notably Marv Johnson, with the Detroit-based Kudo label. Anna Records, a Detroit label run by Berry's sister, Anna Gordy, together with Billy Davis and Gwen Gordy (another sister), will also issue some of Berry's productions until it becomes defunct in 1961.

Jobete Publishing Co. is established by Berry Gordy. The name is a combination of the names of his children, Hazel Joy, Berry, and Terry. The first record of a Jobete song is Herman Griffin's "I Need You" (HOB 112), produced by Berry Gordy.

1959

Marvin Gaye and other members of the Washington, D.C.-based Marquees join Harvey Fuqua's group. They record and tour as Harvey and the Moonglows before disbanding in 1960.

Berry Gordy divorces Thelma (Coleman) Gordy, mother of Hazel Joy, Berry Gordy IV, and Terry. He marries Raynoma Liles later in the year.

January 12
  In Detroit, Berry Gordy borrows $800 from the family loan fund, the Ber-Berry Coop,

in order to found Motown Records. During the year, the first releases of the company will appear on the Tamla label. The name Tamla is a variation on "Tammy," a popular song of the period sung by Debbie Reynolds. The Motown label will be activated early in 1960, although test pressings of the Miracles' "Bad Girl" are made on the Motown label in September 1959. The company's third major label, Gordy, will debut in April 1962.

November 7
  Smokey Robinson marries Claudette Rogers. Both are members of the Miracles.

1960

Berry Gordy starts signing new talent to his company. The Marvelettes are discovered at a talent show at Inkster High School outside of Detroit by Robert Bateman, one of Gordy's producers.

The Miracles' "Shop Around" (Tamla) is the company's first million seller.

The Primettes audition for Berry Gordy, who feels they are too young. They will later become the Supremes.

The Distants are asked into the Hitsville recording studio by Berry Gordy. Their first release for Gordy is on the Miracle label in 1961, as by the Temptations.

Robert Bateman arranges an audition for Mary Wells. Berry signs her immediately and releases "Bye Bye Baby" on the Motown label in December.

Berry Gordy acquires Marvin Gaye's contract from Harvey Fuqua.

1961

"Please Mr. Postman" (The Marvelettes) and "Shop Around" (Miracles) will reach #1 and #2 respectively on the pop charts this year. They are Motown's only entries into the pop Top 10 in 1961.

Jimmy Ruffin signs with Motown.

January
  The Primettes sign with Motown and become the Supremes.

  Berry Gordy establishes the Miracle label, which will only last a year. Jimmy Ruffin and the Temptations will release their first records on this label.

April
  The Supremes first release is on the Tamla label. They will later be switched to

THE MARVELETTES

After recording "Please Mr. Postman" as a quintet, The Marvelettes lost Juanita Cowart. This photo shows lead singer Gladys Horton, Katherine Anderson, Wanda Young, and Georgeanna Tillman.

Photo courtesy Motown Archives, Eastern Michigan University.

TAMLA

PLEASE MR. POSTMAN

TM 228
XCTV 84445

SIDE 1

MARVELETTES

1. ANGEL (Bateman-Saunders-Leverett)
2. I WANT A GUY (Holland-Gordy-Gorman)
3. PLEASE MR. POSTMAN (Brian Bert-Garrett-Dobbins)
4. SO LONG BABY (Holland-Bateman-Young)
5. I KNOW HOW IT FEELS (Holland-Bateman-Bradford-Wylie)

the Motown label.

August

Brian Holland co-produces the Marvelettes' "Please Mr. Postman" with Robert Bateman, who discovered the group in 1960. The song reaches #1 on the pop charts and is Motown's biggest hit to date.

October

Eddie Holland returns to Motown after being under contract to United Artists.

1962

Motown's singles are appealing primarily to the black market, as evidenced by their success on the rhythm & blues charts. In 1962, there will be eleven Top 10 r&b singles. The most popular releases are "Two Lovers" (Mary Wells), "Do You Love Me" (Contours), "You Beat Me To The Punch" (Mary Wells), and "You've Really Got A Hold On Me" (Miracles).

The year 1962 is one in which four Motown singles will reach the Top 10 in the pop market. "Do You Love Me," "Playboy" (Marvelettes), "The One Who Really Loves You" (Mary Wells), and "You Beat Me To The Punch" will "cross over" (to white audiences).

The Gordy label is launched, with the first release by the Temptations. Two additional labels are established this year, Mel-O-Dy and V.I.P.

The Holland-Dozier-Holland songwriting and production team is formed.

Berry Gordy divorces Raynoma (Liles) Gordy, mother of Kerry.

November-December

First national road tour for the Motor Town Revue ends with a ten-day engagement at the Apollo Theatre in New York, December 7-16. The tour was unusual in that Motown took along its own band, unlike most other companies which relied on local house bands. Over forty-five performers made this tour, which started in Boston and went south down the East Coast to Florida.

1963

This year Motown will gross $4.5 million in sales.

Toward end of year, Motown releases in the United Kingdom passed from Oriole to Stateside.

Six Motown releases will reach the Top 10 in the pop charts: "You've Really Got A

Hold On Me" (Miracles); "Pride and Joy" (Marvin Gaye); "Fingertips, Part 2" (Little Stevie Wonder); "Heat Wave" (Martha and the Vandellas); "Mickey's Monkey" (Miracles); and "Quicksand" (Martha and the Vandellas).

The Four Tops are signed to Motown.

Smokey Robinson is named Vice-President of Motown.

Harvey Fuqua joins Motown as a producer, bringing such artists as Junior Walker and the All Stars, the Spinners, and Shorty Long with him from his own labels, Harvey and Tri-Phi.

Marvin Gaye marries Anna Gordy, Berry's sister.

June

Stevie Wonder's "Fingertips, Part 2" becomes Motown's second #1 pop hit.

November

Starting with the November 30, 1963, issue, *Billboard* suspends its "rhythm & blues" chart until January 23, 1965. Thus, r&b chart data for this period is largely based on the *Cashbox* singles charts. Interestingly, it was during this period that Motown began to achieve significant success on the "pop" charts, crossing over to a white audience and achieving greater popularity.

1964

George Clinton and his group, the Parliaments, sign with Motown. Their Motown recordings were never released, and in 1967 they achieved their first chart success with "(I Wanna) Testify" (Revilot 207) on the Detroit-based Revilot label. Motown claimed the rights to the Parliaments' name, forcing George Clinton to rename his group Funkadelic.

Supremes share British television dates in London with the Dave Clark Five.

Berry Gordy signs Brenda Holloway while attending a disc jockey convention in Los Angeles.

Motown will have five Top 10 pop hits this year. Four of them will reach #1 ("My Guy," "Where Did Our Love Go?," "Baby Love," and "Come See About Me"), and the other #2 ("Dancing in the Street").

January

The Supremes break into the Top 40 for the first time with "When The Lovelight Starts Shining."

April

Mary Wells's "My Guy" becomes Motown's

third #1 pop hit.

July

The Supremes start a string of five consecutive #1 pop hits, all written and produced by Holland-Dozier-Holland.

September

"Baby I Need Your Loving," the Four Tops first hit single for Motown, enters the pop charts.

Mary Wells leaves Motown and signs with Twentieth-Century Fox Records.

November

"Baby Love" by the Supremes reaches #1 in the British charts.

Marvin Gaye spends a month in England for television and radio appearances. Accompanying him on his first trip to England are Harvey Fuqua and his wife, Gwen Gordy Fuqua.

December

This year's Christmas shows of the Motor Town Revue at Detroit's Fox Theatre feature Marvin Gaye, the Miracles, the Supremes, Stevie Wonder, the Marvelettes, and the Temptations. The house band is led by Choker Campbell.

December 27

The Supremes first appear on "The Ed Sullivan Show."

1965

Five Motown releases will reach #1 on the pop charts this year: "My Girl" (The Temptations); "Stop! In The Name Of Love" (The Supremes); "Back In My Arms Again" (The Supremes); "I Can't Help Myself" (The Four Tops); and "I Hear A Symphony" (The Supremes). Six other releases will reach the Top 10.

Berry Gordy purchases the Gordy Manor in Detroit this year.

March

Tamla Motown label is launched in the United Kingdom; EMI is the distributor. First release is the Supremes' "Stop! In The Name of Love/I'm In Love Again" (Tamla Motown TMG 501).

Temptations are in England to tape "Ready-Steady-Go" television show.

March 20-April 3

Tour of the United Kingdom by Motown Revue (billed as The Tamla-Motown Show) consisting of the Supremes, Martha & the Vandellas, the Temptations, Stevie Wonder, the Miracles, and the Earl Van Dyke Sextet.

Tour includes Glasgow, Scotland, and ends in Paris. Accompanying the Motown artists is British singer Georgie Fame. The announced purpose of the tour was to celebrate the introduction of the Tamla Motown label in England.

July

Supremes open at the Copa in New York and have a successful engagement, paving the way for other Motown acts to appear at this prestigious nightclub.

August

Brenda Holloway performs with the Beatles on their North American tour.

September

Supremes' television appearances this month include "Hullabaloo" (Sept. 13) and "The Red Skelton Show" (Sept. 21).

Motown releases thirty-three 8-track tapes, the first time this format is used.

October 10

Supremes appear on "The Ed Sullivan Show."

October 18

Supremes appear on "Hullabaloo" again.

November 18

Supremes appear on "The Dean Martin Show."

December

Brian Holland is named a Vice President of Motown.

December 6

Supremes make their third appearance on "Hullabaloo."

1966

Motown introduces a new 8-track cartridge in a book-type, full-color, flip-open package featuring complete album information.

Isley Brothers sign with Motown for the Tamla label.

Gladys Knight & the Pips are signed and record on the Soul label.

(Nick) Ashford and (Valerie) Simpson are signed as staff songwriters after their song, "Let's Go Get Stoned," is a hit for Ray Charles.

Fourteen Motown singles that enter the pop charts in 1966 reach the Top 10, with "You Can't Hurry Love" (The Supremes), "Reach Out I'll Be There" (The Four Tops), and "You Keep Me Hanging On" (The Supremes) attaining the #1 spot.

February

Motown authorizes Ampex to release 4-track reel-to-reel and cassette tapes.

The Supremes record a radio-only single, "Things Are Changing," as part of an Equal Employment Opportunity (EEO) campaign.

February 15 & 17

The Supremes appear on "Anatomy of Pop," an ABC-TV special.

February 16

The Marvelettes make their first appearance on "Hullabaloo." Their current hit is "Don't Mess With Bill."

February 17

The Supremes return to the Copa in New York. Their current hit is "My World Is Empty Without You."

February 20

Supremes appear on "The Ed Sullivan Show."

March

Record World's Rhythm & Blues Awards for 1965 indicate Motown's dominance and influence in r&b. Motown groups finish 1-2-3 in both Male and Female Vocal Groups. Top Male Vocal Group is the Four Tops, followed by the Miracles and the Temptations. The Supremes are chosen Top Female Vocal Group, followed by Martha & the Vandellas and the Marvelettes. The Top Record goes to the Four Tops' "I Can't Help Myself," and Jr. Walker & the All Stars are named Top Instrumental Combo. Other Motown artists mentioned include Marvin Gaye (tied for second in voting for Top Male Vocalist), Stevie Wonder (fifth), Elgins (fifth in Most Promising Male Vocal Group category), and Kim Weston (fourth in voting for Top Female Vocalist).

March

Motown joins industry trade group, the Recording Industry Association of America (RIAA), after a long holdout.

March 4

Supremes appear on "The Sammy Davis Show."

March 24

Supremes appear on "The Dean Martin Show."

April

At the annual BMI awards dinner, Holland-Dozier-Holland receive eight awards, Jobette receives twelve, while Lennon and McCartney receive five.

Schafer Bakeries of Michigan introduces "Supremes Bread." The plastic wrappers feature likenesses of the Supremes and are now collectors items.

April 20

Marvin Gaye makes his Canadian nightclub debut at The Cave in Vancouver, British Columbia. Motown often used Canadian clubs to test their artists before showcasing them in the U.S.

May

Marvin Gaye, Gladys Knight & the Pips, and Brenda Holloway perform at the American Women in Radio & TV (AWRT) conference in Detroit.

May 26

Marvin Gaye begins a two-week engagement at the Whiskey A Go Go in Los Angeles.

June

Marvin Gaye is at the Copa in New York.

Motown announces establishment of a West Coast office, to be managed by Shelly Berger, for expansion into movie production, the securing of film roles for Motown stars, and use of Motown songs in soundtracks. Motown also announces interest in becoming a "Broadway angel" (i.e., a financial backer for Broadway plays).

June 19

Marvin Gaye's first appearance on "The Ed Sullivan Show."

August

Brenda Holloway records "Play It Cool, Stay In School" for WXYZ-AM, a Detroit radio station.

August–October

Motown Mondays at Detroit's Roostertail nightclub feature Four Tops, Jr. Walker & the All-Stars, Marvin Gaye, Martha & the Vandellas, Smokey Robinson & the Miracles, the Marvelettes, and the Temptations.

September

Motown purchases Golden World Records, located at 3246 W. Davison in Detroit, for six figures from Eddie Wingate and Joanne Jackson. Purchase includes recording contracts for Edwin Starr and J.J. Barnes. Barnes, however, signs with another Detroit company, Solid Hitbound Productions, and records for their Groovesville label, although he appears with the Motown Revue at the Fox Theater in Detroit in December 1966. The purchase includes a much-needed recording studio.

October

The Supremes, back from an extensive Far East tour, begin their first Las Vegas appearance at the Flamingo Hotel for three

THE SUPREMES

A candid shot of the original Supremes: (from left) Mary Wilson, Diana Ross, Florence Ballard.

Enlargement of a fan club membership card picturing the new Supremes line-up (1967-1969): (from left) Cindy Birdsong, Diana Ross, Mary Wilson.

weeks.

December

The Motown Revue at Detroit's Fox Theater features the Temptations, Stevie Wonder, Martha & the Vandellas, Gladys Knight & the Pips, Jimmmy Ruffin, the Underdogs, Chris Clark, J.J. Barnes, and the Earl Van Dyke Band.

1967

This year Motown has five major labels active: Motown, Tamla, Gordy, Soul, and V.I.P.

Berry Gordy moves from Detroit to Los Angeles, buying Tommy Smothers' Beverly Hills house for about $500,000.

In 1967, thirteen of Motown's singles will enter the pop charts and reach the Top 10, with "Love Is Here And Now You're Gone" (The Supremes) and "The Happening" (The Supremes) going to #1.

This summer, while touring with Marvin Gaye, Tammi Terrell collapses on-stage during a performance at the Hampden-Sydney College in Virginia. She will be diagnosed as having a brain tumor, and subsequently die on March 16, 1970, at the age of 24.

January

Kim Weston and her husband, producer-songwriter William "Mickey" Stevenson, leave Motown. They both sign with MGM Records.

May

At the annual BMI awards dinner, Jobete receives fourteen awards, Eddie Holland (eight), Lamont Dozier and Brian Holland (six each). Non-Motown artists receiving multiple awards include John Sebastian (five), John Lennon and Paul McCartney (four each), and Mick Jagger and Keith Richards (four each).

July

Florence Ballard is removed from the Supremes and replaced by Cindy Birdsong. Motown's official version is that Flo withdrew from the group "exhausted from the girls' demanding schedule."

August

Motown hosts its first sales convention at the Roostertail in Detroit, "Motown Showcase '68," for 150 distributors. Performing are Diana Ross & the Supremes, Stevie Wonder, Chris Clark, Gladys Knight & the Pips, and the Spinners.

September

Supremes tour Japan.

Chuck Jackson signs with Motown.

November

Stevie Wonder is on a European tour.

December

Ewart Abner, former president of Vee-Jay Records, joins Motown as Director of International Talent Management. He will later be named President of Motown Records.

A special Motown Revue for the handicapped features Smokey Robinson & the Miracles, Stevie Wonder, the Marvelettes, Gladys Knight & the Pips, Chris Clark, Edwin Starr, Willie Tyler & Lester, and the Motown Recording Band.

1968

Motown's officers this year are Berry Gordy, President; Smokey Robinson, Executive Vice President; Esther (Gordy) Edwards, Senior Vice President; Barney Ales, Vice President, Sales; and Brian Holland, Vice President.

The Jackson 5 win an amateur night contest at the Apollo Theater in New York.

Berry Gordy moves to his home to Los Angeles, purchased the previous year.

Temptations are named Top Rhythm & Blues Album Artists in *Billboard*'s annual Who's Who in the World of Music.

Holland-Dozier-Holland leave Motown.

Ten Motown singles reach the Top 10 on the pop charts this year, with "Love Child" (Diana Ross & The Supremes) and "I Heard It Through The Grapevine" (Marvin Gaye) reaching the #1 spot.

February

Far East tour includes Japan, Tokyo, Hong Kong, Manilla, and various U.S. Army bases. Esther Edwards accompanies Stevie Wonder, the Temptations, and Martha Reeves & the Vandellas on this tour.

March

Motown moves its Detroit offices from West Grand Blvd. to new location at 2547 Woodward Avenue and the Fisher Expressway, into what was formerly the Donovan Building.

July

David Ruffin leaves the Temptations for a solo career with Motown.

September

Dennis Edwards makes his first appearance as lead vocalist for the Temptations at the Forum in Los Angeles.

Benefit concert for the youth of Gary, Indiana, at Gilroy Stadium features Gladys Knight & the Pips, Stevie Wonder, Bobby

All photos courtesy Peter Benjaminson.

MARVIN GAYE

Marvin Gaye's biggest hit was the 1968 release,
"I Heard It Through The Grapevine."

Taylor & the Vancouvers, Shorty Long, and Abdulla.

November

Marvin Gaye's version of "I Heard It Through The Grapevine" reaches the top of the pop charts and stays there for nearly two months.

December 20

In Motown's first television special, Diana Ross and the Supremes and the Temptations perform on and host "T.C.B. - Taking Care of Business" on NBC-TV. The soundtrack album is released this month. The Supremes and the Temptations will record several albums together in the future.

1969

Motown celebrates its tenth anniversary with a boat ride on the Thames River in London; performing groups include Martha & the Vandellas.

The Jackson family, including the recently signed Jackson 5, moves from Gary, Indiana, to Los Angeles, living for a time at the homes of Berry Gordy and Diana Ross.

Motown establishes more offices in Los Angeles, furthering a move begun in 1966 that will be made official in 1972.

Berry Gordy and Diana Ross appear to be constant companions during the year.

Motown will have twelve singles in the Top 10 this year, with "I Can't Get Next To You" (The Temptations), "Someday We'll Be Together" (Diana Ross & The Supremes), and "I Want You Back" (Jackson 5) getting to #1 on the pop charts.

May

Jean Terrell signs with Motown as a solo artist. She will replace Diana Ross in the Supremes in January 1970.

Walter "Choker" Campbell establishes Tri-City Recording Co. in Saginaw, Michigan. Labels include Tri-City, Moonville USA, Ultra-City, and Gospel Train.

June

The Holland brothers establish their own labels, Invictus and Hot Wax.

June 29

Shorty Long, composer of "Devil With A Blue Dress," dies in a boating accident on the Detroit River.

August

Motown's Rare Earth label debuts.

September

Jackson 5 debut as new Motown artists at the Daisy Disco in Los Angeles, with Diana Ross.

October

Motown acquires distribution of the Chisa label, founded by Hugh Masekela and Stewart Levine.

October 18

"The Hollywood Palace," an ABC-TV special, features Diana Ross and the Supremes along with the Jackson 5.

November 12

"Diana Ross & the Supremes and the Temptations on Broadway," a musical-comedy television special, is broadcast on NBC-TV.

1970

The West Coast office handles Motown subsidiary labels Chisa, V.I.P., and Rare Earth.

Six of the fourteen Motown singles that will reach the Top 10 in 1970 will also go to #1. They are "ABC" (Jackson 5), "The Love You Save" (Jackson 5), "War" (Edwin Starr), "The Tears Of A Clown" (Smokey Robinson & The Miracles), and "Ain't No Mountain High Enough" (Diana Ross).

January

The Supremes' final performances with Diana Ross as lead singer are given at the Frontier Hotel in Las Vegas. The next month they begin performing with Jean Terrell as lead singer.

February

Jobete and BMI join in a lawsuit against CBS-TV alleging "You've Made Me So Very Happy" was performed on "The Red Skelton Show" without permission.

March

Stevie Wonder performs at the Copa in New York.

March 16

Tammi Terrell dies of a brain tumor.

April

Berry Gordy and Sammy Davis, Jr., form Ecology Records.

June 19

The Jackson 5 draw 18,000 to their first major concert as Motown artists at the Los Angeles Forum.

September 14

Stevie Wonder marries Syreeta Wright (aka Rita Wright) in Detroit.

THE FOUR TOPS

The Fout Tops signed with Motown in 1963 and
scored a #1 hit in 1964 with "Baby, I Need Your
Loving."

October

The Jazz Crusaders join the Chisa label.

Motown's Black Forum label issues its first three albums. The label featured spoken word recordings and was the vehicle for several albums by the Rev. Dr. Martin Luther King, Jr., the first released this month. The other two albums released were by Stokely Carmichael, head of the Student Nonviolent Coordinating Committee (SNCC), and poets Langston Hughes and Margaret Danner. King's WHY I OPPOSE THE WAR IN VIETNAM will win a Grammy for best spoken word album.

November

Diana Ross is reportedly charging $40,000 per week for bookings.

CBS-TV cuts the Supremes' performance of "Stoned Love" from "The Merv Griffin Show" because of possible drug connotations.

November 8

Four Tops appear on "The Ed Sullivan Show." Their current hit is "Still Water (Love)."

November 28

Telephone threats against the Jackson 5 cause cancellation of their concert in Buffalo, NY.

December

Diana Ross wins the NAACP Image Award for Female Entertainer of the Year.

Barney Ales, Motown's Executive Vice President, announces Motown's 1970 gross sales are $39 million.

December 18

"The Smokey Robinson Show," a one-hour musical variety special, is shown on ABC-TV.

1971

The Spinners leave Motown and sign with Atlantic Records. G.C. Cameron stays with Motown as a solo artist.

Berry Gordy buys Red Skelton's Bel Air estate.

Eleven Motown singles will reach the Top 10 this year, with "Just My Imagination (Running Away With Me)" (The Temptations) reaching the #1 spot on the pop charts.

January 20

Diana Ross marries Robert Silberstein, a PR executive, in Las Vegas.

April 18

"Diana!" is shown on ABC-TV. It is Diana Ross's first television special and features

the Jackson 5, Danny Thomas, and Bill Cosby. Motown had issued the soundtrack album at the end of March 1971.

April 30

The new Supremes (Jean Terrell, Cindy Birdsong, and Mary Wilson) appear on "The David Frost Show."

May

The Sterling Ball is held at the Gordy Manor in Detroit to honor the late Loucye Gordy Wakefield; a memorial fund is established in her name.

June

Tom Clay's "What The World Needs Now" is the first release on the Mowest label.

August

The Supremes and the Four Tops tour to promote their album, THE RETURN OF THE MAGNIFICENT SEVEN.

September

Jackson 5 cartoon series is shown on television.

First British release on the Rare Earth label is R. Dean Taylor's "Ain't I A Sad Thing/Back Street" (Rare Earth RES 101).

September 9

Jackson 5 draw 23,000 to the Michigan State Fair.

September 19

"Goin' Back To Indiana," a television special hosted by the Jackson 5, is shown on ABC-TV. Guests include Bill Cosby and Tommy Smothers.

October

Michael Jackson's first solo record, "Got To Be There," is released.

November

Marvin Gaye appears in the film, "Chrome and Hot Leather," an American International Pictures drive-in special.

1972

Suzanne dePasse is named Corporate Director, Creative Production Division. From 1968 to 1972, she was a creative assistant to Berry Gordy. She names Billie Jean Brown Creative Director of the Detroit office.

The Commodores sign with Motown and tour as the opening act for the Jackson 5.

The Four Tops leave Motown and sign with Dunhill Records.

Only four Motown singles reach the Top 10 in the pop charts in 1971, but two of them reach the #1 spot: "Papa Was A Rollin'

GLADYS KNIGHT & THE PIPS

Gladys Knight and The Pips left Motown in 1973.

Stone" (The Temptations) and "Ben" (Michael Jackson).

January

Smokey Robinson and the Miracles begin a tour at the Elmwood Casino in Windsor, Ontario, that will end six months later at the Apollo Theater in New York. It will be Smokey's "farewell tour" with the Miracles, during which he will introduce his replacement, William Griffin.

March

A company newsletter states, "There are no plans at present to phase out the Detroit operations, as many rumors suggest." Rumors were caused by layoffs in Detroit due to the growth of Motown's operations in Los Angeles.

May 1

Marvin Gaye makes a rare concert appearance at the Kennedy Center for the Performing Arts in Washington, D.C., on "Marvin Gaye Day."

June

Motown announces it is closing its Detroit offices and leaving Detroit.

Stevie Wonder opens for the Rolling Stones on their fifty-city North American tour.

September

Two dates at Jesse Jackson's Push Expo '72 in Chicago feature Gladys Knight & the Pips, the Supremes, the Temptations, the Jackson 5, Smokey Robinson, Valerie Simpson, and Thelma Houston.

October

First British releases on Mowest label are by Thelma Houston and Frankie Valli & the Four Seasons.

The film, "Lady Sings The Blues," starring Diana Ross, opens.

November

Jackson 5 are on a European tour.

November 5

"The Jackson 5 Show," a half-hour television special, is shown on CBS-TV.

December

A line of twelve "Supremes Wigs" is introduced in Texas.

1973

In 1973, Motown will gross $46 million in sales.

Gladys Knight & the Pips leave Motown and record the #1 hit, "Midnight Train To Georgia" for Buddah Records.

Motown will have five #1 pop singles in 1973, including "Let's Get It On" (Marvin Gaye), "Keep On Truckin' (Part 1)" (Eddie Kendricks), "Touch Me In The Morning" (Diana Ross), "You Are The Sunshine of My Life" (Stevie Wonder), and "Superstition" (Stevie Wonder).

January

Berry Gordy resigns as President of Motown Records to assume leadership of the new Motown entertainment conglomerate, Motown Industries. He becomes board chairman of Motown Industries, which includes record, motion picture, television, and publishing divisions. Ewart Abner II, a Motown Vice-President for six years, succeeds Berry Gordy as President of Motown Records.

March

At the annual National Academy of Recording Arts and Sciences' awards ceremony, "Papa Was A Rolling Stone" wins three Grammies. These are generally recognized as Motown's first Grammy awards, but the spoken word WHY I OPPOSE THE WAR IN VIETNAM by the Rev. Dr. Martin Luther King, Jr., won a Grammy in 1971; the record was issued on Motown's Black Forum label.

May

"Lady Sings the Blues," starring Diana Ross as Billie Holiday, is shown at the Cannes Film Festival. Diana Ross makes a personal appearance there and performs songs from the film.

June

Black Enterprise magazine lists Motown as the #1 black-owned or managed business, with sales for 1972 reported at $40 million. Ranked at #2 was the Johnson Publishing Co. (*Ebony*, *Jet*, etc.) with sales of $23.1 million for 1972.

August 13

Paul Williams, an original member of the Temptations, dies, an apparent suicide.

December 15

Jermaine Jackson marries Hazel Joy Gordy, Berry Gordy's only daughter, in Beverly Hills, California.

1974

This year Motown will gross $45 million in sales.

Only four Motown singles will reach the Top 10 on the pops charts in 1974, with

THE JACKSON 5

In 1969, Motown linked Diana Ross with the release of
the first Jackson 5 album for publicity reasons.

Stevie Wonder's "You Haven't Done Nothin'" reaching the #1 spot.

Motown assumes distribution for three labels: Manticore (rock-oriented), Melodyland (country-oriented); and CTI (jazz-oriented).

January

Jean Terrell and Lynda Laurence both drop out of the Supremes and are replaced by Scherrie Payne and Cindy Birdsong (who returns as a temporary replacement for Lynda).

March

Stevie Wonder wins five Grammys at the awards ceremony for the album, INNER-VISIONS, and the songs "You Are The Sunshine Of My Life" and "Superstition."

July

The Commodores' first Motown album, MACHINE GUN, is released.

August

Marvin Gaye begins a twenty-city tour in the United States, his first tour since Tammi Terrell collapsed in his arms onstage in 1967.

1975

This year Motown will gross $43.5 million in sales.

Only one Motown release makes the Top 10 on the pop singles charts this year, Stevie Wonder's "Boogie On Reggae Woman."

Motown acquires the Prodigal label through Barney Ales.

March

Stevie Wonder repeats at the Grammy awards and wins another five Grammys, for the album FULFILLINGNESS' FIRST FINALE and songs from it.

April

Smokey Robinson ends his two-year retirement with a performance at the Roxy club in Los Angeles.

May

Jackson 5 leave Motown and sign with Epic Records. Jermaine remains with Motown as a solo artist and is replaced by brother Randy in the renamed Jacksons.

August

Reportedly set to sign a new $13 million contract with Motown, Stevie Wonder holds out for complete artistic control and doesn't sign the contract until April 1976.

September

Ewart Abner II resigns as president of Motown Records. He is replaced temporarily by Berry Gordy. Barney Ales, former Vice President, rejoins the company.

Supremes begin a tour of South Africa; they encounter problems and are asked to leave the country.

1976

This year Motown will gross $50 million in sales.

Rebounding in popularity from a low point in 1975, six Motown releases will reach the Top 10 on the pop charts, including two by the Commodores. Motown will have three #1 pop hits, "Love Hangover" (Diana Ross), "Love Machine (Part 1)" (Miracles), and "Theme From Mahogany (Do You Know Where You're Going To)" (Diana Ross).

February 22

Florence Ballard, former Supreme, dies of cardiac arrest at age thirty-two in Detroit.

May

Motown introduces a country label, Hitsville, featuring such artists as Pat Boone and T.G. Sheppard. The label will fold in 1977.

October

Stevie Wonder's new album, SONGS IN THE KEY OF LIFE, enters the pop charts at #1.

1977

This year Motown will gross $61.4 million in sales.

Motown will have three #1 pop hits this year, including "Sir Duke" (Stevie Wonder), "Got To Give It Up (Part 1)" (Marvin Gaye), and "I Wish" (Stevie Wonder). In addition, two singles by the Commodores will reach the Top 10.

Marvin Gaye and Anna (Gordy) Gaye are divorced after fourteen years of marriage.

The Temptations leave Motown and sign with Atlantic Records, where they will release two albums with Louis Price in place of Dennis Edwards. The group will return to Motown in 1980.

February

Motown files suit against CBS/Epic regarding the Jackson 5 to stop CBS/Epic from using Jermaine Jackson's photo in ads for the weekly variety show, "The Jackson Family." Motown is currently promoting Jermaine as a solo artist. Motown also claims CBS

STEVIE WONDER

Stevie Wonder began recording songs at age eleven; his first hit for Motown was the Tamla-label "Fingertips, Part 2," which peaked at #1 in 1963.

TAMLA

TM 54080
Jobete-BMI
DM V-031304-2
Featuring
Stevie
on Harmonica
& Bongos

Produced By
BERRY
GORDY, JR.
Arr. & Con.
by Clarence
Paul
Time: 2:49

FINGERTIPS - PT 2
(Paul, Cosby)
LITTLE STEVIE WONDER
Taken from album, Tamla 240
"12 Year Old Genius"
(Recorded Live)

announced the signing of the Jackson 5 one year before their contract with Motown expired.

At this year's Grammy awards ceremony, Stevie Wonder receives four Grammys for SONGS IN THE KEY OF LIFE.

March

"An Evening With Diana Ross" is shown on NBC-TV.

Diana Ross and Bob Silberstein are divorced.

May

Motown announces plans for the film "The Wiz," to star Diana Ross.

June

The end of the Supremes is marked by Mary Wilson's "farewell concert" in London, followed by a UK tour consisting of Mary Wilson, Karen Jackson, and Karen Ragland.

September

Berry Gordy and Mike Curb form M.C. Records to record country and western artists.

October

Suzanne dePasse is promoted to Vice President of Motown Industries and assistant to Berry Gordy. Berry Gordy IV is named Vice President of the Creative Division.

December

Mary Wilson of the Supremes files a petition in California, claiming she was a minor in 1961 when she first signed with Motown and charging Motown with conflict of interest as both her agent and employer. Her suit also charges that Motown recorded and released several songs under the group name of "The Supremes" using artists other than herself. Motown denies all charges.

1978

This year Motown will gross $58 million in sales.

Commodores ninety-city U.S. tour grosses over $9 million. Their current hit is "Three Times A Lady."

Smokey Robinson produces the movie, "Big Time." The soundtrack is released on Tamla.

November 21

Berry Gordy, Sr., dies.

December

Diana Ross, Marvin Gaye, Stevie Wonder, and Smokey Robinson record "Pops, We Love You" in honor of Berry Gordy, Sr.

1979

The Commodores' "Still" will be Motown's only #1 pop hit this year. Other popular songs for 1978 from Motown are Stevie Wonder's "Send One Your Love" (#4 on the pop charts) and the Commodores' "Sail On" (#4 on pop charts).

May

Movin' Up, the autobiography of Berry Gordy, Sr., is published by Harper & Row.

1980

Marvin Gaye begins a two-year self-imposed exile in Ostend, Belgium.

Kinsman Dazz, from Cleveland, signs with Motown and becomes the Dazz Band.

The Temptations return to Motown after recording for Atlantic Records. Dennis Edwards is reinstated as lead vocalist.

Motown's pop hits this year include the #1 hit by Diana Ross, "Upside Down," Smokey Robinson's "Cruisin'," "With You I'm Born Again," by Billy Preston and Syreeta, and Stevie Wonder's "Master Blaster (Jammin')."

January 6

Georgeanna Tillman, an original member of the Marvelettes, dies of sickle cell anemia.

May

The lawsuit between Motown and CBS/Epic concerning the Jacksons is settled at the appellate court level. The name, "Jackson 5," remains the property of Berry Gordy and Motown.

October

Stevie Wonder begins his campaign to have the Rev. Dr. Martin Luther King, Jr.'s birthday declared a national holiday.

November

Jay Lasker takes over as President of Motown Records.

1981

Hubert Johnson, formerly with the Contours, commits suicide.

Motown's British distribution changes from EMI to RCA, with much material either deleted or reissued with new labels and covers bearing the RCA logo and address.

Pop hits from Motown this year include the #1 "Endless Love" (Diana Ross and Lionel Richie), "Being With You" (Smokey Robinson), and "Oh No" (Commodores).

January

Reflecting a corporate reorganization, Suzanne dePasse is promoted to President of Motown Productions, a corporate division set up to handle film and television projects.

May

Diana Ross leaves Motown and signs with RCA.

December

"Dreamgirls" opens on Broadway. This successful play is loosely based on the story of the Supremes.

A "Motown Reunion" show is held at Detroit's Madison Theatre, although none of the performers are currently with Motown at the time: Marv Johnson, Martha Reeves, Marvelettes, Mary Wells, Contours, Fantastic Four, and the Falcons (who pre-date Motown and never were signed to Motown).

1982

Marvin Gaye leaves Motown and signs with Columbia Records after Motown releases the album, IN OUR LIFETIME, without his consent.

Lionel Richie leaves the Commodores for a solo career.

Pop hits from Motown this year include the #1 "Truly," by Lionel Richie. Richie scores #1 hits in the next three years as well. Other hits from Motown include "I've Never Been To Me" (Charlene), "That Girl" (Stevie Wonder), and "Let It Whip" (Dazz Band).

May

Diana Ross is given the 1,748th star on Hollywood's Walk of Fame.

The first release of the Motown Latino label is Charlene's "Nunce He Ido A Me," a Spanish version of her "I've Never Been To Me."

June

Temptations reunion tour plays the Fisher Theatre in Detroit. Line-up of seven former and current Temptations includes David Ruffin, Eddie Kendricks, Dennis Edwards, Otis Williams, Melvin Franklin, Richard Street, and Glenn Leonard.

1983

Motown's most popular songs this year are by Lionel Richie, the #1 "All Night Long" and "You Are."

January

Motown acquires the catalog of Hi Records and reissues the company's recordings, the most notable of which are by Al Green.

March

The first album by the Mary Jane Girls is released on the Gordy label. This all-girl group was discovered and introduced by Rick James, who also writes and produces much of their material.

March 25

Motown holds a celebration of their 25th anniversary at the Pasadena Civic Auditorium that will be broadcast by NBC-TV in May.

May

NBC-TV broadcasts "Motown 25: Yesterday, Today, Forever," recorded March 25 at the Pasadena Civic Auditorium. Performing are Smokey Robinson, the Temptations, Stevie Wonder, Marvin Gaye, Lionel Richie (on film), a reunited Michael Jackson and the Jackson 5, and a reunited Diana Ross and the Supremes (Mary Wilson and Cindy Birdsong).

Motown launches a new label, Morocco, standing for the MOtown ROCk COmpany, with first releases due in the summer.

June

Marvin Gaye concert at Joe Louis Arena in Detroit.

August

The 1983 version of the Motown Revue, billed as the 25th Anniversary, plays Detroit's Cobo Hall and features the Four Tops, Temptations, and Mary Wells.

Jr. Walker rejoins Motown following his appearance on their 25th anniversary television special.

1984

Dennis Edwards leaves the Temptations to pursue a solo career. He remains with Motown.

Motown scores two #1 pop hits this year, "I Just Called To Say I Love You" (Stevie Wonder), and "Hello" (Lionel Richie). Other popular hits from Motown include "Somebody's Watching Me" (Rockwell), and "Stuck On You" (Lionel Richie).

January

Rockwell, a new Motown artist, debuts with "Somebody's Watching Me" and an album. It is later revealed that Rockwell is the performing name for Kennedy Gordy, Berry's

THE TEMPTATIONS

Group line-up, 1968-1971: (standing from left) Melvin
Franklin, Paul Williams, Dennis Edwards, Eddie
Kendricks; (seated) Otis Williams.

son (born March 15, 1964).

January 16

Lionel Richie hosts the eleventh annual American Music Awards, shown on ABC-TV. He won the favorite soul single award for "All Night Long," while Michael Jackson took seven awards plus the Award of Merit.

April 1

Marvin Gaye dies from a gunshot wound inflicted by his father.

June

It is announced that Lionel Richie's album, CAN'T SLOW DOWN, is the most successful album in the company's history, having sold over ten million copies worldwide.

"Stevie Wonder Comes Home," a live concert taped in Detroit, is shown on the cable television network, Showtime.

1985

January

For the second year in a row, Lionel Richie hosts the American Music Awards. He wins six awards, including favorite male vocalist in both the pop/rock and black categories, male video artist (black and pop/rock), and video single (both black and pop/rock) for "Hello."

March 25

Stevie Wonder wins an Oscar for Best Original Song for "I Just Called To Say I Love You" from the motion picture, "The Woman In Red."

May 19

"Motown Returns to the Apollo," a three-hour television special, is shown on NBC-TV. The show coincides with the reopening of the newly restored Apollo Theater in Harlem, marking its fiftieth anniversary. The special will win an Emmy for best variety, music, or comedy program.

Summer

Smokey Robinson hosts the "Motown Review," a musical variety series on NBC-TV.

1986

January 20

On the evening of the first U.S. holiday honoring Dr. Martin Luther King, Jr., Stevie Wonder hosts a nationally televised gala featuring a variety of performers.

March

Motown quits RIAA, a recording industry organization, stating that RIAA doesn't adequately represent the interests of an independent record company such as Motown.

August

Motown releases forty-two compact discs containing eighty-four albums of material (two albums by one artist on each disc). They use a new numbering sequence starting at 8000. All of the albums had been previously released.

The Four Tops and the Temptations are featured on the first of several specials devoted to Motown on the Showtime cable network.

December

Rumors abound that Motown is for sale, with MCA named as the most likely buyer. However, Berry Gordy announces at the end of the month that Motown is no longer for sale.

1987

January 21

Smokey Robinson and Marvin Gaye are inducted into the Rock and Roll Hall of Fame. The ceremony is held at the Waldorf Astoria Hotel in New York.

March

Smokey Robinson becomes a member of the Songwriters Hall of Fame.

May

Marvin Gaye is the subject of the second Motown special aired on the Showtime cable network.

July

Martha & the Vandellas, the Four Tops, and Jr. Walker & the All Stars perform at the National Governors Conference in Traverse City, Michigan.

November

Announcements for the January 1988 inductions into the Rock and Roll Hall of Fame are made. Berry Gordy is elected, as are The Supremes. Since the lineup for The Supremes changed over the years, the Hall of Fame specified the group members to be inducted: Diana Ross, Mary Wilson, and Florence Ballard. This lineup prevailed from 1962 to mid-1967 and was responsible for the group's biggest hits.

December 1

As part of the State of Michigan's 150th anniversary celebration, a historical marker is placed in front of the original Hitsville building at 2648 West Grand Blvd. Attending the ceremony are Michigan Governor James Blanchard, Detroit Mayor Coleman A. Young, Motown Vice President Smokey Robinson, and Esther Gordy Edwards, currently president of the Motown Historical Museum, which is located at the site.

TAMLA

1719 Gladstone St., Detroit 6, Mich.

UNBREAKABLE
45 R.P.M.

RECORD NO.
101
(G 1)

Jobete Music
(BMI) Time 2:15

Vocal Accompaniment
By The
RAYBER VOICES

COME TO ME
(Gordy-Johnson)

MARV JOHNSON

TAMLA

2648 W. Grand
Boulevard

Jobete BMI

Detroit 8, Mich.
TR 1-3340

Time 2:49
H-55552

LET YOUR CONSCIENCE BE YOUR GUIDE
(B. Gordy, Jr.)

MARVIN GAYE
Produced By
BERRY GORDY, JR.
T-54041

Four Tamla label designs which gave way to the
familiar "Globes" label (pictured on page 94) and later
designs, including the very first Tamla single (top
left) and Marvin Gaye's first Tamla-label single (top
right).

TAMLA

TAMLA RECORDS, DETROIT, MICHIGAN

45 RPM
RFD-ASCAP
Time 2:20
H 1011

TAMLA 54051
ZTSC 84488
Produced by
Berry Gordy, Jr.

SMALL SAD SAM
(Sunny Skylar and E. V. Deane)
BOB KAYLI

TAMLA

T-54141
© 1966
Jobete BMI
AC-IL-185319
2:57

Produced By
Wm. Stevenson,
H. Cosby
In Album
"Take Two"
T-270

IT TAKES TWO
(Wm. Stevenson, S. Moy)
MARVIN GAYE &
KIM WESTON

A TRADEMARK OF MOTOWN RECORD CORP. © 1966

MISCELLANEOUS
SAMPLE LABEL DESIGNS

PART III

MOTOWN
& RELATED LABELS

The first and only Black Forum 7-inch single.

MISCELLANEOUS
SAMPLE LABEL DESIGNS

Listed below are brief descriptions of the American and British labels on which recordings were issued by the Motown Record Corporation, and for which discographies are included in this book. Also described are five Motown-related Detroit labels that were either purchased by Motown or that discontinued as a result of key personnel joining the Motown organization. The discographies for these five labels (Anna, Golden World, Harvey, Ric-Tic, and Tri-Phi) appear in a separate section of this book.

ANNA Active 1958-1961. A Motown-related Detroit label operated by Berry Gordy's sisters, Anna Gordy and Gwen Gordy, together with Billy Davis (aka Roquel Davis and Tyran Carlo). Harvey Fuqua and Berry Gordy produced records for the label, and future Temptation David Ruffin recorded the next-to-last single released by the label in 1961. As the label was phasing out in 1961, Harvey and Gwen formed their own labels, Tri-Phi and Harvey.

BLACK FORUM Active 1970-1973. Motown's spoken-word label released the speeches of Dr. Martin Luther King, Jr., and others, as well as poetry by such black poets as Langston Hughes and Imanu Amiri Baraka (LeRoi Jones).

BLAZE Active 1969. A short-lived label that created no identity for itself.

CHISA Active 1969-1971. A jazz-oriented label established by Hugh Masekela.

DIVINITY Active 1962-1963. Motown's only gospel-oriented label.

ECOLOGY Established 1970 by Berry Gordy and Sammy Davis, Jr.

FONTANA This was the second British label (London was the first) to issue Motown records in the United Kingdom. Four singles were released during a brief period from December 1961 to March 1962. Subsequent releases of Motown artists in the U.K. appeared on the Oriole label and then on Stateside, before Motown established its own Tamla Motown label in 1965.

GAIEE One single on this label was released in 1975.

GOLDEN WORLD Active 1963-1966. A Mo-town-related Detroit label that was purchased by Motown from Eddie Wingate and Joanne Jackson in 1966. Eddie Wingate's family of labels also included Ric-Tic. The purchase included the recording contracts of Edwin Starr and J.J. Barnes (both of whose records had been released on Ric-Tic), as well as the acquisition a much needed recording studio.

GORDY Established 1962, still active. Two label designs: Gordy 7001-7056 (approximately) are purple with the handwritten Gordy logo in yellow across the top; they carry the slogan, "It's what's in the grooves that counts." The second, current label design is purple with the Gordy logo in a yellow triangle at the side. Following Gordy 7216 (singles) and Gordy 1007 (albums), Motown consolidated the numbering of its three active labels (Gordy, Tamla, Motown), beginning with the number 1600 for singles and number 6000 for albums (see TMG Consolidated Series). Among the artists who have recorded on the Gordy label are the Temptations, the Contours, Marv Johnson, Martha & the Vandellas, Rick James, and the Mary Jane Girls.

HARVEY Active 1961-1963. Established as a subsidiary label of Tri-Phi by Harvey Fuqua and his wife, Gwen Gordy. Jr. Walker & the All Stars released three singles on this label before joining the Motown family.

HITSVILLE Active 1976-1977. Continues the Melodyland label. Both featured a similar label design, and were devoted to country music.

INFERNO A Detroit-based independent label that was briefly associated with Motown in 1968, and which issued garage-band rock 'n' roll. Discography includes only their Motown-related releases.

JU-PAR Two singles were released on this

▲ The first single and the first album on the Motown label. ▲

▼ Early and later Gordy label designs. ▼

MISCELLANEOUS
SAMPLE LABEL DESIGNS

independent label while it was associated with Motown in 1977.

LATINO Active briefly in 1982 as Motown's Hispanic label. Singles appear in the TMG Consolidated Series numerical sequence.

LONDON This major U.K. label issued four singles by Motown artists from 1959 to 1961. During 1961, Motown's British releases were switched from London to Fontana.

MC Active 1977-1978. Berry Gordy and Mike Curb formed this label to release country and western songs.

MELODY Active 1962-1965. Of interest to rhythm and blues collectors for its 1962 releases by Lamont Dozier, the Vells (an early version of Martha & the Vandellas), and the Pirates (a pseudonym for the Temptations). Subsequent releases (Melody 106 onward) were country and western.

MELODYLAND Active 1974-1976. A country and western label that became the Hitsville label after a legal dispute over the name arose.

MIRACLE Active 1961-1962. The first singles by Jummy Ruffin and the Temptations appeared on this short-lived label, which was discontinued when the Gordy label was established in 1962.

MOROCCO Established 1983 and inactive by the end of 1984, this label stands for the MOtown ROCk COmpany. Albums and singles appear in the TMG Consolidated Series numerical sequence.

MOTOWN Established 1961, still active. Two label designs: a striped label was used on the first singles releases (Motown 1000-1011 approximately); subsequent singles bear the now familiar map design in blue and gray. Early albums prior to the introduction of the map design bear an unusual label featuring the word "Motown" in a whimsical 1950s-style lettering. Following Motown 1532 (singles) and Motown 962 (albums), numbering for the Tamla, Motown, and Gordy labels was consolidated into a single sequence starting at 1600 for singles and 6000 for albums (see TMG Consolidated Series). Among the artists

who have recorded for the Motown label are the Supremes, Four Tops, Mary Wells, the Jackson 5, and the Commodores. (NOTE: Motown albums with numbering from M5-101V1 through M8-239M2 and from 5240ML upwards are reissues. See the U.S. record number index for original release numbering.)

MOWEST Active 1971-1973. West Coast-oriented label handled from Motown's Los Angeles office. Roster of artists included the Commodores (before they were switched to the Motown label), Syreeta, G.C. Cameron, Frankie Valli & the Four Seasons, Bobby Taylor, Tom Clay, and Thelma Houston.

NATURAL RESOURCES Active 1972-1973. Used again in 1976 for the novelty group, Gaylord & Holiday, then again in 1978-1979 for a series of reissue and compilation albums, including the FROM THE VAULTS (4014) collection of previously unreleased tracks.

ORIOLE Motown releases in the U.K. began appearing on this label in September 1962 and continued through September 1963, when Stateside picked up Motown for U.K. releases.

PICKWICK This budget-line British label issued a series of fourteen albums by Motown artists in 1982.

PRODIGAL Active 1974-1978. Essentially a pop-rock label that picked up where the Rare Earth label left off. In addition to records by the group Rare Earth, this label included such artists as Gary U.S. Bonds, Charlene, and such novelty acts as Joe Frazier and Gaylord & Holiday.

RARE EARTH Active 1969-1976. Introduced in 1969 at a press conference at Detroit's Roostertail club, the Rare Earth label represented Motown's attempt to capitalize on the psychedelic craze of the late 1960s. The first releases on the label included British acts like the Pretty Things and the Detroit-based Rare Earth group. By mid-1973 the label was practically inactive; the psychedelic craze and "underground rock" were a thing of the past.

RIC-TIC Active 1965-1968. This label began as a Detroit-based competitor to Motown, its biggest hits coming from Edwin Starr ("Agent

MISCELLANEOUS
SAMPLE LABEL DESIGNS

Double-O Soul") and J.J. Barnes ("Real Humdinger"). The contracts for both Edwin Starr and J.J Barnes were purchased from Eddie Wingate and Joanne Jackson in 1966 as part of the purchase of Golden World Records. While Golden World stopped issuing records once it was purchased by Motown, Ric-Tic continued to issue records until 1968. In England, Motown issued several Ric-Tic singles on its Tamla Motown label, and a compilation album (RIC-TIC RELICS) was also released there. Motown also reissued the label's only album, by the San Remo Golden Strings, on the Gordy label.

A variation on the Ric-Tic label design.
(See also page 518)

SOUL Active 1964-1978. Approximately 125 singles and 50 albums were released on this soul and rhythm and blues-oriented label. Two label designs: singles 35001-35019 (approximately) are white with pink lettering on the side; subsequent singles and albums feature a swirl design. Among the artists associated with this label were Shorty Long, Jr. Walker & the All Stars, Gladys Knight & the Pips, Jimmy Ruffin, and the Originals.

STATESIDE This U.K. label issued Motown artists from October 1963 through March 1965, at which time the Tamla Motown label was established in London, England, for all British releases.

TAMLA Established 1959, still active. This was the first label for the Motown Record Corporation, originally slated to be called Tammie after a popular film and song of the period. Various label designs: Tamla singles 101 and 102 show TAMLA in block capital letters across the top of an ochre label; singles 54024-54044 (approximately) have the striped design over a yellow label with a vertical TAMLA to the side; singles 54045-54140 (approximately) are yellow with two globes at the top; singles from 54141 (approximately) to date are yellow with a brown bar across the top. Early albums have a white label with a black and purple logo featuring TAMLA wrapped around a globe. Following single 54333 and album 376, numbering for the Tamla, Motown, and Gordy labels was consolidated into a single sequence starting at 1600 for singles and 6000 for albums (see TMG Consolidated Series). Among the artists who have recorded on Tamla are Marvin Gaye, Smokey Robinson and the Miracles, the Marvelettes, Stevie Wonder, and Eddie Kendricks.

TAMLA MOTOWN Refers to the British label established by Motown in March 1965, once the company had achieved enough popularity and sufficient demand in England. Prior to this, Motown releases in the U.K. had appeared on the London, Fontana, Oriole, and Stateside labels. Tamla Motown would continue as a label until September 1976, when it was changed to Motown. At that time, the black Tamla Motown label was changed to a newly designed blue label with the slogan, "The New Era."

TMG CONSOLIDATED SERIES Starting January 1982, numbering was consolidated for Motown's three active labels: Tamla, Motown, and Gordy. While the three labels each retained their distinctive designs, the numbering for all singles was consolidated into a single sequence beginning at 1600 and for albums at 6000. Also appearing within this sequence are the Latino and Morocco labels. While some compact discs (CDs) appear in the TMG LP sequence, a new consolidated CD sequence was initiated in August 1986, starting at 8000. The 8000 CDs contain two reissued albums on each CD.

The first Soul-label 7-inch single.

Another variation of the Soul singles label.

▼ Two versions of the V.I.P. singles label design. ▼

MISCELLANEOUS
SAMPLE LABEL DESIGNS

TRI-PHI Active 1961-1963. As Anna Records became inactive in 1961, Harvey Fuqua and Gwen Gordy established their own labels, Tri-Phi and Harvey. Tri-Phi was the more active of the two labels. The label's first release was by the Spinners in 1961. The label also released singles by Harvey Fuqua and by the duet of Johnny (Bristol) and Jackey (Beavers), including a version of "Someday We'll Be Together" that later became a hit for Diana Ross.

VIP Active 1964-1972. Approximately sixty-five singles but fewer than ten albums were issued on this subsidiary label, which included on its roster such artists as the Velvelettes, the Spinners, Chris Clark, and Chuck Jackson.

THE HEADLINERS
(V.I.P. label quartet)

The first album on the V.I.P. label.

WEED One album was released on this subsidiary label in 1969 by future Motown executive Chris Clark.

WORKSHOP JAZZ Active 1963-1964. Motown's jazz-oriented label.

YESTERYEAR Motown's reissue label for singles. Each single typically combines two A-sides. Album reissues appear on the regular Tamla, Motown, Gordy, or other labels with new numbers. The single and album reissues are not listed in the main discography of this book.

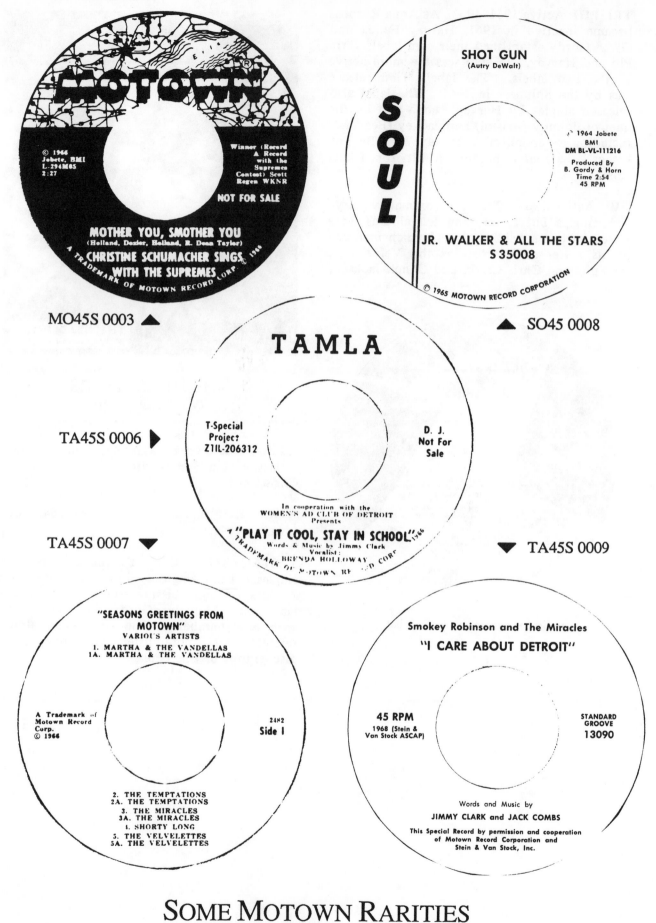

Some Motown Rarities
(See U.S. discography entries for details.)

PART IV

MOTOWN DISCOGRAPHY (UNITED STATES)

KEY TO
U.S. ENTRY NUMBER PREFIXES

ENTRY NUMBER PREFIX	LABEL NAME & RECORD FORMAT	DISCOGRAPHY PAGE NUMBER
BF45	Black Forum 7-inch Singles	169
BFLP	Black Forum Albums	169
BL45	Blaze 7-inch Singles	169
CH45	Chisa 7-inch Singles	169
CHCO	Chisa 7-inch Color Vinyl Singles	170
CHEP	Chisa 7-inch EPs	170
CHLP	Chisa Albums	170
DI45	Divinity 7-inch Singles	170
EC45	Ecology 7-inch Singles	170
GA45	Gaiee 7-inch Singles	170
GO45	Gordy 7-inch Singles	170
GOCO	Gordy 7-inch Color Vinyl Singles	179
GOEP	Gordy 7-inch EPs	180
GOLP	Gordy Albums	180
HI45	Hitsville 7-inch Singles	184
HILP	Hitsville Albums	184
IN45	Inferno 7-inch Singles	184
JU45	Ju-Par 7-inch Singles	185
JULP	Ju-Par Albums	185
MC45	MC 7-inch Singles	185
MCLP	MC Albums	185
ME45	Melody 7-inch Singles	186
MI45	Miracle 7-inch Singles	186
ML45	Melodyland 7-inch Singles	187
MLLP	Melodyland Albums	188
MO12	Motown 12-inch Singles	214
MO45	Motown 7-inch Singles	188
MO45S	Motown 7-inch Special Issues	211
MOCB	Motown Cardboard Singles	212
MOCO	Motown 7-inch Color Vinyl Singles	212
MOEP	Motown 7-inch EPs	213
MOLP	Motown Albums	215
MW45	Mowest 7-inch Singles	227
MWCO	Mowest 7-inch Color Vinyl Singles	229
MWLP	Mowest Albums	229
NA45	Natural Resources 7-inch Singles	230
NALP	Natural Resources Albums	230
PR45	Prodigal 7-inch Singles	231
PRLP	Prodigal Albums	232
RA45	Rare Earth 7-inch Singles	233
RACO	Rare Earth 7-inch Color Vinyl Singles	235
RALP	Rare Earth Albums	235
SO45	Soul 7-inch Singles	237
SOEP	Soul 7-inch EPs	241
SOLP	Soul Albums	242
TA45	Tamla 7-inch Singles	243
TA45S	Tamla 7-inch Special Issues	258
TACO	Tamla 7-inch Color Vinyl Singles	259
TAEP	Tamla 7-inch EPs	259
TALP	Tamla Albums	260
TMG12	TMG Consolidated Series 12-inch Singles	276
TMG45	TMG Consolidated Series 7-inch Singles	265
TMGCD	TMG Consolidated Series Compact Discs	286
TMGLP	TMG Consolidated Series Albums	279
VI45	VIP 7-inch Singles	288
VICO	VIP 7-inch Color Vinyl Singles	291
VILP	VIP Albums	291
WELP	Weed Albums	291
WO45	Workshop Jazz 7-inch Singles	291
WOLP	Workshop Jazz Albums	291

BLACK FORUM 7-INCH SINGLES

BF45 0001 (04/73)	Black Forum B 20000F	Elaine Brown No Time Until We're Free

BLACK FORUM ALBUMS

BFLP 0001 (10/70)	Black Forum BF451L	Dr. Martin Luther King, Jr. WHY I OPPOSE THE WAR IN VIETNAM
BFLP 0002 (10/70)	Black Forum BF452L	Stokely Carmichael FREE HUEY
BFLP 0003 (10/70)	Black Forum BF453L	Langston Hughes & Margaret Danner WRITERS OF THE REVOLUTION
BFLP 0004 (02/72)	Black Forum BF454L	Black Fighting Men Recorded Live in Vietnam GUESS WHO'S COMING HOME
BFLP 0005 (04/72)	Black Forum BF455L	Ossie Davis and Bill Cosby THE CONGRESSIONAL BLACK CAUCUS
BFLP 0006 (04/72)	Black Forum BF456L	Imanu Amiri Baraka BLACK SPIRITS
BFLP 0007 (04/72)	Black Forum BF457L	Imanu Amiri Baraka IT'S NATION TIME
BFLP 0008 (04/73)	Black Forum BF458L	Elaine Brown ELAINE BROWN

BLAZE 7-INCH SINGLES

BL45 0001 (09/69)	Blaze 1107	Jack Ashford and the Sound of New Detroit Do The Choo Choo Pt. 1 Do The Choo Choo Pt. 2

CHISA 7-INCH SINGLES

CH45 0001 (09/69)	Chisa C 8001	Stu Gardener Home On The Range (Everybody Needs A Home) Mend This Generation Note: "A" side also issued on red vinyl.
CH45 0002 (09/69)	Chisa C 8001	Stu Gardener Home On The Range (Everybody Needs A Home) It's A Family Thang
CH45 0003 (09/69)	Chisa C 8002	Monk Montgomery A Place In The Sun Your Love Note: "A" side also issued on red vinyl.
CH45 0004 (10/69)	Chisa C 8003	Arthur Adams It's Private Tonight Let's Make Some Love Note: "A" side also issued on red vinyl. See also Chisa 8011.
CH45 0005 (11/69)	Chisa C 8004	Anonymous Children of Today Can We Talk To You (For A Little While) Love And Peace
CH45 0006 (05/69)	Chisa C 8005	Dorothy, Oma and Zelpha Gonna Put It On Your Mind Henry Blake
CH45 0007 (12/69)	Chisa C 8006	Five Smooth Stones I Will Never Love Another Love Unto Me Note: "A" side also issued on red vinyl.
CH45 0008 (02/70)	Chisa C 8007	Stu Gardener Expressin' My Love I Don't Dream No More
CH45 0009 (04/70)	Chisa C 8008	Arthur Adams My Baby's Love Loving You
CH45 0010 (10/70)	Chisa C 8009	Hugh Masekela and the Union of South Africa You Keep Me Hangin' On Make Me A Potion
CH45 0011 (09/70)	Chisa C 8010	Jazz Crusaders Way Back Home Jackson!
CH45 0012 (02/71)	Chisa C 8011	Arthur Adams Can't Wait To See You Again It's Private Tonight
CH45 0013 (03/71)	Chisa C 8012	Letta I Won't Weep No More You Touched Me
CH45 0014 (06/71)	Chisa C 8013	Jazz Crusaders Pass The Plate Greasy Spoon
CH45 0015 (06/71)	Chisa C 8014	Hugh Masekela and the Union of South Africa Dyambo (Dee-Yambo) Weary Day Is Over Shebeen
CH45 0016	Chisa C 8015	Arthur Adams Uncle Tom Mornin' Train Note: Unissued.

CHISA 7-INCH
COLOR VINYL SINGLES

CHCO 0001	Chisa C 8001 (09/69)	Stu Gardener Home On The Range (Everybody Needs A Home) Note: Red vinyl.
CHCO 0002	Chisa C 8002 (09/69)	Monk Montgomery A Place In The Sun Note: Red vinyl.
CHCO 0003	Chisa C 8003 (10/69)	Arthur Adams It's Private Tonight Note: Red vinyl.
CHCO 0004	Chisa C 8006 (12/69)	The Five Smooth Stones I Will Never Love Another Note: Red vinyl.

CHISA 7-INCH EPS

CHEP 0001	Chisa 60804	The Jazz Crusaders OLD SOCKS, NEW SHOES...NEW SOCKS, OLD SHOES Side 1: Jackson/Hard Times/Why Do You Laugh At Me? - Side 2: Jazz!/Golden Slumbers Note: Manufactured by Little L.P.'s Unlimited of Northfield, Illinois (LLP 135).
CHEP 0002	Chisa 60642 (1968)	Various Artists IN LOVING MEMORY Side 1: Gladys Knight & The Pips...How Great Thou Art/Four Tops...Nobody Knows The Trouble I've Seen - Side 2: Voices Of The Tabernacle...Steal Away/Martha Reeves & The Vandellas...Were You There

CHISA ALBUMS

CHLP 0001	Chisa CS801P (01/70)	Monk Montgomery IT'S NEVER TOO LATE
CHLP 0002	Chisa CS802P	Note: Unissued.
CHLP 0003	Chisa CS803P (07/70)	Hugh Masekela RECONSTRUCTION
CHLP 0004	Chisa CS804P (07/70)	Jazz Crusaders OLD SOCKS NEW SHOES, NEW SOCKS OLD SHOES
CHLP 0005	Chisa CS805P (09/70)	Letta LETTA
CHLP 0006	Chisa CS806P (05/71)	Monk Montgomery BASS ODYSSEY
CHLP 0007	Chisa CS807P (05/71)	Crusaders PASS THE PLATE
CHLP 0008	Chisa CS808P (05/71)	Hugh Masekela and the Union of South Africa HUGH MASEKELA AND THE UNION OF SOUTH AFRICA
CHLP 0009	Chisa CS809P	Letta MOSADI Note: Unissued.

DIVINITY 7-INCH SINGLES

DI45 0001	Divinity 99004 (07/62)	Wright Specials That's What He Is To Me Pilgrim Of Sorrow
DI45 0002	Divinity 99005 (06/63)	Wright Specials Ninety-Nine And A Half Won't Do I Won't Go Back
DI45 0003	Divinity 99006 (07/63)	Gospel Stars Give God A Chance Have You Any Time For Jesus
DI45 0004	Divinity 99007 (05/63)	Burnadettes First You've Got To Recognize God I'm Going Home
DI45 0005	Divinity 99008	Liz Lands We Shall Overcome Trouble In This Land

ECOLOGY 7-INCH SINGLES

EC45 0001	Ecology 1000 (03/71)	Sammy Davis, Jr. In My Own Lifetime I'll Begin Again

GAIEE 7-INCH SINGLES

GA45 0001	Gaiee GA 90001F (04/75)	Valentino I Was Born This Way Liberation

GORDY 7-INCH SINGLES

GO45 0001	Gordy 7001 (04/62)	The Temptations Dream Come True Isn't She Pretty
GO45 0002	Gordy 7002 (05/62)	Lee & The Leopards Come Into My Palace Trying To Make It Note: Also issued on Laurie 3197.
GO45 0003	Gordy 7003 (05/62)	The Valadiers While I'm Away Because I Love Her

GO45 0004	Gordy 7004	Bob Kayli Everybody Was There (I Took Care) Toodle Loo Note: Unissued. "B" side originally released on Carlton 482B. Bob Kayli is a pseudonym for Robert Gordy, one of Berry Gordy's brothers. See also Gordy 7008.
GO45 0005	Gordy 7004	Hattie Littles Back In My Arms Again Is It Love Note: Unissued.
GO45 0006	Gordy 7005 (07/62)	The Contours Do You Love Me Move, Mr. Man
GO45 0007	Gordy 7006 (08/62)	Mike & The Modifiers It's Too Bad I Found Myself A Brand New Baby
GO45 0008	Gordy 7007 (10/62)	Hattie Littles Your Love Is Wonderful Here You Come Note: Vocal accompaniment on "B" side credits The Fayettes.
GO45 0009	Gordy 7008 (11/62)	Bob Kayli Hold on Pearl Toodle Loo Note: See also Gordy 7004B.

GO45 0010	Gordy 7009 (12/62)	LaBrenda Ben & The
		    Beljeans
		The Chaperone
		Camel Walk
		    Note: Originally scheduled to
		be released on Motown 1033 as by
		The Blue Jeans.

GO45 0011	Gordy 7010 (01/63)	The Temptations Paradise Slow Down Heart
GO45 0012	Gordy 7011 (09/62)	Martha And The Vandellas I'll Have To Let Him Go My Baby Won't Come Back
GO45 0013	Gordy 7012 (12/62)	The Contours Shake Sherry You Better Get In Line Note: Promo copies issued with blank "B" side. Also, promo version is alternate take of commercial "Shake Sherry." The running time for promo copy is 2:33, compared to 2:39 for commercial version.
GO45 0014	Gordy 7013 (01/63)	The Valadiers I Found A Girl You'll Be Sorry Someday
GO45 0015	Gordy 7014 (02/63)	Martha & The Vandellas Come And Get These Memories Jealous Lover
GO45 0016	Gordy 7015 (03/63)	The Temptations I Want A Love I Can See The Further You Look The Less You See
GO45 0017	Gordy 7016 (03/63)	The Contours Don't Let Her Be Your Baby It Must Be Love
GO45 0018	Gordy 7017 (04/63)	Bunny Paul We're Only Young Once I'm Hooked
GO45 0019	Gordy 7018 (05/63)	The Stylers Going Steady Anniversary Pushing Up Daisies
GO45 0020	Gordy 7019 (06/63)	The Contours Pa I Need A Car You Get Ugly
GO45 0021	Gordy 7020 (07/63)	The Temptations May I Have This Dance Farewell My Love
GO45 0022	Gordy 7021 (09/63)	Labrenda Ben I Can't Help It, I Gotta Dance Just Be Yourself Note: Vocal accompaniment on "B" side credits The Andantes.
GO45 0023	Gordy 7022 (07/63)	Martha & The Vandellas Heat Wave A Love Like Yours (Don't Come Knocking Everyday)
GO45 0024	Gordy 7023 (10/63)	Rev. Martin Luther King I Have A Dream We Shall Overcome Note: "B" side as by Liz Lands. "B" side vocal accompaniment credits The Voices of Salvation.
GO45 0025	Gordy 7024 (10/63)	The Darnells Too Hurt To Cry, Too Much In Love To Say Goodbye Come On Home
GO45 0026	Gordy 7025 (11/63)	Martha & The Vandellas Quicksand Darling, I Hum Our Song

GO45 0027	Gordy 7026 (12/63)	Liz Lands
		May What He Lived For Live
		He's Got The Whole World In
		    His Hands
		    Note: Promo copies of "A"
		side issued with blank "B" side.
		Vocal accompaniment on both sides
		credits The Voices Of Love.

GO45 0028	Gordy 7027 (01/64)	Martha & The Vandellas Live Wire Old Love (Let's Try It Again)
GO45 0029	Gordy 7028 (01/64)	The Temptations The Way You Do The Things You Do Just Let Me Know

GO45 0030	Gordy 7029 (03/64)	The Contours Can You Do It I'll Stand By You
GO45 0031	Gordy 7030 (03/64)	Liz Lands Midnight Johnny Keep Me 　　Note: Vocal accompaniment on both sides credits The Temptations.
GO45 0032	Gordy 7031 (03/64)	Martha & The Vandellas In My Lonely Room A Tear For The Girl
GO45 0033	Gordy 7032 (04/64)	The Temptations The Girl's Alright With Me I'll Be In Trouble
GO45 0034	Gordy 7033 (07/64)	Martha & The Vandellas Dancing In The Street There He Is (At My Door)
GO45 0035	Gordy 7034 (08/64)	Tommy Good Baby I Miss You Leaving Here
GO45 0036	Gordy 7035 (08/64)	The Temptations Girl (Why You Wanna Make Me 　Blue) Baby, Baby I Need You
GO45 0037	Gordy 7036 (11/64)	Martha & The Vandellas Wild One Dancing Slow
GO45 0038	Gordy 7037 (12/64)	The Contours Can You Jerk Like Me That Day When She Needed 　Me
GO45 0039	Gordy 7038 (12/64)	The Temptations My Girl (Talking 'Bout) Nobody But 　My Baby 　　Note: Issued with black and white picture sleeve.
GO45 0040	Gordy 7039 (02/65)	Martha & The Vandellas Nowhere To Run Motoring
GO45 0041	Gordy 7040 (03/65)	The Temptations It's Growing What Love Has Joined 　Together
GO45 0042	Gordy 7041 (05/65)	Kim Weston A Thrill A Moment I'll Never See My Love Again
GO45 0043	Gordy 7042 (06/65)	Marv Johnson Why Do You Want To Let Me Go I'm Not A Plaything
GO45 0044	Gordy 7043 (06/65)	The Temptations Since I Lost My Baby You've Got to Earn It

GO45 0045	Gordy 7044 (08/65)	The Contours First I Look At The Purse Searching For A Girl
GO45 0046	Gordy 7045 (07/65)	Martha & The Vandellas Love (Makes Me Do Foolish 　Things) You've Been In Love Too 　Long
GO45 0047	Gordy 7046 (09/65)	Kim Weston Take Me In Your Arms (Rock Me 　A Little While) Don't Compare Me With Her
GO45 0048	Gordy 7047 (10/65)	The Temptations My Baby Don't Look Back
GO45 0049	Gordy 7048 (01/66)	Martha & The Vandellas My Baby Loves Me Never Leave Your Baby's 　Side
GO45 0050	Gordy 7049 (02/66)	The Temptations Get Ready Fading Away
GO45 0051	Gordy 7050 (03/66)	Kim Weston Helpless A Love Like Yours (Don't 　Come Knocking Every Day)
GO45 0052	Gordy 7051 (03/66)	Marv Johnson I Miss You Baby (How I Miss You) Just The Way You Are
GO45 0053	Gordy 7052 (03/66)	The Contours Just A Little Misunderstanding Determination
GO45 0054	Gordy 7053 (04/66)	Martha & The Vandellas What Am I Going To Do Without 　Your Love Go Ahead And Laugh
GO45 0055	Gordy 7054 (05/66)	The Temptations Ain't Too Proud To Beg You'll Lose A Precious Love 　　Note: Issued with picture sleeve.
GO45 0056	Gordy 7055 (08/66)	The Temptations Beauty Is Only Skin Deep You're Not An Ordinary Girl 　　Note: Issued with picture sleeve.
GO45 0057	Gordy 7056 (10/66)	Martha & The Vandellas I'm Ready For Love He Doesn't Love Her 　Anymore
GO45 0058	Gordy 7057 (11/66)	The Temptations (I Know) I'm Losing You I Couldn't Cry If I Wanted To
GO45 0059	Gordy 7058 (02/67)	Martha & The Vandellas Jimmy Mack Third Finger, Left Hand

GO45 0060	Gordy 7059 (03/67)	The Contours It's So Hard Being A Loser Your Love Grows More Precious Everyday
GO45 0061	Gordy 7060 (04/67)	San Remo Golden Strings Festival Time Joy Road Note: Previously issued on Ric-Tic 112.
GO45 0062	Gordy 7061 (04/67)	The Temptations All I Need Sorry Is A Sorry Word
GO45 0063	Gordy 7062 (08/67)	Martha & The Vandellas Love Bug Leave My Heart Alone One Way Out Note: "A" side also issued on red vinyl.
GO45 0064	Gordy 7063 (06/67)	The Temptations You're My Everything I've Been Good To You
GO45 0065	Gordy 7064 (06/67)	Rita Wright I Can't Give Back The Love I Feel For You Something On My Mind Note: This is the real name of Syreeta.
GO45 0066	Gordy 7065 (09/67)	The Temptations (Loneliness Made Me Realize) It's You That I Need Don't Send Me Away
GO45 0067	Gordy 7066 (11/67)	Edwin Starr I Want My Baby Back Gonna Keep On Tryin' Till I Win Your Love Note: See also Gordy 7104.
GO45 0068	Gordy 7067 (11/67)	Martha Reeves & The Vandellas Honey Chile Show Me The Way Note: First release as by Martha Reeves and The Vandellas.
GO45 0069	Gordy 7068 (12/67)	The Temptations I Wish It Would Rain I Truly, Truly Believe
GO45 0070	Gordy 7069 (03/68)	Bobby Taylor & The Vancouvers Does Your Mama Know About Me Fading Away Note: Issued with picture sleeve. "A" side also issued on red vinyl.
GO45 0071	Gordy 7070 (04/68)	Martha Reeves & The Vandellas I Promise To Wait My Love Forget Me Not
GO45 0072	Gordy 7071 (04/68)	Edwin Starr I Am The Man For You Baby My Weakness Is You
GO45 0073	Gordy 7072 (04/68)	The Temptations I Could Never Love Another (After Loving You) Gonna Give Her All The Love I've Got
GO45 0074	Gordy 7073 (06/68)	Bobby Taylor & The Vancouvers I Am Your Man If You Love Her
GO45 0075	Gordy 7074 (07/68)	The Temptations Please Return Your Love To Me How Can I Forget
GO45 0076	Gordy 7075 (08/68)	Martha Reeves & The Vandellas I Can't Dance To That Music You're Playing I Tried
GO45 0077	Gordy 7076 (08/68)	Eivets Rednow Alfie More Than A Dream Note: The name is Stevie Wonder spelled backwards.
GO45 0078	Gordy 7077 (09/68)	Marv Johnson I'll Pick A Rose For My Rose You Got The Love I Love
GO45 0079	Gordy 7078 (10/68)	Edwin Starr Way Over There If My Heart Could Tell The Story
GO45 0080	Gordy 7079 (11/68)	Bobby Taylor & The Vancouvers Malinda It's Growing
GO45 0081	Gordy 7080 (10/68)	Martha Reeves & The Vandellas Sweet Darlin' Without You
GO45 0082	Gordy 7081 (10/68)	The Temptations Cloud Nine Why Did She Have To Leave Me (Why Did She Have To Go)
GO45 0083	Gordy 7082 (12/68)	The Temptations Rudolph, The Red Nosed Reindeer Silent Night Note: "A" side also issued on red vinyl.
GO45 0084	Gordy 7083 (01/69)	Edwin Starr Twenty-Five Miles Love Is My Destination Note: "A" side also issued on red vinyl.
GO45 0085	Gordy 7084 (01/69)	The Temptations Run Away Child, Running Wild I Need Your Lovin'
GO45 0086	Gordy 7085 (03/69)	Martha Reeves & The Vandellas (We've Got) Honey Love I'm In Love (And I Know It)

GO45 0087	Gordy 7086 (05/69)	The Temptations Don't Let The Joneses Get You Down Since I've Lost You
GO45 0088	Gordy 7087 (06/69)	Edwin Starr I'm Still A Struggling Man Pretty Little Angel Note: "A" side also issued on red vinyl.
GO45 0089	Gordy 7088	Bobby Taylor Oh, I've Been Bless'd It Should Have Been Me Loving Her Note: Unissued. Released on V.I.P. 25053. See also Gordy 7092.
GO45 0090	Gordy 7089	The Lollipops Cheating Is Telling On You Need Your Love Note: Unissued. Released on V.I.P. 25051.
GO45 0091	Gordy 7090 (07/69)	Blinky & Edwin Starr Oh How Happy Ooo Baby Baby Note: "A" side also issued on red vinyl.
GO45 0092	Gordy 7091	Terry Johnson My Springtime Suzie Note: Unissued. See also Gordy 7095.
GO45 0093	Gordy 7092 (08/69)	Bobby Taylor My Girl Has Gone It Should Have Been Me Loving Her Note: "B" side originally scheduled for release on Gordy 7088B.
GO45 0094	Gordy 7093 (07/69)	The Temptations I Can't Get Next To You Running Away (Ain't Gonna Help You)
GO45 0095	Gordy 7094 (08/69)	Martha Reeves & The Vandellas Taking My Love (And Leaving Me) Heartless
GO45 0096	Gordy 7095 (11/69)	Terry Johnson What 'Cha Gonna Do Suzie Note: "B" side originally scheduled for release on Gordy 7091B.
GO45 0097	Gordy 7096 (12/69)	The Temptations Psychedelic Shack That's The Way Love Is
GO45 0098	Gordy 7097 (02/70)	Edwin Starr Time Running Back and Forth
GO45 0099	Gordy 7098 (03/70)	Martha Reeves & The Vandellas I Should Be Proud Love, Guess Who
GO45 0100	Gordy 7099 (05/70)	The Temptations Ball of Confusion (That's What The World Is Today) It's Summer Note: Issued with picture sleeve. See also Gordy 7109. "A" side also issued on red vinyl.
GO45 0101	Gordy 7100 (05/70)	Buzzie Stone Soul Booster Sandy
GO45 0102	Gordy 7101 (06/70)	Edwin Starr War He Who Picks A Rose
GO45 0103	Gordy 7102 (09/70)	The Temptations Ungena Za Ulimwengu (Unite The World) Hum Along And Dance Note: "A" side also issued on red vinyl.
GO45 0104	Gordy 7103 (10/70)	Martha Reeves & The Vandellas I Gotta Let You Go You're The Loser Now
GO45 0105	Gordy 7104 (12/70)	Edwin Starr Stop The War Now Gonna Keep On Tryin' Till I Win Your Love Note: See also Gordy 7066.
GO45 0106	Gordy 7105 (01/71)	The Temptations Just My Imagination (Running Away With Me) You Make Your Own Heaven And Hell Right Here On Earth
GO45 0107	Gordy 7106 (03/71)	The Undisputed Truth Save My Love For A Rainy Day Since I've Lost You
GO45 0108	Gordy 7107 (04/71)	Edwin Starr Funky Music Sho Nuff Turns Me On Cloud Nine
GO45 0109	Gordy 7108 (06/71)	The Undisputed Truth Smiling Faces Sometimes You Got The Love I Need Note: "A" side also issued on red vinyl.
GO45 0110	Gordy 7109 (07/71)	The Temptations It's Summer I'm The Exception To The Rule Note: "A" side is alternate take to the version on Gordy 7099B. Gordy 7109A runs 2:56, compared to 2:36 for the version on Gordy 7099.

GO45 0111	Gordy 7110 (09/71)	Martha Reeves & The Vandellas Bless You Hope I Don't Get My Heart Broke
GO45 0112	Gordy 7111 (10/71)	The Temptations Superstar (Remember How You Got Where You Are) Gonna Keep On Tryin' Till I Win Your Love
GO45 0113	Gordy 7112 (12/71)	The Undisputed Truth You Make Your Own Heaven And Hell Right Here On Earth Ball Of Confusion (That's What The World Is Today)
GO45 0114	Gordy 7113 (12/71)	Martha Reeves & The Vandellas In And Out Of My Life Your Love Makes It All Worthwhile Note: "A" side also issued on red vinyl.
GO45 0115	Gordy 7114 (02/72)	The Undisputed Truth What It Is California Soul
GO45 0116	Gordy 7115 (02/72)	The Temptations Take A Look Around Smooth Sailing (From Now On)
GO45 0117	Gordy 7116 (04/72)	Eric & The Vikings It's Too Much For Man To Take Too Long Time Don't Wait
GO45 0118	Gordy 7117 (06/72)	The Undisputed Truth Papa Was A Rollin' Stone Friendship Train Note: "A" side also issued on red vinyl.
GO45 0119	Gordy 7118 (05/72)	Martha Reeves & The Vandellas Tear It On Down I Want You Back
GO45 0120	Gordy 7119 (06/72)	The Temptations Mother Nature Funky Music Sho Nuff Turns Me On Note: "A" side also issued on red vinyl.
GO45 0121	Gordy 7120 (08/72)	The Festivals Green Grow The Lilacs So In Love Note: "B" side also issued on Colossus C.122X.
GO45 0122	Gordy 7121 (09/72)	The Temptations Papa Was A Rollin' Stone Papa Was A Rollin' Stone (Instrumental)
GO45 0123	Gordy 7122 (11/72)	The Undisputed Truth Girl You're Alright With A Little Help From My Friends
GO45 0124	Gordy 7123 (12/72)	Jay And The Techniques Robot Man I'll Be Here
GO45 0125	Gordy 7124 (03/73)	The Undisputed Truth Mama I Gotta Brand New Thing (Don't Say No) Gotta Keep On Tryin' Till I Win Your Love
GO45 0126	Gordy 7125	Paul Williams Feel Like Givin' Up Once You Had A Heart Note: Unissued. One of the Temptations, Paul apparently committed suicide just before this single was scheduled to be released.
GO45 0127	Gordy 7126 (02/73)	The Temptations Masterpiece (Vocal) Masterpiece (Instrumental)
GO45 0128	Gordy 7127	Martha Reeves I Won't Be The Fool I've Been Again Baby Don't You Leave Me Note: Unissued.
GO45 0129	Gordy 7128	Luther Allison Little Red Rooster Ragged And Dirty Note: Unissued.
GO45 0130	Gordy 7129 (06/73)	The Temptations Plastic Man Hurry Tommorrow
GO45 0131	Gordy 7130 (06/73)	The Undisputed Truth Law Of The Land Just My Imagination (Running Away With Me)
GO45 0132	Gordy 7131 (08/73)	The Temptations Hey Girl (I Like Your Style) Ma
GO45 0133	Gordy 7132 (09/73)	Eric & The Vikings I'm Truly Yours Where Do You Go (Baby)
GO45 0134	Gordy 7133 (12/73)	The Temptations Let Your Hair Down Ain't No Justice
GO45 0135	Gordy 7134 (04/74)	The Undisputed Truth Help Yourself What's Going On
GO45 0136	Gordy 7135 (02/74)	The Temptations Heavenly Zoom
GO45 0137	Gordy 7136 (05/74)	The Temptations You've Got My Soul On Fire I Need You

GO45 0138 (06/74)	Gordy 7137	Luther Allison Now You Got It Part Time Love
GO45 0139 (12/74)	Gordy 7138	The Temptations Happy People Happy People (Instrumental) Note: "B" side listed as The Temptations Band.
GO45 0140 (07/74)	Gordy 7139	The Undisputed Truth I'm A Fool For You The Girl's Alright With Me
GO45 0141 (10/74)	Gordy 7140	The Undisputed Truth Lil' Red Ridin' Hood Big John Is My Name
GO45 0142	Gordy 7141	The Undisputed Truth Earthquake Shake Spaced Out Note: Unissued. Issued as single-sided "A" side promo only.
GO45 0143 (02/75)	Gordy 7142	The Temptations Shakey Ground I'm A Bachelor
GO45 0144 (04/75)	Gordy 7143	The Undisputed Truth UFO's Got To Get My Hands On Some Lovin'
GO45 0145 (07/75)	Gordy 7144	The Temptations Glasshouse The Prophet
GO45 0146 (09/75)	Gordy 7145	The Undisputed Truth Higher Than High Spaced Out
GO45 0147 (01/76)	Gordy 7146	The Temptations Keep Holding On What You Need Most (I Do Best Of All)
GO45 0148 (03/76)	Gordy 7147	The Undisputed Truth Boogie Bump Boogie I Saw You When You Met Her
GO45 0149	Gordy 7148	Leon Ware Comfort Share Your Love Note: Unissued. Also scheduled for release on Motown 1368, but unissued on this number as well.
GO45 0150 (04/76)	Gordy 7149	Leslie Uggams I Want To Make It Easy For You Two Shoes Note: Originally scheduled to be released on Motown 1391, but release changed to above number at last minute.
GO45 0151 (05/76)	Gordy 7150	The Temptations Up The Creek (Without A Paddle) Darling, Stand By Me (Song For My Woman)
GO45 0152	Gordy 7151	The Temptations Who Are You Darling, Stand By Me (Song For My Woman) Note: Unissued. "A" side issued promotionally as single-sided test pressing only. See also Gordy 7150 and 7152.
GO45 0153 (10/76)	Gordy 7152	The Temptations Who Are You Let Me Count The Ways (I Love You) Note: "A" side originally scheduled for release on Gordy 7151A.
GO45 0154 (01/77)	Gordy 7153	Franki Kah'rl I'm In Love Don't Fan The Flame
GO45 0155 (06/77)	Gordy 7154	21st Creation Tailgate Mr. Disco Radio
GO45 0156 (09/77)	Gordy 7155	High Inergy You Can't Turn Me Off (In The Middle Of Turning Me On) Save It For A Rainy Day
GO45 0157 (09/77)	Gordy 7155	High Inergy You Can't Turn Me Off (In The Middle Of Turning Me On) Let Me Get Close To You
GO45 0158 (05/78)	Gordy 7156	Rick James You And I Hollywood Note: "A" side issued commercially on M-00012D1A as an extended version with running time of 8:04. Also issued promotionally on PR-34 as an extended version with running time of 8:04 on both sides.
GO45 0159 (02/78)	Gordy 7157	High Inergy Love Is All You Need Some Kinda Magic Note: "A" side also issued on yellow vinyl.
GO45 0160 (05/78)	Gordy 7158	21st Creation Girls, Let's Keep Dancing Close Funk Machine
GO45 0161 (07/78)	Gordy 7159	Switch There'll Never Be You Pulled A Switch Note: "A" side also issued on red vinyl.
GO45 0162 (06/78)	Gordy 7160	High Inergy We Are The Future High School
GO45 0163 (08/78)	Gordy 7161	High Inergy Lovin' Fever Beware

GO45 0164	Gordy 7162 (09/78)	Rick James Mary Jane Dream Maker
GO45 0165	Gordy 7163 (12/78)	Switch I Wanna Be Closer Somebody's Watchin' You
GO45 0166	Gordy 7164 (01/79)	Rick James High On Your Love Suite Stone City Band, Hi! Note: Issued with full-color picture sleeve. "A" side issued commercially on M-00012D1B as an extended version with running time of 7:20. Also issued promotionally on PR-45A with extended version running 7:17.
GO45 0167	Gordy 7165 (02/79)	Apollo Astro Disco - Pt. I Astro Disco - Pt. II Note: Issued commercially on M00018D1 as an extended version with running time of 6:50 (vocal) and 10:20 (instrumental).
GO45 0168	Gordy 7166 (03/79)	High Inergy Shoulda Gone Dancin' Peaceland Note: "A" side issued commercially on M-00019D1 as an extended version with running time of 9:47 (vocal) and 8:50 (instrumental).
GO45 0169	Gordy 7167 (04/79)	Rick James Bustin' Out Sexy Lady Note: "A" side issued promotionally on PR-51 as an extended version with running time of 7:20.
GO45 0170	Gordy 7168 (05/79)	Switch Best Beat In Town It's So Real Note: "A" side issued commercially on M-00025D1A as an extended version with running time of 4:45. Also issued promotionally on PR-55B as an extended version with running time of 4:48.
GO45 0171	Gordy 7169 (05/79)	Teena Marie I'm A Sucker For Your Love De Ja Vu (I've Been Here Before) Note: "A" side issued commercially on M-00024D1 as an extended version with running time of 5:54 (vocal) and 5:34 (instrumental).
GO45 0172	Gordy 7170 (06/79)	Mira Waters You Have Inspired Me You Have Inspired Me Note: Issued commercially on M-00030D1 as an extended version with running time of 5:19.
GO45 0173	Gordy 7171 (07/79)	Rick James Fool On The Street Jefferson Ball
GO45 0174	Gordy 7172 (10/79)	High Inergy Come And Get It Midnight Music Man Note: See also Gordy 7174.
GO45 0175	Gordy 7173 (09/79)	Teena Marie Don't Look Back I'm Gonna Have My Cake (And Eat It Too)
GO45 0176	Gordy 7174 (09/79)	High Inergy Skate To The Rhythm Midnight Music Man Note: "A" side issued promotionally on PR-57 as an extended version with running time of 4:03. "B" side previously issued on Gordy 7172B.
GO45 0177	Gordy 7175 (09/79)	Switch I Call Your Name Next To You Note: See also Gordy 7190.
GO45 0178	Gordy 7175 (09/79)	Switch I Call Your Name Best Beat In Town Note: "A" side issued promotionally on PR-55A as an extended version with running time of 7:33. "B" side issued commercially on M-00025D1A as an extended version with running time of 4:45. Also issued promotionally on PR-55B as extended version with running time of 4:48.
GO45 0179	Gordy 7176 (10/79)	Rick James Love Gun Stormy Love Note: "A" side issued promotionally on PR-60 as an extended version with running time of 10:05 (single version on "B" side).
GO45 0180	Gordy 7177 (12/79)	Rick James Come Into My Life (Part 1) Come Into My Life (Part 2) Note: Promo copies of this single issued with both short and long versions.
GO45 0181	Gordy 7178 (01/80)	High Inergy I Love Makin' Love (To The Music) Somebody, Somewhere Note: "A" side issued promotionally on PR-63B as an extended version with running time of 7:44. See also Gordy 7187.
GO45 0182	Gordy 7179 (02/80)	The Stone City Band Strut Your Stuff F.I.M.A. (Funk In Mama Afrika)

Note: "A" side issued
promotionally on PR-63A as an
extended version with running time
of 7:59.

GO45 0183 (02/80)	Gordy 7180	Teena Marie Can It Be Love Too Many Colors (Tee's Interlude)

GO45 0184 (05/80)	Gordy 7181	Switch Don't Take My Love Away Don't Take My Love Away (Instrumental)

GO45 0185 (04/80)	Gordy 7182	The Stone City Band Little Runaway South American Sneeze

GO45 0186 (04/80)	Gordy 7183	The Temptations Power (Vocal) Power (Instrumental)

Note: Issued promotionally on
PR-68A as an extended version
with running time of 6:06. "A" side
also issued on red vinyl.

GO45 0187 (04/80)	Gordy 7184	Teena Marie Behind The Groove You're All The Boogie I Need

Note: A-side issued
promotionally on PR-68B as an
extended version with running time
of 6:04.

GO45 0188 (06/80)	Gordy 7185	Rick James Big Time Island Lady

Note: "A" side issued
promotionally on PR-72B as an
extended version with running time
of 6:27.

GO45 0189 (09/80)	Gordy 7186	Mira Waters Rock And Roll Me You're Moving Out Today

Note: "A" side issued
promotionally on PR-75B1 as an
extended version with running time
of 4:56. "A" side also issued on red
vinyl.

GO45 0190 (08/80)	Gordy 7187	High Inergy Make Me Yours I Love Makin' Love (To The Music)

Note: "A" side issued
promotionally on PR-74B as an
extended version. "B" side
previously issued on Gordy 7178A.

GO45 0191 (07/80)	Gordy 7188	The Temptations Struck By Lightning Twice I'm Coming Home

GO45 0192 (08/80)	Gordy 7189	Teena Marie I Need Your Lovin' Irons In The Fire

Note: "A" side issued
promotionally as an extended
version running 6:28.

GO45 0193 (09/80)	Gordy 7190	Switch My Friend In The Sky Next To You

Note: "B" side previously
issued on Gordy 7175B.

GO45 0194 (09/80)	Gordy 7191	Rick James Summer Love Gettin' It On (In The Sunshine)

GO45 0195 (10/80)	Gordy 7192	High Inergy Hold On To My Love If I Love You Tonight

Note: Originally scheduled to
be released on Gordy 7182, but
issued later with above number.

GO45 0196 (10/80)	Gordy 7193	Switch Love Over And Over Again Keep Movin' On

GO45 0197 (01/81)	Gordy 7194	Teena Marie Young Love First Class Love

GO45 0198 (01/81)	Gordy 7195	Stone City Band All Day And All Of The Night All Day And All Of The Night (Vamp)

Note: "A" side issued
promotionally on PR-80A as an
extended version with running time
of 4:53. "B" side version also
included on PR-80B as an
extended version with running time
of 6:34.

GO45 0199 (03/81)	Gordy 7196	Nolen & Crossley Messin' Up A Good Thing Face On The Photograph

GO45 0200 (03/81)	Gordy 7197	Rick James Give It To Me Baby Don't Give Up On Love

Note: "A" side issued
commercially on 35001V1 as an
extended version with running time
of 5:41 (vocal) and 6:20
(instrumental). Also issued
promotionally on PR-81 with same
running times for vocal and
instrumental versions.

GO45 0201	Gordy 7198	The DeBarges Dance The Night Away

Note: Unissued.

GO45 0202 (04/81)	Gordy 7199	Switch You And I Get Back With You

GO45 0203 (04/81)	Gordy 7200	Stone City Band Freaky Party Girls

Note: "A" side issued
promotionally on PR-80A2 as an
extended version with running time
of 4:58.

GO45 0204	Gordy 7201 (04/81)	High Inergy I Just Wanna Dance With You Take My Life

GO45 0205	Gordy 7202 (06/81)	Teena Marie Square Biz Opus III (Does Anybody Care) Note: "A" side issued commercially on 35000V1 as an extended version with running time of 6:40 (vocal) and 6:39 (instrumental). Also issued on a promotional basis on PR-82A as an extended version with running time of 6:13.

GO45 0206	Gordy 7203 (06/81)	The DeBarges What's Your Name You're So Gentle, So Kind

GO45 0207	Gordy 7204 (07/81)	Tony Travalini This Is It (This Is My Love) Again

GO45 0208	Gordy 7205 (08/81)	Rick James Super Freak (Part I) Super Freak (Part II) Note: Issued commercially on 35002V1 with running time of 3:32 (short version) and 7:05 (long version). Also issued promotionally on PR-83 as an extended version with running time of 7:05 both sides.

GO45 0209	Gordy 7206	Stone City Band Funky Reggae Ganja Note: Unissued. "A" side was issued promotionally on PR-80B2 as an extended version with running time of 5:05.

GO45 0210	Gordy 7207 (08/81)	High Inergy Goin' Through The Motions I Just Can't Help Myself

GO45 0211	Gordy 7208 (08/81)	The Temptations Aiming At Your Heart The Life Of A Cowboy

GO45 0212	Gordy 7209	Nolen & Crossley Change Into the Groove Note: Unissued.

GO45 0213	Gordy 7210	Note: Unissued.

GO45 0214	Gordy 7211 (09/81)	High Inergy Don't Park Your Loving Now That There's You Note: "A" side issued promotionally on PR-88B as an extended version with running time of 6:58.

GO45 0215	Gordy 7212 (10/81)	Teena Marie It Must Be Magic Yes Indeed Note: "A" side issued

promotionally on PR-88A as an extended version with running time of 6:07.

GO45 0216	Gordy 7213 (10/81)	The Temptations Oh, What A Night Isn't The Night Fantastic

GO45 0217	Gordy 7214 (10/81)	Switch I Do Love You Without You In My Life Note: "A" side issued promotionally PR-89B1 as an extended version with running time of 5:05.

GO45 0218	Gordy 7215 (11/81)	Rick James Ghetto Life Below The Funk (Pass The J) Note: "A" side issued promotionally on PR-89A1 as an extended version with running time of 4:20.

GO45 0219	Gordy 7216 (11/81)	Teena Marie Portuguese Love The Ballad Of Cradle Rob And Me

NUMBER SEQUENCE CHANGE

Note: At this point, separate numbering for Tamla, Motown, and Gordy labels was discontinued and, starting in January 1982, was consolidated into a single sequence beginning at number 1600. This new consecutive numbering system was used for all subsequent singles releases, with individual labels retaining their own distinctive designs. Please see "TMG Consolidated Series" for continuation.

GORDY 7-INCH COLOR VINYL SINGLES

GOCO 0001	Gordy 7062 (08/67)	Martha & The Vandellas Love Bug Leave My Heart Alone Note: Red vinyl.

GOCO 0002	Gordy 7069 (03/68)	Bobby Taylor & The Vancouvers Does Your Mama Know About Me Note: Red vinyl.

GOCO 0003	Gordy 7082 (12/68)	The Temptations Rudolph The Red Nosed Reindeer Note: Red vinyl.

GOCO 0004	Gordy 7083 (01/69)	Edwin Starr Twenty-Five Miles Note: Red vinyl.

GOCO 0005	Gordy 7087 (06/69)	Edwin Starr I'm Still A Struggling Man Note: Red vinyl.

GOCO 0006	Gordy 7090 (07/69)	Blinky & Edwin Starr Oh How Happy Note: Red vinyl.
GOCO 0007	Gordy 7099 (05/70)	The Temptations Ball Of Confusion (That's What The World Is Today) Note: Red vinyl.
GOCO 0008	Gordy 7102 (09/70)	The Temptations Ungena Za Ulimwengu (Unite The World) Note: Red vinyl.
GOCO 0009	Gordy 7108 (06/71)	The Undisputed Truth Smiling Faces Sometimes Note: Red vinyl.
GOCO 0010	Gordy 7113 (12/71)	Martha Reeves & The Vandellas In And Out Of My Life Note: Red vinyl.
GOCO 0011	Gordy 7117 (06/72)	The Undisputed Truth Papa Was A Rollin' Stone Note: Red vinyl.
GOCO 0012	Gordy 7119 (06/72)	The Temptations Mother Nature Note: Red vinyl.
GOCO 0013	Gordy 7157 (02/78)	High Inergy Love Is All You Need Note: Yellow vinyl.
GOCO 0014	Gordy 7159 (07/78)	Switch There'll Never Be Note: Red vinyl.
GOCO 0015	Gordy 7183 (04/80)	The Temptations Power Note: Red vinyl.
GOCO 0016	Gordy 7186 (09/80)	Mira Waters Rock And Roll Me Note: Red vinyl.

GORDY 7-INCH EPS

GOEP 0001	Gordy G-60914 (1966)	The Temptations TEMPTIN' TEMPTATIONS Side 1: My Girl/Since I Lost My Baby/Girl (Why You Wanna Make Me Blue) - Side 2: The Girl's Alright With Me/Just Another Lonely Night/Don't Look Back
GOEP 0002	Gordy G-60917 (1966)	Martha & The Vandellas VANDELLAS GREATEST HITS Side 1: Come And Get These Memories/Love Is Like A Heat Wave/Dancing In The Street - Side 2: Love (Makes Me Do Foolish Things)/A Love Like Yours (Don't Come Knocking Everyday)/Nowhere To Run

GOEP 0003	Gordy G-60918 (1966)	The Temptations GETTIN' READY Side 1: Get Ready/Ain't Too Proud To Beg/Say You - Side 2: Not Now (I'll Tell You Later)/Lonely Lonely Man Am I/It's A Lonely World Without Your Love
GOEP 0004	Gordy G-60919 (1967)	The Temptations GREATEST HITS
GOEP 0005	Gordy G-60920 (1967)	Martha & The Vandellas WATCHOUT Side 1: I'm Ready For Love/One Way Out/Jimmy Mack - Side 2: I'll Follow You/No More Tearstained Make Up/Tell Me I'll Never Be Alone
GOEP 0006	Gordy	Various Artists RECORDED LIVE Side 1: The Marvelettes... Locking Up My Heart/Mary Wells...Bye Bye Baby - Side 2: The Miracles...A Love She Can Count On/Marvin Gaye...You Are My Sunshine Note: Side 1: Top of label states "Not For Sale." Number on label shows as JOBETE BMI DM04-0108-1. Side 2: Number on label listed as DM04-0109 V-031307. All cuts taken from the "Recorded Live" albums.

GORDY ALBUMS

GOLP 0001	Gordy G-901 (10/62)	The Contours DO YOU LOVE ME (NOW THAT I CAN DANCE)
GOLP 0002	Gordy G-902 (08/63)	Martha & The Vandellas COME AND GET THESE MEMORIES
GOLP 0003	Gordy G-903 (08/63)	Ralph Sharon MODERN INNOVATIONS ON COUNTRY AND WESTERN THEMES
GOLP 0004	Gordy 904	Note: Unissued.
GOLP 0005	Gordy 905	Note: Unissued.
GOLP 0006	Gordy G-906 (10/63)	Rev. Martin Luther King Jr. THE GREAT MARCH TO FREEDOM
GOLP 0007	Gordy G-907 (09/63)	Martha & The Vandellas HEAT WAVE
GOLP 0008	Gordy G-908 (10/63)	Rev. Martin Luther King and others GREAT MARCH TO WASHINGTON

GOLP 0009	Gordy 909	Note: Unissued.
GOLP 0010	Gordy 910	Note: Unissued.
GOLP 0011	Gordy G-911 (03/64)	The Temptations MEET THE TEMPTATIONS
GOLP 0012	Gordy G-912 (02/65)	The Temptations TEMPTATIONS SING SMOKEY
GOLP 0013	Gordy 913	Note: Unissued.
GOLP 0014	Gordy G-914 (11/65)	The Temptations THE TEMPTIN' TEMPTATIONS
GOLP 0015	Gordy G-915 (05/65)	Martha And The Vandellas DANCE PARTY Note: Original title to have been WILD ONE.
GOLP 0016	Gordy 916	Note: Unissued.
GOLP 0017	Gordy GS-917 (05/66)	Martha And The Vandellas VANDELLAS GREATEST HITS
GOLP 0018	Gordy GS-918 (06/66)	The Temptations GETTIN' READY
GOLP 0019	Gordy GS-919 (11/66)	The Temptations TEMPTATIONS GREATEST HITS
GOLP 0020	Gordy GS-920 (11/66)	Martha & The Vandellas WATCHOUT!
GOLP 0021	Gordy GS-921 (03/67)	The Temptations TEMPTATIONS LIVE!
GOLP 0022	Gordy GS-922 (07/67)	The Temptations THE TEMPTATIONS WITH A LOT O' SOUL
GOLP 0023	Gordy GS-923 (09/67)	The San Remo Golden Strings HUNGRY FOR LOVE Note: Previously released on Ric Tic LSP-901 in 1965.
GOLP 0024	Gordy GS-924 (11/67)	The Temptations THE TEMPTATIONS IN A MELLOW MOOD
GOLP 0025	Gordy GS-925 (09/67)	Martha And The Vandellas MARTHA AND THE VANDELLAS LIVE!
GOLP 0026	Gordy GS-926 (05/68)	Martha Reeves & The Vandellas RIDIN' HIGH
GOLP 0027	Gordy GS-927 (04/68)	The Temptations THE TEMPTATIONS WISH IT WOULD RAIN
GOLP 0028	Gordy GS-928 (06/68)	The San Remo Golden Strings SWING
GOLP 0029	Gordy GS-929 (06/68)	Dr. Martin Luther King Jr. . . . FREE AT LAST
GOLP 0030	Gordy GS-930 (09/68)	Bobby Taylor & The Vancouvers BOBBY TAYLOR AND THE VANCOUVERS
GOLP 0031	Gordy GS-931 (09/68)	Edwin Starr SOUL MASTER
GOLP 0032	Gordy GS-932 (12/68)	Eivets Rednow ALFIE Note: Pseudonym for Stevie Wonder; his name spelled backwards. Reissue contains caption stating this is Stevie Wonder.
GOLP 0033	Gordy GS-933 (07/69)	The Temptations THE TEMPTATIONS SHOW Note: Original TV soundtrack.
GOLP 0034	Gordy GS-934	Kim Weston TAKE ME IN YOUR ARMS Note: Unissued.
GOLP 0035	Gordy GS-935 (01/69)	Various Artists MOTOWN WINNER'S CIRCLE NO. 1 HITS VOL. 1
GOLP 0036	Gordy GS-936 (01/69)	Various Artists MOTOWN WINNER'S CIRCLE NO. 1 HITS VOL. 2
GOLP 0037	Gordy GS-937	Marv Johnson MARV Note: Unissued.
GOLP 0038	Gordy GS-938 (12/68)	The Temptations LIVE AT THE COPA
GOLP 0039	Gordy GS-939 (02/69)	The Temptations CLOUD NINE
GOLP 0040	Gordy GS-940 (04/69)	Edwin Starr 25 MILES
GOLP 0041	Gordy GS-941	Rita Wright RITA WRIGHT Note: Unissued.
GOLP 0042	Gordy GS-942 (07/69)	Bobby Taylor TAYLOR MADE SOUL

GOLP 0043	Gordy GS-943 (07/69)	Various Artists MOTOWN WINNER'S CIRCLE NO. 1 HITS, VOL.3
GOLP 0044	Gordy GS-944 (10/69)	Martha Reeves & The Vandellas SUGAR N' SPICE
GOLP 0045	Gordy GS-945 (10/69)	Edwin Starr & Blinky JUST WE TWO
GOLP 0046	Gordy GS-946 (10/69)	Various Artists MOTOWN WINNER'S CIRCLE NO. 1 HITS, VOL. 4
GOLP 0047	Gordy GS-947 (03/70)	The Temptations PSYCHEDELIC SHACK
GOLP 0048	Gordy GS-948 (08/70)	Edwin Starr WAR & PEACE
GOLP 0049	Gordy GS-949 (09/69)	The Temptations PUZZLE PEOPLE
GOLP 0050	Gordy GS-950 (03/70)	Various Artists MOTOWN WINNER'S CIRCLE NO. 1 HITS VOL. 5
GOLP 0051	Gordy GS-951 (11/70)	The Temptations CHRISTMAS CARD
GOLP 0052	Gordy GS-952 (09/70)	Martha Reeves & The Vandellas NATURAL RESOURCES
GOLP 0053	Gordy GS-953 (08/70)	The Temptations LIVE AT LONDON'S TALK OF THE TOWN
GOLP 0054	Gordy GS-954 (09/70)	The Temptations GREATEST HITS VOLUME 2
GOLP 0055	Gordy G-955L (07/71)	The Undisputed Truth THE UNDISPUTED TRUTH
GOLP 0056	Gordy G-956L (07/71)	Edwin Starr INVOLVED
GOLP 0057	Gordy GS-957 (04/71)	The Temptations SKY'S THE LIMIT
GOLP 0058	Gordy G-958L (02/72)	Martha Reeves & The Vandellas BLACK MAGIC
GOLP 0059	Gordy G-959L (01/72)	The Undisputed Truth FACE TO FACE WITH THE TRUTH
GOLP 0060	Gordy G-960L	Martha Reeves [ALBUM TITLE NOT DETERMINED] Note: Unissued.
GOLP 0061	Gordy G-961L (01/72)	The Temptations SOLID ROCK
GOLP 0062	Gordy G-962L (08/72)	The Temptations ALL DIRECTIONS
GOLP 0063	Gordy G-963L (06/73)	The Undisputed Truth LAW OF THE LAND
GOLP 0064	Gordy G-964L (12/72)	Luther Allison BAD NEWS IS COMING
GOLP 0065	Gordy G-965L (02/73)	The Temptations MASTERPIECE
GOLP 0066	Gordy G-966V1 (12/73)	The Temptations 1990
GOLP 0067	Gordy G-967V1 (03/74)	Luther Allison LUTHER'S BLUES
GOLP 0068	Gordy G6-968S1 (08/74)	The Undisputed Truth DOWN TO EARTH
GOLP 0069	Gordy G6-969S1 (01/75)	The Temptations A SONG FOR YOU
GOLP 0070	Gordy G6-970S1 (03/75)	The Undisputed Truth COSMIC TRUTH
GOLP 0071	Gordy G6-971S1 (03/76)	The Temptations WINGS OF LOVE
GOLP 0072	Gordy G6-972S1 (10/75)	The Undisputed Truth HIGHER THAN HIGH
GOLP 0073	Gordy G-973V1 (11/75)	The Temptations HOUSE PARTY
GOLP 0074	Gordy G6-974S1 (03/76)	Luther Allison NIGHT LIFE
GOLP 0075	Gordy G6-975S1 (08/76)	The Temptations THE TEMPTATIONS DO THE TEMPTATIONS
GOLP 0076	Gordy G6-976P1 (09/76)	Leon Ware MUSICAL MASSAGE Note: Originally scheduled for release on Motown 876, but release changed to the Gordy label.

U.S. DISCOGRAPHY

GOLP 0077	Gordy G6-977S1 (11/76)	Bottom & Co. ROCK BOTTOM
GOLP 0078	Gordy G6-978R1 (10/77)	High Inergy TURNIN' ON
GOLP 0079	Gordy G6-978R1	Dennis Edwards DENNIS EDWARDS Note: Unissued.
GOLP 0080	Gordy G7-979R1 (01/78)	21st Creation BREAK THRU
GOLP 0081	Gordy G7-980R1 (07/78)	Switch SWITCH
GOLP 0082	Gordy G7-980R1	Major Lance MAJOR, JUST MESSIN' AROUND Note: Unissued.
GOLP 0083	Gordy G7-981R1 (04/78)	Rick James COME GET IT Note: Album cover also credits Stone City Band.
GOLP 0084	Gordy G7-982R1 (06/78)	High Inergy STEPPIN' OUT
GOLP 0085	Gordy G7-983R1	21st Creation 21ST CREATION Note: Unissued.
GOLP 0086	Gordy G7-984R1 (01/79)	Rick James BUSTIN' OUT OF L SEVEN
GOLP 0087	Gordy G7-985R1 (03/79)	Apollo APOLLO
GOLP 0088	Gordy G7-986R1 (03/79)	Teena Marie WILD AND PEACEFUL
GOLP 0089	Gordy G7-987R1 (04/79)	High Inergy SHOULDA GONE DANCIN'
GOLP 0090	Gordy G7-988R1 (04/79)	Switch SWITCH II
GOLP 0091	Gordy G7-989R1 (10/79)	High Inergy FRENZY
GOLP 0092	Gordy G8-990M1 (10/79)	Rick James FIRE IT UP
GOLP 0093	Gordy G7-991R1 (01/80)	Stone City Band IN 'N' OUT Note: "Rick James Presents The Stone City Band."
GOLP 0094	Gordy G7-992R1 (02/80)	Teena Marie LADY T
GOLP 0095	Gordy G8-993M1 (03/80)	Switch REACHING FOR TOMORROW
GOLP 0096	Gordy G8-994M1 (04/80)	The Temptations POWER
GOLP 0097	Gordy G8-995M1 (07/80)	Rick James GARDEN OF LOVE
GOLP 0098	Gordy G8-996M1 (08/80)	High Inergy HOLD ON
GOLP 0099	Gordy G8-997M1 (08/80)	Teena Marie IRONS IN THE FIRE
GOLP 0100	Gordy G8-998M1 (10/80)	The Temptations GIVE LOVE AT CHRISTMAS
GOLP 0101	Gordy G8-999M1 (11/80)	Switch THIS IS MY DREAM
GOLP 0102	Gordy G8-1000M1 (01/81)	Nolen & Crossley NOLEN & CROSSLEY
GOLP 0103	Gordy G8-1002M1 (03/81)	Rick James STREET SONGS
GOLP 0104	Gordy G8-1003M1 (03/81)	The DeBarges THE DeBARGES
GOLP 0105	Gordy G8-1004M1 (05/81)	Teena Marie IT MUST BE MAGIC
GOLP 0106	Gordy G8-1005M1 (05/81)	High Inergy HIGH INERGY
GOLP 0107	Gordy G8-1006M1 (08/81)	The Temptations THE TEMPTATIONS
GOLP 0108	Gordy G8-1007M1 (11/81)	Switch SWITCH V

NUMBER SEQUENCE CHANGE

Note: At this point, numbering for Tamla, Motown, and Gordy albums was consolidated into a single sequence starting at 6000. See "TMG Consolidated Series Albums" for continuation.

HITSVILLE 7-INCH SINGLES

HI45 0001 (05/76)	Hitsville 6032	T. G. Sheppard Solitary Man Shame
HI45 0002	Hitsville 6033	Note: Unissued.
HI45 0003	Hitsville 6034	Note: Unissued.
HI45 0004 (06/76)	Hitsville 6035	Rick Tucker I Heard A Song Plans That We Made
HI45 0005	Hitsville 6036	Note: Unissued.
HI45 0006 (06/76)	Hitsville 6037	Pat Boone Texas Woman It's Gone
HI45 0007 (07/76)	Hitsville 6038	Ronnie Dove Tragedy Songs That We Sang As Children
HI45 0008 (07/76)	Hitsville 6039	Kenny Seratt I've Been There Too She Made Me Love You More
HI45 0009 (08/76)	Hitsville 6040	T. G. Sheppard Show Me A Man We Just Live Here (We Don't Love Here Anymore)
HI45 0010 (08/76)	Hitsville 6041	Jerry Naylor The Bad Part Of Me I Hate To Drink Alone
HI45 0011 (09/76)	Hitsville 6042	Pat Boone Oklahoma Sunshine Won't Be Home Tonight
HI45 0012 (10/76)	Hitsville 6043	Jerry Foster I Knew You When One
HI45 0013 (10/76)	Hitsville 6044	Marty Mitchell My Eyes Adored You Devil Woman
HI45 0014 (11/76)	Hitsville 6045	Ronnie Dove Why Daddy The Morning After The Night Before
HI45 0015 (11/76)	Hitsville 6046	Jerry Naylor The Last Time You Love Me Born To Fool Around
HI45 0016 (11/76)	Hitsville 6047	Pat Boone Lovelight Comes A Shining Country Days and Country Nights
HI45 0017 (11/76)	Hitsville 6048	T. G. Sheppard May I Spend Every New Year's With You I'll Always Remember That Song
HI45 0018 (01/77)	Hitsville 6049	Kenny Seratt Daddy, They're Playing A Song About You I Threw Away A Rose
HI45 0019 (01/77)	Hitsville 6050	Wendel Adkins I Will Show Me The Way
HI45 0020 (01/77)	Hitsville 6051	Lloyd Schoonmaker She Gives Me Love Little Sister
HI45 0021 (01/77)	Hitsville 6052	Jerry Foster Family Man Just Another Song Away
HI45 0022 (02/77)	Hitsville 6053	T. G. Sheppard Lovin' On I'll Always Remember That Song
HI45 0023 (02/77)	Hitsville 6054	Pat Boone Colorado Country Morning Don't Want To Fall Away From You
HI45 0024 (03/77)	Hitsville 6055	Wendel Adkins Texas Moon Laid Back Country Picker

HITSVILLE ALBUMS

HILP 0001 (09/76)	Hitsville H6-404S1	T. G. Sheppard SOLITARY MAN
HILP 0002 (09/76)	Hitsville H6-405S1	Pat Boone TEXAS WOMAN
HILP 0003 (01/77)	Hitsville H6-406S1	Wendel Adkins SUNDOWNERS

SERIES DISCONTINUED

Note: See Melodyland for numbers 401-403.

INFERNO 7-INCH SINGLES

IN45 0001 (05/68)	Inferno 5001	Volumes Ain't That Loving You I Love You Baby
IN45 0002 (04/68)	Inferno 5002	Detroit Wheels Linda Sue Dixon Tally Ho

IN45 0003	Inferno 5003 (09/68)	Detroit Wheels Think (About The Good Things) For The Love Of A Stranger

JUPAR 7-INCH SINGLES

JU45 0001	Jupar JP 8001F (02/77)	Flavor Don't Freeze Up Don't Freeze Up (Instrumental)
JU45 0002	Jupar JP 8002F (04/77)	Ju-Par Universal Orchestra Funky Music Time

JUPAR ALBUMS

JULP 0001	Ju-Par JP6-1001S1 (01/77)	Ju-Par Universal Orchestra MOODS AND GROOVES
JULP 0002	Ju-Par JP6-1002S1 (05/77)	Flavor IN GOOD TASTE
JULP 0003	Ju-Par JP6-1003S1 (08/77)	Sly, Slick & Wicked SLY, SLICK AND WICKED

MC 7-INCH SINGLES

MC45 0001	MC MC 5001F (09/77)	Pat Boone Whatever Happened To The Good Old Honky Tonk Ain't Goin' Down In The Ground Before My Time
MC45 0002	MC MC 5002F (10/77)	Wendel Adkins Julieanne (Where Are You Tonight?) She Gives Me Love
MC45 0003	MC MC 5003F (10/77)	Marty Cooper Like a Gypsy $10 Room
MC45 0004	MC MC 5004F (01/78)	Jerry Naylor If You Don't Want To Love Her Love Away Her Memory Tonight
MC45 0005	MC MC 5005F (01/78)	Marty Mitchell You Are The Sunshine Of My Life Yester-Me, Yester-You, Yesterday
MC45 0006	MC MC 5006F (02/78)	Porter Jordan What We Do Two By Two Broken Bones
MC45 0007	MC MC 5007F (02/78)	Kenny Seratt She's The Trip I've Been On (Since You've Been Gone) She Only Made Me Love You More

MC45 0008	MC MC 5008F (03/78)	Wendel Adkins You've Lost That Loving Feeling Show Me The Way
MC45 0009	MC MC 5009F (04/78)	Ernie Payne Neon Riders And Sawdust Gliders The Very Last Love Letter
MC45 0010	MC MC 5010F (04/78)	Jerry Naylor Rave On Lady Would You Like To Dance
MC45 0011	MC MC 5011F (05/78)	Marty Mitchell All Alone In Austin Virginia
MC45 0012	MC MC 5012F (05/78)	E. D. Wofford Baby, I Need Your Lovin' Why Not Try Lovin' Me
MC45 0013	MC MC 5013F (08/78)	Ronnie Dove Angel In Your Eyes (Brings Out The Devil In Me) Songs We Sang As Children
MC45 0014	MC MC 5014F (07/78)	Kay Austin Try Me Big Red Roses (And Little White Lies)
MC45 0015	MC MC 5015F (07/78)	Arthur Blanch The Little Man's Got The Biggest Smile In Town Another Pretty Country Song

MC ALBUMS

MCLP 0001	MC MC6-501S1 (08/77)	Pat Boone THE COUNTRY SIDE OF PAT BOONE
MCLP 0002	MC 502	Jerry Naylor LOVE AWAY HER MEMORY TONIGHT Note: Unissued.
MCLP 0003	MC 503	Jerry Naylor ONCE AGAIN Note: Unissued.
MCLP 0004	MC 504	Porter Jordan PORTER JORDAN SINGS Note: Unissued.
MCLP 0005	MC 505	Pat Boone COUNTRY DAYS AND COUNTRY NIGHTS Note: Unissued.
MCLP 0006	MC 506	Note: Unissued.
MCLP 0007	MC 507	Bob and Penny PRESENTING Note: Unissued.

MCLP 0008	MC 508	Kenny Seratt KENNY SERATT Note: Unissued.
MCLP 0009	MC 509	Note: Unissued.
MCLP 0010	MC 510	Susie Allanson [ALBUM TITLE NOT DETERMINED] Note: Unissued.
MCLP 0011	MC MC6-511S1 (11/77)	Marty Mitchell YOU ARE THE SUNSHINE OF MY LIFE
MCLP 0012	MC 512	Wendell Adkins WENDELL ADKINS Note: Unissued.
MCLP 0013	MC 513	Tucker and Schoonmaker TUCKER AND SCHOONMAKER Note: Unissued.
MCLP 0014	MC 514	Note: Unissued.
MCLP 0015	MC MC6-515S1 (12/77)	Larry Groce PLEASE TAKE ME BACK

MELODY 7-INCH SINGLES

ME45 0001	Melody 101 (07/62)	Creations This Is Our Night You're My Inspiration
ME45 0002	Melody 102 (06/62)	Lamont Dozier Dearest One Fortune Teller Tell Me
ME45 0003	Melody 103 (10/62)	Vels You'll Never Cherish A Love So True ('Till You Lose It) There He Is (At My Door) Note: The Vels recorded as Martha & The Vandellas on the Gordy label, and as the Del-Phis on the Check-Mate label.
ME45 0004	Melody 104	Note: Unissued.
ME45 0005	Melody 105 (09/62)	Pirates Mind Over Matter I'll Love You 'Till I Die Note: Alias for the Temptations.
ME45 0006	Melody 106 (02/63)	Chuck a Luck Sugar Cane Curtain Dingbat Diller
ME45 0007	Melody 107	Jack Haney and "Nikiter" Armstrong Peaceful Summit Chanted Meeting (The Interview) Note: Unissued.

ME45 0008	Melody 108	Note: Unissued.
ME45 0009	Melody 109 (12/63)	Howard Crockett The Big Wheel That Silver Haired Daddy Of Mine
ME45 0010	Melody 110 (01/64)	Gene Henslee Shambles Beautiful Women
ME45 0011	Melody 111 (03/64)	Howard Crockett Bringing In The Gold I've Been A Long Time Leaving
ME45 0012	Melody 112 (03/64)	Bruce Channel Satisfied Mind That's What's Happenin'
ME45 0013	Melody 113 (05/64)	Dorsey Burnette Little Acorn Cold As Usual
ME45 0014	Melody 114 (07/64)	Bruce Channel You Make Me Happy You Never Looked Better
ME45 0015	Melody 115 (05/64)	Howard Crockett My Lil's Run Off Spanish Lace And Memories
ME45 0016	Melody 116 (06/64)	Dorsey Burnette Jimmy Brown Everybody's Angel
ME45 0017	Melody 117 (01/65)	Dee Mullins Love Makes The World Go Round, But Money Greases The Wheel Come On Back (And Be My Love Again)
ME45 0018	Melody 118 (11/64)	Dorsey Burnette Ever Since The World Began Long Long Time Ago
ME45 0019	Melody 119 (12/64)	Howard Crockett Put Me In Your Pocket The Miles
ME45 0020	Melody 120 (03/65)	Hillsiders You Only Pass This Way One Time Rain Is A Lonesome Thing
ME45 0021	Melody 121 (04/65)	Howard Crockett All The Good Times Are Gone The Great Titanic

MIRACLE 7-INCH SINGLES

MI45 0001	Miracle M 1 (01/61)	Jimmy Ruffin Don't Feel Sorry For Me Heart
MI45 0002	Miracle M 2	Little Eva And Band When I Need You Continental Street Note: Unissued. Little Eva is

Raynoma Gordy.

MI45 0003	Miracle M 3	Gino Parks Blibber Blabber Don't Say Bye Bye 　　Note: Unissued.
MI45 0004	Miracle M 4	Andre Williams Rosa Lee Shoo Ooo 　　Note: Unissued.
MI45 0005	Miracle M 5 (07/61)	The Temptations Oh, Mother O Mine Romance Without Finance
MI45 0006	Miracle M 6 (10/61)	The Valadiers Greetings (This Is Uncle Sam) Take A Chance
MI45 0007	Miracle M 7 (09/61)	Equadors Someone To Call My Own You're My Desire
MI45 0008	Miracle M 8 (09/61)	Pete Hartfield Love Me Darling Tonight
MI45 0009	Miracle M 9 (10/61)	Joel Sebastian Angel In Blue Blue Cinderella
MI45 0010	Miracle M 10 (01/61)	Don McKenzie Whose Heart Are You Going To 　Break Now I'll Call You
MI45 0011	Miracle M 11 (10/61)	Freddie Gorman The Day Will Come Just For You
MI45 0012	Miracle M 12 (11/61)	The Temptations Check Yourself Your Wonderful Love

MELODYLAND 7-INCH SINGLES

ML45 0001	Melodyland M 6001F (10/74)	Pat Boone Candy Lips Young Girl 　　Note: See also Melodyland 6005.
ML45 0002	Melodyland M 6002F (11/74)	T. G. Sheppard Devil In The Bottle Rollin With The Flow
ML45 0003	Melodyland M 6003F (11/74)	Jerry Naylor Is This All There Is To A Honky 　Tonk? You're The One
ML45 0004	Melodyland M 6004F (02/75)	Ronnie Dove Please Come To Nashville Pictures On Paper

ML45 0005	Melodyland M 6005F (02/75)	Pat Boone Indiana Girl Young Girl 　　Note: See also Melodyland 6001.
ML45 0006	Melodyland M 6006F (03/75)	T. G. Sheppard Tryin' To Beat The Morning Home I'll Be Satisfied
ML45 0007	Melodyland M 6007F (04/75)	Dorsey Burnette Molly (I Ain't Gettin' Any 　Younger) She's Feelin' Low
ML45 0008	Melodyland M 6008F (04/75)	Karen Kelly The Dessert Annie
ML45 0009	Melodyland M 6009F (04/75)	Terry Stafford Darling Think It Over I Can't Find It
ML45 0010	Melodyland M 6010F (05/75)	Barbara Wyrick Baby, I Love You Too Much You've Been Doing Wrong 　For So Long
ML45 0011	Melodyland M 6011F (05/75)	Ronnie Dove Things Here We Go Again
ML45 0012	Melodyland M 6012F (05/75)	Jerry Naylor He'll Have To Go Once Again
ML45 0013	Melodyland M 6013F (05/75)	Sheila Taylor She Satisfies How Important Can It Be
ML45 0014	Melodyland M 6014F (05/75)	Kenny Seratt If I Could Have It Any Other Way Not Too Old To Cry
ML45 0015	Melodyland M 6015F (05/75)	Jud Strunk The Biggest Parakeets In Town I Wasn't Wrong About You
ML45 0016	Melodyland M 6016F (07/75)	T. G. Sheppard Another Woman I Can't Help Myself (Sugar 　Pie, Honey Bunch)
ML45 0017	Melodyland M 6017F (09/75)	Darla Foster Say Love (Or Don't Say Anything 　At All) He Makes The Wrong Seem 　Right
ML45 0018	Melodyland M 6018F (08/75)	Pat Boone I'd Do It With You Yester-Me, Yester-You, 　Yesterday 　　Note: "B" side as by Pat and Shirley Boone.
ML45 0019	Melodyland M 6019F (08/75)	Dorsey Burnette Lyin' In Her Arms Again Doggone The Dogs

ML45 0020	Melodyland M 6020F (09/75)	Jerry Naylor Prayin' For My Mind What's A Nice Girl Like You Doing In A Honky Tonk
ML45 0021	Melodyland M 6021F (09/75)	Ronnie Dove Drina (Take Your Lady Off For Me) Your Sweet Love
ML45 0022	Melodyland M 6022F	Terry Stafford Reba (She's A) Fire Out Of Control Note: Unissued.
ML45 0023	Melodyland M 6023F (09/75)	Barbara Wyrick Pity Little Billy Jo Crazy Love
ML45 0024	Melodyland M 6024F (09/75)	Kenny Seratt Let's Hold On To What We've Got Truly Great American Blues
ML45 0025	Melodyland M 6025F (10/75)	Joey Martin Anything To Keep From Going Home Rubie Is A Groopie
ML45 0026	Melodyland M 6026F (12/75)	Ernie Payne Take Me (The Way That I Am) Talk To Jeanette
ML45 0027	Melodyland M 6027F (12/75)	Jud Strunk Pamela Brown They're Tearing Down A Town
ML45 0028	Melodyland M 6028F (12/75)	T. G. Sheppard Motels And Memories Pigskin Charade
ML45 0029	Melodyland M 6029F (02/76)	Pat Boone Glory Train U.F.O.
ML45 0030	Melodyland M 6030F (03/76)	Ronnie Dove Right Or Wrong Guns
ML45 0031	Melodyland M 6031F (03/76)	Dorsey Burnette Ain't No Heartbreak I Dreamed I Saw

SERIES DISCONTINUED

Note: Note: See Hitsville for numbers 6032-6035.

MELODYLAND ALBUMS

MLLP 0001	Melodyland ME6-401S1 (05/75)	T. G. Sheppard T. G. SHEPPARD
MLLP 0002	Melodyland ME6-402S1	Note: Unissued.
MLLP 0003	Melodyland ME6-403S1 (03/76)	T. G. Sheppard MOTELS AND MEMORIES

SERIES DISCONTINUED

Note: See Hitsville for numbers 404-406.

MOTOWN 7-INCH SINGLES

MO45 0001	Motown G1/G2 (09/59)	The Miracles Bad Girl I Love You Baby
MO45 0002	Motown TLX2207 (09/59)	The Miracles Bad Girl I Love You Baby Note: Motown G1/G2 and TLX2207 were probably test pressings, as both sides were licensed to Chess Records for release in September 1959 on Chess 1734. Subsequent Miracles' records for Motown were all released on the Tamla label.
MO45 0003	Motown 1000 (02/60)	The Satintones My Beloved Sugar Daddy Note: "A" side version with no strings. No address on label.
MO45 0004	Motown 1000 (02/60)	The Satintones My Beloved Sugar Daddy Note: Version with strings. Has address of 2648 West Grand Blvd on label.
MO45 0005	Motown 1001 (03/60)	Eugene Remus You Never Miss A Good Thing Hold Me Tight Note: "A" side version with no strings.
MO45 0006	Motown 1001 (03/60)	Eugene Remus You Never Miss A Good Thing Gotta Have Your Lovin' Note: "A" side version with strings. Master number in vinyl L8O27990-1A.
MO45 0007	Motown 1001 (03/60)	Eugene Remus You Never Miss A Good Thing Gotta Have Your Lovin' Note: "A" side version with no strings. Master number in vinyl H-55510.
MO45 0008	Motown 1002 (06/60)	Popcorn And The Mohawks Shimmy Gully Custer's Last Man
MO45 0009	Motown 1003 (12/60)	Mary Wells Bye Bye Baby Please Forgive Me

MO45 Motown Sherri Taylor & Singin'
0010 1004 Sammy Ward
(09/60) That's Why I Love You So Much
Lover

MO45 Motown Henry Lumpkin
0011 1005 We Really Love Each Other
(01/61) I've Got A Notion

MO45 Motown Satintones
0012 1006 Tomorrow & Always
(03/61) A Love That Can Never Be
Note: Lead part is
male/female duet with light group
harmony in background. This
version with no strings.

MO45 Motown Satintones
0013 1006 Tomorrow & Always
(03/61) A Love That Can Never Be
Note: Lead on "B" side is
single male with light chorus
backup. Version is with strings.
"Tomorrow & Always" was
released to cash in on the success of
"Will You Still Love Me
Tomorrow" by The Shirelles. Soon
after the second release, the disc
was pulled from the market because
of apparent copyright infringement.

MO45 Motown Satintones
0014 1006 Angel
(04/61) A Love That Can Never Be

MO45 Motown Debbie Dean
0015 1007 Don't Let Him Shop Around
(02/61) A New Girl
Note: Answer record to the
Miracles' "Shop Around" on Tamla.

MO45 Motown The Supremes
0016 1008 I Want A Guy
Never Again
Note: Issued in extremely
limited quantities on a promotional
basis. Matrix numbers in vinyl are
the same as those on the
commercial issue released on Tamla
54038. This is very probably the
rarest single on the Motown label.

MO45 Motown The Contours
0017 1008 Whole Lotta Woman
(02/61) Come On And Be Mine

MO45 Motown Richard Wylie
0018 1009 I'll Still Be Around
(04/61) Money (That's What I Want)

MO45 Motown Satintones
0019 1010 I Know How It Feels
(06/61) My Kind Of Love

MO45 Motown Mary Wells
0020 1011 I Don't Want To Take A Chance
(07/61) I'm So Sorry
Note: First issued with the
pink striped label, then quickly
reissued with the now familiar
Detroit "Map" label. After this

single, all subsequent releases
would be with the "Map" label.
This is also the very first Motown
single issued in a picture sleeve.

MO45 Motown The Contours
0021 1012 Funny
(07/61) The Stretch

MO45 Motown Henry Lumpkin
0022 1013 What Is A Man (Without A
(01/62) Woman)
Don't Leave Me

MO45 Motown Debbie Dean
0023 1014 Itsy Bity Pity Love
(08/61) But I'm Afraid

MO45 Motown Golden Harmoneers
0024 1015 I Am Bound
(08/61) Precious Memories

MO45 Motown Mary Wells
0025 1016 Strange Love
(09/61) Come To Me
Note: Picture sleeve has the
same photo as the one used on
Motown 1011.

MO45 Motown Note: Unissued.
0026 1017

MO45 Motown The All Stars
0027 1018 Disintegrated (Part 1)
Disintegrated (Part 2)
Note: Unissued. Not Jr.
Walker & All Stars!

MO45 Motown Popcorn & The Mohawks
0028 1019 Real Good Lovin'
(10/61) Have I The Right

MO45 Motown Satintones
0029 1020 Zing Went The Strings Of My Heart
(10/61) Faded Letter

MO45 Motown Eddie Holland
0030 1021 Jamie
(10/61) Take A Chance On Me
Note: "A" side issued
promotionally as a one-sided disc
with blank "B" side.

MO45 Motown Twistin' Kings
0031 1022 Xmas Twist
(11/61) White House Twist

MO45 Motown Twistin' Kings
0032 1023 Congo Pt. 1
(12/61) Congo Pt. 2

MO45 Motown Mary Wells
0033 1024 The One Who Really Loves You
(02/62) I'm Gonna Stay
Note: Picture sleeve has same
photo as previously issued on
numbers Motown 1011 and 1016.

MO45 0034	Motown 1025 (03/62)	Debbie Dean Everybody's Talkin' About My Baby I Cried All Night Note: Issued with a picture sleeve.
MO45 0035	Motown 1026 (04/62)	Eddie Holland You Deserve What You Get Last Night I Had A Vision Note: See also Motown 1058.
MO45 0036	Motown 1027 (05/62)	The Supremes Your Heart Belongs To Me (He's) Seventeen Note: Issued with picture sleeve. Issued with alternate versions of "A" side. Master number DM-033209 has no "echo."
MO45 0037	Motown 1028 (06/62)	Herman Griffin Uptight Sleep (Little One)
MO45 0038	Motown 1029 (07/62)	Henry Lumpkin Mo Jo Hanna Break Down And Sing Note: Vocal accompaniment credits The Lovetones.
MO45 0039	Motown 1030 (05/62)	Eddie Holland If Cleopatra Took A Chance What About Me Note: Issued with picture sleeve.
MO45 0040	Motown 1031 (08/62)	Eddie Holland If It's Love (It's Alright) It's Not Too Late
MO45 0041	Motown 1032 (08/62)	Mary Wells You Beat Me To The Punch Old Love (Let's Try It Again) Note: Vocal accompaniment credits The Lovetones.
MO45 0042	Motown 1033	The Blue Jeans Camel Walk The Chaperone Note: Issued later on Gordy 7009 as by La Brenda Ben & The Beljeans.
MO45 0043	Motown 1034 (11/62)	The Supremes Let Me Go The Right Way Time Changes Things Note: See also Motown 1122.
MO45 0044	Motown 1035 (10/62)	Mary Wells Two Lovers Operator
MO45 0045	Motown 1036 (12/62)	Eddie Holland Darling I Hum Our Song Just A Few More Days
MO45 0046	Motown 1037 (02/63)	Linda Griner Envious Good-By Cruel Love

MO45 0047	Motown 1038 (02/63)	Amos Milburn My Baby Gave Me Another Chance I'll Make It Up To You Somehow Note: See also Motown 1046.
MO45 0048	Motown 1039 (02/63)	Mary Wells Laughing Boy Two Wrongs Don't Make A Right Note: "A" side vocal accompaniment credits Andantes & Love-tones.
MO45 0049	Motown 1040 (03/63)	The Supremes My Heart Can't Take It No More You Bring Back Memories
MO45 0050	Motown 1041 (03/63)	Connie Van Dyke Oh Freddie It Hurt Me Too
MO45 0051	Motown 1042 (05/63)	Mary Wells What Love Has Joined Together Your Old Standby
MO45 0052	Motown 1043 (06/63)	Eddie Holland Baby Shake Brenda Note: See also Motown 1052.
MO45 0053	Motown 1044 (06/63)	The Supremes A Breath Taking, First Sight Soul Shaking, One Night Love Making, Next Day Heart Breaking Guy (The Man With The) Rock and Roll Banjo Band
MO45 0054	Motown 1044 (06/63)	The Supremes A Breath Taking Guy (The Man With The) Rock And Roll Banjo Band
MO45 0055	Motown 1045 (08/63)	Holland-Dozier What Goes Up - Must Come Down Come On Home Note: Lamont Dozier and Eddie Holland. "A" side lists vocal accompaniment by The Andantes & Four Tops.
MO45 0056	Motown 1046	The Serenaders If Your Heart Says Yes I'll Cry Tomorrow Note: Unissued. Issued on V.I.P. 25002.
MO45 0057	Motown 1046 (07/63)	Amos Milburn My Daily Prayer I'll Make It Up To You Somehow Note: "B" side previously issued on Motown 1038B.
MO45 0058	Motown 1047 (09/63)	Morrocco Muzik Makers Back To School Again Pig Knuckles

MO45
0059
	Motown
	1048
	(08/63)
		Mary Wells
		What's Easy For Two Is So Hard
		   For One
		You Lost The Sweetest Boy
		     Note: "A" side issued as a
		one-sided promotional single with
		blank "B" side.

MO45 0060	Motown 1049 (10/63)	Eddie Holland I Couldn't Cry If I Wanted To I'm On The Outside Looking In
MO45 0061	Motown 1050 (10/63)	Carolyn Crawford Forget About Me Devil In His Heart

MO45
0062
	Motown
	1051
	(11/63)
		The Supremes
		When The Lovelight Starts Shining
		   Through His Eyes
		Standing At The Crossroads
		   Of Love

MO45 0063	Motown 1052 (12/63)	Eddie Holland Leaving Here Brenda Note: "B" side previously issued on Motown 1043B.
MO45 0064	Motown 1053 (01/64)	Bobby Breen Better Late Than Never How Can We Tell Him
MO45 0065	Motown 1054 (02/64)	The Supremes Run, Run, Run I'm Giving You Your Freedom
MO45 0066	Motown 1055 (03/64)	Sammy Turner Only You Right Now
MO45 0067	Motown 1056 (03/64)	Mary Wells My Guy Oh Little Boy (What Did You Do To Me)

MO45
0068
	Motown
	1057
	(04/64)
		Marvin Gaye & Mary Wells
		Once Upon A Time
		What's The Matter With You
		   Baby
		     Note: Issued with picture
		sleeve.

MO45 0069	Motown 1058 (05/64)	Eddie Holland Just Ain't Enough Love Last Night I Had A Vision Note: "B" side previously issued on Motown 1026B.
MO45 0070	Motown 1059 (05/64)	Bobby Breen Here Comes The Heartache You're Just Like You
MO45 0071	Motown 1060 (06/64)	The Supremes Where Did Our Love Go He Means The World To Me Note: Issued with full-color picture sleeve.
MO45 0072	Motown 1061	Mary Wells When I'm Gone Guarantee (For A Lifetime) Note: Unissued.
MO45 0073	Motown 1062 (07/64)	Four Tops Baby I Need Your Loving Call On Me
MO45 0074	Motown 1063 (08/64)	Eddie Holland Candy To Me If You Don't Want My Love
MO45 0075	Motown 1064 (08/64)	Carolyn Crawford My Smile Is Just A Frown Turned Upside Down I'll Come Running
MO45 0076	Motown 1065	Mary Wells Whisper You Love Me I'll Be Available Note: Unissued.
MO45 0077	Motown 1066 (09/64)	The Supremes Baby Love Ask Any Girl Note: Issued with picture sleeve.
MO45 0078	Motown 1067 (10/64)	The Spinners Sweet Thing How Can I
MO45 0079	Motown 1068 (10/64)	The Supremes Come See About Me Always In My Heart
MO45 0080	Motown 1069 (11/64)	Four Tops Without The One You Love (Life's Not Worthwhile) Love Has Gone
MO45 0081	Motown 1070 (12/64)	Carolyn Crawford When Someone's Good To You My Heart
MO45 0082	Motown 1071 (12/64)	Tony Martin Talkin' To Your Picture Our Rhapsody
MO45 0083	Motown 1072 (12/64)	Choker Campbell's Big Band Come See About Me Pride And Joy
MO45 0084	Motown 1073 (01/65)	Four Tops Ask The Lonely Where Did You Go Note: Issued with picture sleeve.
MO45 0085	Motown 1074 (02/65)	The Supremes Stop! In The Name Of Love I'm In Love Again Note: Issued with picture sleeve. "A" side issued promotionally as one-sided single with blank "B" side.

MO45 0086	Motown 1075 (04/65)	The Supremes Back In My Arms Again Whisper You Love Me Baby Note: Issued with picture sleeve. "A" side issued as one-sided promo single with blank "B" side.
MO45 0087	Motown 1076 (04/65)	Four Tops I Can't Help Myself Sad Souvenirs Note: "A" side issued as one-sided promo single with blank "B" side.
MO45 0088	Motown 1077 (05/65)	Billy Eckstine Had You Been Around Down To Earth
MO45 0089	Motown 1078 (06/65)	The Spinners I'll Always Love You Tomorrow May Never Come
MO45 0090	Motown 1079	The Supremes The Only Time I'm Happy Supreme's Interview Note: Unissued. Special promotional release on the George Alexander label out of New York.
MO45 0091	Motown 1080 (07/65)	The Supremes Nothing But Heartaches He Holds His Own Note: Issued with picture sleeve.
MO45 0092	Motown 1081 (07/65)	Four Tops It's The Same Old Song Your Love Is Amazing
MO45 0093	Motown 1082 (08/65)	Tony Martin The Bigger Your Heart Is (The Harder You'll Fall) The Two Of Us
MO45 0094	Motown 1083 (10/65)	The Supremes I Hear A Symphony Who Could Ever Doubt My Love
MO45 0095	Motown 1084 (10/65)	Four Tops Something About You Darling I Hum Our Song
MO45 0096	Motown 1085 (12/65)	The Supremes Children's Christmas Song Twinkle Twinkle Little Me Note: Issued with picture sleeve. Also issued in red vinyl.
MO45 0097	Motown 1086 (12/65)	Tammi Terrell I Can't Believe You Love Me Hold Me Oh My Darling
MO45 0098	Motown 1087 (12/65)	Barbara McNair The Touch Of Time You're Gonna Love My Baby
MO45 0099	Motown 1088 (01/66)	Tony Martin Ask Any Man Spanish Rose
MO45 0100	Motown 1089 (12/65)	The Supremes My World Is Empty Without You Everything Is Good About You

MO45
0101
	Motown
	1090
	(02/66)
		Four Tops
		Shake Me Wake Me (When It's
		    Over)
		Just As Long As You Need
		    Me

MO45 0102	Motown 1091 (03/66)	Billy Eckstine Slender Thread Wish You Were Here
MO45 0103	Motown 1092 (04/66)	Connie Haines What's Easy For Two Is So Hard For One Walk In Silence
MO45 0104	Motown 1093 (04/66)	The Spinners Truly Yours Where Is That Girl
MO45 0105	Motown 1094 (04/66)	The Supremes Love Is Like An Itching In My Heart He's All I Got
MO45 0106	Motown 1095 (05/66)	Tammi Terrell Come On And See Me Baby Dont'cha Worry
MO45 0107	Motown 1096 (05/66)	Four Tops Loving You Is Sweeter Than Ever I Like Everything About You
MO45 0108	Motown 1097 (07/66)	The Supremes You Can't Hurry Love Put Yourself In My Place Note: Issued with picture sleeve.
MO45 0109	Motown 1098 (08/66)	Four Tops Reach Out I'll Be There Until You Love Someone Note: Issued with picture sleeve.
MO45 0110	Motown 1099 (09/66)	Barbara McNair Everything Is Good About You What A Day
MO45 0111	Motown 1100 (09/66)	Billy Eckstine A Warmer World And There You Were
MO45 0112	Motown 1101 (10/66)	The Supremes You Keep Me Hangin' On Remove This Doubt Note: Issued with picture sleeve.
MO45 0113	Motown 1102 (11/66)	Four Tops Standing In The Shadows Of Love Since You've Been Gone
MO45 0114	Motown 1103 (01/67)	The Supremes Love Is Here And Now You're Gone There's No Stopping Us Now

MO45 0115 (02/67)	Motown 1104	Four Tops Bernadette I Got A Feeling

MO45 0129 (01/68)	Motown 1118	Chuck Jackson (You Can't Let The Boy Overpower) The Man In You Girls, Girls, Girls

MO45 0116 (02/67)	Motown 1105	Billy Eckstine I Wonder Why (Nobody Loves Me) I've Been Blessed

MO45 0130 (01/68)	Motown 1119	Four Tops Walk Away Renee Your Love Is Wonderful

MO45 0117 (03/67)	Motown 1106	Barbara McNair Here I Am Baby My World Is Empty Without You Note: Also issued in red vinyl.

MO45 0131 (01/68)	Motown 1120	Billy Eckstine Is Anyone Here Going My Way Thank You Love

MO45 0118 (03/67)	Motown 1107	The Supremes The Happening All I Know About You

MO45 0132 (02/68)	Motown 1121	Chris Clark Whisper You Love Me Boy The Beginning Of The End Note: "B" side previously issued on Motown 1114B.

MO45 0119 (04/67)	Motown 1108	Paul Peterson Chained Don't Let It Happen To You

MO45 0133 (03/68)	Motown 1122	Diana Ross And The Supremes Forever Came Today Time Changes Things Note: "B" side previously issued on Motown 1034B.

MO45 0120 (04/67)	Motown 1109	The Spinners For All We Know I Cross My Heart

MO45 0121 (05/67)	Motown 1110	Four Tops 7 Rooms Of Gloom I'll Turn To Stone Note: Also issued in red vinyl.

MO45 0134 (03/68)	Motown 1123	Barbara McNair Where Would I Be Without You For Once In My Life Note: "B" side originally scheduled to be released on Motown 1112B.

MO45 0122 (07/67)	Motown 1111	Diana Ross And The Supremes Reflections Going Down For The Third Time Note: Group name changed with this release.

MO45 0135 (04/68)	Motown 1124	Four Tops If I Were A Carpenter Wonderful Baby

MO45 0136	Motown 1125	Diana Ross And The Supremes What The World Needs Now Is Love Your Kiss Of Fire Note: Unissued.

MO45 0123	Motown 1112	Barbara McNair Steal Away Tonight For Once In My Life Note: Unissued. See also Motown 1123.

MO45 0137 (05/68)	Motown 1126	Diana Ross And The Supremes Some Things You Never Get Used To You've Been So Wonderful To Me Note: Also issued in red vinyl.

MO45 0124 (08/67)	Motown 1113	Four Tops You Keep Running Away If You Don't Want My Love

MO45 0125 (09/67)	Motown 1114	Chris Clark From Head To Toe The Beginning Of The End Note: See also Motown 1121.

MO45 0138 (06/68)	Motown 1127	Four Tops For Once In My Life Yesterday's Dreams

MO45 0126 (10/67)	Motown 1115	Tammi Terrell What A Good Man He Is There Are Things

MO45 0139 (06/68)	Motown 1128	Marvin Gaye His Eye Is On The Sparrow Just A Closer Walk With Thee Note: "B" side as by Gladys Knight & The Pips.

MO45 0127 (10/67)	Motown 1116	Diana Ross And The Supremes In And Out Of Love I Guess I'll Always Love You

MO45 0140 (08/68)	Motown 1129	Paul Peterson A Little Bit For Sandy Your Love's Got Me Burnin' Alive

MO45 0128 (11/67)	Motown 1117	The Ones You Haven't Seen My Love Happy Day Note: Also issued on Spirit 0001. Also issued in red vinyl.

MO45 0141 (08/68)	Motown 1130	The Ones Don't Let Me Lose This Dream I've Been Good To You Note: Also issued in red vinyl.

MO45 0142	Motown 1131 (09/68)	Billy Eckstine For Love Of Ivy A Woman
MO45 0143	Motown 1132 (09/68)	Four Tops I'm In A Different World Remember When
MO45 0144	Motown 1133 (09/68)	Barbara McNair You Could Never Love Him (Like I Love Him) Fancy Passes
MO45 0145	Motown 1134 (10/68)	Blinky I Wouldn't Change The Man He Is I'll Always Love You Note: Also issued in red vinyl.
MO45 0146	Motown 1135 (09/68)	Diana Ross And The Supremes Love Child Will This Be The Day Note: Also issued in red vinyl.
MO45 0147	Motown 1136 (11/68)	The Spinners I Just Can't Help But Feel The Pain Bad, Bad Weather (Till You Come Home) Note: See also Motown 1235.
MO45 0148	Motown 1137 (11/68)	Diana Ross & The Supremes & The Temptations I'm Gonna Make You Love Me A Place In The Sun Note: Issued with picture sleeve.
MO45 0149	Motown 1138 (12/68)	Tammi Terrell This Old Heart Of Mine (Is Weak For You) Just Too Much To Hope For
MO45 0150	Motown 1139 (01/69)	Diana Ross & The Supremes I'm Livin' In Shame I'm So Glad I Got Somebody (Like You Around) Note: Also issued in red vinyl.
MO45 0151	Motown 1140 (02/69)	David Ruffin My Whole World Ended (The Moment You Left Me) I've Got To Find Myself A Brand New Baby Note: Also issued in red vinyl.
MO45 0152	Motown 1141 (02/69)	Soupy Sales Muck-Arty Park Green Grow The Lilacs
MO45 0153	Motown 1142 (02/69)	Diana Ross And The Supremes And The Temptations I'll Try Something New The Way You Do The Things You Do Note: Also issued in red vinyl.
MO45 0154	Motown 1143 (03/69)	Billy Eckstine My Cup Runneth Over Ask The Lonely
MO45 0155	Motown 1144 (04/69)	Chuck Jackson Are You Lonely For Me Baby Your Wonderful Love
MO45 0156	Motown 1145	Jonah Jones For Better Or Worse Don't Mess With Bill Note: Unissued.
MO45 0157	Motown 1146 (03/69)	Diana Ross And The Supremes The Composer The Beginning Of The End
MO45 0158	Motown 1147 (04/69)	Four Tops What Is A Man Don't Bring Back Memories
MO45 0159	Motown 1148 (05/69)	Diana Ross And The Supremes No Matter What Sign You Are The Young Folks Note: Also issued in red vinyl.
MO45 0160	Motown 1149 (07/69)	David Ruffin I've Lost Everything I've Ever Loved We'll Have A Good Thing Going On
MO45 0161	Motown 1150 (08/69)	Diana Ross And The Supremes And The Temptations Stubborn Kind Of Fellow Try It Baby
MO45 0162	Motown 1151 (07/69)	Captain Zap & The Motortown Cut-Ups The Luney Take-Off The Luney Landing
MO45 0163	Motown 1152 (09/69)	Chuck Jackson Honey Come Back What Am I Gonna Do Without You
MO45 0164	Motown 1153 (09/69)	Diana Ross And The Supremes And The Temptations The Weight For Better Or Worse
MO45 0165	Motown 1154 (09/69)	Joe Harnell Midnight Cowboy Green Grow The Lilacs Note: See also Motown 1161.
MO45 0166	Motown 1155	The Spinners In My Diary (She's Gonna Love Me) At Sundown Note: Unissued. Release transferred to V.I.P. 25050.
MO45 0167	Motown 1156 (10/69)	Diana Ross And The Supremes Someday We'll Be Together He's My Sunny Boy Note: Background male voice

is by Johhny Bristol.

| MO45
0168 | Motown
1157
(10/69) | The Jackson 5
I Want You Back
Who's Lovin' You
    Note: Also issued in red vinyl. |

| MO45
0169 | Motown
1158
(12/69) | David Ruffin
I'm So Glad I Fell For You
I Pray Everyday You Won't
    Regret Loving Me |

| MO45
0170 | Motown
1159
(11/69) | Four Tops
Don't Let Him Take Your Love
    From Me
The Key |

| MO45
0171 | Motown
1160 | Chuck Jackson
Baby, I'll Get It
The Day The World Stood
    Still
    Note: Unissued. Release
transferred to V.I.P. 25052. |

| MO45
0172 | Motown
1161
(01/70) | Joe Harnell
My Cherie Amour
Green Grow The Lilacs
    Note: "B" side previously
issued on Motown 1154B. |

| MO45
0173 | Motown
1162
(02/70) | The Supremes
Up The Ladder To The Roof
Bill, When Are You Coming
    Back
    Note: First single with Jean
Terrell replacing Diana Ross. |

| MO45
0174 | Motown
1163
(02/70) | The Jackson 5
ABC
The Young Folks
    Note: Also issued in yellow
vinyl. |

| MO45
0175 | Motown
1164
(03/70) | Four Tops
It's All In The Game
Love
    Note: Issued with a picture
sleeve. |

| MO45
0176 | Motown
1165
(04/70) | Diana Ross
Reach Out And Touch
    (Somebody's Hand)
Dark Side Of The World
    Note: Issued with picture
sleeve. Also issued in red vinyl. |

| MO45
0177 | Motown
1166
(05/70) | The Jackson 5
The Love You Save
I Found That Girl
    Note: Also issued in red vinyl. |

| MO45
0178 | Motown
1167
(07/70) | The Supremes
Everybody's Got The Right To
    Love
But I Love You More
    Note: Also issued in red vinyl. |

| MO45
0179 | Motown
1168 | Blinky
How You Gonna Keep It (After
    You Get It)
This Time Last Summer
    Note: Unissued. |

| MO45
0180 | Motown
1168
(04/70) | The Ding Dongs
Gimme Dat Ding
Everything Is Beautiful |

| MO45
0181 | Motown
1169
(07/70) | Diana Ross
Ain't No Mountain High Enough
Can't It Wait Until Tomorrow
    Note: "A" side issued as promo
in short version, as well as long
version. Issued with a picture sleeve. |

| MO45
0182 | Motown
1170
(08/70) | Four Tops
Still Water (Love)
Still Water (Peace)
    Note: Issued with picture
sleeve. Also issued in red vinyl. |

| MO45
0183 | Motown
1171
(08/70) | The Jackson 5
I'll Be There
One More Chance |

| MO45
0184 | Motown
1172
(10/70) | The Supremes
Stoned Love
Shine On Me
    Note: "A" side issued
promotionally with both short and
long versions. Also issued in red
vinyl. |

| MO45
0185 | Motown
1173
(11/70) | The Supremes and Four
    Tops
River Deep, Mountain High
Together We Can Make Such
    Sweet Music |

| MO45
0186 | Motown
1174
(11/70) | The Jackson 5
Santa Claus Is Coming To Town
Christmas Won't Be The
    Same This Year |

| MO45
0187 | Motown
1175
(12/70) | Four Tops
Just Seven Numbers (Can
    Straighten Out My Life)
I Wish I Were Your Mirror
    Note: Issued with picture
sleeve. |

| MO45
0188 | Motown
1176
(12/70) | Diana Ross
Remember Me
How About You
    Note: Issued with picture
sleeve. Also issued in red vinyl. |

| MO45
0189 | Motown
1177
(01/71) | The Jackson 5
Mama's Pearl
Darling Dear
    Note: Issued with picture
sleeve. Also issued in red vinyl. |

| MO45
0190 | Motown
1178
(02/71) | David Ruffin
Don't Stop Loving Me
Each Day Is A Lifetime |

MO45 0191	Motown 1179 (03/71)	The Jackson 5 Never Can Say Goodbye She's Good
MO45 0192	Motown 1180 (04/71)	Gordon Staples & The Motown Strings Strung Out Sounds Of The Zodiac Note: Running time of "A" side different between commercial copy (2:46), and the promo copies (2:58 for mono, 3:16 for stereo). Also issued in red vinyl.
MO45 0193	Motown 1181 (05/71)	The Supremes And The Four Tops You Gotta Have Love In Your Heart I'm Glad About It
MO45 0194	Motown 1182 (04/71)	The Supremes Nathan Jones Happy (Is A Bumpy Road)
MO45 0195	Motown 1183 (04/71)	Bobby Darin Melodie Someday We'll Be Together
MO45 0196	Motown 1184 (04/71)	Diana Ross Reach Out I'll Be There (They Long To Be) Close To You Note: Also issued in red vinyl.
MO45 0197	Motown 1185 (05/71)	Four Tops In These Changing Times Right Before My Eyes
MO45 0198	Motown 1186 (06/71)	The Jackson 5 Maybe Tomorrow I Will Find A Way Note: Printing is in red ink on promo copies.
MO45 0199	Motown 1187 (07/71)	David Ruffin You Can Come Right Back To Me Dinah
MO45 0200	Motown 1188 (07/71)	Diana Ross Surrender I'm A Winner
MO45 0201	Motown 1189 (08/71)	Four Tops MacArthur Park (Part 1) MacArthur Park (Part 2)
MO45 0202	Motown 1190 (09/71)	The Supremes Touch It's So Hard For Me To Say Good-By
MO45 0203	Motown 1191 (10/71)	Michael Jackson Got To Be There Maria (You Were The Only One)
MO45 0204	Motown 1192 (10/71)	Diana Ross I'm Still Waiting A Simple Thing Like Cry
MO45 0205	Motown 1193 (11/71)	Bobby Darin Simple Song Of Freedom I'll Be Your Baby Tonight
MO45 0206	Motown 1194 (11/71)	The Jackson 5 Sugar Daddy I'm So Happy Note: Also issued in blue vinyl.
MO45 0207	Motown 1195 (12/71)	The Supremes Floy Joy This Is The Story
MO45 0208	Motown 1196 (01/72)	Four Tops A Simple Game L.A. (My Town)
MO45 0209	Motown 1197 (02/72)	Michael Jackson Rockin' Robin Love Is Here And Now You're Gone
MO45 0210	Motown 1198 (04/72)	Four Tops I Can't Quit Your Love Happy (Is A Bumpy Road)
MO45 0211	Motown 1199 (04/72)	The Jackson 5 Little Bitty Pretty One If I Have To Move A Mountain
MO45 0212	Motown 1200 (04/72)	The Supremes Automatically Sunshine Precious Little Things
MO45 0213	Motown 1201 (08/72)	Jermaine Jackson That's How Love Goes I Lost My Love In The Big City
MO45 0214	Motown 1202 (05/72)	Michael Jackson I Wanna Be Where You Are We've Got A Good Thing Going Note: Issued with picture sleeve.
MO45 0215	Motown 1203 (05/72)	Bobby Darin Sail Away Something In Her Love Note: See also Motown 1212 and 1217.
MO45 0216	Motown 1204 (06/72)	David Ruffin A Little More Trust A Day In The Life Of A Working Man
MO45 0217	Motown 1205 (06/72)	The Jackson 5 Lookin' Through The Windows Love Song
MO45 0218	Motown 1206 (07/72)	The Supremes Your Wonderful, Sweet Sweet Love The Wisdom Of Time
MO45 0219	Motown 1207 (07/72)	Michael Jackson Ben You Can Cry On My Shoulder

MO45 0220	Motown 1208 (07/72)	The Naturals The Good Things (Where Was I When Love Came By) Me And My Brother

MO45 0221	Motown 1209 (09/72)	Jerry Ross Symposium Duck You Sucker It Happened On A Sunday Morning

MO45 0222	Motown 1210 (08/72)	Four Tops (It's The Way) Nature Planned It I'll Never Change Note: "A" side running time 3:35. Running time on Canadian version 3:50.

MO45 0223	Motown 1211 (12/72)	Diana Ross Good Morning Heartache God Bless The Child Note: Issued with picture sleeve. Also issued with a special label design different than the normal map style.

MO45 0224	Motown 1212 (09/72)	Bobby Darin Average People Something In Her Love Note: "B" side issued previously on Motown 1203B. See also Motown 1217.

MO45 0225	Motown 1213 (10/72)	The Supremes I Guess I'll Miss The Man Over And Over

MO45 0226	Motown 1214 (10/72)	The Jackson 5 The Corner Of The Sky To Know

MO45 0227	Motown 1215 (11/72)	Jerry Ross Symposium Take It Out On Me It's The Same Old Song

MO45 0228	Motown 1216 (11/72)	Jermaine Jackson Daddy's Home Take Me In Your Arms (Rock Me A Little While)

MO45 0229	Motown 1217 (11/72)	Bobby Darin Happy (Love Theme From "Lady Sings The Blues") Something In Her Love Note: "B" side issued previously on Motown 1203B as well as Motown 1212B.

MO45 0230	Motown 1218 (04/73)	Michael Jackson With A Child's Heart Morning Glow

MO45 0231	Motown 1219 (03/73)	Michel Legrand Love Theme From "Lady Sings The Blues" Any Happy Home Note: "B" side as by Gil Askey. Issued with a special label design assigned to all releases from the motion picture "Lady Sings The Blues." Originally scheduled for release on Mowest 5051.

MO45 0232	Motown 1220 (03/73)	The Gil Askey Orchestra Don't Explain C.C. Rider Note: Issued with special label design in conjuction with releases from the movie, "Lady Sings the Blues."

MO45 0233	Motown 1221 (04/73)	Irene "Granny" Ryan No Time At All Time (To Believe In Each Other) Note: Irene Ryan starred in the Broadway musical production of Pippin (Motown album M760L).

MO45 0234	Motown 1222 (05/73)	Willie Hutch Brother's Gonna Work It Out I Choose You Note: "A" side issued as an extended version 12-inch single with a running time of 5:00 on Canadian series MD-6008 as well as U.S. issue 4501MGB with same running time.

MO45 0235	Motown 1223 (04/73)	David Ruffin Blood Donors Needed (Give All You Can) Go On With Your Bad Self

MO45 0236	Motown 1224 (02/73)	The Jackson 5 You Made Me What I Am Hallelujah Day

MO45 0237	Motown 1225 (05/73)	The Supremes Bad Weather Oh Be My Love

MO45 0238	Motown 1226 (06/73)	Vin Cardinal Shame And Scandal In The Family Never Been To Spain Note: See also Motown 1253.

MO45 0239	Motown 1227	Jermaine Jackson [Song titles not determined] Note: Unissued.

MO45 0240	Motown 1228 (06/73)	Reuben Howell I'll See You Through Help The People

MO45 0241	Motown 1229 (03/73)	Martin & Finley Thinkin' 'Bout My Baby Best Friends Note: See also Motown 1242.

MO45 0242	Motown 1230	The Jackson 5 Boogie Man Don't Let Your Baby Catch You Note: Unissued.

MO45 0243	Motown 1231 (04/73)	Irene Ryan I See Your Name Up In Lights When Yesterday Was Tomorrow

MO45 0244	Motown 1232	Note: Unissued.

MO45 0245 (03/73)	Motown 1233	Blinky You Get A Tangle In Your Lifeline This Man Of Mine

MO45 0246 (04/73)	Motown 1234	G. C. Cameron No Matter Where Have I Lost You

MO45
0247
(03/73)
	Motown
	1235
		The Spinners
		Together We Can Make Such
		    Sweet Music
		Bad, Bad Weather (Till You
		    Come Home)
		    Note: "A" side version also
		released on V.I.P. 25057B. Above
		version has strings and runs nine
		seconds longer than the version on
		V.I.P. "B" side was originally
		released on Motown 1136B.

MO45 0248 (04/73)	Motown 1236	Stacie Johnson Woman In My Eyes Every Little Bit Hurts

MO45 0249 (04/73)	Motown 1237	Suzee Ikeda Time For Me To Go Zip-A-Dee Doo-Dah Note: "B" side previously issued on Mowest 5004.

MO45 0250 (06/73)	Motown 1238	Celebration Since I Met You There's No Magic The Circle Again Note: Originally scheduled for release on Mowest 5034.

MO45 0251 (05/73)	Motown 1239	Diana Ross Touch Me In The Morning I Won't Last A Day Without You

MO45
0252
(06/73)
	Motown
	1240
		Severin Browne
		Darling Christina
		All American Boy And His
		    Dog
		    Note: See also Motown 1258.

MO45 0253 (07/73)	Motown 1241	Different Shades of Brown When The Hurt Is Put Back On You Sending Good Vibrations

MO45 0254 (08/73)	Motown 1242	Martin & Finley It's Another Sunday Best Friends Note: "B" side issued previously on Motown 1229B, and scheduled for release on Mowest 5043B.

MO45 0255 (09/73)	Motown 1243	Jimmy Randolph Plainsville, U.S.A. High Road

MO45 0256 (09/73)	Motown 1244	Jermaine Jackson You're In Good Hands Does Your Mama Know About Me

MO45 0257 (09/73)	Motown 1245	Thelma Houston Piano Man I'm Just A Part Of Yesterday Note: Previously issued on Mowest 5050.

MO45
0258
(09/73)
	Motown
	1246
		Art & Honey
		Let's Make Love Now
		(I've Given You) The Best
		    Years Of My Life
		    Note: Originally scheduled for
		release on Mowest 5048.

MO45 0259 (09/73)	Motown 1247	Marbaya Follow Me - Mother Nature And I Thought You Loved Me Note: Originally scheduled for release on Mowest 5044 as by the Music Makers.

MO45 0260 (05/73)	Motown 1248	Stoney Let Me Come Down Easy It's Always Me Note: Originally scheduled for release on Mowest 5045.

MO45 0261 (06/73)	Motown 1249	Earthquire Sunshine Man Soul Long Note: With Tata Vega on lead.

MO45 0262 (07/73)	Motown 1250	Third Creation Rolling Down A Mountainside It's Just A Phase Note: Originally scheduled to be issued on Tamla 54325, but changed to the Motown label instead.

MO45 0263 (07/73)	Motown 1251	Frankie Valli You've Got Your Troubles Listen To Yesterday Note: See also Motown 1279.

MO45 0264 (07/73)	Motown 1252	Willie Hutch Slick Mother's Theme (Mama)

MO45 0265 (07/73)	Motown 1253	Vin Cardinal There'll Be No City On The Hill Never Been To Spain Note: "B" side previously issued on Motown 1226B.

MO45
0266
	Motown
	1254
		Four Tops
		Hey Man - We Got To Get You A
		    Woman
		How Can I Forget You
		    Note: Unissued.

MO45 0267 (05/73)	Motown 1255	Frankie Valli And The Four Seasons How Come? Life and Breath

MO45 0268 (05/73)	Motown 1256	Gloria Jones Why Can't You Be Mine Baby Don'tcha Know (I'm Bleeding For You)

MO45 0269	Motown 1257	Eric & The Vikings Truly Yours Where Do You Go (Baby) Note: Unissued.
MO45 0270	Motown 1258 (06/73)	Severin Browne Darling Christina Snow Flakes Note: "A" side previously issued on Motown 1240A. See also Motown 1303.
MO45 0271	Motown 1259 (07/73)	David Ruffin Common Man Just A Mortal Man

MO45 0272	Motown 1260	Thelma Houston
		No One's Gonna Be A Fool
		    Forever
		Together
		    Note: Unissued. "A" side
		issued as a promotional test
		pressing only in very limited
		quantities. "A" side previously
		released on Mowest 5013.

MO45 0273	Motown 1261 (07/73)	G. C. Cameron Time Let Me Down Easy Note: Also issued in red vinyl.
MO45 0274	Motown 1262 (07/73)	Charlene Duncan Relove Give It One More Try Note: See also Motown 1285.
MO45 0275	Motown 1263 (07/73)	The Devastating Affair That's How It Was (Right From The Start) It's So Sad
MO45 0276	Motown 1264 (08/73)	Puzzle Lady You Make Me Happy
MO45 0277	Motown 1265 (09/73)	Riot God Bless Conchita A Song Of Long Ago
MO45 0278	Motown 1266	Note: Unissued.
MO45 0279	Motown 1267	Note: Unissued.
MO45 0280	Motown 1268 (04/73)	Commodores Are You Happy There's A Song In My Heart Note: See also Motown 1307.
MO45 0281	Motown 1269 (01/74)	Diana Ross & Marvin Gaye My Mistake (Was To Love You) Include Me In Your Life
MO45 0282	Motown 1270	Michael Jackson Doggin' Around Up Again Note: Unissued. See also Motown 1313.

MO45 0283	Motown 1271 (03/74)	Diahann Carroll To A Gentler Time I Can't Give Back The Love I Feel For You
MO45 0284	Motown 1272	C. P. Spencer Still Holding On Say It Like The Children Note: Unissued.
MO45 0285	Motown 1273	Note: Unissued.

MO45 0286	Motown 1274
	(11/73)
		Reuben Howell
		When You Take Another Chance
		    On Love
		You Can't Stop A Man In
		    Love
		    Note: Issued with picture
		sleeve.

MO45 0287	Motown 1275
	(11/73)
		The Sisters Love
		My Love Is Yours (Till The End Of
		    Time)
		You've Got My Mind
		    Note: "B" side also issued on
		Mowest 5030A.

MO45 0288	Motown 1276 (09/73)	Edwin Starr You've Got My Soul On Fire Love (The Lonely People's Prayer)
MO45 0289	Motown 1277 (08/73)	The Jackson 5 Get It Together Touch Note: Also issued in red vinyl.
MO45 0290	Motown 1278 (12/73)	Diana Ross Last Time I Saw Him Save The Children

MO45 0291	Motown 1279
	(11/73)
		Frankie Valli
		The Scalawag Song (And I Will
		    Love You)
		Listen To Yesterday
		    Note: "B" side previously
		issued on Motown 1251B.

MO45 0292	Motown 1280 (09/73)	Diana Ross & Marvin Gaye You're A Special Part Of Me I'm Falling In Love With You
MO45 0293	Motown 1281 (10/73)	Zell Black I'd Hate Myself In The Morning Take My Word
MO45 0294	Motown 1282 (12/73)	Willie Hutch Sunshine Lady I Just Wanted To Make Her Happy
MO45 0295	Motown 1283 (12/73)	Puzzle Mary Mary On With The Show Note: "B" side also issued on Rare Earth 5050A.

MO45 0296	Motown 1284 (02/74)	Edwin Starr Ain't It Hell Up In Harlem Don't It Feel Good To Be Free Note: Originally scheduled to be released on Soul 35112. This number is in the run-out of the record.
MO45 0297	Motown 1285	The Originals Supernatural Voodoo Woman Supernatural Voodoo Woman (Part 2) Note: Unissued. Release transferred to Soul 35112.
MO45 0298	Motown 1285 (01/74)	Charlene Duncan All That Love Went To Waste Give It One More Try Note: "B" side previously issued on Motown 1262B. "A" side taken from the movie "A Touch Of Class."
MO45 0299	Motown 1286 (02/74)	The Jackson 5 Dancing Machine It's Too Late To Change The Time
MO45 0300	Motown 1287 (03/74)	Willie Hutch If You Ain't Got No Money (You Can't Get No Honey) Pt. I If You Ain't Got No Money (You Can't Get No Honey) Pt. II
MO45 0301	Motown 1288 (02/74)	Frankie Valli And The Four Seasons Hickory Charisma
MO45 0302	Motown 1289 (02/74)	Michael Edward Campbell Roxanne (You Sure GOt A Fine Design) Roll It Over
MO45 0303	Motown 1290 (03/74)	Zell Black I Been Had By The Devil Confession (Gotta Get Back To Myself)
MO45 0304	Motown 1291 (04/74)	Bottom & Company You're My Life Gonna Find A True Love
MO45 0305	Motown 1292 (04/74)	Willie Hutch Theme Of Foxy Brown Give Me Some Of That Good Old Love
MO45 0306	Motown 1293 (05/74)	Dan The Banjo Man Dan The Banjo Man Londonderry Note: Pseudonym for Phil Cordell.
MO45 0307	Motown 1294 (04/74)	Martin & Finley White Bird He Still Plays On
MO45 0308	Motown 1295 (04/74)	Diana Ross Sleepin' You
MO45 0309	Motown 1296 (06/74)	Diana Ross & Marvin Gaye Don't Knock My Love Just Say, Just Say
MO45 0310	Motown 1297 (07/74)	Syreeta Come And Get This Stuff Black Magic Note: "B" side also issued on Mowest 5016B.
MO45 0311	Motown 1298 (07/74)	Dickey And The Poseidons Where Were You When The Ship Went Down Tidal Wave
MO45 0312	Motown 1299	Note: Unissued.
MO45 0313	Motown 1300 (06/74)	Edwin Starr Big Papa Like We Used To Do
MO45 0314	Motown 1301 (06/74)	Matrix Streakin' Down The Avenue Commercial Break
MO45 0315	Motown 1302 (06/74)	Puzzle Everybody Wants To Be Somebody State Of Mind
MO45 0316	Motown 1303 (05/74)	Severin Browne Love Song Snow Flakes Note: Issued with full-color picture sleeve. "B" side previously issued on Motown 1258B.
MO45 0317	Motown 1304 (06/74)	Xit I Need Your Love (Give It To Me) Movin' From The City
MO45 0318	Motown 1305 (07/74)	Reuben Howell Rings I'll Be Your Brother
MO45 0319	Motown 1306 (06/74)	Yvonne Fair Funky Music Sho Nuff Turns Me On Let Your Hair Down
MO45 0320	Motown 1307 (05/74)	Commodores Machine Gun There's A Song In My Heart Note: "B" side previously issued on Motown 1268B. Also issued in red vinyl.
MO45 0321	Motown 1308 (10/74)	The Jackson 5 Whatever You Got, I Want I Can't Quit Your Love
MO45 0322	Motown 1309 (11/74)	Bottom & Company Spread The News Love Pains

MO45 0323	Motown 1310 (12/74)	The Jackson 5 I Am Love I Am Love Pt. II
MO45 0324	Motown 1311 (08/74)	G. C. Cameron If You Don't Love Me Topics
MO45 0325	Motown 1312 (10/74)	Riot Just Beyond It's Been Oh So Long Note: See also Motown 1318.
MO45 0326	Motown 1313 (10/74)	Diahann Carroll I've Been There Before I Can't Give Back The Love I Feel For You Note: "B" side previously issued on Motown 1271B.
MO45 0327	Motown 1314 (11/74)	The Pat Boone Family Please Mr. Postman Friend
MO45 0328	Motown 1315 (10/74)	Third Creation Where Do I Belong Penny Annie Fortune Lady
MO45 0329	Motown 1316 (10/74)	Thelma Houston You've Been Doing Wrong For So Long Pick Of The Week Note: "B" side previously issued on Mowest 5008B.
MO45 0330	Motown 1317 (11/74)	Syreeta Heavy Day I'm Goin' Left
MO45 0331	Motown 1318 (10/74)	Riot Put Your Gun Down Brother It's Been Oh So Long Note: "B" side previously issued on Motown 1312B.
MO45 0332	Motown 1319 (10/74)	Commodores I Feel Sanctified It Is As Good As You Make It
MO45 0333	Motown 1320 (10/74)	Xit Renegade Cement Prairie
MO45 0334	Motown 1321 (09/74)	The Devastating Affair You Don't Know (How Hard It Is To Make It) (Vocal) You Don't Know How Hard It Is To Make It (Instrumental)
MO45 0335	Motown 1322	The Allens High Tide Don't Make Me Wait Too Long Note: Unissued. See also Motown 1351.
MO45 0336	Motown 1323 (10/74)	Yvonne Fair Walk Out The Door If You Wanna It Should Have Been Me Note: Issued with picture sleeve. Also issued as an extended

play single on a promotional basis on PR-18 (3:34) for the title of "It Should Have Been Me." See also Motown 1384.

MO45 0337	Motown 1324 (09/74)	The Dynamic Superiors Shoe Shoe Shine Release Me
MO45 0338	Motown 1325 (10/74)	Reuben Howell Constant Disappointment I Believe (When I Fall In Love It Will Be Forever)
MO45 0339	Motown 1326 (11/74)	Edwin Starr Who's Right Or Wrong Lonely Rainy Days In San Diego
MO45 0340	Motown 1327 (11/74)	David Ruffin Me And Rock & Roll (Are Here To Stay) Smiling Faces Sometimes
MO45 0341	Motown 1328 (12/74)	Syreeta Your Kiss Is Sweet Spinnin' And Spinnin'
MO45 0342	Motown 1329 (12/74)	Jimmy Ruffin What Becomes Of The Brokenhearted Baby I've Got It Note: Reissue of Soul 35022.
MO45 0343	Motown 1330 (12/74)	Stephen Cohn Power Is Take It Now
MO45 0344	Motown 1331 (01/75)	Willie Hutch I'm Gonna Stay Woman, You Touched Me
MO45 0345	Motown 1332	David Ruffin Take Me Clear From Here I Just Want To Celebrate Note: Unissued. Test pressings were made of this single, but very few copies are known to exist.
MO45 0346	Motown 1333 (01/75)	Severin Browne Romance The Sweet Sound Of Your Song
MO45 0347	Motown 1334 (01/75)	The Boones When The Lovelight Starts Shining Through His Eyes Viva Espana (Forever A Song In My Heart) Note: See also Motown 1389.
MO45 0348	Motown 1335 (02/75)	Diana Ross Sorry Doesn't Always Make It Right Together Note: Issued with brown and white picture sleeve. See also Motown 1456 and 1496.

MO45 0349	Motown 1336 (03/75)	David Ruffin Superstar (Remember How You Got Where You Are) No Matter Where 　　Note: See also Motown 1393.
MO45 0350	Motown 1337 (03/75)	Bottom & Company Ticket To The Moon Do You Wanna Do A Thing 　　Note: See also Motown 1363.
MO45 0351	Motown 1338 (04/75)	Commodores Slippery When Wet The Bump
MO45 0352	Motown 1339 (02/75)	Willie Hutch Get Ready For The Get Down Don't You Let Nobody Tell 　　You How To Do Your Thing
MO45 0353	Motown 1340 (02/75)	The Allens A Bird In The Hand (Is Worth Two In The Bush) California Music 　　Note: Some copies of "A" side listed as "A Bird In The Hand." See also Motown 1351.
MO45 0354	Motown 1341 (02/75)	Michael Jackson We're Almost There Take Me Back 　　Note: See also Motown 1512.
MO45 0355	Motown 1342 (03/75)	The Dynamic Superiors Leave It Alone One-Nighter 　　Note: See also Motown 1365.
MO45 0356	Motown 1343 (04/75)	Su Shifrin All I Wanna Do For You
MO45 0357	Motown 1344 (04/75)	Yvonne Fair It's Bad For Me To See You You Can't Judge A Book By It's Cover 　　Note: Label shows "It's Cover" rather than "Its." See also Motown 1354.
MO45 0358	Motown 1345 (03/75)	Bob Horn You've Gotta Try A Little Love Static Free
MO45 0359	Motown 1346	Kathe Green Love City What Kind Of Man Are You 　　Note: Unissued. See also Motown 1372 and 1390.
MO45 0360	Motown 1347 (04/75)	G. C. Cameron Tippin' If You're Ever Gonna Love Me 　　Note: See also Motown 1397.
MO45 0361	Motown 1348	Note: Unissued.

MO45 0362	Motown 1349 (04/75)	Michael Jackson Just A Little Bit Of You Dear Michael
MO45 0363	Motown 1350	The Supremes It's All Been Said Before Give Out, But Don't Give Up 　　Note: Unissued. This was to have been the first single featuring Scherrie Payne on lead. See also Motown 1358 and 1374.
MO45 0364	Motown 1351 (05/75)	The Allens High Tide California Music 　　Note: "A" side originally scheduled for release on Motown 1322A. "B" side previously issued on Motown 1340B.
MO45 0365	Motown 1352 (05/75)	Jr. Walker & The All Stars What Does It Take (To Win Your Love) Country Boy 　　Note: "A" side previousy issued on Soul 35062A. "B" side previously issued on Soul 35106B.
MO45 0366	Motown 1353 (06/75)	Syreeta Harmour Love Cause We've Ended As Lovers 　　Note: Issued with orange and brown picture sleeve. Also issued in red vinyl.
MO45 0367	Motown 1354 (07/75)	Yvonne Fair Love Ain't No Toy You Can't Judge A Book By It's Cover 　　Note: "B" side previously issued on 1344B. Also issued with the titles reversed. Label shows "It's" rather than "Its."
MO45 0368	Motown 1355 (06/75)	The Originals Good Lovin' Is Just A Dime Away Nothing Can Take The Place (Of Your Love)
MO45 0369	Motown 1356 (06/75)	The Jackson 5 Forever Came Today All I Do Is Think of You 　　Note: Also issued in red or blue vinyl.
MO45 0370	Motown 1357	The Dynamic Superiors Romeo I Got Away 　　Note: Unissued. See also Motown 1359.
MO45 0371	Motown 1358 (07/75)	The Supremes He's My Man Give Out, But Don't Give Up 　　Note: "B" side originally scheduled to be issued on Motown 1350B, but the release was cancelled. See also Motown 1374.

MO45 0372	Motown 1359 (08/75)	The Dynamic Superiors Nobody's Gonna Change Me I Got Away Note: "B" side originally scheduld for Motown 1357.
MO45 0373	Motown 1360 (08/75)	Willie Hutch Love Power Talk To Me Note: Also issued in yellow vinyl.
MO45 0374	Motown 1361 (09/75)	Commodores This Is Your Life Look What You've Done To Me Note: See also Motown 1443.
MO45 0375	Motown 1362 (09/75)	Magic Disco Machine Control Tower Scratchin
MO45 0376	Motown 1363 (10/75)	Bottom & Company Here For The Party Ticket To The Moon Note: "B" side previously issued on Motown 1337A.
MO45 0377	Motown 1364 (09/75)	G. C. Cameron It's So Hard To Say Goodbye To Yesterday Haulin'+Cold Blooded (Instrumental) Note: Issued with full-color picture sleeve.
MO45 0378	Motown 1365 (10/75)	The Dynamic Superiors Deception One-Nighter Note: "B" side previously issued on Motown 1342B.
MO45 0379	Motown 1366	Commodores Wide Open Note: Unissued. Issued only on a promotional basis.
MO45 0380	Motown 1367 (10/75)	Chip Hand Wait Until September Dreamtime Lover
MO45 0381	Motown 1368	Leon Ware Comfort Share Your Love Note: Unissued. Test pressings exist of this as manufactured by RCA Hollywood. There is a date written on the label of 9-18-75. Titles of the actual A & B side songs are not listed on the label.
MO45 0382	Motown 1369 (10/75)	Lenny Williams Since I Met You Motion
MO45 0383	Motown 1370 (10/75)	The Originals 50 Years Financial Affair
MO45 0384	Motown 1371 (02/76)	Willie Hutch Party Down Just Another Day
MO45 0385	Motown 1372 (11/75)	Kathe Green Beautiful Changes What Kind Of Man Are You Note: "B" side originally scheduled for release on Motown 1346B. See also Motown 1390.
MO45 0386	Motown 1373 (11/75)	William Goldstein Spirit of '76 (A.M. America) Southern Comfort Note: Issued with picture sleeve. Label has special red, white, and blue "Stars & Stripes" type design.
MO45 0387	Motown 1374 (10/75)	The Supremes Where Do I Go From Here Give Out, But Don't Give Up Note: "B" side previously issued on Motown 1358B.
MO45 0388	Motown 1375	The Jackson 5 Body Language (Do The Love Dance) Call Of The Wild Note: Unissued.
MO45 0389	Motown 1376 (10/75)	David Ruffin Walk Away From Love Love Can Be Hazardous To Your Health Note: See also Motown 1388.
MO45 0390	Motown 1377 (10/75)	Diana Ross Theme From Mahogany (Do You Know Where You're Going To) No One's Gonna Be A Fool Forever Note: Issued with full-color picture sleeve. Also issued in yellow vinyl.
MO45 0391	Motown 1378 (11/75)	Joe Frazier First Round Knock-Out Looky Looky (Look At Me Girl) Note: This is the former heavyweight boxing champion.
MO45 0392	Motown 1379 (12/75)	The Originals Everybody's Got To Do Something (Vocal) Everybody's Got To Do Something (Instrumental) Note: Issued promotionally as an extended play single on PR-14 running 6:38.
MO45 0393	Motown 1380	Note: Unissued.
MO45 0394	Motown 1381 (12/75)	Commodores Sweet Love Better Never Than Forever Note: Also issued in yellow vinyl.

MO45 0395	Motown 1382 (02/76)	Stephanie Mills This Empty Place I See You For The First Time
MO45 0396	Motown 1383 (02/76)	Rose Banks Whole New Thing What Am I Gonna Do (With My Life)
MO45 0397	Motown 1384 (03/76)	Yvonne Fair It Should Have Been Me Tell Me Something Good Note: "A" side version three seconds longer than same version on Motown 1323B. Promo version on PR-18 runs 3:34.
MO45 0398	Motown 1385 (03/76)	Thelma Houston The Bingo Long Song (Steal On Home) Razzle Dazzle (Instrumental) Note: Issued with full-color picture sleeve.
MO45 0399	Motown 1386	Jermaine Jackson She's The Ideal Girl I Am So Glad You Chose Me Note: Unissued.
MO45 0400	Motown 1387 (03/76)	Diana Ross I Thought It Took A Little Time (But Today I Fell In Love) After You Note: Issued with brown and yellow picture sleeve. See also Motown 1508.
MO45 0401	Motown 1388 (02/76)	David Ruffin Heavy Love Love Can Be Hazardous To Your Health Note: "B" side previously issued on Motown 1376B.
MO45 0402	Motown 1389 (03/76)	The Boones My Guy When The Love Light Starts Shining Through His Eyes Note: "B" side previously issued on Motown 1334A.
MO45 0403	Motown 1390 (04/76)	Kathe Green Love City What Kind Of Man Are You Note: Originally scheduled to be released on Motown 1346. "B" side previously issued on Motown 1372B.
MO45 0404	Motown 1391	Leslie Uggams I Want To Make It Easy For You Two Shoes Note: Unissued. Released on Gordy 7149.
MO45 0405	Motown 1391 (05/76)	The Supremes I'm Gonna Let My Heart Do The Walking Early Morning Love
MO45 0406	Motown 1392 (03/76)	Diana Ross Love Hangover Kiss Me Now Note: "A" side issued promotionally as an extended play version on PR-15B running 7:49.
MO45 0407	Motown 1393 (05/76)	David Ruffin Everything's Coming Up Love No Matter Where Note: "B" side previously issued on Motown 1336B.
MO45 0408	Motown 1394	Commodores Come Inside Time Note: Unissued.
MO45 0409	Motown 1395	Lena Horne Believe In Yourself (Vocal) Believe In Yourself (Instrumental) Note: Unissued. Issued on oddly numbered Motown 40979. This was one of two numbers issued with an odd number between the cancellation of Melodyland and the start of the Hitsville label.
MO45 0410	Motown 1396 (06/76)	Ronnie McNeir Selling My Heart To The Junkman Love Proposition
MO45 0411	Motown 1397 (07/76)	G. C. Cameron Dream Lady Tippin Note: "B" side previously issued on Motown 1347.
MO45 0412	Motown 1398 (07/76)	Diana Ross One Love In My Lifetime Smile
MO45 0413	Motown 1399	Commodores High On Sunshine Thumpin' Music Note: Unissued. See Motown 1402.
MO45 0414	Motown 1400 (07/76)	William Goldstein & The Magic Disco Machine Midnight Rhapsody (Part 1) Midnight Rhapsody (Part 2) Note: Issued promotionally as an extended play 12-inch single on PR-26 running 6:10 ("A" side). "B" side runs 3:20.
MO45 0415	Motown 1401 (08/76)	Jermaine Jackson Let's Be Young Tonight Bass Odyssey Note: "A" side issued commercially as an extended version 12-inch single on M-00001D1B running 5:07.
MO45 0416	Motown 1402 (08/76)	Commodores Just To Be Close To You Thumpin' Music Note: "A" side issued commercially as an extended 3:22

version as part of PR-39A3. "B" side originally scheduled for release on Motown 1399B.

MO45 0417	Motown 1403 (09/76)	Jerry Butler The Devil In Mrs. Jones Don't Wanna Be Reminded Note: Issued with full-color picture sleeve. See also Motown 1414.
MO45 0418	Motown 1404 (09/76)	Rose Banks Right's Alright Darling Baby
MO45 0419	Motown 1405 (10/76)	David Ruffin On And Off Statue Of A Fool
MO45 0420	Motown 1406 (10/76)	Willie Hutch Let Me Be The One, Baby She's Just Doing Her Thing
MO45 0421	Motown 1407 (10/76)	The Supremes You're My Driving Wheel You're What's Missing In My Life
MO45 0422	Motown 1408 (12/76)	Commodores Fancy Dancer Cebu Note: "A" side issued commercially as an extended version single on M-00002D1B running 6:28.
MO45 0423	Motown 1409 (10/76)	Jermaine Jackson My Touch Of Madness You Need To Be Loved
MO45 0424	Motown 1410 (12/76)	Ronnie McNeir It Won't Be Long (When We're All Gone) Have You Ever Seen Them Shake (Shake It Baby)
MO45 0425	Motown 1411 (12/76)	Willie Hutch Shake It, Shake It I Feel Like We Can Make It Note: "A" side issued commercially as an extended version single on M-00003D1B running 3:33. See also Motown 1433.
MO45 0426	Motown 1412 (03/77)	G. C. Cameron You're What's Missing In My Life Kiss Me When You Want To
MO45 0427	Motown 1413 (01/77)	The Dynamic Superiors I Can't Stay Away (From Someone I Love) Supersensousensation (Try Some Love)
MO45 0428	Motown 1414 (02/77)	Jerry Butler I Wanna Do It To You Don't Wanna Be Reminded Note: "B" side previously issued on Motown 1403B.

MO45 0429	Motown 1415 (02/77)	The Supremes Let Yourself Go You Are The Heart Of Me
MO45 0430	Motown 1416 (03/77)	Willie Hutch We Gonna Have A House Party I Never Had It So Good
MO45 0431	Motown 1417 (04/77)	Jennifer Do It For Me Boogie Boogie Love Note: "A" side issued commercially as an extended version single on M-00005D1 running 5:20. Above single issued with picture sleeve.
MO45 0432	Motown 1418 (05/77)	Commodores Easy Can't Let You Tease Me Note: "A" side issued promotionally as an extended 4:15 version as part of PR-39A4.
MO45 0433	Motown 1419 (06/77)	The Dynamic Superiors Nowhere To Run Pt. 1 Nowhere To Run Pt. 2 Note: Issued commercially as an extended version single on M-10000D1 running 9:07.
MO45 0434	Motown 1420 (07/77)	David Ruffin Just Let Me Hold You For A Night Just Rode By The Place (Where We Used To Stay) Note: See also Motown 1435.
MO45 0435	Motown 1421 (07/77)	Jerry Butler Chalk It Up I Don't Want Nobody To Know Note: "A" side issued commercially as an extended version single on M-00004D1 running 6:11.
MO45 0436	Motown 1422 (09/77)	Thelma Houston & Jerry Butler It's A Lifetime Thing Kiss Me Now
MO45 0437	Motown 1423 (07/77)	Albert Finney Those Other Men What Have They Done (To My Home Town)
MO45 0438	Motown 1424 (08/77)	Willie Hutch We Gonna Party Tonight Precious Pearl
MO45 0439	Motown 1425 (08/77)	Commodores Brick House Captain Quick Draw Note: "A" side issued commercially as an extended version single on M-30000D1 and M-00007D1, both running 6:11 in length.

MO45 0440	Motown 1426 (09/77)	Syreeta & G. C. Cameron Let's Make A Deal Love To The Rescue Note: As by Syreeta and G. C. Cameron
MO45 0441	Motown 1427 (10/77)	Diana Ross Gettin' Ready For Love Confide In Me
MO45 0442	Motown 1428 (10/77)	The Dynamic Superiors You're What I Need Here Comes That Feeling Again
MO45 0443	Motown 1429 (10/77)	Mandre Solar Flight (Opus 1) Money (That's What I Want)
MO45 0444	Motown 1430 (10/77)	Albert Finney A State of Grace When It's Gone
MO45 0445	Motown 1431	Scherrie Payne Fly When I Look At Your Face Note: Unissued.
MO45 0446	Motown 1432 (12/77)	Commodores Too Hot Ta Trot Funky Situation Note: See also Motown 1495.

MO45 0447	Motown 1433 (01/78)	Willie Hutch
		What You Gonna Do After The
		    Party
		I Feel Like We Can Make It
		    Note: "B" side previously issued on Motown 1411B.

MO45 0448	Motown 1434 (01/78)	Mandre Keep Tryin' Third World Calling (Opus II)

MO45 0449	Motown 1435 (01/78)	David Ruffin
		You're My Peace Of Mind
		Rode By The Place (Where
		    We Used To Stay)
		    Note: "B" side previously issued on Motown 1420B.

MO45 0450	Motown 1436 (02/78)	Diana Ross Your Love Is So Good For Me Baby It's Me Note: "A" side issued commercially as an extended version single on M-00010D1B running 6:32.
MO45 0451	Motown 1437 (02/78)	5th Dimension You Are The Reason (I Feel Like Dancing) Slipping Into Something New

MO45 0452	Motown 1438 (02/78)	Carl Bean
		I Was Born This Way
		I Was Born This Way
		    (Instrumental)
		    Note: Both vocal (6:31) and instrumental (5:51) versions issued commercially on M-00008.

MO45 0453	Motown 1439 (03/78)	3 Ounces of Love Star Love I Found The Feeling

MO45 0454	Motown 1440 (03/78)	Cuba Gooding
		Mind Pleaser
		Where Would I Be Without
		    You
		    Note: "A" side issued promotionally as an extended version as part of PR-35A2 running 4:16.

MO45 0455	Motown 1441 (04/78)	Jermaine Jackson
		Castles Of Sand
		I Love Every Little Thing
		    About You
		    Note: "A" side issued promotionally as an extended version as part of PR-35A3 running 5:38.

MO45 0456	Motown 1442 (04/78)	Diana Ross You Got It Too Shy To Say Note: "A" side issued promotionally as an extended version as part of PR-35A1 running 3:55.

MO45 0457	Motown 1443 (05/78)	Commodores
		Three Times A Lady
		Look What You've Done To
		    Me
		    Note: "A" side issued in a short (3:35) and long (4:59) version on a promo single. Also issued as an extended version on PR-39B1 running 6:37. "B" side previously issued on Motown 1361B.

MO45 0458	Motown 1444 (05/78)	Prime Time Good Times Theme Carter Country Theme Note: "A" side promo single issued with both short (2:53) and long (4:14) versions. "A" side also issued promotionally as an extended version on PR-40A running 8:53.
MO45 0459	Motown 1445 (08/78)	Finished Touch Sticks And Stones (But The Funk Won't Never Hurt You) Strokin'

MO45 0460	Motown 1446 (09/78)	Three Ounces Of Love
		Give Me Some Feeling
		Does Your Chewing Gum
		    Lose Its Flavor On The Bedpost
		    Overnight

MO45 0461	Motown 1447 (09/78)	Platinum Hook Hooked For Life Gotta Find A Woman
MO45 0462	Motown 1448 (10/78)	Mandre Fair Game Light Years (Opus IV) Note: "B" side issued

MO45	Motown	Marvin Gaye, Smokey
0471	1455	Robinson, Diana Ross & Stevie
	(11/78)	Wonder

promotionally as an extended
version on PR-38A3 running 7:08.

Pops, We Love You (Vocal)
Pops, We Love You
(Instrumental)
  Note: Issued commercially as
an extended version on M-00015D1
running 6:32. Also issued in a
limited edition heart-shaped red
vinyl single M9-1455F running
3:30 (both vocal and instrumental
versions). Also issued in green vinyl.

| MO45 | Motown | Diana Ross |
| 0463 | 1449 | Top Of The World |

  Note: Unissued. Issued
promotionally with double "A"
sided copies running 3:06.

MO45	Motown	Finished Touch featuring
0464	1449	Kenny Stover
	(10/78)	I Love To See You Dance
		You Danced Into My Life

  Note: "A" side issued
promotionally as an extended play
version on PR-41A running 5:16.
"B" side also issued as an extended
version on PR-41B running 6:01.
"B" side features Larry Brown &
Harold Johnson.

MO45	Motown	Diana Ross
0472	1456	What You Gave Me
	(01/79)	Together

  Note: "A" side issued
commercially as an extended
version on M-00011D1A running
6:06. Also issued promotionally on
PR-42 running 6:06 both sides.
"B" side previously issued on
Motown 1335B. See also Motown
1496.

MO45	Motown	Diana Ross
0465	1450	Lovin', Livin' And Givin'
		Baby Its Me

  Note: Unissued. "A" side
issued commercially on
M-00026D1 running 5:11. "Baby
It's Me" previously issued on
Motown 1436B.

MO45	Motown	Commodores
0473	1457	Say Yeah
		Thumpin' Music

  Note: Unissued. "A" side
issued promotionally as an extended
version on PR-39B4 running 5:44.

MO45	Motown	Bonnie Pointer
0466	1451	Free Me From My Freedom - Tie
	(10/78)	Me To A Tree (Handcuff Me)
		Free Me From My Freedom -
		Tie Me To A Tree (Handcuff Me)
		(Instrumental)

  Note: "A" side vocal issued
commercially as an extended
version on M-00011D1B running
8:25. Above single issued with
picture sleeve. Also issued in red
vinyl.

MO45	Motown	Motown Sounds
0474	1457	Space Dance
	(03/79)	Bad Mouthin'

MO45	Motown	Bloodstone
0475	1458	Just Wanna Get The Feel Of It
	(04/79)	It's Been A Long Time

  Note: "A" side issued
commercially as an extended
version on M-00017D1 running
5:36 (both vocal and instrumental
versions).

MO45	Motown	Commodores
0467	1452	Flying High
	(12/78)	X-Rated Movie

MO45	Motown	5th Dimension
0468	1453	Everybody's Got To Give It Up
	(05/79)	You're My Star

MO45	Motown	Bonnie Pointer
0476	1459	Heaven Must Have Sent You
	(04/79)	Heaven Must Have Sent You
		(LP Version)

  Note: Issued commercially as
an extended version on M-00020D1
running 5:12 (LP version) and
6:59 (New version).

MO45	Motown	Grover Washington, Jr.
0469	1454	Do Dat
	(12/78)	Reed Seed (Trio Tune)

  Note: Also issued in yellow
vinyl.

MO45	Motown	Billy Preston & Syreeta
0477	1460	Go For It
	(04/79)	With You I'm Born Again
		(Instrumental)

  Note: "A" side issued
commercially with extended version
running 8:49 (vocal) and 8:43
(instrumental).

MO45	Motown	Marvin Gaye, Smokey
0470	1455	Robinson, Diana Ross & Stevie
	(12/78)	Wonder
		Pops, We Love You (Vocal)
		Pops, We Love You
		(Instrumental)

  Note: "A" side is alternate
version with the monologue by
Diana Ross omitted.

MO45	Motown	Mandre
0478	1461	Spirit Groove
	(05/79)	M3000 (Opus VI)

  Note: "A" side issued
commercially as an extended
version on M-00022D1A running
6:56. See also Motown 1472.

MO45 Motown   Diana Ross
0479 1462   The Boss
      (05/79)   I'm In The World
                Note: "A" side issued
      commercially as an extended
      version on M-00026D1A running
      7:23. Also coupled with "No One
      Gets The Prize" on M-00035D1B
      running 6:38. Same coupling issued
      promotionally with same running
      time on PR-54A.

MO45 Motown   Finished Touch featuring
0480 1463   Harold Johnson
      (05/79)   The Down Sound Pt. 2
                The Down Sound Pt. 1
                Note: Issued commercially as
      an extended version on
      M-00023D1A running 10:30. Part
      2 is listed as being the "A" side.

MO45 Motown   Platinum Hook
0481 1464   Give Me Time To Say
      (06/79)   Lover What You've Done (To
                Me)

MO45 Motown   Patrick Gammon
0482 1465   Cop An Attitude
      (06/79)   My Song In -G-

MO45 Motown   Commodores
0483 1466   Sail On
      (08/79)   Thumpin' Music
                Note: "A" side issued
      promotionally as an extended
      version on PR-56B running 5:35.
      "B" side previously issued on
      Motown 1402B.

MO45 Motown   Mary Wilson
0484 1467   Red Hot
      (10/79)   Midnight Dancer
                Note: "A" side issued
      promotionally as an extended
      version on PR-58 running (Single
      version 3:53), (Disco version 7:12).
      This was issued on red wax. "A"
      side also issued commercially on
      M-00033D1 with running times
      listed as 6:06 ("A" side Disco
      version) and 3:53 ("B" side Single
      version).

MO45 Motown   Sterling
0485 1468   Roll-Her, Skater
      (10/79)   Roll-Her, Skater
                (Instrumental)
                Note: Issued commercially on
      M-00032D1 as an extended version
      running 7:50 (vocal) and 6:18
      (instrumental).

MO45 Motown   Jermaine Jackson
0486 1469   Let's Get Serious
      (03/80)   Je Vous Aime Beaucoup (I
                Love You)
                Note: "A" side issued
      promotionally as an extended
      version on PR-66 running 3:33
      (short version) and 7:55 (long

version). Also issued in Canada as
PR-68-66 running 7:55. The "B"
side of this is "Power" by The
Temptations. Also issued in red
vinyl.

MO45 Motown   Billy Preston
0487 1470   It Will Come In Time
      (10/79)   All I Wanted Was You
                Note: "A" side has vocal
      accompaniment by Syreeta. See
      also Motown 1477.

MO45 Motown   Diana Ross
0488 1471   It's My House
      (10/79)   Sparkle
                Note: "A" side issued
      promotionally as an extended
      version on PR-54B running 4:29.

MO45 Motown   Mandre
0489 1472   Freakin's Fine
      (10/79)   Spirit Groove
                Note: "A" side issued
      commercially as an extended
      version on M-00022D1B running
      5:55. "B" side previously issued on
      Motown 1461A.

MO45 Motown   Scherrie & Susaye
0490 1473   Leaving Me Was The Best Thing
      (09/79)   You've Ever Done
                When The Day Comes Every
                Night

MO45 Motown   Commodores
0491 1474   Still
      (09/79)   Such A Woman
                Note: "A" side issued
      promotionally as an extended
      version on PR-56 running 5:51.

MO45 Motown   Dr. Strut
0492 1475   Granite Palace
      (10/79)   Blow Top

MO45 Motown   Cook County
0493 1476   Pinball Playboy (Playboy Theme)
      (11/79)   Reach Out For Love

MO45 Motown   Billy Preston & Syreeta
0494 1477   With You I'm Born Again
      (11/79)   All I Wanted Was You
                Note: "B" side is by Billy
      Preston (solo). "B" side also
      previously issued on 1470A.

MO45 Motown   Bonnie Pointer
0495 1478   I Can't Help Myself (Sugar Pie,
      (11/79)   Honey Bunch)
                I Wanna Make It (In Your
                World)

MO45 Motown   Commodores
0496 1479   Wonderland
      (12/79)   Lovin' You
                Note: See also Motown 1527.

MO45 0497	Motown 1480	Lynda Carter The Last Song What's A Little Love Between Friends Note: Unissued. Issued commercially in the U.K. on Tamla Motown TMG-1207.
MO45 0498	Motown 1481 (02/80)	Cook County Little Girls & Ladies Olympiad '84
MO45 0499	Motown 1482 (02/80)	Clifton Dyson Body In Motion (Want Your Body In Motion With Mine) You Gotta Keep Dancin' Note: Issued commercially originally on the All American label as an extended version single AA-373LPD running 7:45 (Side 1) and 5:02 (Side 2). This 12-inch version was somehow picked up by Motown and released on the Motown label on M-00034D1 with the same running times for both sides. It is likely that the people at All American Records (Hollywood, CA) approached Motown Records to distribute this record on a national basis.
MO45 0500	Motown 1483 (03/80)	Dr. Strut Struttin' Blue Lodge
MO45 0501	Motown 1484 (03/80)	Bonnie Pointer Deep Inside My Soul I Love To Sing To You
MO45 0502	Motown 1485 (04/80)	The Planets Break It To Me Gently Secret Note: "A" side also issued promotionally on PR-67A. Previously issued on Rialto 114.
MO45 0503	Motown 1486 (05/80)	Grover Washington, Jr. Snake Eyes Love
MO45 0504	Motown 1487 (07/80)	Ozone Walk On This Is Funkin' Insane
MO45 0505	Motown 1488 (06/80)	Diana Ross & The Supremes Medley of Hits Where Do We Go From Here Note: "B" side as by Diana Ross (solo). "A" side issued commercially as an extended version on M-00035D1A running 10:00. Also issued promotionally as PR-69A with a running time of 5:08 (same as commercial copy). See also Motown 1523.
MO45 0506	Motown 1489 (06/80)	Commodores Old-Fashioned Love Sexy Lady

MO45 0507	Motown 1490 (08/80)	Jermaine Jackson You're Supposed To Keep Your Love For Me Let It Ride
MO45 0508	Motown 1491 (08/80)	Diana Ross I'm Coming Out Give Up
MO45 0509	Motown 1491 (08/80)	Diana Ross I'm Coming Out Friend To Friend Note: "A" side issued promotionally as an extended version on PR-75A running 5:23. "A" side also issued commercially in Canada as an extended version single on the short-lived Canadian 6000 series, numbered MD-6001, running 5:23. See also Motown 1494.
MO45 0510	Motown 1492 (07/80)	Charlene Hungry I Won't Remember Ever Loving You
MO45 0511	Motown 1493 (06/80)	Black Russian Leave Me Now Love's Enough Note: "B" side issued commercially in the Canadian series as M-6000X (the only 7-inch single in this series).
MO45 0512	Motown 1494 (06/80)	Diana Ross Upside Down Friend To Friend Note: "A" side issued promotionally as an extended version on PR-72A running 4:05. Also issued on the Canadian 6000 series as MD-6001A running 4:05. "B" side previously issued on Motown 1491 (second release).
MO45 0513	Motown 1495 (09/80)	Commodores Heroes Funky Situation Note: "B" side previously issued on Motown 1432B.
MO45 0514	Motown 1496 (10/80)	Diana Ross It's My Turn Together Note: "B" side previously issued on Motown 1335B as well as Motown 1456B.
MO45 0515	Motown 1497	Billy Preston & Syreeta Please Stay Signed, Sealed, Delivered (I'm Yours) Note: Unissued. Issued on Tamla 54319.
MO45 0516	Motown 1497 (11/80)	Black Russian Mystified Move Together Note: "A" side issued on the Canadian 6000 series as

M-6000XA.

MO45 0517	Motown 1498 (09/80)	Platinum Hook Words Of Love Ecstasy Paradise

MO45 0518	Motown 1499 (11/80)	Jermaine Jackson Little Girl Don't You Worry We Can Put It Back Together Note: "A" side issued promotionally as an extended version on PR-78B running 4:47. Also issued in red vinyl.

MO45 0519	Motown 1500 (11/80)	Dazz Band Shake It Up Only Love Note: "A" side issued promotionally as an extended version on PR-78A running 5:05.

MO45 0520	Motown 1501 (11/80)	The Temptations Take Me Away There's More Where That Came From

MO45 0521	Motown 1502 (11/80)	Commodores Jesus Is Love Mighty Spirit Note: "A" side issued promotionally as an extended version on PR-70A running 4:26 (short) and 6:04 (long). "B" side also issued as part of PR-70 as "B" side.

MO45 0522	Motown 1503 (02/81)	Jermaine Jackson You Like Me Don't You You Like Me Don't You (Instrumental) Note: Issued promotionally as an extended version on PR-78B running 4:59.

MO45 0523	Motown 1504 (02/81)	Joel Diamond Theme From Raging Bull (Cavalleria Rusticana) Joey's Theme

MO45 0524	Motown 1505 (02/81)	Billy Preston Hope Sock-It, Rocket

MO45 0525	Motown 1506 (02/81)	Midnight Blue I Who Have Nothing (Vocal) I Who Have Nothing (Instrumental)

MO45 0526	Motown 1507 (02/81)	Dazz Band Invitation To Love Magnetized

MO45 0527	Motown 1508 (02/81)	Diana Ross One More Chance After You Note: "B" side previously issued on Motown 1387B.

MO45 0528	Motown 1509	Note: Unissued.

MO45 0529	Motown 1510 (03/81)	Ozone Ozonic Bee Bop The Preacher's Gone Home (Tribute To Cannonball Adderly)

MO45 0530	Motown 1511 (04/81)	Billy Preston A Change Is Gonna Come You

MO45 0531	Motown 1512 (03/81)	Michael Jackson One Day In Your Life Take Me Back Note: "B" side previously issued on Motown 1341B.

MO45 0532	Motown 1513 (05/81)	Diana Ross Cryin' My Heart Out For You To Love Again

MO45 0533	Motown 1514 (06/81)	Commodores Lady (You Bring Me Up) Gettin' It

MO45 0534	Motown 1515 (08/81)	Dazz Band Knock Knock Sooner Or Later

MO45 0535	Motown 1516 (07/81)	Tommy Hill Flame Superstar Of Love (Instrumental)

MO45 0536	Motown 1517 (09/81)	Jose Feliciano Everybody Loves Me The Drought Is Over

MO45 0537	Motown 1518 (06/81)	Ozone Mighty-Mighty Rock And Roll, Pop And Soul Note: "A" side issued promotionally as an extended version on PR-82B running 4:51.

MO45 0538	Motown 1519 (08/81)	Diana Ross and Lionel Richie Endless Love (Vocal) Endless Love (Instrumental)

MO45 0539	Motown 1520 (08/81)	Billy Preston & Syreeta Searchin' Hey You Note: See also Motown 1522.

MO45 0540	Motown 1521 (08/81)	Ozone Gigolette (Vocal) Gigolette (Instrumental) Note: Issued promotionally as an extended version on PR-85B running 6:40 (both vocal and instrumental).

MO45 0541	Motown 1522 (08/81)	Billy Preston & Syreeta Just For You (Put the Boogie In Your Body Hey You Note: "A" side issued promotionally as an extended version on PR-85A running 5:23

(both vocal and instrumental). "B" side previously issued on Motown 1520B.

MO45 0542 (08/81)	Motown 1523	Diana Ross & The Supremes Medley of Hits Where Did We Go Wrong Note: "A" side is a reissue of Motown 1488A with same running time (5:08). "B" side as by Diana Ross (solo).
MO45 0543	Motown 1524	Jose Feliciano I Second That Emotion The Drought Is Over Note: Unissued. Later to be released on Motown 1618 in April 1982 with alternate "B" side. "A" side also issued promotionally as an extended version on PR-91A running 5:35.
MO45 0544 (10/81)	Motown 1525	Jermaine Jackson I'm Just Too Shy All Because Of You
MO45 0545	Motown 1526	Lovesmith Shame On You The Best Of Note: Unissued.
MO45 0546 (09/81)	Motown 1527	Commodores Oh No Lovin' You Note: "B" side previously issued on Motown 1479B.
MO45 0547 (10/81)	Motown 1528	Dazz Band Let The Music Play Hello Girl
MO45 0548	Motown 1529	Ozone Over And Over Again Come On In Note: Unissued.
MO45 0549 (12/81)	Motown 1530	Jose Feliciano I Wanna Be Where You Are Let's Make Love Over The Telephone Note: "A" side issued promotionally as part of PR-91 running 3:58.
MO45 0550 (01/82)	Motown 1531	Diana Ross My Old Piano Now That You're Gone Note: "A" side issued on a promotional basis with special lyric sleeve.
MO45 0551	Motown 1532	Bettye Lavette Right In The Middle (Of Falling In Love) If I Were Your Woman Note: Unissued.

MO45 0552 (01/82)	Motown 1532	Bettye Lavette Right In The Middle (Of Falling In Love) You Seen One You Seen 'Em All Note: "A" side issued promotionally as part of PR-92 running 3:38 (both vocal and instrumental). First issue promo copies list "A" side as taken from the album IT'S A LIE (Motown M8-964M1). Other promo copies list the song as taken from the album BETTYE LAVETTE (Motown 6000ML).

NUMBER SEQUENCE CHANGE

Note: At this point, separate numbering for Tamla, Motown, and Gordy labels was discontinued and, starting in January 1982, was consolidated into a single sequence beginning at number 1600. This new consecutive numbering system was used for all subsequent singles releases, with individual labels retaining their own distinctive designs. Please see "TMG Consolidated Series" for continuation.

MOTOWN 7-INCH SPECIAL ISSUES

MO45S 0001 (09/59)	Motown G1/G2	The Miracles featuring Bill "Smokey" Robinson Bad Girl I Love You Baby Note: See also Motown 2207 below.
MO45S 0002 (09/59)	Motown 2207	The Miracles featuring Bill "Smokey" Robinson Bad Girl I Love You Baby Note: This is a reissue of G1/G2. It is the very first single on the Motown label. It is also considered to be the rarest of the two releases. Both are probably test pressings, as songs are licensed to Chess for commercial release on Chess 1734.
MO45S 0003 (1966)	Motown DM-L-294MO5	The Supremes Mother You, Smother You Mother You, Smother You Note: Christine Schumacher sings with The Supremes. Promotional issue only, pressed in extremely limited quantities for a special promotion on radio WKNR in Dearborn, Michigan. Miss Schumacher was the winner of "Record A Record With The Supremes" contest, hosted by DJ Scott Regan. Issued with regular "Map" label.

MOTOWN CARDBOARD SINGLES

MOCB 0001   Motown 1   (1967)
Diana Ross & The Supremes
Baby Love
Note: Cardboard record.

MOCB 0002   Motown 2   (1967)
Diana Ross & The Supremes
Stop! In The Name Of Love
Note: Cardboard record.

MOCB 0003   Motown 3   (1967)
Diana Ross & The Supremes
Where Did Our Love Go
Note: Cardboard record.

MOCB 0004   Motown 4   (1967)
The Temptations
My Girl
Note: Cardboard record.

MOCB 0005   Motown 5   (1967)
The Four Tops
I Can't Help Myself
Note: Cardboard record.

MOCB 0006   Motown 6   (1967)
Marvin Gaye
How Sweet It Is (To Be Loved By You)
Note: Cardboard record.

MOCB 0007   Motown 7   (1967)
Martha Reeves & The Vandellas
Dancing In The Street
Note: Cardboard record.

MOCB 0008   Motown 8   (1967)
Stevie Wonder
Fingertips-Part II
Note: Cardboard record.

MOCB 0009   Motown 9   (1967)
The Four Tops
Baby I Need Your Loving
Note: Cardboard record.

MOCB 0010   Motown 10   (1967)
Stevie Wonder
Uptight (Everything's Alright)
Note: Cardboard record.

MOCB 0011   Motown 11   (1967)
The Miracles
Shop Around
Note: Cardboard record.

MOCB 0012   Motown 12   (1967)
The Marvelettes
Please Mr. Postman
Note: Cardboard record.

MOCB 0013   Motown 13   (1967)
The Temptations
The Way You Do The Things You Do
Note: Cardboard record.

MOCB 0014   Motown 14   (1967)
Martha Reeves & The Vandellas
Love Is Like A Heatwave
Note: Cardboard record.

MOCB 0015   Motown 15   (1967)
Diana Ross & The Supremes
Come See About Me
Note: Cardboard record.

MOCB 0016   Motown 16   (1967)
Diana Ross & The Supremes
My World Is Empty Without You
Note: Cardboard record.

MOTOWN 7-INCH COLOR VINYL SINGLES

MOCO 0001   Motown 1085   (12/65)
The Supremes
Twinkle Twinkle Little Me
Note: Red vinyl.

MOCO 0002   Motown 1106   (03/67)
Barbara McNair
Here I Am Baby
Note: Red vinyl.

MOCO 0003   Motown 1110   (05/67)
Four Tops
I'll Turn To Stone
Note: Red vinyl.

MOCO 0004   Motown 1117   (11/67)
The Ones
You Haven't Seen My Love
Note: Red vinyl.

MOCO 0005   Motown 1126   (05/68)
Diana Ross & The Supremes
Some Things You Never Get Used To
Note: Red vinyl.

MOCO 0006   Motown 1130   (08/68)
The Ones
Don't Let Me Lose This Dream
Note: Red vinyl.

MOCO 0007   Motown 1134   (10/68)
Blinky
I Wouldn't Change The Man He Is
Note: Red vinyl. Issued with regular blue label.

MOCO 0008   Motown 1135   (09/68)
Diana Ross & The Supremes
Love Child
Note: Red vinyl.

MOCO 0009   Motown 1139   (01/69)
Diana Ross & The Supremes
I'm Livin' In Shame
Note: Red vinyl.

MOCO 0010   Motown 1140   (02/69)
David Ruffin
My Whole World Ended (The Moment You Left Me)
Note: Red vinyl.

MOCO 0011   Motown 1142   (02/69)
Diana Ross & The Supremes & The Temptations
I'll Try Something New
Note: Red vinyl.

MOCO 0012   Motown 1148   (05/69)
Diana Ross & The Supremes
The Young Folks
Note: Red vinyl.

MOCO 0013   Motown 1157   (10/69)
The Jackson 5
I Want You Back
Note: Red vinyl.

MOCO 0014	Motown 1163 (02/70)	Jackson 5 ABC Note: Yellow vinyl.
MOCO 0015	Motown 1165 (04/70)	Diana Ross Reach Out And Touch (Somebody's Hand) Note: Red vinyl.
MOCO 0016	Motown 1166 (05/70)	Jackson 5 The Love You Save Note: Red vinyl.
MOCO 0017	Motown 1167 (07/70)	The Supremes Everybody's Got The Right To Love Note: Red vinyl.
MOCO 0018	Motown 1170 (08/70)	Four Tops Still Water (Love) Note: Red vinyl.
MOCO 0019	Motown 1172 (10/70)	The Supremes Stoned Love Note: Red vinyl.
MOCO 0020	Motown 1176 (12/70)	Diana Ross Remember Me Note: Red vinyl.
MOCO 0021	Motown 1177 (01/71)	Jackson 5 Mama's Pearl Note: Red vinyl.
MOCO 0022	rings 1180 (04/71)	Gordon Staples & The Motown Strings Strung Out Note: Red vinyl.
MOCO 0023	Motown 1184 (04/71)	Diana Ross Reach Out I'll Be There Note: Red vinyl.
MOCO 0024	Motown 1195 (12/71)	The Supremes Floy Joy Note: Blue vinyl.
MOCO 0025	Motown 1261 (07/73)	G. C. Cameron Let Me Down Easy Note: Red vinyl.
MOCO 0026	Motown 1277 (08/73)	The Jackson 5 Get It Together Note: Red vinyl.
MOCO 0027	Motown 1307 (05/74)	Commodores Machine Gun Note: Red vinyl.
MOCO 0028	Motown 1353 (06/75)	Syreeta Harmour Love Note: Red vinyl.
MOCO 0029	Motown 1356 (06/75)	Jackson 5 Forever Came Today Note: Red vinyl.
MOCO 0030	Motown 1356 (06/75)	Jackson 5 Forever Came Today Note: Blue vinyl.

MOCO 0031	Motown 1360 (08/75)	Willie Hutch Love Power Note: Yellow vinyl.
MOCO 0032	Motown 1377 (10/75)	Diana Ross Theme From Mahogany (Do You Know Where You're Going To) Note: Yellow vinyl.
MOCO 0033	Motown 1381 (12/75)	Commodores Sweet Love Note: Yellow vinyl.
MOCO 0034	Motown 1451 (10/78)	Bonnie Pointer Free Me From My Freedom Tie Me To A Tree (Handcuff Me) (Vocal & Instrumental) Note: Issued with regular blue label. Red vinyl.
MOCO 0035	Motown 1454 (12/78)	Grover Washington, Jr. Do Dat Note: Yellow vinyl.
MOCO 0036	Motown 1455 (12/78)	Diana Ross, Marvin Gaye, Smokey Robinson, Stevie Wonder Pops, We Love You Note: Green vinyl.
MOCO 0037	Motown 1455 (11/78)	Diana Ross, Marvin Gaye, Smokey Robinson, Stevie Wonder Pops, We Love You (Vocal) Pops, We Love You (Instrumental) Note: Issued as a limited edition heart-shaped single in a special sleeve.
MOCO 0038	Motown 1469 (03/80)	Jermaine Jackson Let's Get Serious Note: Red vinyl.
MOCO 0039	Motown 1499 (11/80)	Jermaine Jackson Little Girl Don't You Worry Note: Red vinyl.

MOTOWN 7-INCH EPS

MOEP 0001	Motown TME 2001 (04/65)	Various Artists HITSVILLE, U.S.A. NO. 1 Note: Marvin Gaye, Brenda Holloway, Carolyn Crawford, Eddie Holland.
MOEP 0002	Motown TME 2002 (04/65)	The Contours THE CONTOURS
MOEP 0003	Motown TME 2003 (04/65)	The Marvelettes THE MARVELETTES
MOEP 0004	Motown TME 2004 (04/65)	The Temptations THE TEMPTATIONS

MOEP 0005	Motown TME 2005 (04/65)	Kim Weston KIM WESTON
MOEP 0006	Motown TME 2006 (04/65)	Stevie Wonder STEVIE WONDER
MOEP 0007	Motown TME 2007 (05/65)	Mary Wells MARY WELLS
MOEP 0008	Motown TME 2008 (05/65)	The Supremes THE SUPREMES HITS
MOEP 0009	Motown TME 2009 (05/65)	Martha & The Vandellas MARTHA AND THE VANDELLAS
MOEP 0010	Motown TME 2010 (02/66)	The Temptations IT'S THE TEMPTATIONS
MOEP 0011	Motown TME 2011 (02/66)	The Supremes SHAKE
MOEP 0012	Motown TME 2012 (02/66)	The Four Tops THE FOUR TOPS
MOEP 0013	Motown TME 2013 (02/66)	Junior Walker & The All Stars SHAKE AND FINGERPOP
MOEP 0014	Motown TME 2014 (04/66)	Various Artists NEW FACES FROM HITSVILLE Note: Jimmy Ruffin, Chris Clark, Tammi Terrell, the Monitors.
MOEP 0015	Motown TME 2015 (04/66)	Kim Weston ROCK ME A LITTLE WHILE
MOEP 0016	Motown TME 2016 (04/66)	Marvin Gaye MARVIN GAYE
MOEP 0017	Motown TME 2017 (10/66)	Martha And The Vandellas HITTIN'
MOEP 0018	Motown TME 2018 (03/67)	The Four Tops FOUR TOPS HITS
MOEP 0019	Motown TME 2019 (03/67)	Marvin Gaye ORIGINALS FROM MARVIN GAYE
MOEP 0020	Motown TME 2020 (11/76)	Stevie Wonder SONGS IN THE KEY OF LIFE (Bonus disc) Note: Bonus record issued free with "Songs in The Key Of Life." Issued on blue Motown label, in plain sleeve.

MOTOWN 12-INCH SINGLES

MO12 0001	Motown M-00001D1 (1976)	The Originals / Jermaine Jackson Down To Love Town Let's Be Young Tonight
MO12 0002	Motown M-00002D1 (1976)	Thelma Houston / The Commodores Don't Leave Me This Way Fancy Dancer
MO12 0003	Motown M-00003D1 (1976)	Eddie Kendricks / Willie Hutch Going Up In Smoke Shake It, Shake It
MO12 0004	Motown M-10000D1 (1977)	Dynamic Superiors Nowhere To Run Nowhere To Run
MO12 0005	Motown M-20000D1 (1977)	Smokey Robinson Big Time Big Time
MO12 0006	Motown M-30000D1 (1977)	The Commodores Brick House Brick House
MO12 0007	Motown M-00004D1 (1977)	Smokey Robinson / Jerry Butler Vitamin U Chalk It Up
MO12 0008	Motown M-00005D1 (1977)	Jennifer / Syreeta Do It For Me One To One
MO12 0009	Motown M-00006D1 (1977)	21st Creation / Eddie Kendricks Tailgate Born Again
MO12 0010	Motown M-00007D1 (1977)	Commodores Brick House Brick House
MO12 0011	Motown M-00008D1 (1978)	Carl Bean I Was Born This Way (Vocal) I Was Born This Way (Instrumental)
MO12 0012	Motown M-00009D1 (1978)	Ernie Fields Ride A Wild Horse As
MO12 0013	Motown M-00010D1 (1978)	Thelma Houston / Diana Ross I Can't Go On Living Without Your Love Your Love Is So Good For Me
MO12 0014	Motown M-00011D1 (1978)	Diana Ross / Bonnie Pointer What You Gave Me Free Me From My Freedom
MO12 0015	Motown M-00012D1 (1978)	Rick James High On Your Love Suite + One Mo Hit (Of Your Love) You And I

MO12 0016	Motown M-00013D1 (1978)	Thelma Houston Saturday Night, Sunday Morning Saturday Night, Sunday Morning (Instrumental)
MO12 0017	Motown M-00014D1 (1979)	Marvin Gaye A Funky Space Reincarnation A Funky Space Reincarnation (Instrumental)
MO12 0018	Motown M-00015D1 (1979)	Diana Ross, Marvin Gaye, Smokey Robinson, Stevie Wonder Pops We Love You Pops We Love You
MO12 0019	Motown M-00016D1 (1979)	Billy Preston & Syreeta Go For It Go For It (Instrumental)
MO12 0020	Motown M-00017D1 (1979)	Bloodstone Just Wanna Get The Feel Of It Just Wanna Get The Feel Of It (Instrumental)
MO12 0021	Motown M-00018D1 (1979)	Apollo Astro Disco (Vocal) Astro Disco (Instrumental)
MO12 0022	Motown M-00019D1 (1979)	High Inergy Shoulda Gone Dancin' (Vocal) Shoulda Gone Dancin' (Instrumental)
MO12 0023	Motown M-00020D1 (1979)	Bonnie Pointer Heaven Must Have Sent You (New Version) Heaven Must Have Sent You (LP Version)
MO12 0024	Motown M-00021D1 (1979)	Tata Vega I Just Keep Thinking About You Baby Get It Up For Love
MO12 0025	Motown M-00022D1 (1979)	Mandre Spirit Groove Freakin's Fine
MO12 0026	Motown M-00023D1 (1979)	Finished Touch The Down Sound Need To Know You Better
MO12 0027	Motown M-00024D1 (1979)	Teena Marie I'm A Sucker For Your Love I'm A Sucker For Your Love (Instrumental)
MO12 0028	Motown M-00025D1 (1979)	Switch Best Beat In Town We Like To Party...Come On
MO12 0029	Motown M-00026D1 (1979)	Diana Ross The Boss (Disco Version) Lovin', Livin' & Givin'
MO12 0030	Motown M-00027D1 (1979)	Smokey Robinson Get Ready Get Ready (Instrumental)
MO12 0031	Motown M-00028D1 (1979)	Shadee I Just Need More Money I Just Need More Money (Instrumental)
MO12 0032	Motown M-00029D1 (1979)	Platinum Hook Give Me Time To Say Standing On The Verge (Of Getting It On)
MO12 0033	Motown M-00030D1 (1979)	Mira Waters You Have Inspired Me You Have Inspired Me
MO12 0034	Motown M-31000D1 (1979)	Thelma Houston I'm Here Again I'm Here Again
MO12 0035	Motown M-00032D1 (1979)	Sterling Roll-Her, Skater Roll-Her, Skater (Instrumental)
MO12 0036	Motown M-00033D1 (1979)	Mary Wilson Redhot (Disco Version) Redhot (Single Version)
MO12 0037	Motown M-00034D1 (04/80)	Clifton Dyson Body In Motion (Want Your Body In Motion With Mine) You Gotta Keep Dancin'
MO12 0038	Motown M-00035D1 (1979)	Diana Ross & The Supremes / Diana Ross MEDLEY OF HITS Side 1: Stop! In The Name Of Love/Back In My Arms Again/Come See About Me/Love Is Like An Itching In My Heart/Where Did Our Love Go/Baby Love - Side 2: No One Gets The Prize/The Boss
MO12 0039	Motown M 35000V1 (1981)	Teena Marie Square Biz Square Biz (Instrumental)
MO12 0040	Motown M 35001V1 (1981)	Rick James Give It To Me Baby Give It To Me Baby (Instrumental)
MO12 0041	Motown M 35002V1 (08/81)	Rick James Super Freak Super Freak

NUMBER SEQUENCE CHANGE

Note: See "TMG Consolidated Series 12-inch Singles" for continuation.

MOTOWN ALBUMS

MOLP 0001	Motown MLP-600 (11/61)	Mary Wells BYE, BYE BABY, I DON'T WANT TO TAKE A CHANCE

MOLP 0002	Motown MLP-601 (12/61)	Twistin' Kings TWISTIN' THE WORLD AROUND
MOLP 0003	Motown MLP-602	The Satintones THE SATINTONES SING Note: Unissued.
MOLP 0004	Motown MT-603 (05/62)	Various Artists MOTOWN SPECIAL
MOLP 0005	Motown MT-604 (05/62)	Eddie Holland EDDIE HOLLAND
MOLP 0006	Motown MT-605 (09/62)	Mary Wells THE ONE WHO REALLY LOVES YOU
MOLP 0007	Motown MT-606 (12/63)	The Supremes MEET THE SUPREMES Note: Album issued with two different covers. The first version shows the Supremes sitting on stools. The second version depicts the faces of the group. The "faces" cover also exists in at least two versions. One mixes up the identification of Florence Ballard and Mary Wilson; this is corrected on the other, but the song titles for side two are listed incorrectly.
MOLP 0008	Motown MT-607 (02/63)	Mary Wells TWO LOVERS AND OTHER GREAT HITS Note: Title on label give as TWO LOVERS.
MOLP 0009	Motown MT-608 (07/63)	Amos Milburn THE RETURN OF THE BLUES BOSS
MOLP 0010	Motown MT-609 (04/63)	Various Artists MOTOR TOWN REVUE VOL. 1 Note: Recorded live at The Apollo in New York.
MOLP 0011	Motown MLP-610	The Supremes THE SUPREMES SING BALLADS AND BLUES Note: Unissued.
MOLP 0012	Motown MT-611 (09/63)	Mary Wells RECORDED LIVE ON STAGE
MOLP 0013	Motown MLP-612	Note: Unissued.
MOLP 0014	Motown MLP-613 (04/64)	Marvin Gaye & Mary Wells TOGETHER
MOLP 0015	Motown MS-614 (11/63)	Various Artists 16 ORIGINAL BIG HITS VOL. 1 Note: Title on label given as A PACKAGE OF 16 BIG HITS
MOLP 0016	Motown MT-615 (04/64)	Various Artists MOTOR TOWN REVUE VOL. II Note: Recorded live.
MOLP 0017	Motown MS-616 (04/64)	Mary Wells MARY WELLS' GREATEST HITS
MOLP 0018	Motown MLP-617 (05/64)	Mary Wells MY GUY
MOLP 0020	Motown MLP-619 (1966)	Stepin Fetchit MY SON THE SIT-IN
MOLP 0021	Motown MT-620 (03/65)	Choker Campbell and His Big 16 Piece Band HITS OF THE SIXTIES Note: Also released in stereo, MS-620.
MOLP 0022	Motown MT-621 (08/64)	The Supremes WHERE DID OUR LOVE GO Note: Stereo version, MS-621, released October 1964.
MOLP 0023	Motown MS-622 (01/65)	Four Tops FOUR TOPS
MOLP 0024	Motown MS-623 (10/64)	The Supremes A BIT OF LIVERPOOL
MOLP 0025	Motown MS-624 (12/64)	Various Artists 16 ORIGINAL BIG HITS VOL. 3 Note: Title on label given as A COLLECTION OF 16 ORIGINAL BIG HITS VOL. 3.
MOLP 0026	Motown MS-625 (02/65)	The Supremes SUPREMES SING COUNTRY, WESTERN AND POP
MOLP 0027	Motown MS-626	The Supremes LIVE, LIVE, LIVE! Note: Unissued.
MOLP 0028	Motown MS-627 (08/65)	The Supremes MORE HITS BY THE SUPREMES
MOLP 0029	Motown MS-628	The Supremes THERE'S A PLACE FOR US Note: Unissued.
MOLP 0030	Motown MS-629 (04/65)	The Supremes WE REMEMBER SAM COOKE
MOLP 0031	Motown MS-630 (05/65)	Various Artists NOTHING BUT A MAN (SOUNDTRACK)
MOLP 0032	Motown MS-631 (06/65)	Earl Van Dyke & The Soul Brothers THAT MOTOWN SOUND

MOLP 0033	Motown MS-632 (11/65)	Billy Eckstine THE PRIME OF MY LIFE
MOLP 0034	Motown MS-633 (11/65)	Various Artists A COLLECTION OF ORIGINAL 16 BIG HITS VOLUME 4 Note: Title on label given as A COLLECTION OF 16 BIG HITS VOL. 4.
MOLP 0035	Motown MS-634 (11/65)	Four Tops FOUR TOPS SECOND ALBUM
MOLP 0036	Motown MS-635	The Supremes A TRIBUTE TO THE GIRLS Note: Unissued.
MOLP 0037	Motown MS-636 (11/65)	The Supremes SUPREMES AT THE COPA
MOLP 0038	Motown MS-637	Note: Unissued.
MOLP 0039	Motown MS-638 (11/65)	The Supremes MERRY CHRISTMAS
MOLP 0040	Motown MS-639 (08/67)	The Spinners THE ORIGINAL SPINNERS
MOLP 0041	Motown MS-640	Billy Eckstine LIVE AT LAKE TAHOE Note: Unissued.
MOLP 0042	Motown MS-641	Note: Unissued.
MOLP 0043	Motown MT-642 (09/68)	Various Artists IN LOVING MEMORY (TRIBUTE TO MRS. LOUCYE G. WAKEFIELD) Note: See also Motown M 739.
MOLP 0044	Motown MS-643 (02/66)	The Supremes I HEAR A SYMPHONY
MOLP 0045	Motown MS-644 (11/66)	Barbara McNair HERE I AM
MOLP 0046	Motown MS-645 (01/66)	Tony Martin LIVE AT THE AMERICANA
MOLP 0047	Motown MS-646 (11/66)	Billy Eckstine MY WAY
MOLP 0048	Motown MS-647 (08/66)	Four Tops FOUR TOPS ON TOP
MOLP 0049	Motown MS-648	The Supremes PURE GOLD Note: Unissued.
MOLP 0050	Motown MS-649 (08/66)	The Supremes SUPREMES A GO GO
MOLP 0051	Motown MS-650 (01/67)	The Supremes SUPREMES SING HOLLAND - DOZIER - HOLLAND
MOLP 0052	Motown MS-651 (10/66)	Various Artists THE MOTOWN SOUND: A COLLECTION OF ORIGINAL 16 BIG HITS VOL. 5 Note: Title on label given as COLLECTION OF 16 BIG HITS VOL. 5.
MOLP 0053	Motown MS-652 (01/69)	Tammi Terrell IRRESISTIBLE TAMMI TERRELL
MOLP 0054	Motown MS-653 (11/66)	Mary Wells VINTAGE STOCK Note: Original title scheduled as VINTAGE STOCK: THE BEST OF MARY WELLS.
MOLP 0055	Motown MS-654 (11/66)	Four Tops FOUR TOPS LIVE! Note: Recorded live at the upper deck of The Roostertail, Detroit, Michigan.
MOLP 0056	Motown MS-655 (01/67)	Various Artists THE MOTOWN SOUND: A COLLECTION OF ORIGINAL 16 BIG HITS VOL. 6 Note: Title on label given as A COLLECTION OF 16 ORIGINAL BIG HITS VOL. 6.
MOLP 0057	Motown MS-656	The Supremes THE SUPREMES AND THE MOTOWN SOUND Note: Unissued.
MOLP 0058	Motown MS-657 (01/67)	Four Tops FOUR TOPS ON BROADWAY
MOLP 0059	Motown MS-658	Note: Unissued.
MOLP 0060	Motown MS-659 (06/67)	The Supremes SUPREMES SING RODGERS AND HART
MOLP 0061	Motown MS-660 (07/67)	Four Tops FOUR TOPS REACH OUT
MOLP 0062	Motown MS-661 (09/67)	Various Artists THE MOTOWN SOUND: A COLLECTION OF ORIGINAL 16 BIG HITS VOL. 7 Note: Title on label given as COLLECTION OF 16 BIG HITS VOL. 7.

| MOLP 0063 | Motown MS-662 (09/67) | Four Tops FOUR TOPS GREATEST HITS |
| MOLP 0064 | Motown MS-2-663 (09/67) | Diana Ross and The Supremes DIANA ROSS AND THE SUPREMES GREATEST HITS |

MOLP 0064 — Note: Two-album set. Title on label given as SUPREMES GREATEST HITS. The group's name was changed from The Supremes to Diana Ross and the Supremes starting July 1967, when Florence Ballard was replaced by Cindy Birdsong.

MOLP 0065	Motown MS-664 (08/67)	Chris Clark SOUL SOUNDS
MOLP 0066	Motown MS-665 (04/68)	Diana Ross and The Supremes REFLECTIONS
MOLP 0067	Motown MS-666 (12/67)	Various Artists THE MOTOWN SOUND: A COLLECTION OF ORIGINAL 16 BIG HITS VOLUME 8

MOLP 0067 — Note: Title on label given as COLLECTION OF 16 BIG HITS VOL. 8.

| MOLP 0068 | Motown MS-667 (02/68) | Chuck Jackson CHUCK JACKSON ARRIVES! |
| MOLP 0069 | Motown MS-668 (09/68) | Various Artists THE MOTOWN SOUND: A COLLECTION OF 16 ORIGINAL BIG HITS VOL. 9 |

MOLP 0069 — Note: Title on label given as A COLLECTION OF 16 BIG HITS VOL. 9.

MOLP 0070	Motown MS-669 (09/68)	Four Tops YESTERDAY'S DREAMS
MOLP 0071	Motown MS-670 (11/68)	Diana Ross & The Supremes LOVE CHILD
MOLP 0072	Motown MS-671	Note: Unissued.
MOLP 0073	Motown MS-672 (09/68)	Diana Ross & The Supremes DIANA ROSS AND THE SUPREMES SING AND PERFORM "FUNNY GIRL"
MOLP 0074	Motown MS-673	Note: Unissued.
MOLP 0075	Motown MS-674	Note: Unissued.

| MOLP 0076 | Motown MS-675 (06/69) | Four Tops NOW |

MOLP 0076 — Note: Retitled MacARTHUR PARK in 1971.

MOLP 0077	Motown MS-676 (09/68)	Diana Ross & The Supremes DIANA ROSS AND THE SUPREMES 'LIVE' AT LONDON'S TALK OF THE TOWN
MOLP 0078	Motown MS-677 (12/68)	Billy Eckstine FOR LOVE OF IVY
MOLP 0079	Motown MS-678	Note: Unissued.
MOLP 0080	Motown MS-679 (11/68)	Diana Ross & The Supremes & The Temptations DIANA ROSS & THE SUPREMES JOIN THE TEMPTATIONS
MOLP 0081	Motown MS-680 (04/69)	Barbara McNair THE REAL BARBARA McNAIR
MOLP 0082	Motown MS-681 (12/68)	Various Artists MERRY CHRISTMAS FROM MOTOWN

MOLP 0082 — Note: See also Motown MS-725.

| MOLP 0083 | Motown MS-682 (12/68) | Diana Ross & The Supremes with The Temptations T.C.B. |

MOLP 0083 — Note: The original cast soundtrack.

| MOLP 0084 | Motown MS-683 (03/69) | Jonah Jones ALONG CAME JONAH |
| MOLP 0085 | Motown MS-684 (04/69) | Various Artists THE MOTOWN SOUND: COLLECTION OF ORIGINAL 16 BIG HITS VOL. 10 |

MOLP 0085 — Note: Title on label given as A COLLECTION OF 16 ORIGINAL BIG HITS VOL. 10.

MOLP 0086	Motown MS-685 (05/69)	David Ruffin MY WHOLE WORLD ENDED
MOLP 0087	Motown MS-686 (04/69)	Soupy Sales A BAG OF SOUP
MOLP 0088	Motown MS-687 (06/69)	Chuck Jackson GOIN' BACK TO CHUCK JACKSON
MOLP 0089	Motown MS-688 (07/69)	Various Artists MOTORTOWN REVUE LIVE

MOLP 0090	Motown MS-689 (05/69)	Diana Ross & The Supremes LET THE SUNSHINE IN
MOLP 0091	Motown MS-690 (03/70)	Jonah Jones A LITTLE DIS, A LITTLE DAT
MOLP 0092	Motown MS-691 (09/69)	Red Jones STEEERIKES BACK Note: Comedy album on baseball (with Al Ackerman).
MOLP 0093	Motown MS-692 (09/69)	Diana Ross & The Supremes with The Temptations TOGETHER
MOLP 0094	Motown MS-693 (10/69)	Various Artists A COLLECTION OF ORIGINAL 16 BIG HITS VOLUME 11 Note: Title on label given as COLLECTION OF 16 ORIGINAL BIG HITS VOL. 11.
MOLP 0095	Motown MS-694 (11/69)	Diana Ross and The Supremes CREAM OF THE CROP
MOLP 0096	Motown MS-695 (11/69)	Four Tops SOUL SPIN
MOLP 0097	Motown MS-696 (11/69)	David Ruffin FEELIN' GOOD
MOLP 0098	Motown MS-697	The Mynah Birds THE MYNAH BIRDS Note: Unissued. The lead singer for this group was Rick James.
MOLP 0099	Motown MS-698 (12/69)	Joe Harnell MOVING ON
MOLP 0100	Motown MS-699 (11/69)	Diana Ross & The Supremes & The Temptations ON BROADWAY
MOLP 0101	Motown MS-700 (12/69)	The Jackson 5 DIANA ROSS PRESENTS THE JACKSON 5 Note: Originally scheduled to be released under title INTRODUCING THE JACKSON 5.
MOLP 0102	Motown MS-701 (03/70)	Various Artists SHADES OF GOSPEL SOUL
MOLP 0103	Motown MS-702 (01/70)	Diana Ross & The Supremes DIANA ROSS AND THE SUPREMES GREATEST HITS VOLUME 3
MOLP 0104	Motown MS-703 (03/70)	Various Artists MOTOWN AT THE HOLLYWOOD PALACE
MOLP 0105	Motown MS-704 (03/70)	Four Tops STILL WATERS RUN DEEP
MOLP 0106	Motown MS-705 (04/70)	The Supremes RIGHT ON
MOLP 0107	Motown MS-706	Diana Ross TIME AND LOVE Note: Unissued.
MOLP 0108	Motown MS-707 (12/70)	Various Artists MOTOWN CHARTBUSTERS VOL. 1
MOLP 0109	Motown MS2-7088 (05/70)	Diana Ross and The Supremes FAREWELL Note: Two-album set, boxed, issued with booklet.
MOLP 0110	Motown MS-709 (05/70)	The Jackson 5 ABC
MOLP 0111	Motown MS-710 (05/70)	Sammy Davis Jr. SOMETHING FOR EVERYONE
MOLP 0112	Motown MS-711 (06/70)	Diana Ross REACH OUT Note: Originally titled DIANA ROSS, but title changed before release.
MOLP 0113	Motown MS-712	Blinky SUNNY AND WARM Note: Unissued.
MOLP 0114	Motown MS-713 (10/70)	The Jackson 5 CHRISTMAS ALBUM
MOLP 0115	Motown MS-714	Jonah Jones [ALBUM TITLE NOT DETERMINED] Note: Unissued.
MOLP 0116	Motown MS-715 (10/70)	Various Artists MOTOWN CHARTBUSTERS VOL. 2
MOLP 0117	Motown MS-716 (08/70)	The Ding Dongs GIMME DAT DING
MOLP 0118	Motown MS-717 (09/70)	The Supremes & Four Tops THE MAGNIFICENT 7
MOLP 0119	Motown MS-718 (09/70)	The Jackson 5 THIRD ALBUM

MOLP 0120	Motown MS-719 (03/71)	Diana Ross **DIANA**

Note: The original TV soundtrack. Includes songs by The Jackson 5, and segments featuring Bill Cosby and Danny Thomas.

MOLP 0121	Motown MS-720 (10/70)	The Supremes **NEW WAYS BUT LOVE STAYS**
MOLP 0122	Motown MS-721 (09/70)	Four Tops **CHANGING TIMES**
MOLP 0123	Motown MS-722 (10/70)	Gordon Staples & The Motown Strings **STRUNG OUT**
MOLP 0124	Motown MS-723 (07/71)	Diana Ross **SURRENDER**
MOLP 0125	Motown MS-724 (09/70)	Diana Ross **EVERYTHING IS EVERYTHING**
MOLP 0126	Motown MS-725 (11/70)	Various Artists **CHRISTMAS GIFT 'RAP**

Note: This is a reissue of Motown MS-681.

MOLP 0127	Motown. MS-5-726 (03/71)	Various Artists **THE MOTOWN STORY**

Note: Special five-album boxed set with full-color booklet.

MOLP 0128	Motown MS-727 (03/71)	Various Artists **THE MOTOWN STORY VOLUME 1**

Note: Issued as part of a five-album boxed set.

MOLP 0129	Motown MS-728 (03/71)	Various Artists **THE MOTOWN STORY VOLUME 2**

Note: Issued as part of a five-album boxed set.

MOLP 0130	Motown MS-729 (03/71)	Various Artists **THE MOTOWN STORY VOLUME 3**

Note: Issued as part of a five-album boxed set.

MOLP 0131	Motown MS-730 (03/71)	Various Artists **THE MOTOWN STORY VOLUME 4**

Note: Issued as part of a five-album boxed set.

MOLP 0132	Motown MS-731 (03/71)	Various Artists **THE MOTOWN STORY VOLUME 5**

Note: Issued as part of a five-album boxed set.

MOLP 0133	Motown MS-732 (05/71)	Various Artists **MOTOWN CHARTBUSTERS VOL. 3**
MOLP 0134	Motown MS-733	David Ruffin **DAVID**

Note: Unissued.

MOLP 0135	Motown MS-734 (05/71)	Various Artists **MOTOWN CHARTBUSTERS VOL. 4**
MOLP 0136	Motown MS-735 (04/71)	The Jackson 5 **MAYBE TOMORROW**
MOLP 0137	Motown MS-736 (06/71)	The Supremes & The Four Tops **THE RETURN OF THE MAGNIFICENT SEVEN**
MOLP 0138	Motown MS-737 (06/71)	The Supremes **TOUCH**
MOLP 0139	Motown MS-738	Bobby Darin **LIVE AT THE DESERT INN**

Note: Unissued.

MOLP 0140	Motown MS-738L	Bobby Darin **FINALLY**

Note: Unissued.

MOLP 0141	Motown M-739 (04/71)	Various Artists **SOUVENIR ALBUM (1971 STERLING BALL BENEFIT)**

Note: Not issued commercially. Given to attendees of the 1971 Sterling Ball Benefit, held at Gordy Manor in Detroit, to honor Berry Gordy's sister, Loucye Gordy Wakefield, and the memorial scholarship fund established in her name.

MOLP 0142	Motown M-740L (09/71)	Four Tops **GREATEST HITS VOL. 2**
MOLP 0143	Motown M-741L (12/71)	The Jackson 5 **GREATEST HITS**
MOLP 0144	Motown M-742L (09/71)	The Jackson 5 **GOIN' BACK TO INDIANA** Note: Original TV soundtrack.
MOLP 0145	Motown M-743L (10/71)	Various Artists **ROCK GOSPEL: THE KEY TO THE KINGDOM**
MOLP 0146	Motown M-744L (12/71)	Various Artists **MOTOWN CHARTBUSTERS VOL. 5**
MOLP 0147	Motown M-745L (12/71)	The Supremes & The Four Tops **DYNAMITE**
MOLP 0148	Motown M-746L	The Supremes **PROMISES KEPT** Note: Unissued.

MOLP 0149	Motown M-747L (01/72)	Michael Jackson GOT TO BE THERE
MOLP 0150	Motown M-748L (04/72)	Four Tops NATURE PLANNED IT
MOLP 0151	Motown M-749L	Note: Unissued.
MOLP 0152	Motown M-750L (05/72)	The Jackson 5 LOOKIN' THROUGH THE WINDOWS
MOLP 0153	Motown M-751L (05/72)	The Supremes FLOY JOY
MOLP 0154	Motown M-752L (07/72)	Jermaine Jackson JERMAINE
MOLP 0155	Motown M-753L (08/72)	Bobby Darin BOBBY DARIN
MOLP 0156	Motown M-754L (08/72)	The Jerry Ross Symposium THE JERRY ROSS SYMPOSIUM VOL. 2
MOLP 0157	Motown M-755L (08/72)	Michael Jackson BEN
MOLP 0158	Motown M-756L (11/72)	The Supremes THE SUPREMES
MOLP 0159	Motown 757	Jackie Jackson JACKIE JACKSON Note: Unissued. See Motown M-785V1.
MOLP 0160	Motown M-758-D (10/72)	Diana Ross LADY SINGS THE BLUES (SOUNDTRACK) Note: Two-album set.
MOLP 0161	Motown 759 (10/72)	Diana Ross LADY SINGS THE BLUES (SOUNDTRACK) Note: Number allocated to second cassette and 8-track of LADY SINGS THE BLUES, which required two cassettes.
MOLP 0162	Motown M-760L (12/72)	Various Artists PIPPIN (ORIGINAL CAST RECORDING)
MOLP 0163	Motown M-761L (03/73)	The Jackson 5 SKYWRITER
MOLP 0164	Motown M-762L (02/73)	David Ruffin DAVID RUFFIN
MOLP 0165	Motown M-763	Various Artists DETROIT 9000 (SOUNDTRACK) Note: Unissued.
MOLP 0166	Motown M-764-D (04/73)	Four Tops THE BEST OF THE FOUR TOPS Note: Two-album set.
MOLP 0167	Motown 765 (04/73)	Four Tops THE BEST OF THE FOUR TOPS Note: Number allocated to second cassette and 8-track of THE BEST OF THE FOUR TOPS, which required two cassettes.
MOLP 0168	Motown M-766L (04/73)	Willie Hutch THE MACK (SOUNDTRACK)
MOLP 0169	Motown M-767L (04/73)	Michael Jackson MUSIC AND ME
MOLP 0170	Motown M-768L (04/73)	Puzzle PUZZLE
MOLP 0171	Motown M-769L (04/73)	The Spinners THE BEST OF THE SPINNERS
MOLP 0172	Motown M-770L	Blinky SOFTLY Note: Unissued.
MOLP 0173	Motown M-771L (04/73)	Reuben Howell REUBEN HOWELL
MOLP 0174	Motown M-772L (05/73)	Diana Ross TOUCH ME IN THE MORNING
MOLP 0175	Motown 773	Note: Unissued.
MOLP 0176	Motown M774L (05/73)	Severin Browne SEVERIN BROWNE
MOLP 0177	Motown M-775L (05/73)	Jermaine Jackson COME INTO MY LIFE
MOLP 0178	Motown 776	Stacie Johnson STACIE Note: Unissued.
MOLP 0179	Motown M-777L (05/73)	Scatman Crothers BIG BEN SINGS
MOLP 0180	Motown M7-778R2 (09/74)	Martha Reeves & The Vandellas ANTHOLOGY Note: Two-album set.
MOLP 0181	Motown M6-779S1 (11/74)	Severin Browne NEW IMPROVED SEVERIN BROWNE

MOLP	Label	Artist / Title
MOLP 0182	Motown M6-780S1 (09/74)	The Jackson 5 DANCING MACHINE
MOLP 0183	Motown 781	The Devastating Affair THE DEVASTATING AFFAIR Note: Unissued.
MOLP 0184	Motown M-782A3 (08/73)	The Temptations ANTHOLOGY Note: Three-album set. Title on label given as THE TEMPTATIONS' 10th ANNIVERSARY SPECIAL.
MOLP 0185	Motown M-783V1 (09/73)	The Jackson 5 GET IT TOGETHER
MOLP 0186	Motown M-784V1 (09/73)	Willie Hutch FULLY EXPOSED
MOLP 0187	Motown M-785V1 (10/73)	Jackie Jackson JACKIE JACKSON
MOLP 0188	Motown M7-786R2 (07/74)	Jr. Walker & The All Stars ANTHOLOGY Note: Two-album set.
MOLP 0189	Motown 787	Xit RELOCATION Note: Unissued.
MOLP 0190	Motown 788	Frankie Valli INSIDE OUT Note: Unissued.
MOLP 0191	Motown M-789V1 (09/73)	Stephen Cohn STEPHEN COHN
MOLP 0192	Motown M-790V1 (09/73)	Gloria Jones SHARE MY LOVE
MOLP 0193	Motown M9-791A3 (04/74)	Marvin Gaye ANTHOLOGY Note: Three-album set.
MOLP 0194	Motown M-792S2 (01/74)	Gladys Knight & The Pips ANTHOLOGY Note: Two-album set.
MOLP 0195	Motown M793R3 (01/74)	Smokey Robinson & The Miracles ANTHOLOGY Note: Three-album set.
MOLP 0196	Motown M9-794A3 (06/74)	Diana Ross & The Supremes ANTHOLOGY Note: Three-album set.
MOLP 0197	Motown M 795V2 (09/73)	Various Artists A MOTOWN CHRISTMAS Note: Two-album set.
MOLP 0198	Motown M 796V1 (09/73)	The Crusaders AT THEIR BEST
MOLP 0199	Motown M6-797S1 (07/74)	Martin & Finley DAZZLE 'EM WITH FOOTWORK Note: Originally scheduled for Mowest MW-120L.
MOLP 0200	Motown M6-798S1 (07/74)	Commodores MACHINE GUN
MOLP 0201	Motown M6-799S1 (07/74)	Reuben Howell RINGS
MOLP 0202	Motown M 800-R2 (04/74)	Various Artists SAVE THE CHILDREN (ORIGINAL SOUNDTRACK) Note: Two-album set.
MOLP 0203	Motown M6-801S1 (05/74)	Diana Ross DIANA ROSS LIVE AT CAESARS PALACE
MOLP 0204	Motown M 802V1 (01/74)	Edwin Starr HELL UP IN HARLEM (ORIGINAL SOUNDTRACK)
MOLP 0205	Motown M 803V1 (10/73)	Diana Ross & Marvin Gaye DIANA & MARVIN Note: Originally scheduled to be released under title ART & HONEY.
MOLP 0206	Motown M9-804A3 (12/77)	Stevie Wonder LOOKING BACK Note: Three-album set.
MOLP 0207	Motown M6-805S1 (04/74)	Diahann Carroll DIAHANN CARROLL
MOLP 0208	Motown M6-806S1 (04/74)	Riot WELCOME TO THE WORLD OF RIOT
MOLP 0209	Motown M 807V1 (02/74)	Puzzle THE SECOND ALBUM
MOLP 0210	Motown M-808V1 (06/74)	Syreeta STEVIE WONDER PRESENTS SYREETA
MOLP 0211	Motown M9-809A3 (07/74)	Four Tops ANTHOLOGY Note: Three-album set.
MOLP 0212	Motown M6-810S1 (04/74)	Michael Edward Campbell MICHAEL EDWARD CAMPBELL
MOLP 0213	Motown M 811V1 (04/74)	Willie Hutch FOXY BROWN (ORIGINAL SOUNDTRACK FROM AIP'S MOTION PICTURE)

MOLP 0214	Motown M 812V1 (12/73)	Diana Ross LAST TIME I SAW HIM
MOLP 0215	Motown M 813V1 (02/74)	Bobby Darin DARIN 1936-1973
MOLP 0216	Motown M6-814S1 (11/74)	Caston & Majors CASTON & MAJORS
MOLP 0217	Motown M6-815S1 (11/74)	Willie Hutch THE MARK OF THE BEAST
MOLP 0218	Motown 816	The Supremes THE BEST OF THE SUPREMES Note: Unissued.
MOLP 0219	Motown 817	Diana Ross THE BEST OF DIANA ROSS Note: Unissued.
MOLP 0220	Motown M6-818S1 (12/74)	David Ruffin ME 'N ROCK 'N ROLL ARE HERE TO STAY
MOLP 0221	Motown M6-819S1 (11/74)	G. C. Cameron LOVE SONGS & OTHER TRAGEDIES
MOLP 0222	Motown M6-820S1 (03/75)	Commodores CAUGHT IN THE ACT
MOLP 0223	Motown M6-821S1 (05/75)	The Magic Disco Machine DISC-O-TECH Note: Consists of background tracks never fitted to lead parts.
MOLP 0224	Motown M6-822S1 (01/75)	The Dynamic Superiors THE DYNAMIC SUPERIORS
MOLP 0225	Motown 823	Note: Unissued.
MOLP 0226	Motown M6-824S1 (05/75)	Various Artists DISC-O-TECH #1
MOLP 0227	Motown M6-825S1 (01/75)	Michael Jackson FOREVER MICHAEL
MOLP 0228	Motown M6-826S1 (03/75)	The Originals CALIFORNIA SUNSET
MOLP 0229	Motown M7-827R2 (06/75)	The Marvelettes ANTHOLOGY Note: Two-album set.
MOLP 0230	Motown M6-828S1 (06/75)	The Supremes THE SUPREMES

MOLP 0231	Motown M6-829S1 (05/75)	The Jackson 5 MOVING VIOLATION
MOLP 0232	Motown 830	Jermaine Jackson DO UNTO OTHERS Note: Unissued.
MOLP 0233	Motown M6-831S1 (05/75)	Various Artists DISC-O-TECH #2
MOLP 0234	Motown M6-832S1 (07/75)	Yvonne Fair THE BITCH IS BLACK
MOLP 0235	Motown 833	Various Artists MOTOWN 64 ORIGINAL HITS Note: Unissued. Four-album boxed set. Numbers 833 through 837 allocated to the CIMCO marketing organization under license by Motown.
MOLP 0236	Motown 834	Various Artists Unissued. Part of a four-album set.
MOLP 0237	Motown 835	Various Artists Unissued. Part of a four-album set.
MOLP 0238	Motown 836	Various Artists Unissued. Part of a four-album set.
MOLP 0239	Motown 837	Various Artists Unissued. Part of a four-album set.
MOLP 0240	Motown M6-838S1 (06/75)	Willie Hutch ODE TO MY LADY
MOLP 0241	Motown M6-839S1 (09/75)	Various Artists MURPH THE SURF (MOVIE SOUNDTRACK)
MOLP 0242	Motown M7-840R2 (09/75)	Various Artists COOLEY HIGH (SOUNDTRACK) Note: Two-album set.
MOLP 0243	Motown M6-841S1 (07/75)	The Dynamic Superiors PURE PLEASURE Note: Also titled FACE THE MUSIC on some album covers.
MOLP 0244	Motown M6-842S1 (08/76)	Jermaine Jackson MY NAME IS JERMAINE Note: Originally scheduled to be titled COLOR MY WORLD LOVE.
MOLP 0245	Motown M6-843S1 (07/75)	Lenny Williams RISE SLEEPING BEAUTY
MOLP 0246	Motown 844	Syreeta ONE TO ONE Note: Unissued. Later issued on Tamla T-349P1.

MOLP	Motown	Rose Banks
0247	M6-845S1	ROSE
	(05/76)	

MOLP	Motown	Leslie Uggams
0248	M6-846S1	LESLIE UGGAMS
	(09/75)	

MOLP	Motown	Libra
0249	M6-847S1	LIBRA
	(09/75)	

MOLP	Motown	Commodores
0250	M6-848S1	MOVIN' ON
	(10/75)	

MOLP	Motown	David Ruffin
0251	M6-849S1	WHO I AM
	(10/75)	

MOLP	Motown	Jerry Butler
0252	M6-850S1	LOVE'S ON THE MENU
	(06/76)	

MOLP	Motown	Michael Jackson
0253	M6-851S1	THE BEST OF MICHAEL JACKSON
	(08/75)	

MOLP	Motown	Frankie Valli
0254	M6-852S1	INSIDE YOU
	(10/75)	

MOLP	Motown	Various Artists
0255	M6-853S1	DISC-O-TECH NO. 3
	(01/76)	

MOLP	Motown	Willie Hutch
0256	M6-854S1	CONCERT IN BLUES
	(03/76)	

MOLP	Motown	G. C. Cameron
0257	M6-855S1	G. C. CAMERON
	(05/76)	

MOLP	Motown	Kathe Green
0258	M6-856S1	KATHE GREEN
	(01/76)	Note: Also issued on Prodigal 10011.

MOLP	Motown	Motown Magic Disco Machine
0259	M6-857S1	MOTOWN MAGIC DISCO MACHINE VOL. II
	(05/76)	Note: Consists of background tracks never fitted to lead parts.

MOLP	Motown	Diana Ross
0260	M6-858S1	MAHOGANY (ORIGINAL SOUNDTRACK)
	(10/75)	Note: Full title is FROM THE ORIGINAL SOUNDTRACK OF A BERRY GORDY FILM "MAHOGANY" A PARAMOUNT PICTURE.

MOLP	Motown	Stephanie Mills
0261	M6-859S1	FOR THE FIRST TIME
	(10/75)	

MOLP	Motown	Various Artists
0262	M6-860S1	MOTOWN'S ORIGINAL VERSIONS
	(04/76)	

MOLP	Motown	Diana Ross
0263	M6-861S1	DIANA ROSS
	(03/76)	

MOLP	Motown	The Dynamic Superiors
0264	862	SKY'S THE LIMIT
		Note: Unissued.

MOLP	Motown	The Supremes
0265	M6-863S1	HIGH ENERGY
	(04/76)	

MOLP	Motown	Libra
0266	M6-864S1	WINTER DAY'S NIGHTMARE
	(05/76)	

MOLP	Motown	The Jackson 5 featuring Michael Jackson
0267	M6-865S1	JOYFUL JUKEBOX MUSIC
	(10/76)	

MOLP	Motown	David Ruffin
0268	M6-866S1	EVERYTHING'S COMING UP LOVE
	(05/76)	

MOLP	Motown	Commodores
0269	M6-867S1	HOT ON THE TRACKS
	(06/76)	

MOLP	Motown	The Jackson 5
0270	M7-868R3	ANTHOLOGY
	(06/76)	Note: Three-album set.

MOLP	Motown	Diana Ross
0271	M6-869S1	DIANA ROSS' GREATEST HITS
	(08/76)	

MOLP	Motown	Ronnie McNeir
0272	M6-870S1	LOVE'S COMIN' DOWN
	(09/76)	

MOLP	Motown	Willie Hutch
0273	M6-871S1	COLOR HER SUNSHINE
	(10/76)	

MOLP	Motown	Various Artists
0274	M5-872V1	MOTOWN DISC-O-TECH #4
	(10/76)	Note: Also issued as a picture disc.

MOLP	Motown	The Supremes
0275	M6-873S1	MARY, SCHERRIE & SUSAYE
	(10/76)	

MOLP	Motown	Willie Hutch
0276	M6-874S1	HAVIN' A HOUSE PARTY
	(06/77)	

MOLP	Motown	The Dynamic Superiors
0277	M6-875S1	YOU NAME IT
	(10/76)	

MOLP	Motown	Various Artists
0278	M6-876S1	GUYS AND DOLLS (ORIGINAL CAST)
	(12/76)	

MOLP 0279	Motown 876	Leon Ware MUSICAL MASSAGE Note: Unissued. Released on Gordy G-976.
MOLP 0280	Motown M7-877R2 (01/77)	Diana Ross AN EVENING WITH DIANA ROSS Note: Two-album set. Recorded live.
MOLP 0281	Motown M6-878S1 (01/77)	Jerry Butler SUITE FOR THE SINGLE GIRL
MOLP 0282	Motown M6-879S1 (06/77)	The Dynamic Superiors GIVE & TAKE
MOLP 0283	Motown M6-880S1 (01/77)	G. C. Cameron YOU'RE WHAT'S MISSING IN MY LIFE
MOLP 0284	Motown M6-881S1 (03/77)	Various Artists MOTOWN'S PREFERRED STOCK/STOCK OPTION NO. 1
MOLP 0285	Motown M-882S1 (03/77)	Various Artists MOTOWN'S PREFERRED STOCK/STOCK OPTION NO. 2
MOLP 0286	Motown M-883S1 (03/77)	Various Artists MOTOWN'S PREFERRED STOCK/STOCK OPTION NO. 3
MOLP 0287	Motown M7-884R1 (04/77)	Commodores COMMODORES
MOLP 0288	Motown M-885P1 (06/77)	David Ruffin IN MY STRIDE
MOLP 0289	Motown M-886S1 (05/77)	Mandre MANDRE
MOLP 0290	Motown M-887P1 (06/77)	Thelma Houston & Jerry Butler THELMA & JERRY
MOLP 0291	Motown M-888S1 (08/77)	Jermaine Jackson FEEL THE FIRE
MOLP 0292	Motown M-889P1 (07/77)	Albert Finney ALBERT FINNEY'S ALBUM
MOLP 0293	Motown M7-890R1 (09/77)	Diana Ross BABY IT'S ME
MOLP 0294	Motown M6-891S1 (09/77)	Syreeta & G. C. Cameron RICH LOVE, POOR LOVE Note: As by Syreeta and G. C. Cameron
MOLP 0295	Motown M-892S1 (11/77)	Jerry Butler IT ALL COMES OUT IN MY SONG
MOLP 0296	Motown 893	Leon Ware THE WHOLE WORLD IS MY HOME Note: Unissued.
MOLP 0297	Motown M9-894A2 (11/77)	Commodores COMMODORES LIVE! Note: Two-album set.
MOLP 0298	Motown M7-895R1 (01/78)	David Ruffin AT HIS BEST
MOLP 0299	Motown M7-896R1 (01/78)	The Fifth Dimension STAR DANCING
MOLP 0300	Motown M7-897R1 (02/78)	Cuba Gooding THE 1ST CUBA GOODING ALBUM
MOLP 0301	Motown M7-898R1 (02/78)	Jermaine Jackson FRONTIERS
MOLP 0302	Motown M7-899R1 (04/78)	Platinum Hook PLATINUM HOOK
MOLP 0303	Motown M7-900R1 (03/78)	Mandre MANDRE TWO
MOLP 0304	Motown M7-901R1 (05/78)	Three Ounces Of Love THREE OUNCES OF LOVE
MOLP 0305	Motown M7-902R1 (05/78)	Commodores NATURAL HIGH
MOLP 0306	Motown M7-903R1 (07/78)	Thelma Houston & Jerry Butler TWO TO ONE
MOLP 0307	Motown M7-904R1 (07/78)	The Supremes AT THEIR BEST
MOLP 0308	Motown M7-905R1 (08/78)	Prime Time MOTOWN PRESENTS PRIME TIME
MOLP 0309	Motown M7-906R1 (08/78)	Finished Touch NEED TO KNOW YOU BETTER
MOLP 0310	Motown M7-907R1 (09/78)	Diana Ross ROSS
MOLP 0311	Motown M7-908R1 (01/79)	Motown Sounds SPACE DANCE

MOLP 0312	Motown M7-909R1 (01/79)	Bloodstone DON'T STOP!
MOLP 0313	Motown M7-910R1 (09/78)	Grover Washington Jr. REED SEED
MOLP 0314	Motown M7-911R1 (10/78)	Bonnie Pointer BONNIE POINTER
MOLP 0315	Motown M7-912R1 (10/78)	Commodores COMMODORES GREATEST HITS
MOLP 0316	Motown M7-913R1	Jermaine Jackson LIVING Note: Unissued.
MOLP 0317	Motown M7-913R1 (02/79)	T-Boy Ross CHANGES
MOLP 0318	Motown M7-914R1 (01/79)	The 5th Dimension HIGH ON SUNSHINE
MOLP 0319	Motown M7-915R1	Diana Ross DIANA ROSS SINGS SONGS FROM THE "WIZ" Note: Unissued.
MOLP 0320	Motown M7-915R1 (03/79)	Billy Preston & Syreeta MUSIC FROM THE MOTION PICTURE "FAST BREAK"
MOLP 0321	Motown M7-916R1	Finished Touch FINISHED TOUCH Note: Unissued.
MOLP 0322	Motown M7-917R1 (02/79)	Mandre M3000
MOLP 0323	Motown M7-918R1 (04/79)	Platinum Hook IT'S TIME
MOLP 0324	Motown M7-919R1 (04/79)	Cuba Gooding LOVE DANCER
MOLP 0325	Motown M7-920R1 (10/79)	Scherrie & Susaye PARTNERS
MOLP 0326	Motown M7-921R1 (12/78)	Various Artists POPS WE LOVE YOU...THE ALBUM
MOLP 0327	Motown M7-922R1 (05/79)	Patrick Gammon DON'T TOUCH ME
MOLP 0328	Motown M7-923R1 (05/79)	Diana Ross THE BOSS Note: Promo copies issued on gold wax.
MOLP 0329	Motown M7-924R1 (06/79)	Dr. Strut DR. STRUT
MOLP 0330	Motown M7-925K1 (07/79)	Billy Preston LATE AT NIGHT
MOLP 0331	Motown M8-926M1 (07/79)	Commodores MIDNIGHT MAGIC
MOLP 0332	Motown M7-927R1 (09/79)	Mary Wilson MARY WILSON
MOLP 0333	Motown M7-928R1 (10/79)	Jermaine Jackson LET'S GET SERIOUS
MOLP 0334	Motown M7-929R1 (10/79)	Bonnie Pointer BONNIE POINTER
MOLP 0335	Motown M7-930R1 (10/79)	Cook County PINBALL PLAYBOY
MOLP 0336	Motown M7-931R1 (01/80)	Dr. Strut STRUTTIN'
MOLP 0337	Motown M7-932R1 (03/80)	Flight EXCURSION BEYOND
MOLP 0338	Motown M7-933R1 (02/80)	Grover Washington Jr. SKYLARKIN'
MOLP 0339	Motown M7-934R1 (02/80)	The Planets THE PLANETS
MOLP 0340	Motown 935	Note: Unissued.
MOLP 0341	Motown M8-936 (03/80)	Diana Ross DIANA
MOLP 0342	Motown M9-937A2 (03/80)	Various Artists 20/20 TWENTY NO. 1 HITS FROM TWENTY YEARS AT MOTOWN Note: Two-album set.
MOLP 0343	Motown M7-938R1 (04/80)	Ozone WALK ON
MOLP 0344	Motown M8-939M1 (05/80)	Commodores HEROES
MOLP 0345	Motown M9-940A2 (08/80)	Grover Washington Jr. BADDEST Note: All selections previously released on various Kudu albums.

MOLP 0346	Motown M8-941M1 (08/80)	Billy Preston THE WAY I AM
MOLP 0347	Motown M7-942R1 (08/80)	Black Russian BLACK RUSSIAN
MOLP 0348	Motown M8-943M1 (08/80)	Platinum Hook ECSTASY PARADISE
MOLP 0349	Motown M7-944R1 (09/80)	Michael Urbaniak SERENADE FOR THE CITY
MOLP 0350	Motown M7-945R1 (09/80)	Ahmad Jamal NIGHT SONG
MOLP 0351	Motown M8-946M1 (10/80)	Dazz Band INVITATION TO LOVE
MOLP 0352	Motown M8-947M1 (10/80)	Various Artists MUSIC FROM THE ORIGINAL MOTION PICTURE SOUNDTRACK "IT'S MY TURN"
MOLP 0353	Motown M8-948M1 (12/80)	Jermaine Jackson JERMAINE
MOLP 0354	Motown M8-949M1 (12/80)	Various Artists MUSIC FROM THE ORIGINAL MOTION PICTURE SOUNDTRACK "LOVING COUPLES"
MOLP 0355	Motown M8-950M1 (01/81)	Ozone JUMP ON IT
MOLP 0356	Motown M8-951M1 (02/81)	Diana Ross TO LOVE AGAIN
MOLP 0357	Motown M8-952M1 (09/81)	Jermaine Jackson I LIKE YOUR STYLE
MOLP 0358	Motown M8-953M1 (11/81)	Jose Feliciano JOSE FELICIANO
MOLP 0359	Motown M8-954M1	Commodores ANTHOLOGY Note: Unissued. See Motown 6044ML.
MOLP 0360	Motown M8-955M1 (05/81)	Commodores IN THE POCKET
MOLP 0361	Motown M8-956M1 (03/81)	Michael Jackson ONE DAY IN YOUR LIFE
MOLP 0362	Motown M8-957M1 (03/81)	Dazz Band LET THE MUSIC PLAY
MOLP 0363	Motown M8-958M1 (08/81)	Billy Preston & Syreeta BILLY PRESTON & SYREETA
MOLP 0364	Motown M8-959M1 (09/81)	Lovesmith LOVESMITH
MOLP 0365	Motown M13-960C2 (10/81)	Diana Ross ALL THE GREAT HITS Note: Two-album set.
MOLP 0366	Motown M9-961A2 (10/81)	Grover Washington Jr. ANTHOLOGY Note: Two-album set.
MOLP 0367	Motown M8-962M1 (11/81)	Ozone SEND IT

NUMBER SEQUENCE CHANGE

Note: At this point, numbering for Tamla, Motown, and Gordy albums was consolidated into a single sequence starting at 6000. See "TMG Consolidated Series Albums" for continuation.

MOWEST 7-INCH SINGLES

MW45 0001	Mowest MW 5001F (01/72)	Devastating Affair I Want To Be Humble My Place
MW45 0002	Mowest MW 5002F (06/71)	Tom Clay What The World Needs Now Is Love + Abraham, Martin and John The Victors
MW45 0003	Mowest MW 5003F (08/71)	Lodi Happiness I Hope I See It In My Lifetime
MW45 0004	Mowest MW 5004F (10/71)	Suzee Ikeda Zip A Dee Doo Dah Bah Bah Bah Note: "A" side also issued on Motown 1237.
MW45 0005	Mowest MW 5005F (08/71)	G. C. Cameron Act Like A Shotgun Girl, I Really Love You
MW45 0006	Mowest MW 5006F (11/71)	Bobby Taylor Hey Lordy Just A Little Bit Closer
MW45 0007	Mowest MW 5007F (10/71)	Tom Clay Whatever Happened To Love Baby I Need Your Loving
MW45 0008	Mowest MW 5008F (11/71)	Thelma Houston I Want To Go Back There Again Pick Of The Week Note: "B" side also issued on

Motown 1316. "A" side also issued
on blue vinyl.

MW45 0009	Mowest MW 5009F (03/72)	Commodores The Zoo (The Human Zoo) I'm Looking For Love
MW45 0010	Mowest MW 5010F	Note: Unissued.
MW45 0011	Mowest MW 5011F (02/72)	Frankie Valli Love Isn't Here (Like It Used To Be) Poor Fool
MW45 0012	Mowest MW 5012F	G. C. Cameron I'm Gonna Get You Pt. 1 I'm Gonna Get You Pt. 2 Note: Unissued.
MW45 0013	Mowest MW 5013F (03/72)	Thelma Houston Me And Bobby McGee No One's Gonna Be A Fool Forever Note: "A" side also issued on red vinyl.
MW45 0014	Mowest MW 5014F (03/72)	The Sisters Love Mr. Fix-It Man You've Got To Make The Choice
MW45 0015	Mowest MW 5015F (03/72)	G. C. Cameron What It Is, What It Is You Are That Special One
MW45 0016	Mowest MW 5016F (09/72)	Syreeta I Love Every Little Thing About You Black Magic Note: "B" side also issued on Motown 1297.
MW45 0017	Mowest MW 5017F (06/72)	Suzee Ikeda I Can't Give Back The Love I Feel For You Mind Body And Soul
MW45 0018	Mowest MW 5018F (08/72)	Michelle Aller Just Not Gonna Make It Spend Some Time Together
MW45 0019	Mowest MW 5018F	Michelle Aller The Morning After Spend Some Time Together Note: Unissued.
MW45 0020	Mowest MW 5019F (06/72)	Blinky Money (That's What I Want) For Your Precious Love
MW45 0021	Mowest MW 5020F	Blackberries Somebody Up There But I Love Him Note: Unissued.
MW45 0022	Mowest MW 5021F (07/72)	Syreeta To Know You Is To Love You Happiness Note: "A" side also issued on

blue vinyl.

MW45 0023	Mowest MW 5022F (08/72)	Odyssey Our Lives Are Shaped By What We Love Broken Road
MW45 0024	Mowest MW 5023F	The Devastating Affair Where Do You Go Baby Note: Unissued.
MW45 0025	Mowest MW 5024F	Note: Unissued.
MW45 0026	Mowest MW 5025F	Four Seasons The Night Sun Country Note: Unissued.
MW45 0027	Mowest MW 5026F (08/72)	Frankie Valli and the Four Seasons Walk On, Don't Look Back Sun Country
MW45 0028	Mowest MW 5027F	Thelma Houston What If There Is A God Note: Unissued.
MW45 0029	Mowest MW 5028F (10/72)	Crusaders Spanish Harlem Papa Hooper's Barrelhouse Groove
MW45 0030	Mowest MW 5029F (10/72)	Leslie Gore She Said That The Road I Walk
MW45 0031	Mowest MW 5030F (10/72)	The Sisters Love You've Got My Mind Try It, You'll Like It Note: "A" side also issued on Motown 1275.
MW45 0032	Mowest MW 5031F	Repairs Songwriter Fiddler Note: Unissued.
MW45 0033	Mowest MW 5032F	Kubie Glad That You're Not Me Child He Die Note: Unissued.
MW45 0034	Mowest MW 5033F (01/73)	Blinky T'ain't Nobody's Bizness If I Do What More Can I Do
MW45 0035	Mowest MW 5034F	Celebration Since I Met You There's No Magic The Circle Again Note: Unissued. Released on Motown 1238.
MW45 0036	Mowest MW 5034F	Celebration A House Is Not A Home Note: Unissued.

MW45 0037	Mowest MW 5035F	G. C. Cameron and Willie Hutch Come Get This Thang My Woman Note: Unissued. As by G. C. Cameron and Willie Hutch.
MW45 0038	Mowest MW 5036F (01/73)	G. C. Cameron Don't Wanna Play Pajama Games Jesus Help Me Find Another Way Note: "A" side also issued on red vinyl.
MW45 0039	Mowest MW 5037F (02/73)	The Nu Page When The Brothers Come Marching Home A Heart Is A House
MW45 0040	Mowest MW 5038F (01/73)	Commodores Don't You Be Worried Determination
MW45 0041	Mowest MW 5039F (11/72)	Martin and Finley Long Life And Success To The Farmer Half Crazed
MW45 0042	Mowest MW 5040F (01/72)	Michael Campbell Angel Got A Book Today The People In The Valley
MW45 0043	Mowest MW 5041F (01/73)	The Sisters Love (I Could Never Make) A Better Man Than You Give Me Your Love
MW45 0044	Mowest MW 5042F	Leslie Gore Give It To Me Sweet Thing Don't Want To Be One Note: Unissued.
MW45 0045	Mowest MW 5043F	Martin and Finley Thinkin' 'Bout My Baby Best Friends Note: Unissued. Released on Motown 1229.
MW45 0046	Mowest MW 5044F	Music Makers Follow Me - Mother Nature And I Thought You Loved Me Note: Unissued. Released on Motown 1247 as by Marbaya.
MW45 0047	Mowest MW 5045F	Stoney Let Me Come Down Easy It's Always Me Note: Unissued. Released on Motown 1248.
MW45 0048	Mowest MW 5046F	Thelma Houston If It's The Last Thing I Do And I Never Did Note: Unissued.
MW45 0049	Mowest MW 5047F	Stacie Johnson Woman In My Eyes A Carbon Copy Note: Unissued. "A" side released on Motown 1236.
MW45 0050	Mowest MW 5048F	Art and Honey Let's Make Love Now (I've Given You) The Best Years Of My Life Note: Unissued. Released on Motown 1246.
MW45 0051	Mowest MW 5049F	Note: Unissued.
MW45 0052	Mowest MW 5050F (03/73)	Thelma Houston Piano Man I'm Just A Part Of Yesterday Note: Also issued on Motown 1245.

MOWEST 7-INCH COLOR VINYL SINGLES

MWCO 0001	Mowest MW 5008F (11/71)	Thelma Houston I Want To Go Back There Again Note: Blue vinyl.
MWCO 0002	Mowest MW 5013F (03/72)	Thelma Houston Me And Bobby McGee Note: Red vinyl.
MWCO 0003	Mowest MW 5021F (07/72)	Syreeta To Know You Is To Love You Note: Blue vinyl.
MWCO 0004	Mowest MW 5036F (01/73)	G. C. Cameron Don't Wanna Play Pajama Games Note: Red vinyl.

MOWEST ALBUMS

MWLP 0001	Mowest MW 101 (10/72)	Lodi HAPPINESS
MWLP 0002	Mowest MW 102 (07/72)	Thelma Houston THELMA HOUSTON
MWLP 0003	Mowest MW 103-L (07/71)	Tom Clay WHAT THE WORLD NEEDS NOW IS LOVE
MWLP 0004	Mowest MW 104	Note: Unissued.
MWLP 0005	Mowest MW 105	The Devastating Affair [ALBUM TITLE NOT DETERMINED] Note: Unissued.
MWLP 0006	Mowest MW 106	Blackberries [ALBUM TITLE NOT DETERMINED] Note: Unissued.
MWLP 0007	Mowest MW 107	G. C. Cameron 7TH SON Note: Unissued.

MWLP 0008	Mowest MW 108-L (05/72)	Frankie Valli & the 4 Seasons CHAMELEON
MWLP 0009	Mowest MW 109	The Sisters Love [ALBUM TITLE NOT DETERMINED] Note: Unissued.
MWLP 0010	Mowest MW 110	The Commodores [ALBUM TITLE NOT DETERMINED] Note: Unissued.
MWLP 0011	Mowest MW 111	Blinky Williams [ALBUM TITLE NOT DETERMINED] Note: Unissued.
MWLP 0012	Mowest MW 112	Note: Unissued.
MWLP 0013	Mowest MW 113 (06/72)	Syreeta SYREETA
MWLP 0014	Mowest MW 114	Frankie Valli [ALBUM TITLE NOT DETERMINED] Note: Unissued.
MWLP 0015	Mowest MW 115 (05/72)	Odyssey ODYSSEY
MWLP 0016	Mowest MW 116	Note: Unissued.
MWLP 0017	Mowest MW 117 (07/72)	Leslie Gore SOMEPLACE ELSE NOW
MWLP 0018	Mowest MW 118 (07/72)	Crusaders HOLLYWOOD
MWLP 0019	Mowest MW 119 (07/72)	Celebration CELEBRATION
MWLP 0020	Mowest MW 120	Martin and Finley DAZZLE 'EM WITH FOOTWORK Note: Unissued. See Motown M6-797S1.
MWLP 0021	Mowest MW 121 (11/72)	Repairs REPAIRS
MWLP 0022	Mowest MW 122	Kubie KUBIE Note: Unissued.
MWLP 0023	Mowest MW 123	Stacie Johnson [ALBUM TITLE NOT DETERMINED] Note: Unissued.

NATURAL RESOURCES
7-INCH SINGLES

NA45 0001	Natural Res. NR 6001F (12/76)	Gaylord & Holiday Angelina (The Waitress At The Pizzeria) Ramona

NATURAL RESOURCES ALBUMS

NALP 0001	Natural Res. NR-101L (05/72)	Two Friends TWO FRIENDS
NALP 0002	Natural Res. NR-102L (05/72)	Heart HEART Note: Not the group led by the Wilson sisters.
NALP 0003	Natural Res. NR-103L (05/72)	Corliss CORLISS
NALP 0004	Natural Res. NR-104L (07/72)	Gotham PASS THE BUTTER
NALP 0005	Natural Res. NR-105L (07/72)	Road ROAD
NALP 0006	Natural Res. NR-106L (01/73)	Earthquire EARTHQUIRE
NALP 0007	Natural Res. NR-107L (01/73)	Northern Lights VANCOUVER DREAMING
NALP 0008	Natural Res. NR-108S1 (10/76)	Gaylord & Holiday WINE, WOMEN AND SONG
NALP 0009	Natural Res. NR-4001 (03/78)	Various Artists MOTOWN'S GREAT INTERPRETATIONS
NALP 0010	Natural Res. NR-4002 (03/78)	Various Artists MOTOWN INSTRUMENTALS
NALP 0011	Natural Res. NR-4003 (03/78)	Various Artists MOTOWN SHOW TUNES
NALP 0012	Natural Res. NR-4004 (09/78)	Gladys Knight and the Pips SILK N' SOUL Note: Reissue of Soul SS-711.
NALP 0013	Natural Res. NR-4005 (09/78)	Temptations IN A MELLOW MOOD Note: Reissue of Gordy GS-924.
NALP 0014	Natural Res. NR-4006 (09/78)	Diana Ross and the Supremes WHERE DID OUR LOVE GO Note: Reissue of Motown MS-621.

NALP 0015	Natural Res. NR-4007 (09/78)	Marvin Gaye THE SOULFUL MOODS OF MARVIN GAYE Note: Reissue of Tamla TM-221.
NALP 0016	Natural Res. NR-4008 (09/78)	Four Tops REACH OUT Note: Reissue of Motown MS-660.
NALP 0017	Natural Res. NR-4009 (09/78)	Smokey Robinson & the Miracles I'LL TRY SOMETHING NEW Note: Reissue of Tamla TM-230.
NALP 0018	Natural Res. NR-4010 (10/78)	Diana Ross and the Supremes MERRY CHRISTMAS Note: Reissue of Motown MS-638.
NALP 0019	Natural Res. NR-4011 (10/78)	Various Artists WE WISH YOU A MERRY CHRISTMAS
NALP 0020	Natural Res. NR-4012 (01/79)	Various Artists IT TAKES TWO (DUETS)
NALP 0021	Natural Res. NR-4013 (01/79)	Jackson 5 BOOGIE
NALP 0022	Natural Res. NR-4014 (01/79)	Various Artists FROM THE VAULTS
NALP 0023	Natural Res. NR-4015 (05/79)	Various Artists MIGHTY MOTOWN
NALP 0024	Natural Res. NR-4016 (05/79)	Various Artists DISCO PARTY
NALP 0025	Natural Res. NR-4017 (05/79)	Various Artists MOTOWN PARADE OF SONG HITS
NALP 0026	Natural Res. NR-4018 (08/79)	Various Artists IN LOVE
NALP 0027	Natural Res. NR-4019 (08/79)	Various Artists BROKENHEARTED
NALP 0028	Natural Res. NR-4020 (08/79)	Diana Ross and the Supremes with the Temptations T.C.B. Note: Reissue of Motown MS-682.

PRODIGAL 7-INCH SINGLES

PR45 0001	Prodigal 611 (12/74)	Shirley I Hear Those Church Bells Ringing+Chapel Of Love I Do Love You
PR45 0002	Prodigal 612 (01/75)	Gary U.S. Bonds Grandma's Washboard Band Believing You
PR45 0003	Prodigal 613	Note: Unissued.
PR45 0004	Prodigal 614 (03/75)	Ronnie McNair Wendy Is Gone Give Me A Sign
PR45 0005	Prodigal 615 (03/75)	Fox Fire Bump In Your Jeans Such A Long Time
PR45 0006	Prodigal 616 (05/75)	Shirley Alston I'd Rather Not Be Loving You Can't Stop Singin' ('Bout The Boy I Love)
PR45 0007	Prodigal 617 (06/75)	Eddie Parker Body Chains (Vocal) Body Chains (Instrumental)
PR45 0008	Prodigal 618 (07/75)	Softouch After You Give Your All (What Else Is There To Give) Say That You Love Me Boy
PR45 0009	Prodigal 619 (08/75)	Ronnie McNair For Your Love You Better Come On Down
PR45 0010	Prodigal 620 (11/75)	Ronnie McNair Sagittarian Affair You Better Come On Down
PR45 0011	Prodigal 621 (12/75)	Orange Sunshine Who's Cheating On Who I'm In Love
PR45 0012	Prodigal 622 (02/76)	Gaylord & Holiday Eh! Cumpari The Little Shoemaker
PR45 0013	Prodigal 623 (04/76)	Joe Frazier Little Dog Heaven What Ya Gonna Do When The Rain Starts Fallin'
PR45 0014	Prodigal 624 (04/76)	Disco Stan Funky Cocktail (Pt. 1) Funky Cocktail (Pt. 2)
PR45 0015	Prodigal 625	Chip Hand Wait Until September Dreamtime Lover Note: Unissued.
PR45 0016	Prodigal 626 (06/76)	Rita Graham Rich Man, Poor Man I'll Hold Out My Hand

PR45 0017	Prodigal 627 (06/76)	Fantacy Hill Minne Ha Ha Stay With Me
PR45 0018	Prodigal 628	Michael Quatro The Stripper Children Of Tomorrow Note: Unissued.
PR45 0019	Prodigal 629 (01/77)	Dunn & Rubini Imaginary Girl Two
PR45 0020	Prodigal 630 (06/76)	Dunn & Rubini Diggin' It Just Keep Laughin'
PR45 0021	Prodigal 631 (10/76)	Michael Quatro Pure Chopin One By One
PR45 0022	Prodigal 632 (11/76)	Charlene It Ain't Easy Comin' Down On My Way To You
PR45 0023	Prodigal 633 (03/77)	Charlene Freddie Freddie (Instrumental)
PR45 0024	Prodigal 634	Note: Unissued.
PR45 0025	Prodigal 635 (07/77)	Graffiti Orchestra "Star Wars" Theme "Star Wars" Theme (Long Version)
PR45 0026	Prodigal 636 (07/77)	Charlene I've Never Been To Me It's Really Nice To Be In Love Again
PR45 0027	Prodigal 637 (09/77)	Rare Earth Is Your Teacher Cool Crazy Love
PR45 0028	Prodigal 638 (09/77)	Phillip Jarrell Wings Of Time I'm Dyin'
PR45 0029	Prodigal 639 (03/78)	Fresh Just How Does It Feel Feelin' Fresh
PR45 0030	Prodigal 640 (03/78)	Rare Earth Warm Ride Would You Like To Come Along
PR45 0031	Prodigal 641 (06/78)	Fantacy Hill Sanity Baby Your Mama
PR45 0032	Prodigal 642 (06/78)	Fresh Summertime Feelin' Fresh
PR45 0033	Prodigal 643 (06/78)	Rare Earth I Can Feel My Love Risin' S.O.S. (Stop Her On Sight)

PR45 0034	Prodigal 644 (1978)	Stylus Natural Feeling Look At Me
PR45 0035	Prodigal 645 (1978)	Fresh You Never Cared When The Winter Comes
PR45 0036	Prodigal 646 (1978)	Stylus Sweetness Bush Walkin'

PRODIGAL ALBUMS

PRLP 0001	Prodigal PLP-10007 (1975)	Ronnie McNeir RONNIE MCNEIR
PRLP 0002	Prodigal PLP-10008 (1975)	Shirley Alston WITH A LITTLE HELP FROM MY FRIENDS
PRLP 0003	Prodigal PLP-10009 (1975)	Gaylord & Holiday SECOND GENERATION
PRLP 0004	Prodigal 10010 (06/76)	Michael Quatro DANCERS, ROMANCERS, DREAMERS AND SCHEMERS
PRLP 0005	Prodigal P6-10011 (08/76)	Kathe Green KATHE GREEN Note: Also issued on Motown M6-856S1.
PRLP 0006	Prodigal P6-10012 (08/76)	Fantacy Hill FANTACY HILL
PRLP 0007	Prodigal P6-10013 (09/76)	Dunn & Rubini DIGGIN' IT
PRLP 0008	Prodigal P6-10014S1 (09/76)	Tattoo TATTOO
PRLP 0009	Prodigal P6-10015 (11/76)	Charlene CHARLENE
PRLP 0010	Prodigal 10016 (01/77)	Michael Quatro GETTIN' READY
PRLP 0011	Prodigal P6-10017 (02/77)	Delaney Bramlett DELANEY AND FRIENDS - CLASS REUNION
PRLP 0012	Prodigal 10018 (05/77)	Charlene SONGS OF LOVE
PRLP 0013	Prodigal P6-10019S1 (07/77)	Rare Earth RAREARTH

PRLP 0014	Prodigal P6-10020 (09/77)	Phillip Jarrell I SING MY SONGS FOR YOU
PRLP 0015	Prodigal 10021	Note: Unissued.
PRLP 0016	Prodigal P7-10022 (01/78)	Fantacy Hill FIRST STEP
PRLP 0017	Prodigal 10023	Phil Cordell BORN AGAIN Note: Unissued.
PRLP 0018	Prodigal P7-10024 (01/78)	Fresh FEELIN' FRESH
PRLP 0019	Prodigal P7-10025R1 (04/78)	Rare Earth BAND TOGETHER
PRLP 0020	Prodigal P7-10026 (04/78)	Friendly Enemies ROUND ONE
PRLP 0021	Prodigal P7-10027R1 (09/78)	Rare Earth GRAND SLAM
PRLP 0022	Prodigal P7-10028 (10/78)	Fresh OMNIVERSE
PRLP 0023	Prodigal P7-10029R1 (10/78)	Stoney and Meatloaf MEATLOAF
PRLP 0024	Prodigal P7-10030R1 (10/78)	Stylus STYLUS

RARE EARTH 7-INCH SINGLES

RA45 0001	Rare Earth 5005 (07/69)	Pretty Things Private Sorrow Balloon Burning
RA45 0002	Rare Earth 5006 (08/69)	Virgil Brothers Temptation 'Bout To Get Me Look Away
RA45 0003	Rare Earth 5007 (08/69)	Wes Henderson In Bed Reality
RA45 0004	Rare Earth 5008 (09/69)	Sounds Nice Love At First Sight (Je Taime) Love You Too Note: "A" side also issued on red vinyl.
RA45 0005	Rare Earth 5009 (09/69)	Easybeats St. Louis Can't Find Love

RA45 0006	Rare Earth 5010 (11/69)	Rare Earth Generation (Light Up The Sky) Magic Key
RA45 0007	Rare Earth 5011 (11/69)	Rustix Can't You Hear The Music Play I Guess This Is Goodbye
RA45 0008	Rare Earth 5012 (02/70)	Rare Earth Get Ready Magic Key
RA45 0009	Rare Earth 5013 (04/70)	R. Dean Taylor Indiana Wants Me Love's Your Name Note: "A" side also issued on red vinyl.
RA45 0010	Rare Earth 5014 (04/70)	Rustix Come On People Free Again (Non...C'est Rien)
RA45 0011	Rare Earth 5015 (05/70)	Michael Denton Just Another Morning Arma'Geden
RA45 0012	Rare Earth 5016 (06/70)	The Cats Marian Somewhere Up There Note: "A" side also issued on red vinyl.
RA45 0013	Rare Earth 5017 (07/70)	Rare Earth (I Know) I'm Losing You When Joanie Smiles
RA45 0014	Rare Earth 5018 (09/70)	Danny Hernandez and the Ones As Long As I've Got You One Little Teardrop Note: "A" side also issued on red vinyl.
RA45 0015	Rare Earth 5019 (10/70)	Toe Fat Bad Side Of The Moon Just Like Me Note: "A" side also issued on red vinyl.
RA45 0016	Rare Earth 5020 (11/70)	Allan Nichols Coming Apart Let The Music Play
RA45 0017	Rare Earth 5021 (11/70)	Rare Earth Born To Wander Here Comes The Night
RA45 0018	Rare Earth 5022 (01/71)	Brass Monkey Sweet Water You Keep Me Hangin' On
RA45 0019	Rare Earth 5023 (01/71)	R. Dean Taylor Ain't It A Sad Thing Back Street
RA45 0020	Rare Earth 5024 (02/71)	Ken Christie and the Sunday People Don't Pay Me No Mind Listen To Your Soul

RA45 0021	Rare Earth 5015 (02/71)	Kiki Dee Love Makes The World Go Round Jimmy
RA45 0022	Rare Earth 5026 (03/71)	R. Dean Taylor Gotta See Jane Back Street Note: "A" side also issued on red vinyl.
RA45 0023	Rare Earth 5027 (04/71)	Stoney and Meatloaf What You See Is What You Get She's A Lady
RA45 0024	Rare Earth 5028 (04/71)	Impact of Brass Never Can Say Goodbye So Far, So Good
RA45 0025	Rare Earth 5029 (06/71)	Ken Christie and the Sunday People The Rev. John B. Daniels Jesus Is The Key
RA45 0026	Rare Earth 5030 (06/71)	R. Dean Taylor Candy Apple Red Woman Alive Note: "A" side also issued on red vinyl.
RA45 0027	Rare Earth 5031 (06/71)	Rare Earth I Just Want To Celebrate The Seed
RA45 0028	Rare Earth 5032 (07/71)	Messengers That's The Way A Woman Is In The Jungle
RA45 0029	Rare Earth 5033 (07/71)	Stoney and Meatloaf It Takes All Kinds Of People The Way You Do The Things You Do
RA45 0030	Rare Earth 5034 (07/71)	Rustix My Peace Of Heaven Down Down Note: "A" side also issued on blue vinyl.
RA45 0031	Rare Earth 5035 (09/71)	Sunday Funnies Walk Down The Path Of Freedom It's Just A Dream
RA45 0032	Rare Earth 5036 (08/71)	My Friends I'm An Easy Rider Concrete And Clay Note: "A" side also issued on blue vinyl.
RA45 0033	Rare Earth 5037 (11/71)	Rustix We All End Up In Boxes Down Down Note: "A" side also issued on red vinyl.
RA45 0034	Rare Earth 5038 (11/71)	Rare Earth Hey Big Brother Under God's Light
RA45 0035	Rare Earth 5039 (11/71)	Dave Prince The Greatest Man Who Ever Lived A Child Is Waiting
RA45 0036	Rare Earth 5040 (01/72)	Blue Scepter Out In The Night Gypsy Eyes
RA45 0037	Rare Earth 5041 (03/72)	R. Dean Taylor Taos New Mexico Shadow
RA45 0038	Rare Earth 5042 (04/72)	Vincent Dimirco I Can Make It Alone Come Clean
RA45 0039	Rare Earth 5043 (03/72)	Rare Earth What'd I Say Nice To Be With You Note: "A" side also issued on red vinyl and on blue vinyl.
RA45 0040	Rare Earth 5044 (04/72)	Xit Nihaa Shil Hozho (I Am Happy About You) End
RA45 0041	Rare Earth 5045 (04/72)	Howl The Good Long Way From Home Why Do You Cry
RA45 0042	Rare Earth 5046 (05/72)	Chris Holland and T Bone Get Me Some Help If Time Could Stand Still
RA45 0043	Rare Earth 5047 (07/72)	Crystal Mansion Somebody Oughta Turn Your Head Around Earth People
RA45 0044	Rare Earth 5048 (10/72)	Rare Earth Good Time Sally Love Shines Down
RA45 0045	Rare Earth 5049	Wolfe Ballad of the Unloved Tale of Two Cities Note: Unissued.
RA45 0046	Rare Earth 5050	Puzzle It's Not The Last Time On With The Show Note: Unissued.
RA45 0047	Rare Earth 5051 (01/73)	The John Wagner Coalition The Battle Is Over Take Time To Love Me
RA45 0048	Rare Earth 5052 (12/72)	Rare Earth We're Gonna Have A Good Time Would You Like To Come Along
RA45 0049	Rare Earth 5053 (03/73)	Rare Earth Ma (Vocal) Ma (Instrumental) Note: See also Rare Earth 5056.

RA45 0050	Rare Earth 5054 (08/73)	Rare Earth Hum Along And Dance Come With Me
RA45 0051	Rare Earth 5055 (09/73)	Xit Reservation of Education Color Nature Gone
RA45 0052	Rare Earth 5056 (10/73)	Rare Earth Big John Is My Name Ma (vocal) Note: "B" side previously released on Rare Earth 5053.
RA45 0053	Rare Earth 5057 (05/74)	Rare Earth Chained Fresh From The Can
RA45 0054	Rare Earth 5058 (10/75)	Rare Earth It Makes You Happy (But It Ain't Gonna Last Too Long) Boogie With Me Children
RA45 0055	Rare Earth 5059 (08/75)	Rare Earth Keepin' Me Out Of The Storm Let Me Be Your Sunshine
RA45 0056	Rare Earth 5060 (05/76)	Rare Earth Midnight Lady Wallking Schtick

RARE EARTH 7-INCH COLOR VINYL SINGLES

RACO 0001	Rare Earth 5008 (09/69)	Sounds Nice Love At First Sight (Je Taime) Note: Red vinyl.
RACO 0002	Rare Earth 5013 (04/70)	R. Dean Taylor Indiana Wants Me Note: Red vinyl.
RACO 0003	Rare Earth 5016 (06/70)	The Cats Marian Note: Red vinyl.
RACO 0004	Rare Earth 5018 (09/70)	Danny Hernandez And The Ones As Long As I've Got You Note: Red vinyl.
RACO 0005	Rare Earth 5019 (10/70)	Toe Fat Bad Side Of The Moon Note: Red vinyl.
RACO 0006	Rare Earth 5026 (03/71)	R. Dean Taylor Gotta See Jane Note: Red vinyl.
RACO 0007	Rare Earth 5030 (06/71)	R. Dean Taylor Candy Apple Red Note: Red vinyl.
RACO 0008	Rare Earth 5034 (07/71)	Rustix My Peace Of Heaven Note: Blue vinyl.

RACO 0009	Rare Earth 5036 (08/71)	My Friends I'm An Easy Rider Note: Blue vinyl.
RACO 0010	Rare Earth 5037 (11/71)	Rustix We All End Up In Boxes Note: Red vinyl.
RACO 0011	Rare Earth 5043 (03/72)	Rare Earth What'd I Say Note: Red vinyl.
RACO 0012	Rare Earth 5043 (03/72)	Rare Earth What'd I Say Note: Blue vinyl.

RARE EARTH ALBUMS

RALP 0001	Rare Earth RS 505-RS 509 (06/69)	Various Artists AN INTRODUCTION TO RARE EARTH RECORDS Note: Five-album box set consisting of RS 505 through RS 509. Album covers are die-cut with round tops.
RALP 0002	Rare Earth RS 505 (08/69)	Love Sculpture BLUES HELPING Note: Rare Earth albums 505-509 were originally released with die-cut, round-top covers in a boxed set.
RALP 0003	Rare Earth RS 506 (08/69)	Pretty Things S. F. SORROW Note: Rare Earth albums 505-509 were originally released with die-cut, round-top covers in a boxed set.
RALP 0004	Rare Earth RS 507 (08/69)	Rare Earth GET READY Note: Rare Earth albums 505-509 were originally released with die-cut, round-top covers in a boxed set.
RALP 0005	Rare Earth RS 508 (08/69)	Rustix BEDLAM Note: Rare Earth albums 505-509 were originally released with die-cut, round-top covers in a boxed set.
RALP 0006	Rare Earth RS 509 (08/69)	Messengers MESSENGERS Note: Rare Earth albums 505-509 were originally released with die-cut, round-top covers in a boxed set.
RALP 0007	Rare Earth RS 510	Rare Earth GENERATION (Film Soundtrack) Note: Unissued.
RALP 0008	Rare Earth RS 511 (07/70)	Toe Fat TOE FAT

RALP 0009	Rare Earth RS 512 (09/70)	Sounds Nice LOVE AT FIRST SIGHT	RALP 0026	Rare Earth R 529L (09/71)	Impact of Brass DOWN AT THE BRASSWORKS
RALP 0010	Rare Earth RS 513 (07/70)	Rustix COME ON PEOPLE	RALP 0027	Rare Earth R 530L (11/71)	Dennis Stoner DENNIS STONER
RALP 0011	Rare Earth RS 514 (06/70)	Rare Earth ECOLOGY	RALP 0028	Rare Earth R 531L (01/72)	God Squad featuring Leonard Caston JESUS CHRIST'S GREATEST HITS
RALP 0012	Rare Earth RS 515 (09/70)	Pretty Things PARACHUTE	RALP 0029	Rare Earth R 532L (11/71)	Repairs ALREADY A HOUSEHOLD WORD
RALP 0013	Rare Earth RS 516 (09/70)	Power of Zeus THE GOSPEL ACCORDING TO ZEUS	RALP 0030	Rare Earth R 533L (11/71)	Other People HEAD TO HEAD
RALP 0014	Rare Earth RS 517	Easybeats EASY RIDIN' Note: Unissued.	RALP 0031	Rare Earth R 534L (12/71)	Rare Earth IN CONCERT Note: Two-album set.
RALP 0015	Rare Earth RS 518 (09/70)	Lost Nation PARADISE LOST	RALP 0032	Rare Earth 535	Note: Unissued.
RALP 0016	Rare Earth RS 519 (05/70)	Poor Boys AIN'T NOTHIN' IN OUR POCKET BUT LOVE	RALP 0033	Rare Earth R 536L (02/72)	Xit PLIGHT OF THE REDMAN
RALP 0017	Rare Earth RS 520 (06/71)	Rare Earth ONE WORLD	RALP 0034	Rare Earth R 537L (02/72)	Howl the Good HOWL THE GOOD
RALP 0018	Rare Earth RS 521 (09/70)	Cats 45 LIVES	RALP 0035	Rare Earth R 538L (05/72)	Sunday Funnies BENEDICTION
RALP 0019	Rare Earth RS 522 (12/70)	R. Dean Taylor I THINK THEREFORE I AM	RALP 0036	Rare Earth R 539L (05/72)	Keef James ONE TREE OR ANOTHER
RALP 0020	Rare Earth RS 523 (04/71)	Brass Monkey BRASS MONKEY	RALP 0037	Rare Earth R 540L (04/72)	Crystal Mountain THE CRYSTAL MANSION
RALP 0021	Rare Earth RS 524 (04/71)	U.F.O. U.F.O. 1	RALP 0038	Rare Earth R 541L (07/72)	Wolfe WOLFE
RALP 0022	Rare Earth RS 525 (03/71)	Toe Fat TOE FAT TWO	RALP 0039	Rare Earth R 542L (10/72)	Matrix MATRIX
RALP 0023	Rare Earth RS 526 (05/71)	Sunday Funnies SUNDAY FUNNIES	RALP 0040	Rare Earth R 543L (10/72)	Rare Earth WILLIE REMEMBERS
RALP 0024	Rare Earth RS 527 (09/71)	Magic MAGIC	RALP 0041	Rare Earth 544	Puzzle PUZZLE Note: Unissued.
RALP 0025	Rare Earth R 529L (09/71)	Stoney and Meatloaf STONEY AND MEATLOAF	RALP 0042	Rare Earth R 545L (04/73)	Xit SILENT WARRIOR

RALP 0043	Rare Earth R 546L (05/73)	Rare Earth MA Note: Released with black and white poster.
RALP 0044	Rare Earth 547	Note: Unissued.
RALP 0045	Rare Earth R6-548S1 (06/75)	Rare Earth BACK TO EARTH
RALP 0046	Rare Earth 549 (02/76)	Pretty Things REAL PRETTY Note: Two-album set.
RALP 0047	Rare Earth R6-550S1 (03/76)	Rare Earth MIDNIGHT LADY

SOUL 7-INCH SINGLES

SO45 0001	Soul 35001 (03/64)	Shorty Long Devil With The Blue Dress Wind It Up
SO45 0002	Soul 35002 (07/64)	Jimmy Ruffin Since I've Lost You I Want Her Love
SO45 0003	Soul 35003 (08/64)	Jr. Walker & The All Stars Satan's Blues Monkey Jump
SO45 0004	Soul 35004 (08/64)	Sammy Ward Bread Winner You've Got To Change
SO45 0005	Soul 35005 (08/64)	Shorty Long It's A Crying Shame (The Way You Treat A Good Man Like Me) Out To Get You
SO45 0006	Soul 35006 (09/64)	Earl Van Dyke Soul Stomp Hot 'N' Tot
SO45 0007	Soul 35007	The Merced Bluenotes Do The Pig (Part 1) Do The Pig (Part 2) Note: Unissued? It is unclear whether this record was ever released. Others list it as "Thumpin'/Do The Pig."
SO45 0008	Soul 35008 (01/65)	Jr. Walker & The All Stars Shotgun Hot Cha Note: Early copies had the artists incorrectly billed as Jr. Walker & All The Stars, with title as "Shot Gun."
SO45 0009	Soul 35009	Earl Van Dyke & The Soul Brothers All For You Too Many Fish In The Sea Note: Unissued.

SO45 0010	Soul 35010 (03/65)	The Hit Pack Never Say No To Your Baby Let's Dance
SO45 0011	Soul 35011 (03/65)	The Freeman Brothers My Baby Beautiful Brown Eyes
SO45 0012	Soul 35012 (05/65)	Jr. Walker & The All Stars Do The Boomerang Tune Up Note: Later pressings of 35008, 35010, 35011, 35012 had "Distributed By Bell Records, Inc., N.Y.C." at the bottom of the label. This mistake was due to an error at the pressing plant. Rather than scrap an entire batch of singles, Motown decided to cover over the error with a black marker.
SO45 0013	Soul 35013 (07/65)	Jr. Walker & The All Stars Shake And Finger Pop Cleo's Back Note: On Soul LP 701, SHOTGUN, as "Shake and Fingerpop."
SO45 0014	Soul 35014 (1965)	Earl Van Dyke & The Soul Brothers I Can't Help Myself (Sugar Pie, Honey Bunch) How Sweet It Is (To Be Loved By You) Note: Label shows "B" side title without parentheses.
SO45 0015	Soul 35015 (03/66)	Jr. Walker & The All Stars (I'm A) Road Runner Shoot Your Shot
SO45 0016	Soul 35016 (10/65)	Jimmy Ruffin As Long As There Is L-O-V-E (Love) How Can I Say I'm Sorry
SO45 0017	Soul 35017 (12/65)	Jr. Walker & The All Stars Cleo's Mood Baby You Know You Ain't Right Note: "A" side originally issued on Harvey 117.
SO45 0018	Soul 35018 (11/65)	Earl Van Dyke & The Soul Brothers The Flick (Part I) The Flick (Part II)
SO45 0019	Soul 35019	Frank Wilson Sweeter As The Days Go By Do I Love You (Indeed I Do) Note: Unissued. Not released in North America, but issued in United Kingdom on Tamla Motown TMG-1170 (with picture sleeve) on November 9, 1979. The U.K. issue listed "Do I Love You" as the "A" side. Picture sleeve issued with promo copy only. U.S. promo copies are known to exist, but only in small quantities.

SO45 0020	Soul 35020 (03/66)	Frances Nero Keep On Lovin' Me Fight Fire With Fire
SO45 0021	Soul 35021 (09/66)	Shorty Long Function At The Junction Call On Me
SO45 0022	Soul 35022 (07/66)	Jimmy Ruffin What Becomes Of The Broken Hearted Baby I've Got It Note: Reissued in 1974 on Motown 1329 as "What Becomes Of The Brokenhearted."
SO45 0023	Soul 35023 (07/66)	Gladys Knight & The Pips Just Walk In My Shoes Stepping Closer To Your Heart
SO45 0024	Soul 35024 (07/66)	Jr. Walker & The All Stars How Sweet It Is (To Be Loved By You) Nothing But Soul

SO45
0025
	Soul
	35025
	(08/66)
		The Velvelettes
		These Things Will Keep Me Loving
		    You
		Since You've Been Loving Me
		    Note: "B" side scheduled for
		release on V.I.P. 25021B
		(unreleased), but actually released
		on V.I.P. 25030B in November
		1965.

SO45 0026	Soul 35026 (08/66)	Jr. Walker & The All Stars Money (That's What I Want) Part 1 Money (That's What I Want) Part 2
SO45 0027	Soul 35027 (11/66)	Jimmy Ruffin I've Passed This Way Before Tomorrow's Tears
SO45 0028	Soul 35028 (12/66)	Earl Van Dyke & The Motown Brass 6 By 6 There Is No Greater Love
SO45 0029	Soul 35029 (01/67)	The Originals Good Night Irene Need Your Lovin' (Want You Back)
SO45 0030	Soul 35030 (01/67)	Jr. Walker & The All Stars Pucker Up Buttercup Anyway You Wanna
SO45 0031	Soul 35031 (02/67)	Shorty Long Chantilly Lace Your Love Is Amazing

SO45
0032
	Soul
	35032
	(03/67)
		Jimmy Ruffin
		Gonna Give Her All The Love I've
		    Got
		World So Wide, Nowhere To
		    Hide (From Your Heart)

SO45
0033
	Soul
	35033
	(03/67)
		Gladys Knight & The Pips
		Take Me In Your Arms And Love
		    Me
		Do You Love Me Just A
		    Little, Honey

SO45
0034
	Soul
	35034
	(06/67)
		Gladys Knight & The Pips
		Everybody Needs Love
		Stepping Closer To Your
		    Heart
		    Note: "B" side previously
		issued on Soul 35023B.

SO45
0035
	Soul
	35035
	(07/67)
		Jimmy Ruffin
		Don't You Miss Me A Little Bit
		    Baby
		I Want Her Love
		    Note: "B" side previously
		issued on Soul 35002B.

SO45 0036	Soul 35036 (06/67)	Jr. Walker & The All Stars Shoot Your Shot Ain't That The Truth Note: "A" side previously issued on Soul 35015B.
SO45 0037	Soul 35037 (07/67)	Messengers Window Shopping California Soul
SO45 0038	Soul 35038 (08/67)	Barbara Randolph I Got A Feeling You Got Me Hurtin' All Over Note: See also Soul 35050.
SO45 0039	Soul 35039 (09/67)	Gladys Knight & The Pips I Heard It Through The Grapevine It's Time To Go Now
SO45 0040	Soul 35040 (01/68)	Shorty Long Night Fo' Last [Vocal] Night Fo' Last (featuring Shorty Long on the organ)
SO45 0041	Soul 35041 (11/67)	Jr. Walker & The All Stars Come See About Me Sweet Soul
SO45 0042	Soul 35042 (01/68)	Gladys Knight & The Pips The End Of Our Road Don't Let Her Take Your Love From Me
SO45 0043	Soul 35043 (02/68)	Jimmy Ruffin I'll Say Forever My Love Everybody Needs Love
SO45 0044	Soul 35044 (05/68)	Shorty Long Here Comes The Judge Sing What You Wanna
SO45 0045	Soul 35045 (05/68)	Gladys Knight & The Pips It Should Have Been Me You Don't Love Me No More
SO45 0046	Soul 35046 (06/68)	Jimmy Ruffin Don't Let Him Take Your Love From Me Lonely Lonely Man Am I

SO45 0047	Soul 35047 (08/68)	Gladys Knight & The Pips I Wish It Would Rain It's Summer
SO45 0048	Soul 35048 (07/68)	Jr. Walker & The All Stars Hip City (Pt. 1) Hip City (Pt. 2)
SO45 0049	Soul 35049 (07/68)	The Monitors Step By Step (Hand In Hand) Time Is Passin' By Note: Originally scheduled to have been released on V.I.P. 25049, but transferred to the Soul label at the last moment.
SO45 0050	Soul 35050 (08/68)	Barbara Randolph Can I Get A Witness You Got Me Hurtin' All Over Note: "B" side previously issued on Soul 35038B.
SO45 0051	Soul 35051 (09/68)	Abdullah I Comma Zimba Zio (Here I Stand The Mighty One) Why Them, Why Me
SO45 0052	Soul 35052 (09/68)	The Fantastic Four I Love You Madly I Love You Madly (Instrumental) Note: Also issued on Ric-Tic 144.
SO45 0053	Soul 35053 (10/68)	Jimmy Ruffin Gonna Keep On Tryin' Till I Win Your Love Sad And Lonesome Feeling
SO45 0054	Soul 35054 (01/69)	Shorty Long I Had A Dream Ain't No Justice
SO45 0055	Soul 35055 (12/68)	Jr. Walker & The All Stars Home Cookin Mutiny
SO45 0056	Soul 35056 (01/69)	The Originals We've Got A Way Out Love You're The One
SO45 0057	Soul 35057 (02/69)	Gladys Knight & The Pips Didn't You Know (You'd Have To Cry Sometime) Keep An Eye
SO45 0058	Soul 35058 (03/69)	The Fantastic Four I Feel Like I'm Falling In Love Again Pin Point It Down
SO45 0059	Soul 35059 (03/69)	Earl Van Dyke Runaway Child, Running Wild Gonna Give Her All The Love I've Got
SO45 0060	Soul 35060 (01/69)	Jimmy Ruffin Farewell Is A Lonely Sound If You Will Let Me, I Know I Can
SO45 0061	Soul 35061 (04/69)	The Originals Green Grow The Lilacs You're The One
SO45 0062	Soul 35062 (04/69)	Jr. Walker & The All Stars What Does It Take (To Win Your Love) Brainwasher (Part 1) Note: "B" side previously issued on Harvey 117. "A" side reissued in 1975 on Motown 1352A.
SO45 0063	Soul 35063 (05/69)	Gladys Knight & The Pips The Nitty Gritty Got Myself A Good Man
SO45 0064	Soul 35064 (06/69)	Shorty Long A Whiter Shade Of Pale When You Are Available Note: Promo copy lists "Featuring Shorty Long on Vocal and Trumpet" below title of "A Whiter Shade Of Pale."
SO45 0065	Soul 35065 (09/69)	The Fantastic Four Just Another Lonely Night Don't Care Why You Want Me (Long As You Want Me)
SO45 0066	Soul 35066 (09/69)	The Originals Baby, I'm For Real Moment Of Truth
SO45 0067	Soul 35067 (10/69)	Jr. Walker & The All Stars These Eyes I've Got To Find A Way To Win Maria Back
SO45 0068	Soul 35068 (10/69)	Gladys Knight & The Pips Friendship Train Cloud Nine
SO45 0069	Soul 35069 (01/70)	The Originals The Bells I'll Wait For You
SO45 0070	Soul 35070 (01/70)	Jr. Walker & The All Stars Gotta Hold On To This Feeling Clinging To The Thought That She's Coming Back
SO45 0071	Soul 35071 (02/70)	Gladys Knight & The Pips You Need Love Like I Do (Don't You) You're My Everything
SO45 0072	Soul 35072 (03/70)	The Fantastic Four On The Brighter Side Of A Blue World I'm Gonna Carry On
SO45 0073	Soul 35073 (06/70)	Jr. Walker & The All Stars Do You See My Love (For You Growing) Groove And Move
SO45 0074	Soul 35074 (07/70)	The Originals We Can Make It Baby I Like Your Style

SO45 0075	Soul 35075 (06/70)	Yvonne Fair Stay A Little Longer We Should Never Be Lonely My Love
SO45 0076	Soul 35076 (10/70)	David & Jimmy Ruffin Stand By Me Your Love Was Worth Waiting For
SO45 0077	Soul 35077 (12/70)	Jimmy Ruffin Maria (You Were The Only One) Living In A World I Created For Myself
SO45 0078	Soul 35078 (10/70)	Gladys Knight & The Pips If I Were Your Woman The Tracks Of My Tears
SO45 0079	Soul 35079 (11/70)	The Originals God Bless Whoever Sent You Desperate Young Man
SO45 0080	Soul 35080 (01/71)	Joe Hinton Let's All Save The Children You Are Blue
SO45 0081	Soul 35081 (11/70)	Jr. Walker & The All Stars Holly Holy Carry Your Own Load
SO45 0082	Soul 35082 (03/71)	David & Jimmy Ruffin When My Love Hand Comes Down Steppin' On A Dream
SO45 0083	Soul 35083 (05/71)	Gladys Knight & The Pips I Don't Want To Do Wrong Is There A Place (In His Heart For Me)
SO45 0084	Soul 35084 (07/71)	Jr. Walker & The All Stars Take Me Girl, I'm Ready Right On Brothers And Sisters
SO45 0085	Soul 35085 (07/71)	The Originals Keep Me A Man Without Love
SO45 0086	Soul 35086	David & Jimmy Ruffin Lo And Behold The Things We Have To Do Note: Unissued.
SO45 0087	Soul 35087 (09/71)	Popcorn Wylie Funky Rubber Band (Vocal) Funky Rubber Band (Instrumental)
SO45 0088	Soul 35088 (10/71)	Jack Hammer Color Combination Swim
SO45 0089	Soul 35089	Blinky How You Gonna Keep It (After You Get It) This Time Last Summer Note: Unissued. Also unissued on Motown 1168.
SO45 0090	Soul 35090 (11/71)	Jr. Walker & The All Stars Way Back Home (Vocal) Way Back Home (Instrumental)
SO45 0091	Soul 35091 (11/71)	Gladys Knight & The Pips Make Me The Woman That You Go Home To It's All Over But The Shoutin'
SO45 0092	Soul 35092 (12/71)	Jimmy Ruffin Our Favorite Melody You Gave Me Love
SO45 0093	Soul 35093 (01/72)	The Originals I'm Someone Who Cares Once I Have You (I Will Never Let You Go)
SO45 0094	Soul 35094 (03/72)	Gladys Knight & The Pips Help Me Make It Through The Night If You're Gonna Leave (Just Leave)
SO45 0095	Soul 35095 (02/72)	Jr. Walker & The All Stars Walk In The Night I Don't Want To Do Wrong
SO45 0096	Soul 35096 (03/72)	Edwin Starr Take Me Clear From Here Ball Of Confusion (That's What The World Is Today)
SO45 0097	Soul 35097 (06/72)	Jr. Walker & The All Stars Groove Thang Me And My Family
SO45 0098	Soul 35098 (12/72)	Gladys Knight & The Pips Neither One Of Us (Wants To Be The First To Say Goodbye) Can't Give It Up No More
SO45 0099	Soul 35099 (07/72)	Billy Proctor What Is Black I Can Take It All
SO45 0100	Soul 35100 (08/72)	Edwin Starr Who Is The Leader Of The People Don't Tell Me I'm Crazy
SO45 0101	Soul 35101	Bob Rabbit Gospel Truth Running Like A Babbit Note: Unissued.
SO45 0102	Soul 35102 (04/73)	The Originals Be My Love Endlessly Love
SO45 0103	Soul 35103 (05/73)	Edwin Starr There You Go (Vocal) There You Go (Instrumental)
SO45 0104	Soul 35104 (01/73)	Jr. Walker & The All Stars Gimme That Beat (Part 1) Gimme That Beat (Part 2)

SO45 0105	Soul 35105 (04/73)	Gladys Knight & The Pips Daddy Could Swear (I Declare) For Once In My Life
SO45 0106	Soul 35106 (05/73)	Jr. Walker & The All Stars I Don't Need No Reason Country Boy 　　Note: "B" side reissued on Motown 1352B.
SO45 0107	Soul 35107 (07/73)	Gladys Knight & The Pips All I Need Is Time The Only Time You Love Me 　Is When You're Losing Me
SO45 0108	Soul 35108 (07/73)	Jr. Walker & The All Stars Peace And Understanding (Is Hard 　To Find) Soul Clappin' 　　Note: See also Soul 35116.
SO45 0109	Soul 35109 (09/73)	The Originals There's A Chance When You Love 　You'll Lose 1st Lady (Sweet Mother's 　Love) 　　Note: Promo copy has the long (3:57) and short (2:58) versions of "There's A Chance When You Love You'll Lose."
SO45 0110	Soul 35110 (05/74)	Jr. Walker & The All Stars Dancin' Like They Do On Soul 　Train I Ain't That Easy To Lose
SO45 0111	Soul 35111 (06/74)	Gladys Knight & The Pips Between Her Goodbye And My 　Hello This Child Needs Its Father
SO45 0112	Soul 35112	Edwin Starr Ain't It Hell Up In Harlem Don't It Feel Good To Be 　Free 　　Note: Unissued. Release transferred to Motown 1284.
SO45 0113	Soul 35112 (01/74)	The Originals Supernatural Voodoo Woman (Pt. I) Supernatural Voodoo Woman 　(Pt. II) 　　Note: Release was originally scheduled for Motown 1285, but was transferred to this number at the last minute.
SO45 0114	Soul 35113 (07/74)	The Originals Game Called Love Ooh You (Put A Crush On 　Me) 　　Note: See also Soul 35117.
SO45 0115	Soul 35114	Jr. Walker You Are The Sunshine Of My Life Until You Come Back To Me 　(That's What I'm Gonna Do) 　　Note: Unissued.

SO45 0116	Soul 35115 (12/74)	The Originals You're My Only World So Near (And Yet So Far)
SO45 0117	Soul 35116 (12/75)	Jr. Walker I m So Glad Soul Clappin 　　Note: "B" side previously issued on Soul 35108B.
SO45 0118	Soul 35117 (05/76)	The Originals Touch Ooh You (Put A Crush On 　Me) 　　Note: "A" side previously issued on Soul 35113B.
SO45 0120	Soul 35119 (09/76)	The Originals Down To Love Town Just To Be Closer To You
SO45 0121	Soul 35120 (11/76)	Jamal Trice If Love Is Not The Answer Nothing Is Too Good (For 　You Baby)
SO45 0122	Soul 35121	The Originals (Call On Your) Six-Million Dollar 　Man Mother Nature's Best 　　Note: Unissued. Not released due to apparent copyright problem stemming from the television series of the same name. The single does exist as a double-sided "A" side promo copy and test pressing made by Monarch Record Mfg. Co.
SO45 0123	Soul 35122 (08/77)	Jr. Walker Hard Love Whopper Bopper Show 　Stopper
SO45 0124	Soul 35123 (04/78)	Major Lance I Never Thought I'd Be Losing You Chicago Disco

SOUL 7-INCH EPS

SOEP 0001	Soul 60701 (1965)	Jr. Walker & The All Stars SHOTGUN Side 1: Shotgun/(I'm A) Road Runner/Shake And Fingerpop - Side 2: Cleo's Mood/Do The Boomerang/Cleo's Back
SOEP 0002	Soul 60702 (1966)	Jr. Walker & The All Stars SOUL SESSIONS Side 1: Good Rockin'/Shake Everything/Mark Anthony (Speaks) - Side 2: Decidedly/Brainwasher/Three Four Three
SOEP 0003	Soul 60703 (1966)	Jr. Walker & The All Stars ROAD RUNNER Side 1: (I'm A) Road Runner/How Sweet It Is (To Be Loved By You)/Last Call - Side

		2: Pucker Up Buttercup/Baby You Know You Ain't Right/Twist Lackawanna
SOEP 0004	Soul 60704 (1967)	Jimmy Ruffin SINGS TOP TEN Side 1: I've Passed This Way Before/What Becomes Of The Brokenhearted/Gonna Give Her All The Love I've Got - Side 2: As Long As There Is L-O-V-E Love/Since I've Lost You/I Want Her Love

SOUL ALBUMS

SOLP 0001	Soul SS-701 (05/65)	Jr. Walker & The All Stars SHOTGUN
SOLP 0002	Soul S-702 (03/66)	Jr. Walker & The All Stars SOUL SESSION
SOLP 0003	Soul SS-703 (08/66)	Jr. Walker & The All Stars ROAD RUNNER
SOLP 0004	Soul S-704 (01/67)	Jimmy Ruffin TOP TEN
SOLP 0005	Soul S-705 (09/67)	Jr. Walker & The All Stars JR. WALKER & THE ALL STARS LIVE!
SOLP 0006	Soul SS-706 (09/67)	Gladys Knight & The Pips EVERYBODY NEEDS LOVE
SOLP 0007	Soul S-707 (05/68)	Gladys Knight & The Pips FEELIN' BLUESY
SOLP 0008	Soul SS-708 (03/69)	Jimmy Ruffin RUFF' N READY
SOLP 0009	Soul SS-709 (09/68)	Shorty Long HERE COMES THE JUDGE
SOLP 0010	Soul SS-710 (01/69)	Jr. Walker & The All Stars HOME COOKIN'
SOLP 0011	Soul SS-711 (12/68)	Gladys Knight & The Pips SILK N' SOUL
SOLP 0012	Soul 712	Barbara Randolph [ALBUM TITLE NOT DETERMINED] Note: Unissued.
SOLP 0013	Soul S-713 (09/69)	Gladys Knight & The Pips NITTY GRITTY
SOLP 0014	Soul SS-714 (12/68)	The Monitors GREETINGS! . . . WE'RE THE MONITORS
SOLP 0015	Soul SS-715 (09/70)	Earl Van Dyke THE EARL OF FUNK
SOLP 0016	Soul SS-716 (07/69)	The Originals GREEN GROW THE LILACS Note: Reissued using title of hit song, BABY I'M FOR REAL.
SOLP 0017	Soul SS-717 (03/69)	The Fantastic Four BEST OF THE FANTASTIC FOUR
SOLP 0018	Soul SS-718 (08/69)	Jr. Walker & The All Stars JR. WALKER & THE ALL STARS GREATEST HITS
SOLP 0019	Soul SS-719 (11/69)	Shorty Long THE PRIME OF SHORTY LONG
SOLP 0020	Soul SS-720 (11/69)	Various Artists SWITCHED ON BLUES
SOLP 0021	Soul SS-721 (11/69)	Jr. Walker & The All Stars GOTTA HOLD ON TO THIS FEELING Note: Reissued using title of hit song, WHAT DOES IT TAKE TO WIN YOUR LOVE.
SOLP 0022	Soul SS-722	The Fantastic Four HOW SWEET HE IS Note: Unissued.
SOLP 0023	Soul SS-723 (03/70)	Gladys Knight & The Pips GREATEST HITS
SOLP 0024	Soul SS-724 (06/70)	The Originals PORTRAIT OF THE ORIGINALS
SOLP 0025	Soul SS-725 (05/70)	Jr. Walker & The All Stars JR. WALKER & THE ALL STARS LIVE Note: Different songs than those on Soul S-705.
SOLP 0026	Soul SS-726 (09/70)	Jr. Walker & The All Stars A GASSSSSSSSSS
SOLP 0027	Soul SS-727 (09/70)	Jimmy Ruffin THE GROOVE GOVERNOR
SOLP 0028	Soul SS-0728 (10/70)	The Ruffin Brothers Jimmy & David I AM MY BROTHER'S KEEPER
SOLP 0029	Soul SS-729 (10/70)	The Originals NATURALLY TOGETHER

SOLP 0030	Soul SS-730 (10/70)	Gladys Knight & The Pips ALL IN A KNIGHT'S WORK (LIVE)
SOLP 0031	Soul SS-731 (04/71)	Gladys Knight & The Pips IF I WERE YOUR WOMAN
SOLP 0032	Soul S-732L (07/71)	Jr. Walker & The All Stars RAINBOW FUNK
SOLP 0033	Soul S-733L (12/71)	Jr. Walker & The All Stars MOODY JR.
SOLP 0034	Soul S-734L (02/72)	The Originals DEF.I.NI.TIONS
SOLP 0035	Soul S-735L	C. P. Spencer GOIN' FOR MYSELF Note: Unissued.
SOLP 0036	Soul S-736L (12/71)	Gladys Knight & The Pips STANDING OVATION
SOLP 0037	Soul S-737L (02/73)	Gladys Knight & The Pips NEITHER ONE OF US
SOLP 0038	Soul S-738L (04/73)	Jr. Walker & The All Stars PEACE & UNDERSTANDING IS HARD TO FIND
SOLP 0039	Soul S-739L (06/73)	Gladys Knight & The Pips ALL I NEED IS TIME
SOLP 0040	Soul S6-740S1 (08/74)	The Originals GAME CALLED LOVE
SOLP 0041	Soul S-741V1 (02/74)	Gladys Knight & The Pips KNIGHT TIME
SOLP 0042	Soul S6-742S1	Jr. Walker & The All Stars JR. WALKER & THE ALL STARS Note: Unissued. Released in the U.K. on Tamla Motown 11274 in July 1975.
SOLP 0043	Soul 743	The Originals CALIFORNIA SUNSET Note: Unissued.
SOLP 0044	Soul S-744V1 (03/75)	Gladys Knight & The Pips A LITTLE KNIGHT MUSIC
SOLP 0045	Soul S6-745S1 (01/76)	Jr. Walker & The All Stars HOT SHOT
SOLP 0046	Soul S-746P1 (05/76)	The Originals COMMUNIQUE

SOLP 0047	Soul S747S1 (06/76)	Jr. Walker SAX APPEAL
SOLP 0048	Soul S6-748S1 (10/76)	Jr. Walker WHOPPER BOPPER SHOW STOPPER
SOLP 0049	Soul S6-749S1 (01/77)	The Originals DOWN TO LOVE TOWN
SOLP 0050	Soul S7-750R1 (05/78)	Jr. Walker . . . SMOOTH
SOLP 0051	Soul S7-751R1 (08/78)	Major Lance NOW ARRIVING

TAMLA 7-INCH SINGLES

TA45 0001	Tamla 101 (01/59)	Marv Johnson Come To Me Whisper Note: "A" and "B" side vocal accompaniment as by the Rayber Voices. Issued from address 1719 Gladstone Street, Detroit 6, Michigan. Single also issued for national distribution on United Artists 160.
TA45 0002	Tamla 102 (01/59)	Eddie Holland Merry-Go-Round It Moves Me Note: Issued from address 1719 Gladstone Street, Detroit 6, Michigan. Also issued on United Artists 172 for national distribution.
TA45 0003	Tamla 54024 (06/59)	Chico Leverette Solid Sender I'll Never Love Again Note: Pressed in very limited quantities for distribution within the Detroit area.
TA45 0004	Tamla 54024 (06/59)	The Swinging Tigers Snake Walk - Part 1 Snake Walk - Part 2
TA45 0005	Tamla 54025 (08/59)	Ron & Bill It Don't Say Bye-Bye Note: Artists are Ronnie White and Bill "Smokey" Robinson, then both members of The Miracles. Also released on Argo 5350.
TA45 0006	Tamla 54026 (10/59)	The Downbeats Your Baby's Back Request Of A Fool Note: Later issued on Tamla 54056.

TA45 0007	Tamla 54026 (10/59)	The Satintones Motor City Going To The Hop

TA45 0008 — Tamla 54027 (11/59) — Barrett Strong
Money (That's What I Want)
Oh I Apologize
   Note: First pressing has 54027 G1 master number in vinyl, and number 54027 G2 for "B" side. "B" side has fade out at end. Alternate pressing with "A" side master number 54027 G1 in vinyl. "B" side has number DM-066220 in run-out of vinyl. This version runs ten seconds longer than the first pressing and has no fade out. Later pressing with "Globes" label. Bar label with "A" side matrix number 066216 and "B" side number 066220. Licensed and released on Anna 1111 for wider distribution.

TA45 0009 — Tamla 54028 (07/60) — The Miracles
The Feeling Is So Fine
You Can Depend On Me
   Note: This was the Miracles' first Tamla release. It was quickly withdrawn and replaced by "Way Over There." "A" side issued with alternate version. "B" side is alternate take to "Depend On Me."

TA45 0010 — Tamla 54028 (07/60) — The Miracles
Way Over There
Depend On Me
   Note: "A" side master number H55501 issued without strings. Subsequently issued with strings (master number H5501 T-3). The version with strings is the first Tamla record to have national distribution. See also Tamla 54069.

TA45 0011 — Tamla 54029 (07/60) — Barrett Strong
Yes, No, Maybe So
You Knows What To Do
   Note: Back-up vocal accompaniment as by the Rayber Voices on "A" side. Also issued on Anna 1116.

TA45 0012 — Tamla 54030 (08/60) — "Singing" Sammy Ward
What Makes You Love Him
That Child Is Really Wild
   Note: First pressing with "Lines" label.

TA45 0013 — Tamla 54030 (08/60) — "Singing" Sammy Ward
Who's The Fool
That Child Is Really Wild
   Note: With "Globes" label.

TA45 0014 — Tamla 54031 (10/60) — Mable John
Who Wouldn't Love A Man Like That
You Made A Fool Out Of Me
   Note: An alternate take to this "A" side was later issued on Tamla 54081A.

TA45 0015 — Tamla 54032 (11/60) — Herman Griffin
True Love (That's Love)
It's You

TA45 0016 — Tamla 54033 (10/60) — Barrett Strong and Rayber Voices
Whirlwind
I'm Gonna Cry (If You Quit Me)

TA45 0017 — Tamla 54034 (10/60) — The Miracles featuring Bill "Smokey" Robinson
Shop Around
Who's Lovin' You
   Note: "A" side master number 45-H55518 A-2 in vinyl run-out groove. This is an alternate take to what would later be the hit version, which has "A" side master number 45-L13.

TA45 0018 — Tamla 54035 (12/60) — Barrett Strong
Money And Me
You Got What It Takes

TA45 0019 — Tamla 54036 (03/61) — The Miracles
Ain't It Baby
The Only One I Love

TA45 0020 — Tamla 54037 (03/61) — Gospel Stars
He Lifted Me
Behold The Saints Of God
   Note: "Lines" label is first pressing. "A" side master number H-635 1A in vinyl. "B" side master number H-55583 1A in vinyl. Second pressing with "Globes" label. "A" side master number 622 in vinyl. "B" side master number 55583 11L in run-out.

TA45 0021 — Tamla 54038 (04/61) — The Supremes
I Want A Guy
Never Again
   Note: Copies also exist on Motown 1008. Matrix numbers are exactly the same. This number on Motown is extremely rare and only one or two copies are known to exist as a white label promo with "Map" label. At the very last minute, the company decided to release this number on the Tamla label instead of Motown. Only two releases by the Supremes were issued on Tamla, with all subsequent issues on the Motown label.

TA45 0022 — Tamla 54039 (04/61) — Mickey Woods
Poor Sam Jones
They Rode Through The Valley
   Note: Called Mickey Wood on Tamla 54052.

TA45 0023 — Tamla 54040 (05/61) — Mable John
No Love
Looking For A Man
   Note: "A" side has long intro with no horns. Master number

		H-632 in vinyl. Also issued with "A" side having horns with no intro. Master number H-667 in vinyl.
TA45 0024	Tamla 54041 (05/61)	Marvin Gaye Let Your Conscience Be Your Guide Never Let You Go
TA45 0025	Tamla 54042 (06/61)	Gino Parks That's No Lie Same Thing Note: An alternate take to "That's No Lie" later issued as a promotional single on Tamla 54108B.
TA45 0026	Tamla 54043 (06/61)	Barrett Strong Misery Two Wrongs Don't Make A Right Note: "B" side master number H-687 in vinyl. Also issued with "B" side master number H-699 in vinyl. This is alternate take to first release.
TA45 0027	Tamla 54044 (07/61)	The Miracles Broken Hearted Mighty Good Lovin' Note: Issued with full-color picture sleeve. Label design changed to "Globes."
TA45 0028	Tamla 54045 (07/61)	The Supremes Buttered Popcorn Who's Loving You
TA45 0029	Tamla 54046 (08/61)	The Marvelettes Please Mr. Postman So Long Baby
TA45 0030	Tamla 54047 (09/61)	Rev. Columbus Mann Jesus Loves They Shall Be Mine
TA45 0031	Tamla 54048 (10/61)	The Miracles I Can't Believe Everybody's Gotta Pay Some Dues
TA45 0032	Tamla 54049 (10/61)	Sammy Ward What Makes You Love Him Don't Take It Away Note: "A" side is alternate take from Tamla 54030.
TA45 0033	Tamla 54050 (10/61)	Mable John Actions Speak Louder Than Words Take Me Note: Label reads "Mabel John."
TA45 0034	Tamla 54051 (11/61)	Bob Kayli Tie Me Tight Small Sad Sam Note: Real name is Robert Gordy (brother of Berry Gordy). Both sides also issued separately as

		single-sided promotional records with blank "B" sides.
TA45 0035	Tamla 54052 (12/61)	Mickey Wood (They Call Me) Cupid Please Mr. Kennedy Note: Called Mickey Woods on Tamla 54039.
TA45 0036	Tamla 54053 (12/61)	The Miracles What's So Good About Good-By I've Been Good To You Note: Issued with picture sleeve. "A" side also issued as single-sided DJ copy with blank "B" side. "A" side also issued on red vinyl.
TA45 0037	Tamla 54054 (01/62)	The Marvelettes Twistin' Postman I Want A Guy Note: Issued with picture sleeve.
TA45 0038	Tamla 54055 (01/62)	Marvin Gaye Sandman I'm Yours, You're Mine
TA45 0039	Tamla 54056 (02/62)	The Downbeats Your Baby's Back Request Of A Fool Note: Reissue of Tamla 54026.
TA45 0040	Tamla 54057 (03/62)	Singin' Sammy Ward Everybody Knew It Big Joe Moe Note: "B" side master number 034309 in vinyl. Also issued with "B" side master number DM-034379.
TA45 0041	Tamla 54058 (03/62)	Little Otis I Out-Duked The Duke Baby I Need You
TA45 0042	Tamla 54059 (04/62)	The Miracles I'll Try Something New You Never Miss A Good Thing Note: Issued with picture sleeve.
TA45 0043	Tamla 54060 (04/62)	The Marvelettes Playboy All The Love I've Got
TA45 0044	Tamla 54061 (05/62)	Little Stevie Wonder I Call It Pretty Music, But The Old People Call It The Blues, Part I Call It Pretty Music, But The Old People Call It The Blue Part 2 Note: Issued with picture sleeve.
TA45 0045	Tamla 54062	Note: Unissued. Nothing scheduled for this number.

TA45 0046	Tamla 54063 (05/62)	Marvin Gaye Soldier's Plea Taking My Time Note: "A" side vocal accompaniment as by The Lovetones.
TA45 0047	Tamla 54064 (06/62)	Mickey McCullers I'll Cry A Million Tears Same Old Story Note: "A" side vocal accompaniment by The Miracles.
TA45 0048	Tamla 54065 (07/62)	The Marvelettes Beechwood 4-5789 Someday, Someway
TA45 0049	Tamla 54066 (06/62)	Gino Parks For This I Thank You Fire Note: Vocal accompaniment as by the Lovetones.

TA45
0050
	Tamla
	54067
	(07/62)
		Saundra Mallett & The
		    Vandellas
		Camel Walk
		It's Gonna Be Hard Times
		    Note: "A" side backing track
		(Instrumental) portion was taken
		from Gordy 7009. Saundra Mallett
		later went on to sing with The
		Elgins. She was known as Saundra
		Edwards with The Elgins. "B" side
		is the exact same song as released
		on The Elgins album on V.I.P.
		VS-400 ("A" side, song 6).

TA45 0051	Tamla 54068 (07/62)	Marvin Gaye Stubborn Kind Of Fellow It Hurt Me Too Note: "A" side vocal accompaniment by The Vandellas.
TA45 0052	Tamla 54069 (08/62)	The Miracles Way Over There If Your Mother Only Knew Note: See also Tamla 54028.
TA45 0053	Tamla 54070 (10/62)	Little Stevie Wonder La La La La La Little Water Boy Note: "B" side credits both Little Stevie Wonder and Clarence Paul.
TA45 0054	Tamla 54071 (10/62)	Singin' Sammy Ward Someday Pretty Baby Part Time Love

TA45
0055
	Tamla
	54072
	(11/62)
		The Marvelettes
		Strange I Know
		Too Strong To Be Strung
		    Along
		    Note: "A" side also issued as a
		single-sided promotional record
		with blank "B" side.

TA45 0056	Tamla 54073 (11/62)	The Miracles You've Really Got A Hold On Me Happy Landing
TA45 0057	Tamla 54074 (12/62)	Little Stevie Wonder Contract Of Love Sunset
TA45 0058	Tamla 54075 (12/62)	Marvin Gaye Hitch Hike Hello There Angel
TA45 0059	Tamla 54076 (06/63)	Kim Weston Love Me All The Way It Should Have Been Me
TA45 0060	Tamla 54077 (03/63)	The Marvelettes Forever Locking Up My Heart
TA45 0061	Tamla 54078 (03/63)	The Miracles A Love She Can Count On I Can Take A Hint
TA45 0062	Tamla 54079 (04/63)	Marvin Gaye Pride And Joy One Of These Days
TA45 0063	Tamla 54080 (05/63)	Little Stevie Wonder Fingertips - Part 1 Fingertips - Part 2 Note: Issued with picture sleeve.

TA45
0064
	Tamla
	54081
	(06/63)
		Mable John
		Who Wouldn't Love A Man Like
		    That
		Say You'll Never Let Me Go
		    Note: "A" side is alternate
		take to previous release on Tamla
		54031A.

TA45 0065	Tamla 54082 (07/63)	The Marvelettes My Daddy Knows Best Tie A String Around Your Finger
TA45 0066	Tamla 54083 (07/63)	The Miracles Mickey's Monkey Whatever Makes You Happy
TA45 0067	Tamla 54084	Note: Unissued.
TA45 0068	Tamla 54085 (08/63)	Kim Weston Just Loving You Another Train Coming
TA45 0069	Tamla 54086 (09/63)	Little Stevie Wonder Workout Stevie, Workout Money Talk
TA45 0070	Tamla 54087 (09/63)	Marvin Gaye Can I Get A Witness I'm Crazy 'Bout My Baby Note: "A" side back-up by The Supremes.
TA45 0071	Tamla 54088 (10/63)	The Marvelettes As Long As I Know He's Mine Little Girl Blue

TA45 0072	Tamla 54089 (11/63)	The Miracles I Gotta Dance To Keep From Crying Such Is Love, Such Is Life

TA45 0073 — Tamla 54090 (12/63) — Little Stevie Wonder — Castles In The Sand — Thank You (For Loving Me All The Way) — Note: Some copies have no parentheses in "B" side title.

TA45 0074 — Tamla 54091 (01/64) — The Marvelettes — He's A Good Guy (Yes He Is) — Goddess Of Love — Note: "B" side U.S. copies show writers as Holland, Dozier and Gorman, and a running time of 2:30. Canadian label credits writers as Holland, Dozier and Holland, and lists an incorrect running time of 2:39. "A" side also issued as single-sided promotional record under title "Yes He Is."

TA45 0075 — Tamla 54092 (02/64) — The Miracles — (You Can't Let The Boy Overpower) The Man In You — Heartbreak Road

TA45 0076 — Tamla 54093 (02/64) — Marvin Gaye — You're A Wonderful One — When I'm Alone I Cry

TA45 0077 — Tamla 54094 (03/64) — Brenda Holloway — Every Little Bit Hurts — Land Of A Thousand Boys

TA45 0078 — Tamla 54095 (04/64) — Marvin Gaye — Try It Baby — If My Heart Could Sing — Note: Issued with picture sleeve.

TA45 0079 — Tamla 54096 (05/64) — Stevie Wonder — Hey Harmonica Man — This Little Girl — Note: Issued with picture sleeve.

TA45 0080 — Tamla 54097 (06/64) — The Marvelettes — You're My Remedy — A Little Bit Of Sympathy, A Little Bit Of Love — Note: Issued with picture sleeve.

TA45 0081 — Tamla 54098 (06/64) — The Miracles — I Like It Like That — You're So Fine And Sweet — Note: Issued with picture sleeve.

TA45 0082 — Tamla 54099 (07/64) — Brenda Holloway — I'll Always Love You — Sad Song — Note: "A" side also issued as single-sided promotional record with blank "B" side.

TA45 0083 — Tamla 54100 (07/64) — Kim Weston — Looking For The Right Guy — Feel Alright Tonight — Note: "A" side also issued as single-sided promotional record with blank "B" side.

TA45 0084 — Tamla 54101 (08/64) — Marvin Gaye — Baby Don't You Do It — Walk On The Wild Side — Note: Issued with full-color picture sleeve.

TA45 0085 — Tamla 54102 (09/64) — The Miracles — That's What Love Is Made Of — Would I Love You

TA45 0086 — Tamla 54103 (09/64) — Stevie Wonder — Sad Boy — Happy Street

TA45 0087 — Tamla 54104 (09/64) — Marvin Gaye & Kim Weston — What Good Am I Without You — I Want You 'Round

TA45 0088 — Tamla 54105 (10/64) — The Marvelettes — Too Many Fish In The Sea — A Need For Love

TA45 0089 — Tamla 54106 (10/64) — Kim Weston — A Little More Love — Go Ahead And Laugh

TA45 0090 — Tamla 54107 (11/64) — Marvin Gaye — How Sweet It Is (To Be Loved By You) — Forever

TA45 0091 — Tamla 54108 — Stevie Wonder — Pretty Little Angel — Tears In Vain — Note: Issued as promotional copies only, and not issued commercially.

TA45 0092 — Tamla 54108 (11/64) — Gino Parks — Something Will Happen To You — That's No Lie — Note: "B" side previously issued on Tamla 54042. This version is an alternate take to that on Tamla 54042. Issued as promotional copies only.

TA45 0093 — Tamla 54109 (11/64) — The Miracles — Come On Do The Jerk — Baby Don't You Go

TA45 0094 — Tamla 54110 (01/65) — Kim Weston — I'm Still Loving You — Go Ahead And Laugh — Note: "B" side previously issued on Tamla 54106.

TA45 0095 — Tamla 54111 (02/65) — Brenda Holloway — When I'm Gone — I've Been Good To You — Note: Issued with picture sleeve. "A" side also issued as single-sided promotional record with blank "B" side.

TA45 0096	Tamla 54112 (02/65)	Marvin Gaye I'll Be Doggone You've Been A Long Time Coming Note: "A" side also issued as single-sided promotional record with blank "B" side.
TA45 0097	Tamla 54113 (03/65)	The Miracles Ooo Baby Baby All That's Good
TA45 0098	Tamla 54114 (03/65)	Stevie Wonder Kiss Me Baby Tears In Vain Note: "B" side previously issued promotionally on Tamla 54108B.
TA45 0099	Tamla 54115 (05/65)	Brenda Holloway Operator I'll Be Available
TA45 0100	Tamla 54116 (05/65)	The Marvelettes I'll Keep Holding On No Time For Tears
TA45 0101	Tamla 54117 (06/65)	Marvin Gaye Pretty Little Baby Now That You've Won Me
TA45 0102	Tamla 54118 (06/65)	The Miracles The Tracks Of My Tears A Fork In The Road
TA45 0103	Tamla 54119 (08/65)	Stevie Wonder High Heel Sneakers Music Talk
TA45 0104	Tamla 54119 (08/65)	Stevie Wonder High Heel Sneakers Funny How Time Slips Away
TA45 0105	Tamla 54120 (07/65)	The Marvelettes Danger Heartbreak Dead Ahead Your Cheating Ways
TA45 0106	Tamla 54121 (08/65)	Brenda Holloway You Can Cry On My Shoulder How Many Times Did You Mean It
TA45 0107	Tamla 54122 (09/65)	Marvin Gaye Ain't That Peculiar She's Got To Be Real Note: "A" side running time on U.S. copy is 2:50. "A" side running time on Canadian copy is 2:57.
TA45 0108	Tamla 54123 (09/65)	The Miracles My Girl Has Gone Since You Won My Heart
TA45 0109	Tamla 54124 (11/65)	Stevie Wonder Uptight (Everything's Alright) Purple Rain Drops
TA45 0110	Tamla 54125 (11/65)	Brenda Holloway Together 'Til The End Of Time Sad Song Note: "B" side previously issued on Tamla 54099B.
TA45 0111	Tamla 54126 (12/65)	The Marvelettes Don't Mess With Bill Anything You Wanna Do
TA45 0112	Tamla 54127 (12/65)	The Miracles Going To A Go-Go Choosey Beggar Note: Issued with picture sleeve.
TA45 0113	Tamla 54128 (01/66)	Isley Brothers This Old Heart Of Mine (Is Weak For You) There's No Love Left
TA45 0114	Tamla 54129 (01/66)	Marvin Gaye One More Heartache When I Had Your Love
TA45 0115	Tamla 54130 (03/66)	Stevie Wonder Nothing's Too Good For My Baby With A Child's Heart
TA45 0116	Tamla 54131 (04/66)	The Marvelettes You're The One Paper Boy
TA45 0117	Tamla 54132 (04/66)	Marvin Gaye Take This Heart Of Mine Need Your Lovin' (Want You Back) Note: "A" side second issue has back-up chorus less prominent than first pressing. First pressing in mono, second pressing in stereo.
TA45 0118	Tamla 54133 (05/66)	Isley Brothers Take Some Time Out For Love Who Could Ever Doubt My Love Note: "A" side later reissued on Tamla 54182. "B" side originally scheduled to be released on V.I.P. 25020 in July 1965, but never issued on that numbewith that number.
TA45 0119	Tamla 54134 (05/66)	The Miracles Whole Lot Of Shakin' In My Heart (Since I Met You) Oh Be My Love
TA45 0120	Tamla 54135 (06/66)	Isley Brothers I Guess I'll Always Love You I Hear A Symphony Note: "B" side originally scheduled to be released on V.I.P. 25020 in July 1965, but not issued.
TA45 0121	Tamla 54136 (06/66)	Stevie Wonder Blowin' In The Wind Ain't That Asking For Trouble Note: Issued with picture sleeve.

| TA45 0122 | Tamla 54137 (07/66) | Brenda Holloway Hurt A Little Everyday Where Were You |
| | | |

TA45 0123 — Tamla 54138 (07/66) — Marvin Gaye — Little Darling, I Need You — Hey Diddle Diddle
   Note: "A" side title also issued as "Little Darling, (I Need You)." Issued with picture sleeve.

TA45 0124 — Tamla 54139 (10/66) — Stevie Wonder — A Place In The Sun — Sylvia
   Note: Issued with picture sleeve. Also a new label design with this single. "A" side also issued on red vinyl.

TA45 0125 — Tamla 54140 (10/66) — The Miracles — (Come 'Round Here) I'm The One You Need — Save Me
   Note: Issued with full-color picture sleeve.

TA45 0126 — Tamla 54141 (12/66) — Marvin Gaye & Kim Weston — It Takes Two — It's Got To Be A Miracle (This Thing Called Love)

TA45 0127 — Tamla 54142 (11/66) — Stevie Wonder — Some Day At Christmas — The Miracles Of Christmas

TA45 0128 — Tamla 54143 (12/66) — The Marvelettes — The Hunter Gets Captured By The Game — I Think I Can Change You

TA45 0129 — Tamla 54144 — Brenda Holloway — 'Til Johnny Comes — Where Were You
   Note: Unissued. Contrary to the belief that The Miracles' "I Care About Detroit" was to have been assigned this number, the Brenda Holloway sides are the ones Motown listed in their recording sessions to receive this number. "B" side previously released on Tamla 54137B.

TA45 0130 — Tamla 54145 (01/67) — Smokey Robinson & The Miracles — The Love I Saw In You Was Just A Mirage — Come Spy With Me
   Note: "A" side later issued on Tamla 54199 as an alternate version with running time of 2:54. First release as by Smokey Robinson and The Miracles.

TA45 0131 — Tamla 54146 (04/67) — Isley Brothers — Just Ain't Enough Love — Got To Have You Back
   Note: "A" side later issued on Tamla 54182 with running time of 2:17. Time for above version 2:15.

TA45 0132 — Tamla 54147 (02/67) — Stevie Wonder — Travelin' Man — Hey Love

TA45 0133 — Tamla 54148 (04/67) — Brenda Holloway — Just Look What You've Done — Starting The Hurt All Over Again

TA45 0134 — Tamla 54149 (04/67) — Marvin Gaye & Tammi Terrell — Ain't No Mountain High Enough — Give A Little Love

TA45 0135 — Tamla 54150 (04/67) — The Marvelettes — When You're Young And In Love — The Day You Take One, You Have To Take The Other
   Note: "A" side also issued as single-sided promotional record with blank "B" side.

TA45 0136 — Tamla 54151 (05/67) — Stevie Wonder — I Was Made To Love Her — Hold Me

TA45 0137 — Tamla 54152 (05/67) — Smokey Robinson & The Miracles — More Love — Swept For You Baby

TA45 0138 — Tamla 54153 (06/67) — Marvin Gaye — Your Unchanging Love — I'll Take Care Of You

TA45 0139 — Tamla 54154 (07/67) — Isley Brothers — That's The Way Love Is — One Too Many Heartaches

TA45 0140 — Tamla 54155 (08/67) — Brenda Holloway — You've Made Me So Very Happy — I've Got To Find It
   Note: "A" side also issued on red vinyl.

TA45 0141 — Tamla 54156 (08/67) — Marvin Gaye & Tammi Terrell — Your Precious Love — Hold Me Oh My Darling

TA45 0142 — Tamla 54157 (09/67) — Stevie Wonder — I'm Wondering — Everytime I See You I Go Wild

TA45 0143 — Tamla 54158 (11/67) — The Marvelettes — My Baby Must Be A Magician — I Need Someone

TA45 0144 — Tamla 54159 (10/67) — Smokey Robinson & The Miracles — I Second That Emotion — You Must Be Love

TA45 0145 — Tamla 54160 (12/67) — Marvin Gaye — You — Change What You Can

TA45 0146	Tamla 54161 (11/67)	Marvin Gaye & Tammi Terrell If I Could Build My Whole World Around You If This World Were Mine

TA45 0147	Tamla 54162 (02/68)	Smokey Robinson & The Miracles If You Can Want When The Words From Your Heart Get Caught Up In Your Throat

TA45 0148	Tamla 54163 (03/68)	Marvin Gaye & Tammi Terrell Ain't Nothing Like The Real Thing Little Ole Boy, Little Ole Girl

TA45 0149	Tamla 54164 (03/68)	Isley Brothers Take Me In Your Arms (Rock Me A Little While) Why When Love Is Gone

TA45 0150	Tamla 54165 (03/68)	Stevie Wonder Shoo Be Doo Be Doo Da Day Why Don't You Lead Me To Love

TA45 0151	Tamla 54166 (05/68)	The Marvelettes Here I Am Baby Keep Off, No Trespassing

TA45 0152	Tamla 54167 (05/68)	Smokey Robinson & The Miracles Yester Love Much Better Off Note: "B" side also issued on Tamla 54184B.

TA45 0153	Tamla 54168 (06/68)	Stevie Wonder You Met Your Match My Girl

TA45 0154	Tamla 54169 (07/68)	Marvin Gaye and Tammi Terrell You're All I Need To Get By Two Can Have A Party

TA45 0155	Tamla 54170 (08/68)	Marvin Gaye Chained At Last (I Found A Love)

TA45 0156	Tamla 54171 (09/68)	The Marvelettes Destination:Anywhere What's Easy For Two Is So Hard For One

TA45 0157	Tamla 54172 (08/68)	Smokey Robinson & The Miracles Special Occasion Give Her Up

TA45 0158	Tamla 54173 (09/68)	Marvin Gaye & Tammi Terrell Keep On Lovin' Me Honey You Ain't Livin' Till You're Lovin'

TA45 0159	Tamla 54174 (10/68)	Stevie Wonder For Once In My Life Angie Girl

TA45 0160	Tamla 54175 (10/68)	Isley Brothers All Because I Love You Behind A Painted Smile

TA45 0161	Tamla 54176 (11/68)	Marvin Gaye I Heard It Through The Grapevine You're What's Happening (In The World Today) Note: "A" side issued on the BIG CHILL original soundtrack as a remixed extended version with running time of 5:03. Also issued on PR-149 as a promotional 12-inch single with running time of 5:03.

TA45 0162	Tamla 54177 (12/68)	The Marvelettes I'm Gonna Hold On As Long As I Can Don't Make Hurting Me A Habit Note: "A" side also issued with the slightly shortened title, "I'm Gonna Hold On Long As I Can."

TA45 0163	Tamla 54178 (12/68)	Smokey Robinson & The Miracles Baby, Baby Don't Cry Your Mother's Only Daughter

TA45 0164	Tamla 54179 (01/69)	Marvin Gaye & Tammi Terrell Good Lovin' Ain't Easy To Come By Satisfied Feelin'

TA45 0165	Tamla 54180 (01/69)	Stevie Wonder My Cherie Amour Don't Know Why I Love You Note: Canadian "B" side has title listed as "I Don't Know Why." "A" side originally to be titled "Oh My Marcia" (after a former girlfriend of Stevie's). "A" side also issued on red vinyl.

TA45 0166	Tamla 54181 (04/69)	Marvin Gaye Too Busy Thinking About My Baby Wherever I Lay My Hat (That's My Home)

TA45 0167	Tamla 54182 (04/69)	Isley Brothers Just Ain't Enough Love Take Some Time Out For Love Note: "A" side reissue of Tamla 54146A. "A" side master number H-I-T-583M09 in vinyl, and running time of 2:17, compared to the previous release on Tamla 54146 that has master number HIV-188311, and running time of 2:15.

TA45 0168	Tamla 54183 (05/69)	Smokey Robinson & The Miracles Here I Go Again Doggone Right Note: "A" side also issued on red vinyl.
TA45 0169	Tamla 54184 (06/69)	Smokey Robinson & The Miracles Abraham, Martin And John Much Better Off Note: "A" side also issued on red vinyl. "B" side previously issued on Tamla 54167B with same running time (2:49), but different master number. Tamla 54167B has master number W4KM-3826 in vinyl, Tamla 54184 has master number W2-L-1-428M04.
TA45 0170	Tamla 54185 (08/69)	Marvin Gaye That's The Way Love Is Gonna Keep On Tryin' Till I Win Your Love
TA45 0171	Tamla 54186 (10/69)	The Marvelettes That's How Heartaches Are Made Rainy Mourning Note: "A" side also issued on red vinyl.
TA45 0172	Tamla 54187 (11/69)	Marvin Gaye & Tammi Terrell What You Gave Me How You Gonna Keep It (After You Get It)
TA45 0173	Tamla 54188 (09/69)	Stevie Wonder Yester-Me, Yester-You, Yesterday I'd Be A Fool Right Now
TA45 0174	Tamla 54189 (11/69)	Smokey Robinson & The Miracles Point It Out Darling Dear Note: "A" side also issued on red vinyl.
TA45 0175	Tamla 54190 (12/69)	Marvin Gaye Gonna Give Her All The Love I've Got How Can I Forget Note: "A" side also issued on red vinyl.
TA45 0176	Tamla 54191 (01/70)	Stevie Wonder Never Had A Dream Come True Somebody Knows, Somebody Cares
TA45 0177	Tamla 54192 (03/70)	Martin Gaye & Tammi Terrell The Onion Song California Soul Note: "A" side also issued on red vinyl.
TA45 0178	Tamla 54193 (04/70)	Kiki Dee The Day Will Come Between Sunday And Monday My Whole World Ended (The Moment You Left Me) Note: Issued with picture sleeve.
TA45 0179	Tamla 54194 (05/70)	Smokey Robinson & The Miracles Who's Gonna Take The Blame I Gotta Thing For You Note: Also issued with a longer version of "A" side.
TA45 0180	Tamla 54195 (05/70)	Marvin Gaye The End Of Our Road Me And My Lonely Room
TA45 0181	Tamla 54196 (06/70)	Stevie Wonder Signed, Sealed, Delivered I'm Yours I'm More Than Happy (I'm Satisfied) Note: "A" side also issued on red vinyl.
TA45 0182	Tamla 54197 (07/70)	Bob And Marcia Young Gifted And Black Peace Of Mind
TA45 0183	Tamla 54198 (08/70)	The Marvelettes Marionette After All
TA45 0184	Tamla 54199 (09/70)	Smokey Robinson & The Miracles The Tears Of A Clown Promise Me
TA45 0185	Tamla 54199 (09/70)	Smokey Robinson & The Miracles The Tears Of A Clown The Love I Saw In You Was Just A Mirage Note: "B" side is an alternate take to that previously issued on Tamla 54145. The earlier version has a master number U4KM-2652 in vinyl and runs 2:59. Above version has master number T 54199-BO and runs 2:54.
TA45 0186	Tamla 54200 (09/70)	Stevie Wonder Heaven Help Us All I Gotta Have A Song Note: Issued with picture sleeve.
TA45 0187	Tamla 54201 (01/71)	Marvin Gaye What's Going On God Is Love Note: "A" side issued as a special 7-inch promo single on PR-62A with same time as commercial version (3:40).
TA45 0188	Tamla 54202 (02/71)	Stevie Wonder We Can Work It Out Never Dreamed You'd Leave In Summer Note: "A" side also issued on red vinyl.

TA45 0189 | Tamla 54203 (04/71) | Eddie Kendricks
It's So Hard For Me To Say Good-Bye
This Use To Be The Home Of Johnnie Mae
Note: "A" side runs 2:59. "A" side also issued on red vinyl.

TA45 0190 | Tamla 54203 (04/71) | Eddie Kendricks
It's So Hard For Me To Say Good-bye (Short Version)
It's So Hard For Me To Say Good-bye (Long Version)
Note: Issued as a promotional copy only with running times of 3:40 (short version) and 5:04 (long version).

TA45 0191 | Tamla 54203 (04/71) | Eddie Kendricks
This Use To Be The Home Of Johnnie Mae (Short version)
This Use To Be The Home Of Johnnie Mae (Long version)
Note: Issued as a promotional copy only with running times of 3:40 (short version) and 5:40 (long version).

TA45 0192 | Tamla 54204 (07/71) | Valerie Simpson
Back To Nowhere
Can't It Wait Until Tomorrow

TA45 0193 | Tamla 54205 (03/71) | Smokey Robinson & The Miracles
I Don't Blame You At All
That Girl

TA45 0194 | Tamla 54206 (06/71) | Smokey Robinson & The Miracles
Crazy About The La La La
Oh Baby Baby I Love You

TA45 0195 | Tamla 54207 (06/71) | Marvin Gaye
Mercy Mercy Me (The Ecology)
Sad Tomorrows
Note: "A" side issued as a special 7-inch promo single on PR-62B with same running time as commercial version (2:39). Promo issued in 1979.

TA45 0196 | Tamla 54208 (07/71) | Stevie Wonder
If You Really Love Me
Think Of Me As Your Soldier

TA45 0197 | Tamla 54209 (09/71) | Marvin Gaye
Inner City Blues (Make Me Wanna Holler)
Wholly Holy

TA45 0198 | Tamla 54210 (11/71) | Eddie Kendricks
Can I
I Did It All For You
Note: "A" side runs 3:04.

TA45 0199 | Tamla 54210 (11/71) | Eddie Kendricks
Can I (Short version)
Can I (Long version)
Note: Issued in red and blue vinyl promotional copies only with songs running 3:40 (short version)

and 6:05 (long version).

TA45 0200 | Tamla 54211 (11/71) | Smokey Robinson & The Miracles
Satisfaction
Flower Girl
Note: "A" side also issued on red vinyl.

TA45 0201 | Tamla 54212 (10/71) | Virgil Henry
I Can't Believe You're Really Leaving
You Ain't Sayin' Nothin' New
Note: Previously issued on Colossus 115 with alternate "A" side version.

TA45 0202 | Tamla 54213 (11/71) | The Marvelettes
A Breath Taking Guy
You're The One For Me Baby

TA45 0203 | Tamla 54214 (11/71) | Stevie Wonder
What Christmas Means To Me
Bedtime For Toys

TA45 0204 | Tamla 54215 (12/71) | P.J.
T.L.C. (Tender Loving Care)
It Takes A Man To Teach A Woman How To Love
Note: "B" side also issued on V.I.P. 25062. The number M-1181B is shown in the run-out groove on the "B" side.

TA45 0205 | Tamla 54216 (04/72) | Stevie Wonder
Superwoman (Where Were You When I Needed You)
I Love Every Little Thing About You

TA45 0206 | Tamla 54217 (06/72) | The Courtship
It's The Same Old Love
Last Row, First Balcony

TA45 0207 | Tamla 54218 (05/72) | Eddie Kendricks
Eddie's Love
Let Me Run Into Your Lonely Heart

TA45 0208 | Tamla 54219 (05/72) | Different Shades Of Brown
Label Me Love
Life's A Ball (While It Lasts)

TA45 0209 | Tamla 54220 (05/72) | Smokey Robinson & The Miracles
We've Come Too Far To End It Now
When Sundown Comes

TA45 0210 | Tamla 54221 (04/72) | Marvin Gaye
You're The Man (Part 1)
You're The Man (Part 2)
Note: "A" side also issued on red vinyl.

TA45 0211 | Tamla 54222 (08/72) | Eddie Kendricks
If You Let Me
Just Memories

TA45 0212	Tamla 54223 (08/72)	Stevie Wonder Keep On Running Evil
TA45 0213	Tamla 54224 (11/72)	Valerie Simpson Silly Wasn't I I Believe I'm Gonna Take This Ride
TA45 0214	Tamla 54225 (11/72)	Smokey Robinson & The Miracles I Can't Stand To See You Cry With Your Love Came
TA45 0215	Tamla 54226 (10/72)	Stevie Wonder Superstition You've Got It Bad Girl
TA45 0216	Tamla 54227	The Courtship Love Ain't Love (Till You Give It To Somebody) Oops, It Just Slipped Out Note: Unissued. Also issued on Glades 1710.
TA45 0217	Tamla 54228 (11/72)	Marvin Gaye Trouble Man Don't Mess With Mr. "T"
TA45 0218	Tamla 54229	Marvin Gaye I Want To Come Home For Christmas Christmas In The City Note: Unissued.
TA45 0219	Tamla 54230 (01/73)	Eddie Kendricks Girl You Need A Change Of Mind (Part 1) Girl You Need A Change Of Mind (Part 2)
TA45 0220	Tamla 54231	Valerie Simpson Genius II One More Baby Child Born Note: Unissued.
TA45 0221	Tamla 54232 (02/73)	Stevie Wonder You Are The Sunshine Of My Life Tuesday Heartbreak
TA45 0222	Tamla 54233 (06/73)	Smokey Robinson Sweet Harmony Want To Know My Mind
TA45 0223	Tamla 54234 (06/73)	Marvin Gaye Let's Get It On I Wish It Would Rain
TA45 0224	Tamla 54235	Third Creation Rolling Down A Mountainside It's Just A Place Note: Unissued. Issued on Motown 1250.
TA45 0225	Tamla 54235 (07/73)	Stevie Wonder Higher Ground Too High
TA45 0226	Tamla 54236 (06/73)	Eddie Kendricks Darling Come Back Home Loving You The Second Time Around Note: See also Tamla 54249.
TA45 0227	Tamla 54237 (07/73)	The Miracles Don't Let It End ('Til You Let It Begin) Wigs And Lashes Note: First single with William Griffin as lead singer.
TA45 0228	Tamla 54238 (08/73)	Eddie Kendricks Keep On Truckin' (Part 1) Keep On Truckin' (Part 2)
TA45 0229	Tamla 54239 (10/73)	Smokey Robinson Baby Come Close A Silent Partner In A Three-Way Love Affair
TA45 0230	Tamla 54240 (11/73)	The Miracles Give Me Just Another Day I Wanna Be With You Note: See also Tamla 54248.
TA45 0231	Tamla 54241 (10/73)	Marvin Gaye Come Get To This Distant Lover
TA45 0232	Tamla 54242 (10/73)	Stevie Wonder Living For The City Visions
TA45 0233	Tamla 54243 (12/73)	Eddie Kendricks Boogie Down Can't Help What I Am
TA45 0234	Tamla 54244 (01/74)	Marvin Gaye You Sure Love To Ball Just To Keep You Satisfied
TA45 0235	Tamla 54245 (03/74)	Stevie Wonder Don't You Worry 'Bout A Thing Blame It On The Sun Note: "A" side promo copies have shorter version with running time of 3:00, compared to 3:40 for commercial release.
TA45 0236	Tamla 54246 (05/74)	Smokey Robinson It's Her Turn To Live Just My Soul Responding
TA45 0237	Tamla 54247 (04/74)	Eddie Kendricks Son Of Sagittarius Trust Your Heart
TA45 0238	Tamla 54248 (06/74)	The Miracles Do It Baby I Wanna Be With You Note: "B" side previously issued on Tamla 54240.
TA45 0239	Tamla 54249 (07/74)	Eddie Kendricks Tell Her Love Has Felt The Need Loving You The Second Time Around Note: "B" side previously issued on Tamla 54236.

TA45 0240	Tamla 54250 (07/74)	Smokey Robinson Virgin Man Fulfill Your Need
TA45 0241	Tamla 54251 (11/74)	Smokey Robinson I Am I Am The Family Song
TA45 0242	Tamla 54252 (07/74)	Stevie Wonder You Haven't Done Nothin' Big Brother Note: "A" side "Doo Doo Wopsssss" by The Jackson 5.
TA45 0243	Tamla 54253 (09/74)	Marvin Gaye Distant Lover (Edited version) Trouble Man Note: Commercial copy. "A" side runs 3:18.
TA45 0244	Tamla 54253 (09/74)	Marvin Gaye Distant Lover (Live version) Distant Lover (Live version) Note: Promo copy. "A" side master number 62919-M-REI (mono). "B" side master number 62919-S (stereo). Both sides run 3:28.
TA45 0245	Tamla 54253 (09/74)	Marvin Gaye Distant Lover (Edited version) Distant Lover (Edited version) Note: Promo copy. Master number 62919-3C-1-M same on both sides. Running time is 3:18 both sides.
TA45 0246	Tamla 54254 (10/74)	Stevie Wonder Boogie On Reggae Woman Seems So Long
TA45 0247	Tamla 54255 (11/74)	Eddie Kendricks One Tear The Thin Man
TA45 0248	Tamla 54256 (11/74)	The Miracles Don't Cha Love It Up Again
TA45 0249	Tamla 54257 (01/75)	Eddie Kendricks Shoeshine Boy Hooked On Your Love
TA45 0250	Tamla 54258 (02/75)	Smokey Robinson Baby That's Backatcha Just Passing Through Note: See also Tamla 54276.
TA45 0251	Tamla 54259 (04/75)	The Miracles Gemini You Are Love
TA45 0252	Tamla 54260 (06/75)	Eddie Kendricks Get The Cream Off The Top Honey Brown
TA45 0253	Tamla 54261 (08/75)	Smokey Robinson The Agony And The Ecstasy Wedding Song
TA45 0254	Tamla 54262 (10/75)	The Miracles Love Machine (Pt. 1) Love Machine (Pt. 2) Note: Issued on a promotional basis on PR-9 as an extended version 12-inch single with running time of 6:54 both sides.
TA45 0255	Tamla 54263 (09/75)	Eddie Kendricks Happy Deep And Quiet Love
TA45 0256	Tamla 54264 (04/76)	Marvin Gaye I Want You (Long version) I Want You (Instrumental) Note: Long version (vocal) runs 3:53. "A" side also issued on yellow vinyl. Also issued promotionally on PR-16 as a 12-inch extended version with running time 4:33 (vocal) and 4:36 (instrumental).
TA45 0257	Tamla 54264 (04/76)	Marvin Gaye I Want You (Short Version) (Mono) I Want You (Short Version) (Stereo) Note: Issued as promo copies only with running time of 3:15 both sides. Has shorter intro.
TA45 0258	Tamla 54265 (12/75)	Smokey Robinson Quiet Storm Asleep On My Love
TA45 0259	Tamla 54266 (01/76)	Eddie Kendricks He's A Friend All Of My Love Note: Some promos issued on red vinyl.
TA45 0260	Tamla 54267 (04/76)	Smokey Robinson Open Coincidentally Note: See also Tamla 54269.
TA45 0261	Tamla 54268 (05/76)	The Miracles Night Life Smog Note: "B" side on some copies lists artists as "The Miracle Workers."
TA45 0262	Tamla 54269 (05/76)	Smokey Robinson When You Came Coincidentally Note: Issued in Canada only. "B" side previously issued on Tamla 54267, but with shorter running time of 4:22 compared to 4:27 for above version. Also issued promotionally with same number (54269) as an extended version with running time of 5:24.
TA45 0263	Tamla 54270 (06/76)	Eddie Kendricks Get It While It's Hot Never Gonna Leave You

TA45 0264	Tamla 54271 (09/76)	Tata Vega Full Speed Ahead Just As Long As There Is You Note: "A" side issued promotionally as an extended version on PR-21 with running time of 5:04 both sides. Also issued on PR-23B with running time of 5:04.

TA45 0265	Tamla 54272	The Miracles Take It All Note: Unissued. Issued only as a single-sided test pressing; not issued commercially.

TA45 0266	Tamla 54273 (07/76)	Marvin Gaye After The Dance Feel All My Love Inside

TA45 0267	Tamla 54274 (11/76)	Stevie Wonder I Wish You And I

TA45 0268	Tamla 54275 (10/76)	Thelma Houston One Out Of Every Six Pick Of The Week Note: "B" side previously issued on Motown 1316A. Also issued on Mowest 5008.

TA45
0269
	Tamla
	54275
	(10/76)
		Thelma Houston
		One Out Of Every Six (Censored
		Version)
		One Out Of Every Six
		    (Uncensored Version)
		    Note: Issued in promo copies
		only.

TA45 0270	Tamla 54276 (10/76)	Smokey Robinson An Old-Fashioned Man Just Passing Through Note: "B" side previously issued on Tamla 54258B.

TA45 0271	Tamla 54277 (11/76)	Eddie Kendricks Goin' Up In Smoke Thanks For The Memories Note: "A" side issued promotionally on PR-24 as an extended version with running time of 4:30 both sides. Also issued commercially on M-0003D1A as a 12-inch with a running time of 4:30.

TA45
0272
	Tamla
	54278
	(12/76)
		Thelma Houston
		Don't Leave Me This Way
		Today Will Soon Be
		    Yesterday
		    Note: "A" side issued
		commercially on M-00002D1A as
		a 12-inch extended version single
		with running time of 5:40.

TA45
0273
	Tamla
	54278
	(12/76)
		Thelma Houston
		Don't Leave Me This Way (Short
		Version)
		Don't Leave Me This Way
		    (Long Version)
		    Note: Promo issue only. "A"

side has running time of 3:35. "B"
side runs 5:40.

TA45 0274	Tamla 54279 (01/77)	Smokey Robinson There Will Come A Day (I'm Gonna Happen To You) The Humming Song (Lost For Words)

TA45 0275	Tamla 54280 (03/77)	Marvin Gaye Got To Give It Up (Pt. I) Got To Give It Up (Pt. II) Note: Issued with full-color picture sleeve. Also issued promotionally on PR-27 as an extended version with a running time of 11:48 both sides.

TA45 0276	Tamla 54281 (03/77)	Stevie Wonder Sir Duke He's Misstra Know-It-All Note: Issued with black and white picture sleeve.

TA45 0277	Tamla 54282 (04/77)	Tata Vega You'll Never Rock Alone Just When Things Are Getting Good

TA45 0278	Tamla 54283 (04/77)	Thelma Houston If It's The Last Thing I Do If You Won't Let Me Walk On The Water Note: "A" side previously issued on Mowest 5046A.

TA45 0279	Tamla 54284 (06/77)	Smokey Robinson Vitamin U Holly Note: "A" side issued commercially on M-00004D1A as a 12-inch extended version with running time of 4:32.

TA45 0280	Tamla 54285 (07/77)	Eddie Kendricks Born Again Date With The Rain Note: "A" side issued commercially on M-00006D1B as a 12-inch extended version with running time of 4:43. The number T-54284 appears in run-out on both sides of record.

TA45 0281	Tamla 54286 (08/77)	Stevie Wonder Another Star Creepin'

TA45
0282
	Tamla
	54287
	(09/77)
		Thelma Houston
		I'm Here Again
		Sharing Something Perfect
		    Between Ourselves
		    Note: "A" side issued
		promotionally on PR-33 as a
		12-inch extended version with
		running time of 6:31. Also issued
		commercially on M-31000D1 with
		running time of 6:32.

TA45   Tamla   Smokey Robinson
0283   54288   Theme From Big Time Pt. 1
        (09/77)   Theme From Big Time Pt. 2
                        Note: Issued promotionally on
                    PR-29 as a 12-inch extended
                    version with running time of 8:29.
                    Also issued commercially on
                    M-20000D1 with running time of
                    8:29.

TA45   Tamla   Tata Vega
0284   54289   Come In Heaven....Earth Is Calling
                        (Part 1)
                    Come In Heaven....Earth Is
                        Calling (Part 2)
                        Note: Unissued, except as
                    single-sided test pressing.

TA45   Tamla   Eddie Kendricks
0285   54290   Baby
        (12/77)   Intimate Friends

TA45   Tamla   Stevie Wonder
0286   54291   As
        (10/77)   Contusion

TA45   Tamla   Thelma Houston
0287   54292   I Can't Go On Living Without
        (02/78)   Your Love
                    Any Way You Like It
                        Note: "A" side issued
                    commercially on M-00010D1A as
                    a 12-inch extended version with
                    running time of 4:32.

TA45   Tamla   Smokey Robinson
0288   54293   Why You Wanna See My Bad Side
        (03/78)   Daylight & Darkness

TA45   Tamla   Kenny Lupper
0289   54294   Passion Flower
        (03/78)   Kiss Me Now
                        Note: "A" side background
                    vocals by High Inergy.

TA45   Tamla   Thelma Houston
0290   54295   I'm Not Strong Enough To Love
        (09/78)   You Again
                    Triflin'

TA45   Tamla   Smokey Robinson
0291   54296   Shoe Soul
        (10/78)   I'm Loving You Softly

TA45   Tamla   Thelma Houston
0292   54297   Saturday Night, Sunday Morning
        (12/78)   Come To Me
                        Note: "A" side issued
                    commercially on M-00013D1 as a
                    12-inch extended version with
                    running time of 6:19 (vocal) and
                    5:38 (instrumental). Also issued
                    promotionally on PR-45B with
                    running time of 6:22.

TA45   Tamla   Marvin Gaye
0293   54298   A Funky Space Reincarnation
        (12/78)   (Part I)
                    A Funky Space Reincarnation
                        (Part II)
                        Note: Issued commercially on

M-00014D1 as a 12-inch extended
version with running time of 8:15
(vocal) and 8:19 (instrumental).
Also issued promotionally on
PR-46 with running time of 8:15
both sides.

TA45   Tamla   Tata Vega
0294   54299   I Just Keep Thinking About You
        (05/79)   Baby
                    Music In My Heart
                        Note: "A" side issued
                    commercially on M-00021D1A as
                    a 12-inch extended version with
                    running time of 6:01.

TA45   Tamla   Marvin Gaye
0295   54300   Anger
        (06/79)   Time To Get It Together
                        Note: Issued In Canada only.

TA45   Tamla   Smokey Robinson
0296   54301   Get Ready
        (06/79)   Ever Had A Dream
                        Note: "A" side issued
                    commercially on M-00027D1 as a
                    12-inch extended version with
                    running time of 5:43 (vocal) and
                    5:54 (instrumental). See also
                    Tamla 54306.

TA45   Tamla   Shadee
0297   54302   I Just Need More Money (Pt. I)
        (07/79)   I Just Need More Money (Pt.
                        II)

TA45   Tamla   Stevie Wonder
0298   54303   Send One Your Love
        (10/79)   Send One Your Love
                        (Instrumental)
                        Note: Issued with full-color
                    picture sleeve.

TA45   Tamla   Tata Vega
0299   54304   I Need You Now
        (07/79)   In The Morning

TA45   Tamla   Marvin Gaye
0300   54305   Ego Tripping Out
        (09/79)   Ego Tripping Out
                        (Instrumental)

TA45   Tamla   Smokey Robinson
0301   54306   Cruisin'
        (08/79)   Ever Had A Dream
                        Note: "A" side issued
                    promotionally on PR-52A2 as a
                    12-inch extended version with
                    running time of 5:52. "B" side
                    issued previously on Tamla 54301B.

TA45   Tamla   Keith & Darrell
0302   54307   Feel The Fever
        (10/79)   The Things You're Made Of
                        Note: "B" side later reissued
                    in the TMG Consolidated Series on
                    Tamla 1712TFB.

TA45 0303	Tamla 54308 (02/80)	Stevie Wonder Outside My Window Same Old Story Note: Issued with picture sleeve. Also issued on PR-61B2 as a 12-inch promotional version with running time of 5:29.
TA45 0304	Tamla 54309 (02/80)	Keith & Darrell Kickin' It Around I Met This Girl
TA45 0305	Tamla 54310 (02/80)	Quiet Storm Only You (Part I) Only You (Part II) Note: Issued on PR-65 as a promotional 12-inch version with running time of 7:30 (long version) and 3:38 (Part 1).
TA45 0306	Tamla 54311 (03/80)	Smokey Robinson Let Me Be The Clock Travelin' Through
TA45 0307	Tamla 54312 (06/80)	Billy Preston & Syreeta One More Time For Love Dance For Me Children Note: "B" side as by Syreeta.
TA45 0308	Tamla 54313 (06/80)	Smokey Robinson Heavy On Pride (Light On Love) I Love The Nearness Of You
TA45 0309	Tamla 54314 (08/80)	Quiet Storm Heartbreak Graffitti (Part 1) Heartbreak Graffitti (Part II)
TA45 0310	Tamla 54315 (09/80)	Legend Shake It Lady Lay Your Body Down Note: "A" side issued promotionally as part of PR-75 with running time of 3:09. (Same running time as 7-inch version.)
TA45 0311	Tamla 54316 (09/80)	Tata Vega You Keep Me Hangin' On You Better Watch Out Note: Second pressing has titles reversed.
TA45 0312	Tamla 54317 (09/80)	Stevie Wonder Master Blaster (Jammin') Master Blaster (Dub) Note: Issued on PR-76 as a 12-inch promotional extended version with running time of 6:11 ("Jammin'") and 6:27 ("B" side "Dub"). Issued with picture sleeve.
TA45 0313	Tamla 54318 (09/80)	Smokey Robinson Wine, Women And Song I Want To Be Your Love Note: "A" side features Claudette Robinson.
TA45 0314	Tamla 54319 (09/80)	Billy Preston & Syreeta Please Stay Signed, Sealed, Delivered (I'm Yours)
TA45 0315	Tamla 54320 (12/80)	Stevie Wonder I Ain't Gonna Stand For It Knocks Me Off My Feet Note: "A" side issued promotionally as part of PR-77 with same running time as above version (4:39).
TA45 0316	Tamla 54321 (01/81)	Smokey Robinson Being With You What's In Your Life For Me
TA45 0317	Tamla 54322 (02/81)	Marvin Gaye Praise Funk Me
TA45 0318	Tamla 54323 (03/81)	Stevie Wonder Lately If It's Magic
TA45 0319	Tamla 54324	Gary Byrd The Crown (Vocal) The Crown (Instrumental) Note: Unissued. Issued as a 12-inch promotional record (PR-128) featuring a long version (8:43), an edited version (6:49), and an instrumental version (10:49). Issued as a 12-inch commericial release, the first on Stevie Wonder's own label (Wondirection 4507WG), featuring a long version (10:35) and an instrumental (10:40) with a full-color picture sleeve. Also issued in Canada on Wondirection 1000X in stereo and mono versions (both 4:50). Artist given on commercial releases as "Gary Byrd & the G.B. Experience."
TA45 0320	Tamla 54325 (05/81)	Smokey Robinson Aqui Con Tigo Being With You + Aqui Con Tigo Note: "A" side sung in Spanish. "B" side sung half in English, half in Spanish. It is believed that this single was also recorded with a French version, but never released.
TA45 0321	Tamla 54326 (04/81)	Marvin Gaye Heavy Love Affair Far Cry
TA45 0322	Tamla 54327 (05/81)	Smokey Robinson You Are Forever I Hear The Children Singing
TA45 0323	Tamla 54327	Smokey Robinson If You Wanna Make Love (Come 'Round Here) I Hear The Children Singing Note: Unissued.
TA45 0324	Tamla 54328 (07/81)	Stevie Wonder Did I Hear You Say You Love Me As If You Read My Mind Note: "A" side issued promotionally on PR-77A2 as

shorter version with running time of 4:07.

TA45 0325	Tamla 54329 (07/81)	Keith & Darrell You're My Gardener Don't Be Afraid
TA45 0326	Tamla 54330 (07/81)	Quiet Storm When You Came I Let You Go
TA45 0327	Tamla 54331	Stevie Wonder Happy Birthday (Vocal) Happy Birthday (Instrumental)

Note: Unissued. Issued commercially on Motown 4517MGA as a 12-inch extended version with running time of 5:57.

TA45 0328	Tamla 54332 (08/81)	Smokey Robinson Who's Sad Food For Thought
TA45 0329	Tamla 54333 (12/81)	Syreeta Quick Slick I Don't Know

Note: "A" side issued promotionally on PR-90 as slightly shorter version with running time of 3:56.

NUMBER SEQUENCE CHANGE

Note: At this point, separate numbering for Tamla, Motown, and Gordy labels was discontinued and, starting in January 1982, was consolidated into a single sequence beginning at number 1600. This new consecutive numbering system was used for all subsequent singles releases, with individual labels retaining their own distinctive designs. Please see "TMG Consolidated Series" for continuation.

TAMLA 7-INCH SPECIAL ISSUES

TA45S 0001	Tamla 5501F2/5501F1 (05/59)	Nick And The Jaguars Ich-I-Bon #1 Cool And Crazy

Note: A commercial release, but nothing is known as to why this unusual numbering was used.

TA45S 0002	Tamla (1961)	Marvin Gaye Masquerade (Is Over) Witchcraft

Note: Unnumbered. Issued to promote the album THE SOULFUL MOODS OF MARVIN GAYE (TM-221). Issued with "Stripes" label. Name on label given as "Marvin Gay."

TA45S 0003	Tamla EX-009 (11/63)	The Miracles The Christmas Song Christmas Everyday

Note: Issued only on a promotional basis to promote the newest Miracles album, CHRISTMAS WITH THE MIRACLES (Tamla TM-236).

TA45S 0004	Tamla (1966)	Marvin Gaye The Teen Beat Song Loraine Alterman Interviews Marvin Gaye For Teen Beat Readers

Note: Unnumbered. Issued on a promotional basis only for readers of "Teen Beat" magazine. On the "Detroit Free Press" (the action paper) label.

TA45S 0005	Tamla SL4M-3114 (02/66)	The Supremes Things Are Changing

Note: Issued by permission of Motown for "Equal Employment Opportunities Campaign" conducted for Plans For Progress in order to encourage younger blacks in the Detroit area to go out and look for jobs. Issued in a printed cover with "Things Are Changing" in large letters on front of cover.

TA45S 0006	Tamla 211L-206312 (08/66)	Brenda Holloway Play It Cool Stay In School

Note: DJ copy "Special Projects" release "In cooperation with the women's ad club of Detroit."

TA45S 0007	Tamla 2482 (11/66)	Various Artists "Seasons Greetings From Motown"

Note: Side 1. Spoken message from: 1. Martha & The Vandellas. 1A. Martha & The Vandellas. 2. The Temptations. 2A. The Temptations. 3. The Miracles. 3A. The Miracles. 4. Shorty Long. 5. The Velvelettes. 5A. The Velvelettes. See Tamla 2483 for Side 2. Issued only for the Motown fan club in the U.S.

TA45S 0008	Tamla 2483 (11/66)	Various Artists "Seasons Greetings From Motown"

Note: Side 2. Spoken message from: 1. The Spinners. 1A. The Spinners. 2. Four Tops. 2A. Four Tops. 3. The Elgins. 3A. The Elgins. 4. The Supremes. 4A. The Supremes. See Tamla 2482 for Side 1. Issued only for the Motown fan club in the U.S.

TA45S 0009	Tamla 13090 (1967)	Smokey Robinson & The Miracles I Care About Detroit

Note: This is a one-sided disc, issued promotionaly in the summer of 1967 during Detroit's race riots. The main purpose of this single was to try and calm things down at a difficult time for blacks in the city. Issued in two ways. Issue 1 has a yellow label with the notation "Standard Groove" on it, released by permission and with cooperation of Motown. Issue 2 released on the Tamla "Globes" label, but with the same numbering as 1.

| TA45S 0010 | Tamla 54022 | The Miracles
After All
Embraceable You
Note: Unissued. Issued as a bootleg only. The single was released on ten different colors of wax as follows: 1. Clear 2. Pinto 3. Yellow 4. Red 5. Green 6. Blue 7. Black 8. White 9. Black and White Marble Swirl 10. Multi color Swirl. This single not issued by Motown at all. There have been other bootleg releases, but this one is the most significant due to the many colored wax versions. |

TAMLA 7-INCH
COLOR VINYL SINGLES

TACO 0001	Tamla 54053 (12/61)	The Miracles What's So Good About Good-by Note: Red vinyl.
TACO 0002	Tamla 54139 (10/66)	Stevie Wonder A Place In The Sun Note: Red vinyl.
TACO 0003	Tamla 54155 (08/67)	Brenda Holloway You've Made Me So Very Happy Note: Red vinyl.
TACO 0004	Tamla 54180 (01/69)	Stevie Wonder My Cherie Amour Note: Red vinyl.
TACO 0005	Tamla 54183 (05/69)	Smokey Robinson & The Miracles Here I Go Again Note: Red vinyl.
TACO 0006	Tamla 54184 (06/69)	Smokey Robinson & The Miracles Abraham, Martin, And John Note: Red vinyl.
TACO 0007	Tamla 54186 (10/69)	The Marvelettes That's How Heartaches Are Made Note: Red vinyl.
TACO 0008	Tamla 54189 (11/69)	Smokey Robinson & The Miracles Point It Out Note: Red vinyl.
TACO 0009	Tamla 54190 (12/69)	Marvin Gaye Gonna Give Her All The Love I've Got Note: Red vinyl.

TACO 0010	Tamla 54192 (03/70)	Marvin Gaye & Tammi Terrell The Onion Song Note: Red vinyl.
TACO 0011	Tamla 54196 (06/70)	Stevie Wonder Signed, Sealed, Delivered I'm Yours Note: Red vinyl.
TACO 0012	Tamla 54202 (02/71)	Stevie Wonder We Can Work It Out Note: Red vinyl.
TACO 0013	Tamla 54203 (04/71)	Eddie Kendricks It's So Hard For Me To Say Good-bye Note: Red vinyl.
TACO 0014	Tamla 54210	Eddie Kendricks Can I Note: Blue vinyl.
TACO 0015	Tamla 54211 (11/71)	Smokey Robinson & The Miracles Satisfaction Note: Red vinyl.
TACO 0016	Tamla 54221 (04/72)	Marvin Gaye You're The Man Note: Red vinyl.
TACO 0017	Tamla 54264 (04/76)	Marvin Gaye I Want You Note: Yellow vinyl.
TACO 0018	Tamla 54266 (01/76)	Eddie Kendricks He's A Friend Note: Red vinyl.

TAMLA 7-INCH EPS

TAEP 0001	Tamla TM-60252 (1965)	Marvin Gaye GREATEST HITS Side 1: Can I Get A Witness/You're A Wonderful One/Stubborn Kind Of Fellow - Side 2: I'm Crazy 'Bout My Baby/Pride & Joy/Hitch Hike
TAEP 0002	Tamla TM-60253 (1967)	The Marvelettes MARVELETTES GREATEST HITS Side 1: Don't Mess With Bill/Locking Up My Heart/Too Many Fish In The Sea - Side 2: Please Mr. Postman/Forever/Beechwood 4-5789
TAEP 0003	Tamla TM-60254 (1967)	The Miracles GREATEST HITS FROM THE BEGINNING Side 1: Mickey's Monkey/You've Really Got A Hold On Me/I Like It Like That - Side 2: Shop Around/I've Been Good To You/What's So Good About Good Bye

TAEP 0004	Tamla TM-60266 (1966)	Marvin Gaye MOODS OF MARVIN GAYE Side 1: I'll Be Doggone/Little Darling (I Need You)/Take This Heart Of Mine - Side 2: Hey Diddle Diddle/One More Heartache/Ain't That Peculiar
TAEP 0005	Tamla TM-60267 (1966)	Smokey Robinson & The Miracles GOING TO A GO-GO Side 1: The Tracks Of My Tears/Going To A Go-Go/Ooo Baby Baby -Side 2: My Girl Has Gone/Choosey Beggar/In Case You Need Love
TAEP 0006	Tamla TM-60272 (1967)	Stevie Wonder DOWN TO EARTH Side 1: A Place In The Sun/Down To Earth/Thank You Love - Side 2: Sylvia/My World Is Empty Without You/Hey Love
TAEP 0007	Tamla TM-60274 (1967)	The Marvelettes THE MARVELETTES Side 1: The Hunter Gets Captured By The Game/When You're Young And In Love/I Know Better - Side 2: He Was Really Sayin' Somethin'/The Day You Take One (You Have To Take The Other)/Keep Off, No Trespassing Note: The title of "Keep Off, No Trespassing," is listed erroneously on both the cover as well as the label. The song on the record is actually "When I Need You."

TAMLA ALBUMS

TALP 0001	Tamla TM-220 (06/61)	The Miracles HI, WE'RE THE MIRACLES
TALP 0002	Tamla TM-221 (06/61)	Marvin Gaye THE SOULFUL MOODS OF MARVIN GAYE
TALP 0003	Tamla TM-222 (11/61)	Gospel Stars THE GREAT GOSPEL STARS
TALP 0004	Tamla TM-223 (02/62)	The Miracles COOKIN' WITH THE MIRACLES
TALP 0005	Tamla TM-224 (1961)	Various Artists TAMLA SPECIAL #1
TALP 0006	Tamla TM-225	The Downbeats INTRODUCING THE DOWNBEATS Note: Unissued

TALP 0007	Tamla TM-226	Barrett Strong MONEY AND OTHER BIG HITS Note: Unissued.
TALP 0008	Tamla TM-227 (12/62)	Rev. Columbus Mann THEY SHALL BE MINE
TALP 0009	Tamla TM-228 (11/61)	The Marvelettes PLEASE MR. POSTMAN
TALP 0010	Tamla TM-229 (04/62)	The Marvelettes THE MARVELETTES SING
TALP 0011	Tamla TM-230 (09/62)	The Miracles I'LL TRY SOMETHING NEW
TALP 0012	Tamla TM-231 (09/62)	The Marvelettes PLAYBOY
TALP 0013	Tamla TM-232 (07/63)	Little Stevie Wonder TRIBUTE TO UNCLE RAY
TALP 0014	Tamla TM-233 (07/63)	Little Stevie Wonder THE JAZZ SOUL OF LITTLE STEVIE
TALP 0015	Tamla TM-234	The Miracles THE MIRACLES SING MODERN Note: Unissued.
TALP 0016	Tamla TM-235	Note: Unissued.
TALP 0017	Tamla TM-236 (11/63)	The Miracles CHRISTMAS WITH THE MIRACLES
TALP 0018	Tamla TM-237 (05/63)	The Marvelettes MARVELOUS MARVELETTES
TALP 0019	Tamla TM-238 (05/63)	The Miracles THE FABULOUS MIRACLES Note: Two issues of this album. The first was titled THE FABULOUS MIRACLES. When "You've Really Got A Hold On Me" charted, the album was reissued as YOU'VE REALLY GOT A HOLD ON ME, as by the Fabulous Miracles.
TALP 0020	Tamla TM-239 (01/63)	Marvin Gaye THAT STUBBORN KINDA' FELLOW
TALP 0021	Tamla TM-240 (05/63)	Little Stevie Wonder 12 YEAR OLD GENIUS (RECORDED LIVE)
TALP 0022	Tamla TM-241 (05/63)	The Miracles RECORDED LIVE: ON STAGE

TALP 0023	Tamla TM-242 (08/63)	Marvin Gaye RECORDED LIVE: ON STAGE
TALP 0024	Tamla TM-243 (07/63)	The Marvelettes RECORDED LIVE: ON STAGE
TALP 0025	Tamla TM-244	Various Artists RECORDED LIVE AT THE REGAL Note: Unissued.
TALP 0026	Tamla TM-245 (11/63)	The Miracles THE MIRACLES DOIN' MICKEY'S MONKEY
TALP 0027	Tamla TM-246	Note: Unissued.
TALP 0028	Tamla TM-247	Note: Unissued.
TALP 0029	Tamla TM-248	Little Stevie Wonder WORKOUT STEVIE WORKOUT Note: Unissued.
TALP 0030	Tamla TM-249	Note: Unissued.
TALP 0031	Tamla TM-250 (12/63)	Little Stevie Wonder WITH A SONG IN MY HEART
TALP 0032	Tamla TM-251 (04/64)	Marvin Gaye WHEN I'M ALONE I CRY
TALP 0033	Tamla TS-252 (04/64)	Marvin Gaye MARVIN GAYE'S GREATEST HITS
TALP 0034	Tamla TS-253 (02/66)	The Marvelettes MARVELETTES GREATEST HITS
TALP 0035	Tamla TS2-254 (03/65)	The Miracles GREATEST HITS FROM THE BEGINNING Note: Two-album set.
TALP 0036	Tamla TM-255 (07/64)	Stevie Wonder STEVIE AT THE BEACH
TALP 0037	Tamla TS-256 (07/64)	Various Artists A COLLECTION OF 16 ORIGINAL BIG HITS VOL. 2
TALP 0038	Tamla TM-257 (07/64)	Brenda Holloway EVERY LITTLE BIT HURTS
TALP 0039	Tamla TM-258 (01/65)	Marvin Gaye HOW SWEET IT IS TO BE LOVED BY YOU
TALP 0040	Tamla TS-259 (11/64)	Marvin Gaye HELLO BROADWAY

TALP 0041	Tamla 260	Marvin Gaye & Kim Weston MARVIN GAYE & KIM WESTON SIDE BY SIDE Note: Unissued.
TALP 0042	Tamla TS-261 (11/65)	Marvin Gaye A TRIBUTE TO THE GREAT NAT KING COLE
TALP 0043	Tamla 262	Note: Unissued.
TALP 0044	Tamla 263	Note: Unissued.
TALP 0045	Tamla TM-264 (11/65)	Various Artists MOTORTOWN REVUE IN PARIS Note: Recorded live.
TALP 0046	Tamla TS-265 (11/65)	Willie Tyler & Lester HELLO DUMMY
TALP 0047	Tamla TS-266 (05/66)	Marvin Gaye MOODS OF MARVIN GAYE
TALP 0048	Tamla TS-267 (11/65)	Smokey Robinson & The Miracles GOING TO A GO-GO
TALP 0049	Tamla TS-268 (05/66)	Stevie Wonder UP TIGHT Note: Album cover gives title as UP-TIGHT.
TALP 0050	Tamla TS-269 (06/66)	Isley Brothers THIS OLD HEART OF MINE (IS WEAK FOR YOU)
TALP 0051	Tamla TS-270 (08/66)	Marvin Gaye & Kim Weston TAKE TWO
TALP 0052	Tamla TS-271 (11/66)	Smokey Robinson & The Miracles AWAY WE A GO-GO
TALP 0053	Tamla TS-272 (11/66)	Stevie Wonder DOWN TO EARTH
TALP 0054	Tamla 273	Brenda Holloway BRENDA HOLLOWAY Note: Unissued.
TALP 0055	Tamla TS-274 (03/67)	The Marvelettes THE MARVELETTES
TALP 0056	Tamla TS-275 (09/67)	Isley Brothers SOUL ON THE ROCKS
TALP 0057	Tamla TS-276 (09/67)	Smokey Robinson & The Miracles SMOKEY ROBINSON AND THE MIRACLES MAKE IT HAPPEN Note: When "The Tears Of A

Clown" charted, the album was reissued with new title, THE TEARS OF A CLOWN.

TALP 0058	Tamla TS-277 (08/67)	Marvin Gaye & Tammi Terrell UNITED
TALP 0059	Tamla TS-278 (08/67)	Marvin Gaye MARVIN GAYE'S GREATEST HITS VOL. 2
TALP 0060	Tamla TS-279 (09/67)	Stevie Wonder I WAS MADE TO LOVE HER
TALP 0061	Tamla TS-280 (02/68)	Smokey Robinson & The Miracles SMOKEY ROBINSON AND THE MIRACLES GREATEST HITS VOL. 2
TALP 0062	Tamla TS-281 (12/67)	Stevie Wonder SOMEDAY AT CHRISTMAS Note: See also Tamla T7-362R1.
TALP 0063	Tamla TS-282 (03/68)	Stevie Wonder STEVIE WONDER'S GREATEST HITS
TALP 0064	Tamla TS-283	Bob and Marcia YOUNG, GIFTED AND BLACK Note: Unissued.
TALP 0065	Tamla TS-284 (08/68)	Marvin Gaye & Tammi Terrell YOU'RE ALL I NEED
TALP 0066	Tamla TS-285 (08/68)	Marvin Gaye IN THE GROOVE Note: Second and later pressings retitled I HEARD IT THROUGH THE GRAPEVINE.
TALP 0067	Tamla TS-286 (08/68)	The Marvelettes SOPHISTICATED SOUL
TALP 0068	Tamla TS-287 (04/69)	Isley Brothers DOIN' THEIR THING
TALP 0069	Tamla TS-288 (10/69)	The Marvelettes IN FULL BLOOM
TALP 0070	Tamla TS-289 (01/69)	Smokey Robinson & The Miracles LIVE
TALP 0071	Tamla TS-290 (09/68)	Smokey Robinson & The Miracles SPECIAL OCCASION
TALP 0072	Tamla TS-291 (12/68)	Stevie Wonder FOR ONCE IN MY LIFE
TALP 0073	Tamla TS-292 (04/69)	Marvin Gaye M.P.G.
TALP 0074	Tamla TS-293 (05/69)	Marvin Gaye MARVIN GAYE AND HIS GIRLS Note: Includes duets with Mary Wells, Kim Weston, and Tammi Terrell.
TALP 0075	Tamla TS-294 (09/69)	Marvin Gaye & Tammi Terrell EASY
TALP 0076	Tamla TS-295 (07/69)	Smokey Robinson & The Miracles TIME OUT FOR SMOKEY ROBINSON AND THE MIRACLES
TALP 0077	Tamla TS-296 (09/69)	Stevie Wonder MY CHERIE AMOUR
TALP 0078	Tamla TS-297 (11/69)	Smokey Robinson & The Miracles FOUR IN BLUE
TALP 0079	Tamla TS-298 (03/70)	Stevie Wonder LIVE
TALP 0080	Tamla TS-299 (01/70)	Marvin Gaye THAT'S THE WAY LOVE IS
TALP 0081	Tamla TS-300 (09/70)	Marvin Gaye SUPER HITS
TALP 0082	Tamla TS-301 (04/70)	Smokey Robinson & The Miracles WHAT LOVE HAS JOINED TOGETHER
TALP 0083	Tamla TS-302 (05/70)	Marvin Gaye & Tammi Terrell GREATEST HITS
TALP 0084	Tamla TS-303 (07/70)	Kiki Dee GREAT EXPECTATIONS
TALP 0085	Tamla TS-304 (08/70)	Stevie Wonder SIGNED, SEALED & DELIVERED
TALP 0086	Tamla TS-305 (10/70)	The Marvelettes THE RETURN OF THE MARVELETTES
TALP 0087	Tamla TS-306 (09/70)	Smokey Robinson & The Miracles A POCKET FULL OF MIRACLES
TALP 0088	Tamla TS-307 (11/70)	Smokey Robinson & The Miracles THE SEASON FOR MIRACLES

TALP 0089	Tamla TS-308 (04/71)	Stevie Wonder WHERE I'M COMING FROM
TALP 0090	Tamla TS-309 (04/71)	Eddie Kendricks ALL BY MYSELF
TALP 0091	Tamla TS-310 (05/71)	Marvin Gaye WHAT'S GOING ON
TALP 0092	Tamla TS-311 (05/71)	Valerie Simpson EXPOSED
TALP 0093	Tamla T-312L (08/71)	Smokey Robinson & The Miracles ONE DOZEN ROSES
TALP 0094	Tamla T-313L (11/71)	Stevie Wonder GREATEST HITS VOL. 2
TALP 0095	Tamla T-314L (02/72)	Stevie Wonder MUSIC OF MY MIND
TALP 0096	Tamla T-315L (05/72)	Eddie Kendricks PEOPLE...HOLD ON
TALP 0097	Tamla 316	Marvin Gaye YOU'RE THE MAN Note: Unissued.
TALP 0098	Tamla T-317L (07/72)	Valerie Simpson VALERIE SIMPSON
TALP 0099	Tamla T-318L (07/72)	Smokey Robinson & The Miracles FLYING HIGH TOGETHER
TALP 0100	Tamla T-319L (11/72)	Stevie Wonder TALKING BOOK
TALP 0101	Tamla T-320D (12/72)	Smokey Robinson & The Miracles 1957-1972 Note: Two-album set.
TALP 0102	Tamla 321	Smokey Robinson & The Miracles 1957-1972 Note: Number assigned to 8-track and cassette versions of Tamla 320.
TALP 0103	Tamla T-322L (12/72)	Marvin Gaye TROUBLE MAN (SOUNDTRACK)
TALP 0104	Tamla T-323	Marvin Gaye [ALBUM TITLE NOT DETERMINED] Note: Unissued. Christmas album.
TALP 0105	Tamla 324	Note: Unissued.
TALP 0106	Tamla T-325L (04/73)	The Miracles RENAISSANCE Note: First album with William Griffin replacing Smokey Robinson.
TALP 0107	Tamla T-326L (07/73)	Stevie Wonder INNERVISIONS
TALP 0108	Tamla T-327L (05/73)	Eddie Kendricks EDDIE KENDRICKS
TALP 0109	Tamla T-328L (06/73)	Smokey Robinson SMOKEY
TALP 0110	Tamla T-329V1 (08/73)	Marvin Gaye LET'S GET IT ON
TALP 0111	Tamla T-330V1 (02/74)	Eddie Kendricks BOOGIE DOWN!
TALP 0112	Tamla T6-331S1 (03/74)	Smokey Robinson PURE SMOKEY
TALP 0113	Tamla T6-332S1 (07/74)	Stevie Wonder FULFILLINGNESS' FIRST FINALE
TALP 0114	Tamla T6-333S1 (06/74)	Marvin Gaye LIVE
TALP 0115	Tamla T6-334S1 (08/74)	The Miracles DO IT BABY
TALP 0116	Tamla T6-335S1 (12/74)	Eddie Kendricks FOR YOU
TALP 0117	Tamla T6-336S1 (01/75)	The Miracles DON'TCHA LOVE IT
TALP 0118	Tamla T6-337S1 (03/75)	Smokey Robinson A QUIET STORM
TALP 0119	Tamla T6-338S1 (06/75)	Eddie Kendricks THE HIT MAN
TALP 0120	Tamla T6-339S1 (10/75)	The Miracles CITY OF ANGELS
TALP 0121	Tamla T13-340C2 (09/76)	Stevie Wonder SONGS IN THE KEY OF LIFE Note: Includes 7-inch EP (T340EP): Side 1. Saturn 4:54, Ebony Eyes 4:10. Side 2. All Day Sucker 5:06, Easy Goin' Evening

(My Mama's Call) 3:58.

TALP	Tamla		
TALP 0122	Tamla T6-341S1 (02/76)	Smokey Robinson SMOKEY'S FAMILY ROBINSON	
TALP 0123	Tamla T6-342S1 (03/76)	Marvin Gaye I WANT YOU	
TALP 0124	Tamla T6-343S1 (02/76)	Eddie Kendricks HE'S A FRIEND	
TALP 0125	Tamla T6-344S1 (09/76)	The Miracles THE POWER OF MUSIC	
TALP 0126	Tamla T6-345S1 (11/76)	Thelma Houston ANY WAY YOU LIKE IT	
TALP 0127	Tamla T6-346S1 (09/76)	Eddie Kendricks GOIN' UP IN SMOKE	
TALP 0128	Tamla T6-347S1 (08/76)	Tata Vega FULL SPEED AHEAD	
TALP 0129	Tamla T6-348S1 (09/76)	Marvin Gaye GREATEST HITS	
TALP 0130	Tamla T6-349S1 (01/77)	Syreeta ONE TO ONE	
TALP 0131	Tamla T6-350S1 (01/77)	Smokey Robinson DEEP IN MY SOUL	
TALP 0132	Tamla T6-351S1 (01/77)	Valerie Simpson KEEP IT COMIN'	
TALP 0133	Tamla T7-352R2 (03/77)	Marvin Gaye LIVE AT THE LONDON PALLADIUM Note: Two-album set.	
TALP 0134	Tamla T6-353S1 (03/77)	Tata Vega TOTALLY TATA	
TALP 0135	Tamla T6-354S1	Marvin Gaye HERE, MY DEAR Note: Unissued.	
TALP 0136	Tamla T7-354R1 (01/78)	Eddie Kendricks AT HIS BEST	
TALP 0137	Tamla T6-355S1 (07/77)	Smokey Robinson ORIGINAL MUSIC SCORE FROM THE MOTION PICTURE, "BIG TIME"	
TALP 0138	Tamla T6-356S1 (08/77)	Eddie Kendricks SLICK	
TALP 0139	Tamla T6-357S1 (08/77)	The Miracles GREATEST HITS	
TALP 0140	Tamla T7-358R1 (10/77)	Thelma Houston THE DEVIL IN ME	
TALP 0141	Tamla T7-359R1 (02/78)	Smokey Robinson LOVE BREEZE	
TALP 0142	Tamla T7-360R1 (02/79)	Tata Vega TRY MY LOVE	
TALP 0143	Tamla T7-361R1 (10/78)	Thelma Houston READY TO ROLL	
TALP 0144	Tamla T7-362R1 (10/78)	Stevie Wonder SOMEDAY AT CHRISTMAS Note: Previously issued on Tamla TS-281.	
TALP 0145	Tamla T9-363A2 (11/78)	Smokey Robinson SMOKIN' Note: Two-album set, recorded live.	
TALP 0146	Tamla T-364LP2 (12/78)	Marvin Gaye HERE, MY DEAR Note: Two-album set.	
TALP 0147	Tamla T7-365R1 (05/79)	Thelma Houston RIDE TO THE RAINBOW	
TALP 0148	Tamla T7-366R1 (05/79)	Smokey Robinson WHERE THERE'S SMOKE . . .	
TALP 0149	Tamla T8-367M1 (01/80)	Smokey Robinson WARM THOUGHTS	
TALP 0150	Tamla T7-368R1 (06/80)	Shadee I JUST NEED MORE MONEY	
TALP 0151	Tamla T8-369M1	Marvin Gaye LOVE MAN Note: Unissued.	
TALP 0152	Tamla T8-370M1 (09/80)	Tata Vega GIVIN' ALL MY LOVE	
TALP 0153	Tamla T13-371N2 (01/79)	Stevie Wonder STEVIE WONDER'S JOURNEY THROUGH THE SECRET LIFE OF PLANTS Note: Two-album set.	

TALP 0154	Tamla T-372 (04/80)	Syreeta SYREETA
TALP 0155	Tamla T8-373M1 (10/80)	Stevie Wonder HOTTER THAN JULY
TALP 0156	Tamla T8-374M1 (01/81)	Marvin Gaye IN OUR LIFETIME
TALP 0157	Tamla T8-375M1 (02/81)	Smokey Robinson BEING WITH YOU
TALP 0158	Tamla T8-376M1 (11/81)	Syreeta SET MY LOVE IN MOTION

NUMBER SEQUENCE CHANGE

Note: At this point, numbering for Tamla, Motown, and Gordy albums was consolidated into a single sequence starting at 6000. See "TMG Consolidated Series Albums" for continuation.

TMG CONSOLIDATED SERIES 7-INCH SINGLES

TMG45 0001	Motown 1600MF (01/82)	Jermaine Jackson Paradise In Your Eyes I'm My Brother's Keeper
TMG45 0002	Tamla 1601TF (01/82)	Smokey Robinson Tell Me Tomorrow (Part 1) Tell Me Tomorrow (Part 2) Note: Extended version issued promotionally on PR-92A (6:25).
TMG45 0003	Tamla 1602TF (01/82)	Stevie Wonder That Girl All I Do Note: "B" side issued promotionally as an extended version on PR-77B1 (5:06).
TMG45 0004	Gordy 1603GF (01/82)	Switch Call On Me Fallin' Note: "A" side issued promotionally as an extended version on PR-89B2 (5:24).
TMG45 0005	Motown 1604MF (01/82)	Commodores Why You Wanna Try Me X-Rated Movie Note: "A" side issued promotionally as an extended version on PR-87B (4:36).
TMG45 0006	Motown 1605MF (02/82)	Ozone Do What You Wanna Come On In Note: "A" side issued promotionally as an extended version on PR-93B1 (6:10).

TMG45 0007	Gordy 1606GF (02/82)	Nolen & Crossley Change Because Note: "A" side also issued on Gordy 7209.
TMG45 0008	Motown 1607MF (03/82)	Lovesmith I Fooled Ya You're A Fox (Out The Box)
TMG45 0009	Gordy 1608GF (03/82)	Nolen & Crossley Ready Or Not A Place In My Heart Note: "A" side also issued promotionally on PR-93B1.
TMG45 0010	Motown 1609MF (03/82)	Dazz Band Let It Whip Everyday Love Note: Issued comercially as an extended play on the following 12-inch singles: 4503MG (6:22), MD-6007 (Canadian issue) (6:22). Issued promotionally as 12-inch singles in two different formats: PR-93A1 (4:44) and PR-95A (6:22).
TMG45 0011	Tamla 1610TF (03/82)	Syreeta I Must Be In Love Wish Upon A Star
TMG45 0012	Motown 1611MF (03/82)	Charlene I've Never Been To Me Somewhere In My Life Note: "A" side originally issued on Prodigal P-0636.
TMG45 0013	Tamla 1612TF (05/82)	Stevie Wonder Do I Do Rocket Love Note: "Do I Do" issued promotionally with running time of 5:18 (w/Harmonica Solo). Also issued promotionally as a 12-inch on PR-98 (10:27).
TMG45 0014	Gordy 1613GF (04/82)	High Inergy First Impressions Could This Be Love
TMG45 0015	Motown 1614MF (04/82)	Bettye Lavette I Can't Stop Either Way We Lose Note: "A" side issued promotionally as an extended version on PR-96B (5:36).
TMG45 0016	Tamla 1615TF (04/82)	Smokey Robinson Old Fashioned Love Destiny Note: "A" side issued promotionally as an extended version on PR-97B.
TMG45 0017	Gordy 1616GF (04/82)	The Temptations featuring Rick James Standing On The Top (Part 1) Standing On The Top (Part 2) Note: Issued promotionally as an extended version on PR-96A

(9:50).

TMG45 0018	Motown 1617MF (04/82)	Ozone Keep On Dancin' Your Lady Stays On My Mind Note: "A" side issued promotionally as an extended version on PR-93B2 (5:57).

TMG45 0019	Motown 1618MF (04/82)	Jose Feliciano I Second That Emotion Free Me From My Freedom Note: "A" side originally scheduled to be issued as Motown M-1524FA. "A" side issued promotionally as an extended version on PR-91A1 (5:35).

TMG45 0020	Gordy 1619GF (05/82)	Rick James Dance Wit' Me (Part 1) Dance Wit' Me (Part 2) Note: Issued promotionally as an extended version on PR-97A.

TMG45 0021	Motown 1620MF	Jean Carn My Baby Loves Me Completeness Note: Unissued.

TMG45 0022	Motown 1620MF (06/82)	Jean Carn If You Don't Know Me By Now Completeness

TMG45 0023	Motown 1621MF (06/82)	Charlene It Ain't Easy Comin' Down If I Could See Myself Note: "A" side released originally on Prodigal P-0632. See also Motown 1624LF.

TMG45 0024	Motown 1622MF (06/82)	Dazz Band Keep It Live (On The K.I.L.) This Time It's Forever Note: "A" side issued promotionally as an extended version on PR-95B, as well as PR-104B (5:56).

TMG45 0025	Motown 1623MF (06/82)	O.C. Smith Love Changes Got To Know

TMG45 0026	Latino 1624LF (06/82)	Charlene Nunca He Ido A Mi If I Could See Myself Note: "A" side is the Spanish version of "I've Never Been To Me." "B" side previously issued on Motown 1621B. This was the first release on Motown's new Latin-oriented label, Latino.

TMG45 0027	Motown 1625MF (06/82)	Billy Preston I'm Never Gonna Say Goodbye I Love You So

TMG45 0028	Motown 1626MF (07/82)	Diana Ross We Can Never Light That Old Flame Again Old Funky Rolls

Note: Promotional copy issued in a special lyric cover.

TMG45 0029	Motown 1627MF (07/82)	Ozone Li'l Suzy I'm Not Easy Note: "A" side issued as extended version single on the following numbers: 4504MG (6:22), MD-6006 (Canadian numbering) (4:35). Also issued on a promotional format on PR-100 (4:35) as well as PR-104A (6:22).

TMG45 0030	Motown 1628MF (07/82)	Jermaine Jackson Let Me Tickle Your Fancy Maybe Next Time Note: "A" side issued as extended play singles on the following numbers: MD-6003 (Canadian numbering series) (5:05). Also issued as a promotional PR-101B (5:05).

TMG45 0031	Motown 1629MF (08/82)	Regal Funkharmonic Orchestra Strung Out On Motown Strung Out On Commodores Note: Strung Out On Motown: Fingertips/Dancing In The Street/Uptight (Everything's Alright)/I Can't Help Myself (Sugar Pie, Honey Bunch)/The Tears Of A Clown/ABC/I Want You Back/What's Going On/You're The Sunshine Of My Life/Sir Duke/Ain't No Mountain High Enough.

TMG45 0032	Tamla 1630TF (07/82)	Smokey Robinson Yes It's You Lady Are You Still Here

TMG45 0033	Gordy 1631GF (07/82)	The Temptations More On The Inside Money's Hard To Get

TMG45 0034	Gordy 1632GF (07/82)	High Inergy Wrong Man, Right Touch Beware

TMG45 0035	Latino 1633LF	Isela Sotelo Angelito (Angel Baby) Esta Vez Note: Unissued. See Motown 1648MF for release.

TMG45 0036	Gordy 1634GF (07/82)	Rick James Hard To Get My Love Note: "A" side issued commercially on MD-6004. Also issued promotionally as an extended play single on PR-101 (4:07).

TMG45 0037	Gordy 1635GF (08/82)	DeBarge Stop! Don't Tease Me Hesitated

TMG45 0038	Motown 1636MF (09/82)	O. C. Smith I Betcha That's One For Love

TMG45 0039	Motown 1637MF (09/82)	Willie Hutch In And Out The Girl (Can't Help It) Note: "A" side issued commercially on the following numbers: 4501MG (7:17), MD-6008A (7:17).

TMG45 0040	1638	Note: Unissued.

TMG45 0041	Tamla 1639TF (08/82)	Stevie Wonder Ribbon In The Sky Black Orchid

TMG45 0042	1640	Note: Unissued.

TMG45 0043	Gordy 1641GF (09/82)	High Inergy Journey To Love Could This Be Love

TMG45 0044	Tamla 1642TF (01/83)	Gene Van Buren You've Got Me Where I Want You One

TMG45 0045	Motown 1643MF (09/82)	Bobby Nunn She's Just A Groupie Never Seen Anything Like You Note: "A" side issued as an extended play single in the following formats: 4502MG (7:07), MD-6005 (Canadian series) (7:07). Also issued promotionally on PR-105 (7:07).

TMG45 0046	Motown 1644MF (09/82)	Lionel Richie Truly Just Put Some Love In Your Heart

TMG45 0047	Gordy 1645GF (11/82)	DeBarge I Like It Hesitated

TMG45 0048	Gordy 1646GF (10/82)	Rick James She Blew My Mind (69 Times) She Blew My Mind (69 Times) Note: Issued as an extended play single on a promotional basis on PR-107 running 6:30 (vocal) and 7:30 (instrumental).

TMG45 0049	Latino 1647LF (10/82)	Jose Feliciano Samba Pa Ti Malas Costumbres (Evil Ways)

TMG45 0050	Motown 1648MF (10/82)	Isela Sotelo Angelito (Angel Baby) Esta Vez Note: Originally scheduled to be released in July 1982 on Motown's Latino label (Latino 1633LF).

TMG45 0051	Motown 1649MF (10/82)	Jermaine Jackson Very Special Part You're Givin' Me The Runaround Note: "A" side issued promotionally as an extended play single on PR-108 running 6:32 (both vocal and instrumental).

TMG45 0052	Motown 1650MF (10/82)	Charlene & Stevie Wonder Used To Be I Want To Come Back As A Song Note: Promo copies issued in a lyric sheet cover not available with the commercial release. "B" side as by Charlene and Stevie Wonder.

TMG45 0053	Motown 1651MF (11/82)	Commodores Painted Picture Reach High (Instrumental)

TMG45 0054	Gordy 1652GF (11/82)	Bobby Militello featuring Jean Carn Let's Stay Together Charlie's Backbeat

TMG45 0055	Motown 1653MF (11/82)	Bobby Nunn Got To Get Up On It You Need Non-Stop Lovin' Note: Canadian copies feature alternate version of "Got To Get Up On It" with a running time of 4:11 (shown as "B" side.) See also 1671MF. "A" side of Canadian copy listed as "Sexy Sassy" running 3:28. "A" side also issued as an extended play promotional single on PR-111 running 6:01 (vocal) and 4:34 (instrumental).

TMG45 0056	Gordy 1654GF (12/82)	The Temptations Silent Night Everything For Christmas Note: See also Gordy 1713GF.

TMG45 0057	Tamla 1655TF (01/83)	Smokey Robinson I've Made Love To You A Thousand Times Into Each Rain Some Life Must Fall

TMG45 0058	Gordy 1656GF (01/83)	High Inergy So Right Don't Let Up On The Groove Note: See also Gordy 1688GF.

TMG45 0059	Motown 1657MF (01/83)	Lionel Richie You Are You Mean More To Me

TMG45 0060	Gordy 1658GF (01/83)	Rick James Teardrops Throwdown

TMG45 0061	Motown 1659MF (01/83)	Dazz Band On The One For Fun Just Believe In Love Note: "A" side issued as a promotional extended play single on PR-112 running 6:37 (vocal)

and 6:21 (instrumental).

TMG45 0062	Gordy 1660GF (04/83)	DeBarge All This Love I'm In Love With You

TMG45 0063	Motown 1661MF (02/83)	Commodores Reach High Sexy Lady

TMG45 0064	Gordy 1662GF (01/83)	High Inergy He's A Pretender Don't Let Up On The Groove Note: "A" side issued as an extended play single on Motown 4506MG running 5:21 (vocal) and 5:14 (instrumental). Versions with same running times also issued promotionally on PR-113.

TMG45 0065	Motown 1663MF (02/83)	Charlene I Want To Go Back There Again Richie's Song (For Richard Oliver)

TMG45 0066	Motown 1664MF (02/83)	Robert John Bread And Butter If You Don't Want My Love

TMG45 0067	Motown 1665MF (02/83)	Monalisa Young Dancing Machine I'll Be There

TMG45 0068	Gordy 1666GF (03/83)	The Temptations Love On My Mind Tonight Bring Your Body (Exercise Chant)

TMG45 0069	Gordy 1667GF (03/83)	Bobby Militello How Do You Feel Tonight Redliner

TMG45 0070	Motown 1668MF (03/83)	Ozone Strutt My Thang Don't Leave Me Now Note: "A" side issued promotionally as an extended play single on PR-120A1 running 4:49.

TMG45 0071	Motown 1669MF (05/83)	Finis Henderson Skip To My Lou I'd Rather Be Gone Note: "A" side issued promotionally as an extended play single on PR-119A running 5:19.

TMG45 0072	Gordy 1670GF (03/83)	Mary Jane Girls Candy Man (Vocal) Candy Man (Instrumental) Note: Issued as an extended play single on Motown 4509MG running 7:39. Also issued promotionally on PR-115A with same running time.

TMG45 0073	Motown 1671MF (03/83)	Bobby Nunn Sexy Sassy (Vocal) Sexy Sassy (Instrumental) Note: See also Motown 1653MF. This version (3:47)

longer than Canadian issue (3:28).

TMG45 0074	Motown 1672MF (04/83)	Kagny & The Dirty Rats At 15 Dirty Rats Note: "A" side issued promotionally on PR-120B running 6:36 (vocal) and 5:22 (instrumental). "B" side also issued as an alternate take on PR-117B running 4:28.

TMG45 0075	Motown 1673MF (06/83)	Jose Feliciano Balada Del Pianista Volvere Alguna Vez

TMG45 0076	Motown 1674MF	Jose Feliciano Lonely Teardrops Cuidado! Note: Unissued. See Motown 1679MF for release.

TMG45 0077	Motown 1674MF (07/83)	Jose Feliciano Let's Find Each Other Tonight Cuidado! (Instrumental)

TMG45 0078	Tamla 1675TF (04/83)	Syreeta Forever Is Not Enough She's Leaving Home

TMG45 0079	Tamla 1675TF	Syreeta Forever Is Not Enough Wish Upon A Star Note: Unissued.

TMG45 0080	Motown 1676MF (04/83)	Dazz Band Cheek To Cheek Can We Dance

TMG45 0081	Motown 1677MF (04/83)	Lionel Richie My Love Round And Round

TMG45 0082	Tamla 1678TF (04/83)	Smokey Robinson Touch the Sky All My Life's A Lie

TMG45 0083	Motown 1679MF (04/83)	Jose Feliciano Lonely Teardrops Cuidado! (Instrumental) Note: Originally planned for release on Motown 1674MF.

TMG45 0084	Motown 1680MF (06/83)	Dazz Band Party Right Here Gamble With My Love Note: "A" side issued promotionally as an extended play single on PR-125A running 5:12 (vocal) and 4:56 (instrumental).

TMG45 0085	Gordy 1681GF (05/83)	Stone City Band Bad Lady (Vocal) Bad Lady (Instrumental) Note: Issued commercially as an extended play single on Motown 4508MG running 6:44 (vocal) and 6:55 (instrumental).

TMG45 0086	Motown 1682MF	Bobby Nunn The Party Is Over Get It While You Can Note: Unissued. See also Motown 1695MF.
TMG45 0087	Gordy 1683GF (05/83)	The Temptations Surface Thrills Made In America Note: "A" side issued promotionally as an extended play single on PR-119B running 5:15 (vocal) and 4:32 (instrumental).
TMG45 0088	Tamla 1684TF (06/83)	Smokey Robinson & High Inergy / Smokey Robinson Blame It On Love Even Tho'
TMG45 0089	Motown 1685MF (06/83)	Michael Lovesmith Baby I Will What's The Bottom Line Note: "A" side issued promotionally as an extended play single on PR-126 running 5:30 (both vocal and instrumental).
TMG45 0090	1686	Note: Unissued.
TMG45 0091	Gordy 1687GF (07/83)	Rick James Cold Blooded Cold Blooded (Instrumental) Note: Issued commercially as an extended play single on Motown 4511MG running 5:56 (both vocal and instrumental).
TMG45 0092	Gordy 1688GF (07/83)	High Inergy Back In My Arms Again So Right Note: "B" originally issued on Gordy 1656GF-A.
TMG45 0093	Motown 1689MF (08/83)	Jr. Walker Blow The House Down Ball Baby (Instrumental) Note: "A" side issued commercially as an extended play single on Motown 4512MG.
TMG45 0094	Gordy 1690GF (07/83)	Mary Jane Girls All Night Long Musical Love Note: "A" side issued promotionally as an extended play single on PR-118 running 5:34 (vocal).
TMG45 0095	Motown 1691MF (08/83)	Ozone Our Hearts (Will Always Shine) Here I Go Again
TMG45 0096	Morocco 1692CF (08/83)	Sparks Malcolm McDowell Get Crazy Hot Shot Note: First release on Motown's rock-oriented label, Morocco.
TMG45 0097	Gordy 1693GF (09/83)	Stone City Band Ladies Choice (Vocal) Ladies Choice (Instrumental) Note: Issued promotionally as an extended single on PR-124 running 7:18 (vocal) and 7:08 (instrumental).
TMG45 0098	Motown 1694MF (08/83)	Commodores Only You Cebu Note: "B" side previously issued on Motown 1408B.
TMG45 0099	Motown 1695MF (09/83)	Bobby Nunn Private Party Get It While You Can Note: "A" side issued promotionally as an extended play single on PR-127 running 4:52 (vocal) and 6:27 (instrumental). "B" side originally scheduled for release on Motown 1682MFB.
TMG45 0100	Motown 1696MF (08/83)	Finis Henderson Lovers School Girl
TMG45 0101	Motown 1697MF (09/83)	The Motor City Crew Let's Break (Vocal) Let's Break (Instrumental) Note: Issued commercially as an extended play single on Motown 4513MG running 6:38 (both vocal and instrumental).
TMG45 0102	Motown 1697MF	The Motor City Crew Scratch Break (Glove Style) Let's Break (Instrumental) Note: Unissued.
TMG45 0103	Motown 1698MF (09/83)	Lionel Richie All Night Long (All Night) Wandering Stranger Note: "A" side issued as an extended version commercially on the following numbers: Motown 4514MG running 6:22 (vocal) and 6:44 (instrumental). Also Canadian issue MD-4512 running 6:23 (vocal) and 6:42 (instrumental). Issued promotionally in U.S. on PR-132 running 6:22 (vocal) and 6:44 (instrumental).
TMG45 0104	Motown 1699MF (09/83)	Michael Lovesmith Just Say The Word A Promise Is A Promise
TMG45 0105	Tamla 1700TF (10/83)	Smokey Robinson Don't Play Another Love Song Wouldn't You Like To Know
TMG45 0106	Motown 1701MF (10/83)	Dazz Band Joystick Don't Get Caught Up In The Middle

TMG45 0107	Motown 1702MF (01/84)	Rockwell Somebody's Watching Me Somebody's Watching Me (Instrumental) Note: Extended version issued commercially on Motown 4515MG running 4:57 (vocal) and 5:26 (instrumental).
TMG45 0108	Gordy 1703GF (10/83)	Rick James U Bring The Freak Out Money Talks Note: "A" side issued promotionally as an extended version on PR-133B.
TMG45 0109	Gordy 1704GF (10/83)	Mary Jane Girls Boys Boys (Instrumental) Note: Issued promotionally as an extended version on PR-133A.
TMG45 0110	Gordy 1705GF (10/83)	DeBarge Time Will Reveal I'll Never Fall In Love Again
TMG45 0111	Motown 1706MF (10/83)	Four Tops I Just Can't Walk Away Hang
TMG45 0112	Gordy 1707GF (10/83)	The Temptations Miss Busy Body (Get Your Body Busy) Miss Busy Body (Get Your Body Busy) (Part 2) (Instrument Note: Issued promotionally as an extended version on PR-131 running 5:28 (vocal) and 5:32 (instrumental, part 2).
TMG45 0113	Motown 1708MF	Jr. Walker Rise And Shine Closer Than Close Note: Unissued.
TMG45 0114	Motown 1709MF	Monalisa Young Knife Don't Mess With Bill Note: Unissued.
TMG45 0115	Motown 1709MF (02/84)	Monalisa Young Sweet Remedy Don't Mess With Bill
TMG45 0116	Motown 1710MF (11/83)	Lionel Richie Running With The Night Serves You Right Note: "A" side issued promotionally as an extended version on PR-135.
TMG45 0117	Motown 1711MF (12/83)	Bobby Nunn Hangin' Out At The Mall The Lady Killer Note: "A" side issued promotionally as an extended version on PR-136 running 6:22 (vocal) and 5:30 (instrumental).
TMG45 0118	Tamla 1712TF (01/84)	Keith & Darrell Work That Body The Things You're Made Of Note: "A" side issued commercially as an extended version on Motown 4516MG.
TMG45 0119	Gordy 1713GF (12/83)	The Temptations Silent Night Everything For Christmas
TMG45 0120	Gordy 1714GF (11/83)	Rick James & Smokey Robinson / Rick James Ebony Eyes 1, 2, 3, (You, Her And Me)
TMG45 0121	Gordy 1715GF (01/84)	Dennis Edwards featuring Siedah Garrett / Dennis Edwards Don't Look Any Further I Thought I Could Handle It
TMG45 0122	Morocco 1716CF (02/84)	Tiggi Clay Flashes Roses for Lydia
TMG45 0123	Morocco 1717CF (03/84)	Kidd Glove Good Clean Fun Street Angel
TMG45 0124	Motown 1718MF (03/84)	Four Tops Make Yourself At Home Sing A Song Of Yesterday
TMG45 0125	Motown 1719MF (01/84)	Commodores Turn Off The Lights Been Lovin' You
TMG45 0126	Gordy 1720GF (02/84)	Temptations Sail Away Isn't the Night Fantastic Note: "B" side previously issued on Gordy 7213B.
TMG45 0127	Gordy 1721GF (01/84)	Mary Jane Girls Jealousy You Are My Heaven
TMG45 0128	Motown 1722MF (02/84)	Lionel Richie Hello You Mean More To Me Note: "B" side previously issued on Motown 1657MF-B.
TMG45 0129	Gordy 1723GF (02/84)	DeBarge Love Me In A Special Way Dance The Night Away
TMG45 0130	Motown 1724MF (03/84)	Bobby Nunn Do You Look That Good In The Morning Sex Maniac
TMG45 0131	Motown 1725MF (04/84)	Dazz Band Sweep Bad Girl
TMG45 0132	Motown 1726MF (04/84)	Bobby King Lovequake Fall In Love

TMG45 0133	Tamla 1727TF (07/84)	Gene Van Buren You Excite Me I Love You More (Than I Hate What You Do)
TMG45 0134	Morocco 1728CF (04/84)	Tiggi Clay The Winner Gets The Heart Who Shot Zorro
TMG45 0135	Morocco 1729CF (04/84)	Wolf & Wolf Don't Take The Candy War Of Nerves Note: See also Morocco 1754CF.
TMG45 0136	Gordy 1730GF (06/84)	Rick James 17 17 (Instrumental)
TMG45 0137	Motown 1731MF (04/84)	Rockwell Obscene Phone Caller Obscene Phone Caller (Instrumental)
TMG45 0138	Motown 1732MF (04/84)	Michael Lovesmith Gotta Get Out Tonight Sorry Won't Cut It
TMG45 0139	Motown 1733MF (06/84)	KoKo-Pop Baby Sister Baby Sister (Instrumental)
TMG45 0140	Motown 1734MF (07/84)	Charlene We're Both In Love With You I Want The World To Know He's Mine
TMG45 0141	Tamla 1735TF (05/84)	Smokey Robinson And I Don't Love You Dynamite
TMG45 0142	Morocco 1736CF (04/84)	Duke Jupiter Little Lady (I've Got A) Little Black Book
TMG45 0143	Gordy 1737GF (05/84)	Dennis Edwards (You're My) Aphrodisiac Shake Hands (Come Out Dancin')
TMG45 0144	Motown 1738MF (05/84)	Sammy Davis, Jr. Hello Detroit (Vocal) Hello Detroit (Instrumental)
TMG45 0145	Motown 1739MF (05/84)	Michael Jackson Farewell My Summer Love Call On Me
TMG45 0146	1740	Note: Unissued.
TMG45 0147	Gordy 1741GF (05/84)	Mary Jane Girls In My House In My House (Instrumental)
TMG45 0148	Morocco 1742CF (06/84)	Coyote Sisters Straight From The Heart (Into Your Life) Echo
TMG45 0149	Motown 1743MF (09/84)	Sam Harris Sugar Don't Bite You Keep Me Hangin' On
TMG45 0150	Motown 1744MF (08/84)	Kagny Sundown On Sunset Nothin' But Pocket
TMG45 0151	Motown 1745MF (08/84)	Stevie Wonder I Just Called To Say I Love You I Just Called To Say I Love You (Instrumental)
TMG45 0152	Motown 1746MF (06/84)	Lionel Richie Stuck on You Round And Round
TMG45 0153	Motown 1747MF (07/84)	Bobby King with Alfie Silas Close To Me Love In The Fire
TMG45 0154	Morocco 1748CF (07/84)	Duke Jupiter Rescue Me Me and Michelle
TMG45 0155	Motown 1749MF (06/84)	Michael Lovesmith I Can't Give Her Up He Only Looks The Part
TMG45 0156	Morocco 1750CF (07/84)	Jakata Hell Is On The Run Don't Ever Let Go
TMG45 0157	1751	Note: Unissued.
TMG45 0158	Motown 1752MF (08/84)	Vanity Pretty Mess Pretty Mess (Instrumental)
TMG45 0159	1753	Note: Unissued.
TMG45 0160	Morocco 1754CF (09/84)	Wolf & Wolf Talk Of The Town War Of Nerves Note: "B" side previously issued on Morocco 1729CFB.
TMG45 0161	Gordy 1755GF (08/84)	Dennis Edwards Another Place In Time Let's Go Up
TMG45 0162	Tamla 1756TF (08/84)	Smokey Robinson I Can't Find Gimme What You Want
TMG45 0163	Motown 1757MF (08/84)	Michael Jackson Girl You're So Together Touch The One You Love
TMG45 0164	Motown 1758MF (08/84)	Phyllis St. James Candlelight Afternoon Back In The Race
TMG45 0165	Motown 1759MF (09/84)	KoKo-Pop I'm In Love With You On The Beach

TMG45 0166	Motown 1760MF (09/84)	Dazz Band Let It All Blow Now That I Have You

TMG45 0167	Motown 1761MF (09/84)	Charlene Hit And Run Lover The Last Song

TMG45 0168	Motown 1762MF (09/84)	Lionel Richie Penny Lover Tell Me

TMG45 0169   Gordy 1763GF (09/84)   Rick James
You Turn Me On
Fire & Desire
Note: "A" side issued on a promotional basis as an extended version on PR-158 running 5:27 (long version) and 5:30 (long instrumental version).

TMG45 0170   1764   Note: Unissued.

TMG45 0171   Gordy 1765GF (10/84)   The Temptations
Treat Her Like A Lady
Isn't The Night Fantastic
Note: "A" side issued on a promotional basis as an extended version on PR-163A running 6:10 (long version) and 3:45 (short version). "B" side previously issued on Gordy 7231B as well as Gordy 1720GFB.

TMG45 0172   Morocco 1766CF (11/84)   Coyote Sisters
I've Got A Radio
I'll Do It

TMG45 0173   Motown 1767MF (11/84)   Vanity
Mechanical Emotion
Crazy Maybe
Note: "A" side issued on a promotional basis as an extended version on PR-159 running 6:00 (long version) and 6:20 (instrumental version). "A" side also issued commercially on Motown 4526MGB running 5:44 (long version). This commercial release issued with oversize "picture label," with different picture of Vanity on each side.

TMG45 0174   Motown 1768MF (11/84)   Thomas McClary
Thin Walls
Love Will Find A Way

TMG45 0175   Motown 1769MF (11/84)   Stevie Wonder
Love Light In Flight
It's More Than You (Instrumental)
Note: "A" side also issued promotionally as an extended version on PR-161 running 6:30 (Side 1 12-inch version) and 7:38 (instrumental).

TMG45 0176   Gordy 1770GF (01/85)   DeBarge
Rhythm Of The Night
Queen Of My Heart
Note: "A" side also issued commercially on Motown 4532MG as an extended version running 6:45.

TMG45 0177   Motown 1771MF (12/84)   Sam Harris
Hearts On Fire
I Will Wait For You
Note: "A" side issued promotionally as an extended version on PR-162 running 6:40 (Dance mix) and 5:20 (Psycho mix).

TMG45 0178   Motown 1772MF (12/84)   Rockwell
He's A Cobra
Change Your Ways

TMG45 0179   Motown 1773MF (12/84)   Commodores
Nightshift
I Keep Running
Note: 12-inch version issued on Motown 4533MG.

TMG45 0180   Motown 1774MF (01/85)   Stevie Wonder
Don't Drive Drunk
Don't Drive Drunk (Instrumental)
Note: Issued commercially as extended version on Motown 4527MG running 8:18 (long version) and 8:27 (long instrumental version).

TMG45 0181   Motown 1775MF (01/85)   Dazz Band
Heartbeat
Rock With Me
Note: "A" side issued on a promotional basis as extended version on PR-164A running 7:03.

TMG45 0182   Gordy 1776GF (03/85)   Rick James
Can't Stop
Oh What A Night (4 Luv)
Note: Issued commercially as extended version on Motown 4528MG running 6:08 ("A" side long version) and 5:05 ("B" side version).

TMG45 0183   Motown 1777MF (02/85)   Alfie
Star
Keep On Smilin'
Note: Promo copies issued in special lyric sleeve. Issued commercially as extended version on Motown 4530MG running 5:48 ("A" side) and 4:20 ("B" side).

TMG45 0184   Motown 1778MF (03/85)   Jakata
Golden Girl
Light At The End Of The Tunnel
Note: "A" side promo copies issued with versions running 3:56 (short) and 5:01 (long).

TMG45 0185	Motown 1779MF (03/85)	Thomas McClary Man In The Middle Man In The Middle (Instrumental)
TMG45 0186	Motown 1780MF (03/85)	Sam Harris Over The Rainbow I've Heard It All Before
TMG45 0187	Gordy 1781GF (02/85)	The Temptations My Love Is True (Truly For You) Set Your Love Right
TMG45 0188	Motown 1782MF (02/85)	Rockwell Peeping Tom Tokyo (Instrumental) Note: Issued with picture sleeve. Issued commercially with extended versions on Motown 4531MG running 5:50 ("A" side long 12-inch version) and 6:45 ("B" side instrumental).
TMG45 0189	1783	Note: Unissued.
TMG45 0190	Motown 1784MF (03/85)	The Emotions Miss Your Love I Can't Wait To Make You Mine
TMG45 0191	Motown 1785MF (03/85)	Dwight David The Last Dragon The Last Dragon (Instrumental) Note: Title song from Berry Gordy's film, "The Last Dragon."
TMG45 0192	Tamla 1786TF (03/85)	Smokey Robinson & Syreeta First Time On A Ferris Wheel Train Of Thought Note: "B" side by Smokey Robinson (solo). "A" side issued promotionally as 12-inch single on Motown label PR-168B running 3:22.
TMG45 0193	Motown 1787MF (04/85)	Maureen Steele Save The Night For Me Boys Will Be Boys Note: "B" side issued commercially as extended versions on Motown 4542MG running 6:39 ("A" side Club mix) and 3:55 ("B" side Radio Edit of Club Mix).
TMG45 0194	Motown 1788MF (04/85)	Commodores Animal Instinct Lightin' Up The Night Note: "A" side promo copy issued with both short version (4:02), and long version (4:44). Also issued commercially as an extended version on Motown 4535MGA running 9:46 (Club mix).
TMG45 0195	Gordy 1789GF (05/85)	The Temptations How Can You Say That It's Over I'll Keep My Light In My Window Note: See also Gordy 1818GF.

TMG45 0196	Motown 1790MF (05/85)	Four Tops Sexy Ways Body And Soul
TMG45 0197	Motown 1791MF (05/85)	Michael Lovesmith Love In The Combat Zone [Flip side not determined]
TMG45 0198	Motown 1792MF (05/85)	The Emotions If I Only Knew Then (What I Know Now) Eternally
TMG45 0199	Gordy 1793GF (05/85)	DeBarge Who's Holding Donna Now Be My Lady
TMG45 0200	Motown 1794MF (05/85)	Michael Lovesmith Break The Ice Lucky In Love Note: "A" side issued commercially as extended version on Motown 4537MGA running 5:57 (Dance mix).
TMG45 0201	Gordy 1795GF (06/85)	Val Young Mind Games Mind Games (Instrumental) Note: Issued commercially as extended versions on Gordy 4538GG.
TMG45 0202	Gordy 1796GF (05/85)	Rick James Glow Glow (Instrumental) Note: Issued commercially as extended version on Gordy 4539GG running 6:56 ("A" side) and 8:16 (12-inch instrumental).
TMG45 0203	Motown 1797MF (05/85)	Willie Hutch The Glow Keep On Jammin' Note: "A" side issued commercially as extended version on Motown 4534MG running 6:04 (Special 12-inch version).
TMG45 0204	Gordy 1798GF (06/85)	Mary Jane Girls Wild & Crazy Love Wild & Crazy Love (Instrumental) Note: Issued commercially as extended versions on Gordy 4541GG running 6:25 (Club mix), 6:19 (12-inch vocal), and 6:37 (instrumental). Includes picture sleeve.
TMG45 0205	Gordy 1799GF (06/85)	Dennis Edwards Amanda I'm Up For You
TMG45 0206	Motown 1800MF (06/85)	Dazz Band Hot Spot I've Been Waiting Note: 12-inch version issued commercially on Motown 4543MG.

TMG45 0207	Motown 1801MF (06/85)	Lushus Daim & The Pretty Vain More Than You Can Handle More Than You Can Handle (Instrumental) Note: 12-inch version issued promotionally on PR-172.
TMG45 0208	Motown 1802MF (07/85)	Commodores Janet I'm In Love
TMG45 0209	Motown 1803MF (07/85)	KoKo PoP Brand New Beat (Part 1) Brand New Beat (Part 2) Note: 12-inch version issued promotionally on PR-171.
TMG45 0210	Gordy 1804GF (08/85)	El DeBarge with DeBarge You Wear It Well Baby, Won't Cha Come Quick Note: 12-inch version issued commercially on Gordy 4545GG.
TMG45 0211	Gordy 1805GF (08/85)	Dennis Edwards Coolin' Out I Thought I Could Handle It
TMG45 0212	Gordy 1806GF (08/85)	Rick James Spend The Night With Me Spend The Night With Me (Instrumental)
TMG45 0213	Motown 1807MF (08/85)	Maureen Steele Boys Will Be Boys Rock My Heart Note: 12-inch version issued commercially on Motown 4542MG.
TMG45 0214	Tamla 1808TF (08/85)	Stevie Wonder Part-Time Lover Part-Time Lover (Instrumental) Note: 12-inch version issued commercially on Tamla 4548TG.
TMG45 0215	Tamla 1809	Note: Unissued.
TMG45 0216	Motown 1810MF (09/85)	Pal Panic Panic (Instrumental)
TMG45 0217	Motown 1811MF (09/85)	Four Tops Don't Tell Me That It's Over I'm Ready For Love
TMG45 0218	Gordy 1812GF (09/85)	Val Young Seduction Seduction (Instrumental) Note: 12-inch version issued commercially on Gordy 4544GG and promotionally on PR-169.
TMG45 0219	Motown 1813MF (10/85)	Warp 9 Skips A Beat Skips A Beat (Dub) Note: 12-inch version issued commercially on Motown 4555MG.
TMG45 0220	Motown 1814MF (09/85)	Mello-Mackin-D & Mr. Stretch Back To School Back To School (Instrumental) Note: 12-inch version issued commercially on Motown 4546MG.
TMG45 0221	Motown 1815MF (09/85)	Duke Jupiter The Line Of Your Fire Sounds Like Love Note: 12-inch version issued promotionally on PR-173.
TMG45 0222	Gordy 1816GF (09/85)	Mary Jane Girls Break It Up Break It Up (Instrumental) Note: 12-inch version issued commercially on Gordy 4547GG.
TMG45 0223	Tamla 1817TF (11/85)	Stevie Wonder Go Home Go Home (Instrumental) Note: 12-inch version issued commercially on Tamla 4553TG.
TMG45 0224	Gordy 1818GF (10/85)	The Temptations Do You Really Love Your Baby I'll Keep My Light In My Window Note: 12-inch version issued commercially on Gordy 4550GG. See also Gordy 1789GF.
TMG45 0225	Motown 1819MF (11/85)	Lionel Richie Say You, Say Me Can't Slow Down
TMG45 0226	Motown 1820MF (11/85)	Dazz Band When You Needed Roses [Flip side not determined]
TMG45 0227	1821	Note: Unissued.
TMG45 0228	Gordy 1822GF (11/85)	El DeBarge with DeBarge The Heart Is Not So Smart Share My World Note: 12-inch version issued commercially on Gordy 4552GG.
TMG45 0229	1823	Note: Unissued.
TMG45 0230	Motown 1824MF (12/85)	KoKo PoP Lonely Girl, Lonely Boy Make Up Your Mind
TMG45 0231	Motown 1825MF (12/85)	Roq-in' Zoo Frig-o-rator Frig-o-rator (Dub) Note: 12-inch version issued commercially on Motown 4554MG.
TMG45 0232	Motown 1826MF (12/85)	Lushus Daim & The Pretty Vain The One You Love The One You Love (Instrumental)

TMG45 0233	Motown 1827MF (12/85)	Alfie Just Gets Better With Time Keep On Smilin'
TMG45 0234	Tamla 1828TF (01/86)	Smokey Robinson Hold On To Your Love Train Of Thought
TMG45 0235	Motown 1829MF (01/86)	Sam Harris I'd Do It All Again The Rescue Note: 12-inch version issued commercially on Motown 4556MG.
TMG45 0236	Gordy 1830GF (01/86)	Val Young If You Should Ever Be Lonely If You Should Ever Be Lonely (Instrumental) Note: 12-inch version issued commercially on Gordy 4557GG.
TMG45 0237	Motown 1831MF (02/86)	Troy Johnson It's You It's You (Instrumental)
TMG45 0238	Tamla 1832TF (02/86)	Stevie Wonder Overjoyed Overjoyed (Instrumental)
TMG45 0239	Motown 1833MF (02/86)	Vanity Under The Influence Wild Animal Note: 12-inch version issued commercially on Motown 4558MG.
TMG45 0240	Gordy 1834GF (02/86)	The Temptations Touch Set You Right
TMG45 0241	Motown 1835MF (02/86)	The Guinn Family Dreamin' Dreamin' (Instrumental)
TMG45 0242	Tamla 1836TF (03/86)	Marvin Gaye The World Is Rated X The World Is Rated X (Instrumental)
TMG45 0243	Tamla 1836TF-RE1 (04/86)	Marvin Gaye The World Is Rated X No Greater Love
TMG45 0244	Motown 1837MF (03/86)	The Temptations / Smokey Robinson A Fine Mess Wishful Thinking Note: "A" side by the Temptations. "B" side by Smokey Robinson.
TMG45 0245	Motown 0438MF (1986)	Fizzy Qwick Hangin' Out Angels In The Snow
TMG45 0246	Tamla 1839TF (03/86)	Smokey Robinson Sleepless Nights Close Encounters Of The First Kind
TMG45 0247	Motown 1840MF (03/86)	Sam Harris Forever For You The Storm
TMG45 0248	1841	Note: Unissued.
TMG45 0249	Gordy 1842GF (04/86)	El DeBarge / El DeBarge with DeBarge Who's Johnny Love Me In A Special Way Note: "A" side as by El DeBarge, "B" side as by El DeBarge with DeBarge.
TMG45 0250	Motown 1843MF (06/86)	Lionel Richie Dancing On The Ceiling Love Will Find A Way
TMG45 0251	Gordy 1844GF (06/86)	Rick James Sweet And Sexy Thing Sweet And Sexy Thing (Instrumental)
TMG45 0252	Motown 1845MF (06/86)	Rockwell Carme (Part I) Carme (Part II)
TMG45 0253	1846	Note: Unissued.
TMG45 0254	1847	Note: Unissued.
TMG45 0255	Motown 1848MF (06/86)	Vanity Animals Gun Shy
TMG45 0256	1849	Note: Unissued.
TMG45 0257	Motown 1850MF (06/86)	Guinn Open Your Door Sincerely
TMG45 0258	Motown 1851MF (06/86)	Mary Jane Girls Walk Like A Man Shadow Lover
TMG45 0259	Motown 1852MF (06/86)	Burston & Littlejohn Rich & Famous Rich & Famous (Instrumental)
TMG45 0260	Motown 1853MF (06/86)	Nick Jameson Weatherman Casco Bay (Instrumental)
TMG45 0261	Motown 1854MF (06/86)	Four Tops Hot Nights Again
TMG45 0262	Tamla 1855TF (07/86)	Smokey Robinson Because Of You (It's The Best It's Ever Been) Girl I'm Standing There
TMG45 0263	Gordy 1856GF (06/86)	The Temptations Lady Soul Put Us Together Again

TMG45 0264	Gordy 1857GF (07/86)	El DeBarge Love Always The Walls (Came Tumbling Down)
TMG45 0265	Motown 1858MF (08/86)	Chico DeBarge Talk To Me If It Takes All Night
TMG45 0266	Motown 1859MF (08/86)	Stacy Lattislaw Nail It To The Wall Nail It To The Wall (Instrumental)
TMG45 0267	1860	Note: Unissued.
TMG45 0268	1861	Note: Unissued.
TMG45 0269	Gordy 1862GF (09/86)	Rick James Forever And A Day Forever And A Day (Instrumental)
TMG45 0270	Motown 1863MF (08/86)	Rockwell Grow Up Grow Up (Instrumental)
TMG45 0271	Motown 1864MF (09/86)	Fizzy Qwick You Want It Your Way, Always Young, Single And Tough
TMG45 0272	Gordy 1865GF (09/86)	General Kane Crack Killed Applejack Applejack's Theme
TMG45 0273	Motown 1866MF (10/86)	Lionel Richie Love Will Conquer All The Only One
TMG45 0274	Gordy 1867GF (10/86)	El DeBarge Someone Stop Don't Tease Me Note: "B" side as by El DeBarge with DeBarge.
TMG45 0275	1868	Note: Unissued.
TMG45 0276	Gordy 1869GF (11/86)	Bunny DeBarge Save The Best For Me (Best Of Your Lovin') Life Begins With You Note: "B" side as by Bunny DeBarge with DeBarge.
TMG45 0277	Motown 1870MF (10/86)	Billy Preston Since I Held You Close It Don't Get Better Than This
TMG45 0278	Gordy 1871GF (11/86)	The Temptations To Be Continued . . . You're The One
TMG45 0279	Gordy 1872GF (11/86)	General Kane Hairdooz Cuttin' It Up

TMG45 0280	Motown 1873MF (12/86)	Lionel Richie Ballerina Girl Deep River Woman

TMG CONSOLIDATED SERIES 12-INCH SINGLES

TMG12 0001	Motown 4500MG (1982)	Syreeta Can't Shake Your Love (Vocal) + Can't Shake Your Love (Instrumental) Move It, Do It (Vocal) + Move It, Do It (Instrumental)
TMG12 0002	Motown 4501MG (09/82)	Willie Hutch In And Out Brother's Gonna Work It Out
TMG12 0003	Motown 4502MG (09/82)	Bobby Nunn She's Just A Groupie (Vocal) She's Just A Groupie (Instrumental)
TMG12 0004	Motown 4503MG (03/82)	Dazz Band Let It Whip Let It Whip (Instrumental)
TMG12 0005	Motown 4504MG (07/82)	Ozone Li'l Suzy Li'l Suzy (Instrumental)
TMG12 0006	Motown 4505MG (1982)	Smokey Robinson GREATEST HITS MEDLEY Side 1: Being With You/Shop Around/Going To A Go-Go/Get Ready/The Way You Do The Things You Do/The Hunter Gets Captured By The Game/The Tears Of A Clown/I Second That Emotion/My Girl/The Tracks Of My Tears/Don't Mess With Bill/The Love I Saw In You Was Just A Mirage/Ooo Baby Baby/My Guy/More Love/Cruisin'/Being With You/Tell Me Tomorrow/Being With You - Side 2: The Only Game In Town
TMG12 0007	Motown 4506MG (01/83)	High Inergy He's A Pretender (Vocal) He's A Pretender (Instrumental)
TMG12 0008	Wondirection 4507WG (1983)	Gary Byrd And The G. B. Experience The Crown (Vocal) The Crown (Instrumental) Note: First release on Stevie Wonder's Motown distributed label "Wondirection."
TMG12 0009	Motown 4508MG (05/83)	Stone City Band Bad Lady (Vocal) Bad Lady (Instrumental)
TMG12 0010	Motown 4509MG (03/83)	Mary Jane Girls Candy Man Candy Man (Vocal) + Candy Man (Instrumental)

TMG12 0011	Motown 4510MG (1983)	Temptations / Four Tops / Jackson 5 MEDLEY Side 1: Reach Out/I'll Be There/Get Ready/It's The Same Old Song/Ain't Too Proud to Beg/Baby I Need Your Loving/My Girl/I Can't Get Next To You/I Can't Help Myself (Sugar Pie, Honey Bunch)/(I Know) I'm Losing You - Side 2: I Want You Back/ABC/The Love You Save/Dancing Machine/Never Can Say Goodbye/I'll Be There
TMG12 0012	Motown 4511MG (07/83)	Rick James Cold Blooded Cold Blooded (Instrumental)
TMG12 0013	Motown 4512MG (08/83)	Junior Walker Blow The House Down (Vocal) Blow The House Down (Instrumental)
TMG12 0014	Motown 4513MG (09/83)	Motor City Crew Let's Break (Vocal) Let's Break (Instrumental)+ Scratch Break (Glove Style)
TMG12 0015	Motown 4514MG (09/83)	Lionel Richie All Night Long (All Night) (Vocal) All Night Long (All Night) (Instrumental)
TMG12 0016	Motown 4515MG (01/84)	Rockwell Somebody's Watching Me (Vocal) Somebody's Watching Me (Instrumental)
TMG12 0017	Motown 4516MG (01/84)	Keith & Darrell Work That Body (Vocal) Work That Body (Instrumental)
TMG12 0018	Motown 4517MG (11/84)	Stevie Wonder / Rev. Martin Luther King Happy Birthday Greatest Excerpts From His Speeches
TMG12 0019	Motown 4518MG (03/84)	Bobby King Lovequake Midnight Shine
TMG12 0020	Motown 4519MG (05/84)	Sammy Davis Jr. Hello Detroit (Vocal) Hello Detroit (Instrumental)
TMG12 0021	Motown 4520MG (05/84)	Dazz Band Swoop (I'm Yours) Joystick (Vocal)
TMG12 0022	Motown 4521MG (06/84)	Smokey Robinson And I Don't Love You (Vocal) And I Don't Love You (Instrumental)
TMG12 0023	Motown 4522MG (07/84)	Rick James 17 (Vocal) 17 (Instrumental)
TMG12 0024	Motown 4523MG (09/84)	Sam Harris Sugar Don't Bite (New dance mix) Sugar Don't Bite (Instrumental)
TMG12 0025	Motown 4524MG (09/84)	Dazz Band Let It All Blow (Long Version) Let It All Blow (Instrumental)
TMG12 0026	Motown 4525MG (10/84)	Bruni Pagan You Turn Me On (Vocal) You Turn Me On (Instrumental)
TMG12 0027	Motown 4526MG (10/84)	Vanity Pretty Mess (Long Version) Mechanical Emotion (Long Version) Note: Issued with over-size "picture label." A different picture of Vanity on each side of disc.
TMG12 0028	Motown 4527MG (02/85)	Stevie Wonder Don't Drive Drunk (Special 12-inch version) Don't Drive Drunk (Instrumental) + Did I Hear You Say You Love Me
TMG12 0029	Motown 4528MG (01/85)	Rick James Can't Stop (Long Version) Oh What A Night (4 Luv)
TMG12 0030	Motown 4529MG (02/85)	Mary Jane Girls In My House (12-inch version) In My House (Instrumental 12-inch version)
TMG12 0031	Motown 4530MG (02/85)	Alfie Star (Special 12-inch version) Keep On Smilin'
TMG12 0032	Motown 4531MG (02/85)	Rockwell Peeping Tom (Special 12-inch version) Tokyo (12-inch Instrumental version)
TMG12 0033	Motown 4532MG (02/85)	DeBarge Rhythm Of The Night (Long Version) Queen Of My Heart
TMG12 0034	Motown 4533MG (02/85)	The Commodores Nightshift (Edit of Club Mix) Nightshift (Club Mix) + Nightshift (Instrumental mix)
TMG12 0035	Motown 4534MG (04/85)	Willie Hutch The Glow (Special 12-inch version) Keep On Jammin'
TMG12 0036	Motown 4535MG (04/85)	Commodores Animal Instinct (Club Mix) Lightin' Up The Night

TMG12 0037	Motown 4536	Note: Unissued.
TMG12 0038	Motown 4537MG (05/85)	Michael Lovesmith Break The Ice (Dance Mix) Lucky In Love
TMG12 0039	Gordy 4538GG (06/85)	Val Young Mind Games Mind Games
TMG12 0040	Gordy 4539GG (05/85)	Rick James Glow + Glow (Reprise) Glow (12-inch Instrumental)
TMG12 0041	Motown 4540	Note: Unissued.
TMG12 0042	Gordy 4541GG (06/85)	Mary Jane Girls Wild And Crazy Love (Wild & Crazy Club Mix) Wild And Crazy Love (Vocal Mix) + Wild And Crazy Love (Instrumental Mix)
TMG12 0043	Motown 4542MG (07/85)	Maureen Steele Boys Will Be Boys (Club Mix) Rock My Heart (LP Version) + Boys Will Be Boys (Radio Edit of Club Mix)
TMG12 0044	Motown 4543MG (06/85)	Dazz Band Hot Spot (Club Mix) I've Been Waiting
TMG12 0045	Gordy 4544GG (09/85)	Val Young Seduction (12-inch version) Seduction (Instrumental)
TMG12 0046	Gordy 4545GG (08/85)	El DeBarge with DeBarge You Wear It Well (Club Mix) You Wear It Well (Dub Mix) + Baby, Won't Cha Come Quick
TMG12 0047	Motown 4546MG (09/85)	Mello-Mackin-D & Mr. Stretch Back To School (Dance Mix) + Back To School (Long single mix Back To School (Instrumental)
TMG12 0048	Gordy 4547GG (09/85)	Mary Jane Girls Break It Up (12-inch version) Break It Up (Instrumental version)
TMG12 0049	Tamla 4548TG (10/85)	Stevie Wonder Part-Time Lover (12-inch version) Part-Time Lover (Instrumental) Note: Also issued as a special 12-inch single cassette.
TMG12 0050	Motown 4549	Note: Unissued.
TMG12 0051	Gordy 4550GG (10/85)	The Temptations Do You Really Love Your Baby (Club Mix) + Do You Really Love Your Baby (Radio Edit) Do You Really Love Your Baby (Dub Mix) + I'll Keep A
		Light In My Window
TMG12 0052	Motown 4551	Note: Unissued.
TMG12 0053	Gordy 4552GG (11/85)	El DeBarge with DeBarge The Heart Is Not So Smart (Club Mix) The Heart Is Not So Smart (Dub mix) + Share My World
TMG12 0054	Tamla 4553TG (11/85)	Stevie Wonder Go Home (12-inch version) Go Home (Radio Edit of 12-inch Vocal) + Go Home (12-inch Instrumental)
TMG12 0055	Motown 4554MG (1985)	Roq-In Zoo Frig-O-Rator (12-inch Dub Mix) Frig-O-Rator (Dub) + Frig-O-Rator (Edit of Dub Mix)
TMG12 0056	Motown 4555MG (1985)	Warp 9 Skips A Beat (Dub Mix) + Skips A Beat (Radio Edit of Club Mix) Skips A Beat (Dub Mix) + Skips A Beat (Fly-Dubmix)
TMG12 0057	Motown 4556MG (1985)	Sam Harris I'd Do It All Again (Head Mix) I'd Do It All Again (Foot mix) + I'd Do It All Again (Remixed radio edit)
TMG12 0058	Gordy 4557GG (1985)	Val Young If You Should Ever Be Lonely (Club Mix) + If You Should Ever Be Lonely (Radio Edit of Club Mix) If You Should Ever Be Lonely (Street Mix)
TMG12 0059	Motown 4558MG (1986)	Vanity Under The Influence Under The Influence
TMG12 0060	Motown 4559	Note: Unissued.
TMG12 0061	Motown 4560MG (06/86)	Sam Harris The Bells (12-inch version) Forever For You
TMG12 0062	Gordy 4561GG (06/86)	Rick James Sweet And Sexy Thing (12-inch version) Sweet And Sexy Thing (Instrumental) + Sweet And Sexy Thing (Vocal)
TMG12 0063	Motown 4562MG (06/86)	Burston & Littlejohn Rich And Famous (12-inch version) Rich And Famous (Single version) + Rich And Famous (Instrumental)
TMG12 0064	Motown 4563	Note: Unissued.

TMG12 0065	Motown 4564	Note: Unissued.
TMG12 0066	Gordy 4565GG (08/86)	Rick James Forever And A Day (12-inch version) Forever And A Day (12-inch Instrumental)
TMG12 0067	Motown 4566MG (09/86)	Rockwell Grow-Up Grow-Up (Dub) + Grow-Up (Rhythm Mix)
TMG12 0068	Motown 4567MG (09/86)	Chico DeBarge Talk To Me (12-inch version) Talk To Me (LP version) + Talk To Me (Single version)

TMG CONSOLIDATED SERIES ALBUMS

TMGLP 0001	Motown 6000ML (01/82)	Bettye Lavette TELL ME A LIE Note: Originally scheduled to be issued on Motown M8-964M1, but changed to this number at the very last minute.
TMGLP 0002	Tamla 6001TL (01/82)	Smokey Robinson YES IT'S YOU LADY
TMGLP 0003	Tamla 6002TL2 (05/82)	Stevie Wonder ORIGINAL MUSIQUARIUM VOLUMES I AND II Note: Two-album set. Also available on Compact Disc TCD06113TD2.
TMGLP 0004	Gordy 6003GL (03/82)	Nolen & Crossley AMBIENCE
TMGLP 0005	Motown 6004ML (02/82)	Dazz Band KEEP IT LIVE
TMGLP 0006	Gordy 6005GL (05/82)	Rick James THROWIN' DOWN
TMGLP 0007	Gordy 6006GL (04/82)	High Inergy SO RIGHT
TMGLP 0008	Motown 6007ML (09/82)	Lionel Richie LIONEL RICHIE Note: Also issued in compact disc MCD06007MD.
TMGLP 0009	Gordy 6008GL (04/82)	The Temptations REUNION
TMGLP 0010	Motown 6009ML (03/82)	Charlene I'VE NEVER BEEN TO ME
TMGLP 0011	Motown 6010ML (05/82)	Jean Carn TRUST ME
TMGLP 0012	Motown 6011ML (06/82)	Ozone LI'L SUZY
TMGLP 0013	Gordy 6012GL (07/82)	DeBarge ALL THIS LOVE
TMGLP 0014	6013	Note: Unissued.
TMGLP 0015	Motown 6014ML (07/82)	Regal Funkharmonic Orchestra STRUNG OUT ON MOTOWN
TMGLP 0016	Tamla 6015TL (01/83)	Gene Van Buren WHAT'S YOUR PLEASURE
TMGLP 0017	6016	Note: Unissued.
TMGLP 0018	Motown 6017ML (07/82)	Jermaine Jackson LET ME TICKLE YOUR FANCY
TMGLP 0019	Latino 6018LL (06/82)	Jose Feliciano ESCENAS DE AMOR Note: Issued on Motown's Latin subsidiary label, Latino.
TMGLP 0020	Motown 6019ML (05/82)	O. C. Smith LOVE CHANGES
TMGLP 0021	Motown 6020ML (08/82)	Billy Preston PRESSIN' ON
TMGLP 0022	Latino 6021LL (07/82)	Pedro Montero AMOR SECRETO
TMGLP 0023	Motown 6022ML (08/82)	Bobby Nunn SECOND TO NUNN
TMGLP 0024	Gordy 6023GL (10/82)	Bobby Militello BLOW "RICK JAMES PRESENTS BOBBY M"
TMGLP 0025	Motown 6024ML (01/83)	Charlene THE SKY'S THE LIMIT
TMGLP 0026	Motown 6025ML (10/82)	Lawanda Page WATCH IT SUCKER
TMGLP 0027	Motown 6026ML (11/82)	Bill Cosby HIMSELF (ORIGINAL MOTION PICTURE SOUNDTRACK) Note: Also available on compact disc MCD06026MD.

TMGLP 0028	Motown 6027ML (10/82)	Charlene USED TO BE
TMGLP 0029	Motown 6028ML (11/82)	Commodores ALL THE GREAT HITS
TMGLP 0030	Motown 6029ML (11/83)	Monalisa Young KNIFE
TMGLP 0031	Tamla 6030TL (12/82)	Smokey Robinson TOUCH THE SKY
TMGLP 0032	Motown 6031ML (01/83)	Dazz Band ON THE ONE
TMGLP 0033	Gordy 6032GL (02/83)	The Temptations SURFACE THRILLS
TMGLP 0034	Motown 6033ML (11/82)	Stephanie Mills LOVE HAS LIFTED ME
TMGLP 0035	Motown 6034ML (11/82)	Thelma Houston REACHIN' ALL AROUND
TMGLP 0036	Motown 6035ML (03/83)	Jose Feliciano ROMANCE IN THE NIGHT
TMGLP 0037	Motown 6036ML (04/83)	Finis Henderson FINIS
TMGLP 0038	Motown 6037ML (03/83)	Ozone GLASSES
TMGLP 0039	Motown 6038ML (03/83)	Kagny & The Dirty Rats KAGNY & THE DIRTY RATS
TMGLP 0040	Tamla 6039TL (05/83)	Syreeta THE SPELL
TMGLP 0041	Gordy 6040GL (03/83)	Mary Jane Girls MARY JANE GIRLS
TMGLP 0042	Gordy 6041GL (04/83)	High Inergy GROOVE PATROL Note: Includes two songs with Smokey Robinson.
TMGLP 0043	Gordy 6042GL (07/83)	Stone City Band MEET THE STONE CITY BAND "OUT FROM THE SHADOW"
TMGLP 0044	Gordy 6043GL (08/83)	Rick James COLD BLOODED
TMGLP 0045	Motown 6044ML2 (04/83)	Commodores ANTHOLOGY Note: Two-album set. Originally scheduled for Motown 954ML2.
TMGLP 0046	Motown 6045ML (06/83)	Michael Lovesmith I CAN MAKE IT HAPPEN
TMGLP 0047	Morocco 6046CL (05/84)	Wolf & Wolf WOLF & WOLF Note: Issued on Motown's rock subsidiary label, Morocco.
TMGLP 0048	Tamla 6047TL	Stevie Wonder PEOPLE MOVE, HUMAN PLAYS Note: Unissued.
TMGLP 0049	Motown 6048ML5 (05/83)	Various Artists THE MOTOWN STORY: THE FIRST 25 YEARS Note: Issued promotionally as a seven-record boxed set, compared to only the five discs in the commercial issue.
TMGLP 0050	Motown 6049ML2 (05/83)	Diana Ross ANTHOLOGY Note: Two-album set.
TMGLP 0051	6050	Note: Unissued.
TMGLP 0052	Motown 6051ML (09/83)	Bobby Nunn PRIVATE PARTY
TMGLP 0053	Motown 6052ML (01/84)	Rockwell SOMEBODY'S WATCHING ME
TMGLP 0054	Motown 6053ML (07/83)	Jr. Walker BLOW THE HOUSE DOWN
TMGLP 0055	Motown 6054ML (09/83)	Commodores 13
TMGLP 0056	6055	Note: Unissued.
TMGLP 0057	Morocco 6056CL	Paul Sabu KILLER INSTINCT Note: Unissued.
TMGLP 0058	Morocco 6056CL (02/84)	Kidd Glove KIDD GLOVE Note: Promo copies pressed on yellow wax.
TMGLP 0059	Gordy 6057GL (01/84)	Dennis Edwards DON'T LOOK ANY FURTHER
TMGLP 0060	Motown 6058ML (09/83)	Marvin Gaye EVERY GREAT MOTOWN HIT OF MARVIN GAYE

TMGLP 0061	Motown 6059ML (10/83)	Lionel Richie CAN'T SLOW DOWN Note: Also available on compact disc MCD06059MD. Original title scheduled as POSITIVE SPACE.
TMGLP 0062	Morocco 6060CL (08/84)	Jakata LIGHT THE NIGHT
TMGLP 0063	Gordy 6061GL (10/83)	DeBarge IN A SPECIAL WAY
TMGLP 0064	Motown 6062ML (09/83)	Various Artists THE BIG CHILL (ORIGINAL MOTION PICTURE SOUNDTRACK)
TMGLP 0065	Morocco 6063CL (07/84)	The Coyote Sisters THE COYOTE SISTERS
TMGLP 0066	Tamla 6064TL (08/83)	Smokey Robinson BLAME IT ON LOVE AND ALL THE GREAT HITS
TMGLP 0067	Morocco 6065CL (08/83)	Various Artists GET CRAZY (ORIGINAL MOTION PICTURE SOUNDTRACK)
TMGLP 0068	Motown 6066ML (10/83)	Four Tops BACK WHERE I BELONG
TMGLP 0069	Morocco 6067CL (02/84)	Tiggi Clay TIGGI CLAY Note: Promo copies issued on yellow vinyl.
TMGLP 0070	Motown MCD06068MD (02/84)	Commodores COMPACT COMMAND PERFORMANCES: 14 GREATEST HITS Note: compact disc release.
TMGLP 0071	Tamla TCD06069TD (02/84)	Marvin Gaye COMPACT COMMAND PERFORMANCES: 15 GREATEST HITS Note: compact disc release.
TMGLP 0072	Motown MCD06070MD (02/84)	Michael Jackson & The Jackson 5 COMPACT COMMAND PERFORMANCES: 18 GREATEST HITS Note: compact disc release.
TMGLP 0073	Tamla TCD06071TD (02/84)	Smokey Robinson & the Miracles COMPACT COMMAND PERFORMANCES: 18 GREATEST HITS Note: compact disc release.
TMGLP 0074	Motown MCD06072MD (02/84)	Diana Ross COMPACT COMMAND PERFORMANCES: 14 GREATEST HITS Note: compact disc release.
TMGLP 0075	Motown MCD06073MD (02/84)	Diana Ross and the Supremes COMPACT COMMAND PERFORMANCES: 20 GREATEST HITS Note: compact disc release.
TMGLP 0076	Motown 6074MC (10/83)	Commodores MACHINE GUN MOVIN' ON Note: Double cassette release.
TMGLP 0077	Motown 6075MC (10/83)	Four Tops FOUR TOPS REACH OUT Note: Double cassette release.
TMGLP 0078	Motown 6076MC (10/83)	Marvin Gaye LIVE LET'S GET IT ON Note: Double cassette release.
TMGLP 0079	Motown 6077MC (10/83)	Michael Jackson GOT TO BE THERE BEN Note: Double cassette release.
TMGLP 0080	Motown 6078MC (10/83)	Rick James COME GET IT FIRE IT UP Note: Double cassette release.
TMGLP 0081	Motown 6079MC (10/83)	The Temptations MEET THE TEMPTATIONS MASTERPIECE Note: Double cassette release.
TMGLP 0082	Motown 6080MC (10/83)	Grover Washington, Jr. MR. MAGIC FEELS SO GOOD Note: Double cassette release.
TMGLP 0083	Motown 6081MC (10/83)	Stevie Wonder SIGNED, SEALED DELIVERED MY CHERIE AMOUR Note: Double cassette release.
TMGLP 0084	Motown 6082MC (10/83)	Diana Ross TOUCH ME IN THE MORNING LIVE AT CAESAR'S PALACE Note: Double cassette release.
TMGLP 0085	Motown 6083MC (10/83)	Marvin Gaye & Tammi Terrell YOU'RE ALL I NEED UNITED Note: Double cassette release.
TMGLP 0086	Motown 6084ML (11/83)	Dazz Band JOYSTICK Note: Original title scheduled as VIBRATIONS.

TMGLP 0087	Gordy 6085GL (10/83)	The Temptations BACK TO BASICS

TMGLP 0088	Motown 6086ML (12/83)	Various Artists CHRISTINE (ORIGINAL MOTION PICTURE SOUNDTRACK)

TMGLP 0089	6087	Note: Unissued.

TMGLP 0090	Motown 6088ML (04/84)	Bobby King LOVE IN THE FIRE

TMGLP 0091	Tamla 6089TL	Smokey Robinson ESSAR Note: Unissued. See Tamla 6098TL.

TMGLP 0092	Motown 6090ML (07/84)	Charlene HIT & RUN LOVER

TMGLP 0093	Motown 6091ML (03/84)	Various Artists MAKING TRAX (THE GREAT INSTRUMENTALS)

TMGLP 0094	Gordy 6092GL (02/85)	Mary Jane Girls ONLY FOUR YOU Note: Also available on compact disc GCD06092GD.

TMGLP 0095	Motown 6093ML (04/84)	Michael Lovesmith DIAMOND IN THE RAW

TMGLP 0096	Motown 6094ML (04/84)	Various Artists MORE SONGS FROM THE ORIGINAL SOUNDTRACK OF "THE BIG CHILL"

TMGLP 0097	Gordy 6095GL (05/84)	Rick James REFLECTIONS: ALL THE GREATEST HITS Note: Also available on compact disc GCD06095GD.

TMGLP 0098	Motown 6096ML (05/84)	KoKo PoP KOKO POP

TMGLP 0099	Morocco 6097CL (05/84)	Duke Jupiter WHITE KNUCKLE RIDE

TMGLP 0100	Tamla 6098TL (05/84)	Smokey Robinson ESSAR Note: Originally scheduled for release on Tamla 6089TL.

TMGLP 0101	Motown 6099ML (05/84)	Michael Jackson & The Jackson 5 14 GREATEST HITS Note: Issued commercially as a picture disc, along with special white glitter glove. Promo copies on black wax with white label.

TMGLP 0102	Motown 6100MC (05/84)	Michael Jackson & The Jackson 5 16 GREATEST HITS Note: Issued in special cassette format only.

TMGLP 0103	Motown 6101ML (05/84)	Michael Jackson FAREWELL MY SUMMER LOVE Note: First issues have title FAREWELL MY SUMMER LOVE 1984. Date dropped on subsequent pressings.

TMGLP 0104	Motown 6102ML (08/84)	Vanity WILD ANIMAL

TMGLP 0105	Motown 6103ML (08/84)	Sam Harris SAM HARRIS Note: Originally scheduled to be titled OUT OF CONTROL. Also available on compact disc MCD06103MD.

TMGLP 0106	Motown 6104ML (09/84)	Kagny MIND CONTROL

TMGLP 0107	Motown MCD06105MD (09/84)	Diana Ross ALL THE GREAT LOVE SONGS Note: A compact disc release.

TMGLP 0108	Motown MCD06106MD (09/84)	Four Tops COMPACT COMMAND PERFORMANCE: 19 GREATEST HITS Note: A compact disc release.

TMGLP 0109	Motown MCD06107MD (09/84)	Commodores ALL THE GREAT LOVE SONGS Note: A compact disc release.

TMGLP 0110	Motown 6108ML (07/84)	Stevie Wonder SELECTIONS FROM THE ORIGINAL MOTION PICTURE SOUNDTRACK FROM "THE WOMAN IN RED" Note: Music performed by Stevie Wonder and Dionne Warwick.

TMGLP 0111	Motown 6109MD (10/84)	Gladys Knight & The Pips COMPACT COMMAND PERFORMANCES: 17 GREATEST HITS Note: A compact disc release.

TMGLP 0112	Motown MCD06110MD (10/84)	Various Artists MOTOWN GRAMMY RHYTHM & BLUES PERFORMANCES OF THE 1960'S & 1970'S: 16 GREATEST HITS Note: A compact disc release.

TMGLP 0113	Motown MCD06111MD (10/84)	Al Green COMPACT COMMAND PERFORMANCES: 14 GREATEST HITS Note: A compact disc release.

TMGLP 0114	Motown 6112ML (11/84)	Phyllis St. James AIN'T NO TURNIN' BACK

TMGLP 0115	Tamla TCD06113TD2 (01/85)	Stevie Wonder ORIGINAL MUSIQUARIUM VOLS. I AND II

Note: A double compact disc release of Tamla album 6002TL2.

TMGLP 0116	Tamla TCD06114TD	Stevie Wonder ORIGINAL MUSIQUARIUM VOL. 2

Note: Not issued separately. See Tamla TCD06113TD2.

TMGLP 0117	Tamla TCD06115TD2 (01/85)	Stevie Wonder SONGS IN THE KEY OF LIFE VOLS. I AND II

Note: A double compact disc release of Tamla album T13-340C2.

TMGLP 0118	Tamla TCD06116TD	Stevie Wonder SONGS IN THE KEY OF LIFE VOL. 2

Note: Not issued separately. See Tamla TCD06115TD2.

TMGLP 0119	Motown 6117ML (09/84)	Dazz Band JUKEBOX

TMGLP 0120	Motown 6118ML (09/84)	Bobby Nunn FRESH

TMGLP 0121	Gordy 6119GL (10/84)	The Temptations TRULY FOR YOU

TMGLP 0122	Motown MCD06120MD (11/84)	Various Artists THE BIG CHILL (& OTHER CLASSIC HITS)

Note: A compact disc release.

TMGLP 0123	Motown 6121ML (11/84)	Thomas McClary THOMAS McCLARY

TMGLP 0124	Motown 6122ML (01/85)	Rockwell CAPTURED

TMGLP 0125	Gordy 6123GL (01/85)	DeBarge RHYTHM OF THE NIGHT

Note: Also available on compact disc Gordy GCD06123GD.

TMGLP 0126	Motown 6124ML (12/84)	Commodores NIGHTSHIFT

Note: Also available on compact disc Motown MCD06124MD.

TMGLP 0127	Gordy GCD06125GD (03/85)	The Temptations COMPACT COMMAND PERFORMANCES: 17 GREATEST HITS

Note: A compact disc release.

TMGLP 0128	Motown MCD06126MD (03/85)	Grover Washington, Jr. COMPACT COMMAND PERFORMANCES: GROVER WASHINGTON, JR. AT HIS BEST

Note: A compact disc release.

TMGLP 0129	Tamla TCD06127TD2 (03/85)	Stevie Wonder JOURNEY THROUGH THE SECRET LIFE OF PLANTS

Note: A double compact disc release.

TMGLP 0130	Motown 6128ML (03/85)	Various Artists ORIGINAL SOUNDTRACK FROM THE MOTION PICTURE "BERRY GORDY'S THE LAST DRAGON"

Note: Unissued.

TMGLP 0131	6129	

TMGLP 0132	Gordy 6130GL (05/85)	Four Tops MAGIC

TMGLP 0133	Motown 6131ML (12/84)	Various Artists THE FLAMINGO KID (ORIGINAL MOTION PICTURE SOUNDTRACK)

TMGLP 0134	Motown MCD06132MD (04/85)	Various Artists 25 NO. 1 HITS FROM 25 YEARS

Note: A compact disc release.

TMGLP 0135	Motown MCD06133MD (04/85)	Diana Ross ORIGINAL SOUNDTRACK FROM THE MOTION PICTURE "LADY SINGS THE BLUES"

Note: A compact disc release of Motown album M758D.

TMGLP 0136	Tamla 6134TL (10/85)	Stevie Wonder IN SQUARE CIRCLE

Note: Also available on compact disc Tamla TCD06134TD.

TMGLP 0137	Gordy 6135GL (04/85)	Rick James THE GLOW

TMGLP 0138	Motown 6136ML (03/85)	The Emotions IF I ONLY KNEW

TMGLP 0139	Motown MCD06137MD (09/85)	Various Artists 20 GREATEST SONGS IN MOTOWN HISTORY

Note: A compact disc release.

TMGLP 0140	Motown MCD06138MD (07/85)	Various Artists THE GREATEST SONGS WRITTEN BY HOLLAND - DOZIER - HOLLAND

Note: A compact disc release. Title also given as HOLLAND - DOZIER - HOLLAND: THE COMPOSER SERIES.

TMGLP 0141	Motown MCD06139MD (07/85)	Various Artists THE GREATEST SONGS WRITTEN BY SMOKEY ROBINSON Note: A compact disc release. Title also given as SMOKEY ROBINSON: THE COMPOSER SERIES.
TMGLP 0142	Motown MCD06140MD (04/85)	Various Artists THE GREATEST SONGS WRITTEN BY ASHFORD & SIMPSON Note: A compact disc release. Title also given as ASHFORD & SIMPSON: THE COMPOSER SERIES.
TMGLP 0143	Motown 6141ML (04/85)	Maureen Steele NATURE OF THE BEAST
TMGLP 0144	Motown 6142ML (06/85)	Willie Hutch MAKING A GAME OF LIFE
TMGLP 0145	Motown MCD06143MD (07/85)	Commodores and Lionel Richie and Diana Ross LIONEL RICHIE THE COMPOSER: GREAT LOVE SONGS WITH THE COMMODORES AND DIANA ROSS Note: A compact disc release. Includes duets by Lionel Richie and Diana Ross.
TMGLP 0146	Tamla TCD06144TD (07/85)	Stevie Wonder LOVE SONGS: 20 CLASSIC HITS Note: A compact disc release.
TMGLP 0147	Motown 6145ML (05/85)	Michael Lovesmith RHYMES OF PASSION
TMGLP 0148	Motown 6146ML (1986)	Alfie THAT LOOK
TMGLP 0149	Gordy 6147GL (06/85)	Val Young SEDUCTION
TMGLP 0150	Gordy 6148GL (06/85)	Dennis Edwards COOLIN' OUT
TMGLP 0151	Motown 6149ML (06/85)	Dazz Band HOT SPOT
TMGLP 0152	Motown 6150ML (07/85)	Lushus Daim & the Pretty Vain MORE THAN YOU CAN HANDLE Note: Original title scheduled as MIDNIGHT LUST.
TMGLP 0153	Tamla TCD06151TD (07/85)	Stevie Wonder TALKING BOOK Note: A compact disc release.
TMGLP 0154	Tamla TCD06152TD (07/85)	Stevie Wonder INNERVISIONS Note: A compact disc release.
TMGLP 0155	Tamla TCD06153TD (10/85)	Marvin Gaye MARVIN GAYE & HIS WOMEN: 21 CLASSIC DUETS Note: A compact disc release. Duets with Diana Ross, Mary Wells, Kim Weston, and Tammi Terrell.
TMGLP 0156	Motown 6154ML	Nick Jameson A CROWD OF ONE Note: Unissued. See Motown 6210ML.
TMGLP 0157	Motown 6155ML (09/85)	Koko Pop SECRETS OF LONELY BOYS
TMGLP 0158	Tamla 6156TL (10/85)	Smokey Robinson SMOKE SIGNALS
TMGLP 0159	Motown 6157ML (10/85)	Pal PAL
TMGLP 0160	Motown 6158ML (08/86)	Lionel Richie DANCING ON THE CEILING Note: Also available on compact disc Motown MCD06158MD.
TMGLP 0161	Motown MCD06159MD (05/86)	Various Artists GOOD FEELING MUSIC OF THE BIG CHILL GENERATION, VOLUME ONE Note: A compact disc release.
TMGLP 0162	Motown MCD06160MD (05/86)	Various Artists GOOD FEELING MUSIC OF THE BIG CHILL GENERATION, VOLUME TWO Note: A compact disc release.
TMGLP 0163	Motown MCD06161MD (05/86)	Various Artists GOOD FEELING MUSIC OF THE BIG CHILL GENERATION, VOLUME THREE Note: A compact disc release.
TMGLP 0164	Motown 6162ML (10/85)	Duke Jupiter THE LINE OF YOUR LOVE
TMGLP 0165	Motown 6163ML (09/85)	Warp 9 FADE IN, FADE OUT
TMGLP 0166	Gordy 6164GL (11/85)	The Temptations TOUCH ME

TMGLP 0167	Motown 6165ML (12/85)	Sam Harris SAM-I-AM
TMGLP 0168	Motown 6166ML (03/86)	Troy Johnson GETTING A GRIP ON LOVE
TMGLP 0169	Motown 6167ML (02/86)	Vanity SKIN ON SKIN
TMGLP 0170	Motown 6168ML (03/86)	Guinn GUINN
TMGLP 0171	Tamla TCD06169TD (02/86)	The Marvelettes COMPACT COMMAND PERFORMANCES: 23 GREATEST HITS Note: A compact disc release.
TMGLP 0172	Gordy GCD06170GD (02/86)	Martha Reeves & the Vandellas COMPACT COMMAND PERFORMANCES: 26 GREATEST HITS Note: A compact disc release.
TMGLP 0173	Motown MCD06171MD (02/86)	Mary Wells COMPACT COMMAND PERFORMANCES: 22 GREATEST HITS Note: A compact disc release.
TMGLP 0174	Tamla 6172TL (03/86)	Marvin Gaye MOTOWN REMEMBERS MARVIN GAYE
TMGLP 0175	Gordy GCD06173GD (03/86)	DeBarge GREATEST HITS Note: A compact disc release.
TMGLP 0176	Motown MCD06174MD (03/86)	Various Artists MOTOWN'S BIGGEST POP HITS Note: A compact disc release.
TMGLP 0177	6175	Note: Unissued.
TMGLP 0178	6176	Note: Unissued.
TMGLP 0179	Motown MCD06177MD (04/86)	Various Artists ENDLESS LOVE: 15 OF MOTOWN'S GREATEST LOVE SONGS Note: A compact disc release.
TMGLP 0180	Motown 6178ML (06/86)	Rockwell GENIE
TMGLP 0181	Motown 6179ML (06/86)	Fizzy Qwick FIZZY QWICK

TMGLP 0182	Motown 6180ML (04/86)	Various Artists A FINE MESS (ORIGINAL MOTION PICTURE SOUNDTRACK)
TMGLP 0183	Gordy 6181GL (04/86)	El DeBarge EL DEBARGE Note: Also available on compact disc Gordy GCD06181GD.
TMGLP 0184	Gordy GCD06182GD (08/86)	Teena Marie COMPACT COMMAND PERFORMANCES: 14 GREATEST HITS Note: A compact disc release.
TMGLP 0185	Motown MCD06183MD (04/86)	Various Artists 20 HARD-TO-FIND MOTOWN CLASSICS, VOLUME 1 Note: A compact disc release.
TMGLP 0186	Motown MCD06184MD (04/86)	Various Artists 20 HARD-TO-FIND MOTOWN CLASSICS, VOLUME II Note: A compact disc release.
TMGLP 0187	Gordy 6185GL (04/86)	Rick James THE FLAG Note: Also available on compact disc Gordy GCD06185GD.
TMGLP 0188	Motown MCD06186MD (08/86)	Various Artists PIPPIN (ORIGINAL BROADWAY CAST) Note: A compact disc release of Motown album M-760L.
TMGLP 0189	6187	Unissued. Number once given to 8000 series CD.
TMGLP 0190	Motown MCD06188MD2 (08/86)	Four Tops ANTHOLOGY Note: A double compact disc release containing 43 songs.
TMGLP 0191	Motown MCD06189MD2 (08/86)	The Temptations ANTHOLOGY Note: A double compact disc release containing 41 songs.
TMGLP 0192	6190	Note: Unissued.
TMGLP 0193	Tamla TCD06191TD (08/86)	Marvin Gaye LIVE AT THE LONDON PALLADIUM Note: A compact disc release of Tamla album T7-352R2.
TMGLP 0194	Motown MCD06192MD (08/86)	Various Artists YOU CAN'T HURRY LOVE: ALL THE GREAT LOVE SONGS OF THE PAST 25 YEARS Note: A compact disc release.
TMGLP 0195	Motown MCD06193MD (08/86)	The Supremes THE SUPREMES 25TH ANNIVERSARY Note: A double compact disc

		release. Includes songs with the Temptations.
TMGLP 0196	Motown MCD06194MD2 (08/86)	The Jackson 5 ANTHOLOGY Note: A double compact disc release containing 43 songs. Includes some solo cuts by Michael Jackson and Jermaine Jackson.
TMGLP 0197	Motown MCD06195MD2 (08/86)	Michael Jackson ANTHOLOGY Note: A double compact disc release containing 40 songs. Includes some songs recorded with The Jackson 5.
TMGLP 0198	Tamla TCD06196TD2 (08/86)	Smokey Robinson & The Miracles ANTHOLOGY Note: A double compact disc release containing 46 songs. Includes some songs by the Miracles without Smokey Robinson.
TMGLP 0199	Motown MCD06197MD2 (08/86)	Diana Ross ANTHOLOGY Note: A double compact disc release containing 38 songs. Includes some duets with Marvin Gaye and Lionel Richie.
TMGLP 0200	Motown MCD06198MD2 (08/86)	Diana Ross & The Supremes ANTHOLOGY Note: A double compact disc release containing 50 songs. Includes some songs with the Temptations and by the Supremes without Diana Ross.
TMGLP 0201	Motown MCD06199MD2 (08/86)	Marvin Gaye ANTHOLOGY Note: A double compact disc release containing 47 songs. Includes duets with Mary Wells, Kim Weston, and Tammi Terrell.
TMGLP 0202	Motown MCD06200MD2 (08/86)	Gladys Knight & The Pips ANTHOLOGY Note: A double compact disc release containing 40 songs.
TMGLP 0203	Tamla TCD06201TD (08/86)	Marvin Gaye COMPACT COMMAND PERFORMANCES VOLUME II: 20 GREATEST HITS Note: A compact disc release.
TMGLP 0204	Tamla TCD06202TD (08/86)	Smokey Robinson & The Miracles COMPACT COMMAND PERFORMANCES VOLUME II: 22 GREATEST HITS Note: A compact disc release.
TMGLP 0205	Motown MCD06203MD (08/86)	Jr. Walker & The All Stars COMPACT COMMAND PERFORMANCES: 19 GREATEST HITS

		Note: A compact disc release.
TMGLP 0206	Motown MCD06204MD2 (08/86)	The Temptations THE TEMPTATIONS 25TH ANNIVERSARY Note: A double compact disc release.
TMGLP 0207	Tamla TCD06205TD (08/86)	Stevie Wonder HOTTER THAN JULY Note: A compact disc release.
TMGLP 0208	Motown MCD06206MD (08/86)	Jimmy Reed JIMMY REED Note: A compact disc release.
TMGLP 0209	Gordy 6207GL (08/86)	The Temptations TO BE CONTINUED ...
TMGLP 0210	Motown MCD06208MD (08/86)	Little Richard LITTLE RICHARD Note: A compact disc release.
TMGLP 0211	6209	Note: Unissued.
TMGLP 0212	Motown 6210ML (08/86)	Nick Jameson A CROWD OF ONE
TMGLP 0213	Motown 6211ML (08/86)	Four Tops HOT NIGHTS
TMGLP 0214	Motown 6212ML (08/86)	Stacy Lattislaw TAKE ME ALL THE WAY
TMGLP 0215	6213	Note: Unissued.
TMGLP 0216	Motown 6214ML (10/86)	Chico DeBarge CHICO DE BARGE
TMGLP 0217	6215	Note: Unissued.
TMGLP 0218	Gordy 6216GL (10/86)	General Kane IN FULL CHILL

TMG CONSOLIDATED SERIES COMPACT DISCS

TMGCD 0001	Motown MOTD- MCD08000MD (08/86)	Michael Jackson GOT TO BE THERE BEN Note: A compact disc release.
TMGCD 0002	Tamla TAMD- TCD08001TD (08/86)	Smokey Robinson BEING WITH YOU WHERE THERE'S SMOKE Note: A compact disc release.
TMGCD 0003	Motown MOTD- MCD08002MD (08/86)	Diana Ross DIANA THE BOSS Note: A compact disc release.

TMGCD   Gordy GORD-   Teena Marie
0004   GCD08003GD   IRONS IN THE FIRE
        (08/86)   IT MUST BE MAGIC
                        Note: A compact disc release.

TMGCD   Tamla TAMD-   Smokey Robinson
0005   TCD08004TD   & The Miracles
        (08/86)   GOING TO A GO-GO
                      THE TEARS OF A CLOWN
                        Note: A compact disc release.

TMGCD   Motown MOTD- The Supremes
0006   MCD08005MD   WHERE DID OUR LOVE GO
        (08/86)   I HEAR A SYMPHONY
                        Note: A compact disc release.

TMGCD   Tamla TAMD-   Stevie Wonder
0007   TCD08006TD   SIGNED, SEALED, DELIVERED
        (08/86)   MY CHERIE AMOUR
                        Note: A compact disc release.

TMGCD   Motown MOTD- Four Tops
0008   MCD08007MD   REACH OUT
        (08/86)   STILL WATERS RUN
                        DEEP
                        Note: A compact disc release.

TMGCD   Motown MOTD- Gladys Knight &
0009   MCD08008MD   The Pips
        (08/86)   NEITHER ONE OF US
                      ALL I NEED IS TIME
                        Note: A compact disc release.

TMGCD   Motown MOTD- Grover
0010   MCD08009MD   Washington, Jr.
        (08/86)   MR. MAGIC
                      FEELS SO GOOD
                        Note: A compact disc release.

TMGCD   Tamla TAMD-   Marvin Gaye
0011   TCD08010TD   I HEARD IT THROUGH THE
        (08/86)   GRAPEVINE
                      I WANT YOU
                        Note: A compact disc release.
                      First album originally issued as IN
                      THE GROOVE.

TMGCD   Motown MOTD- The Jackson 5
0012   MCD08011MD   THIRD ALBUM
        (08/86)   MAYBE TOMORROW
                        Note: A compact disc release.

TMGCD   Gordy GORD-   Rick James
0013   GCD08012GD   STREET SONGS
        (08/86)   THROWIN' DOWN
                        Note: A compact disc release.

TMGCD   Tamla TAMD-   Marvin Gaye
0014   TCD08013TD   WHAT'S GOING ON
        (08/86)   LET'S GET IT ON
                        Note: A compact disc release.

TMGCD   Motown MOTD- Commodores
0015   MCD08014MD   NATURAL HIGH
        (08/86)   MIDNIGHT MAGIC
                        Note: A compact disc release.

TMGCD   Tamla TAMD-   Marvin Gaye
0016   TCD08015TD   MARVIN GAYE & TAMMI
        (08/86)   TERRELL'S GREATEST HITS
                      DIANA & MARVIN
                        Note: A compact disc release.
                      Duets with Tammi Terrell and
                      Diana Ross.

TMGCD   Gordy GORD-   Temptations
0017   GCD08016GD   CLOUD NINE
        (08/86)   PUZZLE PEOPLE
                        Note: A compact disc release.

TMGCD   Gordy GORD-   Temptations
0018   GCD08017GD   THE TEMPTATIONS
        (08/86)   CHRISTMAS CARD
                      GIVE LOVE AT
                        CHRISTMAS
                        Note: A compact disc release.

TMGCD   Motown MOTD- Al Green
0019   MCD08018MD   LET'S STAY TOGETHER
        (08/86)   I'M STILL IN LOVE WITH
                        YOU
                        Note: A compact disc release.

TMGCD   Motown MOTD- The Jackson 5
0020   MCD08019MD   DIANA ROSS PRESENTS THE
        (08/86)   JACKSON 5
                      ABC
                        Note: A compact disc release.

TMGCD   Gordy GORD-   Edwin Starr
0021   GCD08020GD   25 MILES
        (08/86)   WAR AND PEACE
                        Note: A compact disc release.

TMGCD   Motown MOTD- The Supremes
0022   MCD08021MD   LOVE CHILD
        (08/86)   SUPREMES A GO GO
                        Note: A compact disc release.

TMGCD   Gordy GORD-   Temptations
0023   GCD08022GD   PSYCHEDELIC SHACK
        (08/86)   ALL DIRECTIONS
                        Note: A compact disc release.

TMGCD   Motown MOTD- Jr. Walker & The
0024   MCD08023MD   All Stars
        (08/86)   SHOTGUN
                      ROAD RUNNER
                        Note: A compact disc release.

TMGCD   Motown MOTD- Mary Wells
0025   MCD08024MD   TWO LOVERS
        (08/86)   MY GUY
                        Note: A compact disc release.

TMGCD   Tamla TAMD-   Stevie Wonder
0026   TCD08025TD   FOR ONCE IN MY LIFE
        (08/86)   UP TIGHT
                        Note: A compact disc release.

TMGCD   Motown MOTD- Diana Ross
0027   MCD08026MD   TOUCH ME IN THE MORNING
        (08/86)   BABY IT'S ME
                        Note: A compact disc release.

TMGCD 0028	Motown MOTD-MCD08027MD (08/86)	Four Tops FOUR TOPS FOUR TOPS' SECOND ALBUM Note: A compact disc release.

TMGCD 0029	Tamla TAMD-TCD08028TD (08/86)	Smokey Robinson SMOKEY QUIET STORM Note: A compact disc release.

TMGCD 0030	Motown MOTD-MCD08029MD (08/86)	Diana Ross & The Supremes DIANA ROSS & THE SUPREMES GREATEST HITS, VOLUMES I AND II Note: A compact disc release.

TMGCD 0031	Motown MOTD-MCD08030MD (08/86)	Grover Washington, Jr. SECRET PLACE ALL THE KING'S HORSES Note: A compact disc release.

TMGCD 0032	Motown MOTD-MCD08031MD (08/86)	Gladys Knight & The Pips EVERYBODY NEEDS LOVE IF I WERE YOUR WOMAN Note: A compact disc release.

TMGCD 0033	Motown MOTD-MCD08032MD (08/86)	Diana Ross & The Supremes LET THE SUNSHINE IN CREAM OF THE CROP Note: A compact disc release.

TMGCD 0034	Motown MOTD-MCD08033MD (08/86)	Rare Earth GET READY ECOLOGY Note: A compact disc release.

TMGCD 0035	Motown MOTD-MCD08034MD (08/86)	Various Artists EVERY GREAT MOTOWN SONG: THE FIRST 25 YEARS VOLUMES I AND II Note: A compact disc release.

TMGCD 0036	Gordy GORD-GCD08035GD (08/86)	Temptations A SONG FOR YOU MASTERPIECE Note: A compact disc release.

TMGCD 0037	Tamla TAMD-TCD08036TD (08/86)	Marvin Gaye TROUBLE MAN (ORIGINAL SOUND TRACK) M.P.G. Note: A compact disc release.

TMGCD 0038	Gordy GORD-GCD08037GD (08/86)	Temptations LIVE AT THE COPA WITH A LOT O' SOUL Note: A compact disc release.

TMGCD 0039	Motown MOTD-MCD08038MD (08/86)	Diana Ross & Supremes with The Temptations DIANA ROSS & THE SUPREMES JOIN THE TEMPTATIONS TOGETHER Note: A compact disc release.

TMGCD 0040	Motown MOTD-MCD08039MD (08/86)	Commodores HEROES COMMODORES Note: A compact disc release.

TMGCD 0041	Motown MOTD-MCD08040MD (08/86)	Al Green CALL ME LIVIN' FOR YOU Note: A compact disc release.

TMGCD 0042	Motown MOTD-MCD08041MD (08/86)	Diana Ross & The Supremes / Stevie Wonder MERRY CHRISTMAS SOMEDAY AT CHRISTMAS Note: A compact disc release.

V.I.P. 7-INCH SINGLES

VI45 0001	V.I.P. 25002 (02/64)	The Serenaders If Your Heart Says Yes I'll Cry Tomorrow Note: Originally scheduled for release on Motown 1046, but changed to above number instead.

VI45 0002	V.I.P. 25003 (02/64)	Joanne & The Triangles After The Showers Come Flowers Don't Be A Cry Baby

VI45 0003	V.I.P. 25004 (02/64)	The Hornets Give Me A Kiss She's My Baby

VI45 0004	V.I.P. 25005	Note: Unissued.

VI45 0005	V.I.P. 25006 (1964)	Andantes (Like A) Nightmare If You Were Mine

VI45 0006	V.I.P. 25007 (09/64)	The Velvelettes Needle In A Haystack Should I Tell Them

VI45 0007	V.I.P. 25008 (1964)	Oma Heard Lifetime Man Mr. Lonely Heart

VI45 0008	V.I.P. 25009 (10/64)	Mickey McCullers Same Old Story Who You Gonna Run To Note: "A" side also issued on Tamla 54064.

VI45 0009	V.I.P. 25010	Note: Unissued.

VI45 0010	V.I.P. 25011 (10/64)	The Headliners Tonight's The Night You're Bad News

VI45 0011	V.I.P. 25012 (12/64)	Ray Oddis Randy, The Newspaper Boy Happy Ghoul Tide

VI45 0012	V.I.P. 25013 (12/64)	The Velvelettes He Was Really Sayin' Somethin' Throw A Farewell Kiss

VI45 0013	V.I.P. 25014	Note: Unissued.

VI45 0014	V.I.P. 25015	Note: Unissued.

VI45 0015 — V.I.P. 25016 (05/65) — The Vows — Buttered Popcorn — Tell Me
Note: "Buttered Popcorn" also issued as a promo with blank "B" side.

VI45 0016 — V.I.P. 25017 (05/65) — The Velvelettes — Lonely Lonely Girl Am I — I'm The Exception To The Rule

VI45 0017 — V.I.P. 25018 (05/65) — The Lewis Sisters — He's An Oddball — By Some Chance

VI45 0018 — V.I.P. 25019 (1965) — Danny Day — This Time Last Summer — Please Don't Turn The Lights Out

VI45 0019 — V.I.P. 25020 (1965) — Isley Brothers — I Hear A Symphony — Who Could Ever Doubt My Love
Note: "A" side also issued on Tamla 54135B. "B" side also issued on Tamla 54133B.

VI45 0020 — V.I.P. 25021 — The Velvelettes — A Bird In The Hand (Is Worth Two In The Bush) — Since You've Been Loving Me
Note: Unissued. Released on V.I.P. 25030. "B" side also issued on V.I.P. 25034.

VI45 0021 — V.I.P. 25022 (09/65) — Richard Anthony — I Don't Know What To Do — What Now My Love

VI45 0022 — V.I.P. 25023 (08/65) — Little Lisa — Hang On Bill — Puppet On A String

VI45 0023 — V.I.P. 25024 (09/65) — The Lewis Sisters — You Need Me — Moonlight On The Beach
Note: "(The Singing School Teachers)" under the name of the artists.

VI45 0024 — V.I.P. 25025 (10/65) — The Dalton Boys — I've Been Cheated — Something's Bothering You

VI45 0025 — V.I.P. 25026 (11/65) — The Headliners — We Call It Fun — Voodoo Plan

VI45 0026 — V.I.P. 25027 (11/65) — R. Dean Taylor — Let's Go Somewhere — Poor Girl

VI45 0027 — V.I.P. 25028 (12/65) — The Monitors — Say You — All For Someone
Note: See also V.I.P. 25032.

VI45 0028 — V.I.P. 25029 (12/65) — The Elgins — Darling Baby — Put Yourself In My Place
Note: First pressings as by "The Downbeats."

VI45 0029 — V.I.P. 25030 (11/65) — The Velvelettes — A Bird In The Hand (Is Worth Two In The Bush) — Since You've Been Loving Me
Note: See also V.I.P. 25034.

VI45 0030 — V.I.P. 25031 (12/65) — Chris Clark — Don't Be Too Long — Do Right Baby Do Right
Note: "B" side vocal accompaniment credited to The Lewis Sisters.

VI45 0031 — V.I.P. 25032 (03/66) — The Monitors — Greetings (This Is Uncle Sam) — Say You
Note: "B" side also issued on V.I.P. 25028.

VI45 0032	V.I.P. 25033	Note: Unissued.

VI45 0033 — V.I.P. 25034 (04/66) — The Velvelettes — These Things Will Keep Me Loving You — Since You've Been Loving Me
Note: Also issued on Soul 35025. "B" side previously issued on V.I.P. 25021B and 25030B.

VI45 0034 — V.I.P. 5035 (06/66) — Rick, Robin & Him — Three Choruses Of Despair — Cause You Know Me

VI45 0035 — V.I.P. 25036 (07/66) — The LaSalles — La La La La La — This Is True

VI45 0036 — V.I.P. 25037 (07/66) — The Elgins — Heaven Must Have Sent You — Stay In My Lonely Arms
Note: Later issued on V.I.P. 25065.

VI45 0037 — V.I.P. 25038 (08/66) — Chris Clark — Love's Gone Bad — Put Yourself In My Place
Note: "A" side also issued on red vinyl.

VI45 0038 — V.I.P. 25039 (12/66) — The Monitors — Since I Lost You Girl — Don't Put Off 'Til Tomorrow What You Can Do Today

VI45 0039 — V.I.P. 25040 (01/67) — The Underdogs — Love's Gone Bad — Mo Jo Hanna

VI45 0040	V.I.P. 25041 (02/67)	Chris Clark I Want To Go Back There Again I Love You
VI45 0041	V.I.P. 25042 (04/67)	R. Dean Taylor There's A Ghost In My House Don't Fool Around Note: "B" side later issued on V.I.P. 25045.
VI45 0042	V.I.P. 25043 (06/67)	The Elgins I Understand My Man It's Been A Long Long Time
VI45 0043	V.I.P. 25044 (02/68)	Debbie Dean Why Am I Lovin' You Stay My Love
VI45 0044	V.I.P. 25045 (04/68)	R. Dean Taylor Gotta See Jane Don't Fool Around Note: "A" side also issued on Rare Earth 5004A and 5026A.
VI45 0045	V.I.P. 25046 (04/68)	The Monitors Bring Back The Love The Further You Look, The Less You See
VI45 0046	V.I.P. 25047 (04/68)	The Honest Men Cherie Baby
VI45 0047	V.I.P. 25048	Note: Unissued.
VI45 0048	V.I.P. 25049 (1969)	The Monitors Step By Step (Hand In Hand) Time Is Passin' By Note: Also issued on Soul 35049.
VI45 0049	V.I.P. 25050 (10/69)	The Spinners In My Diary (She's Gonna Love Me) At Sundown Note: Also issued on Motown 1155. "B" side later issued on V.I.P. 25054B.
VI45 0050	V.I.P. 25051 (10/69)	The Lollipops Cheating Is Telling On You Need Your Love
VI45 0051	V.I.P. 25052 (11/69)	Chuck Jackson The Day The World Stood Still Baby, I'll Get It Note: Also issued on Motown 1160.
VI45 0052	V.I.P. 25053 (01/70)	Bobby Taylor Oh, I've Been Bless'd Blackmail Note: "Oh, I've Been Bless'd" was scheduled to be issued as the main side of Gordy 7088, but this single was never released. "A" side also issued on red vinyl.

VI45 0053	V.I.P. 25054 (02/70)	The Spinners Message From A Black Man (She's Gonna Love Me) At Sundown Note: See also V.I.P. 25050.
VI45 0054	V.I.P. 25055 (03/70)	Ivy Jo I Remember When (Dedicated To Beverly) Sorry Is A Sorry Word Note: "A" side also issued on red vinyl.
VI45 0055	V.I.P. 25056 (05/70)	Chuck Jackson Two Feet From Happiness Let Somebody Love Me
VI45 0056	V.I.P. 25057 (07/70)	The Spinners It's A Shame Together We Can Make Such Sweet Music Note: "B" side also released on Motown 1235A. The Motown version is nine seconds longer than above version.
VI45 0057	V.I.P. 25058 (09/70)	Hearts Of Stone It's A Lonesome Road Yesterday's Love Is Over Note: "A" side also issued on red vinyl.
VI45 0058	V.I.P. 25059 (01/71)	Chuck Jackson Pet Names Is There Anything Love Can't Do
VI45 0059	V.I.P. 25060 (12/70)	The Spinners We'll Have It Made My Whole World Ended (The Moment You Left Me) Note: "A" side also issued on red vinyl.
VI45 0060	V.I.P. 25061 (04/71)	King Floyd Heartaches Together We Can Do Anything
VI45 0061	V.I.P. 25062 (04/71)	P.J. (I've Given You) The Best Years Of My Live It Takes A Man To Teach A Woman How To Love Note: "B" side also released on Tamla 54215B.
VI45 0062	V.I.P. 25063 (05/71)	Ivy Jo I'd Still Love You I Can Feel The Pain Note: Both songs taken from the unreleased album IVY JO IS IN THIS BAG (VS-1293).
VI45 0063	V.I.P. 25064 (06/71)	Hearts Of Stone If I Could Give You The World You Gotta Sacrifice (We Gotta Sacrifice)

VI45 0064	V.I.P. 25065 (09/71)	The Elgins Heaven Must Have Sent You Stay In My Lonely Arms Note: Rerelease of V.I.P. 25037.
VI45 0065	V.I.P. 25066 (07/71)	The Stylists What Is Love Where Did The Children Go
VI45 0066	V.I.P. 25067	Chuck Jackson Who You Gonna Run To Forgive My Jealousy Note: Unissued.
VI45 0067	V.I.P. 25068 (11/71)	Tony & Carolyn We've Only Just Begun - I'll Be There I Can Get Away From You (But I Can't Get Over You)
VI45 0068	V.I.P. 25069 (02/72)	Posse Feel Like Givin' Up Take Somebody Like You

V.I.P. 7-INCH COLOR VINYL SINGLES

VICO 0001	V.I.P. 25038 (08/66)	Chris Clark Love's Gone Bad Note: Red vinyl.
VICO 0002	V.I.P. 25053 (01/70)	Bobby Taylor Oh, I've Been Bless'd Note: Red vinyl.
VICO 0003	V.I.P. 25055 (03/70)	Ivy Jo I Remember When (Dedicated To Beverly) Note: Red vinyl.
VICO 0004	V.I.P. 25058 (09/70)	Hearts Of Stone It's A Lonesome Road Note: Red vinyl.
VICO 0005	V.I.P. 25060 (12/70)	Spinners We'll Have It Made Note: Red vinyl.

V.I.P. ALBUMS

VILP 0001	V.I.P. VIPS-400 (10/66)	The Elgins DARLING BABY
VILP 0002	V.I.P. VIPS-401	The Velvelettes THE VELVELETTES Note: Unissued.
VILP 0003	V.I.P. VIPS-402 (1966)	The Abbey Tavern Singers WE'RE OFF TO DUBLIN IN THE GREEN
VILP 0004	V.I.P. VIPS-403 (09/70)	Chuck Jackson TEARDROPS KEEP FALLING ON MY HEART

VILP 0005	V.I.P. VIPS-402 (10/70)	Hearts Of Stone STOP THE WORLD....WE WANNA GET ON
VILP 0006	V.I.P. VIPS-405 (10/70)	The Spinners 2ND TIME AROUND
VILP 0007	V.I.P. VIPS-406	Ivy Jo IVY JO IS IN THIS BAG Note: Unissued.
VILP 0008	V.I.P. VIPS-407 (04/71)	King Floyd HEART OF THE MATTER

WEED ALBUMS

WELP 0001	Weed 801 (11/69)	Chris Clark CC RIDES AGAIN

WORKSHOP JAZZ 7-INCH SINGLES

WO45 0001	Workshop Jazz WSJ 2001 (1962)	Hank & Carol Diamond Exodus I Remember You
WO45 0002	Workshop Jazz WSJ 2002 (1962)	The Earl Washington All Stars Opus No. 3 March Lightly
WO45 0003	Workshop Jazz WSJ 2003 (1962)	Paula Greer I Want To Talk About You So In Love
WO45 0004	Workshop Jazz WSJ 2004 (1963)	Dave Hamilton Mellow In Coli Late Freight
WO45 0005	Workshop Jazz WSJ 2005 (1963)	The Johnny Griffith Trio I'll See You Later I Did
WO45 0006	Workshop Jazz WSJ 2006 (1963)	The George Bohannon Quartet Bobbie El Rig
WO45 0007	Workshop Jazz WSJ 2007 (1963)	Paula Greer I Did Falling In Love With Love

WORKSHOP JAZZ ALBUMS

WOLP 0001	Workshop Jazz WSJ 202 (11/63)	Earl Washington All Stars ALL STAR JAZZ
WOLP 0002	Workshop Jazz WSJ 203 (02/63)	Paula Greer INTRODUCING MISS PAULA GREER

WOLP 0003	Workshop Jazz WSJ 204 (02/63)	Paula Greer and Johnny Griffith Trio DETROIT JAZZ
WOLP 0004	Workshop Jazz WSJ 205 (03/63)	Johnny Griffith Trio JAZZ
WOLP 0005	Workshop Jazz WSJ 206 (03/63)	Dave Hamilton BLUE VIBRATIONS
WOLP 0006	Workshop Jazz WSJ 207 (02/63)	George Bohannon Quartet BOSS BOSSA NOVA
WOLP 0007	Workshop Jazz WSJ 208	Note: Unissued.
WOLP 0008	Workshop Jazz WSJ 209	Note: Unissued.
WOLP 0009	Workshop Jazz WSJ 210	Note: Unissued.
WOLP 0010	Workshop Jazz WSJ 211	Note: Unissued.
WOLP 0011	Workshop Jazz WSJ 212 (06/64)	Lefty Edwards THE RIGHT SIDE OF LEFTY EDWARDS
WOLP 0012	Workshop Jazz WSJ 213 (06/64)	Earl Washington REFLECTIONS
WOLP 0013	Workshop Jazz WSJ 214 (06/64)	George Bohannon Quartet BOLD BOHANNON
WOLP 0014	Workshop Jazz WSJ 215	Note: Unissued.
WOLP 0015	Workshop Jazz WSJ 216	Herbie Williams THE SOUL AND SOUND OF HERBIE WILLIAMS
WOLP 0016	Workshop Jazz WSJ 217	Four Tops BREAKING THROUGH Note: Unissued.
WOLP 0017	Workshop Jazz WSJ 218	Note: Unissued.
WOLP 0018	Workshop Jazz WSJ 219 (08/64)	Pepper Adams COMPOSITIONS OF CHARLIE MINGUS
WOLP 0019	Workshop Jazz WSJ 220 (08/64)	Roy Brooks BEAT

PART V

MOTOWN
DISCOGRAPHY
(UNITED KINGDOM)

KEY TO
U.K. ENTRY NUMBER PREFIXES

ENTRY NUMBER PREFIX	LABEL OR SERIES NAME & RECORD FORMAT	DISCOGRAPHY PAGE NUMBER
DSLP	Deluxe Series Albums	355
FO45	Fontana 7-inch Singles	295
GA45	Gaiee 7-inch Singles	352
HI45	Hitsville 7-inch Singles	352
LO45	London America 7-inch Singles	295
MC45	MC 7-inch Singles	352
MO12	Motown 12-inch Singles	338
MO45	Motown 7-inch Singles	326
MOCD	Motown Compact Discs	351
MOLP	Motown Albums	345
MW45	Mowest 7-inch Singles	352
MWLP	Mowest Albums	353
OR45	Oriole 7-inch Singles	295
OREP	Oriole 7-inch EPs	295
ORLP	Oriole Albums	295
PILP	Pickwick Albums	357
PR45	Prodigal 7-inch Singles	353
PRLP	Prodigal Albums	354
RA45	Rare Earth 7-inch Singles	354
RALP	Rare Earth Albums	355
SILP	16 Big Hits Series Albums	357
SPLP	Special Series Albums	357
SS45	Stateside 7-inch Singles	296
SSEP	Stateside 7-inch EPs	297
SSLP	Stateside Albums	297
TM45	Tamla Motown 7-inch Singles	298
TMEP	Tamla Motown 7-inch EPs	316
TMLP	Tamla Motown Albums	317
TVLP	Television Series Albums	357
X2LP	Two- & Three-Record Album Sets	358

LONDON AMERICA
7-INCH SINGLES

LO45 0001	London America HLM 8998 (11/59)	Paul Gayten The Hunch Hot Cross Buns

                Note: Released in both 78 rpm
       and 45 rpm versions.

LO45 0002	London America HLU 9088 (04/60)	Barrett Strong Money (That's What I Want) Oh I Apologise
LO45 0003	London America HL 9276 (02/61)	The Miracles Shop Around Who's Lovin' You
LO45 0004	London America HL 9366 (06/61)	The Miracles Ain't It Baby The Only One I Love

FONTANA 7-INCH SINGLES

FO45 0001	Fontana H 355 (12/61)	The Marvelettes Please Mr. Postman So Long Baby
FO45 0002	Fontana H 384 (03/62)	The Miracles What's So Good About Goodbye I've Been Good To You
FO45 0003	Fontana H 386 (03/62)	The Marvelettes Twistin' Postman I Want A Guy
FO45 0004	Fontana H 387 (03/62)	Eddie Holland Jamie Take A Chance On Me

ORIOLE 7-INCH SINGLES

OR45 0001	Oriole CBA 1762 (09/62)	Mary Wells You Beat Me To The Punch Old Love (Let's Try It Again)
OR45 0002	Oriole CBA 1763 (09/62)	The Contours Do You Love Me Move Mr. Man
OR45 0003	Oriole CBA 1764 (09/62)	The Marvelettes Beechwood 4-5789 Someday Someway
OR45 0004	Oriole CBA 1775 (10/62)	Mike & The Modifiers I Found Myself A Brand New Baby It's Too Bad
OR45 0005	Oriole CBA 1795 (01/63)	The Miracles You've Really Got A Hold On Me Happy Landing
OR45 0006	Oriole CBA 1796 (01/63)	Mary Wells Two Lovers Operator
OR45 0007	Oriole CBA 1799 (02/63)	The Contours Shake Sherry You Better Get In Line
OR45 0008	Oriole CBA 1803 (02/63)	Marvin Gaye Stubborn Kind Of Fellow It Hurt Me Too
OR45 0009	Oriole CBA 1808 (03/63)	Eddie Holland If It's Love (It's Alright) It's Not Too Late
OR45 0010	Oriole CBA 1809 (03/63)	The Valadiers I Found A Girl You'll Be Sorry Someday
OR45 0011	Oriole CBA 1814 (03/63)	Martha & The Vandellas I'll Have To Let Him Go My Baby Won't Come Back
OR45 0012	Oriole CBA 1817 (04/63)	The Marvelettes Locking Up My Heart Forever
OR45 0013	Oriole CBA 1819 (04/63)	Martha & The Vandellas Come And Get These Memories Jealous Lover
OR45 0014	Oriole CBA 1829 (05/63)	Mary Wells Laughing Boy Two Wrongs Don't Make A Right
OR45 0015	Oriole CBA 1831 (05/63)	The Contours Don't Let Him Be Your Baby It Must Be Love
OR45 0016	Oriole CBA 1846 (07/63)	Marvin Gaye Pride And Joy One Of These Days
OR45 0017	Oriole CBA 1847 (07/63)	Mary Wells Your Old Stand By What Love Has Joined Together
OR45 0018	Oriole CBA 1853 (08/63)	Little Stevie Wonder Fingertips Pt. 2 Fingertips Pt. 1
OR45 0019	Oriole CBA 1863 (09/63)	The Miracles Mickey's Monkey Whatever Makes You Happy

ORIOLE 7-INCH EPS

OREP 0001	Oriole RE 1295 (10/61)	The Miracles SHOP AROUND

ORIOLE ALBUMS

ORLP 0001	Oriole PS 40043 (07/63)	The Contours DO YOU LOVE ME

ORLP 0002	Oriole PS 40044 (07/63)	The Miracles HI! WE'RE THE MIRACLES
ORLP 0003	Oriole PS 40045 (07/63)	Mary Wells TWO LOVERS
ORLP 0004	Oriole PS 40049 (08/63)	Little Stevie Wonder TRIBUTE TO UNCLE RAY
ORLP 0005	Oriole PS 40050 (08/63)	Little Stevie Wonder THE TWELVE-YEAR-OLD GENIUS--LIVE
ORLP 0006	Oriole PS 40051 (08/63)	Mary Wells BYE BYE BABY
ORLP 0007	Oriole PS 40052 (08/63)	Martha & The Vandellas COME AND GET THESE MEMORIES

STATESIDE 7-INCH SINGLES

SS45 0001	Stateside SS 228 (10/63)	Martha & The Vandellas Heatwave A Love Like Yours (Don't Come Knocking Every Day)
SS45 0002	Stateside SS 238 (11/63)	Little Stevie Wonder Workout Stevie, Workout Monkey Talk
SS45 0003	Stateside SS 242 (11/63)	Mary Wells You Lost The Sweetest Boy What's Easy For Two Is Hard For One
SS45 0004	Stateside SS 243 (11/63)	Marvin Gaye Can I Get A Witness I'm Crazy 'Bout My Baby
SS45 0005	Stateside SS 250 (01/64)	Martha & The Vandellas Quicksand Darling, I Hum Our Song
SS45 0006	Stateside SS 251 (01/64)	The Marvelettes As Long As I Know He's Mine Little Girl Blue
SS45 0007	Stateside SS 257 (01/64)	The Supremes When The Lovelight Starts Shining Thru' His Eyes Standing At The Crossroads Of Love
SS45 0008	Stateside SS 263 (02/64)	The Miracles I Gotta Dance To Keep From Crying Such Is Love, Such Is Life
SS45 0009	Stateside SS 272 (03/64)	Martha & The Vandellas Live Wire Old Love (Let's Try It Again)

SS45 0010	Stateside SS 273 (03/64)	The Marvelettes He's A Good Guy (Yes He Is) Goddess Of Love
SS45 0011	Stateside SS 278 (04/64)	The Temptations The Way You Do The Things You Do Just Let Me Know
SS45 0012	Stateside SS 282 (04/64)	The Miracles (You Can't Let The Boy Overpower) The Man In You Heartbreak Road
SS45 0013	Stateside SS 284 (04/64)	Marvin Gaye You're A Wonderful One When I'm Alone I Cry
SS45 0014	Stateside SS 285 (04/64)	Little Stevie Wonder Castles In The Sand Thank You (For Loving Me All The Way)
SS45 0015	Stateside SS 288 (05/64)	Mary Wells My Guy Oh Little Boy (What Did You Do To Me)
SS45 0016	Stateside SS 299 (05/64)	The Contours Can You Do It I'll Stand By You
SS45 0017	Stateside SS 305 (06/64)	Martha & The Vandellas In My Lonely Room A Tear For The Girl
SS45 0018	Stateside SS 307 (06/64)	Brenda Holloway Every Little Bit Hurts Land Of A Thousand Boys
SS45 0019	Stateside SS 316 (07/64)	Mary Wells & Marvin Gaye Once Upon A Time What's The Matter With You Baby
SS45 0020	Stateside SS 319 (07/64)	The Temptations I'll Be In Trouble The Girl's Alright With Me
SS45 0021	Stateside SS 323 (08/64)	Stevie Wonder Hey Harmonica Man This Little Girl
SS45 0022	Stateside SS 324 (08/64)	The Miracles I Like It Like That You're So Fine And Sweet
SS45 0023	Stateside SS 326 (08/64)	Marvin Gaye Try It Baby If My Heart Could Sing
SS45 0024	Stateside SS 327 (08/64)	The Supremes Where Did Our Love Go He Means The World To Me
SS45 0025	Stateside SS 334 (09/64)	The Marvelettes You're My Remedy A Little Bit Of Sympathy, A Little Bit Of Love

SS45 0026	Stateside SS 336 (09/64)	The Four Tops Baby I Need Your Loving Call On Me
SS45 0027	Stateside SS 345 (10/64)	Martha & The Vandellas Dancing In The Street There He Is (At My Door)
SS45 0028	Stateside SS 348 (10/64)	The Temptations (Girl) Why You Wanna Make Me Blue Baby Baby I Need You
SS45 0029	Stateside SS 350 (10/64)	The Supremes Baby Love Ask Any Girl
SS45 0030	Stateside SS 353 (11/64)	The Miracles That's What Love Is Made Of Would I Love You
SS45 0031	Stateside SS 357 (11/64)	Earl Van Dyke Soul Stomp Hot 'N' Tot
SS45 0032	Stateside SS 359 (11/64)	Kim Weston A Little More Love Go Ahead And Laugh
SS45 0033	Stateside SS 360 (11/64)	Marvin Gaye How Sweet It Is (To Be Loved By You) Forever
SS45 0034	Stateside SS 361 (11/64)	The Velvelettes Needle In A Haystack Should I Tell Them
SS45 0035	Stateside SS 363 (12/64)	Marvin Gaye & Kim Weston What Good Am I Without You I Want You Around
SS45 0036	Stateside SS 369 (01/65)	The Marvelettes Too Many Fish In The Sea A Need For Love
SS45 0037	Stateside SS 371 (01/65)	The Four Tops Without The One You Love (Life's Not Worthwhile) Love Has Gone
SS45 0038	Stateside SS 376 (01/65)	The Supremes Come See About Me (You're Gone But) Always In My Heart
SS45 0039	Stateside SS 377 (01/65)	The Miracles Come On Do The Jerk Baby Don't You Go
SS45 0040	Stateside SS 378 (01/65)	The Temptations My Girl (Talking 'Bout) Nobody But My Baby
SS45 0041	Stateside SS 381 (01/65)	The Contours Can You Jerk Like Me That Day When She Needed Me
SS45 0042	Stateside SS 383 (01/65)	Martha & The Vandellas Wild One Dancing Slow
SS45 0043	Stateside SS 384 (02/65)	Carolyn Crawford When Someone's Good To You My Heart
SS45 0044	Stateside SS 387 (02/65)	The Velvelettes He Was Really Sayin' Something Throw A Farewell Kiss
SS45 0045	Stateside SS 394 (03/65)	Tony Martin Talkin' To Your Picture Our Rhapsody

STATESIDE 7-INCH EPS

SSEP 0001	Stateside SE 1009 (01/64)	Various Artists R & B CHARTMAKERS Note: Martha & The Vandellas, the Miracles, the Marvelettes, Marvin Gaye.

SSEP 0002	Stateside SE 1014 (02/64)	Little Stevie Wonder
		I CALL IT PRETTY MUSIC,
		  BUT THE OLD PEOPLE CALL
		  IT THE BLUES

SSEP 0003	Stateside SE 1018 (04/64)	Various Artists R & B CHARTMAKERS NO. 2 Note: The Miracles, Kim Weston, the Supremes, the Marvelettes.
SSEP 0004	Stateside SE 1022 (06/64)	Various Artists R & B CHARTMAKERS NO. 3 Note: Marvin Gaye, the Darnells, Eddie Holland, Martha and the Vandellas.
SSEP 0005	Stateside SE 1025 (09/64)	Various Artists R & B CHARTMAKERS NO. 4 Note: The Supremes, Eddie Holland, the Temptations, the Contours.

STATESIDE ALBUMS

SSLP 0001	Stateside SL 10065 (03/64)	Various Artists ON STAGE
SSLP 0002	Stateside SL 10077 (05/64)	Various Artists SOUND OF THE R & B HITS
SSLP 0003	Stateside SL 10078 (05/64)	Little Stevie Wonder THE JAZZ SOUL OF LITTLE STEVIE WONDER
SSLP 0004	Stateside SL 10095 (09/64)	Mary Wells SINGS MY GUY
SSLP 0005	Stateside SL 10097 (10/64)	Mary Wells & Marvin Gaye TOGETHER

SSLP 0006 (11/64)	Stateside SL 10099	The Miracles FABULOUS MIRACLES
SSLP 0007 (11/64)	Stateside SL 10100	Marvin Gaye MARVIN GAYE
SSLP 0008 (01/65)	Stateside SL 10108	Stevie Wonder HEY HARMONICA MAN
SSLP 0009 (12/64)	Stateside SL 10109	The Supremes MEET THE SUPREMES

TAMLA MOTOWN 7-INCH SINGLES

TM45 0001 (03/65)	Tamla Motown TMG 501	The Supremes Stop! In The Name Of Love I'm In Love Again
TM45 0002 (03/65)	Tamla Motown TMG 502	Martha & The Vandellas Nowhere To Run Motoring
TM45 0003 (03/65)	Tamla Motown TMG 503	The Miracles Ooo Baby Baby All That's Good
TM45 0004 (03/65)	Tamla Motown TMG 504	The Temptations It's Growing What Love Has Joined Together
TM45 0005 (03/65)	Tamla Motown TMG 505	Stevie Wonder Kiss Me Baby Tears In Vain
TM45 0006 (03/65)	Tamla Motown TMG 506	Earl Van Dyke & The Soul Brothers All For You Too Many Fish In The Sea
TM45 0007 (03/65)	Tamla Motown TMG 507	Four Tops Ask The Lonely Where Did You Go
TM45 0008 (04/65)	Tamla Motown TMG 508	Brenda Holloway When I'm Gone I've Been Good To You
TM45 0009 (04/65)	Tamla Motown TMG 509	Junior Walker & The All Stars Shotgun Hot Cha
TM45 0010 (04/65)	Tamla Motown TMG 510	Marvin Gaye I'll Be Doggone You've Been A Long Time Coming
TM45 0011 (04/65)	Tamla Motown TMG 511	Kim Weston I'm Still Loving You Just Loving You

TM45 0012 (05/65)	Tamla Motown TMG 512	Shorty Long Out To Get You It's A Crying Shame
TM45 0013 (05/65)	Tamla Motown TMG 513	The Hit Pack Never Say No To Your Baby Let's Dance
TM45 0014 (05/65)	Tamla Motown TMB 514	The Spinners Sweet Thing How Can I
TM45 0015 (05/65)	Tamla Motown TMG 515	Four Tops I Can't Help Myself Sad Souvenirs
TM45 0016 (05/65)	Tamla Motown TMG 516	The Supremes Back In My Arms Again Whisper You Love Me Boy
TM45 0017 (06/65)	Tamla Motown TMG 517	Choker Campbell's Big Band Mickey's Monkey Pride And Joy
TM45 0018 (06/65)	Tamla Motown TMG 518	The Marvelettes I'll Keep Holding On No Time For Tears
TM45 0019 (06/65)	Tamla Motown TMG 519	Brenda Holloway Operator I'll Be Available
TM45 0020 (07/65)	Tamla Motown TMG 520	Junior Walker & The All Stars Do The Boomerang Tune Up
TM45 0021 (07/65)	Tamla Motown TBM 521	The Velvelettes Lonely Lonely Girl Am I I'm The Exception To The Rule
TM45 0022 (07/65)	Tamla Motown TMG 522	The Miracles The Tracks Of My Tears A Fork In The Road
TM45 0023 (08/65)	Tamla Motown TMG 523	The Spinners I'll Always Love You Tomorrow May Never Come Note: Also released as The Detroit Spinners.
TM45 0024 (08/65)	Tamla Motown TMG 524	Marvin Gaye Pretty Little Baby Now That You've Won Me
TM45 0025 (08/65)	Tamla Motown TMG 525	Marv Johnson Why Do You Want To Let Me Go I'm Not A Plaything
TM45 0026 (08/65)	Tamla Motown TMG 526	The Temptations Since I Lost My Baby You've Got To Earn It
TM45 0027 (08/65)	Tamla Motown TMG 527	The Supremes Nothing But Heartaches He Holds His Own

TM45 0028	Tamla Motown TMG 528 (08/65)	Four Tops It's The Same Old Song Your Love Is Amazing
TM45 0029	Tamla Motown TMG 529 (09/65)	Junior Walker & The All Stars Shake And Fingerpop Cleo's Back
TM45 0030	Tamla Motown TMG 530 (09/65)	Martha & The Vandellas You've Been In Love Too Long Love (Makes Me Do Foolish Things)
TM45 0031	Tamla Motown TMG 531 (09/65)	The Contours First I Look At The Purse Searching For A Girl
TM45 0032	Tamla Motown TMG 532 (09/65)	Stevie Wonder High Heel Sneakers Music Talk
TM45 0033	Tamla Motown TMG 533 (10/65)	Billy Eckstine Had You Been Around Down To Earth
TM45 0034	Tamla Motown TMG 534 (10/65)	Dorsey Burnette Jimmy Brown Everybody's Angel
TM45 0035	Tamla Motown TMG 535 (10/65)	The Marvelettes Danger Heartbreak Dead Ahead Your Cheating Ways
TM45 0036	Tamla Motown TMG 536 (10/65)	The Lewis Sisters You Need Me Moonlight On The Beach
TM45 0037	Tamla Motown TMG 537 (10/65)	Tony Martin The Bigger Your Heart Is (The Harder You'll Fall) The Two Of Us
TM45 0038	Tamla Motown TMG 538 (10/65)	Kim Weston Take Me In Your Arms (Rock Me A Little While) Don't Compare Me With Her
TM45 0039	Tamla Motown TMG 539 (11/65)	Marvin Gaye Ain't That Peculiar She's Got To Be Real
TM45 0040	Tamla Motown TMG 540 (11/65)	The Miracles My Girl Has Gone Since You Won My Heart
TM45 0041	Tamla Motown TMG 541 (11/65)	The Temptations My Baby Don't Look Back
TM45 0042	Tamla Motown TMG 542 (11/65)	Four Tops Something About You Darling, I Hum Our Song
TM45 0043	Tamla Motown TMG 543 (11/65)	The Supremes I Hear A Symphony Who Could Ever Doubt My Love
TM45 0044	Tamla Motown TMG 544 (01/66)	Barbara McNair You're Gonna Love My Baby The Touch Of Time
TM45 0045	Tamla Motown TMG 545 (01/66)	Stevie Wonder Uptight (Everything's Alright) Purple Rain Drops
TM45 0046	Tamla Motown TMG 546 (01/66)	The Marvelettes Don't Mess With Bill Anything You Wanna Do
TM45 0047	Tamla Motown TMG 547 (02/66)	The Miracles Going To A Go-Go Choosey Beggar
TM45 0048	Tamla Motown TMG 548 (02/66)	The Supremes My World Is Empty Without You Everything Is Good About You
TM45 0049	Tamla Motown TMG 549 (02/66)	Martha & The Vandellas My Baby Loves Me Never Leave Your Baby's Side
TM45 0050	Tamla Motown TMG 550 (02/66)	Junior Walker & The All Stars Cleo's Mood Baby You Know You Ain't Right
TM45 0051	Tamla Motown TMG 551 (02/66)	The Elgins Put Yourself In My Place Darling Baby
TM45 0052	Tamla Motown TMG 552 (03/66)	Marvin Gaye One More Heartache When I Had Your Love
TM45 0053	Tamla Motown TMG 553 (03/66)	The Four Tops Shake Me, Wake Me (When It's Over) Just As Long As You Need Me
TM45 0054	Tamla Motown TMG 554 (03/66)	Kim Weston Helpless A Love Like Yours (Don't Come Knocking Every Day)
TM45 0055	Tamla Motown TMG 555 (03/66)	The Isley Brothers This Old Heart Of Mine (Is Weak For You) There's No Love Left
TM45 0056	Tamla Motown TMG 556 (03/66)	Brenda Holloway Together 'Til The End Of Time Sad Song
TM45 0057	Tamla Motown TMG 557 (04/66)	The Temptations Get Ready Fading Away
TM45 0058	Tamla Motown TMG 558 (04/66)	Stevie Wonder Nothing's Too Good For My Baby With A Child's Heart

TM45 0059	Tamla Motown TMG 559 (05/66)	Junior Walker & The All Stars Road Runner Shoot Your Shot
TM45 0060	Tamla Motown TMG 560 (05/66)	The Supremes Love Is Like An Itching In My Heart He's All I Got
TM45 0061	Tamla Motown TMG 561 (05/66)	Tammi Terrell Come On And See Me Baby Don't Cha Worry
TM45 0062	Tamla Motown TMG 562 (05/66)	The Marvelettes You're The One Paper Boy
TM45 0063	Tamla Motown TMG 563 (06/66)	Marvin Gaye Take This Heart Of Mine Need Your Lovin' (Want You Back)
TM45 0064	Tamla Motown TMG 564 (06/66)	The Contours Determination Just A Little Misunderstanding
TM45 0065	Tamla Motown TMG 565 (06/66)	The Temptations Ain't Too Proud To Beg You'll Lose A Precious Love
TM45 0066	Tamla Motown TMG 566 (06/66)	The Isley Brothers Take Some Time Out For Love Who Could Ever Doubt My Love
TM45 0067	Tamla Motown TMG 567 (07/66)	Martha & The Vandellas What Am I Going To Do Without Your Love Go Ahead And Laugh
TM45 0068	Tamla Motown TMS 568 (07/66)	Four Tops Loving You Is Sweeter Than Ever I Like Everything About You
TM45 0069	Tamla Motown TMG 569 (07/66)	The Miracles Whole Lot Of Shakin' In My Heart (Since I Met You)
TM45 0070	Tamla Motown TMG 570 (08/66)	Stevie Wonder Blowin' In The Wind Ain't That Asking For Trouble
TM45 0071	Tamla Motown TMG 571 (08/66)	Junior Walker & The All Stars How Sweet It Is (To Be Loved By You) Nothing But Soul
TM45 0072	Tamla Motown TMG 572 (08/66)	The Isley Brothers I Guess I'll Always Love You I Hear A Symphony
TM45 0073	Tamla Motown TMG 574 (08/66)	Shorty Long Function At The Junction Call On Me
TM45 0074	Tamla Motown TMG 574 (09/66)	Marvin Gaye Little Darling (I Need You) Hey Diddle Diddle
TM45 0075	Tamla Motown TMG 575 (09/66)	The Supremes You Can't Hurry Love Put Yourself In My Place
TM45 0076	Tamla Motown TMG 576 (09/66)	Gladys Knight & The Pips Just Walk In My Shoes Stepping Closer To Your Heart
TM45 0077	Tamla Motown TMG 577 (09/66)	Jimmy Ruffin What Becomes Of The Brokenhearted Baby I've Got It
TM45 0078	Tamla Motown TMG 578 (09/66)	The Temptations Beauty Is Only Skin Deep You're Not An Ordinary Girl
TM45 0079	Tamla Motown TMG 579 (10/66)	Four Tops Reach Out I'll Be There Until You Love Someone
TM45 0080	Tamla Motown TMG 580 (10/66)	The Velvelettes These Things Will Keep Me Loving You Since You've Been Loving Me
TM45 0081	Tamla Motown TMG 581 (11/66)	Brenda Holloway Hurt A Little Everyday Where Were You
TM45 0082	Tamla Motown TMG 582 (11/66)	Martha & The Vandellas I'm Ready For Love He Doesn't Love Her Anymore
TM45 0083	Tamla Motown TMG 583 (11/66)	The Elgins Heaven Must Have Sent You Stay In My Lonely Arms
TM45 0084	Tamla Motown TMG 584 (11/66)	The Miracles (Come 'Round Here) I'm The One You Need Save Me
TM45 0085	Tamla Motown TMG 585 (11/66)	The Supremes You Keep Me Hangin' On Remove This Doubt
TM45 0086	Tamla Motown TMG 586 (12/66)	Junior Walker & The All Stars Money (That's What I Want) Pt. 1 Money (That's What I Want) Pt. 2
TM45 0087	Tamla Motown TMG 587 (12/66)	The Temptations (I Know) I'm Losing You Little Miss Sweetness
TM45 0088	Tamla Motown TMG 588 (12/66)	Stevie Wonder A Place In The Sun Sylvia

TM45 0089	Tamla Motown TMG 589 (01/67)	Four Tops Standing In The Shadows Of Love Since You've Been Gone
TM45 0090	Tamla Motown TMG 590 (01/67)	Marvin Gaye & Kim Weston It Takes Two It's Got To Be A Miracle (This Thing Called Love)
TM45 0091	Tamla Motown TMG 591 (01/67)	Chris Clark Love's Gone Bad Put Yourself In My Place
TM45 0092	Tamla Motown TMG 592 (01/67)	The Originals Goodnight Irene Need Your Lovin' (Want You Back)
TM45 0093	Tamla Motown TMG 593 (02/67)	Jimmy Ruffin I've Passed This Way Before Tomorrow's Tears
TM45 0094	Tamla Motown TMG 594 (02/67)	The Marvelettes The Hunter Gets Captured By The Game I Think I Can Change You
TM45 0095	Tamla Motown TMG 595 (02/67)	The Velvelettes Needle In A Haystack He Was Really Saying Somethin'
TM45 0096	Tamla Motown TMG 596 (02/67)	Junior Walker & The All Stars Pucker Up Buttercup Anyway You Wannta'
TM45 0097	Tamla Motown TMG 597 (02/67)	The Supremes Love Is Here And Now You're Gone There's No Stopping Us Now
TM45 0098	Tamla Motown TMG 598 (03/67)	Smokey Robinson & The Miracles The Love I Saw In You Was Just A Mirage Swept For You Baby
TM45 0099	Tamla Motown TMG 599 (03/67)	Martha & The Vandellas Jimmy Mack Third Finger, Left Hand
TM45 0100	Tamla Motown TMG 600 (03/67)	Shorty Long Chantilly Lace Your Love Is Amazing
TM45 0101	Tamla Motown TMG 601 (03/67)	Four Tops Bernadette I Got A Feeling
TM45 0102	Tamla Motown TMG 602 (03/67)	Stevie Wonder Travelin' Man Hey Love
TM45 0103	Tamla Motown TMG 603 (04/67)	Jimmy Ruffin Gonna Give Her All The Love I've Got World So Wide, Nowhere To Hide (From Your Heart)
TM45 0104	Tamla Motown TMG 604 (04/67)	Gladys Knight & The Pips Take Me In Your Arms And Love Me Do You Love Me Just A Little, Honey
TM45 0105	Tamla Motown TMG 605 (05/67)	The Contours It's So Hard Being A Loser Your Love Grows More Precious Everyday
TM45 0106	Tamla Motown TMG 606 (05/67)	The Isley Brothers Got To Have You Back Just Ain't Enough Love
TM45 0107	Tamla Motown TMG 607 (05/67)	The Supremes The Happening All I Know About You
TM45 0108	Tamla Motown TMG 608 (05/67)	Brenda Holloway Just Look What You've Done Starting The Hurt All Over Again
TM45 0109	Tamla Motown TMG 609 (05/67)	The Marvelettes When You're Young And In Love The Day You Take One (You Have To Take The Other)
TM45 0110	Tamla Motown TMG 610 (05/67)	The Temptations All I Need Sorry Is A Sorry Word
TM45 0111	Tamla Motown TMG 611 (06/67)	Marvin Gaye & Tammi Terrell Ain't No Mountain High Enough Give A Little Love
TM45 0112	Tamla Motown TMG 612 (06/67)	Four Tops 7 Rooms Of Gloom I'll Turn To Stone
TM45 0113	Tamla Motown TMG 613 (06/67)	Stevie Wonder I Was Made To Love Her Hold Me
TM45 0114	Tamla Motown TMG 614 (07/67)	Smokey Robinson & The Miracles More Love Swept For You Baby
TM45 0115	Tamla Motown TMG 614 (07/67)	Smokey Robinson & The Miracles More Love Come Spy With Me Note: Alternative "B" side.
TM45 0116	Tamla Motown TMG 615 (07/67)	The Elgins It's Been A Long Time I Understand My Man
TM45 0117	Tamla Motown TMG 616 (08/67)	Diana Ross & The Supremes Reflections Going Down For The Third Time

TM45 0118	Tamla Motown TMG 617 (08/67)	Jimmy Ruffin Don't You Miss Me A Little Bit Baby I Want Her Love
TM45 0119	Tamla Motown TMG 618 (08/67)	Marvin Gaye Your Unchanging Love I'll Take Care Of You
TM45 0120	Tamla Motown TMG 619 (09/67)	Gladys Knight & The Pips Everybody Needs Love Since I've Lost You
TM45 0121	Tamla Motown TMG 620 (09/67)	The Temptations You're My Everything I've Been Good To You
TM45 0122	Tamla Motown TMG 621 (09/67)	Martha & The Vandellas Love Bug Leave My Heart Alone One Way Out
TM45 0123	Tamla Motown TMG 622 (09/67)	Brenda Holloway You've Made Me So Very Happy I've Got To Find It Note: See also Tamla Motown TMG 700.
TM45 0124	Tamla Motown TMG 623 (10/67)	Four Tops You Keep Running Away If You Don't Want My Love
TM45 0125	Tamla Motown TMG 624 (10/67)	Chris Clark From Head To Toe The Beginning Of The End
TM45 0126	Tamla Motown TMG 625 (10/67)	Marvin Gaye & Tammi Terrell Your Precious Love Hold Me Oh My Darling
TM45 0127	Tamla Motown TMG 626 (10/67)	Stevie Wonder I'm Wondering Every Time I See You I Go Wild
TM45 0128	Tamla Motown TMG 627 (10/67)	Detroit Spinners For All We Know I'll Always Love You
TM45 0129	Tamla Motown TMG 628 (11/67)	Barbara Randolph I Got A Feeling You Got Me Hurtin' All Over
TM45 0130	Tamla Motown TMG 629 (11/67)	Gladys Knight & The Pips I Heard It Through The Grapevine It's Time To Go Now
TM45 0131	Tamla Motown TMG 630 (11/67)	Edwin Starr I Want My Baby Back Gonna Keep On Tryin' Til I Win Your Love
TM45 0132	Tamla Motown TMG 631 (11/67)	Smokey Robinson & The Miracles I Second That Emotion You Must Be Love
TM45 0133	Tamla Motown TMG 632 (11/67)	Diana Ross & The Supremes In And Out Of Love I Guess I'll Always Love You
TM45 0134	Tamla Motown TMG 633 (12/67)	The Temptations (Loneliness Made Me Realise) It's You That I Need I Want A Love I Can See
TM45 0135	Tamla Motown TMG 634 (12/67)	The Four Tops Walk Away Renee Mame
TM45 0136	Tamla Motown TMG 635 (12/67)	Marvin Gaye & Tammi Terrell If I Could Build Me Whole World Around You If This World Were Mine
TM45 0137	Tamla Motown TMG 636 (01/68)	Martha Reeves & The Vandellas Honey Chile Show Me The Way
TM45 0138	Tamla Motown TMG 637 (01/68)	Junior Walker & The All Stars Come See About Me Sweet Soul
TM45 0139	Tamla Motown TMG 638 (01/68)	Chris Clark I Want To Go Back There Again I Love You
TM45 0140	Tamla Motown TMG 639 (01/68)	The Marvelettes My Baby Must Be A Magician I Need Someone
TM45 0141	Tamla Motown TMG 640 (01/68)	Marvin Gaye You Change What You Can
TM45 0142	Tamla Motown TMG 641 (02/68)	The Temptations I Wish It Would Rain I Truly, Truly Believe
TM45 0143	Tamla Motown TMG 642 (02/68)	The Elgins Put Yourself In My Place Darling Baby
TM45 0144	Tamla Motown TMG 643 (02/68)	Rita Wright I Can't Give Back The Love I Feel For You Something On My Mind
TM45 0145	Tamla Motown TMG 644 (02/68)	Shorty Long Night Fo' Last Night Fo' Last (Instrumental
TM45 0146	Tamla Motown TMG 645 (03/68)	Gladys Knight & The Pips The End Of Our Road Don't Let Her Take Your Love From Me
TM45 0147	Tamla Motown TMG 646 (03/68)	Edwin Starr I Am The Man For You Baby My Weakness Is You

TM45 0148	Tamla Motown TMG 647 (03/68)	Four Tops If I Were A Carpenter Your Love Is Wonderful

TM45 0149	Tamla Motown TMG 648 (03/68)	Smokey Robinson & The Miracles If You Can Want When The Words From Your Heart Get Caught Up In Your Throat

TM45 0150	Tamla Motown TMG 649 (03/68)	Jimmy Ruffin I'll Say Forever My Love Everybody Needs Love

TM45 0151	Tamla Motown TMG 650 (04/68)	Diana Ross & The Supremes Forever Came Today Time Changes Things

TM45 0152	Tamla Motown TMG 651 (04/68)	Chuck Jackson Girls, Girls, Girls (You Can't Let The Boy Overpower) The Man In You

TM45 0153	Tamla Motown TMG 652 (04/68)	Isley Brothers Take Me In Your Arms (Rock Me A Little While) Why When Love Has Gone

TM45 0154	Tamla Motown TMG 653 (04/68)	Stevie Wonder Shoo Be Doo Be Doo Da Day Why Don't You Lead Me To Love

TM45 0155	Tamla Motown TMG 654 (05/68)	Bobby Taylor & The Vancouvers Does Your Mama Know About Me Fading Away

TM45 0156	Tamla Motown TMG 655 (05/68)	Marvin Gaye & Tammi Terrell Ain't Nothing Like The Real Thing Little Ole Boy, Little Ole Girl

TM45 0157	Tamla Motown TMG 656 (05/68)	R. Dean Taylor Gotta See Jane Don't Fool Around

TM45 0158	Tamla Motown TMG 657 (05/68)	Martha Reeves & The Vandellas I Promise To Wait My Love Forget Me Not

TM45 0159	Tamla Motown TMG 658 (05/68)	The Temptations I Could Never Love Another (After Loving You) Gonna Give Her All The Love I've Got

TM45 0160	Tamla Motown TMG 659 (06/68)	The Marvelettes Here I Am Baby Keep Off, No Trespassing

TM45 0161	Tamla Motown TMG 660 (06/68)	Gladys Knight & The Pips It Should Have Been Me You Don't Love Me No More

TM45 0162	Tamla Motown TMG 661 (06/68)	Smokey Robinson & The Miracles Yester Love Much Better Off

TM45 0163	Tamla Motown TMG 662 (06/68)	Diana Ross & The Supremes Some Things You Never Get Used To You've Been So Wonderful To Me

TM45 0164	Tamla Motown TMG 663 (07/68)	Shorty Long Here Comes The Judge Sing What You Wanna

TM45 0165	Tamla Motown TMG 664 (07/68)	Jimmy Ruffin Don't Let Him Take Your Love From Me Lonely Lonely Man

TM45 0166	Tamla Motown TMG 665 (08/68)	The Four Tops Yesterday's Dreams For Once In My Life

TM45 0167	Tamla Motown TMG 666 (08/68)	Stevie Wonder You Met Your Match My Girl

TM45 0168	Tamla Motown TMG 667 (09/68)	Junior Walker & The All Stars Hip City (Part 2) Hip City (Part 1)

TM45 0169	Tamla Motown TMG 668 (09/68)	Marvin Gaye & Tammi Terrell You're All I Need To Get By Two Can Have A Party

TM45 0170	Tamla Motown TMG 669 (09/68)	Martha Reeves & The Vandellas I Can't Dance To That Music You're Playing I Tried

TM45 0171	Tamla Motown TMG 670 (09/68)	Paul Petersen A Little Bit For Sandy Your Love Gets Me Burning Alive

TM45 0172	Tamla Motown TMG 671 (10/68)	The Temptations Why Did You Leave Me Darling How Can I Forget

TM45 0173	Tamla Motown TMG 672 (09/68)	Edwin Starr 25 Miles Mighty Good Lovin'

TM45 0174	Tamla Motown TMG 673 (10/68)	Smokey Robinson & The Miracles Special Occasion Give Her Up

TM45 0175	Tamla Motown TMG 674 (10/68)	Gladys Knight & The Pips I Wish It Would Rain It's Summer

TM45 0176	Tamla Motown TMG 675 (11/68)	The Four Tops I'm In A Different World Remember When
TM45 0177	Tamla Motown TMG 676 (11/68)	Marvin Gaye Chained At Last (I Found A Love)
TM45 0178	Tamla Motown TMG 677 (11/68)	Diana Ross & The Supremes Love Child Will This Be The Day
TM45 0179	Tamla Motown TMG 678 (11/68)	Fantastic Four I Love You Madly I Love You Madly (Instrumental)
TM45 0180	Tamla Motown TMG 679 (11/68)	Stevie Wonder For Once In My Life Angie Girl
TM45 0181	Tamla Motown TMG 680 (12/68)	Marv Johnson I'll Pick A Rose For My Rose You Got The Love I Love
TM45 0182	Tamla Motown TMG 681 (01/69)	Marvin Gaye & Tammi Terrell You Ain't Livin' Till You're Lovin' Oh How I'd Miss You
TM45 0183	Tamla Motown TMG 682 (01/69)	Junior Walker & The All Stars Home Cookin' Mutiny
TM45 0184	Tamla Motown TMG 683 (01/69)	Isley Brothers I Guess I'll Always Love You It's Out Of The Question
TM45 0185	Tamla Motown TMG 684 (01/69)	Martha Reeves & The Vandellas Quicksand Dancing In The Street
TM45 0186	Tamla Motown TMG 685 (01/69)	Diana Ross & The Supremes & The Temptations I'm Gonna Make You Love Me A Place In The Sun
TM45 0187	Tamla Motown TMG 686 (02/69)	Marvin Gaye I Heard It Through The Grapevine Need Somebody
TM45 0188	Tamla Motown TMG 687 (02/69)	Smokey Robinson & The Miracles Baby, Baby Don't Cry Your Mother's Only Daughter
TM45 0189	Tamla Motown TMG 688 (02/69)	The Temptations Get Ready My Girl
TM45 0190	Tamla Motown TMG 689 (03/69)	David Ruffin My Whole World Ended (The Moment You Left Me) I've Gotta Find Myself A Brand New Baby
TM45 0191	Tamla Motown TMG 690 (03/69)	Stevie Wonder My Cherie Amour I Don't Know Why (I Love You)
TM45 0192	Tamla Motown TMG 691 (03/69)	Junior Walker & The All Stars Road Runner Shotgun
TM45 0193	Tamla Motown TMG 692 (03/69)	Edwin Starr Way Over There If My Heart Could Tell The Story
TM45 0194	Tamla Motown TMG 693 (04/69)	Isley Brothers Behind A Painted Smile One Too Many Heartaches
TM45 0195	Tamla Motown TMG 694 (03/69)	Martha Reeves & The Vandellas Nowhere To Run Live Wire
TM45 0196	Tamla Motown TMG 695 (04/69)	Diana Ross & The Supremes I'm Living In Shame I'm So Glad I Got Somebody (Like You Around)
TM45 0197	Tamla Motown TMG 696 (04/69)	Smokey Robinson & The Miracles The Tracks Of My Tears Come On Do The Jerk
TM45 0198	Tamla Motown TMG 697 (05/69)	Marvin Gaye & Tammi Terrell Good Lovin' Ain't Easy To Come By Satisfied Feelin'
TM45 0199	Tamla Motown TMG 698 (05/69)	The Four Tops What Is A Man Don't Bring Back Memories
TM45 0200	Tamla Motown TMG 699 (05/69)	The Temptations Ain't Too Proud To Beg Fading Away
TM45 0201	Tamla Motown TMG 700 (06/69)	Brenda Holloway Just Look What You've Done You've Made Me So Very Happy Note: See also Tamla Motown TMG 622.
TM45 0202	Tamla Motown TMG 701 (06/69)	The Marvelettes Reachin' For Something I Can't Have Destination, Anywhere
TM45 0203	Tamla Motown TMB 702 (06/69)	The Originals Green Grow The Lilacs You're The One
TM45 0204	Tamla Motown TMG 703 (07/69)	Jimmy Ruffin I've Passed This Way Before Tomorrow's Tears

TM45 0205	Tamla Motown TMG 704 (07/69)	Diana Ross & The Supremes No Matter What Sign You Are The Young Folks
TM45 0206	Tamla Motown TMG 705 (07/69)	Marvin Gaye Too Busy Thinkin' About My Baby Wherever I Lay My Hat
TM45 0207	Tamla Motown TMG 706 (08/69)	The Honest Men Cherie Baby
TM45 0208	Tamla Motown TMG 707 (08/69)	The Temptations Cloud Nine Why Did She Have To Leave Me (Why Did She Have To Go)
TM45 0209	Tamla Motown TMG 708 (08/69)	The Isley Brothers Put Yourself In My Place Little Miss Sweetness
TM45 0210	Tamla Motown TMG 709 (09/69)	Diana Ross & The Supremes & The Temptations I Second That Emotion The Way You Do The Things You Do
TM45 0211	Tamla Motown TMG 710 (09/69)	The Four Tops Do What You Gotta Do Can't Seem To Get You Out Of My Mind
TM45 0212	Tamla Motown TMG 711 (09/69)	David Ruffin I've Lost Everything I've Ever Loved We'll Have A Good Thing Going On
TM45 0213	Tamla Motown TMG 712 (10/69)	Junior Walker & The All Stars What Does It Take (To Win You Love) Brainwasher
TM45 0214	Tamla Motown TMG 713 (10/69)	Marv Johnson I Miss You Baby (How I Miss You) Bad Girl
TM45 0215	Tamla Motown TMG 714 (10/69)	Gladys Knight & The Pips The Nitty Gritty Got Myself A Good Man
TM45 0216	Tamla Motown TMG 715 (10/69)	Marvin Gaye & Tammi Terrell The Onion Song I Can't Believe You Love Me
TM45 0217	Tamla Motown TMG 716 (11/69)	The Temptations Runaway Child, Running Wild I Need Your Lovin'
TM45 0218	Tamla Motown TMG 717 (11/69)	Stevie Wonder Yester-Me, Yester-You, Yesterday I'd Be A Fool Right Now
TM45 0219	Tamla Motown TMG 718 (11/69)	Marvin Gaye That's The Way Love Is Gonna Keep On Trying Till I Win Your Love
TM45 0220	Tamla Motown TMG 719 (11/69)	Isley Brothers Take Some Time Out For Love Who Could Ever Doubt My Love
TM45 0221	Tamla Motown TMG 720	Blinky & Edwin Starr Oh How Happy Ooo Baby Baby Note: Unissued. Demonstration copies only. See Tamla Motown TMG 748.
TM45 0222	Tamla Motown TMG 721 (11/69)	Diana Ross & The Supremes Someday We'll Be Together He's My Sunny Boy
TM45 0223	Tamla Motown TMG 722 (01/70)	The Temptations I Can't Get Next To You Running Away (Ain't Gonna Help You)
TM45 0224	Tamla Motown TMG 723 (01/70)	The Contours First I Look At The Purse Just A Little Misunderstanding
TM45 0225	Tamla Motown TMG 724 (01/70)	The Jackson Five I Want You Back Who's Loving You
TM45 0226	Tamla Motown TMG 725 (01/70)	Edwin Starr Time Running Back And Forth
TM45 0227	Tamla Motown TMG 726 (02/70)	Jimmy Ruffin Farewell Is A Lonely Sound If You Will Let Me, I Know I Can
TM45 0228	Tamla Motown TMG 727 (02/70)	Junior Walker & The All Stars These Eyes I've Got To Find A Way To Win Maria Back
TM45 0229	Tamla Motown TMG 728 (02/70)	Gladys Knight & The Pips Didn't You Know (You'd Have To Cry Sometime) [Flip side not determined]
TM45 0230	Tamla Motown TMG 729 (03/70)	Chuck Jackson Honey Come Back What Am I Gonna Do Without You
TM45 0231	Tamla Motown TMG 730 (03/70)	Diana Ross & The Supremes & The Temptations Why (Must We Fall In Love) Uptight (Everything's Alright)
TM45 0232	Tamla Motown TMG 731 (03/70)	Stevie Wonder Never Had A Dream Come True Somebody Knows, Somebody Cares

TM45 0233 (03/70)	Tamla Motown TMG 732	The Four Tops I Can't Help Myself Baby I Need Your Lovin'
TM45 0234 (03/70)	Tamla Motown TMG 733	The Originals Baby I'm For Real Moment Of Truth
TM45 0235 (04/70)	Tamla Motown TMG 734	Marvin Gaye Abraham, Martin And John How Can I Forget
TM45 0236 (04/70)	Tamla Motown TMG 735	The Supremes Up The Ladder To The Roof Bill, When Are You Coming Back
TM45 0237 (05/70)	Tamla Motown TMG 736	The Four Tops It's All In The Game Love Is The Answer
TM45 0238 (05/70)	Tamla Motown TMG 737	Marv Johnson So Glad You Chose Me I'm Not A Plaything
TM45 0239 (05/70)	Tamla Motown TMG 738	The Jackson Five ABC The Young Folks
TM45 0240 (05/70)	Tamla Motown TMG 739	Kiki Dee The Day Will Come Between Sunday And Monday My Whole World Ended (The Moment You Left Me)
TM45 0241 (05/70)	Tamla Motown TMG 740	Jimmy Ruffin Everybody Needs Love I'll Say Forever My Love
TM45 0242 (06/70)	Tamla Motown TMG 741	The Temptations Psychedelic Shack That's The Way Love Is
TM45 0243 (06/70)	Tamla Motown TMG 742	Rare Earth Get Ready Magic Key
TM45 0244 (06/70)	Tamla Motown TMG 743	Diana Ross Reach Out And Touch (Somebody's Hand) Dark Side Of The World
TM45 0245 (06/70)	Tamla Motown TMG 744	Stevie Wonder Signed, Sealed, Delivered I'm Yours I'm More Than Happy (I'm Satisfied)
TM45 0246 (07/70)	Tamla Motown TMG 745	Smokey Robinson & The Miracles Tears Of A Clown You Must Be Love
TM45 0247 (07/70)	Tamla Motown TMG 745	Smokey Robinson & The Miracles Tears Of A Clown Who's Gonna Take The Blame Note: Alternate "B" side.
TM45 0248 (07/70)	Tamla Motown TMG 746	The Jackson 5 The Love You Save I Found That Girl
TM45 0249 (07/70)	Tamla Motown TMG 747	The Supremes Everybody's Got The Right To Love But I Love You More
TM45 0250 (08/70)	Tamla Motown TMG 748	Blinky & Edwin Starr Oh How Happy Ooo Baby Baby
TM45 0251 (09/70)	Tamla Motown TMG 749	The Temptations Ball Of Confusion (That's What The World Is Today) It's Summer
TM45 0252 (09/70)	Tamla Motown TMG 750	Junior Walker & The All Stars Do You See My Love (For You Growing) Groove And Move
TM45 0253 (08/70)	Tamla Motown TMG 751	Diana Ross Ain't No Mountain High Enough Can't It Wait Until Tomorrow
TM45 0254 (09/70)	Tamla Motown TMG 752	The Four Tops Still Water (Love) Still Water (Peace)
TM45 0255 (10/70)	Tamla Motown TMG 753	Jimmy Ruffin It's Wonderful (To Be Loved By You) Maria (You Were The Only One)
TM45 0256 (10/70)	Tamla Motown TMG 754	Edwin Starr War He Who Picks A Rose
TM45 0257 (10/70)	Tamla Motown TMG 755	The Motown Spinners It's A Shame Sweet Thing
TM45 0258 (10/70)	Tamla Motown TMG 756	Gladys Knight & The Pips Friendship Train You Need Love Like I Do (Don't You)
TM45 0259 (10/70)	Tamla Motown TMG 757	Stevie Wonder Heaven Help Us All I Gotta Have A Song
TM45 0260 (11/70)	Tamla Motown TMG 758	The Jackson 5 I'll Be There One More Chance
TM45 0261 (11/70)	Tamla Motown TMG 759	Earl Van Dyke 6 By 6 All For You
TM45 0262 (01/71)	Tamla Motown TMG 760	The Supremes Stoned Love Shine On Me

TM45 0263	Tamla Motown TMG 761 (01/71)	Smokey Robinson & The Miracles (Come Round Here) I'm The One You Need We Can Make It We Can
TM45 0264	Tamla Motown TMG 762 (01/71)	Martha Reeves & The Vandellas Forget Me Not I Gotta Let You Go
TM45 0265	Tamla Motown TMG 763 (02/71)	R. Dean Taylor Indiana Wants Me Love's Your Name
TM45 0266	Tamla Motown TMG 764 (02/71)	Edwin Starr Stop The War Now Gonna Keep On Tryin' Till I Win Your Love
TM45 0267	Tamla Motown TMG 765 (06/71)	Gladys Knight & The Pips If I Were Your Woman The Tracks Of My Tears
TM45 0268	Tamla Motown TMG 766 (03/71)	The Motown Spinners Together We Can Make Such Sweet Music Truly Yours
TM45 0269	Tamla Motown TMG 767 (03/71)	Jimmy Ruffin Let's Say Goodbye Tomorrow Living In A World I Created For Myself
TM45 0270	Tamla Motown TMG 768 (03/71)	Diana Ross Remember Me How About You
TM45 0271	Tamla Motown TMG 769 (04/71)	The Jackson 5 Mama's Pearl Darling Dear
TM45 0272	Tamla Motown TMG 770 (04/71)	The Four Tops Just Seven Numbers (Can Straighten Out My Life) I Wish I Were Your Mirror
TM45 0273	Tamla Motown TMG 771 (04/71)	The Elgins Heaven Must Have Sent You Stay In My Lonely Arms
TM45 0274	Tamla Motown TMG 772 (05/71)	Stevie Wonder We Can Work It Out Don't Wonder Why
TM45 0275	Tamla Motown TMG 773 (05/71)	The Temptations Just My Imagination (Running Away With Me) You Make Your Own Heaven And Hell Right Here On Earth
TM45 0276	Tamla Motown TMG 774 (05/71)	Smokey Robinson & The Miracles I Don't Blame You At All That Girl
TM45 0277	Tamla Motown TMG 775 (06/71)	Marvin Gaye What's Going On God Is Love
TM45 0278	Tamla Motown TMG 776 (06/71)	The Undisputed Truth Save My Love For A Rainy Day Since I've Lost You
TM45 0279	Tamla Motown TMG 777 (06/71)	The Supremes & The Four Tops River Deep, Mountain High It's Got To Be A Miracle (This Thing Called Love)
TM45 0280	Tamla Motown TMG 778 (06/71)	The Jackson 5 Never Can Say Goodbye She's Good
TM45 0281	Tamla Motown TMG 779 (07/71)	Stevie Wonder Never Dreamed You'd Leave In Summer If You Really Love Me
TM45 0282	Tamla Motown TMG 780 (07/71)	The Velvelettes These Things Will Keep Me Loving You Since You've Been Loving Me
TM45 0283	Tamla Motown TMG 781 (08/71)	Diana Ross I'm Still Waiting Reach Out I'll Be There
TM45 0284	Tamla Motown TMG 782 (08/71)	The Supremes Nathan Jones Happy (Is A Bumpy Road)
TM45 0285	Tamla Motown TMG 783 (09/71)	The Temptations It's Summer Ungena Za Ulimwengu (Unite The World)
TM45 0286	Tamla Motown TMG 784 (08/71)	Jimmy Ruffin On The Way Out Honey Come Back
TM45 0287	Tamla Motown TMG 785 (09/71)	The Four Tops Simple Game You Stole My Love
TM45 0288	Tamla Motown TMG 786	R. Dean Taylor Ain't It A Sad Thing Back Street Note: Unissued. Rescheduled as Rare Earth RES 101.
TM45 0289	Tamla Motown TMG 787 (09/71)	The Elgins Put Yourself In My Place It's Gonna Be Hard Times
TM45 0290	Tamla Motown TMG 788 (09/71)	Barbara Randolph I Got A Feeling You Got Me Hurtin' All Over
TM45 0291	Tamla Motown TMG 789 (10/71)	The Undisputed Truth Smiling Faces Sometimes You Got The Love I Need

TM45 0292	Tamla Motown TMG 790 (10/71)	Edwin Starr Agent Double O Soul Back Street
TM45 0293	Tamla Motown TMG 791 (10/71)	Rita Wright I Can't Give Back The Love I Feel For You Something On My Mind
TM45 0294	Tamla Motown TMG 792 (10/71)	Diana Ross Surrender I'm A Winner Note: Majority are stereo, though some copies are mono.
TM45 0295	Tamla Motown TMG 793 (11/71)	The Supremes & The Four Tops You Gotta Have Love In Your Heart I'm Glad About It
TM45 0296	Tamla Motown TMG 794 (11/71)	Martha Reeves & The Vandellas Bless You Hope I Don't Get My Heart Broke
TM45 0297	Tamla Motown TMG 795 (11/71)	San Remo Strings Festival Time All Turned On
TM45 0298	Tamla Motown TMG 796 (11/71)	Marvin Gaye Save The Children Little Darling (I Love You)
TM45 0299	Tamla Motown TMG 797 (01/72)	Michael Jackson Got To Be There Maria (You Were The Only One)
TM45 0300	Tamla Motown TMG 798 (01/72)	Stevie Wonder If You Really Love Me Think Of Me As Your Soldier
TM45 0301	Tamla Motown TMG 799 (01/72)	Thelma Houston I Want To Go Back There Again Pick Of The Week
TM45 0302	Tamla Motown TMG 800 (02/72)	The Temptations Superstar (Remember How You Got Where You Are) Gonna Keep On Tryin' Till I Win Your Love
TM45 0303	Tamla Motown TMG 801 (02/72)	Tom Clay What The World Needs Now Is Love + Abraham, Martin And John The Victors
TM45 0304	Tamla Motown TMG 802 (02/72)	Marvin Gaye Mercy Mercy Me (The Ecology) Sad Tomorrows
TM45 0305	Tamla Motown TMG 803 (02/72)	The Four Tops Bernadette I Got A Feeling + It's The Same Old Song
TM45 0306	Tamla Motown TMG 804 (02/72)	The Supremes Floy Joy This Is The Story
TM45 0307	Tamla Motown TMG 805 (03/72)	Gladys Knight & The Pips Make Me The Woman You Go Home To I Don't Want To Do Wrong
TM45 0308	Tamla Motown TMG 806 (03/72)	The Velvelettes Needle In A Haystack I'm The Exception To The Rule
TM45 0309	Tamla Motown TMG 807 (03/72)	San Remo Strings Reach Out I'll Be There Hungry For Love
TM45 0310	Tamla Motown TMG 808 (03/72)	The Temptations Take A Look Around Smooth Sailing From Now On
TM45 0311	Tamla Motown TMG 809 (03/72)	The Jackson 5 Sugar Daddy I'm So Happy
TM45 0312	Tamla Motown TMG 810 (04/72)	Edwin Starr Funky Music Sho Nuff Turns Me On Cloud Nine
TM45 0313	Tamla Motown TMG 811 (04/72)	Smokey Robinson & The Miracles My Girl Has Gone Crazy About the La La La
TM45 0314	Tamla Motown TMG 812 (04/72)	Diana Ross Doobedood'ndoobe, Doobedood'ndoobe, Doobedood'ndoo Keep An Eye
TM45 0315	Tamla Motown TMG 813 (06/72)	Gladys Knight & The Pips Just Walk In My Shoes (I Know) I'm Losing You
TM45 0316	Tamla Motown TMG 814 (05/72)	Earl Van Dyke & The Soul Brothers I Can't Help Myself How Sweet It Is (To Be Loved By You)
TM45 0317	Tamla Motown TMG 815 (05/72)	The Supremes & The Four Tops Without The One You Love Let's Make Love Now
TM45 0318	Tamla Motown TMG 816 (05/72)	Michael Jackson Rockin' Robin Love Is Here And Now You're Gone
TM45 0319	Tamla Motown TMG 817 (05/72)	Marvin Gaye Inner City Blues (Make Me Wanna Holler) Wholly Holy

TM45 0320	Tamla Motown TMG 818 (06/72)	The Undisputed Truth Superstar (Remember How You Got Where You Are) Ain't No Sun Since You've Been Gone
TM45 0321	Tamla Motown TMG 819 (06/72)	Frankie Valli & The Four Seasons You're A Song (That I Can't Sing) Sun Country
TM45 0322	Tamla Motown TMG 820 (06/72)	Mary Wells My Guy You Lost The Sweetest Boy + Two Lovers Note: Maxi-single.
TM45 0323	Tamla Motown TMG 821 (06/72)	The Supremes Automatically Sunshine Precious Little Things
TM45 0324	Tamla Motown TMG 822 (06/72)	The Originals God Bless Whoever Sent You I Like Your Style + Baby I'm For Real Note: Maxi-single.
TM45 0325	Tamla Motown TMG 823 (07/72)	The Four Tops Walk With Me, Talk With Me, Darling L.A. (My Town)
TM45 0326	Tamla Motown TMG 824 (07/72)	Junior Walker & The All Stars Walk In The Night Right On Brothers And Sisters, Gotta Hold On To This Feeling Note: Maxi-single.
TM45 0327	Tamla Motown TMG 825 (09/72)	The Jackson 5 Little Bitty Pretty One Maybe Tomorrow
TM45 0328	Tamla Motown TMG 826 (07/72)	Michael Jackson Ain't No Sunshine I Wanna Be Where You Are
TM45 0329	Tamla Motown TMG 827 (09/72)	Stevie Wonder Superwoman Seems So Long
TM45 0330	Tamla Motown TMG 828 (09/72)	The Sisters Love Mr. Fix-It Man You've Got To Make Your Choice
TM45 0331	Tamla Motown TMG 829 (09/72)	The Four Tops I'll Turn To Stone Love Feels Like Fire
TM45 0332	Tamla Motown TMG 830 (10/72)	Gladys Knight & The Pips Help Me Make It Through The Night If You're Gonna Leave (Just Leave)
TM45 0333	Tamla Motown TMG 831 (09/72)	Laura Lee To Win Your Heart So Will I
TM45 0334	Tamla Motown TMG 832 (10/72)	The Temptations Smiling Faces Sometimes Mother Nature
TM45 0335	Tamla Motown TMG 833 (10/72)	The Jackson 5 Lookin' Through The Windows Love Song
TM45 0336	Tamla Motown TMG 834 (11/72)	Michael Jackson Ben You Can Cry On My Shoulder
TM45 0337	Tamla Motown TMG 835 (11/72)	The Supremes Your Wonderful Sweet, Sweet Love Love It Came To Me This Time
TM45 0338	Tamla Motown TMG 836 (11/72)	The Supremes & The Four Tops Reach Out And Touch (Somebody's Hand) Where Would I Be Without You, Baby
TM45 0339	Tamla Motown TMG 837 (12/72)	The Jackson 5 Santa Claus Is Coming To Town Someday At Christmas + Christmas Won't Be The Same This Year Note: Maxi-single.
TM45 0340	Tamla Motown TMG 838 (12/72)	Jermaine Jackson That's How Love Goes I Lost My Love In The Big City
TM45 0341	Tamla Motown TMG 839 (01/73)	The Temptations Papa Was A Rollin' Stone (Vocal) Papa Was A Rollin' Stone (Instrumental)
TM45 0342	Tamla Motown TMG 840 (01/73)	Junior Walker & The All Stars Take Me Girl, I'm Ready I Don't Want To Do Wrong
TM45 0343	Tamla Motown TMG 841 (01/73)	Stevie Wonder Superstition You've Got It Bad Girl
TM45 0344	Tamla Motown TMG 842 (02/73)	The Jackson 5 Doctor My Eyes My Little Baby
TM45 0345	Tamla Motown TMG 843 (02/73)	Martha Reeves No One There (I've Given You) The Best Years Of My Life
TM45 0346	Tamla Motown TMG 844 (02/73)	Gladys Knight & The Pips The Look Of Love You're My Everything

TM45 0347	Tamla Motown TMG 845 (02/73)	Eddie Kendricks If You Let Me Just Memories
TM45 0348	Tamla Motown TMG 846 (03/73)	Marvin Gaye Trouble Man Don't Mess With Mister "T"
TM45 0349	Tamla Motown TMG 847 (03/73)	Supremes Bad Weather It's So Hard For Me To Say Goodbye
TM45 0350	Tamla Motown TMG 848 (03/73)	Michel Legrand / Gil Askey Love Theme From "Lady Sings The Blues" Any Happy Home
TM45 0351	Tamla Motown TMG 849 (03/73)	Diana Ross Good Morning Heartache God Bless The Child
TM45 0352	Tamla Motown TMG 850 (03/73)	The Four Tops So Deep Within You Happy (Is A Bumpy Road)
TM45 0353	Tamla Motown TMG 851 (04/73)	Jermaine Jackson Daddy's Home Take Me In Your Arms (Rock Me A Little While)
TM45 0354	Tamla Motown TMG 852 (05/73)	Stevie Wonder You Are The Sunshine Of My Life Look Around
TM45 0355	Tamla Motown TMG 853 (04/73)	Smokey Robinson & The Miracles Going To A Go-Go Whole Lotta Shakin' In My Heart (Since I Met You) Yester Love Note: Maxi-single.
TM45 0356	Tamla Motown TMG 854 (04/73)	The Temptations Masterpiece (Vocal) Masterpiece (Instrumental)
TM45 0357	Tamla Motown TMG 855 (05/73)	Gladys Knight & The Pips Neither One Of Us (Wants To Be The First To Say Goodbye) Can't Give It Up No More
TM45 0358	Tamla Motown TMG 856 (05/73)	The Jackson 5 Hallelujah Day To Know
TM45 0359	Tamla Motown TMG 857 (06/73)	Junior Walker & The All Stars Way Back Home (Vocal) Way Back Home (Instrumental) + Country Boy Note: First 20,000 released without "Country Boy."
TM45 0360	Tamla Motown TMG 857 (06/73)	The Four Tops I Can't Quit Your Love I Am Your Man
TM45 0361	Tamla Motown TMG 859 (06/73)	The Supremes Tossin' And Turnin' Oh Be My Love
TM45 0362	Tamla Motown TMG 860 (09/73)	The Marvelettes Reachin' For Something I Can't Have Here I Am Baby
TM45 0363	Tamla Motown TMG 861 (07/73)	Diana Ross Touch Me In The Morning Baby It's Love
TM45 0364	Tamla Motown TMG 862 (08/73)	Willie Hutch Brother's Gonna Work It Out I Choose You
TM45 0365	Tamla Motown TMG 863 (07/73)	Michael Jackson Morning Glow My Girl
TM45 0366	Tamla Motown TMG 864 (08/73)	Gladys Knight & The Pips Take Me In Your Arms And Love Me No One Could Love You More
TM45 0367	Tamla Motown TMG 865 (08/73)	The Jackson Five Skywriter Ain't Nothing Like The Real Thing
TM45 0368	Tamla Motown TMG 866 (08/73)	The Temptations Law Of The Land Funky Music Sho Nuff Turns Me On
TM45 0369	Tamla Motown TMG 867	Martin & Finley It's Another Sunday Best Friends Note: Unissued. Demo only, not released.
TM45 0370	Tamla Motown TMG 868 (08/73)	Marvin Gaye Let's Get It On I Wish It Would Rain
TM45 0371	Tamla Motown TMG 869 (09/73)	Stevie Wonder Higher Ground Too High
TM45 0372	Tamla Motown TMG 870 (09/73)	J. J. Barnes Real Humdinger Please Let Me In + I Ain't Gonna Do It Note: Maxi-single.
TM45 0373	Tamla Motown TMG 871 (12/73)	Detroit Spinners Together We Can Make Such Sweet Music Bad Bad Weather (Till You Come Home)
TM45 0374	Tamla Motown TMG 872 (09/73)	Junior Walker & The All Stars Wholly Holy Peace And Understanding Is Hard To Find

TM45 0375	Tamla Motown TMG 873 (10/73)	Eddie Kendricks Keep On Truckin' (Part 1) Keep On Truckin' (Part 2)
TM45 0376	Tamla Motown TMG 874 (10/73)	Jermaine Jackson The Bigger You Love (The Harder You Fall) I'm In A Different World
TM45 0377	Tamla Motown TMG 875 (10/73)	Edwin Starr You've Got My Soul On Fire Love (The Lonely People's Prayer)
TM45 0378	Tamla Motown TMG 876 (09/73)	Gladys Knight & The Pips Daddy Could Swear, I Declare For Once In My Life
TM45 0379	Tamla Motown TMG 877 (10/73)	Isley Brothers Tell Me It's Just A Rumour Baby Save Me From This Misery
TM45 0380	Tamla Motown TMG 878 (11/73)	The Jackson Five Get It Together Touch
TM45 0381	Tamla Motown TMG 879 (11/73)	Diana Ross & Marvin Gaye You're A Special Part Of Me I'm Falling In Love With You
TM45 0382	Tamla Motown TMG 880 (11/73)	Diana Ross All Of My Life A Simple Thing Like Cry
TM45 0383	Tamla Motown TMG 881 (11/73)	Stevie Wonder Living For The City Visions
TM45 0384	Tamla Motown TMG 882 (01/74)	Marvin Gaye Come Get To This Distant Lover
TM45 0385	Tamla Motown TMG 883 (01/74)	Smokey Robinson Just My Soul Responding Sweet Harmony
TM45 0386	Tamla Motown TMG 884 (01/74)	Supremes I Guess I'll Miss The Man Over And Over
TM45 0387	Tamla Motown TMG 885	Willie Hutch Tell Me Why Our Love Has Turned Cold Mother's Theme (Mama) Note: Release cancelled, no records pressed.
TM45 0388	Tamla Motown TMG 886 (02/74)	The Contours Baby Hit And Run Can You Jerk Like Me
TM45 0389	Tamla Motown TMG 887 (03/74)	The Temptations I Need You Hey Girl (I Like Your Style)
TM45 0390	Tamla Motown TMG 888 (02/74)	Eddie Kendricks Boogie Down Eddie's Love
TM45 0391	Tamla Motown TMG 889 (02/74)	Junior Walker & The All Stars Don't Blame The Children Soul Clappin'
TM45 0392	Tamla Motown TMG 890 (03/74)	Diana Ross & Marvin Gaye You Are Everything Include Me In Your Life
TM45 0393	Tamla Motown TMG 891 (03/74)	The Miracles Don't Let It End (Till You Let It Begin) I Wanna Be With You
TM45 0394	Tamla Motown TMG 892 (04/74)	Stevie Wonder He's Misstra Know-It-All You Can't Judge A Book By Its Cover
TM45 0395	Tamla Motown TMG 893 (04/74)	Diana Ross Last Time I Saw Him Everything Is Everything
TM45 0396	Tamla Motown TMG 894 (04/74)	Junior Walker & The All Stars Gotta Hold On To This Feeling I Ain't Going Nowhere
TM45 0397	Tamla Motown TMG 895 (04/74)	The Jackson 5 The Boogie Man Don't Let The Baby Catch You
TM45 0398	Tamla Motown TMG 896 (05/74)	R. Dean Taylor There's A Ghost In My House Let's Go Somewhere
TM45 0399	Tamla Motown TMG 897 (05/74)	Undisputed Truth Help Yourself What It Is
TM45 0400	Tamla Motown TMG 898 (05/74)	Smokey Robinson Silent Partner In A Three-Way Love Affair Baby Come Close
TM45 0401	Tamla Motown TMG 899 (06/74)	The Contours Do You Love Me Determination
TM45 0402	Tamla Motown TMG 900 (05/74)	Michael Jackson Music And Me Johnny Raven
TM45 0403	Tamla Motown TMG 901 (06/74)	Eddie Kendricks Son Of Sagittarius Can't Help What I Am
TM45 0404	Tamla Motown TMG 902 (07/74)	The Commodores Machine Gun There's A Song In My Heart
TM45 0405	Tamla Motown TMG 903 (06/74)	Gladys Knight & The Pips Didn't You Know (You'd Have To Cry Sometime) Cloud Nine

TM45 0406	Tamla Motown TMG 904 (06/74)	The Jackson Five Dancing Machine It's Too Late To Change The Time
TM45 0407	Tamla Motown TMG 905 (06/74)	Edwin Starr Stop Her On Sight (S.O.S.) Headline News
TM45 0408	Tamla Motown TMG 906 (06/74)	Diana Ross & Marvin Gaye Stop, Look, Listen (To Your Heart) Love Twins
TM45 0409	Tamla Motown TMG 907 (06/74)	The Reflections (Just Like) Romeo And Juliet Can't You Tell By The Look In My Eyes
TM45 0410	Tamla Motown TMG 908 (06/74)	Stevie Wonder Don't You Worry 'Bout A Thing' Do Yourself A Favor
TM45 0411	Tamla Motown TMG 909 (06/74)	R. Dean Taylor Don't Fool Around Poor Girl
TM45 0412	Tamla Motown TMG 910 (07/74)	Gloria Jones Tin Can People So Tired (Of The Way You're Treating Our Love Baby)
TM45 0413	Tamla Motown TMG 911 (07/74)	Jimmy Ruffin What Becomes Of The Brokenhearted Don't You Miss Me A Little Bit Baby
TM45 0414	Tamla Motown TMG 912 (08/74)	Syreeta Spinnin' And Spinnin' Black Maybe
TM45 0415	Tamla Motown TMG 913 (08/74)	Yvonne Fair Funky Music Sho Nuff Turns Me On Let Your Hair Down
TM45 0416	Tamla Motown TMG 914 (08/74)	The Miracles Do It Baby Wigs And Lashes
TM45 0417	Tamla Motown TMG 915 (08/74)	Diana Ross & The Supremes Baby Love Ask Any Girl
TM45 0418	Tamla Motown TMG 916 (09/74)	Eddie Kendricks Girl You Need A Change Of Mind (Part 1) Girl You Need A Change Of Mind (Part 2)
TM45 0419	Tamla Motown TMG 917 (09/74)	Diana Ross Love Me Save The Children
TM45 0420	Tamla Motown TMG 918 (09/74)	R. Dean Taylor Gotta See Jane Candy Apple Red
TM45 0421	Tamla Motown TMG 919 (09/74)	Undisputed Truth I'm A Fool For You Mama I Gotta Brand New Thing (Don't Say No)
TM45 0422	Tamla Motown TMG 920 (10/74)	Diana Ross & Marvin Gaye My Mistake (Was To Love You) Just Say, Just Say
TM45 0423	Tamla Motown TMG 921 (10/74)	Stevie Wonder You Haven't Done Nothin' Happier Than The Morning Sun
TM45 0424	Tamla Motown TMG 922 (10/74)	Jimmy Ruffin Farewell Is A Lonely Sound I Will Never Let You Get Away
TM45 0425	Tamla Motown TMG 923 (11/74)	Marvin Gaye I Heard It Through The Grapevine Chained
TM45 0426	Tamla Motown TMG 924 (11/74)	The Commodores The Zoo (The Human Zoo) I'm Looking For Love
TM45 0427	Tamla Motown TMG 925 (11/74)	Diana Ross & The Supremes Where Did Our Love Go Nothing But Heartaches
TM45 0428	Tamla Motown TMG 926 (11/74)	Syreeta I'm Goin' Left Heavy Day
TM45 0429	Tamla Motown TMG 927 (11/74)	Jackson Five The Life Of The Party Whatever You Got, I Want
TM45 0430	Tamla Motown TMG 928 (12/74)	Stevie Wonder Boogie On Reggae Woman Evil
TM45 0431	Tamla Motown TMG 929 (01/75)	Dynamic Superiors Shoe Shoe Shine Release Me
TM45 0432	Tamla Motown TMG 930 (12/74)	Edwin Starr Who's Right Or Wrong Ain't It Hell Up In Harlem
TM45 0433	Tamla Motown TMG 931 (01/75)	The Temptations / Temptations Band Happy People Happy People (Instrumental)
TM45 0434	Tamla Motown TMG 932 (02/75)	Popcorn Wylie Funky Rubber Band (Vocal) Funky Rubber Band (Instrumental)
TM45 0435	Tamla Motown TMG 933 (01/75)	Syreeta Your Kiss Is Sweet How Many Days
TM45 0436	Tamla Motown TMG 934 (01/75)	Jimmy Ruffin I've Passed This Way Before Sad And Lonesome Feeling

TM45 0437	Tamla Motown TMG 935 (02/75)	The Commodores Superman It Is As Good As You Make It
TM45 0438	Tamla Motown TMG 936 (01/75)	David Ruffin Take Me Clear From Here Blood Donors Needed (Give All You Can)
TM45 0439	Tamla Motown TMG 937 (01/75)	Isley Brothers This Old Heart Of Mine (Is Weak For You) There's No Love Left
TM45 0440	Tamla Motown TMG 938 (02/75)	Caston & Majors Child Of Love No One Will Know
TM45 0441	Tamla Motown TMG 939 (02/75)	The Marvelettes When You're Young And In Love The Day You Take One (You Have To Take The Other)
TM45 0442	Tamla Motown TMG 940 (02/75)	The Miracles Where Are You Going To My Love Up Again
TM45 0443	Tamla Motown TMG 941 (02/75)	Diana Ross Sorry Doesn't Always Make It Right Together
TM45 0444	Tamla Motown TMG 942 (03/75)	The Jackson Five I Am Love I Am Love (Part 2)
TM45 0445	Tamla Motown TMG 943 (03/75)	Undisputed Truth Law Of The Land Lil' Red Riding Hood
TM45 0446	Tamla Motown TMG 944 (03/75)	The Commodores I Feel Sanctified Determination
TM45 0447	Tamla Motown TMG 945 (04/75)	Gladys Knight & The Pips You've Lost That Lovin' Feelin' This Child Needs Its Father
TM45 0448	Tamla Motown TMG 946 (04/75)	Michael Jackson One Day In Your Life With A Child's Heart
TM45 0449	Tamla Motown TMG 947 (05/75)	Eddie Kendricks Shoeshine Boy Hooked On Your Love
TM45 0450	Tamla Motown TMG 948 (05/75)	The Temptations Memories Ain't No Justice
TM45 0451	Tamla Motown TMG 949 (05/75)	Smokey Robinson Baby, That's Backatcha Just Passing Through
TM45 0452	Tamla Motown TMG 950 (08/75)	The Supremes He's My Man Give Out, But Don't Give Up
TM45 0453	Tamla Motown TMG 951 (06/75)	Caston & Majors Sing There's Fear
TM45 0454	Tamla Motown TMG 952 (06/75)	The Commodores Slippery When Wet The Bump
TM45 0455	Tamla Motown TMG 953 (07/75)	Diana Ross & Marvin Gaye Don't Knock My Love I'm Falling In Love With You
TM45 0456	Tamla Motown TMG 954 (06/75)	Syreeta Harmour Love What Love Has Joined Together
TM45 0457	Tamla Motown TMG 955 (06/75)	Gladys Knight & The Pips If I Were Your Woman The Only Time You Love Me Is When You're Losing Me
TM45 0458	Tamla Motown TMG 956 (07/75)	Diana Ross & The Supremes You Can't Hurry Love The Happening
TM45 0459	Tamla Motown TMG 957 (07/75)	Smokey Robinson & The Miracles I'm The One You Need I Second That Emotion
TM45 0460	Tamla Motown TMG 958 (07/75)	The Four Tops 7 Rooms Of Gloom If I Were A Carpenter
TM45 0461	Tamla Motown TMG 959 (07/75)	Stevie Wonder I Was Made To Love Her Never Had A Dream Come True
TM45 0462	Tamla Motown TMG 960 (07/75)	Diana Ross & The Supremes Reflections Love Child
TM45 0463	Tamla Motown TMG 961 (07/75)	Jimmy Ruffin I'll Say Forever My Love It's Wonderful
TM45 0464	Tamla Motown TMG 962 (08/75)	Junior Walker & The All Stars What Does It Take Take Me Girl, I'm Ready
TM45 0465	Tamla Motown TMG 963 (08/75)	The Jackson 5 I Want You Back The Love You Save
TM45 0466	Tamla Motown TMG 964 (08/75)	The Supremes Up The Ladder To The Roof Automatically Sunshine
TM45 0467	Tamla Motown TMG 965 (08/75)	The Four Tops It's All In The Game Bernadette

TM45 0468	Tamla Motown TMG 966 (08/75)	Stevie Wonder Signed, Sealed, Delivered, I'm Yours Fingertips (Part 2)
TM45 0469	Tamla Motown TMG 967 (08/75)	Temptations Ball Of Confusion Take A Look Around
TM45 0470	Tamla Motown TMG 968 (08/75)	Edwin Starr / R. Dean Taylor War Indiana Wants Me
TM45 0471	Tamla Motown TMG 969 (08/75)	The Jackson 5 I'll Be There ABC
TM45 0472	Tamla Motown TMG 970 (08/75)	Diana Ross Remember Me Surrender
TM45 0473	Tamla Motown TMG 971 (08/75)	The Supremes & Four Tops River Deep Mountain High You Gotta Have Love In Your Heart
TM45 0474	Tamla Motown TMG 972 (08/75)	The Four Tops Simple Game Still Water (Love)
TM45 0475	Tamla Motown TMG 973 (08/75)	Michael Jackson / Marv Johnson Got To Be There I Miss You Baby
TM45 0476	Tamla Motown TMG 974 (08/75)	The Supremes Floy Joy Bad Weather
TM45 0477	Tamla Motown TMG 975 (08/75)	The Jackson 5 Lookin' Through The Windows Doctor My Eyes
TM45 0478	Tamla Motown TMG 1000 (08/75)	The Marvelettes / Kim Weston Finders Keepers Losers Weepers Do Like I Do
TM45 0479	Tamla Motown TMG 1001 (09/75)	The Jackson 5 Forever Came Today I Can't Quit Your Love
TM45 0480	Tamla Motown TMG 1002 (09/75)	The Sisters Love I'm Learning To Trust My Man Try It, You'll Like It
TM45 0481	Tamla Motown TMG 1003 (09/75)	Eddie Kendricks If Anyone Can Get The Cream Off The Top
TM45 0482	Tamla Motown TMG 1004 (09/75)	Magic Disco Machine Control Tower Scratchin'
TM45 0483	Tamla Motown TMG 1005 (09/75)	Caston & Majors I'll Keep A Light In My Window Say You Love Me True

TM45 0484	Tamla Motown TMG 1006 (10/75)	Michael Jackson Just A Little Bit Of You Dear Michael
TM45 0485	Tamla Motown TMG 1007 (10/75)	The Commodores Let's Do It Right This Is Your Life
TM45 0486	Tamla Motown TMG 1008 (10/75)	Willie Hutch Love Power Get ready For The Get Down
TM45 0487	Tamla Motown TMG 1009 (10/75)	Gladys Knight & The Pips Neither One Of Us (Wants To Be The First To Say Goodbye) Everybody Needs Love + I Wish It Would Rain Note: Maxi-single.
TM45 0488	Tamla Motown TMG 1010 (10/75)	Diana Ross Theme From Mahagony (Do You Know Where You're Going To) No One's Gonna Be A Fool Forever
TM45 0489	Tamla Motown TMG 1011 (10/75)	The Four Tops Walk Away Renee You Keep Running Away
TM45 0490	Tamla Motown TMG 1012 (11/75)	The Supremes Early Morning Love Where Is It I Belong
TM45 0491	Tamla Motown TMG 1013 (11/75)	Yvonne Fair It Should Have Been Me You Can't Judge A Book By Its Cover
TM45 0492	Tamla Motown TMG 1014 (11/75)	Undisputed Truth Higher Than High Spaced Out
TM45 0493	Tamla Motown TMG 1015 (11/75)	The Miracles Love Machine (Part 1) Love Machine (Part 2)
TM45 0494	Tamla Motown TMG 1016 (11/75)	Dynamic Superiors Deception One-Nighter
TM45 0495	Tamla Motown TMG 1017 (11/75)	David Ruffin Walk Away From Love Love Can Be Hazardous To Your Health
TM45 0496	Tamla Motown TMG 1018 (01/76)	The Commodores Sweet Love Better Never Than Forever
TM45 0497	Tamla Motown TMG 1019 (01/76)	Smokey Robinson Quiet Storm Asleep On My Love
TM45 0498	Tamla Motown TMG 1020 (02/76)	Stephanie Mills This Empty Place If You Can Learn How To Cry Note: There is also a demo for this record with a different "B" side, "I See You For The First Time."

TM45 0499	Tamla Motown TMG 1021 (02/76)	Eddie Kendricks He's A Friend All Of My Love
TM45 0500	Tamla Motown TMG 1022 (03/76)	David Ruffin Heavy Love Me And Rock And Roll (Are Here To Stay)
TM45 0501	Tamla Motown TMG 1023 (02/76)	The Miracles Night Life Overture
TM45 0502	Tamla Motown TMG 1024 (04/76)	Diana Ross Love Hangover Kiss Me Now
TM45 0503	Tamla Motown TMG 1025 (05/76)	Yvonne Fair Its' Bad For Me To See You Walk Out The Door If You Wanna
TM45 0504	Tamla Motown TMG 1026 (04/76)	Marvin Gaye I Want You I Want You (Instrumental)
TM45 0505	Tamla Motown TMG 1027 (05/76)	Junior Walker I'm So Glad Dancin' Like They Do On Soul Train
TM45 0506	Tamla Motown TMG 1028 (04/76)	Edwin Starr Time Running Back And Forth
TM45 0507	Tamla Motown TMG 1029 (05/76)	The Supremes I'm Gonna Let My Heart Do The Walking Color My World Blue
TM45 0508	Tamla Motown TMG 1030 (07/76)	The Boones My Guy When The Lovelight Starts Shining Thru' His Eyes
TM45 0509	Tamla Motown TMG 1031 (06/76)	Eddie Kendricks The Sweeter You Treat Her Happy
TM45 0510	Tamla Motown TMG 1032 (06/76)	Diana Ross I Thought It Took A Little Time (But Today I Fell In Love) After You
TM45 0511	Tamla Motown TMG 1033 (07/76)	G. C. Cameron Me And My Life Act Like A Shotgun
TM45 0512	Tamla Motown TMG 1034 (08/76)	The Commodores High On Sunshine Thumpin' Music
TM45 0513	Tamla Motown TMG 1035 (08/76)	Marvin Gaye After The Dance Feel All My Love Inside
TM45 0514	Tamla Motown TMG 1036 (08/76)	David Ruffin Discover Me Smiling Faces Sometimes

TM45 0515	Tamla Motown TMG 1037 (08/76)	Rose Banks Darling Baby Whole New Thing
TM45 0516	Tamla Motown TMG 1038 (09/76)	The Originals Down To Love Town Just To Be Closer To You
TM45 0517	Tamla Motown TMG 1039 (10/76)	Jerry Butler The Devil In Mrs. Jones I Don't Wanna Be Reminded
TM45 0518	Tamla Motown TMG 1040 (10/76)	Jermaine Jackson Let's Be Young Tonight Bass Odyssey
TM45 0519	Tamla Motown TMG 1041 (09/76)	Diana Ross Touch Me In The Morning I'm Still Waiting Note: Twelve singles, 1041 to 1052, were also issued as a limited edition box set, titled "Motown Singles Collection: 24 Top Hits."
TM45 0520	Tamla Motown TMG 1042 (09/76)	Stevie Wonder Yester-Me, Yester-You, Yesterday Uptight (Everything's Alright) Note: Twelve singles, 1041 to 1052, were also issued as a limited edition box set, titled "Motown Singles Collection: 24 Top Hits."
TM45 0521	Tamla Motown TMG 1043 (09/76)	The Temptations Get Ready Just My Imagination (Running Away With Me) Note: Twelve singles, 1041 to 1052, were also issued as a limited edition box set, titled "Motown Singles Collection: 24 Top Hits."
TM45 0522	Tamla Motown TMG 1044 (09/76)	Diana Ross & The Supremes Baby Love Stop! In The Name Of Love Note: Twelve singles, 1041 to 1052, were also issued as a limited edition box set, titled "Motown Singles Collection: 24 Top Hits."
TM45 0523	Tamla Motown TMG 1045 (09/76)	Marvin Gaye / Diana Ross & The Supremes I Heard It Through The Grapevine I'm Gonna Make You Love Me Note: Twelve singles, 1041 to 1052, were also issued as a limited edition box set, titled "Motown Singles Collection: 24 Top Hits." "B" side as by Diana Ross & The Supremes and The Temptations.
TM45 0524	Tamla Motown TMG 1046 (09/76)	The Supremes Stoned Love Nathan Jones Note: Twelve singles, 1041 to 1052, were also issued as a limited edition box set, titled "Motown Singles Collection: 24 Top Hits."

TM45 0525	Tamla Motown TMG 1047 (09/76)	Diana Ross & Marvin Gaye You Are Everything The Onion Song Note: Twelve singles, 1041 to 1052, were also issued as a limited edition box set, titled "Motown Singles Collection: 24 Top Hits." "B" side as by Marvin Gaye & Tammi Terrell.
TM45 0526	Tamla Motown TMG 1048 (09/76)	Smokey Robinson & The Miracles The Tears Of A Clown Tracks Of My Tears Note: Twelve singles, 1041 to 1052, were also issued as a limited edition box set, titled "Motown Singles Collection: 24 Top Hits."
TM45 0527	Tamla Motown TMG 1049 (09/76)	The Four Tops Reach Out, I'll Be There Standing In The Shadows Of Love Note: Twelve singles, 1041 to 1052, were also issued as a limited edition box set, titled "Motown Singles Collection: 24 Top Hits."
TM45 0528	Tamla Motown TMG 1050 (09/76)	Isley Brothers This Old Heart Of Mine (Is Weak For You) Behind A Painted Smile Note: Twelve singles, 1041 to 1052, were also issued as a limited edition box set, titled "Motown Singles Collection: 24 Top Hits."
TM45 0529	Tamla Motown TMG 1051 (09/76)	Martha Reeves & The Vandellas Jimmy Mack Dancing In The Street Note: Twelve singles, 1041 to 1052, were also issued as a limited edition box set, titled "Motown Singles Collection: 24 Top Hits."
TM45 0530	Tamla Motown TMG 1052 (09/76)	Jimmy Ruffin / Marv Johnson What Becomes Of The Brokenhearted I'll Pick A Rose For My Rose Note: Twelve singles, 1041 to 1052, were also issued as a limited edition box set, titled "Motown Singles Collection: 24 Top Hits."
TM45 0531	Motown TMG 1053 (10/76)	Tata Vega Try Love From The Inside Just As Long As There Is You
TM45 0532	Motown TMG 1054 (11/76)	Stevie Wonder I Wish You And I Note: At this point, Tamla Motown became Motown. The black Tamla label was changed to a newly designed blue label with the slogan, "The New Era." See Motown for continuation.

TAMLA MOTOWN 7-INCH EPS

TMEP 0001	Tamla Motown TME 2001 (04/65)	Various Artists HITSVILLE, U.S.A. NO. 1 Note: Marvin Gaye, Brenda Holloway, Carolyn Crawford, Eddie Holland.
TMEP 0002	Tamla Motown TME 2002 (04/65)	The Contours THE CONTOURS
TMEP 0003	Tamla Motown TME 2003 (04/65)	The Marvelettes THE MARVELETTES
TMEP 0004	Tamla Motown TME 2004 (04/65)	The Temptations THE TEMPTATIONS
TMEP 0005	Tamla Motown TME 2005 (04/65)	Kim Weston KIM WESTON
TMEP 0006	Tamla Motown TME 2006 (04/65)	Stevie Wonder STEVIE WONDER
TMEP 0007	Tamla Motown TME 2007 (05/65)	Mary Wells MARY WELLS
TMEP 0008	Tamla Motown TME 2008 (05/65)	The Supremes THE SUPREMES HITS
TMEP 0009	Tamla Motown TME 2009 (05/65)	Martha & The Vandellas MARTHA AND THE VANDELLAS
TMEP 0010	Tamla Motown TME 2010 (02/66)	The Temptations IT'S THE TEMPTATIONS
TMEP 0011	Tamla Motown TME 2011 (02/66)	The Supremes SHAKE
TMEP 0012	Tamla Motown TME 2012 (02/66)	The Four Tops THE FOUR TOPS
TMEP 0013	Tamla Motown TME 2013 (02/66)	Junior Walker & The All Stars SHAKE AND FINGERPOP
TMEP 0014	Tamla Motown TME 2014 (04/66)	Various Artists NEW FACES FROM HITSVILLE Note: Jimmy Ruffin, Chris Clark, Tammi Terrell, the Monitors.
TMEP 0015	Tamla Motown TME 2015 (04/66)	Kim Weston ROCK ME A LITTLE WHILE
TMEP 0016	Tamla Motown TME 2016 (04/66)	Marvin Gaye MARVIN GAYE

TMEP 0017	Tamla Motown TME 2017 (10/66)	Martha And The Vandellas HITTIN'
TMEP 0018	Tamla Motown TME 2018 (03/67)	The Four Tops FOUR TOPS HITS
TMEP 0019	Tamla Motown TME 2019 (03/67)	Marvin Gaye ORIGINALS FROM MARVIN GAYE
TMEP 0020	Tamla Motown TME 2020 (11/76)	Stevie Wonder A SOMETHING EXTRA BONUS RECORD FOR "SONGS IN THE KEY OF LIFE"

Note: Bonus record issued free with "Songs in The Key Of Life." Issued on blue Motown label, in plain sleeve.

TAMLA MOTOWN ALBUMS

TMLP 0001	Tamla Motown TML 11001 (04/65)	Various Artists A COLLECTION OF 16 TAMLA MOTOWN HITS
TMLP 0002	Tamla Motown TML 11002 (04/65)	The Supremes WITH LOVE FROM US TO YOU
TMLP 0003	Tamla Motown TML 11003 (04/65)	The Miracles I LIKE IT LIKE THAT
TMLP 0004	Tamla Motown TML 11004 (04/65)	Marvin Gaye HOW SWEET IT IS TO BE LOVED BY YOU
TMLP 0005	Tamla Motown TML 11005 (04/65)	Martha & The Vandellas HEAT WAVE
TMLP 0006	Tamla Motown TML 11006 (04/65)	Mary Wells MY BABY JUST CARES FOR ME
TMLP 0007	Tamla Motown TML 11007 (05/65)	Various Artists THE MOTORTOWN REVUE
TMLP 0008	Tamla Motown TML 11008 (05/65)	The Marvelettes THE MARVELLOUS MARVELETTES
TMLP 0009	Tamla Motown TML 11009 (05/65)	The Temptations MEET THE TEMPTATIONS
TMLP 0010	Tamla Motown TML 11010 (06/65)	The Four Tops THE FOUR TOPS
TMLP 0011	Tamla Motown TML 11011 (06/65)	Choker Campbell HITS OF THE SIXTIES

TMLP 0012	Tamla Motown TML 11012 (07/65)	The Supremes WE REMEMBER SAM COOKE
TMLP 0013	Tamla Motown TML 11013 (09/65)	Martha & The Vandellas DANCE PARTY
TMLP 0014	Tamla Motown TML 11014 (09/65)	Earl Van Dyke & Soul Brothers THAT MOTOWN SOUND
TMLP 0015	Tamla Motown TML 11015 (09/65)	Marvin Gaye HELLO BROADWAY
TMLP 0016	Tamla Motown TML 11016 (10/65)	The Temptations THE TEMPTATIONS SING SMOKEY
TMLP 0017	Tamla Motown TML 11017 (10/65)	Junior Walker & The All Stars SHOTGUN
TMLP 0018	Tamla Motown TML 11018 (10/65)	The Supremes THE SUPREMES SING COUNTRY, WESTERN & POP
TMLP 0019	Tamla Motown TML 11019 (12/65)	Various Artists HITSVILLE U.S.A.
TMLP 0020	Tamla Motown TML 11020 (12/65)	The Supremes MORE HITS BY THE SUPREMES
TMLP 0021	Tamla Motown TML 11021 (03/66)	The Four Tops SECOND ALBUM
TMLP 0022	Tamla Motown TML 11022 (02/66)	Marvin Gaye A TRIBUTE TO THE GREAT NAT KING COLE
TMLP 0023	Tamla Motown TML 11023 (03/66)	The Temptations TEMPTIN' TEMPTATIONS
TMLP 0024	Tamla Motown TML 11024 (02/66)	Smokey Robinson & The Miracles GOING TO A GO--GO
TMLP 0025	Tamla Motown TML 11025 (02/66)	Billy Eckstine THE PRIME OF MY LIFE
TMLP 0026	Tamla Motown TML 11026 (02/66)	The Supremes AT THE COPA
TMLP 0027	Tamla Motown TML 11027 (02/66)	Various Artists THE MOTORTOWN REVUE LIVE IN PARIS
TMLP 0028	Tamla Motown TML 11028 (06/66)	The Supremes I HEAR A SYMPHONY

TMLP 0029	Tamla Motown TML 11029 (06/66)	Junior Walker & The All Stars SOUL SESSION
TMLP 0030	Tamla Motown TML 11030 (06/66)	Various Artists MOTOWN MAGIC
TMLP 0031	Tamla Motown TML 11031 (07/66)	The Miracles FROM THE BEGINNING
TMLP 0032	Tamla Motown TML 11032 (07/66)	Mary Wells GREATEST HITS
TMLP 0033	Tamla Motown (S)TML 11033 (10/66)	Marvin Gaye MOODS OF MARVIN GAYE
TMLP 0034	Tamla Motown (S)TML 11034 (10/66)	The Isley Brothers THIS OLD HEART OF MINE (IS WEAK FOR YOU)
TMLP 0035	Tamla Motown (S)TML 11035 (10/66)	The Temptations GETTIN' READY
TMLP 0036	Tamla Motown (S)TML 11036 (10/66)	Stevie Wonder UPTIGHT
TMLP 0037	Tamla Motown (S)TML 11037 (11/66)	The Four Tops FOUR TOPS ON TOP
TMLP 0038	Tamla Motown (S)TML 11038 (12/66)	Junior Walker & The All Stars ROAD RUNNER
TMLP 0039	Tamla Motown (S)TML 11039 (12/66)	The Supremes SUPREMES A-GO-GO
TMLP 0040	Tamla Motown (S)TML 11040 (02/67)	Martha & The Vandellas GREATEST HITS
TMLP 0041	Tamla Motown (S)TML 11041 (02/67)	The Four Tops FOUR TOPS LIVE
TMLP 0042	Tamla Motown (S)TML 11042 (02/67)	The Temptations GREATEST HITS
TMLP 0043	Tamla Motown TML 11043 (02/67)	Various Artists A COLLECTION OF 16 ORIGINAL BIG HITS (VOL. 4)
TMLP 0044	Tamla Motown (S)TML 11044 (03/67)	The Miracles AWAY WE A-GO-GO
TMLP 0045	Tamla Motown (S)TML 11045 (04/67)	Stevie Wonder DOWN TO EARTH
TMLP 0046	Tamla Motown (S)TML 11046 (04/67)	Billy Eckstine MY WAY
TMLP 0047	Tamla Motown (S)TML 11047 (05/67)	The Supremes THE SUPREMES SING MOTOWN
TMLP 0048	Tamla Motown (S)TML 11048 (05/67)	Jimmy Ruffin THE JIMMY RUFFIN WAY
TMLP 0049	Tamla Motown (S)TML 11049 (05/67)	Marvin Gaye & Kim Weston TAKE TWO
TMLP 0050	Tamla Motown TML 11050 (06/66)	Various Artists A COLLECTION OF 16 ORIGINAL BIG HITS (VOL. 5)
TMLP 0051	Tamla Motown (S)TML 11051 (06/67)	Martha & The Vandellas WATCH OUT
TMLP 0052	Tamla Motown (S)TML 11052 (07/67)	The Marvelettes THE MARVELETTES
TMLP 0053	Tamla Motown (S)TML 11053 (07/67)	The Temptations THE TEMPTATIONS LIVE
TMLP 0054	Tamla Motown (S)TML 11054 (07/67)	The Supremes THE SUPREMES SING RODGERS AND HART
TMLP 0055	Tamla Motown (S)TML 11055 (10/67)	Various Artists BRITISH MOTOWN CHARTBUSTERS
TMLP 0056	Tamla Motown (S)TML 11056 (11/67)	The Four Tops REACH OUT
TMLP 0057	Tamla Motown (S)TML 11057 (11/67)	The Temptations WITH A LOT O'SOUL
TMLP 0058	Tamla Motown (S)TML 11058 (01/68)	Gladys Knight & The Pips EVERYBODY NEEDS LOVE
TMLP 0059	Tamla Motown (S)TML 11059 (04/68)	Stevie Wonder I WAS MADE TO LOVE HER
TMLP 0060	Tamla Motown (S)TML 11060 (01/68)	The Detroit Spinners THE DETROIT SPINNERS
TMLP 0061	Tamla Motown (S)TML 11061 (01/68)	The Four Tops FOUR TOPS GREATEST HITS
TMLP 0062	Tamla Motown (S)TML 11062 (01/68)	Marvin Gaye & Tammi Terrell UNITED

TMLP 0063	Tamla Motown (S)TML 11063 (01/68)	Diana Ross & The Supremes GREATEST HITS
TMLP 0064	Tamla Motown TML 11064 (01/68)	Various Artists MOTOWN MEMORIES
TMLP 0065	Tamla Motown (S)TML 11065 (02/68)	Marvin Gaye GREATEST HITS
TMLP 0066	Tamla Motown (S)TML 11066 (02/68)	The Isley Brothers SOUL ON THE ROCKS
TMLP 0067	Tamla Motown (S)TML 11067 (02/68)	Smokey Robinson & The Miracles MAKE IT HAPPEN
TMLP 0068	Tamla Motown (S)TML 11068 (03/68)	The Temptations IN A MELLOW MOOD
TMLP 0069	Tamla Motown (S)TML 11069 (02/68)	Chris Clark SOUL SOUNDS
TMLP 0070	Tamla Motown (S)TML 11070 (04/68)	Diana Ross & The Supremes LIVE AT THE TALK OF THE TOWN
TMLP 0071	Tamla Motown (S)TML 11071 (06/68)	Chuck Jackson CHUCK JACKSON ARRIVES
TMLP 0072	Tamla Motown (S)TML 11072 (06/68)	Smokey Robinson & The Miracles GREATEST HITS
TMLP 0073	Tamla Motown (S)TML 11073 (07/68)	Diana Ross & Supremes REFLECTIONS
TMLP 0074	Tamla Motown (S)TML 11074 (07/68)	Various Artists A COLLECTION OF 16 BIG HITS (VOL. 6)
TMLP 0075	Tamla Motown (S)TML 11075 (08/68)	Stevie Wonder GREATEST HITS
TMLP 0076	Tamla Motown TML 11076 (07/68)	Dr. Martin Luther King, Jr. THE GREAT MARCH TO FREEDOM
TMLP 0077	Tamla Motown TML 11077 (10/68)	Various Artists MOTOWN MEMORIES (VOL. 2)
TMLP 0078	Tamla Motown (S)TML 11078 (08/68)	Martha Reeves & The Vandellas RIDIN' HIGH
TMLP 0079	Tamla Motown (S)TML 11079 (08/68)	The Temptations WISH IT WOULD RAIN
TMLP 0080	Tamla Motown (S)TML 11080 (09/68)	Gladys Knight & The Pips FEELIN' BLUESY
TMLP 0081	Tamla Motown (S)TML 11081 (09/68)	The Elgins DARLING BABY
TMLP 0082	Tamla Motown (S)TML 11082 (11/68)	Various Artists BRITISH MOTOWN CHARTBUSTERS (VOL. 2)
TMLP 0083	Tamla Motown (S)TML 11083 (11/68)	Brenda Holloway THE ARTISTRY OF BRENDA HOLLOWAY
TMLP 0084	Tamla Motown (S)TML 11084 (11/68)	Marvin Gaye & Tammi Terrell YOU'RE ALL I NEED
TMLP 0085	Tamla Motown (S)TML 11085 (12/68)	Stevie Wonder SOMEDAY AT CHRISTMAS
TMLP 0086	Tamla Motown (S)TML 11086 (12/68)	Shorty Long HERE COMES THE JUDGE
TMLP 0087	Tamla Motown (S)TML 11087 (01/69)	The Four Tops YESTERDAY'S DREAMS
TMLP 0088	Tamla Motown (S)TML 11088 (02/69)	Diana Ross & The Supremes SING AND PERFORM FUNNY GIRL
TMLP 0089	Tamla Motown (S)TML 11089 (01/69)	Smokey Robinson & The Miracles SPECIAL OCCASION
TMLP 0090	Tamla Motown (S)TML 11090 (01/69)	The Marvelettes SOPHISTICATED SOUL
TMLP 0091	Tamla Motown (S)TML 11091 (01/69)	Marvin Gaye IN THE GROOVE
TMLP 0092	Tamla Motown (S)TML 11092 (05/69)	Various Artists COLLECTION OF BIG HITS (VOL. 7)
TMLP 0093	Tamla Motown (S)TML 11093 (03/69)	Bobby Taylor & The Vancouvers BOBBY TAYLOR AND THE VANCOUVERS
TMLP 0094	Tamla Motown (S)TML 11094 (02/69)	Edwin Starr SOUL MASTER
TMLP 0095	Tamla Motown (S)TML 11095 (01/69)	Diana Ross & Supremes LOVE CHILD
TMLP 0096	Tamla Motown (S)TML 11096 (01/69)	Diana Ross & The Supremes & The Temptations DIANA ROSS & THE SUPREMES JOIN THE TEMPTATIONS

TMLP 0097	Tamla Motown (S)TML 11097 (02/69)	Junior Walker & The All Stars HOME COOKIN'
TMLP 0098	Tamla Motown (S)TML 11098 (02/69)	Stevie Wonder FOR ONCE IN MY LIFE
TMLP 0099	Tamla Motown (S)TML 11099 (04/69)	Martha Reeves & The Vandellas DANCING IN THE STREET
TMLP 0100	Tamla Motown (S)TML 11100 (04/69)	Gladys Knight & The Pips SILK 'N' SOUL
TMLP 0101	Tamla Motown (S)TML 11101 (07/69)	Billy Eckstine GENTLE ON MY MIND
TMLP 0102	Tamla Motown TML 11102	Note: Unissued.
TMLP 0103	Tamla Motown (S)TML 11103 (05/69)	Tammi Terrell IRRESISTIBLE TAMMI TERRELL
TMLP 0104	Tamla Motown (S)TML 11104 (05/69)	The Temptations LIVE AT THE COPA
TMLP 0105	Tamla Motown (S)TML 11105 (07/69)	The Fantastic Four THE FANTASTIC FOUR
TMLP 0106	Tamla Motown (S)TML 11106 (07/69)	Jimmy Ruffin RUFF 'N' READY
TMLP 0107	Tamla Motown (S)TML 11107 (05/69)	Smokey Robinson & The Miracles LIVE
TMLP 0108	Tamla Motown (S)TML 11108 (07/69)	The Monitors GREETINGS WE'RE THE MONITORS
TMLP 0109	Tamla Motown (S)TML 11109 (09/69)	The Temptations CLOUD NINE
TMLP 0110	Tamla Motown (S)TML 11110 (07/69)	Diana Ross & The Supremes & The Temptations T.C.B.
TMLP 0111	Tamla Motown (S)TML 11111 (07/69)	Marv Johnson I'LL PICK A ROSE FOR MY ROSE
TMLP 0112	Tamla Motown (S)TML 11112 (09/69)	The Isley Brothers BEHIND A PAINTED SMILE
TMLP 0113	Tamla Motown (S)TML 11113 (09/69)	The Four Tops THE FOUR TOPS NOW
TMLP 0114	Tamla Motown (S)TML 11114 (11/69)	Diana Ross & The Supremes LET THE SUNSHINE IN
TMLP 0115	Tamla Motown (S)TML 11115 (09/69)	Edwin Starr 25 MILES
TMLP 0116	Tamla Motown (S)TML 11116 (11/69)	The Originals GREEN GROW THE LILACS
TMLP 0117	Tamla Motown (S)TML 11117 (09/69)	Chuck Jackson GOIN' BACK TO CHUCK JACKSON
TMLP 0118	Tamla Motown (S)TML 11118 (09/69)	David Ruffin MY WHOLE WORLD ENDED
TMLP 0119	Tamla Motown (S)TML 11119 (11/69)	Marvin Gaye M.P.G.
TMLP 0120	Tamla Motown (S)TML 11120 (11/69)	Junior Walker & The All Stars JUNIOR WALKER'S GREATEST HITS
TMLP 0121	Tamla Motown (S)TML 11121 (11/69)	Various Artists MOTOWN CHARTBUSTERS VOLUME 3
TMLP 0122	Tamla Motown (S)TML 11122 (02/70)	Diana Ross & The Supremes & The Temptations TOGETHER
TMLP 0123	Tamla Motown (S)TML 11123 (11/69)	Marvin Gaye MARVIN GAYE AND HIS GIRLS
TMLP 0124	Tamla Motown (S)TML 11124 (11/69)	Various Artists IN LOVING MEMORY
TMLP 0125	Tamla Motown (S)TML 11125 (04/70)	Bobby Taylor TAYLOR MADE SOUL
TMLP 0126	Tamla Motown (S)TML 11126 (11/69)	Various Artists MERRY CHRISTMAS FROM MOTOWN
TMLP 0127	Tamla Motown (S)TML 11127 (02/70)	Various Artists MOTORTOWN REVUE LIVE
TMLP 0128	Tamla Motown (S)TML 11128 (02/70)	Stevie Wonder MY CHERIE AMOUR
TMLP 0129	Tamla Motown (S)TML 11129 (02/70)	Smokey Robinson & The Miracles TIME OUT FOR SMOKEY ROBINSON & THE MIRACLES
TMLP 0130	Tamla Motown (S)TML 11130 (02/70)	Various Artists A COLLECTION OF 16 BIG HITS VOLUME 8

TMLP 0131	Tamla Motown (S)TML 11131 (02/70)	Blinky & Edwin Starr JUST WE TWO
TMLP 0132	Tamla Motown (S)TML 11132 (02/70)	Marvin Gaye & Tammi Terrell EASY
TMLP 0133	Tamla Motown (S)TML 11133 (02/70)	The Temptations PUZZLE PEOPLE
TMLP 0134	Tamla Motown (S)TML 11134 (02/70)	Martha Reeves & The Vandellas SUGAR 'N' SPICE
TMLP 0135	Tamla Motown (S)TML 11135 (02/70)	Gladys Knight & The Pips NITTY GRITTY
TMLP 0136	Tamla Motown (S)TML 11136 (04/70)	Marvin Gaye THAT'S THE WAY LOVE IS
TMLP 0137	Tamla Motown (S)TML 11137 (02/70)	Diana Ross & The Supremes CREAM OF THE CROP
TMLP 0138	Tamla Motown (S)TML 11138 (02/70)	The Four Tops SOUL SPIN
TMLP 0139	Tamla Motown STML 11139 (04/70)	David Ruffin FEELIN' GOOD
TMLP 0140	Tamla Motown STML 11140 (04/70)	Junior Walker & The All Stars THESE EYES
TMLP 0141	Tamla Motown STML 11141 (04/70)	The Temptations LIVE AT THE TALK OF THE TOWN
TMLP 0142	Tamla Motown STML 11142 (04/70)	The Jackson 5 DIANA ROSS PRESENTS THE JACKSON 5
TMLP 0143	Tamla Motown STML 11143 (05/70)	Various Artists MOTOWN MEMORIES VOLUME 3
TMLP 0144	Tamla Motown STML11144 (05/70)	Shorty Long THE PRIME OF SHORTY LONG
TMLP 0145	Tamla Motown STML 11145 (05/70)	The Marvelettes IN FULL BLOOM
TMLP 0146	Tamla Motown STML 11146 (05/70)	Diana Ross & The Supremes GREATEST HITS VOL. 2
TMLP 0147	Tamla Motown STML 11147 (06/70)	The Temptations PSYCHEDELIC SHACK
TMLP 0148	Tamla Motown STML 11148 (06/70)	Gladys Knight & The Pips GREATEST HITS
TMLP 0149	Tamla Motown STML 11149 (06/70)	The Four Tops STILL WATERS RUN DEEP
TMLP 0150	Tamla Motown STML 11150 (06/70)	Stevie Wonder STEVIE WONDER LIVE
TMLP 0151	Tamla Motown STML 11151 (07/70)	Smokey Robinson & The Miracles FOUR IN BLUE
TMLP 0152	Tamla Motown STML 11152 (07/70)	Junior Walker & The All Stars LIVE
TMLP 0153	Tamla Motown STML 11153 (08/70)	Marvin Gaye & Tammi Terrell GREATEST HITS
TMLP 0154	Tamla Motown STML 11154/5 (08/70)	Diana Ross & The Supremes FAREWELL Note: Two-album set.
TMLP 0155	Tamla Motown STML 11156 (08/70)	The Jackson 5 ABC
TMLP 0156	Tamla Motown STML 11157 (08/70)	The Supremes RIGHT ON
TMLP 0157	Tamla Motown STML 11158 (08/70)	Kiki Dee GREAT EXPECTATIONS
TMLP 0158	Tamla Motown STML 11159 (10/70)	Diana Ross DIANA ROSS
TMLP 0159	Tamla Motown STML 11160 (09/70)	Sammy Davis Jr. SOMETHING FOR EVERYONE
TMLP 0160	Tamla Motown STML 11161 (10/70)	Jimmy Ruffin JIMMY RUFFIN - FOREVER
TMLP 0161	Tamla Motown STML 11162 (10/70)	Various Artists MOTOWN CHARTBUSTERS VOLUME 4
TMLP 0162	Tamla Motown STML 11163	Note: Unissued.
TMLP 0163	Tamla Motown STML 11164 (10/70)	Stevie Wonder LIVE AT THE TALK OF THE TOWN
TMLP 0164	Tamla Motown STML 11165 (11/70)	Rare Earth GET READY

TMLP 0165	Tamla Motown STML 11166 (11/70)	Martha Reeves & The Vandellas NATURAL RESOURCES
TMLP 0166	Tamla Motown STML 11167 (11/70)	Junior Walker & The All Stars A GAS
TMLP 0167	Tamla Motown STML 11168 (12/70)	The Jackson 5 CHRISTMAS ALBUM
TMLP 0168	Tamla Motown STML 11169 (12/70)	Stevie Wonder SIGNED, SEALED AND DELIVERED
TMLP 0169	Tamla Motown STML 11170 (12/70)	The Temptations GREATEST HITS VOLUME 2
TMLP 0170	Tamla Motown STML 11171 (01/71)	Edwin Starr WAR AND PEACE
TMLP 0171	Tamla Motown STML 11172 (02/71)	Smokey Robinson & The Miracles SMOKEY ROBINSON AND THE MIRACLES
TMLP 0172	Tamla Motown STML 11173 (03/71)	The Four Tops CHANGING TIMES
TMLP 0173	Tamla Motown STML 11174 (02/71)	The Jackson 5 THIRD ALBUM
TMLP 0174	Tamla Motown STML 11175 (02/71)	The Supremes NEW WAYS BUT LOVE STAYS
TMLP 0175	Tamla Motown STML 11176 (05/71)	David & Jimmy Ruffin I AM MY BROTHER'S KEEPER
TMLP 0176	Tamla Motown STML 11177	Note: Unissued.
TMLP 0177	Tamla Motown STML 11178 (04/71)	Diana Ross EVERYTHING IS EVERYTHING
TMLP 0178	Tamla Motown STML 11179 (05/71)	The Supremes & The Four Tops THE MAGNIFICENT 7
TMLP 0179	Tamla Motown STML 11180 (03/71)	Rare Earth ECOLOGY
TMLP 0180	Tamla Motown STML 11181 (04/71)	Various Artists MOTOWN CHARTBUSTERS VOLUME 5
TMLP 0181	Tamla Motown STML 11182 (04/71)	The Motown Spinners SECOND TIME AROUND
TMLP 0182	Tamla Motown STML 11183 (06/71)	Stevie Wonder WHERE IT'S COMING FROM
TMLP 0183	Tamla Motown STML 11184 (08/71)	The Temptations THE SKY'S THE LIMIT
TMLP 0184	Tamla Motown STML 11185 (08/71)	R. Dean Taylor INDIANA WANTS ME
TMLP 0185	Tamla Motown STML 11186 (09/71)	Eddie Kendricks ALL BY MYSELF
TMLP 0186	Tamla Motown STML 11187 (09/71)	Gladys Knight & The Pips IF I WERE YOUR WOMAN
TMLP 0187	Tamla Motown STML 11188 (10/71)	The Jackson 5 MAYBE TOMORROW
TMLP 0188	Tamla Motown STML 11189 (09/71)	The Supremes TOUCH
TMLP 0189	Tamla Motown STML 11190 (10/71)	Marvin Gaye WHAT'S GOING ON
TMLP 0190	Tamla Motown STML 11191 (10/71)	Various Artists MOTOWN CHARTBUSTERS VOLUME 6
TMLP 0191	Tamla Motown STML 11192 (11/71)	The Supremes & The Four Tops THE RETURN OF THE MAGNIFICENT 7
TMLP 0192	Tamla Motown STML 11193 (10/71)	Diana Ross I'M STILL WAITING
TMLP 0193	Tamla Motown STML 11194 (04/72)	Valerie Simpson EXPOSED
TMLP 0194	Tamla Motown STML 11195 (11/71)	The Four Tops GREATEST HITS VOLUME 2
TMLP 0195	Tamla Motown STML 11196 (02/72)	Stevie Wonder GREATEST HITS VOLUME 2
TMLP 0196	Tamla Motown STML 11197 (02/72)	The Undisputed Truth THE UNDISPUTED TRUTH
TMLP 0197	Tamla Motown STML 11198 (02/72)	Junior Walker & The All Stars RAINBOW FUNK
TMLP 0198	Tamla Motown STML 11199 (02/72)	Edwin Starr INVOLVED

TMLP 0199 (02/72)	Tamla Motown STML 11200	Various Artists MOTOWN MEMORIES (16 NON-STOP TAMLA HITS)
TMLP 0200 (02/72)	Tamla Motown STML 11201	Marvin Gaye THE HITS OF MARVIN GAYE
TMLP 0201 (04/72)	Tamla Motown STML 11202	The Temptations SOLID ROCK
TMLP 0202 (04/72)	Tamla Motown STML 11203	The Supremes & The Four Tops DYNAMITE
TMLP 0203 (05/72)	Tamla Motown STML 11204	Martha Reeves & The Vandellas BLACK MAGIC
TMLP 0204 (05/72)	Tamla Motown STML 11205	Michael Jackson GOT TO BE THERE
TMLP 0205 (06/72)	Tamla Motown STML 11206	The Four Tops NATURE PLANNED IT
TMLP 0206	Tamla Motown STML 11207	Note: Unissued.
TMLP 0207 (07/72)	Tamla Motown STML 11208	Gladys Knight & The Pips STANDING OVATION
TMLP 0208 (09/72)	Tamla Motown STML 11209	Edwin Starr THE HITS OF EDWIN STARR
TMLP 0209 (09/72)	Tamla Motown STML 11210	The Supremes FLOY JOY
TMLP 0210 (08/72)	Tamla Motown STML 11211	Junior Walker & The All Stars MOODY JUNIOR
TMLP 0211 (09/72)	Tamla Motown STML 11212	The Jackson 5 GREATEST HITS
TMLP 0212 (02/73)	Tamla Motown STML 11213	Eddie Kendricks PEOPLE...HOLD ON
TMLP 0213 (10/72)	Tamla Motown STML 11214	The Jackson 5 LOOKIN' THROUGH THE WINDOWS
TMLP 0214 (11/72)	Tamla Motown STML 11215	Various Artists MOTOWN CHARTBUSTERS VOLUME 7
TMLP 0215 (01/73)	Tamla Motown STML 11216	San Remo Strings SAN REMO STRINGS SWING
TMLP 0216 (02/73)	Tamla Motown STML 11217	Various Artists THE MOTOWN SOUND - VOL. 1
TMLP 0217 (11/72)	Tamla Motown STML 11218	The Temptations ALL DIRECTIONS
TMLP 0218 (01/73)	Tamla Motown STML 11219	Valerie Simpson VALERIE SIMPSON
TMLP 0219 (12/72)	Tamla Motown STML 11220	Michael Jackson BEN
TMLP 0220 (01/73)	Tamla Motown STML 11221	Jermaine Jackson JERMAINE
TMLP 0221 (03/73)	Tamla Motown STML 11222	The Supremes PRODUCED AND ARRANGED BY JIMMY WEBB
TMLP 0222 (02/73)	Tamla Motown STML 11223	Martha Reeves & The Vandellas GREATEST HITS VOL. 2
TMLP 0223 (02/73)	Tamla Motown STML 11224	Junior Walker & All Stars GREATEST HITS VOL. 2
TMLP 0224 (02/73)	Tamla Motown STML 11225	Marvin Gaye TROUBLE MAN
TMLP 0225 (02/73)	Tamla Motown STML 11226	Gladys Knight & The Pips HELP ME MAKE IT THROUGH THE NIGHT
TMLP 0226 (04/73)	Tamla Motown STML 11227	Various Artists MOTOWN DISCO CLASSICS VOL. 3
TMLP 0227 (05/73)	Tamla Motown STML 11228	David Ruffin DAVID RUFFIN
TMLP 0228 (07/73)	Tamla Motown STML 11229	The Temptations MASTERPIECE
TMLP 0229 (07/73)	Tamla Motown STML 11230	Gladys Knight & The Pips NEITHER ONE OF US
TMLP 0230 (07/73)	Tamla Motown STML 11231	The Jackson 5 SKYWRITER
TMLP 0231 (08/73)	Tamla Motown STML 11232	Various Artists RIC TIC RELICS
TMLP 0232 (07/73)	Tamla Motown STML 11233	Smokey Robinson & The Miracles GREATEST HITS VOL. 2
TMLP 0233 (07/73)	Tamla Motown STML 11234	Junior Walker & The All Stars PEACE AND UNDERSTANDING IS HARD TO FIND

TMLP 0234	Tamla Motown STML 11235 (07/73)	Michael Jackson MUSIC AND ME
TMLP 0235	Tamla Motown STML 11236 (08/73)	The Detroit Spinners THE BEST OF THE DETROIT SPINNERS
TMLP 0236	Tamla Motown STML 11237 (08/73)	Various Artists THE MOTOWN SOUND VOL. 2
TMLP 0237	Tamla Motown STML 11238 (09/73)	Jermaine Jackson COME INTO MY LIFE
TMLP 0238	Tamla Motown STML 11239 (09/73)	Diana Ross TOUCH ME IN THE MORNING
TMLP 0239	Tamla Motown STML 11240 (09/73)	The Undisputed Truth LAW OF THE LAND
TMLP 0240	Tamla Motown STML 11241	Note: Unissued. See Tamla Motown TMSP 1124.
TMLP 0241	Tamla Motown STML 11242	Note: Unissued. See Tamla Motown TMSP 1124.
TMLP 0242	Tamla Motown STML 11243 (11/73)	The Jackson 5 GET IT TOGETHER
TMLP 0243	Tamla Motown STML 11244 (04/74)	Various Artists MOTOWN DISCO CLASSICS VOL. 4
TMLP 0244	Tamla Motown STML 11245 (10/73)	Eddie Kendricks EDDIE KENDRICKS
TMLP 0245	Tamla Motown STML 11246 (10/73)	Various Artists MOTOWN CHARTBUSTERS VOL. 8
TMLP 0246	Tamla Motown STML 11247 (01/74)	Willie Hutch FULLY EXPOSED
TMLP 0247	Tamla Motown STML 11248 (07/74)	Diana Ross LIVE!
TMLP 0248	Tamla Motown STML 11249 (01/74)	Jackie Jackson JACKIE JACKSON
TMLP 0249	Tamla Motown STML 11250	Note: Unissued.
TMLP 0250	Tamla Motown STML 11251	Note: Unissued. See Tamla Motown TMSP 6001.
TMLP 0251	Tamla Motown STML 11252	Note: Unissued. See Tamla Motown TMSP 6001.
TMLP 0252	Tamla Motown STML 11253	Note: Unissued.
TMLP 0253	Tamla Motown STML 11254 (01/74)	Gloria Jones SHARE MY LOVE
TMLP 0254	Tamla Motown STML 11255 (02/74)	Diana Ross LAST TIME I SAW HIM
TMLP 0255	Tamla Motown STML 11256 (03/74)	The Supremes GREATEST HITS
TMLP 0256	Tamla Motown STML 11257 (07/74)	Diahann Carroll DIAHANN CARROLL
TMLP 0257	Tamla Motown STML 11258 (01/75)	The Marvelettes THE BEST OF THE MARVELETTES
TMLP 0258	Tamla Motown STML 11259 (05/74)	Jimmy Ruffin GREATEST HITS
TMLP 0259	Tamla Motown STML 11260 (05/74)	Edwin Starr HELL UP IN HARLEM
TMLP 0260	Tamla Motown STML 11261	Note: Unissued.
TMLP 0261	Tamla Motown STML 11262	Note: Unissued.
TMLP 0262	Tamla Motown STML 11263	Note: Unissued.
TMLP 0263	Tamla Motown STML 11264 (04/74)	Gladys Knight & The Pips ALL I NEED IS TIME
TMLP 0264	Tamla Motown STML 11265 (06/74)	Smokey Robinson PURE SMOKEY
TMLP 0265	Tamla Motown STML 11266 (04/74)	Eddie Kendricks BOOGIE DOWN
TMLP 0266	Tamla Motown STML 11267	Note: Unissued.
TMLP 0267	Tamla Motown STML 11268 (09/74)	Syreeta STEVIE WONDER PRESENTS SYREETA
TMLP 0268	Tamla Motown STML 11269 (08/74)	Willie Hutch FOXY BROWN
TMLP 0269	Tamla Motown STML 11270 (10/74)	Various Artists MOTOWN CHARTBUSTERS VOL. 9
TMLP 0270	Tamla Motown STML 11271	Note: Unissued. See Tamla Motown TMSP 1127.

TMLP 0271	Tamla Motown STML 11272	Note: Unissued. See Tamla Motown TMSP 1127.
TMLP 0272	Tamla Motown STML 11273 (10/74)	The Commodores MACHINE GUN
TMLP 0273	Tamla Motown STML 11274 (07/75)	Junior Walker & The All Stars JUNIOR WALKER & THE ALL STARS
TMLP 0274	Tamla Motown STML 11275 (11/74)	The Jackson 5 DANCING MACHINE
TMLP 0275	Tamla Motown STML 11276 (12/74)	The Miracles DO IT BABY
TMLP 0276	Tamla Motown STML 11277 (01/75)	The Undisputed Truth DOWN TO EARTH
TMLP 0277	Tamla Motown STML 11278 (12/74)	Various Artists MOTOWN DISCO CLASSICS VOL. 5
TMLP 0278	Tamla Motown STML 11279 (03/75)	Gladys Knight & The Pips KNIGHT TIME
TMLP 0279	Tamla Motown STML 11280 (01/75)	Willie Hutch THE MARK OF THE BEAST
TMLP 0280	Tamla Motown STML 11281	Note: Unissued. See Tamla Motown TMSP 1128.
TMLP 0281	Tamla Motown STML 11282	Note: Unissued. See Tamla Motown TMSP 1128.
TMLP 0282	Tamla Motown STML 11283 (01/75)	David Ruffin ME 'N' ROCK 'N' ROLL ARE HERE TO STAY
TMLP 0283	Tamla Motown STML 11284 (03/75)	Caston and Majors CASTON AND MAJORS
TMLP 0284	Tamla Motown STML 11285	Note: Unissued.
TMLP 0285	Tamla Motown STML 11286 (05/75)	The Commodores CAUGHT IN THE ACT
TMLP 0286	Tamla Motown STML 11287 (06/75)	The Originals CALIFORNIA SUNSET
TMLP 0287	Tamla Motown STML 11288 (06/75)	Smokey Robinson A QUIET STORM
TMLP 0288	Tamla Motown STML 11289 (07/75)	Discotech THE MAGIC DISCO MACHINE
TMLP 0289	Tamla Motown STML 11290 (07/75)	The Jackson 5 MOVING VIOLATION
TMLP 0290	Tamla Motown STML 11291	Note: Unissued. See Tamla Motown TMSP 1129.
TMLP 0291	Tamla Motown STML 11292	Note: Unissued. See Tamla Motown TMSP 1129.
TMLP 0292	Tamla Motown STML 11293 (07/75)	The Supremes THE SUPREMES
TMLP 0293	Tamla Motown STML 12001 (09/75)	Eddie Kendricks THE HIT MAN
TMLP 0294	Tamla Motown STML 12002 (09/75)	Various Artists DISCOTECH
TMLP 0295	Tamla Motown STML 12003 (10/75)	Various Artists MOTOWN GOLD
TMLP 0296	Tamla Motown STML 12004 (12/75)	Diana Ross MAHOGANY
TMLP 0297	Tamla Motown STML 12005 (09/75)	Michael Jackson THE BEST OF MICHAEL JACKSON
TMLP 0298	Tamla Motown STML 12006 (01/76)	The Temptations HOUSE PARTY
TMLP 0299	Tamla Motown STML 12007 (02/76)	The Dynamic Superiors PURE PLEASURE
TMLP 0300	Tamla Motown STML 12008 (11/75)	Yvonne Fair THE BITCH IS BLACK
TMLP 0301	Tamla Motown STML 12009 (11/75)	The Undisputed Truth HIGHER THAN HIGH
TMLP 0302	Tamla Motown STML 12010 (11/75)	The Miracles CITY OF ANGELS
TMLP 0303	Tamla Motown STML 12011 (11/75)	The Commodores MOVIN' ON
TMLP 0304	Tamla Motown STML 12012 (01/76)	David Ruffin WHO AM I?

TMLP 0305	Tamla Motown STML 12013 (01/76)	Gladys Knight & The Pips A LITTLE KNIGHT MUSIC
TMLP 0306	Tamla Motown STML 12014	Note: Unissued. See Motown STMA 8024.
TMLP 0307	Tamla Motown STML 12015 (01/76)	Willie Hutch ODE TO MY LADY
TMLP 0308	Tamla Motown STML 12016 (03/76)	Eddie Kendricks HE'S A FRIEND
TMLP 0309	Tamla Motown STML 12017 (03/76)	Stephanie Mills FOR THE FIRST TIME
TMLP 0310	Tamla Motown STML 12018 (03/76)	Junior Walker & The All Stars HOT SHOT
TMLP 0311	Tamla Motown STML 12019 (03/76)	Various Artists MOTOWN DISCOTECH VOL. 2
TMLP 0312	Tamla Motown STML 12020 (04/76)	The Miracles LOVE MACHINE
TMLP 0313	Tamla Motown STML 12021 (04/76)	Smokey Robinson SMOKEY'S FAMILY ROBINSON
TMLP 0314	Tamla Motown STML 12022 (04/76)	Diana Ross DIANA ROSS
TMLP 0315	Tamla Motown STML 12023 (05/76)	Willie Hutch CONCERT IN BLUES
TMLP 0316	Tamla Motown STML 12024 (07/76)	Rose Banks ROSE BANKS
TMLP 0317	Tamla Motown STML 12025 (03/76)	Marvin Gaye I WANT YOU
TMLP 0318	Tamla Motown STML 12026 (08/76)	Various Artists THE MOTOWN SONGBOOK
TMLP 0319	Tamla Motown STML 12027 (06/76)	The Supremes HIGH ENERGY
TMLP 0320	Tamla Motown STML 12028 (07/76)	Various Artists MOTOWN MAGIC DISCO MACHINE VOL. 2
TMLP 0321	Tamla Motown STML 12029 (08/76)	G. C. Cameron G. C. CAMERON

TMLP 0322	Tamla Motown STML 12030 (06/76)	David Ruffin EVERTHING'S COMING UP LOVE
TMLP 0323	Tamla Motown STML 12031 (06/76)	The Commodores HOT ON THE TRACKS
TMLP 0324	Tamla Motown STML 12032 (06/76)	Jerry Butler LOVE'S ON THE MENU
TMLP 0325	Tamla Motown STML 12033 (08/76)	Junior Walker & The All Stars SAX APPEAL
TMLP 0326	Tamla Motown STML 12034 (09/76)	The Originals COMMUNIQUE
TMLP 0327	Tamla Motown STML 12035 (09/76)	Ronnie McNeir RONNIE McNEIR
TMLP 0328	Tamla Motown STML 12036 (07/76)	Diana Ross GREATEST HITS VOL. 2
TMLP 0329	Tamla Motown STML 12037 (11/77)	Various Artists MOTOWN CHRISTMAS ALBUM
TMLP 0330	Tamla Motown STML 12038 (10/76)	The Miracles THE POWER OF MUSIC
TMLP 0331	Tamla Motown STML 12039 (10/76)	Tata Vega FULL SPEED AHEAD
TMLP 0332	Tamla Motown STML 12040 (10/76)	The Temptations DO THE TEMPTATIONS
TMLP 0333	Tamla Motown STML 12041 (11/76)	Ronnie McNeir LOVE'S COMIN' DOWN
TMLP 0334	Tamla Motown STML 12042 (09/76)	Marvin Gaye THE BEST OF MARVIN GAYE
TMLP 0335	Tamla Motown STML 12043 (11/76)	Eddie Kendricks GOIN' UP IN SMOKE

MOTOWN 7-INCH SINGLES

MO45 0001	Motown TMG 1053 (10/76)	Tata Vega Try Love From The Inside Just As Long As There Is You
MO45 0002	Motown TMG 1054 (11/76)	Stevie Wonder I Wish You And I
MO45 0003	Motown TMG 1055 (10/76)	William Goldstein & The Magic Disco Machine Midnight Rhapsody Midnight Rhapsody (Part 2)

MO45 0004	Motown TMG 1056 (10/76)	Diana Ross One Love In My Lifetime You're Good My Child
MO45 0005	Motown TMG 1057 (10/76)	The Temptations Who Are You Let Me Count The Ways (I Love You)
MO45 0006	Motown TMG 1058 (10/76)	The Commodores Just To Be Close To You Look What You've Done To Me
MO45 0007	Motown TMG 1059 (01/77)	Thelma Houston / William Goldstein The Bingo Long Song (Steal On Home) Razzle Dazzle (Instrumental)
MO45 0008	Motown TMG 1060 (01/77)	Thelma Houston Don't Leave Me This Way Today Will Soon Be Yesterday
MO45 0009	Motown TMG 1061 (01/77)	Eddie Kendricks Goin' Up In Smoke Get It While It's Hot
MO45 0010	Motown TMG 1062 (01/77)	The Commodores Fancy Dancer Cebu
MO45 0011	Motown TMG 1063 (01/77)	The Temptations Shaky Ground I'm A Bachelor
MO45 0012	Motown TMG 1064 (03/77)	The Supremes Love I Never Knew You Could Feel This Good This Is Why I Believe In You
MO45 0013	Motown TMG 1065 (03/77)	Smokey Robinson There Will Come A Day (When I'm Gonna Happen To You) An Old-Fashioned Man
MO45 0014	Motown TMG 1066	The Originals Six-Million Dollar Man Mother Nature's Best Note: Unissued.
MO45 0015	Motown TMG 1067 (04/77)	Jennifer Do It For Me Boogie Boogie Love
MO45 0016	Motown TMG 1068 (03/77)	Stevie Wonder Sir Duke Tuesday Heartbreak
MO45 0017	Motown TMG 1069 (04/77)	Marvin Gaye Got To Give It Up (Part 1) Got To Give It Up (Part 2)
MO45 0018	Motown TMG 1070 (05/77)	Junior Walker & The All Stars I Ain't Going Nowhere What Does It Take (To Win Your Love) + Take Me Girl, I'm Ready

Note: Maxi-single.

MO45 0019	Motown TMG 1071 (05/77)	Dynamic Superiors Stay Away Supersensuousensation (Try Some Love)
MO45 0020	Motown TMG 1072 (05/77)	Tata Vega You'll Never Rock Alone Just When Things Are Getting Good
MO45 0021	Motown TMG 1073 (05/77)	The Commodores Easy Machine Gun + I Feel Sanctified Note: Maxi-single.
MO45 0022	Motown TMG 1074 (07/77)	Thelma Houston & Jerry Butler It's A Lifetime Thing Only The Beginning
MO45 0023	Motown TMG 1075 (06/77)	21st Creation Tailgate Mr. Disco Radio
MO45 0024	Motown TMG 1076 (06/77)	Smokey Robinson Vitamin U Holly
MO45 0025	Motown TMG 1077 (07/77)	Dynamic Superiors Nowhere To Run (Part 1) Nowhere To Run (Part 2)
MO45 0026	Motown TMG 1078 (07/77)	David Ruffin I Can't Stop The Rain My Whole World Ended (The Moment You Left Me)
MO45 0027	Motown TMG 1079 (08/77)	Flavor Don't Freeze Up Don't Freeze Up (Instrumental)
MO45 0028	Motown TMG 1080 (08/77)	Diana Ross & The Supremes Someday We'll Be Together You Keep Me Hangin' On
MO45 0029	Motown TMG 1081 (08/77)	The Jackson 5 Skywriter I Want You Back + The Love You Save Note: Maxi-single.
MO45 0030	Motown TMG 1082 (08/77)	Jerry Butler Chalk It Up I Don't Want Nobody To Know
MO45 0031	Motown TMG 1083 (08/77)	Stevie Wonder Another Star Creepin'
MO45 0032	Motown TMG 1084 (09/77)	Albert Finney Those Other Men What Have They Done (To My Home Town)

MO45 0033	Motown TMG 1085 (09/77)	Smokey Robinson Theme From 'Big Time' (Part 1) Theme From 'Big Time' (Part 2)
MO45 0034	Motown TMG 1086 (09/77)	The Commodores Brick House Sweet Love
MO45 0035	Motown TMG 1087 (10/77)	High Inergy You Can't Turn Me Off (In The Middle Of Turning Me On) Let Me Get Close To You
MO45 0036	Motown TMG 1088 (10/77)	Thelma Houston I'm Here Again Sharing Something Perfect Between Ourselves
MO45 0037	Motown TMG 1089 (10/77)	Mandre Solar Flight (Opus 1) Keep Tryin'
MO45 0038	Motown TMG 1090 (10/77)	Diana Ross Gettin' Ready For Love Stone Liberty
MO45 0039	Motown TMG 1091 (11/77)	Stevie Wonder As Contusion
MO45 0040	Motown TMG 1092 (11/77)	Jermaine Jackson Take Time You Need To Be Loved
MO45 0041	Motown TMG 1093 (11/77)	David Ruffin You're My Peace Of Mind Rode By The Place (Where We Used To Stay)
MO45 0042	Motown TMG 1094 (11/77)	Syreeta & G. C Cameron Let's Make A Deal (Part 1) Let's Make A Deal (Part 2)
MO45 0043	Motown TMG 1095 (11/77)	Gladys Knight & The Pips Help Me Make It Through The Night Daddy Could Swear, I Declare
MO45 0044	Motown TMG 1096 (01/78)	The Commodores Zoom Too Hot Ta Trot
MO45 0045	Motown TMG 1097 (01/78)	Jerry Butler I Wanna Do It To You Let's Go Get Out Of Town
MO45 0046	Motown TMG 1098 (01/78)	Scherrie Payne Fly When I Looked At Your Face
MO45 0047	Motown TMG 1099 (02/78)	Diana Ross Top Of The World Too Shy To Say
MO45 0048	Motown TMG 1100 (02/78)	Mary Wells My Guy What's Easy For Two Is Hard For One
MO45 0049	Motown TMG 1101 (03/78)	5th Dimension You Are The Reason (I Feel Like Dancing) Slipping Into Something New
MO45 0050	Motown TMG 1102 (03/78)	Thelma Houston I Can't Go On Living Without Your Love Any Way You Like It
MO45 0051	Motown TMG 1103 (03/78)	High Inergy Love Is All You Need Save It For A Rainy Day
MO45 0052	Motown TMG 1104 (04/78)	Diana Ross Your Love Is So Good For Me Baby It's Me
MO45 0053	Motown TMG 1105 (03/78)	3 Ounces Of Love Star Love I Found The Feeling
MO45 0054	Motown TMG 1106 (04/78)	Smokey Robinson Madam X The Agony And The Ecstasy
MO45 0055	Motown TMG 1107 (04/78)	Cuba Gooding Mind Pleaser Ain't Nothin' To It
MO45 0056	Motown TMG 1108 (05/78)	Carl Bean I Was Born This Way I Was Born This Way (Instrumental)
MO45 0057	Motown TMG 1109 (05/78)	Major Lance I Never Thought I'd Be Losing You Chicago Disco
MO45 0058	Motown TMG 1110 (05/78)	Rick James You And I Hollywood Note: Issued on a green label, as well as blue label.
MO45 0059	Motown TMG 1111 (06/78)	The Commodores Flying High Funky Situation
MO45 0060	Motown TMG 1112 (07/78)	Diana Ross Lovin', Livin' And Givin' You Got It
MO45 0061	Motown TMG 1113 (07/78)	The Commodores Three Times A Lady Can't Let You Tease Me
MO45 0062	Motown TMG 1114 (07/78)	Smokey Robinson Daylight & Darkness Why You Wanna See My Bad Side
MO45 0063	Motown TMG 1115 (08/78)	Platinum Hook Standing On The Verge (Of Gettin' It On) Til I Met You
MO45 0064	Motown TMG 1116 (09/78)	Mandre Fair Game Light Years (Opus IV)

MO45 0065	Motown TMG 1117 (09/78)	Thelma Houston Don't Pity Me It's Just Me Feeling Good
MO45 0066	Motown TMG 1118 (09/78)	Junior Walker Walk In The Night I Need You Right Now Note: "B" side with Thelma Houston.
MO45 0067	Motown TMG 1119 (09/78)	3 Ounces Of Love Give Me Some Feeling Don't Worry 'Bout My Love
MO45 0068	Motown TMG 1120 (09/78)	The Four Tops I Can't Help Myself It's The Same Old Song
MO45 0069	Motown TMG 1121 (10/78)	Rick James Mary Jane Dream Maker
MO45 0070	Motown TMG 1122 (10/78)	High Inergy Lovin' Fever Beware
MO45 0071	Motown TMG 1123 (10/78)	Switch There'll Never Be You Pulled A Switch
MO45 0072	Motown TMG 1124 (10/78)	The Velvelettes Needle In A Haystack He Was Really Saying Somethin'
MO45 0073	Motown TMG 1125 (10/78)	Bonnie Pointer Free Me From My Freedom - Tie Me To A Tree (Handcuff Me) Free Me From My Freedom - Tie Me To A Tree (Handcuff Me) (Instrumental)
MO45 0074	Motown TMG 1126 (11/78)	Finished Touch I Love To See You Dance Sticks And Stones (But The Funk Won't Ever Hurt You)
MO45 0075	Motown TMG 1127 (11/78)	The Commodores Just To Be Close To You X-Rated Movie
MO45 0076	Motown TMG 1128 (11/78)	Platinum Hook Gotta Find A Woman Hooked For Life
MO45 0077	Motown TMG 1129 (11/78)	Smokey Robinson Shoe Soul I'm Loving You Softly
MO45 0078	Motown TMG 1130 (01/79)	Thelma Houston Saturday Night, Sunday Morning I'm Not Strong Enough (To Love You Again)
MO45 0079	Motown TMG 1131 (01/79)	Grover Washington Do Dat Reed Seed (Trio Tune)
MO45 0080	Motown TMG 1132 (01/79)	Switch We Like To Party...Come On Somebody's Watchin' You
MO45 0081	Tamla Motown TMG 1133 (02/79)	Barbara Randolph I Got A Feeling Can I Get A Witness + You Got Me Hurtin' All Over Note: Maxi-single, released on the black Tamla Motown label in an olive sleeve.
MO45 0082	Motown TMG 1134 (01/79)	Bonnie Pointer Heaven Must Have Sent You I Wanna Make It (In Your World)
MO45 0083	Motown TMG 1135 (02/79)	Diana Ross What You Gave Me Ain't No Mountain High Enough
MO45 0084	Motown TMG 1136 (02/79)	Diana Ross, Marvin Gaye, Stevie Wonder & Smokey Robinson Pops, We Love You Pops, We Love You (Instrumental)
MO45 0085	Motown TMG 1137 (03/79)	Rick James High On Your Love Suite Stone City Band, Hi!
MO45 0086	Motown TMG 1138 (02/79)	Marvin Gaye A Funky Space Reincarnation (Part 1) A Funky Space Reincarnation (Part 2)
MO45 0087	Motown TMG 1139 (04/79)	Billy Preston & Syreeta Go For It With You I'm Born Again (Instrumental) Note: Syreeta on "A" side only.
MO45 0088	Motown TMG 1140 (04/79)	Tata Vega Get It Up For Love I Just Keep Thinking About You Baby
MO45 0089	Motown TMG 1141 (05/79)	Apollo Astro Disco (Part 1) Astro Disco (Part 2)
MO45 0090	Motown TMG 1142 (07/79)	High Inergy Shoulda Gone Dancin' Peaceland
MO45 0091	Motown TMG 1143 (05/79)	Motown Sounds Space Dance Bad Mouthin'
MO45 0092	Motown TMG 1144 (05/79)	Mandre Swang Spirit Groove
MO45 0093	Motown TMG 1145 (07/79)	Bonnie Pointer Heaven Must Have Sent You (New version) My Everything

MO45 0094	Motown TMG 1146 (06/79)	Teena Marie I'm A Sucker For Your Love Deja Vu (I've Been Here Before)
MO45 0095	Motown TMG 1147 (06/79)	Rick James Bustin' Out Sexy Lady
MO45 0096	Motown TMG 1148 (06/79)	Switch Best Beat In Town It's So Real
MO45 0097	Motown TMG 1149 (11/79)	Stevie Wonder Send One Your Love Send One Your Love (Instrumental)
MO45 0098	Motown TMG 1150 (06/79)	Diana Ross The Boss I'm In The World
MO45 0099	Motown TMG 1151 (07/79)	Finished Touch featuring Harold Johnson The Down Sound (Part 1) The Down Sound (Part 2)
MO45 0100	Motown TMG 1152 (07/79)	Smokey Robinson Get Ready Ever Had A Dream
MO45 0101	Motown TMG 1153 (07/79)	Grover Washington Just The Way You Are Loran's Dance
MO45 0102	Motown TMG 1154 (08/79)	Mira Waters You Have Inspired Me You Have Inspired Me (Disco version)
MO45 0103	Motown TMG 1155 (08/79)	The Commodores Sail On Captain Quick Draw
MO45 0104	Motown TMG 1156 (09/79)	Rick James Fool On The Street Jefferson Ball
MO45 0105	Motown TMG 1157 (08/79)	Tata Vega If Love Must Go Come In Heaven (Earth Is Calling)
MO45 0106	Motown TMG 1158 (09/79)	Teena Marie Don't Look Back I'm Gonna Have My Cake (And Eat It Too)
MO45 0107	Motown TMG 1159 (08/79)	Billy Preston & Syreeta With You I'm Born Again Sock-It Rocket Note: Syreeta on "A" side only.
MO45 0108	Motown TMG 1160 (09/79)	Diana Ross No One Gets The Prize Never Say I Don't Love You
MO45 0109	Motown TMG 1161 (09/79)	Patrick Gammon Cop An Attitude My Song In G
MO45 0110	Motown TMG 1162 (09/79)	Sterling Roll-Her, Skater Roll-Her, Skater (Instrumental)
MO45 0111	Motown TMG 1163 (09/79)	Mary Wilson Red Hot Midnight Dancer
MO45 0112	Motown TMG 1164 (09/79)	Smokey Robinson Cruisin' The Humming Song (Lost For Words)
MO45 0113	Tamla Motown TMG 1165 (02/80)	Michael Jackson / Marvin Gaye Ben Abraham, Martin And John Note: Issued on black Tamla Motown label in olive sleeve.
MO45 0114	Motown TMG 1166 (10/79)	The Commodores Still Such A Woman
MO45 0115	Motown TMG 1167 (11/79)	Scherrie & Susaye Leaving Me Was The Best Thing You've Ever Done When The Day Comes Every Night
MO45 0116	Motown TMG 1168 (11/79)	Marvin Gaye Ego Tripping Out Ego Tripping Out (Instrumental)
MO45 0117	Motown TMG 1169 (11/79)	Diana Ross It's My House Sparkle
MO45 0118	Tamla Motown TMG 1170 (11/79)	Frank Wilson Do I Love You (Indeed I Do) Sweeter As The Days Go By Note: Released on black Tamla Motown label in olive sleeve.
MO45 0119	Motown TMG 1171 (01/80)	Bonnie Pointer I Can't Help Myself (Sugar Pie, Honey Bunch) When I'm Gone
MO45 0120	Motown TMG 1172 (01/80)	The Commodores Wonderland Lovin' You
MO45 0121	Motown TMG 1173 (01/80)	Stevie Wonder Black Orchid Blame It On The Sun
MO45 0122	Motown TMG 1174 (01/80)	Rick James Love Gun Stormy Love
MO45 0123	Motown TMG 1175 (02/80)	Billy Preston & Syreeta It Will Come In Time All I Wanted Was You Note: Syreeta on "A" side only.

MO45 0124	Tamla Motown TMG 1176 (01/80)	Martha Reeves & The Vandellas Heatwave Dancing In The Street Note: Issued with picture sleeve on black Tamla Motown label.
MO45 0125	Motown TMG 1177 (02/80)	Mary Wilson Pick Up The Pieces You're The Light That Guides My Way
MO45 0126	Motown TMG 1178 (03/80)	Teena Marie Can It Be Love Too Many Colors (Tee's Interlude)
MO45 0127	Motown TMG 1179 (03/80)	Stevie Wonder Outside My Window Same Old Story
MO45 0128	Tamla Motown TMG 1180 (04/80)	Diana Ross & The Supremes Supremes Medley (Part 1) Supremes Medley (Part 2) Note: Issued on black Tamla Motown label.
MO45 0129	Motown TMG 1181 (04/80)	Stone City Band Strut Your Stuff F.I.M.A. (Funk In Mama Afrika)
MO45 0130	Motown TMG 1182 (04/80)	Smokey Robinson Let Me Be The Clock Travelin' Through
MO45 0131	Motown TMG 1183 (04/80)	Jermaine Jackson Let's Get Serious Je Vous Aime Beaucoup (I Love You)
MO45 0132	Motown TMG 1184 (04/80)	Bonnie Pointer Deep In My Soul I Love To Sing To You
MO45 0133	Motown TMG 1185 (05/80)	Teena Marie Behind The Groove You're All The Boogie I Need
MO45 0134	Motown TMG 1186 (05/80)	Temptations Power Power (Instrumental)
MO45 0135	Motown TMG 1187 (05/80)	Switch Don't Take Your Love From Me Don't Take Your Love From Me (Instrumental)
MO45 0136	Motown TMG 1188 (05/80)	Billy Preston & Syreeta / Billy Preston One More Time For Love Dance For Me Children
MO45 0137	Motown TMG 1189 (05/80)	Detroit Spinners It's A Shame Sweet Thing
MO45 0138	Motown TMG 1190 (06/80)	Dr. Strut Struttin' Blue Lodge
MO45 0139	Motown TMG 1191 (06/80)	Smokey Robinson Heavy On Pride I Love The Nearness Of You
MO45 0140	Motown TMG 1192 (06/80)	Ozone Walk On This Is Funkin! Insane
MO45 0141	Motown TMG 1193 (06/80)	Commodores Old Fashioned Love Sexy Lady
MO45 0142	Motown TMG 1194 (07/80)	Jermaine Jackson Burnin' Hot Castles Of Sand
MO45 0143	Motown TMG 1195 (07/80)	Diana Ross Upside Down Friend To Friend
MO45 0144	Motown TMG 1196 (07/80)	Teena Marie Lonely Desire Aladdin's Lamp
MO45 0145	Motown TMG 1197 (08/80)	Temptations Struck By Lightning Twice I'm Coming Home
MO45 0146	Motown TMG 1198 (08/80)	Rick James Big Time Island Lady
MO45 0147	Motown TMG 1199 (08/80)	Black Russian Mystified Love's Enough
MO45 0148	Motown TMG 1200 (08/80)	Syreeta He's Gone Here's My Love
MO45 0149	Motown TMG 1201 (08/80)	Jermaine Jackson You're Supposed To Keep Your Love For Me Let It Rise
MO45 0150	Motown TMG 1202 (09/80)	Diana Ross My Old Piano Where Did We Go Wrong
MO45 0151	Motown TMG 1203 (09/80)	Teena Marie I Need Your Lovin' Irons In The Fire
MO45 0152	Motown TMG 1204 (09/80)	Stevie Wonder Masterblaster (Jammin) Masterblaster (Dub)
MO45 0153	Motown TMG 1205 (09/80)	High Inergy Make Me Yours I Love Makin' Love
MO45 0154	Motown TMG 1206 (09/80)	Commodores Heroes Don't You Be Worried

MO45 0155	Motown TMG 1207 (10/80)	Lynda Carter Last Song What's A Little Love Between Friends
MO45 0156	Motown TMG 1208 (10/80)	Micheal Urbaniak Nanava Joy
MO45 0157	Motown TMG 1209 (10/80)	Rick James Summer Love Gettin' It On
MO45 0158	Motown TMG 1210 (10/80)	Diana Ross I'm Coming Out Give Up
MO45 0159	Motown TMG 1211 (10/80)	Billy Preston & Syreeta Please Stay Signed Sealed Delivered (I'm Yours)
MO45 0160	Motown TMG 1212 (11/80)	Jermaine Jackson Little Girl Don't You Worry We Can Put It Back Together
MO45 0161	Motown TMG 1213 (11/80)	Dazz Band Shake It Up Only Love
MO45 0162	Motown TMG 1214 (11/80)	High Inergy Hold On To My Love If I Love You Tonight
MO45 0163	Motown TMG 1215 (12/80)	Stevie Wonder I Ain't Gonna Stand For It Knocks Me Off My Feet
MO45 0164	Motown TMG 1216 (12/80)	Temptations Take Me Away There's More Where That Came From
MO45 0165	Motown TMG 1217 (12/80)	Diana Ross It's My Turn Sleepin'
MO45 0166	Motown TMG 1218 (12/80)	Commodores Jesus Is Love Mighty Spirit
MO45 0167	Motown TMG 1219 (01/81)	Tata Vega You Keep Me Hanging On You Better Watch Out
MO45 0168	Motown TMG 1220 (01/81)	Black Russian Leave Me Now Move Together
MO45 0169	Motown TMG 1221 (02/81)	Stone City Band All Day And All Of The Night All Day And All Of The Night (Vamp Version)
MO45 0170	Motown TMG 1222 (02/81)	Jermaine Jackson You Like Me Don't You You Like Me Don't You (Instrumental) Note: Reissued May 1981.

MO45 0171	Motown TMG 1223 (02/81)	Smokey Robinson Being With You What's In Your Life For Me
MO45 0172	Motown TMG 1224 (02/81)	Billy Preston Hope Give It Up
MO45 0173	Motown TMG 1225 (02/81)	Marvin Gaye Praise Funk Me
MO45 0174	Motown TMG 1226 (03/81)	Stevie Wonder Lately If It's Magic
MO45 0175	Motown TMG 1227 (03/81)	Diana Ross One More Chance Confide In Me
MO45 0176	Motown TMG 1228	Note: Unissued.
MO45 0177	Motown TMG 1229 (05/81)	Rick James Give It To Me Baby Don't Give Up On Love
MO45 0178	Motown TMG 1230 (05/81)	Tata Vega Love Your Neighbour There's Love In The World
MO45 0179	Motown TMG 1231 (05/81)	Billy Preston A Change Is Gonna Come You
MO45 0180	Motown TMG 1232 (05/81)	Marvin Gaye Heavy Love Affair Far Cry
MO45 0181	Motown TMG 1233 (05/81)	Diana Ross Cryin' My Heart Out For You To Love Again
MO45 0182	Motown TMG 1234 (06/81)	High Inergy I Just Wanna Dance With You Take My Life
MO45 0183	Motown TMG 1235 (07/81)	Stevie Wonder Happy Birthday Happy Birthday Singalong
MO45 0184	Motown TMG 1236 (07/81)	Teena Marie Square Biz Square Biz (Instrumental)
MO45 0185	Motown TMG 1237 (07/81)	Smokey Robinson You Are Forever I Hear The Children Singing
MO45 0186	Motown TMG 1238 (07/81)	Commodores Lady (You Bring Me Up) Gettin' It
MO45 0187	Motown TMG 1239 (08/81)	Stone City Band Funky Reggae Ganja
MO45 0188	Motown TMG 1240 (09/81)	Diana Ross & Lionel Richie Endless Love Endless Love (Instrumental)

DISTRIBUTION CHANGE

Note: At this point, Motown distribution in Britain passed from EMI to RCA. All of the above singles (1186 to 1240) were effectively 'reissued,' still on the Motown label, but with very minor changes of label design.

MO45 0190	Motown TMG 1241 (11/81)	Rick James Super Freak (Part 1) Super Freak (Part 2)

Note: Reissued on identical number in November 1982, but with "Fire & Desire" as flipside.

MO45 0191	Motown TMG 1242 (11/81)	Jermaine Jackson I'm Just Too Shy All Because Of You
MO45 0192	Motown TMG 1243 (10/81)	Temptations Aiming At Your Heart Life Of A Cowboy
MO45 0193	Motown TMG 1244 (10/81)	Jose Feliciano Everybody Loves Me The Drought Is Over
MO45 0194	Motown TMG 1245 (10/81)	Commodores Oh No Are You Happy
MO45 0195	Motown TMG 1246 (11/81)	Teena Marie It Must Be Magic Yes Indeed
MO45 0196	Motown TMG 1247 (11/81)	Syreeta Quick Slick I Don't Know
MO45 0197	Motown TMG 1248 (12/81)	Diana Ross Tenderness Supremes Medley
MO45 0198	Motown TMG 1249 (11/81)	Ozone Gigolette Gigolette (Instrumental)
MO45 0199	Motown TMG 1250 (01/82)	Rick James Ghetto Life Below The Funk
MO45 0200	Motown TMG 1251 (01/82)	Teena Marie Portuguese Love Ballad Of Cradle Rob
MO45 0201	Motown TMG 1252 (01/82)	Jose Feliciano I Wanna Be Where You Are Let's Make Love On The Telephone
MO45 0202	Motown TMG 1253 (02/82)	Jermaine Jackson Paradise In Your Eyes I'm My Brother's Keeper
MO45 0203	Motown TMG 1254 (01/82)	Stevie Wonder That Girl All I Do

MO45 0204	Motown TMG 1255 (02/82)	Smokey Robinson Tell Me Tomorrow (Part 1) Tell Me Tomorrow (Part 2)
MO45 0205	Motown TMG 1256 (03/82)	Commodores Why You Wanna Try Me? Celebrate
MO45 0206	Motown TMG 1257 (03/82)	Bettye Lavette You Seen One You Seen Them All Right In The Middle
MO45 0207	Motown TMG 1258 (04/82)	Syreeta I Must Be In Love Out The Box
MO45 0208	Motown TMG 1259 (04/82)	Ozone Do Whatcha Wanna Do Come On In
MO45 0209	Motown TMG 1260 (03/82)	Charlene I've Never Been To Me Somewhere In My Life
MO45 0210	Motown TMG 1261 (04/82)	Nolan & Crossley Nolen Or Not A Place In My Heart
MO45 0211	Motown TMG 1262 (05/82)	Smokey Robinson Old Fashioned Love Destiny
MO45 0212	Motown TMG 1263 (05/82)	Temptations Standing On The Top (Part 1) Standing On The Top (Part 2)
MO45 0213	Motown TMG 1264 (05/82)	Jose Feliciano I Second That Emotion Free Me . . .
MO45 0214	Motown TMG 1265 (07/82)	Bettye Lavette I Can't Stop Either Way We Lose
MO45 0215	Motown TMG 1266 (06/82)	Rick James Dance With Me (Part 1) Dance With Me (Part 2)
MO45 0216	Motown TMG 1267 (07/82)	Bobby Womack So Many Sides Of You Just My Imagination
MO45 0217	Motown TMG 1268 (07/82)	High Inergy First Impressions Could This Be Love
MO45 0218	Motown TMG 1269 (05/82)	Stevie Wonder Do I Do Rocket Love
MO45 0219	Motown TMG 1270 (10/82)	The Dazz Band Let It Whip Everyday Love

Note: Reissued October 1982 and January 1983.

MO45 0220	Motown TMG 1271 (07/82)	Jean Carn If You Don't Know Me By Now Completeness

MO45 0221	Motown TMG 1272 (08/82)	Charlene It Ain't Easy Comin' Down Ninca Te Ido Ar Mi (Version 1) Ninca Te Ido Ar Mi (Version 2)
MO45 0222	Motown TMG 1273 (08/82)	Diana Ross Old Funky Roll The Boss
MO45 0223	Motown TMG 1274 (08/82)	Smokey Robinson Cruisin' The Only Game In Town
MO45 0225	Motown TMG 1276 (08/82)	Jermaine Jackson Let Me Tickle Your Fancy Maybe Next Time
MO45 0226	Motown TMG 1277 (08/82)	Rick James Hard To Get My Love
MO45 0227	Motown TMG 1278 (09/82)	Bobby Womack Secrets Stand Up
MO45 0228	Motown TMG 1279 (09/82)	The Dazz Band Keep It Live This Is Forever
MO45 0229	Motown TMG 1280 (09/82)	Stevie Wonder Ribbon In The Sky The Secret Life Of Plants
MO45 0230	Latin TMG 1281 (10/82)	Jose Feliciano Samba Pa Ti No Hay Sombra Que Me Cubra
MO45 0231	Motown TMG 1282 (10/82)	The Commodores Lucy Heaven Knows
MO45 0232	Motown TMG 1283 (10/82)	Billy Preston I'm Never Gonna Say Goodbye I Love You So
MO45 0233	Motown TMG 1284 (11/82)	Lionel Richie Truly Just Put Some Love In Your Heart
MO45 0234	Motown TMG 1285 (11/82)	Willie Hutch In And Out Brother's Gonna Work It Out
MO45 0235	Motown TMG 1286 (11/82)	Jermaine Jackson Very Special Part You're Givin' Me The Run Around
MO45 0236	Motown TMG 1287 (11/82)	Charlene with Stevie Wonder / Charlene Used To Be I Want To Come Back As A Song
MO45 0237	Motown TMG 1288 (01/83)	Bobby M Let's Stay Together Charlie's Backbeat
MO45 0238	Motown TMG 1289 (01/83)	Stevie Wonder Front Line Front Line (Instrumental)
MO45 0239	Motown TMG 1290 (01/83)	Lionel Richie You Are You Mean More To Me
MO45 0240	Motown TMG 1291 (02/83)	Billy Preston & Syreeta New Way To Say I Love You Hey You
MO45 0241	Motown TMG 1292 (02/83)	The Commodores Reach High Reach High (Instrumental)
MO45 0242	Motown TMG 1293 (02/83)	Willie Hutch Party Down Slick
MO45 0243	Motown TMG 1294 (02/83)	High Inergy He's A Pretender (Part 1) He's A Pretender (Part 2)
MO45 0244	Motown TMG 1295 (03/83)	Smokey Robinson I've Made Love To You A Thousand Times Into Each Rain A Little Life Must Fall
MO45 0245	Motown TMG 1296 (03/83)	DeBarge I Like It Hesitated
MO45 0246	Motown TMG 1297 (03/83)	The Temptations Love On My Mind Tonight Bring Your Body Here
MO45 0247	Motown TMG 1298 (03/83)	Robert John Bread & Butter If You Don't Want Me
MO45 0248	Motown TMG 1299 (03/83)	Dazz Band On The One Just Believe In Love
MO45 0249	Motown TMG 1300 (04/83)	Lionel Richie My Love Round And Round
MO45 0250	Motown TMG 1301	Note: Unissued.
MO45 0251	Motown TMG 1302 (04/83)	Monalisa Young Dancing Machine I'll Be There
MO45 0252	Motown TMG 1303 (04/83)	Jermaine Jackson You Moved A Mountain Running
MO45 0253	Motown TMG 1304 (06/83)	Finis Henderson Skip To My Lou I'd Rather Be Gone

MO45 0254	Motown TMG 1305 (05/83)	Jose Feliciano Lonely Teardrops Cuidado
MO45 0255	Motown TMG 1306 (06/83)	Syreeta Forever Is Not Enough He's Leaving Home
MO45 0256	Motown TMG 1307 (05/83)	Smokey Robinson Touch The Sky All My Life's A Lie
MO45 0257	Motown TMG 1308	Note: Unissued.
MO45 0258	Motown TMG 1309	Note: Unissued.
MO45 0259	Motown TMG 1310 (08/83)	Charlene If You Take Away The Pain Until The Morning Rick's Song
MO45 0260	Motown TMG 1311 (07/83)	Michael Lovesmith Baby I Will What's The Bottom Line
MO45 0261	Motown TMG 1312	Note: Unissued.
MO45 0262	Motown TMG 1313 (08/83)	Smokey Robinson & Barbara Mitchell Blame It On Love Even Tho'
MO45 0263	Motown TMG 1314	Note: Unissued.
MO45 0264	Motown TMG 1315 (09/83)	Mary Jane Girls Boys You Are My Heaven
MO45 0265	Motown TMG 1316	Note: Unissued.
MO45 0266	Motown TMG 1317 (09/83)	The Commodores Only You Cebu
MO45 0267	Motown TMG 1318 (10/83)	Junior Walker Blow The House Down Ball Baby
MO45 0268	Motown TMG 1319 (09/83)	Lionel Richie All Night Long Wandering Stranger
MO45 0269	Motown TMG 1320 (10/83)	Temptations with The Four Tops / Temptations Medley Of Hits Papa Was A Rolling Stone
MO45 0270	Motown TMG 1321 (10/83)	Four Tops I Just Can't Walk Away Hang
MO45 0271	Motown TMG 1322 (11/83)	The Commodores Turn Off The Lights Painted Picture
MO45 0272	Motown TMG 1323 (01/84)	Bobby Nunn Don't Knock It Private Party
MO45 0273	Motown TMG 1324 (11/83)	Lionel Richie Running With The Night (Part 1) Running With The Night (Part 2)
MO45 0274	Motown TMG 1325	Note: Unissued.
MO45 0275	Motown TMG 1326	Note: Unissued.
MO45 0276	Gordy TMG 1327 (01/84)	Rick James & Friend Ebony Eyes 1, 2, 3, You, Her & Me
MO45 0277	Motown TMG 1328	Note: Unissued.
MO45 0278	Motown TMG 1329 (03/84)	DeBarge Time Will Reveal I'll Never Fall In Love Again
MO45 0279	Motown TMG 1330 (03/84)	Lionel Richie Hello All Night Long
MO45 0280	Motown TMG 1331 (01/84)	Rockwell Somebody's Watching Me Somebody's Watching Me (Instrumental)
MO45 0281	Motown TMG 1332 (01/84)	Keith & Darrell Work That Body The Things You're Made Of
MO45 0282	Morocco TMG 1333 (04/84)	Tiggi Clay The Winner Gets The Heart Who Shot Zorro?
MO45 0283	Motown TMG 1334 (03/84)	Dennis Edwards featuring Siedah Garrett Don't Look Any Further I Thought I Could Handle It
MO45 0284	Motown TMG 1335 (03/84)	Bobby King Lovequake Fall In Love
MO45 0285	Motown TMG 1336 (03/84)	Rockwell Obscene Phone Caller Obscene Phone Caller (Instrumental)
MO45 0286	Morocco TMG 1337 (03/84)	Kidd Glove Good Clean Fun Street Angel
MO45 0287	Motown TMG 1338 (04/84)	The Dazz Band Swoop I'm Yours Bad Girl
MO45 0288	Motown TMG 1339 (06/84)	Bobby Womack Tell Me Why Through The Eyes Of A Child

MO45 0289	Gordy TMG 1340 (05/84)	Dennis Edwards You're My Aphrodisiac Shake Hands
MO45 0290	Motown TMG 1341 (06/84)	Lionel Richie Stuck On You Round And Round
MO45 0291	Motown TMG 1342 (05/84)	Michael Jackson Farewell My Summer Love Call On Me
MO45 0292	Motown TMG 1343 (06/84)	Duke Jupiter Little Lady (I've Gotta) Little Black Book
MO45 0293	Motown TMG 1344 (06/84)	Smokey Robinson And I Don't Love You Dynamite
MO45 0294	Motown TMG 1345 (07/84)	Rockwell Taxman Wasting Time
MO45 0295	Morocco TMG 1346 (07/84)	Wolf and Wolf Don't Take The Candy War Of Nerves
MO45 0296	Motown TMG 1347 (08/84)	Bobby King featuring Alfie Silas Close To Me Love In The Fire
MO45 0297	Gordy TMG 1348 (07/84)	Rick James 17 17 (Instrumental)
MO45 0298	Motown TMG 1349 (08/84)	Stevie Wonder I Just Called To Say I Love You I Just Called To Say I Love You (Instrumental)
MO45 0299	Motown TMG 1350 (08/84)	The Coyote Sisters Straight From The Heart Echo
MO45 0300	Motown TMG 1351 (09/84)	Sammy Davis Jr. Hello Detroit Hello Detroit (Instrumental)
MO45 0301	Motown TMG 1352 (10/84)	Charlene We're Both In Love With You Richie's Song
MO45 0302	Motown TMG 1353 (09/84)	Bobby Womack Surprise Surprise American Dream
MO45 0303	Motown TMG 1354 (10/84)	Sam Harris Sugar Don't Bite You Keep Me Hangin' On
MO45 0304	Motown TMG 1355 (08/84)	Michael Jackson Girl You're So Together Touch The One You Love
MO45 0305	Motown TMG 1356 (10/84)	Lionel Richie Penny Lover You Are My Love
MO45 0306	Motown TMG 1357 (09/84)	Jakata Hell Is On The Run Don't Ever Let Go
MO45 0307	Motown TMG 1358 (09/84)	Phyllis St. James Candlelight Afternoon Back In The Race
MO45 0308	Gordy TMG 1359 (10/84)	Rick James You Turn Me On Fire And Desire
MO45 0309	Motown TMG 1360 (09/84)	Vanity Pretty Mess Pretty Mess (Instrumental)
MO45 0310	Motown TMG 1361	Note: Unissued.
MO45 0311	Motown TMG 1362 (10/84)	The Coyote Sisters I've Got A Radio I'll Do It
MO45 0312	Motown TMG 1363 (12/84)	Koko-Pop I'm In Love With You On The Beach
MO45 0313	Motown TMG 1364 (11/84)	Stevie Wonder Love Light In Flight It's More Than You
MO45 0314	Motown TMG 1365 (11/84)	The Temptations Treat Her Like A Lady Isn't The Night Fantastic
MO45 0315	Motown TMG 1366 (01/85)	Thomas McClary Thin Walls Love Will Find A Way
MO45 0316	Motown TMG 1367	Note: Unissued.
MO45 0317	Motown TMG 1368 (01/85)	The Dazz Band Heartbreak Heartbreak (Instrumental)
MO45 0318	Motown TMG 1369 (01/85)	Vanity Mechanical Emotion Crazy Maybe
MO45 0319	Motown TMG 1370 (01/85)	Sam Harris Hearts On Fire Over The Rainbow
MO45 0320	Motown TMG 1371 (01/85)	The Commodores Nightshift I Keep Running
MO45 0321	Motown TMG 1372 (12/84)	Stevie Wonder Don't Drive Drunk Don't Drive Drunk (Instrumental)
MO45 0322	Motown TMG 1373 (03/85)	The Temptations My Love Is True I'll Keep A Light In My Window

MO45 0323	Motown TMG 1374 (03/85)	Rockwell He's A Cobra Change Your Ways
MO45 0324	Motown TMG 1375	Note: Unissued.
MO45 0325	Gordy TMG 1376 (03/85)	DeBarge Rhythm Of The Night Queen Of My Heart
MO45 0326	Motown TMG 1377 (02/85)	The Mary Jane Girls In My House In My House (Instrumental)
MO45 0327	Motown TMG 1378 (03/85)	Rick James Can't Stop Oh What A Night (For Luv)
MO45 0328	Motown TMG 1379 (04/85)	Jakata Golden Girl Light At The End Of The Tunnel
MO45 0329	Motown TMG 1380 (04/85)	Diana Ross Love Hangover Remember Me
MO45 0330	Motown TMG 1381 (04/85)	Marvin Gaye Got To Give It Up How Sweet It Is
MO45 0331	Motown TMG 1382 (04/85)	Thelma Houston Don't Leave Me This Way If You Feel It
MO45 0332	Motown TMG 1383 (04/85)	Bonnie Pointer Heaven Must Have Sent You Deep Inside My Soul
MO45 0333	Motown TMG 1384 (04/85)	Stevie Wonder I Wish Sir Duke
MO45 0334	Motown TMG 1385 (04/85)	Teena Marie Behind The Groove I Need Your Lovin'
MO45 0335	Motown TMG 1386 (04/85)	Stevie Wonder Do I Do I Ain't Gonna Stand For It
MO45 0336	Motown TMG 1387 (04/85)	Diana Ross My Old Piano I'm Coming Out
MO45 0337	Motown TMG 1388 (04/85)	Stevie Wonder He's Misstra Know-It-All Boogie On Reggae Woman
MO45 0338	Motown TMG 1389	Note: Unissued.
MO45 0339	Motown TMG 1390 (06/85)	Alfie Star Keep On Smilin'

NUMBER SEQUENCE CHANGE

Note: In April 1985, Motown abandoned their numerical series,

and began using the main RCA computerized numbering sequence.

MO45 0341	Motown ZB 40097 (04/85)	The Commodores Animal Instinct Lighting Up The Night
MO45 0342	Motown ZB 40099 (05/85)	Rockwell Peeping Tom Tokyo
MO45 0343	Motown ZB 40113 (05/85)	The Emotions Miss Your Love I Can't Wait To Make You Mine
MO45 0344	Motown ZB 40159 (06/85)	Maureen Steele Save The Night For Me Rock My Heart
MO45 0345	Motown ZB 40173 (06/85)	Willie Hutch Keep On Jammin' In And Out
MO45 0346	Motown ZB 40201 (06/85)	Jack Jacas Hold Me Hold Me (Instrumental)
MO45 0347	Motown ZB 40213 (06/85)	DeBarge Who's Holding Donna Now Be My Lady
MO45 0348	Motown ZB 40223 (06/85)	Rick James Glow Glow (Instrumental)
MO45 0349	Motown ZB 40271 (08/85)	Mary Jane Girls Wild & Crazy Love Wild & Crazy Love (Instrumental)
MO45 0350	Motown ZB 40273 (07/85)	Michael Lovesmith Break The Ice Lucky In Love
MO45 0351	Motown ZB 40307 (07/85)	The Dazz Band Hot Spot I've Been Waiting
MO45 0352	Motown ZB 40311 (08/85)	The Commodores Janet I'm In Love
MO45 0353	Motown ZB 40343 (09/85)	Maureen Steele Boys Will Be Boys Rock My Heart
MO45 0354	Motown ZB 40345 (08/85)	El DeBarge with DeBarge You Wear It Well Baby Won'tcha Come Quick
MO45 0355	Motown ZB 40351 (09/85)	Stevie Wonder Part-Time Lover Part-Time Lover (Instrumental)
MO45 0356	Motown ZB 40369 (09/85)	Michael Lovesmith Ain't Nothing Like It Fast Girls

MO45 0357	Motown ZB 40401 (04/85)	Koko-Pop Brand New Beat (Part 1) Brand New Beat (Part 2)
MO45 0358	Motown ZB 40421 (11/85)	Lionel Richie Say You, Say Me Can't Slow Down
MO45 0359	Motown ZB 40453 (11/85)	The Temptations Do You Really Love Your Baby I'll Keep A Light In My Window
MO45 0360	Motown ZB 40497 (11/85)	El DeBarge The Heart Is Not So Smart Share My World
MO45 0361	Motown ZB 40501 (11/85)	Stevie Wonder Go Home Go Home (Instrumental)
MO45 0362	Motown ZB 40503 (02/86)	Warp 9 Skips a Beat Skips A Beat (Dub mix)
MO45 0363	Motown ZB 40553 (01/86)	Smokey Robinson Hold On To Your Love Train Of Thought
MO45 0364	Motown ZB 40561 (03/86)	Pal Talk We Don't Talk We Don't (Instrumental)
MO45 0365	Motown ZB 40567 (02/86)	Stevie Wonder Overjoyed Overjoyed (Instrumental)
MO45 0366	Motown ZB 40571 (03/86)	Sam Harris I'd Do It All Again The Rescue
MO45 0367	Gordy ZB 40577 (02/86)	Val Young If You Should Ever Be Lonely If You Should Ever Be Lonely (Instrumental)
MO45 0368	Motown ZB 40609 (04/86)	Vanity Under The Influence Wild Animal
MO45 0369	Motown ZB 40621 (03/86)	The Temptations I'm Fascinated How Can You Say That It's Over
MO45 0370	Tamla Motown ZB 40701 (04/86)	Marvin Gaye I Heard It Through The Grapevine Can I Get A Witness
MO45 0371	Tamla Motown ZB 40709 (04/86)	Diana Ross & The Supremes You Keep Me Hangin' On Come See About Me

MOTOWN 12-INCH SINGLES

MO12 0001	Motown 12TMG 1096 (03/78)	Commodores
		Zoom
		Too Hot Ta Trot
		    Note: Same sleeve as Motown
		    label.

MO12 0002	Motown 12TMG 1104 (04/78)	Diana Ross
		Your Love Is So Good For Me
		Baby It's Me
		    Note: Same sleeve as Motown
		    label.

MO12 0003	Motown 12TMG 1110 (07/78)	Rick James
		You And I
		Hollywood
		    Note: Same sleeve as Motown
		    label.

MO12 0004	Motown 12TMG 1111 (06/78)	Commodores
		Flying High
		Funky Situation
		    Note: Same sleeve as Motown
		    label.

MO12 0005	Motown 12TMG 1115 (08/78)	Platinum Hook
		Standing On The Verge (Of Gettin'
		    It On)
		Til I Met You
		    Note: Same sleeve as Motown
		    label.

MO12 0006	Motown 12TMG 1123 (10/78)	Switch
		There'll Never Be
		You Pulled A Switch
		    Note: Same sleeve as Motown
		    label.

MO12 0007	Motown 12TMG 1132 (01/79)	Switch We Like To Party...Come On Somebody's Watchin' You Note: Issued in picture cover.

MO12 0008	Motown 12TMG 1134 (01/79)	Bonnie Pointer
		Heaven Must Have Sent You
		I Wanna Make It (In Your
		    World)
		    Note: Issued in picture sleeve.

MO12 0009	Motown 12TMG 1135 (02/79)	Diana Ross What You Gave Me Ain't No Mountain High Enough

MO12 0010	Motown 12TMG 1136 (03/79)	Diana Ross, Marvin Gaye,
		    Stevie Wonder & Smokey Robinson
		Pops We Love You (Vocal)
		Pops We Love You
		    (Instrumental)
		    Note: Issued in a picture cover.

MO12 0011	Motown 12TMG 1137 (03/79)	Rick James
		High On Your Love Suite + One
		    Mo Hit (Of Your Love)
		You And I
		    Note: Issued in picture cover.

MO12 0012	Motown 12TMG 1138 (04/79)	Marvin Gaye A Funky Space Reincarnation Got To Give It Up Note: Issued in picture cover.
MO12 0013	Motown 12TMG 1138 (07/79)	Billy Preston & Syreeta Go For It Go For It (Instrumental) Note: Same label design as

U.S. releases. Pressed in a limited
edition in brown vinyl to resemble a
basketball.

MO12 0014	Motown 12TMG 1140 (04/79)	Tata Vega Get It Up For Love I Just Keep Thinking About You Baby Note: Same label design as U.S. releases.
MO12 0015	Motown 12TMG 1141 (05/79)	Apollo Astro Disco Astro Disco (Instrumental) Note: Same label design as U.S. releases.
MO12 0016	Motown 12TMG 1142 (07/79)	High Inergy Shoulda Gone Dancin' Shoulda Gone Dancin' (Instrumental) Note: Same label design as U.S. releases.
MO12 0017	Motown 12TMG 1143 (05/79)	Motown Sounds Space Dance Bad Mouthin' Note: Same label design as U.S. releases.
MO12 0018	Motown 12TMG 1144 (05/79)	Mandre Swang Spirit Groove Note: Same label design as U.S. releases.
MO12 0019	Motown 12TMG 1146 (06/79)	Teena Marie I'm A Sucker For Your Love I'm A Sucker For Your Love (Instrumental) Note: Same label design as U.S. releases.
MO12 0020	Motown 12TMG 1147 (06/79)	Rick James Bustin'Out Bustin' Out (Instrumental) Note: Same label design as U.S. releases.
MO12 0021	Motown 12TMG 1148 (06/79)	Switch Best Beat In Town It's So Real Note: Same label design as U.S. releases.
MO12 0022	Motown 12TMG 1150 (07/79)	Diana Ross The Boss Lovin' Livin' And Givin' Note: Same label design as U.S. releases.
MO12 0023	Motown 12TMG 1158 (09/79)	Teena Marie Don't Look Back I'm Gonna Have My Cake (And Eat It Too) Note: Same label design as U.S. releases.
MO12 0024	Motown 12TMG 1162 (09/79)	Sterling Roll-Her Skater Roll-Her Skater (Instrumental) Note: Same label design as U.S. releases.
MO12 0025	Motown 12TMG 1168 (11/79)	Marvin Gaye Ego Tripping Out What's Going On + What's Happening Brother Note: Same label design as U.S. releases.
MO12 0026	Motown 12TMG 1169 (11/79)	Diana Ross It's My House No One Gets The Prize + The Boss Note: Same label design as U.S. releases.
MO12 0027	Motown 12TMG 1180 (04/80)	Diana Ross & The Supremes / Diana Ross Supremes' Medley Love Hangover
MO12 0028	Motown 12TMG 1183 (05/80)	Jermaine Jackson Let's Get Serious Je Vous Aime Beaucoup (I Love You) Note: Same label design as U.S. releases.
MO12 0029	Motown 12TMG 1186 (05/80)	Temptations Power Power (Instrumental)
MO12 0030	Motown 12TMG 1194 (07/80)	Jermaine Jackson Burnin' Hot Castles Of Sand
MO12 0031	Motown 12TMG 1195 (07/80)	Diana Ross Upside Down Friend To Friend
MO12 0032	Motown TMGT 1198 (08/80)	Rick James Big Time Island Lady
MO12 0033	Motown TMGT 1203 (09/80)	Teena Marie I Need Your Lovin' Behind The Groove
MO12 0034	Motown 12TMG 1204 (09/80)	Stevie Wonder Masterblaster (Jammin) Masterblaster (Dub)
MO12 0035	Motown TMGT 1208 (10/80)	Michael Urbaniak Nanava Joy
MO12 0036	Motown TMGT 1209 (10/80)	Rick James Summer Love Gettin' It On
MO12 0037	Motown 12TMG 1210 (10/80)	Diana Ross I'm Coming Out Give Up

MO12 0038	Motown TMGT 1213 (11/80)	Dazz Band Shake It Up Only Love
MO12 0039	Motown TMGT 1219 (01/81)	Tata Vega You Keep Me Hangin' On You Better Watch Out
MO12 0040	Motown TMGT 1222 (05/81)	Jermaine Jackson You Like Me Don't You You Like Me Don't You (Instrumental) You Like Me Don't You (Vocal remix)
MO12 0041	Motown TMGT 1224 (02/81)	Billy Preston Hope Give It Up Hot
MO12 0042	Motown TMGT 1225 (02/81)	Marvin Gaye Praise Funk Me
MO12 0043	Motown TMGT 1229 (05/81)	Rick James Give It To Me Baby Don't Give Up On Love
MO12 0044	Motown TMGT 1230 (05/81)	Tata Vega Love Your Neighbor There's Love In The World
MO12 0045	Motown TMGT 1231 (05/81)	Billy Preston A Change Is Gonna Come You
MO12 0046	Motown TMGT 1232 (05/81)	Marvin Gaye Heavy Love Affair Far Cry
MO12 0047	Motown TMGT 1235 (07/81)	Stevie Wonder Happy Birthday Happy Birthday Singalong
MO12 0048	Motown TMGT 1236 (07/81)	Teena Marie Square Biz Square Biz (Instrumental)
MO12 0049	Motown TMGT 1238 (07/81)	Commodores Lady (You Bring Me Up) Gettin' It
MO12 0050	Motown TMGT 1241 (11/81)	Rick James Super Freak (Part 1) Super Freak (Part 2) Note: First release with Motown distribution by RCA. Previous 7-inch and 12-inch (1186-1240), originally distributed by EMI, were "reissued with minor label changes." Reissued in November 1982.
MO12 0051	Motown TMGT 1243 (10/81)	Temptations Aiming At Your Heart Life Of A Cowboy
MO12 0052	Motown TMGT 1246 (11/81)	Teena Marie It Must Be Magic Yes Indeed
MO12 0053	Motown TMGT 1247 (11/81)	Syreeta Quick Slick I Don't Know
MO12 0054	Motown TMGT 1248 (12/81)	Diana Ross Tenderness Supremes Medley
MO12 0055	Motown TMGT 1249 (11/81)	Ozone Gigolette Gigolette (Instrumental)
MO12 0056	Motown TMGT 1250 (01/82)	Rick James Ghetto Life Ghetto Life
MO12 0057	Motown TMGT 1251 (01/82)	Teena Marie Portuguese Love Ballad Of Cradle Rob
MO12 0058	Motown TMGT 1255 (02/82)	Smokey Robinson Tell Me Tomorrow Being With You Aqui Con Tigo
MO12 0059	Motown TMGT 1256 (03/82)	Commodores Why You Wanna Try Me? Celebrate
MO12 0060	Motown TMGT 1258 (04/82)	Syreeta I Must Be In Love Out The Box
MO12 0061	Motown TMGT 1259 (04/82)	Ozone Do Whatcha Wanna Do Come On In
MO12 0062	Motown TMGT 1261 (04/82)	Nolen & Crossley Ready Or Not A Place In My Heart
MO12 0063	Motown TMGT 1263 (05/82)	The Temptations Standing On The Top (Full version) Standing On The Top (Part 1) Note: Featuring Rick James.
MO12 0064	Motown TMGT 1266 (06/82)	Rick James Dance With Me (Part 1) Dance With Me (Part 2)
MO12 0065	Motown TMGT 1267 (07/82)	Bobby Womack So Many Sides Of You Just My Imagination
MO12 0066	Motown TMGT 1270 (10/82)	The Dazz Band Let It Whip Everyday Love
MO12 0067	Motown TMGT 1273 (08/82)	Diana Ross Old Funky Roll The Boss
MO12 0068	Motown TMGT 1274 (08/82)	Smokey Robinson Cruisin' The Only Game In Town
MO12 0069	Motown TMGT 1275 (08/82)	Syreeta Can't Shake Your Love Wish Upon A Star

MO12   Motown   Jermaine Jackson
0070   TMGT 1276   Let Me Tickle Your Fancy
          (08/82)   Maybe Next Time

MO12   Motown   Rick James
0071   TMGT 1277   Hard To Get
          (08/82)   My Love
                        Give It To Me

MO12   Motown   The Dazz Band
0072   TMGT 1279   Keep It Live
          (02/83)   This Is Forever

MO12   Motown   Stevie Wonder
0073   TMGT 1280   Ribbon In The Sky
          (09/82)   The Secret Life Of Plants

MO12   Motown   The Commodores
0074   TMGT 1282   Lucy
          (10/82)   Heaven Knows

MO12   Motown   Lionel Richie
0075   TMGT 1284   Truly
          (11/82)   Just Put Some Love In Your
                            Heart

MO12   Motown   Willie Hutch
0076   TMGT 1285   In And Out
          (11/82)   Brother's Gonna Work It Out

MO12   Motown   Jermaine Jackson
0077   TMGT 1286   Very Special Part
          (11/82)   You're Givin' Me The Run
                            Around

MO12   Motown   Bobby M
0078   TMGT 1288   Let's Stay Together
          (01/83)   Charlie's Backbeat

MO12   Motown   Stevie Wonder
0079   TMGT 1289   Front Line
          (01/83)   Front Line (Instrumental)

MO12   Motown   Billy Preston & Syreeta
0080   TMGT 1291   New Way To Say I Love You
          (03/83)   New Way To Say I Love You
                            (Instrumental)
                        One More Time For Love
                        Hey You

MO12   Motown   Willie Hutch
0081   TMGT 1293   Party Down
          (02/83)   Slick

MO12   Motown   High Inergy
0082   TMGT 1294   He's A Pretender
          (02/83)   Don't Let Up On the Groove

MO12   Motown   Smokey Robinson
0083   TMGT 1295   I've Made Love To You A
          (03/83)   Thousand Times
                        Greatest Hits Medley

MO12   Motown   The Temptations
0084   TMGT 1297   Love On My Mind Tonight
          (03/83)   Bring Your Body Here

MO12   Motown   Dazz Band
0085   TMGT 1299   On The One
          (03/83)   Just Believe In Love

MO12   Motown   Lionel Richie
0086   TMGT 1300   My Love
          (04/83)   Round And Round

MO12   Gordy   Mary Jane Girls
0087   TMGT 1301   Candy Man
          (04/83)   Candy Man (Instrumental)

MO12   Motown   Monalisa Young
0088   TMGT 1302   Dancing Machine
          (04/83)   Dancing Machine
                            (Instrumental)

MO12   Motown   Finis Henderson
0089   TMGT 1304   Skip To My Lou
          (06/83)   I'd Rather Be Gone
                        Vina Del Mar

MO12   Motown   Syreeta
0090   TMGT 1306   Forever Is Not Enough
          (06/83)   He's Leaving Home

MO12   Motown   DeBarge
0091   TMGT 1308   All This Love
          (07/83)   I'm In Love With You

MO12   Motown   Mary Jane Girls
0092   TMGT 1309   All Night Long
          (09/83)   Musical Love

MO12   Motown   Michael Lovesmith
0093   TMGT 1311   Baby I Will
          (07/83)   What's The Bottom Line

MO12   Motown   Gary Byrd
0094   TMGT 1312   The Crown (Part 1)
          (07/83)   The Crown (Part 2)

MO12   Motown   Rick James
0095   TMGT 1314   Cold Blooded (Part 1)
          (08/83)   Cold Blooded (Part 2)

MO12   Motown   Mary Jane Girls
0096   TMGT 1315   Boys
          (09/83)   You Are My Heaven
                        All Night Long
                        Candy Man

MO12   Motown   Stone City Band
0097   TMGT 1316   Ladies Choice
          (09/83)   Ladies Choice (Instrumental)

MO12   Motown   Junior Walker
0098   TMGT 1318   Blow The House Down
          (10/83)   Ball Baby

MO12   Motown   The Temptations
0099   TMGT 1320   Medley Of Hits
          (10/83)   Papa Was A Rolling Stone
                            Note: A-side also features The
          Four Tops.

MO12   Motown   The Four Tops
0100   TMGT 1321   I Just Can't Walk Away
          (10/83)   Hang

MO12   Motown   The Commodores
0101   TMGT 1322   Turn Off The Lights
          (11/83)   Painted Picture

MO12 0102	Motown TMGT 1323 (01/84)	Bobby Nunn Don't Knock It Private Party

MO12 0103	Motown TMGT 1324 (11/83)	Lionel Richie Running With The Night All Night Long

MO12 0104	Motown TMGT 1325 (11/83)	The Motor City Crew Scratch Break (Glove style) Let's Break Let's Break (Instrumental)

MO12 0105	Motown TMGT 1326 (01/84)	Stevie Wonder Happy Birthday Extracts From Speeches By Rev. Martin Luther King

MO12 0106	Gordy TMGT 1327 (01/84)	Rick James & Friend Ebony Eyes 1, 2, 3, You, Her & Me Standing On The Top Note: "Standing On The Top" performed by The Temptations featuring Rick James.

MO12 0107	Motown TMGT 1328 (01/84)	The Dazz Band Joystick Don't Get Caught In The Middle

MO12 0108	Motown TMGT 1329 (03/84)	DeBarge Time Will Reveal I'll Never Fall In Love Again All This Love I Like It

MO12 0109	Motown TMGT 1330 (03/84)	Lionel Richie Hello All Night Long Running With The Night

MO12 0110	Motown TMGT 1331 (01/84)	Rockwell Somebody's Watching Me Somebody's Watching Me (Instrumental)

MO12 0111	Motown TMGT 1332 (01/84)	Keith & Darrell Work That Body The Things You're Made Of Work That Body (Extra mix)

MO12 0112	Motown TMGT 1334 (03/84)	Dennis Edwards, featuring Siedah Garrett Don't Look Any Further I Thought I Could Handle It

MO12 0113	Motown TMGT 1335 (03/84)	Bobby King Lovequake Fall In Love

MO12 0114	Motown TMGT 1336 (03/84)	Rockwell Obscene Phone Caller Obscene Phone Caller (Instrumental)

MO12 0115	Motown TMGT 1338 (04/84)	The Dazz Band Swoop I'm Yours Bad Girl

MO12 0116	Motown TMGT 1339 (06/84)	Bobby Womack Tell Me Why Through The Eyes Of A Child

MO12 0117	Gordy TMGT 1340 (05/84)	Dennis Edwards You're My Aphrodisiac Shake Hands

MO12 0118	Motown TMGT 1341 (06/84)	Lionel Richie Stuck On You Round And Round Tell Me

MO12 0119	Motown TMGT 1342 (05/84)	Michael Jackson Farewell My Summer Love Call On Me

MO12 0120	Morocco TMGT 1343 (06/84)	Duke Jupiter Little Lady (I've Gotta) Little Black Book Don't Turn Your Back

MO12 0121	Morocco TMGT 1344 (06/84)	Smokey Robinson And I Don't Love You Dynamite

MO12 0122	Motown TMGT 1345 (07/84)	Rockwell Taxman Wasting Time Change Your Ways

MO12 0123	Motown TMGT 1347 (08/84)	Bobby King, featuring Alfie Silas Close To Me Love In The Fire Midnight Shine

MO12 0124	Gordy TMGT 1348 (07/84)	Rick James 17 17 (Instrumental)

MO12 0125	Motown TMGT 1349 (08/84)	Stevie Wonder I Just Called To Say I Love You I Just Called To Say I Love You (Instrumental)

MO12 0126	Motown TMGT 1350 (08/84)	The Coyote Sisters Straight From The Heart Echo

MO12 0127	Motown TMGT 1351 (09/84)	Sammy Davis, Jr. Hello Detroit Hello Detroit (Instrumental)

MO12 0128	Motown TMGT 1352 (10/84)	Charlene We're Both In Love With You Richie's Song I Want To Go Back There Again

MO12 0129	Motown TMGT 1353 (09/84)	Bobby Womack Surprise Surprise American Dream If You Think You're Lonely Now

MO12 0130	Motown TMGT 1354 (10/84)	Sam Harris Sugar Don't Bite You Keep Me Hangin' On Sugar Don't Bite

(Instrumental)

MO12 0131	Motown TMGT 1355 (08/84)	Michael Jackson Girl You're So Together Touch The One You Love Ben Ain't No Sunshine
MO12 0132	Motown TMGT 1356 (10/84)	Lionel Richie Penny Lover You Are My Love
MO12 0133	Morocco TMGT 1357 (09/84)	Jakata Hell Is On The Run Don't Ever Let Go Hell Is On The Run (Instrumental)
MO12 0134	Motown TMGT 1358 (09/84)	Phyllis St. James Candlelight Afternoon Back In The Race
MO12 0135	Gordy TMGT 1359 (10/84)	Rick James You Turn Me On Fire And Desire
MO12 0136	Motown TMGT 1360 (09/84)	Vanity Pretty Mess Pretty Mess (Instrumental)
MO12 0137	Motown TMGT 1361 (10/84)	The Dazz Band Let It All Blow Now That I Have You Let It All Blow (Instrumental)
MO12 0138	Motown TMGT 1363 (12/84)	KoKo Pop I'm In Love With You On The Beach
MO12 0139	Motown TMGT 1364 (11/84)	Stevie Wonder Love Light In Flight It's More Than You
MO12 0140	Motown TMGT 1365 (11/84)	The Temptations Treat Her Like A Lady Isn't The Night Fantastic
MO12 0141	Motown TMGT 1366 (01/85)	Thomas McClary Thin Walls Love Will Find A Way
MO12 0142	Motown TMGT 1368 (01/85)	The Dazz Band Heartbeat [Flip side not determined]
MO12 0143	Motown TMGT 1369 (01/85)	Vanity Mechanical Emotion Crazy Maybe Mechanical Emotion (Instrumental)
MO12 0144	Motown TMGT 1370 (01/85)	Sam Harris Hearts On Fire Over The Rainbow Hearts On Fire (Remix)
MO12 0145	Motown TMGT 1371 (01/85)	The Commodores Nightshift I Keep Running
MO12 0146	Motown TMGT 1371 (03/85)	The Commodores Nightshift (Remix) I Keep Running Note: Replaces record issued in January 1985.
MO12 0147	Motown TMGT 1372 (12/84)	Stevie Wonder Don't Drive Drunk Don't Drive Drunk (Instrumental)
MO12 0148	Motown TMGT 1373 (03/85)	The Temptations My Love Is True I'll Keep A Light In My Window Treat Her Like A Lady (Remix)
MO12 0149	Motown TMGT 1374 (03/85)	Rockwell He's A Cobra Change Your Ways He's A Cobra (Remix)
MO12 0150	Gordy TMGT 1376 (03/85)	DeBarge Rhythm Of The Night Queen Of My Heart
MO12 0151	Motown TMGT 1377 (02/85)	Mary Jane Girls In My House In My House (Instrumental)
MO12 0152	Motown TMGT 1378 (03/85)	Rick James Can't Stop Oh What A Night (For Luv) Can't Stop (Instrumental)
MO12 0153	Morocco TMGT 1379 (04/85)	Jakata Golden Girl Light At The End Of The Tunnel Golden Girl (Instrumental)
MO12 0154	Motown TMGT 1380 (04/85)	Diana Ross Love Hangover Remember Me
MO12 0155	Motown TMGT 1381 (04/85)	Marvin Gaye Got To Give It Up How Sweet It Is
MO12 0156	Motown TMGT 1382 (04/85)	Thelma Houston Don't Leave Me This Way If You Feel It
MO12 0157	Motown TMGT 1383 (04/85)	Bonnie Pointer Heaven Must Have Sent You Deep Inside My Soul
MO12 0158	Motown TMGT 1384 (04/85)	Stevie Wonder I Wish Sir Duke
MO12 0159	Motown TMGT 1385 (04/85)	Teena Marie Behind The Groove I Need Your Lovin'
MO12 0160	Motown TMGT 1386 (04/85)	Stevie Wonder Do I Do I Ain't Gonna Stand For It

MO12 0161	Motown TMGT 1387 (04/85)	Diana Ross My Old Piano I'm Coming Out
MO12 0162	Motown TMGT 1388 (04/85)	Stevie Wonder He's Misstra Know-It-All Boogie On Reggae Woman
MO12 0163	Motown TMGT 1390 (06/85)	Alfie Star Keep On Smilin'

NUMBER SEQUENCE CHANGE

Note: In April 1985, Motown abandoned their own numerical series and began using the main RCA computerized numbering sequence.

MO12 0165	Motown ZT 40098 (04/85)	The Commodores Animal Instinct Lighting Up The Night
MO12 0166	Motown ZT 40100 (05/85)	Rockwell Peeping Tom Tokyo Peeping Tom (Instrumental)
MO12 0167	Motown ZT 40114 (05/85)	The Emotions Miss Your Love I Can't Wait To Make You Mine
MO12 0168	Motown ZT 40160 (06/85)	Maureen Steele Save The Night For Me Rock My Heart
MO12 0169	Motown ZT 40174 (06/85)	Willie Hutch Keep On Jammin' The Glow In And Out
MO12 0170	Motown ZT 40402 (06/85)	Jack Jacas Hold Me Hold Me (Instrumental)
MO12 0171	Motown ZT 40214 (06/85)	DeBarge Who's Holding Donna Now Be My Lady
MO12 0172	Motown ZT 40224 (06/85)	Rick James Glow Glow (Instrumental)
MO12 0173	Motown ZT 40272 (08/85)	Mary Jane Girls Wild & Crazy Love Wild & Crazy Love (Instrumental) All Night Long
MO12 0174	Motown ZT 40274 (07/85)	Michael Lovesmith Break The Ice Lucky In Love Baby I Will
MO12 0175	Motown ZT 40308 (07/85)	The Dazz Band Hot Spot I've Been Waiting Hot Spot (Club Mix)

MO12 0176	Motown ZT 40312 (08/85)	The Commodores Janet I'm In Love Nightshift (Instrumental)
MO12 0177	Motown ZT 40344 (09/85)	Maureen Steele Boys Will Be Boys Rock My Heart
MO12 0178	Motown ZT 40346 (08/85)	El DeBarge with DeBarge You Wear It Well Baby Won'tcha Come Quick
MO12 0179	Motown ZT 40352 (09/85)	Stevie Wonder Part-Time Lover Part-Time Lover (Instrumental)
MO12 0180	Motown ZT 40370 (09/85)	Michael Lovesmith Ain't Nothin' Like It Fast Girls
MO12 0181	Motown ZT 40402 (04/85)	KoKo Pop Brand New Beat (Part 1) Brand New Beat (Part 2)
MO12 0182	Motown ZT 40422 (11/85)	Lionel Richie Say You, Say Me Can't Slow Down
MO12 0183	Motown ZT 40454 (11/85)	The Temptations Do You Really Love Your Baby (Club mix) Do You Really Love Your Baby (Radio edit) Do You Really Love Your Baby (Dub mix)
MO12 0184	Motown ZT 40498 (11/85)	El DeBarge The Heart Is Not So Smart Share My World You Wear It Well (Dub mix)
MO12 0185	Motown ZT 40502 (11/85)	Stevie Wonder Go Home Go Home (Instrumental)
MO12 0186	Motown ZT 40504 (02/86)	Warp 9 Skips A Beat Skips A Beat (Dub mix)
MO12 0187	Motown ZT 40554 (01/86)	Smokey Robinson Hold On To Your Love Train Of Thought
MO12 0188	Motown ZT 40562 (03/86)	Pal Talk We Don't (Club mix) Talk We Don't (Tribal mix instrumental) Talk We Don't (Safari mix) + Talk We Don't (Jungletalk mix)
MO12 0189	Motown ZT 40568 (02/86)	Stevie Wonder Overjoyed Overjoyed (Instrumental)
MO12 0190	Motown ZT 40572 (03/86)	Sam Harris I'll Do It All Again (Head mix) I'll Do It All Again (Foot mix) The Rescue

MO12 0191	Motown ZT 40578 (02/86)	Val Young If You Should Ever Be Lonely If You Should Ever Be Lonely (Instrumental)
MO12 0192	Motown ZT 40610 (04/86)	Vanity Under The Influence (Mix 1) Under The Influence (Mix 2) Under The Influence (Mix 3) Wild Animal
MO12 0193	Motown ZT 40622 (03/86)	The Temptations I'm Fascinated How Can You Say That It's Over Treat Her Like A Lady (Remix)
MO12 0194	Tamla Motown ZT 40702 (04/86)	Marvin Gaye I Heard It Through The Grapevine Can I Get A Witness That's The Way Love Is You're A Wonderful One
MO12 0195	Tamla Motown ZT 40710 (04/86)	Diana Ross & The Supremes You Keep Me Hangin' On Come See About Me I Hear A Symphony Love Is Like An Itching In My Heart

MOTOWN ALBUMS

MOLP 0001	Motown STML 12044 (12/76)	Various Artists MOTOWN DISCOTECH 3
MOLP 0002	Motown STML 12045 (12/76)	Various Artists COOLEY HIGH
MOLP 0003	Motown STML 12046 (12/76)	The Jackson 5 JOYFUL JUKEBOX MUSIC
MOLP 0004	Motown STML 12047 (12/76)	The Supremes MARY, SCHERRIE AND SUSAYE
MOLP 0005	Motown STML 12048 (12/76)	Junior Walker & The All Stars WHOPPER BOPPER SHOW STOPPER
MOLP 0006	Motown STML 12049 (01/77)	Thelma Houston ANYWAY YOU LIKE IT
MOLP 0007	Motown STML 12050 (02/77)	Leon Ware MUSICAL MASSAGE
MOLP 0008	Motown STML 12051 (02/77)	The Dynamic Superiors YOU NAME IT

MOLP 0009	Motown STML 12052 (03/77)	Jerry Butler SUITE FOR SINGLE GIRL
MOLP 0010	Motown STML 12053 (03/77)	Syreeta ONE TO ONE
MOLP 0011	Motown STML 12054 (04/77)	The Originals DOWN TO LOVE TOWN
MOLP 0012	Motown STML 12055 (04/77)	Smokey Robinson DEEP IN MY SOUL
MOLP 0013	Motown STML 12056 (04/77)	G. C. Cameron YOU'RE WHAT'S MISSING IN MY LIFE
MOLP 0014	Motown STML 12057 (03/77)	The Commodores ZOOM
MOLP 0015	Motown STML 12058 (05/77)	Tata Vega TOTALLY TATA
MOLP 0016	Motown STML 12059 (05/77)	Various Artists A SPECIAL MOTOWN DISCO ALBUM
MOLP 0017	Motown STML 12060 (06/77)	Martha Reeves & The Vandellas ANTHOLOGY
MOLP 0018	Motown STML 12061 (08/77)	The Temptations GREATEST HITS VOL. 3
MOLP 0019	Motown STML 12062 (07/77)	Mandre MANDRE
MOLP 0020	Motown STML 12063 (07/77)	Thelma Houston & Jerry Butler THELMA AND JERRY
MOLP 0021	Motown STML 12064 (07/77)	David Ruffin IN MY STRIDE
MOLP 0022	Motown STML 12065 (09/77)	The Dynamic Superiors NOWHERE TO RUN
MOLP 0023	Motown STML 12066 (08/77)	Flavor IN GOOD TASTE
MOLP 0024	Motown STML 12067 (09/77)	Jermaine Jackson FEEL THE FIRE
MOLP 0025	Motown STML 12068 (09/77)	Smokey Robinson BIG TIME

MOLP 0026	Motown STML 12069 (09/77)	Willie Hutch HAVIN' A HOUSE PARTY	MOLP 0043	Motown STML 12086 (07/78)	Platinum Hook PLATINUM HOOK
MOLP 0027	Motown STML 12070 (10/77)	Various Artists MOTOWN GOLD VOLUME 2	MOLP 0044	Motown STML 12087 (05/78)	The Commodores NATURAL HIGH
MOLP 0028	Motown STML 12071 (11/77)	Eddie Kendricks SLICK	MOLP 0045	Motown STML 12088 (08/78)	Three Ounces Of Love THREE OUNCES OF LOVE
MOLP 0029	Motown STML 12072 (01/78)	Jerry Butler IT ALL COMES OUT IN MY SONG	MOLP 0046	Motown STML 12089 (08/78)	Junior Walker SMOOTH SOUL
MOLP 0030	Motown STML 12073 (11/77)	G. C. Cameron & Syreeta RICH LOVE, POOR LOVE	MOLP 0047	Motown STML 12090 (08/78)	High Inergy STEPPIN' OUT
MOLP 0031	Motown STML 12074 (01/78)	High Inergy TURNIN' ON	MOLP 0048	Motown STML 12091 (09/78)	The Supremes AT THEIR BEST
MOLP 0032	Motown STML 12075 (01/78)	Thelma Houston THE DEVIL IN ME	MOLP 0049	Motown STML 12092 (09/78)	Thelma and Jerry TWO TO ONE
MOLP 0033	Motown STML 12076 (02/78)	Smokey Robinson SMOKEY'S WORLD	MOLP 0050	Motown STML 12093 (10/78)	Diana Ross ROSS
MOLP 0034	Motown STML 12077 (04/78)	Fifth Dimension STAR DANCING	MOLP 0051	Motown STML 12094 (10/78)	Major Lance NOW ARRIVING
MOLP 0035	Motown STML 12078 (04/78)	21st Creation BREAK THRU'	MOLP 0052	Motown STML 12095 (11/78)	Finished Touch NEED TO KNOW YOU BETTER
MOLP 0036	Motown STML 12079 (05/78)	David Ruffin AT HIS BEST	MOLP 0053	Motown STML 12096 (10/78)	Switch SWITCH
MOLP 0037	Motown STML 12080 (05/78)	Eddie Kendricks AT HIS BEST	MOLP 0054	Motown STML 12097 (04/79)	Bloodstone DON'T STOP
MOLP 0038	Motown STML 12081 (05/78)	Smokey Robinson LOVE BREEZE	MOLP 0055	Motown STML 12098 (12/78)	Thelma Houston READY TO ROLL
MOLP 0039	Motown STML 12082 (05/78)	Jermaine Jackson FRONTIERS	MOLP 0056	Motown STML 12099 (12/78)	Grover Washington Jr. REED SEED
MOLP 0040	Motown STML 12083 (05/78)	Cuba Gooding 1ST CUBA GOODING ALBUM	MOLP 0057	Motown STML 12100 (12/78)	The Commodores GREATEST HITS
MOLP 0041	Motown STML 12084 (07/78)	Mandre MANDRE TWO	MOLP 0058	Motown STML 12101 (02/79)	Bonnie Pointer BONNIE POINTER
MOLP 0042	Motown STML 12085 (07/78)	Rick James COME GET IT	MOLP 0059	Motown STML 12102 (02/79)	Various Artists SPECIAL MOTOWN DISCO ALBUM VOL. 2

MOLP 0060	Motown STML 12103 (05/79)	Tata Vega TRY MY LOVE	MOLP 0077	Motown STML 12120 (09/79)	Doctor Strut DOCTOR STRUT

MOLP 0060 Motown STML 12103 (05/79) Tata Vega TRY MY LOVE

MOLP 0061 Motown STML 12104 (03/79) Rick James BUSTIN' OUT OF L SEVEN

MOLP 0062 Motown STML 12105 (03/79) Motown Sounds SPACE DANCE

MOLP 0063 Motown STML 12106 (05/79) Fifth Dimension HIGH ON SUNSHINE

MOLP 0064 Motown STML 12107 (05/79) Billy Preston & Syreeta FAST BREAK

MOLP 0065 Motown STML 12108 (06/79) Apollo APOLLO

MOLP 0066 Motown STML 12109 (06/79) Teena Marie WILD AND PEACEFUL

MOLP 0067 Motown STML 12110 (08/79) Platinum Hook IT'S TIME

MOLP 0068 Motown STML 12111 (08/79) High Inergy SHOULD HAVE GONE DANCIN'

MOLP 0069 Motown STML 12112 (07/79) Switch SWITCH II

MOLP 0070 Motown STML 12113 (08/79) Cuba Gooding LOVE DANCER

MOLP 0071 Motown STML 12114 (06/79) Various Artists POPS WE LOVE YOU

MOLP 0072 Motown STML 12115 (08/79) Smokey Robinson WHERE THERE'S SMOKE

MOLP 0073 Motown STML 12116 (09/79) Billy Preston LATE AT NIGHT

MOLP 0074 Motown STML 12117 (07/79) Thelma Houston RIDE TO THE RAINBOW

MOLP 0075 Motown STML 12118 (07/79) Diana Ross THE BOSS

MOLP 0076 Motown STML 12119 (09/79) Patrick Gammon DON'T TOUCH ME

MOLP 0077 Motown STML 12120 (09/79) Doctor Strut DOCTOR STRUT

MOLP 0078 Motown STML 12121 (09/79) The Jackson 5 20 GOLDEN GREATS

MOLP 0079 Motown STML 12122 (09/79) Gladys Knight & The Pips 20 GOLDEN GREATS

MOLP 0080 Motown STML 12123 (09/79) Various Artists MOTOWN CHARTBUSTERS VOL. 10

MOLP 0081 Motown STML 12124 (09/79) Mary Wilson MARY WILSON

MOLP 0082 Motown STML 12125 (10/79) Various Artists 20 MOD CLASSICS

MOLP 0083 Motown STML 12126 Marvin Gaye LOVE MAN Note: Unissued.

MOLP 0084 Motown STML 12127 (05/80) Jermaine Jackson LET'S GET SERIOUS

MOLP 0085 Motown STML 12128 (12/79) Rick James FIRE IT UP

MOLP 0086 Motown STML 12129 (02/80) Bonnie Pointer BONNIE POINTER II

MOLP 0087 Motown STML 12130 (03/80) Teena Marie LADY TEENA

MOLP 0088 Motown STML 12131 (03/80) Grover Washington Jr. SKYLARKIN'

MOLP 0089 Motown STML 12132 (04/80) Doctor Strut STRUTTIN'

MOLP 0090 Motown STML 12133 (04/80) Various Artists 20 MOD CLASSICS VOL. 2

MOLP 0091 Motown STML 12134 (04/80) Smokey Robinson WARM THOUGHTS

MOLP 0092 Motown STML 12135 (06/80) Switch REACHIN' FOR TOMORROW

MOLP 0093 Motown STML 12136 (06/80) The Temptations POWER

MOLP 0094	Motown STML 12137 (06/80)	Syreeta SYREETA
MOLP 0095	Motown STML 12138 (03/81)	Tata Vega GIVIN' ALL MY LOVE
MOLP 0096	Motown STML 12139 (12/80)	Various Artists MOTOWN CHARTBUSTERS '80
MOLP 0097	Motown STML 12140 (10/80)	The Temptations 20 GOLDEN GREATS
MOLP 0098	Motown STML 12141 (10/80)	Rick James GARDEN OF LOVE
MOLP 0099	Motown STML 12142 (09/80)	Black Russian BLACK RUSSIAN
MOLP 0100	Motown STML 12143 (10/80)	Teena Marie IRONS IN THE FIRE
MOLP 0101	Motown STML 12144 (10/80)	High Inergy HOLD ON
MOLP 0102	Motown STML 12145 (12/80)	Ahmed Jamal NIGHT SONG
MOLP 0103	Motown STML 12146 (12/80)	The Dazz Band INVITATION TO LOVE
MOLP 0104	Motown STML 12147 (12/80)	Jermaine Jackson JERMAINE
MOLP 0105	Motown STML 12148 (04/81)	Billy Preston THE WAY I AM
MOLP 0106	Motown STML 12149 (03/81)	Marvin Gaye IN OUR LIFETIME
MOLP 0107	Motown STML 12150 (03/81)	The Stone City Band THE BOYS ARE BACK
MOLP 0108	Motown STML 12151 (04/81)	Smokey Robinson BEING WITH YOU
MOLP 0109	Motown STML 12152 (04/81)	Diana Ross TO LOVE AGAIN
MOLP 0110	Motown STML 12153 (10/81)	Rick James STREET SONGS
MOLP 0111	Motown STML 12154 (08/81)	Teena Marie IT MUST BE MAGIC
MOLP 0112	Motown STML 12155 (09/81)	Billy Preston & Syreeta BILLY PRESTON & SYREETA
MOLP 0113	Motown STML 12156 (06/81)	The Commodores IN THE POCKET
MOLP 0114	Motown STML 12157 (07/81)	High Inergy HIGH INERGY
MOLP 0115	Motown STML 12158 (07/81)	Michael Jackson ONE DAY IN YOUR LIFE
MOLP 0116	Motown STML 12159 (06/82)	The Temptations THE TEMPTATIONS
MOLP 0117	Motown STML 12160 (10/81)	Jermaine Jackson I LIKE YOUR STYLE
MOLP 0118	Motown STML 12161 (12/81)	Jose Feliciano JOSE FELICIANO
MOLP 0119	Motown STML 12162 (12/81)	Syreeta SEE MY LOVE IN MOTION
MOLP 0120	Motown STML 12163 (03/82)	Diana Ross DIANA'S DUETS
MOLP 0121	Motown STML 12164	Note: Unissued.
MOLP 0122	Motown STML 12165 (03/82)	Smokey Robinson YES IT'S YOU LADY
MOLP 0123	Motown STML 12166 (05/82)	Betty Lavette TELL ME A LIE
MOLP 0124	Motown STML 12167 (06/82)	Rick James THROWIN' DOWN
MOLP 0125	Motown STML 12168 (06/82)	Bobby Womack THE POET
MOLP 0126	Motown STML 12169	Note: Unissued.
MOLP 0127	Motown STML 12170 (08/82)	High Inergy SO RIGHT
MOLP 0128	Motown STML 12171 (07/82)	Charlene I'VE NEVER BEEN TO ME

MOLP 0129	Motown STML 12172 (08/82)	Jean Carn TRUST ME	MOLP 0147	Motown STML 12190 (11/83)	Stone City Band OUT FROM THE SHADOW
MOLP 0130	Motown STML 12173 (09/82)	The Dazz Band KEEP IT LIVE	MOLP 0148	Motown STML 12191 (07/83)	Finis Henderson FINIS
MOLP 0131	Motown STML 12174 (09/82)	Jermaine Jackson LET ME TICKLE YOUR FANCY	MOLP 0149	Motown STML 12192 (09/83)	Michael Lovesmith I CAN MAKE IT HAPPEN
MOLP 0132	Motown STML 12175 (03/83)	Smokey Robinson TOUCH THE SKY	MOLP 0150	Motown STML 12193 (10/83)	Smokey Robinson BLAME IT ON LOVE AND ALL THE GREAT HITS
MOLP 0133	Motown STML 12176 (10/82)	Jose Feliciano ESCENAS DE AMOR	MOLP 0151	Motown STML 12194 (10/83)	Junior Walker BLOW THE HOUSE DOWN
MOLP 0134	Motown STML 12177 (11/82)	Billy Preston PRESSIN' ON	MOLP 0152	Motown STML 12195 (10/83)	Various Artists GET CRAZY (ORIGINAL SOUNDTRACK)
MOLP 0135	Motown STML 12178	Note: Unissued.	MOLP 0153	Motown STML 12196 (11/83)	The Temptations BACK TO BASICS
MOLP 0136	Motown STML 12179 (12/82)	Charlene USED TO BE	MOLP 0154	Motown STML 12197 (11/83)	The Four Tops BACK WHERE I BELONG
MOLP 0137	Motown STML 12180 (12/82)	Bobby M RICK JAMES PRESENTS BOBBY M	MOLP 0155	Motown STML 12198	Note: Unissued.
MOLP 0138	Motown STML 12181 (03/83)	The Dazz Band ON THE ONE	MOLP 0156	Motown STML 12199 (07/84)	Bobby Nunn PRIVATE PARTY
MOLP 0139	Motown STML 12182 (03/83)	The Temptations SURFACE THRILLS	MOLP 0157	Motown STML 12200 (04/84)	DeBarge IN A SPECIAL WAY
MOLP 0140	Motown STML 12183 (04/83)	The Commodores ALL THE GREAT HITS	MOLP 0158	Motown STML 12201 (04/84)	The Dazz Band JOYSTICK
MOLP 0141	Motown STML 12184 (05/83)	Syreeta THE SPELL	MOLP 0159	Motown ZL 72005 (11/85)	Stevie Wonder IN SQUARE CIRCLE
MOLP 0142	Motown STML 12185 (05/83)	Jose Feliciano ROMANCE IN THE NIGHT	MOLP 0160	Motown ZL 72147 (02/84)	Rockwell SOMEBODY'S WATCHING ME
MOLP 0143	Motown STML 12186 (05/83)	Debarge ALL THIS LOVE	MOLP 0161	Motown ZL 72148 (04/84)	Dennis Edwards DON'T LOOK ANY FURTHER Note: On the Gordy label.
MOLP 0144	Motown STML 12187	Note: Unissued.	MOLP 0162	Morocco ZL 72149 (04/84)	Kidd Glove KIDD GLOVE Note: On the Morocco label.
MOLP 0145	Motown STML 12188	Note: Unissued.	MOLP 0163	Morocco ZL 72150	Tiggi Clay TIGGI CLAY Note: On the Morocco label.
MOLP 0146	Motown STML 12189 (06/83)	Mary Jane Girls MARY JANE GIRLS	MOLP 0164	Motown ZL 72151 (04/84)	Bobby King LOVE IN THE FIRE

U.K. DISCOGRAPHY

MOLP 0165	Motown ZL 72152 (07/84)	Smokey Robinson ESSAR
MOLP 0166	Motown ZL 72173 (10/84)	The Coyote Sisters COYOTE SISTERS
MOLP 0167	Motown ZL 72174 (08/84)	Rick James REFLECTIONS OF RICK
MOLP 0168	Motown ZL 72176 (10/84)	Charlene HIT AND RUN LOVER
MOLP 0169	Motown ZL 72177 (04/84)	Wolf & Wolf WOLF & WOLF
MOLP 0170	Motown ZL 72187 (10/84)	Various Artists MAKING TRAX (GREAT INSTRUMENTALS)
MOLP 0171	Motown ZL 72191 (04/85)	KoKo-Pop KOKO-POP
MOLP 0172	Morocco ZL 72193 (10/84)	Duke Jupiter WHITE KNUCKLE RIDE Note: On the Morocco label.
MOLP 0173	Motown ZL 72205 (04/84)	Bobby Womack THE POET II
MOLP 0174	Motown ZL 72227 (08/84)	Michael Jackson FAREWELL MY SUMMER LOVE
MOLP 0175	Motown ZL 72237 (10/84)	Sam Harris SAM HARRIS
MOLP 0176	Motown ZL 72283 (10/84)	Vanity WILD ANIMAL
MOLP 0177	Morocco ZL 72284 (10/84)	Jakata LIGHT THE NIGHT Note: On the Morocco label.
MOLP 0178	Motown ZL 72285 (09/84)	Stevie Wonder THE WOMAN IN RED
MOLP 0179	Latino ZL 72296 (11/84)	Jose Feliciano LOS EXITOS DE JOSE FELICIANO Note: On the Latino label.
MOLP 0180	Motown ZL 72298 (11/84)	Phyllis St. James AIN'T NO TURNIN' BACK
MOLP 0181	Motown ZL 72301 (07/85)	The Four Tops MAGIC
MOLP 0182	Motown ZL 72335 (11/84)	The Dazz Band JUKEBOX
MOLP 0183	Motown ZL 72339 (03/85)	Rockwell CAPTURED
MOLP 0184	Motown ZL 72340 (05/85)	DeBarge RHYTHM OF THE NIGHT
MOLP 0185	Motown ZL 72341 (04/85)	Mary Jane Girls ONLY FOUR YOU
MOLP 0186	Motown ZL 72342 (12/84)	The Temptations TRULY FOR YOU
MOLP 0187	Motown ZL 72343 (02/85)	The Commodores NIGHTSHIFT
MOLP 0188	Motown ZL 72349 (02/85)	Thomas McClary THOMAS McCLARY
MOLP 0189	Motown ZL 72362 (05/85)	Rick James GLOW
MOLP 0190	Motown ZL 72363 (05/85)	Various Artists BERRY GORDY'S "THE LAST DRAGON" (ORIGINAL SOUNDTRACK)
MOLP 0191	Motown ZL 72370 (10/85)	Various Artists THE FLAMINGO KID (ORIGINAL SOUNDTRACK)
MOLP 0192	Motown ZL 72371 (06/85)	Emotions IF I ONLY KNEW
MOLP 0193	Motown ZL 72372 (06/85)	Maureen Steele NATURE OF THE BEAST
MOLP 0194	Motown ZL 72376 (08/85)	Michael Lovesmith RHYMES OF PASSION
MOLP 0195	Motown ZL 72378 (07/85)	Willie Hutch MAKING A GAME OUT OF LOVE
MOLP 0196	Motown ZL 72390 (08/85)	Dennis Edwards COOLIN' OUT
MOLP 0197	Motown ZL 72394 (03/86)	Smokey Robinson SMOKE SIGNALS
MOLP 0198	Motown ZL 72413 (11/85)	The Temptations TOUCH ME

MOTOWN COMPACT DISCS

MOCD 0001	Motown MCD06059MD (05/84)	Lionel Richie CAN'T SLOW DOWN
MOCD 0002	Motown MCD06068MD (05/84)	The Commodores 14 GREATEST HITS
MOCD 0003	Motown MCD06072MD (05/84)	Diana Ross 14 GREATEST HITS
MOCD 0004	Motown MCD06073MD (05/84)	Diana Ross & The Supremes 20 GREATEST HITS
MOCD 0005	Tamla TCD06071TD (05/84)	Smokey Robinson & The Miracles 18 GREATEST HITS
MOCD 0006	Motown ZD 72285 (09/84)	Stevie Wonder THE WOMAN IN RED
MOCD 0007	Gordy ZD 72443 (10/84)	Rick James REFLECTIONS OF RICK
MOCD 0008	Motown ZD 72220 (10/84)	The Four Tops COMPACT COMMAND PERFORMANCES
MOCD 0009	Motown ZD 72221 (10/84)	Diana Ross ALL THE GREAT LOVE SONGS
MOCD 0010	Motown ZD 72222 (10/84)	The Commodores ALL THE GREAT LOVE SONGS
MOCD 0011	Motown ZD 72297 (02/85)	Various Artists GRAMMY R & B SONGS OF THE 1960'S & 1970'S
MOCD 0012	Motown ZD 72366 (04/85)	Grover Washington, Jr. AT HIS BEST
MOCD 0013	Motown ZD 72131 (06/85)	Stevie Wonder SONGS IN THE KEY OF LIFE
MOCD 0014	Motown ZD 72133 (06/85)	Stevie Wonder ORIGINAL MUSIQUARIUM
MOCD 0015	Motown ZD 72145 (06/85)	Stevie Wonder JOURNEY THROUGH THE SECRET LIFE OF PLANTS
MOCD 0016	Motown ZD 72343 (06/85)	The Commodores NIGHTSHIFT
MOCD 0017	Motown ZD 72347 (06/85)	Various Artists THE BIG CHILL Note: Original soundtrack.
MOCD 0018	Motown ZD 72380 (06/85)	Various Artists THE GREATEST SONGS: HOLLAND - DOZIER - HOLLAND
MOCD 0019	Motown ZD 72365 (07/85)	Temptations 17 GREATEST HITS
MOCD 0020	Motown ZD 72379 (07/85)	Various Artists THE GREATEST SONGS: SMOKEY ROBINSON
MOCD 0021	Motown ZD 72237 (08/85)	Sam Harris SAM HARRIS
MOCD 0022	Motown ZD 72383 (10/85)	Various Artists THE GREATEST SONGS: ASHFORD & SIMPSON
MOCD 0023	Motown ZD 72136 (11/85)	Various Artists 25 MOTOWN NO. 1 HITS
MOCD 0024	Motown ZD 72225 (11/85)	Stevie Wonder ORIGINAL MUSIQUARIUM 1
MOCD 0025	Motown ZD 72226 (11/85)	Stevie Wonder ORIGINAL MUSIQUARIUM 2
MOCD 0026	Motown ZD 72363 (11/85)	Various Artists THE LAST DRAGON Note: Original soundtrack.
MOCD 0027	Motown ZD 72005 (11/85)	Stevie Wonder IN SQUARE CIRCLE
MOCD 0028	Motown ZD 72012 (02/86)	Stevie Wonder INNERVISIONS
MOCD 0029	Motown MCD 06007 MD (05/86)	Lionel Richie LIONEL RICHIE
MOCD 0030	Tamla TCD 06069 TD (05/86)	Marvin Gaye 15 GREATEST HITS
MOCD 0031	Motown ZD 72011 (06/86)	Stevie Wonder TALKING BOOK
MOCD 0032	Motown ZD 72389 (06/86)	Stevie Wonder LOVE SONGS
MOCD 0033	Motown ZD 72397 (06/86)	Marvin Gaye MARVIN GAYE AND HIS WOMEN
MOCD 0034	Motown ZD 72400 (06/86)	Various Artists 20 GREATEST SONGS IN MOTOWN HISTORY

MOCD 0035	Motown ZD 72394 (07/86)	Smokey Robinson SMOKE SIGNALS
MOCD 0036	Motown ZD 72129 (08/86)	Diana Ross LADY SINGS THE BLUES
MOCD 0037	Motown ZD 72443 (08/86)	Rick James THE FLAG
MOCD 0038	Motown ZD 72412 (09/86)	Lionel Richie DANCING ON THE CEILING
MOCD 0039	Motown ZD 72341 (10/86)	Mary Jane Girls ONLY FOUR YOU

GAIEE 7-INCH SINGLES

GA45 0001	Gaiee GAE 101 (06/75)	Valentino I Was Born This Way Liberation

HITSVILLE 7-INCH SINGLES

HI45 0001	Hitsville HV 101 (04/77)	T. G. Sheppard Lovin' On We Just Live Here (We Don't Love Here Anymore
HI45 0002	Hitsville HV 102 (05/77)	Wendel Adkins Texas Moon Laid Back Country Picker

MC 7-INCH SINGLES

MC45 0001	MC Records MC 7001 (03/78)	Marty Mitchell You Are The Sunshine Of My Life Yester-Me, Yester-You, Yesterday
MC45 0002	MC Records MC 7002 (05/78)	Jerry Naylor Rave On Lady, Would You Like To Dance

MOWEST 7-INCH SINGLES

MW45 0001	Mowest MW 3001 (10/72)	Thelma Houston No One's Gonna Be A Fool Forever What If
MW45 0002	Mowest YMW 3002 (10/72)	Frankie Valli & The Four Seasons The Night When The Morning Comes Note: See also Mowest YMW 3024.
MW45 0003	Mowest MW 3003 (03/73)	Frankie Valli & The Four Seasons Walk On, Don't Look Back Touch The Rainchild

Note: "B" side also issued on Mowest YMW 3028.

MW45 0004	Mowest YMW 3004	Thelma Houston Black California I'm Letting Go Note: Unissued. Demo copies only.
MW45 0005	Mowest YMW 3005 (10/73)	Thelma Houston Piano Man I'm Just A Part Of Yesterday
MW45 0006	Mowest YMW 3006 (06/73)	Syreeta To Know You Is To Love You Happiness
MW45 0007	Mowest YMW 3007 (07/73)	Hetherington Teenage Love Song That Girl's Alright
MW45 0008	Mowest YMW 3008 (07/73)	Phil Cordell Close To You Londonderry
MW45 0009	Mowest YMW 3009 (09/73)	The Sisters Love I'm Learning To Trust My Man Try It, You'll Like It Note: Reissued on Tamla Motown TMG 1002, September 1975.
MW45 0010	Mowest YMW 3010 (09/73)	The Devastating Affair That's How It Was (Right From The Start) It's So Sad
MW45 0011	Mowest YMW 3011 (09/73)	Phil Cordell Roadie For The Band Twistin' And Jivin'
MW45 0012	Mowest YMW 3012 (11/73)	The Rockits Livin' Without You Love My Love
MW45 0013	Mowest MW 3013 (12/73)	Tom Clay What The World Needs Now Is Love + Abraham, Martin And John The Victors Note: Reissue of Tamla Motown TMG 801.
MW45 0014	Mowest YMW 3014 (04/74)	Bobby Darin Blue Monday Moritat (Mack The Knife)
MW45 0015	Mowest YMW 3015 (05/74)	Phil Cordell Laughter In The Rain If I Don't Get All The Luck
MW45 0016	Mowest YMW 3016 (07/74)	The Rockits Gimme True Love I'm Losing You
MW45 0017	Mowest YMW 3017	Note: Unissued.
MW45 0018	Mowest YMW 3018 (08/74)	Riverhead I Can't Let Maggie Go This Time Around

MW45 0019	Mowest YMW 3019 (08/74)	Reuben Howell Rings I Believe (When I Fall In Love It Will Be Forever)
MW45 0020	Mowest YMW 3020 (09/74)	Severin Browne Love Song Snow Flakes
MW45 0021	Mowest YMW 3021 (09/74)	Phil Cordell Cool Clear Water Everywhere I Go
MW45 0022	Mowest YMW 3022 (11/74)	The Boone Family Please Mr. Postman Friends
MW45 0023	Mowest YMW 3023 (03/75)	Severin Browne Romance The Sweet Sound Of Your Song
MW45 0024	Mowest YMW 3024 (03/75)	Frankie Valli & The Four Seasons The Night When The Morning Comes Note: Reissue of Mowest YMW 3002.
MW45 0025	Mowest YMW 3025 (04/75)	The Boones When The Lovelight Starts Shining Through His Eyes Friends
MW45 0026	Mowest YMW 3026	Phil Cordell Chevy Van Stay With Me Baby Note: Unissued. Demo copies only.
MW45 0027	Mowest YMW 3027 (09/75)	T. G. Sheppard Another Woman I Can't Help Myself (Sugar Pie, Honey Bunch) Note: See also Mowest YMW 3031.
MW45 0028	Mowest YMW 3028 (06/75)	Frankie Valli & The Four Seasons Touch The Rainchild Poor Fool Note: See also Mowest YMW 3003.
MW45 0029	Mowest YMW 3029 (07/75)	The Allens High Tide California Music
MW45 0030	Mowest YMW 3030 (08/75)	Frankie Valli And I Will Love You Sun Country
MW45 0031	Mowest YMW 3031 (09/75)	T. G. Sheppard Another Woman I Can't Help Myself (Sugar Pie, Honey Bunch) Note: See also Mowest YMW 3027.

MW45 0032	Mowest MW 3032 (10/75)	Jud Struk The Biggest Parakeets In Town I Wasn't Wrong About You Note: This is the only Mowest single to have the American release number in the run-out of the record and on the left side of the label.
MW45 0033	Mowest YMW 3033 (03/76)	T. G. Sheppard Motels And Memories Pigskin Charade Note: See also Mowest YMW 3035.
MW45 0034	Mowest YMW 3034 (06/76)	Frankie Valli Life And Breath Thank You
MW45 0035	Mowest YMW 3035 (07/76)	T. G. Sheppard Solitary Man Pigskin Charade Note: See also Mowest YMW 3033.

MOWEST ALBUMS

MWLP 0001	Mowest MWS 7001 (11/72)	Syreeta SYREETA
MWLP 0002	Mowest MWSA 5501 (11/72)	Frankie Valli and the Four Seasons CHAMELEON
MWLP 0003	Mowest MWS 7002 (02/73)	Odyssey ODYSSEY
MWLP 0004	Mowest MWS 7003 (01/73)	Thelma Houston THELMA HOUSTON
MWLP 0005	Mowest MWS 7004 (07/73)	The Crusaders HOLLYWOOD
MWLP 0006	Mowest MWS 7005 (07/75)	Severin Browne LOVE SONGS
MWLP 0007	Mowest MWS 7006 (06/75)	Frankie Valli and the Four Seasons CHAMELEON
MWLP 0008	Mowest MWS 7007 (05/76)	Frankie Valli INSIDE YOU

PRODIGAL 7-INCH SINGLES

PR45 0001	Prodigal PROD 1 (11/76)	Dunn & Rubini Diggin' It Just Keep Laughin'
PR45 0002	Prodigal PROD 2 (02/77)	Charlene It Ain't Easy Comin' Down On My Way To You

PR45 0003	Prodigal PROD 3 (00/77)	Phil Cordell Back In Your Arms Again One Man Show
PR45 0004	Prodigal PROD 4 (08/77)	Charlene I've Never Been To Me Freddie
PR45 0005	Prodigal PROD 5 (08/77)	Graffiti Orchestra Star Wars Theme Star Wars Theme (long version)
PR45 0006	Prodigal PROD 6 (10/77)	Phil Cordell Doin' The Best I Can Cheatin' In The Dark
PR45 0007	Prodigal PROD 7 (11/77)	Rare Earth Is Your Teacher Cool? Crazy Love
PR45 0008	Prodigal PROD 8 (03/78)	Fresh Just How Does It Feel Let Yourself Go
PR45 0009	Prodigal PROD 9 (05/76)	Rare Earth Warm Ride Would You Like To Come Along
PR45 0010	Prodigal PROD 10 (03/79)	Meatloaf featuring Stoney & Meatloaf What You See Is What You Get The Way You Do The Things You Do Note: Reissue of Rare Earth RES 103.

PRODIGAL ALBUMS

PRLP 0001	Prodigal PDL 2001 (10/76)	Michael Quatro DANCERS, ROMANCERS, DREAMERS AND SCHEMERS
PRLP 0002	Prodigal PDL 2002 (11/76)	Dunn & Rubini DIGGIN' IN
PRLP 0003	Prodigal PDL 2003 (01/77)	Tattoo TATTOO
PRLP 0004	Prodigal PDL 2004 (05/77)	Charlene CHARLENE
PRLP 0005	Prodigal PDL 2005 (05/77)	Delaney Bramlett CLASS REUNION
PRLP 0006	Prodigal PDL 2006 (10/77)	Phil Cordell BORN AGAIN
PRLP 0007	Prodigal PDL 2007 (10/77)	Rare Earth RARE EARTH

PRLP 0008	Prodigal PDL 2008 (07/78)	Rare Earth BAND TOGETHER
PRLP 0009	Prodigal PDL 2009 (11/78)	Rare Earth GRAND SLAM
PRLP 0010	Prodigal PDL 2010 (03/79)	Stoney & Meatloaf STONEY & MEATLOAF
PRLP 0011	Prodigal PDL 2011 (07/79)	Stylus STYLUS

RARE EARTH 7-INCH SINGLES

RA45 0001	Rare Earth RES 101 (09/71)	R. Dean Taylor Ain't It A Sad Thing Back Street
RA45 0002	Rare Earth RES 102 (09/71)	Rare Earth I Just Want To Celebrate The Seed
RA45 0003	Rare Earth RES 103 (10/71)	Stoney & Meatloaf What You See Is What You Get The Way You Do The Things You Do Note: Reissued on Prodigal PROD 10 in March 1979.
RA45 0004	Rare Earth RES 104 (01/72)	Rare Earth Hey Big Brother Under God's Light
RA45 0005	Rare Earth RES 105 (04/72)	Rare Earth Born To Wander Here Comes The Night
RA45 0006	Rare Earth RES 106 (06/72)	R. Dean Taylor Taos New Mexico Shadow
RA45 0007	Rare Earth RES 107 (09/72)	Xit I Was Raised End
RA45 0008	Rare Earth YRES 108 (02/73)	Wolfe Dancing In The Moonlight Snarlin' Mama Lion
RA45 0009	Rare Earth YRES 109 (08/73)	Rare Earth Good Time Sally Love Shines Down
RA45 0010	Rare Earth YRES 110 (08/73)	Dan The Banjo Man Dan The Banjo Man Everything Will Rhyme Note: Pseudonym for Phil Cordell.
RA45 0011	Rare Earth YRES 111 (01/74)	Xit Reservation Of Education Young Warrior

RA45 0012	Rare Earth YRES 112 (02/74)	David Alexander Love, Love, Love Missy	
RA45 0013	Rare Earth YRES 113 (06/74)	Dan The Banjo Man Black Magic Londonderry (Instrumental) Note: Pseudonym for Phil Cordell.	
RA45 0014	Rare Earth RES 114 (05/74)	Rare Earth (I Know) I'm Losing You When Joanie Smiles	
RA45 0015	Rare Earth YRES 115 (05/74)	Michael Edwards Campbell Roxanne (You Sure Got A Fine Design) Roll It Over	
RA45 0016	Rare Earth YRES 116 (05/74)	Slowbone And The Wonder Boys Happy Birthday Sweet Sixteen Tales Of A Crooked Man	
RA45 0017	Rare Earth YRES 117 (07/74)	Sonny & The Sovereigns School Is Out Walm Jetz	
RA45 0018	Rare Earth YRES 118 (09/74)	Rough Riders Hot California Beach Do You See Me	
RA45 0019	Rare Earth YRES 119 (10/74)	Slowbone Oh Man Get What You're Given	
RA45 0020	Rare Earth YRES 120 (11/74)	Friendly Persuasion Remember (Sha La La) I'll Always Do The Best I Can	
RA45 0021	Rare Earth YRES 121 (07/74)	Dan The Banjo Man Red River Valley Theme Of Love Note: Pseudonym for Phil Cordell.	

RARE EARTH ALBUMS

RALP 0001	Rare Earth SRE 3001 (10/71)	The Crusaders OLD SOCKS, NEW SHOES	
RALP 0002	Rare Earth SRE 3002 (11/71)	Hugh Masekela HUGH MASEKELA AND THE UNION OF SOUTH AFRICA	
RALP 0003	Rare Earth SRE 3003	Note: Unissued.	
RALP 0004	Rare Earth SRE 3004 (11/71)	Sunday Funnies SUNDAY FUNNIES	
RALP 0005	Rare Earth SRE 3005 (10/72)	Stoney & Meatloaf STONEY & MEATLOAF	

RALP 0006	Rare Earth SREA 4001 (10/71)	Rare Earth ONE WORLD	
RALP 0007	Rare Earth SREA 4002 (09/72)	Xit PLIGHT OF THE RED MAN	
RALP 0008	Rare Earth SRESP 301 (05/72)	Rare Earth IN CONCERT	
RALP 0009	Rare Earth SRE 3006 (01/73)	Road ROAD	
RALP 0010	Rare Earth SRE 3007 (02/73)	Keef James ONE TREE OR ANOTHER	
RALP 0011	Rare Earth SRE 3008 (03/73)	Rare Earth WILLIE REMEMBERS	
RALP 0012	Rare Earth SRE 3009 (04/73)	Corliss CORLISS	
RALP 0013	Rare Earth SRE 3010 (09/73)	Rare Earth MA	
RALP 0014	Rare Earth SRE 3011	Note: Unissued.	
RALP 0015	Rare Earth SRE 3012	Note: Unissued.	
RALP 0016	Rare Earth SRE 3013 (05/76)	Rare Earth MIDNIGHT LADY	

DELUXE SERIES ALBUMS

DSLP 0001	Motown STMA 8001 (11/71)	Diana Ross DIANA! TV SOUNDTRACK	
DSLP 0002	Motown STMA 8002 (05/72)	Stevie Wonder MUSIC OF MY MIND	
DSLP 0003	Motown STMA 8003	Note: Unissued.	
DSLP 0004	Motown STMA 8004 (07/72)	The Undisputed Truth FACE TO FACE WITH THE TRUTH	
DSLP 0005	Motown STMA 8005 (08/72)	Various Artists MOTOWN DISCO CLASSICS VOL. 2	
DSLP 0006	Motown STMA 8006 (10/72)	Diana Ross GREATEST HITS	

DSLP 0007	Motown STMA 8007 (01/73)	Stevie Wonder TALKING BOOK
DSLP 0008	Motown STMA 8008 (04/73)	Smokey Robinson & The Miracles 1957-1972
DSLP 0009	Motown STMA 8009 (08/73)	Willie Hutch THE MACK
DSLP 0010	Motown STMA 8010 (10/73)	The Miracles RENAISSANCE
DSLP 0011	Motown STMA 8011 (10/73)	Stevie Wonder INNERVISIONS
DSLP 0012	Motown STMA 8012 (11/73)	Smokey Robinson SMOKEY
DSLP 0013	Motown STMA 8013 (11/73)	Marvin Gaye LET'S GET IT ON
DSLP 0014	Motown STMA 8014 (11/73)	Original Cast PIPPIN
DSLP 0015	Motown STMA 8015 (01/74)	Diana Ross & Marvin Gaye DIANA AND MARVIN
DSLP 0016	Motown STMA 8016 (02/74)	The Temptations 1990
DSLP 0017	Motown STMA 8017	Note: Unissued.
DSLP 0018	Motown STMA 8018 (09/74)	Marvin Gaye LIVE!
DSLP 0019	Motown STMA 8019 (09/74)	Stevie Wonder FULFILLINGNESS' FIRST FINALE
DSLP 0020	Motown STMA 8020 (01/75)	Eddie Kendricks FOR YOU
DSLP 0021	Motown STMA 8021 (03/75)	The Temptations A SONG FOR YOU
DSLP 0022	Motown STMA 8022 (03/75)	Michael Jackson FOREVER, MICHAEL
DSLP 0023	Motown STMA 8023 (06/75)	The Undisputed Truth COSMIC TRUTH
DSLP 0024	Motown STMA 8024 (02/76)	The Isley Brothers SUPER HITS
DSLP 0025	Motown STMA 8025 (09/76)	The Temptations WINGS OF LOVE
DSLP 0026	Motown STMA 8026 (09/76)	Gladys Knight & The Pips SUPER HITS
DSLP 0027	Motown STMA 8027 (10/76)	Jermaine Jackson MY NAME IS JERMAINE
DSLP 0028	Motown STMA 8028 (11/76)	The Four Tops SUPER HITS
DSLP 0029	Motown STMA 8029 (09/77)	The Undisputed Truth THE BEST OF THE UNDISPUTED TRUTH
DSLP 0030	Motown STMA 8030 (09/77)	Albert Finney ALBERT FINNEY'S ALBUM
DSLP 0031	Motown STMA 8031 (11/77)	Diana Ross BABY IT'S ME
DSLP 0032	Motown STMA 8032 (07/79)	The Commodores MIDNIGHT MAGIC
DSLP 0033	Motown STMA 8033 (05/80)	Diana Ross DIANA
DSLP 0034	Motown STMA 8034 (06/80)	The Commodores HEROES
DSLP 0035	Motown STMA 8035 (11/80)	Stevie Wonder HOTTER THAN JULY
DSLP 0036	Motown STMA 8036 (12/81)	Diana Ross ALL THE GREAT HITS
DSLP 0037	Motown STMA 8037 (11/82)	Lionel Richie LIONEL RICHIE
DSLP 0038	Motown STMA 8038 (09/83)	Rick James COLD BLOODED
DSLP 0039	Motown STMA 8039 (09/83)	The Commodores 13
DSLP 0040	Motown STMA 8040	Stevie Wonder PEOPLE MOVE HUMAN PLAY Note: Release due for November 1983, but cancelled.
DSLP 0041	Motown STMA 8041 (10/83)	Lionel Richie CAN'T SLOW DOWN Note: End of series.

PICKWICK ALBUMS

PILP 0001	Pickwick TMS 3501 (06/82)	Smokey Robinson & The Miracles TEARS OF A CLOWN
PILP 0002	Pickwick TMS 3502 (06/82)	The Four Tops THE FABULOUS FOUR TOPS
PILP 0003	Pickwick TMS 3503 (06/82)	The Jackson 5 THE JACKSON 5
PILP 0004	Pickwick TMS 3504 (06/82)	Stevie Wonder UPTIGHT
PILP 0005	Pickwick TMS 3505 (06/82)	Diana Ross DYNAMIC DIANA
PILP 0006	Pickwick TMS 3506 (06/82)	Gladys Knight & The Pips EVERY BEAT OF MY HEART
PILP 0007	Pickwick TMS 3507 (06/82)	The Temptations GET READY
PILP 0008	Pickwick TMS 3508 (06/82)	Marvin Gaye THE MAGIC OF MARVIN
PILP 0009	Pickwick TMS 3509 (06/82)	Various Artists MOTOWN LOVE SONGS
PILP 0010	Pickwick TMS 3510 (06/82)	Smokey Robinson HOT SMOKEY
PILP 0011	Pickwick TMS 3511 (06/82)	Michael Jackson AIN'T NO SUNSHINE
PILP 0012	Pickwick TMS 3512 (MO/YR)	Note: Unissued.
PILP 0013	Pickwick TMS 3513 (10/82)	Diana Ross & Supremes and The Temptations DIANA ROSS & SUPREMES MEET THE TEMPTATIONS
PILP 0014	Pickwick TMS 3514 (10/82)	The Four Tops HITS OF GOLD

16 BIG HITS SERIES ALBUMS

| SILP 0001 | Motown STMF 7001 (10/82) | Various Artists 16 BIG HITS: EARLY 60s Note: 16 Big Hits series. |
| SILP 0002 | Motown STMF 7002 (10/82) | Various Artists 16 BIG HITS: LATE 60s Note: 16 Big Hits series. End of series. |

SPECIAL SERIES ALBUMS

SPLP 0001	Motown STMX 6001 (03/77)	Diana Ross & The Supremes MOTOWN SPECIAL
SPLP 0002	Motown STMX 6002 (03/77)	The Temptations MOTOWN SPECIAL
SPLP 0003	Motown STMX 6003 (03/77)	Diana Ross & The Supremes & Temptations MOTOWN SPECIAL
SPLP 0004	Motown STMX 6004 (03/77)	The Four Tops MOTOWN SPECIAL
SPLP 0005	Motown STMX 6005 (03/77)	Junior Walker & The All Stars MOTOWN SPECIAL
SPLP 0006	Motown STMX 6006 (03/77)	The Jackson 5 MOTOWN SPECIAL
SPLP 0007	Motown STMX 6007 (03/77)	Various Artists MOTOWN EXTRA SPECIAL

TELEVISION SERIES ALBUMS

TVLP 0001	Motown EMTV5 (08/77)	Diana Ross & The Supremes 20 GOLDEN GREATS Note: TV-promoted album series.
TVLP 0002	Motown EMTV20 (09/79)	Various Artists THE LAST DANCE Note: TV-promoted album series.
TVLP 0003	Motown EMTV21 (11/79)	Diana Ross 20 GOLDEN GREATS Note: TV-promoted album series.
TVLP 0004	Motown EMTV26 (06/80)	The Four Tops 20 GOLDEN GREATS Note: TV-promoted album series.
TVLP 0005	Motown MTV5 (10/81)	Diana Ross & The Supremes 20 GOLDEN GREATS Note: TV-promoted album series.
TVLP 0006	Motown MTV20 (10/81)	Various Artists THE LAST DANCE Note: TV-promoted album series.
TVLP 0007	Motown MTV21 (10/81)	Diana Ross 20 GOLDEN GREATS Note: TV-promoted album series.

TVLP 0008 (10/81)	Motown MTV26	The Four Tops 20 GOLDEN GREATS Note: TV-promoted album series.

TWO- & THREE-RECORD ALBUM SETS

X2LP 0001 (10/73)	Tamla Motown TMSP 1124	The Four Tops THE FOUR TOPS STORY
X2LP 0002	Tamla Motown TMSP 1125	Note: Unissued. See Tamla Motown TMSP 6001.
X2LP 0003	Tamla Motown TMSP 1126	Note: Unissued.
X2LP 0004 (03/74)	Tamla Motown TMSP 1127	Gladys Knight & The Pips ANTHOLOGY
X2LP 0005 (06/74)	Tamla Motown TMSP 1128	Marvin Gaye ANTHOLOGY
X2LP 0006 (10/74)	Tamla Motown TMSP 1129	Junior Walker & The All Stars ANTHOLOGY
X2LP 0007 (03/72)	Tamla Motown TMSP 1130	Various Artists THE MOTOWN STORY
X2LP 0008 (03/73)	Tamla Motown TMSP 1131	Diana Ross LADY SINGS THE BLUES
X2LP 0009	Tamla Motown TMSP 1132	Note: Unissued.
X2LP 0010 (07/74)	Tamla Motown TMSP 1133	Various Artists SAVE THE CHILDREN
X2LP 0011 (01/74)	Tamla Motown 782 A3-1	Temptations ANTHOLOGY
X2LP 0012 (03/74)	Tamla Motown 793 R3-1	Smokey Robinson & The Miracles ANTHOLOGY
X2LP 0013 (09/74)	Tamla Motown 794 A3-1	Diana Ross & The Supremes ANTHOLOGY
X2LP 0014 (10/75)	Tamla Motown TMSP 6001	Diana Ross & The Supremes ANTHOLOGY
X2LP 0015 (10/76)	Tamla Motown TMSP 6002	Stevie Wonder SONGS IN THE KEY OF LIFE

X2LP 0016 (01/76)	Tamla Motown TMSP 6003	The Temptations ANTHOLOGY
X2LP 0017 (01/77)	Motown TMSP 6004	The Jackson 5 ANTHOLOGY
X2LP 0018 (03/77)	Motown TMSP 6005	Diana Ross AN EVENING WITH DIANA ROSS
X2LP 0019 (04/77)	Motown TMSP 6006	Marvin Gaye LIVE AT THE LONDON PALLADIUM
X2LP 0020 (11/77)	Motown TMSP 6007	The Commodores LIVE
X2LP 0021 (01/79)	Motown TMSP 6008	Marvin Gaye HERE MY DEAR
X2LP 0022 (10/79)	Motown TMSP 6009	Stevie Wonder THE SECRET LIFE OF PLANTS
X2LP 0023 (06/80)	Motown TMSP 6010	Various Artists MOTOWN 20TH ANNIVERSARY ALBUM
X2LP 0024 (02/81)	Motown TMSP 6011	Grover Washington Jr. BADDEST
X2LP 0025 (07/82)	Motown TMSP 6012	Stevie Wonder ORIGINAL MUSIQUARIUM
X2LP 0026 (09/82)	Motown TMSP 6013	The Four Tops ANTHOLOGY
X2LP 0027 (09/82)	Motown TMSP 6014	Smokey Robinson & The Miracles ANTHOLOGY
X2LP 0028 (09/82)	Motown TMSP 6015	Grover Washington Jr. ANTHOLOGY
X2LP 0029	Motown TMSP 6016	Note: Unissued.
X2LP 0030 (12/83)	Motown TMSP 6017	Diana Ross THE VERY BEST OF DIANA ROSS
X2LP 0031 (10/83)	Motown TMSP 6018	Various Artists 25 U.S.A. NO. 1 HITS FROM 25 YEARS
X2LP 0032 (11/83)	Motown TMSP 6019	Various Artists THE MOTOWN STORY - THE FIRST 25 YEARS Note: End of series.

PART VI

INDEXES
TO THE U.S.
DISCOGRAPHY

KEY TO
U.S. ENTRY NUMBER PREFIXES

The Abbey Tavern Singers
  VILP 0003
Abdullah
  SO45 0051
Adams, Arthur
  CH45 0004, CH45 0009, CH45 0012,
  CH45 0016, CHCO 0003
Adams, Pepper
  WOLP 0018
Adkins, Wendel
  HI45 0019, HI45 0024, HILP 0003,
  MC45 0002, MC45 0008, MCLP 0012
Alfie
  TMG12 0031, TMG45 0183,
  TMG45 0233, TMGLP 0148
Allanson, Susie
  MCLP 0010
The Allens
  MO45 0335, MO45 0353, MO45 0364
Aller, Michelle
  MW45 0018, MW45 0019
Allison, Luther
  GO45 0129, GO45 0138, GOLP 0064,
  GOLP 0067, GOLP 0074
The All Stars
  MO45 0027, MO45 0365, MOEP 0013,
  MOLP 0188, SO45 0003, SO45 0008,
  SO45 0012, SO45 0013, SO45 0015,
  SO45 0017, SO45 0024, SO45 0026,
  SO45 0030, SO45 0036, SO45 0041,
  SO45 0048, SO45 0055, SO45 0062,
  SO45 0067, SO45 0070, SO45 0073,
  SO45 0081, SO45 0084, SO45 0090,
  SO45 0095, SO45 0097, SO45 0104,
  SO45 0106, SO45 0108, SO45 0110,
  SOEP 0001, SOEP 0002, SOEP 0003,
  SOLP 0001, SOLP 0002, SOLP 0003,
  SOLP 0005, SOLP 0010, SOLP 0018,
  SOLP 0021, SOLP 0025, SOLP 0026,
  SOLP 0032, SOLP 0033, SOLP 0038,
  SOLP 0042, SOLP 0045, TMGCD 0024,
  TMGLP 0205
Alston, Shirley
  PR45 0006, PRLP 0002
Andantes
  GO45 0022, MO45 0048, MO45 0055,
  VI45 0005
Anonymous Children of Today
  CH45 0005
Anthony, Richard
  VI45 0021
Apollo
  GO45 0167, GOLP 0087, MO12 0021
Armstrong, "Nikiter"
  ME45 0007
Art & Honey
  MO45 0258, MW45 0050
Ashford, Jack
  BL45 0001
Ashford, Jack and The Sound Of
    New Detroit
  BL45 0001
Askey, Gil
  MO45 0231, MO45 0232
Austin, Kay
  MC45 0014
Banks, Rose
  MO45 0396, MO45 0418, MOLP 0247
Baraka, Imanu Amiri
  BFLP 0006, BFLP 0007
Bean, Carl
  MO12 0011, MO45 0452

The Beljeans
  GO45 0010
Ben, Labrenda
  GO45 0010, GO45 0022
Ben, Labrenda & The Beljeans
  GO45 0010
Blackberries
  MW45 0021, MWLP 0006
Black Fighting Men Recorded
    Live in Vietnam
  BFLP 0004
Black Russian
  MO45 0511, MO45 0516, MOLP 0347
Black, Zell
  MO45 0293, MO45 0303
Blanch, Arthur
  MC45 0015
Blinky
  GO45 0091, GOCO 0006, GOLP 0045,
  MO45 0145, MO45 0179, MO45 0245,
  MOCO 0007, MOLP 0113, MOLP 0172,
  MW45 0020, MW45 0034, SO45 0089
Blinky & Edwin Starr
  GO45 0091, GOCO 0006
Bloodstone
  MO12 0020, MO45 0475, MOLP 0312
The Blue Jeans
  GO45 0010, MO45 0042
Blue Scepter
  RA45 0036
Bob and Marcia
  TA45 0182, TALP 0064
Bob and Penny
  MCLP 0007
Bohannon, George
  WO45 0006, WOLP 0006, WOLP 0013
Bonds, Gary U.S.
  PR45 0002
Boone, Pat
  HI45 0006, HI45 0011, HI45 0016,
  HI45 0023, HILP 0002, MC45 0001,
  MCLP 0001, MCLP 0005, ML45 0001,
  ML45 0005, ML45 0018, ML45 0029,
  MO45 0327
Boone, Shirley
  ML45 0018
The Boones
  MO45 0347, MO45 0402
Bottom & Company
  GOLP 0077, MO45 0304, MO45 0322,
  MO45 0350, MO45 0376
Bramlett, Delaney
  PRLP 0011
Brass Monkey
  RA45 0018, RALP 0020
Breen, Bobby
  MO45 0064, MO45 0070, MOLP 0019
Bristol, Johnny
  MO45 0167
Brooks, Roy
  WOLP 0019
Brown, Elaine
  BF45 0001, BFLP 0007
Brown, Larry
  MO45 0464
Browne, Severin
  MO45 0252, MO45 0270, MO45 0316,
  MO45 0346, MOLP 0176, MOLP 0181
Burnadettes
  DI45 0004
Burnette, Dorsey
  ME45 0013, ME45 0016, ME45 0018,

ML45 0007, ML45 0019, ML45 0031
Burston & Littlejohn
  TMG12 0063, TMG45 0259
Butler, Jerry
  MO12 0007, MO45 0417, MO45 0428,
  MO45 0435, MO45 0436, MOLP 0252,
  MOLP 0281, MOLP 0290, MOLP 0295,
  MOLP 0306
Buzzie
  GO45 0101
Byrd, Gary
  TA45 0319, TMG12 0008
Byrd, Gary and The G. B.
    Experience
  TMG12 0008
Cameron, G. C.
  MO45 0246, MO45 0273, MO45 0324,
  MO45 0360, MO45 0377, MO45 0411,
  MO45 0426, MO45 0440, MOCO 0025,
  MOLP 0221, MOLP 0257, MOLP 0283,
  MOLP 0294, MW45 0005, MW45 0012,
  MW45 0015, MW45 0037, MW45 0038,
  MWCO 0004, MWLP 0007
Cameron, G. C. and Willie Hutch
  MW45 0037
Campbell, Choker
  MO45 0083, MOLP 0021
Campbell, Choker and His Big 16
    Piece Band
  MOLP 0021
Campbell, Michael
  MW45 0042
Campbell, Michael Edward
  MO45 0302, MOLP 0212
Captain Zap & The Motortown
    Cut-Ups
  MO45 0162
Cardinal, Vin
  MO45 0238, MO45 0265
Carmichael, Stokely
  BFLP 0002
Carn, Jean
  TMG45 0021, TMG45 0022,
  TMG45 0054, TMGLP 0011
Carroll, Diahann
  MO45 0283, MO45 0326, MOLP 0207
Carter, Lynda
  MO45 0497
Caston, Leonard
  RALP 0028
Caston & Majors
  MOLP 0216
The Cats
  RA45 0012, RACO 0003, RALP 0018
Celebration
  MO45 0250, MW45 0035, MW45 0036,
  MWLP 0019
Channel, Bruce
  ME45 0012, ME45 0014
Charlene
  MO45 0510, PR45 0022, PR45 0023,
  PR45 0026, PRLP 0009, PRLP 0012,
  TMG45 0012, TMG45 0023,
  TMG45 0026, TMG45 0052,
  TMG45 0065, TMG45 0140,
  TMG45 0167, TMGLP 0010,
  TMGLP 0025, TMGLP 0028,
  TMGLP 0092
Charlene & Stevie Wonder
  TMG45 0052
Choker Campbell's Big Band
  MO45 0083

Christie, Ken
RA45 0020, RA45 0025
Christie, Ken and The Sunday
    People
RA45 0020, RA45 0025
Chuck a Luck
ME45 0006
Clark, Chris
MO45 0125, MO45 0132, MOLP 0065,
VI45 0030, VI45 0037, VI45 0040,
VICO 0001, WELP 0001
Clay, Tiggi
TMG45 0122, TMG45 0134,
TMGLP 0069
Clay, Tom
MW45 0002, MW45 0007, MWLP 0003
Cohn, Stephen
MO45 0343, MOLP 0191
The Commodores
MO12 0002, MO12 0006, MO12 0010,
MO45 0280, MO45 0320, MO45 0332,
MO45 0351, MO45 0374, MO45 0379,
MO45 0394, MO45 0408, MO45 0413,
MO45 0416, MO45 0422, MO45 0432,
MO45 0439, MO45 0446, MO45 0457,
MO45 0467, MO45 0473, MO45 0483,
MO45 0491, MO45 0496, MO45 0506,
MO45 0513, MO45 0521, MO45 0533,
MO45 0546, MOCO 0027, MOCO 0033,
MOLP 0200, MOLP 0222, MOLP 0250,
MOLP 0269, MOLP 0287, MOLP 0297,
MOLP 0305, MOLP 0315, MOLP 0331,
MOLP 0344, MOLP 0359, MOLP 0360,
MW45 0009, MW45 0040, MWLP 0010,
TMG12 0034, TMG12 0036,
TMG45 0005, TMG45 0053,
TMG45 0063, TMG45 0098,
TMG45 0125, TMG45 0179,
TMG45 0194, TMG45 0208,
TMGCD 0015, TMGCD 0040,
TMGLP 0029, TMGLP 0045,
TMGLP 0055, TMGLP 0070,
TMGLP 0076, TMGLP 0109,
TMGLP 0126, TMGLP 0145
The Commodores and Lionel
    Richie and Diana Ross
TMGLP 0145
The Contours
GO45 0006, GO45 0013, GO45 0017,
GO45 0020, GO45 0030, GO45 0038,
GO45 0045, GO45 0053, GO45 0060,
GOLP 0001, MO45 0017, MO45 0021,
MOEP 0002
Cook County
MO45 0493, MO45 0498, MOLP 0335
Cooper, Marty
MC45 0003
Cordell, Phil
MO45 0306, PRLP 0017
Corliss
NALP 0003
Cosby, Bill
BFLP 0005, MOLP 0120, TMGLP 0027
The Courtship
TA45 0206, TA45 0216
Coyote Sisters
TMG45 0148, TMG45 0172,
TMGLP 0065
Crawford, Carolyn
MO45 0061, MO45 0075, MO45 0081
Creations
ME45 0001

Crockett, Howard
ME45 0009, ME45 0011, ME45 0015,
ME45 0019, ME45 0021
Crothers, Scatman
MOLP 0179
Crusaders
CHLP 0007, MOLP 0198, MW45 0029,
MWLP 0018
Crystal Mansion
RA45 0043
Crystal Mountain
RALP 0037
The Dalton Boys
VI45 0024
Dan The Banjo Man
MO45 0306
Danner, Margaret
BFLP 0003
Darin, Bobby
MO45 0195, MO45 0205, MO45 0215,
MO45 0224, MO45 0229, MOLP 0139,
MOLP 0140, MOLP 0155, MOLP 0215
The Darnells
GO45 0025
David, Dwight
TMG45 0191
Davis, Ossie
BFLP 0005
Davis, Sammy, Jr.
EC45 0001, MOLP 0111, TMG12 0020,
TMG45 0144
Day, Danny
VI45 0018
Dazz Band
MO45 0519, MO45 0526, MO45 0534,
MO45 0547, MOLP 0351, MOLP 0362,
TMG12 0004, TMG12 0021,
TMG12 0025, TMG12 0044,
TMG45 0010, TMG45 0024,
TMG45 0061, TMG45 0080,
TMG45 0084, TMG45 0106,
TMG45 0131, TMG45 0166,
TMG45 0181, TMG45 0206,
TMG45 0226, TMGLP 0005,
TMGLP 0032, TMGLP 0086,
TMGLP 0119, TMGLP 0151
Dean, Debbie
MO45 0015, MO45 0023, MO45 0034,
VI45 0043
DeBarge see also The
DeBarges
DeBarge
TMG12 0033, TMG12 0046,
TMG12 0053, TMG45 0037,
TMG45 0047, TMG45 0062,
TMG45 0110, TMG45 0129,
TMG45 0176, TMG45 0199,
TMG45 0210, TMG45 0228,
TMG45 0249, TMG45 0274,
TMG45 0276, TMGLP 0013,
TMGLP 0063, TMGLP 0125,
TMGLP 0175
DeBarge, Bunny
TMG45 0276
DeBarge, Bunny with DeBarge
TMG45 0276
DeBarge, Chico
TMG12 0068, TMG45 0265,
TMGLP 0216
DeBarge, El
TMG12 0046, TMG12 0053,
TMG45 0210, TMG45 0228,

TMG45 0249, TMG45 0264,
TMG45 0274, TMGLP 0183
DeBarge, El with DeBarge
TMG12 0046, TMG12 0053,
TMG45 0210, TMG45 0228,
TMG45 0249, TMG45 0274
The DeBarges see also
DeBarge
The DeBarges
GO45 0201, GO45 0206, GOLP 0104
Dee, Kiki
RA45 0021, TA45 0178, TALP 0084
Denton, Michael
RA45 0011
Detroit Wheels
IN45 0002, IN45 0003
The Devastating Affair
MO45 0275, MO45 0334, MOLP 0183,
MW45 0001, MW45 0024, MWLP 0005
Diamond, Carol
WO45 0001
Diamond, Hank
WO45 0001
Diamond, Hank & Carol
WO45 0001
Diamond, Joel
MO45 0523
Dickey And The Poseidons
MO45 0311
Different Shades of Brown
MO45 0253, TA45 0208
Dimirco, Vincent
RA45 0038
The Ding Dongs
MO45 0180, MOLP 0117
The Dirty Rats
TMG45 0074, TMGLP 0039
Disco Stan
PR45 0014
Dr. Strut
MO45 0492, MO45 0500, MOLP 0329,
MOLP 0336
Dorothy, Oma and Zelpha
CH45 0006
Dove, Ronnie
HI45 0007, HI45 0014, MC45 0013,
ML45 0004, ML45 0011, ML45 0021,
ML45 0030
The Downbeats
TA45 0006, TA45 0039, TALP 0006,
VI45 0028
Dozier, Lamont
ME45 0002, MO45 0055
Duncan, Charlene
MO45 0274, MO45 0298
Dunn & Rubini
PR45 0019, PR45 0020, PRLP 0007
The Dynamic Superiors
MO12 0004, MO45 0337, MO45 0355,
MO45 0370, MO45 0372, MO45 0378,
MO45 0427, MO45 0433, MO45 0442,
MOLP 0224, MOLP 0243, MOLP 0264,
MOLP 0277, MOLP 0282
Dyson, Clifton
MO12 0037, MO45 0499
Earl Washington All Stars
WO45 0002, WOLP 0001
Earthquire
MO45 0261, NALP 0006
Easybeats
RA45 0005, RALP 0014
Eckstine, Billy

MO45 0088, MO45 0102, MO45 0111,
MO45 0116, MO45 0131, MO45 0142,
MO45 0154, MOLP 0033, MOLP 0041,
MOLP 0047, MOLP 0078

Edwards, Dennis
GOLP 0079, TMG45 0121, TMG45 0143,
TMG45 0161, TMG45 0205,
TMG45 0211, TMGLP 0059,
TMGLP 0150

**Edwards, Dennis featuring Siedah
Garrett**
TMG45 0121

Edwards, Lefty
WOLP 0011

The Elgins
VI45 0028, VI45 0036, VI45 0042,
VI45 0064, VILP 0001

The Emotions
TMG45 0190, TMG45 0198,
TMGLP 0138

Equadors
MI45 0007

Eric & The Vikings
GO45 0117, GO45 0133, MO45 0269

**The Fabulous Miracles see also
The
Miracles**

The Fabulous Miracles
TALP 0019

Fair, Yvonne
MO45 0319, MO45 0336, MO45 0357,
MO45 0367, MO45 0397, MOLP 0234,
SO45 0075

Fantacy Hill
PR45 0017, PR45 0031, PRLP 0006,
PRLP 0016

The Fantastic Four
SO45 0052, SO45 0058, SO45 0065,
SO45 0072, SOLP 0017, SOLP 0022

The Fayettes
GO45 0008

Feliciano, Jose
MO45 0536, MO45 0543, MO45 0549,
MOLP 0358, TMG45 0019, TMG45 0049,
TMG45 0075, TMG45 0076,
TMG45 0077, TMG45 0083,
TMGLP 0019, TMGLP 0036

The Festivals
GO45 0121

Fetchit, Stepin
MOLP 0020

Fields, Ernie
MO12 0012

The Fifth Dimension
MO45 0451, MO45 0468, MOLP 0299,
MOLP 0318

Finished Touch
MO12 0026, MO45 0459, MO45 0464,
MO45 0480, MOLP 0309, MOLP 0321

**Finished Touch featuring Harold
Johnson**
MO45 0480

**Finished Touch featuring Kenny
Stover**
MO45 0464

Finney, Albert
MO45 0437, MO45 0444, MOLP 0292

Five Smooth Stones
CH45 0007, CHCO 0004

Flavor
JU45 0001, JULP 0002

Flight

MOLP 0337

Foster, Darla
ML45 0017

Foster, Jerry
HI45 0012, HI45 0021

The Four Seasons
MO45 0267, MO45 0301, MW45 0026,
MW45 0027, MWLP 0008

The Four Tops
CHEP 0002, MO45 0055, MO45 0073,
MO45 0080, MO45 0084, MO45 0087,
MO45 0092, MO45 0095, MO45 0101,
MO45 0107, MO45 0109, MO45 0113,
MO45 0115, MO45 0121, MO45 0124,
MO45 0130, MO45 0135, MO45 0138,
MO45 0143, MO45 0158, MO45 0170,
MO45 0175, MO45 0182, MO45 0185,
MO45 0187, MO45 0193, MO45 0197,
MO45 0201, MO45 0208, MO45 0210,
MO45 0222, MO45 0266, MOCB 0005,
MOCB 0009, MOCO 0003, MOCO 0018,
MOEP 0012, MOEP 0018, MOLP 0023,
MOLP 0035, MOLP 0048, MOLP 0055,
MOLP 0058, MOLP 0061, MOLP 0063,
MOLP 0070, MOLP 0076, MOLP 0096,
MOLP 0105, MOLP 0118, MOLP 0122,
MOLP 0137, MOLP 0142, MOLP 0147,
MOLP 0150, MOLP 0166, MOLP 0167,
MOLP 0211, NALP 0016, TMG12 0011,
TMG45 0111, TMG45 0124,
TMG45 0196, TMG45 0217,
TMG45 0261, TMGCD 0008,
TMGCD 0028, TMGLP 0068,
TMGLP 0077, TMGLP 0108,
TMGLP 0132, TMGLP 0190,
TMGLP 0213, WOLP 0016

Fox Fire
PR45 0005

Frazier, Joe
MO45 0391, PR45 0013

The Freeman Brothers
SO45 0011

Fresh
PR45 0029, PR45 0032, PR45 0035,
PRLP 0018, PRLP 0022

Friendly Enemies
PRLP 0020

The G. B. Experience
TMG12 0008

Gammon, Patrick
MO45 0482, MOLP 0327

Gardener, Stu
CH45 0001, CH45 0002, CH45 0008,
CHCO 0001

Garrett, Siedah
TMG45 0121

Gaye, Marvin
GOEP 0006, MO12 0017, MO12 0018,
MO45 0068, MO45 0139, MO45 0281,
MO45 0292, MO45 0309, MO45 0470,
MO45 0471, MOCB 0006, MOCO 0036,
MOCO 0037, MOEP 0016, MOEP 0019,
MOLP 0014, MOLP 0193, MOLP 0205,
NALP 0015, TA45 0024, TA45 0038,
TA45 0046, TA45 0051, TA45 0058,
TA45 0062, TA45 0070, TA45 0078,
TA45 0084, TA45 0087, TA45 0090,
TA45 0096, TA45 0101, TA45 0107,
TA45 0114, TA45 0117, TA45 0123,
TA45 0126, TA45 0134, TA45 0138,
TA45 0141, TA45 0145, TA45 0146,
TA45 0148, TA45 0154, TA45 0155,

TA45 0158, TA45 0161, TA45 0164,
TA45 0166, TA45 0170, TA45 0172,
TA45 0175, TA45 0177, TA45 0180,
TA45 0187, TA45 0195, TA45 0197,
TA45 0210, TA45 0217, TA45 0218,
TA45 0223, TA45 0231, TA45 0234,
TA45 0243, TA45 0244, TA45 0245,
TA45 0256, TA45 0257, TA45 0266,
TA45 0275, TA45 0293, TA45 0295,
TA45 0300, TA45 0317, TA45 0321,
TA45S 0002, TA45S 0004,
TACO 0009, TACO 0010, TACO 0016,
TACO 0017, TAEP 0001, TAEP 0004,
TALP 0002, TALP 0020, TALP 0023,
TALP 0032, TALP 0033, TALP 0039,
TALP 0040, TALP 0041, TALP 0042,
TALP 0047, TALP 0051, TALP 0058,
TALP 0059, TALP 0065, TALP 0066,
TALP 0073, TALP 0074, TALP 0075,
TALP 0080, TALP 0081, TALP 0083,
TALP 0091, TALP 0097, TALP 0103,
TALP 0104, TALP 0110, TALP 0114,
TALP 0123, TALP 0129, TALP 0133,
TALP 0135, TALP 0146, TALP 0151,
TALP 0156, TMG45 0242, TMG45 0243,
TMGCD 0011, TMGCD 0014,
TMGCD 0016, TMGCD 0037,
TMGLP 0060, TMGLP 0071,
TMGLP 0078, TMGLP 0085,
TMGLP 0155, TMGLP 0174,
TMGLP 0193, TMGLP 0199,
TMGLP 0201, TMGLP 0203

Gaye, Marvin & Kim Weston
TA45 0087, TA45 0126, TALP 0041,
TALP 0051

Gaye, Marvin & Mary Wells
MO45 0068, MOLP 0014

Gaye, Marvin & Tammi Terrell
TA45 0134, TA45 0141, TA45 0146,
TA45 0148, TA45 0154, TA45 0158,
TA45 0164, TA45 0172, TA45 0177,
TACO 0010, TALP 0058, TALP 0065,
TALP 0075, TALP 0083, TMGLP 0085

Gaylord & Holiday
NA45 0001, NALP 0008, PR45 0012,
PRLP 0003

General Kane
TMG45 0272, TMG45 0279,
TMGLP 0218

George Bohannon Quartet
WO45 0006, WOLP 0006, WOLP 0013

The Gil Askey Orchestra
MO45 0232

**God Squad featuring Leonard
Caston**
RALP 0028

Golden Harmoneers
MO45 0024

Goldstein, William
MO45 0386, MO45 0414

**Goldstein, William & The Magic
Disco Machine**
MO45 0414

Good, Tommy
GO45 0035

Gooding, Cuba
MO45 0454, MOLP 0300, MOLP 0324

Gordy, Raynoma
MI45 0002

Gordy, Robert
GO45 0004, GO45 0009, TA45 0034

Gore, Leslie

MW45 0030, MW45 0044, MWLP 0017
Gorman, Freddie
MI45 0011
Gospel Stars
DI45 0003, TA45 0020, TALP 0003
Gotham
NALP 0004
Graffiti Orchestra
PR45 0025
Graham, Rita
PR45 0016
Green, Al
TMGCD 0019, TMGCD 0041,
TMGLP 0113
Green, Kathe
MO45 0359, MO45 0385, MO45 0403,
MOLP 0258, PRLP 0005
Greer, Paula
WO45 0003, WO45 0007, WOLP 0002,
WOLP 0003
Greer, Paula and Johnny Griffith
Trio
WOLP 0003
Griffin, Herman
MO45 0037, TA45 0015
Griffin, William
TA45 0227, TALP 0106
Griffith, Johnny
WO45 0005, WOLP 0003, WOLP 0004
Griner, Linda
MO45 0046
Groce, Larry
MCLP 0015
Guinn
TMG45 0257, TMGLP 0170
The Guinn Family
TMG45 0241
Haines, Connie
MO45 0103
Hamilton, Dave
WO45 0004, WOLP 0005
Hammer, Jack
SO45 0088
Hand, Chip
MO45 0380, PR45 0015
Haney, Jack
ME45 0007
Haney, Jack and "Nikiter"
Armstrong
ME45 0007
Harnell, Joe
MO45 0165, MO45 0172, MOLP 0099
Harris, Sam
TMG12 0024, TMG12 0057,
TMG12 0061, TMG45 0149,
TMG45 0177, TMG45 0186,
TMG45 0235, TMG45 0247,
TMGLP 0105, TMGLP 0167
Hartfield, Pete
MI45 0008
The Headliners
VI45 0010, VI45 0025
Heard, Oma
VI45 0007
Heart
NALP 0002
Hearts Of Stone
VI45 0057, VI45 0063, VICO 0004,
VILP 0005
Henderson, Finis
TMG45 0071, TMG45 0100,
TMGLP 0037

Henderson, Wes
RA45 0003
Henry, Virgil
TA45 0201
Henslee, Gene
ME45 0010
Hernandez, Danny
RA45 0014, RACO 0004
Hernandez, Danny and The Ones
RA45 0014, RACO 0004
High Inergy
GO45 0156, GO45 0157, GO45 0159,
GO45 0162, GO45 0163, GO45 0168,
GO45 0174, GO45 0176, GO45 0181,
GO45 0190, GO45 0195, GO45 0204,
GO45 0210, GO45 0214, GOCO 0013,
GOLP 0078, GOLP 0084, GOLP 0089,
GOLP 0091, GOLP 0098, GOLP 0106,
MO12 0022, TMG12 0007, TMG45 0014,
TMG45 0034, TMG45 0043,
TMG45 0058, TMG45 0064,
TMG45 0088, TMG45 0092,
TMGLP 0007, TMGLP 0042
Hill, Tommy
MO45 0535
Hillsiders
ME45 0020
Hinton, Joe
SO45 0080
The Hit Pack
SO45 0010
Holland, Chris
RA45 0042
Holland, Chris and T Bone
RA45 0042
Holland, Eddie
MO45 0030, MO45 0035, MO45 0039,
MO45 0040, MO45 0045, MO45 0052,
MO45 0055, MO45 0060, MO45 0063,
MO45 0069, MO45 0074, MOLP 0005,
TA45 0002
Holland-Dozier
MO45 0055
Holloway, Brenda
TA45 0077, TA45 0082, TA45 0095,
TA45 0099, TA45 0106, TA45 0110,
TA45 0122, TA45 0129, TA45 0133,
TA45 0140, TA45S 0006, TACO 0003,
TALP 0038, TALP 0054
The Honest Men
VI45 0046
Horn, Bob
MO45 0358
Horne, Lena
MO45 0409
The Hornets
VI45 0003
Houston, Thelma
MO12 0002, MO12 0013, MO12 0016,
MO12 0034, MO45 0257, MO45 0272,
MO45 0329, MO45 0398, MO45 0436,
MOLP 0290, MOLP 0306, MW45 0008,
MW45 0013, MW45 0028, MW45 0048,
MW45 0052, MWCO 0001, MWCO 0002,
MWLP 0002, TA45 0268, TA45 0269,
TA45 0272, TA45 0273, TA45 0278,
TA45 0282, TA45 0287, TA45 0290,
TA45 0292, TALP 0126, TALP 0140,
TALP 0143, TALP 0147, TMGLP 0035
Houston, Thelma & Jerry Butler
MO45 0436, MOLP 0290, MOLP 0306
Howell, Reuben

MO45 0240, MO45 0286, MO45 0318,
MO45 0338, MOLP 0173, MOLP 0201
Howl the Good
RA45 0041, RALP 0034
Hughes, Langston
BFLP 0003
Hughes, Langston & Margaret
Danner
BFLP 0003
Hutch, Willie
MO12 0003, MO45 0234, MO45 0264,
MO45 0294, MO45 0300, MO45 0305,
MO45 0344, MO45 0352, MO45 0373,
MO45 0384, MO45 0420, MO45 0425,
MO45 0430, MO45 0438, MO45 0447,
MOCO 0031, MOLP 0168, MOLP 0186,
MOLP 0213, MOLP 0217, MOLP 0240,
MOLP 0256, MOLP 0273, MOLP 0276,
MW45 0037, TMG12 0002, TMG12 0035,
TMG45 0039, TMG45 0203,
TMGLP 0144
Ikeda, Suzee
MO45 0249, MW45 0004, MW45 0017
Impact of Brass
RA45 0024, RALP 0026
Isley Brothers
TA45 0113, TA45 0118, TA45 0120,
TA45 0131, TA45 0139, TA45 0149,
TA45 0160, TA45 0167, TALP 0050,
TALP 0056, TALP 0068, VI45 0019
Ivy Jo
VI45 0054, VI45 0062, VICO 0003,
VILP 0007
Jackson, Chuck
MO45 0129, MO45 0155, MO45 0163,
MO45 0171, MOLP 0068, MOLP 0088,
VI45 0051, VI45 0055, VI45 0058,
VI45 0066, VILP 0004
Jackson, Jackie
MOLP 0159, MOLP 0187
Jackson, Jermaine
MO12 0001, MO45 0213, MO45 0228,
MO45 0239, MO45 0256, MO45 0399,
MO45 0415, MO45 0423, MO45 0455,
MO45 0486, MO45 0507, MO45 0518,
MO45 0522, MO45 0544, MOCO 0038,
MOCO 0039, MOLP 0154, MOLP 0177,
MOLP 0232, MOLP 0244, MOLP 0291,
MOLP 0301, MOLP 0316, MOLP 0333,
MOLP 0353, MOLP 0357, TMG45 0001,
TMG45 0030, TMG45 0051,
TMGLP 0018, TMGLP 0196
Jackson, Michael
MO45 0203, MO45 0209, MO45 0214,
MO45 0219, MO45 0230, MO45 0282,
MO45 0354, MO45 0362, MO45 0531,
MOLP 0149, MOLP 0157, MOLP 0169,
MOLP 0227, MOLP 0253, MOLP 0267,
MOLP 0361, TMG45 0145, TMG45 0163,
TMGCD 0001, TMGLP 0079,
TMGLP 0103, TMGLP 0196,
TMGLP 0197
Jackson, Michael & The Jackson 5
TMGLP 0072, TMGLP 0101,
TMGLP 0102
The Jackson 5
MO45 0168, MO45 0174, MO45 0177,
MO45 0183, MO45 0186, MO45 0189,
MO45 0191, MO45 0198, MO45 0206,
MO45 0211, MO45 0217, MO45 0226,
MO45 0236, MO45 0242, MO45 0289,
MO45 0299, MO45 0321, MO45 0323,

MO45 0369, MO45 0388, MOCO 0013,
MOCO 0014, MOCO 0016, MOCO 0021,
MOCO 0026, MOCO 0029, MOCO 0030,
MOLP 0101, MOLP 0110, MOLP 0114,
MOLP 0119, MOLP 0120, MOLP 0136,
MOLP 0143, MOLP 0144, MOLP 0152,
MOLP 0163, MOLP 0182, MOLP 0185,
MOLP 0231, MOLP 0267, MOLP 0270,
NALP 0021, TA45 0242, TMG12 0011,
TMGCD 0012, TMGCD 0020,
TMGLP 0072, TMGLP 0101,
TMGLP 0102, TMGLP 0196,
TMGLP 0197

The Jackson 5 featuring Michael
Jackson
MOLP 0267

The Jaguars
TA45S 0001

Jakata
TMG45 0156, TMG45 0184,
TMGLP 0062

Jamal, Ahmad
MOLP 0350

James, Keef
RALP 0036

James, Rick
GO45 0158, GO45 0164, GO45 0166,
GO45 0169, GO45 0173, GO45 0179,
GO45 0180, GO45 0188, GO45 0194,
GO45 0200, GO45 0208, GO45 0218,
GOLP 0083, GOLP 0086, GOLP 0092,
GOLP 0093, GOLP 0097, GOLP 0103,
MO12 0015, MO12 0040, MO12 0041,
MOLP 0098, TMG12 0012, TMG12 0023,
TMG12 0029, TMG12 0040,
TMG12 0062, TMG12 0066,
TMG45 0017, TMG45 0020,
TMG45 0036, TMG45 0048,
TMG45 0060, TMG45 0091,
TMG45 0108, TMG45 0120,
TMG45 0136, TMG45 0169,
TMG45 0182, TMG45 0202,
TMG45 0212, TMG45 0251,
TMG45 0269, TMGCD 0013,
TMGLP 0006, TMGLP 0044,
TMGLP 0080, TMGLP 0097,
TMGLP 0137, TMGLP 0187

James, Rick & Smokey Robinson
TMG45 0120

Jameson, Nick
TMG45 0260, TMGLP 0156,
TMGLP 0212

Jarrell, Phillip
PR45 0028, PRLP 0014

Jay And The Techniques
GO45 0124

Jazz Crusaders
CH45 0011, CH45 0014, CHEP 0001,
CHLP 0004

Jennifer
MO12 0008, MO45 0431

Jerry Ross Symposium
MO45 0221, MO45 0227, MOLP 0156

Joanne & The Triangles
VI45 0002

John, Mable
TA45 0014, TA45 0023, TA45 0033,
TA45 0064

John, Robert
TMG45 0066

The John Wagner Coalition
RA45 0047

Johnny Griffith Trio
WO45 0005, WOLP 0003, WOLP 0004

Johnson, Harold
MO45 0464, MO45 0480

Johnson, Marv
GO45 0043, GO45 0052, GO45 0078,
GOLP 0037, TA45 0001

Johnson, Stacie
MO45 0248, MOLP 0178, MW45 0049,
MWLP 0023

Johnson, Terry
GO45 0092, GO45 0096

Johnson, Troy
TMG45 0237, TMGLP 0168

Jones, Gloria
MO45 0268, MOLP 0192

Jones, Jonah
MO45 0156, MOLP 0084, MOLP 0091,
MOLP 0115

Jones, Red
MOLP 0092

Jordan, Porter
MC45 0006, MCLP 0004

Ju-Par Universal Orchestra
JU45 0002, JULP 0001

Jupiter, Duke
TMG45 0142, TMG45 0154,
TMG45 0221, TMGLP 0099,
TMGLP 0164

Kagny
TMG45 0074, TMG45 0150,
TMGLP 0039, TMGLP 0106

Kagny & The Dirty Rats
TMG45 0074, TMGLP 0039

Kah'rl, Franki
GO45 0154

Kayli, Bob
GO45 0004, GO45 0009, TA45 0034

Keith & Darrell
TA45 0302, TA45 0304, TA45 0325,
TMG12 0017, TMG45 0118

Kelly, Karen
ML45 0008

Kendricks, Eddie
MO12 0003, MO12 0009, TA45 0189,
TA45 0190, TA45 0191, TA45 0198,
TA45 0199, TA45 0207, TA45 0211,
TA45 0219, TA45 0226, TA45 0228,
TA45 0233, TA45 0237, TA45 0239,
TA45 0247, TA45 0249, TA45 0252,
TA45 0255, TA45 0259, TA45 0263,
TA45 0271, TA45 0280, TA45 0285,
TACO 0013, TACO 0014, TACO 0018,
TALP 0090, TALP 0096, TALP 0108,
TALP 0111, TALP 0116, TALP 0119,
TALP 0124, TALP 0127, TALP 0136,
TALP 0138

Kidd Glove
TMG45 0123, TMGLP 0058

King, Bobby
TMG12 0019, TMG45 0132,
TMG45 0153, TMGLP 0090

King, Bobby with Alfie Silas
TMG45 0153

King, Dr. Martin Luther, Jr.
BFLP 0001, GOLP 0029

King Floyd
VI45 0060, VILP 0008

King, Rev. Martin Luther, Jr.
BFLP 0001, GO45 0024, GOLP 0006,
GOLP 0008, GOLP 0029, TMG12 0018

Knight, Gladys

CHEP 0002, MO45 0139, MOLP 0194,
NALP 0012, SO45 0023, SO45 0033,
SO45 0034, SO45 0039, SO45 0042,
SO45 0045, SO45 0047, SO45 0057,
SO45 0063, SO45 0068, SO45 0071,
SO45 0078, SO45 0083, SO45 0091,
SO45 0094, SO45 0098, SO45 0105,
SO45 0107, SO45 0111, SOLP 0006,
SOLP 0007, SOLP 0011, SOLP 0013,
SOLP 0023, SOLP 0030, SOLP 0031,
SOLP 0036, SOLP 0037, SOLP 0039,
SOLP 0041, SOLP 0044, TMGCD 0009,
TMGCD 0032, TMGLP 0111,
TMGLP 0202

Knight, Gladys & The Pips
CHEP 0002, MO45 0139, MOLP 0194,
NALP 0012, SO45 0023, SO45 0033,
SO45 0034, SO45 0039, SO45 0042,
SO45 0045, SO45 0047, SO45 0057,
SO45 0063, SO45 0068, SO45 0071,
SO45 0078, SO45 0083, SO45 0091,
SO45 0094, SO45 0098, SO45 0105,
SO45 0107, SO45 0111, SOLP 0006,
SOLP 0007, SOLP 0011, SOLP 0013,
SOLP 0023, SOLP 0030, SOLP 0031,
SOLP 0036, SOLP 0037, SOLP 0039,
SOLP 0041, SOLP 0044, TMGCD 0009,
TMGCD 0032, TMGLP 0111,
TMGLP 0202

KoKo Pop
TMG45 0139, TMG45 0165,
TMG45 0209, TMG45 0230,
TMGLP 0098, TMGLP 0157

Kubie
MW45 0033, MWLP 0022

Lands, Liz
DI45 0005, GO45 0024, GO45 0027,
GO45 0031

The LaSalles
VI45 0035

Lattislaw, Stacy
TMG45 0266, TMGLP 0214

Lavette, Bettye
MO45 0551, MO45 0552, TMG45 0015,
TMGLP 0001

Lee & The Leopards
GO45 0002

Legend
TA45 0310

Legrand, Michel
MO45 0231

The Leopards
GO45 0002

Lester
TALP 0046

Letta
CH45 0013, CHLP 0005, CHLP 0009

Leverette, Chico
TA45 0003

The Lewis Sisters
VI45 0017, VI45 0023, VI45 0030

Libra
MOLP 0249, MOLP 0266

Little Eva And Band
MI45 0002

Little Lisa
VI45 0022

Little Otis
TA45 0041

Little Richard
TMGLP 0210

Little Stevie Wonder

TA45 0044, TA45 0053, TA45 0057,
TA45 0063, TA45 0069, TA45 0073,
TALP 0013, TALP 0014, TALP 0021,
TALP 0029, TALP 0031

Littles, Hattie
GO45 0005, GO45 0008

Lodi
MW45 0003, MWLP 0001

The Lollipops
GO45 0090, VI45 0050

Long, Shorty
SO45 0001, SO45 0005, SO45 0021,
SO45 0031, SO45 0040, SO45 0044,
SO45 0054, SO45 0064, SOLP 0009,
SOLP 0019

Lost Nation
RALP 0015

Love Sculpture
RALP 0002

Lovesmith
MO45 0545, MOLP 0364, TMG45 0008

Lovesmith, Michael
TMG12 0038, TMG45 0089,
TMG45 0104, TMG45 0138,
TMG45 0155, TMG45 0197,
TMG45 0200, TMGLP 0046,
TMGLP 0095, TMGLP 0147

The Lovetones
MO45 0038, MO45 0041, MO45 0048,
TA45 0046, TA45 0049

Lumpkin, Henry
MO45 0011, MO45 0022, MO45 0038

Lupper, Kenny
TA45 0289

Lushus Daim & The Pretty Vain
TMG45 0207, TMG45 0232,
TMGLP 0152

McClary, Thomas
TMG45 0174, TMG45 0185,
TMGLP 0123

McCullers, Mickey
TA45 0047, VI45 0008

McDowell, Sparks Malcolm
TMG45 0096

McKenzie, Don
MI45 0010

McNair, Barbara
MO45 0098, MO45 0110, MO45 0117,
MO45 0123, MO45 0134, MO45 0144,
MOCO 0002, MOLP 0045, MOLP 0081

McNeir, Ronnie
MO45 0410, MO45 0424, MOLP 0272,
PR45 0004, PR45 0009, PR45 0010,
PRLP 0001

Magic
RALP 0024

The Magic Disco Machine
MO45 0375, MO45 0414, MOLP 0223

Major Lance
GOLP 0082, SO45 0124, SOLP 0051

Mallett, Saundra
TA45 0050

Mallett, Saundra & The Vandellas
TA45 0050

Mandre
MO12 0025, MO45 0443, MO45 0448,
MO45 0462, MO45 0478, MO45 0489,
MOLP 0289, MOLP 0303, MOLP 0322

Mann, Rev. Columbus
TA45 0030, TALP 0008

Marbaya
MO45 0259, MW45 0046

Martha & The Vandellas
CHEP 0002, GO45 0012, GO45 0015,
GO45 0023, GO45 0026, GO45 0028,
GO45 0032, GO45 0034, GO45 0037,
GO45 0040, GO45 0046, GO45 0049,
GO45 0054, GO45 0057, GO45 0059,
GO45 0063, GO45 0071, GO45 0076,
GO45 0081, GO45 0086, GO45 0095,
GO45 0099, GO45 0104, GO45 0111,
GO45 0114, GO45 0119, GOCO 0001,
GOCO 0010, GOEP 0002, GOEP 0005,
GOLP 0002, GOLP 0007, GOLP 0015,
GOLP 0017, GOLP 0020, GOLP 0025,
GOLP 0026, GOLP 0044, GOLP 0052,
GOLP 0058, MOCB 0007, MOCB 0014,
MOEP 0009, MOEP 0017, MOLP 0180,
TMGLP 0172

Martin & Finley
MO45 0241, MO45 0254, MO45 0307,
MOLP 0199, MW45 0041, MW45 0045,
MWLP 0020

Martin, Joey
ML45 0025

Martin, Tony
MO45 0082, MO45 0093, MO45 0099,
MOLP 0046

The Marvelettes
GOEP 0006, MOCB 0012, MOEP 0003,
MOLP 0229, TA45 0029, TA45 0037,
TA45 0043, TA45 0048, TA45 0055,
TA45 0060, TA45 0065, TA45 0071,
TA45 0074, TA45 0080, TA45 0088,
TA45 0100, TA45 0105, TA45 0111,
TA45 0116, TA45 0128, TA45 0135,
TA45 0143, TA45 0151, TA45 0156,
TA45 0162, TA45 0171, TA45 0183,
TA45 0202, TACO 0007, TAEP 0002,
TAEP 0007, TALP 0009, TALP 0010,
TALP 0012, TALP 0018, TALP 0024,
TALP 0034, TALP 0055, TALP 0067,
TALP 0069, TALP 0086, TMGLP 0171

Mary Jane Girls
TMG12 0010, TMG12 0030,
TMG12 0042, TMG12 0048,
TMG45 0072, TMG45 0094,
TMG45 0109, TMG45 0127,
TMG45 0147, TMG45 0204,
TMG45 0222, TMG45 0258,
TMGLP 0041, TMGLP 0094

Masekela, Hugh
CH45 0010, CH45 0015, CHLP 0003,
CHLP 0008

**Masekela, Hugh and The Union
Of South Africa**
CH45 0010, CH45 0015, CHLP 0008

Matrix
MO45 0314, RALP 0039

Meatloaf
PRLP 0023, RA45 0023, RA45 0029

Mello-Mackin-D & Mr. Stretch
TMG12 0047, TMG45 0220

The Merced Bluenotes
SO45 0007

Messengers
RA45 0028, RALP 0006, SO45 0037

Midnight Blue
MO45 0525

Mike & The Modifiers
GO45 0007

Milburn, Amos
MO45 0047, MO45 0057, MOLP 0009

Militello, Bobby

TMG45 0054, TMG45 0069,
TMGLP 0024

**Militello, Bobby featuring Jean
Carn**
TMG45 0054

Mills, Stephanie
MO45 0395, MOLP 0261, TMGLP 0034

The Miracle Workers
TA45 0261

The Miracles
GOEP 0006, MO45 0001, MO45 0002,
MOCB 0011, MOLP 0195, NALP 0017,
TA45 0009, TA45 0010, TA45 0019,
TA45 0027, TA45 0031, TA45 0036,
TA45 0042, TA45 0047, TA45 0052,
TA45 0056, TA45 0061, TA45 0066,
TA45 0072, TA45 0075, TA45 0081,
TA45 0085, TA45 0093, TA45 0097,
TA45 0102, TA45 0108, TA45 0112,
TA45 0119, TA45 0125, TA45 0130,
TA45 0137, TA45 0144, TA45 0147,
TA45 0152, TA45 0157, TA45 0163,
TA45 0168, TA45 0169, TA45 0174,
TA45 0179, TA45 0184, TA45 0185,
TA45 0193, TA45 0194, TA45 0200,
TA45 0209, TA45 0214, TA45 0227,
TA45 0230, TA45 0238, TA45 0248,
TA45 0251, TA45 0254, TA45 0261,
TA45 0265, TA45S 0003, TA45S 0009,
TA45S 0010, TACO 0001, TACO 0005,
TACO 0006, TACO 0008, TACO 0015,
TAEP 0003, TAEP 0005, TALP 0001,
TALP 0004, TALP 0011, TALP 0015,
TALP 0017, TALP 0019, TALP 0022,
TALP 0026, TALP 0035, TALP 0048,
TALP 0052, TALP 0057, TALP 0061,
TALP 0070, TALP 0071, TALP 0076,
TALP 0078, TALP 0082, TALP 0087,
TALP 0088, TALP 0093, TALP 0099,
TALP 0101, TALP 0102, TALP 0106,
TALP 0115, TALP 0117, TALP 0120,
TALP 0125, TALP 0139, TMGCD 0005,
TMGLP 0073, TMGLP 0198,
TMGLP 0204

**The Miracles featuring Bill
"Smokey" Robinson**
MO45S 0001, MO45S 0002,
TA45 0017

Mr. Stretch
TMG12 0047, TMG45 0220

Mitchell, Marty
HI45 0013, MC45 0005, MC45 0011,
MCLP 0011

The Modifiers
GO45 0007

The Mohawks
MO45 0008, MO45 0028

The Monitors
SO45 0049, SOLP 0014, VI45 0027,
VI45 0031, VI45 0038, VI45 0045,
VI45 0048

Montero, Pedro
TMGLP 0022

Montgomery, Monk
CH45 0003, CHCO 0002, CHLP 0001,
CHLP 0006

Morrocco Muzik Makers
MO45 0058

The Motor City Crew
TMG12 0014, TMG45 0101,
TMG45 0102

The Motortown Cut-Ups

MO45 0162
The Motown Brass
   SO45 0028
Motown Magic Disco Machine
   MOLP 0259
Motown Sounds
   MO45 0474, MOLP 0311
The Motown Strings
   MO45 0192, MOCO 0022, MOLP 0123
Mullins, Dee
   ME45 0017
Music Makers
   MO45 0259, MW45 0046
My Friends
   RA45 0032, RACO 0009
The Mynah Birds
   MOLP 0098
The Naturals
   MO45 0220
Naylor, Jerry
   HI45 0010, HI45 0015, MC45 0004,
   MC45 0010, MCLP 0002, MCLP 0003,
   ML45 0003, ML45 0012, ML45 0020
Nero, Frances
   SO45 0020
Nichols, Allan
   RA45 0016
Nick And The Jaguars
   TA45S 0001
Nolen & Crossley
   GO45 0199, GO45 0212, GOLP 0102,
   TMG45 0007, TMG45 0009,
   TMGLP 0004
Northern Lights
   NALP 0007
Nunn, Bobby
   TMG12 0003, TMG45 0045,
   TMG45 0055, TMG45 0073,
   TMG45 0086, TMG45 0099,
   TMG45 0117, TMG45 0130,
   TMGLP 0023, TMGLP 0052,
   TMGLP 0120
The Nu Page
   MW45 0039
Oddis, Ray
   VI45 0011
Odyssey
   MW45 0023, MWLP 0015
The Ones
   MO45 0128, MO45 0141, MOCO 0004,
   MOCO 0006, RA45 0014, RACO 0004
Orange Sunshine
   PR45 0011
The Originals
   MO12 0001, MO45 0297, MO45 0368,
   MO45 0383, MO45 0392, MOLP 0228,
   SO45 0029, SO45 0056, SO45 0061,
   SO45 0066, SO45 0069, SO45 0074,
   SO45 0079, SO45 0085, SO45 0093,
   SO45 0102, SO45 0109, SO45 0113,
   SO45 0114, SO45 0116, SO45 0118,
   SO45 0120, SO45 0122, SOLP 0016,
   SOLP 0024, SOLP 0029, SOLP 0034,
   SOLP 0040, SOLP 0043, SOLP 0046,
   SOLP 0049
Other People
   RALP 0030
Ozone
   MO45 0504, MO45 0529, MO45 0537,
   MO45 0540, MO45 0548, MOLP 0343,
   MOLP 0355, MOLP 0367, TMG12 0005,
   TMG45 0006, TMG45 0018,

TMG45 0029, TMG45 0070,
   TMG45 0095, TMGLP 0012,
   TMGLP 0038
Pagan, Bruni
   TMG12 0026
Page, Lawanda
   TMGLP 0026
Pal
   TMG45 0216, TMGLP 0159
Parker, Eddie
   PR45 0007
Parks, Gino
   MI45 0003, TA45 0025, TA45 0049,
   TA45 0092
The Pat Boone Family
   MO45 0327
Paul, Bunny
   GO45 0018
Paul, Clarence
   TA45 0053
Payne, Ernie
   MC45 0009, ML45 0026
Payne, Scherrie
   MO45 0363, MO45 0445
Peterson, Paul
   MO45 0119, MO45 0140
The Pips
   CHEP 0002, MO45 0139, MOLP 0194,
   NALP 0012, SO45 0023, SO45 0033,
   SO45 0034, SO45 0039, SO45 0042,
   SO45 0045, SO45 0047, SO45 0057,
   SO45 0063, SO45 0068, SO45 0071,
   SO45 0078, SO45 0083, SO45 0091,
   SO45 0094, SO45 0098, SO45 0105,
   SO45 0107, SO45 0111, SOLP 0006,
   SOLP 0007, SOLP 0011, SOLP 0013,
   SOLP 0023, SOLP 0030, SOLP 0031,
   SOLP 0036, SOLP 0037, SOLP 0039,
   SOLP 0041, SOLP 0044, TMGCD 0009,
   TMGCD 0032, TMGLP 0111,
   TMGLP 0202
Pirates
   ME45 0005
P.J.
   TA45 0204, VI45 0061
The Planets
   MO45 0502, MOLP 0339
Platinum Hook
   MO12 0032, MO45 0461, MO45 0481,
   MO45 0517, MOLP 0302, MOLP 0323,
   MOLP 0348
Pointer, Bonnie
   MO12 0014, MO12 0023, MO45 0466,
   MO45 0476, MO45 0495, MO45 0501,
   MOCO 0034, MOLP 0314, MOLP 0334
Poor Boys
   RALP 0016
Popcorn & The Mohawks
   MO45 0008, MO45 0028
Posse
   VI45 0068
Power of Zeus
   RALP 0013
Preston, Billy
   MO12 0019, MO45 0477, MO45 0487,
   MO45 0494, MO45 0515, MO45 0524,
   MO45 0530, MO45 0539, MO45 0541,
   MOLP 0320, MOLP 0330, MOLP 0346,
   MOLP 0363, TA45 0307, TA45 0314,
   TMG45 0027, TMG45 0277,
   TMGLP 0021
Preston, Billy & Syreeta

MO12 0019, MO45 0477, MO45 0494,
   MO45 0515, MO45 0539, MO45 0541,
   MOLP 0320, MOLP 0363, TA45 0307,
   TA45 0314
Pretty Things
   RA45 0001, RALP 0003, RALP 0012,
   RALP 0046
The Pretty Vain
   TMG45 0207, TMG45 0232,
   TMGLP 0152
Prime Time
   MO45 0458, MOLP 0308
Prince, Dave
   RA45 0035
Proctor, Billy
   SO45 0099
Puzzle
   MO45 0276, MO45 0295, MO45 0315,
   MOLP 0170, MOLP 0209, RA45 0046,
   RALP 0041
Quatro, Michael
   PR45 0018, PR45 0021, PRLP 0004,
   PRLP 0010
Quiet Storm
   TA45 0305, TA45 0309, TA45 0326
Qwick, Fizzy
   TMG45 0245, TMG45 0271,
   TMGLP 0181
Rabbit, Bob
   SO45 0101
Randolph, Barbara
   SO45 0038, SO45 0050, SOLP 0012
Randolph, Jimmy
   MO45 0255
Rare Earth
   PR45 0027, PR45 0030, PR45 0033,
   PRLP 0013, PRLP 0019, PRLP 0021,
   RA45 0006, RA45 0008, RA45 0013,
   RA45 0017, RA45 0027, RA45 0034,
   RA45 0039, RA45 0044, RA45 0048,
   RA45 0049, RA45 0050, RA45 0052,
   RA45 0053, RA45 0054, RA45 0055,
   RA45 0056, RACO 0011, RACO 0012,
   RALP 0004, RALP 0007, RALP 0011,
   RALP 0017, RALP 0031, RALP 0040,
   RALP 0043, RALP 0045, RALP 0047,
   TMGCD 0034
Rayber Voices
   TA45 0001, TA45 0011, TA45 0016
Rednow, Eivets
   GO45 0077, GOLP 0032
Reed, Jimmy
   TMGLP 0208
Reeves, Martha
   CHEP 0002, GO45 0012, GO45 0015,
   GO45 0023, GO45 0026, GO45 0028,
   GO45 0032, GO45 0034, GO45 0037,
   GO45 0040, GO45 0046, GO45 0049,
   GO45 0054, GO45 0057, GO45 0059,
   GO45 0063, GO45 0068, GO45 0071,
   GO45 0076, GO45 0081, GO45 0086,
   GO45 0095, GO45 0099, GO45 0104,
   GO45 0111, GO45 0114, GO45 0119,
   GO45 0128, GOCO 0001, GOCO 0010,
   GOEP 0002, GOEP 0005, GOLP 0002,
   GOLP 0007, GOLP 0015, GOLP 0017,
   GOLP 0020, GOLP 0025, GOLP 0026,
   GOLP 0044, GOLP 0052, GOLP 0058,
   GOLP 0060, MOCB 0007, MOCB 0014,
   MOEP 0017, MOLP 0180, TMGLP 0172
Reeves, Martha & The Vandellas
   CHEP 0002, GO45 0012, GO45 0015,

GO45 0023, GO45 0026, GO45 0028,
GO45 0032, GO45 0034, GO45 0037,
GO45 0040, GO45 0046, GO45 0049,
GO45 0054, GO45 0057, GO45 0059,
GO45 0063, GO45 0068, GO45 0071,
GO45 0076, GO45 0081, GO45 0086,
GO45 0095, GO45 0099, GO45 0104,
GO45 0111, GO45 0114, GO45 0119,
GO45 0128, GOCO 0001, GOCO 0010,
GOEP 0002, GOEP 0005, GOLP 0002,
GOLP 0007, GOLP 0015, GOLP 0017,
GOLP 0020, GOLP 0025, GOLP 0026,
GOLP 0044, GOLP 0052, GOLP 0058,
GOLP 0060, MOCB 0007, MOCB 0014,
MOEP 0017, MOLP 0180, TMGLP 0172

Regal Funkharmonic Orchestra
TMG45 0031, TMGLP 0015

Remus, Eugene
MO45 0005, MO45 0006, MO45 0007

Repairs
MW45 0032, MWLP 0021, RALP 0029

Richie, Lionel
MO45 0538, TMG12 0015, TMG45 0046,
TMG45 0059, TMG45 0081,
TMG45 0103, TMG45 0116,
TMG45 0128, TMG45 0152,
TMG45 0168, TMG45 0225,
TMG45 0250, TMG45 0273,
TMG45 0280, TMGLP 0008,
TMGLP 0061, TMGLP 0145,
TMGLP 0160, TMGLP 0199

Rick, Robin & Him
VI45 0034

Riot
MO45 0277, MO45 0325, MO45 0331,
MOLP 0208

Road
NALP 0005

Robinson, Claudette
TA45 0313

Robinson, Smokey
MO12 0005, MO12 0007, MO12 0018,
MO12 0030, MO45 0470, MO45 0471,
MO45S 0001, MO45S 0002,
MOCO 0036, MOCO 0037, MOLP 0195,
NALP 0017, TA45 0005, TA45 0017,
TA45 0130, TA45 0137, TA45 0144,
TA45 0147, TA45 0152, TA45 0157,
TA45 0163, TA45 0168, TA45 0169,
TA45 0174, TA45 0179, TA45 0184,
TA45 0185, TA45 0193, TA45 0194,
TA45 0200, TA45 0209, TA45 0214,
TA45 0222, TA45 0229, TA45 0236,
TA45 0240, TA45 0241, TA45 0250,
TA45 0253, TA45 0258, TA45 0260,
TA45 0262, TA45 0270, TA45 0274,
TA45 0279, TA45 0283, TA45 0288,
TA45 0291, TA45 0296, TA45 0301,
TA45 0306, TA45 0308, TA45 0313,
TA45 0316, TA45 0320, TA45 0322,
TA45 0323, TA45 0328, TA45S 0009,
TACO 0005, TACO 0006, TACO 0008,
TACO 0015, TAEP 0005, TALP 0048,
TALP 0052, TALP 0057, TALP 0061,
TALP 0070, TALP 0071, TALP 0076,
TALP 0078, TALP 0082, TALP 0087,
TALP 0088, TALP 0093, TALP 0099,
TALP 0101, TALP 0102, TALP 0109,
TALP 0112, TALP 0118, TALP 0122,
TALP 0131, TALP 0137, TALP 0141,
TALP 0145, TALP 0148, TALP 0149,
TALP 0157, TMG12 0006, TMG12 0022,

TMG45 0002, TMG45 0016,
TMG45 0032, TMG45 0057,
TMG45 0082, TMG45 0088,
TMG45 0105, TMG45 0120,
TMG45 0141, TMG45 0162,
TMG45 0192, TMG45 0234,
TMG45 0244, TMG45 0246,
TMG45 0262, TMGCD 0002,
TMGCD 0005, TMGCD 0029,
TMGLP 0002, TMGLP 0031,
TMGLP 0042, TMGLP 0066,
TMGLP 0073, TMGLP 0091,
TMGLP 0100, TMGLP 0158,
TMGLP 0198, TMGLP 0204

Robinson, Smokey & High Inergy
TMG45 0088

Robinson, Smokey & Syreeta
TMG45 0192

Robinson, Smokey & The
Miracles see also The
Miracles

Robinson, Smokey & The Miracles
MOLP 0195, NALP 0017, TA45 0130,
TA45 0137, TA45 0144, TA45 0147,
TA45 0152, TA45 0157, TA45 0163,
TA45 0168, TA45 0169, TA45 0174,
TA45 0179, TA45 0184, TA45 0185,
TA45 0193, TA45 0194, TA45 0200,
TA45 0209, TA45 0214, TA45S 0009,
TACO 0005, TACO 0006, TACO 0008,
TACO 0015, TAEP 0005, TALP 0048,
TALP 0052, TALP 0057, TALP 0061,
TALP 0070, TALP 0071, TALP 0076,
TALP 0078, TALP 0082, TALP 0087,
TALP 0088, TALP 0093, TALP 0099,
TALP 0101, TALP 0102, TMGCD 0005,
TMGLP 0073, TMGLP 0198,
TMGLP 0204

Rockwell
TMG12 0016, TMG12 0032,
TMG12 0067, TMG45 0107,
TMG45 0137, TMG45 0178,
TMG45 0188, TMG45 0252,
TMG45 0270, TMGLP 0053,
TMGLP 0124, TMGLP 0180

Ron & Bill
TA45 0005

Roq-In Zoo
TMG12 0055, TMG45 0231

Ross, Diana
MO12 0013, MO12 0014, MO12 0018,
MO12 0029, MO12 0038, MO45 0122,
MO45 0127, MO45 0133, MO45 0136,
MO45 0137, MO45 0146, MO45 0148,
MO45 0150, MO45 0153, MO45 0157,
MO45 0159, MO45 0161, MO45 0164,
MO45 0167, MO45 0176, MO45 0181,
MO45 0188, MO45 0196, MO45 0200,
MO45 0204, MO45 0223, MO45 0251,
MO45 0281, MO45 0290, MO45 0292,
MO45 0308, MO45 0309, MO45 0348,
MO45 0390, MO45 0400, MO45 0406,
MO45 0412, MO45 0441, MO45 0450,
MO45 0456, MO45 0463, MO45 0465,
MO45 0470, MO45 0471, MO45 0472,
MO45 0479, MO45 0488, MO45 0505,
MO45 0508, MO45 0509, MO45 0512,
MO45 0514, MO45 0527, MO45 0532,
MO45 0538, MO45 0542, MO45 0550,
MOCB 0001, MOCB 0002, MOCB 0003,
MOCB 0015, MOCB 0016, MOCO 0005,
MOCO 0008, MOCO 0009, MOCO 0011,

MOCO 0012, MOCO 0015, MOCO 0020,
MOCO 0023, MOCO 0032, MOCO 0036,
MOCO 0037, MOLP 0064, MOLP 0066,
MOLP 0071, MOLP 0073, MOLP 0077,
MOLP 0080, MOLP 0083, MOLP 0090,
MOLP 0093, MOLP 0095, MOLP 0100,
MOLP 0103, MOLP 0107, MOLP 0109,
MOLP 0112, MOLP 0120, MOLP 0124,
MOLP 0125, MOLP 0160, MOLP 0161,
MOLP 0174, MOLP 0196, MOLP 0203,
MOLP 0205, MOLP 0214, MOLP 0219,
MOLP 0260, MOLP 0263, MOLP 0271,
MOLP 0280, MOLP 0293, MOLP 0310,
MOLP 0319, MOLP 0328, MOLP 0341,
MOLP 0356, MOLP 0365, NALP 0014,
NALP 0018, NALP 0028, TMG45 0028,
TMGCD 0003, TMGCD 0016,
TMGCD 0027, TMGCD 0030,
TMGCD 0033, TMGCD 0039,
TMGCD 0042, TMGLP 0050,
TMGLP 0074, TMGLP 0075,
TMGLP 0084, TMGLP 0107,
TMGLP 0135, TMGLP 0145,
TMGLP 0199, TMGLP 0200

Ross, Diana and Lionel Richie
MO45 0538

Ross, Diana & Marvin Gaye
MO45 0281, MO45 0292, MO45 0309,
MOLP 0205

Ross, Diana and The Supremes
see also The
Supremes

Ross, Diana and The Supremes
MO12 0038, MO45 0122, MO45 0127,
MO45 0133, MO45 0136, MO45 0137,
MO45 0146, MO45 0150, MO45 0157,
MO45 0159, MO45 0167, MO45 0505,
MO45 0542, MOCB 0001, MOCB 0002,
MOCB 0003, MOCB 0015, MOCB 0016,
MOCO 0005, MOCO 0008, MOCO 0009,
MOCO 0012, MOLP 0064, MOLP 0066,
MOLP 0071, MOLP 0073, MOLP 0077,
MOLP 0090, MOLP 0095, MOLP 0103,
MOLP 0109, MOLP 0196, NALP 0014,
NALP 0018, TMGCD 0030, TMGCD 003
TMGCD 0042, TMGLP 0075,
TMGLP 0200

**Ross, Diana and The Supremes
and The Temptations**
MO45 0148, MO45 0153, MO45 0161,
MO45 0164, MOCO 0011, MOLP 0080,
MOLP 0083, MOLP 0093, MOLP 0100,
NALP 0028, TMGCD 0039

**Ross, Diana, Marvin Gaye,
Smokey Robinson, Stevie
Wonder**
MO12 0018, MO45 0470, MO45 0471,
MOCO 0036, MOCO 0037

Ross, Jerry
MO45 0221, MO45 0227, MOLP 0156

Ruffin, David
MO45 0151, MO45 0160, MO45 0169,
MO45 0190, MO45 0199, MO45 0216,
MO45 0235, MO45 0271, MO45 0340,
MO45 0345, MO45 0349, MO45 0389,
MO45 0401, MO45 0407, MO45 0419,
MO45 0434, MO45 0449, MOCO 0010,
MOLP 0086, MOLP 0097, MOLP 0134,
MOLP 0164, MOLP 0220, MOLP 0251,
MOLP 0268, MOLP 0288, MOLP 0298,
SO45 0076, SO45 0082, SO45 0086,
SOLP 0028

MO45 0494, MO45 0515, MO45 0539,
MO45 0541, MOCO 0028, MOLP 0210,
MOLP 0246, MOLP 0320, MOLP 0363,
MW45 0016, MW45 0022, MWCO 0003,
MWLP 0013, TA45 0307, TA45 0314,
TA45 0329, TALP 0130, TALP 0154,
TALP 0158, TMG12 0001, TMG45 0011,
TMG45 0078, TMG45 0079,
TMG45 0192, TMGLP 0040

Syreeta & G. C. Cameron
MO45 0440, MOLP 0294

Tattoo
PRLP 0008

Taylor, Bobby
GO45 0070, GO45 0074, GO45 0080,
GO45 0089, GO45 0093, GOCO 0002,
GOLP 0030, GOLP 0042, MW45 0006,
VI45 0052, VICO 0002

Taylor, Bobby & The Vancouvers
GO45 0070, GO45 0074, GO45 0080,
GOCO 0002, GOLP 0030

Taylor, R. Dean
RA45 0009, RA45 0019, RA45 0022,
RA45 0026, RA45 0037, RACO 0002,
RACO 0006, RACO 0007, RALP 0019,
VI45 0026, VI45 0041, VI45 0044

Taylor, Sheila
ML45 0013

Taylor, Sherri
MO45 0010

**Taylor, Sherri & Singin' Sammy
Ward**
MO45 0010

T Bone
RA45 0042

T-Boy Ross
MOLP 0317

Teena Marie
GO45 0171, GO45 0175, GO45 0183,
GO45 0187, GO45 0192, GO45 0197,
GO45 0205, GO45 0215, GO45 0219,
GOLP 0088, GOLP 0094, GOLP 0099,
GOLP 0105, MO12 0027, MO12 0039,
TMGCD 0004, TMGLP 0184

The Temptations
GO45 0001, GO45 0011, GO45 0016,
GO45 0021, GO45 0029, GO45 0031,
GO45 0033, GO45 0036, GO45 0039,
GO45 0041, GO45 0044, GO45 0048,
GO45 0050, GO45 0055, GO45 0056,
GO45 0058, GO45 0062, GO45 0064,
GO45 0066, GO45 0069, GO45 0073,
GO45 0075, GO45 0082, GO45 0083,
GO45 0085, GO45 0087, GO45 0094,
GO45 0097, GO45 0100, GO45 0103,
GO45 0106, GO45 0110, GO45 0112,
GO45 0116, GO45 0120, GO45 0122,
GO45 0127, GO45 0130, GO45 0132,
GO45 0134, GO45 0136, GO45 0137,
GO45 0139, GO45 0143, GO45 0145,
GO45 0147, GO45 0151, GO45 0152,
GO45 0153, GO45 0186, GO45 0191,
GO45 0211, GO45 0216, GOCO 0003,
GOCO 0007, GOCO 0008, GOCO 0012,
GOCO 0015, GOEP 0001, GOEP 0003,
GOEP 0004, GOLP 0011, GOLP 0012,
GOLP 0014, GOLP 0018, GOLP 0019,
GOLP 0021, GOLP 0022, GOLP 0024,
GOLP 0027, GOLP 0033, GOLP 0038,
GOLP 0039, GOLP 0047, GOLP 0048,
GOLP 0051, GOLP 0053, GOLP 0054,
GOLP 0057, GOLP 0061, GOLP 0062,

GOLP 0065, GOLP 0066, GOLP 0069,
GOLP 0071, GOLP 0073, GOLP 0075,
GOLP 0096, GOLP 0100, GOLP 0107,
ME45 0005, MI45 0005, MI45 0012,
MO45 0148, MO45 0153, MO45 0161,
MO45 0164, MO45 0520, MOCB 0004,
MOCB 0013, MOCO 0011, MOEP 0004,
MOEP 0010, MOLP 0080, MOLP 0083,
MOLP 0093, MOLP 0100, MOLP 0184,
NALP 0013, NALP 0028, TMG12 0011,
TMG12 0051, TMG45 0017,
TMG45 0033, TMG45 0056,
TMG45 0068, TMG45 0087,
TMG45 0112, TMG45 0119,
TMG45 0126, TMG45 0171,
TMG45 0187, TMG45 0195,
TMG45 0224, TMG45 0240,
TMG45 0244, TMG45 0263,
TMG45 0278, TMGCD 0017,
TMGCD 0018, TMGCD 0023,
TMGCD 0036, TMGCD 0038,
TMGCD 0039, TMGLP 0009,
TMGLP 0033, TMGLP 0081,
TMGLP 0087, TMGLP 0121,
TMGLP 0127, TMGLP 0166,
TMGLP 0191, TMGLP 0195,
TMGLP 0200, TMGLP 0206,
TMGLP 0209

**The Temptations featuring Rick
James**
TMG45 0017

Terrell, Jean
MO45 0173

Terrell, Tammi
MO45 0097, MO45 0106, MO45 0126,
MO45 0149, MOLP 0053, TA45 0134,
TA45 0141, TA45 0146, TA45 0148,
TA45 0154, TA45 0158, TA45 0164,
TA45 0172, TA45 0177, TACO 0010,
TALP 0058, TALP 0065, TALP 0075,
TALP 0083, TMGCD 0016, TMGLP 0085,
TMGLP 0201

Third Creation
MO45 0262, MO45 0328, TA45 0224

Thomas, Danny
MOLP 0120

Three Ounces Of Love
MO45 0453, MO45 0460, MOLP 0304

Toe Fat
RA45 0015, RACO 0005, RALP 0008,
RALP 0022

Tony & Carolyn
VI45 0067

Travalini, Tony
GO45 0207

The Triangles
VI45 0002

Trice, Jamal
SO45 0121

Tucker and Schoonmaker
MCLP 0013

Tucker, Rick
HI45 0004

Turner, Sammy
MO45 0066

21st Creation
GO45 0155, GO45 0160, GOLP 0080,
GOLP 0085, MO12 0009

Twistin' Kings
MO45 0031, MO45 0032, MOLP 0002

Two Friends
NALP 0001

Tyler, Willie
TALP 0046

Tyler, Willie & Lester
TALP 0046

U.F.O.
RALP 0021

Uggams, Leslie
GO45 0150, MO45 0404, MOLP 0248

The Underdogs
VI45 0039

The Undisputed Truth
GO45 0107, GO45 0109, GO45 0113,
GO45 0115, GO45 0118, GO45 0123,
GO45 0125, GO45 0131, GO45 0135,
GO45 0140, GO45 0141, GO45 0142,
GO45 0144, GO45 0146, GO45 0148,
GOCO 0009, GOCO 0011, GOLP 0055,
GOLP 0059, GOLP 0063, GOLP 0068,
GOLP 0070, GOLP 0072

The Union Of South Africa
CH45 0010, CH45 0015, CHLP 0008

Urbaniak, Michael
MOLP 0349

The Valadiers
GO45 0003, GO45 0014, MI45 0006

Valentino
GA45 0001

Valli, Frankie
MO45 0263, MO45 0267, MO45 0291,
MO45 0301, MOLP 0190, MOLP 0254,
MW45 0011, MW45 0027, MWLP 0008,
MWLP 0014

**Valli, Frankie and The Four
Seasons**
MO45 0267, MO45 0301, MW45 0027,
MWLP 0008

Van Buren, Gene
TMG45 0044, TMG45 0133,
TMGLP 0016

The Vancouvers
GO45 0070, GO45 0074, GO45 0080,
GOCO 0002, GOLP 0030

The Vandellas
CHEP 0002, GO45 0012, GO45 0015,
GO45 0023, GO45 0026, GO45 0028,
GO45 0032, GO45 0034, GO45 0037,
GO45 0040, GO45 0046, GO45 0049,
GO45 0054, GO45 0057, GO45 0059,
GO45 0063, GO45 0068, GO45 0071,
GO45 0076, GO45 0081, GO45 0086,
GO45 0095, GO45 0099, GO45 0104,
GO45 0111, GO45 0114, GO45 0119,
GOCO 0001, GOCO 0010, GOEP 0002,
GOEP 0005, GOLP 0002, GOLP 0007,
GOLP 0015, GOLP 0017, GOLP 0020,
GOLP 0025, GOLP 0026, GOLP 0044,
GOLP 0052, GOLP 0058, MOCB 0007,
MOCB 0014, MOEP 0009, MOEP 0017,
MOLP 0180, TA45 0050, TA45 0051,
TMGLP 0172

Van Dyke, Connie
MO45 0050

Van Dyke, Earl
MOLP 0032, SO45 0006, SO45 0009,
SO45 0014, SO45 0018, SO45 0028,
SO45 0059, SOLP 0015

**Van Dyke, Earl & The Motown
Brass**
SO45 0028

**Van Dyke, Earl & The Soul
Brothers**
MOLP 0032, SO45 0009, SO45 0014,

Vanity
SO45 0018

Vanity
TMG12 0027, TMG12 0059,
TMG45 0158, TMG45 0173,
TMG45 0239, TMG45 0255,
TMGLP 0104, TMGLP 0169

Various Artists
CHEP 0002, GOEP 0006, GOLP 0035,
GOLP 0036, GOLP 0043, GOLP 0046,
GOLP 0050, MOEP 0001, MOEP 0014,
MOLP 0004, MOLP 0010, MOLP 0015,
MOLP 0016, MOLP 0025, MOLP 0031,
MOLP 0034, MOLP 0043, MOLP 0052,
MOLP 0056, MOLP 0062, MOLP 0067,
MOLP 0069, MOLP 0082, MOLP 0085,
MOLP 0089, MOLP 0094, MOLP 0102,
MOLP 0104, MOLP 0108, MOLP 0116,
MOLP 0126, MOLP 0127, MOLP 0128,
MOLP 0129, MOLP 0130, MOLP 0131,
MOLP 0132, MOLP 0133, MOLP 0135,
MOLP 0141, MOLP 0145, MOLP 0146,
MOLP 0162, MOLP 0165, MOLP 0197,
MOLP 0202, MOLP 0226, MOLP 0233,
MOLP 0235, MOLP 0236, MOLP 0237,
MOLP 0238, MOLP 0239, MOLP 0241,
MOLP 0242, MOLP 0255, MOLP 0262,
MOLP 0274, MOLP 0278, MOLP 0284,
MOLP 0285, MOLP 0286, MOLP 0326,
MOLP 0342, MOLP 0352, MOLP 0354,
NALP 0009, NALP 0010, NALP 0011,
NALP 0019, NALP 0020, NALP 0022,
NALP 0023, NALP 0024, NALP 0025,
NALP 0026, NALP 0027, RALP 0001,
SOLP 0020, TA45S 0007, TA45S 0008,
TALP 0005, TALP 0025, TALP 0037,
TALP 0045, TMGCD 0035, TMGLP 0049,
TMGLP 0064, TMGLP 0067,
TMGLP 0088, TMGLP 0093,
TMGLP 0096, TMGLP 0112,
TMGLP 0122, TMGLP 0130,
TMGLP 0133, TMGLP 0134,
TMGLP 0139, TMGLP 0140,
TMGLP 0141, TMGLP 0142,
TMGLP 0161, TMGLP 0162,
TMGLP 0163, TMGLP 0176,
TMGLP 0179, TMGLP 0182,
TMGLP 0185, TMGLP 0186,
TMGLP 0188, TMGLP 0194

Vega, Tata
MO12 0024, MO45 0261, TA45 0264,
TA45 0277, TA45 0284, TA45 0294,
TA45 0299, TA45 0311, TALP 0128,
TALP 0134, TALP 0142, TALP 0152

Vels
ME45 0003

The Velvelettes
SO45 0025, VI45 0006, VI45 0012,
VI45 0016, VI45 0020, VI45 0029,
VI45 0033, VILP 0002

Virgil Brothers
RA45 0002

The Voices Of Salvation
GO45 0024

Voices Of The Tabernacle
CHEP 0002

Volumes
IN45 0001

The Vows
VI45 0015

Wagner, John
RA45 0047

Walker, Jr.

MO45 0365, MOEP 0013, MOLP 0188,
SO45 0003, SO45 0008, SO45 0012,
SO45 0013, SO45 0015, SO45 0017,
SO45 0024, SO45 0026, SO45 0030,
SO45 0036, SO45 0041, SO45 0048,
SO45 0055, SO45 0062, SO45 0067,
SO45 0070, SO45 0073, SO45 0081,
SO45 0084, SO45 0090, SO45 0095,
SO45 0097, SO45 0104, SO45 0106,
SO45 0108, SO45 0110, SO45 0115,
SO45 0117, SO45 0119, SO45 0123,
SOEP 0001, SOEP 0002, SOEP 0003,
SOLP 0001, SOLP 0002, SOLP 0003,
SOLP 0005, SOLP 0010, SOLP 0018,
SOLP 0021, SOLP 0025, SOLP 0026,
SOLP 0032, SOLP 0033, SOLP 0038,
SOLP 0042, SOLP 0045, SOLP 0047,
SOLP 0048, SOLP 0050, TMG12 0013,
TMG45 0093, TMG45 0113,
TMGCD 0024, TMGLP 0054,
TMGLP 0205

Walker, Jr. & The All Stars
MO45 0365, MOEP 0013, MOLP 0188,
SO45 0003, SO45 0008, SO45 0012,
SO45 0013, SO45 0015, SO45 0017,
SO45 0024, SO45 0026, SO45 0030,
SO45 0036, SO45 0041, SO45 0048,
SO45 0055, SO45 0062, SO45 0067,
SO45 0070, SO45 0073, SO45 0081,
SO45 0084, SO45 0090, SO45 0095,
SO45 0097, SO45 0104, SO45 0106,
SO45 0108, SO45 0110, SOEP 0001,
SOEP 0002, SOEP 0003, SOLP 0001,
SOLP 0002, SOLP 0003, SOLP 0005,
SOLP 0010, SOLP 0018, SOLP 0021,
SOLP 0025, SOLP 0026, SOLP 0032,
SOLP 0033, SOLP 0038, SOLP 0042,
SOLP 0045, TMGCD 0024, TMGLP 0205

Ward, Sammy
SO45 0004, TA45 0032

Ward, "Singing" Sammy
TA45 0012, TA45 0013

Ward, Singin' Sammy
MO45 0010, TA45 0040, TA45 0054

Ware, Leon
GO45 0149, GOLP 0076, MO45 0381,
MOLP 0279, MOLP 0296

Warp 9
TMG12 0056, TMG45 0219,
TMGLP 0165

Washington, Earl
WO45 0002, WOLP 0001, WOLP 0012

Washington, Grover, Jr.
MO45 0469, MO45 0503, MOCO 0035,
MOLP 0313, MOLP 0338, MOLP 0345,
MOLP 0366, TMGCD 0010, TMGCD 0031,
TMGLP 0082, TMGLP 0128

Waters, Mira
GO45 0172, GO45 0189, GOCO 0016,
MO12 0033

Wells, Mary
GOEP 0006, MO45 0009, MO45 0020,
MO45 0025, MO45 0033, MO45 0041,
MO45 0044, MO45 0048, MO45 0051,
MO45 0059, MO45 0067, MO45 0068,
MO45 0072, MO45 0076, MOEP 0007,
MOLP 0001, MOLP 0006, MOLP 0008,
MOLP 0012, MOLP 0014, MOLP 0017,
MOLP 0018, MOLP 0054, TMGCD 0025,
TMGLP 0173, TMGLP 0201

Weston, Kim
GO45 0042, GO45 0047, GO45 0051,

GOLP 0034, MOEP 0005, MOEP 0015,
TA45 0059, TA45 0068, TA45 0083,
TA45 0087, TA45 0089, TA45 0094,
TA45 0126, TALP 0041, TALP 0051,
TMGLP 0201

White, Ronnie
TA45 00051

Williams, Andre
MI45 0004

Williams, Blinky
MWLP 0011

Williams, Herbie
WOLP 0015

Williams, Lenny
MO45 0382, MOLP 0245

Williams, Paul
GO45 0126

Wilson, Frank
SO45 0019

Wilson, Mary
MO12 0036, MO45 0484, MOLP 0332

Wofford, E. D.
MC45 0012

Wolf & Wolf
TMG45 0135, TMG45 0160,
TMGLP 0047

Wolfe
RA45 0045, RALP 0038

Wonder, Little Stevie
TA45 0044, TA45 0053, TA45 0057,
TA45 0063, TA45 0069, TA45 0073,
TALP 0013, TALP 0014, TALP 0021,
TALP 0029, TALP 0031

Wonder, Stevie
GO45 0077, GOLP 0032, MO12 0018,
MO45 0470, MO45 0471, MOCB 0008,
MOCB 0010, MOCO 0036, MOCO 0037,
MOEP 0006, MOEP 0020, MOLP 0206,
TA45 0079, TA45 0086, TA45 0091,
TA45 0098, TA45 0103, TA45 0104,
TA45 0109, TA45 0115, TA45 0121,
TA45 0124, TA45 0127, TA45 0132,
TA45 0136, TA45 0142, TA45 0150,
TA45 0153, TA45 0159, TA45 0165,
TA45 0173, TA45 0176, TA45 0181,
TA45 0186, TA45 0188, TA45 0196,
TA45 0203, TA45 0205, TA45 0212,
TA45 0215, TA45 0221, TA45 0225,
TA45 0232, TA45 0235, TA45 0242,
TA45 0246, TA45 0267, TA45 0276,
TA45 0281, TA45 0286, TA45 0298,
TA45 0303, TA45 0312, TA45 0315,
TA45 0318, TA45 0324, TA45 0327,
TACO 0002, TACO 0004, TACO 0011,
TACO 0012, TAEP 0006, TALP 0036,
TALP 0049, TALP 0053, TALP 0060,
TALP 0062, TALP 0063, TALP 0072,
TALP 0077, TALP 0079, TALP 0085,
TALP 0089, TALP 0094, TALP 0095,
TALP 0100, TALP 0107, TALP 0113,
TALP 0121, TALP 0144, TALP 0153,
TALP 0155, TMG12 0018, TMG12 0028,
TMG12 0049, TMG12 0054,
TMG45 0003, TMG45 0013,
TMG45 0041, TMG45 0052,
TMG45 0151, TMG45 0175,
TMG45 0180, TMG45 0214,
TMG45 0223, TMG45 0238,
TMGCD 0007, TMGCD 0026,
TMGCD 0042, TMGLP 0003,
TMGLP 0048, TMGLP 0083,
TMGLP 0110, TMGLP 0115,

TMGLP 0116, TMGLP 0117,
TMGLP 0118, TMGLP 0129,
TMGLP 0136, TMGLP 0146,
TMGLP 0153, TMGLP 0154,
TMGLP 0207
Wood(s), Mickey
TA45 0022, TA45 0035
Wright, Rita
GO45 0065, GOLP 0041
Wright Specials

DI45 0001, DI45 0002
Wylie, Popcorn
SO45 0087
Wylie, Richard
MO45 0018
Wyrick, Barbara
ML45 0010, ML45 0023
Xit
MO45 0317, MO45 0333, MOLP 0189,
RA45 0040, RA45 0051, RALP 0033,

RALP 0042
Young, Monalisa
TMG45 0067, TMG45 0114,
TMG45 0115, TMGLP 0030
Young, Val
TMG12 0039, TMG12 0045,
TMG12 0058, TMG45 0201,
TMG45 0218, TMG45 0236,
TMGLP 0149

ABC (CD)
TMGCD 0020
ABC (LP)
MOLP 0110
ABC (song)
MO45 0174, MOCO 0014, TMG12 0011
Abraham, Martin And John (song)
MW45 0002, TA45 0169, TACO 0006
Actions Speak Louder Than
Words (song)
TA45 0033
Act Like A Shotgun (song)
MW45 0005
After All (song)
TA45 0183, TA45S 0010
After The Dance (song)
TA45 0266
After The Showers Come Flowers
(song)
VI45 0002
After You (song)
MO45 0400, MO45 0527
After You Give Your All (What
Else Is There To Give) (song)
PR45 0008
Again (song)
GO45 0207, TMG45 0261
The Agony And The Ecstasy
(song)
TA45 0253
Aiming At Your Heart (song)
GO45 0211
Ain't Goin' Down In The Ground
Before My Time (song)
MC45 0001
Ain't It A Sad Thing (song)
RA45 0019
Ain't It Baby (song)
TA45 0019
Ain't It Hell Up In Harlem (song)
MO45 0296, SO45 0112
Ain't No Heartbreak (song)
ML45 0031
Ain't No Justice (song)
GO45 0134, SO45 0054
Ain't No Mountain High Enough
(song)
MO45 0181, TA45 0134
Ain't Nothing Like The Real
Thing (song)
TA45 0148
AIN'T NOTHIN' IN OUR
POCKET BUT LOVE (LP)
RALP 0016
AIN'T NO TURNIN' BACK
(LP)
TMGLP 0114
Ain't That Asking For Trouble
(song)
TA45 0121
Ain't That Loving You (song)
IN45 0001
Ain't That Peculiar (song)
TA45 0107, TAEP 0004
Ain't That The Truth (song)
SO45 0036
Ain't Too Proud To Beg (song)
GO45 0055, GOEP 0003, TMG12 0011
ALBERT FINNEY'S ALBUM
(LP)
MOLP 0292
ALFIE (LP)

GOLP 0032
Alfie (song)
GO45 0077
All Alone In Austin (song)
MC45 0011
All American Boy And His Dog
(song)
MO45 0252
All Because I Love You (song)
TA45 0160
All Because Of You (song)
MO45 0544
ALL BY MYSELF (LP)
TALP 0090
All Day And All Of The Night
(song)
GO45 0198
All Day And All Of The Night
(Vamp) (song)
GO45 0198
ALL DIRECTIONS (CD)
TMGCD 0023
ALL DIRECTIONS (LP)
GOLP 0062
All For Someone (song)
VI45 0027
All For You (song)
SO45 0009
All I Do (song)
TMG45 0003
All I Do Is Think of You (song)
MO45 0369
All I Know About You (song)
MO45 0118
ALL IN A KNIGHT'S WORK
(LIVE) (LP)
SOLP 0030
All I Need (song)
GO45 0062
ALL I NEED IS TIME (CD)
TMGCD 0009
ALL I NEED IS TIME (LP)
SOLP 0039
All I Need Is Time (song)
SO45 0107
All I Wanna Do (song)
MO45 0356
All I Wanted Was You (song)
MO45 0487, MO45 0494
All My Life's A Lie (song)
TMG45 0082
All Night Long (song)
TMG45 0094
All Night Long (All Night) (song)
TMG45 0103
All Night Long (All Night)
(Instrumental) (song)
TMG12 0015
All Night Long (All Night)
(Vocal) (song)
TMG12 0015
All Of My Love (song)
TA45 0259
ALL STAR JAZZ (LP)
WOLP 0001
All That Love Went To Waste
(song)
MO45 0298
All That's Good (song)
TA45 0097
All The Good Times Are Gone
(song)

ME45 0021
ALL THE GREAT HITS (LP)
MOLP 0365, TMGLP 0029
ALL THE GREAT LOVE
SONGS (CD)
TMGLP 0107
ALL THE GREAT LOVE
SONGS (LP)
TMGLP 0109
ALL THE KING'S HORSES
(CD)
TMGCD 0031
All The Love I've Got (song)
TA45 0043
ALL THIS LOVE (LP)
TMGLP 0013
All This Love (song)
TMG45 0062
ALONG CAME JONAH (LP)
MOLP 0084
ALREADY A HOUSEHOLD
WORD (LP)
RALP 0029
Always In My Heart (song)
MO45 0079
Amanda (song)
TMG45 0205
AMBIENCE (LP)
TMGLP 0004
AMOR SECRETO (LP)
TMGLP 0022
And I Don't Love You (song)
TMG45 0141
And I Don't Love You
(Instrumental) (song)
TMG12 0022
And I Don't Love You (Vocal)
(song)
TMG12 0022
And I Never Did (song)
MW45 0048
And I Thought You Loved Me
(song)
MO45 0259, MW45 0046
And There You Were (song)
MO45 0111
Angel (song)
MO45 0014
Angel Got A Book Today (song)
MW45 0042
Angelina (The Waitress At The
Pizzeria) (song)
NA45 0001
Angel In Blue (song)
MI45 0009
Angel In Your Eyes (Brings Out
The Devil In Me) (song)
MC45 0013
Angelito (Angel Baby) (song)
TMG45 0035, TMG45 0050
Angels In The Snow (song)
TMG45 0245
Anger (song)
TA45 0295
Angie Girl (song)
TA45 0159
Animal Instinct (song)
TMG45 0194
Animal Instinct (Club Mix) (song)
TMG12 0036
Animals (song)
TMG45 0255

Annie (song)
ML45 0008
Another Place In Time (song)
TMG45 0161
Another Pretty Country Song
(song)
MC45 0015
Another Star (song)
TA45 0281
Another Train Coming (song)
TA45 0068
Another Woman (song)
ML45 0016
ANTHOLOGY (CD)
TMGLP 0190, TMGLP 0191,
TMGLP 0196, TMGLP 0197,
TMGLP 0198, TMGLP 0199,
TMGLP 0200, TMGLP 0201,
TMGLP 0202
ANTHOLOGY (LP)
MOLP 0180, MOLP 0184, MOLP 0188,
MOLP 0193, MOLP 0194, MOLP 0195,
MOLP 0196, MOLP 0211, MOLP 0229,
MOLP 0270, MOLP 0359, MOLP 0366,
TMGLP 0045, TMGLP 0050
Any Happy Home (song)
MO45 0231
Anything To Keep From Going
Home (song)
ML45 0025
Anything You Wanna Do (song)
TA45 0111
ANY WAY YOU LIKE IT (LP)
TALP 0126
Any Way You Like It (song)
TA45 0287
Anyway You Wanna (song)
SO45 0030
APOLLO (LP)
GOLP 0087
Applejack's Theme (song)
TMG45 0272
Aqui Con Tigo (song)
TA45 0320
Are You Happy (song)
MO45 0280
Are You Lonely For Me Baby
(song)
MO45 0155
Are You Still Here (song)
TMG45 0032
Arma'Geden (song)
RA45 0011
ART & HONEY (LP)
MOLP 0205
As (song)
MO12 0012, TA45 0286
ASHFORD & SIMPSON: THE
COMPOSER SERIES (CD)
TMGLP 0142
As If You Read My Mind (song)
TA45 0324
Ask Any Girl (song)
MO45 0077
Ask Any Man (song)
MO45 0099
Ask The Lonely (song)
MO45 0084, MO45 0154
Asleep On My Love (song)
TA45 0258
As Long As I Know He's Mine
(song)

TA45 0071
As Long As I've Got You (song)
RA45 0014, RACO 0004
As Long As There Is L-O-V-E
Love (song)
SO45 0016, SOEP 0004
Astro Disco (Instrumental) (song)
MO12 0021
Astro Disco (Vocal) (song)
MO12 0021
Astro Disco - Pt. I (song)
GO45 0167
Astro Disco - Pt. II (song)
GO45 0167
At 15 (song)
TMG45 0074
AT HIS BEST (LP)
MOLP 0298, TALP 0136
At Last (I Found A Love) (song)
TA45 0155
AT THEIR BEST (LP)
MOLP 0198, MOLP 0307
Automatically Sunshine (song)
MO45 0212
Average People (song)
MO45 0224
AWAY WE A GO-GO (LP)
TALP 0052
Baby (song)
TA45 0285, VI45 0046
Baby, Baby Don't Cry (song)
TA45 0163
Baby, Baby I Need You (song)
GO45 0036
Baby Come Close (song)
TA45 0229
Baby Don'tcha Know (I'm
Bleeding For You) (song)
MO45 0268
Baby Dont'cha Worry (song)
MO45 0106
Baby Don't You Do It (song)
TA45 0084
Baby Don't You Go (song)
TA45 0093
Baby Don't You Leave Me (song)
GO45 0128
Baby, I'll Get It (song)
MO45 0171, VI45 0051
Baby, I Love You Too Much
(song)
ML45 0010
BABY I'M FOR REAL (LP)
SOLP 0016
Baby, I'm For Real (song)
SO45 0066
Baby I Miss You (song)
GO45 0035
Baby I Need You (song)
TA45 0041
Baby I Need Your Loving (song)
MC45 0012, MO45 0073, MOCB 0009,
MW45 0007, TMG12 0011
BABY IT'S ME (CD)
TMGCD 0027
BABY IT'S ME (LP)
MOLP 0293
Baby It's Me (song)
MO45 0450, MO45 0465
Baby I've Got It (song)
MO45 0342, SO45 0022
Baby I Will (song)

TMG45 0089
Baby Love (song)
MO12 0038, MO45 0077, MO45 0505,
MO45 0542, MOCB 0001
Baby Shake (song)
MO45 0052
Baby Sister (song)
TMG45 0139
Baby Sister (Instrumental) (song)
TMG45 0139
Baby That's Backatcha (song)
TA45 0250
Baby, Won't Cha Come Quick
(song)
TMG12 0046, TMG45 0210
Baby You Know You Ain't Right
(song)
SO45 0017, SOEP 0003
Back In My Arms Again (song)
GO45 0005, MO12 0038, MO45 0086,
MO45 0505, MO45 0542, TMG45 0092
Back In The Race (song)
TMG45 0164
Back Street (song)
RA45 0019, RA45 0022
BACK TO BASICS (LP)
TMGLP 0087
BACK TO EARTH (LP)
RALP 0045
Back To Nowhere (song)
TA45 0192
Back To School (song)
TMG45 0220
Back To School (Dance Mix)
(song)
TMG12 0047
Back To School (Instrumental)
(song)
TMG12 0047, TMG45 0220
Back To School (Long single mix)
(song)
TMG12 0047
Back To School Again (song)
MO45 0058
BACK WHERE I BELONG (LP)
TMGLP 0068
Bad, Bad Weather (Till You
Come Home) (song)
MO45 0147, MO45 0247
BADDEST (LP)
MOLP 0345
Bad Girl (song)
MO45 0001, MO45 0002, MO45S 0001,
MO45S 0002, TMG45 0131
Bad Lady (Instrumental) (song)
TMG12 0009, TMG45 0085
Bad Lady (Vocal) (song)
TMG12 0009, TMG45 0085
Bad Mouthin' (song)
MO45 0474
BAD NEWS IS COMING (LP)
GOLP 0064
The Bad Part Of Me (song)
HI45 0010
Bad Side Of The Moon (song)
RA45 0015, RACO 0005
Bad Weather (song)
MO45 0237
A BAG OF SOUP (LP)
MOLP 0087
Bah-Bah-Bah (song)
MW45 0004

Balada Del Pianista (song)
TMG45 0075
The Ballad Of Cradle Rob And
Me (song)
GO45 0219
Ballad Of The Unloved (song)
RA45 0045
Ball Baby (Instrumental) (song)
TMG45 0093
Ballerina Girl (song)
TMG45 0280
Ball Of Confusion (That's What
The World Is Today) (song)
GO45 0100, GO45 0113, GOCO 0007,
SO45 0096
Balloon Burning (song)
RA45 0001
BAND TOGETHER (LP)
PRLP 0019
BASS ODYSSEY (LP)
CHLP 0006
Bass Odyssey (song)
MO45 0415
The Battle Is Over (song)
RA45 0047
BEAT (LP)
WOLP 0019
Beautiful Brown Eyes (song)
SO45 0011
Beautiful Changes (song)
MO45 0385
Beautiful Women (song)
ME45 0010
Beauty Is Only Skin Deep (song)
GO45 0056
Because (song)
TMG45 0007
Because I Love Her (song)
GO45 0003
Because Of You (It's The Best
It's Ever Been) (song)
TMG45 0262
BEDLAM (LP)
RALP 0005
Bedtime For Toys (song)
TA45 0203
Beechwood 4-5789 (song)
TA45 0048, TAEP 0002
Been Lovin' You (song)
TMG45 0125
The Beginning Of The End (song)
MO45 0125, MO45 0132, MO45 0157
Behind A Painted Smile (song)
TA45 0160
Behind The Groove (song)
GO45 0187
Behold The Saints Of God (song)
TA45 0020
BEING WITH YOU (LP)
TALP 0157
Being With You (song)
TA45 0316, TA45 0320, TMG12 0006
BEING WITH YOU + WHERE
THERE'S SMOKE (CD)
TMGCD 0002
Believe In Yourself (Instrumental)
(song)
MO45 0409
Believe In Yourself (Vocal) (song)
MO45 0409
Believing You (song)
PR45 0002

The Bells (song)
SO45 0069
The Bells (12-inch version) (song)
TMG12 0061
Below The Funk (Pass The J)
(song)
GO45 0218
Be My Lady (song)
TMG45 0199
Be My Love (song)
SO45 0102
BEN (CD)
TMGCD 0001
BEN (LP)
MOLP 0157, TMGLP 0079
Ben (song)
MO45 0219
BENEDICTION (LP)
RALP 0035
Bernadette (song)
MO45 0115
BERRY GORDY'S "THE LAST
DRAGON" (LP)
TMGLP 0130
Best Beat In Town (song)
GO45 0170, GO45 0178, MO12 0028
Best Friends (song)
MO45 0241, MO45 0254, MW45 0045
The Best Of (song)
MO45 0545
THE BEST OF DIANA ROSS
(LP)
MOLP 0219
THE BEST OF MICHAEL
JACKSON (LP)
MOLP 0253
BEST OF THE FANTASTIC
FOUR (LP)
SOLP 0017
THE BEST OF THE FOUR
TOPS (LP)
MOLP 0166, MOLP 0167
THE BEST OF THE SPINNERS
(LP)
MOLP 0171
THE BEST OF THE
SUPREMES (LP)
MOLP 0218
BETTER LATE THAN NEVER
(LP)
MOLP 0019
Better Late Than Never (song)
MO45 0064
Better Never Than Forever (song)
MO45 0394
Between Her Goodbye And My
Hello (song)
SO45 0111
Beware (song)
GO45 0163, TMG45 0034
BIG BEN SINGS (LP)
MOLP 0179
Big Brother (song)
TA45 0242
THE BIG CHILL (& OTHER
CLASSIC HITS) (CD)
TMGLP 0122
THE BIG CHILL (ORIGINAL
MOTION PICTURE
SOUNDTRACK) (LP)
TMGLP 0064
The Bigger Your Heart Is (The

Harder You'll Fall) (song)
MO45 0093
The Biggest Parakeets In Town
(song)
ML45 0015
Big Joe Moe (song)
TA45 0040
Big John Is My Name (song)
GO45 0141, RA45 0052
Big Papa (song)
MO45 0313
Big Red Roses (And Little White
Lies) (song)
MC45 0014
Big Time (song)
GO45 0188, MO12 0005
The Big Wheel (song)
ME45 0009
Bill, When Are You Coming
Back (song)
MO45 0173
BILLY PRESTON & SYREETA
(LP)
MOLP 0363
The Bingo Long Song (Steal On
Home) (song)
MO45 0398
A Bird In The Hand (Is Worth
Two In The Bush) (song)
MO45 0353, VI45 0020, VI45 0029
THE BITCH IS BLACK (LP)
MOLP 0234
A BIT OF LIVERPOOL (LP)
MOLP 0024
BLACK MAGIC (LP)
GOLP 0058
Black Magic (song)
MO45 0310, MW45 0016
Blackmail (song)
VI45 0052
Black Orchid (song)
TMG45 0041
BLACK RUSSIAN (LP)
MOLP 0347
BLACK SPIRITS (LP)
BFLP 0006
Blame It On Love (song)
TMG45 0088
BLAME IT ON LOVE AND
ALL THE GREAT HITS
(LP)
TMGLP 0066
Blame It On The Sun (song)
TA45 0235
Bless You (song)
GO45 0111
Blibber Blabber (song)
MI45 0003
Blood Donors Needed (Give All
You Can) (song)
MO45 0235
Blowin' In The Wind (song)
TA45 0121
BLOW "RICK JAMES
PRESENTS BOBBY M"
(LP)
TMGLP 0024
BLOW THE HOUSE DOWN
(LP)
TMGLP 0054
Blow The House Down (song)
TMG45 0093

Blow The House Down
(Instrumental) (song)
TMG12 0013
Blow The House Down (Vocal)
(song)
TMG12 0013
Blow Top (song)
MO45 0492
Blue Cinderella (song)
MI45 0009
Blue Lodge (song)
MO45 0500
BLUES HELPING (LP)
RALP 0002
BLUE VIBRATIONS (LP)
WOLP 0005
Bobbie (song)
WO45 0006
BOBBY DARIN (LP)
MOLP 0155
BOBBY TAYLOR AND THE
VANCOUVERS (LP)
GOLP 0030
Body And Soul (song)
TMG45 0196
Body Chains (Instrumental) (song)
PR45 0007
Body Chains (Vocal) (song)
PR45 0007
Body In Motion (Want Your
Body In Motion With Mine)
(song)
MO12 0037, MO45 0499
Body Language (Do The Love
Dance) (song)
MO45 0388
BOLD BOHANNON (LP)
WOLP 0013
BONNIE POINTER (LP)
MOLP 0314, MOLP 0334
BOOGIE (LP)
NALP 0021
Boogie Boogie Love (song)
MO45 0431
Boogie Bump Boogie (song)
GO45 0148
BOOGIE DOWN! (LP)
TALP 0111
Boogie Down (song)
TA45 0233
Boogie Man (song)
MO45 0242
Boogie On Reggae Woman (song)
TA45 0246
Boogie With Me Children (song)
RA45 0054
BORN AGAIN (LP)
PRLP 0017
Born Again (song)
MO12 0009, TA45 0280
Born To Fool Around (song)
HI45 0015
Born To Wander (song)
RA45 0017
THE BOSS (CD)
TMGCD 0003
THE BOSS (LP)
MOLP 0328
The Boss (song)
MO12 0038, MO45 0479
The Boss (Disco Version) (song)
MO12 0029

BOSS BOSSA NOVA (LP)
WOLP 0006
Boys (song)
TMG45 0109
Boys (Instrumental) (song)
TMG45 0109
Boys Will Be Boys (song)
TMG45 0193, TMG45 0213
Boys Will Be Boys (Club Mix)
(song)
TMG12 0043
Boys Will Be Boys (Radio Edit of
Club Mix) (song)
TMG12 0043
Brainwasher (song)
SOEP 0002
Brainwasher (Part 1) (song)
SO45 0062
Brand New Beat (Part 1) (song)
TMG45 0209
Brand New Beat (Part 2) (song)
TMG45 0209
BRASS MONKEY (LP)
RALP 0020
Bread And Butter (song)
TMG45 0066
Bread Winner (song)
SO45 0004
Break Down And Sing (song)
MO45 0038
BREAKING THROUGH (LP)
WOLP 0016
Break It To Me Gently (song)
MO45 0502
Break It Up (song)
TMG45 0222
Break It Up (Instrumental) (song)
TMG45 0222, TMG12 0048
Break It Up (12-inch
Instrumental) (song)
TMG12 0048
Break The Ice (song)
TMG45 0200
Break The Ice (Dance Mix) (song)
TMG12 0038
BREAK THRU (LP)
GOLP 0080
A Breath Taking, First Sight Soul
Shaking, One Night Love
Making, Next Day Heart
Breaking Guy (song)
MO45 0053
A Breath Taking Guy (song)
MO45 0054, TA45 0202
Brenda (song)
MO45 0052, MO45 0063
BRENDA HOLLOWAY (LP)
TALP 0054
Brick House (song)
MO12 0006, MO12 0010, MO45 0439
Bring Back The Love (song)
VI45 0045
Bringing In The Gold (song)
ME45 0011
Bring Your Body (Exercise
Chant) (song)
TMG45 0068
Broken Bones (song)
MC45 0006
BROKENHEARTED (LP)
NALP 0027
Broken Hearted (song)

TA45 0027
Broken Road (song)
MW45 0023
Brother's Gonna Work It Out
(song)
MO45 0234, TMG12 0002
The Bump (song)
MO45 0351
Bump In Your Jeans (song)
PR45 0005
Bush Walkin' (song)
PR45 0036
Bustin' Out (song)
GO45 0169
BUSTIN' OUT OF L SEVEN
(LP)
GOLP 0086
But I Love Him (song)
MW45 0021
But I Love You More (song)
MO45 0178
But I'm Afraid (song)
MO45 0023
Buttered Popcorn (song)
TA45 0028, VI45 0015
Bye Bye Baby (song)
GOEP 0006, MO45 0009
BYE, BYE BABY, I DON'T
WANT TO TAKE A
CHANCE (LP)
MOLP 0001
By Some Chance (song)
VI45 0017
C.C. Rider (song)
MO45 0232
California Music (song)
MO45 0353, MO45 0364
California Soul (song)
GO45 0115, SO45 0037, TA45 0177
CALIFORNIA SUNSET (LP)
MOLP 0228, SOLP 0043
CALL ME + LIVIN' FOR YOU
(CD)
TMGCD 0041
Call Of The Wild (song)
MO45 0388
Call On Me (song)
MO45 0073, SO45 0021, TMG45 0004,
TMG45 0145
(Call On Your) Six-Million Dollar
Man (song)
SO45 0122
Camel Walk (song)
GO45 0010, MO45 0042, TA45 0050
Candlelight Afternoon (song)
TMG45 0164
Candy Apple Red (song)
RA45 0026, RACO 0007
Candy Lips (song)
ML45 0001
Candy Man (song)
TMG12 0010
Candy Man (Instrumental) (song)
TMG12 0010, TMG45 0072
Candy Man (Vocal) (song)
TMG12 0010, TMG45 0072
Candy To Me (song)
MO45 0074
Can I (song)
TA45 0198, TACO 0014
Can I (Long version) (song)
TA45 0199

Can I (Short version) (song)
TA45 0199

Can I Get A Witness (song)
SO45 0050, TA45 0070, TAEP 0001

Can It Be Love (song)
GO45 0183

Can't Find Love (song)
RA45 0005

Can't Give It Up No More (song)
SO45 0098

Can't Help What I Am (song)
TA45 0233

Can't It Wait Until Tomorrow
(song)
MO45 0181, TA45 0192

Can't Let You Tease Me (song)
MO45 0432

Can't Shake Your Love
(Instrumental) (song)
TMG12 0001

Can't Shake Your Love (Vocal)
(song)
TMG12 0001

CAN'T SLOW DOWN (CD &
LP)
TMGLP 0061

Can't Slow Down (song)
TMG45 0225

Can't Stop (song)
TMG45 0182

Can't Stop (Long Version) (song)
TMG12 0029

Can't Stop Singin' ('Bout The
Boy I Love) (song)
PR45 0006

Can't Wait To See You Again
(song)
CH45 0012

Can't You Hear The Music Play
(song)
RA45 0007

Can We Dance (song)
TMG45 0080

Can We Talk To You (For A
Little While) (song)
CH45 0005

Can You Do It (song)
GO45 0030

Can You Jerk Like Me (song)
GO45 0038

Captain Quick Draw (song)
MO45 0439

CAPTURED (LP)
TMGLP 0124

A Carbon Copy (song)
MW45 0049

Carme (Part I) (song)
TMG45 0252

Carme (Part II) (song)
TMG45 0252

Carry Your Own Load (song)
SO45 0081

Carter Country Theme (song)
MO45 0458

Casco Bay (Instrumental) (song)
TMG45 0260

Castles In The Sand (song)
TA45 0073

Castles Of Sand (song)
MO45 0455

CASTON & MAJORS (LP)
MOLP 0216

CAUGHT IN THE ACT (LP)
MOLP 0222

Cause We've Ended As Lovers
(song)
MO45 0366

Cause You Know Me (song)
VI45 0034

CC RIDES AGAIN (LP)
WELP 0001

Cebu (song)
MO45 0422, TMG45 0098

CELEBRATION (LP)
MWLP 0019

Cement Prairie (song)
MO45 0333

Chained (song)
MO45 0119, RA45 0053, TA45 0155

Chalk It Up (song)
MO12 0007, MO45 0435

CHAMELEON (LP)
MWLP 0008

Change (song)
GO45 0212, TMG45 0007

A Change Is Gonna Come (song)
MO45 0530

CHANGES (LP)
MOLP 0317

Change What You Can (song)
TA45 0145

Change Your Ways (song)
TMG45 0178

CHANGING TIMES (LP)
MOLP 0122

Chanted Meeting (The Interview)
(song)
ME45 0007

Chantilly Lace (song)
SO45 0031

Chapel Of Love (song)
PR45 0001

The Chaperone (song)
GO45 0010, MO45 0042

Charisma (song)
MO45 0301

CHARLENE (LP)
PRLP 0009

Charlie's Backbeat (song)
TMG45 0054

Cheating Is Telling On You (song)
GO45 0090, VI45 0050

Check Yourself (song)
MI45 0012

Cheek To Cheek (song)
TMG45 0080

Cherie (song)
VI45 0046

Chicago Disco (song)
SO45 0124

CHICO DE BARGE (LP)
TMGLP 0216

Child He Die (song)
MW45 0033

A Child Is Waiting (song)
RA45 0035

Children Of Tomorrow (song)
PR45 0018

Children's Christmas Song (song)
MO45 0096

Choosey Beggar (song)
TA45 0112, TAEP 0005

CHRISTINE (ORIGINAL
MOTION PICTURE

SOUNDTRACK) (LP)
TMGLP 0088

CHRISTMAS ALBUM (LP)
MOLP 0114

CHRISTMAS CARD (LP)
GOLP 0051

Christmas Everyday (song)
TA45S 0003

CHRISTMAS GIFT 'RAP (LP)
MOLP 0126

Christmas In The City (song)
TA45 0218

The Christmas Song (song)
TA45S 0003

CHRISTMAS WITH THE
MIRACLES (LP)
TALP 0017

Christmas Won't Be The Same
This Year (song)
MO45 0186

CHUCK JACKSON ARRIVES!
(LP)
MOLP 0068

The Circle Again (song)
MO45 0250, MW45 0035

CITY OF ANGELS (LP)
TALP 0120

Cleo's Back (song)
SO45 0013, SOEP 0001

Cleo's Mood (song)
SO45 0017, SOEP 0001

Clinging To The Thought That
She's Coming Back (song)
SO45 0070

Close Encounters Of The First
Kind (song)
TMG45 0246

Closer Than Close (song)
TMG45 0113

Close To Me (song)
TMG45 0153

CLOUD NINE (LP)
GOLP 0039

Cloud Nine (song)
GO45 0082, GO45 0108, SO45 0068

CLOUD NINE + PUZZLE
PEOPLE (CD)
TMGCD 0017

Coincidentally (song)
TA45 0260, TA45 0262

Cold As Usual (song)
ME45 0013

COLD BLOODED (LP)
TMGLP 0044

Cold Blooded (song)
TMG12 0012, TMG45 0091

Cold Blooded (Instrumental)
(song)
MO45 0377, TMG12 0012, TMG45 0091

A COLLECTION OF
ORIGINAL 16 BIG HITS
VOLUME 11 (LP)
MOLP 0094

A COLLECTION OF
ORIGINAL 16 BIG HITS
VOLUME 4 (LP)
MOLP 0034

A COLLECTION OF 16
ORIGINAL BIG HITS VOL.
2 (LP)
TALP 0037

Colorado Country Morning (song)

HI45 0023
Color Combination (song)
  SO45 0088
COLOR HER SUNSHINE (LP)
  MOLP 0273
COLOR MY WORLD LOVE
  (LP)
  MOLP 0244
Color Nature Gone (song)
  RA45 0051
Come And Get It (song)
  GO45 0174
COME AND GET THESE
  MEMORIES (LP)
  GOLP 0002
Come And Get These Memories
  (song)
  GO45 0015, GOEP 0002
Come And Get This Stuff (song)
  MO45 0310
Come Clean (song)
  RA45 0038
COME GET IT (LP)
  GOLP 0083, TMGLP 0080
Come Get This Thang (song)
  MW45 0037
Come Get To This (song)
  TA45 0231
Come In Heaven....Earth Is
  Calling (Part 1) (song)
  TA45 0284
Come In Heaven....Earth Is
  Calling (Part 2) (song)
  TA45 0284
Come Inside (song)
  MO45 0408
COME INTO MY LIFE (LP)
  MOLP 0177
Come Into My Life (Part 1) (song)
  GO45 0180
Come Into My Life (Part 2) (song)
  GO45 0180
Come Into My Palace (song)
  GO45 0002
Come On And Be Mine (song)
  MO45 0017
Come On And See Me (song)
  MO45 0106
Come On Back (And Be My Love
  Again) (song)
  ME45 0017
Come On Do The Jerk (song)
  TA45 0093
Come On Home (song)
  GO45 0025, MO45 0055
Come On In (song)
  MO45 0548, TMG45 0006
COME ON PEOPLE (LP)
  RALP 0010
Come On People (song)
  RA45 0010
(Come 'Round Here) I'm The One
  You Need (song)
  TA45 0125
Come See About Me (song)
  MO12 0038, MO45 0079, MO45 0083,
  MO45 0505, MO45 0542, MOCB 0015,
  SO45 0041
Come Spy With Me (song)
  TA45 0130
Come To Me (song)
  MO45 0025, TA45 0001, TA45 0292

Come With Me (song)
  RA45 0050
Comfort (song)
  GO45 0149, MO45 0381
Coming Apart (song)
  RA45 0016
Commercial Break (song)
  MO45 0314
COMMODORES (CD)
  TMGCD 0040
COMMODORES (LP)
  MOLP 0287
COMMODORES GREATEST
  HITS (LP)
  MOLP 0315
COMMODORES LIVE! (LP)
  MOLP 0297
Common Man (song)
  MO45 0271
COMMUNIQUE (LP)
  SOLP 0046
COMPACT COMMAND
  PERFORMANCES: 14
  GREATEST HITS (CD)
  TMGLP 0070, TMGLP 0074,
  TMGLP 0113, TMGLP 0184
COMPACT COMMAND
  PERFORMANCES: 15
  GREATEST HITS (CD)
  TMGLP 0071
COMPACT COMMAND
  PERFORMANCES: 17
  GREATEST HITS (CD)
  TMGLP 0111, TMGLP 0127
COMPACT COMMAND
  PERFORMANCES: 18
  GREATEST HITS (CD)
  TMGLP 0072, TMGLP 0073
COMPACT COMMAND
  PERFORMANCES: 19
  GREATEST HITS (CD)
  TMGLP 0108, TMGLP 0205
COMPACT COMMAND
  PERFORMANCES: 20
  GREATEST HITS (CD)
  TMGLP 0075
COMPACT COMMAND
  PERFORMANCES: 22
  GREATEST HITS (CD)
  TMGLP 0173
COMPACT COMMAND
  PERFORMANCES: 23
  GREATEST HITS (CD)
  TMGLP 0171
COMPACT COMMAND
  PERFORMANCES: 26
  GREATEST HITS (CD)
  TMGLP 0172
COMPACT COMMAND
  PERFORMANCES:
  GROVER WASHINGTON,
  JR. AT HIS BEST (CD)
  TMGLP 0128
COMPACT COMMAND
  PERFORMANCES
  VOLUME II: 20
  GREATEST HITS (CD)
  TMGLP 0203
COMPACT COMMAND
  PERFORMANCES
  VOLUME II: 22
  GREATEST HITS (CD)

TMGLP 0204
Completeness (song)
  TMG45 0021, TMG45 0022
The Composer (song)
  MO45 0157
COMPOSITIONS OF CHARLIE
  MINGUS (LP)
  WOLP 0018
CONCERT IN BLUES (LP)
  MOLP 0256
Concrete And Clay (song)
  RA45 0032
Confession (Gotta Get Back To
  Myself) (song)
  MO45 0303
Confide In Me (song)
  MO45 0441
Congo Pt. 1 (song)
  MO45 0032
Congo Pt. 2 (song)
  MO45 0032
THE CONGRESSIONAL
  BLACK CAUCUS (LP)
  BFLP 0005
Constant Disappointment (song)
  MO45 0338
Continental Street (song)
  MI45 0002
THE CONTOURS (EP)
  MOEP 0002
Contract Of Love (song)
  TA45 0057
Control Tower (song)
  MO45 0375
Contusion (song)
  TA45 0286
COOKIN' WITH THE
  MIRACLES (LP)
  TALP 0004
Cool And Crazy (song)
  TA45S 0001
COOLEY HIGH
  (SOUNDTRACK) (LP)
  MOLP 0242
COOLIN' OUT (LP)
  TMGLP 0150
Coolin' Out (song)
  TMG45 0211
Cop An Attitude (song)
  MO45 0482
CORLISS (LP)
  NALP 0003
The Corner Of The Sky (song)
  MO45 0226
COSMIC TRUTH (LP)
  GOLP 0070
Could This Be Love (song)
  TMG45 0014, TMG45 0043
Country Boy (song)
  MO45 0365, SO45 0106
COUNTRY DAYS AND
  COUNTRY NIGHTS (LP)
  MCLP 0005
Country Days and Country Nights
  (song)
  HI45 0016
THE COUNTRY SIDE OF PAT
  BOONE (LP)
  MCLP 0001
THE COYOTE SISTERS (LP)
  TMGLP 0065
Crack Killed Applejack (song)

SUPREMES JOIN THE
TEMPTATIONS (LP)
MOLP 0080
DIANA ROSS & THE
SUPREMES JOIN THE
TEMPTATIONS +
TOGETHER (CD)
TMGCD 0039
DIANA ROSS AND THE
SUPREMES 'LIVE' AT
LONDON'S TALK OF THE
TOWN (LP)
MOLP 0077
DIANA ROSS AND THE
SUPREMES SING AND
PERFORM "FUNNY
GIRL" (LP)
MOLP 0073
DIANA ROSS' GREATEST
HITS (LP)
MOLP 0271
DIANA ROSS LIVE AT
CAESARS PALACE (LP)
MOLP 0203
DIANA ROSS PRESENTS THE
JACKSON 5 (LP)
MOLP 0101
DIANA ROSS PRESENTS THE
JACKSON 5 + ABC (CD)
TMGCD 0020
DIANA ROSS SINGS SONGS
FROM THE "WIZ" (LP)
MOLP 0319
Did I Hear You Say You Love Me
(song)
TA45 0324
Didn't You Know (You'd Have
To Cry Sometime) (song)
SO45 0057
DIGGIN' IT (LP)
PRLP 0007
Diggin' It (song)
PR45 0020
Dinah (song)
MO45 0199
Dingbat Diller (song)
ME45 0006
Dirty Rats (song)
TMG45 0074
DISCO PARTY (LP)
NALP 0024
DISC-O-TECH (LP)
MOLP 0223
DISC-O-TECH #1 (LP)
MOLP 0226
DISC-O-TECH #2 (LP)
MOLP 0233
DISC-O-TECH NO. 3 (LP)
MOLP 0255
Disintegrated (Part 1) (song)
MO45 0027
Disintegrated (Part 2) (song)
MO45 0027
Distant Lover (song)
TA45 0231
Distant Lover (Edited version)
(song)
TA45 0243, TA45 0245
Distant Lover (Live version)
(song)
TA45 0244
Dr. King's Desired Eulogy (song)

TMG12 0018
DR. STRUT (LP)
MOLP 0329
Do Dat (song)
MO45 0469, MOCO 0035
Does Your Chewing Gum Lose Its
Flavor On The Bedpost
Overnight (song)
MO45 0460
Does Your Mama Know About
Me (song)
GO45 0070, GOCO 0002, MO45 0256
Doggin' Around (song)
MO45 0282
Doggone Right (song)
TA45 0168
Doggone The Dogs (song)
ML45 0019
Do I Do (song)
TMG45 0013
Do I Love You (Indeed I Do)
(song)
SO45 0019
DOIN' THEIR THING (LP)
TALP 0068
DO IT BABY (LP)
TALP 0115
Do It Baby (song)
TA45 0238
Do It For Me (song)
MO12 0008, MO45 0431
Don't Be A Cry Baby (song)
VI45 0002
Don't Be Afraid (song)
TA45 0325
Don't Be Too Long (song)
VI45 0030
Don't Bring Back Memories
(song)
MO45 0158
Don't Care Why You Want Me
(Long As You Want Me)
(song)
SO45 0065
DON'TCHA LOVE IT (LP)
TALP 0117
Don't Cha Love It (song)
TA45 0248
Don't Compare Me With Her
(song)
GO45 0047
Don't Drive Drunk (song)
TMG45 0180
Don't Drive Drunk (Instrumental)
(song)
TMG12 0028, TMG45 0180
Don't Drive Drunk (Special
12-inch version) (song)
TMG12 0028
Don't Ever Let Go (song)
TMG45 0156
Don't Explain (song)
MO45 0232
Don't Fan The Flame (song)
GO45 0154
Don't Feel Sorry For Me (song)
MI45 0001
Don't Fool Around (song)
VI45 0041, VI45 0044
Don't Freeze Up (song)
JU45 0001
Don't Freeze Up (Instrumental)

(song)
JU45 0001
Don't Get Caught Up In The
Middle (song)
TMG45 0106
Don't Give Up On Love (song)
GO45 0200
Don't It Feel Good To Be Free
(song)
MO45 0296, SO45 0112
Don't Knock My Love (song)
MO45 0309
Don't Know Why I Love You
(song)
TA45 0165
Don't Leave Me (song)
MO45 0022
Don't Leave Me Now (song)
TMG45 0070
Don't Leave Me This Way (song)
MO12 0002, TA45 0272
Don't Leave Me This Way (Long
Version) (song)
TA45 0273
Don't Leave Me This Way (Short
Version) (song)
TA45 0273
Don't Let Her Be Your Baby
(song)
GO45 0017
Don't Let Her Take Your Love
From Me (song)
SO45 0042
Don't Let Him Shop Around
(song)
MO45 0015
Don't Let Him Take Your Love
From Me (song)
MO45 0170, SO45 0046
Don't Let It End ('Til You Let It
Begin) (song)
TA45 0227
Don't Let It Happen To You
(song)
MO45 0119
Don't Let Me Lose This Dream
(song)
MO45 0141, MOCO 0006
Don't Let The Joneses Get You
Down (song)
GO45 0087
Don't Let Up On The Groove
(song)
TMG45 0058, TMG45 0064
Don't Let Your Baby Catch You
(song)
MO45 0242
DON'T LOOK ANY
FURTHER (LP)
TMGLP 0059
Don't Look Any Further (song)
TMG45 0121
Don't Look Back (song)
GO45 0048, GO45 0175, GOEP 0001
Don't Make Hurting Me A Habit
(song)
TA45 0162
Don't Make Me Wait Too Long
(song)
MO45 0335
Don't Mess With Bill (song)
MO45 0156, TA45 0111, TAEP 0002,

TMG12 0006, TMG45 0114,
TMG45 0115
Don't Mess With Mr. "T" (song)
TA45 0217
Don't Park Your Loving (song)
GO45 0214
Don't Pay Me No Mind (song)
RA45 0020
Don't Play Another Love Song
(song)
TMG45 0105
Don't Put Off 'Til Tomorrow
What You Can Do Today
(song)
VI45 0038
Don't Say Bye Bye (song)
MI45 0003, TA45 0005
Don't Send Me Away (song)
GO45 0066
DON'T STOP! (LP)
MOLP 0312
Don't Stop Loving Me (song)
MO45 0190
Don't Take It Away (song)
TA45 0032
Don't Take My Love Away (song)
GO45 0184
Don't Take My Love Away
(Instrumental) (song)
GO45 0184
Don't Take The Candy (song)
TMG45 0135
Don't Tell Me I'm Crazy (song)
SO45 0100
Don't Tell Me That It's Over
(song)
TMG45 0217
DON'T TOUCH ME (LP)
MOLP 0327
Don't Wanna Be Reminded (song)
MO45 0417, MO45 0428
Don't Wanna Play Pajama
Games (song)
MW45 0038, MWCO 0004
Don't Want To Be One (song)
MW45 0044
Don't Want To Fall Away From
You (song)
HI45 0023
Don't You Be Worried (song)
MW45 0040
Don't You Let Nobody Tell You
How To Do Your Thing (song)
MO45 0352
Don't You Miss Me A Little Bit
Baby (song)
SO45 0035
Don't You Worry 'Bout A Thing
(song)
TA45 0235
Do Right Baby Do Right (song)
VI45 0030
Do The Boomerang (song)
SO45 0012, SOEP 0001
Do The Choo Choo Pt. 1 (song)
BL45 0001
Do The Choo Choo Pt. 2 (song)
BL45 0001
Do The Pig (Part 1) (song)
SO45 0007
Do The Pig (Part 2) (song)
SO45 0007

DO UNTO OTHERS (LP)
MOLP 0232
Do What You Wanna (song)
TMG45 0006
DOWN AT THE
BRASSWORKS (LP)
RALP 0026
Down Down (song)
RA45 0030, RA45 0033
The Down Sound (song)
MO12 0026
The Down Sound Pt. 1 (song)
MO45 0480
The Down Sound Pt. 2 (song)
MO45 0480
DOWN TO EARTH (EP)
TAEP 0006
DOWN TO EARTH (LP)
GOLP 0068, TALP 0053
Down To Earth (song)
MO45 0088, TAEP 0006
DOWN TO LOVE TOWN (LP)
SOLP 0049
Down To Love Town (song)
MO12 0001, SO45 0120
Do You Look That Good In The
Morning (song)
TMG45 0130
Do You Love Me (song)
GO45 0006
Do You Love Me Just A Little,
Honey (song)
SO45 0033
DO YOU LOVE ME (NOW
THAT I CAN DANCE) (LP)
GOLP 0001
Do You Really Love Your Baby
(song)
TMG45 0224
Do You Really Love Your Baby
(Club Mix) (song)
TMG12 0051
Do You Really Love Your Baby
(Dub Mix) (song)
TMG12 0051
Do You Really Love Your Baby
(Radio Edit) (song)
TMG12 0051
Do You See My Love (For You
Growing) (song)
SO45 0073
Do You Wanna Do A Thing (song)
MO45 0350
Dream Come True (song)
GO45 0001
Dreamin' (song)
TMG45 0241
Dreamin' (Instrumental) (song)
TMG45 0241
Dream Lady (song)
MO45 0411
Dream Maker (song)
GO45 0164
Dreamtime Lover (song)
MO45 0380, PR45 0015
Drina (Take Your Lady Off For
Me) (song)
ML45 0021
The Drought Is Over (song)
MO45 0536, MO45 0543
Drum Major Instinct Sermon
(song)

TMG12 0018
Duck You Sucker (song)
MO45 0221
Dyambo (Dee-Yambo) Weary
Day Is Over (song)
CH45 0015
THE DYNAMIC SUPERIORS
(LP)
MOLP 0224
DYNAMITE (LP)
MOLP 0147
Dynamite (song)
TMG45 0141
Each Day Is A Lifetime (song)
MO45 0190
THE EARL OF FUNK (LP)
SOLP 0015
Early Morning Love (song)
MO45 0405
Earth People (song)
RA45 0043
Earthquake Shake (song)
GO45 0142
EARTHQUIRE (LP)
NALP 0006
EASY (LP)
TALP 0075
Easy (song)
MO45 0432
EASY RIDIN' (LP)
RALP 0014
Ebony Eyes (song)
TMG45 0120
Echo (song)
TMG45 0148
ECOLOGY (CD)
TMGCD 0034
ECOLOGY (LP)
RALP 0011
ECSTASY PARADISE (LP)
MOLP 0348
Ecstasy Paradise (song)
MO45 0517
EDDIE HOLLAND (LP)
MOLP 0005
EDDIE KENDRICKS (LP)
TALP 0108
Eddie's Love (song)
TA45 0207
Ego Tripping Out (song)
TA45 0300
Ego Tripping Out (Instrumental)
(song)
TA45 0300
Eh! Cumpari (song)
PR45 0012
Either Way We Lose (song)
TMG45 0015
ELAINE BROWN (LP)
BFLP 0008
EL DEBARGE (CD & LP)
TMGLP 0183
Embraceable You (song)
TA45S 0010
End (song)
RA45 0040
Endless Love (Instrumental) (song)
MO45 0538
Endless Love (Vocal) (song)
MO45 0538
ENDLESS LOVE: 15 OF
MOTOWN'S GREATEST

TMG45 0169
FIRE IT UP (LP)
GOLP 0092, TMGLP 0080
First Class Love (song)
GO45 0197
THE 1ST CUBA GOODING
ALBUM (LP)
MOLP 0300
First I Look At The Purse (song)
GO45 0045
First Impressions (song)
TMG45 0014
1st Lady (Sweet Mother's Love)
(song)
SO45 0109
First Round Knock-Out (song)
MO45 0391
FIRST STEP (LP)
PRLP 0016
First Time On A Ferris Wheel
(song)
TMG45 0192
First You've Got To Recognize
God (song)
DI45 0004
FIZZY QWICK (LP)
TMGLP 0181
THE FLAG (CD & LP)
TMGLP 0187
Flame (song)
MO45 0535
THE FLAMINGO KID
(ORIGINAL MOTION
PICTURE SOUNDTRACK)
(LP)
TMGLP 0133
Flashes (song)
TMG45 0122
The Flick (Part I) (song)
SO45 0018
The Flick (Part II) (song)
SO45 0018
Flower Girl (song)
TA45 0200
FLOY JOY (LP)
MOLP 0153
Floy Joy (song)
MO45 0207, MOCO 0024
Fly (song)
MO45 0445
Flying High (song)
MO45 0467
FLYING HIGH TOGETHER
(LP)
TALP 0099
Follow Me (song)
MO45 0259, MW45 0046
Food For Thought (song)
TA45 0328
Fool On The Street (song)
GO45 0173
For All We Know (song)
MO45 0120
For Better Or Worse (song)
MO45 0156, MO45 0164
Forever (song)
TA45 0060, TA45 0090, TAEP 0002
Forever And A Day (song)
TMG45 0269
Forever And A Day
(Instrumental) (song)
TMG45 0269

Forever And A Day (12-inch
version) (song)
TMG12 0066
Forever And A Day (12-inch
Instrumental) (song)
TMG12 0066
Forever Came Today (song)
MO45 0133, MO45 0369, MOCO 0029,
MOCO 0030
Forever For You (song)
TMG12 0061, TMG45 0247
Forever Is Not Enough (song)
TMG45 0078, TMG45 0079
FOREVER MICHAEL (LP)
MOLP 0227
Forget About Me (song)
MO45 0061
Forget Me Not (song)
GO45 0071
Forgive My Jealousy (song)
VI45 0066
A Fork In The Road (song)
TA45 0102
FOR LOVE OF IVY (LP)
MOLP 0078
For Love Of Ivy (song)
MO45 0142
FOR ONCE IN MY LIFE (LP)
TALP 0072
For Once In My Life (song)
MO45 0123, MO45 0134, MO45 0138,
SO45 0105, TA45 0159
FOR ONCE IN MY LIFE + UP
TIGHT (CD)
TMGCD 0026
FOR THE FIRST TIME (LP)
MOLP 0261
For The Love Of A Stranger
(song)
IN45 0003
For This I Thank You (song)
TA45 0049
Fortune Teller Tell Me (song)
ME45 0002
45 LIVES (LP)
RALP 0018
FOR YOU (LP)
TALP 0116
For You (song)
MO45 0356
For Your Love (song)
PR45 0009
For Your Precious Love (song)
MW45 0020
FOUR IN BLUE (LP)
TALP 0078
14 GREATEST HITS (LP)
TMGLP 0101
THE FOUR TOPS (EP)
MOEP 0012
FOUR TOPS (LP)
MOLP 0023, TMGLP 0077
FOUR TOPS GREATEST HITS
(LP)
MOLP 0063
FOUR TOPS HITS (EP)
MOEP 0018
FOUR TOPS LIVE! (LP)
MOLP 0055
FOUR TOPS ON BROADWAY
(LP)
MOLP 0058

FOUR TOPS ON TOP (LP)
MOLP 0048
FOUR TOPS + FOUR TOPS'
SECOND ALBUM (CD)
TMGCD 0028
FOUR TOPS REACH OUT (LP)
MOLP 0061
FOUR TOPS SECOND
ALBUM (CD)
TMGCD 0028
FOUR TOPS SECOND
ALBUM (LP)
MOLP 0035
FOXY BROWN (ORIGINAL
SOUNDTRACK FROM
AIP'S MOTION PICTURE)
(LP)
MOLP 0213
Freakin's Fine (song)
MO12 0025, MO45 0489
Freaky (song)
GO45 0203
Freddie (song)
PR45 0023
Freddie (Instrumental) (song)
PR45 0023
Free Again (Non...C'est Rien)
(song)
RA45 0010
...FREE AT LAST (LP)
GOLP 0029
FREE HUEY (LP)
BFLP 0002
Free Me From My Freedom (song)
MO12 0014, MO45 0466, MOCO 0034,
TMG45 0019
FRENZY (LP)
GOLP 0091
FRESH (LP)
TMGLP 0120
Fresh From The Can (song)
RA45 0053
Friend (song)
MO45 0327
Friendship Train (song)
GO45 0118, SO45 0068
Friend To Friend (song)
MO45 0509, MO45 0512
Frig-O-Rator (song)
TMG45 0231
Frig-O-Rator (Dub) (song)
TMG12 0055, TMG45 0231
Frig-O-Rator (Edit of Club Mix)
(song)
TMG12 0055
Frig-O-Rator (12-inch Dub Mix
(song)
TMG12 0055
From Head To Toe (song)
MO45 0125
FROM THE VAULTS (LP)
NALP 0022
FRONTIERS (LP)
MOLP 0301
FULFILLINGNESS' FIRST
FINALE (LP)
TALP 0113
Fulfill Your Need (song)
TA45 0240
FULL SPEED AHEAD (LP)
TALP 0128
Full Speed Ahead (song)

TA45 0264
FULLY EXPOSED (LP)
  MOLP 0186
Function At The Junction (song)
  SO45 0021
Funk Machine (song)
  GO45 0160
Funk Me (song)
  TA45 0317
Funky Cocktail (Pt. 1) (song)
  PR45 0014
Funky Cocktail (Pt. 2) (song)
  PR45 0014
Funky Music (song)
  JU45 0002
Funky Music Sho Nuff Turns Me
  On (song)
  GO45 0108, GO45 0120, MO45 0319
Funky Reggae (song)
  GO45 0209
Funky Rubber Band
  (Instrumental) (song)
  SO45 0087
Funky Rubber Band (Vocal)
  (song)
  SO45 0087
Funky Situation (song)
  MO45 0446, MO45 0513
A Funky Space Reincarnation
  (song)
  MO12 0017
A Funky Space Reincarnation
  (Instrumental) (song)
  MO12 0017
A Funky Space Reincarnation
  (Part I) (song)
  TA45 0293
A Funky Space Reincarnation
  (Part II) (song)
  TA45 0293
Funny (song)
  MO45 0021
Funny How Time Slips Away
  (song)
  TA45 0104
The Further You Look, The Less
  You See (song)
  GO45 0016, VI45 0045
G. C. CAMERON (LP)
  MOLP 0257
Gamble With My Love (song)
  TMG45 0084
GAME CALLED LOVE (LP)
  SOLP 0040
Game Called Love (song)
  SO45 0114
Ganja (song)
  GO45 0209
GARDEN OF LOVE (LP)
  GOLP 0097
A GASSSSSSSSSS (LP)
  SOLP 0026
Gemini (song)
  TA45 0251
GENERATION (Film
  soundtrack) (LP)
  RALP 0007
Generation (Light Up The Sky)
  (song)
  RA45 0006
GENIE (LP)
  TMGLP 0180

Genius II (song)
  TA45 0220
Get Back With You (song)
  GO45 0202
Get Crazy (song)
  TMG45 0096
GET CRAZY (ORIGINAL
  MOTION PICTURE
  SOUNDTRACK) (LP)
  TMGLP 0067
GET IT TOGETHER (LP)
  MOLP 0185
Get It Together (song)
  MO45 0289, MOCO 0026
Get It Up For Love (song)
  MO12 0024
Get It While It's Hot (song)
  TA45 0263
Get It While You Can (song)
  TMG45 0086, TMG45 0099
Get Me Some Help (song)
  RA45 0042
GET READY (LP)
  RALP 0004
Get Ready (song)
  GO45 0050, GOEP 0003, MO12 0030,
  RA45 0008, TA45 0296, TMG12 0006,
  TMG12 0011
Get Ready (Instrumental) (song)
  MO12 0030
Get Ready For The Get Down
  (song)
  MO45 0352
GET READY + ECOLOGY
  (CD)
  TMGCD 0034
Get The Cream Off The Top
  (song)
  TA45 0252
GETTING A GRIP ON LOVE
  (LP)
  TMGLP 0168
Gettin' It (song)
  MO45 0533
Gettin' It On (In The Sunshine)
  (song)
  GO45 0194
GETTIN' READY (EP)
  GOEP 0003
GETTIN' READY (LP)
  GOLP 0018, PRLP 0010
Gettin' Ready For Love (song)
  MO45 0441
Ghetto Life (song)
  GO45 0218
Gigolette (Instrumental) (song)
  MO45 0540
Gigolette (Vocal) (song)
  MO45 0540
GIMME DAT DING (LP)
  MOLP 0117
Gimme Dat Ding (song)
  MO45 0180
Gimme That Beat (Part 1) (song)
  SO45 0104
Gimme That Beat (Part 2) (song)
  SO45 0104
Gimme What You Want (song)
  TMG45 0162
The Girl (Can't Help It) (song)
  TMG45 0039
Girl I'm Standing There (song)

TMG45 0262
Girl, I Really Love You (song)
  MW45 0005
The Girl's Alright With Me (song)
  GO45 0033, GO45 0140, GOEP 0001
Girls, Girls, Girls (song)
  MO45 0129
Girls, Let's Keep Dancing Close
  (song)
  GO45 0160
Girl (Why You Wanna Make Me
  Blue) (song)
  GO45 0036, GOEP 0001
Girl You Need A Change Of Mind
  (Part 1) (song)
  TA45 0219
Girl You Need A Change Of Mind
  (Part 2) (song)
  TA45 0219
Girl You're Alright (song)
  GO45 0123
Girl You're So Together (song)
  TMG45 0163
Give A Little Love (song)
  TA45 0134
GIVE & TAKE (LP)
  MOLP 0282
Give God A Chance (song)
  DI45 0003
Give Her Up (song)
  TA45 0157
Give It One More Try (song)
  MO45 0274, MO45 0298
Give It To Me Baby (song)
  GO45 0200, MO12 0040
Give It To Me Baby
  (Instrumental) (song)
  MO12 0040
Give It To Me Sweet Thing (song)
  MW45 0044
GIVE LOVE AT CHRISTMAS
  (CD)
  TMGCD 0018
GIVE LOVE AT CHRISTMAS
  (LP)
  GOLP 0100
Give Me A Kiss (song)
  VI45 0003
Give Me A Sign (song)
  PR45 0004
Give Me Just Another Day (song)
  TA45 0230
Give Me Some Feeling (song)
  MO45 0460
Give Me Some Of That Good Old
  Love (song)
  MO45 0305
Give Me Time To Say (song)
  MO12 0032, MO45 0481
Give Me Your Love (song)
  MW45 0043
Give Out, But Don't Give Up
  (song)
  MO45 0363, MO45 0371, MO45 0387
Give Up (song)
  MO45 0508
GIVIN' ALL MY LOVE (LP)
  TALP 0152
Glad That You're Not Me (song)
  MW45 0033
GLASSES (LP)
  TMGLP 0038

Glasshouse (song)
　GO45 0145
Glory Train (song)
　ML45 0029
Glow (song)
　TMG12 0040, TMG45 0202
Glow (Instrumental) (song)
　TMG45 0202
Glow (Reprise) (song)
　TMG12 0040
Glow (12-inch instrumental)
　(song)
　TMG12 0040
THE GLOW (LP)
　TMGLP 0137
The Glow (song)
　TMG45 0203
The Glow (Special 12-inch
　version) (song)
　TMG12 0035
Go Ahead And Laugh (song)
　GO45 0054, TA45 0089, TA45 0094
God Bless Conchita (song)
　MO45 0277
God Bless The Child (song)
　MO45 0223
God Bless Whoever Sent You
　(song)
　SO45 0079
Goddess Of Love (song)
　TA45 0074
God Is Love (song)
　TA45 0187
Go For It (song)
　MO12 0019, MO45 0477
Go For It (Instrumental) (song)
　MO12 0019
Go Home (song)
　TMG45 0223
Go Home (Instrumental) (song)
　TMG45 0223
Go Home (Radio Edit of 12-inch
　vocal) (song)
　TMG12 0054
Go Home (12-inch instrumental)
　(song)
　TMG12 0054
Go Home (12-inch version) (song)
　TMG12 0054
GOIN' BACK TO CHUCK
　JACKSON (LP)
　MOLP 0088
GOIN' BACK TO INDIANA
　(LP)
　MOLP 0144
GOIN' FOR MYSELF (LP)
　SOLP 0035
Going Down For The Third Time
　(song)
　MO45 0122
Going Steady Anniversary (song)
　GO45 0019
GOING TO A GO-GO (EP)
　TAEP 0005
GOING TO A GO-GO (LP)
　TALP 0048
Going To A Go-Go (song)
　TA45 0112, TAEP 0005, TMG12 0006
GOING TO A GO-GO + THE
　TEARS OF A CLOWN (CD)
　TMGCD 0005
Going To The Hop (song)

TA45 0007
Goin' Through The Motions (song)
　GO45 0210
GOIN' UP IN SMOKE (LP)
　TALP 0127
Goin' Up In Smoke (song)
　MO12 0003, TA45 0271
Golden Girl (song)
　TMG45 0184
Golden Slumbers (song)
　CHEP 0001
Gonna Find A True Love (song)
　MO45 0304
Gonna Give Her All The Love
　I've Got (song)
　GO45 0073, SO45 0032, SO45 0059,
　SOEP 0004, TA45 0175, TACO 0009
Gonna Keep On Tryin' Till I Win
　Your Love (song)
　GO45 0067, GO45 0105, GO45 0112,
　SO45 0053, TA45 0170
Gonna Put It On Your Mind
　(song)
　CH45 0006
Good-By Cruel Love (song)
　MO45 0046
Good Clean Fun (song)
　TMG45 0123
GOOD FEELING MUSIC OF
　THE BIG CHILL
　GENERATION, VOLUME
　ONE (CD)
　TMGLP 0161
GOOD FEELING MUSIC OF
　THE BIG CHILL
　GENERATION, VOLUME
　TWO (CD)
　TMGLP 0162
GOOD FEELING MUSIC OF
　THE BIG CHILL
　GENERATION, VOLUME
　THREE (CD)
　TMGLP 0163
Good Lovin' Ain't Easy To Come
　By (song)
　TA45 0164
Good Lovin' Is Just A Dime
　Away (song)
　MO45 0368
Good Morning Heartache (song)
　MO45 0223
Good Night Irene (song)
　SO45 0029
Good Rockin' (song)
　SOEP 0002
The Good Things (Where Was I
　When Love Came By) (song)
　MO45 0220
Good Times Theme (song)
　MO45 0458
Go On With Your Bad Self (song)
　MO45 0235
THE GOSPEL ACCORDING
　TO ZEUS (LP)
　RALP 0013
Gospel Truth (song)
　SO45 0101
Got Myself A Good Man (song)
　SO45 0063
Gotta Find A Woman (song)
　MO45 0461
Gotta Get Out Tonight (song)

TMG45 0138
Gotta Have Your Lovin' (song)
　MO45 0006, MO45 0007
GOTTA HOLD ON TO THIS
　FEELING (LP)
　SOLP 0021
Gotta Hold On To This Feeling
　(song)
　SO45 0070
Gotta Keep On Tryin' Till I Win
　Your Love (song)
　GO45 0125
Gotta See Jane (song)
　RA45 0022, RACO 0006, VI45 0044
GOT TO BE THERE (LP)
　MOLP 0149, TMGLP 0079
Got To Be There (song)
　MO45 0203
GOT TO BE THERE + BEN
　(CD)
　TMGCD 0001
Got To Get My Hands On Some
　Lovin' (song)
　GO45 0144
Got To Get Up On It (song)
　TMG45 0055
Got To Give It Up (Pt. I) (song)
　TA45 0275
Got To Give It Up (Pt. II) (song)
　TA45 0275
Got To Have You Back (song)
　TA45 0131
Got To Know (song)
　TMG45 0025
Grandma's Washboard Band
　(song)
　PR45 0002
GRAND SLAM (LP)
　PRLP 0021
Granite Palace (song)
　MO45 0492
Greasy Spoon (song)
　CH45 0014
GREATEST HITS (CD)
　TMGLP 0175
GREATEST HITS (EP)
　GOEP 0004, TAEP 0001
GREATEST HITS (LP)
　MOLP 0143, SOLP 0023, TALP 0083,
　TALP 0129, TALP 0139
GREATEST HITS FROM THE
　BEGINNING (EP)
　TAEP 0003
GREATEST HITS FROM THE
　BEGINNING (LP)
　TALP 0035
GREATEST HITS MEDLEY
　(12-inch)
　TMG12 0006
GREATEST HITS VOL. 2 (LP)
　GOLP 0054, MOLP 0142, TALP 0094
The Greatest Man Who Ever
　Lived (song)
　RA45 0035
THE GREATEST SONGS
　WRITTEN BY ASHFORD &
　SIMPSON (CD)
　TMGLP 0142
THE GREATEST SONGS
　WRITTEN BY HOLLAND -
　DOZIER - HOLLAND (CD)
　TMGLP 0140

THE GREATEST SONGS
WRITTEN BY SMOKEY
ROBINSON (CD)
TMGLP 0141
GREAT EXPECTATIONS (LP)
TALP 0084
THE GREAT GOSPEL STARS
(LP)
TALP 0003
THE GREAT MARCH TO
FREEDOM (LP)
GOLP 0006
GREAT MARCH TO
WASHINGTON (LP)
GOLP 0008
The Great Titanic (song)
ME45 0021
GREEN GROW THE LILACS
(LP)
SOLP 0016
Green Grow The Lilacs (song)
GO45 0121, MO45 0152, MO45 0165,
MO45 0172, SO45 0061
Greetings (This Is Uncle Sam)
(song)
MI45 0006, VI45 0031
GREETINGS! . . . WE'RE THE
MONITORS (LP)
SOLP 0014
Groove And Move (song)
SO45 0073
THE GROOVE GOVERNOR
(LP)
SOLP 0027
GROOVE PATROL (LP)
TMGLP 0042
Groove Thang (song)
SO45 0097
Grow-Up (song)
TMG12 0067, TMG45 0270
Grow-Up (Dub) (song)
TMG12 0067
Grow-Up (Instrumental) (song)
TMG45 0270
Grow-Up (Rhythm Mix) (song)
TMG12 0067
Guarantee (For A Lifetime) (song)
MO45 0072
GUESS WHO'S COMING
HOME (LP)
BFLP 0004
GUINN (LP)
TMGLP 0170
Guns (song)
ML45 0030
Gun Shy (song)
TMG45 0255
GUYS AND DOLLS
(ORIGINAL CAST) (LP)
MOLP 0278
Gypsy Eyes (song)
RA45 0036
Had You Been Around (song)
MO45 0088
Hairdooz (song)
TMG45 0279
Half Crazed (song)
MW45 0041
Hallelujah Day (song)
MO45 0236
Hang (song)
TMG45 0111

Hangin' Out (song)
TMG45 0245
Hangin' Out At The Mall (song)
TMG45 0117
Hang On Bill (song)
VI45 0022
The Happening (song)
MO45 0118
HAPPINESS (LP)
MWLP 0001
Happiness (song)
MW45 0003, MW45 0022
Happy (song)
TA45 0255
Happy Birthday (song)
TMG12 0018
Happy Birthday (Instrumental)
(song)
TA45 0327
Happy Birthday (Vocal) (song)
TA45 0327
Happy Day (song)
MO45 0128
Happy Ghoul Tide (song)
VI45 0011
Happy (Is A Bumpy Road) (song)
MO45 0194, MO45 0210
Happy Landing (song)
TA45 0056
Happy (Love Theme From "Lady
Sings The Blues") (song)
MO45 0229
Happy People (song)
GO45 0139
Happy People (Instrumental)
(song)
GO45 0139
Happy Street (song)
TA45 0086
Hard Love (song)
SO45 0123
Hard Times (song)
CHEP 0001
Hard To Get (song)
TMG45 0036
Harmour Love (song)
MO45 0366, MOCO 0028
Haulin' (song)
MO45 0377
Have I Lost You (song)
MO45 0246
Have I The Right (song)
MO45 0028
Have You Any Time For Jesus
(song)
DI45 0003
Have You Ever Seen Them Shake
(Shake It Baby) (song)
MO45 0424
HAVIN' A HOUSE PARTY
(LP)
MOLP 0276
HEAD TO HEAD (LP)
RALP 0030
HEART (LP)
NALP 0002
Heart (song)
MI45 0001
Heartaches (song)
VI45 0060
Heartbeat (song)
TMG45 0181

Heartbreak Graffitti (Part I)
(song)
TA45 0309
Heartbreak Graffitti (Part II)
(song)
TA45 0309
Heartbreak Road (song)
TA45 0075
A Heart Is A House (song)
MW45 0039
The Heart Is Not So Smart (song)
TMG45 0228
The Heart Is Not So Smart (Club
Mix) (song)
TMG12 0053
The Heart Is Not So Smart (Dub
Mix) (song)
TMG12 0053
Heartless (song)
GO45 0095
HEART OF THE MATTER
(LP)
VILP 0008
Hearts On Fire (song)
TMG45 0177
HEAT WAVE (LP)
GOLP 0007
Heat Wave (song)
GO45 0023
Heaven Help Us All (song)
TA45 0186
Heavenly (song)
GO45 0136
Heaven Must Have Sent You
(song)
MO45 0476, VI45 0036, VI45 0064
Heaven Must Have Sent You (LP
Version) (song)
MO12 0023, MO45 0476
Heaven Must Have Sent You
(New Version) (song)
MO12 0023
Heavy Day (song)
MO45 0330
Heavy Love (song)
MO45 0401
Heavy Love Affair (song)
TA45 0321
Heavy On Pride (Light On Love)
(song)
TA45 0308
He Doesn't Love Her Anymore
(song)
GO45 0057
He Holds His Own (song)
MO45 0091
He Lifted Me (song)
TA45 0020
He'll Have To Go (song)
ML45 0012
Hell Is On The Run (song)
TMG45 0156
Hello (song)
TMG45 0128
HELLO BROADWAY (LP)
TALP 0040
Hello Detroit (Instrumental) (song)
TMG12 0020, TMG45 0144
Hello Detroit (Vocal) (song)
TMG12 0020, TMG45 0144
HELLO DUMMY (LP)
TALP 0046

Hello Girl (song)
MO45 0547

Hello There Angel (song)
TA45 0058

HELL UP IN HARLEM
(ORIGINAL
SOUNDTRACK) (LP)
MOLP 0204

Helpless (song)
GO45 0051

Help Me Make It Through The
Night (song)
SO45 0094

Help The People (song)
MO45 0240

Help Yourself (song)
GO45 0135

He Makes The Wrong Seem Right
(song)
ML45 0017

He Means The World To Me
(song)
MO45 0071

Henry Blake (song)
CH45 0006

He Only Looks The Part (song)
TMG45 0155

Here Comes That Feeling Again
(song)
MO45 0442

Here Comes The Heartache (song)
MO45 0070

HERE COMES THE JUDGE
(LP)
SOLP 0009

Here Comes The Judge (song)
SO45 0044

Here Comes The Night (song)
RA45 0017

Here For The Party (song)
MO45 0376

HERE I AM (LP)
MOLP 0045

Here I Am Baby (song)
MO45 0117, MOCO 0002, TA45 0151

Here I Go Again (song)
TA45 0168, TACO 0005, TMG45 0095

HERE, MY DEAR (LP)
TALP 0135, TALP 0146

Here We Go Again (song)
ML45 0011

Here You Come (song)
GO45 0008

HEROES (LP)
MOLP 0344

Heroes (song)
MO45 0513

HEROES + COMMODORES
(CD)
TMGCD 0040

He's A Cobra (song)
TMG45 0178

HE'S A FRIEND (LP)
TALP 0124

He's A Friend (song)
TA45 0259, TACO 0018

He's A Good Guy (Yes He Is)
(song)
TA45 0074

He's All I Got (song)
MO45 0105

He's An Oddball (song)

VI45 0017

He's A Pretender (song)
TMG45 0064

He's A Pretender (Instrumental)
(song)
TMG12 0007

He's A Pretender (Vocal) (song)
TMG12 0007

He's Got The Whole World In His
Hands (song)
GO45 0027

Hesitated (song)
TMG45 0037, TMG45 0047

He's Misstra Know-It-All (song)
TA45 0276

He's My Man (song)
MO45 0371

He's My Sunny Boy (song)
MO45 0167

(He's) Seventeen (song)
MO45 0036

He Still Plays On (song)
MO45 0307

He Was Really Sayin' Somethin'
(song)
TAEP 0007, VI45 0012

He Who Picks A Rose (song)
GO45 0102

Hey Big Brother (song)
RA45 0034

Hey Diddle Diddle (song)
TA45 0123, TAEP 0004

Hey Girl (I Like Your Style)
(song)
GO45 0132

Hey Harmonica Man (song)
TA45 0079

Hey Lordy (song)
MW45 0006

Hey Love (song)
TA45 0132, TAEP 0006

Hey Man (song)
MO45 0266

Hey You (song)
MO45 0539, MO45 0541

Hickory (song)
MO45 0301

HIGH ENERGY (LP)
MOLP 0265

Higher Ground (song)
TA45 0225

HIGHER THAN HIGH (LP)
GOLP 0072

Higher Than High (song)
GO45 0146

High Heel Sneakers (song)
TA45 0103, TA45 0104

HIGH INERGY (LP)
GOLP 0106

HIGH ON SUNSHINE (LP)
MOLP 0318

High On Sunshine (song)
MO45 0413

High On Your Love Suite (song)
GO45 0166, MO12 0015

High Road (song)
MO45 0255

High School (song)
GO45 0162

High Tide (song)
MO45 0335, MO45 0364

HIMSELF (ORIGINAL

MOTION PICTURE
SOUNTRACK) (CD & LP)
TMGLP 0027

Hip City (Pt. 1) (song)
SO45 0048

Hip City (Pt. 2) (song)
SO45 0048

His Eye Is On The Sparrow (song)
MO45 0139

HIT & RUN LOVER (LP)
TMGLP 0092

Hit And Run Lover (song)
TMG45 0167

Hitch Hike (song)
TA45 0058, TAEP 0001

THE HIT MAN (LP)
TALP 0119

HITS OF THE SIXTIES (LP)
MOLP 0021

HITSVILLE, U.S.A. NO. 1 (EP)
MOEP 0001

HITTIN' (EP)
MOEP 0017

HI, WE'RE THE MIRACLES
(LP)
TALP 0001

Hold Me (song)
TA45 0136

Hold Me Oh My Darling (song)
MO45 0097, TA45 0141

Hold Me Tight (song)
MO45 0005

HOLD ON (LP)
GOLP 0098

Hold On Pearl (song)
GO45 0009

Hold On To My Love (song)
GO45 0195

Hold On To Your Love (song)
TMG45 0234

HOLLAND - DOZIER -
HOLLAND: THE
COMPOSER SERIES (CD)
TMGLP 0140

Holly (song)
TA45 0279

Holly Holy (song)
SO45 0081

HOLLYWOOD (LP)
MWLP 0018

Hollywood (song)
GO45 0158

HOME COOKIN' (LP)
SOLP 0010

Home Cookin (song)
SO45 0055

Home On The Range (Everybody
Needs A Home) (song)
CH45 0001, CH45 0002, CHCO 0001

Honey Brown (song)
TA45 0252

Honey Chile (song)
GO45 0068

Honey Come Back (song)
MO45 0163

Hooked For Life (song)
MO45 0461

Hooked On Your Love (song)
TA45 0249

Hope (song)
MO45 0524

Hope I Don't Get My Heart

Broke (song)
GO45 0111
Hot Cha (song)
SO45 0008
HOT NIGHTS (LP)
TMGLP 0213
Hot Nights (song)
TMG45 0261
Hot 'N' Tot (song)
SO45 0006
HOT ON THE TRACKS (LP)
MOLP 0269
HOT SHOT (LP)
SOLP 0045
Hot Shot (song)
SO45 0119, TMG45 0096
HOT SPOT (LP)
TMGLP 0151
Hot Spot (song)
TMG45 0206
Hot Spot (Club Mix) (song)
TMG12 0044
HOTTER THAN JULY (CD)
TMGLP 0207
HOTTER THAN JULY (LP)
TALP 0155
A House Is Not A Home (song)
MW45 0036
HOUSE PARTY (LP)
GOLP 0073
How About You (song)
MO45 0188
How Can I (song)
MO45 0078
How Can I Forget (song)
GO45 0075, TA45 0175
How Can I Forget You (song)
MO45 0266
How Can I Say I'm Sorry (song)
SO45 0016
How Can We Tell Him (song)
MO45 0064
How Can You Say That It's Over
(song)
TMG45 0195
How Come? (song)
MO45 0267
How Do You Feel Tonight (song)
TMG45 0069
How Great Thou Art (song)
CHEP 0002
How Important Can It Be (song)
ML45 0013
HOWL THE GOOD (LP)
RALP 0034
How Many Times Did You Mean
It (song)
TA45 0106
HOW SWEET HE IS (LP)
SOLP 0022
HOW SWEET IT IS TO BE
LOVED BY YOU (LP)
TALP 0039
How Sweet It Is (To Be Loved
By You) (song)
MOCB 0006, SO45 0014, SO45 0024,
SOEP 0003, TA45 0090
How You Gonna Keep It (After
You Get It) (song)
MO45 0179, SO45 0089, TA45 0172
HUGH MASEKELA AND THE
UNION OF SOUTH

AFRICA (LP)
CHLP 0008
Hum Along And Dance (song)
GO45 0103, RA45 0050
The Humming Song (Lost For
Words) (song)
TA45 0274
Hungry (song)
MO45 0510
HUNGRY FOR LOVE (LP)
GOLP 0023
The Hunter Gets Captured By
The Game (song)
TA45 0128, TAEP 0007, TMG12 0006
Hurry Tommorrow (song)
GO45 0130
Hurt A Little Everyday (song)
TA45 0122
I Ain't Gonna Stand For It (song)
TA45 0315
I Ain't That Easy To Lose (song)
SO45 0110
I Am Bound (song)
MO45 0024
I Am I Am (song)
TA45 0241
I Am Love (song)
MO45 0323
I Am Love Pt. II (song)
MO45 0323
I AM MY BROTHER'S
KEEPER (LP)
SOLP 0028
I Am So Glad You Chose Me
(song)
MO45 0399
I Am The Man For You Baby
(song)
GO45 0072
I Am Your Man (song)
GO45 0074
I Been Had By The Devil (song)
MO45 0303
I Believe I'm Gonna Take This
Ride (song)
TA45 0213
I Believe (When I Fall In Love It
Will Be Forever) (song)
MO45 0338
I Betcha (song)
TMG45 0038
I Call It Pretty Music, But The
Old People Call It The Blues,
Part 1 (song)
TA45 0044
I Call It Pretty Music, But The
Old People Call It The Blues,
Part 2 (song)
TA45 0044
I Call Your Name (song)
GO45 0177, GO45 0178
I Can Feel My Love Risin' (song)
PR45 0033
I Can Feel The Pain (song)
VI45 0062
I Can Get Away From You (But
I Can't Get Over You) (song)
VI45 0067
I Can Make It Alone (song)
RA45 0038
I CAN MAKE IT HAPPEN (LP)
TMGLP 0046

I Can Take A Hint (song)
TA45 0061
I Can Take It All (song)
SO45 0099
I Can't Believe (song)
TA45 0031
I Can't Believe You Love Me
(song)
MO45 0097
I Can't Believe You're Really
Leaving (song)
TA45 0201
I Can't Dance To That Music
You're Playing (song)
GO45 0076
I Can't Find (song)
TMG45 0162
I Can't Find It (song)
ML45 0009
I Can't Get Next To You (song)
GO45 0094, TMG12 0011
I Can't Give Back The Love I
Feel For You (song)
GO45 0065, MO45 0283, MO45 0326,
MW45 0017
I Can't Give Her Up (song)
TMG45 0155
I Can't Go On Living Without
Your Love (song)
MO12 0013, TA45 0287
I Can't Help It, I Gotta Dance
(song)
GO45 0022
I Can't Help Myself (song)
MO45 0087, MOCB 0005, MOCB 0006,
MOCB 0007
I Can't Help Myself (Sugar Pie,
Honey Bunch) (song)
ML45 0016, MO45 0495, SO45 0014,
TMG12 0011
I Can't Quit Your Love (song)
MO45 0210, MO45 0321
I Can't Stand To See You Cry
(song)
TA45 0214
I Can't Stay Away (From
Someone I Love) (song)
MO45 0427
I Can't Stop (song)
TMG45 0015
I Can't Wait To Make You Mine
(song)
TMG45 0190
I Care About Detroit (song)
TA45S 0009
Ich-I-Bon #1 (song)
TA45S 0001
I Choose You (song)
MO45 0234
I Comma Zimba Zio (Here I
Stand The Mighty One) (song)
SO45 0051
I Could Never Love Another
(After Loving You) (song)
GO45 0073
(I Could Never Make) A Better
Man Than You (song)
MW45 0043
I Couldn't Cry If I Wanted To
(song)
GO45 0058, MO45 0060
I Cried All Night (song)

I HEAR A SYMPHONY (CD)
TMGCD 0006
I HEAR A SYMPHONY (LP)
MOLP 0044
I Hear A Symphony (song)
MO45 0094, TA45 0120, VI45 0019
I Heard A Song (song)
HI45 0004
I HEARD IT THROUGH THE
GRAPEVINE (LP)
TALP 0066
I Heard It Through The
Grapevine (song)
SO45 0039, TA45 0161
I HEARD IT THROUGH THE
GRAPEVINE + I WANT
YOU (CD)
TMGCD 0011
I Hear The Children Singing (song)
TA45 0322, TA45 0323
I Hear Those Church Bells
Ringing (song)
PR45 0001
I Hope I See It In My Lifetime
(song)
MW45 0003
I Just Called To Say I Love You
(song)
TMG45 0151
I Just Called To Say I Love You
(Instrumental) (song)
TMG45 0151
I Just Can't Help But Feel The
Pain (song)
MO45 0147
I Just Can't Help Myself (song)
GO45 0210
I Just Can't Walk Away (song)
TMG45 0111
I Just Keep Thinking About You
Baby (song)
MO12 0024, TA45 0294
I JUST NEED MORE MONEY
(LP)
TALP 0150
I Just Need More Money (song)
MO12 0031
I Just Need More Money
(Instrumental) (song)
MO12 0031
I Just Need More Money (Pt. I)
(song)
TA45 0297
I Just Need More Money (Pt. II)
(song)
TA45 0297
I Just Wanna Dance With You
(song)
GO45 0204
I Just Wanted To Make Her
Happy (song)
MO45 0294
I Just Want To Celebrate (song)
MO45 0345, RA45 0027
I Keep Running (song)
TMG45 0179
I Knew You When (song)
HI45 0012
I Know Better (song)
TAEP 0007
I Know How It Feels (song)
MO45 0019

(I Know) I'm Losing You (song)
GO45 0058, RA45 0013, TMG12 0011
I Let You Go (song)
TA45 0326
I Like Everything About You
(song)
MO45 0107
I Like It (song)
TMG45 0047
I Like It Like That (song)
TA45 0081, TAEP 0003
I LIKE YOUR STYLE (LP)
MOLP 0357
I Like Your Style (song)
SO45 0074
I'll Always Love You (song)
MO45 0089, MO45 0145, TA45 0082
I'll Always Remember That Song
(song)
HI45 0017, HI45 0022
I'll Be Available (song)
MO45 0076, TA45 0099
I'll Be Doggone (song)
TA45 0096, TAEP 0004
I'll Begin Again (song)
EC45 0001
I'll Be Here (song)
GO45 0124
I'll Be In Troublee (song)
GO45 0033
I'll Be Satisfied (song)
ML45 0006
I'll Be There (song)
MO45 0183, TMG12 0011, TMG45 0067,
VI45 0067
I'll Be Your Baby Tonight (song)
MO45 0205
I'll Be Your Brother (song)
MO45 0318
I'll Call You (song)
MI45 0010
I'll Come Running (song)
MO45 0075
I'll Cry A Million Tears (song)
TA45 0047
I'll Cry Tomorrow (song)
MO45 0056, VI45 0001
I'll Do It (song)
TMG45 0172
I'll Follow You (song)
GOEP 0005
I'll Have To Let Him Go (song)
GO45 0012
I'll Hold Out My Hand (song)
PR45 0016
I'll Keep A Light In My Window
(song)
TMG12 0051
I'll Keep Holding On (song)
TA45 0100
I'll Keep My Light In My
Window (song)
TMG45 0195, TMG45 0224
I'll Love You 'Till I Die (song)
ME45 0005
I'll Make It Up To You Somehow
(song)
MO45 0047, MO45 0057
I'll Never Change (song)
MO45 0222
I'll Never Fall In Love Again
(song)

TMG45 0110
I'll Never Love Again (song)
TA45 0003
I'll Never See My Love Again
(song)
GO45 0042
I'll Pick A Rose For My Rose
(song)
GO45 0078
I'll Say Forever My Love (song)
SO45 0043
I'll See You Later (song)
WO45 0005
I'll See You Through (song)
MO45 0240
I'll Stand By You (song)
GO45 0030
I'll Still Be Around (song)
MO45 0018
I'll Take Care Of You (song)
TA45 0138
I'LL TRY SOMETHING NEW
(LP)
NALP 0017, TALP 0011
I'll Try Something New (song)
MO45 0153, MOCO 0011, TA45 0042
I'll Turn To Stone (song)
MO45 0121, MOCO 0003
I'll Wait For You (song)
SO45 0069
I Lost My Love In The Big City
(song)
MO45 0213
I Love Every Little Thing About
You (song)
MO45 0455, MW45 0016, TA45 0205
I Love Makin' Love (To The
Music) (song)
GO45 0181, GO45 0190
I Love The Nearness Of You
(song)
TA45 0308
I Love To See You Dance (song)
MO45 0464
I Love To Sing To You (song)
MO45 0501
I Love You (song)
VI45 0040
I Love You Baby (song)
IN45 0001, MO45 0001, MO45 0002,
MO45S 0001, MO45S 0002
I Love You Madly (song)
SO45 0052
I Love You Madly (Instrumental)
(song)
SO45 0052
I Love You More (Than I Hate
What You Do) (song)
TMG45 0133
I Love You So (song)
TMG45 0027
I'm A Bachelor (song)
GO45 0143
I'm A Fool For You (song)
GO45 0140
Imaginary Girl (song)
PR45 0019
I'm An Easy Rider (song)
RA45 0032, RACO 0009
(I'm A) Road Runner (song)
SO45 0015, SOEP 0001, SOEP 0003
I'm A Sucker For Your Love

(song)
GO45 0171, MO12 0027

I'm A Sucker For Your Love
(Instrumental) (song)
MO12 0027

I'm A Winner (song)
MO45 0200

I'm Coming Home (song)
GO45 0191

I'm Coming Out (song)
MO45 0508, MO45 0509

I'm Crazy 'Bout My Baby (song)
TA45 0070, TAEP 0001

I'm Dyin' (song)
PR45 0028

I Met This Girl (song)
TA45 0304

I'm Falling In Love With You
(song)
MO45 0292

I'm Giving You Your Freedom
(song)
MO45 0065

I'm Glad About It (song)
MO45 0193

I'm Going Home (song)
DI45 0004

I'm Goin' Left (song)
MO45 0330

I'm Gonna Carry On (song)
SO45 0072

I'm Gonna Cry (If You Quit Me)
(song)
TA45 0016

I'm Gonna Get You Pt. 1 (song)
MW45 0012

I'm Gonna Get You Pt. 2 (song)
MW45 0012

I'm Gonna Have My Cake (And
Eat It Too) (song)
GO45 0175

I'm Gonna Hold On As Long As I
Can (song)
TA45 0162

I'm Gonna Let My Heart Do The
Walking (song)
MO45 0405

I'm Gonna Make You Love Me
(song)
MO45 0148

I'm Gonna Stay (song)
MO45 0033, MO45 0344

I'm Here Again (song)
MO12 0034, TA45 0282

I'm Hooked (song)
GO45 0018

I'm In A Different World (song)
MO45 0143

I'm In Love (song)
GO45 0154, PR45 0011, TMG45 0208

I'm In Love Again (song)
MO45 0085

I'm In Love (And I Know It)
(song)
GO45 0086

I'm In Love With You (song)
TMG45 0062, TMG45 0165

I'm In The World (song)
MO45 0479

I Miss You Baby (How I Miss
You) (song)
GO45 0052

I'm Just A Part Of Yesterday
(song)
MO45 0257, MW45 0052

I'm Just Too Shy (song)
MO45 0544

I'm Livin' In Shame (song)
MO45 0150, MOCO 0009

I'm Looking For Love (song)
MW45 0009

I'm Loving You Softly (song)
TA45 0291

I'm More Than Happy (I'm
Satisfied) (song)
TA45 0181

I'm My Brother's Keeper (song)
TMG45 0001

I'm Never Gonna Say Goodbye
(song)
TMG45 0027

I'm Not A Plaything (song)
GO45 0043

I'm Not Easy (song)
TMG45 0029

I'm Not Strong Enough To Love
You Again (song)
TA45 0290

I'm On The Outside Looking In
(song)
MO45 0060

I'm Ready For Love (song)
GO45 0057, GOEP 0005, TMG45 0217

I'm So Glad (song)
SO45 0117

I'm So Glad I Fell For You (song)
MO45 0169

I'm So Glad I Got Somebody
(Like You Around) (song)
MO45 0150

I'm So Happy (song)
MO45 0206

I'm Someone Who Cares (song)
SO45 0093

I'm So Sorry (song)
MO45 0020

I'm Still A Struggling Man (song)
GO45 0088, GOCO 0005

I'M STILL IN LOVE WITH
YOU (CD)
TMGCD 0019

I'm Still Loving You (song)
TA45 0094

I'm Still Waiting (song)
MO45 0204

I'm The Exception To The Rule
(song)
GO45 0110, VI45 0016

I'm Truly Yours (song)
GO45 0133

I'm Up For You (song)
TMG45 0205

I Must Be In Love (song)
TMG45 0011

I'm Wondering (song)
TA45 0142

I'm Yours, You're Mine (song)
TA45 0038

IN A MELLOW MOOD (LP)
NALP 0013

In And Out (song)
TMG12 0002, TMG45 0039

In And Out Of Love (song)
MO45 0127

In And Out Of My Life (song)
GO45 0114, GOCO 0010

IN A SPECIAL WAY (LP)
TMGLP 0063

In Bed (song)
RA45 0003

In Case You Need Love (song)
TAEP 0005

Include Me In Your Life (song)
MO45 0281

IN CONCERT (LP)
RALP 0031

Indiana Girl (song)
ML45 0005

Indiana Wants Me (song)
RA45 0009, RACO 0002

I Need Someone (song)
TA45 0143

I Need You (song)
GO45 0137

I Need You Now (song)
TA45 0299

I Need Your Love (Give It To
Me) (song)
MO45 0317

I Need Your Lovin' (song)
GO45 0085, GO45 0192

I Never Had It So Good (song)
MO45 0430

I Never Thought I'd Be Losing
You (song)
SO45 0124

IN FULL BLOOM (LP)
TALP 0069

IN FULL CHILL (LP)
TMGLP 0218

IN GOOD TASTE (LP)
JULP 0002

IN LOVE (LP)
NALP 0026

IN LOVING MEMORY (EP)
CHEP 0002

IN LOVING MEMORY
(TRIBUTE TO MRS.
LOUCYE G. WAKEFIELD)
(LP)
MOLP 0043

In My Diary (song)
MO45 0166, VI45 0049

In My House (song)
TMG45 0147

In My House (Instrumental) (song)
TMG45 0147

In My House (12-inch version)
(song)
TMG12 0030

In My House (12-inch
Instrumental version) (song)
TMG12 0030

In My Lonely Room (song)
GO45 0032

In My Own Lifetime (song)
EC45 0001

IN MY STRIDE (LP)
MOLP 0288

Inner City Blues (Make Me
Wanna Holler) (song)
TA45 0197

INNERVISIONS (CD)
TMGLP 0154

INNERVISIONS (LP)
TALP 0107

IN 'N' OUT (LP)
GOLP 0093
IN OUR LIFETIME (LP)
TALP 0156
INSIDE OUT (LP)
MOLP 0190
INSIDE YOU (LP)
MOLP 0254
IN SQUARE CIRCLE (CD &
LP)
TMGLP 0136
IN THE GROOVE (LP)
TALP 0066
In The Jungle (song)
RA45 0028
In The Morning (song)
TA45 0299
IN THE POCKET (LP)
MOLP 0360
In These Changing Times (song)
MO45 0197
Intimate Friends (song)
TA45 0285
Into Each Rain Some Life Must
Fall (song)
TMG45 0057
Into The Groove (song)
GO45 0212
INTRODUCING MISS PAULA
GREER (LP)
WOLP 0002
INTRODUCING THE
DOWNBEATS (LP)
TALP 0006
INTRODUCING THE
JACKSON 5 (LP)
MOLP 0102
AN INTRODUCTION TO
RARE EARTH RECORDS
(LP)
RALP 0001
INVITATION TO LOVE (LP)
MOLP 0351
Invitation To Love (song)
MO45 0526
INVOLVED (LP)
GOLP 0056
I Out-Duked The Duke (song)
TA45 0041
I Pray Everyday You Won't
Regret Loving Me (song)
MO45 0169
I Promise To Wait My Love (song)
GO45 0071
I Remember When (Dedicated To
Beverly) (song)
VI45 0054, VICO 0003
I Remember You (song)
WO45 0001
IRONS IN THE FIRE (LP)
GOLP 0099
Irons In The Fire (song)
GO45 0192
IRONS IN THE FIRE + IT
MUST BE MAGIC (CD)
TMGCD 0004
IRRESISTIBLE TAMMI
TERRELL (LP)
MOLP 0053
Is Anyone Here Going My Way
(song)
MO45 0131

I Saw You When You Met Her
(song)
GO45 0148
I Second That Emotion (song)
MO45 0543, TA45 0144, TMG12 0006,
TMG45 0019
I See You For The First Time
(song)
MO45 0395
I See Your Name Up In Lights
(song)
MO45 0243
I Should Be Proud (song)
GO45 0099
I SING MY SONGS FOR YOU
(LP)
PRLP 0014
Is It Love (song)
GO45 0005
Island Lady (song)
GO45 0188
Isn't She Pretty (song)
GO45 0001
Isn't The Night Fantastic (song)
GO45 0216, TMG45 0126, TMG45 0171
Is There Anything Love Can't Do
(song)
VI45 0058
Is There A Place (In His Heart
For Me) (song)
SO45 0083
Is This All There Is To A Honky
Tonk? (song)
ML45 0003
Is Your Teacher Cool (song)
PR45 0027
It (song)
TA45 0005
It Ain't Easy Comin' Down (song)
PR45 0022, TMG45 0023
IT ALL COMES OUT IN MY
SONG (LP)
MOLP 0295
It Don't Get Better Than This
(song)
TMG45 0277
It Happened On A Sunday
Morning (song)
MO45 0221
I Think I Can Change You (song)
TA45 0128
I THINK THEREFORE I AM
(LP)
RALP 0019
I Thought I Could Handle It (song)
TMG45 0121, TMG45 0211
I Thought It Took A Little Time
(But Today I Fell In Love)
(song)
MO45 0400
I Threw Away A Rose (song)
HI45 0018
It Hurt Me Too (song)
MO45 0050, TA45 0051
It Is As Good As You Make It
(song)
MO45 0332
It Makes You Happy (But It
Ain't Gonna Last Too Long)
(song)
RA45 0054
It Moves Me (song)

TA45 0002
It Must Be Love (song)
GO45 0017
IT MUST BE MAGIC (CD)
TMGCD 0004
IT MUST BE MAGIC (LP)
GOLP 0105
It Must Be Magic (song)
GO45 0215
I Tried (song)
GO45 0076
I Truly, Truly Believe (song)
GO45 0069
It's A Crying Shame (The Way
You Treat A Good Man Like
Me) (song)
SO45 0005
It's A Family Thang (song)
CH45 0002
It's A Lifetime Thing (song)
MO45 0436
It's All Been Said Before (song)
MO45 0363
It's All In The Game (song)
MO45 0175
It's All Over But The Shoutin'
(song)
SO45 0091
It's A Lonely World Without
Your Love (song)
GOEP 0003
It's A Lonesome Road (song)
VI45 0057, VICO 0004
It's Always Me (song)
MO45 0260, MW45 0047
It's Another Sunday (song)
MO45 0254
It's A Shame (song)
VI45 0056
It's Bad For Me To See You
(song)
MO45 0357
It's Been A Long Long Time
(song)
VI45 0042
It's Been A Long Time (song)
MO45 0475
It's Been Oh So Long (song)
MO45 0325, MO45 0331
It's Gone (song)
HI45 0006
It's Gonna Be Hard Times (song)
TA45 0050
It's Got To Be A Miracle (This
Thing Called Love) (song)
TA45 0126
It's Growing (song)
GO45 0041, GO45 0080
It's Her Turn To Live (song)
TA45 0236
It Should Have Been Me (song)
MO45 0336, MO45 0397, SO45 0045,
TA45 0059
It Should Have Been Me Loving
Her (song)
GO45 0089, GO45 0093
It's Just A Dream (song)
RA45 0031
It's Just A Phase (song)
MO45 0262
It's Just A Place (song)
TA45 0224

It's More Than You
(Instrumental) (song)
TMG45 0175

It's My House (song)
MO45 0488

IT'S MY TURN (LP)
MOLP 0352

It's My Turn (song)
MO45 0514

IT'S NATION TIME (LP)
BFLP 0007

IT'S NEVER TOO LATE (LP)
CHLP 0001

It's Not The Last Time (song)
RA45 0046

It's Not Too Late (song)
MO45 0040

It's Private Tonight (song)
CH45 0004, CH45 0012, CHCO 0003

It's Really Nice To Be In Love
Again (song)
PR45 0026

It's So Hard Being A Loser (song)
GO45 0060

It's So Hard For Me To Say
Good-bye (song)
TA45 0189, TACO 0013, MO45 0202

It's So Hard For Me To Say
Good-bye (Long Version)
(song)
TA45 0190

It's So Hard For Me To Say
Good-bye (Short Version)
(song)
TA45 0190

It's So Hard To Say Goodbye To
Yesterday (song)
MO45 0377

It's So Real (song)
GO45 0170

It's So Sad (song)
MO45 0275

It's Summer (song)
GO45 0100, GO45 0110, SO45 0047

It's The Same Old Love (song)
TA45 0206

It's The Same Old Song (song)
MO45 0092, MO45 0227, TMG12 0011

IT'S THE TEMPTATIONS (EP)
MOEP 0010

(It's The Way) Nature Planned It
(song)
MO45 0222

IT'S TIME (LP)
MOLP 0323

It's Time To Go Now (song)
SO45 0039

It's Too Bad (song)
GO45 0007

It's Too Late To Change The
Time (song)
MO45 0299

It's Too Much For Man To Take
Too Long (song)
GO45 0117

Itsy Bity Pity Love (song)
MO45 0023

It's You (song)
TA45 0015, TMG45 0237

It's You (Instrumental) (song)
TMG45 0237

It Takes All Kinds Of People

(song)
RA45 0029

It Takes A Man To Teach A
Woman How To Love (song)
TA45 0204, VI45 0061

IT TAKES TWO (DUETS) (LP)
NALP 0020

It Takes Two (song)
TA45 0126

It Will Come In Time (song)
MO45 0487

It Won't Be Long (When We're
All Gone) (song)
MO45 0424

I Understand My Man (song)
VI45 0042

I've Been A Long Time Leaving
(song)
ME45 0011

I've Been Blessed (song)
MO45 0116

I've Been Cheated (song)
VI45 0024

I've Been Good To You (song)
GO45 0064, MO45 0141, TA45 0036,
TA45 0095, TAEP 0003

I've Been There Before (song)
MO45 0326

I've Been There Too (song)
HI45 0008

I've Been To The Mountaintop
(song)
TMG12 0018

I've Been Waiting (song)
TMG12 0044, TMG45 0206

(I've Given You) The Best Years
Of My Life (song)
MO45 0258, MW45 0050

(I've Given You) The Best Years
Of My Live (song)
VI45 0061

(I've Got A) Little Black Book
(song)
TMG45 0142

I've Got A Notion (song)
MO45 0011

I've Got A Radio (song)
TMG45 0172

I've Got To Find A Way To Win
Maria Back (song)
SO45 0067

I've Got To Find It (song)
TA45 0140

I've Got To Find Myself A Brand
New Baby (song)
MO45 0151

I've Heard It All Before (song)
TMG45 0186

I've Lost Everything I've Ever
Loved (song)
MO45 0160

I've Made Love To You A
Thousand Times (song)
TMG45 0057

I'VE NEVER BEEN TO ME
(LP)
TMGLP 0010

I've Never Been To Me (song)
PR45 0026, TMG45 0012

I've Passed This Way Before
(song)
SO45 0027, SOEP 0004

IVY JO IS IN THIS BAG (LP)
VILP 0007

I Wanna Be Closer (song)
GO45 0165

I Wanna Be Where You Are
(song)
MO45 0214, MO45 0549

I Wanna Be With You (song)
TA45 0230, TA45 0238

I Wanna Do It To You (song)
MO45 0428

I Wanna Make It (In Your World)
(song)
MO45 0495

I Want A Guy (song)
MO45 0016, TA45 0021, TA45 0037

I Want A Love I Can See (song)
GO45 0016

I Want Her Love (song)
SO45 0002, SO45 0035, SOEP 0004

I Want My Baby Back (song)
GO45 0067

I Want The World To Know He's
Mine (song)
TMG45 0140

I Want To Be Humble (song)
MW45 0001

I Want To Be Your Love (song)
TA45 0313

I Want To Come Back As A Song
(song)
TMG45 0052

I Want To Come Home For
Christmas (song)
TA45 0218

I Want To Go Back There Again
(song)
MW45 0008, MWCO 0001, TMG45 0065,
VI45 0040

I Want To Make It Easy For You
(song)
GO45 0150, MO45 0404

I Want To Talk About You (song)
WO45 0003

I WANT YOU (CD)
TMGCD 0011

I WANT YOU (LP)
TALP 0123

I Want You (song)
TACO 0017

I Want You (Instrumental) (song)
TA45 0256

I Want You (Long version) (song)
TA45 0256

I Want You (Short Version)
(Mono) (song)
TA45 0257

I Want You (Short Version)
(Stereo) (song)
TA45 0257

I Want You Back (song)
GO45 0119, MO45 0168, MOCO 0013,
TMG12 0011

I Want You 'Round (song)
TA45 0087

I Was Born This Way (song)
GA45 0001, MO45 0452

I Was Born This Way
(Instrumental) (song)
MO12 0011, MO45 0452

I Was Born This Way (Vocal)
(song)

MO12 0011

I WAS MADE TO LOVE HER
(LP)
TALP 0060

I Was Made To Love Her (song)
TA45 0136

I Wasn't Wrong About You (song)
ML45 0015

I Who Have Nothing
(Instrumental) (song)
MO45 0525

I Who Have Nothing (Vocal)
(song)
MO45 0525

I Will (song)
HI45 0019

I Will Find A Way (song)
MO45 0198

I Will Never Love Another (song)
CH45 0007, CHCO 0004

I Will Wait For You (song)
TMG45 0177

I Wish (song)
TA45 0267

I Wish It Would Rain (song)
GO45 0069, SO45 0047, TA45 0223

I Wish I Were Your Mirror (song)
MO45 0187

I Wonder Why (Nobody Loves
Me) (song)
MO45 0116

I Won't Be The Fool I've Been
Again (song)
GO45 0128

I Won't Go Back (song)
DI45 0002

I Won't Last A Day Without You
(song)
MO45 0251

I Won't Remember Ever Loving
You (song)
MO45 0510

I Won't Weep No More (song)
CH45 0013

I Wouldn't Change The Man He
Is (song)
MO45 0145, MOCO 0007

JACKIE JACKSON (LP)
MOLP 0159, MOLP 0187

Jackson (song)
CH45 0011, CHEP 0001

Jamie (song)
MO45 0030

Janet (song)
TMG45 0208

JAZZ (LP)
WOLP 0004

Jazz! (song)
CHEP 0001

THE JAZZ SOUL OF LITTLE
STEVIE (LP)
TALP 0014

Jealous Lover (song)
GO45 0015

Jealousy (song)
TMG45 0127

Jefferson Ball (song)
GO45 0173

JERMAINE (LP)
MOLP 0154, MOLP 0353

THE JERRY ROSS
SYMPOSIUM VOL. 2 (LP)

MOLP 0156

JESUS CHRIST'S GREATEST
HITS (LP)
RALP 0028

Jesus Help Me Find Another Way
(song)
MW45 0038

Jesus Is Love (song)
MO45 0521

Jesus Is The Key (song)
RA45 0025

Jesus Loves (song)
TA45 0030

Je Vous Aime Beaucoup (I Love
You) (song)
MO45 0486

Jimmy (song)
RA45 0021

Jimmy Brown (song)
ME45 0016

Jimmy Mack (song)
GO45 0059, GOEP 0005

JIMMY REED (CD)
TMGLP 0208

Joey's Theme (song)
MO45 0523

JOSE FELICIANO (LP)
MOLP 0358

JOURNEY THROUGH THE
SECRET LIFE OF PLANTS
(CD)
TMGLP 0129

Journey To Love (song)
TMG45 0043

JOYFUL JUKEBOX MUSIC
(LP)
MOLP 0267

Joy Road (song)
GO45 0061

JOYSTICK (LP)
TMGLP 0086

Joystick (song)
TMG45 0106

Joystick (Vocal) (song)
TMG12 0021

JUKEBOX (LP)
TMGLP 0119

Julieanne (Where Are You
Tonight?) (song)
MC45 0002

JUMP ON IT (LP)
MOLP 0355

JR. WALKER & THE ALL
STARS (LP)
SOLP 0042

JR. WALKER & THE ALL
STARS GREATEST HITS
(LP)
SOLP 0018

JR. WALKER & THE ALL
STARS LIVE (LP)
SOLP 0005, SOLP 0025

Just A Closer Walk With Thee
(song)
MO45 0139

Just A Few More Days (song)
MO45 0045

Just Ain't Enough Love (song)
MO45 0069, TA45 0131, TA45 0167

Just A Little Bit Closer (song)
MW45 0006

Just A Little Bit Of You (song)

MO45 0362

Just A Little Misunderstanding
(song)
GO45 0053

Just A Mortal Man (song)
MO45 0271

Just Another Day (song)
MO45 0384

Just Another Lonely Night (song)
GOEP 0001, SO45 0065

Just Another Morning (song)
RA45 0011

Just Another Song Away (song)
HI45 0021

Just As Long As There Is You
(song)
TA45 0264

Just As Long As You Need Me
(song)
MO45 0101

Just Believe In Love (song)
TMG45 0061

Just Beyond (song)
MO45 0325

Just Be Yourself (song)
GO45 0022

Just For You (song)
MI45 0011

Just For You (Put the Boogie In
Your Body (song)
MO45 0541

Just Gets Better With Time (song)
TMG45 0233

Just How Does It Feel (song)
PR45 0029

Just Keep Laughin' (song)
PR45 0020

Just Let Me Hold You For A
Night (song)
MO45 0434

Just Let Me Know (song)
GO45 0029

Just Like Men (song)
RA45 0015

Just Look What You've Done
(song)
TA45 0133

Just Loving You (song)
TA45 0068

Just Memories (song)
TA45 0211

Just My Imagination (Running
Away With Me) (song)
GO45 0106, GO45 0131

Just My Soul Responding (song)
TA45 0236

Just Not Gonna Make It (song)
MW45 0018

Just Passing Through (song)
TA45 0250, TA45 0270

Just Put Some Love In Your
Heart (song)
TMG45 0046

Just Rode By The Place (Where
We Used To Stay) (song)
MO45 0434

Just Say, Just Say (song)
MO45 0309

Just Say The Word (song)
TMG45 0104

Just Seven Numbers (Can
Straighten Out My Life) (song)

TMGLP 0018

Let Me Tickle Your Fancy (song)
TMG45 0030

Let's All Save The Children (song)
SO45 0080

Let's Be Young Tonight (song)
MO12 0001, MO45 0415

Let's Break (Instrumental) (song)
TMG12 0014, TMG45 0101,
TMG45 0102

Let's Break (Vocal) (song)
TMG12 0014, TMG45 0101

Let's Dance (song)
SO45 0010

Let's Find Each Other Tonight
(song)
TMG45 0077

LET'S GET IT ON (CD)
TMGCD 0014

LET'S GET IT ON (LP)
TALP 0110, TMGLP 0078

Let's Get It On (song)
TA45 0223

LET'S GET SERIOUS (LP)
MOLP 0333

Let's Get Serious (song)
MO45 0486, MOCO 0038

Let's Go Somewhere (song)
VI45 0026

Let's Go Up (song)
TMG45 0161

Let's Hold On To What We've
Got (song)
ML45 0024

Let's Make A Deal (song)
MO45 0440

Let's Make Love Now (song)
MO45 0258, MW45 0050

Let's Make Love Over The
Telephone (song)
MO45 0549

Let's Make Some Love (song)
CH45 0004

Let Somebody Love Me (song)
VI45 0055

Let's Stay Together (song)
TMG45 0054

LET'S STAY TOGETHER +
I'M STILL IN LOVE WITH
YOU (CD)
TMGCD 0019

LETTA (LP)
CHLP 0005

LET THE MUSIC PLAY (LP)
MOLP 0362

Let The Music Play (song)
MO45 0547, RA45 0016

LET THE SUNSHINE IN (LP)
MOLP 0090

LET THE SUNSHINE IN +
CREAM OF THE CROP
(CD)
TMGCD 0033

Let Your Conscience Be Your
Guide (song)
TA45 0024

Let Your Hair Down (song)
GO45 0134, MO45 0319

Let Yourself Go (song)
MO45 0429

Liberation (song)
GA45 0001

LIBRA (LP)
MOLP 0249

Life And Breath (song)
MO45 0267

Life Begins With You (song)
TMG45 0276

The Life Of A Cowboy (song)
GO45 0211

Life's A Ball (While It Lasts)
(song)
TA45 0208

Lifetime Man (song)
VI45 0007

Light At The End Of The Tunnel
(song)
TMG45 0184

Lightin' Up The Night (song)
TMG12 0036, TMG45 0194

LIGHT THE NIGHT (LP)
TMGLP 0062

Light Years (Opus IV) (song)
MO45 0462

Like a Gypsy (song)
MC45 0003

(Like A) Nightmare (song)
VI45 0005

Like We Used To Do (song)
MO45 0313

Lil' Red Ridin' Hood (song)
GO45 0141

LI'L SUZY (LP)
TMGLP 0012

Li'l Suzy (song)
TMG12 0005, TMG45 0029

Li'l Suzy (Instrumental) (song)
TMG12 0005

Linda Sue Dixon (song)
IN45 0002

The Line Of Your Fire (song)
TMG45 0221

THE LINE OF YOUR LOVE
(LP)
TMGLP 0164

LIONEL RICHIE (CD & LP)
TMGLP 0008

LIONEL RICHIE THE
COMPOSER: GREAT
LOVE SONGS WITH THE
COMMODORES AND
DIANA ROSS (CD)
TMGLP 0145

Listen To Yesterday (song)
MO45 0263, MO45 0291

Listen To Your Soul (song)
RA45 0020

Little Acorn (song)
ME45 0013

A Little Bit For Sandy (song)
MO45 0140

A Little Bit Of Sympathy, A
Little Bit Of Love (song)
TA45 0080

Little Bitty Pretty One (song)
MO45 0211

Little Darling, I Need You (song)
TA45 0123, TAEP 0004

A LITTLE DIS, A LITTLE DAT
(LP)
MOLP 0091

Little Dog Heaven (song)
PR45 0013

Little Girl Blue (song)

TA45 0071

Little Girl Don't You Worry
(song)
MO45 0518, MOCO 0039

Little Girls & Ladies (song)
MO45 0498

A LITTLE KNIGHT MUSIC
(LP)
SOLP 0044

Little Lady (song)
TMG45 0142

The Little Man's Got The Biggest
Smile In Town (song)
MC45 0015

A Little More Love (song)
TA45 0089

A Little More Trust (song)
MO45 0216

Little Ole Boy, Little Ole Girl
(song)
TA45 0148

Little Red Rooster (song)
GO45 0129

LITTLE RICHARD (CD)
TMGLP 0210

Little Runaway (song)
GO45 0185

The Little Shoemaker (song)
PR45 0012

Little Sister (song)
HI45 0020

Little Water Boy (song)
TA45 0053

LIVE (LP)
TALP 0070, TALP 0079, TALP 0114,
TMGLP 0078

LIVE AT CAESAR'S PALACE
(LP)
TMGLP 0084

LIVE AT LAKE TAHOE (LP)
MOLP 0041

LIVE AT LONDON'S TALK
OF THE TOWN (LP)
GOLP 0053

LIVE AT THE AMERICANA
(LP)
MOLP 0046

LIVE AT THE COPA (LP)
GOLP 0038

LIVE AT THE COPA + WITH
A LOT O' SOUL (CD)
TMGCD 0038

LIVE AT THE DESERT INN
(LP)
MOLP 0139

LIVE AT THE LONDON
PALLADIUM (CD)
TMGLP 0193

LIVE AT THE LONDON
PALLADIUM (LP)
TALP 0133

LIVE, LIVE, LIVE! (LP)
MOLP 0027

Live Wire (song)
GO45 0028

LIVIN' FOR YOU (CD)
TMGCD 0041

LIVING (LP)
MOLP 0316

Living For The City (song)
TA45 0232

Living In A World I Created For

Myself (song)
SO45 0077

Lo And Behold (song)
SO45 0086

Locking Up My Heart (song)
GOEP 0006, TA45 0060, TAEP 0002

Londonderry (song)
MO45 0306

(Loneliness Made Me Realize) It's
You That I Need (song)
GO45 0066

Lonely Girl, Lonely Boy (song)
TMG45 0230

Lonely Lonely Girl Am I (song)
VI45 0016

Lonely Lonely Man Am I (song)
GOEP 0003, SO45 0046

Lonely Rainy Days In San Diego
(song)
MO45 0339

Lonely Teardrops (song)
TMG45 0076, TMG45 0083

Long Life And Success To The
Farmer (song)
MW45 0041

Long Long Time Ago (song)
ME45 0018

Long Way From Home (song)
RA45 0041

Look At Me (song)
PR45 0034

Look Away (song)
RA45 0002

LOOKING BACK (LP)
MOLP 0206

Looking For A Man (song)
TA45 0023

Looking For The Right Guy (song)
TA45 0083

LOOKIN' THROUGH THE
WINDOWS (LP)
MOLP 0152

Lookin' Through The Windows
(song)
MO45 0217

Look What You've Done To Me
(song)
MO45 0374, MO45 0457

Looky Looky (Look At Me Girl)
(song)
MO45 0391

Loraine Alterman Interviews
Marvin Gaye For Teen Beat
Readers
TA45S 0004

Love (song)
MO45 0175, MO45 0503

Love Ain't Love (Till You Give It
To Somebody) (song)
TA45 0216

Love Ain't No Toy (song)
MO45 0367

Love Always (song)
TMG45 0264

Love And Peace (song)
CH45 0005

LOVE AT FIRST SIGHT (LP)
RALP 0009

Love At First Sight (Je Taime)
(song)
RA45 0004, RACO 0001

LOVE AWAY HER MEMORY

TONIGHT (LP)
MCLP 0002

Love Away Her Memory Tonight
(song)
MC45 0004

LOVE BREEZE (LP)
TALP 0141

Love Bug Leave My Heart Alone
(song)
GO45 0063, GOCO 0001

Love Can Be Hazardous To Your
Health (song)
MO45 0389, MO45 0401

LOVE CHANGES (LP)
TMGLP 0020

Love Changes (song)
TMG45 0025

LOVE CHILD (LP)
MOLP 0071

Love Child (song)
MO45 0146, MOCO 0008

LOVE CHILD + SUPREMES A
GO GO (CD)
TMGCD 0022

Love City (song)
MO45 0359, MO45 0403

LOVE DANCER (LP)
MOLP 0324

Love, Guess Who (song)
GO45 0099

Love Gun (song)
GO45 0179

Love Hangover (song)
MO45 0406

Love Has Gone (song)
MO45 0080

LOVE HAS LIFTED ME (LP)
TMGLP 0034

Love In The Combat Zone (song)
TMG45 0197

LOVE IN THE FIRE (LP)
TMGLP 0090

Love In The Fire (song)
TMG45 0153

Love Is All You Need (song)
GO45 0159, GOCO 0013

The Love I Saw In You Was Just
A Mirage (song)
TA45 0130, TA45 0185, TMG12 0006

Love Is Here And Now You're
Gone (song)
MO45 0114, MO45 0209

Love Is Like A Heat Wave (song)
GOEP 0002, MOCB 0014

Love Is Like An Itching In My
Heart (song)
MO12 0038, MO45 0105, MO45 0505,
MO45 0542

Love Is My Destination (song)
GO45 0084

Love Isn't Here (Like It Used To
Be) (song)
MW45 0011

Lovelight Comes A Shining (song)
HI45 0016

Love Light In Flight (song)
TMG45 0175

A Love Like Yours (Don't Come
Knocking Everyday) (song)
GO45 0023, GO45 0051, GOEP 0002

Love Machine (Pt. 1) (song)
TA45 0254

Love Machine (Pt. 2) (song)
TA45 0254

Love (Makes Me Do Foolish
Things) (song)
GO45 0046, GOEP 0002

Love Makes The World Go
Round (song)
RA45 0021

Love Makes The World Go
Round, But Money Greases
The Wheel (song)
ME45 0017

LOVE MAN (LP)
TALP 0151

Love Me (song)
MI45 0008

Love Me All The Way (song)
TA45 0059

Love Me In A Special Way (song)
TMG45 0129, TMG45 0249

Love On My Mind Tonight (song)
TMG45 0068

Love Over And Over Again (song)
GO45 0196

Love Pains (song)
MO45 0322

Love Power (song)
MO45 0373, MOCO 0031

Love Proposition (song)
MO45 0410

Lovequake (song)
TMG12 0019, TMG45 0132

Lover (song)
MO45 0010

Lovers (song)
TMG45 0100

Lover What You've Done (To
Me) (song)
MO45 0481

LOVE'S COMIN' DOWN (LP)
MOLP 0272

Love's Enough (song)
MO45 0511

Love's Gone Bad (song)
VI45 0037, VI45 0039, VICO 0001

A Love She Can Count On (song)
TA45 0061

LOVESMITH (LP)
MOLP 0364

Love Song (song)
MO45 0217, MO45 0316

LOVE SONGS & OTHER
TRAGEDIES (LP)
MOLP 0221

LOVE SONGS: 20 CLASSIC
HITS (CD)
TMGLP 0146

LOVE'S ON THE MENU (LP)
MOLP 0252

Love's Your Name (song)
RA45 0009

A Love That Can Never Be (song)
MO45 0012, MO45 0013, MO45 0014

Love (The Lonely People's
Prayer) (song)
MO45 0288

Love Theme From "Lady Sings
The Blues" (song)
MO45 0231

Love To The Rescue (song)
MO45 0440

Love Unto Me (song)

CH45 0007
Love Will Conquer All (song)
TMG45 0273
Love Will Find A Way (song)
TMG45 0174, TMG45 0250
A Love You Can Count On (song)
GOEP 0006
The Love You Save (song)
MO45 0177, MOCO 0016, TMG12 0011
Love You Too (song)
RA45 0004
Lovin' Fever (song)
GO45 0163
LOVING COUPLES (LP)
MOLP 0354
Loving You (song)
CH45 0009
Loving You Is Sweeter Than Ever
(song)
MO45 0107
Loving You The Second Time
Around (song)
TA45 0226, TA45 0239
Lovin', Livin' And Givin' (song)
MO12 0029, MO45 0465
Lovin' On (song)
HI45 0022
Lovin' You (song)
MO45 0496, MO45 0546
Lucky In Love (song)
TMG12 0038, TMG45 0200
The Luney Landing (song)
MO45 0162
The Luney Take-Off (song)
MO45 0162
LUTHER'S BLUES (LP)
GOLP 0067
Lyin' In Her Arms Again (song)
ML45 0019
M.P.G. (CD)
TMGCD 0037
M.P.G. (LP)
TALP 0073
MA (LP)
RALP 0043
Ma (song)
GO45 0132
Ma (Instrumental) (song)
RA45 0049
Ma (Vocal) (song)
RA45 0049, RA45 0052
MacArthur Park (Part 1) (song)
MO45 0201
MacArthur Park (Part 2) (song)
MO45 0201
MACHINE GUN (LP)
MOLP 0200, TMGLP 0076
Machine Gun (song)
MO45 0320, MOCO 0027
THE MACK (SOUNDTRACK)
(LP)
MOLP 0168
Made In America (song)
TMG45 0087
MAGIC (LP)
RALP 0024, TMGLP 0132
Magic Key (song)
RA45 0006, RA45 0008
Magnetized (song)
MO45 0526
THE MAGNIFICENT 7 (LP)
MOLP 0118

MAHOGANY (ORIGINAL
SOUNDTRACK) (LP)
MOLP 0260
MAJOR, JUST MESSIN'
AROUND (LP)
GOLP 0082
Make Me A Potion (song)
CH45 0010
Make Me The Woman That You
Go Home To (song)
SO45 0091
Make Me Yours (song)
GO45 0190
Make Up Your Mind (song)
TMG45 0230
Make Yourself At Home (song)
TMG45 0124
MAKING A GAME OF LIFE
(LP)
TMGLP 0144
MAKING TRAX (THE GREAT
INSTRUMENTALS) (LP)
TMGLP 0093
Malas Costumbres (Evil Ways)
(song)
TMG45 0049
Malinda (song)
GO45 0080
Mama I Gotta Brand New Thing
(Don't Say No) (song)
GO45 0125
Mama's Pearl (song)
MO45 0189, MOCO 0021
MANDRE (LP)
MOLP 0289
MANDRE TWO (LP)
MOLP 0303
Man In The Middle (song)
TMG45 0185
Man In The Middle (Instrumental)
(song)
TMG45 0185
A Man Without Love (song)
SO45 0085
(The Man With The) Rock And
Roll Banjo Band (song)
MO45 0053, MO45 0054
March Lightly (song)
WO45 0002
Marian (song)
RA45 0012, RACO 0003
Maria (You Were The Only One)
(song)
MO45 0203, SO45 0077
Marionette (song)
TA45 0183
Mark Anthony (Speaks) (song)
SOEP 0002
THE MARK OF THE BEAST
(LP)
MOLP 0217
MARTHA AND THE
VANDELLAS (EP)
MOEP 0009
MARTHA AND THE
VANDELLAS LIVE! (LP)
GOLP 0025
MARV (LP)
GOLP 0037
THE MARVELETTES (EP)
MOEP 0003, TAEP 0007
THE MARVELETTES (LP)

TALP 0055
MARVELETTES GREATEST
HITS (EP)
TAEP 0002
MARVELETTES GREATEST
HITS (LP)
TALP 0034
THE MARVELETTES SING
(LP)
TALP 0010
MARVELOUS
MARVELETTES (LP)
TALP 0018
MARVIN GAYE (EP)
MOEP 0016
MARVIN GAYE AND HIS
GIRLS (LP)
TALP 0074
MARVIN GAYE & HIS
WOMEN: 21 CLASSIC
DUETS (CD)
TMGLP 0155
MARVIN GAYE & KIM
WESTON SIDE BY SIDE
(LP)
TALP 0041
MARVIN GAYE & TAMMI
TERRELL'S GREATEST
HITS + DIANA & MARVIN
(CD)
TMGCD 0016
MARVIN GAYE'S GREATEST
HITS (LP)
TALP 0033
MARVIN GAYE'S GREATEST
HITS VOL. 2 (LP)
TALP 0059
Mary Jane (song)
GO45 0164
MARY JANE GIRLS (LP)
TMGLP 0041
Mary Mary (song)
MO45 0295
MARY, SCHERRIE & SUSAYE
(LP)
MOLP 0275
MARY WELLS (EP)
MOEP 0007
MARY WELLS' GREATEST
HITS (LP)
MOLP 0017
MARY WILSON (LP)
MOLP 0332
Masquerade (Is Over) (song)
TA45S 0002
Master Blaster (Dub) (song)
TA45 0312
Master Blaster (Jammin') (song)
TA45 0312
MASTERPIECE (CD)
TMGCD 0036
MASTERPIECE (LP)
GOLP 0065, TMGLP 0081
Masterpiece (Instrumental) (song)
GO45 0127
Masterpiece (Vocal) (song)
GO45 0127
MATRIX (LP)
RALP 0039
Maybe Next Time (song)
TMG45 0030
MAYBE TOMORROW (CD)

TMGCD 0012

MAYBE TOMORROW (LP)
MOLP 0136

Maybe Tomorrow (song)
MO45 0198

May I Have This Dance (song)
GO45 0021

May I Spend Every New Year's
With You (song)
HI45 0017

May What He Lived For Live
(song)
GO45 0027

Me And Bobby McGee (song)
MW45 0013, MWCO 0002

Me And Michelle (song)
TMG45 0154

Me And My Brother (song)
MO45 0220

Me And My Family (song)
SO45 0097

Me And My Lonely Room (song)
TA45 0180

Me And Rock & Roll (Are Here
To Stay) (song)
MO45 0340

MEATLOAF (LP)
PRLP 0023

Mechanical Emotion (song)
TMG45 0173

Mechanical Emotion (Long
Version) (song)
TMG12 0027

MEDLEY (12-inch)
TMG12 0011

MEET THE STONE CITY
BAND "OUT FROM THE
SHADOW" (LP)
TMGLP 0043

MEET THE SUPREMES (LP)
MOLP 0007

MEET THE TEMPTATIONS
(LP)
GOLP 0011, TMGLP 0081

Mellow In Coli (song)
WO45 0004

Melodie (song)
MO45 0195

Mend This Generation (song)
CH45 0001

ME 'N ROCK 'N ROLL ARE
HERE TO STAY (LP)
MOLP 0220

Mercy Mercy Me (The Ecology)
(song)
TA45 0195

MERRY CHRISTMAS (LP)
MOLP 0039, NALP 0018

MERRY CHRISTMAS FROM
MOTOWN (LP)
MOLP 0082

MERRY CHRISTMAS +
SOMEDAY AT
CHRISTMAS (CD)
TMGCD 0042

Merry-Go-Round (song)
TA45 0002

Message From A Black Man
(song)
VI45 0053

MESSENGERS (LP)
RALP 0006

Messin' Up A Good Thing (song)
GO45 0199

MICHAEL EDWARD
CAMPBELL (LP)
MOLP 0212

Mickey's Monkey (song)
TA45 0066, TAEP 0003

Midnight Cowboy (song)
MO45 0165

Midnight Dancer (song)
MO45 0484

Midnight Johnny (song)
GO45 0031

MIDNIGHT LADY (LP)
RALP 0047

Midnight Lady (song)
RA45 0056

MIDNIGHT LUST (LP)
TMGLP 0152

MIDNIGHT MAGIC (CD)
TMGCD 0015

MIDNIGHT MAGIC (LP)
MOLP 0331

Midnight Music Man (song)
GO45 0174, GO45 0176

Midnight Rhapsody (Part 1) (song)
MO45 0414

Midnight Rhapsody (Part 2) (song)
MO45 0414

Midnight Shine (song)
TMG12 0019

Mighty Good Lovin' (song)
TA45 0027

Mighty-Mighty (song)
MO45 0537

MIGHTY MOTOWN (LP)
NALP 0023

Mighty Spirit (song)
MO45 0521

The Miles (song)
ME45 0019

Mind Body And Soul (song)
MW45 0017

MIND CONTROL (LP)
TMGLP 0106

Mind Games (song)
TMG12 0039, TMG45 0201

Mind Games (Instrumental) (song)
TMG45 0201

Mind Over Matter (song)
ME45 0005

Mind Pleaser (song)
MO45 0454

Minne Ha Ha (song)
PR45 0017

THE MIRACLES DOIN'
MICKEY'S MONKEY (LP)
TALP 0026

The Miracles Of Christmas (song)
TA45 0127

THE MIRACLES SING
MODERN (LP)
TALP 0015

Misery (song)
TA45 0026

Miss Busy Body (Get Your Body
Busy) (song)
TMG45 0112

Miss Busy Body (Get Your Body
Busy) (Part 2) (Instrumental)
(song)
TMG45 0112

Miss Your Love (song)
TMG45 0190

Mr. Disco Radio (song)
GO45 0155

Mr. Fix-It Man (song)
MW45 0014

Mr. Lonely Heart (song)
VI45 0007

MR. MAGIC (LP)
TMGLP 0082

MR. MAGIC + FEELS SO
GOOD (CD)
TMGCD 0010

MODERN INNOVATIONS ON
COUNTRY AND
WESTERN THEMES (LP)
GOLP 0003

Mo Jo Hanna (song)
MO45 0038, VI45 0039

Molly (I Ain't Gettin' Any
Younger) (song)
ML45 0007

Moment Of Truth (song)
SO45 0066

Money And Me (song)
TA45 0018

MONEY AND OTHER BIG
HITS (LP)
TALP 0007

Money's Hard To Get (song)
TMG45 0033

Money Talk (song)
TA45 0069

Money Talks (song)
TMG45 0108

Money (That's What I Want)
(song)
MO45 0018, MO45 0443, MW45 0020,
TA45 0008

Money (That's What I Want) Part
1 (song)
SO45 0026

Money (That's What I Want) Part
2 (song)
SO45 0026

Monkey Jump (song)
SO45 0003

MOODS AND GROOVES (LP)
JULP 0001

MOODS OF MARVIN GAYE
(EP)
TAEP 0004

MOODS OF MARVIN GAYE
(LP)
TALP 0047

MOODY JR. (LP)
SOLP 0033

Moonlight On The Beach (song)
VI45 0023

MORE HITS BY THE
SUPREMES (LP)
MOLP 0028

More Love (song)
TA45 0137, TMG12 0006

More On The Inside (song)
TMG45 0033

MORE SONGS FROM THE
ORIGINAL SOUNDTRACK
OF "THE BIG CHILL" (LP)
TMGLP 0096

More Than A Dream (song)
GO45 0077

MORE THAN YOU CAN
HANDLE (LP)
TMGLP 0152
More Than You Can Handle
(song)
TMG45 0207
More Than You Can Handle
(Instrumental) (song)
TMG45 0207
The Morning After (song)
MW45 0019
The Morning After The Night
Before (song)
HI45 0014
Morning Glow (song)
MO45 0230
Mornin' Train (song)
CH45 0016
MOSADI (LP)
CHLP 0009
MOTELS AND MEMORIES
(LP)
MLLP 0003
Motels And Memories (song)
ML45 0028
Mother Nature (song)
GO45 0120, GOCO 0012, MO45 0259,
MW45 0046
Mother Nature's Best (song)
SO45 0122
Mother's Theme (Mama) (song)
MO45 0264
Mother You, Smother You (song)
MO45S 0003
Motion (song)
MO45 0382
Motor City (song)
TA45 0007
Motoring (song)
GO45 0040
MOTORTOWN REVUE IN
PARIS (LP)
TALP 0045
MOTORTOWN REVUE LIVE
(LP)
MOLP 0089
MOTOR TOWN REVUE VOL.
1 (LP)
MOLP 0010
MOTOR TOWN REVUE VOL.
II (LP)
MOLP 0016
MOTOWN AT THE
HOLLYWOOD PALACE
(LP)
MOLP 0104
MOTOWN CHARTBUSTERS
VOL. 1 (LP)
MOLP 0108
MOTOWN CHARTBUSTERS
VOL. 2 (LP)
MOLP 0116
MOTOWN CHARTBUSTERS
VOL. 3 (LP)
MOLP 0133
MOTOWN CHARTBUSTERS
VOL. 4 (LP)
MOLP 0135
MOTOWN CHARTBUSTERS
VOL. 5 (LP)
MOLP 0146
A MOTOWN CHRISTMAS (LP)

MOLP 0197
MOTOWN DISC-O-TECH #4
(LP)
MOLP 0274
MOTOWN GRAMMY
RHYTHM & BLUES
PERFORMANCES OF THE
1960'S & 1970'S: 16
GREATEST HITS (CD)
TMGLP 0112
MOTOWN INSTRUMENTALS
(LP)
NALP 0010
MOTOWN MAGIC DISCO
MACHINE VOL. II (LP)
MOLP 0259
MOTOWN 64 ORIGINAL HITS
(LP)
MOLP 0235
MOTOWN 64 ORIGINAL HITS
VOL. 1 (LP)
MOLP 0236
MOTOWN 64 ORIGINAL HITS
VOL. 2 (LP)
MOLP 0237
MOTOWN 64 ORIGINAL HITS
VOL. 3 (LP)
MOLP 0238
MOTOWN 64 ORIGINAL HITS
VOL. 4 (LP)
MOLP 0239
MOTOWN PARADE OF SONG
HITS (LP)
NALP 0025
MOTOWN PRESENTS PRIME
TIME (LP)
MOLP 0308
MOTOWN REMEMBERS
MARVIN GAYE (LP)
TMGLP 0174
MOTOWN'S BIGGEST POP
HITS (CD)
TMGLP 0176
MOTOWN'S GREAT
INTERPRETATIONS (LP)
NALP 0009
MOTOWN SHOW TUNES (LP)
NALP 0011
MOTOWN'S ORIGINAL
VERSIONS (LP)
MOLP 0262
THE MOTOWN SOUND: A
COLLECTION OF
ORIGINAL 16 BIG HITS
VOL. 5 (LP)
MOLP 0052
THE MOTOWN SOUND: A
COLLECTION OF
ORIGINAL 16 BIG HITS
VOL. 6 (LP)
MOLP 0056
THE MOTOWN SOUND: A
COLLECTION OF
ORIGINAL 16 BIG HITS
VOL. 7 (LP)
MOLP 0062
THE MOTOWN SOUND: A
COLLECTION OF
ORIGINAL 16 BIG HITS
VOLUME 8 (LP)
MOLP 0067
THE MOTOWN SOUND:

COLLECTION OF
ORIGINAL 16 BIG HITS
VOL. 10 (LP)
MOLP 0085
THE MOTOWN SOUND: A
COLLECTION OF 16
ORIGINAL BIG HITS VOL.
9 (LP)
MOLP 0069
MOTOWN SPECIAL (LP)
MOLP 0004
MOTOWN'S PREFERRED
STOCK/STOCK OPTION
NO. 1 (LP)
MOLP 0284
MOTOWN'S PREFERRED
STOCK/STOCK OPTION
NO. 2 (LP)
MOLP 0285
MOTOWN'S PREFERRED
STOCK/STOCK OPTION
NO. 3 (LP)
MOLP 0286
THE MOTOWN STORY (LP)
MOLP 0127
THE MOTOWN STORY: THE
FIRST 25 YEARS (LP)
TMGLP 0049
THE MOTOWN STORY
VOLUME 1 (LP)
MOLP 0128
THE MOTOWN STORY
VOLUME 2 (LP)
MOLP 0129
THE MOTOWN STORY
VOLUME 3 (LP)
MOLP 0130
THE MOTOWN STORY
VOLUME 4 (LP)
MOLP 0131
THE MOTOWN STORY
VOLUME 5 (LP)
MOLP 0132
MOTOWN WINNER'S CIRCLE
NO. 1 HITS VOL. 1 (LP)
GOLP 0035
MOTOWN WINNER'S CIRCLE
NO. 1 HITS VOL. 2 (LP)
GOLP 0036
MOTOWN WINNER'S CIRCLE
NO. 1 HITS, VOL.3 (LP)
GOLP 0043
MOTOWN WINNER'S CIRCLE
NO. 1 HITS, VOL. 4 (LP)
GOLP 0046
MOTOWN WINNER'S CIRCLE
NO. 1 HITS VOL. 5 (LP)
GOLP 0050
Move It, Do It (Instrumental)
(song)
TMG12 0001
Move It, Do It (Vocal) (song)
TMG12 0001
Move, Mr. Man (song)
GO45 0006
Move Together (song)
MO45 0516
Movin' From The City (song)
MO45 0317
MOVING ON (LP)
MOLP 0099
MOVING VIOLATION (LP)

MOLP 0231
MOVIN' ON (LP)
MOLP 0250, TMGLP 0076
M3000 (LP)
MOLP 0322
M3000 (Opus VI) (song)
MO45 0478
Much Better Off (song)
TA45 0152, TA45 0169
Muck-Arty Park (song)
MO45 0152
MURPH THE SURF (MOVIE
SOUNDTRACK) (LP)
MOLP 0241
Musical Love (song)
TMG45 0094
MUSICAL MASSAGE (LP)
GOLP 0076, MOLP 0279
MUSIC AND ME (LP)
MOLP 0169
MUSIC FROM THE MOTION
PICTURE "FAST BREAK"
(LP)
MOLP 0320
MUSIC FROM THE
ORIGINAL MOTION
PICTURE SOUNDTRACK
"IT'S MY TURN" (LP)
MOLP 0352
MUSIC FROM THE
ORIGINAL MOTION
PICTURE SOUNDTRACK
"LOVING COUPLES" (LP)
MOLP 0354
Music In My Heart (song)
TA45 0294
MUSIC OF MY MIND (LP)
TALP 0095
Music Talk (song)
TA45 0103
Mutiny (song)
SO45 0055
My Baby (song)
GO45 0048, SO45 0011
My Baby Gave Me Another
Chance (song)
MO45 0047
My Baby Loves Me (song)
GO45 0049, TMG45 0021
My Baby Must Be A Magician
(song)
TA45 0143
My Baby's Love (song)
CH45 0009
My Baby Won't Come Back
(song)
GO45 0012
My Beloved (song)
MO45 0003, MO45 0004
MY CHERIE AMOUR (CD)
TMGCD 0007
MY CHERIE AMOUR (LP)
TALP 0077, TMGLP 0083
My Cherie Amour (song)
MO45 0172, TA45 0165, TACO 0004
My Cup Runneth Over (song)
MO45 0154
My Daddy Knows Best (song)
TA45 0065
My Daily Prayer (song)
MO45 0057
My Eyes Adored You (song)

HI45 0013
My Friend In The Sky (song)
GO45 0193
My Girl (song)
GO45 0039, GOEP 0001, MOCB 0004,
TA45 0153, TMG12 0006, TMG12 0011
My Girl Has Gone (song)
GO45 0093, TA45 0108, TAEP 0005
MY GUY (CD)
TMGCD 0025
MY GUY (LP)
MOLP 0018
My Guy (song)
MO45 0067, MO45 0402, TMG12 0006
My Heart (song)
MO45 0081
My Heart Can't Take It No More
(song)
MO45 0049
My Kind Of Love (song)
MO45 0019
My Lil's Run Off (song)
ME45 0015
My Love (song)
TMG45 0036, TMG45 0081
My Love Is True (Truly For You)
(song)
TMG45 0187
My Love Is Yours (Till The End
Of Time) (song)
MO45 0287
My Mistake (Was To Love You)
(song)
MO45 0281
THE MYNAH BIRDS (LP)
MOLP 0098
MY NAME IS JERMAINE (LP)
MOLP 0244
My Old Piano (song)
MO45 0550
My Peace Of Heaven (song)
RA45 0030, RACO 0008
My Place (song)
MW45 0001
My Smile Is Just A Frown Turned
Upside Down (song)
MO45 0075
My Song In -G- (song)
MO45 0482
MY SON THE SIT-IN (LP)
MOLP 0020
My Springtime (song)
GO45 0092
Mystified (song)
MO45 0516
My Touch Of Madness (song)
MO45 0423
MY WAY (LP)
MOLP 0047
My Weakness Is You (song)
GO45 0072
MY WHOLE WORLD ENDED
(LP)
MOLP 0086
My Whole World Ended (The
Moment You Left Me) (song)
MO45 0151, MOCO 0010, TA45 0178,
VI45 0059
My Woman (song)
MW45 0037
My World Is Empty Without You
(song)

MO45 0100, MO45 0117, MOCB 0016,
TAEP 0006
Nail It To The Wall (song)
TMG45 0266
Nail It To The Wall
(Instrumental) (song)
TMG45 0266
Nathan Jones (song)
MO45 0194
Natural Feeling (song)
PR45 0034
NATURAL HIGH (LP)
MOLP 0305
NATURAL HIGH +
MIDNIGHT MAGIC (CD)
TMGCD 0015
NATURALLY TOGETHER
(LP)
SOLP 0029
NATURAL RESOURCES (LP)
GOLP 0052
NATURE OF THE BEAST (LP)
TMGLP 0143
NATURE PLANNED IT (LP)
MOLP 0150
A Need For Love (song)
TA45 0088
Needle In A Haystack (song)
VI45 0006
NEED TO KNOW YOU
BETTER (LP)
MOLP 0309
Need To Know You Better (song)
MO12 0026
Need Your Love (song)
GO45 0090, VI45 0050
Need Your Lovin' (Want You
Back) (song)
SO45 0029, TA45 0117
NEITHER ONE OF US (LP)
SOLP 0037
NEITHER ONE OF US + ALL I
NEED IS TIME (CD)
TMGCD 0009
Neither One Of Us (Wants To Be
The First To Say Goodbye)
(song)
SO45 0098
Neon Riders And Sawdust Gliders
(song)
MC45 0009
Never Again (song)
MO45 0016, TA45 0021
Never Been To Spain (song)
MO45 0238, MO45 0265
Never Can Say Goodbye (song)
MO45 0191, RA45 0024, TMG12 0011
Never Dreamed You'd Leave In
Summer (song)
TA45 0188
Never Gonna Leave You (song)
TA45 0263
Never Had A Dream Come True
(song)
TA45 0176
Never Leave Your Baby's Side
(song)
GO45 0049
Never Let You Go (song)
TA45 0024
Never Say No To Your Baby
(song)

SO45 0010
Never Seen Anything Like You
(song)
TMG45 0045
NEW FACES FROM
HITSVILLE (EP)
MOEP 0014
A New Girl (song)
MO45 0015
NEW IMPROVED SEVERIN
BROWNE (LP)
MOLP 0181
NEW WAYS BUT LOVE
STAYS (LP)
MOLP 0121
Next To You (song)
GO45 0177, GO45 0193
Nice To Be With You (song)
RA45 0039
The Night (song)
MW45 0026
Night Fo' Last (featuring Shorty
Long on the organ) (song)
SO45 0040
Night Fo' Last (Vocal) (song)
SO45 0040
NIGHT LIFE (LP)
GOLP 0074
Night Life (song)
TA45 0261
NIGHTSHIFT (CD)
TMGLP 0126
Nightshift (song)
TMG45 0179
Nightshift (Club mix)
TMG12 0034
Nightshift (Edit of Club Mix)
(song)
TMG12 0034
Nightshift (Instrumental mix)
(song)
TMG12 0034
NIGHT SONG (LP)
MOLP 0350
Nihaa Shil Hozho (I Am Happy
About You) (song)
RA45 0040
1957-1972 (LP)
TALP 0101, TALP 0102
1990 (LP)
GOLP 0066
Ninety-Nine And A Half Won't
Do (song)
DI45 0002
NITTY GRITTY (LP)
SOLP 0013
The Nitty Gritty (song)
SO45 0063
Nobody Knows The Trouble I've
Seen (song)
CHEP 0002
Nobody's Gonna Change Me
(song)
MO45 0372
No Greater Love (song)
TMG45 0243
NOLEN & CROSSLEY (LP)
GOLP 0102
No Love (song)
TA45 0023
No Matter What Sign You Are
(song)

MO45 0159
No Matter Where (song)
MO45 0246, MO45 0349, MO45 0407
No More Tearstained Make Up
(song)
GOEP 0005
No One Gets The Prize (song)
MO12 0038
No One's Gonna Be A Fool
Forever (song)
MO45 0272, MO45 0390, MW45 0013
Nothin' But Pocket (song)
TMG45 0150
NOTHING BUT A MAN
(SOUNDTRACK) (LP)
MOLP 0031
Nothing But Heartaches (song)
MO45 0091
Nothing But Soul (song)
SO45 0024
Nothing Can Take The Place (Of
Your Love) (song)
MO45 0368
Nothing Is Too Good (For You
Baby) (song)
SO45 0121
Nothing's Too Good For My
Baby (song)
TA45 0115
No Time (song)
BF45 0001
No Time At All (song)
MO45 0233
No Time For Tears (song)
TA45 0100
Not Now (I'll Tell You Later)
(song)
GOEP 0003
Not Too Old To Cry (song)
ML45 0014
NOW (LP)
MOLP 0076
NOW ARRIVING (LP)
SOLP 0051
Nowhere To Run (song)
GO45 0040, GOEP 0002, MO12 0004
Nowhere To Run Pt. 1 (song)
MO45 0433
Nowhere To Run Pt. 2 (song)
MO45 0433
Now That I Have You (song)
TMG45 0166
Now That There's You (song)
GO45 0214
Now That You're Gone (song)
MO45 0550
Now That You've Won Me (song)
TA45 0101
Now You Got It (song)
GO45 0138
Nunca He Ido A Mi (song)
TMG45 0026
Obscene Phone Caller (song)
TMG45 0137
Obscene Phone Caller
(Instrumental) (song)
TMG45 0137
ODE TO MY LADY (LP)
MOLP 0240
ODYSSEY (LP)
MWLP 0015
Oh Baby Baby I Love You (song)

TA45 0194
Oh Be My Love (song)
MO45 0237, TA45 0119
Oh Freddie (song)
MO45 0050
Oh How Happy (song)
GO45 0091, GOCO 0006
Oh I Apologize (song)
TA45 0008
Oh, I've Been Bless'd (song)
GO45 0089, VI45 0052, VICO 0002
Oh Little Boy (What Did You Do
To Me) (song)
MO45 0067
Oh, Mother O Mine (song)
MI45 0005
Oh My Maria (song)
TA45 0165
Oh No (song)
MO45 0546
Oh, What A Night (song)
GO45 0216
Oh What A Night (4 Luv) (song)
TMG12 0029, TMG45 0182
Oklahoma Sunshine (song)
HI45 0011
Old Fashioned Love (song)
MO45 0506, TMG45 0016
An Old-Fashioned Man (song)
TA45 0270
Old Funky Rolls (song)
TMG45 0028
Old Love (Let's Try It Again)
(song)
GO45 0028, MO45 0041
OLD SOCKS, NEW
SHOES...NEW SOCKS, OLD
SHOES (EP)
CHEP 0001
OLD SOCKS NEW SHOES,
NEW SOCKS OLD SHOES
(LP)
CHLP 0004
Olympiad '84 (song)
MO45 0498
OMNIVERSE (LP)
PRLP 0022
On And Off (song)
MO45 0419
ON BROADWAY (LP)
MOLP 0100
ONCE AGAIN (LP)
MCLP 0003
Once Again (song)
ML45 0012
Once I Have You (I Will Never
Let You Go) (song)
SO45 0093
Once Upon A Time (song)
MO45 0068
Once You Had A Heart (song)
GO45 0126
One (song)
HI45 0012, TMG45 0044
One By One (song)
PR45 0021
ONE DAY IN YOUR LIFE (LP)
MOLP 0361
One Day In Your Life (song)
MO45 0531
ONE DOZEN ROSES (LP)
TALP 0093

The Party Is Over (song)
TMG45 0086
Party Right Here (song)
TMG45 0084
Passion Flower (song)
TA45 0289
PASS THE BUTTER (LP)
NALP 0004
PASS THE PLATE (LP)
CHLP 0007
Pass The Plate (song)
CH45 0014
PEACE & UNDERSTANDING
IS HARD TO FIND (LP)
SOLP 0038
Peace And Understanding (Is
Hard To Find) (song)
SO45 0108
Peaceful Summit (song)
ME45 0007
Peaceland (song)
GO45 0168
Peace Of Mind (song)
TA45 0182
Peeping Tom (song)
TMG45 0188
Peeping Tom (Special 12-inch
version) (song)
TMG12 0032
Penny Annie Fortune Lady (song)
MO45 0328
Penny Lover (song)
TMG45 0168
PEOPLE...HOLD ON (LP)
TALP 0096
The People In The Valley (song)
MW45 0042
PEOPLE MOVE, HUMAN
PLAYS (LP)
TMGLP 0048
Pet Names (song)
VI45 0058
Piano Man (song)
MO45 0257, MW45 0052
Pick Of The Week (song)
MO45 0329, MW45 0008, TA45 0268
Pictures On Paper (song)
ML45 0004
Pig Knuckles (song)
MO45 0058
Pigskin Charade (song)
ML45 0028
Pilgrim Of Sorrow (song)
DI45 0001
PINBALL PLAYBOY (LP)
MOLP 0335
Pinball Playboy (Playboy Theme)
(song)
MO45 0493
Pin Point It Down (song)
SO45 0058
PIPPIN (ORIGINAL
BROADWAY CAST) (CD)
TMGLP 0188
PIPPIN (ORIGINAL CAST
RECORDING) (LP)
MOLP 0162
Pity Little Billy Jo (song)
ML45 0023
A Place In My Heart (song)
TMG45 0009
A Place In The Sun (song)

CH45 0003, CHCO 0002, MO45 0148,
TA45 0124, TACO 0002, TAEP 0006
Plainsville, U.S.A. (song)
MO45 0255
THE PLANETS (LP)
MOLP 0339
Plans That We Made (song)
HI45 0004
Plastic Man (song)
GO45 0130
PLATINUM HOOK (LP)
MOLP 0302
PLAYBOY (LP)
TALP 0012
Playboy (song)
TA45 0043
Play It Cool Stay In School (song)
TA45S 0006
Please Come To Nashville (song)
ML45 0004
Please Don't Turn The Lights Out
(song)
VI45 0018
Please Forgive Me (song)
MO45 0009
Please Mr. Kennedy (song)
TA45 0035
PLEASE MR. POSTMAN (LP)
TALP 0009
Please Mr. Postman (song)
MO45 0327, MOCB 0012, TA45 0029,
TAEP 0002
Please Return Your Love To Me
(song)
GO45 0075
Please Stay (song)
MO45 0515, TA45 0314
PLEASE TAKE ME BACK (LP)
MCLP 0015
PLIGHT OF THE REDMAN
(LP)
RALP 0033
A POCKET FULL OF
MIRACLES (LP)
TALP 0087
Point It Out (song)
TA45 0174, TACO 0008
Poor Fool (song)
MW45 0011
Poor Girl (song)
VI45 0026
Poor Sam Jones (song)
TA45 0022
Pops, We Love You (song)
MO12 0018, MOCO 0036
Pops, We Love You
(Instrumental) (song)
MO45 0470, MO45 0471, MOCO 0037
POPS WE LOVE YOU...THE
ALBUM (LP)
MOLP 0326
Pops, We Love You (Vocal) (song)
MO45 0470, MO45 0471, MOCO 0037
PORTER JORDAN SINGS (LP)
MCLP 0004
PORTRAIT OF THE
ORIGINALS (LP)
SOLP 0024
Portuguese Love (song)
GO45 0219
POSITIVE SPACE (LP)
TMGLP 0061

POWER (LP)
GOLP 0096
Power (song)
GOCO 0015
Power (Instrumental) (song)
GO45 0186
Power (Vocal) (song)
GO45 0186
Power Is (song)
MO45 0343
THE POWER OF MUSIC (LP)
TALP 0125
Praise (song)
TA45 0317
Prayin' For My Mind (song)
ML45 0020
The Preacher's Gone Home
(Tribute To Cannonball
Adderly) (song)
MO45 0529
Precious Little Things (song)
MO45 0212
Precious Memories (song)
MO45 0024
Precious Pearl (song)
MO45 0438
PRESENTING (LP)
MCLP 0007
PRESSIN' ON (LP)
TMGLP 0021
Pretty Little Angel (song)
GO45 0088, TA45 0091
Pretty Little Baby (song)
TA45 0101
Pretty Mess (song)
TMG45 0158
Pretty Mess (Instrumental) (song)
TMG45 0158
Pretty Mess (Long Version) (song)
TMG12 0027
Pride And Joy (song)
MO45 0083, TA45 0062, TAEP 0001
THE PRIME OF MY LIFE (LP)
MOLP 0033
THE PRIME OF SHORTY
LONG (LP)
SOLP 0019
PRIVATE PARTY (LP)
TMGLP 0052
Private Party (song)
TMG45 0099
Private Sorrow (song)
RA45 0001
A Promise Is A Promise (song)
TMG45 0104
Promise Me (song)
TA45 0184
PROMISES KEPT (LP)
MOLP 0148
The Prophet (song)
GO45 0145
PSYCHEDELIC SHACK (LP)
GOLP 0047
Psychedelic Shack (song)
GO45 0097
PSYCHEDELIC SHACK + ALL
DIRECTIONS (CD)
TMGCD 0023
Pucker Up Buttercup (song)
SO45 0030, SOEP 0003
Puppet On A String (song)
VI45 0022

Pure Chopin (song)
PR45 0021
PURE GOLD (LP)
MOLP 0049
PURE PLEASURE (LP)
MOLP 0243
PURE SMOKEY (LP)
TALP 0112
Purple Rain Drops (song)
TA45 0109
Pushing Up Daisies (song)
GO45 0019
Put Me In Your Pocket (song)
ME45 0019
Put Us Together Again (song)
TMG45 0263
Put Your Gun Down Brother
(song)
MO45 0331
Put Yourself In My Place (song)
MO45 0108, VI45 0028, VI45 0037
PUZZLE (LP)
MOLP 0170, RALP 0041
PUZZLE PEOPLE (CD)
TMGCD 0017
PUZZLE PEOPLE (LP)
GOLP 0049
Queen Of My Heart (song)
TMG12 0033, TMG45 0176
Quicksand (song)
GO45 0026
Quick Slick (song)
TA45 0329
QUIET STORM (CD)
TMGCD 0029
Quiet Storm (song)
TA45 0258
A QUIET STORM (LP)
TALP 0118
Ragged And Dirty (song)
GO45 0129
RAINBOW FUNK (LP)
SOLP 0032
Rain Is A Lonesome Thing (song)
ME45 0020
Rainy Mourning (song)
TA45 0171
Ramona (song)
NA45 0001
Randy, The Newspaper Boy
(song)
VI45 0011
RAREARTH (LP)
PRLP 0013
Rave On (song)
MC45 0010
Razzle Dazzle (Instrumental)
(song)
MO45 0398
Reach High (song)
TMG45 0063
Reach High (Instrumental) (song)
TMG45 0053
REACHIN' ALL AROUND (LP)
TMGLP 0035
REACHING FOR
TOMORROW (LP)
GOLP 0095
REACH OUT (LP)
MOLP 0112, NALP 0016
Reach Out (song)
TMG12 0011

Reach Out And Touch
(Somebody's Hand) (song)
MO45 0176, MOCO 0015
Reach Out For Love (song)
MO45 0493
Reach Out I'll Be There (song)
MO45 0109, MO45 0196, MOCO 0023
REACH OUT + STILL
WATERS RUN DEEP (CD)
TMGCD 0008
Ready Or Not (song)
TMG45 0009
READY TO ROLL (LP)
TALP 0143
THE REAL BARBARA
McNAIR (LP)
MOLP 0081
Real Good Lovin' (song)
MO45 0028
Reality (song)
RA45 0003
REAL PRETTY (LP)
RALP 0046
Reba (song)
ML45 0022
RECONSTRUCTION (LP)
CHLP 0003
RECORDED LIVE (EP)
GOEP 0006
RECORDED LIVE AT THE
REGAL (LP)
TALP 0025
RECORDED LIVE ON STAGE
(LP)
MOLP 0012
RECORDED LIVE: ON
STAGE (LP)
TALP 0022, TALP 0023, TALP 0024
Red Hot (song)
MO45 0484
Redhot (Disco Version) (song)
MO12 0036
Redhot (Single Version) (song)
MO12 0036
Redliner (song)
TMG45 0069
REED SEED (LP)
MOLP 0313
Reed Seed (Trio Tune) (song)
MO45 0469
REFLECTIONS (LP)
MOLP 0066, WOLP 0012
Reflections (song)
MO45 0122
REFLECTIONS: ALL THE
GREATEST HITS (CD & LP)
TMGLP 0097
Release Me (song)
MO45 0337
RELOCATION (LP)
MOLP 0189
Relove (song)
MO45 0274
Remember Me (song)
MO45 0188, MOCO 0020
Remember When (song)
MO45 0143
Remove This Doubt (song)
MO45 0112
RENAISSANCE (LP)
TALP 0106
Renegade (song)

MO45 0333
REPAIRS (LP)
MWLP 0021
Request Of A Fool (song)
TA45 0006, TA45 0039
The Rescue (song)
TMG45 0235
Rescue Me (song)
TMG45 0154
Reservation Of Education (song)
RA45 0051
THE RETURN OF THE
BLUES BOSS (LP)
MOLP 0009
THE RETURN OF THE
MAGNIFICENT SEVEN
(LP)
MOLP 0137
THE RETURN OF THE
MARVELETTES (LP)
TALP 0086
REUBEN HOWELL (LP)
MOLP 0173
REUNION (LP)
TMGLP 0009
The Rev. John B. Daniels (song)
RA45 0025
RHYMES OF PASSION (LP)
TMGLP 0147
RHYTHM OF THE NIGHT (CD
& LP)
TMGLP 0125
Rhythm Of The Night (song)
TMG45 0176
Rhythm Of The Night (Long
Version) (song)
TMG12 0033
Ribbon In The Sky (song)
TMG45 0041
Rich And Famous (song)
TMG45 0259
Rich And Famous (Instrumental)
(song)
TMG12 0063, TMG45 0259
Rich And Famous (Single
Version) (song)
TMG12 0063
Rich And Famous (12-inch
version) (song)
TMG12 0063
Richie's Song (For Richard
Oliver) (song)
TMG45 0065
RICH LOVE, POOR LOVE (LP)
MOLP 0294
Rich Man, Poor Man (song)
PR45 0016
Ride A Wild Horse (song)
MO12 0012
RIDE TO THE RAINBOW (LP)
TALP 0147
RIDIN' HIGH (LP)
GOLP 0026
El Rig (song)
WO45 0006
Right Before My Eyes (song)
MO45 0197
Right In The Middle (Of Falling
In Love) (song)
MO45 0551, MO45 0552
Right Now (song)
MO45 0066

RIGHT ON (LP)
  MOLP 0106
Right On Brothers And Sisters
  (song)
  SO45 0084
Right Or Wrong (song)
  ML45 0030
Right's Alright (song)
  MO45 0418
THE RIGHT SIDE OF LEFTY
  EDWARDS (LP)
  WOLP 0011
RINGS (LP)
  MOLP 0201
Rings (song)
  MO45 0318
Rise And Shine (song)
  TMG45 0113
RISE SLEEPING BEAUTY (LP)
  MOLP 0245
RITA WRIGHT (LP)
  GOLP 0041
River Deep, Mountain High (song)
  MO45 0185
ROAD (LP)
  NALP 0005
The Road I Walk (song)
  MW45 0030
ROAD RUNNER (CD)
  TMGCD 0024
ROAD RUNNER (EP)
  SOEP 0003
ROAD RUNNER (LP)
  SOLP 0003
Robot Man (song)
  GO45 0124
Rock And Roll Me (song)
  GO45 0189, GOCO 0016
Rock And Roll, Pop And Soul
  (song)
  MO45 0537
ROCK BOTTOM (LP)
  GOLP 0077
Rocket Love (song)
  TMG45 0013
ROCK GOSPEL: THE KEY TO
  THE KINGDOM (LP)
  MOLP 0145
Rockin' Robin (song)
  MO45 0209
ROCK ME A LITTLE WHILE
  (EP)
  MOEP 0015
Rock My Heart (song)
  TMG45 0213
Rock My Heart (LP Version)
  (song)
  TMG12 0043
Rock With Me (song)
  TMG45 0181
Rode By The Place (Where We
  Used To Stay) (song)
  MO45 0449
Roll-Her, Skater (song)
  MO12 0035, MO45 0485
Roll-Her, Skater (Instrumental)
  (song)
  MO12 0035, MO45 0485
Rolling Down A Mountainside
  (song)
  MO45 0262, TA45 0224
Rollin With The Flow (song)

ML45 0002
Roll It Over (song)
  MO45 0302
Romance (song)
  MO45 0346
ROMANCE IN THE NIGHT
  (LP)
  TMGLP 0036
Romance Without Finance (song)
  MI45 0005
Romeo (song)
  MO45 0370
RONNIE MCNEIR (LP)
  PRLP 0001
Rosa Lee (song)
  MI45 0004
ROSE (LP)
  MOLP 0247
Roses for Lydia (song)
  TMG45 0122
ROSS (LP)
  MOLP 0310
Round And Round (song)
  TMG45 0081, TMG45 0152
ROUND ONE (LP)
  PRLP 0020
Roxanne (You Sure GOt A Fine
  Design) (song)
  MO45 0302
Rubie Is A Groopie (song)
  ML45 0025
Rudolph The Red Nosed Reindeer
  (song)
  GO45 0083, GOCO 0003
RUFF' N READY (LP)
  SOLP 0008
Run Away Child, Running Wild
  (song)
  GO45 0085
Runaway Child, Running Wild
  (song)
  SO45 0059
Running Away (Ain't Gonna
  Help You) (song)
  GO45 0094
Running Back and Forth (song)
  GO45 0098
Running Like A Rabbit (song)
  SO45 0101
Running With The Night (song)
  TMG45 0116
Run, Run, Run (song)
  MO45 0065
S. F. SORROW (LP)
  RALP 0003
S.O.S. (Stop Her On Sight) (song)
  PR45 0033
Sad And Lonesome Feeling (song)
  SO45 0053
Sad Boy (song)
  TA45 0086
Sad Song (song)
  TA45 0082, TA45 0110
Sad Souvenirs (song)
  MO45 0087
Sad Tomorrows (song)
  TA45 0195
Sagittarian Affair (song)
  PR45 0010
Sail Away (song)
  MO45 0215, TMG45 0126
Sail On (song)

MO45 0483
St. Louis (song)
  RA45 0005
Samba Pa Ti (song)
  TMG45 0049
Same Old Story (song)
  TA45 0047, TA45 0303, VI45 0008
Same Thing (song)
  TA45 0025
SAM HARRIS (CD & LP)
  TMGLP 0105
SAM-I-AM (LP)
  TMGLP 0167
Sandman (song)
  TA45 0038
Sandy (song)
  GO45 0101
Sanity Baby (song)
  PR45 0031
Santa Claus Is Coming To Town
  (song)
  MO45 0186
Satan's Blues (song)
  SO45 0003
THE SATINTONES SING (LP)
  MOLP 0003
Satisfaction (song)
  TA45 0200, TACO 0015
Satisfied Feelin' (song)
  TA45 0164
Satisfied Mind (song)
  ME45 0012
Saturday Night, Sunday Morning
  (song)
  MO12 0016, TA45 0292
Saturday Night, Sunday Morning
  (Instrumental) (song)
  MO12 0016
Save It For A Rainy Day (song)
  GO45 0156
Save Me (song)
  TA45 0125
Save My Love For A Rainy Day
  (song)
  GO45 0107
Save The Best For Me (Best Of
  Your Lovin') (song)
  TMG45 0276
SAVE THE CHILDREN
  (ORIGINAL
  SOUNDTRACK) (LP)
  MOLP 0202
Save The Children (song)
  MO45 0290
Save The Night For Me (song)
  TMG45 0193
SAX APPEAL (LP)
  SOLP 0047
Say It Like The Children (song)
  MO45 0284
Say Love (Or Don't Say Anything
  At All) (song)
  ML45 0017
Say That You Love Me Boy
  (song)
  PR45 0008
Say Yeah (song)
  MO45 0473
Say You (song)
  GOEP 0003, VI45 0027, VI45 0031
Say You'll Never Let Me Go
  (song)

TA45 0064
Say You, Say Me (song)
  TMG45 0225
The Scalawag Song (And I Will
    Love You) (song)
  MO45 0291
School Girl (song)
  TMG45 0100
Scratch Break (Glove Style) (song)
  TMG12 0014, TMG45 0102
Scratchin (song)
  MO45 0375
Searchin' (song)
  MO45 0539
Searching For A Girl (song)
  GO45 0045
THE SEASON FOR MIRACLES
    (LP)
  TALP 0088
"Seasons Greetings From
    Motown" (song)
  TA45S 0007, TA45S 0008
THE SECOND ALBUM (LP)
  MOLP 0209
SECOND GENERATION (LP)
  PRLP 0003
2ND TIME AROUND (LP)
  VILP 0006
SECOND TO NUNN (LP)
  TMGLP 0023
Secret (song)
  MO45 0502
SECRET PLACE + ALL THE
    KING'S HORSES (CD)
  TMGCD 0031
SECRETS OF LONELY BOYS
    (LP)
  TMGLP 0157
SEDUCTION (LP)
  TMGLP 0149
Seduction (song)
  TMG45 0218
Seduction (Instrumental) (song)
  TMG12 0045, TMG45 0218
Seduction (12-inch version) (song)
  TMG12 0045
The Seed (song)
  RA45 0027
Seems So Long (song)
  TA45 0246
SELECTIONS FROM THE
    ORIGINAL MOTION
    PICTURE SOUNDTRACK
    FROM "THE WOMAN IN
    RED" (LP)
  TMGLP 0110
Selling My Heart To The
    Junkman (song)
  MO45 0410
Sending Good Vibrations (song)
  MO45 0253
SEND IT (LP)
  MOLP 0367
Send One Your Love (song)
  TA45 0298
Send One Your Love
    (Instrumental) (song)
  TA45 0298
SERENADE FOR THE CITY
    (LP)
  MOLP 0349
Serves You Right (song)

TMG45 0116
SET MY LOVE IN MOTION
    (LP)
  TALP 0158
Set You Right (song)
  TMG45 0240
Set Your Love Right (song)
  TMG45 0187
7 Rooms Of Gloom (song)
  MO45 0121
17 (song)
  TMG45 0136
17 (Instrumental) (song)
  TMG12 0023, TMG45 0136
17 (Vocal) (song)
  TMG12 0023
7TH SON (LP)
  MWLP 0007
SEVERIN BROWNE (LP)
  MOLP 0176
Sex Maniac (song)
  TMG45 0130
Sexy Lady (song)
  GO45 0169, MO45 0506, TMG45 0063
Sexy Sassy (Instrumental) (song)
  TMG45 0073
Sexy Sassy (Vocal) (song)
  TMG45 0073
Sexy Ways (song)
  TMG45 0196
SHADES OF GOSPEL SOUL
    (LP)
  MOLP 0102
Shadow (song)
  RA45 0037
Shadow Lover (song)
  TMG45 0258
SHAKE (EP)
  MOEP 0011
SHAKE AND FINGERPOP
    (EP)
  MOEP 0013
Shake And Fingerpop (song)
  SO45 0013, SOEP 0001
Shake Everything (song)
  SOEP 0002
Shake Hands (Come Out Dancin')
    (song)
  TMG45 0143
Shake It Lady (song)
  TA45 0310
Shake It, Shake It (song)
  MO12 0003, MO45 0425
Shake It Up (song)
  MO45 0519
Shake Me Wake Me (When It's
    Over) (song)
  MO45 0101
Shake Sherry (song)
  GO45 0013
Shakey Ground (song)
  GO45 0143
Shambles (song)
  ME45 0010
Shame (song)
  HI45 0001
Shame And Scandal In The
    Family (song)
  MO45 0238
Shame On You (song)
  MO45 0545
SHARE MY LOVE (LP)

MOLP 0192
Share My World (song)
  TMG12 0053, TMG45 0228
Share Your Love (song)
  GO45 0149, MO45 0381
Sharing Something Perfect
    Between Ourselves (song)
  TA45 0282
Shebeen (song)
  CH45 0015
She Blew My Mind (69 Times)
    (song)
  TMG45 0048
She Gives Me Love (song)
  HI45 0020, MC45 0002
She Made Me Love You More
    (song)
  HI45 0008
She Only Made Me Love You
    More (song)
  MC45 0007
(She's A) Fire Out Of Control
    (song)
  ML45 0022
She Said That (song)
  MW45 0030
She's A Lady (song)
  RA45 0023
She Satisfies (song)
  ML45 0013
She's Feelin' Low (song)
  ML45 0007
(She's Gonna Love Me) At
    Sundown (song)
  MO45 0166, VI45 0049, VI45 0053
She's Good (song)
  MO45 0191
She's Got To Be Real (song)
  TA45 0107
She's Just A Groupie (song)
  TMG45 0045
She's Just A Groupie
    (Instrumental) (song)
  TMG12 0003
She's Just A Groupie (Vocal)
    (song)
  TMG12 0003
She's Just Doing Her Thing (song)
  MO45 0420
She's Leaving Home (song)
  TMG45 0078
She's My Baby (song)
  VI45 0003
She's The Ideal Girl (song)
  MO45 0399
She's The Trip I've Been On
    (Since You've Been Gone)
    (song)
  MC45 0007
Shimmy Gully (song)
  MO45 0008
Shine On Me (song)
  MO45 0184
Shoeshine Boy (song)
  TA45 0249
Shoe Shoe Shine (song)
  MO45 0337
Shoe Soul (song)
  TA45 0291
Shoo Be Doo Be Doo Da Day
    (song)
  TA45 0150

Shoo Ooo (song)
MI45 0004
Shoot Your Shot (song)
SO45 0015, SO45 0036
Shop Around (song)
MOCB 0011, TA45 0017, TAEP 0003,
TMG12 0006
SHOTGUN (EP)
SOEP 0001
SHOTGUN (LP)
SOLP 0001
Shotgun (song)
SO45 0008, SOEP 0001
SHOTGUN + ROAD RUNNER
(CD)
TMGCD 0024
SHOULDA GONE DANCIN'
(LP)
GOLP 0089
Shoulda Gone Dancin' (song)
GO45 0168
Shoulda Gone Dancin'
(Instrumental) (song)
MO12 0022
Shoulda Gone Dancin' (Vocal)
(song)
MO12 0022
Should I Tell Them (song)
VI45 0006
Show Me A Man (song)
HI45 0009
Show Me The Way (song)
GO45 0068, HI45 0019, MC45 0008
SIGNED, SEALED &
DELIVERED (LP)
TALP 0085
SIGNED, SEALED,
DELIVERED (LP)
TMGLP 0083
Signed, Sealed, Delivered (I'm
Yours) (song)
MO45 0515, TA45 0181, TA45 0314,
TACO 0011
SIGNED, SEALED,
DELIVERED + MY
CHERIE AMOUR (CD)
TMGCD 0007
Silent Night (song)
GO45 0083, TMG45 0056, TMG45 0119
A Silent Partner In A Three-Way
Love Affair (song)
TA45 0229
SILENT WARRIOR (LP)
RALP 0042
SILK N' SOUL (LP)
NALP 0012, SOLP 0011
Silly Wasn't I (song)
TA45 0213
A Simple Game (song)
MO45 0208
Simple Song Of Freedom (song)
MO45 0205
A Simple Thing Like Cry (song)
MO45 0204
Since I Held You Close (song)
TMG45 0277
Since I Lost My Baby (song)
GO45 0044, GOEP 0001
Since I Lost You Girl (song)
VI45 0038
Since I Met You (song)
MO45 0382

Since I Met You There's No
Magic (song)
MO45 0250, MW45 0035
Since I've Lost You (song)
GO45 0087, GO45 0107, SO45 0002,
SOEP 0004
Sincerely (song)
TMG45 0257
Since You've Been Gone (song)
MO45 0113
Since You've Been Loving Me
(song)
SO45 0025, VI45 0020, VI45 0029,
VI45 0033
Since You Won My Heart (song)
TA45 0108
Sing A Song Of Yesterday (song)
TMG45 0124
SINGS TOP TEN (EP)
SOEP 0004
Sing What You Wanna (song)
SO45 0044
Sir Duke (song)
TA45 0276
6 By 6 (song)
SO45 0028
16 GREATEST HITS (LP)
TMGLP 0102
16 ORIGINAL BIG HITS VOL.
1 (LP)
MOLP 0015
16 ORIGINAL BIG HITS VOL.
3 (LP)
MOLP 0025
Skate To The Rhythm (song)
GO45 0176
SKIN ON SKIN (LP)
TMGLP 0169
Skips A Beat (song)
TMG45 0219
Skips A Beat (Dub) (song)
TMG45 0219
Skips A Beat (Dub Mix) (song)
TMG12 0056
Skips A Beat (Fly-Dubmix) (song)
TMG12 0056
Skips A Beat (Radio Edit of Club
Mix) (song)
TMG12 0056
Skip To My Lou (song)
TMG45 0071
SKYLARKIN' (LP)
MOLP 0338
SKY'S THE LIMIT (LP)
GOLP 0057, MOLP 0264
THE SKY'S THE LIMIT (LP)
TMGLP 0025
SKYWRITER (LP)
MOLP 0163
Sleepin' (song)
MO45 0308
Sleepless Nights (song)
TMG45 0246
Sleep (Little One) (song)
MO45 0037
Slender Thread (song)
MO45 0102
SLICK (LP)
TALP 0138
Slick (song)
MO45 0264
Slippery When Wet (song)

MO45 0351
Slipping Into Something New
(song)
MO45 0451
Slow Down Heart (song)
GO45 0011
SLY, SLICK AND WICKED
(LP)
JULP 0003
Small Sad Sam (song)
TA45 0034
Smile (song)
MO45 0412
Smiling Faces Sometimes (song)
GO45 0109, GOCO 0009, MO45 0340
Smog (song)
TA45 0261
SMOKE SIGNALS (LP)
TMGLP 0158
SMOKEY (LP)
TALP 0109
SMOKEY + QUIET STORM
(CD)
TMGCD 0029
SMOKEY ROBINSON AND
THE MIRACLES
GREATEST HITS VOL. 2
(LP)
TALP 0061
SMOKEY ROBINSON AND
THE MIRACLES MAKE IT
HAPPEN (LP)
TALP 0057
SMOKEY ROBINSON: THE
COMPOSER SERIES (CD)
TMGLP 0141
SMOKEY'S FAMILY
ROBINSON (LP)
TALP 0122
SMOKIN' (LP)
TALP 0145
. . . SMOOTH (LP)
SOLP 0050
Smooth Sailing (From Now On)
(song)
GO45 0116
Snake Eyes (song)
MO45 0503
Snake Walk - Part 1 (song)
TA45 0004
Snake Walk - Part 2 (song)
TA45 0004
Snow Flakes (song)
MO45 0270, MO45 0316
Sock-It, Rocket (song)
MO45 0524
So Far, So Good (song)
RA45 0024
SOFTLY (LP)
MOLP 0172
So In Love (song)
GO45 0121, WO45 0003
Solar Flight (Opus 1) (song)
MO45 0443
Soldier's Plea (song)
TA45 0046
SOLID ROCK (LP)
GOLP 0061
Solid Sender (song)
TA45 0003
SOLITARY MAN (LP)
HILP 0001

Solitary Man (song)
 HI45 0001
So Long Baby (song)
 TA45 0029
Somebody Knows, Somebody
 Cares (song)
 TA45 0176
Somebody Oughta Turn Your
 Head Around (song)
 RA45 0043
Somebody, Somewhere (song)
 GO45 0181
SOMEBODY'S WATCHING
 ME (LP)
 TMGLP 0053
Somebody's Watching Me (song)
 TMG45 0107
Somebody's Watching Me
 (Instrumental) (song)
 TMG12 0016, TMG45 0107
Somebody's Watching Me (Vocal)
 (song)
 TMG12 0016
Somebody's Watchin' You (song)
 GO45 0165
Somebody Up There (song)
 MW45 0021
SOMEDAY AT CHRISTMAS
 (CD)
 TMGCD 0042
SOMEDAY AT CHRISTMAS
 (LP)
 TALP 0062, TALP 0144
Some Day At Christmas (song)
 TA45 0127
Someday Pretty Baby (song)
 TA45 0054
Someday, Someway (song)
 TA45 0048
Someday We'll Be Together (song)
 MO45 0167, MO45 0195
Some Kinda Magic (song)
 GO45 0159
Someone (song)
 TMG45 0274
Someone To Call My Own (song)
 MI45 0007
SOMEPLACE ELSE NOW (LP)
 MWLP 0017
Something About You (song)
 MO45 0095
SOMETHING FOR
 EVERYONE (LP)
 MOLP 0111
Something In Her Love (song)
 MO45 0215, MO45 0224, MO45 0229
Something On My Mind (song)
 GO45 0065
Something's Bothering You (song)
 VI45 0024
Some Things You Never Get Used
 To (song)
 MO45 0137, MOCO 0005
Something Will Happen To You
 (song)
 TA45 0092
Somewhere In My Life (song)
 TMG45 0012
Somewhere Up There (song)
 RA45 0012
So Near (And Yet So Far) (song)
 SO45 0116

A SONG FOR YOU (LP)
 GOLP 0069
A SONG FOR YOU +
 MASTERPIECE (CD)
 TMGCD 0036
A Song Of Long Ago (song)
 MO45 0277
SONGS IN THE KEY OF LIFE
 (Bonus disc) (EP)
 MOEP 0020
SONGS IN THE KEY OF LIFE
 (LP)
 TALP 0121
SONGS IN THE KEY OF LIFE
 VOL. 2 (CD)
 TMGLP 0118
SONGS IN THE KEY OF LIFE
 VOLS. I AND II (CD)
 TMGLP 0117
SONGS OF LOVE (LP)
 PRLP 0012
Songs That We Sang As Children
 (song)
 HI45 0007
Songs We Sang As Children (song)
 MC45 0013
Songwriter (song)
 MW45 0032
Son Of Sagittarius (song)
 TA45 0237
Sooner Or Later (song)
 MO45 0534
SOPHISTICATED SOUL (LP)
 TALP 0067
SO RIGHT (LP)
 TMGLP 0007
So Right (song)
 TMG45 0058, TMG45 0092
Sorry Doesn't Always Make It
 Right (song)
 MO45 0348
Sorry Is A Sorry Word (song)
 GO45 0062, VI45 0054
Sorry Won't Cut It (song)
 TMG45 0138
THE SOUL AND SOUND OF
 HERBIE WILLIAMS (LP)
 WOLP 0015
Soul Clappin' (song)
 SO45 0108, SO45 0117
THE SOULFUL MOODS OF
 MARVIN GAYE (LP)
 NALP 0015, TALP 0002
Soul Long (song)
 MO45 0261
SOUL MASTER (LP)
 GOLP 0031
SOUL ON THE ROCKS (LP)
 TALP 0056
SOUL SESSION (LP)
 SOLP 0002
SOUL SESSIONS (EP)
 SOEP 0002
SOUL SOUNDS (LP)
 MOLP 0065
SOUL SPIN (LP)
 MOLP 0096
Soul Stomp (song)
 SO45 0006
Sounds Like Love (song)
 TMG45 0221
Sounds Of The Zodiac (song)

MO45 0192
South American Sneeze (song)
 GO45 0185
Southern Comfort (song)
 MO45 0386
SOUVENIR ALBUM (1971
 STERLING BALL
 BENEFIT) (LP)
 MOLP 0141
SPACE DANCE (LP)
 MOLP 0311
Space Dance (song)
 MO45 0474
Spaced Out (song)
 GO45 0142, GO45 0146
Spanish Harlem (song)
 MW45 0029
Spanish Lace And Memories
 (song)
 ME45 0015
Spanish Rose (song)
 MO45 0099
Sparkle (song)
 MO45 0488
SPECIAL OCCASION (LP)
 TALP 0071
Special Occasion (song)
 TA45 0157
THE SPELL (LP)
 TMGLP 0040
Spend Some Time Together (song)
 MW45 0018, MW45 0019
Spend The Night With Me (song)
 TMG45 0212
Spend The Night With Me
 (Instrumental) (song)
 TMG45 0212
Spinnin' And Spinnin' (song)
 MO45 0341
Spirit Groove (song)
 MO12 0025, MO45 0478, MO45 0489
Spirit of '76 (A.M. America)
 (song)
 MO45 0386
Spread The News (song)
 MO45 0322
Square Biz (song)
 GO45 0205, MO12 0039
Square Biz (Instrumental) (song)
 MO12 0039
STACIE (LP)
 MOLP 0178
Stand By Me (song)
 SO45 0076
Standing At The Crossroads Of
 Love (song)
 MO45 0062
Standing In The Shadows Of Love
 (song)
 MO45 0113
Standing On The Top (Part 1)
 (song)
 TMG45 0017
Standing On The Top (Part 2)
 (song)
 TMG45 0017
Standing On The Verge (Of
 Getting It On) (song)
 MO12 0032
STANDING OVATION (LP)
 SOLP 0036
Star (song)

TMG45 0183

Star (Special 12-inch version) (song)
TMG12 0031

STAR DANCING (LP)
MOLP 0299

Star Love (song)
MO45 0453

Starting The Hurt All Over Again (song)
TA45 0133

"Star Wars" Theme (song)
PR45 0025

"Star Wars" Theme (Long Version) (song)
PR45 0025

A State of Grace (song)
MO45 0444

State Of Mind (song)
MO45 0315

Static Free (song)
MO45 0358

Statue Of A Fool (song)
MO45 0419

Stay A Little Longer (song)
SO45 0075

Stay In My Lonely Arms (song)
VI45 0036, VI45 0064

Stay My Love (song)
VI45 0043

Stay With Me (song)
PR45 0017

Steal Away (song)
CHEP 0002

Steal Away Tonight (song)
MO45 0123

STEEERIKES BACK (LP)
MOLP 0092

Step By Step (Hand In Hand) (song)
SO45 0049, VI45 0048

STEPHEN COHN (LP)
MOLP 0191

Stepping Closer To Your Heart (song)
SO45 0023, SO45 0034

Steppin' On A Dream (song)
SO45 0082

STEPPIN' OUT (LP)
GOLP 0084

STEVIE AT THE BEACH (LP)
TALP 0036

STEVIE WONDER (EP)
MOEP 0006

STEVIE WONDER PRESENTS SYREETA (LP)
MOLP 0210

STEVIE WONDER'S GREATEST HITS (LP)
TALP 0063

STEVIE WONDER'S JOURNEY THROUGH THE SECRET LIFE OF PLANTS (LP)
TALP 0153

Sticks And Stones (But The Funk Won't Never Hurt You) (song)
MO45 0459

Still (song)
MO45 0491

Still Holding On (song)
MO45 0284

Still Water (Love) (song)
MO45 0182, MOCO 0018

Still Water (Peace) (song)
MO45 0182

STILL WATERS RUN DEEP (CD)
TMGCD 0008

STILL WATERS RUN DEEP (LP)
MOLP 0105

Stone City Band, Hi! (song)
GO45 0166

Stoned Love (song)
MO45 0184, MOCO 0019

Stone Soul Booster (song)
GO45 0101

Stop! Don't Tease Me (song)
TMG45 0037, TMG45 0274

Stop! In The Name Of Love (song)
MO12 0038, MO45 0085, MO45 0505, MO45 0542, MOCB 0002

Stop The War Now (song)
GO45 0105

STOP THE WORLD....WE WANNA GET ON (LP)
VILP 0005

The Storm (song)
TMG45 0247

Stormy Love (song)
GO45 0179

Straight From The Heart (Into Your Life) (song)
TMG45 0148

Strange I Know (song)
TA45 0055

Strange Love (song)
MO45 0025

Streakin' Down The Avenue (song)
MO45 0314

Street Angel (song)
TMG45 0123

STREET SONGS (LP)
GOLP 0103

STREET SONGS + THROWIN' DOWN (CD)
TMGCD 0013

The Stretch (song)
MO45 0021

The Stripper (song)
PR45 0018

Strokin' (song)
MO45 0459

Struck By Lightning Twice (song)
GO45 0191

STRUNG OUT (LP)
MOLP 0123

Strung Out (song)
MO45 0192, MOCO 0022

Strung Out On Commodores (song)
TMG45 0031

STRUNG OUT ON MOTOWN (LP)
TMGLP 0015

Strung Out On Motown (Medley) (song)
TMG45 0031

STRUTTIN' (LP)
MOLP 0336

Struttin' (song)
MO45 0500

Strutt My Thang (song)
TMG45 0070

Strut Your Stuff (song)
GO45 0182

Stubborn Kind Of Fellow (song)
MO45 0161, TA45 0051, TAEP 0001

Stuck On You (song)
TMG45 0152

STYLUS (LP)
PRLP 0024

Such A Long Time (song)
PR45 0005

Such A Woman (song)
MO45 0491

Such Is Love, Such Is Life (song)
TA45 0072

Sugar Cane Curtain (song)
ME45 0006

Sugar Daddy (song)
MO45 0003, MO45 0004, MO45 0206

Sugar Don't Bite (song)
TMG45 0149

Sugar Don't Bite (Instrumental) (song)
TMG12 0024

Sugar Don't Bite (New dance mix) (song)
TMG12 0024

SUGAR N' SPICE (LP)
GOLP 0044

SUITE FOR THE SINGLE GIRL (LP)
MOLP 0281

Summer Love (song)
GO45 0194

Summertime (song)
PR45 0032

Sun Country (song)
MW45 0026, MW45 0027

SUNDAY FUNNIES (LP)
RALP 0023

SUNDOWNERS (LP)
HILP 0003

Sundown On Sunset (song)
TMG45 0150

SUNNY AND WARM (LP)
MOLP 0113

Sunset (song)
TA45 0057

Sunshine Lady (song)
MO45 0294

Sunshine Man (song)
MO45 0261

Super Freak (song)
MO12 0041

Super Freak (Part I) (song)
GO45 0208

Super Freak (Part II) (song)
GO45 0208

SUPER HITS (LP)
TALP 0081

Supernatural Voodoo Woman (song)
MO45 0297

Supernatural Voodoo Woman (Part 2) (song)
MO45 0297

Supernatural Voodoo Woman (Pt. I) (song)
SO45 0113

Supernatural Voodoo Woman (Pt. II) (song)
SO45 0113

Supersensousensation (Try Some

Love) (song)
MO45 0427

Superstar Of Love (Instrumental)
(song)
MO45 0535

Superstar (Remember How You
Got Where You Are) (song)
GO45 0112, MO45 0349

Superstition (song)
TA45 0215

Superwoman (Where Were You
When I Needed You) (song)
TA45 0205

THE SUPREMES (LP)
MOLP 0158, MOLP 0230

SUPREMES A GO GO (LP)
MOLP 0050

THE SUPREMES AND THE
MOTOWN SOUND (LP)
MOLP 0057

SUPREMES AT THE COPA
(LP)
MOLP 0037

THE SUPREMES HITS (EP)
MOEP 0008

Supreme's Interview
MO45 0090

THE SUPREMES SING
BALLADS AND BLUES
(LP)
MOLP 0011

SUPREMES SING COUNTRY,
WESTERN AND POP (LP)
MOLP 0026

SUPREMES SING HOLLAND,
DOZIER, HOLLAND (LP)
MOLP 0051

SUPREMES SING RODGERS
AND HART (LP)
MOLP 0060

THE SUPREMES 25TH
ANNIVERSARY (CD)
TMGLP 0195

SURFACE THRILLS (LP)
TMGLP 0033

Surface Thrills (song)
TMG45 0087

SURRENDER (LP)
MOLP 0124

Surrender (song)
MO45 0200

Suzie (song)
GO45 0092, GO45 0096

Sweep (song)
TMG45 0131

Sweet And Sexy Thing (song)
TMG45 0251

Sweet And Sexy Thing
(Instrumental) (song)
TMG12 0062, TMG45 0251

Sweet And Sexy Thing (12-inch
version) (song)
TMG12 0062

Sweet And Sexy Thing (Vocal)
(song)
TMG12 0062

Sweet Darlin' (song)
GO45 0081

Sweeter As The Days Go By
(song)
SO45 0019

Sweet Harmony (song)

TA45 0222

Sweet Love (song)
MO45 0394, MOCO 0033

Sweetness (song)
PR45 0036

Sweet Remedy (song)
TMG45 0115

Sweet Soul (song)
SO45 0041

The Sweet Sound Of Your Song
(song)
MO45 0346

Sweet Thing (song)
MO45 0078

Sweet Water (song)
RA45 0018

Swept For You Baby (song)
TA45 0137

Swim (song)
SO45 0088

SWING (LP)
GOLP 0028

SWITCH (LP)
GOLP 0081

SWITCH II (LP)
GOLP 0090

SWITCH V (LP)
GOLP 0108

SWITCHED ON BLUES (LP)
SOLP 0020

Swoop (I'm Yours) (song)
TMG12 0021

Sylvia (song)
TA45 0124, TAEP 0006

SYREETA (LP)
MWLP 0013, TALP 0154

T.C.B. (LP)
MOLP 0083, NALP 0028

T. G. SHEPPARD (LP)
MLLP 0001

T.L.C. (Tender Loving Care)
(song)
TA45 0204

Tailgate (song)
GO45 0155, MO12 0009

T'ain't Nobody's Bizness If I Do
(song)
MW45 0034

Take A Chance (song)
MI45 0006

Take A Chance On Me (song)
MO45 0030

Take A Look Around (song)
GO45 0116

Take It All (song)
TA45 0265

Take It Now (song)
MO45 0343

Take It Out On Me (song)
MO45 0227

Take Me (song)
TA45 0033

TAKE ME ALL THE WAY (LP)
TMGLP 0214

Take Me Away (song)
MO45 0520

Take Me Back (song)
MO45 0354, MO45 0531

Take Me Clear From Here (song)
MO45 0345, SO45 0096

Take Me Girl, I'm Ready (song)
SO45 0084

TAKE ME IN YOUR ARMS
(LP)
GOLP 0034

Take Me In Your Arms And Love
Me (song)
SO45 0033

Take Me In Your Arms (Rock Me
A Little While) (song)
GO45 0047, MO45 0228, TA45 0149

Take Me (The Way That I Am)
(song)
ML45 0026

Take My Life (song)
GO45 0204

Take My Word (song)
MO45 0293

Take Somebody Like You (song)
VI45 0068

Take Some Time Out For Love
(song)
TA45 0118, TA45 0167

Take This Heart Of Mine (song)
TA45 0117, TAEP 0004

Take Time To Love Me (song)
RA45 0047

TAKE TWO (LP)
TALP 0051

Taking My Love (And Leaving
Me) (song)
GO45 0095

Taking My Time (song)
TA45 0046

Tale of Two Cities (song)
RA45 0045

TALKING BOOK (CD)
TMGLP 0153

TALKING BOOK (LP)
TALP 0100

(Talking 'Bout) Nobody But My
Baby (song)
GO45 0039

Talkin' To Your Picture (song)
MO45 0082

Talk Of The Town (song)
TMG45 0160

Talk To Jeanette (song)
ML45 0026

Talk To Me (song)
MO45 0373, TMG45 0265

Talk To Me (LP Version) (song)
TMG12 0068

Talk To Me (Single Version)
(song)
TMG12 0068

Talk To Me (12-inch version)
(song)
TMG12 0068

Tally Ho (song)
IN45 0002

TAMLA SPECIAL #1 (LP)
TALP 0005

Taos New Mexico (song)
RA45 0037

TATTOO (LP)
PRLP 0008

TAYLOR MADE SOUL (LP)
GOLP 0042

Teardrops (song)
TMG45 0060

TEARDROPS KEEP FALLING
ON MY HEART (LP)
VILP 0004

They Shall Be Mine (song)
TA45 0030

Things (song)
ML45 0011

Things Are Changing (song)
TA45S 0005

The Things We Have To Do (song)
SO45 0086

The Things You're Made Of (song)
TA45 0302, TMG45 0118

Think (About The Good Things) (song)
IN45 0003

Thinkin' 'Bout My Baby (song)
MO45 0241, MW45 0045

Think Of Me As Your Soldier (song)
TA45 0196

The Thin Man (song)
TA45 0247

Thin Walls (song)
TMG45 0174

THIRD ALBUM (LP)
MOLP 0119

THIRD ALBUM + MAYBE TOMORROW (CD)
TMGCD 0012

Third Finger, Left Hand (song)
GO45 0059

Third World Calling (Opus II) (song)
MO45 0448

13 (LP)
TMGLP 0055

This Child Needs Its Father (song)
SO45 0111

This Empty Place (song)
MO45 0395

This Is Funkin' Insane (song)
MO45 0504

This Is It (This Is My Love) (song)
GO45 0207

THIS IS MY DREAM (LP)
GOLP 0101

This Is Our Night (song)
ME45 0001

This Is The Story (song)
MO45 0207

This Is True (song)
VI45 0035

This Is Your Life (song)
MO45 0374

This Little Girl (song)
TA45 0079

This Man Of Mine (song)
MO45 0245

THIS OLD HEART OF MINE (IS WEAK FOR YOU) (LP)
TALP 0050

This Old Heart Of Mine (Is Weak For You) (song)
MO45 0149, TA45 0113

This Time It's Forever (song)
TMG45 0024

This Time Last Summer (song)
MO45 0179, SO45 0089, VI45 0018

This Use To Be The Home Of Johnnie Mae (song)
TA45 0189

This Use To Be The Home Of Johnnie Mae (Long Version) (song)

TA45 0191

This Use To Be The Home Of Johnnie Mae (Short Version) (song)
TA45 0191

THOMAS McCLAREY (LP)
TMGLP 0123

Those Other Men (song)
MO45 0437

Three Choruses Of Despair (song)
VI45 0034

Three Four Three (song)
SOEP 0002

THREE OUNCES OF LOVE (LP)
MOLP 0304

Three Times A Lady (song)
MO45 0457

A Thrill A Moment (song)
GO45 0042

Throw A Farewell Kiss (song)
VI45 0012

Throwdown (song)
TMG45 0060

THROWIN' DOWN (CD)
TMGCD 0013

THROWIN' DOWN (LP)
TMGLP 0006

Thumpin' (song)
SO47 0007

Thumpin' Music (song)
MO45 0413, MO45 0416, MO45 0473, MO45 0483

Ticket To The Moon (song)
MO45 0350, MO45 0376

Tidal Wave (song)
MO45 0311

Tie A String Around Your Finger (song)
TA45 0065

Tie Me Tight (song)
TA45 0034

Tie Me To A Tree (Handcuff Me) (song)
MO45 0466

Tie Me To A Tree (Handcuff Me) (Instrumental) (song)
MO45 0466

Tie Me To A Tree (Handcuff Me) (Vocal & Instrumental) (song)
MOCO 0034

TIGGI CLAY (LP)
TMGLP 0069

'Til Johnny Comes (song)
TA45 0129

Time (song)
GO45 0098, JU45 0002, MO45 0273, MO45 0408

TIME AND LOVE (LP)
MOLP 0107

Time Changes Things (song)
MO45 0043, MO45 0133

Time Don't Wait (song)
GO45 0117

Time For Me To Go (song)
MO45 0249

Time Is Passin' By (song)
SO45 0049, VI45 0048

TIME OUT FOR SMOKEY ROBINSON AND THE MIRACLES (LP)
TALP 0076

Time (To Believe In Each Other) (song)
MO45 0233

Time To Get It Together (song)
TA45 0295

Time Will Reveal (song)
TMG45 0110

Tippin' (song)
MO45 0360, MO45 0411

To A Gentler Time (song)
MO45 0283

TO BE CONTINUED . . . (LP)
TMGLP 0209

To Be Continued . . . (song)
TMG45 0278

Today Will Soon Be Yesterday (song)
TA45 0272

TOE FAT (LP)
RALP 0008

TOE FAT TWO (LP)
RALP 0022

TOGETHER (CD)
TMGCD 0039

TOGETHER (LP)
MOLP 0014, MOLP 0093

Together (song)
MO45 0272, MO45 0348, MO45 0472, MO45 0514

Together 'Til The End Of Time (song)
TA45 0110

Together We Can Do Anything (song)
VI45 0060

Together We Can Make Such Sweet Music (song)
MO45 0185, MO45 0247, VI45 0056

To Know (song)
MO45 0226

To Know You Is To Love You (song)
MW45 0022, MWCO 0003

Tokyo (Instrumental) (song)
TMG45 0188

Tokyo (12-inch instrumental version) (song)
TMG12 0032

TO LOVE AGAIN (LP)
MOLP 0356

To Love Again (song)
MO45 0532

Tomorrow & Always (song)
MO45 0012, MO45 0013

Tomorrow May Never Come (song)
MO45 0089

Tomorrow's Tears (song)
SO45 0027

Tonight's The Night (song)
VI45 0010

Too Busy Thinking About My Baby (song)
TA45 0166

Toodle Loo (song)
GO45 0004, GO45 0009

Too High (song)
TA45 0225

Too Hot Ta Trot (song)
MO45 0446

Too Hurt To Cry, Too Much In Love To Say Goodbye (song)

GO45 0025
Too Many Colors (Tee's
   Interlude) (song)
   GO45 0183
Too Many Fish In The Sea (song)
   SO45 0009, TA45 0088, TAEP 0002
Too Shy To Say (song)
   MO45 0456
Too Strong To Be Strung Along
   (song)
   TA45 0055
Topics (song)
   MO45 0324
Top Of The World (song)
   MO45 0463
TOP TEN (LP)
   SOLP 0004
TOTALLY TATA (LP)
   TALP 0134
TOUCH (LP)
   MOLP 0138
Touch (song)
   MO45 0202, MO45 0289, SO45 0118,
   TMG45 0240
TOUCH ME (LP)
   TMGLP 0166
TOUCH ME IN THE
   MORNING (LP)
   MOLP 0174, TMGLP 0084
Touch Me In The Morning (song)
   MO45 0251
TOUCH ME IN THE
   MORNING + BABY IT'S
   ME (CD)
   TMGCD 0027
The Touch Of Time (song)
   MO45 0098
Touch The One You Love (song)
   TMG45 0163
TOUCH THE SKY (LP)
   TMGLP 0031
Touch The Sky (song)
   TMG45 0082
The Tracks Of My Tears (song)
   SO45 0078, TA45 0102, TAEP 0005,
   TMG12 0006
Tragedy (song)
   HI45 0007
Train Of Thought (song)
   TMG45 0192, TMG45 0234
Travelin' Man (song)
   TA45 0132
Travelin' Through (song)
   TA45 0306
Treat Her Like A Lady (song)
   TMG45 0171
A TRIBUTE TO THE GIRLS
   (LP)
   MOLP 0036
A TRIBUTE TO THE GREAT
   NAT KING COLE (LP)
   TALP 0042
TRIBUTE TO UNCLE RAY
   (LP)
   TALP 0013
Triflin' (song)
   TA45 0290
Trouble In This Land (song)
   DI45 0005
Trouble Man (song)
   TA45 0217, TA45 0243
TROUBLE MAN (ORIGINAL

SOUND TRACK) + M.P.G.
   (CD)
   TMGCD 0037
TROUBLE MAN
   (SOUNDTRACK) (LP)
   TALP 0103
True Love (That's Love) (song)
   TA45 0015
Truly (song)
   TMG45 0046
TRULY FOR YOU (LP)
   TMGLP 0121
Truly Great American Blues
   (song)
   ML45 0024
Truly Yours (song)
   MO45 0104, MO45 0269
TRUST ME (LP)
   TMGLP 0011
Trust Your Heart (song)
   TA45 0237
Trying To Make It (song)
   GO45 0002
Tryin' To Beat The Morning
   Home (song)
   ML45 0006
Try It Baby (song)
   MO45 0161, TA45 0078
Try It, You'll Like It (song)
   MW45 0031
Try Me (song)
   MC45 0014
TRY MY LOVE (LP)
   TALP 0142
TUCKER AND
   SCHOONMAKER (LP)
   MCLP 0013
Tuesday Heartbreak (song)
   TA45 0221
Tune Up (song)
   SO45 0012
TURNIN' ON (LP)
   GOLP 0078
Turn Off The Lights (song)
   TMG45 0125
12 YEAR OLD GENIUS
   (RECORDED LIVE) (LP)
   TALP 0021
21ST CREATION (LP)
   GOLP 0085
25 MILES (LP)
   GOLP 0040
Twenty-Five Miles (song)
   GO45 0084, GOCO 0004
25 MILES + WAR AND PEACE
   (CD)
   TMGCD 0021
25 NO. 1 HITS FROM 25
   YEARS (CD)
   TMGLP 0134
20 GREATEST SONGS IN
   MOTOWN HISTORY (CD)
   TMGLP 0139
20 HARD-TO-FIND
   MOTOWN CLASSICS,
   VOLUME 1 (CD)
   TMGLP 0185
20 HARD-TO-FIND
   MOTOWN CLASSICS,
   VOLUME II (CD)
   TMGLP 0186
20/20 - TWENTY NO. 1 HITS

FROM TWENTY YEARS
   AT MOTOWN (LP)
   MOLP 0342
Twinkle Twinkle Little Me (song)
   MO45 0096, MOCO 0001
Twistin' Postman (song)
   TA45 0037
TWISTIN' THE WORLD
   AROUND (LP)
   MOLP 0002
Twist Lackawanna (song)
   SOEP 0003
Two (song)
   PR45 0019
Two Can Have A Party (song)
   TA45 0154
Two Feet From Happiness (song)
   VI45 0055
TWO FRIENDS (LP)
   NALP 0001
Two Lovers (song)
   MO45 0044
TWO LOVERS AND OTHER
   GREAT HITS (LP)
   MOLP 0008
TWO LOVERS + MY GUY (CD)
   TMGCD 0025
The Two Of Us (song)
   MO45 0093
Two Shoes (song)
   GO45 0150, MO45 0404
TWO TO ONE (LP)
   MOLP 0306
Two Wrongs Don't Make A Right
   (song)
   MO45 0048, TA45 0026
U.F.O. (song)
   ML45 0029
U.F.O. 1 (LP)
   RALP 0021
U Bring The Freak Out (song)
   TMG45 0108
UFO's (song)
   GO45 0144
Uncle Tom (song)
   CH45 0016
Under God's Light (song)
   RA45 0034
Under The Influence (song)
   TMG12 0059, TMG45 0239
THE UNDISPUTED TRUTH
   (LP)
   GOLP 0055
Ungena Za Ulimwengu (Unite
   The World) (song)
   GO45 0103, GOCO 0008
UNITED (LP)
   TALP 0058, TMGLP 0085
Until We're Free (song)
   BF45 0001
Until You Come Back To Me
   (That's What I'm Gonna Do)
   (song)
   SO45 0115
Until You Love Someone (song)
   MO45 0109
Up Again (song)
   MO45 0282, TA45 0248
Upside Down (song)
   MO45 0512
Up The Creek (Without A
   Paddle) (song)

GO45 0151

Up The Ladder To The Roof
(song)
MO45 0173

UP TIGHT (CD)
TMGCD 0026

UP TIGHT (LP)
TALP 0049

Uptight (song)
MO45 0037

Uptight (Everything's Alright)
(song)
MOCB 0010, TA45 0109

USED TO BE (LP)
TMGLP 0028

Used To Be (song)
TMG45 0052

VALERIE SIMPSON (LP)
TALP 0098

VANCOUVER DREAMING
(LP)
NALP 0007

VANDELLAS GREATEST
HITS (EP)
GOEP 0002

VANDELLAS GREATEST
HITS (LP)
GOLP 0017

THE VELVELETTES (LP)
VILP 0002

The Very Last Love Letter (song)
MC45 0009

Very Special Part (song)
TMG45 0051

VIBRATIONS (LP)
TMGLP 0086

The Victors (song)
MW45 0002

VINTAGE STOCK: THE BEST
OF MARY WELLS (LP)
MOLP 0054

Virginia (song)
MC45 0011

Virgin Man (song)
TA45 0240

Visions (song)
TA45 0232

Vitamin U (song)
MO12 0007, TA45 0279

Viva Espana (Forever A Song In
My Heart) (song)
MO45 0347

Volvere Alguna Vez (song)
TMG45 0075

Voodoo Plan (song)
VI45 0025

Wait Until September (song)
MO45 0380, PR45 0015

Walk Away From Love (song)
MO45 0389

Walk Away Renee (song)
MO45 0130

Walk Down The Path Of
Freedom (song)
RA45 0031

Walk In Silence (song)
MO45 0103

Walk In The Night (song)
SO45 0095

Walk Like A Man (song)
TMG45 0258

WALK ON (LP)

MOLP 0343

Walk On (song)
MO45 0504

Walk On, Don't Look Back (song)
MW45 0027

Walk On The Wild Side (song)
TA45 0084

Walk Out The Door If You
Wanna (song)
MO45 0336

Wallking Schtick (song)
RA45 0056

The Walls (Came Tumbling
Down) (song)
TMG45 0264

Wandering Stranger (song)
TMG45 0103

Want To Know My Mind (song)
TA45 0222

War (song)
GO45 0102

WAR & PEACE (CD)
TMGCD 0021

WAR & PEACE (LP)
GOLP 0048

A Warmer World (song)
MO45 0111

Warm Ride (song)
PR45 0030

WARM THOUGHTS (LP)
TALP 0149

War Of Nerves (song)
TMG45 0135, TMG45 0160

WATCH IT SUCKER (LP)
TMGLP 0026

WATCHOUT (EP)
GOEP 0005

WATCHOUT! (LP)
GOLP 0020

Way Back Home (song)
CH45 0011

Way Back Home (Instrumental)
(song)
SO45 0090

Way Back Home (Vocal) (song)
SO45 0090

THE WAY I AM (LP)
MOLP 0346

Way Over There (song)
GO45 0079, TA45 0010, TA45 0052

The Way You Do The Things You
Do (song)
GO45 0029, MO45 0153, MOCB 0013,
RA45 0029, TMG12 0006

We All End Up In Boxes (song)
RA45 0033, RACO 0010

We Are The Future (song)
GO45 0162

Weatherman (song)
TMG45 0260

We Call It Fun (song)
VI45 0025

We Can Make It Baby (song)
SO45 0074

We Can Never Light That Old
Flame Again (song)
TMG45 0028

We Can Put It Back Together
(song)
MO45 0518

We Can Work It Out (song)
TA45 0188, TACO 0012

Wedding Song (song)
TA45 0253

We Gonna Have A House Party
(song)
MO45 0430

We Gonna Party Tonight (song)
MO45 0438

We Got To Get You A Woman
(song)
MO45 0266

The Weight (song)
MO45 0164

We Just Live Here (We Don't
Love Here Anymore) (song)
HI45 0009

WELCOME TO THE WORLD
OF RIOT (LP)
MOLP 0208

We Like To Party...Come On
(song)
MO12 0028

We'll Have A Good Thing Going
On (song)
MO45 0160

We'll Have It Made (song)
VI45 0059, VICO 0005

WENDELL ADKINS (LP)
MCLP 0012

Wendy Is Gone (song)
PR45 0004

We Really Love Each Other
(song)
MO45 0011

We're Almost There (song)
MO45 0354

We're Both In Love With You
(song)
TMG45 0140

We're Gonna Have A Good Time
(song)
RA45 0048

WE REMEMBER SAM COOKE
(LP)
MOLP 0030

WE'RE OFF TO DUBLIN IN
THE GREEN (LP)
VILP 0003

We're Only Young Once (song)
GO45 0018

Were You There (song)
CHEP 0002

We Shall Overcome (song)
DI45 0005, GO45 0024

We Should Never Be Lonely My
Love (song)
SO45 0075

We've Come Too Far To End It
Now (song)
TA45 0209

We've Got A Good Thing Going
(song)
MO45 0214

We've Got A Way Out Love
(song)
SO45 0056

(We've Got) Honey Love (song)
GO45 0086

We've Only Just Begun (song)
VI45 0067

WE WISH YOU A MERRY
CHRISTMAS (LP)
NALP 0019

(song)
MO45 0505

Where Do You Go (Baby) (song)
GO45 0133, MO45 0269, MW45 0024

WHERE I'M COMING FROM
(LP)
TALP 0089

Where Is That Girl (song)
MO45 0104

WHERE THERE'S SMOKE . . .
(CD)
TMGCD 0002

WHERE THERE'S SMOKE . . .
(LP)
TALP 0148

Wherever I Lay My Hat (That's
My Home) (song)
TA45 0166

Where Were You (song)
TA45 0122, TA45 0129

Where Were You When The Ship
Went Down (song)
MO45 0311

Where Would I Be Without You
(song)
MO45 0134, MO45 0454

While I'm Away (song)
GO45 0003

Whirlwind (song)
TA45 0016

Whisper (song)
TA45 0001

Whisper You Love Me (song)
MO45 0076

Whisper You Love Me Baby
(song)
MO45 0086

Whisper You Love Me Boy (song)
MO45 0132

White Bird (song)
MO45 0307

White House Twist (song)
MO45 0031

WHITE KNUCKLE RIDE (LP)
TMGLP 0099

A Whiter Shade Of Pale (song)
SO45 0064

Who Are You (song)
GO45 0152, GO45 0153

Who Could Ever Doubt My Love
(song)
MO45 0094, TA45 0118, VI45 0019

WHO I AM (LP)
MOLP 0251

Who Is The Leader Of The People
(song)
SO45 0100

Whole Lot Of Shakin' In My
Heart (Since I Met You) (song)
TA45 0119

Whole Lotta Woman (song)
MO45 0017

Whole New Thing (song)
MO45 0396

THE WHOLE WORLD IS MY
HOME (LP)
MOLP 0296

Wholly Holy (song)
TA45 0197

WHOPPER BOPPER SHOW
STOPPER (LP)
SOLP 0048

Whopper Bopper Show Stopper
(song)
SO45 0123

Who's Cheating On Who (song)
PR45 0011

Whose Heart Are You Going To
Break Now (song)
MI45 0010

Who's Gonna Take The Blame
(song)
TA45 0179

Who's Holding Donna Now (song)
TMG45 0199

Who Shot Zorro (song)
TMG45 0134

Who's Johnny (song)
TMG45 0249

Who's Loving You (song)
TA45 0028

Who's Lovin' You (song)
MO45 0168, TA45 0017

Who's Right Or Wrong (song)
MO45 0339

Who's Sad (song)
TA45 0328

Who's The Fool (song)
TA45 0013

Who Wouldn't Love A Man Like
That (song)
TA45 0014, TA45 0064

Who You Gonna Run To (song)
VI45 0008, VI45 0066

Why Am I Lovin' You (song)
VI45 0043

Why Can't You Be Mine (song)
MO45 0268

Why Daddy (song)
HI45 0014

Why Did She Have To Leave Me
(Why Did She Have To Go)
(song)
GO45 0082

Why Don't You Lead Me To
Love (song)
TA45 0150

Why Do You Cry (song)
RA45 0041

Why Do You Laugh At Me?
(song)
CHEP 0001

Why Do You Want To Let Me
Go (song)
GO45 0043

WHY I OPPOSE THE WAR IN
VIETNAM (LP)
BFLP 0001

Why Not Try Lovin' Me (song)
MC45 0012

Why Them, Why Me (song)
SO45 0051

Why When Love Is Gone (song)
TA45 0149

Why You Wanna See My Bad
Side (song)
TA45 0288

Why You Wanna Try Me (song)
TMG45 0005

Wide Open (song)
MO45 0379

Wigs And Lashes (song)
TA45 0227

Wild And Crazy Love (song)

TMG45 0204

Wild And Crazy Love
(Instrumental) (song)
TMG45 0204

Wild And Crazy Love
(Instrumental Mix) (song)
TMG12 0042

Wild And Crazy Love (Vocal
Mix) (song)
TMG12 0042

Wild And Crazy Love (Wild &
Crazy Club Mix) (song)
TMG12 0042

WILD AND PEACEFUL (LP)
GOLP 0088

WILD ANIMAL (LP)
TMGLP 0104

Wild Animal (song)
TMG45 0239

WILD ONE (LP)
GOLP 0015

Wild One (song)
GO45 0037

WILLIE REMEMBERS (LP)
RALP 0040

Will This Be The Day (song)
MO45 0146

Wind It Up (song)
SO45 0001

Window Shopping (song)
SO45 0037

WINE, WOMEN AND SONG
(LP)
NALP 0008

Wine, Women And Song (song)
TA45 0313

WINGS OF LOVE (LP)
GOLP 0071

Wings Of Time (song)
PR45 0028

The Winner Gets The Heart (song)
TMG45 0134

WINTER DAY'S NIGHTMARE
(LP)
MOLP 0266

The Wisdom Of Time (song)
MO45 0218

Wishful Thinking (song)
TMG45 0244

Wish Upon A Star (song)
TMG45 0011, TMG45 0079

Wish You Were Here (song)
MO45 0102

Witchcraft (song)
TA45S 0002

With A Child's Heart (song)
MO45 0230, TA45 0115

WITH A LITTLE HELP FROM
MY FRIENDS (LP)
PRLP 0002

With A Little Help From My
Friends (song)
GO45 0123

WITH A LOT O' SOUL (CD)
TMGCD 0038

WITH A SONG IN MY HEART
(LP)
TALP 0031

Without The One You Love
(Life's Not Worthwhile) (song)
MO45 0080

Without You (song)

GO45 0081
Without You In My Life (song)
GO45 0217
With You I'm Born Again (song)
MO45 0494
With You I'm Born Again
(Instrumental) (song)
MO45 0477
With Your Love Came (song)
TA45 0214
WOLF & WOLF (LP)
TMGLP 0047
WOLFE (LP)
RALP 0038
A Woman (song)
MO45 0142
Woman Alive (song)
RA45 0026
Woman In My Eyes (song)
MO45 0248, MW45 0049
THE WOMAN IN RED (LP)
TMGLP 0110
Woman, You Touched Me (song)
MO45 0344
Wonderful Baby (song)
MO45 0135
Wonderland (song)
MO45 0496
Won't Be Home Tonight (song)
HI45 0011
Words Of Love (song)
MO45 0517
WORKOUT STEVIE
WORKOUT (LP)
TALP 0029
Workout Stevie, Workout (song)
TA45 0069
Work That Body (song)
TMG45 0118
Work That Body (Instrumental)
(song)
TMG12 0017
Work That Body (Vocal) (song)
TMG12 0017
The World Is Rated X (song)
TMG45 0242, TMG45 0243
The World Is Rated X
(Instrumental) (song)
TMG45 0242
World So Wide, Nowhere To Hide
(From Your Heart) (song)
SO45 0032
Would I Love You (song)
TA45 0085
Wouldn't You Like To Know
(song)
TMG45 0105
Would You Like To Come Along
(song)
PR45 0030, RA45 0048
WRITERS OF THE
REVOLUTION (LP)
BFLP 0003
Wrong Man, Right Touch (song)
TMG45 0034
Xmas Twist (song)
MO45 0031
X-Rated Movie (song)
MO45 0467, TMG45 0005
Yes He Is (song)
TA45 0074
Yes Indeed (song)

GO45 0215
YES IT'S YOU LADY (LP)
TMGLP 0002
Yes It's You Lady (song)
TMG45 0032
Yes, No, Maybe So (song)
TA45 0011
YESTERDAY'S DREAMS (LP)
MOLP 0070
Yesterday's Dreams (song)
MO45 0138
Yesterday's Love Is Over (song)
VI45 0057
Yester Love (song)
TA45 0152
Yester-Me, Yester-You,
Yesterday (song)
MC45 0005, ML45 0018, TA45 0173
You (song)
MO45 0308, MO45 0530, TA45 0145
You Ain't Livin' Till You're
Lovin' (song)
TA45 0158
You Ain't No Ordinary Woman
(song)
SO45 0119
You Ain't Sayin' Nothin' New
(song)
TA45 0201
You And I (song)
GO45 0158, GO45 0202, MO12 0015,
TA45 0267
You Are (song)
TMG45 0059
You Are Blue (song)
SO45 0080
You Are Forever (song)
TA45 0322
You Are Love (song)
TA45 0251
You Are My Heaven (song)
TMG45 0127
You Are My Sunshine (song)
GOEP 0006
You Are That Special One (song)
MW45 0015
You Are The Heart Of Me (song)
MO45 0429
You Are The Reason (I Feel Like
Dancing) (song)
MO45 0451
YOU ARE THE SUNSHINE OF
MY LIFE (LP)
MCLP 0011
You Are The Sunshine Of My Life
(song)
MC45 0005, SO45 0115, TA45 0221
You Beat Me To The Punch
(song)
MO45 0041
You Better Come On Down (song)
PR45 0009, PR45 0010
You Better Get In Line (song)
GO45 0013
You Better Watch Out (song)
TA45 0311
You Bring Back Memories (song)
MO45 0049
You Can Come Right Back To
Me (song)
MO45 0199
You Can Cry On My Shoulder

(song)
MO45 0219, TA45 0106
You Can Depend On Me (song)
TA45 0009
You Can't Hurry Love (song)
MO45 0108
YOU CAN'T HURRY LOVE:
ALL THE GREAT LOVE
SONGS OF THE PAST 25
YEARS (CD)
TMGLP 0194
You Can't Judge A Book By It's
Cover (song)
MO45 0357, MO45 0367
(You Can't Let The Boy
Overpower) The Man In You
(song)
MO45 0129, TA45 0075
You Can't Stop A Man In Love
(song)
MO45 0286
You Can't Turn Me Off (In The
Middle Of Turning Me On)
(song)
GO45 0156, GO45 0157
You Could Never Love Him (Like
I Love Him) (song)
MO45 0144
You Danced Into My Life (song)
MO45 0464
You Deserve What You Got (song)
MO45 0035
You Don't Know How Hard It Is
To Make It (Instrumental)
(song)
MO45 0334
You Don't Know (How Hard It Is
To Make It) (Vocal) (song)
MO45 0334
You Don't Love Me No More
(song)
SO45 0045
You Excite Me (song)
TMG45 0133
You Gave Me Love (song)
SO45 0092
You Get A Tangle In Your
Lifeline (song)
MO45 0245
You Get Ugly (song)
GO45 0020
You Got It (song)
MO45 0456
You Got Me Hurtin' All Over
(song)
SO45 0038, SO45 0050
You Gotta Have Love In Your
Heart (song)
MO45 0193
You Gotta Keep Dancin' (song)
MO12 0037, MO45 0499
You Gotta Sacrifice (We Gotta
Sacrifice) (song)
VI45 0063
You Got The Love I Love (song)
GO45 0078
You Got The Love I Need (song)
GO45 0109
You Got What It Takes (song)
TA45 0018
You Have Inspired Me (song)
GO45 0172, MO12 0033

You Haven't Done Nothin' (song)
  TA45 0242
You Haven't Seen My Love (song)
  MO45 0128, MOCO 0004
You Keep Me Hangin' On (song)
  CH45 0010, MO45 0112, RA45 0018,
  TA45 0311, TMG45 0149
You Keep Running Away (song)
  MO45 0124
You Knows What To Do (song)
  TA45 0011
You Like Me Don't You (song)
  MO45 0522
You Like Me Don't You
  (Instrumental) (song)
  MO45 0522
You'll Be Sorry Someday (song)
  GO45 0014
You'll Lose A Precious Love
  (song)
  GO45 0055
You'll Never Cherish A Love So
  True ('Till You Lose It) (song)
  ME45 0003
You'll Never Rock Alone (song)
  TA45 0277
You Lost The Sweetest Boy (song)
  MO45 0059
You Made A Fool Out Of Me
  (song)
  TA45 0014
You Made Me What I Am (song)
  MO45 0236
You Make Me Happy (song)
  ME45 0014, MO45 0276
You Make Your Own Heaven
  And Hell Right Here On
  Earth (song)
  GO45 0106, GO45 0113
You Mean More To Me (song)
  TMG45 0059, TMG45 0128
You Met Your Match (song)
  TA45 0153
You Must Be Love (song)
  TA45 0144
YOU NAME IT (LP)
  MOLP 0277
You Need Love Like I Do (Don't
  You) (song)
  SO45 0071
You Need Me (song)
  VI45 0023
You Need Non-Stop Lovin' (song)
  TMG45 0055
You Need To Be Loved (song)
  MO45 0423
You Never Cared (song)
  PR45 0035
You Never Looked Better (song)
  ME45 0014
You Never Miss A Good Thing
  (song)
  MO45 0005, MO45 0006, MO45 0007,
  TA45 0042
The Young Folks (song)
  MO45 0159, MO45 0174, MOCO 0012
YOUNG, GIFTED AND
  BLACK (LP)
  TALP 0064
Young Gifted And Black (song)
  TA45 0182
Young Girl (song)

ML45 0001, ML45 0005
Young Love (song)
  GO45 0197
Young, Single And Tough (song)
  TMG45 0271
You Only Pass This Way One
  Time (song)
  ME45 0020
You Pulled A Switch (song)
  GO45 0161
Your Baby's Back (song)
  TA45 0006, TA45 0039
Your Cheating Ways (song)
  TA45 0105
You're A Fox (Out The Box)
  (song)
  TMG45 0008
YOU'RE ALL I NEED (LP)
  TALP 0065, TMGLP 0085
You're All I Need To Get By
  (song)
  TA45 0154
You're All The Boogie I Need
  (song)
  GO45 0187
You're A Special Part Of Me
  (song)
  MO45 0292
You're A Wonderful One (song)
  TA45 0076, TAEP 0001
You're Bad News (song)
  VI45 0010
You're Givin' Me The Runaround
  (song)
  TMG45 0051
You're Gonna Love My Baby
  (song)
  MO45 0098
You're In Good Hands (song)
  MO45 0256
You're Just Like You (song)
  MO45 0070
You're Moving Out Today (song)
  GO45 0189
(You're My) Aphrodisiac (song)
  TMG45 0143
You're My Desire (song)
  MI45 0007
You're My Driving Wheel (song)
  MO45 0421
You're My Everything (song)
  GO45 0064, SO45 0071
You're My Gardener (song)
  TA45 0325
You're My Inspiration (song)
  ME45 0001
You're My Life (song)
  MO45 0304
You're My Only World (song)
  SO45 0116
You're My Peace Of Mind (song)
  MO45 0449
You're My Remedy (song)
  TA45 0080
You're My Star (song)
  MO45 0468
You're Not An Ordinary Girl
  (song)
  GO45 0056
You're So Fine And Sweet (song)
  TA45 0081
You're So Gentle, So Kind (song)

GO45 0206
You're Supposed To Keep Your
  Love For Me (song)
  MO45 0507
You're The Loser Now (song)
  GO45 0104
YOU'RE THE MAN (LP)
  TALP 0097
You're The Man (song)
  TACO 0016
You're The Man (Part 1) (song)
  TA45 0210
You're The Man (Part 2) (song)
  TA45 0210
You're The One (song)
  ML45 0003, SO45 0056, SO45 0061,
  TA45 0116, TMG45 0278
You're The One For Me Baby
  (song)
  TA45 0202
You're What I Need (song)
  MO45 0442
You're What's Happening (In The
  World Today) (song)
  TA45 0161
YOU'RE WHAT'S MISSING IN
  MY LIFE (LP)
  MOLP 0283
You're What's Missing In My Life
  (song)
  MO45 0421, MO45 0426
Your Heart Belongs To Me (song)
  MO45 0036
Your Kiss Is Sweet (song)
  MO45 0341
Your Kiss Of Fire (song)
  MO45 0136
Your Lady Stays On My Mind
  (song)
  TMG45 0018
Your Love (song)
  CH45 0003
Your Love Grows More Precious
  Everyday (song)
  GO45 0060
Your Love Is Amazing (song)
  MO45 0092, SO45 0031
Your Love Is So Good For Me
  (song)
  MO12 0013, MO45 0450
Your Love Is Wonderful (song)
  GO45 0008, MO45 0130
Your Love Makes It All
  Worthwhile (song)
  GO45 0114
Your Love's Got Me Burnin'
  Alive (song)
  MO45 0140
Your Love Was Worth Waiting
  For (song)
  SO45 0076
Your Mama (song)
  PR45 0031
Your Mother's Only Daughter
  (song)
  TA45 0163
Your Old Standby (song)
  MO45 0051
Your Precious Love (song)
  TA45 0141
Your Sweet Love (song)
  ML45 0021

Your Unchanging Love (song)
TA45 0138
Your Wonderful Love (song)
MI45 0012, MO45 0155
Your Wonderful, Sweet Sweet
Love (song)
MO45 0218
You Seen One You Seen 'Em All
(song)
MO45 0552
You Sure Love To Ball (song)
TA45 0234
You Touched Me (song)
CH45 0013
You Turn Me On (song)
TMG45 0169
You Turn Me On (Instrumental)
(song)
TMG12 0026
You Turn Me On (Vocal) (song)
TMG12 0026
You've Been A Long Time
Coming (song)
TA45 0096
You've Been Doing Wrong For So
Long (song)
ML45 0010, MO45 0329
You've Been In Love Too Long
(song)
GO45 0046

You've Been So Wonderful To Me
(song)
MO45 0137
You've Got It Bad Girl (song)
TA45 0215
You've Got Me Where I Want
You (song)
TMG45 0044
You've Got My Mind (song)
MO45 0287, MW45 0031
You've Got My Soul On Fire
(song)
GO45 0137, MO45 0288
You've Gotta Try A Little Love
(song)
MO45 0358
You've Got To Change (song)
SO45 0004
You've Got To Earn It (song)
GO45 0044
You've Got To Make The Choice
(song)
MW45 0014
You've Got Your Troubles (song)
MO45 0263
You've Lost That Loving Feeling
(song)
MC45 0008
You've Made Me So Very Happy
(song)

TA45 0140, TACO 0003
YOU'VE REALLY GOT A
HOLD ON ME (LP)
TALP 0019
You've Really Got A Hold On
Me (song)
TA45 0056, TAEP 0003
You Want It Your Way, Always
(song)
TMG45 0271
You Wear It Well (song)
TMG45 0210
You Wear It Well (Club Mix)
(song)
TMG12 0046
You Wear It Well (Dub Mix)
(song)
TMG12 0046
Zing Went The Strings Of My
Heart (song)
MO45 0029
Zip-A-Dee-Doo-Dah (song)
MO45 0249, MW45 0004
Zoom (song)
GO45 0136
The Zoo (The Human Zoo) (song)
MW45 0009

TA45 0167, TALP 0068, TALP 0073

May 1969
CH45 0006, GO45 0087, MO45 0159,
MOCO 0012, MOLP 0086, MOLP 0090,
SO45 0063, TA45 0168, TACO 0005,
TALP 0074

June 1969
GO45 0088, GOCO 0005, MOLP 0076,
MOLP 0088, RALP 0001, SO45 0064,
TA45 0169, TACO 0006

July 1969
GO45 0091, GO45 0094, GOCO 0006,
GOLP 0033, GOLP 0042, GOLP 0043,
MO45 0160, MO45 0162, MOLP 0089,
RA45 0001, SOLP 0016, TALP 0076

August 1969
GO45 0093, GO45 0095, MO45 0161,
RA45 0002, RA45 0003, RALP 0002,
RALP 0003, RALP 0004, RALP 0005,
RALP 0006, SOLP 0018, TA45 0170

September 1969
BL45 0001, CH45 0001, CH45 0002,
CH45 0003, CHCO 0001, CHCO 0002,
GOLP 0049, MO45 0163, MO45 0164,
MO45 0165, MOLP 0092, MOLP 0093,
RA45 0004, RA45 0005, RACO 0001,
SO45 0065, SO45 0066, SOLP 0013,
TA45 0173, TALP 0075, TALP 0077

October 1969
CH45 0004, CHCO 0003, GOLP 0044,
GOLP 0045, GOLP 0046, MO45 0167,
MO45 0168, MOCO 0013, MOLP 0094,
SO45 0067, SO45 0068, TA45 0171,
TACO 0007, TALP 0069, VI45 0049,
VI45 0050

November 1969
CH45 0005, GO45 0096, MO45 0170,
MOLP 0095, MOLP 0096, MOLP 0097,
MOLP 0100, RA45 0006, RA45 0007,
SOLP 0019, SOLP 0020, SOLP 0021,
TA45 0172, TA45 0174, TACO 0008,
TALP 0078, VI45 0051, WELP 0001

December 1969
CH45 0007, CHCO 0004, GO45 0097,
MO45 0169, MOLP 0099, MOLP 0101,
TA45 0175, TACO 0009

January 1970
CHLP 0001, MO45 0172, MOLP 0103,
SO45 0069, SO45 0070, TA45 0176,
TALP 0080, VI45 0052, VICO 0002

February 1970
CH45 0008, GO45 0098, MO45 0173,
MO45 0174, MOCO 0014, RA45 0008,
SO45 0071, VI45 0053

March 1970
GO45 0099, GOLP 0047, GOLP 0050,
MO45 0175, MOLP 0091, MOLP 0102,
MOLP 0104, MOLP 0105, SO45 0072,
SOLP 0023, TA45 0177, TACO 0010,
TALP 0079, VI45 0054, VICO 0003

April 1970
CH45 0009, MO45 0176, MO45 0180,
MOCO 0015, MOLP 0106, RA45 0009,
RA45 0010, RACO 0002, TA45 0178,
TALP 0082

May 1970
GO45 0100, GO45 0101, GOCO 0007,
MO45 0177, MOCO 0016, MOLP 0109,
MOLP 0110, MOLP 0111, RA45 0011,
RALP 0016, SOLP 0025, TA45 0179,
TA45 0180, TALP 0083, VI45 0055

June 1970

GO45 0102, MOLP 0112, RA45 0012,
RACO 0003, RALP 0011, SO45 0073,
SO45 0075, SOLP 0024, TA45 0181,
TACO 0011

July 1970
CHLP 0003, CHLP 0004, MO45 0178,
MO45 0181, MOCO 0017, RA45 0013,
RALP 0008, RALP 0010, SO45 0074,
TA45 0182, TALP 0084, VI45 0056

August 1970
GOLP 0048, GOLP 0053, MO45 0182,
MO45 0183, MOCO 0018, MOLP 0117,
TA45 0183, TALP 0085

September 1970
CH45 0011, CHLP 0005, GO45 0103,
GOCO 0008, GOLP 0052, GOLP 0054,
MOLP 0118, MOLP 0119, MOLP 0122,
MOLP 0125, RA45 0014, RACO 0004,
RALP 0009, RALP 0012, RALP 0013,
RALP 0015, RALP 0018, SOLP 0015,
SOLP 0026, SOLP 0027, TA45 0184,
TA45 0185, TA45 0186, TALP 0081,
TALP 0087, VI45 0057, VICO 0004,
VILP 0004

October 1970
BFLP 0001, BFLP 0002, BFLP 0003,
CH45 0010, GO45 0104, MO45 0184,
MOCO 0019, MOLP 0114, MOLP 0116,
MOLP 0121, MOLP 0123, RA45 0015,
RACO 0005, SO45 0076, SO45 0078,
SOLP 0028, SOLP 0029, SOLP 0030,
TALP 0086, VILP 0005, VILP 0006

November 1970
GOLP 0051, MO45 0185, MO45 0186,
MOLP 0126, RA45 0016, RA45 0017,
SO45 0079, SO45 0081, TALP 0088

December 1970
GO45 0105, MO45 0187, MO45 0188,
MOCO 0020, MOLP 0108, RALP 0019,
SO45 0077, VI45 0059, VICO 0005

January 1971
GO45 0106, MO45 0189, MOCO 0021,
RA45 0018, RA45 0019, SO45 0080,
TA45 0187, VI45 0058

February 1971
CH45 0012, MO45 0190, RA45 0020,
RA45 0021, TA45 0188, TACO 0012

March 1971
CH45 0013, EC45 0001, GO45 0107,
MO45 0191, MOLP 0120, MOLP 0127,
MOLP 0128, MOLP 0129, MOLP 0130,
MOLP 0131, MOLP 0132, RA45 0022,
RACO 0006, RALP 0022, SO45 0082,
TA45 0193

April 1971
GO45 0108, GOLP 0057, MO45 0192,
MO45 0194, MO45 0195, MO45 0196,
MOCO 0022, MOCO 0023, MOLP 0136,
MOLP 0141, RA45 0023, RA45 0024,
RALP 0020, RALP 0021, SOLP 0031,
TA45 0189, TA45 0190, TA45 0191,
TACO 0013, TALP 0089, TALP 0090,
VI45 0060, VI45 0061, VILP 0008

May 1971
CHLP 0006, CHLP 0007, CHLP 0008,
MO45 0193, MO45 0197, MOLP 0133,
MOLP 0135, RALP 0023, SO45 0083,
TALP 0091, TALP 0092, VI45 0062

June 1971
CH45 0014, CH45 0015, GO45 0109,
GOCO 0009, MO45 0198, MOLP 0137,
MOLP 0138, MW45 0002, RA45 0025,

RA45 0026, RA45 0027, RACO 0007,
RALP 0017, TA45 0194, TA45 0195,
VI45 0063

July 1971
GO45 0110, GOLP 0055, GOLP 0056,
MO45 0199, MO45 0200, MOLP 0124,
MWLP 0003, RA45 0028, RA45 0029,
RA45 0030, RACO 0008, SO45 0084,
SO45 0085, SOLP 0032, TA45 0192,
TA45 0196, VI45 0065

August 1971
MO45 0201, MW45 0003, MW45 0005,
RA45 0032, RACO 0009, TALP 0093

September 1971
GO45 0111, MO45 0202, MOLP 0142,
MOLP 0144, RA45 0031, RALP 0024,
RALP 0025, RALP 0026, SO45 0087,
TA45 0197, VI45 0064

October 1971
GO45 0112, MO45 0203, MO45 0204,
MOLP 0145, MW45 0004, MW45 0007,
SO45 0088, TA45 0201

November 1971
MO45 0205, MO45 0206, MW45 0006,
MW45 0008, MWCO 0001, RA45 0033,
RA45 0034, RA45 0035, RACO 0010,
RALP 0027, RALP 0029, RALP 0030,
SO45 0090, SO45 0091, TA45 0198,
TA45 0199, TA45 0200, TA45 0202,
TA45 0203, TACO 0015, TALP 0094,
VI45 0067

December 1971
GO45 0113, GO45 0114, GOCO 0010,
MO45 0207, MOCO 0024, MOLP 0143,
MOLP 0146, MOLP 0147, RALP 0031,
SO45 0092, SOLP 0033, SOLP 0036,
TA45 0204

January 1972
GOLP 0059, GOLP 0061, MO45 0208,
MOLP 0149, MW45 0001, MW45 0042,
RA45 0036, RALP 0028, SO45 0093

February 1972
BFLP 0004, GO45 0115, GO45 0116,
GOLP 0058, MO45 0209, MW45 0011,
RALP 0033, RALP 0034, SO45 0095,
SOLP 0034, TALP 0095, VI45 0068

March 1972
MW45 0009, MW45 0013, MW45 0014,
MW45 0015, MWCO 0002, RA45 0037,
RA45 0039, RACO 0011, RACO 0012,
SO45 0094, SO45 0096

April 1972
BFLP 0005, BFLP 0006, BFLP 0007,
GO45 0117, MO45 0210, MO45 0211,
MO45 0212, MOLP 0150, RA45 0038,
RA45 0040, RA45 0041, RALP 0037,
TA45 0205, TA45 0210, TACO 0016

May 1972
GO45 0119, MO45 0214, MO45 0215,
MOLP 0152, MOLP 0153, MWLP 0008,
MWLP 0015, NALP 0001, NALP 0002,
NALP 0003, RA45 0042, RALP 0035,
RALP 0036, TA45 0207, TA45 0208,
TA45 0209, TALP 0096

June 1972
GO45 0118, GO45 0120, GOCO 0011,
GOCO 0012, MO45 0216, MO45 0217,
MW45 0017, MW45 0020, MWLP 0013,
SO45 0097, TA45 0206

July 1972
MO45 0218, MO45 0219, MO45 0220,
MOLP 0154, MW45 0022, MWCO 0003,

MWLP 0002, MWLP 0017, MWLP 0018,
MWLP 0019, NALP 0004, NALP 0005,
RA45 0043, RALP 0038, SO45 0099,
TALP 0098, TALP 0099

August 1972
GO45 0121, GOLP 0062, MO45 0213,
MO45 0222, MOLP 0155, MOLP 0156,
MOLP 0157, MW45 0018, MW45 0023,
MW45 0027, SO45 0100, TA45 0211,
TA45 0212

September 1972
GO45 0122, MO45 0221, MO45 0224,
MW45 0016

October 1972
MO45 0225, MO45 0226, MOLP 0160,
MOLP 0161, MW45 0029, MW45 0030,
MW45 0031, MWLP 0001, RA45 0044,
RALP 0039, RALP 0040, TA45 0215

November 1972
GO45 0123, MO45 0227, MO45 0228,
MO45 0229, MOLP 0158, MW45 0041,
MWLP 0021, TA45 0213, TA45 0214,
TA45 0217, TALP 0100

December 1972
GO45 0124, GOLP 0064, MO45 0223,
MOLP 0162, RA45 0048, SO45 0098,
TALP 0101, TALP 0103

January 1973
MW45 0034, MW45 0038, MW45 0040,
MW45 0043, MWCO 0004, NALP 0006,
NALP 0007, RA45 0047, SO45 0104,
TA45 0219

February 1973
GO45 0127, GOLP 0065, MO45 0236,
MOLP 0164, MW45 0039, SOLP 0037,
TA45 0221

March 1973
GO45 0125, MO45 0231, MO45 0232,
MO45 0241, MO45 0245, MO45 0247,
MOLP 0163, MW45 0052, RA45 0049

April 1973
BF45 0001, BFLP 0008, MO45 0230,
MO45 0233, MO45 0235, MO45 0243,
MO45 0246, MO45 0248, MO45 0249,
MO45 0280, MOLP 0166, MOLP 0167,
MOLP 0168, MOLP 0169, MOLP 0170,
MOLP 0171, MOLP 0173, RALP 0042,
SO45 0102, SO45 0105, SOLP 0038,
TALP 0106

May 1973
MO45 0234, MO45 0237, MO45 0251,
MO45 0260, MO45 0267, MO45 0268,
MOLP 0174, MOLP 0176, MOLP 0177,
MOLP 0179, RALP 0043, SO45 0103,
SO45 0106, TALP 0108

June 1973
GO45 0130, GO45 0131, GOLP 0063,
MO45 0238, MO45 0240, MO45 0250,
MO45 0252, MO45 0261, MO45 0270,
SOLP 0039, TA45 0222, TA45 0223,
TA45 0226, TALP 0109

July 1973
MO45 0253, MO45 0262, MO45 0263,
MO45 0264, MO45 0265, MO45 0271,
MO45 0273, MO45 0274, MO45 0275,
MOCO 0025, SO45 0107, SO45 0108,
TA45 0225, TA45 0227, TALP 0107

August 1973
GO45 0132, MO45 0254, MO45 0276,
MO45 0289, MOCO 0026, MOLP 0184,
RA45 0050, TA45 0228, TALP 0110

September 1973

GO45 0133, MO45 0255, MO45 0256,
MO45 0257, MO45 0258, MO45 0259,
MO45 0277, MO45 0288, MO45 0292,
MOLP 0185, MOLP 0186, MOLP 0191,
MOLP 0192, MOLP 0197, MOLP 0198,
RA45 0051, SO45 0109

October 1973
MO45 0293, MOLP 0187, MOLP 0205,
RA45 0052, TA45 0229, TA45 0231,
TA45 0232

November 1973
MO45 0286, MO45 0287, MO45 0291,
TA45 0230

December 1973
GO45 0134, GOLP 0066, MO45 0290,
MO45 0294, MO45 0295, MOLP 0214,
TA45 0233

January 1974
MO45 0281, MO45 0298, MOLP 0194,
MOLP 0195, MOLP 0204, SO45 0113,
TA45 0234

February 1974
GO45 0136, MO45 0296, MO45 0299,
MO45 0301, MO45 0302, MOLP 0209,
MOLP 0215, SOLP 0041, TALP 0111

March 1974
GOLP 0067, MO45 0283, MO45 0300,
MO45 0303, TA45 0235, TALP 0112

April 1974
GO45 0135, MO45 0304, MO45 0305,
MO45 0307, MO45 0308, MOLP 0193,
MOLP 0202, MOLP 0207, MOLP 0208,
MOLP 0212, MOLP 0213, TA45 0237

May 1974
GO45 0137, MO45 0306, MO45 0316,
MO45 0320, MOCO 0027, MOLP 0203,
RA45 0053, SO45 0110, TA45 0236

June 1974
GO45 0138, MO45 0309, MO45 0313,
MO45 0314, MO45 0315, MO45 0317,
MO45 0319, MOLP 0196, MOLP 0210,
SO45 0111, TA45 0238, TALP 0114

July 1974
GO45 0140, MO45 0310, MO45 0311,
MO45 0318, MOLP 0188, MOLP 0199,
MOLP 0200, MOLP 0201, MOLP 0211,
SO45 0114, TA45 0239, TA45 0240,
TA45 0242, TALP 0113

August 1974
GOLP 0068, MO45 0324, SOLP 0040,
TALP 0115

September 1974
MO45 0334, MO45 0337, MOLP 0180,
MOLP 0182, TA45 0243, TA45 0244,
TA45 0245

October 1974
GO45 0141, ML45 0001, MO45 0321,
MO45 0325, MO45 0326, MO45 0328,
MO45 0329, MO45 0331, MO45 0332,
MO45 0333, MO45 0336, MO45 0338,
TA45 0246

November 1974
ML45 0002, ML45 0003, MO45 0322,
MO45 0327, MO45 0330, MO45 0339,
MO45 0340, MOLP 0181, MOLP 0216,
MOLP 0217, MOLP 0221, TA45 0241,
TA45 0247, TA45 0248

December 1974
GO45 0139, MO45 0323, MO45 0341,
MO45 0342, MO45 0343, MOLP 0220,
PR45 0001, SO45 0116, TALP 0116

1975

PRLP 0001, PRLP 0002, PRLP 0003

January 1975
GOLP 0069, MO45 0344, MO45 0346,
MO45 0347, MOLP 0224, MOLP 0227,
PR45 0002, TA45 0249, TALP 0117

February 1975
GO45 0143, ML45 0004, ML45 0005,
MO45 0348, MO45 0352, MO45 0353,
MO45 0354, TA45 0250

March 1975
GOLP 0070, ML45 0006, MO45 0349,
MO45 0350, MO45 0355, MO45 0358,
MOLP 0222, MOLP 0228, PR45 0004,
PR45 0005, SOLP 0044, TALP 0118

April 1975
GA45 0001, GO45 0144, ML45 0007,
ML45 0008, ML45 0009, MO45 0351,
MO45 0356, MO45 0357, MO45 0360,
MO45 0362, TA45 0251

May 1975
ML45 0010, ML45 0011, ML45 0012,
ML45 0013, ML45 0014, ML45 0015,
MLLP 0001, MO45 0364, MO45 0365,
MOLP 0223, MOLP 0226, MOLP 0231,
MOLP 0233, PR45 0006

June 1975
MO45 0366, MO45 0368, MO45 0369,
MOCO 0028, MOCO 0029, MOCO 0030,
MOLP 0229, MOLP 0230, MOLP 0240,
PR45 0007, RALP 0045, TA45 0252,
TALP 0119

July 1975
GO45 0145, ML45 0016, MO45 0367,
MO45 0371, MOLP 0234, MOLP 0243,
MOLP 0245, PR45 0008

August 1975
ML45 0018, ML45 0019, MO45 0372,
MO45 0373, MOCO 0031, MOLP 0253,
PR45 0009, RA45 0055, TA45 0253

September 1975
GO45 0146, ML45 0017, ML45 0020,
ML45 0021, ML45 0023, ML45 0024,
MO45 0374, MO45 0375, MO45 0377,
MOLP 0241, MOLP 0242, MOLP 0248,
MOLP 0249, TA45 0255

October 1975
GOLP 0072, ML45 0025, MO45 0376,
MO45 0378, MO45 0380, MO45 0382,
MO45 0383, MO45 0387, MO45 0389,
MO45 0390, MOCO 0032, MOLP 0250,
MOLP 0251, MOLP 0254, MOLP 0260,
MOLP 0261, RA45 0054, TA45 0254,
TALP 0120

November 1975
GOLP 0073, MO45 0385, MO45 0386,
MO45 0391, PR45 0010

December 1975
ML45 0026, ML45 0027, ML45 0028,
MO45 0392, MO45 0394, MOCO 0033,
PR45 0011, SO45 0117, TA45 0258

1976
MO12 0001, MO12 0002, MO12 0003

January 1976
GO45 0147, MOLP 0255, MOLP 0258,
SOLP 0045, TA45 0259, TACO 0018

February 1976
ML45 0029, MO45 0384, MO45 0395,
MO45 0396, MO45 0401, PR45 0012,
RALP 0046, TALP 0122, TALP 0124

March 1976
GO45 0148, GOLP 0071, GOLP 0074,
ML45 0030, ML45 0031, MLLP 0003,

April 1976
MO45 0397, MO45 0398, MO45 0400,
MO45 0402, MO45 0406, MOLP 0256,
MOLP 0263, RALP 0047, TALP 0123

April 1976
GO45 0150, MO45 0403, MOLP 0262,
MOLP 0265, PR45 0013, PR45 0014,
TA45 0256, TA45 0257, TA45 0260,
TACO 0017

May 1976
GO45 0151, HI45 0001, MO45 0405,
MO45 0407, MOLP 0247, MOLP 0257,
MOLP 0259, MOLP 0266, MOLP 0268,
RA45 0056, SO45 0118, SOLP 0046,
TA45 0261, TA45 0262

June 1976
HI45 0004, HI45 0006, MO45 0410,
MOLP 0252, MOLP 0269, MOLP 0270,
PR45 0016, PR45 0017, PR45 0020,
PRLP 0004, SO45 0119, SOLP 0047,
TA45 0263

July 1976
HI45 0007, HI45 0008, MO45 0411,
MO45 0412, MO45 0414, TA45 0266

August 1976
GOLP 0075, HI45 0009, HI45 0010,
MO45 0415, MO45 0416, MOLP 0244,
MOLP 0271, PRLP 0005, PRLP 0006,
TALP 0128

September 1976
GOLP 0076, HI45 0011, HILP 0001,
HILP 0002, MO45 0417, MO45 0418,
MOLP 0272, PRLP 0007, PRLP 0008,
SO45 0120, TA45 0264, TALP 0121,
TALP 0125, TALP 0127, TALP 0129

October 1976
GO45 0153, HI45 0012, HI45 0013,
MO45 0419, MO45 0420, MO45 0421,
MO45 0423, MOLP 0267, MOLP 0273,
MOLP 0274, MOLP 0275, MOLP 0277,
NALP 0008, PR45 0021, SOLP 0048,
TA45 0268, TA45 0269, TA45 0270

November 1976
GOLP 0077, HI45 0014, HI45 0015,
HI45 0016, HI45 0017, MOEP 0020,
PR45 0022, PRLP 0009, SO45 0121,
TA45 0267, TA45 0271, TALP 0126

December 1976
MO45 0422, MO45 0424, MO45 0425,
MOLP 0278, NA45 0001, TA45 0272,
TA45 0273

1977
MO12 0004, MO12 0005, MO12 0006,
MO12 0007, MO12 0008, MO12 0009,
MO12 0010

January 1977
GO45 0154, HI45 0018, HI45 0019,
HI45 0020, HI45 0021, HILP 0003,
JULP 0001, MO45 0427, MOLP 0280,
MOLP 0281, MOLP 0283, PR45 0019,
PRLP 0010, SOLP 0049, TA45 0274,
TALP 0130, TALP 0131, TALP 0132

February 1977
HI45 0022, HI45 0023, JU45 0001,
MO45 0428, MO45 0429, PRLP 0011

March 1977
HI45 0024, MO45 0426, MO45 0430,
MOLP 0284, MOLP 0285, MOLP 0286,
PR45 0023, TA45 0275, TA45 0276,
TALP 0133, TALP 0134

April 1977
JU45 0002, MO45 0431, MOLP 0287,
TA45 0277, TA45 0278

May 1977
JULP 0002, MO45 0432, MOLP 0289,
PRLP 0012

June 1977
GO45 0155, MO45 0433, MOLP 0276,
MOLP 0282, MOLP 0288, MOLP 0290,
TA45 0279

July 1977
MO45 0434, MO45 0435, MO45 0437,
MOLP 0292, PR45 0025, PR45 0026,
PRLP 0013, TA45 0280, TALP 0137

August 1977
JULP 0003, MCLP 0001, MO45 0438,
MO45 0439, MOLP 0291, SO45 0123,
TA45 0281, TALP 0138, TALP 0139

September 1977
GO45 0156, GO45 0157, MC45 0001,
MO45 0436, MO45 0440, MOLP 0293,
MOLP 0294, PR45 0027, PR45 0028,
PRLP 0014, TA45 0282, TA45 0283

October 1977
GOLP 0078, MC45 0002, MC45 0003,
MO45 0441, MO45 0442, MO45 0443,
MO45 0444, TA45 0286, TALP 0140

November 1977
MCLP 0011, MOLP 0295, MOLP 0297

December 1977
MCLP 0015, MO45 0446, MOLP 0206,
TA45 0285

1978
MO12 0011, MO12 0012, MO12 0013,
MO12 0014, MO12 0015, MO12 0016,
PR45 0034, PR45 0035, PR45 0036

January 1978
GOLP 0080, MC45 0004, MC45 0005,
MO45 0447, MO45 0448, MO45 0449,
MOLP 0298, MOLP 0299, PRLP 0016,
PRLP 0018, TALP 0136

February 1978
GO45 0159, GOCO 0013, MC45 0006,
MC45 0007, MO45 0450, MO45 0451,
MO45 0452, MOLP 0300, MOLP 0301,
TA45 0287, TALP 0141

March 1978
MC45 0008, MO45 0453, MO45 0454,
MOLP 0303, NALP 0009, NALP 0010,
NALP 0011, PR45 0029, PR45 0030,
TA45 0288, TA45 0289

April 1978
GOLP 0083, MC45 0009, MC45 0010,
MO45 0455, MO45 0456, MOLP 0302,
PRLP 0019, PRLP 0020, SO45 0124

May 1978
GO45 0158, GO45 0160, MC45 0011,
MC45 0012, MO45 0457, MO45 0458,
MOLP 0304, MOLP 0305, SOLP 0050

June 1978
GO45 0162, GOLP 0084, PR45 0031,
PR45 0032, PR45 0033

July 1978
GO45 0161, GOCO 0014, GOLP 0081,
MC45 0014, MC45 0015, MOLP 0306,
MOLP 0307

August 1978
GO45 0163, MC45 0013, MO45 0459,
MOLP 0308, MOLP 0309, SOLP 0051

September 1978
GO45 0164, MO45 0460, MO45 0461,
MOLP 0310, MOLP 0313, NALP 0012,
NALP 0013, NALP 0014, NALP 0015,
NALP 0016, NALP 0017, PRLP 0021,
TA45 0290

October 1978
MO45 0462, MO45 0464, MO45 0466,
MOCO 0034, MOLP 0314, MOLP 0315,
NALP 0018, NALP 0019, PRLP 0022,
PRLP 0023, PRLP 0024, TA45 0291,
TALP 0143, TALP 0144

November 1978
MO45 0471, MOCO 0037, TALP 0145

December 1978
GO45 0165, MO45 0467, MO45 0469,
MO45 0470, MOCO 0035, MOCO 0036,
MOLP 0326, TA45 0292, TA45 0293,
TALP 0146

1979
MO12 0017, MO12 0018, MO12 0019,
MO12 0020, MO12 0021, MO12 0022,
MO12 0023, MO12 0024, MO12 0025,
MO12 0026, MO12 0027, MO12 0028,
MO12 0029, MO12 0030, MO12 0031,
MO12 0032, MO12 0033, MO12 0034,
MO12 0035, MO12 0036, MO12 0038

January 1979
GO45 0166, GOLP 0086, MO45 0472,
MOLP 0311, MOLP 0312, MOLP 0318,
NALP 0020, NALP 0022, TALP 0153

February 1979
GO45 0167, MOLP 0317, MOLP 0322,
TALP 0142

March 1979
GO45 0168, GOLP 0087, GOLP 0088,
MO45 0474, MOLP 0320

April 1979
GO45 0169, GOLP 0089, GOLP 0090,
MO45 0475, MO45 0476, MO45 0477,
MOLP 0323, MOLP 0324

May 1979
GO45 0170, GO45 0171, MO45 0468,
MO45 0478, MO45 0479, MO45 0480,
MOLP 0327, MOLP 0328, NALP 0023,
NALP 0024, NALP 0025, TA45 0294,
TALP 0147, TALP 0148

June 1979
GO45 0172, MO45 0481, MO45 0482,
MOLP 0329, TA45 0295, TA45 0296

July 1979
GO45 0173, MOLP 0330, MOLP 0331,
TA45 0297, TA45 0299

August 1979
MO45 0483, NALP 0026, NALP 0027,
NALP 0028, TA45 0301

September 1979
GO45 0175, GO45 0176, GO45 0177,
GO45 0178, MO45 0490, MO45 0491,
MOLP 0332, TA45 0300

October 1979
GO45 0174, GO45 0179, GOLP 0091,
GOLP 0092, MO45 0484, MO45 0485,
MO45 0487, MO45 0488, MO45 0489,
MO45 0492, MOLP 0325, MOLP 0333,
MOLP 0334, MOLP 0335, TA45 0298,
TA45 0302

November 1979
MO45 0493, MO45 0494, MO45 0495

December 1979
GO45 0180, MO45 0496

January 1980
GO45 0181, GOLP 0093, MOLP 0336,
TALP 0149

February 1980
GO45 0182, GO45 0183, GOLP 0094,
MO45 0498, MO45 0499, MOLP 0338,
MOLP 0339, TA45 0303, TA45 0304,

TA45 0305
March 1980
GOLP 0095, MO45 0486, MO45 0500,
MO45 0501, MOCO 0038, MOLP 0337,
MOLP 0341, MOLP 0342, TA45 0306
April 1980
GO45 0185, GO45 0186, GO45 0187,
GOCO 0015, GOLP 0096, MO12 0037,
MO45 0502, MOLP 0343, TALP 0154
May 1980
GO45 0184, MO45 0503, MOLP 0344
June 1980
GO45 0188, MO45 0505, MO45 0506,
MO45 0511, MO45 0512, TA45 0307,
TA45 0308, TALP 0150
July 1980
GO45 0191, GOLP 0097, MO45 0504,
MO45 0510
August 1980
GO45 0190, GO45 0192, GOLP 0098,
GOLP 0099, MO45 0507, MO45 0508,
MO45 0509, MOLP 0345, MOLP 0346,
MOLP 0347, MOLP 0348, TA45 0309
September 1980
GO45 0189, GO45 0193, GO45 0194,
GOCO 0016, MO45 0513, MO45 0517,
MOLP 0349, MOLP 0350, TA45 0310,
TA45 0311, TA45 0312, TA45 0313,
TA45 0314, TALP 0152
October 1980
GO45 0195, GO45 0196, GOLP 0100,
MO45 0514, MOLP 0351, MOLP 0352,
TALP 0155
November 1980
GOLP 0101, MO45 0516, MO45 0518,
MO45 0519, MO45 0520, MO45 0521,
MOCO 0039
December 1980
MOLP 0353, MOLP 0354, TA45 0315
1981
MO12 0039, MO12 0040
January 1981
GO45 0197, GO45 0198, GOLP 0102,
MOLP 0355, TA45 0316, TALP 0156
February 1981
MO45 0522, MO45 0523, MO45 0524,
MO45 0525, MO45 0526, MO45 0527,
MOLP 0356, TA45 0317, TALP 0157
March 1981
GO45 0199, GO45 0200, GOLP 0103,
GOLP 0104, MO45 0529, MO45 0531,
MOLP 0361, MOLP 0362, TA45 0318
April 1981
GO45 0202, GO45 0203, GO45 0204,
MO45 0530, TA45 0321
May 1981
GOLP 0105, GOLP 0106, MO45 0532,
MOLP 0360, TA45 0320, TA45 0322
June 1981
GO45 0205, GO45 0206, MO45 0533,
MO45 0537
July 1981
GO45 0207, MO45 0535, TA45 0324,
TA45 0325, TA45 0326
August 1981
GO45 0208, GO45 0210, GO45 0211,
GOLP 0107, MO12 0041, MO45 0534,
MO45 0538, MO45 0539, MO45 0540,
MO45 0541, MO45 0542, MOLP 0363,
TA45 0328
September 1981
GO45 0214, MO45 0536, MO45 0546,

MOLP 0357, MOLP 0364
October 1981
GO45 0215, GO45 0216, GO45 0217,
MO45 0544, MO45 0547, MOLP 0365,
MOLP 0366
November 1981
GO45 0218, GO45 0219, GOLP 0108,
MOLP 0358, MOLP 0367, TALP 0158
December 1981
MO45 0549, TA45 0329
1982
TMG12 0001, TMG12 0007
January 1982
MO45 0550, MO45 0552, TMG45 0001,
TMG45 0002, TMG45 0003,
TMG45 0004, TMG45 0005,
TMGLP 0001, TMGLP 0002
February 1982
TMG45 0006, TMG45 0007,
TMGLP 0005
March 1982
TMG12 0004, TMG45 0008,
TMG45 0009, TMG45 0010,
TMG45 0011, TMG45 0012,
TMGLP 0004, TMGLP 0010
April 1982
TMG45 0014, TMG45 0015,
TMG45 0016, TMG45 0017,
TMG45 0018, TMG45 0019,
TMGLP 0007, TMGLP 0009
May 1982
TMG45 0013, TMG45 0020,
TMGLP 0003, TMGLP 0006,
TMGLP 0011, TMGLP 0020
June 1982
TMG45 0022, TMG45 0023,
TMG45 0024, TMG45 0025,
TMG45 0026, TMG45 0027,
TMGLP 0012, TMGLP 0019
July 1982
TMG12 0005, TMG45 0028,
TMG45 0029, TMG45 0030,
TMG45 0032, TMG45 0033,
TMG45 0034, TMG45 0036,
TMGLP 0013, TMGLP 0015,
TMGLP 0018, TMGLP 0022
August 1982
TMG45 0031, TMG45 0037,
TMG45 0041, TMGLP 0021,
TMGLP 0023
September 1982
TMG12 0002, TMG12 0003,
TMG45 0038, TMG45 0039,
TMG45 0043, TMG45 0045,
TMG45 0046, TMGLP 0008
October 1982
TMG45 0048, TMG45 0049,
TMG45 0050, TMG45 0051,
TMG45 0052, TMGLP 0024,
TMGLP 0026, TMGLP 0028
November 1982
TMG45 0047, TMG45 0053,
TMG45 0054, TMG45 0055,
TMGLP 0027, TMGLP 0029,
TMGLP 0034, TMGLP 0035
December 1982
TMG45 0056, TMGLP 0031
1983
TA45 0319, TMG12 0008, TMG12 0011
January 1983
TMG12 0007, TMG45 0044,
TMG45 0057, TMG45 0058,

TMG45 0059, TMG45 0060,
TMG45 0061, TMG45 0064,
TMGLP 0016, TMGLP 0025,
TMGLP 0032
February 1983
TMG45 0063, TMG45 0065,
TMG45 0066, TMG45 0067,
TMGLP 0033
March 1983
TMG12 0010, TMG45 0068,
TMG45 0069, TMG45 0070,
TMG45 0072, TMG45 0073,
TMGLP 0036, TMGLP 0038,
TMGLP 0039, TMGLP 0041
April 1983
TMG45 0062, TMG45 0074,
TMG45 0078, TMG45 0080,
TMG45 0081, TMG45 0082,
TMG45 0083, TMGLP 0037,
TMGLP 0042, TMGLP 0045
May 1983
TMG12 0009, TMG45 0071,
TMG45 0085, TMG45 0087,
TMGLP 0040, TMGLP 0049,
TMGLP 0050
June 1983
TMG45 0075, TMG45 0084,
TMG45 0088, TMG45 0089,
TMGLP 0046
July 1983
TMG12 0012, TMG45 0077,
TMG45 0091, TMG45 0092,
TMG45 0094, TMGLP 0043,
TMGLP 0054
August 1983
TMG12 0013, TMG45 0093,
TMG45 0095, TMG45 0096,
TMG45 0098, TMG45 0100,
TMGLP 0044, TMGLP 0066,
TMGLP 0067
September 1983
TMG12 0014, TMG12 0015,
TMG45 0097, TMG45 0099,
TMG45 0101, TMG45 0103,
TMG45 0104, TMGLP 0052,
TMGLP 0055, TMGLP 0060,
TMGLP 0064
October 1983
TMG45 0105, TMG45 0106,
TMG45 0108, TMG45 0109,
TMG45 0110, TMG45 0111,
TMG45 0112, TMGLP 0061,
TMGLP 0063, TMGLP 0068,
TMGLP 0076, TMGLP 0077,
TMGLP 0078, TMGLP 0079,
TMGLP 0080, TMGLP 0081,
TMGLP 0082, TMGLP 0083,
TMGLP 0084, TMGLP 0085,
TMGLP 0087
November 1983
TMG45 0116, TMG45 0120,
TMGLP 0030, TMGLP 0086
December 1983
TMG45 0117, TMG45 0119,
TMGLP 0088
January 1984
TMG12 0016, TMG12 0017,
TMG45 0107, TMG45 0118,
TMG45 0121, TMG45 0125,
TMG45 0127, TMGLP 0053,
TMGLP 0059
February 1984

March 1984
TMG45 0115, TMG45 0122,
TMG45 0126, TMG45 0128,
TMG45 0129, TMGLP 0058,
TMGLP 0069, TMGLP 0070,
TMGLP 0071, TMGLP 0072,
TMGLP 0073, TMGLP 0074,
TMGLP 0075

March 1984
TMG12 0019, TMG45 0123,
TMG45 0124, TMG45 0130,
TMGLP 0093

April 1984
TMG45 0131, TMG45 0132,
TMG45 0134, TMG45 0135,
TMG45 0137, TMG45 0138,
TMG45 0142, TMGLP 0090,
TMGLP 0095, TMGLP 0096

May 1984
TMG12 0020, TMG12 0021,
TMG45 0141, TMG45 0143,
TMG45 0144, TMG45 0145,
TMG45 0147, TMGLP 0047,
TMGLP 0097, TMGLP 0098,
TMGLP 0099, TMGLP 0100,
TMGLP 0101, TMGLP 0102,
TMGLP 0103

June 1984
TMG12 0022, TMG45 0136,
TMG45 0139, TMG45 0148,
TMG45 0152, TMG45 0155

July 1984
TMG12 0023, TMG45 0133,
TMG45 0140, TMG45 0153,
TMG45 0154, TMG45 0156,
TMGLP 0065, TMGLP 0092,
TMGLP 0110

August 1984
TMG45 0150, TMG45 0151,
TMG45 0158, TMG45 0161,
TMG45 0162, TMG45 0163,
TMG45 0164, TMGLP 0062,
TMGLP 0104, TMGLP 0105

September 1984
TMG12 0024, TMG12 0025,
TMG45 0149, TMG45 0160,
TMG45 0165, TMG45 0166,
TMG45 0167, TMG45 0168,
TMG45 0169, TMGLP 0106,
TMGLP 0107, TMGLP 0108,
TMGLP 0109, TMGLP 0119,
TMGLP 0120

October 1984
TMG12 0026, TMG12 0027,
TMG45 0171, TMGLP 0111,
TMGLP 0112, TMGLP 0113,
TMGLP 0121

November 1984
TMG12 0018, TMG45 0172,
TMG45 0173, TMG45 0174,
TMG45 0175, TMGLP 0114,
TMGLP 0122, TMGLP 0123

December 1984
TMG45 0177, TMG45 0178,
TMG45 0179, TMGLP 0126,
TMGLP 0133

1985
TMG12 0055, TMG12 0056,
TMG12 0057, TMG12 0058

January 1985
TMG12 0029, TMG45 0176,
TMG45 0180, TMG45 0181,
TMGLP 0115, TMGLP 0117,

TMGLP 0124, TMGLP 0125

February 1985
TMG12 0028, TMG12 0030,
TMG12 0031, TMG12 0032,
TMG12 0033, TMG12 0034,
TMG45 0183, TMG45 0187,
TMG45 0188, TMGLP 0094

March 1985
TMG45 0182, TMG45 0184,
TMG45 0185, TMG45 0186,
TMG45 0190, TMG45 0191,
TMG45 0192, TMGLP 0127,
TMGLP 0128, TMGLP 0129,
TMGLP 0130, TMGLP 0138

April 1985
TMG12 0035, TMG12 0036,
TMG45 0193, TMG45 0194,
TMGLP 0134, TMGLP 0135,
TMGLP 0137, TMGLP 0142,
TMGLP 0143

May 1985
TMG12 0038, TMG12 0040,
TMG45 0195, TMG45 0196,
TMG45 0197, TMG45 0198,
TMG45 0199, TMG45 0200,
TMG45 0202, TMG45 0203,
TMGLP 0132, TMGLP 0147

June 1985
TMG12 0039, TMG12 0042,
TMG12 0044, TMG45 0201,
TMG45 0204, TMG45 0205,
TMG45 0206, TMG45 0207,
TMGLP 0144, TMGLP 0149,
TMGLP 0150, TMGLP 0151

July 1985
TMG12 0043, TMG45 0208,
TMG45 0209, TMGLP 0140,
TMGLP 0141, TMGLP 0145,
TMGLP 0146, TMGLP 0152,
TMGLP 0153, TMGLP 0154

August 1985
TMG12 0046, TMG45 0210,
TMG45 0211, TMG45 0212,
TMG45 0213, TMG45 0214

September 1985
TMG12 0045, TMG12 0047,
TMG12 0048, TMG45 0216,
TMG45 0217, TMG45 0218,
TMG45 0220, TMGLP 0139,
TMG45 0222, TMGLP 0139,
TMGLP 0157, TMGLP 0165

October 1985
TMG12 0049, TMG12 0051,
TMG45 0219, TMG45 0224,
TMGLP 0136, TMGLP 0155,
TMGLP 0158, TMGLP 0159,
TMGLP 0164

November 1985
TMG12 0053, TMG12 0054,
TMG45 0223, TMG45 0225,
TMG45 0226, TMG45 0228,
TMGLP 0166

December 1985
TMG45 0230, TMG45 0231,
TMG45 0232, TMG45 0233,
TMGLP 0167

1986
TMG12 0059, TMG45 0245,
TMGLP 0148

January 1986
TMG45 0234, TMG45 0235,
TMG45 0236

February 1986
TMG45 0237, TMG45 0238,
TMG45 0239, TMG45 0240,
TMG45 0241, TMGLP 0169,
TMGLP 0171, TMGLP 0172,
TMGLP 0173

March 1986
TMG45 0242, TMG45 0244,
TMG45 0246, TMG45 0247,
TMGLP 0168, TMGLP 0170,
TMGLP 0174, TMGLP 0175,
TMGLP 0176

April 1986
TMG45 0243, TMG45 0249,
TMGLP 0179, TMGLP 0182,
TMGLP 0183, TMGLP 0185,
TMGLP 0186, TMGLP 0187

May 1986
TMGLP 0161, TMGLP 0162,
TMGLP 0163

June 1986
TMG12 0061, TMG12 0062,
TMG12 0063, TMG45 0250,
TMG45 0251, TMG45 0252,
TMG45 0255, TMG45 0257,
TMG45 0258, TMG45 0259,
TMG45 0260, TMG45 0261,
TMG45 0263, TMGLP 0180,
TMGLP 0181

July 1986
TMG45 0262, TMG45 0264

August 1986
TMG12 0066, TMG45 0265,
TMG45 0266, TMG45 0270,
TMGCD 0001, TMGCD 0002,
TMGCD 0003, TMGCD 0004,
TMGCD 0005, TMGCD 0006,
TMGCD 0007, TMGCD 0008,
TMGCD 0009, TMGCD 0010,
TMGCD 0011, TMGCD 0012,
TMGCD 0013, TMGCD 0014,
TMGCD 0015, TMGCD 0016,
TMGCD 0017, TMGCD 0018,
TMGCD 0019, TMGCD 0020,
TMGCD 0021, TMGCD 0022,
TMGCD 0023, TMGCD 0024,
TMGCD 0025, TMGCD 0026,
TMGCD 0027, TMGCD 0028,
TMGCD 0029, TMGCD 0030,
TMGCD 0031, TMGCD 0032,
TMGCD 0033, TMGCD 0034,
TMGCD 0035, TMGCD 0036,
TMGCD 0037, TMGCD 0038,
TMGCD 0039, TMGCD 0040,
TMGCD 0041, TMGCD 0042,
TMGLP 0160, TMGLP 0184,
TMGLP 0188, TMGLP 0190,
TMGLP 0191, TMGLP 0193,
TMGLP 0194, TMGLP 0195,
TMGLP 0196, TMGLP 0197,
TMGLP 0198, TMGLP 0199,
TMGLP 0200, TMGLP 0201,
TMGLP 0202, TMGLP 0203,
TMGLP 0204, TMGLP 0205,
TMGLP 0206, TMGLP 0207,
TMGLP 0208, TMGLP 0209,
TMGLP 0210, TMGLP 0212,
TMGLP 0213, TMGLP 0214

September 1986
TMG12 0067, TMG12 0068,
TMG45 0269, TMG45 0271,
TMG45 0272

October 1986
    TMG45 0273, TMG45 0274,
    TMG45 0277, TMGLP 0216,
    TMGLP 0218

November 1986
    TMG45 0276, TMG45 0278,
    TMG45 0279

December 1986
    TMG45 0280

MOTD-MCD08026MD	MS-641	MS-679	MS-716	MW 102
TMGCD 0027	MOLP 0042	MOLP 0080	MOLP 0117	MWLP 0002
MOTD-MCD08027MD	MS-643	MS-680	MS-717	MW 103-L
TMGCD 0028	MOLP 0044	MOLP 0081	MOLP 0118	MWLP 0003
MOTD-MCD08029MD	MS-644	MS-681	MS-718	MW 104
TMGCD 0030	MOLP 0045	MOLP 0082	MOLP 0119	MWLP 0004
MOTD-MCD08030MD	MS-645	MS-682	MS-719	MW 105
TMGCD 0031	MOLP 0046	MOLP 0083	MOLP 0120	MWLP 0005
MOTD-MCD08031MD	MS-646	MS-683	MS-720	MW 106
TMGCD 0032	MOLP 0047	MOLP 0084	MOLP 0121	MWLP 0006
MOTD-MCD08032MD	MS-647	MS-684	MS-721	MW 107
TMGCD 0033	MOLP 0048	MOLP 0085	MOLP 0122	MWLP 0007
MOTD-MCD08033MD	MS-648	MS-685	MS-722	MW 108-L
TMGCD 0034	MOLP 0049	MOLP 0086	MOLP 0123	MWLP 0008
MOTD-MCD08034MD	MS-649	MS-686	MS-723	MW 109
TMGCD 0035	MOLP 0050	MOLP 0087	MOLP 0124	MWLP 0009
MOTD-MCD08038MD	MS-650	MS-687	MS-724	MW 110
TMGCD 0039	MOLP 0051	MOLP 0088	MOLP 0125	MWLP 0010
MOTD-MCD08039MD	MS-651	MS-688	MS-725	MW 111
TMGCD 0040	MOLP 0052	MOLP 0089	MOLP 0126	MWLP 0011
MOTD-MCD08040MD	MS-652	MS-689	MS-727	MW 112
TMGCD 0041	MOLP 0053	MOLP 0090	MOLP 0128	MWLP 0012
MOTD-MCD08041MD	MS-653	MS-690	MS-728	MW 113
TMGCD 0042	MOLP 0054	MOLP 0091	MOLP 0129	MWLP 0013
MS-2-663	MS-654	MS-691	MS-729	MW 114
MOLP 0064	MOLP 0055	MOLP 0092	MOLP 0130	MWLP 0014
MS2-7088	MS-655	MS-692	MS-730	MW 115
MOLP 0109	MOLP 0056	MOLP 0093	MOLP 0131	MWLP 0015
MS-5-726	MS-656	MS-693	MS-731	MW 116
MOLP 0127	MOLP 0057	MOLP 0094	MOLP 0132	MWLP 0016
MS-614	MS-657	MS-694	MS-732	MW 117
MOLP 0015	MOLP 0058	MOLP 0095	MOLP 0133	MWLP 0017
MS-616	MS-658	MS-695	MS-733	MW 118
MOLP 0017	MOLP 0059	MOLP 0096	MOLP 0134	MWLP 0018
MS-622	MS-659	MS-696	MS-734	MW 119
MOLP 0023	MOLP 0060	MOLP 0097	MOLP 0135	MWLP 0019
MS-623	MS-660	MS-697	MS-735	MW 120
MOLP 0024	MOLP 0061	MOLP 0098	MOLP 0136	MWLP 0020
MS-624	MS-661	MS-698	MS-736	MW 121
MOLP 0025	MOLP 0062	MOLP 0099	MOLP 0137	MWLP 0021
MS-625	MS-662	MS-699	MS-737	MW 122
MOLP 0026	MOLP 0063	MOLP 0100	MOLP 0138	MWLP 0022
MS-626	MS-664	MS-700	MS-738	MW 123
MOLP 0027	MOLP 0065	MOLP 0101	MOLP 0139	MWLP 0023
MS-627	MS-665	MS-701	MS-738L	MW 5001F
MOLP 0028	MOLP 0066	MOLP 0102	MOLP 0140	MW45 0001
MS-628	MS-666	MS-702	MT-603	MW 5002F
MOLP 0029	MOLP 0067	MOLP 0103	MOLP 0004	MW45 0002
MS-629	MS-667	MS-703	MT-604	MW 5003F
MOLP 0030	MOLP 0068	MOLP 0104	MOLP 0005	MW45 0003
MS-630	MS-668	MS-704	MT-605	MW 5004F
MOLP 0031	MOLP 0069	MOLP 0105	MOLP 0006	MW45 0004
MS-631	MS-669	MS-705	MT-606	MW 5005F
MOLP 0032	MOLP 0070	MOLP 0106	MOLP 0007	MW45 0005
MS-632	MS-670	MS-706	MT-607	MW 5006F
MOLP 0033	MOLP 0071	MOLP 0107	MOLP 0008	MW45 0006
MS-633	MS-671	MS-707	MT-608	MW 5007F
MOLP 0034	MOLP 0072	MOLP 0108	MOLP 0009	MW45 0007
MS-634	MS-672	MS-709	MT-609	MW 5008F
MOLP 0035	MOLP 0073	MOLP 0110	MOLP 0010	MW45 0008,
MS-635	MS-673	MS-710	MT-611	MWCO 0001
MOLP 0036	MOLP 0074	MOLP 0111	MOLP 0012	MW 5009F
MS-636	MS-674	MS-711	MT-615	MW45 0009
MOLP 0037	MOLP 0075	MOLP 0112	MOLP 0016	MW 5010F
MS-637	MS-675	MS-712	MT-620	MW45 0010
MOLP 0038	MOLP 0076	MOLP 0113	MOLP 0021	MW 5011F
MS-638	MS-676	MS-713	MT-621	MW45 0011
MOLP 0039	MOLP 0077	MOLP 0114	MOLP 0022	MW 5012F
MS-639	MS-677	MS-714	MT-642	MW45 0012
MOLP 0040	MOLP 0078	MOLP 0115	MOLP 0043	MW 5013F
MS-640	MS-678	MS-715	MW 101	MW45 0013,
MOLP 0041	MOLP 0079	MOLP 0116	MWLP 0001	MWCO 0002

MW 5014F	MW 5048F	P6-10015	RALP 0003	SOLP 0036
MW45 0014	MW45 0050	PRLP 0009	RS 507	S-737L
MW 5015F	MW 5049F	P6-10017	RALP 0004	SOLP 0037
MW45 0015	MW45 0051	PRLP 0011	RS 508	S-738L
MW 5016F	MW 5050F	P6-10019S1	RALP 0005	SOLP 0038
MW45 0016	MW45 0052	PRLP 0013	RS 509	S-739L
MW 5017F	NR-101L	P6-10020	RALP 0006	SOLP 0039
MW45 0017	NALP 0001	PRLP 0014	RS 510	S-741V1
MW 5018F	NR-102L	P7-10022	RALP 0007	SOLP 0041
MW45 0018,	NALP 0002	PRLP 0016	RS 511	S-744V1
MW45 0019	NR-103L	P7-10024	RALP 0008	SOLP 0044
MW 5019F	NALP 0003	PRLP 0018	RS 512	S-746P1
MW45 0020	NR-104L	P7-10025R1	RALP 0009	SOLP 0046
MW 5020F	NALP 0004	PRLP 0019	RS 513	S747S1
MW45 0021	NR-105L	P7-10026	RALP 0010	SOLP 0047
MW 5021F	NALP 0005	PRLP 0020	RS 514	S7-750R1
MW45 0022,	NR-106L	P7-10027R1	RALP 0011	SOLP 0050
MWCO 0003	NALP 0006	PRLP 0021	RS 515	S7-751R1
MW 5022F	NR-107L	P7-10028	RALP 0012	SOLP 0051
MW45 0023	NALP 0007	PRLP 0022	RS 516	SL4M-3114
MW 5023F	NR-108S1	P7-10029R1	RALP 0013	TA45S 0005
MW45 0024	NALP 0008	PRLP 0023	RS 517	SS-0728
MW 5024F	NR-4001	P7-10030R1	RALP 0014	SOLP 0028
MW45 0025	NALP 0009	PRLP 0024	RS 518	SS-701
MW 5025F	NR-4002	PLP-10007	RALP 0015	SOLP 0001
MW45 0026	NALP 0010	PRLP 0001	RS 519	SS-703
MW 5026F	NR-4003	PLP-10008	RALP 0016	SOLP 0003
MW45 0027	NALP 0011	PRLP 0002	RS 520	SS-706
MW 5027F	NR-4004	PLP-10009	RALP 0017	SOLP 0006
MW45 0028	NALP 0012	PRLP 0003	RS 521	SS-708
MW 5028F	NR-4005	R 529L	RALP 0018	SOLP 0008
MW45 0029	NALP 0013	RALP 0025,	RS 522	SS-709
MW 5029F	NR-4006	RALP 0026	RALP 0019	SOLP 0009
MW45 0030	NALP 0014	R 530L	RS 523	SS-710
MW 5030F	NR-4007	RALP 0027	RALP 0020	SOLP 0010
MW45 0031	NALP 0015	R 531L	RS 524	SS-711
MW 5031F	NR-4008	RALP 0028	RALP 0021	SOLP 0011
MW45 0032	NALP 0016	R 532L	RS 525	SS-714
MW 5032F	NR-4009	RALP 0029	RALP 0022	SOLP 0014
MW45 0033	NALP 0017	R 533L	RS 526	SS-715
MW 5033F	NR-4010	RALP 0030	RALP 0023	SOLP 0015
MW45 0034	NALP 0018	R 534L	RS 527	SS-716
MW 5034F	NR-4011	RALP 0031	RALP 0024	SOLP 0016
MW45 0035,	NALP 0019	R 536L	S6-740S1	SS-717
MW45 0036	NR-4012	RALP 0033	SOLP 0040	SOLP 0017
MW 5035F	NALP 0020	R 537L	S6-742S1	SS-718
MW45 0037	NR-4013	RALP 0034	SOLP 0042	SOLP 0018
MW 5036F	NALP 0021	R 538L	S6-745S1	SS-719
MW45 0038,	NR-4014	RALP 0035	SOLP 0045	SOLP 0019
MWCO 0004	NALP 0022	R 539L	S6-748S1	SS-720
MW 5037F	NR-4015	RALP 0036	SOLP 0048	SOLP 0020
MW45 0039	NALP 0023	R 540L	S6-749S1	SS-721
MW 5038F	NR-4016	RALP 0037	SOLP 0049	SOLP 0021
MW45 0040	NALP 0024	R 541L	S-702	SS-722
MW 5039F	NR-4017	RALP 0038	SOLP 0002	SOLP 0022
MW45 0041	NALP 0025	R 542L	S-704	SS-723
MW 5040F	NR-4018	RALP 0039	SOLP 0004	SOLP 0023
MW45 0042	NALP 0026	R 543L	S-705	SS-724
MW 5041F	NR-4019	RALP 0040	SOLP 0005	SOLP 0024
MW45 0043	NALP 0027	R 545L	S-707	SS-725
MW 5042F	NR-4020	RALP 0042	SOLP 0007	SOLP 0025
MW45 0044	NALP 0028	R 546L	S-713	SS-726
MW 5043F	NR 6001F	RALP 0043	SOLP 0013	SOLP 0026
MW45 0045	NA45 0001	R6-548S1	S-732L	SS-727
MW 5044F	P6-10011	RALP 0045	SOLP 0032	SOLP 0027
MW45 0046	PRLP 0005	R6-550S1	S-733L	SS-729
MW 5045F	P6-10012	RALP 0047	SOLP 0033	SOLP 0029
MW45 0047	PRLP 0006	RS 505	S-734L	SS-730
MW 5046F	P6-10013	RALP 0002	SOLP 0034	SOLP 0030
MW45 0048	PRLP 0007	RS 505-RS 509	S-735L	SS-731
MW 5047F	P6-10014S1	RALP 0001	SOLP 0035	SOLP 0031
MW45 0049	PRLP 0008	RS 506	S-736L	T13-340C2

TALP 0060	VIPS-403	00007D1	10000D1	1004M1
TS-280	VILP 0004	MO12 0010	MO12 0004	GOLP 0105
TALP 0061	VIPS-405	00008D1	10007	1005
TS-281	VILP 0006	MO12 0011	PRLP 0001	MO45 0011
TALP 0062	VIPS-406	00009D1	10008	1005M1
TS-282	VILP 0007	MO12 0012	PRLP 0002	GOLP 0106
TALP 0063	VIPS-407	00010D1	10009	1006
TS-283	VILP 0008	MO12 0013	PRLP 0003	MO45 0012,
TALP 0064	WSJ 2001	00011D1	1000M1	MO45 0013,
TS-284	WO45 0001	MO12 0014	GOLP 0102	MO45 0014
TALP 0065	WSJ 2002	00012D1	1001	1006M1
TS-285	WO45 0002	MO12 0015	MO45 0005,	GOLP 0107
TALP 0066	WSJ 2003	00013D1	MO45 0006,	1007
TS-286	WO45 0003	MO12 0016	MO45 0007	MO45 0015
TALP 0067	WSJ 2004	00014D1	10010	1007M1
TS-287	WO45 0004	MO12 0017	PRLP 0004	GOLP 0108
TALP 0068	WSJ 2005	00015D1	10011	1008
TS-288	WO45 0005	MO12 0018	PRLP 0005	MO45 0016,
TALP 0069	WSJ 2006	00016D1	10012	MO45 0017
TS-289	WO45 0006	MO12 0019	PRLP 0006	1009
TALP 0070	WSJ 2007	00017D1	10013	MO45 0018
TS-290	WO45 0007	MO12 0020	PRLP 0007	101
TALP 0071	WSJ 202	00018D1	10014S1	ME45 0001,
TS-291	WOLP 0001	MO12 0021	PRLP 0008	MWLP 0001,
TALP 0072	WSJ 203	00019D1	10015	TA45 0001
TS-292	WOLP 0002	MO12 0022	PRLP 0009	1010
TALP 0073	WSJ 204	00020D1	10016	MO45 0019
TS-293	WOLP 0003	MO12 0023	PRLP 0010	1011
TALP 0074	WSJ 205	00021D1	10017	MO45 0020
TS-294	WOLP 0004	MO12 0024	PRLP 0011	1012
TALP 0075	WSJ 206	00022D1	10018	MO45 0021
TS-295	WOLP 0005	MO12 0025	PRLP 0012	1013
TALP 0076	WSJ 207	00023D1	10019S1	MO45 0022
TS-296	WOLP 0006	MO12 0026	PRLP 0013	1014
TALP 0077	WSJ 208	00024D1	1001S1	MO45 0023
TS-297	WOLP 0007	MO12 0027	JULP 0001	1015
TALP 0078	WSJ 209	00025D1	1002	MO45 0024
TS-298	WOLP 0008	MO12 0028	MO45 0008	1016
TALP 0079	WSJ 210	00026D1	10020	MO45 0025
TS-299	WOLP 0009	MO12 0029	PRLP 0014	1017
TALP 0080	WSJ 211	00027D1	10021	MO45 0026
TS-300	WOLP 0010	MO12 0030	PRLP 0015	1018
TALP 0081	WSJ 212	00028D1	10022	MO45 0027
TS-301	WOLP 0011	MO12 0031	PRLP 0016	1019
TALP 0082	WSJ 213	00029D1	10023	MO45 0028
TS-302	WOLP 0012	MO12 0032	PRLP 0017	101L
TALP 0083	WSJ 214	00030D1	10024	NALP 0001
TS-303	WOLP 0013	MO12 0033	PRLP 0018	102
TALP 0084	WSJ 215	00032D1	10025R1	ME45 0002,
TS-304	WOLP 0014	MO12 0035	PRLP 0019	MWLP 0002,
TALP 0085	WSJ 216	00033D1	10026	TA45 0002
TS-305	WOLP 0015	MO12 0036	PRLP 0020	1020
TALP 0086	WSJ 217	00034D1	10027R1	MO45 0029
TS-306	WOLP 0016	MO12 0037	PRLP 0021	1021
TALP 0087	WSJ 218	00035D1	10028	MO45 0030
TS-307	WOLP 0017	MO12 0038	PRLP 0022	1022
TALP 0088	WSJ 219	009	10029R1	MO45 0031
TS-308	WOLP 0018	TA45S 0003	PRLP 0023	1023
TALP 0089	WSJ 220	0438MF	1002M1	MO45 0032
TS-309	WOLP 0019	TMG45 0245	GOLP 0103	1024
TALP 0090	00001D1	06068MD	1002S1	MO45 0033
TS-310	MO12 0001	TMGLP 0070	JULP 0002	1025
TALP 0091	00002D1	1	1003	MO45 0034
TS-311	MO12 0002	MI45 0001,	MO45 0009	1026
TALP 0092	00003D1	MOCB 0001	10030R1	MO45 0035
VIPS-400	MO12 0003	10	PRLP 0024	1027
VILP 0001	00004D1	MI45 0010,	1003M1	MO45 0036
VIPS-401	MO12 0007	MOCB 0010	GOLP 0104	1028
VILP 0002	00005D1	1000	1003S1	MO45 0037
VIPS-402	MO12 0008	EC45 0001,	JULP 0003	1029
VILP 0003,	00006D1	MO45 0003,	1004	MO45 0038
VILP 0005	MO12 0009	MO45 0004	MO45 0010	102L

TALP 0080	328L	35009	35045	35081
29D1	TALP 0109	SO45 0009	SO45 0045	SO45 0081
MO12 0032	329V1	35010	35046	35082
2D1	TALP 0110	SO45 0010	SO45 0046	SO45 0082
MO12 0002	32D1	35011	35047	35083
3	MO12 0035	SO45 0011	SO45 0047	SO45 0083
MI45 0003,	330V1	35012	35048	35084
MOCB 0003	TALP 0111	SO45 0012	SO45 0048	SO45 0084
300	331S1	35013	35049	35085
TALP 0081	TALP 0112	SO45 0013	SO45 0049	SO45 0085
30000D1	332S1	35014	35050	35086
MO12 0006	TALP 0113	SO45 0014	SO45 0050	SO45 0086
301	333S1	35015	35051	35087
TALP 0082	TALP 0114	SO45 0015	SO45 0051	SO45 0087
302	334S1	35016	35052	35088
TALP 0083	TALP 0115	SO45 0016	SO45 0052	SO45 0088
303	335S1	35017	35053	35089
TALP 0084	TALP 0116	SO45 0017	SO45 0053	SO45 0089
304	336S1	35018	35054	35090
TALP 0085	TALP 0117	SO45 0018	SO45 0054	SO45 0090
305	337S1	35019	35055	35091
TALP 0086	TALP 0118	SO45 0019	SO45 0055	SO45 0091
306	338S1	35020	35056	35092
TALP 0087	TALP 0119	SO45 0020	SO45 0056	SO45 0092
307	339S1	35021	35057	35093
TALP 0088	TALP 0120	SO45 0021	SO45 0057	SO45 0093
308	33D1	35022	35058	35094
TALP 0089	MO12 0036	SO45 0022	SO45 0058	SO45 0094
309	340C2	35023	35059	35095
TALP 0090	TALP 0121	SO45 0023	SO45 0059	SO45 0095
30D1	341S1	35024	35060	35096
MO12 0033	TALP 0122	SO45 0024	SO45 0060	SO45 0096
310	342S1	35025	35061	35097
TALP 0091	TALP 0123	SO45 0025	SO45 0061	SO45 0097
31000D1	343S1	35026	35062	35098
MO12 0034	TALP 0124	SO45 0026	SO45 0062	SO45 0098
311	344S1	35027	35063	35099
TALP 0092	TALP 0125	SO45 0027	SO45 0063	SO45 0099
3114	345S1	35028	35064	350S1
TA45S 0005	TALP 0126	SO45 0028	SO45 0064	TALP 0131
312L	346S1	35029	35065	35100
TALP 0093	TALP 0127	SO45 0029	SO45 0065	SO45 0100
313L	347S1	35030	35066	35101
TALP 0094	TALP 0128	SO45 0030	SO45 0066	SO45 0101
314L	348S1	35031	35067	35102
TALP 0095	TALP 0129	SO45 0031	SO45 0067	SO45 0102
315L	349S1	35032	35068	35103
TALP 0096	TALP 0130	SO45 0032	SO45 0068	SO45 0103
316	34D1	35033	35069	35104
TALP 0097	MO12 0037	SO45 0033	SO45 0069	SO45 0104
317L	35000V1	35034	35070	35105
TALP 0098	MO12 0039	SO45 0034	SO45 0070	SO45 0105
318L	35001	35035	35071	35106
TALP 0099	SO45 0001	SO45 0035	SO45 0071	SO45 0106
319L	35001V1	35036	35072	35107
TALP 0100	MO12 0040	SO45 0036	SO45 0072	SO45 0107
320D	35002	35037	35073	35108
TALP 0101	SO45 0002	SO45 0037	SO45 0073	SO45 0108
321	35002V1	35038	35074	35109
TALP 0102	MO12 0041	SO45 0038	SO45 0074	SO45 0109
322L	35003	35039	35075	35110
TALP 0103	SO45 0003	SO45 0039	SO45 0075	SO45 0110
323	35004	35040	35076	35111
TALP 0104	SO45 0004	SO45 0040	SO45 0076	SO45 0111
324	35005	35041	35077	35112
TALP 0105	SO45 0005	SO45 0041	SO45 0077	SO45 0112,
325L	35006	35042	35078	SO45 0113
TALP 0106	SO45 0006	SO45 0042	SO45 0078	35113
326L	35007	35043	35079	SO45 0114
TALP 0107	SO45 0007	SO45 0043	SO45 0079	35114
327L	35008	35044	35080	SO45 0115
TALP 0108	SO45 0008	SO45 0044	SO45 0080	35115

54057	54093	54127	54162	TA45 0179
TA45 0040	TA45 0076	TA45 0112	TA45 0147	54195
54058	54094	54128	54163	TA45 0180
TA45 0041	TA45 0077	TA45 0113	TA45 0148	54196
54059	54095	54129	54164	TA45 0181,
TA45 0042	TA45 0078	TA45 0114	TA45 0149	TACO 0011
54060	54096	54130	54165	54197
TA45 0043	TA45 0079	TA45 0115	TA45 0150	TA45 0182
54061	54097	54131	54166	54198
TA45 0044	TA45 0080	TA45 0116	TA45 0151	TA45 0183
54062	54098	54132	54167	54199
TA45 0045	TA45 0081	TA45 0117	TA45 0152	TA45 0184,
54063	54099	54133	54168	TA45 0185
TA45 0046	TA45 0082	TA45 0118	TA45 0153	541L
54064	540L	54134	54169	RALP 0038
TA45 0047	RALP 0037	TA45 0119	TA45 0154	54200
54065	54100	54135	54170	TA45 0186
TA45 0048	TA45 0083	TA45 0120	TA45 0155	54201
54066	54101	54136	54171	TA45 0187
TA45 0049	TA45 0084	TA45 0121	TA45 0156	54202
54067	54102	54137	54172	TA45 0188,
TA45 0050	TA45 0085	TA45 0122	TA45 0157	TACO 0012
54068	54103	54138	54173	54203
TA45 0051	TA45 0086	TA45 0123	TA45 0158	TA45 0189,
54069	54104	54139	54174	TA45 0190,
TA45 0052	TA45 0087	TA45 0124,	TA45 0159	TA45 0191,
54070	54105	TACO 0002	54175	TACO 0013
TA45 0053	TA45 0088	54140	TA45 0160	54204
54071	54106	TA45 0125	54176	TA45 0192
TA45 0054	TA45 0089	54141	TA45 0161	54205
54072	54107	TA45 0126	54177	TA45 0193
TA45 0055	TA45 0090	54142	TA45 0162	54206
54073	54108	TA45 0127	54178	TA45 0194
TA45 0056	TA45 0091,	54143	TA45 0163	54207
54074	TA45 0092	TA45 0128	54179	TA45 0195
TA45 0057	54109	54144	TA45 0164	54208
54075	TA45 0093	TA45 0129	54180	TA45 0196
TA45 0058	54110	54145	TA45 0165,	54209
54076	TA45 0094	TA45 0130	TACO 0004	TA45 0197
TA45 0059	54111	54146	54181	54210
54077	TA45 0095	TA45 0131	TA45 0166	TA45 0198,
TA45 0060	54112	54147	54182	TA45 0199,
54078	TA45 0096	TA45 0132	TA45 0167	TACO 0014
TA45 0061	54113	54148	54183	54211
54079	TA45 0097	TA45 0133	TA45 0168,	TA45 0200,
TA45 0062	54114	54149	TACO 0005	TACO 0015
54080	TA45 0098	TA45 0134	54184	54212
TA45 0063	54115	54150	TA45 0169,	TA45 0201
54081	TA45 0099	TA45 0135	TACO 0006	54213
TA45 0064	54116	54151	54185	TA45 0202
54082	TA45 0100	TA45 0136	TA45 0170	54214
TA45 0065	54117	54152	54186	TA45 0203
54083	TA45 0101	TA45 0137	TA45 0171,	54215
TA45 0066	54118	54153	TACO 0007	TA45 0204
54084	TA45 0102	TA45 0138	54187	54216
TA45 0067	54119	54154	TA45 0172	TA45 0205
54085	TA45 0103,	TA45 0139	54188	54217
TA45 0068	TA45 0104	54155	TA45 0173	TA45 0206
54086	54120	TA45 0140,	54189	54218
TA45 0069	TA45 0105	TACO 0003	TA45 0174,	TA45 0207
54087	54121	54156	TACO 0008	54219
TA45 0070	TA45 0106	TA45 0141	54190	TA45 0208
54088	54122	54157	TA45 0175,	54220
TA45 0071	TA45 0107	TA45 0142	TACO 0009	TA45 0209
54089	54123	54158	54191	54221
TA45 0072	TA45 0108	TA45 0143	TA45 0176	TA45 0210,
54090	54124	54159	54192	TACO 0016
TA45 0073	TA45 0109	TA45 0144	TA45 0177,	54222
54091	54125	54160	TACO 0010	TA45 0211
TA45 0074	TA45 0110	TA45 0145	54193	54223
54092	54126	54161	TA45 0178	TA45 0212
TA45 0075	TA45 0111	TA45 0146	54194	54224

PART VII

INDEXES
TO THE U.K.
DISCOGRAPHY

KEY TO
U.K. ENTRY NUMBER PREFIXES

Flavor
DSLP 0030, MO45 0032

Flavor
MO45 0027, MOLP 0023

The Four Seasons
MW45 0002, MW45 0003, MW45 0024,
MW45 0028, MWLP 0002, MWLP 0007,
TM45 0321

The Four Tops
DSLP 0028, MO12 0099, MO12 0100,
MO45 0068, MO45 0269, MO45 0270,
MOCD 0008, MOLP 0154, MOLP 0181,
PILP 0002, PILP 0014, SPLP 0004,
SS45 0026, SS45 0037, TM45 0007,
TM45 0015, TM45 0028, TM45 0042,
TM45 0053, TM45 0068, TM45 0079,
TM45 0089, TM45 0101, TM45 0112,
TM45 0124, TM45 0135, TM45 0148,
TM45 0166, TM45 0176, TM45 0199,
TM45 0211, TM45 0233, TM45 0237,
TM45 0254, TM45 0272, TM45 0279,
TM45 0287, TM45 0295, TM45 0305,
TM45 0317, TM45 0325, TM45 0331,
TM45 0338, TM45 0352, TM45 0360,
TM45 0460, TM45 0467, TM45 0473,
TM45 0474, TM45 0489, TM45 0527,
TMEP 0012, TMEP 0018, TMLP 0010,
TMLP 0021, TMLP 0037, TMLP 0041,
TMLP 0056, TMLP 0061, TMLP 0087,
TMLP 0113, TMLP 0138, TMLP 0149,
TMLP 0172, TMLP 0178, TMLP 0191,
TMLP 0194, TMLP 0202, TMLP 0205,
TVLP 0004, TVLP 0008, X2LP 0001,
X2LP 0026

Fresh
PR45 0008

Friendly Persuasion
RA45 0020

Gammon, Patrick
MO45 0109, MOLP 0076

Garrett, Siedah
MO12 0112, MO45 0283

Gaye, Marvin
DSLP 0013, DSLP 0015, DSLP 0018,
MO12 0010, MO12 0012, MO12 0025,
MO12 0042, MO12 0046, MO12 0155,
MO12 0194, MO45 0017, MO45 0084,
MO45 0086, MO45 0113, MO45 0116,
MO45 0173, MO45 0180, MO45 0330,
MO45 0370, MOCD 0030, MOCD 0033,
MOLP 0083, MOLP 0106, OR45 0008,
OR45 0016, PILP 0008, SS45 0004,
SS45 0013, SS45 0019, SS45 0023,
SS45 0033, SS45 0035, SSEP 0001,
SSEP 0004, TMEP 0001, SSLP 0005,
SSLP 0007, TM45 0010, TM45 0024,
TM45 0039, TM45 0052, TM45 0063,
TM45 0074, TM45 0090, TM45 0111,
TM45 0119, TM45 0126, TM45 0136,
TM45 0141, TM45 0156, TM45 0169,
TM45 0177, TM45 0182, TM45 0187,
TM45 0198, TM45 0206, TM45 0216,
TM45 0219, TM45 0235, TM45 0277,
TM45 0298, TM45 0304, TM45 0319,
TM45 0348, TM45 0370, TM45 0381,
TM45 0384, TM45 0392, TM45 0408,
TM45 0422, TM45 0425, TM45 0455,
TM45 0504, TM45 0513, TM45 0523,
TM45 0525, TMEP 0016, TMEP 0019,
TMLP 0004, TMLP 0015, TMLP 0022,
TMLP 0033, TMLP 0049, TMLP 0062,
TMLP 0065, TMLP 0084, TMLP 0091,
TMLP 0119, TMLP 0123, TMLP 0132,
TMLP 0136, TMLP 0153, TMLP 0189,
TMLP 0200, TMLP 0224, TMLP 0317,
TMLP 0334, X2LP 0005, X2LP 0019,
X2LP 0021

Gaye, Marvin & Kim Weston
SS45 0035, TM45 0090, TMLP 0049

Gaye, Marvin & Tammi Terrell
TM45 0111, TM45 0126, TM45 0136,
TM45 0156, TM45 0169, TM45 0182,
TM45 0198, TM45 0216, TM45 0525,
TMLP 0062, TMLP 0084, TMLP 0132,
TMLP 0153

Gayten, Paul
LO45 0001

Goldstein, William
MO45 0003, MO45 0007

**Goldstein, William & The Magic
  Disco Machine**
MO45 0003

Gooding, Cuba
MO45 0055, MOLP 0040, MOLP 0070

Graffiti Orchestra
PR45 0005

Harris, Sam
MO12 0130, MO12 0144, MO12 0190,
MO45 0303, MO45 0319, MO45 0366,
MOCD 0021, MOLP 0175

Henderson, Finis
MO12 0089, MO45 0253, MOLP 0148

Hetherington
MW45 0007

High Inergy
MO12 0016, MO12 0082, MO45 0035,
MO45 0051, MO45 0070, MO45 0090,
MO45 0153, MO45 0162, MO45 0182,
MO45 0217, MO45 0243, MOLP 0031,
MOLP 0047, MOLP 0068, MOLP 0101,
MOLP 0114, MOLP 0127

The Hit Pack
TM45 0013

Holland, Eddie
FO45 0004, OR45 0009, SSEP 0004,
SSEP 0005, TMEP 0001

Holloway, Brenda
SS45 0018, TM45 0008, TM45 0019,
TM45 0056, TM45 0081, TM45 0108,
TM45 0123, TM45 0201, TMEP 0001,
TMLP 0083

The Honest Men
TM45 0207

Houston, Thelma
MO12 0156, MO45 0007, MO45 0008,
MO45 0022, MO45 0036, MO45 0050,
MO45 0065, MO45 0066, MO45 0078,
MO45 0331, MOLP 0006, MOLP 0020,
MOLP 0032, MOLP 0049, MOLP 0055,
MOLP 0074, MW45 0001, MW45 0004,
MW45 0005, MWLP 0004, TM45 0301

Houston, Thelma & Jerry Butler
MO45 0022, MOLP 0020

Howell, Reuben
MW45 0019

Hutch, Willie
DSLP 0009, MO12 0076, MO12 0081,
MO12 0169, MO45 0234, MO45 0242,
MO45 0345, MOLP 0026, MOLP 0195,
TM45 0364, TM45 0387, TM45 0486,
TMLP 0246, TMLP 0268, TMLP 0279,
TMLP 0307, TMLP 0315

The Isley Brothers
DSLP 0024, TM45 0055, TM45 0066,
TM45 0072, TM45 0106, TM45 0153,

TM45 0184, TM45 0194, TM45 0209,
TM45 0220, TM45 0379, TM45 0439,
TM45 0528, TMLP 0034, TMLP 0066,
TMLP 0112

Jacas, Jack
MO12 0170, MO45 0346

Jackson, Chuck
TM45 0152, TM45 0230, TMLP 0071,
TMLP 0117

Jackson, Jackie
TMLP 0248

Jackson, Jermaine
DSLP 0027, MO12 0028, MO12 0030,
MO12 0040, MO12 0070, MO12 0077,
MO45 0040, MO45 0131, MO45 0142,
MO45 0149, MO45 0160, MO45 0170,
MO45 0191, MO45 0202, MO45 0225,
MO45 0235, MO45 0252, MOLP 0024,
MOLP 0039, MOLP 0084, MOLP 0104,
MOLP 0117, MOLP 0131, TM45 0340,
TM45 0353, TM45 0376, TM45 0518,
TMLP 0220, TMLP 0237

Jackson, Michael
DSLP 0022, MO12 0119, MO12 0131,
MO45 0113, MO45 0291, MO45 0304,
MOLP 0115, MOLP 0174, PILP 0011,
TM45 0299, TM45 0318, TM45 0328,
TM45 0336, TM45 0365, TM45 0402,
TM45 0448, TM45 0475, TM45 0484,
TMLP 0204, TMLP 0219, TMLP 0234,
TMLP 0297

The Jackson 5
MO45 0029, MOLP 0003, MOLP 0078,
PILP 0003, SPLP 0006, TM45 0225,
TM45 0239, TM45 0248, TM45 0260,
TM45 0271, TM45 0280, TM45 0311,
TM45 0327, TM45 0335, TM45 0339,
TM45 0344, TM45 0358, TM45 0367,
TM45 0380, TM45 0397, TM45 0406,
TM45 0429, TM45 0444, TM45 0465,
TM45 0471, TM45 0477, TM45 0479,
TMLP 0142, TMLP 0155, TMLP 0167,
TMLP 0173, TMLP 0187, TMLP 0211,
TMLP 0213, TMLP 0230, TMLP 0242,
TMLP 0274, TMLP 0289, X2LP 0017

Jakata
MO12 0133, MO12 0153, MO45 0306,
MO45 0328, MOLP 0177

Jamal, Ahmed
MOLP 0102

James, Keef
RALP 0010

James, Rick
DSLP 0038, MO12 0003, MO12 0011,
MO12 0020, MO12 0032, MO12 0036,
MO12 0043, MO12 0050, MO12 0056,
MO12 0063, MO12 0064, MO12 0071,
MO12 0095, MO12 0106, MO12 0124,
MO12 0135, MO12 0152, MO12 0172,
MO45 0058, MO45 0069, MO45 0085,
MO45 0095, MO45 0104, MO45 0122,
MO45 0146, MO45 0157, MO45 0177,
MO45 0190, MO45 0199, MO45 0215,
MO45 0226, MO45 0297, MO45 0308,
MO45 0327, MO45 0348, MOCD 0007,
MOCD 0037, MOLP 0042, MOLP 0061,
MOLP 0085, MOLP 0098, MOLP 0110,
MOLP 0124, MOLP 0167, MOLP 0189

James, Rick & Friend
MO12 0106, MO45 0276

Jennifer
MO45 0015

John, Robert
  MO45 0247
Johnson, Harold
  MO45 0099
Johnson, Marv
  TM45 0025, TM45 0181, TM45 0214,
  TM45 0238, TM45 0475, TM45 0530,
  TMLP 0111
Jones, Gloria
  TM45 0412, TMLP 0253
Jupiter, Duke
  MO12 0120, MO45 0292, MOLP 0172
Keith & Darrell
  MO12 0111, MO45 0281
Kendricks, Eddie
  DSLP 0020, MO45 0009, MOLP 0028,
  MOLP 0037, TM45 0347, TM45 0375,
  TM45 0390, TM45 0403, TM45 0418,
  TM45 0449, TM45 0481, TM45 0499,
  TM45 0509, TMLP 0185, TMLP 0212,
  TMLP 0244, TMLP 0265, TMLP 0293,
  TMLP 0308, TMLP 0335
Kidd Glove
  MO45 0286, MOLP 0162
King, Bobby
  MO12 0113, MO12 0123, MO45 0284,
  MO45 0296, MOLP 0164
King, Bobby featuring Alfie Silas
  MO12 0123, MO45 0296
King, Dr. Martin Luther, Jr.
  TMLP 0076
Knight, Gladys
  DSLP 0026, MO45 0043, MOLP 0079,
  PILP 0006, TM45 0076, TM45 0104,
  TM45 0120, TM45 0130, TM45 0146,
  TM45 0161, TM45 0175, TM45 0215,
  TM45 0229, TM45 0258, TM45 0267,
  TM45 0307, TM45 0315, TM45 0332,
  TM45 0346, TM45 0357, TM45 0366,
  TM45 0378, TM45 0405, TM45 0447,
  TM45 0457, TM45 0487, TMLP 0058,
  TMLP 0080, TMLP 0100, TMLP 0135,
  TMLP 0148, TMLP 0186, TMLP 0207,
  TMLP 0225, TMLP 0229, TMLP 0263,
  TMLP 0278, TMLP 0305, X2LP 0004
Knight, Gladys & The Pips
  DSLP 0026, MO45 0043, MOLP 0079,
  PILP 0006, TM45 0076, TM45 0104,
  TM45 0120, TM45 0130, TM45 0146,
  TM45 0161, TM45 0175, TM45 0215,
  TM45 0229, TM45 0258, TM45 0267,
  TM45 0307, TM45 0315, TM45 0332,
  TM45 0346, TM45 0357, TM45 0366,
  TM45 0378, TM45 0405, TM45 0447,
  TM45 0457, TM45 0487, TMLP 0058,
  TMLP 0080, TMLP 0100, TMLP 0135,
  TMLP 0148, TMLP 0186, TMLP 0207,
  TMLP 0225, TMLP 0229, TMLP 0263,
  TMLP 0278, TMLP 0305, X2LP 0004
KoKo Pop
  MO12 0138, MO12 0181, MO45 0312,
  MO45 0357, MOLP 0171
Lavette, Bettye
  MO45 0206, MO45 0214, MOLP 0123
Lee, Laura
  TM45 0333
Legrand, Michel
  TM45 0350
The Lewis Sisters
  TM45 0036
Little Stevie Wonder
  OR45 0018, ORLP 0004, ORLP 0005,

SS45 0002, SS45 0014, SSEP 0002,
SSLP 0003
Long, Shorty
  TM45 0012, TM45 0073, TM45 0100,
  TM45 0145, TM45 0164, TMLP 0086,
  TMLP 0144
Lovesmith, Michael
  MO12 0093, MO12 0174, MO12 0180,
  MO45 0260, MO45 0350, MO45 0356,
  MOLP 0149, MOLP 0194
M, Bobby
  MO12 0078, MO45 0237, MOLP 0137
McClary, Thomas
  MO12 0141, MO45 0315, MOLP 0188
McNair, Barbara
  TM45 0044
McNeir, Ronnie
  TMLP 0327, TMLP 0333
The Magic Disco Machine
  MO45 0003, TM45 0482
Major Lance
  MO45 0057, MOLP 0051
Mandre
  MO12 0018, MO45 0037, MO45 0064,
  MO45 0092, MOLP 0019, MOLP 0041
Martha & The Vandellas
  OR45 0011, OR45 0013, ORLP 0007,
  SS45 0001, SS45 0005, SS45 0009,
  SS45 0017, SS45 0027, SS45 0042,
  SSEP 0001, SSEP 0004, TM45 0002,
  TM45 0030, TM45 0049, TM45 0067,
  TM45 0082, TM45 0099, TM45 0122,
  TMEP 0009, TMEP 0017, TMLP 0005,
  TMLP 0013, TMLP 0040, TMLP 0051
Martin & Finley
  TM45 0369
Martin, Tony
  SS45 0045, TM45 0037
The Marvelettes
  FO45 0001, FO45 0003, OR45 0003,
  OR45 0012, SS45 0006, SS45 0010,
  SS45 0025, SS45 0036, SSEP 0001,
  SSEP 0003, TM45 0018, TM45 0035,
  TM45 0046, TM45 0062, TM45 0094,
  TM45 0109, TM45 0140, TM45 0160,
  TM45 0202, TM45 0362, TM45 0441,
  TM45 0478, TMEP 0003, TMLP 0008,
  TMLP 0052, TMLP 0090, TMLP 0145,
  TMLP 0257
Mary Jane Girls
  MO12 0087, MO12 0092, MO12 0096,
  MO12 0151, MO12 0173, MO45 0264,
  MO45 0326, MO45 0349, MOCD 0039,
  MOLP 0146, MOLP 0185
Masekela, Hugh
  RALP 0002
Meatloaf
  PR45 0010, PRLP 0010, RA45 0003,
  RALP 0005
Meatloaf featuring Stoney &
  Meatloaf
  PR45 0010
Mike & The Modifiers
  OR45 0004
Militello, Bobby
  MO12 0078, MO45 0237, MOLP 0137
Mills, Stephanie
  TM45 0498, TMLP 0309
The Miracles
  DSLP 0008, DSLP 0010, FO45 0002,
  LO45 0003, LO45 0004, MOCD 0005,
  OR45 0005, OR45 0019, OREP 0001,

ORLP 0002, PILP 0001, SS45 0008,
SS45 0012, SS45 0022, SS45 0030,
SS45 0039, SSEP 0001, SSEP 0003,
SSLP 0006, TM45 0003, TM45 0022,
TM45 0040, TM45 0047, TM45 0069,
TM45 0084, TM45 0098, TM45 0114,
TM45 0115, TM45 0132, TM45 0149,
TM45 0162, TM45 0174, TM45 0188,
TM45 0197, TM45 0246, TM45 0247,
TM45 0263, TM45 0276, TM45 0313,
TM45 0355, TM45 0393, TM45 0416,
TM45 0442, TM45 0459, TM45 0493,
TM45 0501, TM45 0526, TMLP 0003,
TMLP 0024, TMLP 0031, TMLP 0044,
TMLP 0067, TMLP 0072, TMLP 0089,
TMLP 0107, TMLP 0129, TMLP 0151,
TMLP 0171, TMLP 0232, TMLP 0275,
TMLP 0302, TMLP 0312, TMLP 0330,
X2LP 0012, X2LP 0027
Mitchell, Barbara
  MO45 0262
Mitchell, Marty
  MC45 0001
The Modifiers
  OR45 0004
The Monitors
  TMEP 0014, TMLP 0108
The Motor City Crew
  MO12 0104
Motown Sounds
  MO12 0017, MO45 0091, MOLP 0062
The Motown Spinners   see also
  The
  Spinners
The Motown Spinners
  TM45 0257, TM45 0268, TMLP 0181
Naylor, Jerry
  MC45 0002
Nolen & Crossley
  MO45 0210, MO12 0062
Nunn, Bobby
  MO12 0102, MO45 0272, MOLP 0156
Odyssey
  MWLP 0003
The Originals
  MO45 0014, MOLP 0011, TM45 0092,
  TM45 0203, TM45 0234, TM45 0324,
  TM45 0516, TMLP 0116, TMLP 0286,
  TMLP 0326
Ozone
  MO12 0055, MO12 0061, MO45 0140,
  MO45 0198, MO45 0208
Pal
  MO12 0188, MO45 0364
Payne, Scherrie
  MO45 0046
Petersen, Paul
  TM45 0171
The Pips
  DSLP 0026, MO45 0043, MOLP 0079,
  PILP 0006, TM45 0076, TM45 0104,
  TM45 0120, TM45 0130, TM45 0146,
  TM45 0161, TM45 0175, TM45 0215,
  TM45 0229, TM45 0258, TM45 0267,
  TM45 0307, TM45 0315, TM45 0332,
  TM45 0346, TM45 0357, TM45 0366,
  TM45 0378, TM45 0405, TM45 0447,
  TM45 0457, TM45 0487, TMLP 0058,
  TMLP 0080, TMLP 0100, TMLP 0135,
  TMLP 0148, TMLP 0186, TMLP 0207,
  TMLP 0225, TMLP 0229, TMLP 0263,
  TMLP 0278, TMLP 0305, X2LP 0004

TM45 0255, TM45 0269, TM45 0286,
TM45 0413, TM45 0424, TM45 0436,
TM45 0463, TM45 0530, TMEP 0014,
TMLP 0048, TMLP 0106, TMLP 0160,
TMLP 0175, TMLP 0258

St. James, Phyllis
MO12 0134, MO45 0307, MOLP 0180

San Remo Strings
TM45 0297, TM45 0309, TMLP 0215

Scherrie & Susaye
MO45 0115

Sheppard, T. G.
HI45 0001, MW45 0027, MW45 0031,
MW45 0033, MW45 0035

Silas, Alfie
MO12 0123, MO45 0296

Simpson, Valerie
TMLP 0193, TMLP 0218

The Sisters Love
MW45 0009, TM45 0330, TM45 0480

Slowbone
RA45 0016, RA45 0019

Slowbone And The Wonder Boys
RA45 0016

Sonny & The Sovereigns
RA45 0017

The Soul Brothers
TM45 0006, TM45 0316, TMLP 0014

The Sovereigns
RA45 0017

The Spinners see also Detroit
Spinners; The Motown
Spinners

The Spinners
TM45 0014, TM45 0023

Starr, Edwin
TM45 0131, TM45 0147, TM45 0173,
TM45 0193, TM45 0221, TM45 0226,
TM45 0250, TM45 0256, TM45 0266,
TM45 0292, TM45 0312, TM45 0377,
TM45 0407, TM45 0432, TM45 0470,
TM45 0506, TMLP 0094, TMLP 0115,
TMLP 0131, TMLP 0170, TMLP 0198,
TMLP 0208, TMLP 0259

Steele, Maureen
MO12 0168, MO12 0177, MO45 0344,
MO45 0353, MOLP 0193

Sterling
MO12 0024, MO45 0110

Stone City Band
MO12 0097, MO45 0129, MO45 0169,
MO45 0187, MOLP 0107, MOLP 0147

Stoney
PR45 0010, PRLP 0010, RA45 0003,
RALP 0005

Stoney & Meatloaf
PR45 0010, PRLP 0010, RA45 0003,
RALP 0005

Strong, Barrett
LO45 0002

Struk, Jud
MW45 0032

Stylus
PRLP 0011

Sunday Funnies
RALP 0004

The Supremes
MO12 0027, MO12 0195, MO45 0012,
MO45 0028, MO45 0128, MO45 0371,
MOCD 0004, MOLP 0004, MOLP 0048,
PILP 0013, SPLP 0001, SPLP 0003,
SS45 0007, SS45 0024, SS45 0029,

SS45 0038, SSEP 0003, SSEP 0005,
SSLP 0009, TM45 0001, TM45 0016,
TM45 0027, TM45 0043, TM45 0048,
TM45 0060, TM45 0075, TM45 0085,
TM45 0097, TM45 0107, TM45 0117,
TM45 0133, TM45 0151, TM45 0163,
TM45 0178, TM45 0186, TM45 0196,
TM45 0205, TM45 0210, TM45 0222,
TM45 0231, TM45 0236, TM45 0249,
TM45 0262, TM45 0279, TM45 0284,
TM45 0295, TM45 0306, TM45 0317,
TM45 0323, TM45 0337, TM45 0338,
TM45 0349, TM45 0361, TM45 0386,
TM45 0417, TM45 0427, TM45 0452,
TM45 0458, TM45 0462, TM45 0466,
TM45 0473, TM45 0476, TM45 0490,
TM45 0507, TM45 0522, TM45 0523,
TM45 0524, TMEP 0008, TMEP 0011,
TMLP 0002, TMLP 0012, TMLP 0018,
TMLP 0020, TMLP 0026, TMLP 0028,
TMLP 0039, TMLP 0047, TMLP 0054,
TMLP 0063, TMLP 0070, TMLP 0073,
TMLP 0088, TMLP 0095, TMLP 0096,
TMLP 0110, TMLP 0114, TMLP 0122,
TMLP 0137, TMLP 0146, TMLP 0154,
TMLP 0156, TMLP 0174, TMLP 0178,
TMLP 0188, TMLP 0191, TMLP 0202,
TMLP 0209, TMLP 0221, TMLP 0255,
TMLP 0292, TMLP 0319, TVLP 0001,
TVLP 0005, X2LP 0013, X2LP 0014

The Supremes & The Four Tops
TM45 0279, TM45 0295, TM45 0317,
TM45 0338, TM45 0473, TMLP 0178,
TMLP 0191, TMLP 0202

Susaye
MO45 0115

Switch
MO12 0006, MO12 0007, MO12 0021,
MO45 0071, MO45 0080, MO45 0096,
MO45 0135, MOLP 0053, MOLP 0069,
MOLP 0092

Syreeta
MO12 0013, MO12 0053, MO12 0060,
MO12 0069, MO12 0080, MO12 0090,
MO45 0042, MO45 0087, MO45 0107,
MO45 0123, MO45 0136, MO45 0148,
MO45 0159, MO45 0196, MO45 0207,
MO45 0224, MO45 0240, MO45 0255,
MOLP 0010, MOLP 0030, MOLP 0064,
MOLP 0094, MOLP 0112, MOLP 0119,
MOLP 0141, MW45 0006, MWLP 0001,
TM45 0414, TM45 0428, TM45 0435,
TM45 0456, TMLP 0267

Syreeta & G. C Cameron
MO45 0042

Tattoo
PRLP 0003

Taylor, Bobby
TM45 0155, TMLP 0093, TMLP 0125

Taylor, Bobby & The Vancouvers
TM45 0155, TMLP 0093

Taylor, R. Dean
RA45 0001, RA45 0006, TM45 0157,
TM45 0265, TM45 0288, TM45 0398,
TM45 0411, TM45 0420, TM45 0470,
TMLP 0184

Teena Marie
MO12 0019, MO12 0023, MO12 0033,
MO12 0048, MO12 0052, MO12 0057,
MO12 0159, MO45 0094, MO45 0106,
MO45 0126, MO45 0133, MO45 0144,
MO45 0151, MO45 0184, MO45 0195,

MO45 0200, MO45 0334, MOLP 0066,
MOLP 0087, MOLP 0100, MOLP 0111

The Temptations
DSLP 0016, DSLP 0021, DSLP 0025,
MO12 0029, MO12 0051, MO12 0063,
MO12 0084, MO12 0099, MO12 0106,
MO12 0140, MO12 0148, MO12 0183,
MO12 0193, MO45 0005, MO45 0011,
MO45 0134, MO45 0145, MO45 0164,
MO45 0192, MO45 0212, MO45 0246,
MO45 0269, MO45 0314, MO45 0322,
MO45 0359, MO45 0369, MOCD 0019,
MOLP 0018, MOLP 0093, MOLP 0097,
MOLP 0116, MOLP 0139, MOLP 0153,
MOLP 0186, MOLP 0198, PILP 0007,
PILP 0013, SPLP 0002, SPLP 0003,
SS45 0011, SS45 0020, SS45 0028,
SS45 0040, SSEP 0005, TM45 0004,
TM45 0026, TM45 0041, TM45 0057,
TM45 0065, TM45 0078, TM45 0087,
TM45 0110, TM45 0121, TM45 0134,
TM45 0142, TM45 0159, TM45 0172,
TM45 0186, TM45 0189, TM45 0200,
TM45 0208, TM45 0210, TM45 0217,
TM45 0223, TM45 0231, TM45 0242,
TM45 0251, TM45 0275, TM45 0285,
TM45 0302, TM45 0310, TM45 0334,
TM45 0341, TM45 0356, TM45 0368,
TM45 0389, TM45 0433, TM45 0450,
TM45 0469, TM45 0521, TM45 0523,
TMEP 0004, TMEP 0010, TMLP 0009,
TMLP 0016, TMLP 0023, TMLP 0035,
TMLP 0042, TMLP 0053, TMLP 0057,
TMLP 0068, TMLP 0079, TMLP 0096,
TMLP 0104, TMLP 0109, TMLP 0110,
TMLP 0122, TMLP 0133, TMLP 0141,
TMLP 0147, TMLP 0169, TMLP 0183,
TMLP 0201, TMLP 0217, TMLP 0228,
TMLP 0298, TMLP 0332, X2LP 0011,
X2LP 0016

The Temptations Band
TM45 0433

**The Temptations with The Four
Tops**
MO45 0269

Terrell, Tammi
TM45 0061, TM45 0111, TM45 0126,
TM45 0136, TM45 0156, TM45 0169,
TM45 0182, TM45 0198, TM45 0216,
TM45 0525, TMEP 0014, TMLP 0062,
TMLP 0084, TMLP 0103, TMLP 0132,
TMLP 0153

Thelma and Jerry
MOLP 0049

Three Ounces Of Love
MO45 0053, MO45 0067, MOLP 0045

21st Creation
MO45 0023, MOLP 0035

The Undisputed Truth
DSLP 0004, DSLP 0023, DSLP 0029,
TM45 0278, TM45 0291, TM45 0320,
TM45 0399, TM45 0421, TM45 0445,
TM45 0492, TMLP 0196, TMLP 0239,
TMLP 0276, TMLP 0301

Urbaniak, Michael
MO12 0035, MO45 0156

The Valadiers
OR45 0010

Valentino
GA45 0001

Valli, Frankie
MW45 0002, MW45 0003, MW45 0024,

MW45 0028, MW45 0030, MW45 0034,
MWLP 0002, MWLP 0007, MWLP 0008,
TM45 0321

Valli, Frankie & The Four Seasons
MW45 0002, MW45 0003, MW45 0024,
MW45 0028, MWLP 0002, MWLP 0007,
TM45 0321

The Vancouvers
TM45 0155, TMLP 0093

The Vandellas
MO45 0124, MOLP 0017, OR45 0011,
OR45 0013, ORLP 0007, SS45 0001,
SS45 0005, SS45 0009, SS45 0017,
SS45 0027, SS45 0042, SSEP 0001,
SSEP 0004, TM45 0002, TM45 0030,
TM45 0049, TM45 0067, TM45 0082,
TM45 0099, TM45 0122, TM45 0137,
TM45 0158, TM45 0170, TM45 0185,
TM45 0195, TM45 0264, TM45 0296,
TM45 0529, TMEP 0009, TMEP 0017,
TMLP 0005, TMLP 0013, TMLP 0040,
TMLP 0051, TMLP 0078, TMLP 0099,
TMLP 0134, TMLP 0165, TMLP 0203,
TMLP 0222

Van Dyke, Earl
SS45 0031, TM45 0006, TM45 0261,
TM45 0316, TMLP 0014

**Van Dyke, Earl & The Soul
   Brothers**
TM45 0006, TM45 0316, TMLP 0014

Vanity
MO12 0136, MO12 0143, MO12 0192,
MO45 0309, MO45 0318, MO45 0368,
MOLP 0176

Various Artists
DSLP 0005, MOCD 0011, MOCD 0017,
MOCD 0018, MOCD 0020, MOCD 0022,
MOCD 0023, MOCD 0026, MOCD 0034,
MOLP 0001, MOLP 0002, MOLP 0016,
MOLP 0027, MOLP 0059, MOLP 0071,
MOLP 0080, MOLP 0082, MOLP 0090,
MOLP 0096, MOLP 0152, MOLP 0170,
MOLP 0190, MOLP 0191, PILP 0009,
SILP 0001, SILP 0002, SPLP 0007,
SSEP 0001, SSEP 0003, SSEP 0004,
SSEP 0005, SSLP 0001, SSLP 0002,
TMEP 0001, TMEP 0014, TMLP 0001,
TMLP 0007, TMLP 0019, TMLP 0027,
TMLP 0030, TMLP 0043, TMLP 0050,
TMLP 0055, TMLP 0064, TMLP 0074,
TMLP 0077, TMLP 0082, TMLP 0092,
TMLP 0121, TMLP 0124, TMLP 0126,
TMLP 0127, TMLP 0130, TMLP 0143,
TMLP 0161, TMLP 0180, TMLP 0190,
TMLP 0199, TMLP 0214, TMLP 0216,
TMLP 0226, TMLP 0231, TMLP 0236,
TMLP 0243, TMLP 0245, TMLP 0269,
TMLP 0277, TMLP 0294, TMLP 0295,
TMLP 0311, TMLP 0318, TMLP 0320,
TMLP 0329, TVLP 0002, TVLP 0006,
X2LP 0007, X2LP 0010, X2LP 0023,
X2LP 0031, X2LP 0032

Vega, Tata
MO12 0014, MO12 0039, MO12 0044,
MO45 0001, MO45 0020, MO45 0088,
MO45 0105, MO45 0167, MO45 0178,

MOLP 0015, MOLP 0060, MOLP 0095,
TM45 0531, TMLP 0331

The Velvelettes
MO45 0072, SS45 0034, SS45 0044,
TM45 0021, TM45 0080, TM45 0095,
TM45 0282, TM45 0308

Walker, Junior
MO12 0098, MO45 0018, MO45 0066,
MO45 0267, MOLP 0005, MOLP 0046,
MOLP 0151, SPLP 0005, TM45 0009,
TM45 0020, TM45 0029, TM45 0050,
TM45 0059, TM45 0071, TM45 0086,
TM45 0096, TM45 0138, TM45 0168,
TM45 0183, TM45 0192, TM45 0213,
TM45 0228, TM45 0252, TM45 0326,
TM45 0342, TM45 0359, TM45 0374,
TM45 0391, TM45 0396, TM45 0464,
TM45 0505, TMEP 0013, TMLP 0017,
TMLP 0029, TMLP 0038, TMLP 0097,
TMLP 0120, TMLP 0140, TMLP 0152,
TMLP 0166, TMLP 0197, TMLP 0210,
TMLP 0223, TMLP 0233, TMLP 0273,
TMLP 0310, TMLP 0325, X2LP 0006

Walker, Junior & The All Stars
MO45 0018, MOLP 0005, SPLP 0005,
TM45 0009, TM45 0020, TM45 0029,
TM45 0050, TM45 0059, TM45 0071,
TM45 0086, TM45 0096, TM45 0138,
TM45 0168, TM45 0183, TM45 0192,
TM45 0213, TM45 0228, TM45 0252,
TM45 0326, TM45 0342, TM45 0359,
TM45 0374, TM45 0391, TM45 0396,
TM45 0464, TMEP 0013, TMLP 0017,
TMLP 0029, TMLP 0038, TMLP 0097,
TMLP 0120, TMLP 0140, TMLP 0152,
TMLP 0166, TMLP 0197, TMLP 0210,
TMLP 0223, TMLP 0233, TMLP 0273,
TMLP 0310, TMLP 0325, X2LP 0006

Ware, Leon
MOLP 0007

Warp 9
MO12 0186, MO45 0362

Washington, Grover
MO45 0079, MO45 0101

Washington, Grover, Jr.
MOCD 0012, MOLP 0056, MOLP 0088,
X2LP 0024, X2LP 0028

Waters, Mira
MO45 0102

Wells, Mary
MO45 0048, OR45 0001, OR45 0006,
OR45 0014, OR45 0017, ORLP 0003,
ORLP 0006, SS45 0003, SS45 0015,
SS45 0019, SSLP 0004, TM45 0322,
TMEP 0007, TMLP 0006, TMLP 0032

Wells, Mary & Marvin Gaye
SS45 0019, SSLP 0005

Weston, Kim
SS45 0032, SS45 0035, SSEP 0003,
TM45 0011, TM45 0038, TM45 0054,
TM45 0090, TM45 0478, TMEP 0005,
TMEP 0015, TMLP 0049

Wilson, Frank
MO45 0118

Wilson, Mary
MO45 0111, MO45 0125, MOLP 0081

Wolf & Wolf
MO45 0295, MOLP 0169

Wolfe
RA45 0008

Womack, Bobby
MO12 0065, MO12 0116, MO12 0129,
MO45 0216, MO45 0227, MO45 0288,
MO45 0302, MOLP 0125, MOLP 0173

The Wonder Boys
RA45 0016

Wonder, Little Stevie
OR45 0018, ORLP 0004, ORLP 0005,
SS45 0002, SS45 0014, SSEP 0002,
SSLP 0003

Wonder, Stevie
DSLP 0002, DSLP 0007, DSLP 0011,
DSLP 0019, DSLP 0035, DSLP 0040,
MO12 0010, MO12 0034, MO12 0047,
MO12 0073, MO12 0079, MO12 0105,
MO12 0125, MO12 0139, MO12 0147,
MO12 0158, MO12 0160, MO12 0162,
MO12 0179, MO12 0185, MO12 0189,
MO45 0002, MO45 0016, MO45 0031,
MO45 0039, MO45 0084, MO45 0097,
MO45 0121, MO45 0127, MO45 0152,
MO45 0163, MO45 0174, MO45 0183,
MO45 0203, MO45 0218, MO45 0229,
MO45 0236, MO45 0238, MO45 0298,
MO45 0313, MO45 0321, MO45 0333,
MO45 0335, MO45 0337, MO45 0355,
MO45 0361, MO45 0365, MOCD 0006,
MOCD 0013, MOCD 0014, MOCD 0015,
MOCD 0024, MOCD 0025, MOCD 0027,
MOCD 0028, MOCD 0031, MOCD 0032,
MOLP 0159, MOLP 0178, PILP 0004,
SS45 0021, SSLP 0008, TM45 0005,
TM45 0032, TM45 0045, TM45 0058,
TM45 0070, TM45 0088, TM45 0102,
TM45 0113, TM45 0127, TM45 0154,
TM45 0167, TM45 0180, TM45 0191,
TM45 0218, TM45 0232, TM45 0245,
TM45 0259, TM45 0274, TM45 0281,
TM45 0300, TM45 0329, TM45 0343,
TM45 0354, TM45 0371, TM45 0383,
TM45 0394, TM45 0410, TM45 0423,
TM45 0430, TM45 0461, TM45 0468,
TM45 0520, TM45 0532, TMEP 0006,
TMEP 0020, TMLP 0036, TMLP 0045,
TMLP 0059, TMLP 0075, TMLP 0085,
TMLP 0098, TMLP 0128, TMLP 0150,
TMLP 0163, TMLP 0168, TMLP 0182,
TMLP 0195, X2LP 0015, X2LP 0022,
X2LP 0025

Wright, Rita
TM45 0144, TM45 0293

Wylie, Popcorn
TM45 0434

Xit
RA45 0007, RA45 0011, RALP 0007

Young, Monalisa
MO12 0088, MO45 0251

Young, Val
MO12 0191, MO45 0367

ABC (LP)
TMLP 0155
ABC (song)
TM45 0239, TM45 0471
Abraham, Martin And John (song)
MO45 0113, MW45 0013, TM45 0235,
TM45 0303
Act Like A Shotgun (song)
TM45 0511
After The Dance (song)
TM45 0513
After You (song)
TM45 0510
Agent Double O Soul (song)
TM45 0292
The Agony And The Ecstasy
(song)
MO45 0054
Aiming At Your Heart (song)
MO12 0051, MO45 0192
Ain't It A Sad Thing (song)
RA45 0001, TM45 0288
Ain't It Baby (song)
LO45 0004
Ain't It Hell Up In Harlem (song)
TM45 0432
Ain't No Justice (song)
TM45 0450
Ain't No Mountain High Enough
(song)
MO12 0009, MO45 0083, TM45 0111,
TM45 0253
AIN'T NO SUNSHINE (LP)
PILP 0011
Ain't No Sunshine (song)
MO12 0131, TM45 0328
Ain't No Sun Since You've Been
Gone (song)
TM45 0320
Ain't Nothing Like It (song)
MO12 0180, MO45 0356
Ain't Nothing Like The Real
Thing (song)
TM45 0156, TM45 0367
Ain't Nothin' To It (song)
MO45 0055
AIN'T NO TURNIN' BACK
(LP)
MOLP 0180
Ain't That Asking For Trouble
(song)
TM45 0070
Ain't That Peculiar (song)
TM45 0039
Ain't Too Proud To Beg (song)
TM45 0065, TM45 0200
Aladdin's Lamp (song)
MO45 0144
ALBERT FINNEY'S ALBUM
(LP)
DSLP 0030
All Because Of You (song)
MO45 0191
ALL BY MYSELF (LP)
TMLP 0185
All Day And All Of The Night
(song)
MO45 0169
All Day And All Of The Night
(Vamp Version) (song)
MO45 0169
ALL DIRECTIONS (LP)

TMLP 0217
All For You (song)
TM45 0006, TM45 0261
All I Do (song)
MO45 0203
All I Know About You (song)
TM45 0107
All I Need (song)
TM45 0110
ALL I NEED IS TIME (LP)
TMLP 0263
All I Wanted Was You (song)
MO45 0123
All My Life's A Lie (song)
MO45 0256
All Night Long (song)
MO12 0092, MO12 0096, MO12 0103,
MO12 0109, MO12 0173, MO45 0268,
MO45 0279
All Of My Life (song)
TM45 0382
All Of My Love (song)
TM45 0499
All That's Good (song)
TM45 0003
ALL THE GREAT HITS (LP)
DSLP 0036, MOLP 0140
ALL THE GREAT LOVE
SONGS (CD)
MOCD 0009, MOCD 0010
ALL THIS LOVE (LP)
MOLP 0143
All This Love (song)
MO12 0091, MO12 0108
All Turned On (song)
TM45 0297
American Dream (song)
MO12 0129, MO45 0302
And I Don't Love You (song)
MO12 0121, MO45 0293
And I Will Love You (song)
MW45 0030
Angie Girl (song)
TM45 0180
Animal Instinct (song)
MO12 0165, MO45 0341
Another Star (song)
MO45 0031
Another Woman (song)
MW45 0027, MW45 0031
ANTHOLOGY (LP)
MOLP 0017, X2LP 0004, X2LP 0005,
X2LP 0006, X2LP 0011, X2LP 0012,
X2LP 0013, X2LP 0014, X2LP 0016,
X2LP 0017, X2LP 0026, X2LP 0027,
X2LP 0028
Any Happy Home (song)
TM45 0350
Anything You Wanna Do (song)
TM45 0046
ANYWAY YOU LIKE IT (LP)
MOLP 0006
Any Way You Like It (song)
MO45 0050
Anyway You Wannta' (song)
TM45 0096
APOLLO (LP)
MOLP 0065
Aqui Con Tigo (song)
MO12 0058
Are You Happy (song)
MO45 0194

THE ARTISTRY OF BRENDA
HOLLOWAY (LP)
TMLP 0083
As (song)
MO45 0039
Ask Any Girl (song)
SS45 0029, TM45 0417
Ask The Lonely (song)
TM45 0007
Asleep On My Love (song)
TM45 0497
As Long As I Know He's Mine
(song)
SS45 0006
Astro Disco (song)
MO12 0015
Astro Disco (Instrumental) (song)
MO12 0015
Astro Disco (Part 1) (song)
MO45 0089
Astro Disco (Part 2) (song)
MO45 0089
AT HIS BEST (CD)
MOCD 0012
AT HIS BEST (LP)
MOLP 0036, MOLP 0037
At Last (I Found A Love) (song)
TM45 0177
AT THE COPA (LP)
TMLP 0026
AT THEIR BEST (LP)
MOLP 0048
Automatically Sunshine (song)
TM45 0323, TM45 0466
AWAY WE A-GO-GO (LP)
TMLP 0044
Baby (song)
TM45 0207
Baby, Baby Don't Cry (song)
TM45 0188
Baby Baby I Need You (song)
SS45 0028
Baby Come Close (song)
TM45 0400
Baby Don't Cha Worry (song)
TM45 0061
Baby Don't You Go (song)
SS45 0039
Baby Hit And Run (song)
TM45 0388
Baby I'm For Real (song)
TM45 0234, TM45 0324
Baby I Need Your Lovin' (song)
SS45 0026, TM45 0233
Baby It's Love (song)
TM45 0363
BABY IT'S ME (LP)
DSLP 0031
Baby It's Me (song)
MO12 0002, MO45 0052
Baby I've Got It (song)
TM45 0077
Baby I Will (song)
MO12 0093, MO12 0174, MO45 0260
Baby Love (song)
SS45 0029, TM45 0417, TM45 0522
Baby, That's Backatcha (song)
TM45 0451
Baby Won'tcha Come Quick
(song)
MO12 0178, MO45 0354
Baby You Know You Ain't Right

SONG & RECORD TITLE INDEX (U.K.)

RALP 0012
COSMIC TRUTH (LP)
  DSLP 0023
Could This Be Love (song)
  MO45 0217
Country Boy (song)
  TM45 0359
COYOTE SISTERS (LP)
  MOLP 0166
Crazy About The La La La (song)
  TM45 0313
Crazy Love (song)
  PR45 0007
Crazy Maybe (song)
  MO12 0143, MO45 0318
CREAM OF THE CROP (LP)
  TMLP 0137
Creepin' (song)
  MO45 0031
The Crown (Part 1) (song)
  MO12 0094
The Crown (Part 2) (song)
  MO12 0094
Cruisin' (song)
  MO12 0068, MO45 0112, MO45 0223
Cryin' My Heart Out For You
  (song)
  MO45 0181
Cuidado (song)
  MO45 0254
Daddy Could Swear, I Declare
  (song)
  MO45 0043, TM45 0378
Daddy's Home (song)
  TM45 0353
Dance For Me Children (song)
  MO45 0136
DANCE PARTY (LP)
  TMLP 0013
DANCERS, ROMANCERS,
  DREAMERS AND
  SCHEMERS (LP)
  PRLP 0001
Dance With Me (Part 1) (song)
  MO12 0064, MO45 0215
Dance With Me (Part 2) (song)
  MO12 0064, MO45 0215
Dancing In The Moonlight (song)
  RA45 0008
DANCING IN THE STREET
  (LP)
  TMLP 0099
Dancing In The Street (song)
  MO45 0124, SS45 0027, TM45 0185,
  TM45 0529
DANCING MACHINE (LP)
  TMLP 0274
Dancing Machine (song)
  MO12 0088, MO45 0251, TM45 0406
Dancing Machine (Instrumental)
  (song)
  MO12 0088
DANCING ON THE CEILING
  (CD)
  MOCD 0038
Dancing Slow (song)
  SS45 0042
Dancin' Like They Do On Soul
  Train (song)
  TM45 0505
Danger Heartbreak Dead Ahead
  (song)

TM45 0035
Dan The Banjo Man (song)
  RA45 0010
Dark Side Of The World (song)
  TM45 0244
DARLING BABY (LP)
  TMLP 0081
Darling Baby (song)
  TM45 0051, TM45 0143, TM45 0515
Darling Dear (song)
  TM45 0271
Darling, I Hum Our Song (song)
  SS45 0005, TM45 0042
DAVID RUFFIN (LP)
  TMLP 0227
Daylight & Darkness (song)
  MO45 0062
The Day Will Come Between
  Sunday And Monday (song)
  TM45 0240
The Day You Take One (You
  Have To Take The Other)
  (song)
  TM45 0109, TM45 0441
Dear Michael (song)
  TM45 0484
Deception (song)
  TM45 0494
DEEP IN MY SOUL (LP)
  MOLP 0012
Deep In My Soul (song)
  MO45 0132
Deep Inside My Soul (song)
  MO12 0157, MO45 0332
Deja Vu (I've Been Here Before)
  (song)
  MO45 0094
Destination, Anywhere (song)
  TM45 0202
Destiny (song)
  MO45 0211
Determination (song)
  TM45 0064, TM45 0401, TM45 0446
THE DETROIT SPINNERS (LP)
  TMLP 0060
THE DEVIL IN ME (LP)
  MOLP 0032
The Devil In Mrs. Jones (song)
  TM45 0517
DIAHANN CARROLL (LP)
  TMLP 0256
DIANA (LP)
  DSLP 0033
DIANA! (TV SOUNDTRACK)
  (LP)
  DSLP 0001
DIANA AND MARVIN (LP)
  DSLP 0015
DIANA ROSS (LP)
  TMLP 0158, TMLP 0314
DIANA ROSS & SUPREMES
  MEET THE
  TEMPTATIONS (LP)
  PILP 0013
DIANA ROSS & THE
  SUPREMES JOIN THE
  TEMPTATIONS (LP)
  TMLP 0096
DIANA ROSS PRESENTS THE
  JACKSON 5 (LP)
  TMLP 0142
DIANA'S DUETS (LP)

MOLP 0120
Didn't You Know (You'd Have
  To Cry Sometime) (song)
  TM45 0229, TM45 0405
DIGGIN' IN (LP)
  PRLP 0002
Diggin' It (song)
  PR45 0001
DISCOTECH (LP)
  TMLP 0294
Discover Me (song)
  TM45 0514
Distant Lover (song)
  TM45 0384
Doctor My Eyes (song)
  TM45 0344, TM45 0477
DOCTOR STRUT (LP)
  MOLP 0077
Do Dat (song)
  MO45 0079
Does Your Mama Know About
  Me (song)
  TM45 0155
Do I Do (song)
  MO12 0160, MO45 0218, MO45 0335
Do I Love You (Indeed I Do)
  (song)
  MO45 0118
Doin' The Best I Can (song)
  PR45 0006
DO IT BABY (LP)
  TMLP 0275
Do It Baby (song)
  TM45 0416
Do It For Me (song)
  MO45 0015
Do Like I Do (song)
  TM45 0478
Don't Drive Drunk (song)
  MO12 0147, MO45 0321
Don't Blame The Children (song)
  TM45 0391
Don't Bring Back Memories
  (song)
  TM45 0199
Don't Compare Me With Her
  (song)
  TM45 0038
Don't Drive Drunk (Instrumental)
  (song)
  MO12 0147, MO45 0321
Don't Ever Let Go (song)
  MO12 0133, MO45 0306
Don't Fool Around (song)
  TM45 0157, TM45 0411
Don't Freeze Up (Instrumental)
  (song)
  MO45 0027
Don't Freeze Up (song)
  MO45 0027
Don't Get Caught In The Middle
  (song)
  MO12 0107
Don't Give Up On Love (song)
  MO12 0043, MO45 0177
Don't Knock It (song)
  MO12 0102, MO45 0272
Don't Knock My Love (song)
  TM45 0455
Don't Leave Me This Way (song)
  MO12 0156, MO45 0008, MO45 0331
Don't Let Her Take Your Love

From Me (song)
TM45 0146
Don't Let Him Be Your Baby
(song)
OR45 0015
Don't Let Him Take Your Love
From Me (song)
TM45 0165
Don't Let It End (Till You Let It
Begin) (song)
TM45 0393
Don't Let The Baby Catch You
(song)
TM45 0397
Don't Let Up On the Groove
(song)
MO12 0082
DON'T LOOK ANY
FURTHER (LP)
MOLP 0161
Don't Look Any Further (song)
MO12 0112, MO45 0283
Don't Look Back (song)
MO12 0023, MO45 0106, TM45 0041
Don't Mess With Bill (song)
TM45 0046
Don't Mess With Mister "T"
(song)
TM45 0348
Don't Pity Me (song)
MO45 0065
DON'T STOP (LP)
MOLP 0054
Don't Take The Candy (song)
MO45 0295
Don't Take Your Love From Me
(song)
MO45 0135
Don't Take Your Love From Me
(Instrumental) (song)
MO45 0135
DON'T TOUCH ME (LP)
MOLP 0076
Don't Turn Your Back (song)
MO12 0120
Don't Wonder Why (song)
TM45 0274
Don't Worry 'Bout My Love
(song)
MO45 0067
Don't You Be Worried (song)
MO45 0154
Don't You Miss Me A Little Bit
Baby (song)
TM45 0118, TM45 0413
Don't You Worry 'Bout A Thing'
(song)
TM45 0410
Doobedood'ndoobe,
Doobedood'ndoobe,
Doobedood'ndoo (song)
TM45 0314
Do The Boomerang (song)
TM45 0020
DO THE TEMPTATIONS (LP)
TMLP 0332
Do Whatcha Wanna Do (song)
MO12 0061, MO45 0208
Do What You Gotta Do (song)
TM45 0211
The Down Sound (Part 1) (song)
MO45 0099

The Down Sound (Part 2) (song)
MO45 0099
DOWN TO EARTH (LP)
TMLP 0045, TMLP 0276
Down To Earth (song)
TM45 0033
DOWN TO LOVE TOWN (LP)
MOLP 0011
Down To Love Town (song)
TM45 0516
DO YOU LOVE ME (LP)
ORLP 0001
Do You Love Me (song)
OR45 0002, TM45 0401
Do You Love Me Just A Little,
Honey (song)
TM45 0104
Do You Really Love Your Baby
(song)
MO45 0359
Do You Really Love Your Baby
(Club mix) (song)
MO12 0183
Do You Really Love Your Baby
(Dub mix) (song)
MO12 0183
Do You Really Love Your Baby
(Radio edit) (song)
MO12 0183
Do Yourself A Favor (song)
TM45 0410
Do You See Me (song)
RA45 0018
Do You See My Love (For You
Growing) (song)
TM45 0252
Dream Maker (song)
MO45 0069
The Drought Is Over (song)
MO45 0193
DYNAMIC DIANA (LP)
PILP 0005
DYNAMITE (LP)
TMLP 0202
Dynamite (song)
MO12 0121, MO45 0293
Early Morning Love (song)
TM45 0490
EASY (LP)
TMLP 0132
Easy (song)
MO45 0021
Ebony Eyes (song)
MO12 0106, MO45 0276
Echo (song)
MO12 0126, MO45 0299
ECOLOGY (LP)
TMLP 0179
EDDIE KENDRICKS (LP)
TMLP 0244
Eddie's Love (song)
TM45 0390
Ego Tripping Out (song)
MO12 0025, MO45 0116
Ego Tripping Out (Instrumental)
(song)
MO45 0116
18 GREATEST HITS (CD)
MOCD 0005
Either Way We Lose (song)
MO45 0214
End (song)

RA45 0007
Endless Love (song)
MO45 0188
Endless Love (Instrumental) (song)
MO45 0188
The End Of Our Road (song)
TM45 0146
ESCENAS DE AMOR (LP)
MOLP 0133
ESSAR (LP)
MOLP 0165
AN EVENING WITH DIANA
ROSS (LP)
X2LP 0018
Even Tho' (song)
MO45 0262
Ever Had A Dream (song)
MO45 0100
EVERTHING'S COMING UP
LOVE (LP)
TMLP 0322
EVERY BEAT OF MY HEART
(LP)
PILP 0006
Everybody Loves Me (song)
MO45 0193
EVERYBODY NEEDS LOVE
(LP)
TMLP 0058
Everybody Needs Love (song)
TM45 0120, TM45 0150, TM45 0241,
TM45 0487
Everybody's Angel (song)
TM45 0034
Everybody's Got The Right To
Love (song)
TM45 0249
Everyday Love (song)
MO12 0066, MO45 0219
Every Little Bit Hurts (song)
SS45 0018
EVERYTHING IS
EVERYTHING (LP)
TMLP 0177
Everything Is Everything (song)
TM45 0395
Everything Is Good About You
(song)
TM45 0048
Everything Will Rhyme (song)
RA45 0010
Every Time I See You I Go Wild
(song)
TM45 0127
Everywhere I Go (song)
MW45 0021
Evil (song)
TM45 0430
LOS EXITOS DE JOSE
FELICIANO (LP)
MOLP 0179
EXPOSED (LP)
TMLP 0193
Extracts From Speeches By Rev.
Martin Luther King
MO12 0105
F.I.M.A. (Funk In Mama Afrika)
(song)
MO45 0129
THE FABULOUS FOUR TOPS
(LP)
PILP 0002

MO45 0317
Heartbreak (Instrumental) (song)
  MO45 0317
Heartbreak Road (song)
  SS45 0012
The Heart Is Not So Smart (song)
  MO12 0184, MO45 0360
Hearts On Fire (song)
  MO12 0144, MO45 0319
Hearts On Fire (Remix) (song)
  MO12 0144
HEAT WAVE (LP)
  TMLP 0005
Heatwave (song)
  MO45 0124, SS45 0001
Heaven Help Us All (song)
  TM45 0259
Heaven Knows (song)
  MO12 0074, MO45 0231
Heaven Must Have Sent You
    (song)
  MO12 0008, MO12 0157, MO45 0082,
  MO45 0332, TM45 0083, TM45 0273
Heaven Must Have Sent You
    (New version) (song)
  MO45 0093
Heavy Day (song)
  TM45 0428
Heavy Love (song)
  TM45 0500
Heavy Love Affair (song)
  MO12 0046, MO45 0180
Heavy On Pride (song)
  MO45 0139
He Doesn't Love Her Anymore
    (song)
  TM45 0082
He Holds His Own (song)
  TM45 0027
Hell Is On The Run (song)
  MO12 0133, MO45 0306
Hell Is On The Run
    (Instrumental) (song)
  MO12 0133
Hello (song)
  MO12 0109, MO45 0279
HELLO BROADWAY (LP)
  TMLP 0015
Hello Detroit (song)
  MO12 0127, MO45 0300
Hello Detroit (Instrumental) (song)
  MO12 0127, MO45 0300
HELL UP IN HARLEM (LP)
  TMLP 0259
Helpless (song)
  TM45 0054
HELP ME MAKE IT
    THROUGH THE NIGHT
    (LP)
  TMLP 0225
Help Me Make It Through The
    Night (song)
  MO45 0043, TM45 0332
Help Yourself (song)
  TM45 0399
He Means The World To Me
    (song)
  SS45 0024
HERE COMES THE JUDGE
    (LP)
  TMLP 0086
Here Comes The Judge (song)

TM45 0164
Here Comes The Night (song)
  RA45 0005
Here I Am Baby (song)
  TM45 0160, TM45 0362
HERE MY DEAR (LP)
  X2LP 0021
Here's My Love (song)
  MO45 0148
HEROES (LP)
  DSLP 0034
Heroes (song)
  MO45 0154
He's A Cobra (song)
  MO12 0149, MO45 0323
He's A Cobra (Remix) (song)
  MO12 0149
HE'S A FRIEND (LP)
  TMLP 0308
He's A Friend (song)
  TM45 0499
He's A Good Guy (Yes He Is)
    (song)
  SS45 0010
He's All I Got (song)
  TM45 0060
He's A Pretender (song)
  MO12 0082
He's A Pretender (Part 1) (song)
  MO45 0243
He's A Pretender (Part 2) (song)
  MO45 0243
He's Gone (song)
  MO45 0148
Hesitated (song)
  MO45 0245
He's Leaving Home (song)
  MO12 0090, MO45 0255
He's Misstra Know-It-All (song)
  MO12 0162, MO45 0337, TM45 0394
He's My Man (song)
  TM45 0452
He's My Sunny Boy (song)
  TM45 0222
He Was Really Saying Somethin'
    (song)
  MO45 0072, SS45 0044, TM45 0095
He Who Picks A Rose (song)
  TM45 0256
Hey Big Brother (song)
  RA45 0004
Hey Diddle Diddle (song)
  TM45 0074
Hey Girl (I Like Your Style)
    (song)
  TM45 0389
HEY HARMONICA MAN (LP)
  SSLP 0008
Hey Harmonica Man (song)
  SS45 0021
Hey You (song)
  MO12 0080, MO45 0240
HIGH ENERGY (LP)
  TMLP 0319
Higher Ground (song)
  TM45 0371
HIGHER THAN HIGH (LP)
  TMLP 0301
Higher Than High (song)
  TM45 0492
High Heel Sneakers (song)
  TM45 0032

HIGH INERGY (LP)
  MOLP 0114
HIGH ON SUNSHINE (LP)
  MOLP 0063
High On Sunshine (song)
  TM45 0512
High On Your Love Suite (song)
  MO12 0011, MO45 0085
High Tide (song)
  MW45 0029
Hip City (Part 1) (song)
  TM45 0168
Hip City (Part 2) (song)
  TM45 0168
HIT AND RUN LOVER (LP)
  MOLP 0168
THE HIT MAN (LP)
  TMLP 0293
THE HITS OF EDWIN STARR
    (LP)
  TMLP 0208
HITS OF GOLD (LP)
  PILP 0014
THE HITS OF MARVIN GAYE
    (LP)
  TMLP 0200
HITS OF THE SIXTIES (LP)
  TMLP 0011
HITSVILLE U.S.A. (LP)
  TMLP 0019
HITSVILLE, U.S.A. NO. 1 (EP)
  TMEP 0001
HITTIN' (EP)
  TMEP 0017
HI! WE'RE THE MIRACLES
    (LP)
  ORLP 0002
Hold Me (song)
  MO12 0170, MO45 0346, TM45 0113
Hold Me (Instrumental) (song)
  MO12 0170, MO45 0346
Hold Me Oh My Darling (song)
  TM45 0126
HOLD ON (LP)
  MOLP 0101
Hold On To My Love (song)
  MO45 0162
Hold On To Your Love (song)
  MO12 0187, MO45 0363
Holly (song)
  MO45 0024
HOLLYWOOD (LP)
  MWLP 0005
Hollywood (song)
  MO12 0003, MO45 0058
HOME COOKIN' (LP)
  TMLP 0097
Home Cookin' (song)
  TM45 0183
Honey Chile (song)
  TM45 0137
Honey Come Back (song)
  TM45 0230, TM45 0286
Hooked For Life (song)
  MO45 0076
Hooked On Your Love (song)
  TM45 0449
Hope (song)
  MO12 0041, MO45 0172
Hope I Don't Get My Heart
    Broke (song)
  TM45 0296

Hot (song)
MO12 0041

Hot California Beach (song)
RA45 0018

Hot Cha (song)
TM45 0009

Hot Cross Buns (song)
LO45 0001

Hot 'N' Tot (song)
SS45 0031

HOT ON THE TRACKS (LP)
TMLP 0323

HOT SHOT (LP)
TMLP 0310

HOT SMOKEY (LP)
PILP 0010

Hot Spot (song)
MO12 0175, MO45 0351

Hot Spot (Club Mix) (song)
MO12 0175

HOTTER THAN JULY (LP)
DSLP 0035

HOUSE PARTY (LP)
TMLP 0298

How About You (song)
TM45 0270

How Can I (song)
TM45 0014

How Can I Forget (song)
TM45 0172, TM45 0235

How Can You Say That It's Over
(song)
MO12 0193, MO45 0369

How Many Days (song)
TM45 0435

How Sweet It Is (song)
MO12 0155, MO45 0330

HOW SWEET IT IS TO BE
LOVED BY YOU (LP)
TMLP 0004

How Sweet It Is (To Be Loved
By You) (song)
SS45 0033, TM45 0071, TM45 0316

HUGH MASEKELA AND THE
UNION OF SOUTH
AFRICA (LP)
RALP 0002

The Humming Song (Lost For
Words) (song)
MO45 0112

The Hunch (song)
LO45 0001

Hungry For Love (song)
TM45 0309

The Hunter Gets Captured By
The Game (song)
TM45 0094

Hurt A Little Everyday (song)
TM45 0081

I Ain't Going Nowhere (song)
MO45 0018, TM45 0396

I Ain't Gonna Do It (song)
TM45 0372

I Ain't Gonna Stand For It (song)
MO12 0160, MO45 0163, MO45 0335

I Am Love (song)
TM45 0444

I Am Love (Part 2) (song)
TM45 0444

I AM MY BROTHER'S
KEEPER (LP)
TMLP 0175

I Am The Man For You Baby
(song)
TM45 0147

I Am Your Man (song)
TM45 0360

I Believe (When I Fall In Love It
Will Be Forever) (song)
MW45 0019

I CALL IT PRETTY MUSIC,
BUT THE OLD PEOPLE
CALL IT THE BLUES (EP)
SSEP 0002

I CAN MAKE IT HAPPEN (LP)
MOLP 0149

I Can't Believe You Love Me
(song)
TM45 0216

I Can't Dance To That Music
You're Playing (song)
TM45 0170

I Can't Get Next To You (song)
TM45 0223

I Can't Give Back The Love I
Feel For You (song)
TM45 0144, TM45 0293

I Can't Go On Living Without
Your Love (song)
MO45 0050

I Can't Help Myself (song)
MO45 0068, MO45 0119, MW45 0027,
MW45 0031, TM45 0233, TM45 0316

I Can't Let Maggie Go (song)
MW45 0018

I Can't Quit Your Love (song)
TM45 0360, TM45 0479

I Can't Stop (song)
MO45 0214

I Can't Stop The Rain (song)
MO45 0026

I Can't Wait To Make You Mine
(song)
MO12 0167, MO45 0343

I Choose You (song)
TM45 0364

I Could Never Love Another
(After Loving You) (song)
TM45 0159

I'd Be A Fool Right Now (song)
TM45 0218

I'd Do It All Again (song)
MO45 0366

I Don't Blame You At All (song)
TM45 0276

I Don't Know (song)
MO12 0053, MO45 0196

I Don't Know Why (I Love You)
(song)
TM45 0191

I Don't Wanna Be Reminded
(song)
TM45 0517

I Don't Want Nobody To Know
(song)
MO45 0030

I Don't Want To Do Wrong (song)
TM45 0307, TM45 0342

I'd Rather Be Gone (song)
MO12 0089, MO45 0253

If Anyone Can (song)
TM45 0481

I Feel Sanctified (song)
MO45 0021, TM45 0446

If I Could Build Me Whole World
Around You (song)
TM45 0136

If I Don't Get All The Luck (song)
MW45 0015

If I Love You Tonight (song)
MO45 0162

IF I ONLY KNEW (LP)
MOLP 0192

If It's Love (It's Alright) (song)
OR45 0009

If It's Magic (song)
MO45 0174

If I Were A Carpenter (song)
TM45 0148, TM45 0460

IF I WERE YOUR WOMAN
(LP)
TMLP 0186

If I Were Your Woman (song)
TM45 0267, TM45 0457

If Love Must Go (song)
MO45 0105

If My Heart Could Sing (song)
SS45 0023

If My Heart Could Tell The Story
(song)
TM45 0193

I Found A Girl (song)
OR45 0010

I Found Myself A Brand New
Baby (song)
OR45 0004

I Found That Girl (song)
TM45 0248

I Found The Feeling (song)
MO45 0053

If This World Were Mine (song)
TM45 0136

If You Can Learn How To Cry
(song)
TM45 0498

If You Can Want (song)
TM45 0149

If You Don't Know Me By Now
(song)
MO45 0220

If You Don't Want Me (song)
MO45 0247

If You Feel It (song)
MO12 0156, MO45 0331

If You Let Me (song)
TM45 0347

If You Really Love Me (song)
TM45 0281, TM45 0300

If You're Gonna Leave (Just
Leave) (song)
TM45 0332

If You Should Ever Be Lonely
(song)
MO12 0191, MO45 0367

If You Should Ever Be Lonely
(Instrumental) (song)
MO12 0191, MO45 0367

If You Take Away The Pain
Until The Morning (song)
MO45 0259

If You Think You're Lonely Now
(song)
MO12 0129

If You Will Let Me, I Know I Can
(song)
TM45 0227

I Got A Feeling (song)
MO45 0081, TM45 0101, TM45 0129,
TM45 0290, TM45 0305
I Gotta Dance To Keep From
Crying (song)
SS45 0008
I Gotta Have A Song (song)
TM45 0259
I Gotta Let You Go (song)
TM45 0264
I Guess I'll Always Love You
(song)
TM45 0072, TM45 0133, TM45 0184
I Guess I'll Miss The Man (song)
TM45 0386
I HEAR A SYMPHONY (LP)
TMLP 0028
I Hear A Symphony (song)
MO12 0195, TM45 0043, TM45 0072
I Heard It Through The
Grapevine (song)
MO12 0194, MO45 0370, TM45 0130,
TM45 0187, TM45 0425, TM45 0523
I Hear The Children Singing (song)
MO45 0185
I Just Called To Say I Love You
(song)
MO12 0125, MO45 0298
I Just Can't Walk Away (song)
MO12 0100
I Just Called To Say I Love You
(Instrumental) (song)
MO12 0125, MO45 0298
I Just Can't Walk Away (song)
MO45 0270
I Just Keep Thinking About You
Baby (song)
MO12 0014, MO45 0088
I Just Wanna Dance With You
(song)
MO45 0182
I Just Want To Celebrate (song)
RA45 0002
I Keep Running (song)
MO12 0145, MO12 0146, MO45 0320
(I Know) I'm Losing You (song)
RA45 0014, TM45 0087, TM45 0315
I Like Everything About You
(song)
TM45 0068
I Like It (song)
MO12 0108, MO45 0245
I LIKE IT LIKE THAT (LP)
TMLP 0003
I Like It Like That (song)
SS45 0022
I LIKE YOUR STYLE (LP)
MOLP 0117
I Like Your Style (song)
TM45 0324
I'll Always Do The Best I Can
(song)
RA45 0020
I'll Always Love You (song)
TM45 0023, TM45 0128
I'll Be Doggone (song)
TM45 0010
I'll Be In Trouble (song)
SS45 0020
I'll Be There (song)
MO45 0251, TM45 0260, TM45 0471
I'll Do It (song)

MO45 0311
I'll Do It All Again (Foot mix)
(song)
MO12 0190
I'll Do It All Again (Head mix)
(song)
MO12 0190
I'll Have To Let Him Go (song)
OR45 0011
I'll Keep A Light In My Window
(song)
MO12 0148, MO45 0322, MO45 0359,
TM45 0483
I'll Keep Holding On (song)
TM45 0018
I'll Never Fall In Love Again
(song)
MO12 0108, MO45 0278
I'LL PICK A ROSE FOR MY
ROSE (LP)
TMLP 0111
I'll Pick A Rose For My Rose
(song)
TM45 0181, TM45 0530
I'll Say Forever My Love (song)
TM45 0150, TM45 0241, TM45 0463
I'll Stand By You (song)
SS45 0016
I'll Take Care Of You (song)
TM45 0119
I'll Turn To Stone (song)
TM45 0112, TM45 0331
I Lost My Love In The Big City
(song)
TM45 0340
I Love Makin' Love (song)
MO45 0153
I Love The Nearness Of You
(song)
MO45 0139
I Love To See You Dance (song)
MO45 0074
I Love To Sing To You (song)
MO45 0132
I Love You (song)
TM45 0139
I Love You Madly (Instrumental)
(song)
TM45 0179
I Love You Madly (song)
TM45 0179
I Love You So (song)
MO45 0232
I'm A Bachelor (song)
MO45 0011
I'm A Fool For You (song)
TM45 0421
I'm A Sucker For Your Love
(song)
MO12 0019, MO45 0094
I'm A Sucker For Your Love
(Instrumental) (song)
MO12 0019
I'm A Winner (song)
TM45 0294
I'm Coming Home (song)
MO45 0145
I'm Coming Out (song)
MO12 0037, MO12 0161, MO45 0158,
MO45 0336
I'm Crazy 'Bout My Baby (song)
SS45 0004

I'm Falling In Love With You
(song)
TM45 0381, TM45 0455
I'm Fascinated (song)
MO12 0193, MO45 0369
I'm Glad About It (song)
TM45 0295
I'm Goin' Left (song)
TM45 0428
I'm Gonna Have My Cake (And
Eat It Too) (song)
MO12 0023, MO45 0106
I'm Gonna Let My Heart Do The
Walking (song)
TM45 0507
I'm Gonna Make You Love Me
(song)
TM45 0186, TM45 0523
I'm Here Again (song)
MO45 0036
I'm In A Different World (song)
TM45 0176, TM45 0376
I'm In Love (song)
MO12 0176, MO45 0352
I'm In Love Again (song)
TM45 0001
I'm In Love With You (song)
MO12 0091, MO12 0138, MO45 0312
I'm In The World (song)
MO45 0098
I Miss You Baby (song)
TM45 0214, TM45 0475
I'm Just A Part Of Yesterday
(song)
MW45 0005
I'm Just Too Shy (song)
MO45 0191
I'm Learning To Trust My Man
(song)
MW45 0009, TM45 0480
I'm Letting Go (song)
MW45 0004
I'm Living In Shame (song)
TM45 0196
I'm Looking For Love (song)
TM45 0426
I'm Losing You (song)
MW45 0016
I'm Loving You Softly (song)
MO45 0077
I'm More Than Happy (I'm
Satisfied) (song)
TM45 0245
I'm My Brother's Keeper (song)
MO45 0202
I'm Never Gonna Say Goodbye
(song)
MO45 0232
I'm Not A Plaything (song)
TM45 0025, TM45 0238
I'm Not Strong Enough (To Love
You Again) (song)
MO45 0078
I'm Ready For Love (song)
TM45 0082
I'm So Glad (song)
TM45 0505
I'm So Glad I Got Somebody
(Like You Around) (song)
TM45 0196
I'm So Happy (song)
TM45 0311

I'm Still Loving You (song)
TM45 0011
I'M STILL WAITING (LP)
TMLP 0192
I'm Still Waiting (song)
TM45 0283, TM45 0519
I'm The Exception To The Rule
(song)
TM45 0021, TM45 0308
I'm The One You Need (song)
TM45 0459
I Must Be In Love (song)
MO12 0060, MO45 0207
I'm Wondering (song)
TM45 0127
IN A MELLOW MOOD (LP)
TMLP 0068
In And Out (song)
MO12 0076, MO12 0169, MO45 0234,
MO45 0345
In And Out Of Love (song)
TM45 0133
IN A SPECIAL WAY (LP)
MOLP 0157
Include Me In Your Life (song)
TM45 0392
IN CONCERT (LP)
RALP 0008
INDIANA WANTS ME (LP)
TMLP 0184
Indiana Wants Me (song)
TM45 0265, TM45 0470
I Need Someone (song)
TM45 0140
I Need You (song)
TM45 0389
I Need You Right Now (song)
MO45 0066
I Need Your Lovin' (song)
MO12 0033, MO12 0159, MO45 0151,
MO45 0334, TM45 0217
I Never Thought I'd Be Losing
You (song)
MO45 0057
IN FULL BLOOM (LP)
TMLP 0145
IN GOOD TASTE (LP)
MOLP 0023
IN LOVING MEMORY (LP)
TMLP 0124
In My House (song)
MO12 0151, MO45 0326
In My House (Instrumental) (song)
MO12 0151, MO45 0326
In My Lonely Room (song)
SS45 0017
IN MY STRIDE (LP)
MOLP 0021
Inner City Blues (Make Me
Wanna Holler) (song)
TM45 0319
INNERVISIONS (CD)
MOCD 0028
INNERVISIONS (LP)
DSLP 0011
IN OUR LIFETIME (LP)
MOLP 0106
INSIDE YOU (LP)
MWLP 0008
IN SQUARE CIRCLE (CD)
MOCD 0027
IN SQUARE CIRCLE (LP)

MOLP 0159
IN THE GROOVE (LP)
TMLP 0091
IN THE POCKET (LP)
MOLP 0113
Into Each Rain A Little Life
Must Fall (song)
MO45 0244
INVITATION TO LOVE (LP)
MOLP 0103
INVOLVED (LP)
TMLP 0198
I Promise To Wait My Love (song)
TM45 0158
IRONS IN THE FIRE (LP)
MOLP 0100
Irons In The Fire (song)
MO45 0151
IRRESISTIBLE TAMMI
TERRELL (LP)
TMLP 0103
I Second That Emotion (song)
MO45 0213, TM45 0132, TM45 0210,
TM45 0459
I See You For The First Time
(song)
TM45 0498
Island Lady (song)
MO12 0032, MO45 0146
Isn't The Night Fantastic (song)
MO12 0140, MO45 0314
Is Your Teacher Cool? (song)
PR45 0007
It Ain't Easy Comin' Down (song)
MO45 0221, PR45 0002
IT ALL COMES OUT IN MY
SONG (LP)
MOLP 0029
I Think I Can Change You (song)
TM45 0094
I Thought I Could Handle It (song)
MO12 0112, MO45 0283
I Thought It Took A Little Time
(But Today I Fell In Love)
(song)
TM45 0510
It Hurt Me Too (song)
OR45 0008
It Is As Good As You Make It
(song)
TM45 0437
It Must Be Love (song)
OR45 0015
IT MUST BE MAGIC (LP)
MOLP 0111
It Must Be Magic (song)
MO12 0052, MO45 0195
I Tried (song)
TM45 0170
I Truly, Truly Believe (song)
TM45 0142
It's A Crying Shame (song)
TM45 0012
It's A Lifetime Thing (song)
MO45 0022
It's All In The Game (song)
TM45 0237, TM45 0467
It's Another Sunday (song)
TM45 0369
It's A Shame (song)
MO45 0137, TM45 0257
Its' Bad For Me To See You

(song)
TM45 0503
It's Been A Long Time (song)
TM45 0116
It's Gonna Be Hard Times (song)
TM45 0289
It's Got To Be A Miracle (This
Thing Called Love) (song)
TM45 0090, TM45 0279
It's Growing (song)
TM45 0004
It Should Have Been Me (song)
TM45 0161, TM45 0491
It's Just Me Feeling Good (song)
MO45 0065
It's More Than You (song)
MO12 0139, MO45 0313
It's My House (song)
MO12 0026, MO45 0117
It's My Turn (song)
MO45 0165
It's Not Too Late (song)
OR45 0009
It's Out Of The Question (song)
TM45 0184
It's So Hard Being A Loser (song)
TM45 0105
It's So Hard For Me To Say
Goodbye (song)
TM45 0349
It's So Real (song)
MO12 0021, MO45 0096
It's So Sad (song)
MW45 0010
It's Summer (song)
TM45 0175, TM45 0251, TM45 0285
It's The Same Old Song (song)
MO45 0068, TM45 0028, TM45 0305
IT'S THE TEMPTATIONS (EP)
TMEP 0010
IT'S TIME (LP)
MOLP 0067
It's Time To Go Now (song)
TM45 0130
It's Too Bad (song)
OR45 0004
It's Too Late To Change The
Time (song)
TM45 0406
It's Wonderful (song)
TM45 0463
It's Wonderful (To Be Loved By
You) (song)
TM45 0255
It Takes Two (song)
TM45 0090
It Will Come In Time (song)
MO45 0123
I Understand My Man (song)
TM45 0116
I've Been Good To You (song)
FO45 0002, TM45 0008, TM45 0121
I've Been Waiting (song)
MO12 0175, MO45 0351
(I've Given You) The Best Years
Of My Life (song)
TM45 0345
I've Got A Radio (song)
MO45 0311
I've Gotta Find Myself A Brand
New Baby (song)
TM45 0190

(I've Gotta) Little Black Book
(song)
  MO12 0120, MO45 0292
I've Got To Find A Way To Win
Maria Back (song)
  TM45 0228
I've Got To Find It (song)
  TM45 0123
I've Lost Everything I've Ever
Loved (song)
  TM45 0212
I've Made Love To You A
Thousand Times (song)
  MO12 0083, MO45 0244
I'VE NEVER BEEN TO ME
(LP)
  MOLP 0128
I've Never Been To Me (song)
  MO45 0209, PR45 0004
I've Passed This Way Before
(song)
  TM45 0093, TM45 0204, TM45 0436
I Wanna Be Where You Are
(song)
  MO45 0201, TM45 0328
I Wanna Be With You (song)
  TM45 0393
I Wanna Do It To You (song)
  MO45 0045
I Wanna Make It (In Your World)
(song)
  MO12 0008, MO45 0082
I Want A Guy (song)
  FO45 0003
I Want A Love I Can See (song)
  TM45 0134
I Want Her Love (song)
  TM45 0118
I Want My Baby Back (song)
  TM45 0131
I Want To Come Back As A Song
(song)
  MO45 0236
I Want To Go Back There Again
(song)
  MO12 0128, TM45 0139, TM45 0301
I WANT YOU (LP)
  TMLP 0317
I Want You (song)
  TM45 0504
I Want You (Instrumental) (song)
  TM45 0504
I Want You Around (song)
  SS45 0035
I Want You Back (song)
  MO45 0029, TM45 0225, TM45 0465
I Was Born This Way
(Instrumental) (song)
  MO45 0056
I Was Born This Way (song)
  GA45 0001, MO45 0056
I WAS MADE TO LOVE HER
(LP)
  TMLP 0059
I Was Made To Love Her (song)
  TM45 0113, TM45 0461
I Wasn't Wrong About You (song)
  MW45 0032
I Was Raised (song)
  RA45 0007
I Will Never Let You Get Away
(song)

TM45 0424
I Wish (song)
  MO12 0158, MO45 0002, MO45 0333,
  TM45 0532
I Wish It Would Rain (song)
  TM45 0142, TM45 0175, TM45 0370,
  TM45 0487
I Wish I Were Your Mirror (song)
  TM45 0272
JACKIE JACKSON (LP)
  TMLP 0248
THE JACKSON 5 (LP)
  PILP 0003
Jamie (song)
  FO45 0004
Janet (song)
  MO12 0176, MO45 0352
THE JAZZ SOUL OF LITTLE
STEVIE WONDER (LP)
  SSLP 0003
Jealous Lover (song)
  OR45 0013
Jefferson Ball (song)
  MO45 0104
JERMAINE (LP)
  MOLP 0104, TMLP 0220
Jesus Is Love (song)
  MO45 0166
Je Vous Aime Beaucoup (I Love
You) (song)
  MO12 0028, MO45 0131
Jimmy Brown (song)
  TM45 0034
Jimmy Mack (song)
  TM45 0099, TM45 0529
JIMMY RUFFIN - FOREVER
(LP)
  TMLP 0160
THE JIMMY RUFFIN WAY
(LP)
  TMLP 0048
Johnny Raven (song)
  TM45 0402
JOSE FELICIANO (LP)
  MOLP 0118
JOURNEY THROUGH THE
SECRET LIFE OF PLANTS
(CD)
  MOCD 0015
Joy (song)
  MO12 0035, MO45 0156
JOYFUL JUKEBOX MUSIC
(LP)
  MOLP 0003
JOYSTICK (LP)
  MOLP 0158
Joystick (song)
  MO12 0107
JUKEBOX (LP)
  MOLP 0182
JUNIOR WALKER AND THE
ALL STARS (LP)
  TMLP 0273
JUNIOR WALKER'S
GREATEST HITS (LP)
  TMLP 0120
Just Ain't Enough Love (song)
  TM45 0106
Just A Little Bit Of You (song)
  TM45 0484
Just A Little Misunderstanding
(song)

TM45 0064, TM45 0224
Just As Long As There Is You
(song)
  MO45 0001, TM45 0531
Just As Long As You Need Me
(song)
  TM45 0053
Just Believe In Love (song)
  MO12 0085, MO45 0248
Just How Does It Feel (song)
  PR45 0008
Just Keep Laughin' (song)
  PR45 0001
Just Let Me Know (song)
  SS45 0011
(Just Like) Romeo And Juliet
(song)
  TM45 0409
Just Look What You've Done
(song)
  TM45 0108, TM45 0201
Just Loving You (song)
  TM45 0011
Just Memories (song)
  TM45 0347
Just My Imagination (song)
  MO12 0065, MO45 0216
Just My Imagination (Running
Away With Me) (song)
  TM45 0275, TM45 0521
Just My Soul Responding (song)
  TM45 0385
Just Passing Through (song)
  TM45 0451
Just Put Some Love In Your
Heart (song)
  MO12 0075, MO45 0233
Just Say, Just Say (song)
  TM45 0422
Just Seven Numbers (Can
Straighten Out My Life) (song)
  TM45 0272
Just The Way You Are (song)
  MO45 0101
Just To Be Closer To You (song)
  TM45 0516
Just To Be Close To You (song)
  MO45 0006, MO45 0075
Just Walk In My Shoes (song)
  TM45 0076, TM45 0315
JUST WE TWO (LP)
  TMLP 0131
Just When Things Are Getting
Good (song)
  MO45 0020
Keep An Eye (song)
  TM45 0314
KEEP IT LIVE (LP)
  MOLP 0130
Keep It Live (song)
  MO12 0072, MO45 0228
Keep Off, No Trespassing (song)
  TM45 0160
Keep On Jammin' (song)
  MO12 0169, MO45 0345
Keep On Smilin' (song)
  MO12 0163, MO45 0339
Keep On Truckin' (Part 1) (song)
  TM45 0375
Keep On Truckin' (Part 2) (song)
  TM45 0375
Keep Tryin' (song)

MO45 0037
KIDD GLOVE (LP)
MOLP 0162
KIM WESTON (EP)
TMEP 0005
Kiss Me Baby (song)
TM45 0005
Kiss Me Now (song)
TM45 0502
KNIGHT TIME (LP)
TMLP 0278
Knocks Me Off My Feet (song)
MO45 0163
KOKO-POP (LP)
MOLP 0171
L.A. (My Town) (song)
TM45 0325
Ladies Choice (Instrumental)
(song)
MO12 0097
Ladies Choice (song)
MO12 0097
LADY SINGS THE BLUES (CD)
MOCD 0036
LADY SINGS THE BLUES (LP)
X2LP 0008
LADY TEENA (LP)
MOLP 0087
Lady, Would You Like To Dance
(song)
MC45 0002
Lady (You Bring Me Up) (song)
MO12 0049, MO45 0186
Laid Back Country Picker (song)
HI45 0002
Land Of A Thousand Boys (song)
SS45 0018
THE LAST DANCE (LP)
TVLP 0002, TVLP 0006
THE LAST DRAGON (CD)
MOCD 0026
Last Song (song)
MO45 0155
LAST TIME I SAW HIM (LP)
TMLP 0254
Last Time I Saw Him (song)
TM45 0395
LATE AT NIGHT (LP)
MOLP 0073
Lately (song)
MO45 0174
Laughing Boy (song)
OR45 0014
Laughter In The Rain (song)
MW45 0015
LAW OF THE LAND (LP)
TMLP 0239
Law Of The Land (song)
TM45 0368, TM45 0445
Leave Me Now (song)
MO45 0168
Leaving Me Was The Best Thing
You've Ever Done (song)
MO45 0115
Let It All Blow (song)
MO12 0137
Let It All Blow (Instrumental)
(song)
MO12 0137
Let It Rise (song)
MO45 0149
Let It Whip (song)

MO12 0066, MO45 0219
Let Me Be The Clock (song)
MO45 0130
Let Me Count The Ways (I Love
You) (song)
MO45 0005
Let Me Get Close To You (song)
MO45 0035
LET ME TICKLE YOUR
FANCY (LP)
MOLP 0131
Let Me Tickle Your Fancy (song)
MO12 0070, MO45 0225
Let's Be Young Tonight (song)
TM45 0518
Let's Break (song)
MO12 0104
Let's Break (Instrumental) (song)
MO12 0104
Let's Dance (song)
TM45 0013
Let's Do It Right (song)
TM45 0485
LET'S GET IT ON (LP)
DSLP 0013
Let's Get It On (song)
TM45 0370
LET'S GET SERIOUS (LP)
MOLP 0084
Let's Get Serious (song)
MO12 0028, MO45 0131
Let's Go Get Out Of Town (song)
MO45 0045
Let's Go Somewhere (song)
TM45 0398
Let's Make A Deal (Part 1) (song)
MO45 0042
Let's Make A Deal (Part 2) (song)
MO45 0042
Let's Make Love Now (song)
TM45 0317
Let's Make Love On The
Telephone (song)
MO45 0201
Let's Say Goodbye Tomorrow
(song)
TM45 0269
Let's Stay Together (song)
MO12 0078, MO45 0237
LET THE SUNSHINE IN (LP)
TMLP 0114
Let Your Hair Down (song)
TM45 0415
Let Yourself Go (song)
PR45 0008
Liberation (song)
GA45 0001
Life And Breath (song)
MW45 0034
Life Of A Cowboy (song)
MO12 0051, MO45 0192
The Life Of The Party (song)
TM45 0429
Light At The End Of The Tunnel
(song)
MO12 0153, MO45 0328
Lighting Up The Night (song)
MO12 0165, MO45 0341
LIGHT THE NIGHT (LP)
MOLP 0177
Light Years (Opus IV) (song)
MO45 0064

Lil' Red Riding Hood (song)
TM45 0445
LIONEL RICHIE (CD)
MOCD 0029
LIONEL RICHIE (LP)
DSLP 0037
A Little Bit For Sandy (song)
TM45 0171
A Little Bit Of Sympathy, A
Little Bit Of Love (song)
SS45 0025
Little Bitty Pretty One (song)
TM45 0327
Little Darling (I Love You) (song)
TM45 0298
Little Darling (I Need You) (song)
TM45 0074
Little Girl Blue (song)
SS45 0006
Little Girl Don't You Worry
(song)
MO45 0160
A LITTLE KNIGHT MUSIC
(LP)
TMLP 0305
Little Lady (song)
MO12 0120, MO45 0292
Little Miss Sweetness (song)
TM45 0087, TM45 0209
A Little More Love (song)
SS45 0032
Little Ole Boy, Little Ole Girl
(song)
TM45 0156
LIVE (LP)
DSLP 0018, TMLP 0107, TMLP 0152,
TMLP 0247, X2LP 0020
LIVE AT THE COPA (LP)
TMLP 0104
LIVE AT THE LONDON
PALLADIUM (LP)
X2LP 0019
LIVE AT THE TALK OF THE
TOWN (LP)
TMLP 0070, TMLP 0141, TMLP 0163
Live Wire (song)
SS45 0009, TM45 0195
Living For The City (song)
TM45 0383
Living In A World I Created For
Myself (song)
TM45 0269
Livin' Without You (song)
MW45 0012
Locking Up My Heart (song)
OR45 0012
Londonderry (song)
MW45 0008
Londonderry (Instrumental) (song)
RA45 0013
(Loneliness Made Me Realise) It's
You That I Need (song)
TM45 0134
Lonely Desire (song)
MO45 0144
Lonely Lonely Girl Am I (song)
TM45 0021
Lonely Lonely Man (song)
TM45 0165
Lonely Teardrops (song)
MO45 0254
Look Around (song)

TM45 0354

LOOKIN' THROUGH THE
WINDOWS (LP)
TMLP 0213

Lookin' Through The Windows
(song)
TM45 0335, TM45 0477

The Look Of Love (song)
TM45 0346

Look What You've Done To Me
(song)
MO45 0006

Loran's Dance (song)
MO45 0101

Love Bug Leave My Heart Alone
(song)
TM45 0122

Love Can Be Hazardous To Your
Health (song)
TM45 0495

LOVE BREEZE (LP)
MOLP 0038

LOVE CHILD (LP)
TMLP 0095

Love Child (song)
TM45 0178, TM45 0462

LOVE DANCER (LP)
MOLP 0070

Love Feels Like Fire (song)
TM45 0331

Love Gun (song)
MO45 0122

Love Hangover (song)
MO12 0027, MO12 0154, MO45 0329,
TM45 0502

Love Has Gone (song)
SS45 0037

Love I Never Knew You Could
Feel This Good (song)
MO45 0012

LOVE IN THE FIRE (LP)
MOLP 0164

Love In The Fire (song)
MO12 0123, MO45 0296

Love Is All You Need (song)
MO45 0051

The Love I Saw In You Was Just
A Mirage (song)
TM45 0098

Love Is Here And Now You're
Gone (song)
TM45 0097, TM45 0318

Love Is Like An Itching In My
Heart (song)
MO12 0195, TM45 0060

Love Is The Answer (song)
TM45 0237

Love It Came To Me This Time
(song)
TM45 0337

Love Light In Flight (song)
MO12 0139

A Love Like Yours (Don't Come
Knocking Every Day) (song)
SS45 0001, TM45 0054

Love, Love, Love (song)
RA45 0012

LOVE MACHINE (LP)
TMLP 0312

Love Machine (Part 1) (song)
TM45 0493

Love Machine (Part 2) (song)

TM45 0493

Love (Makes Me Do Foolish
Things) (song)
TM45 0030

LOVE MAN (LP)
MOLP 0083

Love Me (song)
TM45 0419

Love My Love (song)
MW45 0012

Love On My Mind Tonight (song)
MO12 0084, MO45 0246

Love Power (song)
TM45 0486

Lovequake (song)
MO12 0113, MO45 0284

LOVE'S COMIN' DOWN (LP)
TMLP 0333

Love's Enough (song)
MO45 0147

Love's Gone Bad (song)
TM45 0091

Love Shines Down (song)
RA45 0009

Love Song (song)
MW45 0020

LOVE SONGS (CD)
MOCD 0032

LOVE SONGS (LP)
MWLP 0006

Love Song (song)
TM45 0335

LOVE'S ON THE MENU (LP)
TMLP 0324

Love's Your Name (song)
TM45 0265

Love (The Lonely People's
Prayer) (song)
TM45 0377

Love Theme From "Lady Sings
The Blues" (song)
TM45 0350

Love Twins (song)
TM45 0408

Love Will Find A Way (song)
MO12 0141, MO45 0315

Love Your Neighbor (song)
MO12 0044, MO45 0178

The Love You Save (song)
MO45 0029, TM45 0248, TM45 0465

Lovin' Fever (song)
MO45 0070

Loving You Is Sweeter Than Ever
(song)
TM45 0068

Lovin', Livin' And Givin' (song)
MO12 0022, MO45 0060

Lovin' On (song)
HI45 0001

Lovin' You (song)
MO45 0120

Lucky In Love (song)
MO12 0174, MO45 0350

Lucy (song)
MO12 0074, MO45 0231

M.P.G. (LP)
TMLP 0119

MA (LP)
RALP 0013

MACHINE GUN (LP)
TMLP 0272

Machine Gun (song)

MO45 0021, TM45 0404

THE MACK (LP)
DSLP 0009

Madam X (song)
MO45 0054

MAGIC (LP)
MOLP 0181

THE MAGIC DISCO MACHINE
(LP)
TMLP 0288

Magic Key (song)
TM45 0243

THE MAGIC OF MARVIN (LP)
PILP 0008

THE MAGNIFICENT 7 (LP)
TMLP 0178

MAHOGANY (LP)
TMLP 0296

MAKE IT HAPPEN (LP)
TMLP 0067

Make Me The Woman You Go
Home To (song)
TM45 0307

Make Me Yours (song)
MO45 0153

MAKING A GAME OUT OF
LOVE (LP)
MOLP 0195

MAKING TRAX (GREAT
INSTRUMENTALS) (LP)
MOLP 0170

Mama I Gotta Brand New Thing
(Don't Say No) (song)
TM45 0421

Mama's Pearl (song)
TM45 0271

Mame (song)
TM45 0135

MANDRE (LP)
MOLP 0019

MANDRE TWO (LP)
MOLP 0041

Maria (You Were The Only One)
(song)
TM45 0255, TM45 0299

THE MARK OF THE BEAST
(LP)
TMLP 0279

MARTHA AND THE
VANDELLAS (EP)
TMEP 0009

THE MARVELETTES (EP)
TMEP 0003

THE MARVELETTES (LP)
TMLP 0052

THE MARVELLOUS
MARVELETTES (LP)
TMLP 0008

MARVIN GAYE (EP)
TMEP 0016

MARVIN GAYE (LP)
SSLP 0007

MARVIN GAYE AND HIS
GIRLS (LP)
TMLP 0123

MARVIN GAYE AND HIS
WOMEN (CD)
MOCD 0033

Mary Jane (song)
MO45 0069

MARY JANE GIRLS (LP)
MOLP 0146

MARY, SCHERRIE AND
　　SUSAYE (LP)
　　MOLP 0004
MARY WELLS (EP)
　　TMEP 0007
MARY WILSON (LP)
　　MOLP 0081
Masterblaster (Dub) (song)
　　MO12 0034, MO45 0152
Masterblaster (Jammin) (song)
　　MO12 0034, MO45 0152
MASTERPIECE (LP)
　　TMLP 0228
Masterpiece (Instrumental) (song)
　　TM45 0356
Masterpiece (Vocal) (song)
　　TM45 0356
Maybe Next Time (song)
　　MO12 0070, MO45 0225
MAYBE TOMORROW (LP)
　　TMLP 0187
Maybe Tomorrow (song)
　　TM45 0327
Me And My Life (song)
　　TM45 0511
Me And Rock And Roll (Are
　　Here To Stay) (song)
　　TM45 0500
Mechanical Emotion (song)
　　MO12 0143, MO45 0318
Mechanical Emotion
　　(Instrumental) (song)
　　MO12 0143
Medley Of Hits (song)
　　MO12 0099, MO45 0269
MEET THE SUPREMES (LP)
　　SSLP 0009
MEET THE TEMPTATIONS
　　(LP)
　　TMLP 0009
Memories (song)
　　TM45 0450
ME 'N' ROCK 'N' ROLL ARE
　　HERE TO STAY (LP)
　　TMLP 0282
Mercy Mercy Me (The Ecology)
　　(song)
　　TM45 0304
MERRY CHRISTMAS FROM
　　MOTOWN (LP)
　　TMLP 0126
Mickey's Monkey (song)
　　OR45 0019, TM45 0017
Midnight Dancer (song)
　　MO45 0111
MIDNIGHT LADY (LP)
　　RALP 0016
MIDNIGHT MAGIC (LP)
　　DSLP 0032
Midnight Rhapsody (song)
　　MO45 0003
Midnight Rhapsody (Part 2) (song)
　　MO45 0003
Midnight Shine (song)
　　MO12 0123
Mighty Good Lovin' (song)
　　TM45 0173
Mighty Spirit (song)
　　MO45 0166
Mind Pleaser (song)
　　MO45 0055
Miss Your Love (song)

MO12 0167, MO45 0343
Missy (song)
　　RA45 0012
Mr. Disco Radio (song)
　　MO45 0023
Mr. Fix-It Man (song)
　　TM45 0330
Moment Of Truth (song)
　　TM45 0234
Money (That's What I Want)
　　(song)
　　LO45 0002
Money (That's What I Want) Pt.
　　1 (song)
　　TM45 0086
Money (That's What I Want) Pt.
　　2 (song)
　　TM45 0086
Monkey Talk (song)
　　SS45 0002
MOODS OF MARVIN GAYE
　　(LP)
　　TMLP 0033
MOODY JUNIOR (LP)
　　TMLP 0210
Moonlight On The Beach (song)
　　TM45 0036
MORE HITS BY THE
　　SUPREMES (LP)
　　TMLP 0020
More Love (song)
　　TM45 0114, TM45 0115
Moritat (Mack The Knife) (song)
　　MW45 0014
Morning Glow (song)
　　TM45 0365
Motels And Memories (song)
　　MW45 0033
Mother Nature (song)
　　TM45 0334
Mother Nature's Best (song)
　　MO45 0014
Mother's Theme (Mama) (song)
　　TM45 0387
Motoring (song)
　　TM45 0002
THE MOTORTOWN REVUE
　　(LP)
　　TMLP 0007
MOTORTOWN REVUE LIVE
　　(LP)
　　TMLP 0127
THE MOTORTOWN REVUE
　　LIVE IN PARIS (LP)
　　TMLP 0027
MOTOWN CHARTBUSTERS
　　'80 (LP)
　　MOLP 0096
MOTOWN CHARTBUSTERS
　　VOLUME 3 (LP)
　　TMLP 0121
MOTOWN CHARTBUSTERS
　　VOLUME 4 (LP)
　　TMLP 0161
MOTOWN CHARTBUSTERS
　　VOLUME 5 (LP)
　　TMLP 0180
MOTOWN CHARTBUSTERS
　　VOLUME 6 (LP)
　　TMLP 0190
MOTOWN CHARTBUSTERS
　　VOLUME 7 (LP)

TMLP 0214
MOTOWN CHARTBUSTERS
　　VOLUME 8 (LP)
　　TMLP 0245
MOTOWN CHARTBUSTERS
　　VOLUME 9 (LP)
　　TMLP 0269
MOTOWN CHARTBUSTERS
　　VOLUME 10 (LP)
　　MOLP 0080
MOTOWN CHRISTMAS
　　ALBUM (LP)
　　TMLP 0329
MOTOWN DISCO CLASSICS
　　VOL. 2 (LP)
　　DSLP 0005
MOTOWN DISCO CLASSICS
　　VOL. 3 (LP)
　　TMLP 0226
MOTOWN DISCO CLASSICS
　　VOL. 4 (LP)
　　TMLP 0243
MOTOWN DISCO CLASSICS
　　VOL. 5 (LP)
　　TMLP 0277
MOTOWN DISCOTECH 3 (LP)
　　MOLP 0001
MOTOWN DISCOTECH VOL.
　　2 (LP)
　　TMLP 0311
MOTOWN EXTRA SPECIAL
　　(LP)
　　SPLP 0007
MOTOWN GOLD (LP)
　　TMLP 0295
MOTOWN GOLD VOLUME 2
　　(LP)
　　MOLP 0027
MOTOWN LOVE SONGS (LP)
　　PILP 0009
MOTOWN MAGIC (LP)
　　TMLP 0030
MOTOWN MAGIC DISCO
　　MACHINE VOL. 2 (LP)
　　TMLP 0320
MOTOWN MEMORIES (LP)
　　TMLP 0064, TMLP 0199
MOTOWN MEMORIES (VOL.
　　2) (LP)
　　TMLP 0077
MOTOWN MEMORIES
　　VOLUME 3 (LP)
　　TMLP 0143
THE MOTOWN SONGBOOK
　　(LP)
　　TMLP 0318
THE MOTOWN SOUND -
　　VOL. 1 (LP)
　　TMLP 0216
THE MOTOWN SOUND VOL.
　　2 (LP)
　　TMLP 0236
MOTOWN SPECIAL (LP)
　　SPLP 0001, SPLP 0002, SPLP 0003,
　　SPLP 0004, SPLP 0005, SPLP 0006
THE MOTOWN STORY (LP)
　　X2LP 0007
THE MOTOWN STORY - THE
　　FIRST 25 YEARS (LP)
　　X2LP 0032
MOTOWN 20TH
　　ANNIVERSARY ALBUM

(LP)
X2LP 0023
Move Mr. Man (song)
OR45 0002
Move Together (song)
MO45 0168
MOVING VIOLATION (LP)
TMLP 0289
MOVIN' ON (LP)
TMLP 0303
Much Better Off (song)
TM45 0162
Musical Love (song)
MO12 0092
MUSICAL MASSAGE (LP)
MOLP 0007
MUSIC AND ME (LP)
TMLP 0234
Music And Me (song)
TM45 0402
MUSIC OF MY MIND (LP)
DSLP 0002
Music Talk (song)
TM45 0032
Mutiny (song)
TM45 0183
My Baby (song)
TM45 0041
MY BABY JUST CARES FOR
ME (LP)
TMLP 0006
My Baby Loves Me (song)
TM45 0049
My Baby Must Be A Magician
(song)
TM45 0140
My Baby Won't Come Back
(song)
OR45 0011
MY CHERIE AMOUR (LP)
TMLP 0128
My Cherie Amour (song)
TM45 0191
My Everything (song)
MO45 0093
My Girl (song)
SS45 0040, TM45 0167, TM45 0189,
TM45 0365
My Girl Has Gone (song)
TM45 0040, TM45 0313
My Guy (song)
MO45 0048, SS45 0015, TM45 0322,
TM45 0508
My Heart (song)
SS45 0043
My Little Baby (song)
TM45 0344
My Love (song)
MO12 0071, MO12 0086, MO45 0226,
MO45 0249
My Love Is True (song)
MO12 0148, MO45 0322
My Mistake (Was To Love You)
(song)
TM45 0422
MY NAME IS JERMAINE (LP)
DSLP 0027
My Old Piano (song)
MO12 0161, MO45 0150, MO45 0336
My Song In G (song)
MO45 0109
Mystified (song)

MO45 0147
MY WAY (LP)
TMLP 0046
My Weakness Is You (song)
TM45 0147
MY WHOLE WORLD ENDED
(LP)
TMLP 0118
My Whole World Ended (The
Moment You Left Me) (song)
MO45 0026, TM45 0190, TM45 0240
My World Is Empty Without You
(song)
TM45 0048
Nanava (song)
MO12 0035, MO45 0156
Nathan Jones (song)
TM45 0284, TM45 0524
NATURAL HIGH (LP)
MOLP 0044
NATURAL RESOURCES (LP)
TMLP 0165
NATURE OF THE BEAST (LP)
MOLP 0193
NATURE PLANNED IT (LP)
TMLP 0205
A Need For Love (song)
SS45 0036
Needle In A Haystack (song)
MO45 0072, SS45 0034, TM45 0095,
TM45 0308
Need Somebody (song)
TM45 0187
NEED TO KNOW YOU
BETTER (LP)
MOLP 0052
Need Your Lovin' (Want You
Back) (song)
TM45 0063, TM45 0092
NEITHER ONE OF US (LP)
TMLP 0229
Neither One Of Us (Wants To Be
The First To Say Goodbye)
(song)
TM45 0357, TM45 0487
Never Can Say Goodbye (song)
TM45 0280
Never Dreamed You'd Leave In
Summer (song)
TM45 0281
Never Had A Dream Come True
(song)
TM45 0232, TM45 0461
Never Leave Your Baby's Side
(song)
TM45 0049
Never Say I Don't Love You
(song)
MO45 0108
Never Say No To Your Baby
(song)
TM45 0013
NEW FACES FROM
HITSVILLE (EP)
TMEP 0014
NEW WAYS BUT LOVE
STAYS (LP)
TMLP 0174
New Way To Say I Love You
(song)
MO12 0080, MO45 0240
New Way To Say I Love You

(Instrumental) (song)
MO12 0080
The Night (song)
MW45 0002, MW45 0024
Night Fo' Last (song)
TM45 0145
Night Fo' Last (Instrumental
(song)
TM45 0145
Night Life (song)
TM45 0501
NIGHTSHIFT (CD)
MOCD 0016
NIGHTSHIFT (LP)
MOLP 0187
Nightshift (song)
MO12 0145, MO45 0320
Nightshift (Instrumental) (song)
MO12 0176
Nightshift (Remix) (song)
MO12 0146
NIGHT SONG (LP)
MOLP 0102
Ninca Te Ido Ar Mi (song)
MO45 0221
1957-1972 (LP)
DSLP 0008
1990 (LP)
DSLP 0016
NITTY GRITTY (LP)
TMLP 0135
The Nitty Gritty (song)
TM45 0215
No Hay Sombra Que Me Cubra
(song)
MO45 0230
No Matter What Sign You Are
(song)
TM45 0205
No One Could Love You More
(song)
TM45 0366
No One Gets The Prize (song)
MO12 0026, MO45 0108
No One's Gonna Be A Fool
Forever (song)
MW45 0001, TM45 0488
No One There (song)
TM45 0345
No One Will Know (song)
TM45 0440
Nothing But Heartaches (song)
TM45 0027, TM45 0427
Nothing But Soul (song)
TM45 0071
Nothing's Too Good For My
Baby (song)
TM45 0058
No Time For Tears (song)
TM45 0018
NOW ARRIVING (LP)
MOLP 0051
Nowhere To Run (song)
TM45 0002, TM45 0195
NOWHERE TO RUN (LP)
MOLP 0022
Nowhere To Run (Part 1) (song)
MO45 0025
Nowhere To Run (Part 2) (song)
MO45 0025
Now That I Have You (song)
MO12 0137

Now That You've Won Me (song)
TM45 0024

Obscene Phone Caller (song)
MO12 0114, MO45 0285

Obscene Phone Caller
(Instrumental) (song)
MO12 0114, MO45 0285

ODE TO MY LADY (LP)
TMLP 0307

ODYSSEY (LP)
MWLP 0003

Oh Be My Love (song)
TM45 0361

Oh How Happy (song)
TM45 0221, TM45 0250

Oh How I'd Miss You (song)
TM45 0182

Oh I Apologise (song)
LO45 0002

Oh Little Boy (What Did You Do
To Me) (song)
SS45 0015

Oh Man (song)
RA45 0019

Oh No (song)
MO45 0194

Oh What A Night (For Luv)
(song)
MO12 0152, MO45 0327

Old Fashioned Love (song)
MO45 0141, MO45 0211

An Old-Fashioned Man (song)
MO45 0013

Old Funky Roll (song)
MO12 0067, MO45 0222

Old Love (Let's Try It Again)
(song)
OR45 0001, SS45 0009

OLD SOCKS, NEW SHOES (LP)
RALP 0001

Once Upon A Time (song)
SS45 0019

ONE DAY IN YOUR LIFE (LP)
MOLP 0115

One Day In Your Life (song)
TM45 0448

One Love In My Lifetime (song)
MO45 0004

One Man Show (song)
PR45 0003

One Mo Hit (Of Your Love)
(song)
MO12 0011

One More Chance (song)
MO45 0175, TM45 0260

One More Heartache (song)
TM45 0052

One More Time For Love (song)
MO12 0080, MO45 0136

One-Nighter (song)
TM45 0494

One Of These Days (song)
OR45 0016

One Too Many Heartaches (song)
TM45 0194

ONE TO ONE (LP)
MOLP 0010

ONE TREE OR ANOTHER
(LP)
RALP 0010

1, 2, 3, You, Her & Me (song)
MO12 0106, MO45 0276

One Way Out (song)
TM45 0122

ONE WORLD (LP)
RALP 0006

The Onion Song (song)
TM45 0216, TM45 0525

ONLY FOUR YOU (CD)
MOCD 0039

ONLY FOUR YOU (LP)
MOLP 0185

The Only Game In Town (song)
MO12 0068, MO45 0223

Only Love (song)
MO12 0038, MO45 0161

The Only One I Love (song)
LO45 0004

Only The Beginning (song)
MO45 0022

The Only Time You Love Me Is
When You're Losing Me (song)
TM45 0457

Only You (song)
MO45 0266

On My Way To You (song)
PR45 0002

ON STAGE (LP)
SSLP 0001

On The Beach (song)
MO12 0138, MO45 0312

ON THE ONE (LP)
MOLP 0138

On The One (song)
MO12 0085, MO45 0248

On The Way Out (song)
TM45 0286

Ooo Baby Baby (song)
TM45 0003, TM45 0221, TM45 0250

Operator (song)
OR45 0006

ORIGINAL MUSIQUARIUM
(CD)
MOCD 0014

ORIGINAL MUSIQUARIUM 1
(CD)
MOCD 0024

ORIGINAL MUSIQUARIUM 2
(CD)
MOCD 0025

ORIGINAL MUSIQUARIUM
(LP)
X2LP 0025

ORIGINALS FROM MARVIN
GAYE (EP)
TMEP 0019

Our Rhapsody (song)
SS45 0045

OUT FROM THE SHADOW
(LP)
MOLP 0147

Outside My Window (song)
MO45 0127

Out The Box (song)
MO12 0060, MO45 0207

Out To Get You (song)
TM45 0012

Over And Over (song)
TM45 0386

Overjoyed (song)
MO12 0189, MO45 0365

Overjoyed (Instrumental) (song)
MO12 0189, MO45 0365

Over The Rainbow (song)

MO12 0144, MO45 0319

Overture (song)
TM45 0501

Painted Picture (song)
MO12 0101, MO45 0271

Papa Was A Rollin' Stone (song)
MO12 0099, MO45 0269

Papa Was A Rollin' Stone
(Instrumental) (song)
TM45 0341

Papa Was A Rollin' Stone
(Vocal) (song)
TM45 0341

Paper Boy (song)
TM45 0062

Paradise In Your Eyes (song)
MO45 0202

Part-Time Lover (song)
MO12 0179, MO45 0355

Part-Time Lover (Instrumental)
(song)
MO12 0179, MO45 0355

Party Down (song)
MO12 0081, MO45 0242

PEACE AND
UNDERSTANDING IS
HARD TO FIND (LP)
TMLP 0233

Peace And Understanding Is Hard
To Find (song)
TM45 0374

Peaceland (song)
MO45 0090

Peeping Tom (song)
MO12 0166, MO45 0342

Peeping Tom (Instrumental) (song)
MO12 0166

Penny Lover (song)
MO12 0132, MO45 0305

PEOPLE...HOLD ON (LP)
TMLP 0212

PEOPLE MOVE HUMAN
PLAY (LP)
DSLP 0040

Piano Man (song)
MW45 0005

Pick Of The Week (song)
TM45 0301

Pick Up The Pieces (song)
MO45 0125

Pigskin Charade (song)
MW45 0033, MW45 0035

PIPPIN (LP)
DSLP 0014

A Place In My Heart (song)
MO12 0062, MO45 0210

A Place In The Sun (song)
TM45 0088, TM45 0186

PLATINUM HOOK (LP)
MOLP 0043

Please Let Me In (song)
TM45 0372

Please Mr. Postman (song)
FO45 0001, MW45 0022

Please Stay (song)
MO45 0159

PLIGHT OF THE RED MAN
(LP)
RALP 0007

THE POET (LP)
MOLP 0125

THE POET II (LP)

MOLP 0173
Poor Fool (song)
  MW45 0028
Poor Girl (song)
  TM45 0411
POPS WE LOVE YOU (LP)
  MOLP 0071
Pops, We Love You (song)
  MO45 0084
Pops, We Love You
  (Instrumental) (song)
  MO12 0010, MO45 0084
Pops, We Love You (Vocal) (song)
  MO12 0010
Portuguese Love (song)
  MO12 0057, MO45 0200
POWER (LP)
  MOLP 0093
Power (song)
  MO12 0029, MO45 0134
Power (Instrumental) (song)
  MO12 0029, MO45 0134
THE POWER OF MUSIC (LP)
  TMLP 0330
Praise (song)
  MO12 0042, MO45 0173
Precious Little Things (song)
  TM45 0323
PRESSIN' ON (LP)
  MOLP 0134
Pretty Little Baby (song)
  TM45 0024
Pretty Mess (song)
  MO12 0136, MO45 0309
Pretty Mess (Instrumental) (song)
  MO12 0136, MO45 0309
Pride And Joy (song)
  OR45 0016, TM45 0017
THE PRIME OF MY LIFE (LP)
  TMLP 0025
THE PRIME OF SHORTY
  LONG (LP)
  TMLP 0144
PRIVATE PARTY (LP)
  MOLP 0156
Private Party (song)
  MO12 0102, MO45 0272
PRODUCED AND
  ARRANGED BY JIMMY
  WEBB (LP)
  TMLP 0221
PSYCHEDELIC SHACK (LP)
  TMLP 0147
Psychedelic Shack (song)
  TM45 0242
Pucker Up Buttercup (song)
  TM45 0096
PURE PLEASURE (LP)
  TMLP 0299
PURE SMOKEY (LP)
  TMLP 0264
Purple Rain Drops (song)
  TM45 0045
Put Yourself In My Place (song)
  TM45 0051, TM45 0075, TM45 0091,
  TM45 0143, TM45 0209, TM45 0289
PUZZLE PEOPLE (LP)
  TMLP 0133
Queen Of My Heart (song)
  MO12 0150, MO45 0325
Quicksand (song)
  SS45 0005, TM45 0185

Quick Slick (song)
  MO12 0053, MO45 0196
A QUIET STORM (LP)
  TMLP 0287
Quiet Storm (song)
  TM45 0497
RAINBOW FUNK (LP)
  TMLP 0197
R & B CHARTMAKERS (EP)
  SSEP 0001
R & B CHARTMAKERS NO. 2
  (EP)
  SSEP 0003
R & B CHARTMAKERS NO. 3
  (EP)
  SSEP 0004
R & B CHARTMAKERS NO. 4
  (EP)
  SSEP 0005
RARE EARTH (LP)
  PRLP 0007
Rave On (song)
  MC45 0002
Razzle Dazzle (Instrumental)
  (song)
  MO45 0007
Reach High (song)
  MO45 0241
Reach High (Instrumental) (song)
  MO45 0241
Reachin' For Something I Can't
  Have (song)
  TM45 0202, TM45 0362
REACHIN' FOR TOMORROW
  (LP)
  MOLP 0092
REACH OUT (LP)
  TMLP 0056
Reach Out And Touch
  (Somebody's Hand) (song)
  TM45 0244, TM45 0338
Reach Out I'll Be There (song)
  TM45 0079, TM45 0283, TM45 0309,
  TM45 0527
Ready Or Not (song)
  MO12 0062, MO45 0210
READY TO ROLL (LP)
  MOLP 0055
Real Humdinger (song)
  TM45 0372
Red Hot (song)
  MO45 0111
Red River Valley (song)
  RA45 0021
REED SEED (LP)
  MOLP 0056
Reed Seed (Trio Tune) (song)
  MO45 0079
REFLECTIONS (LP)
  TMLP 0073
Reflections (song)
  TM45 0117, TM45 0462
REFLECTIONS OF RICK (CD)
  MOCD 0007
REFLECTIONS OF RICK (LP)
  MOLP 0167
Release Me (song)
  TM45 0431
Remember Me (song)
  MO12 0154, MO45 0329, TM45 0270,
  TM45 0472
Remember (Sha La La) (song)

RA45 0020
Remember When (song)
  TM45 0176
Remove This Doubt (song)
  TM45 0085
RENAISSANCE (LP)
  DSLP 0010
The Rescue (song)
  MO12 0190, MO45 0366
Reservation Of Education (song)
  RA45 0011
THE RETURN OF THE
  MAGNIFICENT 7 (LP)
  TMLP 0191
RHYMES OF PASSION (LP)
  MOLP 0194
RHYTHM OF THE NIGHT (LP)
  MOLP 0184
Rhythm Of The Night (song)
  MO12 0150, MO45 0325
Ribbon In The Sky (song)
  MO12 0073, MO45 0229
Richie's Song (song)
  MO12 0128, MO45 0301
RICH LOVE, POOR LOVE (LP)
  MOLP 0030
RICK JAMES PRESENTS
  BOBBY M (LP)
  MOLP 0137
Rick's Song (song)
  MO45 0259
RIC TIC RELICS (LP)
  TMLP 0231
RIDE TO THE RAINBOW (LP)
  MOLP 0074
RIDIN' HIGH (LP)
  TMLP 0078
Right In The Middle (song)
  MO45 0206
RIGHT ON (LP)
  TMLP 0156
Right On Brothers And Sisters
  (song)
  TM45 0326
Rings (song)
  MW45 0019
River Deep, Mountain High (song)
  TM45 0279, TM45 0473
ROAD (LP)
  RALP 0009
Roadie For The Band (song)
  MW45 0011
ROAD RUNNER (LP)
  TMLP 0038
Road Runner (song)
  TM45 0059, TM45 0192
Rocket Love (song)
  MO45 0218
Rockin' Robin (song)
  TM45 0318
ROCK ME A LITTLE WHILE
  (EP)
  TMEP 0015
Rock My Heart (song)
  MO12 0168, MO12 0177, MO45 0344,
  MO45 0353
Rode By The Place (Where We
  Used To Stay) (song)
  MO45 0041
Roll-Her, Skater (song)
  MO12 0024, MO45 0110
Roll-Her, Skater (Instrumental)

(song)
MO12 0024, MO45 0110
Roll It Over (song)
RA45 0015
Romance (song)
MW45 0023
ROMANCE IN THE NIGHT
(LP)
MOLP 0142
RONNIE McNEIR (LP)
TMLP 0327
ROSE BANKS (LP)
TMLP 0316
ROSS (LP)
MOLP 0050
Round And Round (song)
MO12 0086, MO12 0118, MO45 0249,
MO45 0290
Roxanne (You Sure Got A Fine
Design) (song)
RA45 0015
RUFF 'N' READY (LP)
TMLP 0106
Runaway Child, Running Wild
(song)
TM45 0217
Running (song)
MO45 0252
Running Away (Ain't Gonna
Help You) (song)
TM45 0223
Running Back And Forth (song)
TM45 0226, TM45 0506
Running With The Night (song)
MO12 0103, MO12 0109
Running With The Night (Part 1)
(song)
MO45 0273
Running With The Night (Part 2)
(song)
MO45 0273
Sad And Lonesome Feeling (song)
TM45 0436
Sad Song (song)
TM45 0056
Sad Tomorrows (song)
TM45 0304
Sail On (song)
MO45 0103
Samba Pa Ti (song)
MO45 0230
Same Old Story (song)
MO45 0127
SAM HARRIS (CD)
MOCD 0021
SAM HARRIS (LP)
MOLP 0175
SAN REMO STRINGS SWING
(LP)
TMLP 0215
Santa Claus Is Coming To Town
(song)
TM45 0339
Satisfied Feelin' (song)
TM45 0198
Saturday Night, Sunday Morning
(song)
MO45 0078
Save It For A Rainy Day (song)
MO45 0051
Save Me (song)
TM45 0084

Save Me From This Misery (song)
TM45 0379
Save My Love For A Rainy Day
(song)
TM45 0278
SAVE THE CHILDREN (LP)
X2LP 0010
Save The Children (song)
TM45 0298, TM45 0419
Save The Night For Me (song)
MO12 0168, MO45 0344
SAX APPEAL (LP)
TMLP 0325
Say You Love Me True (song)
TM45 0483
Say You, Say Me (song)
MO12 0182, MO45 0358
School Is Out (song)
RA45 0017
Scratch Break (Glove style) (song)
MO12 0104
Scratchin' (song)
TM45 0482
Searching For A Girl (song)
TM45 0031
SECOND ALBUM (LP)
TMLP 0021
SECOND TIME AROUND (LP)
TMLP 0181
THE SECRET LIFE OF
PLANTS (LP)
X2LP 0022
The Secret Life Of Plants (song)
MO12 0073, MO45 0229
Secrets (song)
MO45 0227
The Seed (song)
RA45 0002
Seems So Long (song)
TM45 0329
SEE MY LOVE IN MOTION
(LP)
MOLP 0119
Send One Your Love (song)
MO45 0097
Send One Your Love
(Instrumental) (song)
MO45 0097
7 Rooms Of Gloom (song)
TM45 0112, TM45 0460
17 (song)
MO12 0124, MO45 0297
17 (Instrumental) (song)
MO12 0124, MO45 0297
17 GREATEST HITS (CD)
MOCD 0019
Sexy Lady (song)
MO45 0095, MO45 0141
Shadow (song)
RA45 0006
SHAKE (EP)
TMEP 0011
SHAKE AND FINGERPOP
(EP)
TMEP 0013
Shake And Fingerpop (song)
TM45 0029
Shake Hands (song)
MO12 0117, MO45 0289
Shake It Up (song)
MO12 0038, MO45 0161
Shake Me, Wake Me (When It's

Over) (song)
TM45 0053
Shake Sherry (song)
OR45 0007
Shaky Ground (song)
MO45 0011
SHARE MY LOVE (LP)
TMLP 0253
Share My World (song)
MO12 0184, MO45 0360
Sharing Something Perfect
Between Ourselves (song)
MO45 0036
She's Good (song)
TM45 0280
She's Got To Be Real (song)
TM45 0039
Shine On Me (song)
TM45 0262
Shoeshine Boy (song)
TM45 0449
Shoe Shoe Shine (song)
TM45 0431
Shoe Soul (song)
MO45 0077
Shoó Be Doo Be Doo Da Day
(song)
TM45 0154
Shoot Your Shot (song)
TM45 0059
SHOP AROUND (EP)
OREP 0001
Shop Around (song)
LO45 0003
SHOTGUN (LP)
TMLP 0017
Shotgun (song)
TM45 0009, TM45 0192
Shoulda Gone Dancin' (song)
MO12 0016, MO45 0090
Shoulda Gone Dancin'
(Instrumental) (song)
MO12 0016
SHOULD HAVE GONE
DANCIN' (LP)
MOLP 0068
Should I Tell Them (song)
SS45 0034
Show Me The Way (song)
TM45 0137
SIGNED, SEALED AND
DELIVERED (LP)
TMLP 0168
Signed, Sealed, Delivered (I'm
Yours) (song)
MO45 0159, TM45 0245, TM45 0468
Silent Partner In A Three-Way
Love Affair (song)
TM45 0400
SILK 'N' SOUL (LP)
TMLP 0100
Simple Game (song)
TM45 0287, TM45 0474
A Simple Thing Like Cry (song)
TM45 0382
Since I Lost My Baby (song)
TM45 0026
Since I've Lost You (song)
TM45 0120, TM45 0278
Since You've Been Gone (song)
TM45 0089
Since You've Been Loving Me

(song)
TM45 0080, TM45 0282
Since You Won My Heart (song)
TM45 0040
Sing (song)
TM45 0453
SING AND PERFORM
FUNNY GIRL (LP)
TMLP 0088
SINGS MY GUY (LP)
SSLP 0004
Sing What You Wanna (song)
TM45 0164
Sir Duke (song)
MO12 0158, MO45 0016, MO45 0333
6 By 6 (song)
TM45 0261
Six-Million Dollar Man (song)
MO45 0014
16 BIG HITS: EARLY 60s (LP)
SILP 0001
16 BIG HITS: LATE 60s (LP)
SILP 0002
Skips A Beat (song)
MO12 0186, MO45 0362
Skips A Beat (Dub mix) (song)
MO12 0186, MO45 0362
Skip To My Lou (song)
MO12 0089, MO45 0253
SKYLARKIN' (LP)
MOLP 0088
THE SKY'S THE LIMIT (LP)
TMLP 0183
SKYWRITER (LP)
TMLP 0230
Skywriter (song)
MO45 0029, TM45 0367
Sleepin' (song)
MO45 0165
SLICK (LP)
MOLP 0028
Slick (song)
MO12 0081, MO45 0242
Slippery When Wet (song)
TM45 0454
Slipping Into Something New
(song)
MO45 0049
Smiling Faces Sometimes (song)
TM45 0291, TM45 0334, TM45 0514
SMOKE SIGNALS (CD)
MOCD 0035
SMOKE SIGNALS (LP)
MOLP 0197
SMOKEY (LP)
DSLP 0012
SMOKEY ROBINSON AND
THE MIRACLES (LP)
TMLP 0171
SMOKEY'S FAMILY
ROBINSON (LP)
TMLP 0313
SMOKEY'S WORLD (LP)
MOLP 0033
Smooth Sailing From Now On
(song)
TM45 0310
SMOOTH SOUL (LP)
MOLP 0046
Snarlin' Mama Lion (song)
RA45 0008
Snow Flakes (song)

MW45 0020
Sock-It Rocket (song)
MO45 0107
So Deep Within You (song)
TM45 0352
So Glad You Chose Me (song)
TM45 0238
Solar Flight (Opus 1) (song)
MO45 0037
SOLID ROCK (LP)
TMLP 0201
Solitary Man (song)
MW45 0035
So Long Baby (song)
FO45 0001
So Many Sides Of You (song)
MO12 0065, MO45 0216
Somebody Knows, Somebody
Cares (song)
TM45 0232
SOMEBODY'S WATCHING
ME (LP)
MOLP 0160
Somebody's Watching Me (song)
MO12 0110, MO45 0280
Somebody's Watching Me
(Instrumental) (song)
MO12 0110, MO45 0280
Somebody's Watchin' You (song)
MO12 0007, MO45 0080
SOMEDAY AT CHRISTMAS
(LP)
TMLP 0085
Someday At Christmas (song)
TM45 0339
Someday Someway (song)
OR45 0003
Someday We'll Be Together (song)
MO45 0028, TM45 0222
Something About You (song)
TM45 0042
A SOMETHING EXTRA
BONUS RECORD FOR
"SONGS IN THE KEY OF
LIFE" (EP)
TMEP 0020
SOMETHING FOR
EVERYONE (LP)
TMLP 0159
Something On My Mind (song)
TM45 0144, TM45 0293
Some Things You Never Get Used
To (song)
TM45 0163
Somewhere In My Life (song)
MO45 0209
A SONG FOR YOU (LP)
DSLP 0021
SONGS IN THE KEY OF LIFE
(CD)
MOCD 0013
SONGS IN THE KEY OF LIFE
(LP)
X2LP 0015
Son Of Sagittarius (song)
TM45 0403
SOPHISTICATED SOUL (LP)
TMLP 0090
SO RIGHT (LP)
MOLP 0127
Sorry Doesn't Always Make It
Right (song)

TM45 0443
Sorry Is A Sorry Word (song)
TM45 0110
So Tired (Of The Way You're
Treating Our Love Baby)
(song)
TM45 0412
Soul Clappin' (song)
TM45 0391
SOUL MASTER (LP)
TMLP 0094
SOUL ON THE ROCKS (LP)
TMLP 0066
SOUL SESSION (LP)
TMLP 0029
SOUL SOUNDS (LP)
TMLP 0069
SOUL SPIN (LP)
TMLP 0138
Soul Stomp (song)
SS45 0031
SOUND OF THE R & B HITS
(LP)
SSLP 0002
So Will I (song)
TM45 0333
SPACE DANCE (LP)
MOLP 0062
Space Dance (song)
MO12 0017, MO45 0091
Spaced Out (song)
TM45 0492
Sparkle (song)
MO45 0117
A SPECIAL MOTOWN DISCO
ALBUM (LP)
MOLP 0016
SPECIAL MOTOWN DISCO
ALBUM VOL. 2 (LP)
MOLP 0059
SPECIAL OCCASION (LP)
TMLP 0089
Special Occasion (song)
TM45 0174
THE SPELL (LP)
MOLP 0141
Spinnin' And Spinnin' (song)
TM45 0414
Spirit Groove (song)
MO12 0018, MO45 0092
Square Biz (song)
MO12 0048, MO45 0184
Square Biz (Instrumental) (song)
MO12 0048, MO45 0184
Standing At The Crossroads Of
Love (song)
SS45 0007
Standing In The Shadows Of Love
(song)
TM45 0089, TM45 0527
Standing On The Top (song)
MO12 0106
Standing On The Top (Full
version) (song)
MO12 0063
Standing On The Top (Part 1)
(song)
MO12 0063, MO45 0212
Standing On The Top (Part 2)
(song)
MO45 0212
Standing On The Verge (Of

Gettin' It On) (song)
MO12 0005, MO45 0063

STANDING OVATION (LP)
TMLP 0207

Stand Up (song)
MO45 0227

Star (song)
MO12 0163, MO45 0339

STAR DANCING (LP)
MOLP 0034

Star Love (song)
MO45 0053

Starting The Hurt All Over Again
(song)
TM45 0108

Star Wars Theme (song)
PR45 0005

Star Wars Theme (Long version)
(song)
PR45 0005

Stay Away (song)
MO45 0019

Stay In My Lonely Arms (song)
TM45 0083, TM45 0273

Stay With Me Baby (song)
MW45 0026

Stepping Closer To Your Heart
(song)
TM45 0076

STEPPIN' OUT (LP)
MOLP 0047

STEVIE WONDER (EP)
TMEP 0006

Stevie Wonder Flight (song)
MO45 0313

STEVIE WONDER LIVE (LP)
TMLP 0150

STEVIE WONDER PRESENTS
SYREETA (LP)
TMLP 0267

Sticks And Stones (But The Funk
Won't Ever Hurt You) (song)
MO45 0074

Still (song)
MO45 0114

Still Water (Love) (song)
TM45 0254, TM45 0474

Still Water (Peace) (song)
TM45 0254

STILL WATERS RUN DEEP
(LP)
TMLP 0149

Stone City Band, Hi! (song)
MO45 0085

Stoned Love (song)
TM45 0262, TM45 0524

Stone Liberty (song)
MO45 0038

STONEY & MEATLOAF (LP)
PRLP 0010, RALP 0005

Stop Her On Sight (S.O.S.) (song)
TM45 0407

Stop! In The Name Of Love (song)
TM45 0001, TM45 0522

Stop, Look, Listen (To Your
Heart) (song)
TM45 0408

Stop The War Now (song)
TM45 0266

Stormy Love (song)
MO45 0122

Straight From The Heart (song)

MO12 0126, MO45 0299

Street Angel (song)
MO45 0286

STREET SONGS (LP)
MOLP 0110

Struck By Lightning Twice (song)
MO45 0145

STRUTTIN' (LP)
MOLP 0089

Struttin' (song)
MO45 0138

Strut Your Stuff (song)
MO45 0129

Stubborn Kind Of Fellow (song)
OR45 0008

Stuck On You (song)
MO12 0118, MO45 0290

STYLUS (LP)
PRLP 0011

Such A Woman (song)
MO45 0114

Such Is Love, Such Is Life (song)
SS45 0008

Sugar Daddy (song)
TM45 0311

Sugar Don't Bite (song)
MO12 0130, MO45 0303

Sugar Don't Bite (Instrumental)
(song)
MO12 0130

SUGAR 'N' SPICE (LP)
TMLP 0134

SUITE FOR SINGLE GIRL (LP)
MOLP 0009

Summer Love (song)
MO12 0036, MO45 0157

Sun Country (song)
MW45 0030, TM45 0321

SUNDAY FUNNIES (LP)
RALP 0004

Super Freak (Part 1) (song)
MO12 0050, MO45 0190

Super Freak (Part 2) (song)
MO12 0050, MO45 0190

SUPER HITS (LP)
DSLP 0024, DSLP 0026, DSLP 0028

Superman (song)
TM45 0437

Supersensuousensation (Try Some
Love) (song)
MO45 0019

Superstar (Remember How You
Got Where You Are) (song)
TM45 0302, TM45 0320

Superstition (song)
TM45 0343

Superwoman (song)
TM45 0329

THE SUPREMES (LP)
TMLP 0292

SUPREMES A-GO-GO (LP)
TMLP 0039

THE SUPREMES HITS (EP)
TMEP 0008

Supremes Medley (song)
MO12 0027, MO12 0054, MO45 0197

Supremes Medley (Part 1) (song)
MO45 0128

Supremes Medley (Part 2) (song)
MO45 0128

THE SUPREMES SING
COUNTRY, WESTERN &

POP (LP)
TMLP 0018

THE SUPREMES SING
MOTOWN (LP)
TMLP 0047

THE SUPREMES SING
RODGERS AND HART (LP)
TMLP 0054

SURFACE THRILLS (LP)
MOLP 0139

Surprise Surprise (song)
MO12 0129, MO45 0302

Surrender (song)
TM45 0294, TM45 0472

Swang (song)
MO12 0018, MO45 0092

Sweeter As The Days Go By
(song)
MO45 0118

The Sweeter You Treat Her (song)
TM45 0509

Sweet Harmony (song)
TM45 0385

Sweet Love (song)
MO45 0034, TM45 0496

Sweet Soul (song)
TM45 0138

The Sweet Sound Of Your Song
(song)
MW45 0023

Sweet Thing (song)
MO45 0137, TM45 0014, TM45 0257

Swept For You Baby (song)
TM45 0098, TM45 0114

SWITCH (LP)
MOLP 0053

SWITCH II (LP)
MOLP 0069

Swoop I'm Yours (song)
MO12 0115, MO45 0287

Sylvia (song)
TM45 0088

SYREETA (LP)
MOLP 0094, MWLP 0001

T.C.B. (LP)
TMLP 0110

Tailgate (song)
MO45 0023

Take A Chance On Me (song)
FO45 0004

Take A Look Around (song)
TM45 0310, TM45 0469

Take Me Away (song)
MO45 0164

Take Me Clear From Here (song)
TM45 0438

Take Me Girl, I'm Ready (song)
MO45 0018, TM45 0342, TM45 0464

Take Me In Your Arms And Love
Me (song)
TM45 0104, TM45 0366

Take Me In Your Arms (Rock Me
A Little While) (song)
TM45 0038, TM45 0153, TM45 0353

Take My Life (song)
MO45 0182

Take Some Time Out For Love
(song)
TM45 0066, TM45 0220

Take This Heart Of Mine (song)
TM45 0063

Take Time (song)

Tie Me To A Tree (Handcuff Me)
(song)
MO45 0073
Tie Me To A Tree (Handcuff Me)
(Instrumental) (song)
MO45 0073
TIGGI CLAY (LP)
MOLP 0163
Til I Met You (song)
MO12 0005, MO45 0063
Time (song)
TM45 0226, TM45 0506
Time Changes Things (song)
TM45 0151
TIME OUT FOR SMOKEY
ROBINSON & THE
MIRACLES (LP)
TMLP 0129
Time Will Reveal (song)
MO12 0108, MO45 0278
Tin Can People (song)
TM45 0412
Today Will Soon Be Yesterday
(song)
MO45 0008
TOGETHER (LP)
SSLP 0005, TMLP 0122
Together (song)
TM45 0443
Together 'Til The End Of Time
(song)
TM45 0056
Together We Can Make Such
Sweet Music (song)
TM45 0268, TM45 0373
To Know (song)
TM45 0358
To Know You Is To Love You
(song)
MW45 0006
Tokyo (song)
MO12 0166, MO45 0342
TO LOVE AGAIN (LP)
MOLP 0109
To Love Again (song)
MO45 0181
Tomorrow May Never Come
(song)
TM45 0023
Tomorrow's Tears (song)
TM45 0093, TM45 0204
Too Busy Thinkin' About My
Baby (song)
TM45 0206
Too High (song)
TM45 0371
Too Hot Ta Trot (song)
MO12 0001, MO45 0044
Too Many Colors (Tee's
Interlude) (song)
MO45 0126
Too Many Fish In The Sea (song)
SS45 0036, TM45 0006
Too Shy To Say (song)
MO45 0047
Top Of The World (song)
MO45 0047
Tossin' And Turnin' (song)
TM45 0361
TOTALLY TATA (LP)
MOLP 0015
Touch (song)

TM45 0380
TOUCH (LP)
TMLP 0188
TOUCH ME (LP)
MOLP 0198
TOUCH ME IN THE
MORNING (LP)
TMLP 0238
Touch Me In The Morning (song)
TM45 0363, TM45 0519
The Touch Of Time (song)
TM45 0044
Touch The One You Love (song)
MO12 0131, MO45 0304
Touch The Rainchild (song)
MW45 0003, MW45 0028
TOUCH THE SKY (LP)
MOLP 0132
Touch The Sky (song)
MO45 0256
To Win Your Heart (song)
TM45 0333
The Tracks Of My Tears (song)
TM45 0022, TM45 0197, TM45 0267,
TM45 0526
Train Of Thought (song)
MO12 0187, MO45 0363
Travelin' Through (song)
MO45 0130
Treat Her Like A Lady (song)
MO12 0140, MO45 0314
Treat Her Like A Lady (Remix)
(song)
MO12 0148, MO12 0193
A TRIBUTE TO THE GREAT
NAT KING COLE (LP)
TMLP 0022
TRIBUTE TO UNCLE RAY
(LP)
ORLP 0004
TROUBLE MAN (LP)
TMLP 0224
Trouble Man (song)
TM45 0348
Truly (song)
MO12 0075, MO45 0233
TRULY FOR YOU (LP)
MOLP 0186
Truly Yours (song)
TM45 0268
TRUST ME (LP)
MOLP 0129
Try It Baby (song)
SS45 0023
Try It, You'll Like It (song)
MW45 0009, TM45 0480
Try Love From The Inside (song)
MO45 0001, TM45 0531
TRY MY LOVE (LP)
MOLP 0060
Tuesday Heartbreak (song)
MO45 0016
Tune Up (song)
TM45 0020
TURNIN' ON (LP)
MOLP 0031
Turn Off The Lights (song)
MO12 0101, MO45 0271
THE TWELVE-YEAR-OLD
GENIUS--LIVE (LP)
ORLP 0005
25 MILES (LP)

TMLP 0115
25 Miles (song)
TM45 0173
25 MOTOWN NO. 1 HITS (CD)
MOCD 0023
25 U.S.A. NO. 1 HITS FROM 25
YEARS (LP)
X2LP 0031
20 GOLDEN GREATS (LP)
MOLP 0078, MOLP 0079, MOLP 0097,
TVLP 0001, TVLP 0003, TVLP 0004,
TVLP 0005, TVLP 0007, TVLP 0008
20 GREATEST HITS (CD)
MOCD 0004
20 GREATEST SONGS IN
MOTOWN HISTORY (CD)
MOCD 0034
20 MOD CLASSICS (LP)
MOLP 0082
20 MOD CLASSICS VOL. 2 (LP)
MOLP 0090
Twistin' And Jivin' (song)
MW45 0011
Twistin' Postman (song)
FO45 0003
Two Can Have A Party (song)
TM45 0169
TWO LOVERS (LP)
ORLP 0003
Two Lovers (song)
OR45 0006, TM45 0322
The Two Of Us (song)
TM45 0037
TWO TO ONE (LP)
MOLP 0049
Two Wrongs Don't Make A Right
(song)
OR45 0014
Under God's Light (song)
RA45 0004
Under The Influence (song)
MO45 0368
Under The Influence (Mix 1)
(song)
MO12 0192
Under The Influence (Mix 2)
(song)
MO12 0192
Under The Influence (Mix 3)
(song)
MO12 0192
THE UNDISPUTED TRUTH
(LP)
TMLP 0196
Ungena Za Ulimwengu (Unite
The World) (song)
TM45 0285
UNITED (LP)
TMLP 0062
Until You Love Someone (song)
TM45 0079
Up Again (song)
TM45 0442
Upside Down (song)
MO12 0031, MO45 0143
Up The Ladder To The Roof
(song)
TM45 0236, TM45 0466
UPTIGHT (LP)
PILP 0004, TMLP 0036
Uptight (Everything's Alright)
(song)

TM45 0045, TM45 0231, TM45 0520

USED TO BE (LP)
MOLP 0136

Used To Be (song)
MO45 0236

VALERIE SIMPSON (LP)
TMLP 0218

THE VERY BEST OF DIANA
ROSS (LP)
X2LP 0030

Very Special Part (song)
MO12 0077, MO45 0235

The Victors (song)
MW45 0013, TM45 0303

Vina Del Mar (song)
MO12 0089

Visions (song)
TM45 0383

Vitamin U (song)
MO45 0024

Walk Away From Love (song)
TM45 0495

Walk Away Renee (song)
TM45 0135, TM45 0489

Walk In The Night (song)
MO45 0066, TM45 0326

Walk On (song)
MO45 0140

Walk On, Don't Look Back (song)
MW45 0003

Walk Out The Door If You
Wanna (song)
TM45 0503

Walk With Me (song)
TM45 0325

Walm Jetz (song)
RA45 0017

Wandering Stranger (song)
MO45 0268

War (song)
TM45 0256, TM45 0470

WAR AND PEACE (LP)
TMLP 0170

Warm Ride (song)
PR45 0009

WARM THOUGHTS (LP)
MOLP 0091

War Of Nerves (song)
MO45 0295

Wasting Time (song)
MO12 0122, MO45 0294

WATCH OUT (LP)
TMLP 0051

Way Back Home (Instrumental)
(song)
TM45 0359

Way Back Home (Vocal) (song)
TM45 0359

THE WAY I AM (LP)
MOLP 0105

Way Over There (song)
TM45 0193

The Way You Do The Things You
Do (song)
PR45 0010, RA45 0003, SS45 0011,
TM45 0210

We Can Make It We Can (song)
TM45 0263

We Can Put It Back Together
(song)
MO45 0160

We Can Work It Out (song)

TM45 0274

We Just Live Here (We Don't
Love Here Anymore (song)
HI45 0001

We Like To Party...Come On
(song)
MO12 0007, MO45 0080

We'll Have A Good Thing Going
On (song)
TM45 0212

We're Both In Love With You
(song)
MO12 0128, MO45 0301

WE REMEMBER SAM COOKE
(LP)
TMLP 0012

What Am I Going To Do Without
Your Love (song)
TM45 0067

What Am I Gonna Do Without
You (song)
TM45 0230

What Becomes Of The
Brokenhearted (song)
TM45 0077, TM45 0413, TM45 0530

What Does It Take (song)
TM45 0464

What Does It Take (To Win You
Love) (song)
TM45 0213

What Does It Take (To Win Your
Love) (song)
MO45 0018

Whatever Makes You Happy
(song)
OR45 0019

Whatever You Got, I Want (song)
TM45 0429

What Good Am I Without You
(song)
SS45 0035

What Have They Done (To My
Home Town) (song)
MO45 0032

What If (song)
MW45 0001

What Is A Man (song)
TM45 0199

What It Is (song)
TM45 0399

What Love Has Joined Together
(song)
OR45 0017, TM45 0004, TM45 0456

What's A Little Love Between
Friends (song)
MO45 0155

What's Easy For Two Is Hard For
One (song)
MO45 0048, SS45 0003

WHAT'S GOING ON (LP)
TMLP 0189

What's Going On (song)
MO12 0025, TM45 0277

What's Happening Brother (song)
MO12 0025

What's In Your Life For Me (song)
MO45 0171

What's So Good About Goodbye
(song)
FO45 0002

What's The Bottom Line (song)
MO12 0093, MO45 0260

What's The Matter With You
Baby (song)
SS45 0019

What The World Needs Now Is
Love (song)
MW45 0013, TM45 0303

What You Gave Me (song)
MO12 0009, MO45 0083

What You See Is What You Get
(song)
PR45 0010, RA45 0003

When I Had Your Love (song)
TM45 0052

When I Looked At Your Face
(song)
MO45 0046

When I'm Alone I Cry (song)
SS45 0013

When I'm Gone (song)
MO45 0119, TM45 0008

When Joanie Smiles (song)
RA45 0014

When Someone's Good To You
(song)
SS45 0043

When The Day Comes Every
Night (song)
MO45 0115

When The Lovelight Starts
Shining Thru' His Eyes (song)
MW45 0025, SS45 0007, TM45 0508

When The Morning Comes (song)
MW45 0002, MW45 0024

When The Words From Your
Heart Get Caught Up In Your
Throat (song)
TM45 0149

When You're Young And In Love
(song)
TM45 0109, TM45 0441

Where Are You Going To My
Love (song)
TM45 0442

Where Did Our Love Go (song)
SS45 0024, TM45 0427

Where Did We Go Wrong (song)
MO45 0150

Where Did You Go (song)
TM45 0007

Where Is It I Belong (song)
TM45 0490

WHERE IT'S COMING FROM
(LP)
TMLP 0182

WHERE THERE'S SMOKE (LP)
MOLP 0072

Wherever I Lay My Hat (song)
TM45 0206

Where Were You (song)
TM45 0081

Where Would I Be Without You,
Baby (song)
TM45 0338

Whisper You Love Me Boy (song)
TM45 0016

WHITE KNUCKLE RIDE (LP)
MOLP 0172

WHO AM I? (LP)
TMLP 0304

Who Are You (song)
MO45 0005

Who Could Ever Doubt My Love

(song)
TM45 0043, TM45 0066, TM45 0220
Whole Lotta Shakin' In My Heart
(Since I Met You) (song)
TM45 0069, TM45 0355
Whole New Thing (song)
TM45 0515
Wholly Holy (song)
TM45 0319, TM45 0374
WHOPPER BOPPER SHOW
STOPPER (LP)
MOLP 0005
Who's Gonna Take The Blame
(song)
TM45 0247
Who's Holding Donna Now (song)
MO12 0171, MO45 0347
Who Shot Zorro? (song)
MO45 0282
Who's Lovin' You (song)
LO45 0003, TM45 0225
Who's Right Or Wrong (song)
TM45 0432
Why Did She Have To Leave Me
(Why Did She Have To Go)
(song)
TM45 0208
Why Did You Leave Me Darling
(song)
TM45 0172
Why Don't You Lead Me To
Love (song)
TM45 0154
Why Do You Want To Let Me
Go (song)
TM45 0025
Why (Must We Fall In Love)
(song)
TM45 0231
Why When Love Has Gone (song)
TM45 0153
Why You Wanna See My Bad
Side (song)
MO45 0062
Why You Wanna Try Me? (song)
MO12 0059, MO45 0205
Wigs And Lashes (song)
TM45 0416
Wild & Crazy Love (song)
MO12 0173, MO45 0349
Wild & Crazy Love (Instrumental)
(song)
MO12 0173, MO45 0349
WILD AND PEACEFUL (LP)
MOLP 0066
WILD ANIMAL (LP)
MOLP 0176
Wild Animal (song)
MO12 0192, MO45 0368
Wild One (song)
SS45 0042
WILLIE REMEMBERS (LP)
RALP 0011
Will This Be The Day (song)
TM45 0178
WINGS OF LOVE (LP)
DSLP 0025
The Winner Gets The Heart (song)
MO45 0282
WISH IT WOULD RAIN (LP)
TMLP 0079
Wish Upon A Star (song)

MO12 0069, MO45 0224
With A Child's Heart (song)
TM45 0058, TM45 0448
WITH A LOT O'SOUL (LP)
TMLP 0057
WITH LOVE FROM US TO
YOU (LP)
TMLP 0002
Without The One You Love (song)
SS45 0037, TM45 0317
With You I'm Born Again (song)
MO45 0107
With You I'm Born Again
(Instrumental) (song)
MO45 0087
WOLF & WOLF (LP)
MOLP 0169
THE WOMAN IN RED (CD)
MOCD 0006
THE WOMAN IN RED (LP)
MOLP 0178
Wonderland (song)
MO45 0120
Workout Stevie, Workout (song)
SS45 0002
Work That Body (song)
MO12 0111, MO45 0281
Work That Body (Extra mix)
(song)
MO12 0111
World So Wide, Nowhere To Hide
(From Your Heart) (song)
TM45 0103
Would I Love You (song)
SS45 0030
Would You Like To Come Along
(song)
PR45 0009
X-Rated Movie (song)
MO45 0075
Yes Indeed (song)
MO12 0052, MO45 0195
YES IT'S YOU LADY (LP)
MOLP 0122
YESTERDAY'S DREAMS (LP)
TMLP 0087
Yesterday's Dreams (song)
TM45 0166
Yester Love (song)
TM45 0162, TM45 0355
Yester-Me, Yester-You,
Yesterday (song)
MC45 0001, TM45 0218, TM45 0520
You (song)
MO12 0045, MO45 0179, TM45 0141
You Ain't Livin' Till You're
Lovin' (song)
TM45 0182
You And I (song)
MO12 0003, MO12 0011, MO45 0002,
MO45 0058, TM45 0532
You Are (song)
MO45 0239
You Are Everything (song)
TM45 0392, TM45 0525
You Are Forever (song)
MO45 0185
You Are My Heaven (song)
MO12 0096, MO45 0264
You Are My Love (song)
MO12 0132, MO45 0305
You Are The Reason (I Feel Like

Dancing) (song)
MO45 0049
You Are The Sunshine Of My Life
(song)
MC45 0001, TM45 0354
You Beat Me To The Punch
(song)
OR45 0001
You Better Get In Line (song)
OR45 0007
You Better Watch Out (song)
MO12 0039, MO45 0167
You Can Cry On My Shoulder
(song)
TM45 0336
You Can't Hurry Love (song)
TM45 0075, TM45 0458
You Can't Judge A Book By Its
Cover (song)
TM45 0394, TM45 0491
(You Can't Let The Boy
Overpower) The Man In You
(song)
SS45 0012, TM45 0152
You Can't Turn Me Off (In The
Middle Of Turning Me On)
(song)
MO45 0035
You Don't Love Me No More
(song)
TM45 0161
You Got It (song)
MO45 0060
You Got Me Hurtin' All Over
(song)
MO45 0081, TM45 0129, TM45 0290
You Gotta Have Love In Your
Heart (song)
TM45 0295, TM45 0473
You Got The Love I Love (song)
TM45 0181
You Got The Love I Need (song)
TM45 0291
You Have Inspired Me (song)
MO45 0102
You Have Inspired Me (Disco
version) (song)
MO45 0102
You Haven't Done Nothin' (song)
TM45 0423
You Keep Me Hangin' On (song)
MO12 0039, MO12 0130, MO12 0195,
MO45 0028, MO45 0167, MO45 0303,
MO45 0371, TM45 0085
You Keep Running Away (song)
TM45 0489
You Like Me Don't You (song)
MO12 0040, MO45 0170
You Like Me Don't You
(Instrumental) (song)
MO12 0040, MO45 0170
You Like Me Don't You (Vocal
remix) (song)
MO12 0040
You'll Be Sorry Someday (song)
OR45 0010
You'll Lose A Precious Love
(song)
TM45 0065
You'll Never Rock Alone (song)
MO45 0020
You Lost The Sweetest Boy (song)

SS45 0003, TM45 0322

You Make Your Own Heaven
And Hell Right Here On
Earth (song)
TM45 0275

You Mean More To Me (song)
MO45 0239

You Met Your Match (song)
TM45 0167

You Moved A Mountain (song)
MO45 0252

You Must Be Love (song)
TM45 0132, TM45 0246

YOU NAME IT (LP)
MOLP 0008

You Need Love Like I Do (Don't
You) (song)
TM45 0258

You Need Me (song)
TM45 0036

You Need To Be Loved (song)
MO45 0040

The Young Folks (song)
TM45 0205, TM45 0239

Young Warrior (song)
RA45 0011

You Pulled A Switch (song)
MO12 0006, MO45 0071

Your Cheating Ways (song)
TM45 0035

YOU'RE ALL I NEED (LP)
TMLP 0084

You're All I Need To Get By
(song)
TM45 0169

You're All The Boogie I Need
(song)
MO45 0133

You're A Song (That I Can't Sing)
(song)
TM45 0321

You're A Special Part Of Me
(song)
TM45 0381

You're A Wonderful One (song)
MO12 0194, SS45 0013

You're Givin' Me The Run
Around (song)
MO12 0077, MO45 0235

(You're Gone But) Always In My
Heart (song)
SS45 0038

You're Gonna Love My Baby
(song)
TM45 0044

You're Good My Child (song)
MO45 0004

You're My Aphrodisiac (song)
MO12 0117, MO45 0289

You're My Everything (song)
TM45 0121, TM45 0346

You're My Peace Of Mind (song)
MO45 0041

You're My Remedy (song)
SS45 0025

You're Not An Ordinary Girl
(song)
TM45 0078

You're So Fine And Sweet (song)
SS45 0022

You're Supposed To Keep Your
Love For Me (song)
MO45 0149

You're The Light That Guides
My Way (song)
MO45 0125

You're The One (song)
TM45 0062, TM45 0203

YOU'RE WHAT'S MISSING IN
MY LIFE (LP)
MOLP 0013

Your Kiss Is Sweet (song)
TM45 0435

Your Love Gets Me Burning
Alive (song)
TM45 0171

Your Love Grows More Precious
Everyday (song)
TM45 0105

Your Love Is Amazing (song)
TM45 0028, TM45 0100

Your Love Is So Good For Me
(song)
MO12 0002, MO45 0052

Your Love Is Wonderful (song)
TM45 0148

Your Mother's Only Daughter
(song)
TM45 0188

Your Old Stand By (song)
OR45 0017

Your Precious Love (song)
TM45 0126

Your Unchanging Love (song)

TM45 0119

Your Wonderful Sweet, Sweet
Love (song)
TM45 0337

You Seen One You Seen Them
All (song)
MO45 0206

You Stole My Love (song)
TM45 0287

You Turn Me On (song)
MO12 0135, MO45 0308

You've Been A Long Time
Coming (song)
TM45 0010

You've Been In Love Too Long
(song)
TM45 0030

You've Been So Wonderful To Me
(song)
TM45 0163

You've Got It Bad Girl (song)
TM45 0343

You've Got My Soul On Fire
(song)
TM45 0377

You've Got To Earn It (song)
TM45 0026

You've Got To Make Your
Choice (song)
TM45 0330

You've Lost That Lovin' Feelin'
(song)
TM45 0447

You've Made Me So Very Happy
(song)
TM45 0123, TM45 0201

You've Really Got A Hold On
Me (song)
OR45 0005

You Wear It Well (song)
MO12 0178, MO45 0354

You Wear It Well (Dub mix)
(song)
MO12 0184

ZOOM (LP)
MOLP 0014

Zoom (song)
MO12 0001, MO45 0044

The Zoo (The Human Zoo) (song)
TM45 0426

November 1959
  LO45 0001
April 1960
  LO45 0002
February 1961
  LO45 0003
June 1961
  LO45 0004
October 1961
  OREP 0001
December 1961
  FO45 0001
March 1962
  FO45 0002, FO45 0003, FO45 0004
September 1962
  OR45 0001, OR45 0002, OR45 0003
October 1962
  OR45 0004
January 1963
  OR45 0005, OR45 0006
February 1963
  OR45 0007, OR45 0008
March 1963
  OR45 0009, OR45 0010, OR45 0011
April 1963
  OR45 0012, OR45 0013
May 1963
  OR45 0014, OR45 0015
July 1963
  OR45 0016, OR45 0017, ORLP 0001,
  ORLP 0002, ORLP 0003
August 1963
  OR45 0018, ORLP 0004, ORLP 0005,
  ORLP 0006, ORLP 0007
September 1963
  OR45 0019
October 1963
  SS45 0001
November 1963
  SS45 0002, SS45 0003, SS45 0004
January 1964
  SS45 0005, SS45 0006, SS45 0007,
  SSEP 0001
February 1964
  SS45 0008, SSEP 0002
March 1964
  SS45 0009, SS45 0010, SSLP 0001
April 1964
  SS45 0011, SS45 0012, SS45 0013,
  SS45 0014, SSEP 0003
May 1964
  SS45 0015, SS45 0016, SSLP 0002,
  SSLP 0003
June 1964
  SS45 0017, SS45 0018, SSEP 0004
July 1964
  SS45 0019, SS45 0020
August 1964
  SS45 0021, SS45 0022, SS45 0023,
  SS45 0024
September 1964
  SS45 0025, SS45 0026, SSEP 0005,
  SSLP 0004
October 1964
  SS45 0027, SS45 0028, SS45 0029,
  SSLP 0005
November 1964
  SS45 0030, SS45 0031, SS45 0032,
  SS45 0033, SS45 0034, SSLP 0006,
  SSLP 0007
December 1964
  SS45 0035, SSLP 0009

January 1965
  SS45 0036, SS45 0037, SS45 0038,
  SS45 0039, SS45 0040, SS45 0041,
  SS45 0042, SSLP 0008
February 1965
  SS45 0043, SS45 0044
March 1965
  SS45 0045, TM45 0001, TM45 0002,
  TM45 0003, TM45 0004, TM45 0005,
  TM45 0006, TM45 0007
April 1965
  TM45 0008, TM45 0009, TM45 0010,
  TM45 0011, TMEP 0001, TMEP 0002,
  TMEP 0003, TMEP 0004, TMEP 0005,
  TMEP 0006, TMLP 0001, TMLP 0002,
  TMLP 0003, TMLP 0004, TMLP 0005,
  TMLP 0006
May 1965
  TM45 0012, TM45 0013, TM45 0014,
  TM45 0015, TM45 0016, TMEP 0007,
  TMEP 0008, TMEP 0009, TMLP 0007,
  TMLP 0008, TMLP 0009
June 1965
  TM45 0017, TM45 0018, TM45 0019,
  TMLP 0010, TMLP 0011
July 1965
  TM45 0020, TM45 0021, TM45 0022,
  TMLP 0012
August 1965
  TM45 0023, TM45 0024, TM45 0025,
  TM45 0026, TM45 0027, TM45 0028
September 1965
  TM45 0029, TM45 0030, TM45 0031,
  TM45 0032, TMLP 0013, TMLP 0014,
  TMLP 0015
October 1965
  TM45 0033, TM45 0034, TM45 0035,
  TM45 0036, TM45 0037, TM45 0038,
  TMLP 0016, TMLP 0017, TMLP 0018
November 1965
  TM45 0039, TM45 0040, TM45 0041,
  TM45 0042, TM45 0043
December 1965
  TMLP 0019, TMLP 0020
January 1966
  TM45 0044, TM45 0045, TM45 0046
February 1966
  TM45 0047, TM45 0048, TM45 0049,
  TM45 0050, TM45 0051, TMEP 0010,
  TMEP 0011, TMEP 0012, TMEP 0013,
  TMLP 0022, TMLP 0024, TMLP 0025,
  TMLP 0026, TMLP 0027
March 1966
  TM45 0052, TM45 0053, TM45 0054,
  TM45 0055, TM45 0056, TMLP 0021,
  TMLP 0023
April 1966
  TM45 0057, TM45 0058, TMEP 0014,
  TMEP 0015, TMEP 0016
May 1966
  TM45 0059, TM45 0060, TM45 0061,
  TM45 0062
June 1966
  TM45 0063, TM45 0064, TM45 0065,
  TM45 0066, TMLP 0028, TMLP 0029,
  TMLP 0030, TMLP 0050
July 1966
  TM45 0067, TM45 0068, TM45 0069,
  TMLP 0031, TMLP 0032
August 1966
  TM45 0070, TM45 0071, TM45 0072,
  TM45 0073

September 1966
  TM45 0074, TM45 0075, TM45 0076,
  TM45 0077, TM45 0078
October 1966
  TM45 0079, TM45 0080, TMEP 0017,
  TMLP 0033, TMLP 0034, TMLP 0035,
  TMLP 0036
November 1966
  TM45 0081, TM45 0082, TM45 0083,
  TM45 0084, TM45 0085, TMLP 0037
December 1966
  TM45 0086, TM45 0087, TM45 0088,
  TMLP 0038, TMLP 0039
January 1967
  TM45 0089, TM45 0090, TM45 0091,
  TM45 0092
February 1967
  TM45 0093, TM45 0094, TM45 0095,
  TM45 0096, TM45 0097, TMLP 0040,
  TMLP 0041, TMLP 0042, TMLP 0043
March 1967
  TM45 0098, TM45 0099, TM45 0100,
  TM45 0101, TM45 0102, TMEP 0018,
  TMEP 0019, TMLP 0044
April 1967
  TM45 0103, TM45 0104, TMLP 0045,
  TMLP 0046
May 1967
  TM45 0105, TM45 0106, TM45 0107,
  TM45 0108, TM45 0109, TM45 0110,
  TMLP 0047, TMLP 0048, TMLP 0049
June 1967
  TM45 0111, TM45 0112, TM45 0113,
  TMLP 0051
July 1967
  TM45 0114, TM45 0115, TM45 0116,
  TMLP 0052, TMLP 0053, TMLP 0054
August 1967
  TM45 0117, TM45 0118, TM45 0119
September 1967
  TM45 0120, TM45 0121, TM45 0122,
  TM45 0123
October 1967
  TM45 0124, TM45 0125, TM45 0126,
  TM45 0127, TM45 0128, TMLP 0055
November 1967
  TM45 0129, TM45 0130, TM45 0131,
  TM45 0132, TM45 0133, TMLP 0056,
  TMLP 0057
December 1967
  TM45 0134, TM45 0135, TM45 0136
January 1968
  TM45 0137, TM45 0138, TM45 0139,
  TM45 0140, TM45 0141, TMLP 0058,
  TMLP 0060, TMLP 0061, TMLP 0062,
  TMLP 0063, TMLP 0064
February 1968
  TM45 0142, TM45 0143, TM45 0144,
  TM45 0145, TMLP 0065, TMLP 0066,
  TMLP 0067, TMLP 0069
March 1968
  TM45 0146, TM45 0147, TM45 0148,
  TM45 0149, TM45 0150, TMLP 0068
April 1968
  TM45 0151, TM45 0152, TM45 0153,
  TM45 0154, TMLP 0059, TMLP 0070
May 1968
  TM45 0155, TM45 0156, TM45 0157,
  TM45 0158, TM45 0159
June 1968
  TM45 0160, TM45 0161, TM45 0162,
  TM45 0163, TMLP 0071, TMLP 0072

July 1968
TM45 0164, TM45 0165, TMLP 0073, TMLP 0074, TMLP 0076

August 1968
TM45 0166, TM45 0167, TMLP 0075, TMLP 0078, TMLP 0079

September 1968
TM45 0168, TM45 0169, TM45 0170, TM45 0171, TM45 0173, TMLP 0080, TMLP 0081

October 1968
TM45 0172, TM45 0174, TM45 0175, TMLP 0077

November 1968
TM45 0176, TM45 0177, TM45 0178, TM45 0179, TM45 0180, TMLP 0082, TMLP 0083, TMLP 0084

December 1968
TM45 0181, TMLP 0085, TMLP 0086

January 1969
TM45 0182, TM45 0183, TM45 0184, TM45 0185, TM45 0186, TMLP 0087, TMLP 0089, TMLP 0090, TMLP 0091, TMLP 0095, TMLP 0096

February 1969
TM45 0187, TM45 0188, TM45 0189, TMLP 0088, TMLP 0094, TMLP 0097, TMLP 0098

March 1969
TM45 0190, TM45 0191, TM45 0192, TM45 0193, TM45 0195, TMLP 0093

April 1969
TM45 0194, TM45 0196, TM45 0197, TMLP 0099, TMLP 0100

May 1969
TM45 0198, TM45 0199, TM45 0200, TMLP 0092, TMLP 0103, TMLP 0104, TMLP 0107

June 1969
TM45 0201, TM45 0202, TM45 0203

July 1969
TM45 0204, TM45 0205, TM45 0206, TMLP 0101, TMLP 0105, TMLP 0106, TMLP 0108, TMLP 0110, TMLP 0111

August 1969
TM45 0207, TM45 0208, TM45 0209

September 1969
TM45 0210, TM45 0211, TM45 0212, TMLP 0109, TMLP 0112, TMLP 0113, TMLP 0115, TMLP 0117, TMLP 0118

October 1969
TM45 0213, TM45 0214, TM45 0215, TM45 0216

November 1969
TM45 0217, TM45 0218, TM45 0219, TM45 0220, TM45 0222, TMLP 0114, TMLP 0116, TMLP 0119, TMLP 0120, TMLP 0121, TMLP 0123, TMLP 0124, TMLP 0126

January 1970
TM45 0223, TM45 0224, TM45 0225, TM45 0226

February 1970
TM45 0227, TM45 0228, TM45 0229, TMLP 0122, TMLP 0127, TMLP 0128, TMLP 0129, TMLP 0130, TMLP 0131, TMLP 0132, TMLP 0133, TMLP 0134, TMLP 0135, TMLP 0137, TMLP 0138

March 1970
TM45 0230, TM45 0231, TM45 0232, TM45 0233, TM45 0234

April 1970

TM45 0235, TM45 0236, TMLP 0125, TMLP 0136, TMLP 0139, TMLP 0140, TMLP 0141, TMLP 0142

May 1970
TM45 0237, TM45 0238, TM45 0239, TM45 0240, TM45 0241, TMLP 0143, TMLP 0144, TMLP 0145, TMLP 0146

June 1970
TM45 0242, TM45 0243, TM45 0244, TM45 0245, TMLP 0147, TMLP 0148, TMLP 0149, TMLP 0150

July 1970
TM45 0246, TM45 0247, TM45 0248, TM45 0249, TMLP 0151, TMLP 0152

August 1970
TM45 0250, TM45 0253, TMLP 0153, TMLP 0154, TMLP 0155, TMLP 0156, TMLP 0157

September 1970
TM45 0251, TM45 0252, TM45 0254, TMLP 0159

October 1970
TM45 0255, TM45 0256, TM45 0257, TM45 0258, TM45 0259, TMLP 0158, TMLP 0160, TMLP 0161, TMLP 0163

November 1970
TM45 0260, TM45 0261, TMLP 0164, TMLP 0165, TMLP 0166

December 1970
TMLP 0167, TMLP 0168, TMLP 0169

January 1971
TM45 0262, TM45 0263, TM45 0264, TMLP 0170

February 1971
TM45 0265, TM45 0266, TMLP 0171, TMLP 0173, TMLP 0174

March 1971
TM45 0268, TM45 0269, TM45 0270, TMLP 0172, TMLP 0179

April 1971
TM45 0271, TM45 0272, TM45 0273, TMLP 0177, TMLP 0180, TMLP 0181

May 1971
TM45 0274, TM45 0275, TM45 0276, TMLP 0175, TMLP 0178

June 1971
TM45 0267, TM45 0277, TM45 0278, TM45 0279, TM45 0280, TMLP 0182

July 1971
TM45 0281, TM45 0282

August 1971
TM45 0283, TM45 0284, TM45 0286, TMLP 0183, TMLP 0184

September 1971
RA45 0001, RA45 0002, TM45 0285, TM45 0287, TM45 0289, TM45 0290, TMLP 0185, TMLP 0186, TMLP 0188

October 1971
RA45 0003, RALP 0001, RALP 0006, TM45 0291, TM45 0292, TM45 0293, TM45 0294, TMLP 0187, TMLP 0189, TMLP 0190, TMLP 0192

November 1971
DSLP 0001, RALP 0002, RALP 0004, TM45 0295, TM45 0296, TM45 0297, TM45 0298, TMLP 0191, TMLP 0194

January 1972
RA45 0004, TM45 0299, TM45 0300, TM45 0301

February 1972
TM45 0302, TM45 0303, TM45 0304, TM45 0305, TM45 0306, TMLP 0195,

TMLP 0196, TMLP 0197, TMLP 0198, TMLP 0199, TMLP 0200

March 1972
TM45 0307, TM45 0308, TM45 0309, TM45 0310, TM45 0311, X2LP 0007

April 1972
RA45 0005, TM45 0312, TM45 0313, TM45 0314, TMLP 0193, TMLP 0201, TMLP 0202

May 1972
DSLP 0002, RALP 0008, TM45 0316, TM45 0317, TM45 0318, TM45 0319, TMLP 0203, TMLP 0204

June 1972
RA45 0006, TM45 0315, TM45 0320, TM45 0321, TM45 0322, TM45 0323, TM45 0324, TMLP 0205

July 1972
DSLP 0004, TM45 0325, TM45 0326, TM45 0328, TMLP 0207

August 1972
DSLP 0005, TMLP 0210

September 1972
RA45 0007, RALP 0007, TM45 0327, TM45 0329, TM45 0330, TM45 0331, TM45 0333, TMLP 0208, TMLP 0209, TMLP 0211

October 1972
DSLP 0006, MW45 0001, MW45 0002, RALP 0005, TM45 0332, TM45 0334, TM45 0335, TMLP 0213

November 1972
MWLP 0001, MWLP 0002, TM45 0336, TM45 0337, TM45 0338, TMLP 0214, TMLP 0217

December 1972
TM45 0339, TM45 0340, TMLP 0219

January 1973
DSLP 0007, MWLP 0004, RALP 0009, TM45 0341, TM45 0342, TM45 0343, TMLP 0215, TMLP 0218, TMLP 0220

February 1973
MWLP 0003, RA45 0008, RALP 0010, TM45 0344, TM45 0345, TM45 0346, TM45 0347, TMLP 0212, TMLP 0216, TMLP 0222, TMLP 0223, TMLP 0224, TMLP 0225

March 1973
MW45 0003, RALP 0011, TM45 0348, TM45 0349, TM45 0350, TM45 0351, TM45 0352, TMLP 0221, X2LP 0008

April 1973
DSLP 0008, RALP 0012, TM45 0353, TM45 0355, TM45 0356, TMLP 0226

May 1973
TM45 0354, TM45 0357, TM45 0358, TMLP 0227

June 1973
MW45 0006, TM45 0359, TM45 0360, TM45 0361

July 1973
MW45 0007, MW45 0008, MWLP 0005, TM45 0363, TM45 0365, TMLP 0228, TMLP 0229, TMLP 0230, TMLP 0232, TMLP 0233, TMLP 0234

August 1973
DSLP 0009, RA45 0009, RA45 0010, TM45 0364, TM45 0366, TM45 0367, TM45 0368, TM45 0370, TMLP 0231, TMLP 0235, TMLP 0236

September 1973
MW45 0009, MW45 0010, MW45 0011,

October 1973
RALP 0013, TM45 0362, TM45 0371,
TM45 0372, TM45 0374, TM45 0378,
TMLP 0237, TMLP 0238, TMLP 0239

October 1973
DSLP 0010, DSLP 0011, MW45 0005,
TM45 0375, TM45 0376, TM45 0377,
TM45 0379, TMLP 0244, TMLP 0245,
X2LP 0001

November 1973
DSLP 0012, DSLP 0013, DSLP 0014,
MW45 0012, TM45 0380, TM45 0381,
TM45 0382, TM45 0383, TMLP 0242

December 1973
MW45 0013, TM45 0373

January 1974
DSLP 0015, RA45 0011, TM45 0384,
TM45 0385, TM45 0386, TMLP 0246,
TMLP 0248, TMLP 0253, X2LP 0011

February 1974
DSLP 0016, RA45 0012, TM45 0388,
TM45 0390, TM45 0391, TMLP 0254

March 1974
TM45 0389, TM45 0392, TM45 0393,
TMLP 0255, X2LP 0004, X2LP 0012

April 1974
MW45 0014, TM45 0394, TM45 0395,
TM45 0396, TM45 0397, TMLP 0243,
TMLP 0263, TMLP 0265

May 1974
MW45 0015, RA45 0014, RA45 0015,
RA45 0016, TM45 0398, TM45 0399,
TM45 0400, TM45 0402, TMLP 0258,
TMLP 0259

June 1974
RA45 0013, TM45 0401, TM45 0403,
TM45 0405, TM45 0406, TM45 0407,
TM45 0408, TM45 0409, TM45 0410,
TM45 0411, TMLP 0264, X2LP 0005

July 1974
MW45 0016, RA45 0017, RA45 0021,
TM45 0404, TM45 0412, TM45 0413,
TMLP 0247, TMLP 0256, X2LP 0010

August 1974
MW45 0018, MW45 0019, TM45 0414,
TM45 0415, TM45 0416, TM45 0417,
TMLP 0268

September 1974
DSLP 0018, DSLP 0019, MW45 0020,
MW45 0021, RA45 0018, TM45 0418,
TM45 0419, TM45 0420, TM45 0421,
TMLP 0267, X2LP 0013

October 1974
RA45 0019, TM45 0422, TM45 0423,
TM45 0424, TMLP 0269, TMLP 0272,
X2LP 0006

November 1974
MW45 0022, RA45 0020, TM45 0425,
TM45 0426, TM45 0427, TM45 0428,
TM45 0429, TMLP 0274

December 1974
TM45 0430, TM45 0432, TMLP 0275,
TMLP 0277

January 1975
DSLP 0020, TM45 0431, TM45 0433,
TM45 0435, TM45 0436, TM45 0438,
TM45 0439, TMLP 0257, TMLP 0276,
TMLP 0279, TMLP 0282

February 1975
TM45 0434, TM45 0437, TM45 0440,
TM45 0441, TM45 0442, TM45 0443

March 1975
DSLP 0021, DSLP 0022, MW45 0023,

MW45 0024, TM45 0444, TM45 0445,
TM45 0446, TMLP 0278, TMLP 0283

April 1975
MW45 0025, TM45 0447, TM45 0448

May 1975
TM45 0449, TM45 0450, TM45 0451,
TMLP 0285

June 1975
DSLP 0023, GA45 0001, MW45 0028,
MWLP 0007, TM45 0453, TM45 0454,
TM45 0456, TM45 0457, TMLP 0286,
TMLP 0287

July 1975
MW45 0029, MWLP 0006, TM45 0455,
TM45 0458, TM45 0459, TM45 0460,
TM45 0461, TM45 0462, TM45 0463,
TMLP 0273, TMLP 0288, TMLP 0289,
TMLP 0292

August 1975
MW45 0030, TM45 0452, TM45 0464,
TM45 0465, TM45 0466, TM45 0467,
TM45 0468, TM45 0469, TM45 0470,
TM45 0471, TM45 0472, TM45 0473,
TM45 0474, TM45 0475, TM45 0476,
TM45 0477, TM45 0478

September 1975
MW45 0027, MW45 0031, TM45 0479,
TM45 0480, TM45 0481, TM45 0482,
TM45 0483, TMLP 0293, TMLP 0294,
TMLP 0297

October 1975
MW45 0032, TM45 0484, TM45 0485,
TM45 0486, TM45 0487, TM45 0488,
TM45 0489, TMLP 0295, X2LP 0014

November 1975
TM45 0490, TM45 0491, TM45 0492,
TM45 0493, TM45 0494, TM45 0495,
TMLP 0300, TMLP 0301, TMLP 0302,
TMLP 0303

December 1975
TMLP 0296

January 1976
TM45 0496, TM45 0497, TMLP 0298,
TMLP 0304, TMLP 0305, TMLP 0307,
X2LP 0016

February 1976
DSLP 0024, TM45 0498, TM45 0499,
TM45 0501, TMLP 0299

March 1976
MW45 0033, TM45 0500, TMLP 0308,
TMLP 0309, TMLP 0310, TMLP 0311,
TMLP 0317

April 1976
TM45 0502, TM45 0504, TM45 0506,
TMLP 0312, TMLP 0313, TMLP 0314

May 1976
MWLP 0008, PR45 0009, RALP 0016,
TM45 0503, TM45 0505, TM45 0507,
TMLP 0315

June 1976
MW45 0034, TM45 0509, TM45 0510,
TMLP 0319, TMLP 0322, TMLP 0323,
TMLP 0324

July 1976
MW45 0035, TM45 0508, TM45 0511,
TMLP 0316, TMLP 0320, TMLP 0328

August 1976
TM45 0512, TM45 0513, TM45 0514,
TM45 0515, TMLP 0318, TMLP 0321,
TMLP 0325

September 1976
DSLP 0025, DSLP 0026, TM45 0516,

TM45 0519, TM45 0520, TM45 0521,
TM45 0522, TM45 0523, TM45 0524,
TM45 0525, TM45 0526, TM45 0527,
TM45 0528, TM45 0529, TM45 0530,
TMLP 0326, TMLP 0327, TMLP 0334

October 1976
DSLP 0027, MO45 0001, MO45 0003,
MO45 0004, MO45 0005, MO45 0006,
PRLP 0001, TM45 0517, TM45 0518,
TM45 0531, TMLP 0330, TMLP 0331,
TMLP 0332, X2LP 0015

November 1976
DSLP 0028, MO45 0002, PR45 0001,
PRLP 0002, TM45 0532, TMEP 0020,
TMLP 0333, TMLP 0335

December 1976
MOLP 0001, MOLP 0002, MOLP 0003,
MOLP 0004, MOLP 0005

1977
PR45 0003

January 1977
MO45 0007, MO45 0008, MO45 0009,
MO45 0010, MO45 0011, MOLP 0006,
PRLP 0003, X2LP 0017

February 1977
MOLP 0007, MOLP 0008, PR45 0002

March 1977
MO45 0012, MO45 0013, MO45 0016,
MOLP 0009, MOLP 0010, MOLP 0014,
SPLP 0001, SPLP 0002, SPLP 0003,
SPLP 0004, SPLP 0005, SPLP 0006,
SPLP 0007, X2LP 0018

April 1977
HI45 0001, MO45 0015, MO45 0017,
MOLP 0011, MOLP 0012, MOLP 0013,
X2LP 0019

May 1977
HI45 0002, MO45 0018, MO45 0019,
MO45 0020, MO45 0021, MOLP 0015,
MOLP 0016, PRLP 0004, PRLP 0005

June 1977
MO45 0023, MO45 0024, MOLP 0017

July 1977
MO45 0022, MO45 0025, MO45 0026,
MOLP 0019, MOLP 0020, MOLP 0021

August 1977
MO45 0027, MO45 0028, MO45 0029,
MO45 0030, MO45 0031, MOLP 0018,
MOLP 0023, PR45 0004, PR45 0005,
TVLP 0001

September 1977
DSLP 0029, DSLP 0030, MO45 0032,
MO45 0033, MO45 0034, MOLP 0022,
MOLP 0024, MOLP 0025, MOLP 0026

October 1977
MO45 0035, MO45 0036, MO45 0037,
MO45 0038, MOLP 0027, PR45 0006,
PRLP 0006, PRLP 0007

November 1977
DSLP 0031, MO45 0039, MO45 0040,
MO45 0041, MO45 0042, MO45 0043,
MOLP 0028, MOLP 0030, PR45 0007,
TMLP 0329, X2LP 0020

January 1978
MO45 0044, MO45 0045, MO45 0046,
MOLP 0029, MOLP 0031, MOLP 0032

February 1978
MO45 0047, MO45 0048, MOLP 0033

March 1978
MC45 0001, MO12 0001, MO45 0049,
MO45 0050, MO45 0051, MO45 0053,
PR45 0008

April 1978
MO12 0002, MO45 0052, MO45 0054, MO45 0055, MOLP 0034, MOLP 0035

May 1978
MC45 0002, MO45 0056, MO45 0057, MO45 0058, MOLP 0036, MOLP 0037, MOLP 0038, MOLP 0039, MOLP 0040, MOLP 0044

June 1978
MO12 0004, MO45 0059

July 1978
MO12 0003, MO45 0060, MO45 0061, MO45 0062, MOLP 0041, MOLP 0042, MOLP 0043, PRLP 0008

August 1978
MO12 0005, MO45 0063, MOLP 0045, MOLP 0046, MOLP 0047

September 1978
MO45 0064, MO45 0065, MO45 0066, MO45 0067, MO45 0068, MOLP 0048, MOLP 0049

October 1978
MO12 0006, MO45 0069, MO45 0070, MO45 0071, MO45 0072, MO45 0073, MOLP 0050, MOLP 0051, MOLP 0053

November 1978
MO45 0074, MO45 0075, MO45 0076, MO45 0077, MOLP 0052, PRLP 0009

December 1978
MOLP 0055, MOLP 0056, MOLP 0057

January 1979
MO12 0007, MO12 0008, MO45 0078, MO45 0079, MO45 0080, MO45 0082, X2LP 0021

February 1979
MO12 0009, MO45 0081, MO45 0083, MO45 0084, MO45 0086, MOLP 0058, MOLP 0059

March 1979
MO12 0010, MO12 0011, MO45 0085, MOLP 0061, MOLP 0062, PR45 0010, PRLP 0010

April 1979
MO12 0012, MO12 0014, MO45 0087, MO45 0088, MOLP 0054

May 1979
MO12 0015, MO12 0017, MO12 0018, MO45 0089, MO45 0091, MO45 0092, MOLP 0060, MOLP 0063, MOLP 0064

June 1979
MO12 0019, MO12 0020, MO12 0021, MO45 0094, MO45 0095, MO45 0096, MO45 0098, MOLP 0065, MOLP 0066, MOLP 0071

July 1979
DSLP 0032, MO12 0013, MO12 0016, MO12 0022, MO45 0090, MO45 0093, MO45 0099, MO45 0100, MO45 0101, MOLP 0069, MOLP 0074, MOLP 0075, PRLP 0011

August 1979
MO45 0102, MO45 0103, MO45 0105, MO45 0107, MOLP 0067, MOLP 0068, MOLP 0070, MOLP 0072

September 1979
MO12 0023, MO12 0024, MO45 0104, MO45 0106, MO45 0108, MO45 0109, MO45 0110, MO45 0111, MO45 0112, MOLP 0073, MOLP 0076, MOLP 0077, MOLP 0078, MOLP 0079, MOLP 0080, MOLP 0081, TVLP 0002

October 1979
MO45 0114, MOLP 0082, X2LP 0022

November 1979
MO12 0025, MO12 0026, MO45 0097, MO45 0115, MO45 0116, MO45 0117, MO45 0118, TVLP 0003

December 1979
MOLP 0085

January 1980
MO45 0119, MO45 0120, MO45 0121, MO45 0122, MO45 0124

February 1980
MO45 0113, MO45 0123, MO45 0125, MOLP 0086

March 1980
MO45 0126, MO45 0127, MOLP 0087, MOLP 0088

April 1980
MO12 0027, MO45 0128, MO45 0129, MO45 0130, MO45 0131, MO45 0132, MOLP 0089, MOLP 0090, MOLP 0091

May 1980
DSLP 0033, MO12 0028, MO12 0029, MO45 0133, MO45 0134, MO45 0135, MO45 0136, MO45 0137, MOLP 0084

June 1980
DSLP 0034, MO45 0138, MO45 0139, MO45 0140, MO45 0141, MOLP 0092, MOLP 0093, MOLP 0094, TVLP 0004, X2LP 0023

July 1980
MO12 0030, MO12 0031, MO45 0142, MO45 0143, MO45 0144

August 1980
MO12 0032, MO45 0145, MO45 0146, MO45 0147, MO45 0148, MO45 0149

September 1980
MO12 0033, MO12 0034, MO45 0150, MO45 0151, MO45 0152, MO45 0153, MO45 0154, MOLP 0099

October 1980
MO12 0035, MO12 0036, MO12 0037, MO45 0155, MO45 0156, MO45 0157, MO45 0158, MO45 0159, MOLP 0097, MOLP 0098, MOLP 0100, MOLP 0101

November 1980
DSLP 0035, MO12 0038, MO45 0160, MO45 0161, MO45 0162

December 1980
MO45 0163, MO45 0164, MO45 0165, MO45 0166, MOLP 0096, MOLP 0102, MOLP 0103, MOLP 0104

January 1981
MO12 0039, MO45 0167, MO45 0168

February 1981
MO12 0041, MO12 0042, MO45 0169, MO45 0170, MO45 0171, MO45 0172, MO45 0173, X2LP 0024

March 1981
MO45 0174, MO45 0175, MOLP 0095, MOLP 0106, MOLP 0107

April 1981
MOLP 0105, MOLP 0108, MOLP 0109

May 1981
MO12 0040, MO12 0043, MO12 0044, MO12 0045, MO12 0046, MO45 0177, MO45 0178, MO45 0179, MO45 0180, MO45 0181

June 1981
MO45 0182, MOLP 0113

July 1981
MO12 0047, MO12 0048, MO12 0049, MO45 0183, MO45 0184, MO45 0185,

March 1983
MO45 0186, MOLP 0114, MOLP 0115

August 1981
MO45 0187, MOLP 0111

September 1981
MO45 0188, MOLP 0112

October 1981
MO12 0051, MO45 0192, MO45 0193, MO45 0194, MOLP 0110, MOLP 0117, TVLP 0005, TVLP 0006, TVLP 0007, TVLP 0008

November 1981
MO12 0050, MO12 0052, MO12 0053, MO12 0055, MO45 0190, MO45 0191, MO45 0195, MO45 0196, MO45 0198

December 1981
DSLP 0036, MO12 0054, MO45 0197, MOLP 0118, MOLP 0119

January 1982
MO12 0056, MO12 0057, MO45 0199, MO45 0200, MO45 0201, MO45 0203

February 1982
MO12 0058, MO45 0202, MO45 0204

March 1982
MO12 0059, MO45 0205, MO45 0206, MO45 0209, MOLP 0120, MOLP 0122

April 1982
MO12 0060, MO12 0061, MO12 0062, MO45 0207, MO45 0208, MO45 0210

May 1982
MO12 0063, MO45 0211, MO45 0212, MO45 0213, MO45 0218, MOLP 0123

June 1982
MO12 0064, MO45 0215, MOLP 0116, MOLP 0124, MOLP 0125, PILP 0001, PILP 0002, PILP 0003, PILP 0004, PILP 0005, PILP 0006, PILP 0007, PILP 0008, PILP 0009, PILP 0010, PILP 0011

July 1982
MO12 0065, MO45 0214, MO45 0216, MO45 0217, MO45 0220, MOLP 0128, X2LP 0025

August 1982
MO12 0067, MO12 0068, MO12 0069, MO12 0070, MO12 0071, MO45 0221, MO45 0222, MO45 0223, MO45 0224, MO45 0225, MO45 0226, MOLP 0127, MOLP 0129

September 1982
MO12 0073, MO45 0227, MO45 0228, MO45 0229, MOLP 0130, MOLP 0131, X2LP 0026, X2LP 0027, X2LP 0028

October 1982
MO12 0066, MO12 0074, MO45 0219, MO45 0230, MO45 0231, MO45 0232, MOLP 0133, PILP 0013, PILP 0014, SILP 0001, SILP 0002

November 1982
DSLP 0037, MO12 0075, MO12 0076, MO12 0077, MO45 0233, MO45 0234, MO45 0235, MO45 0236, MOLP 0134

December 1982
MOLP 0136, MOLP 0137

January 1983
MO12 0078, MO12 0079, MO45 0237, MO45 0238, MO45 0239

February 1983
MO12 0072, MO12 0081, MO12 0082, MO45 0240, MO45 0241, MO45 0242, MO45 0243

March 1983
MO12 0080, MO12 0083, MO12 0084,

April 1983
MO12 0085, MO45 0244, MO45 0245, MO45 0246, MO45 0247, MO45 0248, MOLP 0132, MOLP 0138, MOLP 0139

April 1983
MO12 0086, MO12 0087, MO12 0088, MO45 0249, MO45 0251, MO45 0252, MOLP 0140

May 1983
MO45 0254, MO45 0256, MOLP 0141, MOLP 0142, MOLP 0143

June 1983
MO12 0089, MO12 0090, MO45 0253, MO45 0255, MOLP 0146

July 1983
MO12 0091, MO12 0093, MO12 0094, MO45 0260, MOLP 0148

August 1983
MO12 0095, MO45 0259, MO45 0262

September 1983
DSLP 0038, DSLP 0039, MO12 0092, MO12 0096, MO12 0097, MO45 0264, MO45 0266, MO45 0268, MOLP 0149

October 1983
DSLP 0041, MO12 0098, MO12 0099, MO12 0100, MO45 0267, MO45 0269, MO45 0270, MOLP 0150, MOLP 0151, MOLP 0152, X2LP 0031

November 1983
MO12 0101, MO12 0103, MO12 0104, MO45 0271, MO45 0273, MOLP 0147, MOLP 0153, MOLP 0154, X2LP 0032

December 1983
X2LP 0030

January 1984
MO12 0102, MO12 0105, MO12 0106, MO12 0107, MO12 0110, MO12 0111, MO45 0272, MO45 0276, MO45 0280, MO45 0281

February 1984
MOLP 0160

March 1984
MO12 0108, MO12 0109, MO12 0112, MO12 0113, MO12 0114, MO45 0278, MO45 0279, MO45 0283, MO45 0284, MO45 0285, MO45 0286

April 1984
MO12 0115, MO45 0282, MO45 0287, MOLP 0157, MOLP 0158, MOLP 0161, MOLP 0162, MOLP 0164, MOLP 0169, MOLP 0173

May 1984
MO12 0117, MO12 0119, MO45 0289, MO45 0291, MOCD 0001, MOCD 0002, MOCD 0003, MOCD 0004, MOCD 0005

June 1984
MO12 0116, MO12 0118, MO12 0120,

MO12 0121, MO45 0288, MO45 0290, MO45 0292, MO45 0293

July 1984
MO12 0122, MO12 0124, MO45 0294, MO45 0295, MO45 0297, MOLP 0156, MOLP 0165

August 1984
MO12 0123, MO12 0125, MO12 0126, MO12 0131, MO45 0296, MO45 0298, MO45 0299, MO45 0304, MOLP 0167, MOLP 0174

September 1984
MO12 0127, MO12 0129, MO12 0133, MO12 0134, MO12 0136, MO45 0300, MO45 0302, MO45 0306, MO45 0307, MO45 0309, MOCD 0006, MOLP 0178

October 1984
MO12 0128, MO12 0130, MO12 0132, MO12 0135, MO12 0137, MO45 0301, MO45 0303, MO45 0305, MO45 0308, MO45 0311, MOCD 0007, MOCD 0008, MOCD 0009, MOCD 0010, MOLP 0166, MOLP 0168, MOLP 0170, MOLP 0172, MOLP 0175, MOLP 0176, MOLP 0177

November 1984
MO12 0139, MO12 0140, MO45 0313, MO45 0314, MOLP 0179, MOLP 0180, MOLP 0182

December 1984
MO12 0138, MO12 0147, MO45 0312, MO45 0321, MOLP 0186

January 1985
MO12 0141, MO12 0142, MO12 0143, MO12 0144, MO12 0145, MO45 0315, MO45 0317, MO45 0318, MO45 0319, MO45 0320

February 1985
MO12 0151, MO45 0326, MOCD 0011, MOLP 0187, MOLP 0188

March 1985
MO12 0146, MO12 0148, MO12 0149, MO12 0150, MO12 0152, MO45 0322, MO45 0323, MO45 0325, MO45 0327, MOLP 0183

April 1985
MO12 0153, MO12 0154, MO12 0155, MO12 0156, MO12 0157, MO12 0158, MO12 0159, MO12 0160, MO12 0161, MO12 0162, MO12 0165, MO12 0181, MO45 0328, MO45 0329, MO45 0330, MO45 0331, MO45 0332, MO45 0333, MO45 0334, MO45 0335, MO45 0336, MO45 0337, MO45 0341, MO45 0357, MOCD 0012, MOLP 0171, MOLP 0185

May 1985
MO12 0166, MO12 0167, MO45 0342,

MO45 0343, MOLP 0184, MOLP 0189, MOLP 0190

June 1985
MO12 0163, MO12 0168, MO12 0169, MO12 0170, MO12 0171, MO12 0172, MO45 0339, MO45 0344, MO45 0345, MO45 0346, MO45 0347, MO45 0348, MOCD 0013, MOCD 0014, MOCD 0015, MOCD 0016, MOCD 0017, MOCD 0018, MOLP 0192, MOLP 0193

July 1985
MO12 0174, MO12 0175, MO45 0350, MO45 0351, MOCD 0019, MOCD 0020, MOLP 0181, MOLP 0195

August 1985
MO12 0173, MO12 0176, MO12 0178, MO45 0349, MO45 0352, MO45 0354, MOCD 0021, MOLP 0194, MOLP 0196

September 1985
MO12 0177, MO12 0179, MO12 0180, MO45 0353, MO45 0355, MO45 0356

October 1985
MOCD 0022, MOLP 0191

November 1985
MO12 0182, MO12 0183, MO12 0184, MO12 0185, MO45 0358, MO45 0359, MO45 0360, MO45 0361, MOCD 0023, MOCD 0024, MOCD 0025, MOCD 0026, MOCD 0027, MOLP 0159, MOLP 0198

January 1986
MO12 0187, MO45 0363

February 1986
MO12 0186, MO12 0189, MO12 0191, MO45 0362, MO45 0365, MO45 0367, MOCD 0028

March 1986
MO12 0188, MO12 0190, MO12 0193, MO45 0364, MO45 0366, MO45 0369, MOLP 0197

April 1986
MO12 0192, MO12 0194, MO12 0195, MO45 0368, MO45 0370, MO45 0371

May 1986
MOCD 0029, MOCD 0030

June 1986
MOCD 0031, MOCD 0032, MOCD 0033, MOCD 0034

July 1986
MOCD 0035

August 1986
MOCD 0036, MOCD 0037

September 1986
MOCD 0038

October 1986
MOCD 0039

STMA 8010	(S)TML 11035	(S)TML 11074	(S)TML 11113	STML 11149
DSLP 0010	TMLP 0035	TMLP 0074	TMLP 0113	TMLP 0149
STMA 8011	(S)TML 11036	(S)TML 11075	(S)TML 11114	STML 11150
DSLP 0011	TMLP 0036	TMLP 0075	TMLP 0114	TMLP 0150
STMA 8012	(S)TML 11037	(S)TML 11078	(S)TML 11115	STML 11151
DSLP 0012	TMLP 0037	TMLP 0078	TMLP 0115	TMLP 0151
STMA 8013	(S)TML 11038	(S)TML 11079	(S)TML 11116	STML 11152
DSLP 0013	TMLP 0038	TMLP 0079	TMLP 0116	TMLP 0152
STMA 8014	(S)TML 11039	(S)TML 11080	(S)TML 11117	STML 11153
DSLP 0014	TMLP 0039	TMLP 0080	TMLP 0117	TMLP 0153
STMA 8015	(S)TML 11040	(S)TML 11081	(S)TML 11118	STML 11154/5
DSLP 0015	TMLP 0040	TMLP 0081	TMLP 0118	TMLP 0154
STMA 8016	(S)TML 11041	(S)TML 11082	(S)TML 11119	STML 11156
DSLP 0016	TMLP 0041	TMLP 0082	TMLP 0119	TMLP 0155
STMA 8017	(S)TML 11042	(S)TML 11083	(S)TML 11120	STML 11157
DSLP 0017	TMLP 0042	TMLP 0083	TMLP 0120	TMLP 0156
STMA 8018	(S)TML 11044	(S)TML 11084	(S)TML 11121	STML 11158
DSLP 0018	TMLP 0044	TMLP 0084	TMLP 0121	TMLP 0157
STMA 8019	(S)TML 11045	(S)TML 11085	(S)TML 11122	STML 11159
DSLP 0019	TMLP 0045	TMLP 0085	TMLP 0122	TMLP 0158
STMA 8020	(S)TML 11046	(S)TML 11086	(S)TML 11123	STML 11160
DSLP 0020	TMLP 0046	TMLP 0086	TMLP 0123	TMLP 0159
STMA 8021	(S)TML 11047	(S)TML 11087	(S)TML 11124	STML 11161
DSLP 0021	TMLP 0047	TMLP 0087	TMLP 0124	TMLP 0160
STMA 8022	(S)TML 11048	(S)TML 11088	(S)TML 11125	STML 11162
DSLP 0022	TMLP 0048	TMLP 0088	TMLP 0125	TMLP 0161
STMA 8023	(S)TML 11049	(S)TML 11089	(S)TML 11126	STML 11163
DSLP 0023	TMLP 0049	TMLP 0089	TMLP 0126	TMLP 0162
STMA 8024	(S)TML 11051	(S)TML 11090	(S)TML 11127	STML 11164
DSLP 0024	TMLP 0051	TMLP 0090	TMLP 0127	TMLP 0163
STMA 8025	(S)TML 11052	(S)TML 11091	(S)TML 11128	STML 11165
DSLP 0025	TMLP 0052	TMLP 0091	TMLP 0128	TMLP 0164
STMA 8026	(S)TML 11053	(S)TML 11092	(S)TML 11129	STML 11166
DSLP 0026	TMLP 0053	TMLP 0092	TMLP 0129	TMLP 0165
STMA 8027	(S)TML 11054	(S)TML 11093	(S)TML 11130	STML 11167
DSLP 0027	TMLP 0054	TMLP 0093	TMLP 0130	TMLP 0166
STMA 8028	(S)TML 11055	(S)TML 11094	(S)TML 11131	STML 11168
DSLP 0028	TMLP 0055	TMLP 0094	TMLP 0131	TMLP 0167
STMA 8029	(S)TML 11056	(S)TML 11095	(S)TML 11132	STML 11169
DSLP 0029	TMLP 0056	TMLP 0095	TMLP 0132	TMLP 0168
STMA 8030	(S)TML 11057	(S)TML 11096	(S)TML 11133	STML 11170
DSLP 0030	TMLP 0057	TMLP 0096	TMLP 0133	TMLP 0169
STMA 8031	(S)TML 11058	(S)TML 11097	(S)TML 11134	STML 11171
DSLP 0031	TMLP 0058	TMLP 0097	TMLP 0134	TMLP 0170
STMA 8032	(S)TML 11059	(S)TML 11098	(S)TML 11135	STML 11172
DSLP 0032	TMLP 0059	TMLP 0098	TMLP 0135	TMLP 0171
STMA 8033	(S)TML 11060	(S)TML 11099	(S)TML 11136	STML 11173
DSLP 0033	TMLP 0060	TMLP 0099	TMLP 0136	TMLP 0172
STMA 8034	(S)TML 11061	(S)TML 11100	(S)TML 11137	STML 11174
DSLP 0034	TMLP 0061	TMLP 0100	TMLP 0137	TMLP 0173
STMA 8035	(S)TML 11062	(S)TML 11101	(S)TML 11138	STML 11175
DSLP 0035	TMLP 0062	TMLP 0101	TMLP 0138	TMLP 0174
STMA 8036	(S)TML 11063	(S)TML 11103	STML 11139	STML 11176
DSLP 0036	TMLP 0063	TMLP 0103	TMLP 0139	TMLP 0175
STMA 8037	(S)TML 11065	(S)TML 11104	STML 11140	STML 11177
DSLP 0037	TMLP 0065	TMLP 0104	TMLP 0140	TMLP 0176
STMA 8038	(S)TML 11066	(S)TML 11105	STML 11141	STML 11178
DSLP 0038	TMLP 0066	TMLP 0105	TMLP 0141	TMLP 0177
STMA 8039	(S)TML 11067	(S)TML 11106	STML 11142	STML 11179
DSLP 0039	TMLP 0067	TMLP 0106	TMLP 0142	TMLP 0178
STMA 8040	(S)TML 11068	(S)TML 11107	STML 11143	STML 11180
DSLP 0040	TMLP 0068	TMLP 0107	TMLP 0143	TMLP 0179
STMA 8041	(S)TML 11069	(S)TML 11108	STML11144	STML 11181
DSLP 0041	TMLP 0069	TMLP 0108	TMLP 0144	TMLP 0180
STMF 7001	(S)TML 11070	(S)TML 11109	STML 11145	STML 11182
SILP 0001	TMLP 0070	TMLP 0109	TMLP 0145	TMLP 0181
STMF 7002	(S)TML 11071	(S)TML 11110	STML 11146	STML 11183
SILP 0002	TMLP 0071	TMLP 0110	TMLP 0146	TMLP 0182
(S)TML 11033	(S)TML 11072	(S)TML 11111	STML 11147	STML 11184
TMLP 0033	TMLP 0072	TMLP 0111	TMLP 0147	TMLP 0183
(S)TML 11034	(S)TML 11073	(S)TML 11112	STML 11148	STML 11185
TMLP 0034	TMLP 0073	TMLP 0112	TMLP 0148	TMLP 0184

MO12 0073	MO12 0109	MO12 0145,	TML 11019	TML 11055
TMGT 1282	TMGT 1331	MO12 0146	TMLP 0019	TMLP 0055
MO12 0074	MO12 0110	TMGT 1372	TML 11020	TML 11056
TMGT 1284	TMGT 1332	MO12 0147	TMLP 0020	TMLP 0056
MO12 0075	MO12 0111	TMGT 1373	TML 11021	TML 11057
TMGT 1285	TMGT 1334	MO12 0148	TMLP 0021	TMLP 0057
MO12 0076	MO12 0112	TMGT 1374	TML 11022	TML 11058
TMGT 1286	TMGT 1335	MO12 0149	TMLP 0022	TMLP 0058
MO12 0077	MO12 0113	TMGT 1376	TML 11023	TML 11059
TMGT 1288	TMGT 1336	MO12 0150	TMLP 0023	TMLP 0059
MO12 0078	MO12 0114	TMGT 1377	TML 11024	TML 11060
TMGT 1289	TMGT 1338	MO12 0151	TMLP 0024	TMLP 0060
MO12 0079	MO12 0115	TMGT 1378	TML 11025	TML 11061
TMGT 1291	TMGT 1339	MO12 0152	TMLP 0025	TMLP 0061
MO12 0080	MO12 0116	TMGT 1379	TML 11026	TML 11062
TMGT 1293	TMGT 1340	MO12 0153	TMLP 0026	TMLP 0062
MO12 0081	MO12 0117	TMGT 1380	TML 11027	TML 11063
TMGT 1294	TMGT 1341	MO12 0154	TMLP 0027	TMLP 0063
MO12 0082	MO12 0118	TMGT 1381	TML 11028	TML 11064
TMGT 1295	TMGT 1342	MO12 0155	TMLP 0028	TMLP 0064
MO12 0083	MO12 0119	TMGT 1382	TML 11029	TML 11065
TMGT 1297	TMGT 1343	MO12 0156	TMLP 0029	TMLP 0065
MO12 0084	MO12 0120	TMGT 1383	TML 11030	TML 11066
TMGT 1299	TMGT 1344	MO12 0157	TMLP 0030	TMLP 0066
MO12 0085	MO12 0121	TMGT 1384	TML 11031	TML 11067
TMGT 1300	TMGT 1345	MO12 0158	TMLP 0031	TMLP 0067
MO12 0086	MO12 0122	TMGT 1385	TML 11032	TML 11068
TMGT 1301	TMGT 1347	MO12 0159	TMLP 0032	TMLP 0068
MO12 0087	MO12 0123	TMGT 1386	TML 11033	TML 11069
TMGT 1302	TMGT 1348	MO12 0160	TMLP 0033	TMLP 0069
MO12 0088	MO12 0124	TMGT 1387	TML 11034	TML 11070
TMGT 1304	TMGT 1349	MO12 0161	TMLP 0034	TMLP 0070
MO12 0089	MO12 0125	TMGT 1388	TML 11035	TML 11071
TMGT 1306	TMGT 1350	MO12 0162	TMLP 0035	TMLP 0071
MO12 0090	MO12 0126	TMGT 1390	TML 11036	TML 11072
TMGT 1308	TMGT 1351	MO12 0163	TMLP 0036	TMLP 0072
MO12 0091	MO12 0127	TML 11001	TML 11037	TML 11073
TMGT 1309	TMGT 1352	TMLP 0001	TMLP 0037	TMLP 0073
MO12 0092	MO12 0128	TML 11002	TML 11038	TML 11074
TMGT 1311	TMGT 1353	TMLP 0002	TMLP 0038	TMLP 0074
MO12 0093	MO12 0129	TML 11003	TML 11039	TML 11075
TMGT 1312	TMGT 1354	TMLP 0003	TMLP 0039	TMLP 0075
MO12 0094	MO12 0130	TML 11004	TML 11040	TML 11076
TMGT 1314	TMGT 1355	TMLP 0004	TMLP 0040	TMLP 0076
MO12 0095	MO12 0131	TML 11005	TML 11041	TML 11077
TMGT 1315	TMGT 1356	TMLP 0005	TMLP 0041	TMLP 0077
MO12 0096	MO12 0132	TML 11006	TML 11042	TML 11078
TMGT 1316	TMGT 1357	TMLP 0006	TMLP 0042	TMLP 0078
MO12 0097	MO12 0133	TML 11007	TML 11043	TML 11079
TMGT 1318	TMGT 1358	TMLP 0007	TMLP 0043	TMLP 0079
MO12 0098	MO12 0134	TML 11008	TML 11044	TML 11080
TMGT 1320	TMGT 1359	TMLP 0008	TMLP 0044	TMLP 0080
MO12 0099	MO12 0135	TML 11009	TML 11045	TML 11081
TMGT 1321	TMGT 1360	TMLP 0009	TMLP 0045	TMLP 0081
MO12 0100	MO12 0136	TML 11010	TML 11046	TML 11082
TMGT 1322	TMGT 1361	TMLP 0010	TMLP 0046	TMLP 0082
MO12 0101	MO12 0137	TML 11011	TML 11047	TML 11083
TMGT 1323	TMGT 1363	TMLP 0011	TMLP 0047	TMLP 0083
MO12 0102	MO12 0138	TML 11012	TML 11048	TML 11084
TMGT 1324	TMGT 1364	TMLP 0012	TMLP 0048	TMLP 0084
MO12 0103	MO12 0139	TML 11013	TML 11049	TML 11085
TMGT 1325	TMGT 1365	TMLP 0013	TMLP 0049	TMLP 0085
MO12 0104	MO12 0140	TML 11014	TML 11050	TML 11086
TMGT 1326	TMGT 1366	TMLP 0014	TMLP 0050	TMLP 0086
MO12 0105	MO12 0141	TML 11015	TML 11051	TML 11087
TMGT 1327	TMGT 1368	TMLP 0015	TMLP 0051	TMLP 0087
MO12 0106	MO12 0142	TML 11016	TML 11052	TML 11088
TMGT 1328	TMGT 1369	TMLP 0016	TMLP 0052	TMLP 0088
MO12 0107	MO12 0143	TML 11017	TML 11053	TML 11089
TMGT 1329	TMGT 1370	TMLP 0017	TMLP 0053	TMLP 0089
MO12 0108	MO12 0144	TML 11018	TML 11054	TML 11090
TMGT 1330	TMGT 1371	TMLP 0018	TMLP 0054	TMLP 0090

MO45 0008	MO45 0041	11026	TMLP 0058	TMLP 0090
1061	1094	TMLP 0026	11059	11091
MO45 0009	MO45 0042	11027	TMLP 0059	TMLP 0091
1062	1095	TMLP 0027	1106	11092
MO45 0010	MO45 0043	11028	MO45 0054	TMLP 0092
1063	1096	TMLP 0028	11060	11093
MO45 0011	MO12 0001,	11029	TMLP 0060	TMLP 0093
1064	MO45 0044	TMLP 0029	11061	11094
MO45 0012	1097	1103	TMLP 0061	TMLP 0094
1065	MO45 0045	MO45 0051	11062	11095
MO45 0013	1098	11030	TMLP 0062	TMLP 0095
1066	MO45 0046	TMLP 0030	11063	11096
MO45 0014	1099	11031	TMLP 0063	TMLP 0096
1067	MO45 0047	TMLP 0031	11064	11097
MO45 0015	110	11032	TMLP 0064	TMLP 0097
1068	RA45 0010	TMLP 0032	11065	11098
MO45 0016	1100	11033	TMLP 0065	TMLP 0098
1069	MO45 0048	TMLP 0033	11066	11099
MO45 0017	11001	11034	TMLP 0066	TMLP 0099
107	TMLP 0001	TMLP 0034	11067	111
RA45 0007	11002	11035	TMLP 0067	RA45 0011
1070	TMLP 0002	TMLP 0035	11068	1110
MO45 0018	11003	11036	TMLP 0068	MO12 0003,
1071	TMLP 0003	TMLP 0036	11069	MO45 0058
MO45 0019	11004	11037	TMLP 0069	11100
1072	TMLP 0004	TMLP 0037	1107	TMLP 0100
MO45 0020	11005	11038	MO45 0055	11101
1073	TMLP 0005	TMLP 0038	11070	TMLP 0101
MO45 0021	11006	11039	TMLP 0070	11102
1074	TMLP 0006	TMLP 0039	11071	TMLP 0102
MO45 0022	11007	1104	TMLP 0071	11103
1075	TMLP 0007	MO12 0002,	11072	TMLP 0103
MO45 0023	11008	MO45 0052	TMLP 0072	11104
1076	TMLP 0008	11040	11073	TMLP 0104
MO45 0024	11009	TMLP 0040	TMLP 0073	11105
1077	TMLP 0009	11041	11074	TMLP 0105
MO45 0025	1101	TMLP 0041	TMLP 0074	11106
1078	MO45 0049	11042	11075	TMLP 0106
MO45 0026	11010	TMLP 0042	TMLP 0075	11107
1079	TMLP 0010	11043	11076	TMLP 0107
MO45 0027	11011	TMLP 0043	TMLP 0076	11108
108	TMLP 0011	11044	11077	TMLP 0108
RA45 0008	11012	TMLP 0044	TMLP 0077	11109
1080	TMLP 0012	11045	11078	TMLP 0109
MO45 0028	11013	TMLP 0045	TMLP 0078	1111
1081	TMLP 0013	11046	11079	MO12 0004,
MO45 0029	11014	TMLP 0046	TMLP 0079	MO45 0059
1082	TMLP 0014	11047	1108	11110
MO45 0030	11015	TMLP 0047	MO45 0056	TMLP 0110
1083	TMLP 0015	11048	11080	11111
MO45 0031	11016	TMLP 0048	TMLP 0080	TMLP 0111
1084	TMLP 0016	11049	11081	11112
MO45 0032	11017	TMLP 0049	TMLP 0081	TMLP 0112
1085	TMLP 0017	1105	11082	11113
MO45 0033	11018	MO45 0053	TMLP 0082	TMLP 0113
1086	TMLP 0018	11050	11083	11114
MO45 0034	11019	TMLP 0050	TMLP 0083	TMLP 0114
1087	TMLP 0019	11051	11084	11115
MO45 0035	1102	TMLP 0051	TMLP 0084	TMLP 0115
1088	MO45 0050	11052	11085	11116
MO45 0036	11020	TMLP 0052	TMLP 0085	TMLP 0116
1089	TMLP 0020	11053	11086	11117
MO45 0037	11021	TMLP 0053	TMLP 0086	TMLP 0117
109	TMLP 0021	11054	11087	11118
RA45 0009	11022	TMLP 0054	TMLP 0087	TMLP 0118
1090	TMLP 0022	11055	11088	11119
MO45 0038	11023	TMLP 0055	TMLP 0088	TMLP 0119
1091	TMLP 0023	11056	11089	1112
MO45 0039	11024	TMLP 0056	TMLP 0089	MO45 0060
1092	TMLP 0024	11057	1109	11120
MO45 0040	11025	TMLP 0057	MO45 0057	TMLP 0120
1093	TMLP 0025	11058	11090	11121

TMLP 0121	11154/5	11188	1122	TMLP 0249
11122	TMLP 0154	TMLP 0187	MO45 0070	11251
TMLP 0122	11156	11189	11220	TMLP 0250
11123	TMLP 0155	TMLP 0188	TMLP 0219	11252
TMLP 0123	11157	1119	11221	TMLP 0251
11124	TMLP 0156	MO45 0067	TMLP 0220	11253
TMLP 0124	11158	11190	11222	TMLP 0252
11125	TMLP 0157	TMLP 0189	TMLP 0221	11254
TMLP 0125	11159	11191	11223	TMLP 0253
11126	TMLP 0158	TMLP 0190	TMLP 0222	11255
TMLP 0126	1116	11192	11224	TMLP 0254
11127	MO45 0064	TMLP 0191	TMLP 0223	11256
TMLP 0127	11160	11193	11225	TMLP 0255
11128	TMLP 0159	TMLP 0192	TMLP 0224	11257
TMLP 0128	11161	11194	11226	TMLP 0256
11129	TMLP 0160	TMLP 0193	TMLP 0225	11258
TMLP 0129	11162	11195	11227	TMLP 0257
1113	TMLP 0161	TMLP 0194	TMLP 0226	11259
MO45 0061	11163	11196	11228	TMLP 0258
11130	TMLP 0162	TMLP 0195	TMLP 0227	1126
TMLP 0130	11164	11197	11229	MO45 0074,
11131	TMLP 0163	TMLP 0196	TMLP 0228	X2LP 0003
TMLP 0131	11165	11198	1123	11260
11132	TMLP 0164	TMLP 0197	MO12 0006,	TMLP 0259
TMLP 0132	11166	11199	MO45 0071	11261
11133	TMLP 0165	TMLP 0198	11230	TMLP 0260
TMLP 0133	11167	112	TMLP 0229	11262
11134	TMLP 0166	RA45 0012	11231	TMLP 0261
TMLP 0134	11168	1120	TMLP 0230	11263
11135	TMLP 0167	MO45 0068	11232	TMLP 0262
TMLP 0135	11169	11200	TMLP 0231	11264
11136	TMLP 0168	TMLP 0199	11233	TMLP 0263
TMLP 0136	1117	11201	TMLP 0232	11265
11137	MO45 0065	TMLP 0200	11234	TMLP 0264
TMLP 0137	11170	11202	TMLP 0233	11266
11138	TMLP 0169	TMLP 0201	11235	TMLP 0265
TMLP 0138	11171	11203	TMLP 0234	11267
11139	TMLP 0170	TMLP 0202	11236	TMLP 0266
TMLP 0139	11172	11204	TMLP 0235	11268
1114	TMLP 0171	TMLP 0203	11237	TMLP 0267
MO45 0062	11173	11205	TMLP 0236	11269
11140	TMLP 0172	TMLP 0204	11238	TMLP 0268
TMLP 0140	11174	11206	TMLP 0237	1127
11141	TMLP 0173	TMLP 0205	11239	MO45 0075,
TMLP 0141	11175	11207	TMLP 0238	X2LP 0004
11142	TMLP 0174	TMLP 0206	1124	11270
TMLP 0142	11176	11208	MO45 0072,	TMLP 0269
11143	TMLP 0175	TMLP 0207	X2LP 0001	11271
TMLP 0143	11177	11209	11240	TMLP 0270
11144	TMLP 0176	TMLP 0208	TMLP 0239	11272
TMLP 0144	11178	1121	11241	TMLP 0271
11145	TMLP 0177	MO45 0069	TMLP 0240	11273
TMLP 0145	11179	11210	11242	TMLP 0272
11146	TMLP 0178	TMLP 0209	TMLP 0241	11274
TMLP 0146	1118	11211	11243	TMLP 0273
11147	MO45 0066	TMLP 0210	TMLP 0242	11275
TMLP 0147	11180	11212	11244	TMLP 0274
11148	TMLP 0179	TMLP 0211	TMLP 0243	11276
TMLP 0148	11181	11213	11245	TMLP 0275
11149	TMLP 0180	TMLP 0212	TMLP 0244	11277
TMLP 0149	11182	11214	11246	TMLP 0276
1115	TMLP 0181	TMLP 0213	TMLP 0245	11278
MO12 0005,	11183	11215	11247	TMLP 0277
MO45 0063	TMLP 0182	TMLP 0214	TMLP 0246	11279
11150	11184	11216	11248	TMLP 0278
TMLP 0150	TMLP 0183	TMLP 0215	TMLP 0247	1128
11151	11185	11217	11249	MO45 0076,
TMLP 0151	TMLP 0184	TMLP 0216	TMLP 0248	X2LP 0005
11152	11186	11218	1125	11280
TMLP 0152	TMLP 0185	TMLP 0217	MO45 0073,	TMLP 0279
11153	11187	11219	X2LP 0002	11281
TMLP 0153	TMLP 0186	TMLP 0218	11250	TMLP 0280

11282	MO12 0017,	MO45 0119	TMLP 0293	12034
TMLP 0281	MO45 0091	1172	12002	TMLP 0326
11283	1144	MO45 0120	TMLP 0294	12035
TMLP 0282	MO12 0018,	1173	12003	TMLP 0327
11284	MO45 0092	MO45 0121	TMLP 0295	12036
TMLP 0283	1145	1174	12004	TMLP 0328
11285	MO45 0093	MO45 0122	TMLP 0296	12037
TMLP 0284	1146	1175	12005	TMLP 0329
11286	MO12 0019,	MO45 0123	TMLP 0297	12038
TMLP 0285	MO45 0094	1176	12006	TMLP 0330
11287	1147	MO45 0124	TMLP 0298	12039
TMLP 0286	MO12 0020,	1177	12007	TMLP 0331
11288	MO45 0095	MO45 0125	TMLP 0299	1204
TMLP 0287	1148	1178	12008	MO12 0034,
11289	MO12 0021,	MO45 0126	TMLP 0300	MO45 0152
TMLP 0288	MO45 0096	1179	12009	12040
1129	1149	MO45 0127	TMLP 0301	TMLP 0332
MO45 0077,	MO45 0097	118	1201	12041
X2LP 0006	115	RA45 0018	MO45 0149	TMLP 0333
11290	RA45 0015	1180	12010	12042
TMLP 0289	1150	MO12 0027,	TMLP 0302	TMLP 0334
11291	MO12 0022,	MO45 0128	12011	12043
TMLP 0290	MO45 0098	1181	TMLP 0303	TMLP 0335
11292	1151	MO45 0129	12012	12044
TMLP 0291	MO45 0099	1182	TMLP 0304	MOLP 0001
11293	1152	MO45 0130	12013	12045
TMLP 0292	MO45 0100	1183	TMLP 0305	MOLP 0002
113	1153	MO12 0028,	12014	12046
RA45 0013	MO45 0101	MO45 0131	TMLP 0306	MOLP 0003
1130	1154	1184	12015	12047
MO45 0078,	MO45 0102	MO45 0132	TMLP 0307	MOLP 0004
X2LP 0007	1155	1185	12016	12048
1131	MO45 0103	MO45 0133	TMLP 0308	MOLP 0005
MO45 0079,	1156	1186	12017	12049
X2LP 0008	MO45 0104	MO12 0029,	TMLP 0309	MOLP 0006
1132	1157	MO45 0134	12018	1205
MO12 0007,	MO45 0105	1187	TMLP 0310	MO45 0153
MO45 0080,	1158	MO45 0135	12019	12050
X2LP 0009	MO12 0023,	1188	TMLP 0311	MOLP 0007
1133	MO45 0106	MO45 0136	1202	12051
MO45 0081,	1159	1189	MO45 0150	MOLP 0008
X2LP 0010	MO45 0107	MO45 0137	12020	12052
1134	116	119	TMLP 0312	MOLP 0009
MO12 0008,	RA45 0016	RA45 0019	12021	12053
MO45 0082	1160	1190	TMLP 0313	MOLP 0010
1135	MO45 0108	MO45 0138	12022	12054
MO12 0009,	1161	1191	TMLP 0314	MOLP 0011
MO45 0083	MO45 0109	MO45 0139	12023	12055
1136	1162	1192	TMLP 0315	MOLP 0012
MO12 0010,	MO12 0024,	MO45 0140	12024	12056
MO45 0084	MO45 0110	1193	TMLP 0316	MOLP 0013
1137	1163	MO45 0141	12025	12057
MO12 0011,	MO45 0111	1194	TMLP 0317	MOLP 0014
MO45 0085	1164	MO12 0030,	12026	12058
1138	MO45 0112	MO45 0142	TMLP 0318	MOLP 0015
MO12 0012,	1165	1195	12027	12059
MO12 0013,	MO45 0113	MO12 0031,	TMLP 0319	MOLP 0016
MO45 0086	1166	MO45 0143	12028	1206
1139	MO45 0114	1196	TMLP 0320	MO45 0154
MO45 0087	1167	MO45 0144	12029	12060
114	MO45 0115	1197	TMLP 0321	MOLP 0017
RA45 0014	1168	MO45 0145	1203	12061
1140	MO12 0025,	1198	MO12 0033,	MOLP 0018
MO12 0014,	MO45 0116	MO12 0032,	MO45 0151	12062
MO45 0088	1169	MO45 0146	12030	MOLP 0019
1141	MO12 0026,	1199	TMLP 0322	12063
MO12 0015,	MO45 0117	MO45 0147	12031	MOLP 0020
MO45 0089	117	120	TMLP 0323	12064
1142	RA45 0017	RA45 0020	12032	MOLP 0021
MO12 0016,	1170	1200	TMLP 0324	12065
MO45 0090	MO45 0118	MO45 0148	12033	MOLP 0022
1143	1171	12001	TMLP 0325	12066

PART VIII

APPENDIX
MOTOWN-RELATED
LABEL DISCOGRAPHIES

ANNA 7-INCH SINGLES

AN45 0001	Anna 101 (1958)	Voice Masters Hope And Pray Oops I'm Sorry
AN45 0002	Anna 102	Voice Masters Needed (For Lovers Only) Needed
AN45 0003	Anna 1103	Hill Sisters Hit And Run Away Love Advertising For Love
AN45 0004	Anna 1104	Bob Kayli Never More Peppermint (You Know What To Do) Note: Pseudonym of Robert Gordy, brother of Berry Gordy, Jr.
AN45 0005	Anna 1105	Greg Tracey All I Want Is You Take Me Back
AN45 0006	Anna 1106	Paul Gayten Hot Cross Buns The Hunch
AN45 0007	Anna 1107 (1959)	Paul Gayten Hot Cross Buns The Hunch
AN45 0008	Anna 1108	Johnny & Jackey Let's Go To A Movie Baby Lonely And Blue Note: Johnny Bristol and Jackey Beavers.
AN45 0009	Anna 1109	Larry Darnell With Tears In My Eyes I'll Get Along Somehow
AN45 0010	Anna 1110	Falcons Just For Your Love This Heart Of Mine
AN45 0011	Anna 1111 (1959)	Barrett Strong Money (That's What I Want) Oh! I Apologize Note: Originally released on Tamla 54027.
AN45 0012	Anna 1112	Paul Gayten and his Orchestra Beatnick Beat Scratch Back
AN45 0013	Anna 1113	Letha Jones I Need You Black Clouds
AN45 0014	Anna 1114	Ty Hunter / Voice Masters Everything About You Orphan Boy
AN45 0015	Anna 1115	Herman Griffin / Mello-Dees Do You Want To See My Baby Hurry Up And Marry Me
AN45 0016	Anna 1116	Barrett Strong Yes, No, Maybe So You Know What To Do
AN45 0017	Anna 1117	Ruben Forte I Feel It So Good
AN45 0018	Anna 1118	Allen "Bo" Story Blue Moon Don't
AN45 0019	Anna 1119	Joe Tex All I Could Do Was Cry Pt. 1 All I Could Do Was Cry Pt. 2
AN45 0020	Anna 1120	Johnny & Jackey Hoy Hoy No One Else But You Note: Johnny Bristol and Jackey Beavers.
AN45 0021	Anna 1121	Bill Murray and George Copeland Big Time Spender Pt. 1 Big Time Spender Pt. 2 Note: Bill "Winehead Willy" Murray and George "Sweet Lucy" Copeland.
AN45 0022	Anna 1122	Cap'tans I'm Afraid Tight Skirts & Crazy Sweaters
AN45 0023	Anna 1123	Ty Hunter and the Voice Masters Every Time I'm Free
AN45 0024	Anna 1124	Joe Tex I'll Never Break Your Heart, Pt. 1 I'll Never Break Your Heart, Pt. 2
AN45 0025	Anna 1125 (02/61)	Lamont Anthony Let's Talk It Over Benny The Skinny Man Note: Pseudonym of Lamont Dozier. "B" side originally issued as "Popeye," then withdrawn under pressure from King Features.
AN45 0026	Anna 1126 (1960)	Wreg Tracey All I Want For Christmas Take Me Back
AN45 0027	Anna 1127 (02/61)	David Ruffin I'm In Love One Of These Days
AN45 0028	Anna 1128 (1961)	Joe Tex Ain't It A Mess Baby, You're Right

GOLDEN WORLD 7-INCH SINGLES

GW45 0001	Golden World 1	Willie Kendrick Stop This Train Fine As Wine

GW45 0002	Golden World 2	Sue Perrin Candy Store Man Recipe Of Love
GW45 0003	Golden World 3	Note: Unissued?
GW45 0004	Golden World 4	Adorables Deep Freeze Daddy Please
GW45 0005	Golden World 5	Note: Unissued?
GW45 0006	Golden World 6	Patti Gilson Pulling Petals Don't You Tell A Lie
GW45 0007	Golden World 7	Leroy Smalley Ain't It A Shame Girls Are Sentimental
GW45 0008	Golden World 8 (03/64)	Reflections (Just Like) Romeo & Juliet Can't You Tell By The Look In My Eyes
GW45 0009	Golden World 9	Note: Unissued?
GW45 0010	Golden World 10	Adorables Be School's All Over
GW45 0011	Golden World 11	Elliott Baron Man To Man The Spare Rib
GW45 0012	Golden World 12 (06/64)	Reflections Like Columbus Did Lonely Girl
GW45 0013	Golden World 13	Note: Unissued?
GW45 0014	Golden World 14	Manhattans Just A Little Loving Beautiful Brown Eyes
GW45 0015	Golden World 15	Reflections Oowee Now Talkin 'Bout My Girl
GW45 0016	Golden World 16	Reflections Henpecked Guy Don't Do That To Me
GW45 0017	Golden World 17	Debonaires A Little Too Long Please Don't Say
GW45 0018	Golden World 18	Juanita Williams Baby Boy You Knew What You Was Gettin'
GW45 0019	Golden World 19	Reflections You're My Baby Shabby Little Hut
GW45 0020	Golden World 20 (02/65)	Reflections Poor Man's Son Comin' At You
GW45 0021	Golden World 21 (05/65)	Barbara Mercer Hey Can't Stop Loving You Baby
GW45 0022	Golden World 22	Reflections Wheelin' & Dealin' Deborah Ann
GW45 0023	Golden World 23	Carl Carlton I Love True Love Nothin' No Sweeter Than Love
GW45 0024	Golden World 24	Reflections Out Of The Picture June Bride
GW45 0025	Golden World 25	Adorables Ooh Boy! Devil In His Eyes
GW45 0026	Golden World 26	Debonaires Eenie Meenie Gypsaleenie Please Don't Say We're Through
GW45 0027	Golden World 27	Barbara Mercer The Things We Do Together Hungry For Love
GW45 0028	Golden World 28	Barbara Mercer Doin' Things Together With You Hungry For Love
GW45 0029	Golden World 29	Reflections Girl In The Candy Store Your Kind Of Love
GW45 0030	Golden World 30	Note: Unissued?
GW45 0031	Golden World 31	Sunliners The Swingin' Kind All Alone
GW45 0032	Golden World 32	Gino Parks My Sophiscated Lady Talkin' About My Baby
GW45 0033	Golden World 33	Rose Batiste Sweetheart Darling That's What He Told Me
GW45 0034	Golden World 34	Note: Unissued?
GW45 0035	Golden World 35	Note: Unissued?
GW45 0036	Golden World 36 (03/66)	Holidays I'll Love You Forever Makin' Up Time
GW45 0037	Golden World 37	Larry Knight and the Upsetters Everything's Gone Wrong Hurt Me

GW45 0038	Golden World 38	Debonaires
		Big Time Fun
		How's Your New Love
		   Treating You
		      Note: See also Golden World
		44.

GW45 0039	Golden World 39	Note: Unissued?
GW45 0040	Golden World 40	Tamiko Jones Am I Glad Now I'm Spellbound
GW45 0041	Golden World 41	Tony Michaels Picture Me & You I Love The Life I Live
GW45 0042	Golden World 42	Pat Lewis Let's Get Together Can't Shake It Together
GW45 0043	Golden World 43	Theresa Lindsey Daddy-O I'll Bet You
GW45 0044	Golden World 44	Debonaires C.O.D. How's Your New Love Treating You?
GW45 0045	Golden World 45	Willie Kendrick Fine As Wine Stop The Train
GW45 0046	Golden World 46 (1966)	Parliaments That Was My Girl Heart Trouble
GW45 0047	Golden World 47 (06/66)	Holidays No Greater Love Watch Out Girl
GW45 0048	Golden World 101 (1966)	Sue Perrin I Wonder Put A Ring On My Finger

HARVEY 7-INCH SINGLES

HA45 0001	Harvey 111 (10/61)	Eddie Burns Orange Driver Hard Hearted Woman Note: See also Harvey 118.
HA45 0002	Harvey 112	Loe & Joe Little Ole Boy That's How I Am Without You
HA45 0003	Harvey 113 (05/62)	Jr. Walker & The All Stars Twist Lackawanna Willie's Blues
HA45 0004	Harvey 114	Five Quails It's Been A Long Time Get To School On Time

HA45 0005	Harvey 115	Eddie Burns Mean And Evil (Baby) Thing To Do
HA45 0006	Harvey 116	Five Quails My Love Never Felt Like This Before
HA45 0007	Harvey 117	Jr. Walker & The All Stars Cleo's Mood Brainwasher Note: See also Harvey 119.
HA45 0008	Harvey 118	Eddie Burns Orange Driver Messing With My Bread
HA45 0009	Harvey 119	Jr. Walker & The All Stars Brainwasher Good Rockin'
HA45 0010	Harvey 120	Five Quails I Thought Over The Hump
HA45 0011	Harvey 121	Harvey & Ann Will I Do What Can You Do Now

RIC-TIC 7-INCH SINGLES

RI45 0001	Ric-Tic 100	Gino Washington Gino Is A Coward Puppet On A String
RI45 0002	Ric-Tic 101	Freddie Gorman In A Bad Way There Can Be Too Much
RI45 0003	Ric-Tic 102	Freddie Gorman Can't Get It Out Of My Mind Take Me Back
RI45 0004	Ric-Tic 103 (07/65)	Edwin Starr Agent Double-O Soul (Vocal) Agent Double-O Soul (Instrumental)
RI45 0005	Ric-Tic 104 (08/65)	San Remo Golden Strings Hungry For Love All Turned On Note: "B" side as by Bob Wilson & The San Remo Quartet.
RI45 0006	Ric-Tic 105	Rose Batiste That's What He Told Me Holding Hands
RI45 0007	Ric-Tic 106	J. J. Barnes I Think I Found A Love Please Let Me In
RI45 0008	Ric-Tic 107 (10/65)	Edwin Starr Back Street (Vocal) Back Street (Instrumental)
RI45 0009	Ric-Tic 108 (10/65)	San Remo Golden Strings I'm Satisfied Blueberry Hill

RI45 0010	Ric-Tic 109 (01/66)	Edwin Starr Stop Her On Sight (S.O.S.) I Have Faith In You
RI45 0011	Ric-Tic 109X (1966)	Edwin Starr Scott's On Swingers (S.O.S.) Note: Promotional release for Detroit-area disc jockey Scot Regan of WKNR-AM.
RI45 0012	Ric-Tic 110	J. J. Barnes Real Humdinger I Ain't Gonna Do It
RI45 0013	Ric-Tic 111 (1966)	Laura Lee To Win Your Heart So Will I
RI45 0014	Ric-Tic 112	San Remo Golden Strings Festival Time Joy Road

RI45 0015	Ric-Tic 113	Fantastic Four
		Can't Stop Looking For My Baby
		  Pt 1
		Can't Stop Looking For My
		  Baby Pt 2
		   Note: Unissued. See also
		Ric-Tic 121.

RI45 0016	Ric-Tic 114 (04/66)	Edwin Starr Headline News Harlem
RI45 0017	Ric-Tic 115	J. J. Barnes Day Tripper Don't Bring Me Bad News
RI45 0018	Ric-Tic 116	San Remo Golden Strings International Love Theme Quanto Sei Bella
RI45 0019	Ric-Tic 117	J. J. Barnes Deeper In Love Say It
RI45 0020	Ric-Tic 118	Edwin Starr Girls Are Getting Prettier It's My Turn Now
RI45 0021	Ric-Tic 119	Fantastic Four Girl Have Pity (I'm Gonna) Live Up To What She Thinks
RI45 0022	Ric-Tic 120	Edwin Starr You're My Mellow My Kind Of Woman
RI45 0023	Ric-Tic 121	Fantastic Four Can't Stop Looking For My Baby Just The Lonely
RI45 0024	Ric-Tic 122 (02/67)	Fantastic Four The Whole World Is A Stage Ain't Love Wonderful
RI45 0025	Ric-Tic 123 (1967)	Al Kent The Way You Been Acting Lately The Way You Been Acting Lately (Instrumental)
RI45 0026	Ric-Tic 124 (1967)	Andre Williams You Got It And I Want It I Can't Stop Crying
RI45 0027	Ric-Tic 125 (1967)	Willie "G" Meet Me Halfway (Loving Me Is Like) Money In The Bank
RI45 0028	Ric-Tic 126	Note: Unissued.
RI45 0029	Ric-Tic 127 (06/67)	Al Kent Where Do I Go From Here You've Got To Pay The Price

RI45 0030	Ric-Tic 128 (04/67)	Fantastic Four
		You Gave Me Something (And
		  Everything's Alright)
		Let's Have A Love-In
		  (Instrumental)

RI45 0031	Ric-Tic 129 (1967)	Flaming Embers /
		  Wingate's Love-In Strings
		Let's Have A Love-In
		Let's Have A Love-In
		  (Instrumental)

RI45 0032	Ric-Tic 129 (1967)	Flaming Embers /
		  Wingate's Love-In Strings
		She's A Real Live Wire
		Let's Have A Love-In
		  (Instrumental)

RI45 0033	Ric-Tic 130 (08/67)	Fantastic Four As Long As I Live (I Live For You) To Share Your Love
RI45 0034	Ric-Tic 132 (1967)	Flaming Embers Hey Mama (What'cha Got Good) Let's Have A Love-In
RI45 0035	Ric-Tic 133 (1967)	Al Kent Orchestra Finders Keepers Ooh! Pretty Lady
RI45 0036	Ric-Tic 134 (1968)	Fantastic Four As Long As The Feeling Is There Goddess Of Love Note: See also Ric-Tic 136.
RI45 0037	Ric-Tic 135 (02/68)	Detroit Emeralds Showtime Showtime (Instrumental)
RI45 0038	Ric-Tic 136 (1968)	Fantastic Four Love Is A Many Splendored Thing Goddess Of Love Note: See also Ric-Tic 134.
RI45 0039	Ric-Tic 137 (1968)	Fantastic Four No Love Like Your Love Man In Love
RI45 0040	Ric-Tic 138 (1968)	Detroit Emeralds Shades Down Ode To Billy Joe

RI45 0041	Ric-Tic 139 (1968)	**Fantastic Four** I've Got To Have You Win Or Lose
RI45 0042	Ric-Tic 140 (1968)	**Flaming Embers / Al Kent** Bless You (My Love) Bless You My Love (Instrumental)
RI45 0043	Ric-Tic 141 (1968)	**Detroit Emeralds** I'm An Ordinary Man I'll Keep On Coming Back
RI45 0044	Ric-Tic 142 (1968)	**Little Ann** Going Down A One-Way Street I'd Like To Know You Better
RI45 0045	Ric-Tic 143 (1968)	**Flaming Embers** Children Children (Instrumental)
RI45 0046	Ric-Tic 144 (1968)	**Fantastic Four** I Love You Madly I Love You Madly (Instrumental)
RI45 0047	Ric-Tic 145 (1968)	**Flaming Embers** Tell It Like It Is Just Like Children

RIC-TIC ALBUMS

RILP 0001	Ric-Tic LSP-901 (1965)	**San Remo Golden Strings** HUNGRY FOR LOVE Note: Reissued on Gordy GS-923 in 1967.

TRI-PHI 7-INCH SINGLES

TR45 0001	Tri-Phi 1001 (06/61)	**Spinners** That's What Girls Are Made For Heebie Jeebies
TR45 0002	Tri-Phi 1002	**Johnny & Jackey** Carry Your Own Load So Disappointing Note: Johnny Bristol and Jackey Beavers. See also Tri-Phi 1016.
TR45 0003	Tri-Phi 1003 (09/61)	**Lorri Rudolph** Don't Let Them Tell Me (Tell Them Yourself) Grieving About A Love
TR45 0004	Tri-Phi 1004 (11/61)	**Spinners** Love (I Am So Glad I Found You) Sudbuster
TR45 0005	Tri-Phi 1005 (11/61)	**Johnny & Jackey** Someday We'll Be Together She Don't Play Note: Johnny Bristol and Jackey Beavers.
TR45 0006	Tri-Phi 1006 (01/62)	**Shorty Long** I'll Be There Bad Willie Note: See also Tri-Phi 1015.

TR45 0007	Tri-Phi 1007 (12/61)	**Spinners** What Did She Use Itching For My Baby But I Don't Know Where To Scratch
TR45 0008	Tri-Phi 1008	**Davenport Sisters** You've Got Me Crying Again Hoy Hoy
TR45 0009	Tri-Phi 1009	**Jordan Harmonizers** Do You Know Him I Won't Mind
TR45 0010	Tri-Phi 1010 (03/62)	**Spinners** She Loves Me So Whistling About You
TR45 0011	Tri-Phi 1010	**Harvey Fuqua** She Loves Me So Whistling About You Note: Unissued. See also Tri-Phi 1017.
TR45 0012	Tri-Phi 1011	**Merced Blue Notes** Midnite Sessions Pt. 1 Midnite Sessions Pt. 2
TR45 0013	Tri-Phi 1012 (06/62)	**Challengers III** Stay Honey Honey Honey
TR45 0014	Tri-Phi 1013 (1962)	**Spinners** I've Been Hurt I Got Your Water Boiling Baby (I'm Gonna Cook Your Goose)
TR45 0015	Tri-Phi 1014 (1962)	**Ervin Sisters** Changing Baby Do It Right
TR45 0016	Tri-Phi 1015 (10/62)	**Shorty Long** I'll Be There Too Smart
TR45 0017	Tri-Phi 1016	**Johnny & Jackey** Do You See My Love For You Growing Carry Your Own Load Note: Johnny Bristol and Jackey Beavers.
TR45 0018	Tri-Phi 1017	**Harvey Fuqua** She Loves Me So Any Way You Wanta
TR45 0019	Tri-Phi 1018 (1962)	**Spinners** She Don't Love Me To Young, Too Much, Too Soon
TR45 0020	Tri-Phi 1019	**Johnny & Jackey** Baby Don'tcha Worry Stop What You're Saying Note: Johnny Bristol and Jackey Beavers.

TR45 0021	Tri-Phi 1020	Challengers III Every Day I Hear An Echo
TR45 0022	Tri-Phi 1021 (03/63)	Shorty Long What's The Matter Going Away
TR45 0023	Tri-Phi 1022 (1963)	Ervin Sisters Why I Love Him Every Day's A Holiday

| TR45 0024 | Tri-Phi 1023 (1963) | Merced Blue Notes Whole Lotta Nothin Fragile |
| TR45 0025 | Tri-Phi 1024 (1963) | Harvey Fuqua Memories Of You Come On And Answer Me |